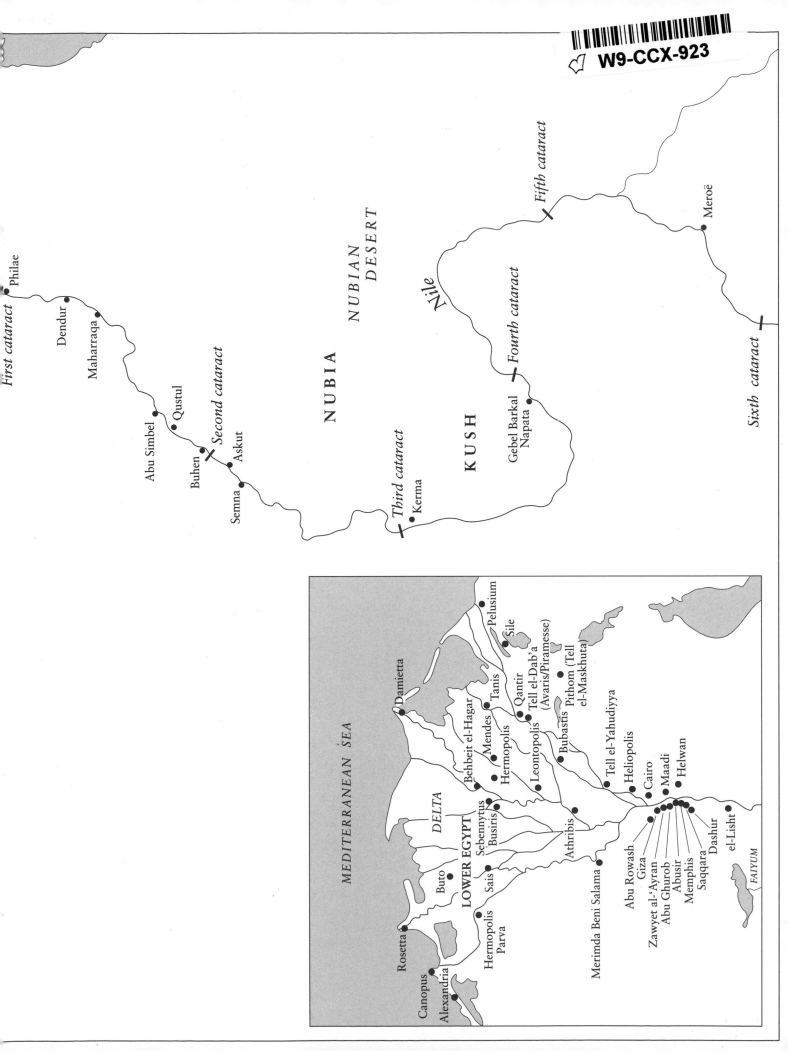

First cataract

Philae

Dendur

Maharraqa

Abu Simbel

Qustul

Buhen

Second cataract

Askut

Semna

Third cataract

Kerma

NUBIA

NUBIAN

DESERT

Nile

KUSH

Gebel Barkal

Napata

Fourth cataract

Fifth cataract

Meroë

Sixth cataract

MEDITERRANEAN SEA

Damietta

Pelusium

Sile

Tanis

Qantir

Tell el-Dab'a
(Avaris/Piramesse)

Behbeit el-Hagar

Mendes

Hermopolis

Leontopolis

Bubastis

Pithom (Tell
el-Maskhuta)

Tell el-Yahudiyya

Heliopolis

Cairo

Maadi

Helwan

DELTA

Sebennytus

Busiris

LOWER EGYPT

Athribis

Buto

Sais

Abu Rowash

Giza

Zawyet al-'Ayran

Abu Ghurob

Abusir

Memphis

Saqqara

Dashur

el-Lisht

FAIYUM

Merimda Beni Salama

Rosetta

Hermopolis
Parva

Canopus

Alexandria

# THE OXFORD ENCYCLOPEDIA OF ANCIENT EGYPT

# THE OXFORD ENCYCLOPEDIA OF

# ANCIENT EGYPT

DONALD B. REDFORD

EDITOR IN CHIEF

VOLUME 1

OXFORD

UNIVERSITY PRESS

2001

# OXFORD
## UNIVERSITY PRESS

Oxford   New York
Athens  Auckland  Bangkok  Bogotá  Buenos Aires  Calcutta
Cape Town  Chennai  Dar es Salaam  Delhi  Florence  Hong Kong  Istanbul
Karachi  Kuala Lumpur  Madrid  Melbourne  Mexico City  Mumbai
Nairobi  Paris  São Paulo  Shanghai  Singapore  Taipei  Tokyo  Toronto  Warsaw

and associated companies in
Berlin   Ibadan

Copyright © 2001 by Oxford University Press, Inc.

Published by Oxford University Press, Inc.
198 Madison Avenue, New York, New York 10016
www.oup.com

Oxford is a registered trademark of Oxford University Press

Library of Congress Cataloging-in-Publication Data
The Oxford Encyclopedia of Ancient Egypt / Donald B. Redford, editor in chief.
p.   cm.
Includes bibliographical references and index.
ISBN 0-19-510234-7 (set)—ISBN 0-19-513821-X (v. 1) —
ISBN 0-19-513822-8 (v. 2)—ISBN 0-19-513823-6 (v. 3)
1. Egypt—Civilization—To 332 B.C.—Encyclopedias.
2. Egypt—Civilization—332 B.C.–638 A.D.—Encyclopedias.
3. Egypt—Antiquities—Encyclopedias.
I. Redford, Donald B.
DT58 .O94   2000
932—dc21      99-054801

The photographs and line drawings used herein were supplied by contributors to the work,
members of the Editorial Board, major museums, and by commercial photographic archives.
The publisher has made every effort to ascertain that necessary permissions to reprint materials have
been secured. Sources of all photographs and line drawings are given in captions to illustrations.

### EDITORIAL AND PRODUCTION STAFF

*Commissioning Editor:* Christopher Collins
*Project Editor:* Eugene Romanosky
*Development Editors:* Donald B. Spanel, Marion Osmun
*Copy Chief:* Martha Goldstein
*Copyeditors:* Jane McGary, Martin Ahermaa, Betty Leigh Hutcheson,
Mark La Flaur, Wendy Raver
*Proofreaders:* Karen Fraley, Ellen Thorn, Walter Saxon, Carol Wengler
*Translators:* Julia Harvey, Susan Romanosky, Elizabeth Schwaiger,
Sabine H. Seiler, Robert E. Shillenn, Jennifer Worth
*Bibliographic Researcher:* Melinda Hartwig
*Photo Researcher:* Elena Pischikova
*Indexers:* Carol Roberts and Kay Wosewick
*Cartographer:* Bill Nelson
*Book Designer:* Joan Greenfield

*Publisher:* Karen Casey

3 5 7 9 8 6 4 2
Printed in the United States of America
on acid-free paper

# CONTENTS

# EDITORIAL BOARD

# PREFACE

*The Oxford Encyclopedia of Ancient Egypt* provides students, scholars, and the merely curious with the latest information on the civilization that developed and flourished in the Nile Valley. It presents the prehistoric, predynastic, and dynastic phases of that civilization within the context of its contiguous and sometimes conquering neighbors, tracing its history through the Islamic conquest of 642 CE—although the focus is on dynastic Egypt and its cultural complexity.

Although modern Egyptology originally grew out of the Enlightenment's emphasis on rational and systematic methodologies, it was not until well into the twentieth century that the field developed into a mature multidisciplinary endeavor that combined both a number of the humanities and social sciences with *scientific* archaeology. Before this maturation, any investigations termed "archaeological" frequently turned out to be fiercely nationalistic, rough-and-ready treasure hunts on a grand scale. In fact, many early Egyptologists were judged by the number of objects they had discovered, and frequently the first and most important task of the researcher was assumed to be the sketching, listing, and describing of sculpture, painting, and architecture, as well as the deciphering of inscriptions. Not a few early "Histories" of ancient Egypt are actually little more than catalogs of *objets d'art*, coupled with paraphrases of textual sources, as, for example, A. Wiedemann's, *Ägyptische Geschichte* (1884) or W. M. Flinders Petrie's *A History of Egypt* (1898).

In the twentieth century, particularly after World War II, students of ancient Egypt began to realize that the application of new testing techniques, such as neutron activation, thermoluminescence, and accelerated radiocarbon (C-14) dating, could potentially resolve many perennial questions in the field; that tightly controlled stratigraphic archaeology and artifactual seriation were entirely possible and desirable; and that survey and remote-sensing strategies brought valuable scholarly dividends. Archaeologists and anthropologists with science-oriented experience in Europe or the Americas have since become deeply involved in Egyptological research. Although purists have sometimes sought to exclude these non-Egyptologists from active research, their expert contributions are clearly of great value.

Yet archaeology has supplied only the most visible scientific tools that aid in the systematic recovery of ancient Egypt. An interdisciplinary approach that includes historical, literary, and religious studies has increasingly engaged the field with provocative questions and possible answers, while many other scholarly endeavors have emerged against a backdrop of political science, economic history, and sociology. For example, scholars have applied literary theory to ancient Egyptian texts, and the study of myth and cult is being used to place ancient

Egyptian belief systems under close and valuable scrutiny. While the hieroglyphic script has been deciphered for nearly two centuries, studies in Egyptian language have labored under the handicaps of lack of vocalization, haphazard preservation, and traditional linguistic analysis. Since the 1960s, however, modern linguists have wrought a revolution in our knowledge and appreciation of the ancient Egyptian language.

Even as our scholarly tools have been honed and improved in the twentieth century, the pace of data recovery has accelerated. The 1980s and 1990s have produced significant discoveries at nearly every site in Egypt, and scholarly publications have found it hard to keep pace with this flood of new discoveries. Such reports in periodicals glossed by the terms "Notes and News," "News in Brief," "Prosopographica," and "Nuntii" help, to a limited degree, to convey discoveries quickly to scholar and layman alike, but they cannot present a detailed statement on Egyptology and where it stands at present.

Side-by-side with the advances of a more scientific Egyptology and the continuing flood of new discoveries, a plethora of various "Egyptomanias" in the second half of the twentieth century have both heightened and misled the general public's interest in ancient Egypt. While some of these popular expressions may be intriguing to some, the vast majority of enthusiasts display a wholesale ignorance of the academic disciplines involved in Egyptology, as well as a profound lack of familiarity with the vast array of evidence that scholars take for granted. The result is a widespread image of ancient Egypt in the popular imagination that is seriously flawed and at variance with the current understanding of the field.

All these considerations combined and made it increasingly obvious that an authoritative statement regarding ancient Egypt was much needed. Continental Europeans have produced some works that satisfy such requirements: G. Posener's *Dictionnaire de la Civilization Egyptienne* (Paris, 1959), W. Helck's and E. Otto's *Kleines Wörterbuch der Ägyptologie* (Wiesbaden, 1956), P. Vernus and J. Yoyotte's *Dictionnaire des pharaons* (Paris, 1988), and the substantial treatment of Egypt in the *Handbuch der Orientalistik* (volumes on Egypt, 1952–1968). While these well-received compendia were conceived on a modest scale for the general reader, the scholar was served by the monumental six-volume *Lexikon der Ägyptologie* (Wiesbaden, 1972–1986). Although most Egyptologists have been able to use this German *Lexikon*, English-speaking general readers have not had an authoritative encyclopedia covering all aspects of ancient Egypt.

With this gap in mind, Oxford University Press decided in 1994 to develop and publish an encyclopedic work on ancient Egypt that would describe in detail where Egyptology stands, as a whole, at the turn of the millennium. The encyclopedia would differ from others by the extent of its illustrations, including plans and maps, and by the extensive annotated bibliographies appended to each signed entry. A most important feature informing the whole would be the comprehensive treatment afforded to all branches of research subsumed under the rubric of Egyptology: archaeology, anthropology, architecture, linguistics, literary studies, epigraphy, papyrology, history, art history, religion, economics, ecology, geomorphology, and the life sciences. Experts in each field were recruited to contribute up-to-date and authoritative entries on the topics of their expertise. While word limits were assigned to all entries, contributors were left free to expand or reduce their pieces within reasonable parameters. In the case of particularly broad or important subjects, as, for example, "Administration," "New Kingdom," and "Sculpture," composite entries bring together several articles, treating the most important aspects of those topics.

In some periods of Egyptian history, debate continues to rage over such basic issues as order of kings, chronology, and the extent and nature of regimes. Nothing is more detrimental to the pedagogic mission of a work such as this than to have the reader deceived into thinking that one view is paramount, or that debate does not exist. Consequently, in such problem areas as the Second Intermediate Period and the Hyksos rule or the chronological and spatial distribution of political power in the Third Intermediate Period, the editors have welcomed the expression of all views, however discordant, while requesting that contributors observe a common chronology for the sake of editorial uniformity (see the king list which, along with a map of Egypt and its neighbors, is printed on the endpapers of each volume). Also, a certain degree of redundancy has been tolerated to provide readers with ease of access to information. This will be detected, for example, in the treatment of such linked themes as "Myths," "Tombs," and "Funerary Literature." A consistent and intended reduplication of information appears as well in entries on the dynasties, in which the regime is viewed as a whole, and in the entries for individual reigns within a dynasty, in which some of the same material may be treated again.

Although a comprehensive approach has been the primary aim of the project, it may appear to the specialist that gaps occur in the entry terms. The editorial staff has presented the most significant names and terms, reasoning that the inclusion of a greater number would transform the work into a *dictionnaire géographique* or a *prosopographica*. Most, if not all, of the seemingly "missing" content has been intentionally subsumed into larger articles and is listed, as appropriate, in a blind entry and/or in the topical index of the final volume. Also a synoptic outline of contents has been included there to help lead readers through related and pertinent concepts.

## Transliteration and Chronology

Several of the conventions that inform the encyclopedia are deliberate choices for which no apology can or will be offered. The transcription and vocalization of Egyptian words follow a long-established pattern that is neither dependent on contemporary vocalization (almost wholly of hypothetical reconstruction) or the classical forms in Greek. Transliteration adheres to Alan H. Gardiner's system as conveyed in his *Egyptian Grammar* (originally published in 1927; 3d ed., 1957), except where the vocalized form of a word has become common English (as with *ba, ka, maat,* and the names of people, places, or things).

In selecting an absolute chronology, the editors entered a world of uncertainty and acrimonious debate. At one time, the prospect appeared bright that a critical evaluation of king lists and offering lists, coupled with the results of accelerated radiocarbon testing, would solve the problem once and for all; such hopes are now apparently illusory. The late John Wilson, introducing a lecture on the Armana Age, once declared, "I have before me all the current chronologies suggested for this period, and I don't believe any of them." While the same could be said today with equal skepticism, it would ill serve the pedagogic and synthetic overview purposes of the present work to allow each contributor to decide on his or her own schema. An editorial decision has therefore been made to select one of the current chronological schemes circulating in the scholarly world, modifying it appropriately where new evidence has become available (e.g., the length of such reigns as those of Sneferu, Raneferef, Horemheb, Ramesses VII and VIII, and Shabtaqa, to name but a few). In terms of the "High," "Middle," and "Low" dating options confronting Egyptologists in the New Kingdom, the chronology presented would be classed as "High"; for earlier periods, it falls into line, for the most part, with the currently promoted chronologies of Nicolas Grimal and Jürgen von Beckerath.

*Acknowledgments*

Finally, in the pursuance of the task of Editor in Chief, I have been placed in the debt of a number of people. When, on 27 September 1994, I was approached by Christopher Collins, now an executive editor at Oxford University Press, with the proposal for the present work, I was quite unaware of the burden acceptance would place upon me—but I was also unaware of the generous support that O.U.P. would provide. Chris and Claude Conyers, then editorial director of the Scholarly and Professional Reference Department, gave invaluable advice, especially in the formative stages, when conceptual organization was paramount. Without their drive and guidance, this work would never have been completed. I am also very much indebted to Donald Spanel, then an associate curator at the Brooklyn Museum of Art, who was largely responsible for the project's development phase. Under the supervision of O.U.P., Donald shouldered the complex and substantial burden of producing the detailed plans that eventually became the encyclopedia's database. Later, an amazingly industrious and talented group of area editors reviewed manuscripts as they materialized over three years, and their scholarly judgment is largely responsible for the high standards the work now reflects. Initially, the subject matter was to be divided as follows: Edward Bleiberg, history and economics; John L. Foster, language and literature; Rita E. Freed, art and archaeology; Gerald E. Kadish, Old Kingdom and history; Ronald J. Leprohon, Middle Kingdom and history; and David P. Silverman, religion. As the project moved forward, however, these broad categories began to blur and the entire editorial board graciously agreed to enlarge their supervisory responsibilities when and where required.

Extensive support to the entire operation has been given by the staff of the Scholarly and Professional Reference Department of Oxford University Press. First and foremost, I must thank the project editors, Rhoda Terry and (latterly) Gene Romanosky. They were charged with the day-to-day administration of the project and acted as the liaison between contributors, editors, and O.U.P. staff. Gene, in particular, has intrepidly assumed principal responsibility for managing a seemingly boundless number of project variables in the face of a very tight production schedule. Martha Goldstein, copy chief, and Jane McGary, copy-editor, have painstakingly read and regularized the terminology and styling of an immense amount of complicated and specialized copy—some 620 articles. For the preparation of many of the photographs, we are much indebted to Elena Pischikova. Also, David P. Silverman and Dieter and Dorothea Arnold generously furnished us with their personal photographs. For the index, a *sine qua non* of any encyclopedic publication, thanks must be extended to Carol Roberts.

Encyclopedias, by their very nature and intent, anticipate future updated and revised editions. We have, to the best of our abilities, presented to the reader and researcher the vast tableaux of Egyptology as it is constituted at the turn of the century and millennium. That the grand picture will change, and is changing as I write, is as certain as anything is in this world. One can only hope that the encyclopedic project herewith begun will enjoy periodic renewal. *Velut Arbor Aevo!*

Donald B. Redford
*University Park, Pennsylvania*

# THE OXFORD ENCYCLOPEDIA OF ANCIENT EGYPT

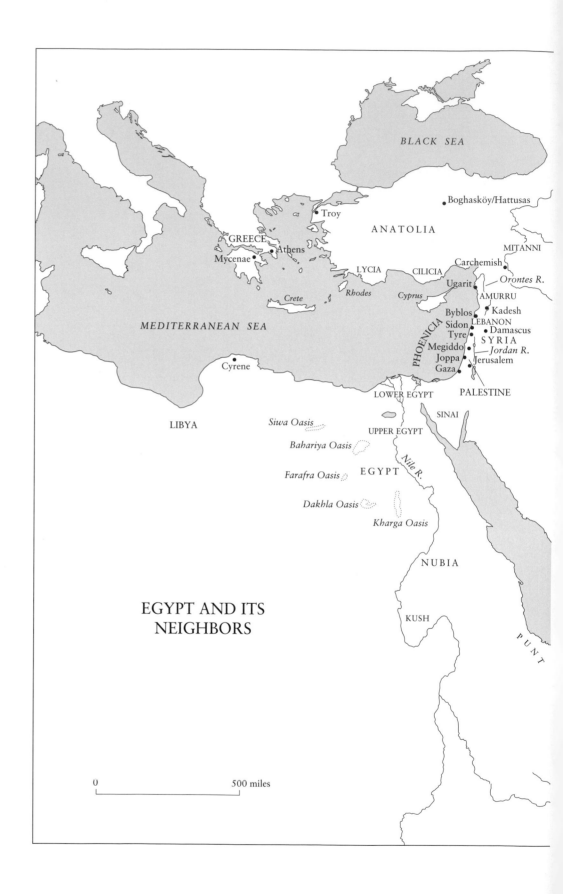

BLACK SEA

• Boghasköy/Hattusas

ANATOLIA

Troy

GREECE
Athens
Mycenae •

MITANNI

LYCIA     CILICIA     Carchemish •
                                        Orontes R.
                          Ugarit •
Crete     Rhodes     Cyprus          AMURRU
                                        • Kadesh
MEDITERRANEAN SEA          Byblos •
                          Sidon • LEBANON
                          Tyre •   • Damascus
                          PHOENICIA   SYRIA
                          Megiddo •   Jordan R.
                          Joppa •   Jerusalem
Cyrene •                  Gaza •
                          PALESTINE
                LOWER EGYPT
                                        SINAI
LIBYA     Siwa Oasis
                          UPPER EGYPT
          Bahariya Oasis
                                        Nile R.
          Farafra Oasis     EGYPT

          Dakhla Oasis
                Kharga Oasis

                          NUBIA

                KUSH
                                        P U N T

EGYPT AND ITS
NEIGHBORS

0                    500 miles

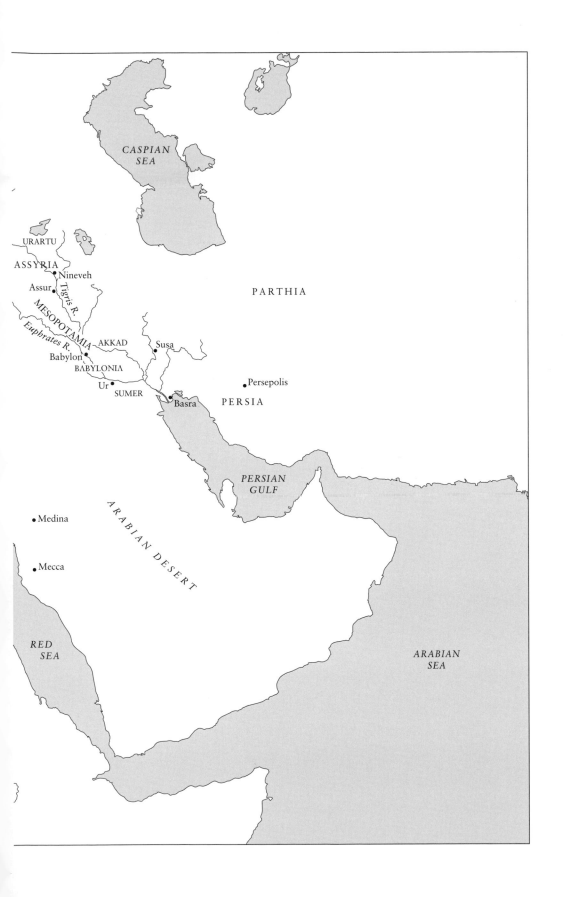

# A

**ABU GHUROB,** a New Kingdom site, situated in Middle Egypt at the edge of the Faiyum, 3.75 kilometers (about 2.5 miles) due west of the point where the Bahr Yussuf branch of the Nile River starts to turn northwest toward Medinet Faiyum. The site is on desert land, some 30 meters (about 100 feet) above sea level, but it lies within the alluvial area of the Nile's ancient deposits.

From the eighteenth to the twentieth dynasties, the town of Mi-wer, as Abu Ghurob was then named, provided a palace or a residence and harem for the convenience and entertainment of royalty, who wanted to indulge in the sports of fishing and fowling in the marshy and fertile Faiyum Depression. The principal monuments include a temple, constructed in the reign of Thutmose III (r.1504–1452 BCE), an associated palace and harem, and the royal docking place. All were institutions in which the ruler's administrators, officials, and workers, such as craftsmen, servants, and laborers, were employed. Their housing formed part of the town site and, outside the town, various cemetery areas were established for both the wealthy and the poor inhabitants. Mi-wer was occupied until the reign of Ramesses V (1160–1156 BCE) and was probably abandoned soon after.

Abu Ghurob is of archaeological and cultural significance as one of the few settlement sites of the New Kingdom to have been excavated. The finds comprised a wide range of domestic and funerary items. Artifacts relating to the spinning, weaving, and sewing of linen are of particular interest, since papyrus fragments reveal that the manufacture of textiles came under the authority of the harem. The royal wives and concubines supervised such work, but they undertook any fine sewing themselves, since cloth and garments were distributed to the various royal residences. Finds also indicate that fishing and associated crafts such as net-making were important, both for leisure purposes and for providing a valuable food source.

Excavations at Abu Ghurob were conducted for about thirty-two years. The first work there was by William Matthew Flinders Petrie from 1888 to 1890; he concentrated on the temple and its surrounding area, and he investigated part of the cemeteries. In 1900, Émile Chassinat heard about discoveries from a tomb, which he was able to trace and study; this turned out to be a communal grave of women from the harem that dated to the early part of the reign of Akhenaten (1372–1355 BCE). In the 1903–1904 season, Leonard Loat mainly investigated the animal cemeteries. In 1905, Ludwig Borchardt acquired a small wooden head of Queen Tiye (coregent r.1410–1372 BCE) from a dealer and discovered that it had come from Abu Ghurob. He visited the site and saw the remains of a large building, which he concluded was a palace of the late eighteenth dynasty. In 1920, a final three-month excavation was carried out by Guy Brunton and Reginald Engelbach. By that time, much of the site had been destroyed by illicit digging. They devoted their main efforts to the cemeteries but also reexamined the temple area, and their report was published in 1927.

## BIBLIOGRAPHY

Borchardt, Ludwig. *Der Porträtkopf der Königin Teje: Ausgrabungen der Deutschen Orient-Gesellschaft im Tell el-Amarna*, vol. 1. Leipzig, 1911.

Brunton, Guy, and Reginald Engelbach. *Gurob*. British School of Archaeology in Egypt, 41. London, 1927.

Chassinat, Émile. "Une Tombe inviolée de la XVIIIe Dynastie découverte aux environs de Médinet el-Gorab dans le Fayoûm." *Bulletin de l'Institut français d'archéologie orientale* 1 (1901), 225–234.

Murray, Margaret A. *Saqqara Mastabas*: part 1, *Gurob* by L. Loat. British School of Archaeology in Egypt, 10. London, 1905.

Petrie, W. M. F. *Kahun, Gurob and Hawara*. London, 1890.

Petrie, W. M. F. *Illahun, Kahun and Gurob*. London, 1891.

Thomas, Angela P. *Gurob: A New Kingdom Town*. Egyptology Today, 5. Warminster, 1981.

ANGELA P. THOMAS

**ABU ROWASH,** located in the continuation of Gebel el-Ghigiga, the western fringe of the Nile Valley (30°2′N, 31°4′E). The archaeological area of Abu Rowash, which belongs to the very northern part of the necropolis at Memphis, joins various sites together, which date from the Early Dynastic period to the Coptic period. The elevation called Gebel Abu Rowash is limited in the north, by the depression of Wadi Qarun and, in the south, by Wadi el-Hassanah, where a section of the desert route leads from Cairo on the Nile River to Alexandria on the Mediterranean coast. At a height of about 150 meters (500 feet), the elevation owes its name to the vicinity of the village of Abu Rowash, located 8 kilometers (5 miles) north of the Giza pyramids and 15 kilometers (10 miles) west of Cairo. The funerary complex of Djedefre, the third ruler of the fourth dynasty (c.2584–2576 BCE), was built

ABU ROWASH. *The central section of the foundation level and the cleared descending ramp.* (Photograph by M. Vallogia, 1997)

at the top of this escarpment, on the plateau of Gaa. The location of this pyramid has been known since the nineteenth century from the descriptions of Howard Vyse (*The Pyramids of Gizeh in 1837*, vol. 3, London, 1842, pp. 8–9), of W. M. Flinders Petrie (*The Pyramids and Temples of Gizeh*, London, 1883, pp. 53–55), and of Richard Lepsius (*Denkmäler aus Aegypten und Aethiopien*, vol. 1, Berlin, 1897, pp. 21–24).

Excavations at the site were begun by the French Institute of Oriental Archaeology in Cairo. Between 1900 and 1902, Émile Chassinat discovered the remains of a funerary settlement, a boat pit, and numerous statuary fragments that had the name of Didoufri (an early reading of Djedefre), which allowed for the identification of the tomb's owner. In 1912 and 1913, the French Institute, then under the direction of Pierre Lacau, continued the work and cleared new structures to the east of the pyramid. In connection with those excavations, Pierre Montet was asked to explore two sections of the huge Thinite necropolis and one of the fourth dynasty, located to the southeast of the village of Abu Rowash. In this cemetery, on a northern spur, Fernand Bisson de la Roque, between 1922 and 1924, excavated *mastaba* tombs of the fifth and sixth dynasties. In the southern part of the site, burials of the first and fifth dynasties and of the Middle Kingdom were surveyed by Adolf Klasens, between 1957 and 1959, under the patronage of the Museum of Antiquities of Leiden, the Netherlands.

In the north, in Wadi Qarun, many sites have been worked archaeologically since the beginning of the twentieth century: Charles Palanque, at the turn of the century, excavated the Coptic monastery of El-Deir el-Nahya; Pierre Lacau identified in 1913 a necropolis of the third and fourth dynasties; and in the 1920s, Bisson de la Roque sampled numerous borings in galleries that in the Late period served as burial sites for sacred crocodiles. In the 1930s, Rizkallah Macramallah discovered some solid remains of a Middle Kingdom fortress. In 1980, Zahi Hawass found a necropolis of the Early Dynastic period.

In 1995, a joint mission of the French Institute and the University of Geneva, with the collaboration of the Supreme Council of Antiquities, initiated a new program at the funerary complex of Djedefre. This monumental complex, like all the tomb complexes of the Old Kingdom, was built with a harbor on the Nile and several buildings in sequence. There was a temple at the foot of an ascending causeway that led to a funerary temple next to the royal pyramid; there was also a satellite pyramid, with one or more solar barks. The whole settlement was surrounded by a precinct wall. This funerary complex began to suffer desecration at the beginning of the Roman period, serving as a quarry from antiquity to modern times. This may help explain why Egyptologists who inventoried the various elements of the funerary complexes lacked so much data. It may also explain the marginalization of the site in the attempts at historic reconstructions of the fourth dynasty. The new program aims at a reevaluation of the reign of Djedefre. In the early 1900s, the discovery of a large number of broken royal statues had actually allowed Chassinat to suspect signs of a *damnatio memoriae* (Lat., to be stricken from the memory), connected with an illegitimacy in the claim to power by Didoufri/Djedefre. Today, however, a few stratigraphic sections demonstrated that those ancient destructions traced back only to the Roman period, when the site was occupied for a very long time. In the northeastern part of the complex, one can actually find reused remains that testify to a Roman presence. The site had an exceptionally strategic location, overlooking crossroads and offering the opportunity for the easy collection of already cut-and-dressed granite and limestone. Quarrying of the site materials, which occurred until the nineteenth century, left a smashed and open pyramid base. Its interior shows elements arranged in the form of a T, including a north–south descending ramp and, perpendicular to it, a shaft, which should contain the royal tomb.

According to the first results, the size of the pyramid was nearly the same as that of Menkaure: 106.20 meters (315 feet) on each side, with an estimated height of about 65.50 meters (200 feet), and the angle of slope being 51°57′. At foundation level, the foundation courses have lopsided beds of 12°. These become incrementally horizontal in their angles especially at the place of the foundation deposits. In the pyramid's interior, the excavation of the descending passage yielded, apart from a copper-ax deposit, guide markings on the rock, which determined that the original passage slope leading to the funerary apartment was 28°. Some graffiti left by quarrymen yielded the name of Djedefre *in situ*, as well as the mention of the first year of his reign (2584 BCE). In the central shaft, only the foundation level was saved; nevertheless, the discovery of a few architectural fragments of limestone and granite described the location of the royal burial. As of the 1990s, this substructure seems to show marked similarity with that of the northern pyramid of Zawiyet el-Aryan.

## BIBLIOGRAPHY

Chassinat, Émile. "A propos d'une tête en grès rouge du roi Didoufrî (IVe dynastie) conservée au Musée du Louvre." *Monuments et mémoires publiés par l'académie des inscriptions et belles-lettres* 25 (1921–1922), 53–75. Presentation of the work carried out on the site and description of the discovered material, followed by a historical interpretation.

Grimal, Nicolas. "Travaux de l'IFAO en 1994–1995, Abou Rawash." *Bulletin de l'Institut français d'archéologie orientale* 95 (1995), 545–551. Summary of the preliminary report on the first excavation season.

Grimal, Nicholas. "Travaux de l'IFAO en 1995–1996, Abou Rawash." *Bulletin de l'Institut français d'archéologie orientale* 96 (1996), 494–499. Summary of the 1996 preliminary report.

Maragioglio, Vito, and Celeste Rinaldi. *L'architettura delle piramidi menfite*, vol. 5. Rapallo, 1966. Architectural description of the pyramids of Djedefre and Khafre.

Marchand, Sylvie, and Michel Baud. "La céramique miniature d'Abou Rawash. Un dépôt à l'entrée des enclos orientaux." *Bulletin de l'Institut français d'archéologie orientale* 96 (1996), 255–288. Analysis of the pottery discovered in 1995 and 1996.

Müller, Hans W. "Der Gute Radjedef, Sohn des Rê." *Zeitschrift für die Ägyptische Sprache und Altertumskunde* 91 (1964), 129–133. Presentation of the inscribed statuary fragments, kept in Munich, in the Staatliche Sammlung Ägyptischer Kunst.

Valloggia, Michel. "Le complexe funéraire de Radjedef à Abou-Roasch: état de la question et perspectives de recherches." *Bulletin de la Société française d'Égyptologie: Réunions trimestrielles et communications d'archéologie* 130 (1994), 5–17. General presentation of the archaeological and historical aspects of the site that seem problematical.

Valloggia, Michel. "Fouilles archéologiques à Abu Rawash (Égypte). Rapport préliminaire de la campagne 1995." *Genava*, n.s. 43 (1995), 65–72. Description of the work of the first season.

Valloggia, Michel. "Fouilles archéologiques à Abu Rowash (Égypte):

Rapport préliminaire de la campagne 1996." *Genava* n.s. 44 (1996), 51–59.

Valloggia, Michel. "Fouillés archéologiques à Abu Rowash (Égypte). Rapport préliminaire de la campagne 1997." *Genava* n.s. 45(1997), 125–132.

MICHEL VALLOGGIA

**ABU SIMBEL,** site south of Aswan, on the western bank of the Nile River in what was Nubia (now near Egypt's border with Sudan). It has two rock-cut temples from the nineteenth dynasty reign of Ramesses II (22°21′N, 31°38′E). First noted in European literature by Johann Burckhardt in 1819, Abu Simbel has since become one of the most famous of monuments in the Nile Valley. Following the decision to build a new High Dam at Aswan in the early 1960s, the temples were dismantled and relocated in 1968 on the desert plateau 64 meters (about 200 feet) above and 180 meters (600 feet) west of their original site.

The ancient name for the region, Meha, was first documented in the late eighteenth dynasty, when the pharaohs Ay and Horemheb had rock-cut chapels hewn in the hills just to the south of Abu Simbel, at Gebel Shems and Abahuda. The original concept behind the Abu Simbel temples was also of eighteenth dynasty origin, the model being the temples of Amenhotpe III at Soleb and his Queen Tiye at Sedeinga. The Great Temple at Abu Simbel was the first of a series of four temples built during the reign of Ramesses II, which formed a unit, and each was dedicated to one of the four state gods: Amun-Re, Re-Horakhty, Ptah, and the divine manifestation of the pharaoh; the three other temples were built at Wadi-es-Sebua (the domain of Amun), Derr (the domain of Re-Horakhty), and Gerf Hussein (the domain of Ptah). The temples at Abu Simbel were begun in the early years of the reign and were completed by its twenty-fifth year.

No precinct wall, or *dromos*, now survives in front of the Great Temple; that such a precinct wall may originally have existed has been suggested by the brick wall to the northern side of the temple, with a pylon and gateway that lead toward the Small Temple and the mud-brick walls that enclose the entrance to the chapel on the south side. The ramp to the terrace is flanked by two large stelae. Along the terrace, statues of both the living and the mummified king alternate with images of falcon deities. An open solar chapel, with an altar (the baboons and obelisks are now in the Cairo Museum), stands at the northern end of the terrace; at its southern end is inscribed a version of the "Marriage Stela," which recorded Ramesses II's marriage with a Hittite princess, dated to Year 34 of the king's reign.

ABU SIMBEL. *The Great Temple of Ramesses II, nineteenth dynasty.* (Courtesy Dieter Arnold)

The rock-cut façade, shaped like a pylon, is dominated by four colossal seated statues of the king, each 22 meters (67 feet) high; these are flanked by much smaller standing images of his mother and wife, with very small figures of sons or daughters standing between his feet. An earthquake in antiquity damaged the colossal figures flanking the doorway; the upper part of the southern colossus fell, but the northern figure suffered less damage and was restored in the reign of Sety II. Above the main entrance, a massive niche contains a personification of the king's name. The left doorjamb has a lengthy cryptic inscription of the king's titulary.

The temple was entirely cut in the rock cliff, which necessitated some adaptations of the classic temple plan. The entrance opens onto a hall lined by eight square pillars, with standing statues of the king; this indicates an equivalency to an open festival court, of the type found in analogous temples at Thebes (e.g., the Ramesseum) and in Nubia (e.g., es-Sebua). Reliefs of the Battle of Kadesh cover the northern wall, with other military scenes in relief on the southern wall. The Kadesh reliefs are unusual in that they were signed by the chief sculptor, Piaay, son of Khanefer. The scenes flanking the door into the hall depict the king, standing in front of Amun and Mut, on one side, with Re-Horakhty and Ius-aas on the other; in both scenes, the seated image of the deified king was added, between the two deities, and this alteration indicates that the deification of Ramesses II occurred during the construction of the temple (the image of the divine king being integral to the decoration of the inner rooms). Four suites of rooms, usually called treasuries, lie off this hall. Two falcon-headed sphinxes were in front of the doorway that led to the second hall, and they, along with a statue of the viceroy of Nubia, Paser II, were removed to the British Museum in London. A hall with four square columns has religious scenes. Beyond it lies the sanctuary, with four rock-cut statues of the presiding deities: Amun-Re and Ramesses are flanked by Ptah and Re-Horakhty. The axis of the temple is arranged so that, on two days of the year (21 February; 21 October), the rising sun illuminates the king's image. The decoration of the main rooms is in sunken relief, with rich polychrome painting, but the side chambers are not so fine and the color scheme is limited.

Immediately to the south of the Great Temple is another single rock-cut chamber, with remains of a preceding brick court or hall; this is designated the birth-house in its inscriptions. The two main walls carry depictions of sacred barks; one is the bark of Thoth of Amun-hery-ib (Abahuda), and the other is the sacred bark of Ramesses II.

The Small Temple lies a short distance to the north. Its façade takes the form of a double pylon with six colossal standing statues 10 meters (33 feet) in height, carved from the rock; there are also two of Nefertari and four of Ramesses II, each flanked by small figures of their children. The hall has six square pillars, and the faces on the central aisle were carved with Hathor-headed sistra in high relief. A narrow vestibule carries a unique scene of the coronation of Nefertari by the goddesses Isis and Hathor. The statue in the sanctuary is of the goddess Hathor, in the form of a cow, emerging from the rock, with a small statue of the king in front of her. The reliefs on the sanctuary walls depict Ramesses II worshipping himself and Nefertari: in this temple, Nefertari appears as a manifestation of the goddess Hathor. Throughout the temple, the relief is of good quality, depicting rather slender, attenuated figures. The whole was colored in a scheme in which white and gold predominate. The cliff surrounding both temples carries numerous rock inscriptions made for viceroys and other high officials of the reign.

## BIBLIOGRAPHY

Christophe, Louis A. *Abou-Simbel et l'épopée de la découverte*. Brussels, 1965. A history of the temple since the earliest European visitors.

Desroches-Noblecourt, Christiane, and C. Kuentz. *Le Petit Temple d'Abou Simbel*. 2 vols. Cairo, 1968.

Säve-Söderbergh, Torgny, ed. *Temples and Tombs of Ancient Nubia: The International Rescue Campaign at Abu Simbel, Philae and Other Sites*. London, 1987. An account of the rescue of Abu Simbel and other Nubian monuments.

ROBERT MORKOT

**ABUSIR,** an archaeological locality on the western bank of the Nile River, approximately 25 kilometers (15 miles) southwest of Cairo (29°56'N, 31°13'E). Its name was derived from the Egyptian Per-Usire, in Greek, Busiris, meaning "the place of worship of the god Osiris," ruler of the land of the dead.

Although Abusir had already been inhabited by hunters in the Middle Paleolithic and was settled in the Neolithic, it became especially important in the fifth dynasty, when the first ruler, Userkaf (ruled c.2513–2506 BCE), built the sun temple Nekhen-Re there and his successor, Sahure (ruled c.2506–2492 BCE), founded a royal cemetery. Sahure was the first to build himself a pyramid complex that is regarded as a milestone in the development of royal tombs; the dimensions of his pyramid were smaller than those of the fourth dynasty pyramids, but his mortuary and valley temples achieved greater importance. The mortuary temple was designed with finely worked building materials: red granite was used for the palm columns that stood in an open court; walls of white limestone were decorated with superb polychrome scenes in low relief, which mainly showed mythical scenes of the ruler victorious in battle against Egypt's traditional enemies; hunting scenes; and ships.

ABUSIR. *Eastern end of Sahure's Causeway.* (Courtesy Dieter Arnold)

Sahure's valley temple on the edge of the desert served as a landing place, linked to the Nile by a canal. A causeway led from this temple to the mortuary temple; some fragments of the causeway's relief decoration included scenes of the completion celebrations buildings, starving Bedouins, and other scenes.

The pyramid complex of Sahure's successor, Kakai (ruled c.2492–2482 BCE), was located on the most elevated site in the cemetery. The pyramid, which was changed in the course of construction from a stepped into a true pyramid, rose to a height of approximately 74 meters (225 feet). The casing was, however, left unfinished, like the remaining parts of the complex, as a result of the ruler's premature death. His mortuary temple was constructed of mud bricks and wood by his sons and heirs, Neferefre Kakai and Newoserre Any. At the end of the nineteenth century, tomb robbers discovered a papyrus archive (called the First Abusir Archive) in the storage rooms of the mortuary temple. These records date from the last part of the fifth dynasty to the end of the sixth.

On the southern side of Neferirkare Kakai's pyramid is the smaller pyramid complex of his wife, Khentkawes II. Valuable finds from the queen's mortuary temple have included numerous papyrus fragments (the Second Abusir Archive) and other materials that throw new light on complex problems related to the ending of the fourth dynasty and the beginning of the fifth—in particular, the role played by the two queen mothers, Khentkawes I and Khentkawes II.

Neferirkare Kakai's eldest son Neferefre ruled for only a brief period, perhaps two years. His unfinished pyramid was changed into a *mastaba*, and before its eastern side, an architecturally unique mortuary temple was built of mud bricks. The finds there have included stone statue fragments of the ruler, as well as papyri from yet another temple archive (the Third Abusir Archive), roughly the same age as the Second Abusir Archive. A cult abattoir, known as "the Sanctuary of the Knife," was connected with that mortuary temple. Fragments of pyramid foundations have been uncovered between Sahure's pyramid and Userkaf's sun temple (and those have been hypothetically attributed to Neferefre Kakai's ephemeral successor[?] Shepseskare).

To remain near his family, the next fifth dynasty ruler, Newoserre Any, built his pyramid at the northeastern corner of the pyramid of Neferirkare Kakai, appropriating the unfinished foundations of its valley temple and a part of its causeway for his own complex. The open courtyard of Newoserre Any's mortuary temple was adorned with papyrus-form columns of red granite, with relief decoration that in many respects resembled that of Sahure; but the normal, rectangular temple plan had to be abandoned in favor of an L-shaped outline, for lack of space.

Newoserre Any's wife, Reputnub, does not appear to be buried in the vicinity of her husband's tomb. Her tomb may be one of the pyramid complexes (marked "no. XXIV" and "no. XXV" on the Lepsius archaeological map) that were demonstrably constructed in that time. Excavations in pyramid 24 ("no. XXIV") have provided valuable information about its mode of construction, but the name of its owner remains unknown. Newoserre Any's successor, Mekauhor, abandoned the Abusir necropolis.

Other members of the royal family and courtiers and officials of that time were also buried in the vicinity of the pyramids. The largest of their tombs belonged to the vizier Ptahshepses, Newoserre Any's son-in-law; that twice-extended *mastaba* almost rivaled the royal complexes in size, architectural plan, and quality of decorative relief. Its eight-stemmed lotus-form columns of fine limestone are unique. Not far from this is the *mastaba* of the princesses Khamerernebty and Meretites, two daughters of Newoserre Any. Nearby are the *mastaba*s of the princesses Khekeretnebty and Hetjetnub, daughters of Isesi.

A large cemetery, with tombs of dignitaries from the third dynasty to the sixth was discovered on the southern edge of Abusir; these include the partially intact tomb of the vizier Kar and his family, from the time of Pepy I. Also situated in this part of Abusir is the tomb of Fetekti, built at the end of the fifth dynasty. At the northern edge, there is a fifth dynasty burial ground with tombs of those from lower social ranks.

During the First Intermediate Period, there were no royal mortuary cults at Abusir. Although briefly revived at the beginning of the Middle Kingdom, from this period to the Late period, Abusir became increasingly a cemetery for the common people. A cemetery in southwestern Abusir was built to contain huge shaft tombs that were dated to the end of the twenty-sixth dynasty and the beginning of the twenty-seventh. Among them was the tomb of Udjahorresnet, chancellor of Egypt's Persian kings, Cambyses and Darius I (of the First Persian Occupation). His tomb was constructed with a cunning system of linked shafts, filled with sand; this was supposed to prevent access to the burial chamber. The southwestern excavation also uncovered the intact tomb of Iufaa, director of the palace.

The history of archaeological research in Abusir, in which Germans, French, Swiss, Egyptians, and Czechs have participated, began in the 1830s. Yet only two expeditions have carried out long-term and extensive excavations there—that of the German Oriental Society, headed by Ludwig Borchardt, from the beginning of the twentieth century, and the ongoing expedition of the Czech Institute of Egyptology, which began in the 1960s.

## BIBLIOGRAPHY

Borchardt, Ludwig. *Das Grabdenkmal des Königs Ne-user-reʿ.* 2 vols. Leipzig, 1907 and 1908.
Borchardt, Ludwig. *Das Grabdenkmal des Königs Saʒhu-reʿ,* vol. 1: *Der Bau.* Leipzig, 1910; vol. 2: *Die Wondbilder.* Leipzig, 1913.
Verner, Miroslav. *Forgotten Pharaohs, Lost Pyramids: Abusir.* Prague, 1994. A comprehensive, richly illustrated account of the history of Abusir, its main features and artifacts, and the history of their excavation.
Verner, Miroslav. *Abusir III: The Pyramid Complex of Khentkaus.* Prague, 1995.

MIROSLAV VERNER

**ABYDOS,** a site, ancient *ʒbḏw,* situated in the ancient Thinite nome (eighth Upper Egyptian nome) in southern Egypt (26°11′N 31°55′E). On the western side of the Nile, the site is on the edge of the low desert, 15 kilometers (9.5 miles) from the river. Greater Abydos spreads over 8 square kilometers (5 square miles) and is composed of archaeological remains from all phases of ancient Egyptian civilization. Abydos was significant in historical times as the main cult center of Osiris, ancient Egypt's primary funerary god. Many cult structures were dedicated to Osiris, and vast cemetery fields were developed, incorporating not only the regional population but also nonlocal people who chose to build tombs and commemorative monuments at Abydos. In the Predynastic and Early Dynastic periods, Abydos may have functioned primarily as a satellite funerary center for the nome capital of Thinis, which is perhaps to be located in the vicinity of the modern town of Girga or Balliana at the edge of the Nile. The significance of Abydos, however, exceeded that of a provincial burial center. It was the burial place of the first kings of Early Dynastic times (first and second dynasties), and during the subsequent Old and Middle Kingdoms Abydos evolved into a religious center of great importance.

The most striking buildings standing at Abydos are the well-preserved New Kingdom temples of Sety I and Ramesses II (nineteenth dynasty); the Early Dynastic funerary enclosure of King Khasekhemwy (second dynasty); and the walled enclosure called the Kom es-Sultan, which was the location of the early town and the main temple dedicated to Osiris. The greater part of the site, however, remains concealed beneath the sand, a fact recognized in the Arabic name of the modern town: Arabah el-Madfunah ("the buried Arabah"). Abydos can be discussed in terms of its major areas.

**North Abydos.** The area includes the Kom es-Sultan, the temple precinct, Umm el-Gaab, funerary enclosures, and cemeteries.

***Kom es-Sultan and the temple precinct of Osiris-Khentyamentiu.*** North Abydos was the major focal point of early activity, and it was here that an early town and

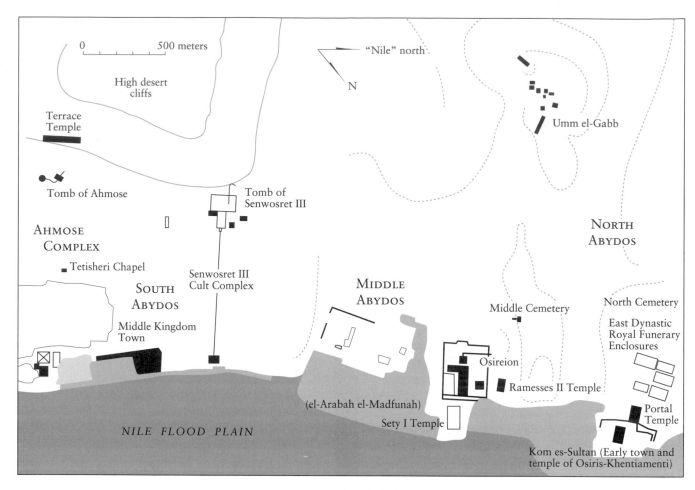

ABYDOS. *Plan of Abydos.*

temple site developed in the Predynastic period on the desert fringe at the locale now called the Kom es-Sultan ("Mound of the Ruler" in Arabic). Meager remnants of the Predynastic and Early Dynastic settlement were exposed in 1902–1903 by W. M. Flinders Petrie, who conducted the first extensive recorded excavation in the Kom es-Sultan. However, most of the early town lies covered by remains of later periods and beneath the level of modern groundwater.

Petrie's work produced evidence for the existence of a cult structure dedicated to the canid deity Khentyamentiu ("Foremost of the Westerners") during the Early Dynastic period. A temple dedicated to that god is likely to have formed the primary ritual center of Abydos in the Predynastic and Early Dynastic periods. During the Old Kingdom, Khentyamentiu was syncretized with the newly important funerary deity, Osiris. A temple dedicated to Osiris-Khentyamentiu existed from the time of the late Old Kingdom and is referred to on many stelae and private votive objects from the Old Kingdom and later peri-

ods. Petrie's work also exposed a series of royal cult buildings erected by kings from the Old Kingdom through New Kingdom. These structures are probably royal cult buildings (*ka*-chapels) built in proximity to the main temple of Osiris-Khentyamentiu, the remains of which are yet to be exposed. Beginning in the Old Kingdom, the temple precinct and core town area was provided with a town wall, which was modified and extended into the Late period, creating the large walled *temenos* visible there today. Research on the Kom es-Sultan has resumed under the University of Pennsylvania–Yale–New York University Expedition to Abydos. Work in 1979 and 1991 by D. O'Connor and M. Adams examined parts of the late Old Kingdom and First Intermediate Period town.

***Umm el-Gaab.*** At the locale now called Umm el-Gaab ("Mother of Pots" in Arabic) excavation undertaken first by E. Amélineau (1895–1898) and then by Petrie (1899–1900) exposed an extensive royal cemetery dating to the Predynastic and Early Dynastic periods. Plundered in antiquity but still preserving a significant sample of their original contents, several large Early Dynastic tombs were identified as the burial places of the earliest kings of the historic period. Subsequent to Petrie's work at Abydos, excavations at North Saqqara by W. Emery exposed a cemetery consisting of large *mastabas* of the first and second dynasties. This led many scholars to interpret the Abydos royal tombs as "cenotaphs," or symbolic tombs built by the early kings in an ancestral burial ground for religious reasons. More recently, scholars have accepted Abydos as the burial place of the earliest kings of dynastic times, whose roots were in the Thinite nome.

Renewed archaeological work since 1973 by the German Archaeological Institute, directed by G. Dreyer, has recorded in detail the development of a royal cemetery beginning in the Naqada I period. The history of this cemetery at Umm el-Gaab (covering much of the fourth millennium BCE), provides evidence for the increasing wealth and complexity of society in the late Predynastic period. Umm el-Gaab is especially important because of the evidence it provides for the emergence of political power culminating in pharaonic kingship and the associated centralized state around the beginning of dynastic times (c.3100 BCE). In a locality designated Cemetery U, royal tombs of late Naqada II and Naqada III display the differentiation associated with a stratified society and the existence of powerful kings who controlled considerable resources. Inscribed labels from the largest Predynastic tomb (tomb U-J, dating to the Naqada IIIa period) provide the earliest evidence for use of the hieroglyphic writing system in Egypt.

In the Early Dynastic period, Umm el-Gaab was the burial place of the first pharaohs of the historic dynasties (as well as their immediate Dynasty "0" predecessors). All the rulers of the first dynasty, as well as two kings of the second dynasty (Peribsen and Khasekhemwy), were buried at Abydos, a phenomenon which expresses the continued importance of dynastic associations between the first kings of the historic period and their Predynastic forebears. Tombs at Umm el-Gaab of the first and second dynasties are much larger than those of the Predynastic period and typically consist of a central burial chamber surrounded by storerooms and subsidiary burials. The tombs from the Predynastic were subterranean, with little more than a mound and upright stelae marking locations.

***Early Dynastic funerary enclosures.*** The primary aboveground structures associated with the Early Dynastic royal tombs were the funerary enclosures, which were built not at Umm el-Gaab but rather adjacent to the Kom es-Sultan. From the time of the early first dynasty, these structures consisted of large, rectangular mud-brick enclosures employing the "palace-façade" style of architecture. Two still stand today: the enclosure of Khasekhemwy and that of Qaa (now occupied by the Coptic village of Deir Sitt Damiana). After initial excavation by Petrie, work in 1986–1991 by D. O'Connor reexamined parts of the interiors of these structures and exposed twelve buried boats on the east side of the Khasekhemwy enclosure. The specific functions of these funerary enclosures remain an issue of debate, but they probably played a role in both the funerary ceremony itself and the long-term maintenance of a royal cult. Architectural elements articulated in the funerary enclosure of Khasekhemwy suggest continuity of form and religious function with the Step Pyramid complex of Djoser (third dynasty) at Saqqara.

***Development of the cult of Osiris.*** The burial place of the first kings at Umm el-Gaab was of supreme importance in the later development of Abydos. By the time of the Old Kingdom, Abydos was already understood as the burial place of Osiris, ruler of the netherworld and personification of the deceased pharaoh reborn into rulership in the afterlife. During the Old Kingdom, Osiris merged with Khentyamentiu. By the time of the early Middle Kingdom, there is evidence that Umm el-Gaab was understood as the burial place of Osiris himself; one tomb in particular, that of King Djer, appears to have been thought to be the deity's tomb. A yearly procession from the temple of Osiris-Khentyamentiu in the Kom es-Sultan reenacted the myth of the god's murder by Seth and his burial and rebirth as ruler of the netherworld. This procession, in which the god's image was carried aboard the sacred *neshmet* bark, progressed from the Kom es-Sultan through a low desert wadi leading up to Umm el-Gaab. The offerings presented to Osiris by pilgrims, especially in the New Kingdom and later periods, created the vast pottery-covered mounds that gave Umm el-Gaab its Arabic name.

***North and Middle cemeteries.*** From the time of the late Old Kingdom, the temple and cult of Osiris-Khentyamentiu created the impetus for the development of large cemeteries immediately west of the Kom es-Sultan and flanking the route of the Osiris procession to Umm el-Gaab. Excavation of the Northern and Middle cemeteries by a series of archaeologists—Mariette (1858), Peet (1909–1913), Garstang (1898–1899), Petrie (early 1900s), and Frankfort (1925–1926), among others—produced a large volume of objects; material from the North and Middle cemeteries constitutes an important body of funerary material in collections throughout the world.

The North Cemetery developed on the northern side of the wadi around the area of the Early Dynastic royal funerary enclosures and extends westward for one-half kilometer in the direction of Umm el-Gaab. Its development is associated primarily with the Middle Kingdom and later periods. An important area associated with the cult of Osiris lies adjacent to the west side of the Kom es-Sultan; there, large clusters of tombs as well as private

ABYDOS. *Central Hall of the Osireion, viewed from the west.* (Courtesy Dieter Arnold)

offering chapels (cenotaphs) were erected beginning in the Middle Kingdom. These chapels were intended to provide an eternal association between the deceased and the god Osiris, and the area of the North Cemetery closest to the Kom es-Sultan was called *rwd n ntr '3* ("Terrace of the Great God"). This area has produced an immense number of inscribed stelae and statues, especially in the second half of the nineteenth century through the work of G. Maspero, A. Mariette, and antiquities dealers such as Anastasi. More recent archaeological work was undertaken by the Pennsylvania–Yale Expedition codirected by D. O'Connor and W. K. Simpson. The Middle Cemetery extends along the southern side of the wadi, also running nearly a kilometer toward Umm el-Gaab; it was developed from the Old Kingdom onward.

Flanked on north and south by the extensive nonroyal burial grounds of the North and Middle cemeteries, the sacred processional route to Umm el-Gaab was protected by royal decree from burials and other development. A series of royal stelae set up at the terminal ends of the processional route by the time of the Middle Kingdom demarcated this sacred area. Recent work in 1996 by M. A. Pouls has discovered a limestone chapel of Thutmose III, which may be part of the formalized layout of the processional route during the New Kingdom.

**Middle Abydos.** The area includes the Sety I temple and the Osireion.

**Temple of Sety I.** Standing one kilometer to the south of the Kom es-Sultan and at the northern edge of the area often called "Middle Abydos," the temple of Sety I is the largest well-preserved building of the New Kingdom at Abydos. The L-shaped limestone temple was named "The Mansion of Millions of Years of King Menmaatre Who Is Contented in Abydos." The building consists of the two hypostyle halls that front seven sanctuaries, in sequence from south to north dedicated to Sety, Ptah, Re-Horakhty, Amun-Re, Osiris, Isis, and Horus. The southern sanctuary, dedicated to Sety himself, celebrates his deification as a deceased king. To the south of the Sety sanctuary, the King's Gallery contains a list of Sety's predecessors on the throne of Egypt. While including veneration of Egypt's principal deities, the Sety temple is most explicitly focused on the king's associations with Osiris and his deified predecessors, fully within the tradition of New Kingdom royal mortuary temples. The temple proper is set within a large brick enclosure (220 × 350 meters/700 × 102 feet) containing two open forecourts, as well as rows of mud-brick storage magazines on the south. A rear gateway set within a brick pylon is oriented to the site of the archaic royal cemetery at Umm el-Gaab; like the temple complex in the Kom es-Sultan, the Sety temple was linked both conceptually and through actual ritual processions with the putative burial place of Osiris.

*Osireion.* In addition to the Sety temple's orientation to Umm el-Gaab, behind the temple stands a subterranean structure, the Osireion, which functioned as a symbolic tomb or cenotaph of Osiris. The structure was excavated primarily in 1902–1903 by M. Murray, working with Petrie. The main central chamber contains a central platform and ten monolithic red granite piers. The architecture is intentionally archaizing in style (mimicking the monolithic architecture of the fourth dynasty) and was perhaps intended to provide a suitable burial structure for Osiris. The central platform is surrounded by water channels meant to represent the primeval mound of creation surrounded by the waters of Nun. Attached to the main chamber are other chambers and passages containing scenes and texts from the *Book of Gates* and *Book of Going Forth by Day* (*Book of the Dead*), standard elements of Ramessid royal tombs. Adjacent to the Sety temple was a smaller one-room chapel dedicated to Sety's father Ramesses I, now in the Metropolitan Museum, New York. Farther north stand the well-preserved remains of a temple built by Ramesses II. Remains of other Ramessid royal buildings lie along the desert edge between the Sety temple and the Kom es-Sultan.

The area of Middle Abydos south of the Sety temple is the least-known area of the site because the modern town of Arabah el-Madfunah covers most of the surface of this part of Abydos. In all likelihood, this was the location of the major concentration of settlement from the New Kingdom onward. Remnants of architectural elements and inscribed temple blocks from a number of periods suggest that remnants of more cult buildings are yet to be exposed south of the Sety temple.

**South Abydos.** South Abydos covers about 2 square kilometers (1.25 square miles) of low desert in a strip approximately 1 kilometer (a half mile) wide between the cultivation and high desert cliffs. In early times, the area was used for Predynastic habitation and cemeteries; however, the major development of this area of Abydos occurred in the Middle Kingdom, when the first of a series of royal cult complexes was established by Senwosret III.

*Complex of Senwosret III.* Extending between the cliffs and cultivation, the Senwosret III mortuary complex consists of a massive subterranean tomb with a royal mortuary temple. It was initially examined by D. Randall-MacIver and A. Weigall of the Egypt Exploration Fund between 1899 and 1902, and renewed work during the 1990s by the University of Pennsylvania, directed by J. Wegner, has excavated the mortuary temple, which is dedicated to the deceased Senwosret III and celebrates his unification with Osiris. A large planned settlement just south of the mortuary complex is similar in scale and organization to the town at Illahun that is attached to the pyramid complex of Senwosret II. Work in 1997 identified the name of this temple–town foundation as "Enduring are the Places of Khakaure Justified in Abydos."

*Complex of Ahmose.* One-half kilometer south of the Senwosret III complex stand the remains of a series of monuments erected by the eighteenth dynasty king Ahmose, which were initially examined by A. Mace and C. T. Currelly for the Egypt Exploration Fund. A pyramid and temple situated at the edge of cultivation are associated with a subterranean tomb near the base of the desert cliffs. This was the last royal pyramid to be erected in Egypt. In 1993, S. Harvey reexamined the pyramid temple and exposed remains of a small temple stamped with the titulary of Queen Ahmose-Nefertari and possibly dedicated to her cult. Between the Ahmose pyramid and underground tomb is a small chapel dedicated to Ahmose's grandmother, Queen Tetisheri. A well-preserved stela, now in the Cairo Museum, was discovered in the Tetisheri chapel. A final monument belonging to the Ahmose complex is the terrace temple, on the lower part of the hill; it appears to be incomplete, and its function remains unclear.

**BIBLIOGRAPHY**

Calverley, A. M., and M. F. Broome. *The Temple of King Sethos I at Abydos.* 4 vols. London, 1933–1958.

David, Rosalie. *A Guide to Religious Ritual at Abydos.* Warminster, 1981.

Dreyer, Günter, et al. Preliminary Reports on Work at Umm el-Gaab. *Mitteilungen des Deutschen Archäologische Instituts Kairo* (1986, 1990, 1991, 1993, 1995, 1998).

Dreyer, Günter. *Umm el-Qaab I.* Mainz, 1998.

Griffiths, J. Gwyn. *The Origins of Osiris.* Leiden, 1980.

Harvey, Stephen. "The Monuments of Ahmose at Abydos." *Egyptian Archaeology* 4 (1995), 3–5.

Kemp, Barry. "Abydos and the Royal Tombs of the First Dynasty." *Journal of Egyptian Archaeology* 52 (1966), 13–22.

Kemp, Barry. "The Egyptian First Dynasty Royal Cemetery." *Antiquity* 41 (1967), 22–32.

Kemp, Barry. "The Osiris Temple at Abydos." *Mitteilungen des Deutsches Archaeologisches Institute Kairo* 23 (1968), 138–155.

Murray, Margaret. *The Osireion.* London, 1904.

O'Connor, David. "The 'Cenotaphs' of the Middle Kingdom at Abydos." *Mélanges Gamal Eddin Mokhtar* (1985), 161–178.

O'Connor, David. "Boat Graves and Pyramid Origins." *Expedition* 33 (1991), 5–17.

Otto, Eberhard. *Egyptian Art and the Cults of Osiris and Amun.* London, 1968.

Petrie, W. M. F. *The Royal Tombs of the First Dynasty.* 2 vols. London, 1900–1901.

Petrie, W. M. F. *Abydos.* 2 vols. London, 1902.

Simpson, William K. *The Terrace of the Great God at Abydos: The Offering Chapels of Dynasties 12 and 13.* New Haven and Philadelphia, 1974.

Spiegel, Joachim. *Die Götter von Abydos: Studien zum ägyptischen Synkretismus,* Gottinger Orientforschungen, 4. Wiesbaden, 1973.

Wegner, Josef. "Old and New Excavations at the Abydene Complex of Senwosret III." *K.M.T.: A Modern Journal of Ancient Egypt* 6.2 (1996), 59–71.

Wegner, Josef. "Excavations at the Town of *Enduring-are-the-Places-of-Khakaure-Maa-Kheru-in-Abydos.*" *Journal of the American Research Center in Egypt* 35 (1998), 1–44.

JOSEF W. WEGNER

**ABYDOS LIST.** *See* King Lists.

**ACACIA.** *See* Flora.

**ACHAEMENIDS.** The last pharaoh of the twenty-sixth dynasty, Psamtik III (526–525 BCE), was conquered and captured by the Persian king Cambyses, son of Cyrus II, after the Battle of Pelusium in 525 BCE. Egypt, together with Cyprus and Phoenicia, then formed the sixth satrapy of the Persian Empire. The satrap (Pers., "protector of the reign"), who represented the king of Persia, resided at Memphis with his chancellery. The garrison posts remained at Mareotis, Daphnis, and Elephantine (where a Jewish colony with a temple to Yahweh had existed on the island since the time of Apries; it was destroyed in 410 BCE).

Besides Cambyses, the First Persian domination (Manetho's Dynasty 27) includes the rulers Darius I (521–486 BCE), Xerxes (486–466 BCE), Artaxerxes I (465–424 BCE), Darius II (423–405 BCE), and Artaxerxes II (405–359 BCE). This regime was recognized in Egypt at least until 402 BCE. According to an inscription on a stela from the Serapeum, (from the sepulchre for the Apis bulls) dated to the sixth year of Cambyses' reign, the king had assumed the Egyptian royal epithet *mswty R'*, as we know from the autobiography of Wedjahorresene, court doctor during the reigns of Cambyses and Darius I. Incised on Wedjahorresene's naophorus (block) statue, now in the Vatican Museum, is a depiction of him in Persian dress with Persian-made bracelets; there is a depiction in the same manner of another official, the treasurer Ptahhotep on another Serapeum stela, now in the Brooklyn Museum of Art. Egyptian hatred of Cambyses, referred to by the Greeks (Herodotus 3.27–38; Diodorus Siculus 1.46; Strabo 107.27; Plutarch *On Isis and Osiris* 44), derived not only from the impact of the military conquests but also from the resentment of the Egyptian clergy to Cambyses' decree limiting the royal concessions to the temples (Demotic Papyrus 215, verso, Bibliothèque Nationale, Paris). The three military expeditions on which he embarked (against Carthage, the oasis of the Libyan desert, and Nubia) were serious failures. Cambyses died in 522 BCE in Syria on his way home. His successor, Darius I, abrogated Cambyses' unpopular decree. He constructed an immense temple to Amun Re in the Kharga Oasis, and he succeeded in dredging the navigable route from the Nile to the Red Sea (from Bubastis across the Wadi Tummilat to Lake Timsah at the Bitter Lakes), which he marked with large stelae bearing commemorative inscriptions in hieroglyphs and cuneiform. Diodorus lists Darius I as the sixth and last legislator; he is better called a codifier, since (Demotic Papyrus, 215, verso, Bibliothèque Nationale, Paris) he had the laws that were in force transcribed on papyrus in both Egyptian (Demotic) and Aramaic (the official language of the empire) until Amasis' final year.

Aryandes, the first satrap of Egypt, was executed for being a rebel. He was followed by Pherendates and then by Achemenes (one of Xerxes' brothers), who died in the Battle of Papremis in the Nile Delta during the rebellion of 460 BCE, which was led by Inaros, son of Psamtik (Thucydides 1.104). Arsames held the office of satrap during the reign of Darius II.

Three indigenous dynasties (the twenty-eighth, twenty-ninth, and thirtieth) existed in Egypt from 402 BCE until Artaxerxes conquered Nektanebo II. Egypt then endured the Second Persian Occupation, from 343 to 332 BCE. The ephemeral Pharaoh Khababash (known from the "stela of the satrap Ptolomey") was probably removed in 344/343 BCE. The satrap Sabace (Arrian *Anabasis* 2.11) died in the Battle of Issus, where Sematauwrytefnakhte, an Egyptian doctor from the court of Darius III, was also present; the latter also survived the "battle of the Greeks" (as known from his autobiography, inscribed in hieroglyphs on a stela now in the Naples Museum). The last satrap, Mazakes (Arrian *Anabasis* 3.102), handed Egypt over to Alexander the Great in 322 BCE.

[*See also* Late Period; *overview article and article on the* Thirty-first Dynasty; *and* Persia.]

**BIBLIOGRAPHY**

Bresciani, E. "Persian Occupation of Egypt." In *Cambridge History of Iran,*" vol. 2. Cambridge, 1985.

Briant, P. "Etnoclasse dominante et populations soumises: le cas de l'Egypte." In *Achaemenid History*, vol. 3, pp. 137–173. Leiden, 1988.

Dandamaev, M. *A Political History of the Achaemenid Empire.* Leiden, 1989.

Lloyd, A. H. "Herodotus on Cambyses; Some Thoughts on Recent Work." *Achaemenid History*, vol. 3, pp. 55–66. Leiden, 1988.

Posener G. *La première domination perse en Egypte.* Cairo, 1936.

EDDA BRESCIANI
Translated from Italian by Jennifer Worth

**ADMINISTRATION.** *This is a three-part article covering* State Administration, Provincial Administration, *and* Temple Administration.

## State Administration

Administration is the socioeconomic institution installed to control resources within a defined terrain, the estate. In *state administration*, control operates at the national level, and in Egypt its client is the royal court. Control is a function of technological development. Ancient technologies, particularly those of communication, do not permit instant response across large distances. Sources on the subject indicate a journey time of about three weeks for a ship traveling from the Nile Delta upriver to southern Upper Egypt; this creates a response lag of about six weeks, short for the ancient world but not comparable to modern conditions. The premodern state characteristically enjoyed only limited administrative reach into the lives of the inhabitants of its territory. Such differences necessitate careful translation and interpretation in areas like security (army and the border) and revenues (defining rent and tax). The sources are not explicit on the system of land rights in Egypt; in most documents, the frequency and basis of revenue collection are not stated. The apparent monopoly of Egypt's royal court in many areas may reflect its dominance in economic or ideological terms, more than juridical regime.

From its invention in the late fourth millennium BCE, writing technology (script and material) played a major role in administration. Nonetheless, administration is first a practice based on social relations, rather than a set of documents. The texts provide extensive data on administration, but this remains a partial view of the reasons and methods of any social control of resources. Archaeological evidence may help to complete the picture in the case of urban storage, building, and quarrying expeditions, but it has not yet enlightened us on irrigation or rural organization.

The Egyptians distinguished between local and national levels of administration by prefixing to a title a phrase invoking royal authority: in the Middle Kingdom it was "seal-bearer [?] of the reigning [?] king," and in the New Kingdom it was "king's scribe." In general, these phrases denoting national office seem confined to high officials in the royal court. When a provincial governor prefixed the phrase to his main title, it might indicate that he had been promoted to that inner group of national officials. A seventeenth dynasty royal decree records a "king's seal-bearer, mayor of Coptos," at a time when the king ruled from nearby Thebes over only southern Egypt. Often the royal prefix-title distinguished national treasurers or overseers of estates and workforces from men with identical function at a lower level, in one province, or on one estate. Coordination between national and provincial levels of administration seems to have fallen to the *ṯȝty* ("highest official"), a title conventionally translated "vizier" in Egyptology. It is less easy to identify court officials responsible in each period for connections between Egypt and foreign dominions.

Ancient Egypt had two centers: an ideal personalized center—the king; and an institutional center—offices of revenue and expenditure (notably military and monumental). The personal center had always to be on the move, to maintain the unity of the state. Royal travel was a religious motif, cast in the Early Dynastic period as the Following of Horus. In the Middle Kingdom textual record, the king travels to different places always with a religious mission, to establish or renew cult in specific localities. Simultaneous military and economic objectives may be discerned; royal visits to the First Cataract of the Nile in the sixth dynasty and to Medamud in the thirteenth dynasty included the reception of foreign rulers. Since divine kingship united religious, military, and economic terrain, the historian cannot assume precedence for one of the three in revenue-raising and expenditure. The depersonalized center of ancient Egypt was the sum of buildings and staff involved in maintaining the royal court. Few locations are known for these, even at Amarna, the best-preserved of the royal cities. The administrations did not form one complex at a single place of royal residence. The Old Egyptian term *ẖnw* ("the residence") denoted a fixed location for the central offices of state, but it did not exist in every period. The Old Kingdom figures in later literary texts as the "period of the residence," but it is not known whether this was a single place or a new palace for each reign. In the Middle Kingdom, there seems to have been no residence until Amenemhet I founded a fortified residence, called Itjtawyamenemhat ("Amenemhat secures the Two Lands," abbreviated to Itjtawy) probably near his pyramid at el-Lisht. In the New Kingdom, there again seems to be no residence in the eighteenth dynasty until Akhenaten founded his capital, Akhetaten, with nearby royal tomb, the southernmost point from which the Two Lands were governed. In the nineteenth and twentieth dynasties, the residence was in the northeastern Delta at Piramesse; it was abandoned in favor of the still more northerly site of Tanis in the twenty-first dynasty. The next secure evidence for a residence comes in the late fourth century BCE, when Alexander the Great founded Alexandria, on the Mediterranean, at the westernmost edge of the Delta. In the late Middle Kingdom, when official titles were most precise, and the residence at Itjtawy was still functioning, special phrases identify some high stewards and overseers of sealers as "following the king" or "who is in the palace." Presumably the existence of a fixed residence for the ever-traveling king made it necessary to share a position between two men, one accompanying the king around the country, the other responsible for the fixed head office.

By the standards of modern state budgets, the requirements of the early state were minimal, with none of the vast industrialized enterprises of warfare and welfare. Translations of ancient offices as "departments" of defense, trade, or agriculture constitute an anachronism that may distort a reconstruction of the revenue-raising and -spending patterns of the early state. The bureau of an Egyptian high official lies between the two poles of informal/personal and formal/depersonalized in the development of the modern state. Even where the term *ḥз* ("bureau") was used, it may refer physically to the reception rooms in the palatial home of the particular official. Five great officials of state may be noted: vizier, treasurer, general, royal documents scribe, and chief lector-priest. After the vizier, who was key coordinator of the system, the treasurer seems to be the leading official of state. His responsibility for revenue covers two areas, each governed by a separate national official. One bore the title "overseer of sealers" (the men responsible for items of high value in small scale, requiring sealing), the other was "high steward" (responsible for other commodities: for the "stewards," literally "overseers of estates," see below). The "overseer of fields" was another national official in the area of revenue, who was involved in calculating estate values. The general (literally "taskforce overseer") seems at the national level to cover security rather than building or quarrying; the latter, in particular, always included a military dimension, as an activity in wild terrain. Little is known of documentation and storage, which presumably formed the core duties of the royal documents scribe, another official at the highest level. High status fell in the religious domain to the high priests of Heliopolis and Memphis (later also of Thebes) and to the chief lector-priest. Lectors (literally "holders of the festival roll") would have been competent in reading hieroglyphs, since the festival rituals were written until the late Middle Kingdom in that sacred script rather than in ordinary longhand (Hieratic). The chief lector presumably supervised the copying and composing of hieroglyphic texts for royal inscriptions in the domains of eternity: the temples and cemeteries. Inscriptions of Amenemhet III and Hatshepsut record that chief lectors under divine inspiration provided the four sacred throne-names added at accession by the king to his birth-name. The presence of chief lectors at the highest level emphasizes the importance of the religious dimension of the early state in Egypt.

In managing royal concerns nationwide, holders of different titles might perform the same functions. This applies in particular to overseers of construction, quarrying, or mining, and to the judicial aspect of officialdom. In the Old Kingdom, the tasks of an "overseer of works" might fall to a vizier or a "chief of directors of craftsmen" (the latter becoming the designation for the high priest of Ptah at Memphis). There seems to have been no separate archi-tectural or engineering division of the administration any more than there was a separate judiciary. The title *sзb* is often translated "judge," but it seems to be a generic term for "official" when applied to a named individual, in contrast to the term *sr*, which is the generic term for "official" in the indefinite. As coordinator of the administration, the vizier most often held the responsibility of "overseer of the six great mansions," a term that covered at the national level all centers of royal authority. One Middle Kingdom security official, an "overseer of disputes" held the variant "overseer of the six mansions in Itjtawy," expressing from a different angle authority over places of judgment at the residence. The administration of justice formed an important aspect of all officialdom and land ownership; this is reflected in the literary *Story of Khuninpu* (the "Eloquent Peasant" of Egyptological literary studies), where a traveler robbed on the land of a high steward petitions that high official directly at his town house.

Revenue collection may be divided into periodic and sporadic. Rent cannot be distinguished from taxation unless the property rights are known for the items collected. In most instances, underlying ownership is not recorded, and it is probably wiser to adopt the broad term "dues" in preference to the term "tax," which assumes specific relations between revenue collector and payer. Similarly, in the delivery of foreign goods, the broad Egyptian term *inw* ought to be translated first as "deliveries," rather than (as is often the case in modern histories) as "tribute." Goods collected may be raw materials or worked products; they may be divided first into foods and others, then into staples and luxuries. Even simple homes may have nonstaples. Ancient Egyptian economy and demography are little known, but it seems reasonable to assume majority dependence on local agriculture and animal husbandry, as opposed to hunting-gathering (still an important element of early states) or urban commerce. There is little if any evidence for centralized intervention in irrigation or animal and plant domestication. Irrigation networks in the Nile Valley depended on regional basins, not a national system of control. Irrigation may have played a role in the consolidation of oligarchic power at some stage of the Predynastic, but there is no precise data for effective control of high and low annual Nile floods in relation to forming or maintaining the unified state. Nearly all texts refer to centralized interest in produce rather than in the maintenance of lands, and land assessment by officials relates to harvest yield, not to irrigation repairs. One of the most explicit texts on irrigation works is the twelfth dynasty composition inscribed on tomb figurines called *shawabti*s (the meaning is unknown). The oldest version orders the figure to substitute for the deceased in any of these four tasks in the afterlife: on replacement land (the meaning is unknown); removal of a sector; ferrying earth from riverbank lands; and ploughing new lands for the reigning king. The fourth implies royal expansion (but not maintenance) of irrigation, using conscripted labor.

The existence of royal land would have given court officials specific interests throughout Egypt. The proportion of those to other lands is not known, and the relation of the Egyptian term *pr nswt* ("royal domain") to other domains is problematic. The twelfth dynasty inscription of Nebipusenusret assigns officials to "royal domain" or "temple," but that refers to function rather than to salary source. The scale of the surviving Old and Middle Kingdom temple architecture does not suggest an important role for it in the state economy, but the archaeological record may be misleading, since the national religious centers at Memphis and Heliopolis are little known. From the New Kingdom, religious architecture is better preserved, and it apparently was conceived in different form, which included vast enclosures surrounded by massive walls. Temple enclosures seem the most secure nonmilitary structures in the New Kingdom and Late period landscape. In a nonmonetary but partly urbanized economy, grain is currency, and granaries are the principal banks. The regional temple granaries may form local points of royal power. New Kingdom temple economy may then be the result of a restructured state economy, under a complex system of resource management. The relationship between royal domain and temple is additionally obscured because royal cult centers lay within temple domains. The principal center of the royal cult, near the burial place of the king at Thebes, was "in the Amun domain." This religious expression would not have given the Amun priesthood any additional resources; temple officials were appointed by the king, and "temple lands" could be managed by high court officials. The longest Egyptian manuscript, Papyrus Harris I, records massive donations by Ramesses III of the twentieth dynasty to his own cult, centered at Medinet Habu "in the Amun domain." High officials managed the Ramesses III cult estates, and their resources flowed into the temple of the king, not the households of the priests. The civil war at the end of the twentieth dynasty may have centered on control of the national bank—the granaries in the Amun domain at Thebes. The viceroy of Kush needed these to pay for his troops and seems to have wrested control by force from their usual state official, the high priest of Amun; in response, the Delta-based court of Ramesses XI had to enlist the help of Libyan settlers to restore order. The death of Ramesses XI left a new Libyan king ruling Egypt from the North, a Libyan general governing Upper Egypt from Thebes (legitimated by taking the title "High Priest of Amun"), with the viceroy independent in Nubia.

In these struggles, as in the general question about relations between separate "domains," using the European concepts of Clergy and State is inappropriate. Behind the Egyptian religious title of an estate, the economic and political structures emerge only in precise data on goods, their origins, and their destinations. The Abusir Papyri from the Old Kingdom indicate a complex web of estates, passing "on paper" goods from one estate via others to a final destination. The royal court accounts in Papyrus Boulaq 18 from the early thirteenth dynasty present a similar banking system of dues from various departments and places. The New Kingdom festival list of Ramesses III confirms the web of rights and obligations from which the accountant calculated the actual destination of a product.

Egypt as a central state raised revenues in kind from the local areas, but the basis, frequency, and regularity of the collections are not known. To raise revenues efficiently and fairly, the central administration required a national record of property; one part of that is preserved indirectly in hieroglyphic references to the "time of the count of cattle and people." Livestock and labor force form two naturally variable resources, and their calculation was the basis for the assessment of estates. Middle Kingdom official documents from Illahun recorded household populations—in one case a soldier with his family, in another a lector with a large household. For accuracy in herd counts, a new census would fall every first, second, or third year after the preceding one (not necessarily fixed as biennial, as is often stated). During the Old Kingdom, Egyptians used the count to calculate time in general, and the recurrent "year of count" became the term for consecutive "year of reign" by the First Intermediate Period. The assessment of estates also depended on records of land ownership; indirect evidence for these survives in legal cases in which the parties resort to state records, most notably in the hieroglyphic inscription from the tomb-chapel of Mes, a Ramessid official. Transfers of ownership underwent official approval in the bureau of the vizier as "deeds of conveyance" (literally "house contents"), according to the *Duties of the Vizier* (as preserved in eighteenth dynasty tomb-chapels) and to earlier documents from Illahun (late Middle Kingdom). The near-total destruction of Egypt's state records obscures an implied gargantuan scale of assessment.

In periods of unity, Egypt occupied and administered neighboring lands. Excavations at Buhen in Lower Nubia revealed an Egyptian copper-working station of the Old Kingdom, established by the fourth dynasty; there is as yet little indication of the early military and administrative organization of such outposts. During the Middle Kingdom, at least one town on the eastern Mediterranean coast, Byblos, traded with Egypt to such an extent that its rulers occasionally used the Egyptian language and hieroglyphic script, with the self-description "mayor of Byblos"; however, there is no evidence for an Egyptian military settlement in the Near East or for separate ad-

Valley. With the exception of the nomarchs of the fifteenth Upper Egyptian nome who, in the late Old Kingdom, were also responsible for leading expeditions to Hatnub (the alabaster or calcite quarries), the oversight of such undertakings did not fall within the competence of provincial administrators. The epithets of nomarchs make reference to their legal jurisdiction (at the lower level), which can also be shown for the New Kingdom.

The tasks in the provinces were carried out in close cooperation with the central authorities, under the control of the highest executive official of the land, the vizier. The nomarchs were subject to the instructions of the vizier and had to answer to him. The assessments of taxes and the calculations of the number of corvée laborers to be provided were made in the central offices. The tasks assigned were then executed in each locality under the direction of the nomarch, according to the directives of the central authority, as communicated through the regional authorities. These very complex administrative procedures can be most clearly seen in the texts of the exemption decrees for provincial temples of the Old Kingdom. These decrees released any temple, for which they were issued, from performing every kind of duty for the state. In addition, they were removed from the jurisdiction of the provincial officials. These decrees show that tax collection and the corvée were organized by nomes and that the nomes were administrative units.

In the second half of the fifth dynasty, the office of "Supervisor of Upper Egypt" was created; this official functioned as the representative of the vizier in Upper Egypt and, as the authority to whom the nomarchs were subordinated, took on part of the oversight duties of viziers over the nomarchs. The headquarters of this official was in Abydos, and besides him, there were other officials who were responsible for only one part of a region in Upper Egypt. So, at one time, there was a supervisor of Upper Egypt in Meir for the middle nomes and one in Akhmim for the northern nomes (those north of Abydos). As to whether there were established supraregional subdivisions of the office of "Supervisor of Upper Egypt" for any significant period cannot be proved. In the late Old Kingdom, even nomarchs bore this title—and so they became independent of the supraregional officials, likely gaining greater autonomy with respect to the recruitment of corvée labor or the disposition of the taxes that were collected. This suggests, for example, a possible early form of the title borne by nomarchs "Overseer of the Barley of Upper Egypt." A Lower Egyptian counterpart to this supraregional office in Upper Egypt cannot be attested for this period.

The city of Elephantine seems to have held a special position in Upper Egypt. There is still no evidence that this island in the Nile was part of the first Upper Egyptian

nome or the administrative seat of that nome. (Rather, we ought to look to Kom Ombo to locate the nomarchial seat.) The officials who resided in Elephantine during the sixth dynasty were responsible for local administration and for relations with Nubia.

In the late Old Kingdom, the nomarchs were in many cases also directors of the local temple administrations, particularly the provincial temple, which was located at their administrative seat. As a result, two originally separate administrative offices were brought together under the control of a single person. Toward the end of the Old Kingdom, the central power of the state declined in importance. This led to a degree of *de facto* autonomy for the individual regions in the province that was quite far-reaching. Those who held power in the regions took over for their own areas tasks that were previously reserved to the central power. They laid claim to complete discretionary power over taxes and corvée labor, something that had begun in the late sixth dynasty. They also had their own troops and engaged in battles against their local rivals. As a result, at least in southern Upper Egypt, the old traditional nomes no longer existed. In many places, the temple administration was the actual local or regional administrative constant, as seen when the title "Great Head of the Nome" declined in significance and the high priests functioned as the leaders of the provincial administrations.

During the First Intermediate Period, new areas of power or administrative districts gradually took shape. The ancient nomes were replaced by so-called city districts, the area of which, at least in Egypt's south, was often smaller than that of the older nomes. After the reunification, under the kings of the eleventh dynasty, and the founding of the Middle Kingdom, the city districts became the new nomes. Characteristically, their names (as in the later Greco-Roman period) were formed from the name of each regional seat of administration, the capital of the nome.

An obvious exception in Middle Egypt was the fifteenth and sixteenth Upper Egyptian nomes, where, even in the early Middle Kingdom, the nomarchs used the title "Great Head of a Nome" and designated their administrative region with the ancient nome emblem. The area of the sixteenth Upper Egyptian nome was, however, reduced in size when Amenemhet I redrew the nome boundaries and created a separate district on the eastern bank of the Nile. For this new district, a new form of the name and the new nomarch title of $h3ty$-' was used; it had already been introduced during the eleventh dynasty to the south of that area.

The title $h3ty$-' is usually translated as "mayor," and since this designation falsely suggests a leadership function in an (urban) settlement, it will not be used here. The evidence shows that officials with that title were usually also responsible for the surrounding rural area and for the collection of taxes on agricultural products. The "city" that they administered was an extensive area, with fields and waterways, as can be seen from the description of the reordering of the provinces in the twelfth dynasty, under Chnumhotep in Beni Hasan. These were nomes. To what extent this situation also applies to the pyramid cities—whose mayors are known in the late Middle Kingdom—must remain open. The only thing that is certain is that, within the state administrative structure, they had a status that corresponded to that of the nomes. No "mayors" of the two capital cities Itjtawi and Thebes are yet documented. That the title was a functional one is attested to by the fact that it was written twice in complete lists of titles, where it occurs a second time outside the series of rank titles.

The nomarchs of the Middle Kingdom were also responsible for the collection of taxes and the recruitment of the population liable for corvée labor. From Middle Egypt, the documentation shows that they had a large staff of coworkers to help carry out their duties. In that respect, the provincial administration was organized according to the model of the national state administration. Among other things, there is evidence of a "Speaker of the Nomarch," whose function corresponded to that of the vizier on the national level, as well as a treasurer and a director of the nome's office of records (usually understood as a prison). Under the "speaker," there was an official who was in charge of the irrigation canals of the region (*ḳnbty n w*), which had meanwhile been introduced. Then there was a series of scribes who belonged to the middle level of the administration. For other regions of Egypt, less evidence of this kind of complex administrative structure exists in primary sources; however, such a structure can be inferred from the so-called tax list in the tomb of Rekhmire, a more recent copy of an older text.

As in the Old Kingdom, the provincial administration was under the authority of the vizier. For the southern part of Upper Egypt, the supraregional administrative unit (*w'rt*) of the "southern head" (*tp rsy*), was set up in the time of Senwosret I; it was under the authority of the "speaker" (who must be differentiated from the "nome speakers"), who functioned as the representative of the vizier. He took over the duties that had been the responsibility of the governor of Upper Egypt, and his administrative seat was Thebes, which during the Middle Kingdom had become co-capital with Itjtawy, the royal residence in the North.

The postulated major administrative reform of the Middle Kingdom by Senwosret III must be viewed with greater skepticism than has been the case. Beyond question, the large and sumptuously decorated tombs of the nomarchs—known from Aswan, Middle Egypt, and northern Upper Egypt—were no longer constructed toward the end of the twelfth dynasty. Whether this finding can be used to infer a radical internal political change, consisting of the elimination of the so-called nome princedoms, is less certain. First, it must be determined that these tomb complexes were not ended abruptly under this king. Second, the existence of such tombs cannot be proven for other regions, even for the earlier period, although the existence of nomarchs is documented in those places. Third, the situation in Aswan, well known from the numerous finds there, does not show this radical break in the administrative structure. Therefore, a general administrative reform that affected the whole of Egypt did not take place.

As for the lack of tomb complexes in later times, religious reasons might also be cited. Even for the officials who exercised supraregional activity like the "speaker" in Thebes, no large decorated tombs can be found. The existence of nomarchs was later documented for the thirteenth dynasty and also the seventeenth dynasty. Among these, some cases are documented in which a son took over the father's office, so that no radical break can be shown with respect to the inheritance of offices. In contrast, earlier nomarchs of the twelfth dynasty, in order to take over their father's or grandfather's office, needed legitimization by the king; only he installed them in the position their fathers had held. They were, by law, royal officials—not princes in their own right. In their inscriptions, despite many instances of usurping formerly royal attributes, they are at pains to present themselves as loyal servants of the king.

Typically the nomarchs of the Middle Kingdom were often also at the same time high priests at the local temples. As to whether this was the case for all regions of Egypt cannot be determined for lack of sources. Following the model of Egypt proper, a nomarch was also put in place in Nubia on the southern limit of the territory then ruled by Egypt. According to the sources, this nomarch was in charge of the entire area of the Second Cataract along with its forts.

The New Kingdom provincial administration was similar to that of the Middle Kingdom. The nomarchs bore the same official title, and nomes continued to be called by the name of their capital, as this was true for both Upper and Lower Egypt. The personal bond of the nomarchs to the local temple administrations soon became looser, and generally, they were no longer high priests of these temples. Their responsibility for the collection of taxes remained, and until the rule of Thutmose III, they were responsible for the recruiting of those compelled to perform state labor. The nome prince of Elkab was also in charge of the gold mines of the Eastern Desert. For the Ramessid era, the sources concerning provincial administration are rather poor. No tombs are known for members of the provincial administration. Wilbour Papyrus shows that they were responsible for overseeing state lands, and according to the Haremheb Decree, the nomarchs were responsible for the king's supplies during his visit to Luxor for the Opet festival; with priests of the local temples, nomarchs comprised the district court of justice. Hardly anything more is known about other members of the provincial administration subordinate to the nomarchs; the administrative structure had been greatly simplified.

While the nomarchs of Egypt proper continued to be subject to the vizier, those in Nubia were under the authority of the viceroy of Kush. For a long time this also applied to the nomarchs of Elephantine, when the southern part of Upper Egypt belonged to the Nubian administrative region; for a time its northern border was near Hierakonpolis.

In the eighteenth dynasty, the nome was still designated as a city district (*nìwt*), while in the Ramessid era, it was replaced by the term *ḳ'ḥt*. After the New Kingdom, nomes were called *t3š*. For the period after the New Kingdom, the Third Intermediate Period, little is known about provincial administration. The splintering of the state into various independent Libyan princedoms in Middle and Lower Egypt led to a situation in which the provincial administration no longer played any major role—since the character of the territorial state had, in many instances, been lost. Frequently, there was no hinterland, no province in the strict sense of the word, located at any distance from the seat of the ruler. Therefore the question of its administration became moot. Still, for larger contiguous areas, there remains documentation for leaders of the regional administration who held the title *ḥ3ty-'* ("nomarch"). Nothing is known about the functions and duties of this official or even about the structure of the administration under him. In the inscription of King Piya, in keeping with his idea of a new unitary state, the independent princes were also designated as nomarchs. The title *ḥ3ty-'* has also been documented for the Theban theocratic state. Under these officials there were nome scribes; this situation can be traced to the period of the Ptolemies.

From the period of the First Persian Occupation, the twenty-seventh dynasty, nomarchs of Coptos are known from inscriptions in the Wadi Hammamat. Since they had Persian names, they may have been members of the foreign ruling class. As to whether this was the rule for holding the office during that period, the lack of additional sources make it impossible to say with certainty. From Greek sources, the complex provincial administrations of the Ptolemaic and Roman periods are known. At first, nomarchs headed the nomes but later *strategoi* were appointed. For the supraregional administration, an *epi-*

*strategos* was responsible; his position is similar to that of the "speaker" in the administration of the "southern head," during the Middle Kingdom.

The lists of nomes of the Egyptian temples from the Ptolemaic and Roman periods do not reflect the administrative reality of their own times, since they show the administrative situation of the Old Kingdom. The twenty-two Upper Egyptian nomes from that ancient period are well documented; for a large portion of the Lower Egyptian nomes, this was also the case. Nomes were added to these lists for Lower Egypt, to create an archaic effect, so they are thereby anachronistic.

[*See also* Administration, *article on* State Administration; Officials; *and* Taxation.]

**BIBLIOGRAPHY**

A brief overview of provincial administration in ancient Egypt is afforded by F. Gomáa, R. Müller-Wollermann, and W. Schenkel in *Mittelägypten zwischen Samalut und dem Gabal Abu Sir* (Beihefte TAVO, series B, number 69, pp. 5–19), Wiesbaden, 1991. They deal with its development from earliest times to the Coptic period.

W. Helck describes the nomes as administrative districts in *Die altägyptischen Gaue* (Beihefte TAVO, series B, no. 5), Wiesbaden, 1974. He demonstrates the evolution of provincial administration to the Greco-Roman period. (This book has the drawback of having used the lists of the nomes from the Greco-Roman period as its ordering principle, so for most of the periods of Egyptian history, this is an anachronism.)

For the Old Kingdom and the First Intermediate Period, the following are available: E. Martin-Pardey, *Untersuchungen zur ägyptischen Provinzialverwaltung bis zum Ende des Alten Reiches* (Hildesheimer Ägyptologische Beiträge, 1), Hildesheim, 1976; and H. G. Fischer, *Dendera in the Third Millennium B.C.*, Locust Valley, N. Y., 1968. Fischer's work, along with statements that apply to the provinces in general, contains an exemplary description of a province in Upper Egypt.

The most reliable published description of the circumstances of provincial administration in the Middle Kingdom is provided by Dietlef Franke in *Das Heiligtum des Heqaib auf Elephantine* (Studien zur Archäologie und Geschichte Altägyptens, 9), Heidelberg, 1994.

For the Middle Kingdom and the New Kingdom, with a brief overview of the following period, W. Helck's is still the basic work, *Zur Verwaltung des Mittleren und Neuen Reiches*, Leiden and Cologne, 1958.

A study of provincial administration after the New Kingdom has not yet been published.

EVA PARDEY
Translated from German by Robert E. Shillenn

## Temple Administration

From Old Kingdom times to the beginning of the Roman period, temples had a prominent role in ancient Egyptian society. Temples were not only religious institutions but economic ones as well, having their own resources and their priestly, administrative, and productive personnel. Textual and archaeological sources show that many different types of temples existed, ranging from large temples in the main religious centers (notably Thebes, Abydos, Memphis, and Heliopolis) to modest shrines in the countryside. A basic distinction should be made between (1) the cult temples of local deities (though acknowledged throughout Egypt), whose buildings and provisions were, ideally, added to by each king, and (2) the funerary (or memorial) temples that were the personal foundations of a king. These two types of institutions had essential differences in their administrations during both the Old and Middle Kingdoms. During the New Kingdom, the administrative status of the memorial temple, which was no longer part of the royal tomb complex, came to resemble that of local cult temples. The cult temples had religious and economic ties with the memorial foundations in their vicinity. No separate memorial temples are known for the pharaohs of the Late and Greco-Roman periods, but new sanctuaries were built in these periods for the increasingly popular worship of sacred animals.

**Temple Estates.** The religious duty of the pharaoh, as son of the gods, was to build his divine father and/or mother a house, and to provide them with food and luxury items. According to temple inscriptions, the way to do this was to give the temples their own means of production, as well as part of the materials and objects required. The concept "give," however, stands for different and complex processes in economic reality. In the Old Kingdom, the endowments of land for local cult temples were modest and emphatically meant for the upkeep of the priests. More is known about the funerary temples of this period, which were assigned their proper domains throughout the country. Yet the temples did not collect the revenues from these domains; this was done by the royal residence, which kept part of the products and passed on the rest to the funerary temples. A further intermediate stage was the solar temple, to which a funerary temple was economically attached, and only that solar temple had sufficient facilities to produce and store the offerings required for its own cult and for that of the funerary temple. Middle Kingdom documents also mention offerings being transferred to royal funerary foundations from nearby cult temples.

Only from the New Kingdom onward was there a great degree of autonomy within the temples, with regard to their economic sources. In the Ramessid period, the temples in prominent religious centers had their own estates, many of which were of a considerable size. The endowments made by King Ramesses III, for example, to his newly founded temples are thought to comprise 13 to 18 percent of the arable land and about 2.5 percent of the Egyptian population (estimated at about three million in that period). To his new temple in Western Thebes, Ramesses "gave" 62,626 persons; and to the Theban temples, he "gave" 2,382 square kilometers of cultivable land

(which, however, means nothing more than that those people and fields were somehow attached to the temples in question). The numbers quoted might include many fields actually leased out for cultivation, as well as their tenants.

The temples' agricultural domains were of two types: those worked by temple cultivators and those worked by private tenants or by other institutions (including other temples). The crops of the second type were shared between the temple (which received only a small part) and the cultivating party. Surprisingly, many of the domains cultivated by the temples themselves came under the authority of functionaries without any titles relating to temple administration. Besides their own fields, the temples also administrated royal domains, from which they may have received partial revenues, the rest being collected by government officials. The main products of the temple and the domains were emmer wheat, barley, flax, and fodder. Vegetables, fruit, olives, and grapes (for wine) were grown in the temple gardens or vineyards. In addition to their fields, gardens, and personnel, the temples also had their own granaries, treasuries, workshops, fowlyards, cowsheds, slaughterhouses, and boats. Together, these resources constituted the temple estate. Such an estate, which could be further enriched by minor donations on behalf of the king or private individuals, was called "divine offering," in perfect agreement with the reason for the Egyptian temple as an economic institution. Much of the produce of the estate was presented on the altars of the gods, to be redistributed afterward among the priests and temple administrators. A considerable part of the annual temple revenues, however, may have been used to support the temple personnel in a more direct way, while the crops of some types of domains had to be paid to other parties as described above. Temples might also trade their products for precious materials, such as oil or silver.

The Persian conqueror Cambyses (r. 525–522 BCE) reduced Egyptian temple revenues, but he was more careful with regard to the most important sanctuaries. The Ptolemaic kings also tried to reduce the temple estates, introducing a new tax (Gr., the *syntaxis*) as an alternative source of temple revenue. Despite this development, the temples remained rich and important economic institutions until they lost their estates under the Roman emperor Augustus (r. 30 BCE–14 CE) and came to depend entirely on taxes levied by the state.

**Temple Administrators.** Although the long history of the Egyptian temples saw many changes in the organization of their personnel, some basic features remained. One such feature was the distinction between the priests, supervisors, and scribes and the lower productive and administrative personnel. The distinction was not so much between priestly and nonpriestly functions: priests might be concerned with everyday economic affairs, and temple craftsmen could also be part-time priests. The two groups, rather, represented different social classes. Official inscriptions emphasized that priests and temple officials were appointed from prominent local families or from the ranks of high state officials, whereas productive personnel were usually referred to in the same texts as "slaves" or "serfs," who were collectively assigned ("given") to the temples, rather than appointed.

During the Old Kingdom, the priests of funerary temples bore the titles of *wʿb* ("pure one"), lector-priest, god's servant, and the somewhat enigmatic title *ḫnty-š*. God's servants and *ḫnty-š* were organized in shifts, each shift having its own supervisors. All priests were responsible for temple property and the daily offerings. The *ḫnty-š* are also mentioned as holders of fields, but it is unclear whether that was their administrative duty. To the regular temple priesthood must be added the priests who officiated in private funerary cults. Such cults were often attached to temples, and their priests shared in the temple offerings. The nonpriestly personnel included agricultural workers and the personnel of workshops and storehouses (which were collectively referred to as "serfs"), as well as craftsmen, scribes, and guards. The local cult temple was supervised by a "high priest" or by an "overseer of priests," who also managed the temple's economic affairs. Toward the end of the Old Kingdom, the title "Overseer of Priests" was held by mayors and provincial governors, who thus supervised the temples in their districts. During the Middle Kingdom, the mayors were also "overseer of priests" or "temple overseers" of royal funerary foundations.

In a New Kingdom temple, the main body of priests comprised men who bore the lower priestly title of *wab*. They performed their religious duties in shifts, which probably explains how *wʿb*-priests could at the same time be administrators and craftsmen. Together with the god's servants, god's fathers, and lector-priests, they were supervised by the high priest, who also had administrative responsibilities. An "overseer of priests of Upper and Lower Egypt" was responsible for all the priests of all the Egyptian temples. Throughout most of the New Kingdom, this title was held by the high priest of the Temple of Amun at Karnak, but at times it was held also by the high priests of other temples or by the vizier.

The high priest shared his responsibilities with the temple steward ("overseer of the house"), as well as with the scribes and overseers of the temple workshops, granaries, treasuries, and cattle. The estates of the larger temples of this period were immense, and huge numbers of personnel were involved in the production, administra-

tion, and transport of their revenues. The titles of temple stewards and overseers were often held by functionaries who were otherwise engaged in quite different fields of administration; most of these were high government or army officials, who probably received their temple functions as additional sources of income. They were probably seldom to be seen in the temple area, but they were represented on the spot by deputies and scribes.

Ideally speaking, priests were appointed by the king—since, in theory, they replaced the pharaoh as the performer of temple rituals. In practice, however, priestly offices were usually passed on within the same families, which led to the existence of veritable priestly dynasties, especially well known from the New Kingdom and later periods. At the end of the twentieth dynasty, things took an exceptional turn in Thebes—the main religious center of New Kingdom Egypt. The accumulation of priestly offices by a few families, the concentration of power in the person of the high priest of Amun at Karnak (who then also became responsible for the affairs of other Theban temples), and the royal status claimed by the high priest and general Herihor and his successors, all led to the development of a "state within the state" that rivaled the waning Ramessid dynasty and the succeeding dynasties in the North of Egypt. An important person from that time onward was the "Divine Consort" (or "Divine Adoratrice") of Amun; the ancient title (also held by New Kingdom queens and princesses) became applied to a celibate woman of royal and priestly status who headed a vast estate.

Apart from the exceptional office of "Divine Consort," women are seldom attested as priests: Old and Middle Kingdom texts contained references to female "god's servants" and *wab*-priests, mainly for female deities, Hathor in particular. The temples also had chantresses and female musicians, and in later periods, these were the only temple functions held by women. Although such titles indicated their high social status, women never appeared in documents as temple administrators.

The Late period brought an increase in the number of priestly offices, among them a new office with supreme administrative responsibility: that of the *lesonis*. According to documents from the time of the First Persian Occupation and the Ptolemaic period, that priest was elected by the temple priesthood, perhaps annually, and appointed by the government. In the Ptolemaic period, the *lesonis* was subordinate to an *epistates*, who supervised the temple on behalf of the government administration. Priests are well represented in the Greek and Demotic texts of the Ptolemaic period, as collectors of taxes and as the holders of temple fields; with regard to cultic and economic temple affairs, royal proclamations reflect the decisions of priestly synods. The priests lost their administrative power in the Roman period, however, when the temple estates were dissolved.

**State and Temple.** The economic traffic between the Old Kingdom funerary temples and the royal residence, as well as the later Ptolemaic and Roman temple taxes, demonstrate that the state and temple administrations were closely interrelated. Throughout pharaonic history, however, the protection of temple property or personnel from interference by other institutions was the subject of special royal decrees. Since such "immunity charters" were always concerned with specific temples or specific circumstances, it is difficult to establish to what extent such protection was a matter of course. Even the seemingly autonomous temples of the New Kingdom had their obligations toward government administration. As discussed above, part of their agricultural production was collected by state officials on account of *khato* domains, and there are other indications for taxes to be paid to the king or his representatives. Reference has also been made to the supervision of temple domains by officials who had no titles relating to temple administration. The temples were also subject to inspections by officials of the royal treasury, concerning temple property or misbehavior of temple personnel.

Although considerable portions of Egypt's economic resources became part of temple estates, those resources remained available to society as a whole. Many people benefited from them—as priests or temple officials, who were entitled to share in the divine offerings, or as tenants of temple fields. Thus the temples played an active, integrative role in the national economy while retaining a distinct administrative identity.

[*See also* Priesthood; Royal Roles; Taxation; *and* Temples.]

## BIBLIOGRAPHY

Evans, J. A. S. "A Social and Economic History of an Egyptian Temple in the Greco-Roman Period." *Yale Classical Studies* 17 (1961), 143–283. History of the temples in that period, exemplified by the fortunes of the temple of the god Soknebtunis in the Faiyum Oasis.

Goedicke, H. "Cult Temple and 'State' during the Old Kingdom in Egypt." In *State and Temple Economy in the Ancient Near East*, vol. 1, pp. 113–131. Orientalia Lovaniensa Analecta, 5, edited by E. Lipinski. Leuven, 1979. On the endowments of land to temples by the Old Kingdom pharaohs.

Haring, B. J. J. *Divine Households. Administrative and Economic Aspects of the New Kingdom Royal Memorial Temples in Western Thebes*. Egyptologische Uitgaven, 12. Leiden, 1997. Case study of the administrative structure and economic significance of the temples founded by the pharaohs of the New Kingdom on the western bank of the Nile, opposite present-day Luxor.

Helck, W. *Materialien zur Wirtschaftsgeschichte des Neuen Reiches*. 6 vols. Akademie der Wissenschaften und der Literatur. Abhand-
lungen der geistes- und sozialwissenschaftlichen Klasse (1960, nos. 10 and 11; 1963, nos. 2 and 3; 1964, no. 4; 1969, no. 4). Wiesbaden, 1961–1969. Extensive collection of economic data from New Kingdom documents, including various aspects of temple administration (mainly in vols. 1–3).

Janssen, J. J. "The Role of the Temple in the Egyptian Economy during the New Kingdom." In *State and Temple Economy in the Ancient Near East*, vol. 2, pp. 505–515. Orientalia Lovaniensa Analecta, 6, edited by E. Lipinski. Leuven, 1979. General discussion, with specific remarks on the Theban memorial temples.

Kemp, B. J. "Temple and Town in Ancient Egypt." In *Man, Settlement and Urbanism*, edited by P. J. Ucko, R. Tringham, and G. W. Dimbleby, pp. 657–680. London, 1972. Fundamental essay on the economic role of temples in ancient Egyptian society, especially as the centers of settlements.

Kemp, B. J. *Ancient Egypt: Anatomy of a Civilization*. London and New York, 1989. History of the ancient Egyptian society until the end of the New Kingdom; also deals with the economic role of temples.

Kitchen, K. A. "The Vintages of the Ramesseum." In *Studies in Pharaonic Religion and Society in Honour of J. Gwyn Griffiths*. Occasional Publications 8, edited by A. B. Lloyd, pp. 115–123. London, 1992. Reconstruction of the location and administration of vineyards of a New Kingdom memorial temple.

Meeks, D. "Les donations aux temples dans l'Egypte du Ier millénaire avant J.-C." In *State and Temple Economy in the Ancient Near East*, vol. 2, pp. 605–687. Orientalia Lovaniensa Analecta, 6, edited by E. Lipinski. Leuven, 1979. Concentrates on the donations of land to temples by private individuals in the Late period.

O'Connor, D. "The Social and Economic Organization of Ancient Egyptian Temples." In *Civilizations of the Ancient Near East*, vol. 1, edited by J. M. Sasson, pp. 319–329. New York, 1995. Discusses the historical development of Old, Middle, and New Kingdom temples; attention is given to the socioeconomic context.

Posener-Kriéger, P. "Les papyrus d'Abousir et l'économie des temples funéraires de l'Ancien Empire." In *State and Temple Economy in the Ancient Near East*, vol. 1, pp. 133–151. Orientalia Lovaniensa Analecta, 5, edited by E. Lipinski. Leuven, 1979. Expert description of the intricate relationships between the residence and the royal funerary temples of the fifth dynasty.

Sauneron, S. *The Priests of Ancient Egypt*. New York, 1960. Classic study of the priests and their place in Egyptian society throughout the pharaonic and Greco-Roman periods. Translation of *Les prêtres de l'ancienne Egypte* (Paris, 1957; 2d ed., Paris, 1988).

Spalinger, A. J. "A Redistributive Pattern at Assiut." *Journal of the American Oriental Society* 105 (1985), 7–20. On the circulation of offerings in a Middle Kingdom cult temple.

Spalinger, A. J. "Some Revisions of Temple Endowments in the New Kingdom." *Journal of the American Research Center in Egypt* 28 (1991), 21–39. On temple inspections as the background of royal decrees with regard to temple property.

Stead, M. "A Model to Facilitate the Study of Temple Administration in Graeco-Roman Egypt." In *Atti del XVII Congresso Internazionale di Papirologia*, 3. Naples, 1984. Brief outline of temple revenues and expenses.

BEN HARING

**ADMINISTRATIVE TEXTS** result from a selective deployment of writing in control of resources on estates. Most surviving ancient Egyptian administrative texts derive from the two spheres of the state economy: royal domain and temple. The Egyptians used the same word, *pr,* for "house" and "estate." In the increased precision of official positions in the late Middle Kingdom, the basic title "estate overseer" was modified by supplementary phrases to specify particular areas of responsibility. Four of these provide us with the sections into which the Egyptians themselves divided estate resources:

1. accountant of manpower;
2. accountant of livestock;
3. accountant of grain; and
4. accountant of shipping.

Item 1 involves time calculation; items 1 and 2 require periodic recalculation of resources affected by birth and death rates; and items 2 and 3 require calculation of land area and type. The fourth item is all-important in the Nile Valley, where river boats remained the principal means of transport until the nineteenth century CE.

To these principal economic concerns may be added the supplementary categories of natural nonstaples, nonedible raw materials, and artificial products. The distinction between staples and luxuries depends on the criteria of scale of production and access. In organization it is complemented by the contrast in processing and storage between edibles and other goods. Some goods occupy an anomalous position in this scheme, such as the luxury edibles (meat, honey, wine, and oil). The large Egyptian house seems to have comprised two conceptually and physically distinct areas: the provisioning sector (Eg., *šnꜥ*), where food and drink were prepared, and the reception rooms *(ḥ3)* and family rooms *(ipt),* where the owner lived. The precise late Middle Kingdom titles specify for the *(šnꜥ)* officials the following segments *(ꜥt):* bread; beer; other liquids; meat; fat; fruits; fish and birds.

Goods other than edibles formed the stock of the treasury (literally "white house") and seem to have been designated as "sealed goods." These are above all the products of craftsmen. The late Middle Kingdom titles specify the following professions after the basic title overseer of a "sector" *(wꜥrt):* coppersmiths, goldsmiths, glaze workers, jewelers (literally "drillers of semiprecious stones"), furniture-makers, sculptors, draftsmen, necropolis workers (for production of stelae and offering-tables—i.e., sculptors in two-dimensional relief). Less ornamented crafts included the key industries of pottery and textile production. With clay and flax products, there is greater scope for household production.

In managerial positions, written calculation is the key skill, and "accountant" seems a more accurate rendering for the Egyptian title conventionally translated "scribe" *(sš).* This position seems always to have been held by men. Although little evidence survives for schools, formal training in writing may have been specifically for men entering the administration. The script learned for this was not hieroglyphic, but rather the cursive forms Hieratic (in the Old to New Kingdoms), Abnormal Hieratic (developed in the Third Intermediate Period), and Demotic (in the Late period, and retained, though secondary to Greek, in the Macedonian, Ptolemaic, and Roman periods). The longest surviving mathematical manual (the Papyrus Rhind, late Second Intermediate Period, c.1550 BCE) would have provided a trainee with rather more calculating skills than he would need for daily estate records. The New Kingdom literary text known as the *Satirical Letter* (Papyrus Anastasi I) also provides perhaps overextensive coverage of practical problems faced by the administrator.

Administrative texts, defined as those produced in and for estate management, may be separated from the related categories of judicial texts and business letters. Those may include short accountancy texts, and may be copied into longer estate records or "journals." However, they form discrete bodies of text in subject matter, headings, and format. They present a body of text with verbal sentences and, often, narrative passages, whereas administrative texts favor nominal forms, often in tabular layout or with guidelines. Different centers across the country may have adopted local practices in orthography and handwriting, or even in idiom, but this is rarely documented in the surviving fragments of administrative textual production. Indications of regional variation surface in the northern and southern sections of Papyrus Harris I (see the discussion following the list below) and in the late adoption of the Demotic script in Upper Egypt.

**List of Administrative Documents.** The principal surviving administrative documents are here summarized in chronological order.

**1.** *Abusir Papyri.* These are fragmentary temple business papers from three centers of royal cult at the northern end of the Abusir–Saqqara–Dahshur cemeteries: the pyramid complex of Neferirkare, the pyramid complex of Neferefre, and the cult complex of a queen Khentkawes. They include tables recording work shifts for temple personnel, lists of cult apparel including detailed notes of repairs, accounts for income, and passes issued to allow entry into restricted areas.

**2.** *Old Kingdom papyri from provincial towns.* Fewer documents survive from the third millennium BCE outside the Memphite area, and these are difficult to date. They include early Old Kingdom (fourth or fifth dynasty) cloth accounts from Gebelein in southern Upper Egypt, and unpublished date and grain accounts from Sharuna in northern Middle Egypt (Berlin Papyrus 10500), as well as papyri from Elephantine (published judicial and epistolary examples, unpublished accounts fragments).

**3.** *Hekanakhte Papyri and other early Middle Kingdom accounts.* The Hekanakhte papyri are a group of letters and accounts concerning farms in Upper Egypt, managed by Hekanakhte, a funerary priest. The identity of the estate is uncertain, but it may be the fields supporting the funerary estate of a high official (one correspondent is a general). The texts provide much of the surviving detail on Middle Kingdom agriculture. Writing-boards preserve additional data, such as name lists of servants, but without context.

**4.** *Reisner Papyri.* The four papyri are named after the American excavator who discovered them on a coffin in the cemetery at Nag el-Deir, on the eastern bank of the Nile in the region of Abydos (Simpson 1963–1986). They contain accounts of the labor time, materials, and tools (including repairs) in a building project involving the vizier Intefiqer, of the reign of Senwosret I of the twelfth dynasty. Traces of erased accounts on part of the group deal with textile production by women recruited from certain towns.

**5.** *Lahun Papyri.* Under this heading may be grouped three collections of fragmentary papyri from the area of the modern village Illahun (el-Lahun), at the entrance to Faiyum province: (1) Valley Temple business papers from the pyramid complex of Senwosret II (most now preserved in Berlin); (2) miscellaneous items from the large town site adjacent to the pyramid complex (most now preserved in University College, London); and (3) a smaller number of papyri retrieved from the late Middle Kingdom tombs at Haraga, across the fields from Illahun on a sand island.

The Valley Temple papyri recall the range of the Abusir Papyri, with tables of duty, inventories, and accounts of goods required for festival offerings, or labor required from the temple community for state works; however, there is also a substantial correspondence between the mayor of the nearest town and the temple scribe. These letters deal largely with the problems of offering supplies and labor requirements. Numerous items were copied onto a *hryt* ("journal"), including copies of business letters as well as records of deliveries and expenditure. The group does not contain any religious texts (liturgies, hymns, ritual guides, incantations, or funerary texts).

The papyri from the large town site appear much more heterogeneous, reflecting their diverse find-spots in larger and smaller houses. The largest group (labeled Lot VI by the excavator and first editor) includes numerous accounts that concentrate on royal building works but also include herds management, two similar lists of "goods taken in a levy(?)," and provisioning-sector accounts. A separate item preserves part of a "calculation of fields," and another set of large fragments comes from consecutive items of account at the town (not recorded every day, so not strictly a journal). The judicial texts include the only surviving *wpwt* "household listings," presumably used by the administration to calculate wealth. The larger unpublished fragments include a group of accounts concerning timber, textiles, and fish, some of which mention the early thirteenth dynasty treasurer Senebsumai.

The Haraga papyri include the only surviving Middle Kingdom fragment of land assessment for the Bureau of Fields.

**6.** *Papyrus Boulaq 18.* This name is given to two accountancy texts from a late Middle Kingdom tomb at Thebes, which was discovered with the intact burial of the scribe of the main works enclosure, Neferhotep. The longer presents a daily record of income and expenditure for the royal court over a period of two weeks, apparently during a visit by the king to Medamud. The shorter series involves the estate of the vizier and was apparently written up by or for Neferhotep himself.

**7.** *Other Middle Kingdom papyri.* The box of papyri found in a reused tomb beneath the Ramesseum precinct contained literary and religious manuscripts, but some of these bore secondary texts such as grain accounts, a granary plan, and a time-check of seventy days in ten equal sections (possibly for mummification). The judicial texts on the Brooklyn Papyrus (35.1446) include a list of runaway workers by city from south to north, with references to types of land and work obligations.

**8.** *Papyrus Louvre 3226.* This, one of the longest surviving eighteenth dynasty administrative papyri, records the movements of two cargo ships traveling along the Nile Valley and dealing in dates and grain.

**9.** *Ostraca from eighteenth dynasty work projects at Deir el-Bahri.* This is the earliest surviving large group of ostraca; earlier examples are isolated finds from Old and Middle Kingdom cemeteries and building sites, and the late seventeenth or early eighteenth dynasty potsherds from the palace at Deir el-Ballas, between Thebes and Dendera. The Deir el-Bahri items have not been published in full and are divided between several museums; they include records of work and supplies at the temple for Queen Hatshepsut as king and at the tomb of one of her high officials, Senenmut.

**10.** *Memphite palace accounts papyri of the eighteenth dynasty.* Of three related papyri, one records expenditure on shipbuilding (Papyrus British Museum 10056). Another concerns work in ivory and ebony for the domain of Thutmose III and the boat of the king (Papyrus Hermitage 1116B). A third preserves grain accounts involving the estates of the treasurer and the "God's Adoratrice," and includes payments to foreign envoys (Papyrus Hermitage 1116A).

**11.** *Accounts from the reign of Sety I.* This set of papyri preserves highly detailed accounts of baking and brewing. These involve at least in part army rations, and perhaps relate to the Asian campaigns of Sety I. The records specify amounts down to tiny fractions, in a bureaucratic exercise reminiscent of the extreme precision in late third millennium BCE Iraq (accountancy texts of the Ur III period).

**12.** *Memphite shipping logs, nineteenth dynasty.* Two shipping logs preserve details of estate management on the Nile. They are connected with the estate of the high priest at Memphis, Prince Khaemwaset, of the early years of Ramesses II.

**13.** *Ramesseum Ostraca.* Ostraca from the temple for Ramesses II on the western bank of the Nile at Thebes include accountancy texts. Four record ship deliveries of sandstone blocks for the construction of the temple (Kitchen 1991).

**14.** *Papyrus Amiens.* This substantial account of transport ships involves the collection of grain from various temple domains in the tenth province of Upper Egypt and elsewhere (Gardiner 1948, vi–vii, no. 1). Jac Janssen has identified the Papyrus British Museum 10061 as the lower half of this manuscript. This fixes provenance at Asyut, the strategic point midway between Memphis and Thebes.

**15.** *Gurob Papyri.* Petrie retrieved a substantial number of fragmentary Ramessid accounts papyri from the palace town near modern Gurob, at the entrance to the Faiyum. These deal in large part with the palace of the royal family, including deliveries of textiles from the palace to the royal residence at Piramesse in the eastern Delta (Gardiner 1948, viii–xiii, nos. 2–16). Future study of these texts may clarify the extent to which the Gurob palace functioned as a specialist textile factory. A few manuscripts of the same date were found in New Kingdom levels at the nearby Middle Kingdom townsite north of modern Illahun.

**16.** *Wilbour Papyrus.* This manuscript, preserved in the Brooklyn Museum, is by far the most extensive and important land census to survive. Despite its length of more than 10 meters (32 feet), the precise object of the assessment remains unclear (Janssen 1975). The assessors covered an area of northern Middle Egypt, but it is unclear whether they examined all lands, or whether the grain yields refer to the main harvest or a second crop. The relationship between the sets of figures is also uncertain, making it difficult to identify a "tax" on, for example, temple domains. The papyrus includes the professions of those responsible for cultivating.

**17.** *Papyrus Harris, Harem Conspiracy Papyri, Tomb Robbery Papyri.* See the discussion after the list of administrative papyri.

**18.** *Deir el-Medina papyri and ostraca.* Deir el-Medina is the modern name for a walled area of houses in the desert on the western bank of the Nile at Thebes, a site known in Egyptian texts simply as "the Settlement." Here lived, with their families, the craftsmen of the king's tomb

in the Valley of the Kings. The nineteenth and twentieth dynasty royal tomb took the form of a long corridor, decorated along its full length; its creation therefore required a considerable number of skilled draftsmen, competent in canonical art with hieroglyphic script. In effect, it is a key royal workshop of draftsmen, and therefore has a higher proportion of literate men, living in desert conditions where texts survive well, in contrast to the river valley. The Deir el-Medina papyri and ostraca constitute the largest mass of text from a single community of the Bronze Age, with few premodern rivals in scale. The largest of these came to light in the first modern clearance of the site, for the antiquities collection of Bernardino Drovetti (today preserved in the Egyptian Museum, Turin). The Journal of the Necropolis was the central mechanism of control. The extant portions display the same features of copying and summary as found in Middle Kingdom compilations of accounts. Of other papyri from the site, the Turin Taxation Papyrus is among the most complete; it records on the front side (*recto*) grain deliveries to Thebes from towns in southern Upper Egypt (Gardiner 1948, xiii, no. 17). The accountant is the necropolis scribe Thutmose, writing in Year 12 of the reign of Ramesses XI. The Deir el-Medina material also includes the earliest record of work stoppages, the Turin Strike Papyrus, from regnal Years 29–30 of Ramesses III. A valuable but broken series of revenue accounts occupies the back (verso) of the king list known as the Turin Royal Canon; despite its condition, it includes contexts for several technical terms of importance to the question of "tax" (see below).

**19.** *Land accounts of the Third Intermediate Period.* Different collections preserve a series of highly fragmentary documents, perhaps from a single find. Extant portions record fields in the tenth nome (province) of Upper Egypt (capital at modern Qau). Despite their poor condition, they provide one of the main blocks of data on land assessment. There are few other documents for either this period or this region (Vleeming 1993; note that the Oxford group figures in Gardiner 1948, xxi, no. 23).

In the Late period, accounts were in Demotic, and, in contrast to Demotic judicial texts, few of these have been identified, studied or published.

**Other Sources.** Other administrative notes were applied directly in ink to the surface of an object to record immediate information. Notes of date and work gang occur on building blocks in Old and Middle Kingdom royal pyramid complexes (Arnold 1990). At all periods there are commodity "labels," usually the name and quantity of a commodity written onto its container. Concentrations of "labels" include Old Kingdom tomb goods on the western bank at Aswan, and wares in the late eighteenth dynasty palace cities of Malqata and Amarna, in the tomb of Tutankhamun, in the Ramesseum, and at Deir el-Medina.

These may be related to the substantial body of different kinds of incised or painted potmarks from the Early Dynastic to the Late period. However, the potmarks themselves, on the border of literacy and illiteracy, remain largely enigmatic.

Judicial texts and letters include numerous details on estate management, and often provide a narrative context for technical terms left unexplained in accountancy papyri. They may also cite excerpts from administrative documents. A special class of judicial text is the *sipty wr* ("great revision"). In these, state officials inspect local conditions preparatory to a major overhaul. The most important attested revisions are reviews of temple domains, involving the maintenance of cults from estates. Any major new cult foundation would require such a review. The procedure survives more in hieroglyphic texts than in original manuscript sources. An exception is Papyrus Abbott, which preserves the inspection of all royal tombs at Thebes outside the Valley of the Kings; the review was prompted by a trial of tomb robbers. This is one of a group of documents recording cases of treason, perhaps buried and found together (Tomb Robbery Papyri and Harem Conspiracy Papyri). The greatest of these is Papyrus Harris I (British Museum 9999), the longest surviving papyrus roll at over 40 meters (128 feet). This bears a meticulous list of all donations throughout Egypt by Ramesses III to temple domains, in a prayer to the gods to install his son Ramesses IV safely on the throne as his successor. It has often been interpreted as a cession of crown land to the priesthood, but this rests on a misreading of the category "temple domain." Nearly all the donations are to the cult of Ramesses III himself "in the Amun domain," that is, to the temple for his eternal cult at Medinet Habu on the western bank at Thebes. State officials rather than temple staff manage his cult estates, and the revenues go to the royal cult, not to the Amun priests. The document therefore gives details not of a loss of royal power, but of the practical results of a "great revision." Like any king, Ramesses III would need to review revenues, including temple lands, in order to construct the temples to his own cult and fund it in perpetuity; the succeeding kings would presumably do the same, again reviewing all estates, including those for the cult of Ramesses III. The practical functioning of this system over time remains to be studied, as do the proportion of state to private land and the precise scope of the reviews. Though a "religious" document, Papyrus Harris contains essential evidence on estate formation and management.

Other nondocumentary manuscripts may also supply details of the management of estates. Literary letters such as the Late Egyptian Miscellanies exaggerate the disadvantages of life outside the scribal profession, and include vivid accounts of farming and border patrols (Caminos 1954). In addition to these manuscript sources, carved inscriptions in Hieratic and hieroglyphic provide evidence for the administration. Even where these appear to be direct copies on stone from manuscript originals, such inscriptions are secondary rather than primary sources. Their context in an inaccessible or sacred location, and often in the sacred script, sets the direct administrative data in the frame of religious monument and eternity. One of the largest groups consists of Middle Kingdom expedition inscriptions in Sinai, Wadi Hammamat, Wadi el-Hudi and Toshka. In contrast to inscriptions at other quarries and of other periods, these, mainly hieroglyphic records record times, numbers of men and commodities involved in the expedition. Most of the more detailed inscriptions date to the reigns of Senwosret I (Wadi Hammamat and Wadi el-Hudi) and Amenemhet III (Sinai).

Hieroglyphic sources include royal annals preserving substantial economic data, often recorded with mathematical precision. The earliest of these are basalt fragments of one or more fifth dynasty monuments (Palermo Stone and related fragments). A series of twelfth dynasty quartzite and granite blocks appears to belong to court annals of Amenemhet II, reused in later monuments at Memphis and Cairo. Far better preserved are the campaign annals of Thutmose III and other inscriptions of the same reign in the Amun temple at Karnak, and the great festival list of Ramesses III at Medinet Habu. Royal stelae often include details of revenue or expenditure as part of the narrative of royal triumph; the accuracy of figures in such texts must be assessed against the purpose of the inscription.

For the study of administration, one of the most revealing classes of hieroglyphic text is the exemption decree. These are attested already in the Old Kingdom, where temples received, and copied on stone, royal exemption from levies on produce or labor. A thousand years later, the Decree of Horemheb preserves measures against exaggerated demands by state officials on local resources. Not long after this, Sety I issued a decree to protect the income of the Abydos temple to his cult; it survives in a copy carved on the rock at Nauri, 35 kilometers (22 miles) north of the Third Cataract. A hieroglyphic inscription carved under Siptah and Tawosret records the establishment and protection of an estate to support a cult of Amun (stela from Bilgai, in the central Delta). Several New Kingdom royal decrees derive from a "great revision" entailing the diversion of funds. Surviving examples include a *sed*-festival decree of Amenhotep III, the establishment of the new royal cult of the Aten under Akhenaten, the restoration decree of Tutankhamun, and decrees of Merenptah and Ramesses III. They include protection clauses in terms similar to those of the exemption decrees.

Numerous Third Intermediate Period and Late period stelae bear hieroglyphic donation texts citing field areas. Already in the New Kingdom land donations are recorded, as in the tomb-chapel of Penniut at Aniba in Nubia. These give insight into land ownership and management. The Endowment Stela of Psamtik I provides details of the journey of his daughter Nitiqret from the Delta to Thebes; it records the sources of income for the royal party on its way south, together with the funds for her new position as priestess at the Amun temple.

From the Old and Middle Kingdoms, several tomb-chapel hieroglyphic inscriptions survive with records of inheritance; as with legal manuscripts, these may shed light on property rights and estate management. One of the principal sources in this field is the chapel of Djefai-hapy at Asyut. Kemp (1989) has compared these to the modern Islamic *waqf,* or pious foundation; any donation in perpetuity would certainly require religious expression to have a chance of surviving economic pressures. In the case of ancient Egypt, religious objections could presumably be met by the tactic of *wedjeb khet* ("reversion of offerings"), whereby revenue from one estate "turned" to another, as it were, to a second divine recipient after the first had partaken of the offerings.

The Theban tomb-chapels of mid-eighteenth dynasty viziers preserve the hieroglyphic text that seems closest to an Egyptian treatise on the administration, known today as the *Duties of the Vizier.* This is of disputed origin, but it may be copied from a late Middle Kingdom original; it is accompanied by a pictorial version of the proportions of dues levied in Upper Egypt.

The various sources attest to revenues under different names. Their debated meanings are crucial to determining the nature of private property, taxation, foreign revenue, and slavery in ancient Egypt. The word *inw* is often translated "tribute," but it has in fact a neutral, technical sense in accountancy texts. In the late Middle Kingdom Papyrus Boulaq 18, for example, it is clear that estate revenue is termed *ʿkw* in general, but can be divided into *iḫw* and *ʒnw.* The distinguishing criterion is the source, or, more particularly, the place where the raw material is worked; *ʿkw* is produced in the *šnʿ* ("provisioning-quarters") of the estate, and *inw* (literally, "supplements") covers anything added to the daily estate production. Thus, *ʿkw* denotes the regular revenue, and *inw* the special extras. "Tribute" is a mistranslation which introduces assumed sociopolitical relations extraneous to the Egyptian word. Similar caution must be applied to words translated "tax." Late Middle Kingdom accounts papyri use the terms *tʒ-r-tʒ, bʒkw,* and *ḥtr.* Although rare, *tʒ-r-tʒ,* might be translated literally "grain taken against land"; the correct levy would be calculated from the known acreage and type of land, and the known size of household, a labor force for harvest; *bʒkw* denotes produce of labor, implying use of labor force but not necessarily a fixed regular yield such as rent or tax; *ḥtr* means literally "yoked," and is used for payments obligatory for a fixed time or destination, on grounds that are not stated. In the Illahun Valley Temple papyri, it is the term for deliveries expected for specific festivals, again leaving unclear whether it is a rent or a tax. In the Late Egyptian texts of the late New Kingdom, new terms appear, and the old terms are likely to have different technical meanings. In addition to *bʒkw* and *ḥtr* the terms *šʒgt* and *tp-drt* apply to estate revenues, while *tʒ-r-tʒ* is no longer found; *tp-drt* means "upon the hand," suggesting a levy fixed for a particular individual, perhaps by title or office; *šʒgt* means "amounts due," but again the criteria and frequency for this and the other levies require further research. Until a databank of these terms becomes available, their meaning remains obscure, and with it the entire relation between state and individual in ancient Egypt.

## BIBLIOGRAPHY

Arnold, Felix. *The Control Notes and Team Marks. The Metropolitan Museum of Art Egyptian Exhibition. The South Cemeteries of Lisht,* vol. 2. New York, 1990. Key reference work for the Middle Kingdom texts written on stone blocks between the quarry and the building-site.

Breasted, J. H. *Ancient Records of Egypt.* 5 vols. Chicago, 1906. Despite its age, the series remains a useful reference source, and often the only published English translation, for numerous hieroglyphic inscriptions, and several cursive manuscripts such as Papyrus Harris I.

Caminos, Ricardo A. *Late Egyptian Miscellanies.* Oxford, 1954. Translations and commentary of the satirical and realistic literary paragraphs used to encourage apprentice scribes; these provide narrative contexts for details of administrative procedure, including informal methods not otherwise recorded in the surviving sources.

Gardiner, A. H. *Ramesside Administrative Documents.* Oxford, 1948. Provides hieroglyphic transcriptions for a series of late New Kingdom and Third Intermediate Period texts, with brief introduction to their contents.

Gardiner, A. H., T. E. Peet, and J. Černy. *The Inscriptions of Sinai,* vol. 2. Egypt Exploration Society Memoir, 55. London, 1955. Translations of the extant inscriptions in Sinai, including the main Middle Kingdom corpus.

James, T. G. H. *The Hekanakhte Papers and Other Middle Kingdom Documents.* New York, 1962. The first edition and principal reference source, with photographs, transliteration, and translation of early Middle Kingdom accounts papyri and letters.

Janssen, Jac J. "Prolegomena to the Study of Egypt's Economic History during the New Kingdom." *Studien zur Altägyptischen Kultur* 3 (1975), 127–185. Although only available in a specialized journal, this is the fundamental essay on problems of interpreting Egyptian administrative texts; it includes a summary of the principal administrative New Kingdom texts.

Kemp, Barry J. *Ancient Egypt: Anatomy of a Civilization.* London and New York, 1989. An excellent introduction to the Old to New Kingdoms, this is one of the only works to combine archaeological with textual evidence in the study of the Egyptian economy.

Kitchen, K. "Building the Ramesseum." *Cahier de Recherches de l'In-*

*stitut de Papyrologie et d'Egyptologie de Lille* 13 (1991), 85–93. A succinct study of four Ramesseum ostraca, recording cargoes of sandstone blocks.

Quirke, S. *The Administration of Egypt in the Late Middle Kingdom: The Hieratic Documents.* New Malden, 1991. Discussion of Papyrus Boulaq 18 and other textual sources for reconstructing state administration at that period.

Simpson, William K. *Papyrus Reisner, I–IV.* Boston, 1963–1986. Includes the first edition of the papyri found by Reisner in a Middle Kingdom tomb at Nag el-Deir; also translations and full discussions.

Spalinger, A. J. "Some Revisions of Temple Endowments in the New Kingdom." *Journal of the American Research Center in Egypt* 28 (1991), 21–39. Basic study highlights the importance of the periodic royal "great revision" of temple domains.

Spalinger, A. J. "From Local to Global: The Extension of an Egyptian Bureaucratic Term to the Empire." *Studien zur Altägyptischen Kultur* 23 (1996), 353–376. Discusses *bȝk*, *ḥtr*, and *inw* in New Kingdom texts, with reference to the sources of other periods.

Vleeming, Sven. *Papyrus Reinhardt. An Egyptian Land-list of the Tenth Century BC.* Berlin, 1993. The first edition of one of the most important surviving, if highly fragmentary, accounts papyri of the Third Intermediate Period; it includes discussions of the terms for types of land, as well as a listing of the other accounts texts surviving from the early first millennium BCE.

Ward, William A. *Index of Egyptian Administrative and Religious Titles of the Middle Kingdom.* Beirut, 1982. Despite its limitations, this remains the only available single listing of formal titles and self-descriptive phrases for the period; includes, though it does not distinguish, the rigorously precise official titles used in the late Middle Kingdom.

STEPHEN G. J. QUIRKE

**AEGEAN.** *See* Mediterranean Area.

**AFROCENTRISM** is a general approach to scholarly research that attempts to avoid the values and assumptions imposed by the European tradition, and, where possible, to look at questions from an African perspective. In historical research, in particular, the effect is to focus on Africans and the peoples of the African diaspora as active agents in history, rather than viewing them as the passive pawns of social forces at the periphery of historical events, as the European historical tradition has tended to do. The approach has the dual goals of reducing the distortions in historical reconstructions and, as a consequence, correcting distortions in the perception of people of African heritage in their own eyes and in the eyes of society in general. In this second, more political goal lies an inherent danger of the Afrocentric approach: that, in its effort to counteract negative distortions, it will simply substitute new distortions for the old.

Related to (and to some extent a reaction against) the French *Négritude* movement, the Afrocentric approach has several sub-approaches, each with its own proponents. Several of these approaches are related to the history of people of African heritage who live in societies with larger populations of European heritage; they may focus on the religions of West Africa, for example, or the lives of Africans within the institution of slavery. However, probably the most popular variety of Afrocentrism is the approach that Russell Adams (1993) has labeled "Nile-Valley Afrocentrism," which centers on the ancient Egyptian and, to a lesser extent, the ancient Nubian civilizations; and it is this aspect of the movement that concerns Egyptology and Egyptologists.

The basic tenets of Nile-Valley Afrocentrism are a reaction to the prejudiced view sometimes encountered in societies of predominantly European heritage, that all important social, intellectual, and technical achievements are European in origin. This view has as corollaries the contention that there has never been a great African civilization, and that people of African heritage are incapable of great achievements. The Afrocentrism that focuses on the Nile Valley attempts to refute this by pointing out that ancient Egyptian civilization was an African culture, and that the ancient Egyptians would be identified by modern Europeans and Americans as "black." These claims have been argued particularly by Cheik Anta Diop (1981) and I. von Sertima (1989), supported by some depictions of Egyptians in Egyptian art; counter-arguments based on classical terminology for Egyptians and other African peoples have been put forward by Frank Snowden (in Lefkowitz and Rodgers 1996). The opinion of physical anthropologists on the question is far from unanimous, but they generally avoid the question by arguing that race is a social rather than a biological categorization.

The view that the ancient Egyptians were black is often supported by the contention that one of the ancient names of Egypt, *Kmt*, is to be translated "land of the black people" rather than "the black land," as Egyptologists generally translate it. For this reason, many Afrocentric writers prefer to use the term "Kemet" rather than "Egypt," "Kemetology" rather than "Egyptology," "Kemetian" rather than "Egyptian," and "Kemetic" rather than "hieroglyphic writing." Two major objections to this understanding of the word *Kmt* are its failure to deal with the similarly construed term *Dšrt*, "the red land," which clearly does not refer to red people; and the grammatical objection that, had the Egyptians wanted to write "land of the black people," they would have used a nominalized nisbe formation on the nominalized adjective *kmwyt/kmtyt*—that is, *kmw* or the feminine collective *kmt* ("black ones") + *y* (pertaining to them) + *t* (place), followed by human determinatives and plural strokes. Such forms are unattested.

A second type of claim by Afrocentric writers is that the ancient Egyptian culture was considerably more advanced than Egyptological scholarship allows. Such claims have included technological advances, such as the contention that the Egyptians built a primitive glider that allowed them to fly and that they had learned to harness the power of electricity. Their knowledge of mathematics has been extended to include the value of $\pi$ (*pi*) and the Pythagorean Theorem. Claims for philosophical and ethical development have also been made—for example, by Maulana Karenga (1996), whose discussions of Egyptian ethical beliefs are both modest and generally well supported by the ancient evidence. More common, however, are claims of mental and spiritual knowledge that surpass those of any recorded culture, including telepathy, levitation, and prophecy. Many of the technological claims, and all the mental claims, for the ancient Egyptians are more extreme than the claims of race, because they are much less a matter of modern perceptions.

Perhaps the most widely debated of the Afrocentric claims is the assertion that Greek culture, the revered root of Western civilization, either was Egyptian in origin or borrowed many of its achievements from ancient Egypt. Particularly prominent is the contention that the Greeks, and Aristotle in particular, "stole" their philosophical ideas from the Egyptians, which was first propounded in George James's *Stolen Legacy* (1954). James's book has severe chronological problems (Aristotle is said to have stolen much of his *oeuvre* from the library of Alexandria, which was founded some time after his death), but more recently Afrocentric scholars have tried to argue a more general borrowing by attempting to find philosophical concepts in Egyptian religious literature. Related claims are made by other writers who identify famous Greek people (Socrates, and with only slightly more justice, Cleopatra) as Egyptian.

The debate about the relationship between Egypt and Greece has centered around the work of Martin Bernal (1987–1991) who does not consider himself an Afrocentrist, but who seems to support many of the same goals as Afrocentrists. His books claim that much of Greek culture originated in Egypt, whence it was communicated through a kind of cultural imperialism, backed up by military force in the Middle and New Kingdoms. His arguments are almost entirely based on classical texts; they include the Greek accounts of Egyptians that claim them as ancestors, the Athenian versions of myths which often ascribe foreign origins to other cities, and superficial similarities between numerous Greek words and those of Egyptian and Semitic languages. An uneven but cumulatively devastating collection of critiques of Bernal's arguments has been compiled by Mary Lefkowitz and Guy Rodgers (1996).

The fourth claim of Afrocentrists is related to the previous one. In addition to having initiated or dominated ancient Greek culture, the ancient Egyptians are credited with all known African civilizations. This contention that Egyptian civilization spread throughout all parts of the continent is often supported by citations from nineteenth-century scholars, who attributed any monument or work of art found on the African continent to Egyptian influence, as P. L. Shinnie (1971) has pointed out. The most prominent proponent of these ideas is the late Senegalese scholar Cheik Anta Diop (1981), who claimed that close parallels between the Egyptian language and Wolof, as well as the religious beliefs of both cultures, point to Egyptian origins for his own culture. Egyptian origins have been claimed for African cultures as far distant in space and time as the builders of Great Zimbabwe, a third-to-fifteenth century stone fortress and town in southeastern Africa. For members of the African diaspora, these claims have the advantage of allowing all peoples of African origin to trace their origins to the ancient Egyptian culture.

Finally, and most troublesome to Egyptologists, many Nile-Valley Afrocentrists claim that there has been a conspiracy among non-African scholars to obscure ancient Egypt's African characteristics, its great achievements, its formative role in Greek philosophy and culture, and its close relationship with other African cultures. The most common of these claims is that there has been a concerted effort to knock off the noses of ancient Egyptian statues (most notably the Sphinx) to disguise their African appearance. This accusation is most often leveled at Napoleon Bonaparte, who is said to have shot the nose off the Sphinx—a claim that is manifestly incorrect, not only because earlier Western representations of the Sphinx depict it with its nose missing (for example, the drawing published in 1755 by Frederick Norden) but also because medieval Arabic texts attribute the damage to a Muslim fanatic in the fourteenth century CE (see Haarmann 1980). Other statuary and relief art is said to have been mutilated as well. Moreover, any attempts Egyptologists have made to refute some of the unsubstantiated claims about foreign conquests, Egyptian origins, and exaggerated Egyptian achievements are identified as part of this conspiracy.

It cannot be denied that many Egyptologists of previous generations shared the racist views that were endemic in their societies, and their work has often reflected this. In some cases, this racism had the effect of denigrating the achievements of the Egyptians (as can be seen, for example, in some of the condescending descriptions of Egyptian religious beliefs or thought processes); in other cases, the solution was to consider the Egyptians as entirely unconnected with the rest of Africa, an argument that can be supported by the geographical isolation of the lower Nile Valley, but only to a limited extent. One of the valuable contributions of the Afrocentric movement is that it has made Egyptologists aware of the extent to which their generally held beliefs may be distorted by racist assumptions.

The initial formation of the field of Egyptology was based on philology: the desire to read the hieroglyphic texts on Egyptian monuments. The hope of early scholars was that these texts would prove to contain confirmation and elaboration of the events recorded in the Hebrew scriptures and the New Testament. Their background knowledge about Egypt was based on classical and biblical sources, and their primary concern was to address the questions that those sources raised. In addition, their research was often dependent on the support of the general public, and it was thus necessary to relate it to things the public already knew about, again classical writers or biblical events. The search for connections between Egypt and other cultures was therefore oriented almost entirely toward the cultures of the Mediterranean and the Near East. Not only were these cultures more interesting to scholars who already had a background knowledge of classics and the Bible, but they were also literate, so contacts among them could easily be traced.

Connections with African cultures were less interesting to early Egyptologists for the same reasons; most of these scholars had little knowledge of the African cultures to the south and west of Egypt. Even when Nubian culture became better known, it was viewed as a pale and inaccurate imitation of Egypt. Since much of its art obviously was related to the pharaonic tradition, it was evaluated primarily in terms of the accuracy with which the Egyptian forms were copied; there was little appreciation of its distinctive Nubian characteristics and the creativity with which the borrowed forms were manipulated to serve the purposes of a very different culture. Moreover, the Nubian and Libyan cultures with which the Egyptians interacted had no written language—it is not even certain what kinds of languages they spoke. Therefore, it is impossible to trace influences such as loanwords, stories, borrowed divinities, names, and the like. To see such connections, it is necessary to see both sides of the equation: one needs to compare the Libyan or Nubian version to the Egyptian version to determine whether they are sufficiently similar to support an argument for connection. But there are no contemporary Libyan or Nubian versions to compare.

The lack of information about adjacent African cultures, their lack of written languages, and the strong formative influence of classical studies and the Bible, when combined with the racist assumptions of the society in which early Egyptologists lived, resulted in a very strong eurocentric bias in Egyptology at the most basic levels.

This Eurocentrism has been pointed out by the Afrocentrists, and the reexamination of many of these fundamental questions that is currently taking place in the field is to some degree attributable to their influence.

Not all effects of Afrocentrism are equally useful, however. The movement has many problematic aspects. Afrocentrists, too, are products of the Western intellectual tradition, and they have usually adopted the values of Western culture no less than the Egyptologists they criticize. Indeed, the very focus of Nile-Valley Afrocentrists on Egyptian culture betrays their acceptance of the Western tradition that admires Egypt but neglects most other African cultures. There is also the problem of Afrocentrism's assumption that the African continent is the only logical geographical category to which Egypt can belong, when in fact "Africa" is largely an arbitrary, modern *Western* conceptual category no less arbitrary than the category of race. The Egyptians saw themselves as surrounded by three peoples: the "Asiatics" (a broad category encompassing all the cultures to the north and east), the Libyans, and the Nubians. There is no evidence that the Egyptians defined themselves as "African" or felt themselves more closely connected to their Libyan or Nubian neighbors than to their neighbors in Western Asia or (later) Europe. The concept of "Africa" that groups Egypt geographically with other African cultures and separates it from "Western Asia" or "Asia" is only an artifact of the Western concept of "continents."

Other problems with Afrocentrism are methodological. Because the real impetus behind Afrocentric contentions is the hope that people of African descent will better appreciate the achievements of their people, the analyses of Egyptian evidence tend to emphasize (and sometimes exaggerate) evidence that suggests the superiority of Egyptian developments in ethics, technology, politics, philosophy, and the like. Evidence that would argue against these claims is disparaged and, if possible, discredited. Such tendentious reasoning obviously is undesirable in scholarship.

Despite these flaws, the Afrocentric approach has considerable currency in modern education, particularly in elementary education in the United States, usually in areas with large African-American populations. The curriculum most often taken as a model is the *Portland Baseline Essays*, a collection of materials that was prepared for the school system in Portland, Oregon. Many of these materials, particularly the science sections, are seriously flawed, but they have sometimes been adopted, nonetheless, in the belief that the increased self-esteem of the African-American students and their consequent improved levels of achievement will outweigh the inaccuracies of the materials.

The ultimate role that Afrocentrism will play in the field of Egyptology is yet to be decided. A positive and stimulating synthesis will be possible only to the degree that Egyptologists and Afrocentrists are willing to be open-minded and work together in accordance with accepted scholarly standards.

[*See also* Interpretation of Evidence; People; Race; *and* Wisdom Tradition.]

### BIBLIOGRAPHY

Adams, Russell. "African-American Studies and the State of the Art." In *Africana Studies: A Survey of Africa and the African Diaspora*, edited by Mario Azevdo, pp. 25–45. Durham, N. C., 1993. The author distinguishes and describes various types of Afrocentrism in addition to what he calls "Nile Valley Afrocentrism."

Bernal, Martin. *Black Athena: The Afroasiatic Roots of Classical Civilization.* 2 vols. New Brunswick, N.J., 1987–1991.

Diop, Cheik Anta. "The Origin of the Ancient Egyptians." In *General History of Africa II: Ancient History of Africa*, edited by G. Mokhtar, pp. 27–57. Paris, 1981. A summary of many of Diop's positions.

Haarmann, Ulrich. "Regional Sentiment in Medieval Islamic Egypt." *Bulletin of the Society for Oriental and African Studies* 43 (1980), 55–66. A study of medieval Egyptian attitudes toward the pharaonic past, including the episode of the damage to the Sphinx.

James, George. *Stolen Legacy.* New York, 1954. A problematic work much cited by Afrocentrists, claiming that Greek philosophy was taken from Egypt.

Lefkowitz, Mary, and Guy Rodgers, eds. *Black Athena Revisited.* Chapel Hill, N. C., and London, 1996. Essays criticizing the claims of Martin Bernal's *Black Athena*.

Roth, Ann Macy. "Building Bridges to Afrocentrism: A Letter to my Egyptological Colleagues." *Newsletter of the American Research Center in Egypt* 167 and 168 (1995), 1, 14–17 and 1, 12–15.

Shinnie, P. L. "The Legacy to Africa." *The Legacy of Egypt*, edited by J. R. Harris, pp. 435–455. Oxford, 1971.

von Sertima, Ivan, ed. *Egypt Revisited*. New Brunswick and London, 1989. A collection of essays (many reprinted from other sources) by authors writing from Afrocentric positions or whose views accord with Afrocentrism.

ANN MACY ROTH

**AFTERLIFE.** Belief in the afterlife is among the fundamental concepts of Egyptian culture. Since late prehistoric times, the Egyptians found means to ensure eternal life in comfort after death. These practices underwent continuous development into Roman times. That the afterlife was of paramount importance for the Egyptians can be seen from the number of richly furnished tombs found in the Nile Valley, the most extensive remains preserved from ancient Egypt. In fact, the Egyptians invested a large portion of their wealth in the afterlife—more than any other culture in the world. The afterlife was a luxury commodity which only the king and the elite could afford. For the royal household and the higher officials, the highest values in life were the favor of the king and a happy afterlife. In the Egyptian conception, people were as unequal in the afterlife as in earthly life, and existing documents disclose no interest in what happened to ordinary people after death. Anyone who wanted a good afterlife had to do much during life to achieve it. First, one had to have a tomb built and had to acquire a large number of objects thought to be needed in the afterlife. In addition, it was necessary to ensure that one's heirs would mummify the body and carry out the funeral ritual. Finally, a regular schedule for offerings at the tomb had to be organized. The best way to accomplish this was to set up a mortuary foundation by designating the income from a given parcel of land for that purpose.

The sources from which we learn how the Egyptians conceived of the afterlife are extraordinarily rich and span four and one-half millennia. They include the objects the deceased took along into the tomb (from the mid-fifth millennium onward); the tomb as a building (from the Predynastic period); the images applied to the walls of tombs (from the third dynasty); and the texts that describe the afterlife (from the late fifth dynasty).

The basic conception of the afterlife held that the body must be preserved. The deceased was just as dependent on nourishment—food and drinks—as on earth. According to the Egyptians' conception, human life, whether in time or in eternity, supposed individual consciousness. The formulation that the literature of the dead found for this was that the deceased individual always wanted to remember his own name. However, it was clearly the body that was the bearer of the individual's consciousness. Besides the body, a human being had other elements which accompanied the body invisibly and represented different aspects of its vitality. The Egyptian terms for these—*ka, ba,* and *akh*—are not easy to translate, though often rendered as "soul." After death, this situation was reversed: the body was an immobile mummy, but the "souls" could leave it on occasion and wander around. Life in the afterworld was thus not appreciably different from a person's former life on earth, except that it was conducted in a different place. Since the late Old Kingdom, tomb inscriptions refer to the starry heaven as well as "the beautiful west," that is the mountains on the western bank of the Nile where the sun sets, as the regions of the dead. There, in the place where the gods dwelt, the deceased was very near the gods and attained a state of being like theirs. A king became an actual god upon his death, and his afterlife was entirely like that of the gods; indeed, from the time of the Middle Kingdom, nonroyal persons too could become divinities of a kind in the afterlife.

It was, however, a fundamental principle that the afterlife of a king was quite different from that of ordinary mortals, because the king descended from the gods. We must therefore consider separately the ways kings and nonroyal persons were thought to live after death.

In the last part of the prehistoric period, from the middle of the fifth millennium until the late fourth millennium BCE, a rich burial culture first developed in Egypt. From this we can conclude that a wealthy elite intended to extend into the afterlife the standard of living to which they had become accustomed on earth. The finds point to two major themes: the body had to be nourished in the afterlife, and it had to be kept fresh and beautiful by means of cosmetic objects which symbolize eternal rejuvenation. The high artistic quality of these objects reflects a strong aesthetic sense. This was the beginning of a long-standing characteristic of Egyptian culture: the beauty of the objects and images in the tomb elevated the quality of life in the afterworld.

With the beginning of dynastic times, tombs, which had previously been reinforced shafts, evolved into buildings made of mud brick. Kings and members of their households had rectangular buildings erected, which had an ever-increasing number of storerooms to accommodate furnishings and supplies: huge quantities of food in ceramic jars, luxurious stoneware dishes, tools, household furniture, and game boards. In addition, the tomb contained a stela that had the appearance of a door, in front of which the mortuary priests and family members were expected to place food and drink offerings. Already at this time there were one or more statues of the deceased, in which he could take material shape. Provisions for the afterlife now took on the definitive form that was to continue into the Roman period. The deceased was provided with a house befitting his high status, with all the accessories and provisions required by a large household with family and servants. The false door symbolized the ability of the deceased to leave the tomb at will and take up the offerings. The false door and tomb statues reflect the principle that an artfully crafted model could fulfill the same purpose as the real object; however, the model does not replace the real object but instead supplements it. In Egypt, there was no separation between material and immaterial existence; rather, they continuously and imperceptibly merged.

At the beginning of the Old Kingdom stone masonry was developed, and from this time on the tomb complexes of kings and those of high officials differ sharply. The kings of the third through sixth dynasties built huge pyramid complexes. The cult spaces contained extensive cycles of wall reliefs, and in the chamber for the coffin, from the end of the fifth dynasty, the Pyramid Texts were inscribed. Thus, for the first time, comprehensive information is available about the conception of the king's life in the afterworld. The only protagonist in the reliefs is the king. We see him seated at the table, looking over an endless abundance of food. He is also depicted as a child being nursed by a goddess; this ensures his sustenance and

rejuvenation. He is shown carrying out several important official acts: he celebrates this coronation jubilee at which all the gods and courtiers pay homage to him. When he encounters the gods, he does so as an equal. A flourishing economy is depicted by the arrival of a fleet of trading ships. He slays his enemies and traitors, both real and symbolic, in that he locates dangerous animals in the desert or in the marshes of the Nile Delta. Through these symbolic acts, both his own life force and that of the whole country are regenerated, and his power over rebels and his dominance over the world are confirmed.

The Pyramid Texts ensure the difficult passage from the death of the king to his divine existence in the afterlife. A major theme is the bountiful provision of the deceased king with food and drink. In addition, the crown goddesses give birth to him anew every day, nurse him at their breasts, and never wean him; thus, the king experiences a symbolic rejuvenation for all eternity, as depicted in the reliefs. However, the Pyramid Texts also recount a story different from the reliefs: the king must be awakened from the sleep of death and ascend to heaven as a god. This he can do, because he is descended from the creator god. In the beginning, the sun god, Re, who came into being spontaneously, created Shu and Tefnet, or air and moisture. They in turn begot the sky goddess Nut and the earth god Geb, parents of the two divine pairs Osiris and Isis and Seth and Nephthys. Seth killed his brother Osiris; however, after Re awakened him, Osiris became the lord of the realm of the dead, and his son Horus succeeded him as king on earth. In life, every pharaoh was the son of Osiris and the son of Re, and in death he became Osiris and Re themselves. The nine most ancient gods therefore represent the closest relatives of the king. Over and over again, the Pyramid Texts describe how the king is awakened and his body kept whole and incorruptible through the cultic purification; how he receives his raiment and crown; and how his Osiric family, the third generation of gods, helps him in these acts. Also essential is the idea that he descends from Re, which is always invoked to reinforce his claim to rule. When the king has risen from the dead as Osiris and the court of the gods confirms his claim to the throne, he is able to ascend into heaven. This is perilous, because he needs the aid of the heavenly ferryman, who transports to Re only a king who convinces him of his power. Therefore, the king must associate his arrival in heaven with an impressive demonstration of power. His coming is announced by earthquakes and thunder; the gods tremble when they glimpse the sword in his hand. Now he captures even the gods; he cooks and devours them in order to incorporate their cumulative power. Finally, he journeys like the sun god across the heavens or becomes a star like Orion. Like the sun, he is swallowed up every evening by the goddess of heaven, Nut, and reborn at daybreak. It is typical that the texts describe the unending existence of the king—his cyclical renewal—using a great variety of metaphors, such as the sun in its course, one of the circumpolar stars, the daily-reborn child of the goddess of heaven or of the crown goddesses.

The pyramid complexes make the statement that the deceased king is now definitively a god who must have his own temple and cult so that he, like the other major gods, may be effective in blessing the country. The texts witness his integration into his divine family. The reliefs reflect his specific role as a god: the rites of victory over enemies and those for the renewal of life are the tasks of the king who rules and regenerates the earthly world, in analogy with the sun god, who rules and regenerates the cosmos. This is the meaning of the huge investments that he mobilized for his tomb complex during life.

The reliefs in the tombs of high officials depict life in the hereafter as a mirror image of life on earth. Here too, a central idea is the provision of food and drink. But in contrast to the king, who becomes a god and enters the divine family, the entombed official lives with his actual family in the afterlife. He goes hunting in desert and marsh, but primarily he oversees economic life—agricultural and cattle-raising, the production and transport of goods, all carefully depicted in many scenes. The passage of the deceased into the afterlife is described not by texts but rather by the representations of the burial ritual. From the sparse inscriptions, we learn only that he wants to "walk on the beautiful ways of the west." The deceased official is not a god but rather an *akh*-spirit who has generative powers: he causes the work in fields and workshops to bring blessed prosperity; he keeps in motion the same segment of the world that was assigned to him in life.

The royal tomb complexes of the Middle Kingdom are so poorly preserved that we can learn nothing new from them about concepts of the afterlife in that period. By contrast, officials and local princes now had their own collection of texts that supplied them with necessary information—the so-called Coffin Texts. These are derived from the Pyramid Texts, and the deceased is now addressed as Osiris, just like the king. This thinking remained normative well into Roman times: the deceased shared the fate of the god who ruled over the dead and who died and rose again. The Egyptians had a distinctive conception of the boundaries of the individual. These boundaries were not fixed; the dead person could be transformed or permeated; he was able to transpose himself into different gods and act like them; he could borrow a divine personality while at the same time remaining himself. Existence with Re and with Osiris was desired and was described as being of equal value. Along with

this, the dead person wanted to be free to leave the tomb and go into the sunlight, to be transformed into various gods, to feast in paradisiacal fields of offerings, or to be cared for by goddesses.

First, however, he had to be acquitted by the court of justice. Justification functioned according to the paradigm of Horus and Seth: Seth was the mythical rebel who went against the order established by the gods by murdering his brother with the intention of usurping Horus's place as the rightful heir. Likewise, the deceased received vindication against his enemies who seek to challenge his place in the afterworld. He mobilizes all his magical power and knowledge in order to ward off his enemies' attack. If he failed, he might end up in the fishnets cast by the demons or in their slaughterhouse. He was at particular pains to avoid being forever numbered among the damned, who had to walk upside down, eat feces, and drink urine. This is the epitome of the dreadful fate that befalls the rebel. The justification of the deceased did not involve his personal ethical behavior; rather, it was a matter of never having been disobedient and having always submitted unconditionally to the order established by the gods and the king.

Court officials of this period inscribed the Pyramid Texts in their tombs, formerly the privilege of kings. The reliefs and paintings in their tombs deal with the same themes as in the Old Kingdom, but a few new episodes from the lives of the tomb-owners—often local princes—begin to appear, such as the transport of colossal statues of themselves. Such scenes reflect their increased political autonomy.

At the beginning of the New Kingdom, a sudden development occurred with respect to conceptions of the afterlife. Everything changed, including the tomb architecture and the images and texts that were placed inside. The domain of the king and that of the officials still developed along separate paths. For the first time, the afterlife was depicted. The tombs of the kings are underground tunnels, the walls of which are decorated with the so-called Underworld Books. These contain a precise report of how the sun god, Re, traveled through the underworld during the twelve hours of the night and what took place there. Texts and pictures complement one another, somewhat like a modern comic strip. Re sails in the "bark of the millions" in which the blessed dead are seated, on a river along which Osiris dwells with innumerable gods, demons, and the dead, both blessed and damned. The sun god allows favors to be bestowed on the good dead, while the damned must endure hellish tortures. When he has sailed on, everything once again lies in darkness and the sleep of death. Every night those who rebel against the order established by the creator god lie in wait on his path, embodied in the serpent Apophis, but they are al-

AFTERLIFE. *Deceased and his wife working in the underworld.* Detail of the copy by C. K. Wilkinson of a painting in the tomb of Senedjem at Thebes, nineteenth dynasty. (The Metropolitan Museum of Art, 30.4.2)

ways slain. After Re has been rejuvenated in the serpent which embodies time, he rises renewed on the eastern horizon. The daily rebirth of the sun was for the Egyptians the paradigm of eternal regeneration, in which humans, kings, gods, and all of creation partook.

Most of the books of the underworld do not mention the king explicitly; only the Litany of Re portrays his fate in the afterworld. The new concept of the existence of the king in the afterworld affirms that he is one both with Re and with Osiris, and that every night Re and Osiris enter into one another. Despite this proud equating of the king with the gods, the king runs the risk of falling into the hands of demons who could slay him, tearing him limb from limb, and annihilate him. The text gives no reason for this astonishing threat; clearly some skepticism about

the divine nature of the king is filtering through here, even as this belief is still being strongly asserted. In the New Kingdom, the mortuary temple became separated from the tomb and no longer served only as the place of worship of the king; instead, it was also open to other gods. Owing to this fusion of cults, the king lived there in eternity in the company of his divine family.

The *Book of Going Forth by Day* (the so-called *Book of the Dead*) is a collection of sayings that provided deceased nonroyals with all the necessary knowledge about life in the afterworld. It is composed of both texts and pictures, which can appear on papyrus or on tomb walls. The deceased wanted to be able to venture forth from the tomb and move about freely. He wanted to be able to assume any form and to be in the retinue of Osiris or Re. Another desired place was the field of offerings, where the dead live fully, move, eat, and beget. One characteristic of the *Book of Going Forth by Day* is the multiplicity of tests that the deceased must pass in order to ward off the attacks of the demons who seek to hand them over to eternal torment. What is most important is the judgment in which the deceased counts up all the conceivable evil deeds that he has not committed. Here for the first time the deceased assumes ethical responsibility for his or her conduct during life on earth. Evil deeds are subject to punishment, but people rely on the power of the litany of denial. The text is full of exacting theological considerations about Re and Osiris and their relationship to each other. Here, too, a certain skepticism can be detected as to whether the words and the images will adduce the hoped-for effect. It must be asserted with ever greater insistence and ever more words that the deceased is as unscathed and unassailable as a god.

The tomb reliefs and paintings of the early New Kingdom spread before us an abundance of scenes from life on earth. High court officials tended to depict the official actions that they carry out in the presence of the king. The tombs are also abundantly equipped with beautiful cosmetic articles, symbolizing eternal rejuvenation. In time, illustrations from the *Book of Going Forth by Day* become more common, until scenes of daily life practically disappear. This development shows that people no longer attributed any beneficial effect to pictures of life on earth, either for the deceased or for his surviving posterity.

Toward the end of the second millennium BCE, conceptions of the afterlife drastically changed once again with the Third Intermediate Period. Of royal tombs, only those of the twenty-second and twenty-third dynasties at Tanis remain, and these are much smaller than previous ones and include only a few excerpts from the royal Underworld Books. In general, what stands out is that there was no longer any difference between the afterlife of kings and that of other individuals. The royal books were now available to everyone. From the eleventh century to the eighth there are no tombs with murals; depictions and texts about life in the afterlife instead appear on painted coffins and papyri. These consist of quotations from the *Book of Going Forth by Day* and the *Book of That Which Is in the Underworld*, ever more richly illustrated until little more than pictures remains. From the late twenty-fifth dynasty (c. 700 BCE) onward, sumptuous officials' tombs with wall reliefs and inscriptions once again appear. Some of these are enormous palaces that surpass anything before them. Their owners were scholars who had significant historical knowledge and used this learning to introduce a collection of quotations from the full range of older pictorial themes and texts.

From the Persian period (fifth century BCE) we have no evidence of funerary practices. In the Ptolemaic and Roman periods, however, the tradition of tombs decorated with images was resumed, partly in Egyptian style but increasingly in a mixed Egyptian-Hellenistic style. The Underworld Books are found on stone sarcophagi, and spells from the *Book of Going Forth by Day* are painted directly onto the wrappings of mummies. Two new texts were created which opened up new prospects for life in the hereafter: the deceased had the air needed for breathing (i.e., everlasting life) supplied to him by decree of the gods; and he or she gained access to earthly life in order to partake in the feasts offered to the gods in the temples. In the second century CE, the old conceptions of the afterlife disappeared as Christianity spread.

The images and texts that the ancient Egyptians created in general present no emotion, so it is not easy to say what their attitude toward death was. From the Middle Kingdom (about 2000 BCE) on, however, in many tombs we find an inscription addressed to visitors that reads "O you who love to live and hate to die." In fact, from all periods there are sayings suggesting that a long life was seen as the highest good on earth. In the New Kingdom, there are more bitter laments over the darkness and loneliness that prevail in the afterworld. Especially starting around 1000 BCE, there is formulated the sad certainty that a deceased person loses individual consciousness and lingers on in a gloomy state of slumber. However, this notion did not lead to a new concept of life in the hereafter; rather, the old beliefs persisted. People learned to live with the conflict between skepticism and confidence in the ancient magical means which promised a conscious life in a beautiful afterworld.

[*See also* Book of Going Forth by Day; Book of That Which Is In the Underworld; Coffin Texts; Judgment of the Dead; Paradise; *and* Pyramid Texts.]

## BIBLIOGRAPHY

*General Works*

Bierbrier, M. L., ed. *Portraits and Masks: Burial Customs in Roman Egypt.* London, 1997. Essays dealing chiefly with the lifelike mummy portraits of the Roman period.

D'Auria, Sue, Peter Lacovara, and Catharine H. Roehrig. *Mummies and Magic: The Funerary Arts of Ancient Egypt.* Boston, 1988. Informative overview of all major aspects of funerary customs and conceptions of the afterlife, tracing development and meaning of mortuary objects from prehistoric to Coptic times; an exhibition catalogue with good bibliography.

Emery, Walter B. *A Funerary Repast in an Egyptian Tomb of the Archaic Period.* Leiden, 1962. A rare example of an unplundered tomb of this early date.

Forman, Werner, and Stephen Quirke. *Hieroglyphs and the Afterlife in Ancient Egypt.* London, 1996. An account of texts, from the Old Kingdom to the Roman period, intended to guarantee life after death, with concise interpretation of themes and copious illustrations.

Hoffmann, Michael. *Egypt before the Pharoahs: The Prehistoric Foundations of Egyptian Civilization.* London, Melbourne, and Henley, 1984. Since cemeteries constitute nearly the only remains from this period, funeral customs and burial objects are emphasized in this work.

Hornung, Erik. *Valley of the Kings: Horizon of Eternity.* Translated by D. Warburton. New York, 1990. Interpretation of inscriptions and depictions in New Kingdom royal tombs that recount the nightly journey of the deceased king with the sun god.

Lauer, Jean-Philippe. *Saqqara, the Royal Cemetery of Memphis: Excavations and Discoveries since 1850.* London, 1978. Short description of the most important tombs, principally of the Old Kingdom, by a leading authority.

Leclant, Jean. "Earu-Gefilde." In *Lexikon der Ägyptologie,* 1: 1156–1160. Wiesbaden, 1975. Discusses the fields of the dead, including an unproven hypothesis of early Egyptologists that the Greek "Elysion" derives from Egyptian *sht j3rw.*

Morenz, Siegfried. *Egyptian Religion.* London, 1973. The chapter "Death and the Dead" thoroughly covers Egyptian attitudes.

Quirke, Stephen. *Ancient Egyptian Religion.* London, 1992. Includes an important chapter on death and afterlife, covering attitudes toward death, burial customs, and conceptions of the afterlife expressed in texts and tomb paintings.

Spencer, Alan Jeffrey. *Death in Ancient Egypt.* Harmondsworth, 1982. Good information about some important aspects, including mummification, burial goods, coffins, and tomb structures.

Vandier, Jacques. *Manuel d'archéologie égyptienne.* 6 vols. Paris, 1952–1978. The only handbook that includes general iconography from nonroyal tombs.

*Translations of Source Texts*

Faulkner, Raymond O. *The Ancient Egyptian Pyramid Texts.* Warminster, 1969.

Faulkner, Raymond O. *The Ancient Egyptian Coffin Texts.* 3 vols. Warminster, 1973–1978. This and the preceding are excellent translations of two of the most difficult corpora of religious texts, with the earliest descriptions of nonroyal and royal afterlife, respectively.

Faulkner, Raymond O. *The Ancient Egyptian Book of the Dead.* Edited by Carol Andrews. Rev. edn, London, 1985. Includes glossary and a fine set of illustrations from the best copy (in the British Museum), though lacks an index.

Hornung, Erik. *Die Unterweltsbücher der Ägypter.* New edn., Zurich and Munich, 1992. Complete translations of all royal guides to the afterworld from the New Kingdom, with line drawings of illustrations and summary introduction.

Lichtheim, Miriam. *Ancient Egyptian Autobiographies Chiefly of the Middle Kingdom: A Study and an Anthology.* Freiburg and Göttingen, 1988. Translation and commentary of sixty autobiographical texts from the Old and Middle Kingdoms; these texts contain the subjects' wishes for their afterlife.

MAYA MÜLLER
Translated from German by Robert E. Shillenn
and Jane McGary

**AGRICULTURE** was the basis of the economy in dynastic Egypt, but it was first a modest supplement to hunting and gathering in the Nile Valley. How it came to Egypt from the Near East and how it was transformed from a minor economic sideline into a sophisticated and highly productive farming system are still poorly understood. Egypt's archaeological record from the Predynastic to the Early Dynastic period is meager, offering the barest outline. Through the later pharaonic textual, artistic, and other evidence, however, a wealth of detail has been amassed about food production, although the data are by no means complete. Many questions remain about the cultivation of fruits, vegetables, fodder crops, and pulses, as well as the identities and characteristics of some of these crops.

**Prehistoric Agriculture.** The first traces of farming in Egypt come from a series of Neolithic sites on the northern Faiyum Basin (the Faiyum A culture) as well as the site of Merimde Beni-Salame in the western Nile Delta. These are small seasonal camps, nearly identical to hunter-gatherer settlements from the Upper Paleolithic and Mesolithic, except for traces of crude pottery, crops, and livestock. Egypt's first farmers were hunter-gatherers who also herded a few animals and planted a few crops. They included emmer wheat, barley, lentils, peas, and flax, as well as cattle, sheep, goats, and pigs—the remains of which were all found in the oldest levels of Merimde (c.4800 BCE). In the Faiyum, barley and emmer wheat grains, along with wild seeds, were found in storage pits at the Upper K site (5145 ± 155 calibrated BCE); at other sites, the bones of sheep, goat, and cattle have been found.

Both the crops and livestock were most probably introduced from the Near East, where they had first been domesticated several millennia earlier; but possibly, before those introductions, some groundwork for farming in Egypt had led to efforts to protect, tame, or raise indigenous plants and/or animals. Cattle, for example, *may* have been independently domesticated in Egypt, since the wild progenitor of domestic cattle, a native of the Nile Valley, had been hunted there. Then, too, several native Egyptian crops that were grown in pharaonic times *may* have been cultivated earlier; however, there is as yet almost no archaeological data from the Nile Valley's crucial period preceding agriculture. The agricultural techniques of Egypt's first farmers almost certainly did not come from the Near East but probably were developed in the Nile Valley. Egyptian farmers relied on crops grown in the wake of annual summer floods; winter rains or perennial irrigation were used in the Near East, since flooding occurred in the spring but was not seasonally reliable.

From the modest beginnings of agriculture at Merimde (and probably many other sites in the Delta that have either been destroyed or buried under Nile silts) farming villages quickly developed. The settlement at Merimde, from the second level on, developed into a substantial town, which relied increasingly on crops and livestock. At the same time, small farming settlements were started in the Nile Valley, first at El-Omari near Helwan (4110 ± 260 calibrated BCE) and Maadi (3900–3500 BCE), and then in

Middle Egypt in the Matmar region (c.4000 BCE). By 3800 BCE, farming communities were thriving in Middle Egypt and becoming established in Upper Egypt—in Armant, the Naqada region, and at Hierakonpolis.

Because Predynastic archaeology has been focused primarily on cemeteries, there is little information about farming, besides the remains of field crops and other plants. Among the latter are grapes, watermelons, and melons; the sycomore fig, dom palm, and Christ's thorn, indigenous to the Nile Valley, have also been found at Predynastic sites, although probably wild at that time. While little is known about cultivation practices, Late Predynastic cemeteries and other evidence reflect a complex society, with wealth and social stratification. Egyptian farming, therefore, was probably highly productive by that time, and the basic practices of flood-basin agriculture were probably well established. Some sort of flood control was underway too, as one of the last Predynastic kings is shown ceremonially breaching a levee or dike with a hoe on the Scorpion mace head.

**Pharaonic Agriculture.** Egyptologists have been writing about Egyptian food production for about 150 years, relying almost entirely on texts and artistic evidence. The texts, which include literary and administrative documents, private letters, and household accounts, are a treasure trove of details about prices, wages, taxes, land tenure, crop yields, and cereal trade. Artistic evidence comes primarily from carved reliefs and scene paintings in Old, Middle, and New Kingdom private tombs, as well as from small models of everyday activities (in ceramic, wood, and other materials) placed in tombs. Many of the paintings and reliefs, often beautifully rendered, depict scenes of everyday life, such as sowing and harvesting; they are frequently supplemented with explanatory captions. As comprehensive as these two sources seem, they are nonetheless limited in several significant ways. The representations were not intended as "photorealistic" depictions or treatises but are idealized creations, prepared according to the canons of the funerary cult, to serve the deceased. They are laden with standard themes and scenes that were copied repeatedly; sometimes ambiguous, they can be difficult to interpret and are occasionally contradictory (the same sequence of scenes has sometimes been interpreted in radically different ways by different scholars).

While texts offer rich details, sometimes enlivened by human emotion, they provide only a glimpse into particular aspects of farming. Linguistic data may be elusive, since many terms are poorly understood or have not yet been translated. Texts may also be colored by political agendas, boasts, and propaganda, which may be misleading. In addition, the interpretation of both texts and artistic evidence has suffered from the preconceived notions of the interpreter. Historical observations, such as those by the Classical-era authors Herodotus and Pliny, have supplemented Egyptian texts and tomb scenes. While they have been useful for understanding some agricultural practices of Greco-Roman times, their observations may not apply to earlier periods; Egypt's economy went through major transformations under the Greeks and Romans, profoundly changing many aspects of Nile Valley agriculture, including the staple crops and irrigation practices.

Archaeological evidence has made only a relatively small contribution to the current understanding of pharaonic agriculture. With an emphasis on burials and temples, excavated remains of farming were reflected mainly in activities related to mortuary practices. The food offerings in tombs were carefully chosen species and are unlikely to be representative of ancient Egyptian crops as a whole; for example, pulses, which were probably an important source of protein, are rarely found in tombs. Settlement sites, however, yield a fuller record of agricultural practices, with the traces of many everyday activities well preserved. Remains of tools and facilities—such as querns, hearths, ovens, and granaries—as well as plant and animal remains in various stages of processing have been recovered. Still, relatively few settlements have been excavated in Egypt until recently, so information on subsistence is only now being systematically collected and analyzed. In the 1980s and 1990s, there has been a quiet revolution in the study of ancient Egyptian agriculture. Although texts and picture-based research still provide the bulk of knowledge, some Egyptologists and archaeologists are focusing on food production, using archaeological approaches that have been routine in most areas of prehistoric research. Settlement sites are now being targeted for excavation. Plant remains are deemed valuable artifacts in their own right and are being systematically and extensively recovered. A variety of intensive retrieval methods, such as flotation and fine sieving, are being employed to recover large collections of materials. Analyses are going beyond simple species lists or first occurrences, to probe a wide range of issues—processing methods, field conditions, water regimens, crop contaminants, fodder crops, fuels, and possible weeding practices. Many of the approaches are integrated studies, drawing on ethnographic, ecological, and experimental data, in addition to using the texts and tomb scenes. Remains of plants and food residues are examined with scanning electron microscopy, infrared spectroscopy, and various chemical analyses. While much of this analysis is still in its infancy in Egyptology, it already offers the needed balance to the text and picture-based studies.

**Farming Systems.** Several cultivation systems were employed in Egyptian agriculture to fill the different economic and ecological niches. Large-scale field agriculture,

AGRICULTURE. *Nakht, an official, supervising agricultural estate activities.* Detail of a copy by
N. de G. Davies and L. Crane of the southern part of the eastern wall in the tomb of Nakht at
Thebes, eighteenth dynasty, reign of Thutmose IV. (The Metropolitan Museum of Art, 15.5.19b)

devoted to the subsistence crops, dominated the natural
flood basins. Covered by the annual floodwaters, which
left fertile silts behind, these lands required neither perennial irrigation nor extensive soil preparation. Gardens,
orchards, and plantations were situated on high ground
and on marginal lands, which required both perennial
irrigation and extensive land development. Planted with
vegetables, vines, and fruit trees, these labor-intensive
agricultural lands produced foods primarily destined for
the market, the mortuary cult, and wealthy households.
Peasants, however, probably raised some fruits and vegetables for their own consumption.

The Wilbour Papyrus and some other texts document
complex landholding patterns that are not fully understood. All of Egypt theoretically belonged to the crown,
but much of the land was parcelled out through endowments to temples, foundations, officials, and private indi-

viduals. During the New Kingdom, the land was divided
into large estates and small holdings (in a pattern resembling medieval European manors); this practice was continued into Egypt's Late period. The small farms were
granted to soldiers and to individuals working for institutions; worked for subsistence and rent, the small farms
averaged 5 arouras (about 1.25 hectares), enough to support a family. Large estate lands were worked by a staff or
rented out. Land was also bought and sold. New Kingdom
documents indicate that people of all occupations owned
or rented farm land, both for field crops and vegetable
plots. Texts also suggest that small and large holdings
were scattered widely, rather than consolidated into a
single location for each owner.

The ancient Egyptian agricultural year was divided
into three periods—inundation; coming forth, or growth;
and drought. Nearly all of Egypt's annual crops were

planted in the fall, after the inundation. They were winter crops, adapted to grow through the cooler winter months, to ripen in the spring. The only crops that grew in the warm spring or hot summer, besides trees and vines, were probably some annual fruits and vegetables. There is very little evidence for them, however, apart from the ancient plants themselves and some artistic records of summer cultivation.

**Field Agriculture.** The field crops included emmer wheat and barley, which are well documented, as well as flax, for which there is some documentation, and the pulses, for which there is almost none. The cereals were the staples, for bread and beer; they were paid as wages and collected as taxes. Flax was raised for its fibers, used to make linen, string, and rope, and for its seed, an important source of oil. The pulses were probably the poor man's "meat."

**The cereals.** Emmer wheat (*Triticum dicoccum*), called *bdt*, was the only wheat of any significance in Predynastic and pharaonic Egypt. With its grains tightly enveloped in a husk (a hull), it is considered a primitive wheat. Emmer was initially the major cereal grain throughout the ancient world, but it was gradually displaced by the free-threshing wheats, durum (*Triticum durum*) and bread wheat (*Triticum aestivum*). These two are easier to process, since the grains fall freely away during threshing, whereas emmer's chaff can only be removed with laborious processing. For reasons not yet understood, Egyptians continued raising emmer as their major cereal long after its decline elsewhere; not until after Alexander's conquest in 332 BCE was emmer replaced by the free-threshing wheats.

Other wheats have been associated with ancient Egypt, but they played a minor role, if any, in the economy. Some free-threshing wheats have been claimed as an ancient Egyptian cereal, on the basis of the term *swt*, translated as "naked wheat," but their rare and isolated finds suggest that they may have been nothing more than field weeds. Another possible field weed is einkorn wheat (*Triticum monococcum*), which has also been recovered in extremely small quantities. Spelt wheat (*Triticum spelta*) appears in the literature about ancient Egypt, but it was probably never grown in the Nile Valley; adapted to conditions in northern Europe, it would have been ill suited to Egypt's climate. The English name for spelt wheat, however, is similar to the German term for hulled wheats in general, *Spelzen* or *Spelzweizen*, so this is likely the source of the confusion.

Most of the barley, called *it* in ancient Egypt, was the six-row (*Hordeum vulgare* subsp. *hexastichum*) variety, although the primitive two-row barley (*Hordeum vulgare* subsp. *distichum*) has also been found at Egyptian sites. A four-row barley has also been identified among Egyptian plant remains, but it is most likely a lax-eared variety of six-row barley.

**Pulses.** The pulses (peas and lentils) rarely occur as tomb offerings; they are not in Egyptian tomb paintings or often mentioned in texts. In historic times and up to the present, however, pulses have been a staple for the bulk of Egypt's population. They were likely of equal importance in pharaonic times but endured a lowly status that condemned them to obscurity. Lentils (*Lens culinaris*), called *'ršn*, occur more frequently in archaeological contexts than any other pulse, but the archaeological record is still too poor to conclude that they were the most important pulse. Lentils and peas (*Pisum sativum*), called *thw3*, were both known from the beginnings of farming in Egypt. Fava or faba beans (*Vicia faba* var. *minor*), called *pr* or *pa-l*, are first known from the fifth dynasty. Chickpeas (*Cicer arietinum*), called *hrw-bjk*, are known from the eighteenth dynasty, but they may have been cultivated much earlier.

**Irrigation and the Flood.** The alluvial flats where the field crops were raised were originally segmented into discrete flood basins by the natural levees and hillocks, as well as by old Nile channels. The annual flood, the sole source of water, moved through the basins by natural gravitational flow. Efforts to guide and control this free-flooding Nile began in the Predynastic period and continued throughout the pharaonic period. By the end of that time, a system of dikes and canals regulated flooding and drainage. All administered on the local level, this rudimentary irrigation regime, together with an extension of a canal system, increased the land area; it also improved growing conditions for annual crops, by retaining water for longer periods, if necessary. The inundation began in July in southern Egypt and reached the northernmost basin four to six weeks later. The flood waters were directed into the basins, retained for a sufficient period, and then released back into the river. Occasionally, the floods were disastrously low, leaving whole areas of the Nile Valley dry and the economy devastated. When the floods were late, planting was delayed which threatened the harvest. Normally, the flood basins were drained by early October in southern Egypt and by mid- to late November in the northernmost basins.

After the flood receded, it left behind a layer of silt that spared farmers any extensive soil preparation. Because the flood effectively fertilized the soil with new silts and washed away damaging salts, fertilizers and fallowing were generally unnecessary. Textual records of fallowing deal primarily with land unintentionally set aside, owing to low floods, damage from animals, and the death of landowners. With the flood waters drained, dikes and canals were refurbished and boundary markers were repositioned. The land was then ready for planting, often without further preparation. On freshly deposited silts, little tilling, if any, was required; however, plowing may have been necessary on virgin lands, fallowed soil, or lands left too long after draining. A hoe was used or a shallow-ploughing ard, pulled by cattle or men.

**Cereal Cultivation.** Grains were planted by broadcast sowing; on fresh silts, they were immediately incorporated into the soil by ploughing or trampling. The close association of ploughing and tilling is suggested by the Egyptian word for "plough" (*sk3*), which can also mean, "till," or "cultivate." Trampling was done by flocks of sheep, occasionally by donkeys, and during the New Kingdom, by pigs. Once sown, the cereals were probably left nearly unattended until harvest, except for a government survey used to determine taxes. There is no textual or artistic evidence of weeding, and archaeological remains of cereals suggest that they came from the fields laden with weeds. Although weeds competed with crops, they may have provided food and other useful products. Some became domesticates that were planted for their own properties.

Emmer and barley usually ripen about six months after sowing, placing the harvest between February and May, with barley maturing a few weeks before emmer. The main tool for harvesting was a hand-held sickle, originally made of chipped stone blades set in a wooden handle or sometimes an animal's jawbone. Copper and then bronze sickles came into use in pharaonic times, although stone blades were used continuously throughout this period. Some question whether cereals were cut off just below the ear or lower down on the straw. Old Kingdom tomb scenes show the cereals bundled into sheaves with a long length of straw. In the New Kingdom scenes, however, the harvested grains are depicted loose in baskets or woven carriers. Noting this change in the scenes, some have suggested that it may indicate a change in harvesting methods. Whether cereal straw was harvested with the grains or separately, it was an important product in its own right, valuable as fodder, as fuel, and as temper for mud bricks, plaster, and pottery. Perhaps a growing demand for straw was responsible for the (possible) change in harvesting methods during the New Kingdom.

Threshing was done soon after the harvest to separate the emmer spikelets and barley grains from the straw. Hoofed animals, usually cattle, were driven over the cereal crop, thickly laid on the threshing floor. Workers winnowed out the remaining straw and chaff by tossing the grains in the air with winnowing fans, small wooden scoops. After additional cleaning through sieves, the barley grains and emmer spikelets were ready to be measured and stored.

**Pulse Cultivation.** Little is known of how pulses were cultivated, but extrapolating from Egyptian practices common early in the twentieth century, lentils, chickpeas, and peas were probably broadcast sown while faba beans may have been pressed into holes. All would have been harvested by uprooting the plant, which was then threshed to separate the beans from the pods. Peas may also have been hand picked, as tender garden vegetables.

**Fodder Crops.** Leguminous fodder crops—such as grass pea (*Lathyrus sativus*), bitter vetch (*Vicia ervilia*), and *berseem*, or Egyptian clover (*Trifolium alexandrinum*)—may have been cultivated in pharaonic Egypt as field crops; however the first records of them appear only during Greco-Roman times. In a land of such limited grazing, fodder was no doubt very important for maintaining herds and flocks, particularly during the inundation. From Old Kingdom and later settlement sites, small leguminous seeds have been recovered in great quantities. Because they appear to be derived from dung cakes burned as fuel, the seeds have been interpreted as possible fodder. It has been difficult to determine if these legumes are wild or domesticated. *Berseem* is particularly interesting, since it probably was originally domesticated in Egypt.

**Oil Crop Cultivation.** Flax (*Linum usitatissimum*) was called *mhj* and is known from Predynastic sites; it was broadcast sown and harvested by uprooting, as was often shown in tomb scenes. If fibers were wanted, the plants were placed close together, to encourage tall growth. Varieties grown for seed were planted more thinly, to promote branching and flowering. The stalks harvested for fibers were retted, a process in which the stalks are left in water, making it easier to strip away the long fibers. When flax plants were harvested for seed, the dried plants were threshed.

During the New Kingdom, two other plants were grown for oil: sesame (*Sesamum indicum*) and safflower (*Carthamus tinctorius*). Seeds of both were found among offerings in Tutankhamun's tomb but are otherwise poorly documented. Safflower blossoms were used to dye linen and were incorporated in mummy garlands, possibly as early as the eighteenth dynasty.

**Gardens, Orchards, and Plantations.** Unlike field agriculture, orchards and plantations required both frequent irrigation and extensive land preparation. Because perennial crops had to be planted out of the flood's reach, orchards were usually located on high ground either along the river or in the flood plain, or they were on marginal lands, such as the desert edge. Garden plots were often planted with orchards or in similar habitats beyond the flood. Before planting, garden and orchard lands had to be cleared of scrub growth and improved with fertilizers, such as manure, organic midden matter, and/or Nile silts dredged from canals. Garden and orchard crops had to be watered continuously through the year, a labor-

AGRICULTURE. *Wooden funerary model of a man plowing with a yoke of oxen, early twelfth dynasty.* (The Metropolitan Museum of Art, 36.5)

ious manual task that effectively limited the size of plots. Tomb scenes often show gardeners hand watering with pots. If the lands were near the Nile, water could be drawn from the river. But many gardens and orchards were probably irrigated with water from wells and ponds dug down to the water table. The *shadoof,* a simple water-lifting device that was introduced during the New Kingdom, may have eased the gardener's burden, but watering still remained an arduous chore. The *saqiya,* the first device that could lift significant amounts of water efficiently, was not introduced until Ptolemaic times.

Garden plots and fruit trees were maintained by peasants as well as by the elite. The plots ranged from small household kitchen gardens to large plantations. At the desert site of the workmen's village of Amarna, traces were found of small gardens, evidently irrigated with water drawn from a large well at the edge of the city. Peasant farmers may have maintained a few fruit trees on high

ground in the flood plain or around their village. Orchards, usually with accompanying gardens and ponds, were labor intensive to build and maintain; thus they were established only on the estates of high officials and institutions. Small garden plots were probably for subsistence, while gardens on estates provided both produce and pleasure. During the Old and Middle Kingdoms, production seems to have been stressed; vegetable gardens and vineyards are depicted in tomb scenes in the context of a productive landscape. Formal pleasure gardens, valued both for their aesthetic and symbolic presence, became an essential feature of New Kingdom temples and private estates.

Gardens, orchards, and plantations served an important role in the economy by placing less productive lands into cultivation. In the Faiyum, in Middle Egypt, and in the Delta, lands unsuitable for grains were gradually developed as orchards and plantations. During the New

Kingdom, even low-lying lands in the Delta, apparently protected with dikes, were put into production with vines and fruit/seed oil trees. Vegetable plots might have also have been planted late in the season in low-lying river-bank areas or in waterlogged lands in the flood plain. The pools dug to water gardens and orchards were doubly productive, since they could also support fish, waterfowl, trees, vegetables, and flowers. In the commercial gardens and orchards, the high labor costs of land development and water were justified by the high value of the crops. Fruits and vegetables were part of the trade and market economy, rather than subsistence goods, although vegetables were sporadically paid as wages. Vines, fruit/seed oil trees, and fruits were raised as cash crops and as offerings for the temples; flowers were also produced for the temples. Plantations far from centers of population specialized in crops that could be stored and transported easily, such as wine and oil. During the Old Kingdom, the Delta had become an area of specialized wine production. By the New Kingdom, olive trees (*Olea europaea*) were apparently cultivated in the Faiyum and Delta. Olives (*d̲.t*) were used for pickling and some oil production, although the bulk of ancient Egypt's olive oil was probably imported. Other seed-oil trees included the moringa (*Moringa peregrina*), balanos (*Balanites aegyptiaca*), almond (*Prunus dulcis*), and castor tree (*Ricinus communis*).

Estate gardens and orchards are most often depicted as walled, with a rectangular pool or another source of standing water. Flowers were grown around the pool, along with vines and neat rows of trees, often planted in pits. The most common flowers in New Kingdom gardens were the cornflower (*Centaurea depressa*), mandrake (*Mandrogora officinarum*), poppy (*Papaver rhoeas*), and lotus (*Nymphea lotus, N. caerulea*). Grape vines (*Vitis vinifera*), often combined with trees, were a constant feature of gardens as early as the Predynastic. Grapes were pressed into wine from very early in the Old Kingdom, if not earlier. The common trees in New Kingdom garden scenes were a combination of local and introduced species—dom palms, sycomore figs, common figs, dates, and pomegranates. The dom palm (*Hyphaene thebaica*) and the sycomore fig (*Ficus sycomorus*) were known from the Predynastic and probably domesticated in the Nile Valley, as was the native *nabkh* (*Ziziphus spina-christi*), a small apple-like fruit. Adapted to the conditions of the Nile Valley, these trees were probably the most common fruit species in the gardens of small holders and around villages.

From the Old Kingdom, the common fig (*Ficus carica*), the persea tree (*Mimusops laurifolia*), and occasionally the Egyptian plum (*Cordia myxa*) are shown in scenes or mentioned in texts. The date palm (*Phoenix dactylifera*)—its leaves, fiber, and wood—was used in the Old Kingdom, but the fruits were rare until the Middle Kingdom and

only abundant in post-pharaonic sites. The horticultural use of artificial pollination, probably beginning during the Middle Kingdom, would have increased fruit quantity and quality. With Egyptian expansion during the empire-building of the eighteenth dynasty, there was great interest in foreign plants, such as the pomegranate tree (*Punica granatum*) and the carob tree (*Ceratonia siliqua*).

Little is known about vegetable garden practices, except for the tomb scenes that depict garden plots on estates as a grid of miniature square basins. Vegetables may also have been intercropped with fruits and vines. The identity of all the vegetable crops grown is not clear, since some are known only through linguistic terms with uncertain translations. Others are known only from artistic representations that are not precise enough for identification. The archaeobotanical record—from seeds, stems, fruits, other plant parts, and pollen—provides the best direct evidence for the identification of these crops: Melons (*Citrullus melo*), watermelons (*Citrullus lanatus*), and chufa (*Cyperus esculentus*) are documented from the Predynastic on by archaeological evidence and also by artistic representations; it is unclear, however, when chufa, or yellow nutgrass, was actually put into cultivation. A sedge with edible tubers, chufa was domesticated in Egypt from a wild variety native to the Nile Valley. Chufa was probably the most successful summer crop in pharaonic Egypt, since this hardy plant needed little care.

From the Old Kingdom, onions (*Allium cepa*), lettuce (*Lactuca sativa*), and the chate melon (*Cucumis melo* var. *chate*) were depicted in tomb scenes, although their identity was not always certain. For example, there are as yet no confirmed archaeological remains of lettuce from pharaonic times, yet there is some linguistic and artistic evidence for the plant, such as tomb scenes depicting gardeners planting a long-leafed lettuce; also, Min, the deity of vegetation and procreation is shown in fields of stylized lettuce. Since there are no other indications of lettuce until Greco-Roman times, this variety may have been domesticated in Egypt. The term *iskt* dates from the sixth dynasty and is translated as "leek," but the Egyptian plant was more probably the kurrat (*Allium ampeloprasum* var. *kurrat*) rather than the European garden leek (*Allium ampeloprasum* var. *porrum*). Since the two are closely related, artistic representations usually identified as leeks might be the kurrat or even the long-leafed onion. Thus far, the only archaeological remains identified as kurrat date from the twentieth to twenty-sixth dynasty, while there are none of leeks. In Egypt today, the kurrat is referred to as "local kurrat" while the leek is "foreign kurrat." The chate melon, a green nonsweet variety of African melon, is elongated and curved, more closely resembling a cucumber than a sweet melon. Models and depictions of this fruit have frequently been interpreted as cucumber;

however, the cucumber (*Cucumis sativus*), first cultivated in India, was probably not introduced to Egypt until Greco-Roman times.

Whether celery and radish were known in pharaonic times is questionable. The only celery (*Apium graveolens*) from ancient Egypt, found in funeral garlands, is wild. The cultivated vegetable did not appear in Egypt until the fourteenth or fifteenth century CE. Although linguistic evidence for radish has been cited for the pharaonic period, the first well-dated archaeological evidence for Egyptian radish (*Raphanus sativus* var. *aegyptiacus*) is later, from the Roman period. Condiments, used for flavorings and medicine, were not commonly known in Egypt until New Kingdom times. Archaeological remains of coriander (*Coriandrum sativum*), black cumin (*Nigella sativa*), cumin (*Cuminum cyminum*), and dill (*Anethum graveolens*) are first known from the eighteenth dynasty. Fenugreek (*Trigonella foenum-graecum*) and garlic (*Allium sativum*) have been identified in Predynastic contexts, but they are not confirmed again until the New Kingdom.

**Conclusions.** Although the details of crops and farming practices are important, the context and wider implications of agriculture must also be considered. Ancient Egypt was an agrarian-based society, thus almost everyone was in some way involved in farming, from the pharaoh, who ultimately owned the land, to the peasant who toiled in the fields. Many religious rituals were performed to assure fertility and a rich harvest. Agricultural produce was a societal and private source of prestige and wealth. After death, the well-to-do were surrounded with colorful farming scenes as well as rich offerings of cereals, fruits, and vegetables for the afterlife. Several millennia later, we are only beginning to understand the sophistication and skill of ancient Egyptian farmers.

[*See also* Animal Husbandry; Economy; Hunting; Irrigation; Landholding; *and* Technology and Engineering.]

**BIBLIOGRAPHY**

Butzer, K. *Early Hydraulic Civilization in Egypt: A Study in Cultural Ecology.* Chicago, 1976. Study of the Nile Valley and Egyptian irrigation, based on texts and geology.

Darby, W. J., P. Ghalioungui, and L. Grivetti. *Food: The Gift of Osiris II.* London, 1977. A compendium of foods, with discussions based on traditional text and picture-based research.

Eyre, C. J. "The Water Regimes for Orchards and Plantations in Pharaonic Egypt." *Journal of Egyptian Archaeology* 80 (1994), 57–80. Discusses land preparation and irrigation systems for plantations and gardens, using texts and artistic evidence.

Germer, R. *Flora des pharaonischen Ägypten.* Deutsches Archäologisches Institut Abteilung Kairo, Sonderschrift, 14. Mainz, 1985. A comprehensive catalog of plants found in Egypt, with discussions of all plant finds as well as the biology of the plants.

Hepper, F. N. *Pharaoh's Flowers: The Botanical Treasures of Tutankhamun.* London, 1990. Written for the lay public, an interesting discussion of plants found in the tomb.

Manniche, L. *An Ancient Egyptian Herbal.* Austin, 1989. Primarily a discussion of medicinal uses of plants, written for a general audience.

Moens, M.-F. "The Ancient Egyptian Garden in the New Kingdom: A Study of Representations." *Orientalia Lovaniensia Periodica* 15 (1984), 11–53. Discusses the New Kingdom formal garden and its significance, using primarily the artistic record.

Moens, M.-F., and W. Wetterstrom. "The Agricultural Economy of an Old Kingdom Town in Egypt's West Delta: Insights from the Plant Remains." *Journal of Near Eastern Studies* 47.3 (1988), 159–173. The authors reconstruct aspects of the economy, using a large collection of archaeobotanical remains collected by flotation; they also draw upon textual and artistic evidence.

Murray, M. A. "Cereal Production and Processing." In *Ancient Egyptian Materials and Technology,* edited by P. Nicholson and I. Shaw. Cambridge, in press. The most up-to-date discussion of cereal processing prepared for this new version of a classic text.

Murray, M. A. "Fruits, Vegetables, Pulses and Condiments." In *Ancient Egyptian Materials and Technology,* edited by P. Nicholson and I. Shaw. Cambridge, in press. The most up-to-date discussion of the subject prepared for this new version of a classic text.

Murray, M. A. "Viticulture and Wine Production." In *Ancient Egyptian Materials and Technology,* edited by P. Nicholson and I. Shaw. Cambridge, in press. The most up-to-date discussion of the subject prepared for this new version of a classic text.

Samuel, D. "Ancient Egyptian Cereal Processing: Beyond the Artistic Record." *Cambridge Archaeological Journal* 3.2 (1993), 276–283. Shows the limitations of relying only on artistic representations for understanding ancient processing methods.

Täckholm, V., G. Täckholm, and M. Drar. *Flora of Egypt,* vol. 1: *Bulletin of the Faculty of Science Fouad I University.* Cairo, 1941. A classic; in the sections on *Triticum* and *Hordeum,* there is a detailed discussion of ancient Egyptian cereals and all finds published up to that time.

Vandier, J. *Scéne de la Vie agricole: Manuel d'archéologie égyptienne,* vol. 6. Paris, 1978. Egyptian agriculture as seen through the artistic record.

Wetterstrom, W. "Foraging and Farming in Egypt: The Transition from Hunting and Gathering to Horticulture in the Nile Valley." In *The Archaeology of Africa: Food, Metals and Towns,* edited by T. Shaw, P. Sinclair, B. Andah, and A. Okpoko, pp.165–226. London, 1993. Review article of the transition to agriculture, which analyzes the archaeological data and also considers ecological and ethnographic data.

Zohary, D., and M. Hopf. *Domestication of Plants in the Old World: The Origin and Spread of Cultivated Plants in West Asia, Europe and the Nile Valley.* 2d ed. Oxford, 1993. A comprehensive review of archaeological and other evidence for the domestication and spread of cultivated plants.

WILMA WETTERSTROM AND
MARY ANNE MURRAY

**A-GROUP,** the archaeological designation for an indigenous Nubian culture; the term "A-Group" was introduced by George A. Reisner (1910) in his chronological model of the Nubian cultures, but it came into general use much later, in connection with the 1960s salvage archaeology of the Nile region that would become flooded by the soon-to-be-built Aswan High Dam. The cultural designations "Archaic," "Protodynastic," or "Early Dynastic" had been preferred for it before that time. The term "A Horizon" was first proposed for it by William Y. Adams (1977).

The A-Group emerged in Lower Nubia in the territory adjacent to the Nile River between the First Cataract and the Second, during the Predynastic period in Egypt. It reached its climax about the time of the Egyptian unification c.3000 BCE. A-Group remains have been found between Kubanniya, 10 kilometers (6 miles) to the north of Aswan, and Saras East in Batn el-Hagar, 30 kilometers (20 miles) to the south of the Second Cataract. The rocky tract at Semna and Kumma might have constituted its southern border.

The chronological framework of the Nubian A-Group consists of three phases (Nordström 1972 and as of 1999 in press). The *Early A-Group* inhabited the northern part of Lower Nubia and was contemporary with the latter part of Egypt's Amratian culture and early Gerzean (called in Werner Kaiser's 1957 chronology, Naqada Ic and IIa–c); the Early A-Group was also coexistent with an indigenous Neolithic culture called the Abkan, which dominated the southern part of Lower Nubia and Batn el-Hagar, with the Second Cataract area as a center. Archaeological finds also indicate contacts at this time between Egypt and all of Lower Nubia. During the *Middle A-Group*, the second cultural phase, coexistent with Egypt's middle Gerzean (Naqada IId and IIIa), the communities in Lower Nubia and the northern part of Batn el-Hagar developed a uniform culture, characterized by lively contacts with Egypt but also with communities to their south. Cultural and economic exchange was intensified during the third phase, the *Terminal A-Group*, a period of prosperity and population growth that was coexistent with Egypt's unification stage (Naqada IIIb) and the initial part of the first dynasty.

The A-Group was basically a prehistoric culture with no written sources of its own, yet with a distinct Nubian identity; there are a few contemporary textual remains of Egyptian origin that are directly relevant in this context. "The Nubian land" or "the land of the bow" (*t3-sty*) was the Egyptian name for Lower Nubia, and the oldest known evidence with this designation is a first dynasty tablet of King Aha (c.2920 BCE). It shows a prisoner with a Nubian bow, and a *sty*-sign (Old Egyptian for "bow"), and it may have commemorated the king's conquest of the originally Nubian district between Gebel es-Silsila and the First Cataract, which established the border at Aswan (Elephantine). Another document is a relief (now in Khartoum) cut on a rock at Gebel Sheikh Suleiman on the western bank of the Nile in the district of Wadi Halfa, showing slain enemies and Nubian prisoners, one of them tied to the prow of a boat; presumably it is of Early Dynastic origin but its date has been disputed.

The most important source material of the A-Group is archaeological and came from some seventy-five village cemeteries situated on or above the narrow floodplain, systematically excavated during the various salvage expeditions. They have yielded rich and varied funeral offerings of both Egyptian and indigeneous objects (see below). Only a small proportion of the finds originated from settlements, such as house structures or camp sites, and these have been less systematically recorded and published. The osteological (bone) material has been thoroughly studied, however.

The general characteristics of the A-Group can be summarized as follows. The population, estimated at less than ten thousand, lived in small communities along the Nile's floodplain. Structural remains of houses have been found only occasionally, most notably stone foundations at Afia. The A-Group people practiced agriculture; they grew cereal grains and leguminous plants. Animal husbandry, primarily cattle raising, formed the basis of their economy; this was concluded by abundant finds of cowhides in their graves and from cattle dung mixed into the potter's clay as temper. Fishing, hunting, and food gathering were probably complementary parts of their subsistence economy.

They buried their dead in cemeteries, usually in oval or subrectangular pits that were dug into the alluvium, and placed the body in a contracted position with the head toward the south (the upstream direction of the Nile). The burials were commonly furnished with offerings of various kinds. The richer graves yielded collections of fine imported Egyptian objects: open bowls, pottery jars (many with signs of having been used in daily life), stone vessels, incense burners, cylinder seals, slate palettes, copper implements, amulets, and stone beads. The greater part of the finds, however, were of Nubian origin, and those consisted of an array of pottery types (the finest were thin-walled bowls with red-painted geometric designs), and of locally made stone palettes, ivory bracelets, and beads; there were also local pottery figurines, feather fans, and remains of leather clothing. Mollusk shells from the Red Sea (or Indian Ocean) were common. On the whole, the material culture of the A-Group has displayed a blending of Egyptian and Sudanese designs and influences. The distribution of the funerary remains indicates a social inequality that became strongly emphasized during the Terminal phase.

The control of trade and exchange might have become the decisive factor in the development of the A-Group's socioeconomic and political structure. The leaders of the A-Group communities probably played an important intermediary role among the fast-developing Egyptian economy, the communities in Upper Nubia, and those in surrounding regions, furnishing raw materials of various kinds, including ivory, hardwoods, precious stones, and gold, perhaps also cattle.

An advanced chiefdom that controlled at least the southern part of Lower Nubia may have been formed during Terminal A-Group times, perhaps the result of a consolidation process parallel to that of Egypt. The center was at Qustul, near the present-day border of Egypt and Sudan, where an elite cemetery with funerary offerings of outstanding quality has been located. Other focal points were Sayala and Dakka farther north. The complete breakdown of the A-Group's structure came abruptly—when the Egyptian kings of the first dynasty decided to take full control of the southern trade and the flow of raw materials. After the reign of Djer of the first dynasty (c.2900 BCE) through the fifth dynasty (c.2374 BCE) the A-Group was practically nonexistant; traces of permanent A-Group settlements dating in that period were scarce in Lower Nubia, and only a few scattered graves have been unearthed.

The *B-Group* had been proposed as an early archaeological designation for an indigenous culture in Lower Nubia. It had been identified by George A. Reisner (1910) and some other scholars as perhaps contemporary with Egypt's Old Kingdom. The B-Group, however, is no longer accepted as a cultural entity by archaeologists; the burials formerly attributed to it are now considered to be either Early A-Group or to belong to a poor social stratum of the Terminal A-Group.

[*See also* Nubia.]

**BIBLIOGRAPHY**

Adams, William Y. *Nubia: Corridor to Africa.* Princeton, 1977.

Kaiser, Werner. "Zur inneren Chronologie der Naqadakultur." *Archaeologia Geographica* 6 (1957), 69–77.

Nordström, Hans-Åke. *Neolithic and A-Group Sites.* Scandinavian Joint Expedition to Sudanese Nubia, 3. Stockholm, 1972.

Nordström, Hans-Åke. "The Nubian A-Group: Perceiving a Social Landscape." In *Proceedings of the Ninth International Conference of Nubian Studies.* Boston (in press, 1999).

O'Connor, David. *Ancient Nubia: Egypt's Rival in Africa.* Philadelphia, 1993.

Reisner, George A. *The Archaeological Survey of Nubia. Report for 1907–1908.* 2 vols. Cairo, 1910.

Smith, Harry S. "The Development of the 'A-Group' Culture in Northern Lower Nubia." In *Egypt and Africa: Nubia from Prehistory to Islam,* edited by W. V. Davies, pp. 92–111. London, 1991.

Trigger, Bruce G. *History and Settlement in Lower Nubia.* Yale University Publications in Anthropology, 69. New Haven, 1965.

Williams, Bruce B. *The A-Group Royal Cemetery at Qustul: Cemetery L. Excavations between Abu Simbel and the Sudan Frontier.* The University of Chicago, Oriental Institute Nubian Expedition, 3. Chicago, 1986.

HANS-ÅKE NORDSTRÖM

**AHMOSE** (ruled c.1569–c.1545 BCE), first king of the eighteenth dynasty and the founder of the New Kingdom. The son of Sekenenre Ta'o and the powerful queen Ahhotep, he succeeded to the throne upon the death of his brother Kamose. As he was probably about ten years old at the time, his mother Ahhotep served as regent until he was about sixteen. When his mother died, he provided fine jewelry for her funerary treasure. His wife was Ahmose-Nefertari, who was most likely the daughter of Kamose, his brother; she wielded considerable influence and was the object of a posthumous cult.

Having assumed power, he immediately took steps to drive the Hyksos out of Northern Egypt, and he achieved his goal within the first decade of his reign, thereby completing the task that his father and his brother had begun. The details of this campaign are recorded in the biographical texts inscribed in the tombs of two officers who fought under him (both also named Ahmose): Ahmose, son of Ebana, and Ahmose Pennekheb. King Ahmose first launched a successful attack on Avaris, the Hyksos capital in the Nile Delta. The city having fallen, he chased his enemies into southern Palestine and subdued them. He then settled an insurrection to the south, in Nubia. With Egypt now secure, he guaranteed its safety by returning to deal one final blow to the Hyksos in Palestine and southern Phoenicia. The testimonies of the two officers previously mentioned give evidence of the great respect that his soldiers had for their king (who was only about twenty years old at the time of his victory).

Although his greatest fame derived from those military exploits, Ahmose's domestic achievements are also notable. He reformed and strengthened the internal administration so that it could effectively carry out his orders. The limestone quarries at Tura were reopened, and the construction of monumental royal and temple buildings was resumed. Although there are few remains of these structures, what does exist reveals generally high craftsmanship. Temple remains give evidence that he fostered the cult of the Theban god Amun-Re. Also during his reign, Egypt renewed the foreign contacts that had been broken when the Hyksos ruled. Trade took place with the Near East, Byblos, Crete, and Nubia.

Ahmose was buried near his seventeenth dynasty ancestors at Dra Abul Naga at Thebes, and he was honored with a cult at Abydos throughout the eighteenth dynasty. He bequeathed to his son Amenhotpe I a unified, strong, and free Egypt that went on to flourish in the New Kingdom.

[*See also* Ahmose-Nefertari.]

**BIBLIOGRAPHY**

Grimal, Nicolas. *A History of Ancient Egypt.* Oxford, 1992.

Vandersleyen, Claude. "Une tempête sous le règne d'Amosis." Revue d'Égyptologie 19 (1967), 123–159.

Vandersleyen, Claude. *Les guerres d'Amosis, fondateur de la XVIIIe dynastie.* Monographies Reine Elisabeth, 1. Brussels, 1971.

EUGENE ROMANOSKY

**AHMOSE-NEFERTARI,** wife of the founder of the eighteenth dynasty, New Kingdom, Ahmose (r.1569–1545 BCE), and the mother of his son and successor, Amenhotpe I (r.1545–1525 BCE). She died at some point during the reign of Thutmose I (c.1525–1516 BCE). There are some indications that she played an important role in the succession from Amenhotpe I to Thutmose I, especially since the latter king was not related to the family that had founded the dynasty. Possibly, she had served some twenty years earlier as queen regent for Amenhotpe I after the death of her husband. She is known from various New Kingdom documents and representations; in particular, the text from a damaged stela discovered at Karnak recounts in considerable detail a formal transaction between her and King Ahmose.

Ahmose-Nefertari's mortuary temple is situated on the western bank of the Nile across from Thebes; however, it has all but vanished. Her probable tomb is not far away at Dra Abul Naga, and her sarcophagus and mummy were discovered hidden in an ancient cache of royal remains at Deir el-Bahri.

During the centuries after her death, Ahmose-Nefertari was usually represented in scenes with other members of the royal families of the New Kingdom—the so-called king lists. She was also frequently depicted with her son Amenhotpe I because of the reverence in which their memory was held by Egyptians in the area of the workers' village at Deir el-Medina, near the Valley of the Kings. The cult of the deified Amenhotpe I and that of his mother were very important there.

[*See also* Ahmose; *and* Amenhotpe I.]

### BIBLIOGRAPHY

Gitton, Michel. *L'épouse du dieu Ahmes Néfertary.* Paris, 1975. The principal study of the historical figure.

Valbelle, Dominique. *Les ouvriers de la tombe.* Cairo, 1985. Provides a good overview of the workers' village at Deir el-Medina.

DAVID A. BERG

**AKH** (Eg., *ꜣḫ*), a term that occurs regularly throughout ancient Egyptian secular and religious texts, represented by the crested ibis hieroglyph. The *akh*-concept appears to have no intrinsic relation to the bird, to which it might only have been related phonetically. The fundamental meaning of *akh* was "effectiveness," whether in daily affairs or during the afterlife. In the afterlife, *akh* designated a transfigured deceased who, capable of unhindered movement and full physical functioning, would be an effective deceased. Unlike *ba* and *ka* forms, the *akh* individual was often identified with light.

In the mortuary sphere, *akh* denoted the deceased who became an effective being by virtue of having the proper offerings and knowing the efficacious spells. One was made an *akh* after burial through a mortuary ritual that "caused one to become an *akh*" (*sꜣḫ*), which had been performed as early as the Early Dynastic period by a *sekhen-akh* priest (*sḫn-ꜣḫ;* "an *akh*-seeker"). The divine source of *akh*-transformation was unseen, reflecting what Karl Jansen-Winkeln (1996) called an invisible *akh*-effectiveness, its hidden nature being part of its power.

In the living sphere, *akh* commonly referred to "the effectiveness" of kings, officials, or townsmen who acted on behalf of their gods, kings, lords, or one another. Members of all levels of society could be *akh*-effective or perform *akhu*-effective deeds, which were not simply glorious or useful things, as often translated, but concrete acts that affected eternity. For example, in the twelfth dynasty, Senwosret I, in his filial role of Horus, built monuments for his divine father and supplied his offerings, "doing that which is *akh*-effective." Sety I, in the nineteenth dynasty, after completing a chapel at Abydos for his deceased earthly father, said, "I have performed *akhut* ['that which is *akh*'] for you [since] I built for you a temple for your *ka*." In the twenty-seventh dynasty, a nonroyal individual, Oudjahorresne, performed *akhu*-deeds on behalf of his townspeople, defending the feeble, saving the fearful, and doing all *akhu*-acts for them as a father acts for his son. The nature of *akhu*-deeds was thus closely allied to the maintenance of societal *maat* ("justice").

In virtually all the periods of ancient Egypt's religious and secular texts, the concept of *akh* operated in a reciprocal relationship between god and king, between father and son. In the Pyramid Texts, the king as Horus became *akh* through his father Osiris, just as Osiris became *akh* through his son Horus: "It is through you [Osiris] that he [Horus] has become *akh*." In a Coffin Text, the son became *akh* by the father and the father by the son. In the *Book of Going Forth by Day* (*Book of the Dead*), each embraces the other "that he might be an *akh* thereby." The same reciprocity obtained in nonmortuary literature: Senwosret I of the twelfth dynasty constructed a temple for his divine father, providing for his altars, and doing all that which was *akh*-effective; Akhenaten named himself "son of eternity who came forth from the Aten [his father], *akh* for him who is *akh* for him" (Sandman, 1938, p. 91).

Cosmic, primordial notions of luminous power were allied to the concept of *akh*. Whether the concept of *akh*-effectiveness was projected from pragmatic, daily affairs into the cosmic sphere, or the reverse, has become a point of debate. Gertie Englund (1978) opted for the latter and considered the primary meaning of *akh* to be a form of primordial creative power related to the birth of light. Indeed, *akh* often denoted forms of effective light—such as the circumpolar stars (especially in the Pyramid Texts), the solar eye, and sunbeams—which are all intensified forms of celestial effectiveness; sunlight is effectiveness *par excellence*, since light in the mortuary texts daily brings forth and maintains creation. In the Coffin Texts, Atum created Shu and Tefnut with his *akhu*-power; the deceased, the product of *akh*-creation is an *akh*, lord of *akhu*, who himself created an *akh* at his will and who is lord of *seshep* light (*sšp*). This same "lord of *seshep* light" appellation was used in the *Book of Going Forth by Day* for the sun god Re. Light, which produces creation, is by definition effective.

The luminous associations of *akh* were reflected on the understanding of the *akh*-deceased, who would be transfigured in light. In the Coffin Texts, the deceased said, "Re does it [various things] for me and his *akh* is in me" and "as for any *akh* that knows the name of the shining sun, he knows his own name." The *Book of Going Forth by Day* states that Re looks on this *akh* as himself, so the *akh*-deceased can be seen as the very beams of Re. The *akh* thus became both Re and his emanation of light, thus at once creator and creation. Yet *akh*-power can also denote nonsolar forms of effective power, as in the creative speech of the gods, or even the milk full of *akhu* that Hathor, in cow form, imparts when suckling her daughter Hatshepsut.

The ability to function as an *akh* in the netherworld depended, in part, on having material sustenance. Early Dynastic cylinder seals denoted the deceased, hieroglyphically, as an *akh*-bird with head turned back toward a table of food offerings. A number of fourth and fifth dynasty tombs at Giza show the tomb owner, probably understood as a statue, in a funerary cult ceremony labeled "the feeding of the *akh*" (*snmt ȝḫ*), in which offerings were laid down by priests, including the embalmer priest. "Feeding the *akh*" reflected a concrete view of the deceased *akh*, without notions of transfiguration or bodily transformation; this understanding was echoed in Old Kingdom autobiographical tomb inscriptions, in which the owner asserted that he or she is an *akh iker* (*ȝḫ iḳr*; "an able/effective *akh*") or an *akh aper* (*ȝḫ ʿpr*; "an equipped *akh*")—the effective, equipped status based on having the proper tomb goods, knowledge of magical spells, and food goods.

Letters to the dead, during the Old Kingdom and the First Intermediate Period, were often written on offering vessels and were sometimes addressed to the *akh* or *akh iker* and left at his or her offering slab, similarly reflecting an image of the *akh*-deceased as an effective being without overtones of luminosity. Those are *akh*-beings who, though dead, can still act for or against the living and exist with them in a reciprocal arrangement. A group of New Kingdom stelae were dedicated to the deceased as

an *akh iker en Ra* (*ȝḫ iḳr n Rʿ*); these able or effective *akhs* of the sun god Re were depicted as seated individuals (again, probably statues), who were recently deceased ancestors of the dedicators. The purpose of the *akh iker en Ra* dead was to intercede on behalf of their worshipers. Anthropoid busts, sometimes found in conjunction with *akh iker en Ra* stelae and related offering tables, may actually be abbreviated statue forms of *akhs* in that New Kingdom ancestor worship.

**BIBLIOGRAPHY**

Demarée, Robert J. *The ȝḫ iḳr n Rʾ-Stelae. On Ancestor Worship in Ancient Egypt.* Leiden, 1983. A group of New Kingdom stelae dedicated to the "able/effective *akh* of Re" (or the "*akh* who is able/effective on behalf of Re," as Alan Schulman suggested in *Bibliotheca Orientales* 43.3–4 [1986], 317). The *akh*-beings are the dedicators' recently dead relatives who are asked to intercede positively in the lives of the living.

Englund, Gertie. *Akh—une notion religieuse dans l'Égypte pharaonique.* Uppsala, 1978. Examines the meaning and usage of *akh* in the major mortuary texts throughout Egyptian history and rejects the idea that the concept of effectiveness in the secular texts had any application in the mortuary ones.

Friedman, Florence. "On the Meaning of Akh (*ȝḫ*) in Egyptian Mortuary Texts." Ph.D. diss., Brandeis University, 1981. A study of the meaning of *akh* in the Pyramid Texts, the Coffin Texts, and the *Book of Going Forth by Day*, from which the conclusion on its fundamental meaning is "effectiveness."

Friedman, Florence. "The Root Meaning of *ȝḫ*: Effectiveness or Luminosity?" *Serapis* 8 (1984–1985), 39–46. The basic meaning of *akh* as "effectiveness," evidenced in texts since the Old Kingdom, was secondarily applied to the circumpolar stars, the solar eye, and other solar manifestations that were understood as intensified forms of celestial effectiveness.

Friedman, Florence. "On the Meaning and Use of Some Anthropoid Busts from Deir el Medina." *Journal of Egyptian Archaeology* 71 (1985), 82–97, pls. 5 and 6: Suggests that the anthropoid busts from Deir el-Medina represent a form of the *akh iker* and, as such, were a focus of appeals for protection and other petitions.

Jansen-Winkeln, Karl. "'Horizont' und 'Verklärtheit': Zur Bedeutung der Wurzel *ȝḫ*." *Studien zur Altägyptischen Kultur* 23 (1996), 201–215. Akh is a form of invisible effectiveness with horizon origin. All *akhu*-beings, as well as the *akh*-deceased, are effective in the afterlife, owing to an unseen power that is inaccessible to human knowledge; the archetype of such *akh*-effectiveness is the Sun in the *akhet*-horizon, where the Sun becomes *akh*-effective while it cannot yet be seen.

Sandman, M. *Texts from the Time of Akhenaten.* Brussels, 1938.

FLORENCE DUNN FRIEDMAN

**AKHENATEN** (r. 1372–1355 BCE), originally Amenhotpe IV, tenth king of the eighteenth dynasty, New Kingdom. He succeeded his father Amenhotpe III. Commonly known nowadays as the "heretic king," at his accession Akhenaten bore the same personal name as his father. His mother was Queen Tiye, the Great Royal Wife of Amenhotpe III. Akhenaten's own principal queen was Nefertiti, who bore him six daughters. Another daughter issued from his union with Kiya, a well-documented secondary wife. The names of the mother(s) of his putative sons and consecutive successors, Smenkhkare and Tutankhamun, are not known. The thesis that Akhenaten married his daughters and sired his own grandchildren with them is controversial.

Egyptologists continue to be divided on many aspects of Akhenaten's reign besides his sex life. Two of his recent "biographers," Cyril Aldred (1988) and Donald B. Redford (1984), arrive at diametrically opposed estimates of his character. One among many contested questions is whether Akhenaten and his father shared the throne for a time before Amenhotpe III's death; the present account presumes that there was no coregency.

The earlier, Theban phase of Akhenaten's reign witnessed the realization of an ambitious building program at the Karnak temple which aimed to appropriate the cult center of the state god Amun for the worship of a solar deity favored by Akhenaten. The king's vision of this god evolved rapidly during his Theban period—from a falcon-headed man labeled "Re-Horus of the Two Horizons" to the aniconic image of a sun disk (*aten*; in Egyptian, *itn*) whose rays end in hands. These hands fondle the king and queen proffering to them, and them alone, hieroglyphs meaning "life" and "prosperity."

Akhenaten gave his sun god a programmatic name which, in his third regnal year, came to be written in cartouches that had traditionally been used for royal names. Implicit in this innovation was the notion that the disk reigned like a king. By this time the institutions of the traditional gods had been economically subordinated to Aten's cult. The reliefs that Akhenaten commissioned at Karnak show that ritual was reduced to the presentation of offerings. New iconography introduced to replace traditional cult scenes included the royal chariot procession between palace and temple, and scenes showing king and queen at the "window of appearances," themes that were elaborated in the course of the reign. Another series of reliefs at Karnak showed Akhenaten celebrating the *sed-*festival.

The king's personal name was altered from Amenhotpe ("Amun is satisfied") to Akhenaten ("Beneficial for Aten") by early Year 5 at the latest. At that time he commanded the foundation of a new capital city in middle Egypt devoted to the exclusive worship of the disk. The king's plans for building and embellishing Akhetaten ("Horizon of Aten"), the name he gave to this new capital, were outlined in proclamations issued when it was founded and on the first anniversary of this event. In these texts, sacral structures take precedence, but royal residences and provisions for the burial of the king, Nefertiti, and their old-

AKHENATEN. *Fragment of the face of Akhenaten, eighteenth dynasty.* It was found by W. M. Flinders Petrie during the 1891–1892 field season in a rubble heap near the Temple of Aten at Tell el-Amarna. (The Metropolitan Museum of Art, Gift of Edward S. Harkness, 1926. [26.7.1395])

est daughter are also mentioned. As actually built, Akhetaten served as a vast stage for the conspicuous "display" of the royal family—elaborately orchestrated progresses to and from the temple, feasts on occasions such as the awarding of honors to members of the elite, and pageants staged to demonstrate the ruler's omnipotence. (Archeological evidence supports occupation of the city for a time following Akhenaten's death, but it effectively ceased to be an administrative and cult center shortly after Tutankhamun's accession, when the court was removed to Memphis and the temple of Amun at Thebes reinstated as the focus of the official religion.)

Earlier generations of Egyptologists, influenced by political events in the first half of the twentieth century, labeled Akhenaten a pacifist whose ineptitude in foreign policy supposedly had disastrous consequences for Egypt's imperial status. Nowadays a different picture emerges, primarily as a result of continuing reassessment of international correspondence recorded on cuneiform tablets found at Akhetaten (the Amarna Letters). Accordingly, Egyptian diplomacy in Asia was characterized by efforts to balance one power against another. This policy was in large measure successful until quite late in Akhenaten's reign, when the Hittites defeated Egypt's allies, the Mitanni. To the south, the Nubian viceroy suppressed a rebellion in Year 12 or 13.

Akhenaten's "revolution from above" was conservative and aimed at reasserting the pharaoh's absolute authority over the elite, which had eroded over the centuries. Akhenaten's "theology" facilitated the achievement of this goal. Sweeping away the old cults effectively eliminated their priesthoods, and with the priests went the established families who also supplied the officials of the bureaucracy. To replace them, Akhenaten promoted "new men" who pledged loyalty to him. Analysis of the decoration of nonroyal tombs at Akhetaten shows that the king exercised more control over the destiny of the elite than at any earlier time.

The term "monotheism" can be applied with some justification to the fully developed religion as practiced at Akhetaten by the king and queen. Solar religion was, however, not new to Egypt; even the god Amun was associated with the sun god, as Amun-Re, from his earliest attestation at Thebes in the eleventh dynasty. Fundamental differences between Akhenaten's religion and the traditional solar cults were the former's lack of mythology, its exclusivity, and an emphasis on light as the defining essence of the deity. The uniqueness of both Aten and his "perfect little man-child" Akhenaten was repeatedly stressed. The population at large was denied access to the god; the disk was approachable only indirectly, through the king and, to a lesser extent, through the queen. Aten's remoteness was characterized by an absence of discourse. Only a single text, cut into the king's granite sarcophagus, preserves an utterance of Aten, whereas speeches of traditional gods were regularly inscribed beside their images on temple walls.

A hymn whose composition is traditionally ascribed to the king codifies the "theology" of the disk and its relationship to Akhenaten. This text, which described the quickening of all life at sunrise (among other things), was "illustrated" among the reliefs of Akhenaten's solar temples at Karnak and on the wall of the burial chamber in his tomb at Akhetaten.

The disk's name was reformulated in the later years of the reign. However, unlike the erasure and revision that accompanied the earlier change of the king's name from Amenhotpe to Akhenaten, pre-existing usages of Aten's "old" name were not emended; both forms are found in the inscriptions on the king's own sarcophagus. It is moot whether active suppression of other divinities—first and foremost the state god Amun and his consort Mut—began at this time or somewhat earlier. The desecration of Amun's and Mut's figures and of their names, even as they occurred in proper names of earlier kings and nonroyal persons alike, was widespread by the end of the reign. The consistency with which other deities were proscribed has not yet been adequately studied.

Akhenaten's penchant for novelty and display will have impressed the elite in a variety of ways. Of the innovations introduced in the visual arts, the manner in which the king himself was depicted retains its shock value down to the present. The king's physiognomy (his hanging chin, thick lips, sunken cheeks and slanting eyes) and "effeminate" body (narrow shoulders, fleshy chest, swelling thighs, pendulous abdomen, and full buttocks, in marked contrast to spindly limbs and a scrawny neck), especially as embodied in the colossi commissioned for the Karnak temple, have raised questions about his physical and mental health. But aberrations from previously accepted norms need not reflect his actual appearance. They are better understood as stylistic and iconographic devices chosen to stress Akhenaten's uniqueness. To suppose that the king proposed or even designed these images himself is speculative. In any case, the radical, exaggerated forms characteristic of the Theban phase were significantly moderated during the later years of the reign.

When Akhenaten died, he was buried in the tomb that had been begun for him in accordance with the stipulations of the decree founding Akhetaten, but he did not long rest undisturbed. Early in the reign of Tutankhamun, an officially sanctioned campaign of defamation was undertaken against Akhenaten. His works at Karnak were pulled down, and eventually the official buildings at Akhetaten were demolished too, with the quarried stone at both sites appropriated for reuse. Akhenaten's figure and name, along with Nefertiti's, were hacked out of reliefs and their statuary smashed. The royal tomb provides unequivocal evidence for the thoroughness with which Akhenaten's monuments were attacked, making it highly unlikely that his mummy survived. In effect, Akhenaten's reign was excised from public record.

The king was rediscovered toward the middle of the nineteenth century when early Egyptologists visited the site of his ruined capital. From that time on, Akhetaten was known as Tell el-Amarna, or simply Amarna, while the term "Amarna period" came to be used somewhat misleadingly to designate all of Akhenaten's reign. The excavation of the city continues down to the present under the auspices of the Egypt Exploration Society (London), while Akhenaten's monuments at Karnak have been the subject of intensive study since the 1970s. The jury on the king, perhaps the most controversial figure in all of Egyptian history, will be out for some time to come.

[*See also* Amarna, Tell el-; Aten; Monotheism; *and* Nefertiti.]

### BIBLIOGRAPHY

Aldred, Cyril. *Akhenaten, King of Egypt.* London, 1988.

*Amarna Letters: Essays on Ancient Egypt ca. 1390–1310 B.C.* KMT Communications, 3. San Francisco, 1994. Contains two articles refuting recent arguments in favor of an Amenhotpe III/IV coregency and an "addendum" amounting to a retraction by a proponent.

Assmann, Jan. *Akhanyati's Theology of Light and Time.* Proceedings of the Israel Academy of Sciences and Humanities, 7.4. Jerusalem, 1992. Description of Akhenaten's religion by the leading authority on the subject.

Burridge, A. L. "Akhenaten: A New Perspective; Evidence of a Genetic Disorder in the Royal Family of 18th Dynasty Egypt." *Journal of the Society for the Study of Egyptian Antiquities* 23 (1993), 63–74. An attempt to explain Akhenaten's appearance in art in pathological terms.

Eaton-Krauss, Marianne. "Akhenaten versus Akhenaten." *Bibliotheca Orientalis* 47 (1990), 541–559. Article reviewing and contrasting the "biographics" of Aldred and Redford.

Johnson, W. Raymond. "Amenhotep III and Amarna: Some New Considerations." *Journal of Egyptian Archaeology* 82 (1996), 65–82. The leading proponent of a coregency between Akhenaten and his father offers new arguments to support his view.

Kemp, Barry J., ed. *Amarna Reports.* Vol. 6. Egypt Exploration Society Occasional Publication 10. London, 1995. Latest volume in the series of "preliminary" reports on continuing archeological exploration by the Egypt Exploration Society at Akhenaten's capital. See the critical review by Marianne Eaton-Krauss, *Bibliotheca Orientalis* 54(1997), 612–616.

Martin, Geoffrey Thorndike. *The Royal Tomb at El-'Amarna.* Vol. 1: *The Objects.* Vol. 2: *The Reliefs, Inscriptions and Architecture.* London, 1974, 1989.

Martin, Geoffrey Thorndike. *A Bibliography of the Amarna Period and Its Aftermath: The Reigns of Akhenaten, Smenkhkare, Tutankhamun and Ay (c.1350–1321 B.C.).* London and New York, 1991.

Murnane, William J. *Texts from the Amarna Period in Egypt.* Atlanta, 1995. English translations of the most important texts.

Redford, Donald B. *Akhenaten. The Heretic King.* Princeton, 1984.

Redford, Donald B. *The Akhenaten Temple Project.* Vol. 1: *Initial Discoveries.* With Ray Winfield Smith. Warminster, 1976. Vol. 2: *Rwd-mnw, Foreigners and Inscriptions.* Toronto, 1988. Results to date of a North American mission's work on Akhenaten's structures at the Karnak temple.

Vergnieux, Robert, and Michel Gondran. *Aménophis IV et les pierres du soleil: Akhénaten retrouvé.* Paris, 1997. Update on the work of the joint Franco-Egyptian mission at Karnak on the blocks from Akhenaten's structures. Pp. 106–107 illustrate Christian E. Loeben's reconstruction of the scene "depicting" Akhenaten's solar hymn.

MARIANNE EATON-KRAUSS

**AKHMIM,** a site known in ancient Egypt as *Ipw* or *ḫnt-mnw,* and an important cult center for the fertility god Min (26°40′N, 31°45′E). The information from this site, like many others, is extremely limited since it lies under a mound occupied by the densely populated modern village. An accidental discovery there during the excavation to lay a new building foundation led the Egyptian Supreme Council of Antiquities to uncover a temple built by Ramesses II. Large statues of the king and his daughter Meritamun were found, and the layout of part of the temple was discerned. When Christianity became the official religion of the Roman Empire, many monasteries were built throughout Egypt. One of the most important was the White Monastery at Akhmim, also called the Monastery of Saint Shenoute, the construction of which in the fourth century CE used many decorated stones removed from ancient Egyptian temples.

Attention has been given in recent years to the cemeteries around Akhmim. Although the prehistory of the province is little known, two cemeteries that were dated to the Old Kingdom have been systematically excavated and the data published by the Australian Centre for Egyptology. Hawawish on the eastern bank of the Nile River was the metropolitan cemetery; it contained 884 rock-cut tombs, of which sixty retained most or part of their decoration. Many stelae, coffins, statues, and other materials have also come from the cemetery and are today in various museums, providing information on at least ten successive generations, or some four hundred years in the latter part of the Old Kingdom. The tomb owners included viziers, governors, and priests. The tombs of Memi and Hem-Min (from the end of the fifth dynasty) show a clever architectural design that concealed the true burial chambers of their owners; the latter tomb is one of the largest single-roomed chapels, at 20.2 × 9.2 meters (61 × 28 feet) and 3.9 meters (12 feet) in height.

The governors of Akhmim had interests in art, and one decorated his own father's tomb. Later governors employed a gifted artist, Seni, who decorated the tombs of Tjeti-iker and Kheni and left an inscription claiming that he worked alone. Scenes at Akhmim depicted various daily activities and entertainments, where bullfighting seemed favored. The tombs of Hagarsa on the western bank of the Nile are of smaller size than those on the eastern, but they provide valuable information on the closing years of the Old Kingdom. One tomb belongs to Wahi, the overseer of the army, and another to Hefefi and his family, where six individuals were buried together in one room, presumably as a result of some fighting in the region.

Nothing is known about Akhmim in the Middle Kingdom, with the exception of a stela erected by governor Intef, but the province produced many important personages during the latter part of the eighteenth dynasty. The parents of Queen Tiye (wife of Amenhotpe III)—Yuya and Tuya—were known to have come from Akhmim, as did Sennedjem (the overseer of tutors for King Tutankh-

AKHMIM. *Statue of Meritamun, daughter of Ramesses II, at the Temple of Isis at Akhmim.* (Courtesy Donald B. Redford)

AKHMIM. *The White Monastery.* (Courtesy Donald B. Redford)

amun), who left a large rock-cut tomb at Awlad-Azzaz, recorded by the Australian Centre for Egyptology. King Ay (r.1346–1343 BCE) is also believed to have originated in Akhmim and, as a proud native of the town, he restored its temples and erected a new rock-cut temple for Min at the mountain of el-Salamuni, following the end of the Amarna period and ancient Egypt's return to polytheism. Ay's temple was recorded by the German Institute of Archaeology, and the mountain was found to have a number of tombs that were dated to the Greco-Roman period.

### BIBLIOGRAPHY

Kanawati, Naguib. *The Rock Tombs of El-Hawawish: The Cemetery of Akhmim.* 10 vols. Sydney, 1980–1992. A complete record of all decorated and some undecorated tombs in this cemetery, which were dated to the Old Kingdom and the First Intermediate Period.

Kanawati, Naguib. *The Tombs of El-Hagarsa,* 3 vols. Australian Centre for Egyptology Reports, 4–6. Sydney, 1993–1995. A record of a second cemetery on the southern boundary of the province with Abydos. The tombs contain interesting information on the hostilities that caused the fall of the Old Kingdom.

Kuhlmann, Klaus P. "Der Felstempel des Eje bei Ackmim." *Mitteilungen des Deutschen Archäologischen Instituts, Abteilung Kairo* 35 (1979), 165–188. A description of an unusual rock temple, constructed by King Ay and dedicated to his city of origin.

Kuhlmann, Klaus P. *Materialien zur Archäologie und Geschichte des Raumes von Achmim.* Mainz, 1983. An excellent survey of the history and monuments of Akhmim, based on archaeological evidence as well as that reported by past historians and travelers.

Ockinga, Boyo. *A Tomb from the Reign of Tutankhamun at Awlad Azzaz-Akhmim.* Warminster, 1997. Although deliberately damaged, this large tomb belongs to a period when the royal family had special links with Akhmim.

NAGUIB KANAWATI

**ALABASTER.** *See* Calcite.

**ALEXANDER** (356–323 BCE), of Macedon, called the Great, was the son of Philip II of Macedon. Alexander came to the throne in 336 BCE and carried forward his father's plan of a campaign against the Persian Empire, creating his own vast empire that extended from Greece to Egypt to northern India. His conquests helped spread Greek civilization throughout the ancient world. Alexander spent the first two years as king subduing opposition in Greece, then campaigning in the Danube area; in 334 BCE, he entered Asia by crossing the Hellespont.

After two successful battles against Persian forces and campaigns against cities in western Turkey and on the Levantine coast, he and his forces arrived in Egypt in October of 332. He met no opposition from the Egyptians, who were already hostile to Persian occupation, and even the Persian garrison greeted Alexander with gifts. He was crowned pharaoh at Memphis in 332, remaining in Egypt until April of 331, longer than he had stayed in any other place during his long campaign. In Egypt, as he would do in many foreign lands, he was careful to observe the local religious rituals with public sacrifices to the Egyptian gods. He also made administrative arrangements that aimed at securing his control of the land while solidifying the support of the Egyptian people.

After his recognition as the divine pharaoh, he proceeded to the Siwa Oasis, where the priests greeted him as "Son of Amun" and "Lord of the Two Lands." Within the sanctuary, he received an oracle, which he never revealed in detail to anyone, although he declared himself satisfied with what he had learned. Returning from the Libyan Desert, he founded the city of Alexandria on the Mediterranean coast, the official founding date being 7 April 331 BCE. He then returned to Memphis, where he set up the framework for his rule in Egypt.

As would the Ptolemaic dynasty that ruled after him, Alexander relied heavily on the established bureaucracy to channel revenues and taxes from the countryside to the Macedonian treasury. He divided the land for administrative purposes between two Egyptian officials, Doloaspis and Pietesis, nomarchs of the upper echelon, although Doloaspis became sole administrator when Pietesis declined to serve. Security was maintained by military forces, under the command of mainly Macedonian officers; some were garrisoned at Memphis and Pelusium with Greek commanders over the mercenary and ancillary troops. The numerous commands were aimed at preventing a concentration of all the power of Egypt in just one man.

Alexander left Egypt in April of 331, never to return. His arrangements for maintaining the security of Macedonian control were successful. He had been accepted into the pantheon by the priesthood, and his cartouche became part of the official formulary in Egyptian inscriptions. Although his plan for division of authority foundered when Kleomenes of Naukratis gained control of the country as Alexander's loyal agent, there was never any threat to Alexander's authority. When Alexander died, on 10 June 323, having conquered the Persian Empire and having won control of the vast terrain reaching east to the Hindu Kush, Egypt was still his. It passed, as a Macedonian possession, to Alexander's general, Ptolemy, who governed as satrap of Egypt until 285 BCE, when he abdicated in favor of his son.

[*See also* Ptolemaic Period.]

### BIBLIOGRAPHY

All modern works on Alexander are based on a limited number of extensive ancient sources, supplemented by minor ancient works, and all were written at least three hundred years after Alexander's death; most are available in many translations. The most respected is Arrian's *Anabasis of Alexander, and Indica;* other extensive ancient works include Diodorus Siculus' *Library of History,* book 17; Curtius

Rufus Quintus' *History of Alexander;* and Plutarch's *Life of Alexander* (all four are available in translation in the Loeb Classical Library). Of value also is the Pseudo Callisthenes, the so-called Alexander Romance, attributed to Callisthenes; also Justin's epitome of Pompeius Trogus' *Historiae Philippicae.*

ALAN E. SAMUEL

**ALEXANDRIA,** capital of Ptolemaic Egypt, a seaport on the Mediterranean coast founded by Alexander the Great in 331 BCE (31°11′N, 29°54′E). Surviving archaeological monuments are rare in Alexandria, and travelers of the nineteenth century, hoping to find the famous buildings described in the ancient texts, were quick to record their disappointment (see *Description de l'Egypte,* series A, vol. 5, Alexandria, 1817). The tourists of today are in little better situation. Despite one hundred years of archaeological exploration and excavation, there is little to be seen *in situ.*

Only one monument has remained in place since antiq-

uity, resisting the numerous earthquakes that have struck the city during its twenty-three centuries of existence. This is a monolith, a column of red Aswan granite, 30 meters (100 feet) tall, dedicated to the Roman emperor Diocletian in 299 CE, after his violent retaking of the town from a usurper of the imperial throne. The height of this monolith, probably the largest of its type in the Greco-Roman world, only serves to emphasize the absence of other monuments. The tomb of Alexander the Great has disappeared in spite of some 139 exploratory missions. Ancient sources recount that, during a financial crisis, Ptolemy IV Philopator plundered Alexander's tomb and placed the body in a glass sarcophagus surrounded by the corpses of the other Ptolemies. This would suggest that there was some sort of collective royal vault, and the visit of Augustus to the tomb would tend to confirm this idea. According to the first-century CE Roman historian Suetonius in his *Alexander,* when Augustus was asked if he would also like to see the Ptolemies, who must therefore have been nearby, he replied that he had come to see

ALEXANDRIA. *Diorama reconstruction of the city in the Ptolemaic era.* (Courtesy of the American Museum of Natural History)

a king and not cadavers. Knowledge of the monument's emplacement was lost during the second half of the third century CE, and Saint John Chrysostom could exclaim in the fourth century that a certain affair was as uncertain as the situation of Alexander's tomb. The disappearance of the site from the collective memory probably occurred after the terrible destruction caused by the conquest of the city by Queen Zenobia of Palmyra in 259 CE and its subsequent retaking by the Roman emperor Aurelian. Ammianus Marcellinus describes the Brucheion district as a desert, and Alexandria's famed library and museum must have disappeared at this time as well as, perhaps, a part of the royal palace complex. Ancient writers, especially the early first-century CE Greek geographer Strabo, mentioned those monuments, but their descriptions were too summary to give any precise idea of architectural form. Nevertheless, an archaeological dig in the early part of the twentieth century revealed an alabaster (calcite) construction whose architectural style allowed for a dating to the early Hellenistic period. Achille Adriani, a former director of the Graeco-Roman Museum, saw this as an antechamber to Alexander's tomb and, while the idea may be tempting, it is unlikely that there will ever be formal proof. A seemingly unbridgeable gap remains between textual sources and the evidence unearthed by archaeologists.

In the western district of Rhakotis, the great sanctuary of Sarapis once stood on one of the few elevations of the city. Rufinus has left a quite detailed description from the fourth century CE. He wrote of colonnades, *exedrae*, and priests' cells built around the temple, whose walls were sheathed in marble and sheets of precious metal. Inside stood a colossal statue of the god. The only other Alexandrian monument that was the subject of an equally developed description was the Caesareum. In the first century CE, Philo wrote of the sanctuary:

> a temple to Caesar on shipboard, situated on an eminence facing the harbours . . . huge and conspicuous, fitted on a scale not found elsewhere with dedicated offerings, around it a girdle of pictures and statues in silver and gold, forming a precinct of vast breadth, embellished with porticoes, libraries, chambers, groves, gateways and wide open courts and everything which lavish expenditure could produce to beautify it.
> (*The Embassy to Gaius*, §151)

Those are the most precise descriptions that exist, and yet they say nothing of the architectural style of the buildings. Another early first-century CE source, the Roman scholar Pliny the Elder, recorded a list of those monuments that must have appeared thoroughly exotic in the eyes of the Greeks and Romans—the numerous obelisks of Alexandria. He pointed out that a pair were erected in front of the Caesareum to mark the entrance, as was also the case

for the temple of Arsinoe. Those obelisks have now disappeared from Alexandria—the first pair despatched—one to London in 1877, the other to Central Park, New York, in 1879. One of the second pair had been moved to Rome during antiquity; however, aside from the precise indication by Pliny, there were engravings and even photographs showing the obelisks, called "Cleopatra's Needles," still in place. They were a first and interesting sign of an Egyptianized decoration of the town.

The *membra disjecta* (discards) of Alexandrian archaeology are generally made up of columns, bases, and capitals in the Greek orders: Doric, Ionic, and Corinthian. Similarly, the remains of the colonnade of the Canopic Way, the city's principal east–west artery, are Greek in style, as might be expected in a city founded by Greeks and where the status of full citizen was reserved for Greeks. Yet archaeologists have recently uncovered a considerable number of pharaonic pieces that were dated from long before the city's foundation. During the underwater excavation at the site of the Pharos lighthouse, one of the Seven Wonders of the Ancient World, just off Fort Qait Bay, twenty-five sphinxes were found that were dated between the time of Senwosret III (twelfth dynasty) and Psamtik II (twenty-sixth dynasty), also three obelisks inscribed to Sety I, and six papyriform columns, some of which bear the cartouche of Ramesses II. Certain of those blocks have been reworked and were clearly destined to serve as building material for later constructions. Others, although sometimes broken into several fragments, are in a good state of preservation. Such is the case of two quartzite obelisks of Sety I, the bases of which were also discovered; they probably once stood as decorative elements within the city. That does not, however, change the history of Alexandria, since the inscriptions on them all refer to the sanctuary of Heliopolis. The Ptolemies, and thereafter the Roman emperors, took those elements from the site, which was then being quarried, as was attested by Strabo about 25 BCE and by an inscription on one of the four bronze crabs unearthed at the base of one of Cleopatra's Needles as it was being dismantled before shipment to New York.

This was not the first time that pharaonic elements were found in Alexandria. A lintel inscribed to Ramesses II and columns of Aswan granite were also discovered during a dig in the Brucheion district. Those finds gave a certain idea of the urban form of Alexandria—a Greek town with touches of Egyptian decoration, in the form of sphinxes and obelisks. Aside from those splashes of local color, the question remains as to whether there were complete buildings in pharaonic style, and only continued archaeological exploration can provide the answer.

The Pharos lighthouse excavations have also added some Egyptianized pieces of Ptolemaic manufacture to

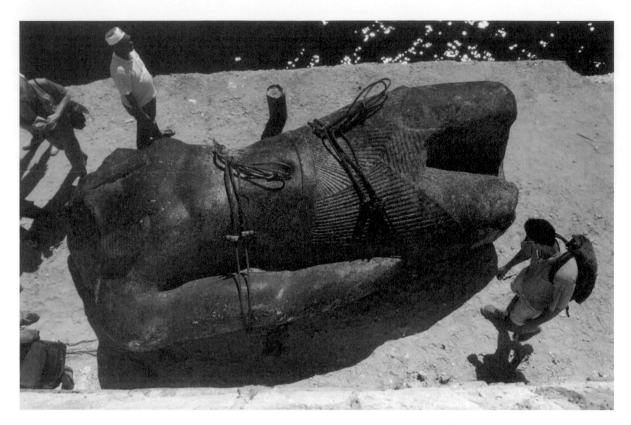

ALEXANDRIA. *Colossus of a Ptolemy as pharaoh, just after it was removed from the sea.*
(Courtesy of the Centre National de la Recherche Scientifique, Centre d'Etudes Alexandrines)

the conundrum. For example, there is the fragment of an obelisk inscribed to a Ptolemy and a series of colossal red Aswan granite statues, about 12 meters high (almost 40 feet) including the base, which probably stood at the foot of the lighthouse. Two of these were found lying side by side, just below their pedestals, and are thus more or less *in situ*. In total there appears to be an ensemble of three royal couples, with the Ptolemy represented as pharaoh and the queen as Isis. In an act of royal propaganda, the Ptolemies wished to associate themselves with the very emblem of their town—the pharaonic form demonstrated to all arriving in Alexandria by sea that they were not simply masters of the greatest city of the Hellenistic world but also of an entire country.

Of the Pharos lighthouse itself—the Seventh Wonder of the Ancient World—the excavations have revealed few elements. All the same, it should be remarked that the massive architectural elements discovered—the jambs and lintels (the largest of which weighs 70 tons and measures about 11.5 meters [36 feet]), are of Aswan granite. Thus, to build that enormous structure, there was a need to call upon Egyptian expertise. Without radically changing the current image of that tower, the excavations dem-

onstrate an Egyptian angle that was hitherto not appreciated.

Aside from the underwater work, archaeological excavations on land have principally been in domestic sites. Digs in the areas of the Caesareum and Brucheion have revealed both Hellenistic architecture and urban form. At least in those districts, the lifestyle of the inhabitants resembled more that of the Greeks of Delos or Athens than that of the Egyptians of the hinterland. The explorations of the necropolises have yielded different information, however. The tombs of Mustafa Kamel, in the eastern necropolis, were dated to the third century BCE. They are Greek in style with Macedonian touches, such as a fresco above the entry to a tomb that shows a horseman in three-quarter profile. Yet against the columns of the central court, four limestone sphinxes seem to root Alexandria in Egypt. In the district of Anfushi, on what was the Isle of Pharos, at the bottom of the stairway of a first-century BCE tomb, a fresco represents Isis and, within, a painted geometric pattern has panels bearing the *pschent*-crown (Gr., ψχεντ; Eg., *p3 shmty*). It would appear, if an allusion from Caesar's *De Bello Alexandrino* (Concerning the Alexandrian War) is to be accepted, that this quarter had been inhabited by Egyptians, which would explain the decorations. From the first century CE, there is the evidence of the catacombs of Kom el Shuqafa. Although the complex was discovered in 1892, previously unrecorded paintings were noted above two sarcophagi in the 1990s. They were executed on two panels, one above the other. The upper scene presents the embalming of Osiris in the rigid style of pharaonic tradition; in the scene below, there is a sense of movement in a Greek painting about the abduction of Persephone, whose clothes seem to swirl and whose gestures are fluid. Those two images, expressing the hope for a future life—the resurrection of Osiris on the one hand and the return of Persephone from the underworld on the other—demonstrate that an Alexandrian could indeed express his faith in two eschatologies, that of the pharaohs and that of Greek mythology.

In Alexandria, emergency excavations have been on the increase as a result of a redevelopment of the city center. There have been digs close to the Caesareum and to the Library, and there is ongoing work in a part of the immense necropolis to the west of the city, but since the modern city sits atop the ancient, the archaeologist must await the opportunity to undertake salvage work that might lead to the discovery of the monuments of Alexandria. At the same time, such monuments may be in a ruined state that precludes their proper identification.

### BIBLIOGRAPHY

Empereur, Jean-Yves. *Alexandria Rediscovered.* New York, 1998.

Empereur, Jean-Yves. *La Gloire d'Alexandrie.* Paris, 1998.

Empereur, Jean-Yves. *Le Phare d'Alexandrie.* Paris, 1998.

Fraser, Peter M. *Ptolemaic Alexandria.* 3 vols. Oxford, 1972.

Grimm, Günter. *Alexandria, die erste Königsstadt der hellenistischen Welt: bilder aus der Nilmetropole von Alexander dem Grossen bis Kleopatra VII.* Mainz, 1998.

Haas, Christopher. *Alexandria in Late Antiquity: Topography and Social Conflict.* Baltimore, 1997.

JEAN-YVES EMPEREUR
Translated from French by Colin Clement

**ALLEGORY** is a word of Greek origin, meaning literally "speaking differently." Normally, it involves seeking a second and deeper meaning behind that which is at first apparent in a mythological account. In the ancient world, the idea appears in several other literary traditions. In Hebrew, the term *midrash* ("investigation") denotes a process that often leads to explanations on allegorical lines. In Egyptian, the expression used most often to introduce an alternative explanation was *ky djed* (*ky ḏd;* "another saying"). The resulting ideas often imply types of metaphor and symbolism. A related form is the parable.

No particular literary form is, however, tied to the use of allegory. The expressions used—as for instance in the Egyptian and Greek examples cited—seem fairly close, but the literary types may range widely.

**Motivation.** In the ancient cultures, allegory was not a normal feature of the earliest literary texts. It belongs, rather, to the later phases, when the understanding of those texts posited certain difficulties and challenges. A reflective approach to traditional ideologies was thus involved, and in Egypt the first profusion of allegorical explanations occurred during the New Kingdom, in the *Book of Going Forth by Day* (*Book of the Dead*). During the sixth century BCE and later, several Greek philosophers, including Pherecydes of Syros and Theagenes of Rhegium, used allegory in a way that revealed their motivations. They were concerned to achieve rational explanations in matters relating to conceptions of the gods, particularly those portrayed in the works of Homer and Hesiod. At the same time, some philosophers went beyond their critique of religion, notably Xenophanes, famed for his dictum: "If oxen, horses and lions had hands or could paint, then the horses would make horse-like images of the gods, and the oxen would make ox-like images, and fashion the gods' bodies in their own likeness." He also said that "Homer and Hesiod have attributed to the gods everything which brings shame and reproach among men: theft, adultery, and fraud" (see Edward Hussey, *The Presocratics*, London, 1972, p. 13).

Among those who were later prepared to use allegory was Plato, whose parable of the Cave in his *Republic* is an attractive example. Later still, Plutarch often followed Plato; his treatment of Egyptian material shows a variety of method. The Stoics were keen allegorists, and among their proposals was an attempt to gloss over Homer's account of the adultery of Aphrodite, the wife of Hephaestus, with Ares. According to the Stoics that episode should not be taken literally; the basic meaning was astral, signifying the coming together of two planets, those of Aphrodite and Ares. Plutarch was rather scornful of this, and he defended Homer, arguing that Homer was giving a moral lesson on the perils of licentious conduct.

Although Egyptian religion was, in general, deeply concerned with ethical issues—as can be seen in the importance ascribed to the judgment of the dead and to the all-pervasive influence of *maat* (*m3ʿt;* "justice"), the motivation behind its use of allegory seems to relate rather to the quest for valid and correct information about religious matters, often with the sense that this information may be somehow hidden and that access to it must be urgently sought. Spell 17 of the *Book of the Dead* is replete with allegory, and throughout its questions and answers this urgency is tensely conveyed. The text's earliest form is known from the Coffin Texts, Spell 335, "renowned for its glosses," as M. Heerma van Voss remarked in his masterly study of 1963, in which he assigned the text to the ninth or tenth dynasty. In it, we constantly meet the Egyptian expression, *ky djed*, cited above. Its use varies. Sometimes it introduces a different reading; at other times it adduces explanations by way of a commentary; and among those explanations some are allegorical. The New Kingdom versions are more detailed in their annotations, which often follow a question, such as "What is this?" A striking example occurs with a vignette showing two lions, back to back, beneath the sign of the horizon.

Middle Kingdom texts read:

To me belongs Yesterday; I know Tomorrow. This is Osiris. As for Yesterday, this is Osiris. As for Tomorrow, this is Re.

New Kingdom versions read:

What, then, is this? As for Yesterday, this is Osiris. As for Tomorrow, this is Re, on that day when the enemies of the lord of all will be destroyed and when his son Horus will be established as ruler.

This is the day when we shall remain in festival. This is the disposal of the burial of Osiris by his father Re.

The two lions below the sign of the horizon also carry the symbolism of Yesterday and Tomorrow as applied to Osiris and Re. A feature of allegory is the inclusion of an interplay between the abstract and the concrete, that metaphysical ideas, in this case referring to time and eternity, are incorporated into the symbols.

The *Book of the Dead* has provided many examples of particular objects being allegorized in mythical terms. In Spell 99, many nautical objects are treated in this way. It is said of a vessel for baling out water: "Thy name is the hand of Isis wiping out the blood from the Eye of Horus"; and the phrase "knowing the souls" in several spells implies a knowledge of many secret second meanings.

**Ritual and Narrative.** Symbolism is a part of every religion; and religious ritual imparts to acts, sayings, and objects a number of ideas relating to myth or history. The Ramesseum Dramatic Papyrus, a work from the early Middle Kingdom, gives instructions for ritual proceedings in which objects and actions were often assigned second meanings that were connected with royal ceremony and the myth of Osiris.

Egypt has provided a number of narrative compositions that clearly belong to the category of allegory. For example, the Late period Egyptian story, "The Blinding of Truth," was edited by Alan H. Gardiner. Although the papyrus is marred by missing material, especially the opening section, three main characters appear: Truth, his younger brother Falsehood, and Truth's unnamed son. The story began with the statement that Truth borrowed an elaborate knife from Falsehood and then lost or damaged it. Falsehood reported the matter to the Ennead, with the demand that Truth should be blinded and made

his doorkeeper. That demand was accepted and enacted by the Ennead. Then, a sensual lady enabled Truth's son to be procreated, born, and educated; yet his schoolmates taunted him as having no father. Truth's son proceeded to seek revenge by charging Falsehood, his uncle, before the Ennead with the offence of stealing his wonderful ox. The Ennead endorsed the charge. The end of the story then refers to the blinding of Falsehood, so a just retribution seems thus to be achieved. Since the two main characters were presented as personified abstractions, in his analysis Gardiner was led to claim that "surely this must be the earliest example of allegory in the manner of John Bunyan." Bunyan's *The Pilgrim's Progress* (1678 and 1684) certainly used this technique, with figures like Giant Despair, Mr. Wordly Wiseman, Hopeful, and Ignorance, and a similar mode applied to places.

Gardiner is clearly right in seeing the theme as "a but thinly disguised version of the legend of Osiris," with Truth in the role of Osiris, Falsehood in that of Seth, and Truth's son in that of Horus. The Sensual Lady, he admits, is quite unlike Isis, unless we recall the procreative initiative of Isis, even in the context of death. What Gardiner missed was the closer parallel in the feud of Horus and Seth; the part played by the Ennead points to the similar situation in *The Contendings of Horus and Seth*, which treats the ancient myth with a touch of burlesque. Unlike the story about Truth and Falsehood, the *Contendings* does not bear the stamp of allegory; "The Blinding of Truth" is partly allegorical, because it abandons the simple telling of the myth.

The "Tale of the Two Brothers" derives from the nineteenth dynasty. A feature of the story is a false charge of adultery, made by the wife of one of the brothers against the other. Anubis and Bata are the names of the brothers, and both were divine names in Egypt, but the mythological details are not otherwise known. John A. Wilson referred to the story as a folktale, while Helmuth Jacobsohn was able to find in it a plethora of traditional beliefs. It is indeed a gripping tale, adorned with marvelous metamorphoses. Wilson maintained that "it served for entertainment"; no deeper purpose was apparent. In contrast, "The Quarrel of the Head and the Belly," a short work from the twenty-second dynasty, is plainly didactic and allegorical, using the interdependence of parts of the body in its plea for cooperation. The theme also appears later, in the Roman author Livy, in the speech of Menenius Agrippa before the Roman Senate; it is also in the Aesopic fable about the quarrel of the Belly and the Feet; and it even appears in the Pauline doctrine (*1 Cor.* 12.12) of the early Christian church, to emphasize a community of members of one body.

Almost in a class of its own is "Astarte and the Tribute of the Sea," which has been shown to belong to a basic myth prevalent in the maritime cities of the eastern Mediterranean, reflecting the struggle between land and sea. The Egyptian tale would be "a translation of one version of the story . . . owing much to the foreign community in Memphis" (Redford, 1992).

**The Animal Fable.** A veritable richesse of the animal fable genre is offered by Egypt and by the cultures of the Near East. Several instances were transmitted to Europe through the medium of Aesop, the Greek writer of the sixth century BCE. Their influence reached as far as the seventeenth-century French fables of Jean de La Fontaine and the eighteenth-century Russian fables of Ivan Andreyevich Krylov; and, in a wider sense, even to *Animal Farm* (1946) by George Orwell. That animal fables are intrinsically allegorical is shown by their aim, not at the life of animals, but at the human predicament. The Egyptians lived very close to their domesticated animals and had a long tradition of hunting wild animals in the desert and the Nile Delta. Moreover, their worship of various animal deities was based in their religious experience; this did not prevent them indulging in a playful and satiric approach to the animal world.

A feature of the abundant animal fable material left by the ancient Egyptians is its often combined pictorial and literary qualities. The pictures frequently show animals performing in the manner of human beings, as in the charming scene from the Satirical Papyrus, now in the British Museum, where an antelope and a lion are shown playing a board game; the lion raises a playing piece with an expression of triumph. This material often revels in the reversal of roles, showing, for example, cats serving a mouse-lady or foxes guarding a herd of goats.

At times, the fable has been drawn from mythology but was given a didactic emphasis. Such is the fable of the "Lion and the Mouse," which is part of a Demotic work that relates the return of the sun god from Nubia. It tells that a lion spared the life of a mouse and was, in return, when caught in a hunter's net, helped by the mouse to escape, as the mouse gnawed through the bonds. The moral allegory is stressed: do unto others as you would have others do unto you—even the weakest can help the strongest. The story is found also in the Aesopic corpus, but Emma Brunner-Traut (1989) has been able to demonstrate the priority of the Egyptian form.

"The War of the Frogs and Mice" is attested in Egypt in pictorial form only, with cats replacing the frogs. It is likely that a literary text existed too, one parallel to the Greek *Batrachomyomachia*, a post-Homeric parody of the *Iliad*. The Egyptian depictions are amusingly composed, especially that of a mouse-pharaoh in his chariot attacking a formidable cat-fortress. The folly of war is suggested, but the tone is lighthearted rather than didactic.

**Hieroglyphic Writing.** In the Hellenistic and Roman eras, allegory in its Greek form had a tremendous impact on the development of the major religions. Philo of Alexandria was a whole-hearted allegorist, as was Origen, also in Alexandria; in each case, the main impetus was in line with the moral urge of the earlier Greek innovators—a desire to guard the integrity of writings regarded as canonical. At that time, both the Hebrew Bible and the early Christian writings needed some defense. Gnostic and Hermetic writings, then, also contained allegorical explanations, but in their cases, Egyptian influence must be assessed as well.

A striking feature of the approach developed by Greek authors was the belief that Egyptian hieroglyphic writing was essentially allegorical in principle. A suggestion of this may be seen in Plutarch's comparison of proverbial sayings, as used by Pythagoras and the mode of hieroglyphic writing. The proverbial sayings are figurative in style (e.g., "Do not sit on a bushel"), and this implies that hieroglyphs employ pictures metaphorically. No such implication is given by Herodotus, who described two types of writing, the hieroglyphic and the Demotic, but with no hint of a symbolical theory. When we reach Diodorus Siculus, the first-century BCE Greek historian, however, a clear statement appears that the basic principle of the hieroglyphs was allegorical. By and large, the same was true of Plutarch, but his more than thirty linguistic references to Egyptian show some complexities. Sometimes he was thinking of ideograms, which can stand by themselves. Like Diodorus and later writers, Plutarch ignored the basic phonetic element.

This position was consolidated by Plotinus, Porphyry, and Iamblichus, all Neoplatonists. Books dealing specifically with hieroglyphs included one by a much earlier writer, Chaeremon, who became a tutor of the Roman emperor Nero. His book gave examples only by scattered quotations. His example from Psellus included the dictum rendered as "Egyptian wisdom is to say all things symbolically." This was typical of accepted opinion even in the first century CE, and Chaeremon was an "Egyptian Priest and Stoic Philosopher."

The *Hieroglyphica* of Horapollo was first published in Greek in 1505 CE. Deriving probably from the fifth century CE, the book deals with each hieroglyph separately, explaining the sign and its meaning along accepted allegorical lines. Despite this initial obstacle, the work is by no means entirely misleading. On occasion, it is absolutely correct, as when it says that the sign for a fish denotes "hate"; sometimes it appears as an ideogram for the Egyptian *bwt*, with that meaning.

Remarkably, the symbolical theory proved persistent. One reason was its apparent agreement with Neoplatonist thought, which was still flourishing in Europe during the Renaissance. In the fifteenth century, Ficino's Hermetic translations were published, and Hermes Trismegistus confirmed the European interest in Egypt. In spite of some misleading ideas, this interest appealed strongly to the German artist Albrecht Dürer, who produced in about 1517 his splendid triumphal arch to honor Maximilian I, the German emperor, and to the Italian artist, Pinturicchio, who depicted Osiris, Isis, and Apis for the Borgia rooms in the Vatican.

Providing texts for European art works based on Egyptian obelisks has caused some problems. In later centuries, the Rosicrucians and Freemasons claimed to follow Egyptian ritual modes, which resulted in anti-Christian accusations; yet they still flourish today as secret societies. Wolfgang Amadeus Mozart's opera *Die Zauberflöte* (*The Magic Flute*, 1791) has close links with the Masonic movement and the mysteries of Isis. As for the allegorical basis of hieroglyphs, Jean-François Champollion, the founder of modern Egyptology, ended all that in 1822 with his translation of the Rosetta Stone.

[*See also* Egyptomania; Scripts, *article on* Hieroglyphs; Symbols; *and* Wisdom Tradition.]

## BIBLIOGRAPHY

Assmann, Jan. *Zeit und Ewigkeit im alten Ägypten.* Heidelberg, 1975. Deals with the Two Lions depicted in *Book of the Dead*, Spell 17, but examines the concepts in great detail.

Brunner-Traut, Emma. *Altägyptische Märchen.* 8th ed. Munich, 1989. Offers translations and commentary and includes the best introduction to the Egyptian animal fable.

Clark, R. T. Rundle. *Myth and Symbol in Ancient Egypt.* London, 1959.

Gardiner, Alan H. *Hieratic Papyri in the British Museum.* 3d series. London, 1935. Contains much commentary.

Griffiths, John Gwyn. "The Tradition of Allegory in Egypt." In *Religions en Égypte hellénistique et romaine*, edited by P. Derchain. Paris, 1969.

Griffiths, John Gwyn. *Plutarch's De Iside et Osiride.* Cardiff, 1970.

Heerma van Voss, M. S. H. G. *De oudste Versie van Dodenboek 17a.* Leiden, 1963. Deals with the earliest form, that in the Coffin Texts.

Hersman, Anne B. *Studies in Greek Allegorical Interpretation.* Chicago, 1906.

Iversen, Erik. *The Myth of Egypt and Its Hieroglyphs in European Tradition.* Copenhagen, 1961; repr. Princeton, 1993. An impressive study, much used here for the postclassical era.

Iversen, Erik. *Egyptian and Hermetic Doctrine.* Copenhagen, 1984. Makes several new contributions.

Jacobsohn, Helmuth. *Die dogmatische Stellung des Königs in der Theologie der alten Ägypter.* Ägyptologische Forschungen, 8. Glückstadt, 1939, repr. 1955.

Lichtheim, Miriam. *Ancient Egyptian Literature.* 3 vols. Berkeley, 1973–1980. Volumes 2 and 3 contain the tales.

Lloyd, Alan B. *Herodotus.* 3 vols. Leiden, 1975–1988.

Morenz, Siegfried. *Die Begegnung Europas mit Ägypten.* Berlin, 1968. Covers roughly the same ground as Iversen's *Myth of Egypt*, but is less trenchant in criticism of the classical tradition.

Naville, Edouard. *Das Aegyptische Todtenbuch der XVIII.bis XX. Dynastie.* 3 vols. Berlin, 1886, repr. Graz, 1971.

Redford, Donald B. *Egypt, Canaan, and Israel in Ancient Times.* Princeton, 1992.

Wente, Edward F. "Late Egyptian Stories." In *The Literature of Ancient Egypt*, edited by W. K. Simpson. New Haven, 1972. Offers translations and comments.

Wilson, John A. "Translations of Egyptian Texts." In *Ancient Near Eastern Texts Relating to the Old Testament* (ANET), edited by James B. Pritchard, 3d ed. with supplement. Princeton, 1969.

J. GWYN GRIFFITHS

**AMARNA, TELL EL-,** site of the New Kingdom capital of the eighteenth dynasty king Amenhotpe IV/Akhenaten (r. 1372–1355 BCE), built to honor his sole god Aten, located in Middle Egypt (27°38′N, 30°53′E). The large mud-brick and stone expanse of the city, as well as the cuneiform clay tablets found there within a state archival office, have made Tell el-Amarna important to archaeologists and essential to historians of the Near East interested in the Late Bronze Age.

**Identification.** The remains of Tell el-Amarna today stretch some 10 kilometers (7 miles) north to south on the eastern side of the Nile River. The ancient city and environs occupied nearly twice that distance on both sides of the river and were together called *Akhetaten*, "the Horizon of the Aten [sun disk]." The name was given by the city's founder, Akhenaten, on a series of boundary stelae placed to delimit Tell el-Amarna. The city within Akhetaten may have had a separate designation or more than one, and the monumental buildings that Akhenaten had built within the city also had discreet appellations (for some of these see below).

The name Tell el-Amarna is a misnomer, for the site has no visible mound that characterizes tells in the Near East generally. Modern names and spellings have shifted since Western expeditions arrived there in the late eighteenth century. First designated El-Tell by the Napoleonic expedition of 1798, the site was called by several names (for example, Till Bene Amran, used by Robert Hay in 1829). European travelers conflated the villages of et-Tell (or Till) and el-Amariya with a tribe settled in the region called Ben Amran. The name Tel(l) el-Amarna first appeared on a publication by John Gardner Wilkinson, who mapped the site and published his map in 1830.

**Occupational History.** Tell el-Amarna, or el-Amarna as it is now more commonly termed, consists principally of the capital built for King Akhenaten, about 1360 BCE, on land that he believed to be previously unsettled. (Son of Amenhotpe III, Akhenaten had ascended to the throne as Amenhotpe IV in 1372 BCE but changed his name a few years later.) Some areas of the site had been occupied, however, during other ancient eras. The earliest remains are known from several Paleolithic areas, with flint concentrations, and a few Neolithic (Predynastic) artifacts suggest pre-third millennium occupation in the region.

Akhenaten's city within Akhetaten was largely aban-

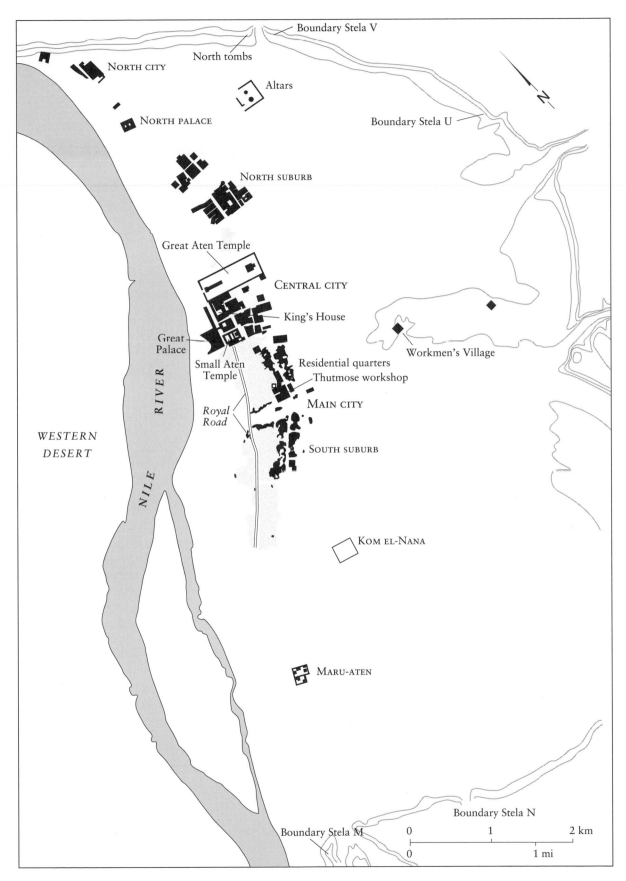

Boundary Stela V

North tombs

NORTH CITY

Altars

NORTH PALACE

Boundary Stela U

NORTH SUBURB

Great Aten Temple

CENTRAL CITY

King's House

Great
Palace

Workmen's Village

Small Aten
Temple

Residential quarters

Thutmose workshop

Royal
Road

MAIN CITY

WESTERN
DESERT

SOUTH SUBURB

NILE RIVER

KOM EL-NANA

MARU-ATEN

Boundary Stela N

Boundary Stela M

0          1          2 km

0                    1 mi

AMARNA, TELL EL-. *Plan of Tell el-Amarna.*

doned within a dozen years of his death in 1355 BCE. The ruler who succeeded Akhenaten for a year or two, Smenkhkare, appears to have resided in el-Amarna, and Tutankhaten, who soon changed his name to the more familiar Tutankhamun, is well attested at the site for at least another two years. Building activity is documented also in a workers' village in the period following Tutankhamun's abandonment of Middle Egypt and return to the region of Thebes. The full seventeen years of Akhenaten's reign, together with the dozen or so years comprising Smenkhkare's, Tutankhamun's, and Ay's rules, are often referred to as the "Amarna period," although el-Amarna was not inhabited during all of it.

In one region of southern el-Amarna, near the Nile, are the remains of a town that survived the abandonment of the main city. Fragmentary architecture of late New Kingdom date or later are mixed there with potsherds of the Amarna period. Although originally identified as the "river temple," the bits of structures have recently been relabeled as house remains. A few burials of the twenty-second and twenty-third dynasties were found in the early 1920s near the workers' village, and in 1984 a burial of the twentieth to twenty-first dynasties was excavated in the same area. Sherds of the Late period (end of eighth century–332 BCE) were found near the southern tombs of Akhenaten's nobles. These may have belonged to burials of a population that lived in the general vicinity (possibly the river town) or may indicate transient activity through the area for various purposes, possibly even illicit ones, that is, tomb robbery. In the Roman period, several settlements existed at the site of el-Amarna, and Coptic Christians later converted tombs there for housing and worship.

**Research and Excavation.** The largest of the few preserved Egyptian cities, el-Amarna has been frequently explored and studied. Recent surveys and comparisons with the earliest maps of the region indicate that el-Amarna has always been visible to interested visitors. Areas destroyed by illicit digging appear to have been only slightly less disturbed in the mid-1800s than today.

As early as 1714, Father Claude Sicard, a French Jesuit missionary, published a drawing of Amarna Boundary Stela A at Tuna el-Gebel. The Napoleonic scientific expedition visited the region in 1799, and Edmé Jomard produced a plan of El-Tell in the pioneering study *Description de l'Égypte*, published in 1817. John Gardner Wilkinson visited el-Amarna in 1824 and 1826 to draw, plan, and copy the buildings and tombs, and he produced plans of the entire city. Other travelers in the 1820s and 1830s, such as Robert Hay, James Burton, and Nestor L'Hôte, made copies of the tombs of Akhenaten's nobles. The royal Prussian expedition led by Richard Lepsius drew plans of the city of el-Amarna between 1843 and 1845.

The first modern archaeological work at el-Amarna took place in 1891–1892 when William Matthew Flinders Petrie opened excavations in a variety of locations at the site. Several expeditions followed in rapid succession, culminating in the methodical survey and excavations of Ludwig Borchardt (1907, 1911–1914), carried out for the Deutsche Orient-Gesellschaft. Some of the best-known works of Amarna art were uncovered during that period, including the famous bust of Nefertiti, which is now in the Egyptian Museum in Berlin (Charlottenburg), and numerous other statues found in the house and workshop of the sculptor Thutmose in the main city/south suburb. The Egypt Exploration Fund (EEF; now Society) of London copied and published the private tombs and boundary stelae between 1901 and 1907. They resumed work at the site in 1921 under a succession of well-known directors, including Thomas Eric Peet, Henri Frankfort, Francis Llewellyn Griffith, and John D. S. Pendlebury. The EEF explored nearly all the areas of the site, moving from peripheral regions such as the workers' village, the "river temple," and the northern palace to later extensive excavations in the central city that lasted until 1936.

In the early 1970s, Geoffrey T. Martin reinvestigated the royal tomb at el-Amarna and published on the numerous but fragmentary objects associated there with Akhenaten and Nefertiti. In 1977, the Egypt Exploration Society resumed work under the direction of Barry J. Kemp and has worked at the site since. Kemp commenced excavation at the workers' village that once housed artisans employed in the royal tomb. His team found that the village may have been abandoned and then reinhabited in the time of Tutankhamun by guardians of the royal and private necropolises. Research has focused on identifying patterns of activity sited within the village, as well as the interdependence between the village and the central city. Kemp has moved his investigations into the main city area since 1987 but continues to be interested in the interrelationships between public and private buildings and their peripheral economic dependencies.

**Remains.** The fifteen boundary stelae of Akhenaten delimiting the territory of el-Amarna, like the remains of the city they describe, are important monuments. Some of these boundary markers consist only of a stela and others of an actual rock shrine containing statuary. They provide further information about the site, however, for three preserve the text of a proclamation made by Akhenaten in the first months of his fifth regnal year, in which he describes and names numerous buildings and complexes to be constructed at Akhetaten. Some of these (e.g., the great Aten temple, the "mansion of the Aten," the royal tomb) can be identified with excavated structures; some cannot with certainty (e.g., the "house of rejoicing and sunshade of the great queen"), and some others appear never to

AMARNA, TELL EL-. *View of Tell el-Amarna.* (Courtesy of David P. Silverman)

have been completed (e.g., the tomb of the Mnevis bull of Heliopolis). The identifiable buildings correspond to complexes and tombs built throughout much of the 10-kilometer north–south stretch of el-Amarna, a fact that confirms the original design of the city as a long narrow town accommodated to the Nile and the eastern bay of limestone cliffs by a royal road. This road was later redirected in part but remained the primary route linking north areas to the central city.

At its northern end, el-Amarna had a mud-brick northern river palace oriented on its western side to the royal road that travels southward for 6 kilometers (3.7 miles). This palace may have been the principal residence of the king. A group of administrative buildings lies just south of it along with a residential quarter also oriented to the road. Farther south is the northern palace, also built to face the royal road—a tourist attraction today. There, around courts with pools and shaded garden porticoes, lived at least two queens, including Meritaten, Akhenaten's daughter, who resided there after a predecessor, perhaps Nefertiti or Kiya.

The northern suburb is located to the east of the royal road orientation, and the parts excavated (those farthest north from the central city) appear to have been a late addition. Areas of residence between the northern suburb and the central city have not been excavated but could

reveal in time whether this is a natural northern extension from the central city or grew up later in a separate but parallel fashion.

The central city contains most of the buildings whose material remains, architecture, and preserved decoration may suggest a center planned for state administration and worship. Oriented to the royal road, it contained from north to south, the enormous precinct of the great Aten temple ("house" or "estate of the Aten"); the king's house, connected by a bridge to the great palace; the smaller Aten temple (the "Mansion of the Aten"); and the Smenkhkare hall. On the eastern side of the road, the king's house and smaller Aten temple were the westernmost of a complex of buildings that were crucial to state functions. Kemp considers the king's house to be the most likely siting for the "window of appearance" pictured in numerous private tombs of Akhenaten's officials (Kemp and Garfi 1993, p. 59). A series of scribal offices lay east of the king's house, including one identified by stamped bricks as the "place of the pharaoh's correspondence." In this archival office were found the majority of the Amarna Letters, famous as the correspondence between the Egyptian rulers Amenhotpe III, Akhenaten, and Tutankhamun with kings and city-state rulers from Mesopotamia and the Levant. To the east of the offices lies a garrison block with animal stalls and barracks, as well as separate storage areas for rations. This security complex is not oriented toward the royal road. Being on the eastern edge of the city, it may have had more association with the desert and the wadi due east, leading to the royal tomb.

The best-known compound in the central city, the great Aten temple, likewise comprised several structures. The Gempaaten ("the Aten is found") was a multicourted stone building near the western end of the temple precinct. It was entered from a western gateway through high pylons giving on to stone colonnades that themselves led to a series of unroofed courtyards. Within and beside these courts were arranged bread-offering altars, made of stone (within the courts) or brick (south of the courts). More than 750 altars were placed within the Gempaaten, and some 920 brick tables lay to the south of the building. Another 920 may once have existed on the northern side. The formal colonnaded setting appears to have been the primary offering area for Aten state worship but not the actual sanctuary of the temple. Between Gempaaten and a second stone structure to the east, the sanctuary, was a "butcher's yard" with tethering stones and an enormous open area. A separate northern entrance to the open area before the sanctuary was elaborated as a gateway pavilion. A stela of quartzite, perhaps evoking the Heliopolitan *benben* stone, was set up on a line with this entrance. The sanctuary building was flanked to the north by more bread-offering altars, but excavations to the south of the building and just outside the enclosure wall have revealed indications of different ritual activities as well. In a dump, Petrie and Pendlebury found plain everted-rim bowls with burnt resins inside. In 1986, Kemp confirmed that the bowls with burned "incense" were common in the dump area along with "beer-jar" shapes and other offering vessel types (Kemp 1989, vol. 4, pp. 116–121). Kemp found fragments of storage jars, and Pendlebury had found seals and labels in the area. Kemp has identified this dump as a significant locale for the sanctuary's refuse. It provides evidence for the libations and offerings of incense made within the neighboring building. Kemp has noted the placement of large bakeries on the southern side of the enclosure wall opposite the Gempaaten. The hundreds of altars there would have held loaves from those bakeries; Kemp believes that a segment of the city's populace offered to the Aten on the brick tables to the south of the Gempaaten while the king and family officiated inside the temple proper (Kemp and Garfi 1993, p. 55). Despite Kemp's contributions, the ritual connection between the sanctuary and the Gempaaten, as well as the use patterns for the complex generally, remain uncertain.

In the main city or south suburb are residential and administrative quarters. Large-scale unexcavated complexes of undoubted administrative nature lie in this sector, largely to the west of more domestic structures. The state and temple institutions operated their own economies and necessarily housed the resources, both perishable and nonperishable. Kemp believes that government workshops may have been situated in those large centers, but he also notes that large institutions appear to have been made up of a number of complexes, often not located together. The designation of industrial centers without inscription as "royal," "temple," or "private" thus becomes problematic (Kemp and Garfi 1993, pp. 67–69; Kemp 1989, vol. 5, pp. 56–63).

The house and workshop of the sculptor Thutmose, famous for the many statues and plaster masks of royal family, are located in the south suburb near other sculptors' shops. Thutmose's precise economic and administrative association with his patrons is difficult to ascertain. Whether individual artisans were contracted directly by the court, through court-sanctioned patrons, or both, is unknown. For example, some obviously nonroyal estates appear to have housed royal workshops, perhaps as a subcontract from the crown.

Architecture is not always a clear indicator of function. Archaeological research has demonstrated the often diverse patterns of use for both residences and specialized buildings, such as "magazines," which, as Kemp has found, were used both for production and for storage (Kemp and Garfi 1993, pp. 67–69). Nearly all areas of el-Amarna held residences (royal, temple, private), and those residences nearly always contained separate storage facilities, wells, often industrial centers. The degree to which these separate facilities indicate independent economic behavior is unknown.

To the south of the main city/south suburb is Kom el-Nana, oriented to the original royal road since it was laid out before the growth of the main city. Kom el-Nana is a temple complex with supporting buildings for food production and storage. Kemp believes that this is the third of three major institutions described in the early proclamation, the "sunshade of the great queen" (Kemp and Garfi 1993, p. 79). Even farther south and entirely isolated is the Maruaten, a site that houses enclosures with altars and shrines along with pools and surrounding gardens. It is clearly linked with queens, including Akhenaten's daughter Meritaten.

Other areas of southern el-Amarna include the abovementioned river settlement, which is a residential area, and el-Hawata in the far south, also near the Nile. Little remains in this sector. On the opposite end of the site are a number of architectural remains not part of the city proper. Three large desert altars in the northeastern desert, nearly opposite the northern palace, are oriented toward the royal road. These mud-brick structures with ramps once held pavilions, perhaps for large-scale royal receptions of dignitaries, such as are pictured in two private tombs. Above these altars are the northern tombs of private residents of el-Amarna. A second set of such tombs exists in the southern cliffs. A total of forty-three tombs was excavated in whole or part. The most elaborate had colonnaded inner halls, and in those that were decorated (many were left incomplete) the royal family and the architecture of Akhetaten figured prominently in painted relief sculpture.

The royal tomb and a few uninscribed smaller tombs were located in a wadi reached through a larger wadi running eastward opposite the central city. Unusual relief scenes of mourning over corpses on beds appear on the walls of the royal burial chamber and on a side chamber used for the burial of Akhenaten's daughter, who may have died in childbirth. The royal funerary goods left at the site were smashed into pieces, but remains of the royal sarcophagus and canopic box have been studied (Martin 1974). At the mouth of the eastern wadi was the workers' village, which was apparently used for the building of the royal tomb and later, during the reign of Tutankhamun, for guarding the same area. The villagers in the time of Tutankhamun had not only self-sufficient residences but also shrines where families gathered to eat and commune with recently deceased relatives. These shrines would also have been memorial chapels for a household or several related households. The second phase in the workers' village is one of the latest excavated, representing the later reign of Akhenaten through the reign of Tutankhamun, including the time after the court's departure from el-Amarna. The activity of the guards living in the village in the last phase therefore reflects a mixture of religious beliefs with various traditional gods reappearing in shrine images. Following the abandonment of the workers' village, the city of Amarna was both used as a quarry, especially for the Ramessid temple at Hermopolis, and deliberately mutilated. Statuary was destroyed *in situ* or dragged away and dumped. A similar pattern of reuse and destruction can be seen in the earlier complex at East Karnak, which Akhenaten built both before and after his change of name from Amenhotpe.

## BIBLIOGRAPHY

Aldred, Cyril. *Akhenaten, Pharaoh of Egypt: A New Study*. London, 1968. Pioneering historical and art historical study of the ruler, presenting Aldred's arguments for a prolonged coregency between Akhenaten and his father Amenhotpe III. Revised and reissued in 1988.

Bomann, Ann H. *The Private Chapel in Ancient Egypt: A Study of the Chapels in the Workmen's Village at El Amarna with Special Reference to Deir el Medina and Other Sites*. London, 1991. Identifies the close relationship between el-Amarna chapels and Deir el-Medina private chapels used for personal cult worship, differentiating these from chapels strictly attached to tombs, which the author considers to be for the *ka* of the deceased.

Kemp, Barry J. *Amarna Reports*. 5 vols. London, 1984–1989. Annual reports of work by the Egypt Exploration Society under Kemp's direction. Each volume includes contributions by expedition members on topics such as pottery analysis, ancient wells, survey work, ancient ovens, faunal and botanical remains, etc. Kemp's offerings are always written with the reader in mind, but some authors allow the technical side to dominate.

Kemp, Barry J. "Tell el-Amarna." In *Lexikon der Ägyptologie*, 6: 309–319. Wiesbaden, 1985. Encyclopedia article encapsulating work at the site, with references to 1985.

Kemp, Barry J. *Ancient Egypt: Anatomy of a Civilization*. London, 1989. General work on the cultural life of ancient Egypt, with a lengthy chapter using el-Amarna as "Egypt in microcosm." Contains analysis of work up to 1988.

Kemp, Barry J., and Salvatore Garfi. *A Survey of the Ancient City of El-'Amarna*. London, 1993. Survey sheets of the site with accompanying text. Kemp offers a number of recent thoughts, particularly on provisioning within el-Amarna, and provides summaries of earlier analyses within the technical descriptions of the sheets.

Martin, Geoffrey T. *The Royal Tomb at el-Amarna I*. London, 1974. The tomb objects from museums all over the world gathered together for study.

Martin, Geoffrey T. *A Bibliography of the Amarna Period and Its Aftermath*. London, 1991.

Moran, William L. *The Amarna Letters*. Baltimore, 1992. Retranslation and annotation of the famous correspondence between the rulers of el-Amarna, Mesopotamia, and the Levant. Eminently readable.

Murnane, William J., and Charles C. Van Siclen III. *The Boundary Stelae of Akhenaten*. London, 1993. Publication of the refound, recollated, and researched boundary stelae, forming an important reference work for historians and philologists of el-Amarna.

Redford, Donald B. *Akhenaten the Heretic King*. Princeton, 1984. Chapter 7 contains Redford's summation of the city. Archaeologically much has been revised since that time, but Redford has a spirited style and links the site with East Karnak, where he excavated Akhenaten's early temples.

Van de Walle, Baudouin. "La découverte d'Amarna et d'Akhenaton." *Revue d'Égyptologie* 28 (1976), 7–24. History of the early researches at el-Amarna.

BETSY M. BRYAN

**AMARNA LETTERS.** In 1887, Egyptian peasants rummaging in ruins on the plain of Amarna found inscribed clay tablets. The script was Near Eastern cuneiform—at the time, a startling and unprecedented discovery. The site was the city of Akhetaten, founded by Amenhotpe IV (Akhenaten) of the eighteenth dynasty, and the find-spot proved to be the "Place of the Letters of the Pharaoh," the storehouse of Egypt's diplomatic correspondence with its Near Eastern neighbors along the Fertile Crescent—another startling discovery. Eventually, the corpus of letters, with four attached inventories, would number 350. Discovered elsewhere on the site were thirty-two more tablets in a miscellany of genres.

The language of the Amarna Letters, with a few exceptions in Assyrian, Hurrian, and Hittite, is Babylonian, but not the standard language of contemporary Babylonia. It is, rather, a provincial language that had become a lingua

AMARNA LETTERS. *Clay tablet of a letter in Akkadian cuneiform from King Ashur-Uballit I of Assyria to Akhenaten, eighteenth dynasty.* The letter states that the ambassador who bears it is sent with greetings and a gift of one splendid chariot, two horses, and some lapis lazuli. It stipulates that the embassy is not to make a long stay in Egypt. (The Metropolitan Museum of Art, 24.2.11)

franca, a language of international diplomacy and trade. Within this language are two principal traditions. One is called "Hurro-Akkadian," a name that reflects the role of the Hurrians in the formation and diffusion of the language. This was the usual language of correspondence of the major powers. The other tradition is confined to the Levant, southern Syria, and Palestine, and it is radically different. The transforming influence of the underlying Canaanite speech of the area is everywhere, manifest and profound, especially in morphology and syntax. The Babylonian component is mainly lexical and therefore relatively superficial, whereas the grammar is radically Canaanitized. These Amarna Letters are therefore an important source for the reconstruction of early Canaanite dialects such as Proto-Hebrew.

Correspondence with independent powers to the north is attested from late (about the thirtieth year) in the reign of Amenhotpe III to early in the reign of Tutankhamun, a period of about twenty-five years. It should be read in the light of a central and pervasive metaphor that goes back about a millennium: the household. Allies were members of the same household and were therefore "brothers," hence the dominance of the themes of the love and friendship that bind the "brothers," and of gifts, the visible expression of this bond. "Send me much gold, and you, for your part, whatever you want from my country, write me so that it may be taken to you" (the king of Babylonia to the pharaoh). The notion that they hold all in common is the ideal; the reality includes squabbles, misunderstandings, and disappointments with gifts, all frankly expressed.

The correspondence with vassals in Syria and Palestine, about three hundred letters, tells us much about the Egyptian administration, but a number of major problems remain. How many provinces were there—two, three, or four? What was the pharaoh's role and the nature and frequency of his intervention? Were these troops in transit, on an annual tour, or on their way to a great campaign in the north? Answers to these questions are fundamental to the interpretation of a large part of the vassal correspondence.

This much is clear, however: Egypt's claims of service were total and absolute, denying the vassal all autonomy and receiving his ready acknowledgment. Just as clearly, vassals pursued their own goals of expansion and self-interest. A healthy pragmatism provided a *modus vivendi*. Practically, Egypt accepted limits to its power, and the vassals continued to acknowledge an absolute power that no longer existed, if indeed it ever had.

**BIBLIOGRAPHY**

Knudtzon, J. A. *Die El-Amarna-Tafeln.* Vorderasiatische Bibliotek, 2. Leipzig, 1908–1915; reprint, Aalen, 1964. A classic, still the only reliable version of the cuneiform text.

Moran, William L. *The Amarna Letters.* Baltimore, 1992. The only up-to-date translation of the entire corpus.

Rainey, Anson F. *El Amarna Tablets 359–379.* 2d. ed. Alter Orient und Altes Testament, 8. Kevelaer und Neukirchen-Uluyn, 1978. A careful edition and translation of the post-Knudtzon Amarna tablets.

WILLIAM L. MORAN

**AMARNA PERIOD.** *See* New Kingdom, *article on* Amarna Period and the End of the Eighteenth Dynasty.

**AMASIS** (r. 569–526 BCE), fifth king of the Saite or twenty-sixth dynasty, Late period. Although not descended from the royal line begun by Psamtik I (r. 664–610 BCE), Amasis was an army general of uncertain but probably Libyan ancestry, selected by Egyptian troops to replace his predecessor, Apries (r. 589–570 BCE). Apries had been accused of cowardice while unsuccessfully attempting to invade the Greek city of Cyrene in North Africa, originally the capital of Cyrenaica. Information on the circumstances surrounding that usurpation is contradictory. Some accounts tell of Apries's death in battle with the forces of Amasis after Apries had fled Egypt in 570 BCE, to return three years later with a Babylonian army; others relate that Amasis imprisoned and later executed Apries after the coup of 570 BCE. The Greek historians Herodotus and Diodorus Siculus, as well as Egyptian sources (a fragmentary Demotic story) portray Amasis as a plebeian who drank too much and did not act in a properly regal manner. Although those characterizations were probably true, Amasis had a very productive reign, proved himself capable of making both domestic and foreign-policy decisions, and demonstrated great acumen as a statesman.

Egypt, during the Saite dynasty, was a country greatly dependent on foreign trade and involved in *realpolitik*—at a time when it was not the dominant power in the area. When the twenty-sixth dynasty was founded by Psamtik I, he began his reign as a virtual Assyrian vassal. Yet the Babylonians (Chaldeans) had become the most influential force in the area by the time of Amasis, and their king, Nebuchadrezzar, was vigorously engaging the Hebrews in Palestine—a struggle that provoked some feeble and fruitless attempts at intervention by the Egyptian kings who had preceded Amasis. That situation faced Amasis at the beginning of his reign. Like his predecessors, he maintained a strong naval presence to protect Egyptian trade routes and an army powerfully reinforced by Greek mercenaries. Notwithstanding those precautionary measures, consistent with his military experience, he was an astute diplomat who forged numerous foreign alliances to support his country's interests. Most of the alliances were with the various Greek states with which Egypt traded and on which Egypt depended for mercenary troops. Amasis was careful not to provoke the Babylonians, although some of his treaties with the Greek states were clearly meant to deflect a possible invasion by them.

Amasis was equally successful with domestic affairs, reforming Egypt's juridical system and relocating the main body of Greek mercenaries away from a potentially harmful border position, where they might have been subverted, thereby opening Egypt to invaders. He married a woman who was possibly the daughter of a Greek (Lydian?) family residing in Egypt. Presuming that his marriage had political overtones, it would have served his desire to maintain a good relationship with an influential minority, who supported him despite the substantial taxes levied on the Hellenistic community in Egypt. The reign of Amasis was marked by massive building projects and a high level of prosperity throughout the land. In many ways, he was the most successful pharaoh of the Saite dynasty, rivaled only by its founder, Psamtik I.

His long reign ended with his death and the succession of his son Psamtik III. His tomb is presumably located in the eastern Delta city of Sais, the capital of the twenty-sixth dynasty, but no trace of it has yet been found. A single inscribed sphinx bearing his name (now in Rome, in the Museo Capitoline) is the only unquestionable example of a three-dimensional representation of him, although there is a group of fragmentary anthropomorphic statues probably depicting Amasis. They have long faces and eyes set high up on the head, features usually associated in the region with Libyans and perhaps revealing his ancestry. Most of the information about the reign of Amasis comes from the Greek historian, Herodotus, who visited Egypt less than a century after his death; but biblical sources, fragmentary Egyptian stone inscriptions, and papyri supplement our limited knowledge of this pharaoh.

### BIBLIOGRAPHY

De Meulenaere, Herman. "Amasis." In *Lexikon der Ägyptologie*, 1:181–182. Wiesbaden, 1975.

Josephson, Jack A. *Egyptian Royal Sculpture of the Late Period, 400–246 B.C.* Mainz, 1997.

Lloyd, A. B. "The Late Period." *Ancient Egypt: A Social History.* Cambridge, 1983.

Myśliwiec, Karol. *Royal Portraiture of the Dynasties XXI–XXX.* Mainz, 1988.

Spalinger, Anthony. "Egypt and Babylonia: A Survey (c. 620 B.C.–550 B.C.)." *Studien zur Altägyptischen Kultur* 5 (1977), 221–244.

Spalinger, Anthony. "The Concept of Monarchy during the Saite Epoch—An Essay of Synthesis." *Orientalia*, NS 47 (1978), 12–36.

JACK A. JOSEPHSON

**AMENEMHAT OF BENI HASAN** (fl. 1950 BCE). Amenemhat, the short form of whose name was Ameni, was the "Great Overlord of the Oryx nome" (the sixteenth Egyptian nome [province]) and the owner of tomb number 2 at Beni Hasan. The autobiography in his tomb states that he began his career as a "Great Overseer of the Army," accompanying his king with local troops to subdue the Nubian country of Kush. This was most probably the expedition of the eighteenth year in Senwosret I's reign. Further expeditions led Amenemhat again to the South, bringing gold via caravan to the city of Coptos for his king. His twenty-five years of service in the nome are fixed chronologically by a double date, to the period between the eighteenth and forty-third year of Senwosret I. Priestly titles also attach him to the temples of the deities Horus and Khnum in cities on the western bank of the Nile. His autobiography stresses his benign role, as provider and promoter of prosperity in his nome, even during years of famine, as well as his efficient care of the nome's cattle on behalf of the government.

His tomb's ground plan differs from the prior tombs in the Beni Hasan cemetery, indicating that he did not belong to the old nomarchic family clan. His tomb has a causeway; a portico with two proto-Doric octagonal columns; and a square main chamber, with four sixteen-sided columns in two rows, parallel to the axis, leading to a shrine with an overlifesize seated statue of Amenemhat flanked by two smaller standing figures (his wife, Hetepet, and his mother, Khenu).

The walls of his tomb are decorated with superb paintings: they show crafts (on the western wall); Amenemhat supervising the yearly cattle count (on the northern wall); long rows of wrestling men and an attack on a fortress—both themes have a special tradition in the cemetery—above a solemn riverine procession to the holy cities of Abydos and Busiris (on the eastern wall); and, for the benefit of Amenemhat and his wife, a long offering list with priests performing the offering rituals (on the southern wall).

[*See also* Beni Hasan.]

**BIBLIOGRAPHY**

Hölzl, Christian. "The Rock-tombs of Beni Hasan: Architecture and Sequence." In *VI Congresso internazionale di egittologia: Atti*. Proceedings of the 6th International Congress of Egyptology, Turin, Italy, September 1–8, 1991, vol. 1, pp. 279–283. Turin, 1992.

Lichtheim, Miriam. *Ancient Egyptian Autobiographies Chiefly of the Middle Kingdom: A Study and an Anthology*. Orbis biblicus et orientalis, 84. Freiburg-Göttingen, 1988. Translation of Amenemhat's autobiography and other inscriptions.

Newberry, Percy E. *Beni Hasan*. London, 1893. Principal publication of Amenemhat's tomb.

Obsomer, Claude. *Sésostris Ier: Étude chronologique et historique du règne*. Bruxelles, 1995. About Amenemhat's Nubian campaign; complete and annotated translation of his autobiography.

Shedid, Abdel Ghaffar. *Die Felsgräber von Beni Hassan in Mittelägypten*. Mainz, 1994. Beautiful photographs of the restored tombs at Beni Hasan, with a history of the cemetery and a discussion of techniques, art, and style.

DETLEF FRANKE

**AMENEMHET I** (r. 1991–1962 BCE), first king of the twelfth dynasty, Middle Kingdom. In the fictitious prophecy of Amenemhet I's accession, as told by the sage Neferti at King Sneferu's court, Amenemhet is styled as the savior of his country and a terminator of the alleged chaotic conditions that prevailed before he attained kingship; there are no hard facts beneath the text, however. Amenemhet I's attestation in history is meager: he was not the son of his predecessor Montuhotep III, and Egyptologists assume that Montuhotep's vizier, Amenemhet, is identical with this founder of the twelfth dynasty.

Amenemhet I's throne name Sehtepibre means "who pacifies the heart of the sun god Re," and his Horus name is similarly modeled: Sehtepibtowy means "who pacifies the heart of the Two Lands." The reconciliation theme was felt appropriate, but it had its forerunner in the titulary of Teti, the first king of the sixth dynasty (Sehoteptowy, "who pacifies the Two Lands"). Amenemhet I's reign should be understood as a continuation of the glorious past but, at the same time, as a new beginning. That idea was condensed into his second Horus name, Wehem-meswet ("repeater of births"), which labeled his reign as one of renaissance and restoration.

The change of the king's titulary could be hypothetically combined with a change of royal residence: the majority of his reign was spent at Thebes, where he began preparations for his tomb, but later he moved his court north to el-Lisht, to a place called *Itjtawy* (*Itt-t3wy;* "[Amenemhet] is-he-who seizes the Two Lands"). The new residence marked the end of the Thebes-centered policy of his predecessors. At Itjtowy, the royal precinct became the place for his new pyramid and burial.

Amenemhet I launched activities in the temples of Tod, Armant, Karnak, Coptos, Dendera, Medinet el-Faiyum, Memphis, and Bubastis, as well as in the Qantir region. Only one government expedition to the Wadi Hammamat quarries is known for his reign. He devoted significant efforts toward establishing a royal presence in the Nile

AMENEMHET I. *Lintel depicting Amenemhet at his* sed-*festival, twelfth dynasty*. The king is represented running, flanked by four deities who offer him symbols of life and power. Painted limestone. (The Metropolitan Museum of Art, Rogers Fund, 1908. [08.200.5])

Delta and in strengthening the Egyptian frontiers; although known only from textual evidence, in the eastern Delta he initiated the "Walls of the Ruler," a fortification designed to prevent intrusion by adjacent countries. He did the same in the western Delta against the Libyans; at Qaret el-Dahr, to the south of the Wadi Natrun, a monumental temple gate has been found, once part of a frontier fortress. Military expeditions to the south to vanquish Lower Nubia were recorded for his last year of reign, his twenty-ninth. Their organization was due to the vizier Antefoqer, and the *Story of Sinuhe* reports a military raid against the Libyans led by the king's son, Senwosret I. Just before Amenemhet I's *sed*-festival, he was killed as a victim of a harem conspiracy, and the attack on him was reflected in his *Instructions of Amenemhet* to his son. There, the king, speaking in the hereafter, advised his son from his own bad experience with courtiers. Scholars still debate whether a ten-year coregency existed for Amenemhet I with his son Senwosret I.

[*See also* Instructions of Amenemhet.]

## BIBLIOGRAPHY

Allen, James P. "Some Theban Officials of the Early Middle Kingdom." In *Studies in Honor of William Kelly Simpson*, edited by Peter Der Manuelian, vol. 1, pp. 1–26. Boston, 1996.

Arnold, Dorothea. "Amenemhat I and the early Twelfth Dynasty at Thebes." *Metropolitan Museum Journal* 26 (1991), 5–48. Ascribes the unfinished royal tomb in the valley northwest of the Ramesseum to Amenemhet's Theban years; study of the early twelfth dynasty's history, art, ceramics, and other materials.

Berman, Lawrence M. "Amenemhet I." Ph.D. diss., Yale University, 1985. Collection of relevant sources, but somewhat out of date.

Franke, Detlef. "The Middle Kingdom in Egypt." In *Civilizations of the Ancient Near East*, edited by J. M. Sasson et al., vol. 2, pp. 735–738. New York, 1995. General outline of Amenemhet's reign, with bibliography.

Vandersleyen, Claude. *L'Égypte et la vallée du Nil.* 2 vols. Paris, 1995. Archaeological and textual sources of the reigns of Montuhotep III and Amenemhet I, in volume 2.

DETLEF FRANKE

**AMENEMHET III** (r. 1843–1797 BCE), sixth king of the twelfth dynasty, Middle Kingdom. He was the son of Senwosret III (r. 1878–1843 BCE), with whom he shared the throne for an unknown length of time. His father's aggressive administrative and military policies left Amenemhet III a country that enjoyed an internal as well as an external peace that had not existed for centuries.

Internally, Senwosret III's removal of the great nomarchical families (the provincial governors who had ruled their own nomes of Egypt since the days of the Old Kingdom) meant that Amenemhet III was in charge of a highly centralized government. The crown therefore attained easy access to resources, both goods and labor, for which earlier it would have been in competition with the provincial rulers. In fact, the increased number of commemorative stelae for that period left at the pilgrimage site of Abydos indicates the rise of a middle class of petty bureaucrats, who were part of the burgeoning central administration.

Senwosret III's military conquests meant that Egypt had complete control of all river traffic and of the desert trade routes from the Sinai Peninsula to the Second Cataract of the Nile in Nubia. The Sinai yielded valuable copper and turquoise and Nubia had large quantities of gold, all of which were desirable materials, eagerly exploited by the central authorities. With that additional wealth channelled into the royal coffers, Amenemhet III was able to devote much of his energies to vast building projects.

Consequently, remains dated to his reign are known throughout Egypt. In the Sinai, the temple that had been dedicated to the goddess Hathor was expanded. In the Nile Delta, monuments have been found in Khatana, Tell el-Yahudiyya, and Tell Basta (Bubastis). The Memphis area has yielded many finds, from Memphis itself, to the site of the king's first pyramid at Dahshur, to the capital city at el-Lisht; but it is the Faiyum area that brought Amenemhet III his lasting fame. Remains there include temples at Medinet el-Faiyum and Medinet Maadi, two seated colossi at Biahmu, and a second pyramid at Hawara after the one at Dahshur had suffered a partial collapse. The Hawara pyramid's funerary temple was so large that it was regarded by some classical authors as a labyrinth. Although those authors credited Amenemhet III with the excavation of Lake Moeris in the Faiyum, it is more likely that his fame in the area during Greco-Roman times and his subsequent deification as King Lamarres (or Marres) derived from the many instances of his name on the many monuments found there. While most of the twelfth dynasty kings were attested in the Faiyum, when the local people looked for a venerable ancestor to whom they could ascribe the greatest feats, they chose the most visible: Amenemhet III. To a lesser degree, the king also built in Middle Egypt, but evidence for his building activities is especially plentiful in Upper Egypt, from Abydos to Coptos and from Karnak to Elkab and Aswan. Amenemhet III's reign is also renowned for the many graffiti left by the members of his expeditions who worked at mines and quarries throughout Egypt.

After a reign of forty-six years, Amenemhet III was buried in his pyramid at Hawara, leaving the country in the hands of two of his children, first King Amenemhet IV, then Queen Sobekneferu.

## BIBLIOGRAPHY

Leprohon, Ronald J. "The Reign of Amenemhet III." Ph.D. Diss. University of Toronto, 1980. A complete study of the reign of Amenemhet III, it is currently being revised for publication.

Matzker, Ingo. *Die letzten Könige der 12. Dynastie.* Frankfurt, 1986. A scholarly study of much of the documentation from the late twelfth dynasty.

AMENEMHET III. *The king's pyramid at Dahshur, twelfth dynasty.* (Courtesy Dieter Arnold)

Quirke, Stephen. *The Administration of Egypt in the Late Middle Kingdom: The Hieratic Documents.* New Malden, 1990. Many of the documents included date to the reign of Amenemhet III.

RONALD J. LEPROHON

**AMENHOTEP, SON OF HAPU** (c.1430–1345?), famous courtier during the reign of Amenhotpe III of the eighteenth dynasty. Amenhotep, son of Hapu, was born into a modest family during the reign of Thutmose III, in Athribis (in the Nile Delta). There were three phases to his career, which were described in his funerary inscriptions. They included "royal scribe under the king's [Amenhotpe III's] immediate supervision"; "royal scribe at the head of the recruits," a position concerned with logistics, not with war; and "chief of all the king's works." There was a logic to those steps in his career: first with intellectual development; then with experience in calculating, organizing, and leading men; and finally with ability to run large-scale works. This last included supervision of the carving, transporting, and erecting of huge statues, among them the Colossi of Memnon and the 20-meter (62-foot) colossus in front of the Tenth Pylon at Karnak.

Nothing is known of him during his first fifty years, which preceded Amenhotpe III's reign. In fact, the documentation concerning him begins in Year 30 of Amenhotpe III, when he was already in his late seventies. He never had important titles, such as vizier or "first prophet of Amun," yet he was the person closest to the king because of his intellectual and moral qualities. He did play an important part in the king's first *sed*-festival (*ḥb-sd;* the thirty-year jubilee for renewing the king's potency), and he was steward to Satamon, Amenhotpe III's daughter and wife. His funeral temple, built among those of the pharaohs, is the most obvious sign of his outstanding position. In Karnak, two statues represented him at the time of his death as a mediator between humans and the gods. During the Ramessid era, he was depicted in two tombs at the end of a line of famous kings, queens, and princes. Thousands of years later, he was worshiped as a healing god, comparable to Asklepios, with a principal shrine at Deir el-Bahri.

**BIBLIOGRAPHY**

Murnane, William J. "Power behind the Throne: Amenhotep son of Hapu." *K.M.T.: A Modern Journal of Ancient Egypt* 22 (Summer, 1991), 8–13, 57–59.

Varille, Alexandre. *Inscriptions concernant l'architecte Amenhotep fils de Hapou.* Bibliothèque d'études, 44. Cairo, 1968.

Wildung, Dietrich. *Egyptian Saints: Deification in Pharaonic Egypt.* New York, 1977.

CLAUDE A. P. VANDERSLEYEN

**AMENHOTPE I** (r. 1545–1525 BCE), second king of the eighteenth dynasty, New Kingdom. Although certainly the son of the previous king Ahmose (r. 1569–1545 BCE) and his wife Ahmose-Nefertari, his other family ties remain vaguely documented. Ahotpe II, once believed to be his wife and sister, is now thought to have been his grandmother. Merit-Amun I remains as his "Great-King's Wife," but significantly she was not a "King's Mother." Another wife, Sitkamose, is attested on stelae of the nineteenth dynasty. No children can be convincingly attributed to Amenhotpe I. Thutmose I's wife Ahmose is thought by some to have been Amenhotpe I's sister, but this was unlikely since she was not a "Daughter of a King." Her sole relationship was with Thutmose I, and she was most probably his sister and wife.

Amenhotpe I must have consolidated and strengthened his father's accomplishments, but the reign is very poorly documented. The Greco-Egyptian historian Manetho (c.305–285 BCE) assigned him twenty years and seven months, which accords well with his highest known regnal date of Year 21. There is no convincing evidence of a coregency with his father Ahmose or with his successor Thutmose I. A *sed*-festival, usually celebrated in the thirtieth year of the reign, was mentioned in the biography of the court official Amenemhet; but this claim must have been a polite fiction or a jubilee celebrated earlier than the thirtieth year.

Military campaigns for Amenhotpe I are attested in Nubia and in the Near East, but the details are not clear. Most likely the king was consolidating his father's success in both areas. The Near Eastern campaign can be deduced from a gate inscription found at the Karnak temple.

Amenhotpe I's building activities were better documented. In Karnak, he built the alabaster (calcite) chapel called "Amun with Enduring Monuments." In Deir el-Bahri and in Dra Abul Naga, he built bark stations; in Elkab, there is a temple to Nekhbet. At Abydos, he finished Ahmose's temple. At Kom Ombo, Elephantine, Shatt el-Rigal, and Gebel es-Silsila, some single blocks inscribed with his name remain.

Egypt enjoyed a rich cultural life during Amenhotpe I's reign. Both science and the arts flourished. The Ebers Papyrus, a list of medical diagnoses and prescriptions, was written at that time. Amenhotpe I also founded the artisan's village of Deir el-Medina attached to the necropolis at Thebes. Ironically, there are few contemporary representations of this patron of the arts known today, although many images made in the Ramessid era survive.

Amenhotpe I was the first king of Egypt to separate his tomb and his mortuary temple in an effort to mislead looters. His destroyed mortuary temple might actually have been located in Deir el-Bahri, where a House of Amenhotpe in the Garden was located within Hatshepsut's mortuary temple. Two uninscribed tombs in the Valley of the Kings have been attributed to Amenhotpe I, but neither accords with the description of his tomb in the Abbott Papyrus. The king's mummy was reburied by priests of the twenty-first dynasty after the tomb was robbed. It was discovered with other royal mummies at Deir el-Bahri.

Later generations of Egyptians venerated Amenhotpe I at Deir el-Medina. There, he was treated as a local god, as was his mother. He was also known as a source of oracles. He was represented in three forms: Amenhotpe of the Town; Amenhotpe Beloved of Amun; and Amenhotpe of the Forecourt. Many feasts of the year honored him.

### BIBLIOGRAPHY

James, T. G. H. "Egypt from the Expulsion of the Hyksos to Amenophis I." Chapter 8 in *Cambridge Ancient History*, vol. 2. Cambridge, 1965. An older but still valuable account of political and cultural developments during the reign.

Redford, Donald B. "A Gate Inscription from Karnak." *Journal of the American Oriental Society* 99.2 (1979), 270–287. On the campaign in the Near East.

Robins, Gay. "Amenhotpe I and the Child Amenemhat." *Göttinger Miszellen* 20 (1978), 71–75. Disproves the connection between them.

Robins, Gay. "A Critical Examination of the Theory That the Right to the Throne of Ancient Egypt Passed through the Female Line in the 18th Dynasty." *Göttinger Miszellen* 62 (1983), 67–77. Shows that this older theory must not be true.

EDWARD BLEIBERG

**AMENHOTPE II** (r. 1454–1419 BCE), sixth king of the eighteenth dynasty, New Kingdom. He was the son and successor of Thutmose III. Amenhotpe II's mother was Hatshepsut, the last Great Royal Wife of Thutmose III. Amenhotpe II apparently came to the throne as coregent with his father (for a period of two years and four months). The length of Amenhotpe II's reign was in excess of twenty-five years (from his highest attested date) with a maximum of thirty-five years of independent rule. He was likely making preparations for the celebration of a second *sed*-festival at the time of his death. Amenhotpe II was buried in the Valley of the Kings (tomb 35), where his mummy was found still resting in its own sarcophagus (although reburied there in the late New Kingdom). In addition to appearing on his own monuments, Amenhotpe II or his name also appears on monuments of his contemporaries, both during the coregency period and during the period of his sole rule. Amenhotpe II was succeeded by Thutmose IV, his son by his wife Tiye, although no certain monument exists naming her as queen during his reign.

The early years of the reign of Amenhotpe II included several military campaigns in the Levant—first during the coregency period by Year 3, and later independently during Years 7 and 9. According to surviving sources (Amada and Elephantine stelae, Memphis and Karnak stelae), these campaigns were victories, but they probably merely served to reinforce the hegemony of Egypt over the region established by his father Thutmose III. Amenhotpe II was also known for his physical prowess as a huntsman, charioteer, and archer—themes that recur on a number of his monuments (stelae from Giza, Medamud, and Karnak).

While not ranked as one of the major kings of Egypt, Amenhotpe II appeared in his proper place in subsequent king lists (at Saqqara and Abydos), and his existence and relative position in Egyptian history have not been in much dispute. As with many of the kings of the eighteenth dynasty, his identity in the king list of the Greco-Egyptian historian Manetho is problematic. The monuments of Amenhotpe II are often fragmentary and not well known; they are found throughout Egypt and Nubia, but they are centered at ancient Thebes (now Luxor). The monuments at Western Thebes include his tomb and mortuary temple, as well as the completion of—or additions to—two temples started by his father. In Thebes proper, he worked at North Karnak (a garden, a palace, two bark shrines, and a chapel for incense); in Central Karnak (shrines in calcite [Egyptian alabaster], red granite, and sandstone; a *sed*-festival court before the Eighth Pylon; various cycles of carved reliefs within the main temple; a shrine to the goddess Ipy [Opet]; a granary); and at Luxor (a bark shrine). Outside of Thebes, his monuments include temples and other buildings at Tell Basta, Heliopolis, Giza, Hermopolis, Abydos, Coptos, Ombos, Medamud, Armant, Tod, er-Rezeikat, Elkab, Esna, Elephantine, Seheil, Kalabsha, Amada, Uronarti, Aniba, Buhen, Semna-Kumma, and Sail. Small finds with the king's name and monuments of his officials were found throughout Egypt. Amenhotpe II also had work done in the Sinai, at Serabit el-Kadim. Curiously, faience apes with the cartouche of Amenhotpe II were found at Mycenae and in Greece, at Tiryns.

### BIBLIOGRAPHY

Daressy, Georges. *Fouilles de la vallée des rois (1898–1899).* Catalogue général des antiquités égyptiennes du Musée du Caire. Cairo, 1902. The formal report on the objects from the tomb of Amenhotpe II.

Manuelian, Peter Der. *Studies in the Reign of Amenophis II.* Hildesheimer Ägyptologischer Beiträge, 26. Hildesheim, 1987. The only study to attempt a look at various aspects of the reign, with good documentation of the published materials.

Petrie, W. M. Flinders. *Six Temples at Thebes, 1896.* London, 1897. The basic study of the king's mortuary temple (as of 1998, there has been renewed work at the site).

Redford, Donald B., "The Coregency of Tuthmosis III and Amenophis II." *Journal of Egyptian Archaeology* 51 (1965), 107–122. This is the basic work on the coregency between Amenhotpe II and his father.

Van Siclen, Charles C., III. *The Alabaster Shrine of King Amenhotep II.* San Antonio, 1986. A study of one of the many "lost" monuments of the king; it includes a list of his Theban monuments.

Van Siclen, Charles C., III. "Amenhotep II's Bark Chapel for Amun at North Karnak," *Bulletin de l'Institut français d'archéologie orientale* 86 (1986), 353–359, pls. 43–61. A preliminary report on the "lost" temple of Amenhotpe II.

Van Siclen, Charles C., III. "Preliminary Report on the Epigraphic Work Done in the Edifice of Amenhotpe II, Seasons of 1988–89 and 1989–90." *Varia Aegyptiaca* 6 (1990), 75–90. A report on a "lost" structure of the king; as of 1999, the work was still ongoing and had expanded to the court south of the Eight Pylon at Karnak.

CHARLES C. VAN SICLEN

**AMENHOTPE III** (r. 1410–1372 BCE), ninth king of the eighteenth dynasty, New Kingdom. One of the wealthiest and best-attested rulers, Amenhotpe III, governed Egypt for more than thirty-eight years. Presumably the chosen heir of his father Thutmose IV, Amenhotpe probably became king before the age of twelve. Monuments dated to the first ten years of Amenhotpe III's reign can be counted in single digits, perhaps an indication of the king's youth. A punitive expedition to Nubia in the fifth year of his reign was carried out by the king's army and may have taken the troops as far south as the Shendi reach of the Nile River, above the Fifth Cataract. Three stelae, at Aswan and Sai Island near the Third Cataract, commemorate this expedition; another, left by the viceroy of Nubia, Merymose, at the fortress of Semna may refer to another expedition in lower Nubia, north of the Second Cataract. Sometime later in his reign, Amenhotpe III ordered the construction of a temple and fort a little to the south of Sai Island at Soleb.

Although the kings of the eighteenth dynasty primarily ruled from Memphis, Amenhotpe III built a residential complex on the western bank of the Nile at Thebes, at a site now called Malqata. Jar labels, primarily from festival provisions of food and drink, attest to the king's occupation of Malqata from after his Year 20 through the end of his reign. Whether Amenhotpe lived at Malqata year-round or spent the hotter months in the North is unknown. However, his complex at Thebes included houses for his family and close court associates. During the second half of his reign, the king oversaw, personally or through advisors, a near transformation of the existing religious monuments in Thebes, and he added to them his enormous funerary temple at Kom el-Hetan. Amenhotpe III celebrated the *sed*-festivals that rejuvenated the king, guaranteeing his continued fitness to rule, in his Years 30/31, 33/34, and 37. The festivals took place in Thebes and, particularly for the all-important first *sed*-festival, Amenhotpe conducted the rituals to ensure the favor of the gods, especially the solar deities.

Amenhotpe III's primary wife was Queen Tiye, to whom he was married in Year 2. The daughter of a court noble with land holdings near modern Akhmim, Tiye shared Amenhotpe's throne and produced his heir Amenhotpe IV, along with a number of male and female children. Among the women whom Amenhotpe III married were three of

AMENHOTPE III. *Statue of Amenhotpe III at the Luxor Museum.* (Courtesy David P. Silverman)

his daughters, one of whom, Sitamun, bore the chief title "Great Royal Wife." It remains a possibility that the title "King's Wife" was, in the case of the daughters, merely a rank title, conferred as a courtesy to ensure revenues. In any case, it is unclear exactly what roles these princesses fulfilled as royal wives, but they did not unseat their mother. In religious and royal ideology of the reign, Tiye was considered to be the mother sky goddess, while the daughters were treated as the consorts or daughters of the sun god.

The diplomatic correspondence of Amenhotpe III and his contemporary Near Eastern rulers is partially preserved in the Amarna Letters, cuneiform tablets found at Amarna. The gold wealth of the king was envied by the rulers of Babylonia and Mitanni, and Amenhotpe used his affluence to bring the princesses from those countries to Egypt as his wives; he negotiated marriage with princesses from Arzawa, Syria, and Mitanni. No doubt the prestige attached to Amenhotpe's diplomatic marriages was considerable, but whatever alliance may have existed between Egypt and Mitanni, it did not help the Syrian ruler fend off a fatal attack by the Hittites. Amenhotpe III's second Mitanni marriage negotiation was completed by his son and successor Amenhotpe IV, with Queen Tiye serving as an intermediary.

Amenhotpe's sobriquet, while he lived, was "the Dazzling Sundisk," and his court became proverbial for luxury. His courtiers and administrators came from old noble families, in conformity with his explicit policy of not choosing any but "blue bloods." One, Amenhotep, son of Hapu the labor minister, became the subject of legend after his death—revered a thousand years later as a god of healing (sometimes identified with Asklepios).

The heir apparent during the early years of the reign was the little-known Thutmose, presumably Amenhotpe III's firstborn. He disappears from the record, however, by the fourth decade and presumably met a premature death. His younger brother, named Amenhotep after his father, was then promoted to crown prince. Although it is certain that Amenhotpe IV (who became Akhenaten) succeeded his father, scholars remain divided on whether there was a coregency between the two rulers and whether such a joint rule would have been of two or twelve years. Given the numerous Near Eastern rulers and vassals known from the Amarna Letters, a twelve-year shift in the chronology of the correspondence means that their historical circumstances must remain unclear for many events.

[*See also* Tiye.]

### BIBLIOGRAPHY

Berman, Lawrence, ed. *The Art of Amenhotep III: Art Historical Analysis*. Cleveland, 1990. Proceedings of a symposium held in 1987, with important contributions.

Kondo, Jiro, "A Preliminary Report on the Re-clearance of the Tomb of Amenophis III (WV 22)." In *After Tutankhamun: Research and Excavation in the Royal Necropolis at Thebes*, edited by C.N. Reeves, pp. 41–54. London, 1992. New finds and indications of the uses of the tomb.

Kozloff, Arielle, and Betsy M. Bryan, with Lawrence M. Berman. *Egypt's Dazzling Sun Amenhotep III and his World*. Cleveland, 1992. Essays and catalog of an exhibition on the reign.

O'Connor, David, and Eric H. Cline, eds. *Amenhotep III: Perspectives on His Reign*. Ann Arbor, 1998. This superb volume contains the viewpoints of a number of leading researchers.

Topozada, Z. "Les deux campagnes d'Amenhotep III en Nubie." *Bulletin de l'Institut français d'archéologie orientale* 88 (1988), 153–165.

BETSY M. BRYAN

**AMETHYST.** *See* Gems.

**AMPHIBIANS AND REPTILES.** The Nile River, the Nile Valley, and the surrounding deserts were filled with a variety of amphibians and reptiles—crocodiles, snakes, lizards, and frogs—which inspired a mixture of awe and dread among the ancient Egyptians.

The ancient Egyptian word for crocodile, *msḥ* (*Crocodilus niloticus*), has survived in the Egyptian Arabic *timsāḥ*. Its distribution and frequency today are not as great as in ancient times. They are frequently depicted in Nilotic scenes in tombs, laying eggs, as prey of hunters, or lying in wait to devour baby hippopotami. The crocodile posed a particular threat to young children and people who worked in the water—boatmen, water-carriers, fishermen, washermen, and boatbuilders—as well as to the

cattle in charge of herdsmen, who used a special apotropaic gesture against the animals and recited magical formulas to keep them at bay. The ibis and ichneumon were considered threats to crocodiles because these animals reputedly ate their eggs.

In a religious context, crocodiles played an ambivalent role. The crocodile was worshipped as the god Sobek, particularly at Kom Ombo and in the Faiyum, and crocodile mummies have been unearthed at cult sites all over Egypt. The crocodile could be identified with the good god Osiris or with his evil brother, Seth. While Egyptians expressed the wish to be transformed into crocodiles after death, a crocodile-headed demon consumed the souls of the dead who had not lived virtuous lives, and they needed spells to protect themselves from crocodiles in the afterlife. Crocodile statuettes were worn as amulets and the animal was often depicted on scarabs. A magic spell against headache was recited over a mud crocodile figurine. In the story of *King Khufu and the Magicians*, a man exacts revenge on the adulterer engaged in an affair with his wife by having a magician form a wax crocodile which turns into a full-sized animal that carries off the adulterer. Crocodile dung, fat, and eyes were used in medical prescriptions, but there is limited evidence for their consumption as food.

Snakes (*ḥf3w* was the most common Egyptian term for the members of the suborder *Ophidia*) were found throughout Egypt in the desert, fields, pastures, and houses, and around the Nile. Poisonous snakes posed a serious threat. A papyrus manual for the treatment of snakebite lists the names of thirty-seven types of snake distinguished by the ancient Egyptians. It gives a physical description of each snake and its habitat, along with precise descriptions of symptoms, whether or not the wound is mortal, and the name of the god or goddess of which the snake is considered to be a manifestation. Following the list of snakes is a list of remedies. One of the snakes the Egyptians had to contend with was the horned viper (*Cerastes cornutus*), whose rasping coils make a sound like the letter *f*; hence, its image was used as the hieroglyph to write this letter (*fy* was the Egyptian word for "viper").

The snake god Apophis was considered the enemy of order, and images of Apophis were subjected to various tortures during special rituals designed to ensure the triumph of Re and Maat over chaos. Other snake deities had positive aspects. The goddess Renenutet was associated with the fertility of crops and had close ties with weaving and linen. She was worshipped throughout Egypt, but her cult was of particular significance in the Faiyum. The snake goddess Meretseger may have been an object of a domestic cult in the village of the royal tomb-builders and their families at Deir el-Medina. Certainly, nonpoisonous snakes would have been considered beneficial to the house, as they are sometimes regarded today in Egypt, because they ate rodents.

The *uraeus* worn at the front of the king's headdress depicts the Egyptian cobra (*Naja haje*). It represented the snake goddess Wadjet, associated with the Lower Egyptian sanctuary of Buto. The *uraeus* came to be considered a protector of kingship.

Snakes appear in several Egyptian literary works. The central character in the *Story of the Shipwrecked Sailor* is a cobra who saves the shipwrecked sailor, and the eponymous character of the *Story of the Doomed Prince* escapes one of the fates that had been decreed for him at birth after his wife puts out some beer to attract the threatening snake out of its hole. The snake drinks it, passes out, and is hacked up by the woman.

Several dozen species of lizards (*ḥntȝsw*) are still found in Egypt today. Geckos were common, and the hieroglyph which means "many" (*'šȝ*) probably represented the fan-footed gecko (*Ptyodactylus hasselquistii*) or the white-spotted gecko (*Tarentola annularis*). Members of the genus *Uromastyx* are also depicted in art. All Egyptian lizards, including geckos, are harmless, and are found outdoors and in houses. The ancient Egyptians, however, regarded them with dread, as do modern Egyptians, who commonly consider them capable of poisoning food and causing skin diseases. Religious texts and coffins, including the *Book of Going Forth by Day* (*Book of the Dead*), contain vignettes in which protective deities are depicted holding geckos, along with other harmful objects such as knives and snakes. The gecko was also said to be the enemy of the sun god Re and was associated with the god Anubis. A medical text contains prescriptions to keep lizards out of the house, while cooked lizards were used in a magic potion meant to cause skin disease. The final entry in the aforementioned manual is a "poisonous" legged reptile, which its publisher identifies as a chameleon, but which may actually be a gecko.

The most famous association of frogs with Egypt is as the second plague recounted in the Old Testament. Egyptian frogs and toads (*'bḥn* or *qrr*) are of the species *Rana mascareniensis* and various *Bufo* species. This ubiquitous resident of the Nile marshes probably inspired the Egyptians to use a hieroglyph of the tadpole (*ḥfn*) to designate the number 100,000. The birth goddess Heqat is depicted as a frog, or frog-headed. Frogs also appear frequently on amulets and as figurines.

[*See also* Crocodiles; Frogs; *and* Snakes.]

### BIBLIOGRAPHY

Anderson, John. *Zoology of Egypt*, vol. 1: *Reptilia and Batrachia*. London, 1898. Contains systematic descriptions of a number of reptile and amphibian species.

Broekhuis, Jan. *De Godin Renenwetet*. Bibliotheca Classica Vangor-cumiana, 19. Assen, 1971. Publication of a dissertation, in Dutch, on the snake goddess Renenutet, with English summary, pp. 149–152.

Brunner-Traut, Emma. "Eidechse." In *Lexikon der Ägyptologie*, 1: 1204–1205. Wiesbaden, 1975. Short article on lizards contains fair bibliography.

Brunner-Traut, Emma. "Krokodil." In *Lexikon der Ägyptologie*, 3: 791–801. Wiesbaden, 1980. Overview of crocodiles in Egypt, with extensive bibliography.

Dolzani, Claudia. *Il dio Sobk*. Memorie della Accademia Nazionale dei Lincei, Classe di Scienze Morali, Storiche e Filologiche, ser. 8, v. 10, fasc. 4. Rome, 1961. On the crocodile god Sobek.

Houlihan, Patrick F. *The Animal World of the Pharaohs*. Cairo, 1996. This easily accessible, richly illustrated book has an excellent bibliography.

Johnson, Sally B. *The Cobra Goddess of Ancient Egypt*. London and New York, 1990. An overview of the *uraeus* and a typological study of *uraei* during the Predynastic through Old Kingdom periods.

Kákosy, László. "Frosch." In *Lexikon der Ägyptologie*, 2: 334–336. Wiesbaden, 1977. Brief article on frogs.

Keimer, Ludwig. "Sur quelques représentations de caméléon de l'ancienne Égypte." *Bulletin de l'Institut français d'archéologie Orientale* 35 (1936–1937), 85–95. On the few representations of chameleons in Egyptian art.

Keimer, Ludwig. *Histoire de serpents dans l'Égypte ancienne et moderne*. Memoires de l'Institut de l'Égypte, 50. Cairo, 1947. About snake charming and worship in ancient and modern Egypt.

Leitz, Christian. *Die Schlangennamen in den ägyptischen und griechischen Giftbüchern*. Mainz, 1997. Lexicographic study of names of Egyptian snakes in Egyptian and Greek.

Marx, Hymen. *Checklist of the Reptiles and Amphibians of Egypt*. Cairo, 1968. The most complete list published to date.

Sauneron, Serge. "Une description égyptienne du caméléon." *Revue d'Égyptologie* 24 (1972), 160–164. Identifies the legged reptile in the Brooklyn Papyrus as a chameleon.

Sauneron, Serge. *Un traité égyptien d'ophiologie*. Cairo, 1989. Publication of the Brooklyn Papyrus, identifying snakes and the treatment of their bites.

NICOLE B. HANSEN

**AMRATIAN PERIOD.** *See* Predynastic Period.

**AMULETS** and jewelry that incorporated amuletic elements were an essential adornment worn by ancient Egyptians at every level of society, both in life and in the hereafter; even sacred animals wore them. Royalty, however, were rarely depicted wearing individual amulets; they wore amuletic forms that had been incorporated into jewelry, such as pectorals, bracelets, or bangles.

Three of the four words translated as "amulet" came from verbs meaning "to guard" or "to protect," confirming that the primary purpose of these personal ornaments was to provide magical protection, although in many instances the wearer clearly hoped to be endowed, in addition, with magical powers or capabilities. A fourth word meant essentially "well-being."

The amulet's shape, the material from which it was

AMULETS. *Various amulets*. From Aniba, Middle Kingdom through New Kingdom. (University of Pennsylvania Museum, Philadelphia. Neg. # S4–141977)

made, and its color were crucial to its meaning. Many types of material—precious metal, semiprecious stones, glazed composition (a sand core with a vitreous alkaline glaze), glass, and organic matter—were employed in the production of amulets, and most had an underlying symbolism. For example, lapis lazuli was the color of the dark blue, protective night sky; green turquoise and feldspar were like the life-bringing waters of the Nile River. Green jasper was the color of new vegetation, symbolizing new life; red jasper and carnelian were like blood, the basis of life. Gold represented the sun with all its inherent life-promoting properties and connotations of daily renewal; silver was the color of the monthly reborn moon. All those materials could be imitated by like-colored glass, glazed composition, glaze, or paint. Although a particular amulet's material might have been specified in texts, almost any material, as long as its color was appropriate to the symbolism, could be substituted.

Most provenanced amulets came from burials or were found on bodies; however, the distinction between amu-

lets for the living and funerary amulets is often problematic, since amulets worn in life for their magical properties could be taken to the tomb for use in life after death. Funerary amulets were made specifically for burials. They were placed on the corpse to give aid and protection during the perilous journey to the netherworld and to supply and supplement the requirements of the afterlife. Ancient sources provide the most information about funerary amulets. The forms of certain funerary amulets were prescribed by chapters of the *Book of Going Forth by Day* (*Book of the Dead*). In those chapters, the material to be used was stipulated, the spell to be recited was provided, the desired result was stated, and the amulet's appearance was illustrated in an accompanying vignette. The *Book of Going Forth by Day* was placed in the tomb and functioned as a funerary amulet, since its spells were aimed at helping its deceased owner reach the netherworld and obtain a comfortable life there.

Other sources of information for funerary amulets include a list from the Ptolemaic era of 104 amulets from the temple of Hathor at Dendera. These amulets were depicted without written description on a doorway of the temple's roof in the western Osiris complex. The verso of a contemporary funerary text, the MacGregor Papyrus, contains images of seventy-five amulets, usually with names. In addition, the text of a wooden tablet of New Kingdom date (now in the Berlin Museum) specifies the materials of a select group of amulets, and a Late period sheet-gold plaque (now in the British Museum) is embossed with a selection of amuletic forms.

Funerary texts usually specified where on the corpse an amulet should be placed. From the New Kingdom until later dynastic times, the exact positioning was important. Some rare diagrams on Late period papyri provided a schematic layout for the positioning of amulets on mummies, although contemporary bodies had amulets scattered over them in a random fashion. During the nineteenth century, when many mummies were unwrapped but not recorded, information about the positioning of amulets was lost. The pioneering recording work in this field by W. M. Flinders Petrie (conveniently republished in his *Amulets*, London, 1914) was restricted to mummies that were dated to the very end of dynastic times. In the latter twentieth century, however, information provided by modern X-ray techniques on still-wrapped corpses, careful documentation of new finds, and reassessment of existing evidence, constantly add to the current state of knowledge.

Amulets were worn on the body in several ways. A means of suspension or holes for attachment were not essential for funerary amulets since they were often laid on the body, but in rare instances amulets on their original stringing have survived. From the First Intermediate Period, twisted flax fibers were knotted between widely spaced amulets. Two thousand years later, this tradition of stringing survived on the chests of Roman mummies, worn in rows of well-spaced amulets, on flax threads, attached to palm-fiber frames. In all other instances, the order of restringing was arbitrary. Depictions of strings of amulets and surviving, still-strung examples show that the living wore individual amulets combined with strings of beads on either gold chains or wire.

Recognizable amulets have been dated as early as the Predynastic Badarean period, some fifteen centuries before the first dynasty. Most take the form of a living creature or part of a living creature (with the part representing the whole). Though all came from burials, they were intended to function as a magical aid to the living and were taken to the grave subsequently. Some, such as a hobbled hippopotamus made of shell and pierced to be worn upside down, were meant to work apotropaically—to ward off an evil or dangerous force by its very representation. (Throughout Egyptian history the male hippopotamus was feared for its unpredictable savagery and became linked with the demonized form of the god Seth.) Amulets of the head of a dog, bull, panther or lioness, gazelle or antelope could also have been used apotropaically, but they might have been intended to transfer the animal's particular qualities or characteristic behavior to the wearer by sympathetic magic—to confer the wild dog's swiftness or cunning, the bull's virility or strength, leonine savagery, or the desert creature's agility and speed. W. M. Flinders Petrie, in his seminal work on amulets (1914), attempted to classify into five broad categories (homopoeic, ktematic, dynatic, theophoric, and phylactic) the 275 types of amulets known to him, based on the amulet's function. He termed such examples *homopoeic*, that is, the amulets, shaped like living creatures (or their parts) with special characteristics or capabilities that their owner wished to acquire by assimilation.

The fly amulet, which first appeared in the Predynastic-period, had significance until the Third Intermediate Period, but whether it was worn apotropaically, to ward off Egypt's most prevalent pest, or to endow its wearer by sympathetic magic with its unrivaled powers of reproduction, is uncertain. A Predynastic amulet's specific function may, in most instances, only be surmised. When of New Kingdom date and made of precious metal, especially gold, a fly was considered representative of a royal award, originally for bravery in the field, perhaps for persistence in attacking the enemy, based on the insect's characteristic behavior. Other Predynastic amulets depict the reclining jackal and crouched falcon. (Although both animals represented a specific deity in dynastic times, the historical identities of Anubis and Horus are not attributable retrospectively to Predynastic amulets). Natural objects, such as shells and birds' claws, were also used amuletically in Predynastic times, and their forms were retained well into the pharaonic era, imitated in other materials.

Although only a few amulets and pieces of amuletic jewelry can be securely dated to the Early Dynastic period, the expanded range of materials and manufacturing techniques used is exemplified by a bracelet that was found in the tomb of the first dynasty pharaoh Djer at Abydos. It is comprised of alternating gold and turquoise *serekh*-beads surmounted by crouched falcons that were identified with the living king—and were presumably his protector. One of three contemporary gold amulets from a woman's burial at Naga ed-Deir in Upper Egypt was shaped like an elaterid beetle, sacred to the warlike goddess Neith of Sais; its top was also inlaid with her emblem. Although, the amulet placed its wearer under Neith's protection, it might also have been the insignia of her priestess. During the succeeding period, the Old Kingdom, a woman buried at Giza wore some fifty gold elaterids around her neck.

By the end of the Old Kingdom, the range of amuletic

types was expanded; many took the form of living creatures. The earliest firmly dated scarab (dung beetle) was made of ivory and the find was excavated in a sixth dynasty burial at Abydos. Its appearance marked the beginning of an amuletic form that was to become the most prevalent in ancient Egypt. Ancient misapprehensions about the insect's characteristic behavior—that baby beetles were spontaneously generated from a ball of dung rolled about by an adult—led to its consideration as a symbol of new life, regeneration, and resurrection. Other new forms, such as turtles, scorpions, and crocodiles, which appeared in numbers at that time, were apotropaic, worn to ward off the evil or danger they represented.

Within the history of ancient Egyptian mythology, the turtle remained a creature of darkness, waiting in the waters of the underworld to impede the nightly progress of the sun god's bark. The harmful powers of the scorpion, however, later came to be harnessed for good as the goddess Serket (who wore the venomous creature on her head), who—with Isis, Neith, and Nephthys—became an amuletic protectress of the dead, linked with the embalmed internal organs. Yet throughout dynastic times, scorpion-form amulets continued to be used apotropaically. Amulets of crocodiles, which predate the first dynasty, also exemplify this strangely ambiguous attitude. Throughout the pharaonic period, they were worn to ward off this most feared creature which, in eating its victim, denied a person the chance of an afterlife. At the same time, the crocodile was revered as the deity Sobek who, thus propitiated, in theory could do no harm. The amulet of a crowned crocodile, or of a man with a crocodile's head, represented Sobek and could be worn as a sign of the god's patronage and protection. As early as the Old Kingdom, amulets of a standing hippopotamus probably depicted the beneficent Taweret as the goddess of childbirth; a horned cow's head probably represented the goddess Hathor as the archetypal mother; and a vulture probably symbolized Nekhbet as the patroness of Upper Egypt. It is not certain that the frog was then associated with the goddess Heket who assisted Khnum at mankind's creation. Because of its apparent self-generation from mud in teeming numbers, the frog always had connotations of fertility and resurrection.

Other amulets of living creatures that first appeared in the late Old Kingdom pose greater problems of classification. Does the duckling represent a food offering to be a magical supplier of offerings not presented at the tomb? If this is its function, it would belong to Petrie's *ktematic* class (from Greek for "property") of amulets representing items connected with the funerary cult. Other amulets in this category functioned as substitutes for funerary goods taken to the tomb for use in the afterlife but which might be stolen or destroyed: they take the form of various types of jewelry, clothing, and *shawabti* servant figures. Then, too, the duckling might be interpreted as a forerunner of the duck-form amulet with head turned back as though in sleep, awaiting awakening, which symbolized resurrection. A new amulet form, one shaped like a *bolti* fish, certainly had connotations of regeneration because of its habit of hiding its young in its mouth when danger threatened, spitting them out later to reappear as though reborn. The simian-shaped amulets may have represented the vervet, guarantor of its wearer's sexuality, or they were forerunners of a sacred baboon.

The couchant hare as amulet had a long history, and was especially popular in the Late period. It is unclear, however, whether it was expected to endow its wearer with the creature's legendary speed, awareness, or fecundity, or to guarantee the same victory over death that it achieved by surviving in the inhospitable desert, death's domain. Another amulet new to the Old Kingdom, which also enjoyed its greatest popularity in the Late period, represented in its developed form, two back-to-back couchant lions. The sun rose each dawn over their backs, and the amulet would afford its owner a similar daily rebirth. Uncertain, however, is whether a single couchant lion form was intended to bestow fierceness or to afford protection.

The first animal-headed human deity as amulet occurred in the Old Kingdom as a jackal-headed man, undoubtedly Anubis, the god of mummification. Perhaps the chief embalmer as early as that time donned a jackal's mask to carry out his work and thus initiated the iconography. Like the crocodile, the black jackal was a dangerous force that had to be propitiated; since its main activity was prowling desert cemeteries for bones to crunch, and since destruction of the body prevented an afterlife, the jackal was deified as the god of embalming, assigned to protect the very corpse it would by nature attack. A new amuletic form, one of a kneeling man with a palm rib in each outstretched hand, exhibits the unchanging iconography of Heh, god of millions, bestower of eternity. The significance is unknown, however, from the considerable extant examples of human-form amulets of men, women, and children; these are distinguished by various postures and children are always identified by the characteristic pose, with a finger to the mouth.

Some of the best known, in the form of inanimate objects, made a first appearance in the Old Kingdom. Most belong to Petrie's *dynatic* category: amulets that were invested with particular powers whose use could be transferred to their wearers. Although the *ankh*, the T-shaped cross with a loop handle later adopted by the Copts (representing pictorially a sandal's tie-straps) appeared early, few amuletic examples have survived from any period of pharaonic history. The hieroglyph *ankh* was used to write the words "life," "to live," "living," and "alive." The *ankh*, however, was employed far more as an element of design, in a hieroglyphic context, and as a large scepterlike emblem carried by deities and offered to the favored.

New, too, was the *djed*-pillar amulet, in the form of the hieroglyph meaning "enduring" and "stable," originally representing a stylized tree trunk with lopped-off branches. It was associated first with Sokar, funerary god of Saqqara (near Memphis), and later with Ptah, the creator god of Memphis. It was already becoming linked with Osiris, the god of the dead during that time, and henceforth represented his backbone with ribs. Once it became a prescribed funerary amulet in the early New Kingdom, chapter 155 of the *Book of Going Forth by Day* associated it solely with Osiris. Although its specified material was gold, most examples of this form were made of green or blue materials having regenerative connotations.

The *wedjat* ("sound one") also made its first appearance in the Old Kingdom; it took the form of the eye of the falcon sky god Horus. The Eye of Horus was considered the most powerful of protective amulets. Abundant examples with many variant forms and materials have survived from all subsequent dynastic periods. Its basic shape resembles a human eye with eyebrow, but beneath the eye it has a drop and a curl, markings of the lanner falcon (*Falco biarmicus*). It is usually considered to represent the left "lunar" eye, plucked out by Seth and restored to Horus by Thoth—a reference to the moon being "injured" as it wanes and "restored" as it waxes each month. Yet the term might also apply to the right "solar" eye that was never injured; interestingly, right *wedjat* amulets also exist.

During the First Intermediate Period, the number and range of amuletic forms noticeably increased. A new category of funerary amulets that represented royal regalia and divine emblems, once only of use to royalty in the life after death, became available to everyone as a result of the democratization of funerary beliefs and practices already in evidence. Henceforth, any burial might have contained amulets of the most royal of all protective creatures, the human-headed, lion-bodied sphinx. Other examples include the Red Crown or Double Crown; the vulture and cobra, emblems of Upper and Lower Egypt respectively; and the *uraeus* (upreared cobra), solar protector of royalty, which in life was worn only by the pharaoh. Other forms of amulet that fall within Petrie's dynatic classification were not added to the repertory for commoners until the Late period. Examples include the royal beard and headdress, the White Crown, and the crook and flail; some divine emblems, such as the animal-headed *was*-scepter, bestower of dominion; the cord-formed *shen*, which granted solar protection; the tall feather plumes, emblem of divine majesty; and cosmic forms, such as the sun and moon, symbolic of a celestial afterlife to which only the pharaoh once had access.

Unique to the First Intermediate Period was a category of funerary amulet in the shape of various parts of the human anatomy. These were intended to bestow their particular functions and capabilities on their dead owner and physically substitute for those bodily parts should they be damaged or destroyed. The hand, fist, or arm with fist would endow their wearer with manual dexterity and the capability for forceful action; the leg with foot would bestow the power of movement; the eye would give sight; and the face would provide the use of the senses in general. Perhaps most of them came to be considered inessential later because improvements in mummification methods made limbs less likely to become detached or injured. Body-part amulets demonstrate the problem of attempted classification into only five broad categories; their function is essentially homopoeic, but by providing a substitution, they are ktematic.

During the Middle Kingdom, the range of amuletic types widened, although some were to prove not only characteristic of, but virtually exclusive to, the period. Curiously, most were intended for use by women. Such is the case for the protective cylinder amulet, whether solid or of hollow precious metal, and for the amulet shaped like an oyster shell, also frequently of precious metal, which guaranteed the wearer's good health—and whose name (*wedja*) came to be one of the generic words for an amulet. Although actual cowrie shells were worn amuletically far earlier, only in the Middle Kingdom were they made of precious metals or semiprecious stones and strung as girdle elements, intended to ward off harm from the female genitalia they were thought to resemble. (The New Kingdom development of the shape is so unlike the original as to be termed "wallet-bead.") The bird's claw, too, was imitated during the Middle Kingdom in inlaid precious metal or in semiprecious stone, and this amulet was attached to anklets to bestow swiftness and grace to a dancer's steps. Cloisonné-work clasps that spelled hieroglyphic good wishes to their royal wearers are found only during the Middle Kingdom. Exceptionally, a typical Middle Kingdom form, the hunched, squatting female human-headed sphinx (the proto-*ba*) of amethyst or turquoise was developed by the end of the New Kingdom into a seated cat whose human female head sported the stranded hairstyle characteristic of Nubia, which has been linked with childbirth and nursing. Virtually unique to the Middle Kingdom as an amulet, although commonplace throughout dynastic times as a protective decorative element, is the *s3* (used as hieroglyph to write the word "protection"); it is shaped like the reed protector worn as a life jacket by marsh dwellers.

Scarabs appeared in increasing numbers during the Middle Kingdom, and their amuletic properties were enhanced by texts and decorative images on their undersides, although some examples were employed as seals and were inscribed with the name and titles of their owner. Often the scarab seal acted as the bezel of a finger ring and was attached to the ring's shank so that it could revolve. During the New Kingdom, when scarabs as seals were superseded by metal signet rings, their amuletic function became all-important once more. The range of decoration on the underside of the scarab was enormous, from religious and royal scenes, texts, mottoes, and good luck signs to geometric and floral patterns and cryptography. Exactly contemporary with fully developed scarab amulets, and having an identical function were the scaraboids. Those forms have the same flat, oval, decorated underside, but instead of the insect's body, the back takes the shape of almost any living creature, often in multiples. These carved in high relief or free standing included kneeling antelopes, reclining lions, standing hedgehogs, recumbent ducks, reclining hippopotami, crocodiles back to back, *bolti* fish, baboons, and monkeys. A deviant form is the cowroid, a scaraboid with an elongated base and a back that resembles a stylized cowrie shell.

One particular form of scarab, the heart scarab, was to become the funerary amulet *par excellence*, so-called because it was made solely to be placed over the mummy's heart. Ideally shaped from a specified (but unidentified) green stone, its underside bore the heart scarab formula (chapter 30B of the *Book of Going Forth by Day*). Its function was to bind the heart to silence while it was being weighed in the underworld, so as to ascertain its deceased owner's worthiness to enter the Egyptian version of paradise. The heart was weighed and left in place during mummification (as the only internal organ to remain in the body) because it was believed to be the seat of intelligence, the originator of all feelings and actions, and the storehouse of memory. Consequently, four chapters of the *Book of Going Forth by Day* were concerned with preventing the deceased from being deprived of the heart in the afterlife. Heart-shaped amulets (substitutes for the organ should the unthinkable occur) were occasionally inscribed with the heart scarab formula. The earliest were contemporary with their first depiction as a prescribed funerary amulet in early New Kingdom books of *Going Forth by Day* and were made only of materials with regenerative symbolism or with connotations of eternity. Their characteristic shape resembled a pot with a neck and two lug handles, rather than the organ in question, but their ability to represent the very essence of their owner was demonstrated by forms with human heads. The earliest dated heart scarab bearing chapter 30B belonged to Nebankh, a thirteenth dynasty official of Sobekhotpe IV. It predates the earliest royal example to survive, which belonged to the seventeenth dynasty pharaoh Sobkemsaf II by more than a century. Generally, such innovations appeared among nonroyalty only after an earlier introduction for royalty.

Royal heart scarabs of the New Kingdom and later were frequently incorporated into a pectoral and supplied with inlaid wings, an acknowledgment that the dung beetle could fly and a visualization of the concept of resurrection. For commoners in the Late period, the same imagery was conveyed by a large flat-based winged scarab of glazed composition used for stitching to the mummy wrappings or for incorporation into the bead netting that enveloped contemporary mummies. A less well-known type of Late period funerary scarab has relief legs clasped to a highly convex belly that was pierced or had a loop for attachment to mummy wrappings. Sometimes the insect's head was replaced by that of a ram, falcon, or bull—presumably having connotations of solar rebirth.

Another prescribed New Kingdom funerary amulet was the *tyet* or Girdle of Isis, representing an open loop of cloth with a bound lower end and a long hanging sash that is flanked by two folded loops. Its specified material was red jasper, the color of the goddess's blood, and it conferred her protection. Papyrus exemplified green vegetation (considered symbolic of new life) and as the *wadj*, or papyrus scepter, it became another example of prescribed funerary amulets. Made predominantly of green material, it occurred first in the eighteenth dynasty; some Late period examples had two plants carved side by side on a plaque.

Surprisingly few amulets of deities, whether in human, animal-headed, or sacred animal form, predate the New Kingdom. Even then, the number of examples was not great and the repertory remains restricted. By far the most popular forms were the minor household deities connected with birth who would help with rebirth in the afterlife. The goddess Taweret—a composite of a hippopotamus with fearsome teeth, always in upright posture but with the pendulous breasts and swollen stomach of a pregnant woman, and with a crocodile's tail—aided woman in childbirth. Her attendant Bes was a good-natured genie, who warded off evil influences at the moment of birth by noisy music-making or by wielding a knife. This dwarflike deity had a lion's mane surrounding leonine features, a lion's tail, and bandy legs and was usually depicted naked, except for tall plumes on his head. During the New Kingdom, the major deities as amulets were the falcon-form sun god, Isis suckling Horus, Hathor as cow, Thoth as baboon, the ram-headed creator Khnum, and a divine child (Horus or the infant sun). Unique to the Ramessid period was an amulet depicting the god Seth with a long curved snout and tall squared-off ears. Although patron of the Ramessid pharaohs, his amuletic form would only be worn in life as a sign of devotion; in the afterlife, Osiris was king. After his demonization, in the Late period, amulets

AMULETS. *Bronze amulet*. The form is an Oxyrhynchus fish, Ptolemaic period, fourth century BCE. (University of Pennsylvania Museum, Philadelphia, Neg. # S8–61855)

were made showing Seth in hippopotamus form being harpooned by Horus, thus protecting the owner against evil.

From the end of the New Kingdom, amulets of deities became numerous and more diverse in subject. Most of the great gods and goddesses and their animal manifestations, as well as some obscure deities were represented during this time. Examples of those in completely human form were Amun-Re, king of the gods; Ptah, the Memphite creator; the lotus god Nefertum; Shu, god of air; Maat, goddess of cosmic order; Hathor with cow's horns and disk; and Mut, Amun-Re's wife, first appeared early in the Third Intermediate Period, as did Hatmehit, the local goddess of Mendes who wears a fish on her head. Not until the twenty-sixth dynasty, however, were there amulets that depicted the ancient war goddess Neith; the Theban lunar god Khonsu; Imhotep, the deified architect of the Step Pyramid at Saqqara; and the local hunter god Inhert. Amulets of the Apis bull, Ptah's earthly animal manifestation, were, surprisingly, introduced at that late date.

Numerous falcon-headed deities first occurred as amulets during the Third Intermediate Period. Such were Horus of Edfu, Horus-the-Elder, Horus, son of Osiris, the Theban war god Montu, and a secondary form of lunar Khnosu. More obscure amuletic deities for this period were the snake-headed Nehebkau who symbolized invincible living power, and Mayhes, the only lion god who appeared as amulet. Maned, lion-headed goddesses, however, were particularly popular during the Third Intermediate Period. Those included Bastet, patroness of the Libyan dynasties; Sekhmet, symbolizing the destroying heat of the sun; Tefnut of Heliopolis; Wadjyt, protectress of Lower Egypt; and local deities, such as Mehyt and Pakhet. It was also usually a lion goddess's head which surmounted the broad collar of the protective *aegis* amulet. Amulets of Bastet as a cat were proliferate. Petrie had classified all amulets of deities as theophoric (better theomorphic), but in function most can be allotted to his phylactic (protective) category or to his homopoeic category, for the wearer wished to assimilate the deity's particular powers or characteristics.

First occuring in the Third Intermediate Period and characteristic of it, were amulets of the Four Sons of Horus, the canopic deities who guarded the embalmed internal organs. At that time, a change in mummification practices caused the canopic packages to be returned to the body cavity, each with an amulet of the relevant deity attached, shown full length and mummiform. Even when the packages were placed in canopic jars, an amuletic set containing falcon-headed Kebehsenuef, baboon-headed Hapy, human-headed Imsety, and jackal-headed Duamutef would still be supplied for stitching to the mummy wrappings or for incorporation into the bead netting that enveloped contemporary mummies.

During the Saite period, funerary amulets were used in significantly increased number and form. Types which had previously been found only in royal burials were now made available to all. The *weres*-amulet, in the shape of a headrest, the preferred support for the head during sleep and usually made from hematite, became characteristic of Late period burials. Its primary purpose was to raise the deceased's head magically in resurrection, just as the sun was raised over the eastern horizon each dawn. The *pss-kf* amulet with a bifurcated end was used in the Opening of the Mouth ceremony, which reincorporated the spirit into the corpse on the day of burial. It reappeared in the New Kingdom form at this time. The carnelian or red jasper snake's head, which protected the dead against snake bites and gave refreshment to the throat, was manufactured only for royalty and the highest officials during the New Kingdom.

New forms were invented during the Saite period, perhaps to fill a perceived lack. The two-fingers amulet, always of a dark material (obsidian or black glass), perhaps represented the index finger and the second digit of the embalmer, and was invariably found near the embalming wound. It might have been intended to confirm the embalming process or to give protection to the most vulnerable area of the corpse. Amulets in the form of the carpenter's set, square, and plummet, which bestowed eternal rectitude and everlasting equilibrium; the writing tablet amulet, which gave access to magical formulas; and the *sma*-sign, which represented an animal's lungs and windpipe, symbolizing unification, were unique to the period. These examples belong to Petrie's *dynatic* category but are representative of a state or condition that the owner wished to enjoy in the afterlife.

The amuletic form of the triad of the Osirian holy family—comprised of Isis and Nephthys flanking the child Horus—has not been dated earlier than the Saite period. Always made of glazed composition, the figures are almost invariably shown in frontal raised relief against a plaque. The goddesses would bestow to the deceased the same protection that they afforded their dead brother Osiris and his infant son Horus. It is noteworthy that amulets of the god of the dead continued to be extremely few in number. Earlier, Osiris was depicted only as a pectoral element in the company of family deities. Most of the tiny

bronzes of Late period date that characteristically depict him in mummiform not only have suspension loops but also show tangs below the feet and were not intended to be worn as a personal ornament.

[*See also* Jewelry; *and* Symbols.]

### BIBLIOGRAPHY

Andrews, Carol. *Amulets of Ancient Egypt*. London, 1994. The most up-to-date, comprehensive account of the subject; fully illustrated from the large and mostly unpublished collection of the British Museum's Egyptian Department.

Müller-Winkler, C. *Die Ägyptischen Objekt-Amulette*. Orbis Biblicus et Orientalis, Series Archaeologica, 5. Freiburg, 1987. A comprehensive listing of all published examples of amulets of inanimate form; their materials and dimensions are tabulated, their stylistic development noted, and their dating discussed. An illustrated catalog of the Freiburg University collection of such amulets is included.

Petrie, W. M. Flinders. *Amulets*. London, 1914. The seminal work on the subject; his general classification system remains usable and his illustrations of the positioning of amulets on twenty-four Late period mummies is of great value. The chief drawback is that it predates most of the site reports that are sources for well-dated and closely identified examples. (For example, Tutankhamun's treasures and the royal burials of Tanis were unknown to Petrie.)

Reisner, G. A. *Amulets (Catalogue général des Antiquités égyptiennes du Musée du Caire)*. 2 vols. Cairo, 1907/1958. Photographs and line drawings show many of the objects, but the text has minimal catalog entries.

CAROL A. R. ANDREWS

**AMUN AND AMUN-RE.** The god Amun, who later became Amun-Re, was the focus of the most complex theological system of ancient Egypt. In his developed form, Amun-Re combined within himself the two opposite realities of divinity—the hidden and the revealed. The name Amun (Eg., *Imn*) indicated his essential being, for its meaning was "the hidden one" or "the secret one." According to myth, his true name was unknown, thus indicating his unknowable essence. This imperceptibility owed to the absolute otherness or holiness of the deity, and it attested that he was totally different from all other beings and transcendent of the created universe. The second element in his name, *Re*, was the common Egyptian term for "the sun." In this *Re* element, which was also the name of the sun god of Heliopolis, Amun was revealed—thus, Amun-Re.

Amun was known at an early date, since a few references in the Pyramid Texts (from the Old Kingdom) attest to his antiquity. Although those references are scanty, they show him as a primeval deity, a symbol of the creative force. Amun was also known as one of the eight Heh gods of the Ogdoad of Hermopolis, where he was paired with his original spouse, Amaunet, as a symbol of hiddenness and mystery. Since he was an element in the Hermopolitan Ogdoad, that might indicate Hermopolis as his place

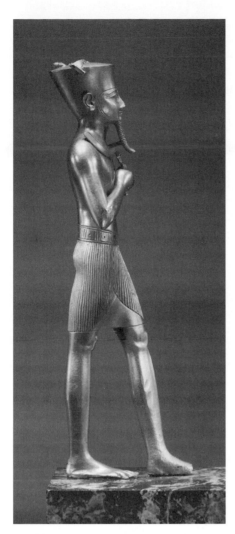

AMUN AND AMUN-RE. *The Gold Amun, twenty-second dynasty.* This solid-gold statue of the solar god Amun is an extremely rare example of ancient Egyptian precious statuary. Found in Karnak, it may have been a part of the royal offerings to the temple. (The Metropolitan Museum of Art, Gift of Edward S. Harkness, 1926. [26.7.1412])

of origin, although another possibility makes him an ancient deity of the area around Thebes. It was at Thebes that Amun's power developed, although he was, at first, less important than Montu, the war deity and the original chief god of the city. As the power of Thebes grew during the latter decades of the First Intermediate Period, Amun grew along with it. Even at that early date, Amun's nature tended toward syncretism, and the name Amun-Re appeared on a stela erected by the governor Intef of Thebes before 2000 BCE. Amun's growth was accelerated when Amenemhet I seized power in Thebes and founded the twelfth dynasty in 1991 BCE.

The hidden aspect of Amun enabled him to be easily syncretized and associated with other deities. Amun was identified with Montu and he soon replaced Montu as protector of Thebes. As the power of Thebes increased, Amun's identification with Re became more pronounced. That identification was probably encouraged by the moving of Egypt's capital from Thebes to Itjtawy, at the apex of the Nile Delta, under Amenemhet I (r.1991–1962 BCE). Amun and Re were thereby placed in closer contact, and a syncretism of the two would have been very astute, both theologically and politically. The syncretism did not imply the absorption of one deity by the other; nor did it imply the creation of yet another god. Amun and Re still remained as separate hypostatic deities, but their syncretism was an expression of the unity of divine power. Associations with other deities were also found, and Amun soon came to bear such designations as Amun-Re-Atum, Amun-Re-Montu, Amun-Re-Horakhty, and Min-Amun.

In the middle of the sixteenth century BCE, the expulsion of the Hyksos as rulers, provided an impetus to Amun's growth, for that event was a vindication of both Egyptian power and Amun-Re. Temples to him were erected throughout Egypt, the two most significant being that in the heart of ancient Thebes, present-day Luxor, and the Great Temple at Karnak, the major shrine of Amun-Re, on the outskirts of the present city. The importance of those shrines is evident in the extravagant manner in which they were enlarged and enriched over the centuries by rulers of Egypt who were eager to express their devotion to Amun-Re, who had become the state god. At Thebes, the annual Opet festival was celebrated in his honor. During the Opet festival, the statue of Amun was conveyed by boat from the Karnak temple to that at Luxor. The festival was a celebration of Amun's marriage to Mut in his aspect of *Ka-mut-ef* (*K3 mwt.f*; "bull of his mother")—a recognition of his procreative function—but it was also the festival of the Egyptian state, for Amun-Re had become the protecting deity of Egypt and the monarchy. During the New Kingdom, Amun-Re received the title of "king of the gods," and the growth of the empire transformed him into a universal deity. By the twenty-fifth (Nubian) dynasty, Amun-Re was even chief god of the Nubian kingdom of Napata.

The might of Amun-Re and the strength of the royal throne were not seen as competing powers. Essentially, they were two sides of the same coin: the monarchy supporting Amun-Re, and the god being the mainstay of royal power. Such interdependence of state and religion was underscored by the official mythology that made Amun-Re the physical father of the pharaoh. According to myth, Amun-Re could take the form of the ruling monarch to impregnate the chief royal wife with his successor—a tradition first recorded in New Kingdom times, under Hatshepsut, but most probably was more ancient. Furthermore, according to official state theology, Egypt was ruled by Amun-Re through the pharaoh, with the god revealing his will through oracles. Amun-Re was concerned with the maintenance of *maat* (*mȝ't*; "truth," "justice," "goodness"), not only on the wider scale but even at the level of the individual. He became the champion of the poor and a focus of personal piety. The magnitude of Amun-Re's spiritual and political power helped transform ancient Egypt into a theocracy, and his priesthood became one of the largest and most influential. That situation was beneficial both to the political powers and to the spiritual power for as long as each supported the other. At times, however, conflict arose, as happened during the eighteenth dynasty reign of Amenhotpe IV (Akhenaten). The most obvious proof of the political power of Amun-Re and his temple was the emergence of the Theban priest-kings during the twenty-first dynasty.

Amun-Re was the Egyptian creator deity *par excellence*. His association with the air as an invisible force facilitated his development as supreme creator. According to Egyptian myth and theology, he was self-created, thus without mother or father. His creative role, stressed during the Middle Kingdom (and even as early as the Pyramid Texts of the Old Kingdom), developed fully during the New Kingdom, when he became the greatest expression of a transcendent creator ever known in Egyptian theology. He was not immanent within creation, and creation was not an extension of himself. He remained apart from his creation, totally different from it, and fully independent of it. As with the creator deity of the Hebrew scriptures, Amun-Re carried out his creative action in virtue of his supreme power; he did not physically engender the universe, as had happened in the creation myth of Re-Atum at Heliopolis.

During the New Kingdom, the theology of Amun-Re at Thebes became very complex. His position as king of the gods increased to a point that approached monotheism. In Amun-Re's most advanced theological expressions, the other gods became symbols of his power or manifestations of him—he himself being the one and only supreme divine power. This absolute supremacy of Amun-Re was eloquently expressed in the sun hymns found in the eighteenth dynasty tombs at Thebes. As Amun, he was secret, hidden, and mysterious; but as Re, he was visible and revealed. Although for centuries Egyptian religion had been flexible and open to contradictory mythological expressions, the Theban theology of Amun-Re came close to establishing a standard of orthodoxy in doctrine.

Although the daily ritual in the temple of Amun-Re was essential for the maintenance of political and universal order, elaborate public rituals occurred only at the great festivals, when the focus was on the revelation of the god in the cult statue. His temple was not the gathering place for common worship but, rather, the abode of the god and the point of contact between the divine realm and this world. The daily cult was celebrated as a mystery, within the temple, although this did not imply that its rituals were totally unknown. The performance of the daily ritual was a necessity, for by means of it the deity was imbued with new life, purified, anointed, clothed, and presented with the figure of the goddess Maat as a symbol of universal order; the performance of those rituals constituted an assurance that the cosmic and political orders would endure. An essential component of the ritual was the chanting of hymns to Amun-Re, for not only did they express the theology of the deity but their articulation was also an actualization of their content. Theoretically, it was the pharaoh who conducted the rituals, but for practical reasons their performance was delegated to the priesthood.

Like many gods, Amun was frequently expressed in association with a triad. The triad at Thebes was Amun, his spouse Mut, and their son Khons, a moon god. (Mut was originally a vulture goddess of Thebes, who replaced Amun's first spouse, Amaunet, after Amun came to power.) The sacred animal of Amun had originally been the goose and, like Geb, he was sometimes known as the "Great Cackler." The ram, as a symbol of fertility, later became the major theriomorphic symbol of Amun, and the goose symbol was suppressed. Yet Amun was always portrayed in anthropomorphic form, never as a ram or as a man with a ram's head. His association with fertility was symbolized by statues of him with an erect penis. When depicted as king of the gods, Amun-Re was usually shown as wearing a crown of two plumes, a symbol borrowed from Min of Coptos.

With the possible exception of Osiris, Amun-Re is the most widely documented of all Egyptian deities. His textual materials and iconography are too numerous to list, and the wide variety of sun hymns and theological texts have provided ample material for the exposition of his nature and function.

[*See also* Hymns, *article on* Solar Hymns.]

**BIBLIOGRAPHY**

Allen, James P. *Genesis in Egypt: The Philosophy of Ancient Egyptian Creation Accounts.* Yale Egyptological Studies, 2. New Haven, 1988. Pages 48–55 are valuable for an insight into the theology of Amun in his aspect as creator, the author translates and comments on a number of key passages from Papyrus Leiden I 350.

Assmann, Jon. *Egyptian Solar Religion in the New Kingdom.* Translated from German by Anthony Alcock. London, New York, 1995. (Original *Re und Amun*, Freiburg, 1983.) Contains a wealth of very valuable information and theological insights into the nature of Amun-Re.

David, A. Rosalie. *Religious Ritual at Abydos (c.1300 B.C.)* Warminster, 1973.

David, A. Rosalie. *The Ancient Egyptian: Religious Beliefs and Practices.* London and Boston, 1982. A general work on Egyptian religion, but pages 120–171 concentrate on the New Kingdom and on Amun-Re; a fine introduction to the religion and myth of Egypt.

Hornung, Erik. *Conceptions of God in Ancient Egypt: The One and the Many.* Translated from German by John Baines. London, 1983. Materials on Amun and Amun-Re are incorporated at a number of points; more important, the book provides a fine insight into the Egyptian concept of gods and divinity.

Kemp, Barry J. *Ancient Egypt: Anatomy of a Civilization.* London and New York, 1989. A book of very wide scope, containing some excellent material devoted to Amun-Re and his rituals.

Lalouette, Claire. *Thèbes ou la naissance d'un Empire.* Paris, 1986. Although concerned mainly with the history of the Theban state, important materials are provided for placing Amun-Re in his historical context.

Lichtheim, Miriam. *Ancient Egyptian Literature: A Book of Readings.* 2 vols. Berkeley, 1976. Volume II contains translations of several important hymns and prayers to Amun-Re, including the famous hymn of Suti and Hor dating from the eighteenth dynasty.

Morenz, Siegfried. *Egyptian Religion.* Translated from German by Ann E. Keep. Ithaca, 1973. Contains numerous references to Amun and Amun-Re; valuable for an understanding of the god within the wider context of the Egyptian religious system.

Moret, Alexandre. *Le Rituel du culte divin journalier en Égypte d'après les papyrus de Berlin et les textes du tempte de Séti 1er à Abydos.* Geneva, 1988. A reprint; although written at the beginning of the twentieth century, and available only in French, very useful for its ritual texts and line drawings, especially texts from the temple of Sety I at Abydos.

Otto, Eberhard. *Ancient Egyptian Art: The Cults of Osiris and Amon.* Translated from German by Kate Bosse-Griffiths. New York, 1967. An excellent study of the cults of the two deities.

Redford, Donald B. *Akhenaten: The Heretic King.* Princeton, 1984. Very useful for an understanding of the conflict between the religion of Amun-Re and the religion of the Aten, as promulgated by Akhenaten. Although ill-disposed toward Akhenaten and regarding his movement a heresy, the author is very informative and the book contains a wealth of information.

Wainwright, Gerald A. "Some Aspects of Amun." *Journal of Egyptian Archaeology* 20 (1934), 139–153.

Watterson, Barbara. *The Gods of Ancient Egypt.* New York, 1984. Contains a brief chapter that very clearly outlines the historical development of Amun-Re; a very good account for the general reader.

VINCENT ARIEH TOBIN

**ANATOLIA.** *See* Hittites; *and* Mediterranean Area.

**ANCESTOR CULTS.** *See* Cults, *article on* Private Cults.

**ANCIENT HISTORIANS.** The earliest extant classical writer to mention Egypt is the Greek epic poet Homer. He says little, but his comments had a considerable effect in orienting interest and confirming attitudes: Egypt is a rich and distant land, full of marvels which are sometimes of enormous size, and it is associated with wisdom and scientific expertise—all qualities destined to play a major part in developing the image of Egypt in subsequent literature. Epic writers of the Hesiodic school also contributed to the tradition through their accounts of such legends as the conflict of Danaus and Aegyptus. More practical concerns appeared in the *periploi*, a genre of navigation texts, literally "voyages around the coast," that provided information, sometimes fanciful, on the geography of Mediterranean lands and beyond, including Egypt.

Hecataeus of Miletus (born in the late sixth century BCE) marked a major advance both in developing the legendary record on Egypt and in geography, producing two major studies: the *Genealogies* and the *Periodos gēs* ("Circuit of the Earth"). The first attempted to bring coherence into Greek mythological and legendary traditions, whereas the second was a geographical survey in which cartography, ethnography, botany, and a variety of "marvels" were discussed. Both survive only in fragments or summaries which reflect the interests of the exceptors and therefore give a very partial view of the originals, but they were certainly quarried by numerous later authors.

The fifth-century BCE Greek historian Herodotus provides the consummation of all earlier efforts. In books II and III of his *History of the Persian War,* he offers a vivid account of Egypt. His portrayal of the customs and achievements of the Egyptians is dominated by a perception of their radical difference from other nations. This attitude leads him to focus on a wide range of features: shipping, the status of women, weaving, urinating and defecation, religious practice, priestly organization, care for the elderly, mourning rituals, mortuary practice, food and food preparation, kneading of mud/clay, circumcision, writing, medicine, prophecy, marriage customs, oil production, class structure, and methods of coping with mosquitoes. Although the strangeness of Egypt dominates much of his thinking, another strong element is the belief in the cultural dependence of Greece on Egypt; for example, he claims that the Greeks owe to Egypt their religion, the calendar, sculpture, geometry, and the laws of Solon. In the account of Egyptian history (II, 99 ff: III, 1–66 ff.) we encounter a parallel phenomenon in that the rulers discussed operate in a very alien environment but do not inhabit anything approaching an Egyptian moral and intellectual universe: Amasis (III, 39–43) expresses impeccably Greek sentiments, and Psamtik I and Necho II betray a striking, if implausible, Hellenic spirit of inquiry.

With Hecataeus of Abdera (late fourth century BCE), the idealizing view of Egyptian civilization begins to assert itself strongly. He produced a highly influential *History of Egypt,* now lost, but in evaluating its impact we must remember that he was preeminently a philosopher. As in his work *On the Hyperboreans,* he was concerned to produce a picture of the ideal society and state, and his agenda was determined by such works as the *Republic* of Plato and the many philosophically oriented studies of kingship in vogue from the fourth century BCE onward. Therefore, Hecataeus used what he saw and knew of Egypt as raw material to serve a philosophical purpose and not to provide an accurate record of Egypt's past or present. The capacity of this work to mislead must have been considerable and has not always been recognized, either by ancient or by modern writers.

Manetho of Sebennytus, approximately contemporary with Hecataeus, was a very different phenomenon: he was an Egyptian high priest who achieved high status in the Alexandrian court during the early Ptolemaic period (late fourth century–early third century BCE). Deeply versed in traditional learning, he wrote a number of works, the most influential of which was a history of Egypt in Greek in three books, produced at the instigation of Ptolemy II. This compilation began with the dynasties of the gods and ended with the thirtieth dynasty, though an account of the thirty-first dynasty was subsequently added by another hand. The original is lost, but we have examples of its use as the chronological framework for Egyptian history in early Christian writers such as Africanus and Eusebius. There are also a very few quotations, like that in Josephus' *Contra Apionem* describing the Hyksos invasion of Egypt. Manetho evidently used Egyptian documentation and with its aid produced a chronology that continues to underpin our perceptions of Egyptian history, despite the corruption of his tradition and its manifest methodological deficiencies. For Greek-speakers who cared to look, he provided access to native Egyptian material, though sadly they usually preferred more exciting and less accurate books.

Chronologically, the next extant author to deal with Egypt is Polybius (c.200–118 BCE). One of the greatest of ancient historians, he explored the rise of Rome in his *Histories* and in the process provided invaluable information on the earlier history of the Ptolemaic dynasty. However, it is Diodorus Siculus (first century BCE) who continued the broad Herodotean perspective on pharaonic Egypt. He wrote a world history entitled the *Historical Library* in forty books, of which only fifteen survive intact. His chronological framework derives from Apollodorus (second century BCE), and he then builds up his narrative of periods or events by taking one or two major sources and supplementing them, as appropriate, from other material. Book I is largely devoted to Egypt, covering religion, Egyptian colonies (all unhistorical), geography (particularly the Nile), botany, zoology, history, kingship, administration, manners and customs, and famous Greeks who were alleged to have visited Egypt. His authorities have been much discussed. Hecataeus of Abdera and Agatharcides were once widely held to be the major sources, but more recent research suggests a more complex picture, and we must make allowance for the possible direct or indirect influence of, for example, Hellanicus, Herodotus, Manetho, Eudoxus, and Posidonius. The idealizing tendencies of Hecataeus of Abdera and Helle-

nistic theorists are certainly much in evidence, and Herodotus's ideas on cultural diffusion from Egypt are taken much further, as are contrasts with Greek practice. Outside Book I, Diodorus has much to say on fifth- and fourth-century Egyptian history, for which his main source was Ephorus (c.405–330 BCE). Here, as elsewhere, Diodorus emerges as a third-rate historian, and his intellectual deficiencies are aggravated by the rhetorical, moralistic, and sensationalist tendencies of Hellenistic historiography, as well as by considerable chronological ineptitude. He must, therefore, always be used with caution, and only after careful appraisal of his data. Nevertheless, he does preserve good information, and, since for fifth- and fourth-century Egyptian history he is sometimes the only consecutive narrative we have, he cannot be ignored.

With Strabo, who was born in Asia Minor around 64 BCE, we are back in the world of the *periplous*. He visited Egypt in the company of the Roman imperial prefect Aelius Gallus about 25 BCE. His one surviving work, the *Geographika*, is a *periplous* in seventeen books, of which the first section of book XVII is devoted to Egypt. He discusses the Nile, the organization, manners, and customs of the country, economy, geography, Alexandria, the history of the Ptolemies to the Roman conquest, and a wealth of sites which give him many opportunities for comment on botany, zoology, and all the other topics traditionally covered by writers on Egypt. Strabo's value to the Egyptologist lies in his descriptions of localities and ethnography, particularly since he sometimes describes sites that are wholly or partly irrecoverable; for example, his account of Alexandria is the starting point for all major reconstructions of the city.

In the first century CE, another Egyptian succeeded in making his mark at the highest level; Chaeremon, who was a tutor of Emperor Nero, is mentioned by Josephus in the same breath as Manetho. He was a Stoic philosopher who also features as a *hierogrammateus* ("lector-priest"), and he wrote a work on hieroglyphs as well as a *History of Egypt*. Although he was well placed to gain good information on Egypt's past, the signs are that this work was a Stoic counterpart of the history of Hecataeus of Abdera.

Plutarch of Chaeronea (c.50–c.120 CE) was a polymath with an enormous range of interests. His best-known work on Egypt is *De Iside et Osiride*, a Hellenized narrative in Greek (although always cited with the Latin title) of the myth of Osiris and Isis, which forms the only detailed consecutive account of the myth extant in any language. For this work he drew on many writers varying greatly in date and value, including Hellanicus, Manetho, Hecataeus of Abdera, and Eudoxus, as well as Egyptian sources, though he did not know Egyptian. Platonic and Stoic influence is unmistakable, and there is equally clear evidence of misinterpretation based on the assumptions that foreign deities were really Greek gods in disguise, and that Egyptian myths and rituals could be interpreted to reveal underlying truths of relevance to the Greeks. The result is a monograph that is not entirely reliable, but, used in conjunction with Egyptian data, much can be gained from it. In addition to *De Iside et Osiride*, we should also mention Plutarch's *Parallel Lives*, in particular the *Life of Agesilaus*. These can provide valuable thumbnail sketches of individuals or events important in late Egyptian history, and they also offer a control on Diodorus Siculus, who frequently deals with the same events. The moralistic focus of the *Lives* and the lack of interest in chronological niceties mean that they are not as valuable as they might be expected to be.

Among later pagan Greek writers, "Horapollo" is perhaps the most interesting. He is supposed to have written a work in Egyptian entitled *Hieroglyphica*, which was then translated into Greek by someone called Philip. This claim, like Horapollo himself, is almost certainly fictitious. The author of the *Hieroglyphica* was probably a Greek who knew something of the script and wrote about it from a Neoplatonist point of view, arguing that the signs were symbols of ideas and gave the key to ultimate reality. While the work contains some accurate information, its views did great damage in pointing the early decipherers of hieroglyphs in quite the wrong direction.

Pagan Latin writers infrequently added information not found in extant Greek sources, but their attitudes and subject matter are very much a continuation of Greek preoccupations. Thus, Pomponius Mela (early first century CE) produced a *periplous* including Egypt which is little more than a scholarly exercise; Pliny (23–79 CE) refers frequently to aspects of Egypt in his *Naturalis Historia*; Apuleius (born c.125 CE) incorporated a heavily hellenized account of the rites of Isis at Cenchreae in book XI of his novel *Metamorphoses*; and Ammianus Marcellinus (c.330–395 CE) provides a somewhat unreliable description of Egypt and the Egyptians in book XXII of his history of the late Roman Empire, as well as incidental comments elsewhere.

The conversion of the classical world to Christianity saw no waning of interest in Egypt, but the focus of attention shifts to two main issues: first, authors like Eusebius devote much effort to chronology in an attempt to correlate biblical history with that of the pagan world, and in the process they report much of value on Egyptian history; second, many writers—such as Clement of Alexandria, Dio Chrysostom, Porphyry, and Lactantius—discuss aspects of Egyptian religion against the background of Christianity, frequently with some distaste. With their work the ancient tradition on Egypt concludes.

The classical tradition shows little understanding of the ethos of Egyptian civilization and is distorted by fundamental errors that continue to mislead, but it did preserve much good information on externals and kept knowledge of pharaonic culture alive until Egyptian texts again became accessible during the nineteenth century.

[*See also* Herodotus; Manetho; *and* Plutarch.]

## BIBLIOGRAPHY

Ball, J. *Egypt in the Classical Geographers.* Cairo, 1942. A useful key to the material, but lacking in penetration.

Burton, Anne. *Diodorus Siculus Book I: A Commentary.* Études préliminaires aux religions orientales dans l'empire romain, 29. Leiden, 1972. The introduction comments well on sources and methods. The commentary is useful but variable.

Drews, R. *The Greek Accounts of Eastern History.* Washington, D.C., 1973. Much perceptive comment on Herodotus, but his predecessors are also well discussed.

Froidefond, C. *Le Mirage égyptien dans la littérature grecque d'Homère à Aristote.* Publications universitaires des lettres et sciences humaines d'Aix-en-Provence. Aix-en-Provence, 1971. A brilliant examination of the development of the Greek tradition and the mistaken ideas it so often developed and disseminated.

Godley, A. D. *Herodotus.* Loeb Classical Library. 4 vols. London and New York, 1920–1924. A reliable translation with facing Greek text and some notes.

Griffiths, John Gwyn. *Plutarch's De Iside et Osiride.* Cardiff, 1970. Introduction, Greek text, translation, and commentary. This work gives access to all aspects of this important text.

Griffiths, John Gwyn. *Apuleius of Madauros: The Isis Book (Metamorphoses, Book XI).* Études préliminaires aux religions orientales dans l'empire romain, 39. Leiden, 1975. Introduction, Latin text, translation, and commentary by a world authority on Late Egyptian religion.

Lloyd, Alan B. *Herodotus Book II.* Études préliminaires aux religions orientales dans l'empire romain, 43. 3 vols. Leiden, 1975–1993. The introduction contains a detailed discussion of the pre-Herodotean tradition and Herodotus's sources and methods. The commentary addresses all aspects of Herodotus's discussion of Egypt.

Lloyd, Alan B. "Manetho and the Thirty-first Dynasty." In *Pyramid Studies and Other Essays presented to I. E. S. Edwards,* edited by John Baines et al., pp. 154–160. Egypt Exploration Society Occasional Publications, 7. London, 1988. A discussion of the non-Manethonian tradition on the thirty-first dynasty and an attempt to explain its anomalies.

Mosshammer, A. A. *The Chronicle of Eusebius and Greek Chronographic Tradition.* Lewisburg and London, 1979. Much valuable comment on Christian chronography.

Murray, Oswyn. "Hecataeus of Abdera and Pharaonic Kingship." *Journal of Egyptian Archaeology* 56 (1970), 141–171. An authoritative discussion of Hecataeus' work and its impact.

Oldfather, C. H., et al. *Library of History.* Loeb Classical Library. 12 vols. London, 1933–1967. Translation with facing Greek text and some notes.

Pearson, L. *Early Ionian Historians.* Oxford, 1939. Still valuable on Hecataeus, despite its age, and other early historians are also discussed.

Sacks, K. *Diodorus Siculus and the First Century.* Princeton, 1990. Not specifically on the Egyptian sections of his work, but an enlightening attempt to place Diodorus in his first-century intellectual context, which needs to be understood if the Egyptian data are to be properly evaluated.

Waddell, W. G. *Manetho.* Loeb Classical Library. London and Cambridge, Mass., 1940. Contains a good general introduction and a collection of the fragments with facing English translation and some notes.

West, Stephanie. "Herodotus' Portrait of Hecataeus." *Journal of Hellenic Studies* 111 (1991), 144–160. Deals with the relationship between Hecataeus of Miletus and Herodotus.

                                        ALAN B. LLOYD

**ANIBA,** ancient Miam *(Mj'm)*, was founded during the Middle Kingdom, perhaps under Senwosret I (22°40′N, 32°01′E). During the New Kingdom, it served as the administrative capital of colonized Wawat (Lower Nubia) and the residence of one of the Deputies *(jdnw)* of the viceroy of Kush, the colonial official in charge of Upper and Lower Nubia. Miam was centered on one of three fertile stretches of floodplain that marked Lower Nubian native polities, each of which was the focus of a principality during the New Kingdom. The Ramessid-era occupation, including the rock-cut tomb of Pennut saved during the Aswan High Dam salvage campaign, provided important evidence for the later colonial occupation of Nubia, refuting the idea of depopulation after the eighteenth dynasty. It remained a key center during this period, serving as a base for the powerful Viceroy Panhesy, who retreated here after his unsuccessful attempt to wrest control of kingship from Ramesses XI (r. 1111–1081 BCE).

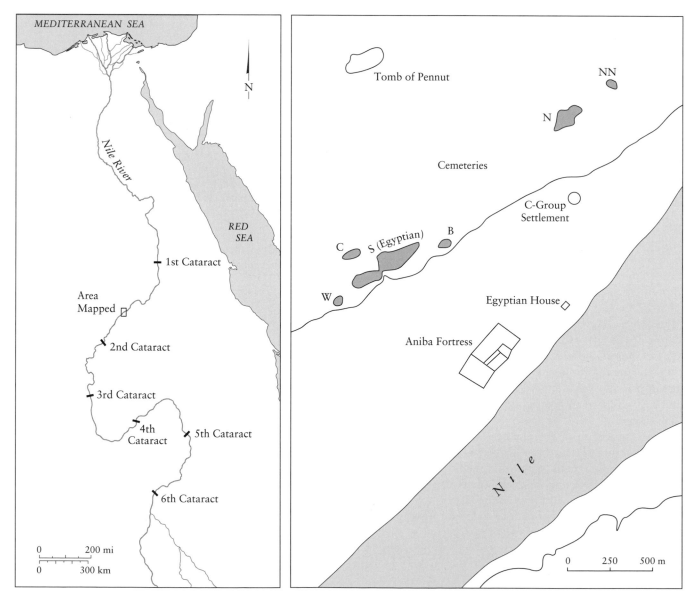

ANIBA. *Plan of Aniba.* The map shows the location of the site and the Cataracts of the Nile. (Courtesy Stewart Tyson Smith and David Lawson)

Survey and excavations by Arthur Weigall, C. Leonard Woolley, Walter B. Emery and L. P. Kirwan, Georg Steindorff, and Abdel Moneim abu Bakr revealed the remains of a large fortified town that underwent several expansions from the Middle Kingdom to the New Kingdom, eventually reaching a size of 8 hectares (about 20 acres). Major discoveries included the remains of a stone temple dedicated to Horus, Lord of Miam; a building identified by the excavators as a treasury; and a set of storage magazines to the north of the city with inscribed door jambs, naming Nehi, viceroy under Thutmose III (r. 1504–1452 BCE). Nearby was a rare example of a Nubian C-Group settlement of round, semisubterranean houses with stone foundations.

A small A-Group cemetery and a major C-Group cemetery with more than one thousand graves were found to the north of the fortress. The C-Group cemetery was important for understanding the evolution of C-Group tombs through the Second Intermediate Period; the mix of Egyptian with native tomb architecture and burial practices shed light on the process of interaction that preceded acculturation in the New Kingdom. David O'Connor in *Ancient Nubia: Egypt's Rival in Africa* (Philadelphia, 1993, pp. 33–36) has argued that evidence for social stratification in the later phases of that cemetery, including the use of monolithic stelae and the differential size of tumuli, indicated that Aniba was the center of a C-Group polity that ruled all of Lower Nubia (although a lack of comparable evidence from other sites hampers his argument).

The extensive Egyptian cemetery to the south of city provided information on the Egyptian colony from the late Middle Kingdom through the New Kingdom. Aniba also provided many excellent examples of New Kingdom tomb superstructures, including both rectilinear and pyramid chapels of mud brick, which were similar to contemporary examples at Dier el-Medina and Dra Abul Naga in the Theban necropolis. Numerous inscriptions on stelae and grave goods indicated that Aniba was an important center for the exploitation of Nubian gold during the New Kingdom; the titles inscribed included those for gold workers, chiefs of gold workers, scribe-reckoners of gold, and overseers of the treasury. Another title revealed that Aniba had its own branch of the royal treasury. The burials provided important evidence for the range of Egyptian colonial society, documenting both Egyptianization and the use of local administrators in high posts during the New Kingdom.

### BIBLIOGRAPHY

Moneim abu Bakr, Abdel. *Fouilles en Nubie.* 2 vols. Cairo, 1963 and 1967. Preliminary reports on the final excavations at Aniba during the Aswan High Dam Salvage Campaign.

Simpson, William Kelly. *Heka-Nefer and the Dynastic Material from Toshka and Arminna.* New Haven and Philadelphia, 1963. Discussion and report on the tombs of the Princes of Miam and associated sites.

Steindorff, Georg. *Aniba.* 2 vols. Hamburg, 1935 and 1937. The most substantial publication on the site, with reports on the major excavations undertaken at Aniba from 1929 to 1934.

Vercoutter, Jean. "The Gold of Kush." *Kush* 7 (1959), 120–153. Detailed discussion of the organization of gold production in Nubia during the New Kingdom, in which Aniba played a key role.

STUART TYSON SMITH

**ANIMAL HUSBANDRY.** No development has had a greater effect on human history than the domestication of plants and animals. Domestication allowed for a controllable economic base and a need for complex social interactions that led to plant and animal husbandry and, ultimately, to the earliest civilizations. Animal domestication occurred independently in several regions of the world (e.g., the Near East, China, and Mesoamerica, among others), but archaeological evidence from the Near East has established it as the cradle of earliest domestication and husbandry. Egypt, to its southwest, similarly based its economy on husbandry and farming and became the site of one of the earliest great civilizations.

Numerous definitions for *domestication* have been offered by concerned scholars, and all seem to have avid followers as well as critics. Taking into account both anthropological and biological criteria, one of the more comprehensive definitions for a *domesticated animal* is the following: one whose genetic make-up (and thus whose gene pool) has been altered to satisfy the vital needs of humans, such that if it were released into its natural environment, it would be at a selective disadvantage when competing against its wild counterparts. In other words, an animal is a domesticate when human actions have resulted in genetically altering a group of animals so that they become dependent on humans for survival; then if returned to the wild, they would most likely perish before comparable wild animals of their kind.

Although examples do exist of domesticates returning to natural habitats, their descendants have taken on the behavior and appearance of their wild counterparts (e.g., wild boar, American mustang), demonstrating that domestication does not create a new species but selects particular traits that already exist in the wild species. In domestication, the forces of natural selection have, in a sense, been superseded by human selection.

The earliest morphological (appearance) changes that were associated with domestication and animal husbandry might not, however, have necessarily been a function of conscious human selection. Each animal species has its own evolutionary path, so some changes may be purely coincidental with changed conditions. What actually takes place when wild animals are adopted and dominated by humans is the same process as that of adaptation, which occurs to animals in the wild—but, in this case, the adaptation is for fitness into a cultural niche. The cultural niche offers different selective pressures than those that occur in the natural habitat. Thus, some characteristics, which may not have been important in the wild, may prove advantageous in a domestic context. For example, the supply and type of foods available to captive animals would differ from those of wild animals, because human groups would likely have different seasonal priorities than the captive animals' wild counterparts. Those that would not be able to adapt to the new niche—either because they will not submit to human dominance or cannot adapt to the new selective pressures—get culled out of the breeding population through natural or human-induced attrition. Some may even return to the wild; but those that have a selective advantage for survival in the cultural niche gain the best chance of passing on their characteristics to the next generation and ensuring the perpetuation of their genotype.

As a rule, the success in subjugating a species and creating a successful domestic form has depended on the presence of certain innate characteristics. For example, domesticated animals were generally gregarious and possessed, in the wild state, a discernible social order. This is not to say that all gregarious animals were predisposed to domestication and husbandry, as failed experiments by the ancient Egyptians with hyena and gazelles demonstrated, but that those animals that were successfully domesticated held such traits in common.

Although domestication was a process (rather than an event) leading to husbandry, certain points along the continuum may be identified as important stages in the growing influence of human selective forces. In the initial stage of animal domestication, the organisms were genetically the same as their wild counterparts, but they were behaviorally conditioned, or tamed, to accept the dominant position of humans. Their breeding habits, however, were not curtailed; an animal might even breed with wild members of the species. The second stage in the process included the presence of a restricted breeding population; control, whether intentional or otherwise, was attained over potential breeding partners by fencing or otherwise excluding wild members of the species. The second stage has often been correlated with early husbandry, and it is marked by morphological changes in the animal, such as a reduction in body or horn size, changes in hair color, or a reduction in the chewing apparatus. The third stage was the beginning of true husbandry, identified by the intentional development of discernible characteristics in the stock. Size management or the suppression of horn growth would be examples of early stage three; advanced stage three would be indicated by the development of breeds (subspecies), with specifically developed morpho-

economic characteristics (such as plentiful milk or non-shedding wool or year-round egg production).

**Hunter-Gatherers and Early Farmers.** Any discussion of the inception of animal husbandry in Egypt must consider the popular misconceptions about the lifestyle of early farmers and hunting-gathering societies. Ethnographic studies on hunter-gatherers and groups practicing simple, nonmechanized agriculture have shown that many of our still-evident Victorian conceptions are incorrect. For example, observations about the life of present-day hunter-gatherer groups, even those living in harsh and arid environments, suggest that their daily life is not a constant struggle and is composed of considerable leisure time (e.g., Hadza of Tanzania, the !Kung San of South Africa). Among the !Kung San, food sufficient to feed a family of four for three days, on the average, could be collected by one woman in a six-hour period. In contrast, present-day populations involved in nonmechanized agriculture work endless hours for the same level of caloric reward. Furthermore, life in crowded villages is often characterized by unsanitary conditions, which pose increased chances for the spread of disease.

The negative physical effects of a life devoted to farming, as opposed to hunting-gathering, can be further exemplified by evidence compiled from the study of ancient skeletal remains. Although the physical effects on humans who were associated with the shift to a domestic-based economy has not been well documented in Egypt, a recent study on the remains of a sample of Predynastic and Old Kingdom Egyptians showed that all groups suffered from anemia, with the exception of individuals recovered from elite tombs. Such widespread anemia was attributed to poor hygienic conditions, particularly to parasitic infestations that still characterize crowded agricultural communities. A separate study, centered in Nubia, showed a similar pattern. The development of a domestic-based economy there led to nutritional deficiencies that were manifested in the form of slow bone development, anemia, microdefects in dentition, and premature osteoporosis in juveniles and in young, adult females.

Information available on hunter-gatherers and early agriculturalists, exemplified by the few cases presented here, should help dispel the traditional Western myth of the hunter-gatherer life always near the brink of starvation but the early agricultural life as one of leisure. In fact, it may raise the question of why animal husbandry flourished in an environment as rich as that of the Nile Valley.

**Origin of Egyptian Animal Husbandry.** Researchers have postulated that changes in the environment, in the biological makeup of the animals, or in human populations (cultures) might have singly or together produced the needed impetus behind the adoption of animal (and plant) husbandry in Egypt. It seems impossible, however,

ANIMAL HUSBANDRY. *Wooden funerary model of a cattle stable from Thebes, found in the tomb of Meketra, early twelfth dynasty.* (The Metropolitan Museum of Art, Museum Excavations, 1919–1920; Rogers Fund supplemented by contribution of Edward S. Harkness; 20.3.9)

to delineate which, if any, was the primary cause. Various stimuli from each of these spheres no doubt functioned together in this transformation, and the evidence from Egypt appears to support this.

In many early Holocene epoch sites (9800 to 8900 BCE), the lack or rarity of faunal remains and the difficulty involved in determining whether, on the basis of fragmentary remains, these organisms were domesticated are serious problems in attempting to trace the origins of Egyptian animal husbandry. From three types of data, criteria are generally used to identify examples of prehistoric animal husbandry. The first type employs physical characteristics of the organisms involved, such as size, morphology, and color. The second concerns assessments of the ecological fitness of the animal to the local paleobiotype or the sudden appearance of a new species into the area.

Studying the demography, ecology, and biogeography of exploited animal populations often involves the comparison of the sex ratios or mortality and survivorship patterns between recovered archaeological materials and a documented wild population. Artifacts and artistic scenes are the third source of information.

Unlike the plants and animals of the Levant and Near East, there is no definitive evidence that the wild progenitors that formed the basis of Egypt's domestic economy (i.e., pig, sheep, goat, but see the entry on *Cattle*) were ever native to the Nile Valley. Consequently, many scholars believe that Paleolithic Egyptians learned the concept of domestication and husbandry from their eastern and, perhaps, western neighbors and that many of the domestic species raised in Egypt originated in those areas. Few scholars, however, have critically evaluated the established concept of a Near Eastern center for domestic origins. (In fact, it might be argued that the Near Eastern regional center for domestication may be the result of intensive scholarly research; traditionally, that area received so much attention that new discoveries continued to be compiled at a faster rate than in Egypt.)

A second, more important factor, however, may lead to the illusion of a Near Eastern center for domestication. Because domestic-based systems, like all biological systems, adhere to evolutionary principles, successful systems expand and come to dominate and replace less successful systems. The Near Eastern complex—of barley, wheat, legumes, sheep, goats, and pigs—is an example of a very successful system that spread throughout the Mediterranean region, westward and up the Danube and Rhine basins, as well as eastward to the Indus Valley. The success of that complex in Egypt does not automatically imply that when those domesticated species were first introduced they filled a niche unoccupied by other domesticates; it is possible that the Near Eastern complex simply outcompeted an already established, but less successful system that incorporated indigenous cultivated or proto-domesticated animals (and plants). Finds in the Sahara, Egypt's Western Desert, of two bones, believed to represent domesticated cattle, found in context with materials dated to about 6000 BCE, as well as bones believed to be those of domesticated cattle from Bir Kiseiba dated to 8000 BCE, lend some credence to just such a supposition.

Regardless of the initial date, the adoption of animal husbandry in the Sahara was most probably related to its desiccation and to the frequent variability in regional rainfall patterns, which were especially aggravated during periods of severe aridity. Modern studies in the eastern Sahara have shown that annual rainfall totals vary considerably from site to site and from year to year. Work conducted by zoologists, archaeologists, and geologists suggests that in the early and mid-Holocene climatic variability was even greater than that occurring today. Such variable conditions, it is hypothesized, may have led to serious attempts to manage wild animal resources. The resource management may have begun simply, by moving young captured animals to areas where water and vegetation were more immediately available. Such an explanation is, however, a simple summary of a complex set of processes.

Evidence from the Faiyum suggests that the lifestyles of the late Paleolithic, Neolithic, and Predynastic peoples of the area were similar. In general, a mobile hunting-gathering way of life was maintained, but during the Neolithic, animal husbandry was added to the system; that is, domesticated animals were added to an already broad and diversified, mobile hunter-gatherer lifestyle. This additional resource served as insurance against an increasingly unpredictable food supply, brought about by changing environmental conditions. A complete reliance on domesticates, however, was not practical west of the Nile, because of the potential fluctuations in vegetal productivity brought on by unpredictable rainfall. Any group that would have fully adopted domesticates in place of wild resources would, in the long run, have eventually been forced to abandon such a lifestyle. It therefore seems that a balance of wild and domestic resources was best suited to the local environmental conditions (and to long-established patterns); this prevailed until the advent of large-scale irrigation from the Nile during the Middle Kingdom lessened the potential for failure.

A mixed strategy, such as that outlined for the Faiyum, is thought to have existed in other areas of the Western Desert as well. Initially, cattle were herded and, later, sheep and goats; crops were planted in those areas where they could be sustained. Groups were not sedentary, but practiced seasonal migration, so that they could take advantage of the different resources in different areas as they became available. Studies of Egypt's paleoenvironment suggest that conditions became increasingly less hospitable during the early-to-mid Holocene. Evidence from geologic, climatologic, and faunal studies indicates that from c.8000 to 3000 BCE (roughly the time from the inception of domesticates in the Egyptian region to the rise of the first dynasty), the environment of North Africa became increasingly more arid, accompanied by decreased Nile flooding and increased variability in winter temperature and precipitation. If these ecological assessments are accurate, Egypt's early and mid-Holocene inhabitants were faced with an increasingly less productive (or at least a less predictable) resource base; undoubtedly, some cultural adjustments had to be made.

Evidence from the archaeological record supports this ecological scenario. Winter rains had been important, affecting the vegetal productivity of desert margins and oases, which were used as grazing sites by wild animals and the newly domesticated herds. Coinciding with the increasing trend toward aridity, those fertile areas would have become less productive, so cultural groups depending on these resources would have had to adjust their settlement and subsistence strategies. The archaeological record has provided evidence that during the early-to-mid Holocene, the frequency of sites with Saharan-type artifacts increased dramatically along the Nile. Studies of regional settlement patterns in the Nile floodplain have also indicated a corresponding increase in the number and size of sites along the river (from c.10,000 to 4500 BCE). The associated faunal record has demonstrated that a decreasing emphasis was placed on the large animals characteristic of more open terrains (e.g., wild cattle, hartebeest, and red-fronted gazelle); an increasingly strong emphasis was placed on Nile resources. Additionally, the type of domesticates known from the Sahara and the Faiyum in the early Holocene (c.5000 BCE) were the same as those that occurred after 5000 BCE in the Nile Valley: cattle, sheep, goats, and (perhaps) grain.

The apparent adoption of Saharan domesticates by Nile groups enabled them to produce and store surplus food, as was evidenced by the discovery of food-storage facilities at both Merimde and the Faiyum. In turn, humans were able to alter their immediate environment so that the restrictions imposed by a mobile hunting-and-gathering lifestyle became less relevant. Food supplies, in the long run, became more stable and human populations slowly increased.

**Animal Husbandry.** Dynastic Egyptians utilized a variety of wild animals throughout their long history. In time, some of them became domesticated; others remained genetically wild but were nurtured and tamed for use in both religious and secular activities. Cattle, sheep, goats, and pigs comprised the main source of domesticant protein throughout most of Egyptian history. Cattle (genus *Bos*) and, perhaps, sheep (genus *Ovis*) were intentionally bred, eventually resulting in identifiable breeds. Egyptian herdsmen were aware of fundamental breeding practices, because special bulls were known to be kept for breeding purposes. Herdsmen understood how to assist the cows in calving. The bovine life cycle, from birth to mating to death, was displayed in tomb art from all periods and provinces. Some tombs included scenes of calving, grazing, drawing ploughs, and butchering.

Based on tomb scenes from all periods and provinces, the Egyptians had special personnel to select beasts for sacred and secular butchery, to direct the killings in accordance with the sacred rites, and to examine the flesh for any marks of disease or impurity. Butchers were portrayed as commoners and were probably not supervised by priests or priest-physicians. Cattle were slain by cutting their throats with a knife; they were then bled and skinned. Scenes show priest-physicians inspecting the blood to make pronouncements on its purity. A paragraph in the Ebers Papyrus suggests that a dish was made of cooked blood. After the animal was bled, it was skinned, disemboweled, and then dismembered. Select pieces were presented as offerings or they were exhibited as filets or joints suspended in meat shops. Diverse parts were also used in medicinal prescriptions. Representations of butchers in association with meat shops were made during the Old, Middle, and New Kingdoms. The brains were also eaten. Cattle skulls recovered from a sixteenth dynasty animal cemetery were split along the median (basocranial) axis, to permit access to the brain.

Although ancient Egyptians were exceptionally fond of dining on fowl, only two forms were clearly domesticated,

the greylag goose and the white-fronted goose. The wild bird resources of Egypt were so great that the widespread domestication of bird species may not have been as practical or efficient as hunting and trapping. Nevertheless, many species of birds have been depicted in aviaries and pens and, like other important food resources, were managed.

The origin of beekeeping is still a mystery, but Egypt is one of the earliest cultures known to have kept bees and may have pioneered ancient apiculture. As early as the fifth dynasty, apiculture as a profession was illustrated. A bas-relief in the Chamber of Seasons of Newoserre Any's solar temple at Abu Ghurob clearly shows a man working with bees. The presence of royal, or state-controlled, hives was suggested by the Middle Kingdom titles of a man named Intet, "Nomarch, Royal Acquaintance, and Overseer of Beekeepers," and another Middle Kingdom title, "Overseer of Beekeepers of the Entire Land." By the Ptolemaic period, both royal and private bee farms existed.

Household pets, such as dogs and cats, were common in Egypt. Several breeds of dogs were present, and some were clearly products of selective breeding, especially the greyhound and the soluki. Animals such as monkeys, ibex, and even hyenas were also kept for various purposes. Although a great variety of individual animals were tamed (not bred) for religious and secular purposes—ostriches, ibex, gazelle, and others—and as pets, particularly among the fashionable upper classes, such animals remained genetically wild.

[*See also* Agriculture; Bees and Honey; Cattle; Equines; Pigs; Poultry; *and* Sheep and Goats.]

## BIBLIOGRAPHY

Bökönyi, Sandor. "Archaeological Problems and Methods of Recognizing Domestication." In *The Domestication and Exploitation of Plants and Animals*, edited by P. Ucko and G. Dimbleby, pp. 219–230. Chicago, 1969. Outlines a series of morphological, as well as cultural, criteria considered when inspecting skeletal remains that might represent domestic forms.

Brewer, Douglas. *Fishermen, Hunters and Herders: Zoo Archaeology in the Fayum, Egypt (ca. 8200–5000 bp)*. British Archaeological Reports, International Series, 478. Oxford, 1989. One of the first works (in Egypt) to look at an archaeological problem from the perspective of the animal remains. The conclusions indicate that Neolithic Faiyum peoples practiced a mobile lifestyle little changed from the peoples of the preceding Upper Paleolithic.

Brewer, Douglas, Donald B. Redford, and Susan Redford. *Domestic Plants and Animals: The Ancient Egyptian Origins*. Warminster, 1992. A survey of ancient Egyptian domesticates, their origins and uses; provides an introduction that defines *domestication*.

Lovell, Nancy. "Anemia in the Nile and Indus Valleys: Evidence and Interpretation." In *Comparative and Intersocietal Perspectives: The Indus Valley, Mesopotamia and Egypt*, edited by R. Wright (forthcoming). Demonstrates the afflictions that can be directly traced to Neolithic living conditions, such as overcrowding, nutritional stress, and diseases.

Morey, Darcy. "Cranial Allometry and the Evolution of the Domestic

Dog." Ph.D. diss., University of Tennessee, 1990. Good review of how domestication might have proceeded for animals in general and the dog in particular.

Redford, Donald. *Egypt and Canaan in the New Kingdom.* Beer Seva, 1990.

Redman, Charles L. *The Rise of Civilization: From Early Farmers to Urban Society in the Ancient Near East.* San Francisco, 1978. The impact of domestication on settled peoples; how it offered a new lifestyle, leading to complex societies.

Wendorf, F., A. Close, R. Schild, K. Wasylikowa, R. Housley, J. Harlan, and H. Królik. "Saharan Exploitation of Plants 8000 BP." *Nature* 359 (1992), 721–724. A review of possible climatic shifts, as recorded in the Western Desert of Egypt.

Zeuner, F. E. *A History of Domesticated Animals.* New York, 1963. Classic work on domesticated animals, outlining their origins and wild progenitors.

DOUGLAS J. BREWER

**ANKH.** *See* Amulets.

**ANKHSHESHONQY.** The *Instructions of Ankhsheshonqy* is the name given to a collection of aphorisms preserved in a Demotic manuscript dating to the first century BCE (British Museum EA 10508). The text was found near Akhmim in Middle Egypt. Comprising twenty-eight columns of writing, it is divided into two parts: the aphorisms proper and an introductory narrative that purports to describe the circumstances in which these were set down.

The introduction identifies the author of the maxims as a man named Ankhsheshonqy, the son of Tjanefer. It recounts how a group of conspirators plotted to murder the king. Ankhsheshonqy learned of their plan but did not inform the authorities. The plot failed and the conspirators were duly executed. Ankhsheshonqy was punished for his silence by a sentence of imprisonment. Realizing that he would be separated from his son, he requested the authorities to allow him to write down a series of instructions for the youth's moral guidance.

This account takes up the first five columns of the British Museum manuscript. The remainder of that roll is devoted to the actual maxims that Ankhsheshonqy is supposed to have composed for his son's benefit. These mix advice on practical matters relating to agriculture, with guidance on behavior toward the gods, one's superiors and inferiors, as well as the members of one's family. Although the tone of the aphorisms is often cynical, revealing a somewhat jaundiced view of human nature, what underlies them, in common with other Wisdom Literature written in Demotic script was a belief in a principle of causality—the idea that there is a fixed and certain connection between a deed and its effect: good acts result in good for the doer, and evil acts in evil, in accordance with the laws of *maat* (principle of justice and harmony).

Some of the maxims are preserved in other Demotic papyri, not always in their order of occurrence in the British Museum manuscript. The earliest date to the second century BCE. This raises the question of whether the British Museum text is an original work or a compilation of existing sayings from various sources. A slightly different version of the narrative prologue is attested in a manuscript from Tebtunis in the Faiyum written in the second century CE. It omits the actual maxims. Some think that the prologue and the collection of aphorisms that it introduces may originally have been separate works. Others maintain that the two were composed by the same person, as parts of a whole. Opinion is also divided as to when this might have happened. On the basis of the names of certain characters who figure in the prologue, some would date the text's genesis as early as the sixth century BCE. Whereas others view it as a product of the late Ptolemaic period. If the prologue and the body of the text were written at separate times, then an early date of composition for the prologue would not preclude a later date for the rest.

Whatever the case, with a manuscript tradition extending over four centuries, the *Instructions of Ankhsheshonqy* was evidently an important work for the ancient Egyptians. For us, the text is significant as well, since it and the nearly contemporary Insinger Papyrus are the two longest and best-preserved specimens of Demotic Wisdom Literature extant.

BIBLIOGRAPHY

Glanville, S. R. K. *The Instructions of 'Onchsheshonqy (British Museum Papyrus 10508).* Catalogue of Demotic Papyri in the British Museum, 1. London, 1955. Standard edition of the text.

Lichtheim, Miriam. *Late Egyptian Wisdom Literature in the International Context. A Study of Demotic Instructions.* Orbus Biblicus et Orientalis, 52. Freiburg and Göttingen, 1983. Most recent English translation, with discussion of the work's main themes, on pp. 13–92.

Smith, H. S. "The Story of 'Onchsheshonqy." *Serapis* 6 (1980), 133–156. Re-edition of the initial columns of the text.

Smith, M. "Weisheit, demotische." In *Lexikon der Ägyptologie*, 6: 1200–1201. Wiesbaden, 1986. Annotated list of editions, translations, and studies of the text (in English).

MARK SMITH

**ANKHTIFI OF MO'ALLA,** nomarch of the third Upper Egyptian nome, is known from the inscriptions in the chapel of his rock-cut tomb situated in Mo'alla (ancient Hefat, about 40 kilometers/25 miles south of Luxor, on the eastern bank of the Nile). The events described date back to the ninth Herakleopolitan dynasty, probably to its third king, Neferkare (c.2100 BCE); at that time, the first political disorders developed that presaged the conflict between the Herakleopolitan kingdom and the rising power of Thebes. Ankhtifi's main titles were "Great Overlord of the Nome," "Overseer of Priests," and "General."

Inspired by the god Horus and under the nominal authority of his sovereign, Ankhtifi extended his influence over the second Upper Egyptian nome, Edfu, for which he also became nomarch, and then over the first nome of Upper Egypt, Elephantine. He then led several military expeditions against a coalition formed by the nomes of Thebes and Coptos, the fourth and fifth Upper Egyptian nomes, respectively. He first fought in the region of Hermonthis, against the Thebans and their allies, the Coptites, and then in the Theban nome, where intimidation operations took place.

The interest in those inscriptions far exceeds their mere historical facts. They express Ankhtifi's pride in acting on his own initiative and in proving both his military valor and his sound judgment during his administration. In accordance with the phraseology used in the First Intermediate Period, they also tell us how well the nomarch looked after his city and his nome—in particular, how he provided it with grain. Moreover, the prosperity of his administration enabled him, at a time when famine struck Upper Egypt, to have the surplus of his own grain production sent as far as the cities of Dendera and Abydos to the north, and Elephantine to the south. They also contain a description of the various parts of the chapel of his tomb, with curses against those who might be tempted to desecrate them, as well as a description of the doorway leading to it. A final inscription, although fragmentary, seems to allude to the new year's rites and to a nautical celebration, also represented on a wall of the tomb and associated with the falcon god Hemen of Mo'alla, where the hippopotamus of myth was overcome.

## BIBLIOGRAPHY

*Tomb Publication*
Vandier, Jacques. *Mo'alla: La tombe d'Ankhtifi et la tombe de Sebekhotep.* Bibliothèque d'Étude, 18. Cairo, 1950.

*Translations of Chapel Inscriptions*
Lichtheim, Miriam. *Ancient Egyptian Literature: A Book of Readings,* vol. 1, *The Old and Middle Kingdoms,* pp. 85–86. Berkeley, 1973.
Lichtheim, Miriam. *Ancient Egyptian Autobiographies Chiefly of the Middle Kingdom: A Study and Anthology,* pp. 24–26. Orbis Biblicus et Orientalis, 84. Freiburg and Göttingen, 1988.
Schenkel, Wolfgang. *Memphis. Herakleopolis, Theben. Die Epigraphischen Zeugnisse der 7.–11: Dynastie Ägyptens,* pp. 45–57. Ägyptologische Abhandlungen, 12. Wiesbaden, 1965.
Schenkel, Wolfgang. *Die Bewässerungsrevolution im Alten Ägypten,* pp. 42–44. Mainz, 1978.

*Commentaries on Chapel Inscriptions*
Doret, Éric. "Ankhtifi and the Description of His Tomb at Mo'alla." In *For His Ka: Essays Offered in the Memory of Klaus Baer,* edited by David Silverman, pp. 79–86. Studies in Oriental Civilization, 55. Chicago, 1994.

Fecht, Gerhard. "Zu den Inschriften des ersten Pfeilers im Grab des Anchtifi (Mo'alla)." In *Festschrift für Siegfried Schott zu seinem 70. Geburtstag am 20. August 1967,* edited by Wolfgang Helck, pp. 50–60. Wiesbaden, 1968.
Fischer, Henry G. "Notes on the Mo'alla Inscriptions and Some Contemporaneous Texts." *Wiener Zeitschrift für die Kunde des Morgenlandes* 57 (1961), 59–77.
Goedicke, Hans. "Ankhtyfy's Threat." In *Individu, société et spiritualité dans l'Égypte pharaonique et copte: Mélanges égyptologiques offerts au Professeur Aristide Théodoridès,* edited by C. Cannuyer and J. M. Kruchten, pp. 111–121. Athens, 1993.
Goedicke, Hans. "Administrative Notions in the First Intermediate Period." *Chronique d'Égypte* 70 (1995), 41–51.
Goedicke, Hans. "Ankhtyfy's Fight." *Chronique d'Égypte* 73 (1998), 29–41.
Kees, Hermann. "Aus den Notjahren der Thebais." *Orientalia,* n.s. 21 (1952), 86–97.
Posener, George. "La tombe d'Anchtifi à Mo'alla." *Journal des Savants* (1952), 115–126.
Spanel, Donald. "The Date of Ankhtifi of Mo'alla. *Göttinger Miszellen* 78 (1984), 87–94.
Willems, Harco. "Crime, Cult and Capital Punishment (Mo'alla Inscription 8)." *Journal of Egyptian Archaeology* 76 (1990), 27–54.

ERIC DORET

**ANNALS,** the translation usually given for Egyptian *gnwt* (plural of *gnt*), a word whose cognates suggest an object inscribed on soft material such as wood or ivory (cf. *gnwty,* "carver in wood"). The term presumably derives from those rectangular wooden or ivory "labels" that occur in such abundance in mortuary contexts from the late Naqada III through the Early Dynastic period. The evidence of these labels begins to fail at the beginning of the second dynasty, to be replaced by the "publication" of the sequence of year rectangles during the later Old Kingdom in the form of the Palermo Stone, the Memphite fragments, and the reused block (sarcophagus) from South Saqqara.

The earliest examples (specifically from Abydos) were intended for the identification of commodities (and sometimes their sources) within storage facilities; but shortly, in the evolution of the form, the need to date securely the act of storage began to take precedence over all other considerations. Labels from the beginning of the first dynasty give prominence to the king's Horus-name (sometimes accompanied by the *nb.ty* name) with the mention of an event or events that signal a particular year. The whole is either freely distributed over the surface of the label or is arranged horizontally in two to four registers provided with "ground" lines. The events commemorated, which range from three to eight or nine in number, are confined to the upper registers, while the lowest is reserved for the notation of some commodity and its amount. It became customary to list on the extreme left, behind the king's name, the titles and name of an official (responsible for the item in question?). The extant labels, coming as they do from storage areas in a tomb context, are thus commodity-specific. But they are presumably merely adapted copies of a set of archetypal year labels, composed at the royal residence for various uses in the administration. These "master" versions of the *gn(w)t* for a given year would not require such specificity, and the Palermo Stone suggests that the bottom register in the archetype was occupied by a datum crucial to the running of the state as a whole—the height of the annual inundation.

Throughout the Old Kingdom, both contents and format of the annals evolved rapidly. By the reign of Wadji a prominent *rnpt*-sign was inscribed on the right side, enclosing the registers and indicating a single year's span. The reign of Den introduced a bifurcation of the field into two vertical blocks, that on the right containing the events in multiple registers, and that on the left naming the king, official, and commodity. By the close of the first dynasty, the columnar format was beginning to dominate at the expense of the vertical registers. While for the first dynasty the recording scribe chose to commemorate a variety of event types, such as cultic acts, cult-statue carving, construction, battles, progresses, and taxation, by the second dynasty the need was clearly felt to regularize the content. To provide a sort of *aide-mémoire* in the growing sequence of *gnwt*, the scribes listed the biennial cattle count and royal progress in alternating year-rectangles, while the intervening years were signalized by noting another biennial event, a species of royal séance called the "Appearance of the King of Upper and Lower Egypt." This event seems temporarily to have been dispensed with under Sneferu and was only sporadically revived by his successors, but reference to the cattle-count in all years became common: thus "the *x*th time of the [cattle]-count and "year after the *x*th time of the [cattle]-count." No later than the reign of Khufu, the formula *ir.n.f m mnw.f* ("he made [it] as his monument") appears and is used to introduce the king's bequests to the gods, such as gifts, chattels, endowments, statuary, and buildings. While the records of military campaigns and construction continue occasionally to appear, by the fifth dynasty it is the acts listed under the *ir.n.f m mnw.f* formula that multiply to such an extent that a much-expanded rectangle is needed. Thus, the format has become a vehicle to keep account of the disbursement of the king's largesse, and at the same time to promote his piety and his upholding of *maat*, while year-identification and sequence have declined in importance, to be covered by what is in reality a regnal year numbering in embryo.

Toward the close of the fifth dynasty, one or more kings—we may not be dealing with a single instance—chose to inscribe on stone the accumulated sequence of year rectangles, clearly available in the archives from the inception of the genre, perhaps for temple display. The result was a monument which, although it might have had value for practical reference, stressed the ideological truths of the continuum of the royal line (and thus divine favor), and the piety of later kings in honoring the gods.

Evidence as to how the *gnwt* were evolving as a genre begins to peter out before the close of the third millennium BCE. To judge from the reuse of a block containing an inscription of annals even before the close of the sixth dynasty, it would appear that monumental publication and display of *gnwt* had fallen into abeyance before the end of the Old Kingdom. The practice of keeping concise records of a year's events in the original rectangular format may itself have passed into obsolescence at this time.

Arguably the *gnwt* of the Old Kingdom, in whatever form they had survived, formed the basis of the true king list tradition. The latter, the presence of which is attested no later than the early twelfth dynasty, drew on a version of the *gnwt* that had already undergone some revision and midrashic embellishment. Reign lengths could not always be ascertained (compare the shortening of the fourth dynasty *floruits* of Sneferu, Khufu, and Khafre), and certain unhistorical constructs (for example, the "Ennead" principle) had begun to be brought to bear on the ordering and numbering of reigns.

The word *gnwt*, however, continues to appear in Egyptian texts until Greco-Roman times, albeit with restricted application. Its most frequent use is in scenes of royal legitimation (divine approbation [= "coronation"] or *išd*-tree scenes) in which some god, usually Thoth, promises the king many *gnwt*. To underscore this statement, which is tantamount to the prediction of a long reign, the god is often seen marking a notched *rnpt* frond, or writing the promises with a pen. Less common, though couched in a well-attested cliché, *gnwt* may be found in a trope which stresses negatively the uniqueness of a contemporary event: "[They] made a search in the annals of the most ancient kings . . . (but) nothing like this which happened to His Majesty had happened to them." That the annals of the Old Kingdom remained available to scribes centuries later, possibly in derived copies on papyrus, can be argued on the basis of occasional and candid comments on the difficulty of reading the archaic diction. Manetho seems to have disposed of a garbled version of an archaic document which may have been based ultimately on the annals of the first and second dynasties.

The term "annals" is sometimes applied to types of records that deal with needs other than year identification and event commemoration. Already in the Old Kingdom, landowning institutions such as temple estates regulated their affairs by recourse to such account texts as office directories, service regulation books, and salary sheets, all organized within a calendrical as well as an annual framework. By the Middle Kingdom governmental (treasury, granary, etc.), temple, and judicial institutions were employing the daybook or journal (*ḥrwyt*) as a means to record day-to-day accounts (income and disbursements) and events (arrivals, departures, civil and military matters, court cases, etc.). These documents were sometimes excerpted to provide the skeleton of a hieroglyphic inscription, especially in the case of military exploits. (See, for example, the Tod inscription of Senwosret I, the "Annus mirabilis" of Amenemhet II, the "Annals" of Thutmose III, the triumph stelae of Amenophis II, and the Bubastite fragment of Thutmose IV.) The daybook of the king's house may also prove to be in part the source of the formal list on a stela of benefactions to the gods in the form of gifts, offerings, and endowments (although in some reigns the "inventory"—*ipty*—provided an additional source). Inasmuch as this genre of inscription belongs within the *ir.n.f m mnw.f* type of text, the list of benefactions as a genre descends from and perpetuates the latest motivation behind the true *gnwt* before its obsolescence.

While it is safe to say that *gnwt* were no longer being produced by the Middle Kingdom, the word continues to be used in contexts with a religious connotation. The *gnwt* are said to be deposited in the "House of Life" or the *sd* pavilion, or under the *išd*-tree, and to enjoy the aegis of a particular deity. While some of the writings thus labeled may ultimately derive, at several removes, from the annals of the Old Kingdom, the "historicization" of the realm of the gods probably involved an artificial extension of the annals of the ancestors backward into the time of the gods. Thus, the "annals (*gnwt*) of the gods," which are said to be copied out in the House of Life, probably encompass mythological stories such as are preserved piecemeal in a wide variety of genres, beatification spells, "Underworld" books, magical incantations, mythological inventories, etc. The loose usage of the Late period probably coupled these texts, "the mighty acts of the gods" (in one Greek papyrus), with tales of the ancestors in a single, all-inclusive genre. It was this type of literature, at several removes from the true *gnwt*, that Manetho had access to in fleshing out his basic king list and writing up his *Aegyptiaca* in the third century BCE.

**BIBLIOGRAPHY**

Barta, W. "Die Chronologie der 1. bis 5. Dynastie nach den Angaben des rekonstruierten Annalensteins." *Zeitschrift für Ägyptische Sprache und Altertumskunde* 108 (1981), 11–23.

Borchardt, L. *Die Annalen und die zeitliche Festlegung des Alten Reiches der aegyptischen Geschichte.* Berlin, 1917.

Dobrev, V., and M. Baud. "Les annales royales de la VIᵉ dynastie recemment identifiées au musée du Caire." *Comptes Rendues de l'Académie des Inscriptions et Belles Lettres* (1995), 415–426.

Helck, W. "Bemerkungen zum Annalenstein." Mitteilungen des Deutschen Archäologischen Instituts, Abteilung Kairo 30 (1974), 31–35.

Helck, W. *Untersuchungen zur Thinitenzeit.* Wiesbaden, 1987.

O'Mara, P. *The Palermo Stone.* 2 vols. La Canada, Calif., 1979–1980.

Redford, D. B. "The Meaning and Use of the Term *gnwt*, 'Annals'." In *Studien zu Sprache und Religion Aegyptens*, edited by F. Junge, vol. 1, pp. 327–342. Gottingen, 1984.

Redford, D. B. *Pharaonic King-lists, Annals and Day-books.* Mississauga, Ont., 1986.

DONALD B. REDFORD

**ANUBIS.** The most important of Egypt's canine gods, Anubis (*Inpw*) was the patron of embalmers and protector of the necropolis, who guided the deceased and participated in the divine judgment. During the embalming and Opening of the Mouth rituals, priests wore masks representing Anubis.

Anubis's role as god of the cemetery probably originated from the observation of animals scavenging among burials. Although he has features of a wild dog, he was probably intended to be a jackal, as indicated by his long, drooping, club-shaped tail. He is usually shown lying on his stomach on a shrine-shaped chest, sometimes wearing a collar, with a flail upright on his back. From the New Kingdom on, he is depicted as a jackal-headed human, rarely appearing in fully human form. Like Wepwawet and Khentyamentiu, the other canine gods of the necropolis, Anubis is black, a color symbolic of the afterlife and fertility. Anubis is represented by the *imy-wt* fetish, a headless animal skin hanging from a pole.

The etymology of the name *Inpw* is unclear; Kurt Sethe (1930, sec. 17) and others derive it from the Egyptian word for "puppy," although previous scholars have suggested a derivation from the terms for "to putrefy" or "prince." Anubis's most common epithets relate to his funerary role, including "He Who Is upon His Mountain"; "Lord of the Sacred Land"; "He Who Is before the Divine Booth"; "He Who Is in the Mummy Wrappings"; and "Undertaker."

Anubis originated as Egypt's principal funerary god. Old Kingdom offering prayers invoke primarily him. The Pyramid Texts portray him as the judge of the dead, and the deceased king is said to have the body of Atum and the face of Anubis. When Osiris supplanted him in the Middle Kingdom, Anubis was credited with aiding Isis and embalming Osiris, while remaining a guide, protector, and judge of the dead. He appears in the vignettes accompanying chapter 125 of the *Book of Going Forth by Day* (*Book of the Dead*), where he weighs the heart of the deceased against *maat*. Tombs of the New Kingdom and later show him attending the mummy and holding it upright during the Opening of the Mouth ceremony. In the Ptolemaic period, Anubis was transformed into a cosmic deity, and in his funerary role was identified with that of

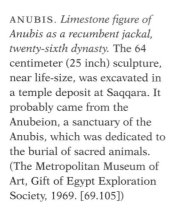

ANUBIS. *Limestone figure of Anubis as a recumbent jackal, twenty-sixth dynasty.* The 64 centimeter (25 inch) sculpture, near life-size, was excavated in a temple deposit at Saqqara. It probably came from the Anubeion, a sanctuary of the Anubis, which was dedicated to the burial of sacred animals. (The Metropolitan Museum of Art, Gift of Egypt Exploration Society, 1969. [69.105])

Hermes Psychopompos. In Roman times, he gained popularity as Isis's companion and protector.

Originally the local god of the seventeenth Upper Egyptian nome, the Greek Cynopolis, Anubis was eventually worshipped throughout Egypt. As Anubis-Horus, he had a sanctuary at the site of Hut-nesut, probably Sharuna, in the eighteenth nome. At Memphis, he presided over the cemeteries with Sokar, and he had a sanctuary at Tura. At Heliopolis, where extensive dog cemeteries of the Late and Ptolemaic periods have been excavated, he was identified with Horus. The predominance of Anubis in the embalmers' area at Saqqara has given it the name "the Anubeion."

Anubis's parentage is uncertain. The Pyramid Texts call both the cow-goddess Hesat and the cat-goddess Bastet his mother. Later sources call him the son of Nephthys by Re, Osiris, or Seth. According to Plutarch, his birth resulted from an extramarital liaison between Nephthys and Osiris, but Isis then raised him as her own son. A Demotic magical papyrus calls Osiris and Isis-Sekhmet his parents. The Pyramid Texts identify Anubis as the father of the serpent goddess Kebehut, who assisted him in the purification of the dead.

[*See also* Canines.]

### BIBLIOGRAPHY

Altenmüller, Birgitte. "Anubis." In *Lexikon der Ägyptologie*, 1: 327–333. Wiesbaden, 1975.

Griffiths, J. G. *Plutarch's De Iside et Osiride.* Cardiff, 1970.

Hart, George. *A Dictionary of Egyptian Gods and Goddesses.* London, 1986. See pp. 21–26.

Sethe, Kurt. *Urgeschichte und älteste Religion der Ägypter.* Leipzig, 1930.

Spence, Lewis. *Ancient Egyptian Myths and Legends.* New York, 1990. See pp. 103–106. Reprinted from an original publication of 1915, this book presents a summary that is somewhat out of date but still useful.

Watterson, Barbara. *The Gods of Ancient Egypt.* London, 1984. See pp. 173–175.

DENISE M. DOXEY

**APIS.** *See* Bull Gods; *and* Cults, *article on* Animal Cults.

**APPEAL TO THE LIVING.** *See* Offerings, *article on* Offering Formulas and Lists.

**APRIES** (r. 589–570 BCE), fourth king of the twenty-sixth or Saite dynasty, Late period. The historical framework for Apries' reign is provided by the fifth-century BCE Greek historian Herodotus and the partly dependent account by the first-century BCE historian Diodorus Siculus. Some details for the account were provided by Hebrew scriptures, Babylonian references, and Egyptian texts. Comparison of those sources indicates the classical narrative as seriously defective in the account of the end of Apries' reign. The main foreign-policy issue during his time was the containment of Chaldean expansion from the Near East. In 589 BCE, Apries attempted to end the Chaldean siege of Jerusalem but was defeated and driven south. In 582 BCE, Nebuchadrezzar II, Chaldean king of Babylonia, invaded Egypt after military successes in Syria-Palestine, but that incursion left little impact on historical sources. Apries' successful campaigns (c.574–571 BCE) against Tyre, Sidon, and Cyprus should be seen against that background; for they would have assisted him in blocking Chaldean progress southward, and they probably enhanced the economic resources needed to sustain the war.

Operations against Cyrene (571–570 BCE) brought further Chaldean involvement in Egypt, but unexpectedly: Apries dispatched an expedition against Cyrene (a Greek city in eastern Libya, on the Mediterranean), probably motivated by Cyrene's encroachment on Libyan territory, which would, in turn, have threatened Egypt's western frontier. That army was defeated, and the disaster led immediately to a revolt of the *machimoi*, the native Egyptian warrior class, who had suffered severely in the encounter and who were resentful of the favor shown by the crown to foreign mercenaries, particularly Carians and Ionians. The rebels, led by Amasis, an erstwhile officer of Apries, defeated Apries in 570 BCE at Momemphis (probably the present-day Kom el-Hisn), but Apries escaped. Whether he remained in Egypt or went immediately to Babylonia in search of support from Nebuchadrezzar is unclear. Nebuchadrezzar, however, launched an invasion of Egypt in 567 BCE, which included Apries and was probably intended to reestablish the deposed pharaoh as a Babylonian puppet. That force was defeated by a combination of bad weather and Egyptian military action, and Apries was drowned. He was buried with full honors in the royal cemetery at the temple of Neith at Sais.

The historical sources reveal much less about Apries' internal policies than his foreign relations, but his policies conformed to a standard practice. The erection of a Memphite stela of his thirteenth regnal year and his generosity to the ram of Mendes demonstrated a determination to keep the temple organizations on his side. He continued the policy of controlling the Theban priesthood through the appointment of royal women as divine votaresses of Amun-Re; Ankhnesneferibre succeeded Nitocris in that capacity in 584 BCE. The Memphite stela also explicitly expressed his determination to operate on the basis of ancestral custom. Apries' known building activities were few but were preeminently exemplified through the Palace of Apries at Memphis, which must have been a most impressive structure. The spectacular palace at Sais mentioned by Herodotus may have been another example, but it is not clear whether Apries built this structure or merely lived in it.

### BIBLIOGRAPHY

Boardman, J. et al., eds. *The Cambridge Ancient History*, 2d ed. Vol 3: *The Assyrian and Babylonian Empires and Other States of the Near East from the Eighth to the Sixth Centuries B.C.* Cambridge, 1991. An excellent survey of the twenty-sixth dynasty, including much on Apries.

Leahy, M. A. "The Earliest Dated Monument of Amasis and the End of the Reign of Apries." *Journal of Egyptian Archaeology* 74 (1988), 183–199.

Lloyd, Alan B. *Herodotus Book II*. Etudes préliminaires aux religions orientales dans l'empire romain, 43. 3 vols. Leiden, 1975–1993. A discussion of the Herodotean data on Apries in the light of all other evidence.

Lloyd, Alan B. "The Late Period, 664–323 BC." In *Ancient Egypt: A Social History*, edited by B. G. Trigger et al. Cambridge, 1983. Apries placed firmly within the history of the twenty-sixth dynasty.

ALAN B. LLOYD

# ARCHAEOLOGICAL AND RESEARCH INSTITUTIONS.

A diverse group of institutions have been established in Egypt and in other countries for the study of ancient Egypt; some are official branches of various governments, but others are private, nonprofit foundations or organizations sponsored by their members (see table 1).

Organized, foreign archaeological research in Egypt began in 1798 with the establishment of the Institut d'Égypte, founded by French scholars of the Commission for Arts and Sciences of the Army of the Orient. They had accompanied Napoleon Bonaparte's military expedition to Egypt in that year. In 1799, they had organized field expeditions throughout Egypt to record the ancient monuments, continuing their work until the French army was defeated by the British in 1801; they were then evacuated from Egypt, and the institute was disbanded. Returning to France, members of the expedition begin to publish accounts and memoirs. Most notably, in 1802, Dominique Vivant Denon published *Voyage dans la Basse et la Haute Égypte pendant les campagnes du général Bonaparte*. The official publication of the expedition was the encyclopedic and lavishly illustrated *Description de l' Égypte;* begun in 1803, the first volume appeared in 1808 and the final volume in 1826. The completed publication comprised ten volumes of text, ten folio volumes of plates, and three elephant folios of maps and plates. The institute was reorganized as the Institut égyptien in 1862 in Cairo, under the patronage of the khedive of Egypt, and it became again the Institut d'Égypte in 1918. It served as a forum for its scholar members, both foreign and Egyptian, who presented their research and published their work in its *Bulletin* and *Mémoires*. After 1955, its activities were greatly reduced, although the building and library containing some fifteen thousand volumes remain.

During the first half of the nineteenth century, a number of scientific expeditions had been dispatched to Egypt by European governments and universities to record, study, and collect. In 1858, an official antiquities service was established by the khedive of Egypt, and he named as

TABLE 1. *Foreign Research Centers in Egypt*

| Date | Institution | Sponsoring Country |
|------|-------------|--------------------|
| 1798 | Institut d'Égypte | France |
| 1880 | Institut Français d'archéologie orientale du Caire | France |
| 1882 | Egypt Exploration Society | United Kingdom |
| 1907 | Deutsches Archäologisches Institut, Abteilung Kairo | Germany |
| 1923 | Fondation Égyptologique Reine Élisabeth | Belgium |
| 1923 | Société Française d'Égyptologie | France |
| 1924 | The Epigraphic Survey of the Oriental Institute, the University of Chicago | United States |
| 1931 | Schweizerisches Institut für ägyptische Bauforschung und Altertumskunde | Switzerland |
| 1939 | Griffith Institute | United Kingdom |
| 1948 | American Research Center in Egypt | United States |
| 1955 | Centre d'Études et de documentation sur l'ancienne Égypte, Collection Scientifique | Egypt |
| 1958 | Czech Institute of Egyptology | Czech Republic |
| 1959 | Polish Center of Mediterranean Archaeology | Poland |
| 1967 | Centre Franco-Égyptian d'Étude des Temples de Karnak | Egypt and France |
| 1971 | Netherlands Institute for Archaeology and Arabic Studies in Cairo | The Netherlands |
| 1971 | Austrian Archaeological Institute | Austria |
| 1970s | Archaeological Section, Italian Cultural Institute | Italy |
| 1979 | Canadian Institute in Egypt | Canada |
| 1989 | Australian Centre for Egyptology | Australia |
| 1993 | Institute for Nautical Archaeology—Egypt | United States |
| 1994 | McDonald Institute for Archaeological Research | United Kingdom |

director Auguste Mariette, a French Egyptologist. Not until 1880 was another permanent research institute established in Egypt. At the prompting of Gaston Maspero, an Egyptologist who soon succeeded Mariette as head of the antiquities service, the French government established the École Française du Caire. In 1898, it was renamed the Institut français d'archéologie orientale du Caire (IFAO) and was moved to the historic Mounira Palace in Cairo.

Under Maspero, who remained until 1883, the scholars of the École had begun a program of copying texts and drawing and photographing monuments, and their first publication appeared in 1883. Under the succeeding director, Émile Chassinat, who remained until 1911, the institute began an extensive program of excavations all over Egypt and established its press. This press has now published more than seven hundred volumes, in twenty-five series, on ancient and modern Egypt, as well as several annual bulletins dedicated to specific aspects of the institute's research. Excavations and documentation projects have included the complete temples of Edfu, Esna, Deir el-Shelwit, and Dendera, the village and tombs at Deir el-Medina, excavations at the temples of Medamud, Tod, and Karnak North, and at several sites in the oases of the Western Desert. As part of the UNESCO campaign for the salvage of the Nubian monuments, the institute has excavated the temple of Ramesses II at Wadi es-Sebua. The institute headquarters includes a library of more than sixty thousand volumes, the buildings of the institute's press, and the support facilities for the field expeditions. Young scholars, called *pensionnaires*, are appointed to the institute for multiyear fellowships, which allow them to do research in Egypt. Fieldwork is carried out by the *chargés de mission*—professional archaeologists, architects, and Egyptologists attached to the institute.

In 1882, to take advantage of excavation opportunities in Egypt that were provided by the establishment of the antiquities service, the Egypt Exploration Society was founded by Amelia Edwards, an English novelist and journalist, with Reginald Stuart Poole, a numismatist and nephew of Edward Lane, the great scholar of modern Egypt. Through the subscription of its members, the society provided support for excavations and recording in Egypt and for the publication of this research. It sponsored the work of Édouard Naville at Deir el-Bahri, John Pendlebury and Henri Frankfort at Tell el-Amarna, Amice Calverley at the temple of Sety I at Abydos, Bernard Grenfell and Arthur Hunt at Oxyrhynchus, Walter B. Emery at the Middle Kingdom fortresses of Nubia and the Early Dynastic cemetery at Saqqara, and William Matthew Flinders Petrie at many sites in Egypt. The society continues to work at Memphis, Saqqara, Amarna, and at Qasr Ibrim, south of Aswan on an island in Lake Nasser. Headquartered in London, the society established a Cairo office for the first time in 1993. It also maintains a permanent expedition house at Saqqara. The London office includes a library of twenty-five thousand volumes and expedition archives. The publications of the society include the *Journal of Egyptian Archaeology*, which was begun in 1914, and the popular magazine *Egyptian Archaeology*, which was begun in 1991, as well as more than two hundred scholarly reports and studies in five series.

The Deutsches Archäologisches Institut, Abteilung Kairo, was founded in 1907 as the Imperial German Institute for Egyptian Archaeology, with Ludwig Borchardt as its first director. Borchardt had been carrying out research in Egypt since 1899, as scientific attaché for Egyptology at the German embassy. Research before World War I and between the two world wars focused on Thebes, Tell el-Amarna, and the prehistoric site of Merimde. The institute, whose library and archives were dispersed during World War II, was reestablished in 1957 in a new headquarters in Cairo, with the donation of the library and archives of Ludwig Keimer. This facility serves as a base for the fieldwork of the institute at Dahshur, Thebes, Elephantine, Abydos, Buto, and Abu Mina; work also continues in the study and restoration of Islamic monuments in Egypt. During the Nubian Salvage Campaign, the institute supervised the study and relocation of the Kalabsha temple. The institute publishes an annual journal, the *Mitteilungen des Deutsches Archäologisches Institut, Abteilung Kairo*, and the results of its research and excavations in several series: the Sonderschriften, the Abhandlungen, and the Archäologische Veröffentlichungen.

The 1922 discovery of the tomb of Tutankhamun spurred the activities of other foreign Egyptologists, resulting in the foundation, soon after, of other research institutes. In 1923, Jean Capart, the Belgian Egyptologist and art historian, established the Fondation Égyptologique Reine Élisabeth at the request of Queen Élisabeth of Belgium after she had visited Tutankhamun's tomb. Headquartered in Brussels, where it maintains a library of Egyptology and papyrology, it has sponsored excavations in Thebes and at Elkab, a major temple site south of Thebes. In addition to an annual journal, *Chronique d'Égypte*, the foundation has published more than fifty volumes on the art, archaeology, and literature of ancient Egypt and more than thirty volumes on papyrology and Christian Egypt.

The Société Française d'Égyptologie was founded in 1923 by Étienne Drioton, with its headquarters at the Collège de France. Like the Institut d'Égypte, it meets several times each year for the presentation of papers by its members; these are published in the bulletin of the society, which was begun in 1955. It also publishes the scholarly journal *Revue d'Égyptologie*, established in 1933.

The Epigraphic Survey of the Oriental Institute, the University of Chicago (popularly known as Chicago House), was established in Luxor in 1924 by James Henry Breasted. It was organized to record the inscriptions and scenes on the monuments of Thebes that, owing to human and natural factors, were rapidly decaying. It worked first on the temple of Ramesses III at Medinet Habu and developed a method of recording that combined the use of large-format photography and line drawings by a team of artists and Egyptologist-epigraphers to record large-scale reliefs and produce precise facsimiles. This has become known as the Chicago House Method and is particularly suited to monuments for which tracing would be impractical or for those with substantial changes and alterations. In addition, archaeological and architectural surveys were also carried out on monuments that required excavation as part of the recording process. That survey has produced eighteen volumes, many of them large folios, recording the mortuary temple of Ramesses III at Medinet Habu. It has also recorded reliefs and inscriptions in the temples of Karnak and Luxor and the Theban tomb of Kheruef. As part of the Nubian salvage campaign, it recorded the temple at Beit el-Wali. Present work involves the cleaning and conservation of monuments that are also being recorded. At its headquarters in Luxor, called Chicago House, it maintains a library of more than fourteen thousand volumes, the only Egyptological library south of Cairo, as well as an archive of some sixteen thousand negatives and about twenty thousand prints.

The Schweizerisches Institut für ägyptische Bauforschung und Altertumskunde was founded in Cairo in 1931, by Ludwig Borchardt, who had also been the first director of the Imperial German Institute. Administered by a private foundation, it maintains a headquarters and library in Cairo. Under Borchardt, a research program was established that emphasized the excavation, documentation, and study of the architectural remains of ancient Egypt. The institute has excavated at Elephantine (jointly with the German Institute) since 1969, at the funerary temple of Merenptah in Thebes since 1971, and at Pelusium in the Nile Delta. Documentation projects have included Philae, Syene/Aswan, and Lake Moeris in the Faiyum. The institute publishes its research in its series *Beiträge fur ägyptische Bauforschung und Altertumskunde* and in collaboration with the German Institute.

The Griffith Institute, located in the Ashmolean Museum at the University of Oxford, was founded in 1939 by the bequest of Francis Llewellyn Griffith, the noted British philologist and translator of Egyptian texts. Its library of more than thirty thousand volumes is based on the libraries of Griffith, Walter E. Crum, A. H. Sayce, and Alan Gardiner. Its archives include the original records of Howard Carter's excavation of the tomb of Tutankhamun as well as the papers of Alan Gardiner, Battiscombe Gunn, and Jaroslav Černý. Its influential publication program has produced the *Topographical Bibliography of Ancient Egyptian Hieroglyphic Texts, Reliefs and Paintings,* which continues to appear in revised editions. Alan Gardiner's *Egyptian Grammar* and R. O. Faulkner's *A Concise Dictionary of Middle Egyptian* are used by most students who learn ancient Egyptian. Its *Tut'ankhamun's Tomb Series* has made available many aspects of the finds from the tomb that remained unpublished at Carter's death in 1939.

With the advent of World War II, large-scale excavations by universities and museums ended, such as those by New York's Metropolitan Museum of Art and Boston's Museum of Fine Arts. The war sharply curtailed the activities of the foreign research institutes of both Europe and Egypt. After the war ended, an American research institute was established in Egypt to take the place of the prewar museum excavations. This, the American Research Center in Egypt (ARCE), was founded in 1948 by a consortium of museums and universities to provide a base for work in Egypt. The center in Cairo assists the expeditions of its member institutions, provides a fellowship program both for students and advanced scholars, and publishes the *Journal of the American Research Center in Egypt,* a newsletter, and field reports. Expeditions working from the center have excavated throughout Egypt at Thebes, Hierakonpolis, Giza, Abydos, Mendes, Kom el-Hisn, and many other sites. The center was expanded to include scholarly work in medieval and modern Egypt and is now actively involved in the conservation of Egyptian monuments, both ancient and medieval, throughout Egypt. At the Cairo center, it maintains a library of more than fifteen thousand volumes and a computer center.

In 1955, with the threat of the Nile's inundation of the Nubian monuments, which would result from the new Aswan High Dam, a research institute was founded in Cairo, the Centre d'Études et de documentation sur l'ancienne Égypte, Collection Scientifique (CEDAE). It was established jointly by the Egyptian government and UNESCO. Mobilized to study, document, and salvage the archaeological remains of Nubia—and working in collaboration with international scholars—this center has studied and recorded the temples of Nubia, including Abu Simbel, Amada, Debod, Derr, Garf Hussein, Dendur, and Kalabsha. Its scholars have also documented the graffiti of the Theban area, the mortuary temple of Ramesses II—the Ramesseum—and several tombs in the Valley of the Queens. Through its publication program, it has produced more than seventy-five volumes on this research.

In 1958, the Czech Institute of Egyptology was founded by the Ministry of Culture of the Czechoslovak Republic. From its base in the Czech embassy in Cairo, it has worked almost exclusively at the site of Abusir, the royal necropolis of the fifth dynasty, particularly at the great *mastaba* of the vizier Ptah-shepses. In Nubia, it helped to document the ancient rock inscriptions. At Charles University's Czech Institute of Egyptology in Prague, its resources include the eleven-thousand-volume Jaroslav Černý Library, as well as archives of field records. It has published the results of its excavations at Abusir, as well as studies on the Egyptian antiquities kept in Czech museums and collections.

The Polish Center of Mediterranean Archaeology of the University of Warsaw was established in 1959 by Kazimierz Michalowski, a specialist in the art of ancient Egypt. It maintains a permanent mission in Cairo and has worked closely with the Egyptian antiquities authorities on long-term joint projects of documentation, excavation, and restoration, most notably the restoration of the temples of Hatshepsut and Thutmose III at Deir el-Bahri in Thebes; it also works in the Delta, at the sites of Tell Atrib and Marina el-Alamein, and in the seaport of Alexandria, conducting both excavations and restoration projects. It has published the reports of its work at Deir el-Bahri and at Alexandria, and its journal *Polish Archaeology in the Mediterranean* was begun in 1989.

In 1967, the Centre Franco-Égyptien d'Étude des Temples de Karnak was established jointly by the Egyptian antiquities authorities and the Centre national de la recherche scientifique (CNRS), the French national scientific organization. Devoted solely to the restoration, study, and preservation of the Great Temple complex of the god Amun at Karnak in Thebes, its permanent staff includes not only Egyptologists but also architects, engineers, conservators, artists, and photographers. In consolidating the Ninth and Tenth Pylons of the temple, they recovered thousands of blocks with relief decoration (*talatat*) from the dismantled temples of the Amarna period. In addition, they have reconstructed other monuments within the complex, excavated areas that now appear to be vacant, and studied the effects on the monuments of climate, a rising water table, and human action. The results of their work are published in the *Cahiers de Karnak.*

In 1971, Leiden University established the Netherlands Institute for Archaeology and Arabic Studies in Cairo. It is now supported by a consortium of Dutch and Flemish universities, and it maintains a center in Cairo with a library and support facilities for scholars. Like the American Research Center, the Netherlands institute enables its member institutions and students to conduct research and excavations in Egypt. It provides academic programs in Egypt for students from its member universities and has supported excavations and research projects at Tell Ibrahim Awad in the Delta, at Berenike on the Red Sea, at Saqqara, and in the Wadi Natrun. It also assists the Tutankhamun Clothing Project and the Multilingual Egyptological Thesaurus Project. In 1996, it established a new publication series in collaboration with Leiden University.

The interests of Italian Egyptologists, museums, and universities are facilitated by the Archaeological Section of the Italian Cultural Institute in Cairo. Established in the 1970s, it maintains an archaeological library of six thousand volumes available to scholars, and it sponsors both lectures and exhibitions at the institute.

The Austrian Archaeological Institute in Cairo was founded in 1971 by Manfred Bietak. It has committed itself to long-term excavations of Tell ed-Dabʻa in the Delta. The identification of Tell ed-Dabʻa as the site of the Hyksos capital, Avaris, has made important contributions to the understanding of the Hyksos rule of Egypt and with Egypt's relationship to its neighbors in the Levant and the Aegean. The institute has also excavated at Tell el-Hebua in Sinai and at Thebes, surveying the monumental tombs of the Late period. At its offices in Cairo, it has a library of five thousand volumes and support facilities for affiliated scholars. Through the Austrian Archaeological Institute in Vienna, it publishes the results of its fieldwork; in 1990, it established the new journal *Ägypten und Levante*.

The Canadian Institute in Egypt was established in 1979 by Geoffrey E. Freeman and the Society for the Study of Egyptian Antiquities, under the auspices of the Canadian Mediterranean Institute. It provides assistance to scholars and expeditions from Canadian museums and universities. Its members have conducted long-term excavations and archaeological surveys in the Dakhla Oasis, in the Wadi Tumilat, at Pithom (Tell el-Maskhuta), at East Karnak, the site of the dismantled temples of the Amarna period, at Mendes in the Delta, and in the Dongola Reach in Sudan. Preliminary reports of these expeditions are published in the *Journal of the Society for the Study of Egyptian Antiquities*.

The Australian Centre for Egyptology was founded in 1989. Based at Macquarie University in Sydney, it maintains a branch in Egypt, which promotes and coordinates the Egyptological research of the various Australian institutions working in Egypt. It also publishes their results in the *Bulletin* that was established in 1989 and in two series of excavation reports and research monographs. The center's scholars have excavated a number of important cemeteries: el-Hammamiya and el-Hagarsa near Sohag in Upper Egypt; in the necropolis at Thebes; and in the Teti pyramid cemetery at Saqqara.

The Institute for Nautical Archaeology–Egypt established a branch in Egypt in 1993. Egypt has rich, largely unexplored resources for underwater archaeology, both in the Mediterranean and on the Red Sea coast. The institute has converted five buildings at the National Maritime Museum in Alexandria to the Alexandria Conservation Laboratory for Submerged Antiquities. The Institute of Nautical Archaeology is a U.S.-based research organization that was founded in 1973 by George Bass, who founded the field of underwater archaeology in the Middle East.

New research institutes continue to establish programs in Egypt. The McDonald Institute for Archaeological Research, established at the University of Cambridge in 1994, places particular emphasis on collaborative and multidisciplinary scientific research in archaeology. Egyptologists working with the McDonald Institute are conducting research and excavation at Tell el-Amarna, Saqqara, and Memphis. This research is supported by the institute's laboratories for geoarchaeology, archaeozoology, and bioarchaeology as well as the study collections of the University Museum of Archaeology and Anthropology and the Department of Archaeology at Cambridge.

Research and excavation in Egypt has not been limited to the activities of these institutes and centers. Scholarly work is also being done by professionals from other foreign museums and universities, including those of Spain and Japan.

[*See also* Educational Institutions; Egyptology; Museums; *and biographies of Carter, Champollion, and Petrie.*]

## BIBLIOGRAPHY

American Research Center in Egypt. *Forty Years of Bridging Time and Culture*, New York, 1987. Brochure giving a history of the organization and an overview of its activities.

Beaucour, Fernand, Yves Laissus, and Chantal Orgogozo. *The Discovery of Egypt: Artists, Travellers and Scientists*. Paris, 1990. A well-illustrated account of the French scholars who accompanied Napoleon to Egypt.

Bell, Lanny. "New Kingdom Epigraphy." In *The American Discovery of Ancient Egypt: Essays*, edited by Nancy Thomas, pp. 97–108. Los Angeles, 1996. An account by a former director of the history of Chicago House and its epigraphic method.

Bierbrier, Morris L. *Who Was Who in Egyptology*. 3d rev. ed. London, 1995. A comprehensive biographical resource of scholars and travelers who studied ancient Egypt.

Breasted, Charles. *Pioneer to the Past: The Story of James Henry Breasted*. New York, 1943. A biography of the founder of the Oriental Institute of the University of Chicago and the Epigraphic Survey of the Oriental Institute, popularly known as Chicago House.

Desroches Noblecourt, Christiane. *La Grande Nubiade ou le parcours d'une égyptologue*. Paris, 1992. An account by one of the participating Egyptologists of the founding of both the Centre d'Études et de documentation sur l'ancienne Égypte and the Centre Franco-Égyptien d'Étude des Temples de Karnak.

Dunham, Dows. *Recollections of an Egyptologist*. Boston, 1972. A brief account by one of its founders of how and why ARCE was established.

James, T. G. H., ed. *Excavating in Egypt: The Egypt Exploration Society 1882–1982*. Chicago, 1982. The official history of the society as prepared for its centenary.

Lauffray, Jean, and Serge Sauneron. "La Création d'un Centre Franco-Égyptien pour l'Étude des Temples de Karnak." *Kêmi* 18 (1968), 103–104. Provides a summary of the reasons for its establishment and the organizational program.

McDonald Institute for Archaeological Research. *Archaeology at Cambridge.* Cambridge, 1994. Brochure describing the institute's multi-disciplinary archaeological and scientific research.

Netherlands Institute for Archaeology and Arabic Studies in Cairo. Cairo, 1996. Brochure prepared for the twenty-fifth anniversary of the institute.

Roemer, Hans Robert. "Relations in the Humanities between Germany and Egypt: On the Occasion of the Seventy-fifth Anniversary of the German Institute of Archaeology in Cairo (1907–1982)." In *Ägypten: Dauer und Wandel,* pp. 1–6. Sonderschrift 18, Deutsches Archäologisches Institut, Abteilung Kairo. Mainz, 1985.

Säve-Söderbergh, Torgny. *Temples and Tombs of Ancient Nubia: The International Rescue Campaign at Abu Simbel, Philae and Other Sites.* London, 1987. An account of the founding of the Centre d'Études et de documentation sur l'ancienne Égypte at the beginning of the Nubian Salvage Campaign.

Vercoutter, Jean. "Introduction." *Le Livre du Centenaire de l'Institut Français d'Archéologie Orientale du Caire 1880–1980.* Mémoires publiés par les membres de l'Institut Français d'Archéologie Orientale du Caire, 104, pp. vii–xxv. Cairo, 1980. The official history of the institute as prepared for its centenary.

Whitehouse, Helen, and Jaromir Malek. "A Home for Egyptology in Oxford." *The Ashmolean* 16 (1989), 8–9. Article on the fiftieth anniversary of the opening of the Griffith Institute.

SUSAN J. ALLEN

**ARCHAEOLOGY.** The history of archaeological work in Egypt may conveniently be divided into five rather arbitrary phases of unequal length, each of very different character. The first phase consisted of ancient interest in Egypt's past. The second did not transpire until the seventeenth century CE. The third took place in the nineteenth century. Both the fourth and fifth occurred in the twentieth century.

**Phase One: From Antiquity to the Seventeenth Century.** More than four thousand years ago, ancient Egyptians themselves excavated parts of their archaeological patrimony. Most of the work was motivated by practical concerns: a pharaoh could show his love of the gods and respect for their priests by restoring temples. He could demonstrate his own legitimacy by preserving the monuments of his ancestors. In the twelfth dynasty, for example, Senwosret (Sesostris) III removed two sarcophagi from beneath the third dynasty Step Pyramid and placed them in the foundation deposits of his own pyramid complex as a means of demonstrating a historical affinity with Egypt's more ancient kings. In the nineteenth dynasty, Khaemwese, a son of Ramesses II, carefully explored necropolises from Saqqara north to Giza, cleaning and restoring many ancient monuments. He considered his actions to be both pious and historically important. Greeks and Romans, too (Egypt was under their control from 332

BCE to 337 CE), took an antiquarian interest in Egyptian monuments and restored or rebuilt those that played significant roles in their own religious ritual.

These early ventures into Egypt's past were harmless; some even protected the monuments. By the end of the Roman period, however, the treatment of Egyptian antiquities had become much more brutal. Perhaps it was because they no longer had meaning or cultural relevance: by the fifth century CE, the last Egyptian temples had closed, the last priests had died, and knowledge of the Egyptian language had died out. It was also because two new and jealous religions, Christianity and Islam, which dominated Egypt in turn beginning in the third century CE, saw Egyptian monuments as threats to man's relationship with the True God, best used only as convenient sources of building material. Local villagers plowed artifacts into the mud, burned papyri as fuel for bread ovens, hacked out pagan images on temple walls, and tore out stone blocks for new construction. The ancient Egyptians had sometimes abandoned or dismantled monuments; the Romans had carted several obelisks back to Rome, but there had not been destruction of this magnitude before.

Such destruction has continued into recent times. European travelers, who had begun visiting Egypt in numbers in the sixteenth century, were not concerned with archaeological preservation. Early pilgrims carried off Christian objects, anxious to acquire relics that would confirm their religious beliefs and offer proof of biblical history. They too destroyed figures that they could no longer understand or that seemed threatening. Medieval travelers picked over ancient sites, collecting mementos of their visits and carving their names on temple walls. Renaissance entrepreneurs dug for mummies that could be shipped to Europe and ground into what many believed were efficacious medicines. In all these instances, the digging was primitive and random, the record-keeping nonexistent, and the destruction of what we today would consider essential information nearly total.

Until the nineteenth century, Europeans derived most of their knowledge about ancient Egypt from classical sources (especially Herodotus, Diodorus Siculus, Horapollo, and Pliny the Elder), biblical texts and exegeses, and the often fraudulent writings of travel writers such as John Mandeville (who, in fact, had never visited Egypt). Rarely accurate, these descriptions of Egypt and its monuments conspired to convince European scholars that Egypt was a truly exceptional country whose culture and history followed none of the rules that had governed the rest of human development. For example, both Pliny and Mandeville claimed that Egypt was a country inhabited by one-legged human beings who hopped about cultivated fields so fertile that frogs spontaneously generated in the mud, whose people drank from a Nile so potent

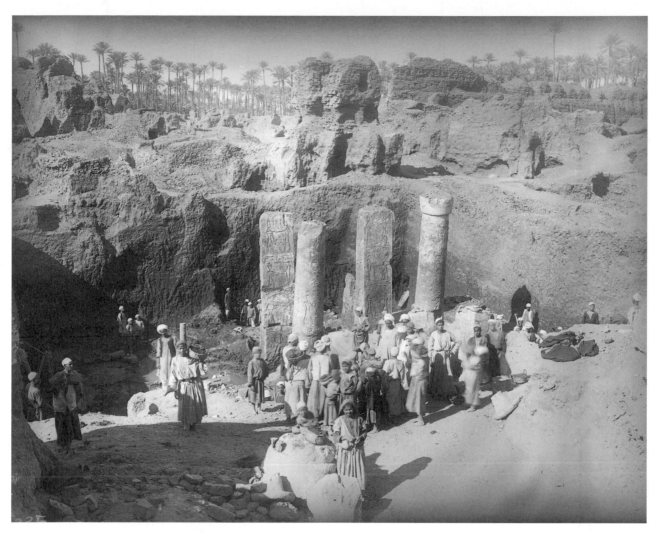

ARCHAEOLOGY. *Photo from Eckley B. Coxe Jr.'s expedition to Memphis, May 1915.* Shown here is the excavation of the Merenptah building no. 100–101, nineteenth dynasty. (University of Pennsylvania Museum, Philadelphia. Neg. # S4–141815)

it instantly made women pregnant, a people who built temples and pyramids with the direct assistance of God and the angels. Egypt was said to be the site of the garden of Eden, the earthly model of paradise. Surely, Europeans argued, the usual rules could not be applied there. Egypt was thus considered a unique country that had appeared suddenly, fully developed, with no predecessors, survived for three thousand years, and disappeared, leaving no obvious descendants.

Gradually, this view was expanded as tales about Egypt assumed an ever greater role in European myth and art. That the ancient Egyptians possessed knowledge far greater than modern humans was a popular opinion. This belief was regularly confirmed by the misinformation published in Europe about the magical powers of Egyp-

tian objects, the potency of Egyptian symbols, and the special relationship between Egypt and the supernatural. For example, Europeans had long believed that the bodies of Christian saints, unlike those of ordinary mortals, were incorruptible. If their corpses were exhumed, it was claimed, they would be as perfectly whole and sweet-smelling as a living person's. How saintly, then, must the ancient Egyptians have been because thousands of perfectly preserved bodies (mummies) were found there every year! The whole population must have sat at the right hand of God!

**Phase Two: Seventeenth- and Eighteenth-Century Collecting.** By the late seventeenth century, Egyptian artifacts were to be seen throughout Europe. At that time museums were first established, and *cabinets des curiosités*

ARCHAEOLOGY. *Excavations of Dieter Arnold at el-Lisht, 1989.* Repair work on the western side of Imhotep's *mastaba.* (Courtesy Dieter Arnold)

could be found in the homes of the well-to-do. These Egyptian collections exerted a profound influence on Europe's views and on its own decorative arts and architecture. People wanted to possess Egyptian "things," the older, the more mysterious, the better. From the late 1600s onward, European collectors enthusiastically sought after Egyptian *objêts*, and agents happily ran an antiquities trade to satisfy them. In a short time, not only were small amulets, statuettes, and mummies being shipped abroad but even monumental sculptures, obelisks, whole tombs, and temple walls. The peculiar features of Egyptian art that these collections displayed—human figures with animal heads, elaborate pieces of golden jewelry, and fascinating but unreadable texts—only confirmed the Egyptians' special status.

**Phase Three: Nineteenth-Century Exploration.** The distorted European picture of ancient Egypt did not begin to change until early in the nineteenth century. The first step toward a more accurate representation resulted from the Napoleonic expedition of 1798–1802. Bonaparte had brought 175 "savants" with his army—a committee of artists and scholars—whose task was to prepare as complete a record of the country as possible. The result was the *Description de l'Égypte* (1809–1828), a stunning record of Egypt's archaeological monuments, natural history, and local cultures, published in twenty-one volumes of text, maps, and plates. The *Description*'s elaborate illustrations gave Europeans their first accurate view of the country and its monuments. For almost the first time, Europeans could see the real Egypt, not the fanciful country that earlier sources had described.

In 1799, Napoleon's men found what was later to be called the Rosetta Stone while digging coastal defenses near the Rosetta branch of the Nile. It was immediately recognized as a possible source for the decipherment of Egyptian hieroglyphic script. Although the Rosetta Stone was confiscated by the British after the Battle of Waterloo (it is now in the British Museum), copies had been made, and, working from them in France, Jean-François Champollion declared in 1822 that the key to ancient Egyptian had been found. With that announcement, it became possible for the first time in fourteen hundred years to read ancient texts and to learn about Egypt from the ancients themselves. Almost overnight, a vast new source of information was available, and there was a scramble to acquire inscribed materials to study.

This desire for texts, either the originals or copies, led to numerous expeditions to the Nile Valley. Champollion

ARCHAEOLOGY. *Careful recording necessitates measurements.* A theodolite, a surveying instrument, measures vertical and horizontal angles, as used at the excavations of Dieter Arnold in el-Lisht, 1989. (Courtesy Dieter Arnold)

visited Egypt in 1828 to copy texts, and a dozen other scholars from throughout Europe went as well. The most important was Richard Lepsius (1810–1884), whose thirteen-volume *Denkmäler aus Aegypten und Aethiopien* (1849–1859) included hundreds of folio plates of ancient texts, relief scenes, and temple plans. Today, Lepsius's work is still a rich source of information for Egyptologists; then, it and the *Description* were the most reliable and comprehensive sources available. So too were the superb watercolors of David Roberts (1796–1864), and the works of Sir John Gardner Wilkinson, whose brilliant three-volume *Manners and Customs of the Ancient Egyptians* (1837) provided descriptions and explanations of nearly every aspect of the ancient culture.

As positive as the contributions of these descriptive publications may have been, they had unintended negative impact too. Although in the nineteenth century, in other parts of the world, archaeology was rapidly developing new techniques of excavation, dating, and interpretation, in Egypt these were being pushed into the background of scholarship. Egyptologists, most of them philologists by training, considered archaeological data merely footnotes to the story told by the written word.

Archaeology's goal, it was argued, should simply be to find more texts. Archaeological context was ignored, and objects were saved only if they were deserving of display in museums. Excavators felt perfectly justified in plowing through sites (not habitation sites, but cemeteries or temples, for they were the ones known to contain the treasures), saving only inscribed objects and pieces of aesthetic appeal, and tossing the rest into the Nile. Not only would the texts reveal all that one needed to know, scholars claimed, but also there would be more to dig. Egypt was an archaeological cornucopia that could never be exhausted. By the late nineteenth century, dozens of expeditions were at work on sites from the Mediterranean to Aswan. It was an exciting time: excavators plundered tombs, dynamited temples, committed piracy, and shot their competitors in order to assemble great collections. Enactment of antiquities laws (the first in 1835), the founding of the Egyptian Antiquities Service, and the establishment of a national museum (1863) did little to reduce the scale of pillaging.

**Phase Four: Early Twentieth-Century Excavation.** Not until the beginning of the twentieth century were excavations properly controlled in Egypt. These rare early projects, in which careful digging was accompanied by proper recording procedures and contextual analyses, were the work of William Matthew Flinders Petrie (1853–1942) and George Andrew Reisner (1867–1942). Petrie's work on artifact typologies, seriation, and sequence dating demonstrated that even without associated texts, archaeological material could provide important information and not just pretty objects. His numerous publications, particularly of Predynastic materials, helped set new standards for the analysis of archaeological data. Similarly, Reisner's meticulous excavations of cemeteries at Giza and at Naga ed-Deir established new chronological guidelines for Early Dynastic and Old Kingdom artifacts.

Unfortunately, Petrie's and Reisner's emphases and methods were slow to influence other excavators' techniques. What we today consider "proper" excavations remained the exception. The first half of the twentieth century was a time of spectacular archaeological discoveries in Egypt, including the tomb of Tutankhamun (excavated by Howard Carter), the treasures of Illahun and Thebes (The Metropolitan Museum of Art, New York); the Early Dynastic cemeteries at Saqqara (Walter B. Emery); and the Giza cemeteries (Reisner and Hermann Junker). Yet, important and well-executed as these projects were, they indicate that Egyptologists still preferred clearing tombs and stone temples to sifting through habitation debris or working with mud brick, still preferred well-preserved sites along the desert edge to the complex remains in the Nile Valley and Delta. The excavations of the necropolis at Tanis (a Delta site dug by Pierre Montet) and the long-term projects at Tell el-Amarna and Deir el-Medina (both townsites) were among the few exceptions. Thus, there were few attempts in the early twentieth century to work at sites being threatened by new irrigation schemes, growing towns, new roads, or expanding agriculture, so many of these sites are gone. This bias in favor of desert and stone continues to be an increasingly serious problem even today.

**Phase Five: Modern Analysis.** One of the most significant changes in the character of Egyptian archaeology occurred during the Nubian Salvage Campaign in the 1960s. Deeply concerned about the hundreds of sites that would be destroyed by rising Nile waters when the new Aswan High Dam was completed, Egypt and UNESCO issued a joint appeal to archaeologists from around the world to conduct salvage archaeological projects in the area south of Aswan. Although in ancient times this area, which was part of Nubia, did not belong to Egypt culturally, excavations there had traditionally been conducted by Egyptologists (among them, Reisner, Junker, and Emery). Now, dozens of archaeologists, many of them trained in fields very different from Egyptology, came to work. With backgrounds in European prehistory and North

American archaeology, they brought with them more rigorous approaches to excavation and analysis than Egyptian archaeology had ever developed. Lithics and ceramics were subjected to detailed study; typologies were created; chronological schemes were expanded and refined; and such disciplines as palynology, botany, zoology, chemistry, and statistics were used to reveal changing patterns of climate, describe minute details of lifestyle, and track changes in culture.

When the Nubian campaign ended, many of these archaeologists turned their attentions farther north to Egyptian sites, bringing a whole new approach to Egyptian materials. They took an interest in urban sites. These archaeologists gave emphasis to finds that earlier generations of Egyptological excavators had considered worthless: for example, animal bones, vegetation, stone tools, potsherds, soils, and mud-brick architecture. They were eager to work in areas formerly though to be impossible, in the Delta, the Nile alluvium, and the oases. They gave to archaeological data an interpretive emphasis formerly reserved only for textual evidence. They also asked new questions about subjects as diverse as health and disease, social stratification, the influence of climatic change on agriculture and trade, the development of ceramic technology, and the origins of complex society.

Today, archaeological work in Egypt is increasingly more anthropological rather than object or text oriented. Not surprisingly, many of its practitioners have as much social science in their backgrounds as traditional Egyptology. Karl Butzer, for example, is a geographer and anthropologist who has examined the impact of the environment on ancient Egyptian culture and on the development of irrigation in the Nile Valley. Bruce Trigger is an anthropologist interested in the origins of civilization and its dynamics. Fekri Hassan is a prehistorian with a longstanding interest in the origins of Egyptian society and the theoretical framework for its study. William Y. Adams is a prehistorian by training, whose Nubian ceramic studies are benchmarks that have put Nubian chronology on a solid footing. Barry Kemp is an Egyptologist and archaeologist who has studied the dynamics of Egyptian society as revealed by the archaeological record; his work at Tell el-Amarna and his processual approach to dynastic culture have had major impact. The activities of these and other scholars provide examples of archaeological analysis and interpretation as good as any in the world today. Furthermore, excavations—the long-term work at Hierakonpolis; Mark Lehner's studies of the Giza plateau; Robert Wenke's surveys and excavations in the Faiyum and the Delta; Manfred Bietak's superb studies of the site of Tell ed-Dab'a (ancient Avaris); and those of the Germans and Swiss at Elephantine, to name a few examples—are truly state-of-the-art projects. No longer is the emphasis on pretty objects or simple description; there is a commitment to problem-oriented excavations, to the utilization of appropriate techniques, and to cross-cultural comparisons that extract the maximum amount of information from Egyptian sites.

It has taken several centuries, but Egyptologists today recognize that ancient Egyptian culture is not a unique phenomenon that can only be explained by suspending the rules and invoking the gods. Egyptian culture *is* very special and very impressive, but by acknowledging that it *is* the work of humans, it can best be understood. When studied like other civilizations, ancient Egypt has relevance to our understanding of human development. Such newfound relevance has come at a critical time. Without carefully planned archaeological work coupled with meticulous conservation and recording, Egypt's cultural patrimony will not survive. Egypt's archaeological sites are being seriously threatened today, from pollution, agriculture, growing population, theft, and other insidious forces. These threats make it even more crucial that we treat Egypt's archaeological remains not as the inexhaustible curiosities we once thought they were, but as fragile and finite resources.

[*See also* Archaeological and Research Institutions; Educational Institutions; Egyptology; Epigraphy; Museums; *and the biographies of Champollion, Lepsius, and Petrie.*]

### BIBLIOGRAPHY

Assmann, Jan, et al., eds. *Problems and Priorities in Egyptian Archaeology*. London, 1987. Series of reports on some of the current archaeological work being conducted in Egypt, especially in the Nile Delta.

Bietak, Manfred. "Avaris and Piramesse: Archaeological Exploration in the Eastern Nile Delta." *Proceedings of the British Academy* 65 (1979), 225–290. Accessible introduction to Bietak's excellent work at an important Delta site; also published as a separate volume (Oxford, 1981). More recent information on his work there, and on other Egyptian projects, may be found listed and abstracted in the *Annual Egyptological Bibliography* (Leiden, 1947–).

Butzer, Karl W. *Early Hydraulic Civilization in Egypt: A Study in Cultural Ecology*. Chicago, 1976.

*Description de l'Égypte*. 21 vols. Paris, 1809–1828.

Greener, Leslie. *The Discovery of Egypt*. London, 1966. The most readable account of Egyptology's early history to 1855.

Kemp, Barry J. "In the Shadow of Texts: Archaeology in Egypt." *Archaeological Review from Cambridge* 3 (1984), 19–28.

Lepsius, Richard. *Denkmäler aus Aegypten und Aethiopien*. 13 vols. Berlin, 1849–1859.

Reeves, C. Nicholas. *After Tut'ankhamun: Research and Excavation in the Royal Necropoleis at Thebes*. London, 1992. Examples of the kind of archaeological work currently being done in the Valley of the Kings.

Trigger, Bruce G. *A History of Archaeological Thought*. Cambridge, 1989. General work with occasional discussion of Egyptian data.

Trigger, Bruce G. *Early Civilizations: Ancient Egypt in Context*. Cairo, 1993. Good example of how current anthropological theory is making use of Egyptian archaeological data.

Weeks, Kent R., ed. *Egyptology and the Social Sciences: Five Studies*. Cairo, 1979. Egyptologists discuss the future needs of Egyptian historical, anthropological, and archaeological studies.

Weeks, Kent R. *An Historical Bibliography of Egyptian Prehistory*. American Research Center in Egypt, 6. Winona Lake, Ind., 1985. Useful source for work done on Paleolithic through Early Dynastic Egyptian sites.

Wilkinson, John Gardner. *Manners and Customs of the Ancient Egyptians*. 3 vols. London, 1837.

KENT R. WEEKS

**ARCHAIC PERIOD.** *See* Early Dynastic Period.

**ARCHAISM.** To an Egyptologist, an *archaism* (also called "antiquarianism" by C. Aldred and having "classicistic tendencies" according to B. V. Bothmer) refers to a deliberate attempt to reproduce a style of sculpture, painting, language, literature, architecture, or other material or intangible cultural artifact from an earlier period. A more general definition of an *archaism* is the survival or presence of something from the past that was not necessarily preconceived. Therefore, its use in describing certain aspects of ancient Egyptian culture requires qualification, because virtually every element of that civilization reached back in time for its inspiration. Much of that emulation consisted of sustaining and continuing some traditions, including statue poses, the presence of back pillars, hair styles, royal regalia, and, most importantly, religion. These and numerous other aspects of Egyptian civilization remained largely unchanged throughout pharaonic times, reflecting the overwhelming need of those people to maintain their society in a largely unaltered state. Despite that compulsion, there were substantial alterations of styles during those three thousand years, and those stylistic revisions usually permit art historians to date fragmentary remains found outside the archaeological contexts—although an archaism can cause scholars confusion in making attributions.

A fine line separates an archaism from the prolongation of a static state or a stasis. An archaism requires a conscious and purposeful effort to imitate a particular style, individual, scene, or use of language, among other things, that serves to associate one historical period with a determinate moment of the past. According to J. Baines (1989, p. 137), "archaism describes instances where there is some extra meaning in these practices." It must also include a substantial gap in time to constitute an archaism. To describe a continuation of style directly following the original in time, Bothmer used the word "archaistic." The studied consistency of Egyptian cultural traditions was increasingly interrupted by foreign influence toward the end of its history, but it persisted well after the beginning of Roman domination in 30 BCE.

The most obvious explanation for an archaism is to assume that the ancient Egyptians, desirous of restoring past glories, imitated styles prevalent during the reigns of their greatest rulers, which was usually, but not always, true. Visual access to works from more ancient eras was a necessity, along with the requisite materials, artistic skills, and in some cases, sufficient labor. The great pharaohs of the Middle Kingdom revived pyramid building but usually had them constructed with mud bricks, rather than with the large limestone blocks used during the Old Kingdom of several hundred years earlier; the country was no longer able to supply the large labor force needed to copy the monumental architectural works of the earlier kings. The sole exception was the pyramid of Amenemhet I (r. 1991–1962 BCE), the first pharaoh of the twelfth dynasty, which was composed of limestone blocks taken from Old Kingdom sites. In other cases of archaisms, we do not know why the style of one particular king was copied and another, of commensurate importance, was not. For example, the image of the eighteenth dynasty pharaoh Thutmose III (r. 1504–1452 BCE) was a frequent model for later imitators, but portraits of the successful rulers from the twelfth dynasty were not.

**Sculpture.** The earliest acknowledged example of an archaism occurs in the sixth dynasty tomb of Nisutnefer in Giza, just south of present-day Cairo, which directly borrows from that of Shepseskaf of the Fourth dynasty. The scholar H. Brunner, however, disclaims any evidence for an archaism before the nineteenth dynasty (*Lexikon der Ägyptologie*, vol. 1, col. 388. [Wiesbaden, 1976]), a concept with which few, if any, other scholars agree. Later, archaisms became manifest during the Middle Kingdom reign of Senwosret I (c.1971–1928 BCE) whose fragmentary dyad statue portraying him with the goddess Hathor recalls those of Menkaure (r. 2551–2523 BCE) from the fourth dynasty. A statue of Senwosret II (r. 1897–1877 BCE) shows the position of the hands of the king as similar to those of Khafre (r. 2576–2551 BCE), also from the fourth dynasty. Relief decoration in the pyramid complex of Senwosret I was strongly influenced by the sanctuary of Pepy II (r. 2300–2206 BCE) in Saqqara, the necropolis of Memphis; this is an instance of copying from a pharaoh whose reign ended the Old Kingdom and whose rule was not nearly as productive as those of the frequently imitated kings of the fourth dynasty. It appears that archaisms were inspired by an appreciation of artistic merit as well as an admiration of political and economic successes.

Sculpture from the New Kingdom demonstrates archaisms that recall both the Old and Middle Kingdoms. Although these classicistic tendencies are most obvious during the reign of Amenhotpe III (r. 1410–1372 BCE), a statue of Amenhotpe II (r. 1454–1419 BCE) in the collection of University College, London (U.C. no. 14665), displays a falcon protecting the king in the fashion of the famous fourth dynasty statue of Khafre in the Cairo Museum (JE 10062). Even earlier in the eighteenth dynasty, is a group of statues of Amenhopte I (r. 1545–1525 BCE), identified by R. Tefnin (1968) and J. Romano (1976), which have close stylistic affinities to eleventh dynasty royal representations, particularly those of Montuhotep. Perhaps the most intriguing example of an archaism from the reign of Amenhotpe III is a scribe statue of Amenhotep, son of Hapu, as an aged man (Cairo, CG 42127). This portrait of a private man later deified—considered one of the finest sculptures of the New Kingdom—so closely emulated the style of the Middle Kingdom that at least one eminent Egyptologist, D. Wildung (1984), believed that it was usurped from the earlier period, with the inscription added during the eighteenth dynasty. His view is not generally accepted, but it demonstrates how carefully the artist imitated the style of a period almost five hundred years old at the time of the subject's portrayal. The statue wears a wig with pointed ends copied with great fidelity from Middle Kingdom models and has heavily lidded eyes that also imitated a style unused for centuries. Only the elegantly shaped eyebrows are unmistakably traceable to the reign of Amenhotpe III (Russmann 1989). This accuracy of imitation leaves little doubt that well-preserved sculpture from earlier eras of Egypt was available to artisans in the New Kingdom.

Relief decoration in the New Kingdom also took inspiration from Old and Middle Kingdom models. As Donald Spanel (1988) noted, relief portraits of Amenhotpe I show the influence of eleventh and early twelfth dynasty monarchs, thus revealing the desire of the eighteenth dynasty's founding king to advertise himself as the latest in a line of Theban defenders of the realm. The reliefs in the Theban tomb of Kharuef (tomb 192) recall the aesthetics of two earlier eras. A. Kozloff and B. Bryan (1992) described the stiff quality of the figures portrayed in ritual combat and dance scenes in that tomb as reminiscent of Old and Middle Kingdom action scenes.

Notwithstanding abundant examples of archaisms during the Middle and New Kingdoms, the Late period (1070–343 BCE) contained the greatest measure of revisiting the past. The beginning of that era, the Third Intermediate Period (1081–711 BCE), was a time of relative instability; the empire was divided into two kingdoms, one in Upper and one in Lower Egypt. The pharaohs, no longer descendants of a royal line, reverted to early eighteenth dynasty models for inspiration in their desire to establish royal legitimacy. Depictions from this time of Thutmose III were so carefully copied from the originals that they still create confusion about their dating. The literature of Egyptology often refers to this studied imitation as an integral part of the art of that time.

Examples of uncertain attributions from that time include an extraordinary gold statuette of Amun, originally attributed by Howard Carter to the reign of Thutmose III, and subsequently to the twenty-second dynasty by Aldred (1960). Another statue fragment in The Metropolitan Museum of Art, New York, was initially assigned to the early eighteenth dynasty and is now dated to the Third Intermediate Period, perhaps the twenty-third dynasty (Josephson and Stanwick, forthcoming). Seipel (1992) dates two sculptures to the Third Intermediate Period: one is in Vienna, a statue of a god originally thought to be Ramessid, and the second, in London, of just a head, is usually also attributed to the New Kingdom. An article by T. G. H. James (1994), however, persuasively argues against the attribution of the Vienna statue to this later period. Archaisms in relief sculpture were also pronounced during the Third Intermediate Period. Richard Fazzini (1988, 1997) has concluded that many echo Old and New Kingdom paradigms.

In the Kushite and Saite dynasties of the Late period (the twenty-fifth and twenty-sixth dynasties, c.755–525 BCE), archaism reached full bloom. The twenty-fifth dynasty was founded by Nubian invaders who conquered Egypt, revitalized, and reunited it. They embarked on an ambitious building program unprecedented since the reign of Ramesses II, deliberately evoking the past for legitimization of their kingships. The latter part of the Middle Kingdom provided models for sculpture in the round to such a pronounced degree that there is still considerable difficulty in separating the two styles. Bothmer's classic study (1960) of the sculpture of the Late period contained three statues that the author attributed to the twenty-fifth dynasty, which now can, with reasonable certainty, be dated to the Middle Kingdom (Josephson 1997). The massive private tomb of Harwa in Thebes, built during the Kushite domination, showed considerable copying from Memphite Old Kingdom tombs, demonstrating not only archaisms but the utilization of inspirational material that originated in that ancient and distant capital of Egypt.

By the twenty-sixth dynasty and the return to native rule under Psamtik I in 664 BCE, sculptors turned more to the New Kingdom for their ideals. There was a ten-year transition period in Thebes in Upper Egypt, during which Mentuemhet, governor of upper Egypt under the Nubians, continued to maintain his position under the new king; this circumstance may have contributed to the remarkable archaizing evident in his splendid Theban tomb (tomb 34). It probably was constructed during the time that straddled the Kushite and Saite dynasties and, therefore, reflected influences derived from both the Old and New Kingdoms. A similar blending of Old and New Kingdom conventions is seen in the slightly later Theban tomb of Ibi (tomb 36); interestingly, the Old Kingdom influence in this monument has been traced to a fifth dynasty tomb

of a man with the same name. Soon after Mentuemhet's death, sculpture and relief in Thebes tended to revert to the New Kingdom conventions expressed earlier in the Third Intermediate Period. A unique portrait of Psamtik I in The Metropolitan Museum of Art, New York, is hardly distinguishable from its Ramessid-era precedents (Josephson 1996).

The use of archaisms in sculpture continued unabated, even after Egypt was conquered and occupied by the Persians in 525 BCE and the Greeks in 332 BCE. Native workshops carried on well-established traditions that included selecting paradigms from the past. During the thirtieth dynasty (380–343 BCE), the ultimate period of native rule, artists chose to emulate the work of the New Kingdom. A relief fragment, now in the Greco-Roman Museum in Alexandria, from the tomb of Zanofer, a fourth century BCE dignitary, was carefully derived in the details and poses of its figures from that considerably earlier period. It incorporates a blind harpist and female offering bearers, standard in the eighteenth dynasty, although a new realism was imparted to the faces of the participants in the scene. The portraiture of the fourth century BCE demonstrated a dichotomy that existed between the naturalistic portrayals of private persons and the very idealized features of the kings, whose faces reflect Saite origins (Josephson 1997).

The Greeks, after the conquest of Egypt by Alexander the Great in 332 BCE, established Egypt's new capital city, Alexandria, a seaport on the Mediterranean coast. Their pharaohs, all named Ptolemy, maintained the Egyptian religion and built numerous temples dedicated to Egyptian gods. In so doing, they conformed to ancient traditions in decoration, and they opted, at least at the beginning of this era, to imitate the royal sculpture of the thirtieth dynasty, an action that Bothmer characterized as "archaistic." Even the Roman emperors, who displaced the Ptolemies in 30 BCE, continued to have statues carved of themselves in Egyptian royal regalia—then thousands of years old—a clear demonstration of archaisms used for propagandizing purposes.

**Architecture.** Obvious demonstrations of archaisms may be seen in the royal and monumental architecture of ancient Egypt. The building remains from the earliest times are tombs. Their significance to their eventual occupants was awe-inspiring. More than simply memorials, they were abodes for the deceased's afterlife, serving to shelter the corpse and burial goods, thus insuring its inhabitant immortality in the afterlife. Evolving from simple graves in the Predynastic period to impressive royal pyramids in the third dynasty, a spectacular and never again duplicated size was reached in the fourth dynasty. Although pyramid building was continued to the end of the Old Kingdom (c.2200 BCE), it had ceased thereafter until the great pharaohs of the twelfth dynasty revived that practice. Amenemhet I erected at el-Lisht, south of Saqqara, a substantial pyramid with subsidiary structures that carefully duplicated Old Kingdom models. His successors in that dynasty continued to build their monuments in el-Lisht and Dashur, near Saqqara, and were the last pharaohs to do so, although the use of small pyramidal structures were associated with private tombs during the eighteenth and nineteenth dynasties in the Theban necropolis. During the reign of the first king of the Middle Kingdom, Nebhepetre Montuhotep I (2061–2011 BCE), column capitals of the Old Kingdom were imitated by architects, although other details were derived from the preceding First Intermediate Period. The funerary temple of Montuhotep in Deir el-Bahri, located in the Theban necropolis on the western bank of the Nile across from modern Luxor, served as the inspiration for that of the queen who became the female pharaoh Hatshepsut (r. 1502–1482 BCE) of the early eighteenth dynasty. Hatshepsut urgently needed to establish her legitimacy, having usurped the throne from her stepson, Thutmose III. In this example of archaism, the two temples are immediately adjacent to each other, showing both political motivation and visual accessability as inspiration for the copy.

Almost from the beginning of the Old Kingdom, stone masons copied plant forms when carving columns. By the reign of King Djoser of the third dynasty, these artisans imitated the shape of the papyrus plant to make distinctive and highly decorative pillars. It is not surprising that the reign of the first of the pyramid builders had many architectural innovations—his architect was the genius Imhotep. Fluted columns were another invention of that early Old Kingdom savant and their use largely vanished from then until the Middle Kingdom. The use of a column resembling the stalk and spreading head of a papyrus plant, common in Djoser's constructions at Saqqara, also vanished, reappearing in the nineteenth dynasty, the time of Ramesses II (Clark and Engelbach 1990). Pillars resembling palm trees are first attested from Abusir at the temple of Sahure of the fifth dynasty. They are rarely seen again until Ptolemaic times (305–31 BCE), when they were textured to imitate the palm tree's bark. Archaisms in conception and execution were used abundantly in the architecture and interior decoration of the Asasif tombs of the Theban necropolis during the twenty-fifth and twenty-sixth dynasties.

**Painting.** Wall paintings dating to the Late Gerzean period (c.3500 BCE) have been found south of Thebes in the Predynastic city of Hierakonpolis (tomb 100). A crudely rendered funerary scene painted on a plastered brick wall, apparently from a tomb, is perhaps the earliest illustration of the king smiting his enemies with a mace—a gesture that later became accepted as a symbol of the pharaoh's might. By the third dynasty, the art of wall painting became highly sophisticated, showing elaborately organized and realistic scenes. The best known of this genre is a painting of ducks rising from a marsh found in the tomb of Itet at Meidum. It is part of a scene showing the sons of the deceased casting a net over a marshland pond, trapping the birds, and according to Aldred (1980, p. 66), "an essential theme of all later representations of country life, especially with its ritual overtones of the destruction of evil manifestations." During the Middle Kingdom, painting replaced relief decoration in many tombs, particularly in the Middle Egyptian sites of Beni Hasan, Bersheh, and Meir; the wall paintings in these tombs rely on the Old Kingdom for inspiration, in both size and subject matter, although there is also an ample amount of contemporary innovation.

During the New Kingdom, wall painting reached its highest level of artistry and greatest amount of use. The early part of that dynasty, particularly the reign of Thutmose III (r. 1504–1452 BCE), was a time in which the style and the choice of subject matter was largely influenced by Middle Kingdom traditions. Within a short period of time, an age of luxury and opulence had arrived in Egypt. The influx of new styles and innovations replaced, to a large extent, the archaisms that are prominent earlier in the dynasty. Despite this onrush of new ideas and techniques, the use of paste fillings on wall scenes in Amarna, the new capital built by Amenhotpe IV (r. 1372–1355 BCE), emulated its use in the Old and Middle Kingdoms. Although wall painting remained in the repertory of decorative schemes, it was not a prominent feature in tombs after the New Kingdom and comparatively few examples are known from later periods.

**Language.** Hieroglyphically formulated language was at the core of cultural and religious expression in ancient Egyptian civilization, and unlike the cuneiform writing of ancient Mesopotamia, did not need to be reinvented as a literary vehicle. The earliest hieroglyphs predated the first dynasty and remained in use until the end of the fourth century CE. For some four thousand years, the language and its exercise evolved from simple descriptive inscriptions on slate palettes to complicated treatises covering the full range of human thought and endeavors. During the fifth dynasty, religious texts, now known as the Pyramid Texts, appeared as inscriptions on the interior walls of those great structures. They were placed there for the benefit of the buried king, thus imparting to him eternal protection. These incantations were copied by early Middle Kingdom nobles and painted on their coffins. The reason for this expression of archaism is obvious, but it is notable that they followed the Old Kingdom style of writing, despite the substantial advances in the language achieved during the Middle Kingdom. These coffins also had spells painted on them, now identified as the Coffin Texts. These special charms disappeared until the Saite dynasty, almost fifteen hundred years later, whose scribes copied the Middle Kingdom style of writing.

Examples of archaisms from earlier literary and religious texts found on temple walls and papyri were ubiquitous in ancient Egypt; an illustration may be seen copied on a Ramessid ostracon (Simpson 1958). It seems certain that the purpose of maintaining writings in religious institutions was to preserve them rather than to effect their diffusion (see Riccati 1997). Regardless of that design, their availability was obvious, and they were widely copied—a tendency conforming to a desire to continue the traditions of the Egyptian civilization in a static state and to relive the past. Clearly, this emulation was the focal point of demonstrating veneration for their ancestors.

This worshipful attitude for their antecedents reached a peak in the writings of the Kushite and Saite dynasties, as it did with other forms of archaisms. The Nubian invaders of the twenty-fifth dynasty and the Libyan colonists who became the rulers of Egypt in the twenty-sixth dynasty, felt a pressing need to promote their legitimacy as kings. The Nubians, whose language was different from ancient Egyptian, returned to the Old Kingdom Pyramid Texts, although they combined them with contemporary phrases. In another example of an archaism, the Nubian pharaoh Taharqa had copied a replica of an Old Kingdom papyrus onto a basalt slab, now called the Memphite Theology. Their immediate successors, the Saite kings, liberally used Middle Kingdom writing—a form much employed throughout that period. Riccati (1997) avers that this dynasty witnessed the revival of scholarly research—with the gathering of quotations from ancient monuments, the collecting of rare works, and the reproduction of ancient examples. The worship of earlier dignitaries—as Imhotep, the great builder and physician of the third dynasty; Amenhotep, son of Hapu; and Prince Khaemwase, who restored many ancient monuments in the nineteenth dynasty and was one of the sons of Ramesses II—was dramatically expanded during the Saite period. These examples provide an additional indication of a preoccupation with Egypt's distant past and a heightened awareness of its notables, owing to an exploration of ancient documents.

### BIBLIOGRAPHY
Aldred, C. "The Carnarvon Statuette of Amun." *Journal of Egyptian Archaeology* 46 (1960).
Aldred, C. *Egyptian Art.* London, 1980.
Assmann, J. *Ägypten: Eine Sinngeschichte.* Vienna and Munich, 1996.
Baines, J. "Ancient Egyptian Concepts and Uses of the Past: 3rd to 2nd Millennium Evidence." In *Who Needs the Past? Indigenous Values and Archaeology,* edited by R. Layton. London, 1989.
Bothmer, B. V. *Egyptian Sculpture of the Late Period: 700 B. C. to A. D. 100.* Brooklyn, 1960.
Bothmer, Bernard. *Karnak V, 1970–1971.* Cairo, 1975.

Brunner, H. "Zum Verständnis der archaierenden Tendezen in der ägptischen Spätzeit" *Saeculum* 21 (1970), 151–161.
Clark, S., and E. Engelbach. *Ancient Egyptian Construction and Architecture.* New York, 1990.
Der Manuelian, P. "Prolegomena zur Untersuchung saitischer 'Kopien.'" *Studien zur Altägyptischen Kultur* 10 (1983), 221–245.
Fazzini, Richard. *Egypt Dynasty XXII-XXV.* Leiden, 1988.
Fazzini, Richard. "Several Objects and Some Aspects of the Art of the Third Intermediate Period." In *C. Aldred Festschrift.* Toronto and New York, 1997.
James, T. G. H. "A Ramesside Divine Sculpture at Kingston Lacy." In *A. F. Shore Festschrift.* London, 1994.
Josephson, J. A. "A Portrait Head of Psamtik I?" In *W.K. Simpson Festschrift.* Boston, 1996.
Josephson, J. A. "Egyptian Sculpture of the Late Period Revisited." *Journal of the American Research Center in Egypt* 34 (1997).
Josephson, J. A. *Royal Egyptian Sculpture of the Late Period, 400–246 B.C.* Mainz, 1997.
Josephson, J., and P. Stanwick. *Royal Images from the Late Period at The Metropolitan Museum of Art.* New York, forthcoming.
Kozloff, A., and B. Bryan. *Egypt's Dazzling Sun.* Cleveland, 1992.
Kuhlmann, K. "Eine Beschreibung der Grabedekoration mit der Aufforerung su kopieren und zum Hinterlassen von Besucherinschriften aus saitischer Zeit." *Mitteilungen des Deutschen Archaologischen Institute, Abteilung Kairo* 29 (1973), 205–213.
Neureiter, S. "Eine neue Interpretation des Archaismus." *Studien zur Altagyptischen Kultur* 21 (1994), 219–254.
Riccati, A. *The Egyptians.* Chicago, 1997.
Romano, J. "Observations on Early Eighteenth Dynasty Royal Sculpture." *Journal of the American Research Center in Egypt* 13 (1976), 97.
Russmann, E. R. *Egyptian Sculpture: Cairo and Luxor.* Austin, 1989.
Seipel, W. *Gott·Mensch·Pharoah.* Vienna, 1992.
Simpson, W. K. "Allusions to the 'Shipwrecked Sailor' and the 'Eloquent Peasant' in a Ramesside Text." *Journal of the American Oriental Society* 78 (1958).
Spanel, Donald. *Through Ancient Eyes: Egyptian Portraiture.* Birmingham, 1988.
Tefnin, R. "Contribution à l'iconographie d'Aménophis I." In *Annuaire de l'Institute de Philologie et d' Histoire Orientales et Slaves,* vol. 20, 1968–1972.
Vernus, P. *Essais sur la consience de l'histoire dans l'Égypte pharonique.* Paris, 1995.
Wildung, D. *L'âge d'or de l'Égypte, le Moyen Empire.* Fribourg, 1984.

JACK A. JOSEPHSON

**ARCHERY.** *See* Sports.

**ARCHITECTURE.** One of the most impressive human achievements, and a fundamental manifestation of ancient Egyptian culture, was the architecture, from late prehistoric (3000 BCE) to late Roman imperial times (250 CE). Egyptian structure was based on the principles of order and measure, frontality, parallelism, and symmetry, as well as on the dualism between the abstract, geometrical forms of the inorganic realm and the floral but stylized forms of the organic. The styles of Egyptian architecture, however, did gradually change through three

ARCHITECTURE. *Remains of the mortuary temple of Nebhepetre Montuhetep I, at Deir el-Bahri, eleventh dynasty.* (Courtesy Dieter Arnold)

millennia. Because of the predominance of permanent or monumental structures, semipermanent styles have rarely been recognized or studied by Egyptologists, but they did exist. All Egyptian styles display the creative capacities of their designers in the selection of prototypes, shapes, dimensions, and proportions, and in the organization of those elements.

**Early Egypt.** Architecture was developed relatively late in the Nile Valley as compared to its development in the ancient Near East. In Mesopotamia, cities and temples were built as early as the fourth millennium BCE, yet Egyptian building before 3100 BCE consisted of modest domestic structures; only perishable materials were used, such as reeds, wood, and some unfired brick. Significant brick architecture became important from about 3100 to 2630 BCE—during the time of Egypt's ideological consolidation of government, religion, and art. That period, dating from the mythic unification of the Two Lands and the ensuing Thinite rulers of the Early Dynastic period, was especially meaningful for the creation of the images and ideas that determined the future of Egyptian art and architecture. In the Early Dynastic phase, as in other early cultures, the architecture became a royal or governmental domain. Under the divine rulership of Egypt's

Horus kings and the new centralized government, architecture became a means of establishing and immortalizing the ideology of the Egyptian cosmos. The architecture of that period, therefore, concentrated on huge palaces, *mastaba* tombs, and royal funerary complexes of brick, which displayed the structural and stylistic features that were to be unmistakenly "Egyptian."

The main achievement of the architecture of Early Dynastic Egypt was the formation of the palace type for the Horus king, of a monumental brick enclosure with an elaborate system of projections and recesses, similar to some early Mesopotamian temples. The Egyptian palace was probably not only the king's residence but also an arena for the display of royal power; it was also the meeting place for his followers and the gods. Except for the remains of a paneled gateway at Hierakonpolis, no remains of those early buildings have been found—but full-scale models of such palaces, to be used by the rulers in the afterlife, were preserved at Abydos and Hierakonpolis. Their enormous dimensions reveal one of the key properties of early Egyptian architecture—monumentality. Many features of later Egyptian architecture, from the Old Kingdom onward, have their roots in the Early Dynastic palaces. Such features include the paneled wall and the so-called palace façade, the form of the decorated *mastaba*, the false door, the wall decoration of the royal funerary crypt, and the decoration of sarcophagi.

The tombs of the kings at Abydos and those of their families and high officials at Memphis, Tarkhan, Helwan, and some other sites consist of subterranean burial chambers and storerooms for enormous quantities of grave goods. The open-pit construction required lavish timber ceilings of cedar beams imported from Lebanon, which carried the enormous weight of the superstructure—a huge rectangular massif of brick or rubble—the *mastaba*. Their slightly slanting exterior walls were either plain or, in imitation of the royal palace, paneled. In general, no cult installations were provided.

By the end of the second dynasty, stone was used for the first time in private tomb building, at the cemetery of Helwan, c.2700 BCE. It was introduced into the construction of royal cult complexes of Djoser, first king of the third dynasty, at Saqqara, c.2650 BCE. That grandiose complex marked both the climax and the end of the development of such early building in Egypt, yet its meaning is, lacking inscriptions, open to hypothesis. Its planning is attributed to the famous architect and scholar Imhotep, who united the basic elements of the royal funerary architecture at Abydos with the traditions of Memphis. Djoser's monument was walled by a 277 by 544 meter (900 × 1,700 foot) stone enclosure with one true gate at the southern end of the eastern wall and fourteen false gates, copying older brick prototypes. Unlike the funerary enclosures at Abydos, the walls have projecting towers articulated by shallow, vertical grooves. Two royal tombs were enclosed: the northern main tomb was built under Djoser's Step Pyramid, while the southern tomb was built under a monumental *mastaba* along the southern wall of the enclosure. The subterranean chambers of both tombs are similar in size and architectural expenditure and seem to belong to the same ruler, providing an important example, the multiple burial, a typical trait of Egyptian funerary monuments. Underground galleries in both tombs were decorated with green faience tiles that imitated reed structures; they are believed to represent a prehistoric-style residence that the king would use in the next world. The original superstructure of Djoser's tomb was based on the flat shape of a *mastaba*, it was later transformed into the first stepped *mastaba*, suggesting that the idea of a stepped tomb was only then created. The enormous size and the newly created shape point not only to an increasing demand for a monumental manifestation of kingship but also to new ideas about the royal afterlife. The *sed*-festival court along the eastern side of the complex was an element with conceptual origins in the ancient tradition of assembling the gods of the Two Lands within the fortress of the gods. Some thirty shrines of at least three chapel types—probably of different local traditions—surrounded the courtyard. The Djoser complex is the greatest example of Egyptian architecture with symbolic structures that cannot be entered or used by the living; they were meant instead for spiritual use in a different world. Since the first major stone construction was built relatively late in Egypt's creative development, some basic architectural forms had already been devised for perishable materials, which were then translated into stone. Still, the Djoser complex displays several forms arranged in a cluster, which serves to characterize the creative, early phases of the known architecture.

Domestic construction in early ancient Egypt left no conspicuous remains, so it was relatively insubstantial. From the prehistoric period, several examples of primitive dwellings are known, simple reed shelters from about 5000 to 3600 BCE, when oval-shaped semisubterranean wattle-and-daub houses were built. Houses of mud brick were built near the end of the prehistoric period, in the Gerzean phase of the Neolithic. Despite primitive house construction, vast townlike clusters of such shelters were built at Merimde, at Beni Salame (c.4800 BCE), and at Maadi (c.3600 BCE). During the wars of the unification of the Two Lands after 3500 BCE, towns were developed surrounded by round or oval enclosures and fortified by towers.

**Old Kingdom.** Little is known of the architecture of the major towns of the Nile Valley or their temples during the Old Kingdom, including those at Memphis, Heliopolis, Buto, and Sais. The main source of information has been the monumental cemeteries—those mainly at Giza, Abusir, Saqqara, and Dahshur—with their royal cult complexes and attached private tombs. Nevertheless the main building activity was concentrated, for ideological reaons, on constructing the royal cult complex. After Djoser, the royal cult complexes of the later third dynasty (Sekhemkhet at Saqqara, and an anonymous king at Zawyet el-Aryan) were simplified, heralding a new concept for the funerary structures of the fourth to the sixth dynasties. The architects of the fourth dynasty pyramid complex of King Sneferu at Meidum (c.2580) transformed an older stepped building into the first true pyramid, a building form that would house the burial chambers of pharaohs until the end of the Middle Kingdom. In the time of Sneferu, the role of the ruler expanded so that he was no longer simply a manifestation of the god Horus. Instead, he became identified with the sun god and joined in that daily cycle of death and resurrection. Egyptian belief that the most sacred and dramatic action occured when the sun set—or underground, in the interior of the pyramid and without the help of priests or rituals—may help to explain why the cult places attached to the eastern side of Sneferu's pyramids at Meidum and the Bent Pyramid at

ARCHITECTURE. *The "Botanical Garden" in the Festival Temple of Thutmose III at Karnak, eighteenth dynasty.* (Courtesy Dieter Arnold)

Dahshur were modest structures. In front of the eastern side of the two pyramids a rather modest cult installation was built, consisting of an enclosure that contained an altar flanked by two round-topped stelae of 4.2 meters (13.5 feet). Rather than the usual north–south axis of the third dynasty complexes, the new complex was oriented east–west. The rituals may have been directed to the pyramid itself, as a form of manifesting the king, but the ceremonies might also have been those of an early mortuary cult, which addressed the spirit of the king as it left the tomb. The realignment from facing the northern sky to facing the eastern sky might indicate that the sun and its movements had become ever more important to the new ideology. The pyramid complex of Sneferu at Meidum and the two complexes at Dahshur were marked by an enormous increase in pyramid size, causing unprecedented technical problems for the builders. Systems for the production of the massive quarried stone, its transport, and its lifting had to be developed, and measures had to be found to counter sagging foundations and cracking chamber roofs. These requirements generated a major development in Egyptian building technology.

Based on the great achievements of Sneferu's pyramid builders, the architects of the succeeding kings, Khufu (Cheops), Khafre, and Menkaure, created most ingenious cult complexes at Giza. Their three pyramids were, for millennia to come, the largest building projects to be completed. The construction of those giants, up to 146 meters high (450 feet) was such a technical accomplishment that we still have difficulty explaining their building methods. A new feature was the construction of a statue temple at the side of the causeway leading to the Bent Pyramid of Sneferu. The large limestone building (27 × 48 meters/90 × 150 feet) contained an open court with a portico of pillars protecting six shrines at the rear for sculptures of Sneferu. Parts of the building were decorated with wall relief. Not coincidentally, the cult of statues also appeared in private *mastaba* tombs of the period, housed in chamberlike niches in the core masonry. From the time of Khufu onward, similar statue temples replaced the stelae chapels at the eastern side of the pyramids and formed the nucleus of the development of the pyramid temples of the later Old Kingdom. The pyramid temples of Khufu and Khafre included a vast courtyard, surrounded by monolithic pillars, with narrow statue shrines behind them. The combination of a pillared court and a door niche that led to a statue shrine behind would be consistently repeated in Egyptian funerary architecture, used until the tombs of the Late period. The floors were of basalt, calcite (Egyptian alabaster), or granite. The pillars and lower parts of the walls were of granite and the upper parts of the walls were of limestone, for decoration with painted reliefs.

Another architectural element to be developed from the early fourth dynasty onward was the valley temple. Only those of Khafre and Menkaure are known. Located on the bank of a canal, the valley temple of Khafre consisted of an enormous quay and platform that allowed boats to land in front of the building, a transverse entrance hall with two gates, and a T-shaped interior pillared hall. Sockets in the pavement along the walls indicate the installation of at least twenty-three statues. The traditional explanation, that a valley temple served as a landing stage and embalming house for the body of a deceased king, is no longer accepted. Although, for geographical reasons, the valley temple and the pyramid complex had to be separated, the conceptual and ritual unity of the complex was maintained by the connecting link of a causeway. The linking of temples in the valley to the royal cult complex by monumental causeways began with Sneferu and continued until the New Kingdom. Unlike the sphinx avenues of the New Kingdom, however, the causeways were narrow, roofed (and thus rather dark inside), and had decorated walls.

The architecture of the pyramid age was the purest expression of Egyptian building principles; it was marked by simplicity and monumentality. The precise geometrical shapes were emphasized by the use of hard stone with sharp edges and polished surfaces. The harsh angular form of the giant pyramids dwarfed the human viewer. Long rows of pillars, with huge slightly inclined and undecorated limestone surfaces, were delineated by direct sunshine. For the first time, the principles of linear, symmetrical organization dominated ground plans. Under Menkaure and his successors, there was a great reduction in the size of the pyramid and an accentuation of the pyramid temple, which indicates a changed attitude toward the cult of the king. To allow the king's continued existence, the monument had to be provided with a new structure, a real funerary chapel attached directly to the eastern side of the pyramid casing—that room had a false door on its western wall. False doors rarely imitated real doors but showed a door slit within a stepped recess, often topped with a *cavetto* (cornice). Private tombs often used a profusely decorated ceremonial false door that depicted the royal palace façade.

For the first time, the king was perceived as a mortal who needed food and supplies, a development suggesting a diminishing of the king's godliness. In the pyramid temples, granite pillars were replaced by granite palm columns and, to a lesser degree, by the bundled-lotus column. Another achievement of the later Old Kingdom was the detailed Egyptian *cavetto*, a decorative element that accentuated, from the late fourth dynasty onward, practically every pharaonic building. The 5-meter- (16-foot-) wide offering hall and the entrance halls of the pyramid temples were covered with technically interesting, huge false limestone vaults (true limestone vaults had been constructed in the early fourth dynasty at Dahshur). The offering and entrance halls are the first known examples of large-scale interior spaces. From the mid-fifth dynasty onward, the elements of the pyramid temples were fully elaborated, so the temple designs of the later fifth and the sixth dynasties were changed very little.

The new spirit and naturalistic elements that characterized the reliefs of the pyramid temple of Userkaf, founder of the fifth dynasty—as well as those of the contemporary private *mastaba* tombs—reflected the increasing importance of the cult of Re, the sun god. Solar aspects had played an important role in the deification of the king, from the beginning of the fourth dynasty, but by the beginning of the fifth dynasty the tendency had become so important that at royal tombs the solar cult installations needed independent structures, separated from the funerary complexes. Userkaf was the first king to build a separate sun temple near the royal cult complex at Abusir, creating a tradition that lasted to the end of the fifth dynasty. The sun temples of Userkaf and of Any were based on the prototype of the (now lost) temple of Re-Horakhty at Heliopolis, having a gigantic freestanding obelisk surrounded by a wide courtyard. The valley temple and causeway near them approximated the arrangement of a pyramid complex.

The appearance of a cult for a god (Re) other than the king (Horus) suggests that in the course of the fifth and sixth dynasties, temples for other deities must also have developed. Since, except for later reused building blocks, nothing was preserved of those buildings, it has been thought that no temples of the gods existed during the Old Kingdom. At Bubastis and other sites, reused building elements suggest the existence of Old Kingdom gods' temples, some of considerable dimensions. In addition, the royal sanctuaries to Nekhbet at Hierakonpolis and to Wadjet at Buto, and to other deities, go back into earliest Egyptian times. Those types of sanctuaries were amplified during the sixth dynasty by the introduction of royal *ka* chapels, for kings who sought to be near the protective sanctuaries of the gods. In those small temples, the royal statue participated in the cultic activities of the temple of the local gods. The creation of a cult site for the king under the protection of a god was innovative and a foreshadowing of the development of the royal cult during the Middle Kingdom. The *ka* chapel of Pepy I of the sixth dynasty, at Abydos, was a small temple with a pillared court and five parallel statue shrines, similar in plan to those for the cults in the pyramid temples. Stone columns of floral shapes—palm, papyrus, lotus—as used for the porches and courts of the pyramid temples of the fifth dynasty, introduced soft, organic forms. From that time, they were to contrast with the sharp-edged inorganic forms common to Egyptian architecture.

The early tradition of private *mastaba* building from the first three dynasties was continued throughout the Old Kingdom—but it made use of the new building material, stone. Since paneled exteriors could be produced in stone only by great labor, just a few *mastaba* builders maintained that tradition into the Middle Kingdom. In the fourth dynasty, the plain *mastaba*, with two cult chapels at the eastern side, was usual. During the later Old Kingdom, the original idea of a *mastaba* as a massive stylized burial mound was distorted by the extension of the cult chapel into a complicated multiroom installation. The central offering hall was supplemented by statue rooms (*serdab*) and other features, some of them based on royal cult temples. In the fourth dynasty, rock-cut tombs were used at Giza and in numerous Middle and Upper Egyptian cemeteries, dug or cut horizontally into the sloping limestone or sandstone cliffs. Their two parts, the first set in a public cult area, and the second, inaccessible burial chambers, established prototypes for the later private rock-cut tomb tradition of the Middle and New Kingdoms.

The Old Kingdom "house for the dead" differed considerably from the houses of the living; compared with the extraordinary investments in tomb buildings, private dwellings remained modest mud-brick structures. The best preserved examples would be a few priests' houses in the funerary complex of Queen Khentkawes from the end of the fourth dynasty. They had solid walls, long and narrow vaulted rooms, and a coiled ground plan. Palace remains have not yet been located for the period.

**Middle Kingdom.** The decline of the concept of the solar king plus the collapse of the centralized government of the Old Kingdom allowed a much broader based development of the arts throughout the nomes (provinces) of the First Intermediate Period. In the eleventh dynasty, the area around Thebes was studded with the *saff*-tombs (row tombs) of Theban kings and officials. They consisted of huge, open sunken courtyards dug into the flat desert surface. The courtyard's rear was emphasized by rows of pillars that probably recalled a house façade. The courtyards are impressive examples of the creation of vast, depressed base planes. In contrast, the cult and burial rooms were

relatively insignificant. The founder of the eleventh dynasty, Nebhepetre Montuhotep I, overcame this provincial tradition by creating an innovative terraced temple tomb, at Deir el-Bahri, with a huge forecourt and a two-storied façade of open-pillared halls; the deliberate elevation of the floor planes, to enhance the image of the building within its landscape, seems to be an Upper Egyptian contribution. The frontal approach, though a straight axial causeway of 1 kilometer (about half a mile), led directly to the visual goal, the temple gate. A generation later, with the transfer of the royal court under Amenemhet I to el-Lisht near Memphis, that Upper Egyptian experiment ended, to be revived only in the New Kingdom under Hatshepsut.

The kings of the twelfth dynasty who succeeded Amenemhet I revived for their funerary installations the early Memphite tradition; they imitated the prototypes of the Old Kingdom pyramid complexes at el-Lisht, Illahun, Dahshur, and Hawara. The main building material for pyramids became, perhaps for cultic reasons, brick cased with limestone. The original vast pyramid temples were gradually reduced to become modest funerary chapels, and the reduced size was compensated for in the addition of a new temple type, which seems to have placed the cult of the deceased king under the protection of the gods of Egypt: the main examples are the southern temple of Senwosret III at Dahshur and the so-called labyrinth of Amenemhet III at Hawara.

Many Middle Kingdom temples were still built mainly in brick with some stone elements, such as door frames and columns. Some temples were built entirely in stone, which began the gradual process of the "petrification" of brick temples (as at Medinet Maadi, Qasr el-Sagha, Medamud, Karnak, Tod, and Elephantine). The main example was Senwosret I's temple of Amun-Re at Karnak, which today can only be judged from some magnificent elements that were used in the construction of later buildings. From such elements, Senwosret's "white chapel" could be entirely reassembled, a pillared bark station standing on a high podium. The small stone temples of Medinet Maadi and Qasr el-Sagha consist of a row of several parallel statue shrines that open onto a broad offering hall. Although some large stone temples existed in the towns of the Nile Delta, in general, their dimensions were smaller than those at the royal cult complexes.

The eleventh and twelfth dynasties produced many rock-cut tombs for the nomarchs of Middle and Upper Egypt, at Beni Hasan, Bersheh, Meir, Rifeh, and Qurna, in which some elements of temple building were combined with the plan for the house of the dead. Cut into the cliff, steep stairs, ramps, and terraces led to tomb façades, which were often formed as a portico with fluted (wrongly so-called) proto-Doric pillars or lotiform columns. Inside, a templelike and elaborately decorated cult chapel led to the statue niche, and lotiform columns supported the ceiling. Some multiroomed rock-cut tombs at Asyut, Qaw el-Kebir, and Aswan had the dimensions of major temples; they displayed for the first time the Egyptian way of organizing underground space—a linear plan, with a series of spaces that differed both in size and form. With the end of nomarchic rule (provincial governors) under Senwosret III came the end of large rock-cut tombs. Nevertheless, private *mastaba* tombs were still built in the tradition of the Old Kingdom (as at Saqqara, Dahshur, el-Lisht, and Illahun), some even creating the ancient pattern of paneled exterior walls.

Substantial remains of twelfth dynasty settlements have been excavated, and they reveal for the first time the overall picture of Egyptian dwellings. The houses reflect the status of the occupants more by dimension than by building expenditure, revealing considerable class distinctions. Farmers and people living in the community as priests, soldiers, workers, or miners were often quartered in rows of small buildings. In those houses, a court led to a central living room and a separate master bedroom. Only the elite class of high priests and officials owned mansions of great dimensions; in those buildings, sometimes several apartments for the women and other relatives were combined in a larger unit. The main hall was often distinguished by a dais for the master, who also used the house as his office or for receiving visitors. Rural installations, such as stables and granaries, were a regular component even of elite mansions. The walls and floors were made of unfired bricks, which were whitewashed. More luxury was added by painting the wall dado black and the upper parts of the walls white or yellow, divided by colorful borders. Figural decoration was rare. The roof was constructed of brick vaults or of flat wooden beams with attached reed matting. Larger rooms required wooden columns on stone bases. In more elegant houses, the columns were decorated and they carried floral capitals. Occasionally, small stairs led to the rooftop, which could be used for storage or for sleeping on hot nights. Air funnels on the roof brought fresh air into the master bedroom. Stone door sills and door frames, rare before the Middle Kingdom, became common during the New Kingdom. The interior courts were sometimes sheltered against the winds and sun by a columned hall; at the center of the court was a small pool or fountain. Occasionally a side room contained a bathing basin. The houses of the twelfth dynasty suggest local differences, especially those of Tell ed-Dab'a, Dahshur, el-Lisht, Illahun, and Elephantine; the palaces differ as well, as far as we can judge, from the few remaining at Tell ed-Dab'a, Bubastis, and Dahshur.

The Middle Kingdom excelled at military building. A chain of spectacular fortresses—the Second Cataract forts—protected the trade route to the southern Nile Valley against the kingdom of Kush. These buildings, of unique value for the history of military architecture, were still standing into the 1960s but, without proper exploration, were inundated by the new Aswan High Dam project that produced Lake Nasser. Some were small but strong castles, defended by thick brick walls, with battlements and towering entrance gates; others were fortresses with dimensions of up to 250 by 600 meters (750 × 1850 feet), more fortified large camps and cities.

**New Kingdom.** Liberation from the Hyksos, who ruled during the Second Intermediate Period, and Egypt's consequent political recovery produced building activity all over the country, with a new cultic center at Thebes on the Nile River. It began with the eighteenth dynasty temple for the joint cult of Hatshepsut, Thutmose I, and Amun-Re at Deir el-Bahri; apparently influenced by the Middle Kingdom building of Nebhepetre Montuhotep I, it revived local stylistic tendencies, favoring open-columned fronts and gradually rising terraces. Its overall disposition was, however, determined by new cultic requirements. A monumental causeway flanked by huge sphinxes and vast courts on three levels, offered space for the reception of the pompous processions of the divine barks from Karnak. The same principles dominated the residence of the sun god Amun-Re, directly opposite at Karnak. There, a huge temple complex was built around the modest Middle Kingdom temple, by continuous addition of new buildings along the axis of orientation. The temple thereby displays, with its rigid axial arrangement and symmetry, the basic principles of Egyptian architecture. There, also, the requirements of the "eternal wandering" (see Sigfried Gideon's *The Eternal Present: The Beginnings of Architecture*, 1957) of the divine barks were met, transforming the temples into processional stations that were connected with one another by processional alleys. The temple front was the stage for the god's theatrical appearance; as the visual goal of the procession, it was enhanced by huge pylons, which had suddenly emerged, architecturally, from modest Middle Kingdom beginnings. Celebrations of the god's appearance required large festival courts and hypostyle halls, as the first resting place of the divine bark after leaving the sanctuary. From Thutmose III onward, such halls were often shaped like a basilica, with high central nave and low flanking aisles, which created the effect of a protective canopy surrounded by the colonnades of a court. The basilica type was one of the major architectural contributions of the New Kingdom, only to be replaced in the Late period by the *pronaos* type. The residence for the cult images was a simple group of rooms at the back of the temple, often consisting of a triple shrine for the local triad of deities.

ARCHITECTURE. *Temple of Sety I at Qurna, nineteenth dynasty.* (Courtesy Dieter Arnold)

The eighteenth dynasty reign of Amenhotpe III favored gigantic building projects, such as the Luxor temple, the royal so-called mortuary temple, the temple of Montu at Karnak, and the temple of Soleb, with large colonnaded courts, hypostyle halls, and rows of extraordinary statue pillars. A majestic creation was the elongated entrance colonnade of the Luxor temple, with seven pairs of papyrus columns; this gigantic bark station probably created the prototype for the even greater hypostyle hall of Karnak. Still during the eighteenth dynasty, the buildings of Akhenaten at Karnak and at Tell el-Amarna marked a unique reappearance of sun temples, thereby redefining the image of an ancient solar sanctuary according to New Kingdom building ideas. Series of pylons, seen as sun gates and images of the mountains at sunrise, included vast altar courts that were open to the rays of Aten. Accessible high altars surrounded by screen walls were developed into a special building type. The predominant role of the king was emphasized by long rows of colossal statues. Still, an astonishing number of period building elements disappeared during the succeeding Ramessid era, only to be revived in the Late period (e.g., entrance porches, kiosks, composite columns, screen walls, broken lintels).

The traditional royal cult continued to be associated with those of the major local gods in temples termed "Mansions for Millions of Years." Examples are the temples of Amun-Re in Western Thebes and of Osiris at Abydos. Gradually developing in the eighteenth dynasty from twelfth dynasty prototypes, such temple building reached its peak with the work of Amenhotpe III, Sety I (Qurna and Abydos), Ramesses II (the Ramesseum), and Ramesses III (Medinet Habu). The Theban examples followed a ground plan and a decoration program that included separate cult arrangements for the deities Amun-Re, Hathor, Re-Horakhty, and the Osiris-king. The two well-preserved temples for Sety I and Ramesses II at Abydos were fitted to the local requirements of the Osiris cult. Sety I's temple incorporated an enormous underground Osiris tomb in the style of the Old Kingdom. In Ramessid-era Lower Nubia, the rock-temple type that had been created in the eighteenth dynasty was developed into monumental forms and dimensions; the axial room organization was based on prototypes created for rock-cut tombs of the twelfth dynasty. The sequence of the rock-cut pillared hall/offering hall/sanctuary was dictated by contemporary temple plans. The most fascinating examples, the temples of Ramesses II and his queen at Abu Simbel, emphasized the devine character of the royal couple with enormous rock-cut statues at the temple façade.

The Theban rock-cut tombs of the New Kingdom profited from the nearby prototypes of the Middle Kingdom and often imitated their pillared façades. A main feature was the T-shaped ground plan, with a broad entrance hall and a deep corridor leading to the statue niche. Lavish decoration in the form of wall paintings or reliefs, overshadowed the architectural achievements, which were minor compared to the harmonious pillared halls of the earlier twelfth dynasty. Only some Thutmose-era tombs—such as the Theban tombs of Senenmut (tomb 71), Puiemre (tomb 39), and the vizier Rekhmire (tomb 100)—displayed some compelling interior spaces. Tombs of high officials of the New Kingdom in the cemetery of Saqqara were faithful copies of contemporary temples for the gods, with a pylon, colonnaded forecourt, deep hall, interior colonnaded court, and a triple shrine.

The New Kingdom's vast array of private houses, uncovered at Tell el-Amarna and at Deir el-Medina, attest to a refined lifestyle. The elite houses at Tell el-Amarna seem to be villas; set within gardens, they were embellished with grand entrance and reception halls. Also from the New Kingdom onward, townhouses are known; models and representations have depicted buildings of three or four floors, with workshops or storage magazines on the ground floor and the master apartment on the top floor. During the New Kingdom, settlements of large size developed around the temple compounds; these occupied a quarter or more of the area and thereby divided the town, by their numerous processional roads, into separate quarters. Other points of town orientation were the directions of the river or any canals and the cardinal points. In Late New Kingdom cities, a rigid quartering of nationalities was reported. Many questions about the operation of cities are as yet unanswered, because no public or market squares, storehouses, and other features have been located. A population density of 625 persons per hectare has been assumed, so a town of one million square meters would have had about fifty thousand inhabitants.

The considerable remains of the New Kingdom royal palaces at Malqata and Tell el-Amarna suggest a clear separation of the king's dwelling apartments from the vast and complex ceremonial structures for public presentation. As in major private houses, the royal reception hall with the throne dais, the master bedroom, and subsidiary apartments for family members or court officials were special; floors, walls, and ceilings were profusely painted, the supports shaped into fantastic composite columns of wood. The enormous ceremonial buildings of the palace complex of Tell el-Amarna have not yet been satisfactorily explained. A special royal building type of the late eighteenth dynasty is the royal throne canopy, in which all elements of imperial claims and luxury were blended.

From the eighteenth to the twentieth dynasty, a special palace type was attached to the so-called royal mortuary temples. Such palaces were modeled on a real palace; they had the columned throne room, the bedroom and bathroom of the king, and several apartments for the royal family or high officials—but they were probably symbolic and not meant to be used as a royal dwelling. Remains of the Ramessid palaces at Qantir stress the military nature of the royal residence.

A considerable number of Ramessid fortresses protected Egyptian borders—along the Mediterranean in the west against the Libyans, and in the east against the Canaanites. The Nubian forts that had been built during the Middle Kingdom at the Nile cataracts were also revived, with small castellated structures, dwelling towers, and large fortified settlements. A most spectacular architectural achievement was the heavily buttressed barbican (tower) of Buhen, with its northern parallel in the shape of the Migdol towers of the Nile Delta and Palestine. An example of a magnificent late Ramessid fortification was the enclosure of the temple of Ramesses III at Medinet Habu. Although more fortresses were built during the restless Third Intermediate Period, none could withstand the ferocity of the attacks by the Assyrians from 671 to 661 BCE.

**Twenty-first to the Thirtieth Dynasty.** Official buildings of the Late period retained many New Kingdom characteristics. Yet lessened construction and the disappearance of the major temples of this period at Tanis may bias the assessment toward a less creative phase. The major monument still standing is the forecourt built under Sheshonq I at Karnak.

The twenty-fifth (Kushite) dynasty initiates not only a cultural recovery but a new archaism, as was demonstrated by the copying of Old Kingdom reliefs. Prominent columned halls and kiosks were attached to Theban pylons and temple entrances, the most spectacular example being the kiosk of king Taharqa in the forecourt of the temple of Amun at Karnak. Despite the non-Egyptian origin of the dynasty, no Kushite elements have been detected in their buildings within Egypt. The Kushite period did produce major architectural achievements in tomb building, with Theban rock-cut tombs of the twenty-fifth dynasty (and the twenty-sixth) showing magnificent examples of the copying of older prototypes adapted to a new concept. Their three-part plans recall the divine temples that were graced with a huge festival courtyard, a deeply sunken sacrificial courtyard, interior cult rooms, and elaborate burial systems. The tombs of the Memphite area explored new possibilities; for example, a burial chamber beneath a gigantic shaft filled with pure sand, meant to deter tomb robbers. That new burial type was further developed in the twenty-ninth and thirtieth dynasty.

Temples of the twenty-sixth dynasty have left little in physical remains. Yet the temples of Sais and other Lower Egyptian cities must be understood as prototypical for the buildings of the thirtieth dynasty and the Ptolemaic period. The temples were smaller than those of their predecessors but built in hard stone, for eternity. No open courts and frontal columned halls were added; the house of the god became introverted. It enclosed a huge, monolithic hard stone *naos* for the god. The *pronaos*, one of the great innovations of the Late period, was a hypostyle hall with a colonnaded front half enclosed by screen walls. A major contribution to the creation of the new style was the innovative composite capitals during the twenty-sixth dynasty reign of Psamtik II—the first new type created since the New Kingdom and an important element in the fashioning of future kiosks and *pronaoi*. In contrast to the composite column of the late eighteenth dynasty (the Amarna period's creation), with an assembled use of different capital types, the new composite capital united a variety of plants on the same capital. Close connections with the Greek world followed, at the time of Egypt's kings Necho, Apries, and Amasis, which aided in the importation of Egyptian building ideas.

Egypt's twenty-ninth and thirtieth dynasties created an immensely important temple-building phase, a new beginning for the imperial building style. It was ended by the Persian invasion of 343 BCE. In the Late period, based on the achievements of the Old and Middle Kingdoms, a new temple type emerged, which survived the Second Persian Occupation, to be used by the early Ptolemies. Late period temples continued to be ideally constructed of hard stone, the freestanding bark shrine for the major god of the temple was a new development, and the form of the *pronaos* was further developed. New too, was the definition of a special building type for the birth-house, a new home for the cult of the king that flourished mainly in the Ptolemaic and Roman periods. The Late period's preference for female deities especially supported the development of sanctuaries for the goddess Isis.

Enormous efforts were undertaken by the kings of both the twenty-sixth and the thirtieth dynasty to fortify Egyptian temples and towns in the North against the Persians. Brick enclosure walls, 15 to 20 meters (45 to 65 feet) thick and 20 meters (65 feet) high, surrounded almost all the Delta sites and even some sanctuaries, such as the temples of Amun-Re, Mut, and Khons at Thebes. Nevertheless, none could resist the Persian siege strategies of 525 BCE or 343 BCE.

**Ptolemaic Period.** After the founding of the Mediterranean seaport of Alexandria by Alexander the Great in 332 BCE, the expansion of that city—the new capital of their Egyptian domain—was of prime importance to the Ptolemies. Under those new Greek rulers, numerous city building projects (the royal palace, the Museion, the Pharos lighthouse, and the columned streets) were designed in the Hellenistic style of the period. Some (the number is not known) were finished with architectonic elements copied from or removed from older sites—obelisks, pharaonic sculpture, and other decorative elements—all used to emphasize either an ideological background or to provide pleasure for the eye. Both the Serapeum and the Caesareum displayed such features. Gradually, pharaonic motifs and elements were integrated into Classical-era style, creating a distinct Ptolemaic branch of Hellenistic construction; they were mainly characterized by illusionist and even baroque tendencies. What cannot be overestimated is the importance of Ptolemaic architecture, as both a stylistic blend and the origin of later stylistic ideas. The building type of the Ptolemeion—with flat segmented pediments, kiosklike structures, screen walls, and *cavetto* copings—was introduced, via the city of Alexandria, into Roman and then sometime later into European architecture.

The Ptolemies soon discovered the importance of building religious pharaonic-style architecture as a means of cultivating their relationship with the local populace and priesthood. The early Ptolemaic era, from Ptolemy I to Ptolemy V (350–180 BCE), had building activity that was commenced cautiously and according to the style of the thirtieth dynasty, retaining pharaonic tradition. Such

ARCHITECTURE. *Late New Kingdom Temple of Khonsu at Karnak, with the entrance porch of Taharqa, twenty-fifth dynasty.* (Courtesy Dieter Arnold)

stylistic dependence is not surprising, since many buildings left unfinished from the thirtieth dynasty needed completion. Examples of that period include the two gates of Ptolemy III Euergetes at Karnak; the temple houses of Deir el-Medina, Esna, and Edfu; the small temple of Esna-North; and the temples of Isis at Aswan and on Philae. The mid-Classical period is represented by the reigns of Ptolemy VI to Ptolemy XI (180–80 BCE), during which an increasing number of new temple buildings defined the accomplished Ptolemaic architectural style. A rigid structure and a dignified harmony characterized, for example, the *pronaoi* of Edfu and the inner court and hypostyle of the temple of Isis on Philae. Some buildings, such as the temple of Opet at Karnak, display the style's stronger articulation of the façade. Other typical buildings of the period include the *pronaos* of Medamud, the birth-house of Edfu, and the temple house of Kom Ombo. The mature Ptolemaic phase began under Ptolemy X. It characterized the buildings of Ptolemy XII and Cleopatra VII and continued into the early Roman imperial period, from 80 BCE to the turn of the millennium. It was marked by capital shapes that were lavish, strongly plastic, and far overhanging the slender but widely spaced columns of uncustomary heights and proportions. In addition, the surfaces

of Ptolemaic temple façades revealed a pronounced rhythm—with the projections, recesses, toruses, and *cavettos* of their intricate screen walls. Heavily protruding and receding articulations of the edges covered the surface with light and shadow effects, which defined the plane of the wall reliefs. Such means of architectural expression brought about a bombastic but majestic effect that may be described as baroque, and the style should be seen as directly connected with the similar tendencies of contemporary Hellenistic architecture in Greece; good examples include the theatrical-picturesque forms of the birth-house of Armant; the *pronaoi* at Kom Ombo and Bigga; and, in the Augustan period, the *pronaos* and hypostyle of the Kalabsha temple and the kiosk on Philae. In the latter phase, the overflowing forms of temple reliefs succeeded in opening up the hitherto intact visual surfaces of Egyptian temple walls.

The interior plan of a typical Ptolemaic temple was based on the older concept of the bark shrine that was surrounded on all sides by an ambulatory. Its huge dimensions prevented the impression of a building mass that stood within a wide space; rather the viewer stood between the bark shrine and the surrounding chapel ring. This central building's volume was enveloped by several layers of space, some gradually added during temple enlargements. The *pronaos* and entrance kiosks embraced, with their side walls and roof, the front of the actual temple house, which penetrated deeply into the *pronaos*. An appealing connection of spacial elements may be seen in the birth-houses of the Ptolemaic period; the wide space between the contained sanctuary and the protecting "tent-roof," their contrasting shapes, and the openings between the enclosing columns all served to accentuate the formal autonomy of both building masses.

Excavations of Ptolemaic towns in the Faiyum, Tebtunis, and Dime disclosed important details of house building in later times. Some tall, three-storied townhouses with vaulted cellars have been found there, still standing.

**Roman Period.** Besides military installations, Roman building activity mainly promoted nonsacred structures of urban value—bathhouses, theaters, hippodromes, basilicas, forums, new settlements, and the embellishment of towns with columned streets and triumphal arches. Such expensive building activity in Egyptian provincial towns (in the Faiyum, Oxyrhynchus, Antinoöpolis, Hermopolis Magna) even created new building types, such as the komasterion (an assembly hall for participants in processions) and the tetrastylos (a four-column monument).

Until the second century CE, the Roman emperor Augustus and his successors supported a considerable building program that kept the old-fashioned local style, but it was restricted to the Middle and Upper Egyptian provinces, south of the Delta. Most of the projects there were, however, enlargements of existing temples, and very few new buildings were undertaken. That early Roman buildings continued the late Ptolemaic style is not surprising. The main buildings preserved from the Roman period are the *pronaos* and birth-house at Dendera, the *pronaos* at Esna, the forecourt and kiosk on Philae, the temples of Shanhur, Deir el-Shelwit, Kalabsha, Taffeh, Dendur, and Maharraqa. In the course of the first century CE, the energetic Ptolemaic and early Roman styles were simplified, and this cannot be overlooked; the forms appear flat and remain on the surface. The centralized control of temple building enhanced the retaining of existing styles and types—nevertheless, some interesting new local temple types were developed in the Faiyum as well as in the western oases as late as the second century CE. In the politically and economically troubled third century CE, pharaonic-style architecture was gradually abandoned.

During Egypt's recovery under the Eastern Roman emperors Constantine the Great (r. 306–337 CE) and Theodosius I (r. 379–395 CE), pharaonic religion and culture was affected by early Christianity, resulting in an architectural style with its main roots in the Roman architecture of the Near East, from which Christianity came to Egypt. The rigid separation between pharaonic and Classical-era forms gradually disappeared in Egypt, leading to some bizarre style mixes. The mixing stopped just short of a distinct Egyptian-Roman style, clearly observable in Alexandria in the Roman crypts of Kom el-Shukafa.

The new cultural cohesion under the late Roman government eased Egyptian building motifs and elements throughout the empire—to both the Western and Eastern Roman realms. Temples for Isis and Serapis were, for example, built in numerous towns beyond Egypt; they were built in Classical-era style, tinged with "exotic" pharaonic features, and embellished with sphinxes, obelisks, and Egyptianized statues. In an early form of Egyptomania, Roman parks were decorated with "Canopic" sites. Officials built pyramids in the city of Rome, and Egyptian building materials were transported both to Rome and to imperial sites from Egypt's quarries. Most important, however, was the influence of the Egyptianized Hellenistic architecture of Alexandria on Roman construction, both in the provinces and in the Italian peninsula. From Alexandria, and then via Italy, the last shadowy descendants of pharaonic elements entered the Christian church architecture of Europe; the motif of the columned canopy survived not only in the basic early Christian basilica with a transept but also in the *ciborium*, which glorified an altar or a saint's tomb. The *cavetto*, the screen wall, the spiral staircase, and the flat segmented pediment were also elements with their roots in Egypt.

[*See also* Bricks and Brick Architecture; Egyptomania; *and* Stoneworking.]

**BIBLIOGRAPHY**

Arnold, Dieter. *Building in Egypt: Pharaonic Stone Masonry.* New York, 1991.

Arnold, Dieter. *Lexikon der ägyptischen Baukunst.* Zurich, 1994.

Badawy, Alexander. *Le dessin architectural chez les anciens égyptiens.* Cairo, 1948.

Badawy, Alexander. *A History of Egyptian Architecture.* 3 vols. Berkeley, 1966–1968.

Clark, Somers, and R. Engelbach. *Ancient Egyptian Masonry: The Building Craft.* London, 1930.

*Description de l'Égypte.* 19 vols. Paris, 1809–1828; reprint, Princeton, 1987.

Haeny, Gerhard. *Basilikale Anlagen in der ägyptischen Baukunst des Neuen Reiches.* Beiträge zur ägyptischen Bauforschung und Alterumskunde, 9. Wiesbaden, 1970.

Jéquier, Gustave. *L'architecture et la décoration dans l'ancienne Égypte.* 3 vols. Paris, 1911, 1920, 1924.

Jéquier, Gustave. *Manuel d'archéologie égyptienne: Les éléments de l'architecture.* Paris, 1924.

Müller, H. W. "Gedanken zur Entstehung, Interpretation und Rekonstruktion ältester ägyptischer Monumentalarchitektur." In *Ägypten, Dauer und Wandel: Symposium anlässlich des 75. jährigen Bestehens des Deutschen Archäologischen Instituts, Kairo am 10. und 11. October, 1982,* pp. 7–33. Mainz, 1985.

Prisse d'Avennes, Émile. *Histoire de l'art égyptien d'après les monuments depuis les temps les plus reculés jusqu'à la domination romaine.* Paris, 1878.

Ricke, Herbert. *Bemerkungen zur ägyptischen Baukunst des Alten Reiches.* 2 vols. Vol 1: Zurich, 1944; Vol. 2: Cairo, 1950.

Smith, Earl Baldwyn. *Egyptian Architecture as Cultural Expression.* New York, 1938; reprint, Watkins Glen, N. Y., 1968.

Smith, William Stevenson. *The Art and Architecture of Ancient Egypt.* London, 1958; rev. ed., 1965, and 1981.

Spencer, A. J. *Brick Architecture in Ancient Egypt.* Warminster, 1979.

Vandier, J. *Manuel d'archéologie égyptienne.* Vol. 1, pt. 2, *Les époques de formation: Les trois premières dynasties.* Paris, 1952.

Vandier, J. *Manuel d'archéologie égyptienne.* Vol. 2, pt. 1, *Les grandes époques: L'architecture funéraire.* Paris, 1954.

Vandier, J. *Manuel d'archéologie égyptienne.* Vol. 2, pt. 2, *Les grandes époques: L'architecture religieuse et civil.* Paris, 1955.

Wildung, Dietrich. *Egypt from Prehistory to the Romans.* New York, 1997.

*Mastabas*

Brinks, J. "Mastaba." In *Lexikon der Ägytologie,* 3: 1214–1231. Wiesbaden, 1980.

Cherpion, Nadine. *Mastabas et hypogées d'ancien empire: La problème de la datation.* Brussels, 1989.

Junker, Hermann. *Giza.* 12 vols. Vienna, 1929–1955.

Kaiser, W. "Zu Entwicklung und Vorformen der frühzeitlichen Gräber mit reichgegliederter Oberbaufassade." In *Mélanges Gamal Eddin Mokhtar,* edited by Paule Posener-Kriéger, pp. 25–38. Cairo, 1985.

Reisner, George A. *The Development of the Egyptian Tomb down to the Accession of Cheops.* Cambridge, Mass., 1935.

Reisner, George A. "The History of the Egyptian Mastaba." In *Mélanges Maspero,* vol. 1, pp. 579–584. Mémoires publiés par les membres de l'Institut Francaise d'archéologie orientale du Caire, 66. Cairo, 1935–1938.

Vandier, J. *Manuel d'archéologie égyptienne.* Vol. 2, pt. 1, *Les grandes époques: L'architecture funéraire,* pp. 251–294. Paris, 1954.

*Rock Tombs*

Assmann, Jan. "Das Grab mit gewundenem Abstieg: Zum Typenwandel des Privat-Felsgrabes im Neuen Reich." *Mitteilungen des Deutschen Archäologischen Instituts, Abteilung Kairo* 40 (1984), 277–290.

Brunner, Hellmut. *Die Anlage der ägyptischen Felsgräber bis zum Mittleren Reich.* Glückstadt, 1936.

Dziobek, Eberhard. "Eine Grabpyramide des frühen Neuen Reiches in Theben." *Mitteilungen des Deutschen Archäologischen Instituts, Abteilung Kairo* 45 (1989), 109–132.

Eigner, Dieter. "Das thebanische Grab des Amenhotep, Wesir von Unterägypten: die Architektur." *Mitteilungen des Deutschen Archäologischen Instituts, Abteilung Kairo* 39 (1983), 39–50.

Eigner, Dieter. *Die monumentalen Grabbauten der Spätzeit in der thebanischen Nekropole.* 2 vols. Vienna, 1984.

Martin, Geoffrey T. *The Hidden Tombs of Memphis: New Discoveries from the Time of Tutankhamun and Ramesses the Great.* London, 1991.

Müller, Hans-Wolfgang. *Die Felsengräber der Fürsten von Elephantine aus der Zeit des Mittleren Reiches.* Glückstadt, 1940.

Schenkel, W. "Zur Typologie des Felsgrabes." In *Thebanische Beamtennekropolen: Neue Perspektiven archäologischer Forschung Internationales Symposium Heidelberg 9.–13.6. 1993,* edited by Jan Assmann, et al., pp. 169–183. Studien zur Archäologie und Geschichte Altägyptens, 12. Heidelberg, 1995.

Seyfried, K. J. "Bemerkungen zur Erweiterung der unterirdischen Anlagen einiger Gräber des Neuen Reiches in Theben." *Annales du service des antiquités de l'Égypte* 71 (1987), 229–249.

Vandier, J. *Manuel d'archéologie égyptienne.* Vol. 2, pt. 1, *Les grandes époques: L'architecture funéraire,* pp. 293–386. Paris, 1954.

*Houses*

Anus, P. "Habitations de prêtres dan le temple d'Amon à Karnak." *Karnak (1968–1969),* pp. 217–238. Kêmi, 21. Paris, 1971.

Arnold, Felix. "A Study of Egyptian Domestic Buildings." *Varia Aegyptiaca* 5 (1989), 75–93.

Bietak, M. "An Iron Age Four-Room House in Ramesside Egypt." *Eretz-Israel* 23 (1992), 9–12.

Boak, Arthur E. R. *Soknopaiou Nesos: The University of Michigan Excavations at Dimê in 1931–1932.* Ann Arbor, 1935.

Borchardt, Ludwig, and Herbert Ricke. *Die Wohnhäuser in Tell El-Amarna.* Berlin, 1980.

Endruweit, Albrecht. *Städischer Wohnbau in Ägypten: Klimagerechte Lehmarchitektur in Amarna.* Berlin, 1994.

Kemp, Barry J. "Large Middle Kingdom Granary Buildings." *Zeitschrift für Ägyptische Sprache und Alterumskunde* 113 (1986), 120–136.

Kemp, Barry J. "The Amarna Workmen's Village in Retrospect." *Journal of Egyptian Archaeology* 73 (1987), 21–50.

Rodziewicz, Mieczyslaw. *Les habitations romaines tradives d'Alexandrie.* Alexandrie, 3. Warsaw, 1984.

Tietze, Ch. "Amarna. Analyse der Wohnhäuser und soziale struktur der Stadtbewohner." *Zeitschrift für Ägyptische Sprache und Alterumskunde* 112 (1985), 48–84.

Tietze, Ch. "Amarna (Teil II). Analyse der ökonomischen Beziehungen der Stadtbewohner." *Zeitschrift für Ägyptische Sprache und Alterumskunde* 113 (1986), 55–78.

Traunecker, C. "Les maisons du domaine d'Aton à Karnak." In *Sociétés urbaines en Égypte et au Soudan,* pp. 73–93. Cahier de recherches de l'Institut de papyrologie et d'égyptologie de Lille, 10. Lille, 1988.

*Settlements*

Kemp, Barry J. "The City of el-Amarna as a Source for the Study of Urban Society in Ancient Egypt." *World Archaeology* 9 (1977–1978), 123–139.

Ucko, P. J., ed. *Man, Settlement and Urbanism.* London, 1972.

Ucko, P. J. "The Early Development of Towns in Egypt." *Antiquity* 5 (1977), 185–200.

Uphill, Eric P. *Egyptian Towns and Cities.* Shire Egyptology, 8. Aylesbury, 1988.

Valbelle, Dominique. "L'Égypte pharaonique." In *Naissance des Cités,* edited by Jean-Louis Huot, et al., pp. 255–322. Paris, 1990.

Ziermann, Martin. *Befestigungsanlagen und Stadtentwicklung in der Frühzeit und im frühe Alten Reich.* Mainz, 1992.

*Palaces*

Assmann, Jan. "Palast oder Tempel." *Journal of Near Eastern Studies* 31 (1972), 143–155.

Bietak, M. *Eine Palastanlage aus der Zeit des späten Mittleren Reichs und andere Forschungsergebnisse aus dem östlichen Nildelta (Tell el-Dab'a, 1979–1984),* pp. 325–332. Vienna, 1985.

Kemp, Barry J. "The Palace of Apries at Memphis." *Mitteilungen des Deutschen Archäologischen Instituts, Abteilung Kairo* 33 (1977), 101–108.

Kemp, Barry J. "The Harim-Palace at Medinet el-Ghurab." *Zeitschrift für Ägyptische Sprache und Alterumskunde* 105 (1978), 122–133.

O'Connor, David. "City and Palace in New Kingdom Egypt." *Sociétés urbaines en Égypte et au Soudan,* pp. 73–87. Cahier de recherches de l'Institut de papyrologie et d'égyptologie de Lille, 11. Lille, 1989.

O'Connor, David. "Mirror of the Cosmos: The Palace of Merenptah." In *Fragments of a Shattered Visage,* edited by Edward Bleiberg and Rita Freed, pp. 167–197. Memphis, Tenn., 1993.

Stadelmann, Rainer. "Tempelpalast und Erscheinungsfenster in den Thebanischen Totentempeln." *Mitteilungen des Deutschen Archäologischen Instituts, Abteilung Kairo* 29 (1973), 221–242.

Uphill, Eric P. "The Concept of the Egyptian Palace as a 'Ruling Machine.'" In *Man, Settlement and Urbanism,* edited by P. Ucko, pp. 721–734. London, 1972.

DIETER ARNOLD

ARMANT. *View of Armant.*

**ARMANT** (Gr., Hermonthis), a site located about 12 kilometers (7.5 miles) southwest of present-day Luxor, on the western bank of the Nile (25°37′N, 32°32′E). Armant was probably the original capital and the most important cult center of the god Montu in the fourth Upper Egyptian nome (province). Armant's ancient Egyptian name was *Iwny*, and from the New Kingdom onward was found written *Iwnw*. The similarity with the name of the Lower Egyptian city of Heliopolis, or On *(Iwnw)*, led the Egyptians to clarify Armant as *Iwnw Mntw* ("On-of-Montu"), or even *Iwnw Šmꜣw* ("Heliopolis-of-the-South"), a term also, and ambiguously, applied in later periods to Thebes.

Cemeteries from prehistoric into Christian times have been discovered at Armant, but no temple blocks have been found predating the eleventh dynasty. A reference, however, to "Montu, Lord of Armant" in the sixth dynasty Theban tomb of the nomarch Ihy verified the contemporary existence of a Montu cult center in Armant, despite the lack of monumental remains from the Old Kingdom. Blocks dating to the Middle Kingdom were reused in later Ptolemaic-era temple construction, so no plan is recoverable for the original eleventh dynasty Montu structure. After being neglected during the Second Intermediate Period, Montu's temple received lavish attention from its inception during the eighteenth dynasty—the New King-

dom temple being constructed to the south and in front of the earlier structures. It included a pylon, a forecourt, and a colonnade to the core sanctuary—primarily the work of Thutmose III (r. 1504–1452 BCE). The temple remained much the same until its destruction, possibly by the Persians, during the Late period. The reconstruction of the entire complex may have been started in the reign of Nektanebo II of the thirtieth dynasty, but it was principally a project of the Ptolemies. For example, Cleopatra VII (r. 44–33 BCE) and her son Caesarion contributed a birth-house and a sacred lake.

At Armant, the god Montu was accompanied by two divine consorts: the goddesses Iunyt and Tjenenyet. Iunyt, first seen in reliefs that were dated to the reign of Montuhotep III in the eleventh dynasty (r. 2000–1998 BCE), was probably the primordial goddess of the city, inasmuch as her name means "she-of-Armant." Tjenenyet was first mentioned by name on blocks from the twelfth dynasty. Although the two goddesses and Montu form a triad, their precise familial relationship to one another is uncertain. In the Ramessid period of the New Kingdom, Tjenenyet began to eclipse her partner, and another goddess appeared: Rettawy ("female-Re-of-the-Two-Lands"). Rather than being a new deity, Rettawy may represent a solar aspect of Iunyt, who is attested in the New Kingdom with the epithet "Daughter of Re." It has been proposed that Rettawy is an epithet of Tjenenyet, but those two goddesses have been portrayed together in the same context, whereas Rettawy and Iunyt have not.

In the reign of Nektanebo II (360–343 BCE), the Buchis bulls, sacred to the cult of Montu at Armant, were buried for the next 650 years in the Bucheum, built at the desert's edge 6 kilometers (4 miles) west of the city. The mummified "Mother of Buchis" cows were interred 400 meters (about 1300 feet) north of the Bucheum.

[*See also* Montu.]

### BIBLIOGRAPHY

Eggebrecht, Arne. "Armant." In *Lexikon der Ägyptologie*, 1:435–441. Wiesbaden, 1975. Scholarly essay in German, with extensive references.

Mond, Robert, and Oliver H. Myers. *Temples of Armant*. London, 1940. Report by the principal excavators of the site under the auspices of the Egypt Exploration Society.

Porter, Bertha, and Rosalind L. B. Moss. *Topographical Bibliography of Ancient Egyptian Hieroglyphic Texts, Reliefs and Paintings*, vol. 5, *Upper Egypt: Sites*. Oxford, 1937. The site of Armant is covered on pp. 151–160.

EDWARD K. WERNER

**ART.** The ancient Egyptians "depicted in their temples what was beautiful and how it was beautiful . . . it had long been recognized that the arts must be of the highest quality," wrote Hekataois of Miletos some twenty-five hundred years ago. In fact, "beautiful, appealing, or of more than ordinary significance," one dictionary's definition of *art*, aptly describes much of the sculpture, relief, painting, and small objects of daily life that were produced for more than three millennia of Egyptian culture. For its aesthetic appeal, monumentality, spirituality, and political message, it was not only revered and copied in its own time by its own people, but it also provided a philosophical and practical foundation for later Western art.

**Sources and Function.** Like many other ancient cultures, the Egyptians created what the modern world admires as art for practical purposes—for worship, for daily use, or to serve for eternity. The vast majority of Egyptian artists' works were never meant to be seen; royal and private tombs, sealed and inaccessible after burial, have provided scholars the greatest source of their art. Because a tomb functioned both as an abstract reproduction of a house on earth and a stage for the mortuary rites that guaranteed eternal life, scenes of ritual and daily life were carved or painted on tomb walls. In addition, statuary of the deceased and his family were produced in his (or her) likeness as substitute bodies and homes for the soul, and the tombs were equipped with this life's pleasures and necessities for the afterlife. All were brought to life, magically, through the Opening of the Mouth ceremony. The cre-

ation of funerary items, which were of the highest quality the owner could afford, became a veritable industry.

The gods of Egypt also required their own houses for eternity—the temples—and these form the second-largest source of art. Reliefs on temple walls portrayed the magical rites that took place within and depicted the temple's riches. The most sacred object in a temple was its cult statue, namely the image of the deity to whom the temple was dedicated; often in precious metal, it was housed inside the temple's inner sanctuary and served as the focus of worship. Statues of kings and, to a lesser extent, private individuals were also placed inside temples to guarantee an owner's eternal presence before the gods and to insure that they received a share of the gods' wealth. All this art was largely inaccessible to Egypt's multitudes, because the general public was not permitted beyond a temple's outer courtyard.

Domestic structures, both royal and private, are an additional source of art; because they were built mainly of mud bricks, relatively little is left. Palace remains, best preserved at Tell el-Amarna, featured walls and floors lavishly painted with scenes from nature and daily life. Private dwellings occasionally displayed brightly painted border decorations or images of deities associated with fertility and household protection. Few objects not strictly utilitarian have been found in houses, probably because prized possessions became part of the owner's tomb equipment or were passed along to descendants.

**Artists.** The needs of temples, tombs, and houses kept ancient Egyptian artists in demand. Although their monuments and written records show they enjoyed a comfortable lifestyle and were well treated, relatively few are known by name. Even more rarely can a specific artist be associated with his work (and art was men's work; women do not seem to have been employed in that area). In fact, more than one artist was likely to have worked on any given statue or relief, with each responsible for a different aspect, such as rough cutting, fine detailing, or polishing. Groups of artists worked together in workshops, which were generally affiliated with temples, palaces, or estates of wealthy landowners. Egyptian art was functional, and although it was intended to be pleasing to the eye, as ancient Greek writers asserted, the concept of "art for art's sake" really did not exist; nor was there a word for "art" in ancient Egypt. With relatively few exceptions, the individuality of both the artist and his product were coincidental. Artists, including sculptors, outline draftsmen, and painters were regarded as technicians, who were instructed to follow very specific rules, known as the canon of proportion. According to the canon, throughout most of Egyptian history the human body was divided into eighteen equal units, and each body part was on or near a specific unit. [*See* Grid Systems.] In this way, the human body was reproduced in the same manner regardless of its size or maker; a specific figure rendered in small scale on papyrus or on a fragment of limestone could thereby be enlarged to fill a temple or tomb wall. The canon also imparted a specific look to things Egyptian, one that changed little through the dynasties.

To date, the richest source of information about sculptors' studios comes from Akhenaten's city of Akhetaten (Tell el-Amarna), which yielded several. Both masters and apprentices lived and worked in the same structures, which were composed of small rooms grouped around courtyards. Separate areas seem to have been reserved for those working in the various mediums. Some spaces within workshops served for storage and the viewing of finished products.

Seldom was a statue an accurate portrait; rather, it provided an ideal image of the way its owner wished to be remembered for eternity, regardless of actual age or appearance. Individuality and identity were provided by the name incised or painted on the base or back pillar—thereby a new owner, whether king or commoner, might claim a statue, tomb, or temple simply by changing the name on it. "Usurpation," as this practice was called, began as early as the Old Kingdom.

**Materials.** The permanence of stone made it a favored material for sculpture; limestone, sandstone, and granite, all easily accessible in quarries close to the Nile River, were the stones most commonly used. Others, including quartzite, diorite, basalt, and anhydrite were less plentiful and less accessible but desirable because of their color, their hardness, or the high gloss achieved when polished. Color and rarity also made some semiprecious stones appealing, such as turquoise (green-blue), amethyst (violet), and lapis lazuli (deep blue). These were imported from the Sinai, Nubia, and Afghanistan, respectively, and were used primarily as inlays for royal jewelry and weaponry.

Some of Egypt's most sensitively modeled sculptures were of wood. How common wood sculpture was remains unclear; much of it has not survived, because of susceptibility to insects and dry rot. Local woods were soft and insubstantial; the best woods for sculpture—cedar, yew, and ebony—were imported from sub-Saharan Africa and the Levant.

Although metal sculpture was relatively uncommon prior to the Late period, the few surviving pieces indicate that the Egyptians were superb metalsmiths. As early as the Old Kingdom, life-size and lifelike statues were made of copper that was hammered over a core. Hollow-casting of copper-bronze during the Middle Kingdom produced sculptural masterworks with portraitlike qualities. Large-scale, hollow-cast bronzes became a high point of Third Intermediate Period sculpture; by the Late period, small-scale bronzes, particularly of deities, were mass pro-

duced. A few statues of gods made out of precious metal (gold and silver) are known; most likely, they were cult statues. Gold and silver were also used in jewelry.

**Predynastic Art.** Many of the principles that define Egyptian art evolved during its formative years and, as previously noted, remained largely unchanged for more than three millennia. One of these qualities was the ability and the desire on the part of the artists, from the very beginnings of Egyptian culture in the fourth millennium BCE, to transform something utilitarian into an object of beauty, such as the pottery or cosmetic articles placed in the graves of the early Predynastic period, where simple shapes or surfaces had often been embellished for no apparent reason other than to make them more attractive. From the Naqada I (4000–3500 BCE) period, for example, gracefully shaped bowls and beakers, handmade by the coil method, were coated with a red slip, burnished, and then further enhanced with white paint. The painted decoration, usually consisting of parallel lines, might feature simple geometric shapes, depictions of vegetation, entire landscapes, or narrative scenes. In all such representations, the meaning was conveyed in the most succinct manner possible, a quality that would continue into dynastic times.

Particularly in the early representation of animals and humans, those elements and aspects considered critical were always rendered, although function often took precedence over accuracy, as may be clearly seen in a Naqada I period bowl. There, three hippopotamuses, with bodies shown in profile, swim between a central pool and a mountain range depicted in aerial perspective. Although its profile identified the animal, its ability to function was predicated on its having two eyes and two ears, all of which were shown, but neither in proper profile nor in appropriate positions. Rather, they were shown in a line atop the head. A sense of whimsy was often apparent in Naqada I cosmetic items, such as combs made of ivory or bone; because the teeth mimicked animal legs, the comb backs were carved in zoomorphic shapes. Hardly practical, at times this practice rendered the combs more susceptible to breakage.

Some of Egypt's earliest human sculpture (from the Neolithic and Badarian periods) likewise shows the depiction of essential aspects reduced to their most basic shapes. Simple cones and cylinders of clay joined together form graceful, naturalistic torsos; facial features consisting of no more than holes poked or pinched into clay succeed in conveying believable emotion. In somewhat later human images (from the Naqada II period) naturalism gave way to abstraction as salient aspects—such as heads, hips, or sexual attributes—were emphasized, and nonessential areas, including limbs and torsos, were reduced to mere suggestions. That very abstract quality

Obverse.

Reverse.

ART. *Drawing of the Narmer Palette, a slate palette from the first dynasty.* The obverse depicts King Narmer smiting an enemy, while on the reverse the king inspects decapitated enemies.

characterized Egypt's first known colossal images of the fertility god Min, the largest of which was originally well over 2 meters (6.5 feet) high. The torso and legs were reduced to stone cylinders, and hands carved in low relief embrace a large phallus made of another stone and inserted in place. Simple but powerful even in their damaged state, the message of the Min sculptures was clear.

The end of the Predynastic period (Naqada II–III times) was marked by an explosion of creativity, owing, in part, to higher population, abundant food, greater social organization, and increased specialization. Egypt's trade with Nubia and the Near East brought in new ideas and new raw materials. In addition, familiar types of objects acquired new functions; for example, the slate palettes used for grinding eye paint, which had been carved in simple geometric or zoomorphic shapes, were made larger and more ornate, since the softness of slate made it easy to work. On them, tentative beginnings of relief carving soon resulted in their surfaces covered completely with animated humans, animals, and hybrids. Although no longer useful for their original purpose, the symbolic

nature of some of the representations and their discovery in the temple precinct at Hierakonpolis suggest new ritual significance.

**Early Dynastic Art.** The Narmer Palette, the most famous of the slate palettes, is not only an art historical milestone but also an important monument for the study of Egyptian history, religion, and language. Many of the canons and principles that were to define Egyptian art for the next three thousand years were expressed on it: for example, readable scenes were organized on registers; the most important person, King Narmer, was also the largest; the main side featured a smiting scene, the same subject that would dominate temple walls into the Roman period (here, Narmer's upraised right arm grasped a mace and his left held a kneeling captive by the hair—although the next action was clear, what is represented captured for eternity the moment before the mace crashed down). Rarely was Egyptian art violent, although the prelude and aftermath of violence were frequent subjects, particularly on temple walls. Postaction violence was shown on the reverse side of the Narmer Palette, where Narmer's decapitated and bound enemies were shown with their heads between their legs.

King Narmer's representation exemplified the standard for the depiction of human figures in relief. Profile and frontal views were combined so that the most characteristic aspect of each feature was represented. Narmer faced right, the dominant orientation, and his left foot was forward, thereby conveying a sense of stability and forward motion. Only those details that were considered essential, such as the bulging muscles of the legs and forearms that advertised the king's strength, were included. Although composed before the aid of the later eighteen-square canon (grid system), Narmer's body proportions were rendered close to those that employed it. Narmer wore the standard attributes of kingship, including the tall, conical crown of Upper Egypt (Nile Valley) on the main side and the flat-topped crown of Lower Egypt (Delta) on the reverse. In addition, he wore an artificial beard and a bull's tail hanging from his belt. The tail represents an example of the incorporation of animal attributes into the office of kingship; here, the unbridled power of the bull, symbolized by its tail, is equated with royalty. On the reverse of the palette, a bull representing the king breaks into a walled enclosure and subdues an enemy just as the human king on the obverse overcomes a captive. The falcon, also identified with kingship because of its domination of the sky, symbolically conquers the North, by hooking the nose of a human face that is emerging from a plant that grows in the Nile Delta.

Early Dynastic sculpture shows that the artists struggled to liberate human and animal forms from a stone matrix. The body was often little more than a cubic mass with limbs closely adhering. Emphasis was placed on the head or facial features by making them disproportionately large. Because it was vulnerable to breakage, the neck was reduced in size and strengthened by means of a heavy wig, crown, or headdress. The results of those naive attempts are often powerful but haunting.

**Old Kingdom.** The explosion of monumental stone architecture during the Pyramid Age and the evolution of religious thought was accompanied by an increased demand for sculpture. Life-size and larger images of fourth dynasty kings and queens furnished mortuary temples. Brought to life by means of the Opening of the Mouth ceremony, they served as eternal recipients of the royal cults; they also housed the *ka* (life force) and other aspects of the soul of the deceased. In these royal statues, best preserved from the pyramid precincts of Khafre and Menkaure, the Egyptian ideal for sculpture in the round was first perfected.

A sculpture of Menkaure, beside a queen from the king's valley temple, embodies this ideal. Immobile and impassive, the king stands with his left foot forward and hands at his sides. Beside him, the queen places her arm around his waist, a gesture of association, but one that conveys no emotional attachment; faces gaze directly ahead betraying no feelings. Both figures show the Egyptian ideal body form, similar to that seen in relief on the Narmer Palette. Menkaure's broad shoulders taper to a trim waist and muscular legs; his pectoral muscles give definition to an otherwise taut expanse of chest. The female has smaller shoulders, modest breasts, a narrow waist, and small hips. The absence of fat on her body is so pronounced that, despite a sheath dress, her ribs, navel, and pubic triangle are visible. Regardless of their actual ages or true appearance at the time the statue was made, that was the way they, as well as subsequent kings and commoners, generally chose to be represented for eternity. Other statues from the same complex show the king in the company of anthropomorphic deities, both male and female. King and gods share not only the same body form but also the same facial features, thereby emphasizing the divine nature of kingship.

The Great Sphinx at Giza, the largest of a statue type that was originated in the fourth dynasty and was continued into the Roman period, exemplifies another aspect of the divinity of the royal office. By combining the head of the reigning monarch with the massive and powerful body of a lion, later associated with the sun god, the king sent a message of his invincibility. The sphinx form also illustrates the Egyptian fondness for combining anthropomorphic and zoomorphic attributes in the same sculpture, another tradition that would endure for millennia.

For their tombs, often constructed near the royal tomb by permission of the king, Old Kingdom high court officials also required statuary. The most common form of private statue also showed its male owner standing with left foot forward or he might be seated. Statuary of women from the Old Kingdom was more rare. A group statue, however, might include the tomb owner's wife or wife and children, often on a scale much smaller than reality. Occasionally, the same person was shown more than once in the same group statue (pseudo-group), but wearing a different garment or holding different titles. Private sculpture was similar to royal sculpture in that it represented an idealized likeness of its owner, rather than a true-to-life picture, and facial features copied those of the king. With few exceptions, the name written on a statue, rather than its portraitlike details, gave it an identity and individuality.

Although most Old Kingdom private sculpture conformed to the standard youthful ideal, another type showed the owner with a heavily jowled, mature face and a torso marked with rolls of fat. Most likely, such an image was one of prosperity and abundance, although it might also have portrayed the actual appearance of the owner—and in some cases they definitely did. Occasionally, disabilities such as dwarfism or kyphosis (humpback)

ART. *Two red-breasted geese, fourth dynasty.* Part of a painted plaster panel from the tomb of Nefermat and Atet, from Meidum, now in the Egyptian Museum, Cairo. (Giraudon /Art Resource, NY)

were depicted in statuary. For example, the statue of a dwarf was discovered in a tomb at Giza, and the owner's anatomical remains confirmed his dwarfism.

Relief decoration offered tremendous opportunities for artistic expression during the Old Kingdom. Reliefs in tombs expanded from simple fourth dynasty depictions of the deceased at his funerary meal to more than thirty rooms covered with idealized scenes from the owner's life and the activities of his estate by the sixth dynasty. Some subjects, such as the owner fishing and fowling, not only reflected important daily activities, but also symbolically showed his mastery over malevolent forces. Although a standard theme near the entryway of every large tomb, it still afforded the artist room for individual creativity. For example, the cycle of life and death was nowhere better reflected than in the fishing scene in the tomb of Vizier Mereruka, where beneath the Nile waters a hippopotamus gave birth into the waiting jaws of a crocodile. Fish were so accurately depicted that not only their genus but also their species may be identified.

In the inner rooms of the *mastaba* tomb, where narrow registers feature workmen engaged in food production or crafts, active poses provided a stark contrast to the stiff formality of the tomb owner, who was shown on a much larger scale. Although multiple figures engaged in the same activity were often shown in the same pose and even rhythmically overlapping, depth and perspective were lacking. When the standard combination of profile and frontal view proved inadequate, artists creatively folded the body inward at the shoulder into the appropriate position; that allowed them to abide by the rules but often produced awkward results. Frontality was avoided at all costs, and true profiles were used only when statues were depicted.

Although most sculpture and relief was brightly painted, time and changing climatic conditions have caused much

of the color to fade or disappear. Tantalizing traces show a rich palette of natural earth tones and a fondness for intricate interior detail in contrasting colors. Toward the end of the Old Kingdom, a number of tombs were only painted and not carved in relief. Many displayed the spindly limbs and overall awkwardness that marked the era's end.

**First Intermediate Period.** With the decline in central authority at the end of the Old Kingdom, royal sponsorship of art in the capital declined. Power reverted to the nomes (provinces), and nomarchs commissioned local artists to paint, or carve reliefs, and sculpt for their tombs. Attempts to copy earlier models often resulted in ill-proportioned, often humorous imitations. In time, local styles developed, particularly in Dendera, Naga ed-Deir, Gebelein, and Saqqara. At some of those sites, the entire decorative program of the tomb was reduced to what could fit on a single stela.

**Middle Kingdom.** With the reunification of the country in the eleventh dynasty, royal sponsorship of schools of sculpture and relief resumed as the necessary adjunct to the large-scale building projects in the new capital, Thebes. Artists once again gained access to earlier models and, within a few decades, succeeded in mimicking them so well, particularly in relief, that at times it is difficult for Egyptologists to differentiate between certain Old and Middle Kingdom works. Sculpture in the round of the eleventh dynasty exhibited a heavy, brutal quality; that soon gave way to the earlier, idealizing, youthful forms during the early twelfth dynasty, when the capital was moved back North. The deliberate copying of Old Kingdom models was, in part, the result of a direct attempt by the rulers to promote themselves as legitimate heirs of earlier kings and to recapture their absolute power.

Middle Kingdom proliferation of temples throughout Egypt, and particularly the increasing importance of Osiris, god of the netherworld, created a need for new

ART. *Ivory dancing dwarves, Middle Kingdom.* They are now on display in the Egyptian Museum, Cairo. (Courtesy David P. Silverman)

types of statuary and relief. Royal sculptures appeared in temple contexts for the first time on a large scale, and there they provided reminders of the king's omnipresence, power, and proximity to the gods. In the private realm, the so-called block or cuboid statue—a representation of the owner, always male, seated with his knees to his chest and his arms crossed—first appeared at the beginning of the twelfth dynasty in tomb contexts. It soon became temple sculpture *par excellence*, the smooth planes of the compact body serving as ideal surfaces for inscribed prayers of supplication. The increased number and size of statues and stelae of women—by themselves, both royal and nonroyal—may correspond with an increased visibility and importance of women in Egyptian society.

A major artistic upheaval accompanied governmental reforms of the mid-twelfth dynasty, under King Senwosret III. Beginning in the reign of his predecessor, Senwosret II, a subtle change became evident both in the royal and nonroyal physiognomy, in both sculpture and relief. Perhaps the timeless, eternally youthful face that was perfectly suited for the eternity of a tomb conveyed an inadequate message when brought outside into temple contexts; so a sterner, more mature visage replaced it. The late twelfth dynasty face was marked by deep furrows, heavily lidded eyes sunken deep in their sockets, and a mouth curved downward into a frown or projected outward in a pout. The decline of royal power was paralleled by a decline in the quality of royal sculpture and, by the thirteenth dynasty, much of the finest art was for the private sphere.

Some of the most beautifully crafted, sophisticated, and aesthetically pleasing of Egypt's minor arts date from the Middle Kingdom. The exploitation of new mines and the expansion of trade with Nubia, sub-Saharan Africa, and the Sinai brought Egypt exotic materials, such as ivory, ebony, amethyst, and turquoise, which skilled artisans turned into cloisonné jewelry, inlaid and veneered furniture, or objects whose sole purpose may have been for amusement. Three ivory dwarfs with upraised hands, who danced when strings were pulled through their communal base, still delight the observer. Not only was the object clever but the details, ranging from chubby bowed legs to ecstatic facial expressions, were superbly captured.

**Second Intermediate Period.** A weakened central government at the end of the thirteenth dynasty collapsed when the Near Eastern group, known as the Hyksos, entered Egypt through the eastern Delta and took control. The Hyksos are recognizable through their distinctive burial customs, pottery types, and scarabs. Although they added their names to many of their predecessors' monu-

ART. *Colossal statue of Akhenaten from Karnak, eighteenth dynasty.* It is now on exhibit in the Egyptian Museum, Cairo. (Courtesy David P. Silverman)

ments, they are not known to have produced any of their own. [*See* Hyksos.]

**New Kingdom.** Native control of Egypt was reestablished at the end of the seventeenth dynasty by a family from Thebes, and again the arts began to flourish. Artisans at first produced statuary that copied great works of earlier dynasties, particularly those immediately available to them. As a result, in Thebes the sculptures of Amenhotpe I, the first king of the eighteenth dynasty, were modeled on the statuary of Senwosret I, a king of the twelfth dynasty, who had also built extensively in Thebes. Original and copy were so similar that the two have been confused.

For the first time, kings conquered and occupied territory beyond Egypt's borders. As the empire grew, wealth increased through tribute and trade, and the demand for monuments burgeoned. Soon, a distinctively New Kingdom style evolved. In the reign of Hatshepsut (1502–1482 BCE), the queen and regent who ruled as an eighteenth dynasty king, several hundred statues of the monarch in various guises were commissioned for her funerary temple at Deir el-Bahri alone. The majority portray her with male attributes, including a muscular chest, kilt, royal beard, and left-foot-forward pose; in a few, she has a feminine body and wears a sheath dress. Her sweet unlined face, arched eyes and brows, aquiline nose, and lips drawn up in a slight smile then set the standard for later New Kingdom rulers.

As the treasury profited from the new-found wealth of the empire, kings added colossal statuary, pylons, and other auxiliary structures to Amun's temple at Karnak and to other temples throughout the land—in a demonstration of devotion and a statement of power. A growing bureaucratic class also demanded sculpture for temples and tombs, so private art proliferated. Individuals commissioned innovative works to meet their specific needs. For example, although it would have been unseemly for a private individual to touch the pharaoh, Senenmut, Hatshepsut's architect and the tutor of her daughter, did so cryptically, by embracing a three-dimensional rebus of his monarch's name. In other statuary, Hatshepsut's young daughter is shown on Senenmut's lap or in his arms. Such close association between royalty and private individuals was seldom repeated.

The New Kingdom was the great age of painting, a medium that found its most eloquent expression in funerary arts of all types, including palace and tomb walls, coffins, and papyri. Through gradations of color or minute strokes of the brush, paint lent itself to subtleties that were unthinkable in relief or sculpture. A rich and diverse repertory of subjects challenged the rules of representation, and artists met the challenge through experiments with innovative positions, use of space, emotion, and perspective, particularly in representations of servants or scenes of daily life.

In the course of Amenhotpe III's long and prosperous reign of thirty-seven years, in both Egypt and Nubia, he erected more temples and commissioned more and larger statuary than any of his predecessors, much of it in celebration of his three jubilee festivals. Over the years, his image of himself changed, perhaps in conjunction with his increasing devotion to the sun god, Aten. For the first time in Egyptian history, and most likely during the final years of his life, the king is shown in a less than ideal manner, with pudgy cheeks, flaccid breasts, and a protruding belly—decidedly overweight. Then all the rules of artistic representation were changed during the reign of his son and successor, Amenhotpe IV, who changed his name to Akhenaten. His belief that the light of the sun, Aten, was the world's sole god—who expressed himself only through the king and his wife Nefertiti—inspired a social revolution and one reflected in artistic representation. In a series of colossal statues erected early in his reign at Karnak, the image of Akhenaten transcended reality, to shock the viewer. A narrow and grossly elongated face and facial features, an emaciated upper torso with a suggestion of breasts swelling into a pendant belly, and voluptuous hips blurred the distinction between man and woman. His wife Nefertiti and their daughters were shown in similar fashion, in the reliefs in temples built by the king at Karnak.

The eccentricities of the new image lessened somewhat after Akhenaten abandoned Thebes in favor of the city that he established to honor Aten, called Akhetaten (Tell el-Amarna). The emphasis on life in all its aspects gave rise to a new naturalism in artistic representation. The absence of images of the traditional gods resulted in the creation of a whole new artistic vocabulary; the focus was the royal family in its role as intermediary between Aten and the populace. King and queen were depicted in relaxed, intimate poses, playing with their daughters, who eventually numbered six, or traveling between palace and temple in the state chariot in a panoply of royal display. Private sculpture was rare. Shortly after Akhenaten's death, during the reign of Tutankhamun, the new city was abandoned and the old gods were restored to prominence. Artisans returned, for the most part, to the traditional, formal methods of figural representation, particularly those of deities and kings. A tendency toward greater naturalism in the rendering of facial features, and a baroque attention to detail became part of Amarna's artistic legacy.

Ramessid kings of the next two dynasties defended Egypt's empire and depicted their military exploits in panoramic narratives on temple walls throughout Egypt and Nubia. Temples were furnished, inside and out, with statuary of all sizes, particularly by Ramesses II ("the Great"). What his artisans did not create, they usurped, by adding Ramesses' name; at times, they even resculpted earlier pieces in his image. Private sculpture again proliferated, and innovative statue types and poses demonstrated the personal relationship between man and god.

**Third Intermediate Period.** Expressions of personal piety dominated the art of the Third Intermediate Period, possibly in response to governmental turmoil. Block statues with facial features reminiscent of the mid-eighteenth dynasty were deposited in temples in record numbers, and images of gods covered funerary equipment, including coffins, papyri, and stelae. The period is noteworthy for its unplundered twenty-first and twenty-second dynasty royal tombs at Tanis, which contained a trove of jewelry made of gold and semiprecious stones.

When Nubian kings invaded in the twenty-fifth dynasty and proclaimed themselves rightful heirs to the Egyptian throne, they depicted themselves with pharaonic accoutrements, augmented by distinctive Nubian trappings. Those included a cap crown, adorned with two *uraei* (coiled serpents) at the front and images of Amun, symbolized by the head of a ram at the shoulders and neck. Round, compact faces with bolder features reflected their Nubian heritage.

**Late Period.** The nationalism that accompanied the expulsion of the Nubians and the return to native rule found expression in the art of the twenty-sixth dynasty. Both in sculpture and reliefs, there was a deliberate attempt to copy the styles of earlier eras, particularly, but not exclusively, the Old Kingdom, out of a desire to iden-

ART. *Wall-painting of the Seven Celestial Cows and the Sacred Bull, nineteenth dynasty, tomb of Nefertari, Valley of the Queens, Thebes.* (Giraudon / Art Resource, NY)

tify with periods of Egypt's strength. The favored sculpture types included block statues, which were deposited in temples, or naophorous statues, which also demonstrated the devotion between man and god. With a Greek settlement at Naukratis and other foreign groups living and trading in Egypt's major cities and ports, the country and its art were becoming increasingly cosmopolitan. Frequent contact with Greece may have inspired Egyptian artists to experiment with more anatomically detailed representations of the human face and body, which nevertheless still fell within traditional parameters. Highly polished, hard dark stones were a favored medium for such sculptures. The thirtieth dynasty, the last period of native rule, produced some of Egypt's finest and most sophisticated works.

**Ptolemaic Period.** The dynasty founded by Alexander the Great's general, Ptolemy, depicted its rulers in alternatively Egyptian or Greek style, with the appropriate accoutrements; it also produced some of the best monumental architecture extant in Egypt today. Although those

buildings are Egyptian in style and content, the Hellenistic Greek overlay is most apparent in the relief decoration, which exhibits a bold, voluptuous modeling of the human figure, both male and female. That body form was also used in the contemporary sculpture, which, despite the foreign rulers, maintained the same function and format as it had in pharaonic times.

**Roman Rule.** Although traditional pharonic ideals were maintained and the arts thrived during Ptolemaic rule, under the succeeding Roman control, support for the arts diminished along with the general impoverishment of the country. The Roman emperors depicted themselves in Egyptian garb in sculpture or as worshipping Egyptian gods on temples, but that diminished in time. Private sculpture was comparatively rare. Perhaps the best examples of the intermingling of Egyptian and Roman ideals was attempted in the funerary arts; Roman and Egyptian styles were juxtaposed but not combined in paintings on tomb walls. Funerary masks, one of the most traditional and long-lived of Egyptian art forms, exhibited either the most traditional of Egyptian imagery or classically attired figures, whose penetrating and direct gaze forecast the finest of Byzantine works.

[*See also* Archaism; Architecture; Artists and Artisans; Beauty; Bronze; Bronze Statuettes; Calcite; Captions; Ceramics; Color Symbolism; Diorite and Related Rocks; Faience; Gems; Gesture; Glass; Gold; Granite; Grid Systems; Ivory; Jewelry; Limestone; Masks; Models; Painting; Palettes; Portraiture; Relief Sculpture; Royal Tomb Painting; Silver; Sphinx; Vessels; *and the composite article on* Sculpture.]

## BIBLIOGRAPHY

Aldred, C. *Akhenaten and Nefertiti.* New York, 1973. Detailed analysis of art in the Amarna period for 1973 exhibition.

Aldred, C. *Egyptian Art: In the Days of the Pharaohs, 3100–320 B.C.* New York, 1980. Very readable overview of stylistic development of Egyptian art.

Arnold, D. *The Royal Women of Amarna: Images of Beauty from Ancient Egypt.* New York, 1996. Critical reexamination of Amarna sculpture and relief.

Bothmer, B. V. *Egyptian Sculpture of the Late Period.* New York, 1960. Pioneering attempt to analyze and date Egyptian sculpture and relief from the twenty-fifth dynasty through Roman times.

Brovarski, E., S. Doll, and R. Freed, eds. *Egypt's Golden Age—The Art of Living in the New Kingdom.* Boston, 1982. Exhibition catalog of Egypt's finest nonroyal minor arts of the New Kingdom; essays and entries by multiple authors.

D'Auria, S., P. Lacovara, and C. Roehrig. *Mummies and Magic.* Boston, 1988. Exhibition catalog about the art of burial; multiple authors for entries and essays.

Donadoni Roveri, A. M. *Egyptian Civilization—Daily Life, Religious Beliefs, Monumental Art.* Turin, 1988/89. Catalog of the Egyptian Museum, Turin, Italy, in three volumes.

Evers, H. G. *Staat aus dem Stein—Denkmaler, Geschichte und Bedeutung der aegyptischen Plastik während des mittleren Reichs.* Munich, 1929. First detailed analysis of Middle Kingdom art.

Freed, R., Y. Markowitz, and S. D'Auria, eds. *Pharaohs of the Sun: Akhenaten, Nefertiti, Tutankhamen.* Boston, 1999. Copiously illustrated essays and entries on Amarna period objects by a variety of scholars.

Hayes, W. C. *The Scepter of Egypt.* 2 vols. New York, 1953; 1959. Overview of Egyptian collection in the Metropolitan Museum of Art, New York.

Josephson, J. *Egyptian Royal Sculpture of the Late Period, 400–246 B.C.* Mainz, 1997. Well-written analysis of royal material from the twenty-eighth dynasty through the early Ptolemaic period.

Kozloff, A., and B. Bryan. *Egypt's Dazzling Sun: Amenhotep III and His World.* Cleveland, 1992. Exhaustive compendium and analysis of material from Amenhotpe III's reign.

Mekhitarian, A. *Egyptian Painting.* New York, 1954. Analysis of the style and methods of ancient Egyptian painters.

Robins, G. *The Art of Ancient Egypt.* Cambridge, Mass., 1997. Thematic approach to Egyptian art.

Russman, E. *Egyptian Sculpture. Cairo and Luxor.* Austin, 1989. Beautifully written overview and stylistic analysis of key pieces from the Egyptian Museum, Cairo, and Luxor Museum.

Saleh, M., and H. Sourouzian. *The Egyptian Museum, Cairo: Official Catalogue.* Mainz, 1987. Rich source of information and photographs on objects in the Egyptian Museum, Cairo.

Schäfer, H. *Principles of Egyptian Art.* Translated by J. Baines. Oxford,
1986; 1st ed. Leipzig, 1919. Pioneering analysis of Egyptian art theory.

Smith, W. S. *A History of Egyptian Sculpture and Painting in the Old Kingdom.* London, 1946. Overview of art of the Old Kingdom, copiously illustrated; somewhat out of date, but still a standard reference work.

Smith, W. S. *The Art and Architecture of Ancient Egypt,* revised by W. K. Simpson. New Haven and London, 1998. Detailed overview of the topic, recently revised, with extensive photographs and footnotes.

Vandersleyen, C., ed. *Das Alte Aegypten.* Berlin, 1975. Collection of essays and entries on Egyptian sculpture and relief by various scholars; includes 440 plates.

Vandier, J. *Manuel d'archéologie égyptienne.* Paris, 1952–1978. Six volumes of analysis of Egyptian sculpture and relief.

Wildung, D. *Sesostris und Amenemhat: Aegypten im Mittleren Reich.* Munich, 1984. Development of Middle Kingdom sculpture.

RITA E. FREED

**ARTISTS AND ARTISANS.** Egyptologists long debated whether the statuary, painting, and relief created during the three millennia of pharaonic history could properly be considered art, since those products were intended to serve an essentially utilitarian purpose in the context of Egyptian civilization, above all in the funerary cult. Nowadays, specialists agree that the Egyptians did indeed make art. The related issue of whether those who produced art may be accurately called artists is a question of definition, for there can be no doubt that a wealth of masterpieces are preserved to attest the inspiration and technical skill of artistic genius. Among the extensive documentation, there is no evidence for women working as sculptors, draftsmen, or painters. The rare application of the title "scribe/painter" to a woman identified her as a cosmetician, a face painter. Weaving, with which this article is not concerned, was the only handicraft traditionally open to women.

In this article, the term *artist* will be reserved for men who produced fine art: the sculptors, draftsmen, and painters. Focus is on those professions, especially on sculptors working in stone, who have attracted more scholarly attention than other artists. Their statues and the reliefs carved in stone are hallmarks of ancient Egypt. Men involved in metal-working and stone-vessel manufacture, cabinetmakers, joiners, and jewelers—called artisans or craftsmen here—will figure in comparison with or contrast to artists. The Egyptian language did not make this distinction, for there was no word *artist* distinct from *ḥmwtj* ("artisan" or "craftsman").

Neither artists nor artisans were free agents in ancient Egypt but were attached to an official institution—the court or a temple. Yet some freelance work was possible within that framework in all periods. Sculptors and painters might be sent from one place to another by the king, with a specific commission, or delegated to work temporarily for a favored official, but they did not travel on their own from place to place in search of work.

**Status.** Representational and textual sources make it clear that artists of the courts and temples enjoyed a higher status than the men who made coffins, furniture, stone vessels, and similar goods. In common with all professions, however, the highest prestige among both artists and craftsmen attached to those who achieved the rank of administrator ("overseer" or "controller") over their colleagues. Whether artistic and/or organizational expertise were decisive factors in advancement is not known. Here, two pieces of evidence relating to the logistical skills required in connection with statue manufacture can be cited: in a tomb dated to c.1850 BCE at Bersheh in Middle Egypt, a team of 172 men was shown towing a colossal calcite (Egyptian alabaster) statue of the tomb owner, the nomarch Djehuty-hotep; the "controller of works on this statue" figured among the officials involved in the transport of the figure.

Some 450 years later Amenhotep, son of Hapu—perhaps the most influential official of his age—took pride in claiming responsibility for the transport of a pair of seated quartzite colossi of his king, Amenhotpe III, from the "Red Mountain," near Memphis in Lower Egypt, some 700 kilometers (almost 435 miles) upstream to Thebes. The prestige associated with that feat rivaled the achievement of the sculptor who oversaw the carving of the figures.

Pertinent data on the status of artisans in comparison to artists are provided by the labels accompanying workshop scenes in nonroyal tombs of the Old Kingdom and by the inscriptions from all periods on stelae and statues and in tombs that belonged to artists. During the Old Kingdom, men who were depicted carving and painting statues were, with few exceptions, the only figures in workshop scenes whose labels included names that supplemented titles. Such personalization attests their elevated status above smiths, jewelers, carpenters, and others in adjacent scenes. There, prestige stood in direct relationship to the importance of the product, since statues were prerequisites for the continued existence of the owner in the afterlife.

More than a millennium later, toward the end of the eighteenth dynasty, a seemingly insignificant object found at King Akhenaten's capital city of Amarna confirmed the enduring prestige of the sculptor's profession. A blinker (a flap on a bridle that keeps a horse from seeing to the side) inscribed for the "Sculptor and Superintendent of Works" Thutmose, provided not only the name of the master who ran the extensive compound where it was excavated—complete with living and working quarters for himself, his

assistants, and apprentices—it also showed that Thutmose owned horses and drove a chariot, privileges reserved for the elite.

The Egyptian word for "painter" was the same as "scribe," the most prestigious of all professions in ancient Egypt. Draftsmen, too, were among the literate few.

**Training and Organization of Work.** As in other professions, a son often followed in his father's footsteps. That tradition is exemplified by the genealogy of the draftsman-painter Dedia, who was charged by Sety I of the nineteenth dynasty with restoring several temples at Thebes in the aftermath of the Amarna period. Dedia belonged to the sixth generation of "Superintendants of Draftsmen," and names borne by his ancestors have revealed the Levantine origin of Dedia's family, showing that foreign birth was no hindrance to entering the profession and rising to a position of authority in it.

Artists and artisans alike served a period of apprenticeship. Although tools and techniques were simple—with form stipulated by a canon and content restricted by rules of decorum—it can hardly have been that "pharaonic art style . . . was relatively easy to pick up" (Barry J. Kemp, *Ancient Egypt, Anatomy of a Civilization.* London and New York, 1989, p. 84), since no amount of material incentives suffice if talent and skills are lacking.

Texts are silent on the role of aesthetic criteria in the judgment of an artist. Descriptions of monuments might include the information that they were "beautiful," which was synonymous with "perfect," costly (i.e., made of precious materials), and large (i.e., impressive), but those estimations were intended to reflect on the prestige of the commissioning authority or the owner—whether king, commoner, or god—rather than to furnish a commentary on the proficiency of the person(s) who made them.

The intervention of the patron in the creative process is equivocal. One phrase among the titles and epithets of the sculptor Bak, who worked for King Akhenaten of the eighteenth dynasty, described the artist as "a disciple whom His Majesty Himself instructed." That statement has been interpreted to imply that Akhenaten was personally responsible for creating the radical art style characteristic of the earlier years of his reign. Yet the phrase is neither unique to Bak nor to the Amarna period, and it seems to be related to the rank called "Overseer of Works," which Bak also held, rather than to his role as sculptor.

Statuary, reliefs, and paintings were the products of teamwork. Wall decoration, for example, was laid out by men called "outline draftsmen," carved by relief sculptors, then painted. Analysis of unfinished work has revealed specialists (such as the sculptor whose skill qualified him to carve the heads and faces of the king and the gods) and painters who executed fine details, while inexperienced or

ARTISTS AND ARTISANS. *Fifth dynasty sculptors, from the tomb of Ty at Saqqara.*

less skilled colleagues laid down broad areas of flat color and painted in the background.

In a temple, several teams of artists and craftsmen might be at work simultaneously under the supervision of one or more "masters" (which method of production did not differ fundamentally from well-documented practices in the ateliers of the Renaissance and Baroque eras of western Europe).

Raw materials were at the disposition of the employer, since quarrying and mining, as well as the importation of various materials (like coniferous wood from the Levant and the gemstone lapis lazuli from farther afield) were under the control of the crown and its sometime rival the temple. Tools, too, were not normally owned by the men who wielded them, but were state or temple property, to be issued as needed.

**Self-Assessment.** Ancient Egyptian artists were not accustomed to claim credit for specific works. Comparatively few "artists' signatures" are attested, so artistic personalities, familiar in Western Art especially from the Renaissance onward, are lacking. Nevertheless, Egyptologists have been tempted to associate iconographic and stylistic innovations with known individuals. For example, Senenmut, the architect of Queen Hatshepsut's mortuary temple at Deir el-Bahri, has been credited with creating new genres in statuary, since they are first attested among his own scultptures. Colossi in the "radical" style, which characterized the earlier, Theban phase of Akhenaten's reign, have been attributed to Bak, a sculptor who claims responsibility for "very large monuments of the king in the Aten temple at Amarna." Tangible evidence is, however, lacking to support these and similar claims made by Egyptologists on behalf of other artists. Certainly, innovations originated in and were disseminated from the major royal and temple ateliers, either directly by the artists or through the medium of their works.

Texts have seldom been informative about an artist's attitude toward his own proficiency. In one remarkable document (the stela Louvre C 14, dated c.2025 BCE), the owner—a sculptor, painter, and overseer of craftsmen—laid claim to secret knowledge, before he launched into a detailed, boastful account of his accomplishments. More than seven centuries later, an overseer of works and sculptor named Userhat-Hatiay similarly claimed access to secrets, implying a role for them in the practice of his profession, which included the manufacture of cult images for the temples of the gods. Such secret information might refer to temple archives, where specifications for divine statues and pattern books for reliefs and paintings were presumably kept, although evidence for that is scant.

Many of the higher ranking artists simultaneously occupied positions in the priesthood, and depictions of them on their own monuments showed them like other important men: receiving offerings or worshiping deities, not working at their professions.

**The Workplace: Historical Review.** Workshop scenes in nonroyal tombs of the Old Kingdom show artists and craftsmen at work, side by side, on the estate of the tomb owner. Leatherworkers might have been needed on a regular basis to supply sandals and apparel for a large household, and joiners were needed to make and keep furniture in good repair. The sculptors would be only on temporary loan from the king, for the purposes of preparing statues that were required for the funerary equipment of the tomb owner and his family.

From the later Old Kingdom, the practice of sending artists from the capital at Memphis to decorate tombs of favored officials in the provinces has been documented. That local workshops also existed is proved by the proliferation of local styles that emerged with the breakdown of central authority toward the end of the sixth dynasty. Detailed analysis of finds from some sites in northern Upper Egypt has identified iconographic and paleographic peculiarities that evolved in relative isolation during the period that followed.

When a Theban royal family succeeded in reuniting the country, contact was reestablished with the "classical" art of the Old Kingdom, as represented in the necropolis of the Memphis region. Within a few decades, at about 2000 BCE, a uniform style again existed throughout Egypt. The role of artists based at the Residence, which was again located near Memphis, was paramount in this development. Inscriptions confirm the evidence of the monuments themselves; for example, an official at Elephantine on Egypt's southern border recorded that Senwosret I sent artists from the Residence to decorate his tomb. An almost contemporary biographical inscription of a sculptor relates the way he began his career at the Residence before being sent to Abydos, the cult center of the god of the dead, Osiris, to work on the king's projects there.

Local ateliers working under the intermittent influence of such artists existed at both Elephantine and Abydos. Around Thebes, such a workshop is presumed to have served the needs of temples in a number of towns, as well as in the provincial capital of Thebes itself.

Tanis, in the northeastern Nile Delta, was long considered the site of a major contemporaneous atelier—an idea that arose because many royal sculptures of Middle Kingdom kings were discovered there. Those statues, however, were brought to Tanis centuries after the fall of the Middle Kingdom. A number of them can be confidently traced back to the once vast temple precinct at Heliopolis, some 40 kilometers (25 miles) north of Memphis. Most likely, Heliopolis—the center of the solar cult from earliest times—possessed its own atelier as early as the Old Kingdom, but neither archaeological nor textual evidence has yet come to light to substantiate this supposition.

The major stylistic divide in Middle Kingdom art separates works produced to furnish temples of the gods from those created for royal funerary establishments. Presumably, an atelier was in existence for several generations near the sites of the kings' pyramids, which were all located in the general vicinity of Memphis; there, draftsmen and sculptors working in a continuous tradition made statuary and decorated the temples of royal funerary complexes, as well as the tombs of favored officials in the associated cemeteries. Those men and their Old Kingdom predecessors may have been affiliated with the cult of Ptah—the patron god of craftsmen—which was centered at Memphis. Ptah's high priest was called "Greatest of Craftsmen." The assumption of an atelier in physical proximity to the temple is reasonable, but there are few named craftsmen whose titles associated them explicitly with Ptah's temple, and they lived during the New Kingdom.

Karnak, Amun's cult center at Thebes, is the only religious institution whose claim to extensive workshops and ateliers is well supported. From the New Kingdom, a wealth of onomastic (name-related) data exists for smiths, carpenters, sculptors, and draftsmen attached to the temple treasury. That information is supplemented by the decoration of contemporaneous tombs, where there are depictions of the manufacture of a variety of items in temple workshops—from elaborate cult vessels, jewelry, and gilded openwork shrines to colossal statuary.

Carpenters, smiths, and jewelers worked in ateliers located near the temple (with its treasury), from which they obtained their tools and raw materials. Relief sculptors, draftsmen, and painters worked of necessity at the wall—whether at the temple or tomb. The presence of ateliers for the manufacture of statues raises a more complex question, for the medium determined where statuary was made. Sculptors who created small, portable cult images could have worked close to Karnak, to facilitate access to (and effective control over) the precious metals, imported woods, and semiprecious stones requisitioned from the treasury.

Study focusing on the sculpture of Amenhotpe III (c.1390 BCE) of the eighteenth dynasty has confirmed that ateliers for stone statuary existed at quarry sites. From the following reign—that of Akhenaken—a number of workshops for stone statuary have been located at the site of Akhenaten's capital. One was beside the great Aten temple in the city center, but the famous atelier belonging to the master sculptor Thutmose, where archaeologists excavated the painted bust of Queen Nefertiti along with several other masterpieces, was situated within a residential quarter, among other large estates.

**Workmen's Villages.** Special communities, housing workmen employed on royal building projects, are known from the Old Kingdom onward. One such settlement, associated with the pyramid plateau of Giza is under excavation by Egyptian archaeologists. Such villages are not identical with the so-called pyramid towns, where the personnel lived who served the cult of the deceased king.

The best-known workmen's village is the New Kingdom settlement of Deir el-Medina at Western Thebes. Overwhelming site data comes from the period that followed the reestablishment of the community after the Amarna period. The walled village at Tell el-Amarna accommodated the workmen who cut and decorated the rock-cut tombs at the site, but the village's brief existence ended as a billet for those who policed the cemetery. The exceptional, indeed privileged, status of the artists and artisans who lived and worked at Deir el-Medina derived from their association with the king and his fate, for they were responsible for cutting and decorating the royal tombs located in the cliffs of Western Thebes. The debris of the settlement yielded copious written documentation concerned with the daily life and religious beliefs of the community; aside from figured limestone ostraca, remarkably little archaeological evidence related to the crafts pursued by the site's inhabitants in their spare time.

**Payment.** Prior to the New Kingdom, information on remuneration for artists and artisans is limited. Inscriptions left by those for whom tombs and their decoration were commissioned in Old Kingdom times are concerned with assuring posterity that proper payment (unspecified) was made for the work and the craftsmen "satisfied." Such inscriptions were intended to document the good character and generosity of the tomb owner. Study of both the inscriptions and the representations that accompany a few of them suggests that the standard payment in the form of victuals (food) was supplemented in some cases by "wages," paid in lengths of linen cloth, a valuable commodity in all periods.

The Ramessid workmen's village of Deir el-Medina provides a surfeit of information on prices and payment. For their regular work in the service of the state, the inhabitants received grain rations monthly, according to their profession and rank. Any surplus that remained after baking and brewing for the family might be traded within the community. The state also provided oil, cloth, seasonal products (fruit, vegetables), and some luxuries. Supplementary income derived from freelancing among the community. Craftsmen worked not only for each other to order but they also accumulated stock, as witnessed, for example, by finds of *shawabtis* that lack only the name of the owner (and it would have been added when the figurine was sold). A wooden statue cost about twice the monthly grain ration of a draftsman. The charge for decorating a coffin exceeded the price of the coffin itself—attesting to the higher value placed on the work of a draftsman over a joiner.

[*See also* Art; Painting, *overview article;* Scribes; *and* Sculpture, *overview article.*]

### BIBLIOGRAPHY

Aldred, Cyril. "Some Royal Portraits of the Middle Kingdom in Egypt." *Metropolitan Museum Journal* 3 (1970), 27–50. See especially pages 37–39, on which doubt is expressed that geographically specific styles existed in royal sculpture of the Middle Kingdom.

Arnold, Dorothea. *The Royal Women of Amarna: Images of Beauty from Ancient Egypt.* Exhibiton catalog, The Metropolitan Museum of Art. New York, 1996. Includes a chapter devoted to the workshop of the sculptor Thutmose.

Baines, John. "Techniques of Decoration in the Hall of Barques in the Temple of Sethos I at Abydos." *Journal of Egyptian Archaeology* 75 (1989), 13–28.

Baines, John. "On the Status and Purposes of Ancient Egyptian Art." *Cambridge Archaeological Journal* 4. 1 (1994), 67–94. Pages 67–74 present the role of artists and their status.

Barta, Winfried. *Das Selbstzeugnis eines altägyptischen Künstlers (Stele Louvre C 14).* Berlin, 1970. Publication on the stela, with detailed commentary.

Dijk, Jacobus van. "Maya's Chief Sculptor Userhat-Hatiay." *Göttinger Miszellen* 148 (1995), 29–34.

Dorman, Peter F. *The Monuments of Senenmut: Problems in Historical Methodology.* London and New York, 1988. Reviews on Senenmut's statues; argues against his personal involvement in creating them.

Eyre, Christopher J. "Work and Organization of Work in the Old Kingdom" and "Work and the Organization of Work in the New Kingdom." In *Labor in the Ancient Near East,* edited by Marvin A. Powell, pp. 5–47 and 167–221 (respectively). New Haven, 1987.

Fischer, Henry George. *Dendera in the Third Millennium.* Locust Valley, N. Y., 1968. One of several studies by Fischer detailing the evolution of a local style during the First Intermediate Period.

Franke, Detlef. *Das Heiligtum des Heqaib auf Elephantine. Geschichte eines Provinzheiligtums im Mittleren Reich.* Heidelberg, 1994. Chapter 3 is devoted to the relationship between the royal craftsmen and local ateliers at Elephantine.

Freed, Rita E. "The Development of Middle Kingdom Egyptian Sculptural Schools of Late Dynasty XI, with an appendix on trends of Early Dynasty XII (2040–1878 BCE)." Ph.D. diss., Institute of Fine Arts, New York University, 1984. Available from University Microfilms International, Ann Arbor, Mich. (#8421510).

Kozloff, Arielle P., and Betsy M. Bryan. *Egypt's Dazzling Sun: Amenhotep III and His World.* Exhibition Catalog, Cleveland Museum of Art, 1992. See Bryan's comments on statue production on pages 136–146.

Krauss, Rolf. "Der Oberbildhauer Bak und sein Denkstein in Berlin." *Jahrbuch der Berliner Museen* n. F. 28 (1986), 5–46. Thorough study of Bak, Akhenaten's "Chief Sculptor."

Lowle, D. A. "A Remarkable Family of Draughtsmen-Painters from Early Nineteenth-Dynasty Thebes." *Oriens Antiquus* 15 (1976), 91–106. Discussion of Dedia's monuments.

Roth, Ann Macy. "The Practical Economics of Tomb Building in the Old Kingdom: A Visit to the Necropolis in a Carrying Chair." In *For his Ka: Essays Offered in Memory of Klaus Baer,* edited by David P. Silverman, pp. 227–240. Chicago, 1994.

Steinmann, Frank. "Untersuchungen zu den in der handwerklich-künstlerischen Produktion beschäftigten Personen und Berufsgruppen des Neuen Reiches." *Zeitschrift für ägyptische Sprache und Altertumskunde* 118 (1991), 149–161. Last of five articles devoted to analyzing the professions of ancient Egyptian artists and artisans, from a socioeconomic standpoint.

Vercoutter, Jean. "Le rôle des artisans dans la naissance de la civilisation égyptienne." *Chronique d'Égypte* 68 (1993), 70–83. Covers the relationship of the god Ptah to artists and artisans, with particular reference to the formative phase of Egyptian civilization.

MARIANNE EATON-KRAUSS

**ASASIF,** one of the principal areas of the Theban necropolis, located on the eastern bank of the Nile River (25°44′N, 32°36′E). The exact meaning of the Arabic term *al-ʿasasif* is not known, although the translation "passages interconnecting under the ground" has been suggested. More likely, however, the term is a plural of *al-ʿassaf,* which is attested as a personal name. Thus the term may refer to a tribe or clan that claimed descent from a certain individual al-ʿAssaf. Topographically, the area known as the Asasif stretches from the edge of the cultivation in the southeast to (and including) the tomb and temple of Nebhepetre Montuhotep I and the terrace temple of Hatshepsut at Deir el-Bahri in the northwest. Besides these two temples, the most visible landmarks in the area today are huge, towerlike mud-brick buildings (pylons) that form the superstructures of large private tombs of the Saite period (the twenty-sixth dynasty, 664–525 BCE).

ASASIF. *Pylons from the tomb of Montuemhat.* (Courtesy Dieter Arnold)

The Asasif was first used as a royal and private cemetery during the second half of the eleventh dynasty (c.2050 BCE), when Nebhepetre Montuhotep I built there instead of at the necropolis of his predecessors (Antef I, Antef II, and Antef III) in el-Tarif. On virgin ground, he had constructed for himself an ambitious and innovative royal tomb-and-temple complex. When excavated, that complex contained the main burial of the king, as well as several additional burial shafts for royal princesses and wives of the king. High officials of his court had their tombs built in the cliffs overlooking the Asasif and at Deir el-Bahri; lower court officials had their tombs cut in the plain. The prevailing type of private tomb during this period was the *saff*-tomb, whose architecture was strongly influenced by that of the royal tombs in el-Tarif (e.g., the tomb of Antef, tomb 386 in Western Thebes). Most of this period's tombs have their central axis oriented toward the long artificial causeway that connected the temple of Nebhepetre with an (unknown) valley temple on the edge of the cultivation. After the first decades of the twelfth dynasty, when the king and his court moved to the new capital, Itjtawy, in northern Egypt, the Asasif was abandoned as a major burial ground for more than four hundred years.

At the beginning of the eighteenth dynasty (c.1569 BCE), the Asasif again became the scene of extensive building activity. Amenhotpe I had a small structure (a pyramid?) erected to the north of the temple of Nebhepetre Montuhotep I. Less than fifty years later, Hatshepsut (r. 1502–1482 BCE) chose a nearby location as the place for her mortuary temple. Her famous terrace temple in Deir el-Bahri, which combined architectural features from Nebhepetre's temple with those of the *saff*-tombs, continued to be one of the most important sacred places in the Theban necropolis until Greco-Roman times. For the construction of the temple's causeway, which was at least partially flanked by sphinxes, several earlier buildings and *saff*-tombs at Asasif had to be destroyed or covered. Close to the causeway and the enclosure wall of the temple lies the "hidden" private tomb of Senenmut (tomb 353), who was, in part, responsible for the construction of Hatshepsut's mortuary temple. The tombs of some other high officials of that time were located in the nearby hills of Khokhah, and Qurna, and they were oriented to Hatshepsut's causeway (e.g., those of Puimre, tomb 39; Nebamun, tomb 65; Hapuseneb, tomb 67; Senenmut, tomb 71; and his brother, Senimen, tomb 252). During the remaining time of the eighteenth dynasty to the twentieth, the main private cemeteries were shifted to other areas in the Theban necropolis (to Qurna, Khokhah, and Dra Abul Naga). The temple and causeway of Hatshepsut, however, remained the center for a number of highly important festivals and ceremonies (e.g., the Valley feast), and court officials occasionally used the Asasif as a burial ground (e.g., the tombs in the Kharuef complex).

In the twentieth dynasty, Ramesses IV (r.1166–1160 BCE) initiated the construction of his gigantic mortuary temple complex near the southeastern edge of the Asasif. The size of that temple would have surpassed by far that of Ramesses III at Medinet Habu, but the ambitious project never progressed beyond the initial stage. For the construction of the temple's foundations, a large section of Nebhepetre's causeway had to be dismantled. In addition, a number of earlier tombs of that period were either destroyed or entirely covered. For nearly four hundred years after the end of the twentieth dynasty (c.1075–690 BCE), no major building activities are known for the Asasif. As the twenty-fifth dynasty became the twenty-sixth, it once again became the focus of the Theban necropolis. Partly, this was due to the increasing importance of the goddess Hathor, whose main center of worship at that time seems to have been the mortuary temple of Hatshepsut. Then, too, the highest officials of the Theban administration created large subterranean tomb complexes there, known as the Saite tombs, whose main architectural features were huge towerlike superstructures (pylons) and large open sun courts. Some of the Saite tombs exceed, both in their dimensions and in the quality of their decoration, most of the earlier royal tombs in the Valley of the Kings and are among the largest private funerary monuments ever built in Egypt (e.g., those of Sheshonq, tomb 27; Harwa, tomb 37; Montuemhat, tomb 34; and Pabasa, tomb 279). The contents of the decoration program and the style of the limestone reliefs frequently and consciously referred to earlier periods (the Middle Kingdom and the eighteenth dynasty). The elaborate subterranean parts of the Saite tombs made them an ideal burial ground for later periods and, in fact, they were frequently reused for intrusive burials until and throughout Greco-Roman times.

The first systematic exploration of the Asasif was in the earlier part of the twentieth century and is mainly connected with the Egyptian Expedition of The Metropolitan Museum of Art, New York. Under Herbert E. Winlock and Ambrose Lansing, the museum expedition spent more than two decades at the Asasif, during which time it unearthed the unfinished mortuary temple of Ramesses IV and a large number of Middle Kingdom and later tombs. Since the late 1960s, several excavation projects began to work in the central area. The American, Austrian, Belgian, German, and Italian projects have concentrated their efforts mainly on the Saite tombs.

[*See also* Deir el-Bahri; Theban Necropolis; *and the article on* Montuhotep I, Nebhepetre.]

**BIBLIOGRAPHY**

Arnold, Dieter. *Das Grab des Jni-jtj.f. Die Architektur.* Archäologische Veröffentlichungen, Deutsches Archäologisches Institut, Abteilung Kairo, 4. Mainz, 1971.

Bietak, Manfred. "Theban-West (Luqsor), Vorbericht über die ersten vier Grabungskampagnen (1969–71)." *Sitzungsberichte der Österreichischen Akademie der Wissenschaften,* 278 (1972), 7–26.

Bietak, Manfred, and Elfriede Haslauer. *Das Grab des Anch-Hor, Obersthofmeister der Goltesgamahl Nitokris.* Untersuchungen der Zweigstelle Kairo des Österreichischen Archäologischen Instituts, 4–5. Vienna, 1978–1982. Exemplary publication of a Late period tomb in the Asasif region.

Dorman, Peter F. *The Tombs of Senenmut: The Architecture and Decoration of Tombs 71 and 353.* Publications of The Metropolitan Museum of Art. Egyptian Expedition, 24. New York, 1991.

Eigner, Diethelm. *Die monumentalen Grabbauten der Spätzeit in der Thebanischen Nekropole.* Untersuchungen der Zweigstelle Kairo des Österreichischen Archäologischen Instituts, 6. Vienna, 1984. Comprehensive and detailed study of the large private tombs of the Late period in Thebes.

Kampp, Friederike. *Die Thebanische Nekropole.* Theben, 13. Mainz, 1996. Standard publication of the private tombs of Thebes, with up-to-date bibliography.

Porter, Bertha, and Rosalind L. B. Moss. *Topographical Bibliography of Ancient Egyptian Hieroglyphic Texts Reliefs and Paintings.* Oxford, 1960–1972.

Thomas, Nancy K. "A Typological Study of Saite Tombs at Thebes." Ph.D. diss. University of California, Los Angeles, 1980.

Winlock, Herbert E. *Excavations at Deir el Bahri 1911–1931.* New York, 1942.

DANIEL C. POLZ

**ASHMUNEIN.** *See* Hermopolis.


**ASSYRIA.** *See* Mesopotamia.


**ASTROLOGY.** During Predynastic and pharaonic times, astronomy was almost entirely devoted to keeping track of time and making calendars, with the primary purpose of predicting the time of sunrise, the appearance of the stellar deities, the celebration of the feasts for particular gods, and the eschatological connection between the spirits of the deities and the pharaoh (also later of the ordinary Egyptian). Astrology, in the modern sense of computing horoscopes (the relative positions of the Sun, Moon, and planets with respect to background constellations of the zodiac and the use of that information as a predictor of the human condition) was *not* an Egyptian development. Instead there emerged, in association with the rather intricate development of Egyptian religion, a series of special times to be heeded, usually referred to as the calendar of lucky and unlucky days. Each month of the lunar-based religious calendar contained both lucky days, propitious to the average person, and unlucky days, harbingers of misfortune. These were based on the fortunes or misfortunes of a specific deity or a group of deities who were associated with the particular day or days of the month, as recounted in Egyptian legends.

When the Greek Ptolemies became the rulers of Egypt (304–30 BCE), both Hellenistic and Babylonian cultures soon strongly influenced the character of Egyptian astronomy, which has been evident in the surviving temples, monuments, and papyri. The twelve ecliptic constellations of the zodiac first appeared on temples and monuments during the Ptolemaic period. Although the traditional Egyptian constellations as well as their names were also used, the basic pictorial elements of today's zodiacal signs (such as the Capricorn goat-fish, the double-headed archer of Sagittarius, and the ear of corn representing Virgo) were Babylonian in origin. Similarly, the underlying astrological notion connected with the "exaltations" (the ordering of particular planets into certain zodiacal signs that produced special influences on the human condition) was derived from Babylonian astrology. Conversely, the concept we know to be connected with the "houses" (the association of a given planet with a given constellation to produce the greatest influence) seems to be of Greek origin, based on the arrangement of planets according to their orbital periods, since a different ordering of the planets was used in Babylonian astrology.

Of the zodiacs found in Egypt, six come from ceilings in temples; six or seven from Roman-era coffin lids; and eight from ceilings in private tombs. The best known is the zodiac in the round sky map of the temple of Hathor at Dendera, now displayed in Paris, at the Louvre. Zodiacal signs were not specifically named in any of the scenes, so our information comes from horoscopes on ostraca (Neugebauer and Parker 1968) and from planetary tables, in which Demotic names for single signs were direct translations from Greek. In some cases, iconographic relationships existed between the zodiacal signs and similar pharaonic-era signs. An example would be the Ox Leg called *Meskhetiu* (*msḥtyw*), which is our Big Dipper.

Some Greek and Demotic papyri and ostraca contain astrological horoscopes and, sometimes, Babylonian-like omens. Owing to the brevity of the texts, the latter were mostly incomplete; yet the stated planetary positions were usually sufficient to permit scholars to compute a date. Most referred to Roman times, with the oldest dated to the reign of Cleopatra VII (Neugebauer and Parker 1968). Inscriptions, however, were very often written long after the event described in the texts.

A statue of the astronomer/astrologer Harkhebi, dating to the early third century BCE, contains a brief text that summarized his accomplishments and provided some cultural information about his duties, which were inherited from his forebears. Several excerpts are quoted below (taken from the translation given by Otto Neugebauer and Richard Parker 1969); the commentary on them reflects some of the concepts mentioned in this article:

> who announces rising and setting at their times, with the gods who foretell the future.

These two clauses refer to Harkhebi's casting of horoscopes. The "gods who foretell the future" are the planets, so that the announcement of rising and setting times must refer to the constellations of the zodiac. Then there is:

> for which he purified himself in their days when Akh rose heliacally beside Benu from earth and he contented the lands with his utterances.

The name *Akh* (*ȝḥ*) is one of the thirty-six Decans and *Benu* (*bnw*) is one of the names for Venus. The phrase indicates a particular configuration that appears on the eastern horizon in early morning light. The actual star is not known; but the heliacal rising reference indicates that it is the star's first appearance after a long period of ab-

ASTROLOGY. *Nineteenth dynasty star chart of the North Pole of the sky.* From the tomb of Sety I, Valley of the Kings, Thebes.

sence from the sky. That Venus is the nearby morning star at that moment suggests an exaltation; because of the rarity of the event, perhaps it is even an occurrence in a "house." Either interpretation is indicative of the astrological nature of the phrase. The word *utterances* probably refers to any associated predictions. There is also:

> who observes the culmination of every star in the sky, who knows the heliacal rising of every . . . in a good year, and who foretells the heliacal rising of Sothis at the beginning of the year.

The lacuna is undoubtedly the word *star*. This phrase apparently implies that knowledge of when certain stars reach the prime meridian could be used for the prediction of heliacal risings of other stars. Accumulated observational experience by a trained observer of such culminations has been used in other cultures to predict the heliacal rising of stars. The preeminent star for the Egyptians was Sirius (called by them Sothis), the heliacal rising of which marked the beginning of the lunar year, because of their early association of this event with the onset of the annual Nile River flood.

> He observes her (i.e., Sothis) on the day of her first festival, knowledgeable in her course at the times of designating therein, observing what she does daily, all she has foretold is in her charge.

These phrases reflect the importance attached to determining the time of the major heliacal rising festival each year. The last part, "all she has foretold is in her charge," seems to indicate that the prediction depends on the positions of the Moon and planets in the zodiac. A late papyrus does contain specific positions of the Moon and planets in relation to a Sothic rising that would be consistent with this interpretation. In the following:

> knowing the northing and southing of the sun, announcing all its wonders and appointing for them a time, he declares when they have occurred, coming at their times,

this reference is associated with Harkhebi's ability to predict the summer and winter solstices, again with the positions of the Moon and planets (wonders) in the zodiac as the principal indicators. The important winter-solstice festival was celebrated in Egypt as the birthday of Re. The phrase

> who divides the hours for the two times (day and night) without going into error at night,

indicates that two methods of telling time were used. During the day, the hour was measured by a shadow clock, which was quite inaccurate for the first hour or so after sunrise and before sunset, because of the lengthy shadows cast. At night, a water clock was used, which was ac-

curately calibrated to account for longer winter night hours and shorter summer night hours. Finally, in the phrases

> knowledgeable in everything which is seen in the sky, for which he has waited, skilled with respect to their conjunctions and their regular movements,

the Egyptian word for "conjunction" (*ḫnm; khenem*) also means "unite," so that the last part of the phrase clearly refers to following the planets as they approached the Sun from one side, disappeared, and then emerged on the other side during the course of a few weeks (Wells 1985). The reference to "regular movements" includes the fact that planets also have retrograde motions. The phrase, "he travels backwards," is sometimes encountered in reference to the planets.

The inscription from Harkhebi's statue, more than any other document, informs us of the wide-ranging nature of the duties expected of an Egyptian astronomer/astrologer/priest of his time.

[*See also* Astronomy; *and* Calendars.]

**BIBLIOGRAPHY**

Allen, James P. "The Celestial Realm." In *Ancient Egypt*, edited by David P. Silverman, pp. 114–131. New York, 1997.

Britton, J., and Christopher Walker. "Astronomy and Astrology in Mesopotamia." In *Astronomy before the Telescope*, edited by Christopher Walker, pp. 42–67. London, 1996.

Neugebauer, Otto, and Richard A. Parker. "Two Demotic Horoscopes." *Journal of Egyptian Archaeology* 54 (1968), 231–235. Examples of two horoscopes written on ostraca; the omens are missing, but the positioning of the Sun and Moon in Taurus and Capricorn, respectively, as well as the planets in some of the other constellations, plus a date in both the civil and lunar calendars, permitted the authors to date the horoscope to 4 May 38 BCE, during the reign of Cleopatra VII. The article demonstrates the difficulties faced in interpreting our few surviving documents.

Neugebauer, Otto, and Richard A. Parker. *Egyptian Astronomical Texts, vol. III: Decans, Planets, Constellations and Zodiacs.* Brown Egyptological Studies, 3. Providence, 1969. This last of three volumes requires a knowledge of Egyptian grammar and some background in positional astronomy for full appreciation.

Toomer, G. J. "Ptolemy and His Greek Predecessors." In *Astronomy before the Telescope*, edited by Christopher Walker, pp. 68–91. London, 1996.

Wells, Ronald A. "Sothis and the Satet Temple on Elephantine: A Direct Connection." *Studien zur Altägyptischen Kultur* 12 (1985), 255–302. Figure 11 and associated discussion (pp. 275–277) describe the iconography found on the unique depiction of the crown of Satet, dating to Ptolemaic times; it shows a scorpion, holding in its claws the sun sign, containing a star, which is a symbol for the heliacal rising of Sothis. The scorpion holding the sun symbol in its claws indicates Egyptian recognition of the ecliptic passing through Libra (claws of the scorpion) and Scorpio, based on careful observation of the constellations before sunrise and after sunset. Similar observation would be required for the planetary conjunctions.

RONALD A. WELLS

**ASTRONOMY.** The oldest possibly astronomically in-spired monuments on record consist of a series of aligned megalithic structures and stone circles found adjacent to Middle and Late Neolithic (7000–5000 BCE) settlements at Nabta in the Western Desert of Egypt just north of Sudan. One of these, a 4-meter (12-foot) circle of small upright and recumbent stone slabs, also contains four sets of nar-rower pillar-like stones arranged in pairs that form slots at opposite ends of a diameter that appears to have been aligned along the summer solstice sunrise–sunset line of about 6000 BCE. In addition, two similar opposing pairs of uprights marked the north–south axis of the monument (Malville, Wendorf, et al. 1998).

To the ancient Egyptians, astronomy became integrated into their concept of self-identity. Their observations of moving star patterns in the night sky more than seven thousand years ago resulted in a variety of myths that in-fluenced their religious beliefs. Their principal deities were specific heavenly bodies, whose actions governed many aspects of daily Egyptian life. People, institutions, and the state were considered reflections of the greater cosmos from which they evolved and toward which they aspired. That relationship was a consequence of the abil-ity of those early sky watchers to predict the time and place of their gods' appearances. They developed an ele-mentary form of positional astronomy that led to an annual time unit of 365 days; the division of night into segments that predicted the time of sunrise; and the formation of a relatively complicated lunar calendar, used to determine recurrent times of feasts and offerings to their gods. As the cohesiveness of the state strengthened, economic progress forced the simplification of this reli-gious calendar into a secular one that the ordinary Egyp-tian could use for business transactions. It comprised twelve 30-day months with a special 5-day unit added to bring the total to 365 days. Known as the civil calendar, it is the earliest predecessor of our modern Western coun-terpart. These early evolutionary trends and their effect on later generations are summarized here.

**Predynastic Astronomy.** The preeminent Egyptian god was the sun god Re. The early Egyptians therefore followed the annual motion of the sun disk along the hori-zon at sunrise and sunset, the northern and southernmost turning points of which are called the summer and winter solstices, respectively. Much of Egyptian astronomy and religion can ultimately be traced back to that simple movement of the Sun along the horizon.

Two principal collections of Predynastic legends had a profound effect on Egyptian culture. One was the re-nowned myth of the sky goddess Nut giving birth to Re, which catalyzed both timekeeping and calendar develop-ment and endowed the concept of divine royalty. The other, a compilation of stories related to the safe passage of Re through the underworld, referred to as the *Book of Gates*, became the first markers of the night intervals that were used to predict the time of sunrise for daily morning offerings to Re. The specific effects of each of these leg-ends are discussed below.

***The mythology of Nut and the birth of Re.*** The god-dess Nut was depicted as a naked female stretching across the sky between the horizons. The Sun is shown passing into her mouth, coursing through her star speckled body, and emerging again from her birth canal. The faint outer arm of the Milky Way fortuitously resembles a female and was clearly perceived by early Egyptians as the goddess Nut. An expansion of the star patches in the vicinity of the constellation Gemini forms her head. A division in the star patterns at the cross shape of the constellation Cyg-nus represents her legs; this particular location of Cygnus, reminiscent of primitive female figurines marked with cross-shaped genitalia, provides the female identification in the heavenly image. Cygnus' principal bright star, De-neb, coincides with the birth canal's exit.

The apparent path of the Sun in the sky is directed through Gemini, in an area of the Milky Way that corre-sponds with the head's mouth. After twilight on the vernal (spring) equinox, the head of Nut may be seen dropping below the horizon, with her face upward and her mouth open at or very close to the position where the Sun had set earlier. This configuration must have impressed early Egyptians as a faintly glowing head on the horizon that just consumed the Sun.

The Egyptian perception of the Sun emerging from Nut at birth occurred at winter solstice sunrise, 272 days later. The lower half of the goddess then reached a point where a great circle from the north celestial pole drawn through Deneb would intersect the horizon at exactly the spot where the Sun would appear. This great circle marked the shortest path that the infant Re would follow after birth, from Deneb to the point of its appearance on the horizon at sunrise. That picture reflected the ancient Egyptian method of birthing, where the woman assumed a squatting position with her feet supported on bricks, to deposit the infant directly onto the ground. This particu-lar winter solstice geometry does not repeat on any other day, since the sunrise horizon point would then be farther north. The correlation is supported by the number of days between the vernal equinox and the winter solstice, which is also the period of human gestation.

Two related aspects of Egyptian culture have been clar-ified by the astronomical associations discussed above. The first is the religious aspect, that Re was considered to be a self-creating god; Re does enter Nut at sunset on the vernal equinox, at which time the goddess presumably conceives. Oral conception was implied, but that is not an unusual belief in a primitive society. Nut then gives birth to Re nine months later, on the morning of the winter solstice. The second aspect is the assistance of the goddess Nut in performing the task of self-creation, which appears to have later governed the behavior of Egyptian kings, who maintained that their origin was divine—a result of the sun god intervening in the form of the reigning pharaoh to impregnate the queen to produce the next heir to the throne. Therefore, the king and queen might justify the line of succession throughout dynastic times as a reflection of the ancient tradition incorporated in the Nut cosmogony (Wells 1992).

**The hours of night and the Book of Gates.** The stories of the nocturnal passage of Re in his solar bark through the twelve portals of the underworld were also related to time-keeping (Wells, 1993). The *Book of Gates* was concerned with his safety on this voyage. Each gate, corresponding to one of the 12 hours of night, was in the charge of a demonic gatekeeper and several attendants. Re had to recite correctly the names of the gate, the gatekeeper, and his assistants in a spell before he could pass on to the next one. In later periods, both the deceased pharaoh and even his subjects were expected to utter the recitations correctly in order to reach the immortal gods.

Although the earliest form of the *Book of Gates* is unknown, it probably originated as a device for telling the time at night, by using stars to predict the time of sunrise. A particularly bright star would have been noticed to rise a given interval ahead of the Sun in sufficient time to permit the daily offering preparations before sunrise. A single star would be an inadequate herald of sunrise, since its interval would continuously increase—because stars rise 4 minutes later each night. As an example, for a star clock to work for the whole year, with 12 assumed equal hours of 60 minutes each, a series of twenty-four bright stars would be required. Each star, spaced across the sky in equal hourly intervals, would serve 15 days in turn as the marker of the hour before sunrise. The 4-minute delay would then shift it to spend 15 days marking the previous hour, and so on, in turn, until that star returned to its duty as the herald of sunrise again, a year later.

Bright stars may be difficult to distinguish from one another at rising. As part of a recognizable configuration of three or four other, fainter ones, however, which rose a few minutes before the principal bright star, the star pattern might forewarn the bright star's rising. The ancient Egyptians would have identified the faint stars as the attendants; the bright star as the gatekeeper; and the place of their appearance, the gate itself. The recitation requiring the names of all the gates and the demigods was just a mnemonic device to ensure that each star group would be recognized and remembered in the correct sequence. Only the group just rising would be at the horizon gate, marking the current hour. Others would be distributed overhead, toward the western horizon, while the remainder would still be in the underworld. As each group dominated the horizon gate, the gate would be associated with the stories that characterized the order of the sequence. Later, when the Egyptians wrote down those narratives, they depicted each group as having its own separate gate. Since twelve star groups came out of the underworld during the night, then the underworld would be illustrated as having twelve gates. Variants of the *Book of Gates* also have eight, ten, or other numbers of gates, which reflect the different number of patterns used in the different star clocks. Such differences indicate that the first Egyptian "hours" were of unequal length, since they depended on the sizes of the star configurations.

**Astronomical Origin of Egyptian Calendars.** Although specific documented predynastic evidence is lacking, the astronomical origin of the two myths discussed above along with the surviving structure of the later lunar calendar both serve as important guidelines in the reconstruction of the way the precursor calendar system might have been originated (Wells 1994).

Calendars are usually based on Earth's orbital period. One sacrosanct cycle for the Egyptians was the time required for Re to return to his birthplace on the southeastern horizon each year, at the winter solstice. The accurate determination of this period as 365 days, by a simple counting procedure—probably using wooden stakes, cords, and shadows—can be dated to sometime around 4500 BCE. At that time, the mouth area of Nut in Gemini was aligned more directly to the west; due west was interpreted by the ancient Egyptians as the entrance to the underworld, a concept that probably originated because of this alignment of Nut's mouth.

A desire to know when to celebrate the annual Birth of Re festival, which the Egyptians called *mswt R'*, would be a strong incentive for the creation of a calendar. The calendar was probably originated in Lower Egypt, where the chief cult center was later established at Heliopolis, by counting the number of lunar months (i.e., the occurrences of a specific lunar phase) between each winter solstice. Normally, there would be twelve 29- or 30-day months, the first one beginning after the festival had occurred. Because such a calendar averages only 354 days, whenever the first day of a new year occurred within 11 days after a winter solstice feast, an intercalary thirteenth month would have to be placed at its beginning, so that the next celebration of the festival would occur within the last month, which was named for the feast. Such intercalations were necessary about once every 2 or 3 years. In this manner, although the festival might occur on different days during the last month, the embarrassment of having to celebrate the festival in a differently named month would be avoided.

Because of the agrarian dependence of Upper Egypt on the Nile River floods, a different lunar calendar appears to have originated in the South. Instead of the Birth of Re festival, its regulating factor was the heliacal rising of the star Sirius—the first appearance of this star at dawn, just prior to sunrise, after an absence from the sky of about 70 days. Sirius rose heliacally in 4500 BCE, near the time the Nile itself began to rise. The Egyptians called this rising *prt spdt* ("the going forth of Sothis"), and it became a marker associated with the variable onset of the flood because its period of 365 days was easier to count. The cult center was at the temple of Satet (Sothis) on the island of Elephantine, in the Nile, near the present-day town of Aswan (Wells 1985); this was the fabled source of the Nile, according to ancient Egyptian tradition. The lunar calendar of Upper Egypt, therefore, appears to have used the festival celebrating *prt spdt* as the principal feast in its last month, governing the intercalation scheme.

The dynastic lunar calendar, from which recorded dates survive, was apparently the product of the political consolidation of Upper and Lower Egypt. The relationships between the northern "lunisolar" and the southern "lunistellar" calendars made their combining relatively easy. The key factors behind the religious festivals that regulated both calendars were theologically related—the star Sirius was equated with the deity Isis, the daughter of the sun god Re. At the beginning of the first dynasty, on their festival days, they rose within 2 degrees of each other on the horizon, although these occurred 6 months apart. During the merging of Upper and Lower Egypt, the use of the southern calendar spread northward, to usurp many of the functions of the northern calendar. Although the newly combined lunar calendar was regulated by Sirius, the name of its last month, normally derived from its principal festival, instead retained the old northern name, *mswt Rˁ*, in deference to the "Birth of Re."

This dynastic Egyptian lunar calendar was impractical for use by the general public. It contained either 12 or 13 months, and the beginnings of each had to be determined by observation. A special class of priests, called the "Overseers of the Hours," were needed to ensure its regulation. Yet as the ability to write spread throughout Egypt during the early dynasties, the need for dated records, for business transactions, forced the adoption of a simpler calendrical method. It rounded the numbers evenly to 12 months of 30 days each, none beginning observationally. This new civil calendar was divided into three 4-month seasons—corresponding to the periods of growth, harvest, and inundation—just like the lunar calendar, which was not abandoned but was used to regulate the observance of religious feasts. Since the civil calendar's total was only 360 days, a special interval of 5 days, known as the epagomenal days, preceded the onset of each year; the ancient Egyptians called them "the 5 days upon the year."

**The Old Kingdom.** By the onset of the Old Kingdom, observations of the Sun, Moon, and stars had led to a so-

phisticated time-keeping system intimately bound with a series of religious orders. Both contributed to the massive building programs of the Old Kingdom pharaohs, which promoted a growing economy. Astronomical/religious zeal reached an apex with the pyramids and sun temples of the fourth dynasty and the fifth.

The pyramids were stone pathways to the gods, conduits by which the soul of the deceased pharaoh could reach the northern circumpolar stars, identified as the immortal gods. The Egyptians called these stars *ikhemu-sek* ("the ones not knowing destruction"), an indication that they understood their circumpolar nature—or rather, perhaps, recognized that they did not pass into the underworld, as did the stars that rose and set. The sanctity of the circumpolar stars was apparently incorporated into the Giza pyramids, all of which had northern entrances with corridors sloping downward at an angle such that the circumpolar stars were visible from the interior (Edwards 1993). Consequently, it is easy to explain the peculiar northeastern–southwestern diagonal orientation of these three pyramids with respect to one another; they were simply offset away from the river, each by one full width, so that their northern faces did not block another's view toward the circumpolar stars.

Of the nine fifth dynasty kings, six built huge sun temples, expressly to honor Re, and they incorporated the title "Son of Re" into their official names, to acknowledge their divine origin according to the cosmogony of Nut (Edwards 1994). Their temples were important not only for religious reasons but also because the administration of their vast temple estates had a significant influence on the state economy. Two of the temples have been excavated, revealing a special architectural design, which facilitated the measurement of night hours for the prediction of sunrise.

The lower (so-called valley) temples in the priests' towns, located below the main sun temples, were each axially oriented toward a separate series of stars on the northeastern horizon; in that way, their roofs could have been used as observation platforms for marking the hours at night. Analysis of the stars (Wells 1993) has shown that they measured unequal segments of the night. In addition, Userkaf's temple, the first one of the six built, was associated with a series containing Deneb as its brightest star, appropriately the one from which Re himself was born. The Overseers of the Hours would have sighted the stars with an instrument called the *bay* (a palm rib with a notch cut into one end). The *bay*, with another instrument called the *merkhet* (essentially a plumb bob for determining the local vertical), would also have been used to ascertain the orientation of the building and the axial line on the roof. Similar devices were probably used to determine the orientation of pyramids.

These six temples from the fifth dynasty eventually operated simultaneously and, judging from the different orientations of the associated two known valley temples, each probably used different series of stars to predict the time of sunrise (Wells 1993). One king's priests probably did not want to usurp the ritual duties of another king's; this circumstance suggests that at one point there were six local times (i.e., nocturnal "hours" of differing lengths not having synchronous onsets). Yet since the communities were separated, and their clocks had the common purpose of predicting sunrise, these differences would not have mattered.

**The Middle Kingdom.** Primary knowledge of Middle Kingdom astronomy has been provided by a series of ninth and tenth dynasty wooden coffins, on whose interior lids were painted tables of rising stars. Those tables suggest that attempts had been made to regularize the measurement of hours with portable written records.

The surviving coffin lid tables record thirty-six rising stars, each successively marking an "hour" for an interval of 10 days; those hours were, however, only of a duration of forty minutes (24/36 × 60). Referred to as the "Decans," the thirty-six stars were located in a belt south of the ecliptic, all having the same invisible interval of seventy days prior to their heliacal rising, the property of the principal star in the group, Sirius (Neugebauer and Parker 1960). This new method of denoting the night hours was based on combining only those stars that behaved like Sirius with 10-day weeks of the civil calendar. In that way, one star's heliacal rising was replaced by the next after 10 days; alternatively, they were spaced in forty-minute intervals across the sky. (In other words, 18 decanal hours × 40/60 = 12 of our standard hours.) Although 18 Decans marked the period from sunset to sunrise, three Decans were assigned to each interval of twilight, leaving 12 Decans to mark the hours of total darkness. The 12-unit division of the night may, therefore, have originated in this combination of Decan stars with the civil calendar decades.

Although having a specific Egyptian name, the only one of the Decans unambiguously identified today is Sirius (*Sepdet*). The constellation of Orion (*Sah*) is also identifiable, although the association of names with its individual stars remains undetermined. Some of the coffin-lid vignettes depict the seven stars of the Big Dipper (Ursa Major), in approximately the known configuration. The Egyptians also depicted this star pattern as the hind leg of an ox, called it *Meskhetiu*, and identified it with the goddess Hathor.

Scholars usually refer to the coffin-lid tables as diagonal star clocks, because a given star appears one line higher in adjacent decade columns, marking an earlier hour. Consulting one of these decanal tables while viewing the night sky at a given moment, the time would be known by noting the tabular position of a specific star. The tables included an extra entry to account for the five epagomenal days of the civil calendar. Nevertheless, they failed to utilize an extra day for leap year. Every 4 years, the tables were therefore one day in error; after 120 years, they were off by a whole month. The Egyptians apparently attempted to solve this problem by shifting the star names by the appropriate amounts, which reset the clock with the civil calendar. Yet that procedure appears to have been abandoned by the time of the New Kingdom, when new observational procedures were instituted.

**The New Kingdom.** Astronomy during the New Kingdom was characterized by more complicated meridional transits, which required calibration by the newly introduced water clock. A variety of tomb paintings has provided this information. Two new elements appeared in these tomb scenes. One depicted men, facing the viewer and seated in front of grid patterns that contained stars, with the star names to the side; the other is an arrangement of zodiac-like representations of star groups, in the form of animals and deities.

Those stellar groupings have as yet defied attempts at decipherment, except for the already known examples of *Sepdet*, *Sah*, and *Meskhetiu*. Although certain vague relationships are evident, correct identifications cannot be made without independent, contemporary texts that would have similar descriptive elements.

The star grids behind seated priests in the tombs of Ramesses VI, VII, and IX, however, represent the last major stage in telling time with stars. Instead of using the rising stars, the new procedure involved any stars that were transiting both the meridian and the several adjacent pre- and postmeridional lines. The technique was derived from earlier tables of transiting decanal stars that were found in the cenotaph of Sety I and in the tomb of Ramesses IV. The Ramesses IV example consisted of twelve Decans in thirty-six tables that transited only the local meridian, thereby measuring equal "hours" during the night. The final stage exhibited in the later Ramessid tombs, however, was not limited to decanal stars. It consisted of thirteen stars (one marking the beginning of night), in twenty-four tables, and used transits over three lines that were parallel with the meridian on either side, in addition to the meridian; that resulted in unequal "hours," depending on the altitude of the star—hardly an observational improvement.

Actual observation of the stars required two priests, with one seated facing north, who performed the function of the *bay*, and the other seated facing the one watching the stars behind him. The viewer of the tomb scene figure was assumed to be the pharaoh's spirit, which would be able to move safely from hour to hour, as with the *Book of Gates*. The inscriptions listed particular stars for the

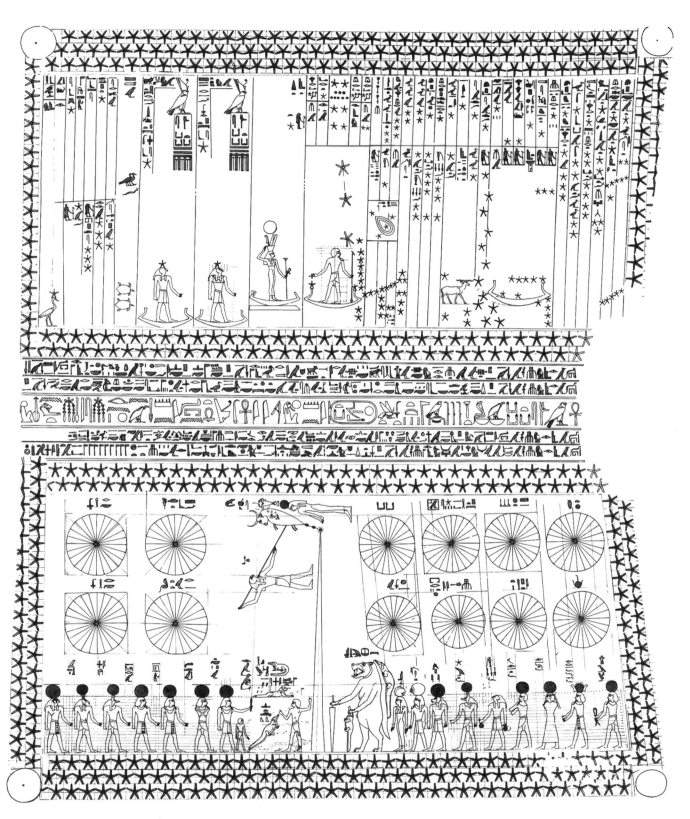

ASTRONOMY. *Astronomical scenes based on a star clock.* The twelve discs represent the months. This is a copy by C. K. Wilkinson of the ceiling painting in the tomb of Senenmut, eighteenth dynasty, reign of Hatshepsut. (The Metropolitan Museum of Art.)

beginning and the twelve hours of the night, and they indicated that the stars might be seen "over the left shoulder," "over the right shoulder," "over the left ear," "over the right ear," and so on. The vertical lines in the grid denoted those same positions, both before and after the meridian transit. The horizontal grid lines denoted the hours of night.

The Ramessid tables suggest that a water clock was probably required to regulate which of the transiting stars should be used. An inscription dated to about 1520 BCE, written by Amenemhet, a nobleman under Amenhotpe I, is the earliest description of the use of a water clock. Those devices were shaped like vases, with a scale on the inside to denote hours. The base had a plug with an exit hole no larger than one made by a needle (Cotterell, Dickson, and Kamminga 1986). They were filled with water that escaped through this tiny hole. Hours were measured against the scale as the water level dropped.

In daylight, time was measured by shadow clocks, a device probably dating to the earliest periods of telling time. The extant examples all resemble the *merkhet* surveying instrument, which probably served dual purposes. When facing the Sun, it could be quickly leveled by hand with the aid of the plumb bob, so that the short L-shaped upright arm, or a small crossbeam attached to it, would accurately cast its shadow to the "hour" mark on the long arm. A text from the cenotaph of Sety I indicates that it could measure 4 "hours" before and after noon but that there was an "hour" after sunrise and another before sunset during which it could not be used. Shadows would be too long at that time, because of the low Sun angle, making the instrument unwieldy. There was then an hour of twilight before sunrise and again after sunset. Those numbers divided the day period, including twilight, into 12 "hours." Hence, the day division into twelve segments is probably at least as old as the night division into twelve, which has been traced to the diagonal star-clock tables of the Middle Kingdom.

**The Ptolemaic Period.** The character of Egyptian astronomy changed significantly when the Ptolemies became the rulers of Egypt (304–30 BCE). Both Greek and Babylonian influences were soon visible in the temples, monuments, and papyri that are known. The Greco-Babylonian zodiac was incorporated into Egyptian stylistic art, to appear on temples and monuments, and Greek and Demotic papyri included astrological horoscopes and Babylonian-like omens.

[*See also* Astrology; *and* Calendars.]

### BIBLIOGRAPHY

Clagett, M. *Ancient Egyptian Science*, vol. 2: *Calendars, Clocks, and Astronomy*. American Philosophical Society, Philadelphia, 1995. A treatise by a historian of science, with volume I consisting of two books that deal with science and engineering. Volume II provides source material and discusses interpretations of some of the problems related to calendar studies.

Cotterell, B., F. P. Dickson, and J. Kamminga. "Ancient Egyptian Water-Clocks: A Reappraisal." *Journal of Archaeological Science* 14(1986), 31–50. The only technical engineering study of the workings of Egyptian outflow clocks.

Edwards, I. E. S. *The Pyramids of Egypt*. Rev. ed. Harmondsworth, 1993. Still the standard work on Egyptian pyramids.

Edwards, I. E. S. "Do the Pyramid Texts Suggest an Explanation for the Abandonment of the Subterranean Chamber of the Great Pyramid?" In *Hommages à Jean Leclant*, edited by C. Berger, G. Clerc, and N. Grimal. *Bibliothèque d'Étude* 106.1 (1994), 159–167. Discusses, among other things, the title "Son of Re" from Khufu onward.

Malville, J. McKim, Fred Wendorf, et al. "Megaliths and Neolithic Astronomy in Southern Egypt." *Nature* 392 (1998), 488–491. Discussion of Nabta settlements and megaliths, with several good photos of a stone circle.

Mengoli, P. "Some Considerations of Egyptian Star-Clocks." *Archiv der Geschichte der Naturwissenschaften*, 22/23/24 (1988), 1127–1150. A good summary (in English) of the manner in which Egyptian star clocks worked.

Neugebauer, O. *The Exact Sciences in Antiquity*. New York, Dover edition, 1969. The revised, published version of his six 1949 Cornell lectures; easier reading than the 1960 volumes.

Neugebauer, O. *A History of Ancient Mathematical Astronomy*, 3 vols. New York, Heidelberg, Berlin, 1975. Not for the casual reader (background in mathematics and astronomy, as well as historical background in several ancient cultures are recommended). The short section on Egypt is of interest from a purely mathematical, as opposed to a cultural, viewpoint; the general discussions on chronological concepts, calendars, and the year provide useful interrelationships.

Neugebauer, O., and R. A. Parker. *Egyptian Astronomical Texts*. vol. 1: *The Early Decans*. Providence (1960); vol. 2: *The Ramesside Star Clocks*. Providence (1964); vol. 3: *Decans, Planets, Constellations and Zodiacs*. Providence (1969). Specialist books, requiring a knowledge of Egyptian grammar and a minimal background in positional astronomy for full appreciation.

Parker, R. A. *The Calendars of Ancient Egypt*. Oriental Institute of Chicago, Studies in Ancient Oriental Civilization, No. 26. Chicago, 1950. Knowledge of Egyptian grammar and some background in positional astronomy and calendrics are needed for comprehension; some sections are dated, but many basic concepts are still valid.

Quirke, S. *Ancient Egyptian Religion*. British Museum Press, London, 1992. A valuable reader on the intricacies of Egyptian religion.

Wells, R. A. "Sothis and the Satet Temple on Elephantine: A Direct Connection." *Studien zur Altägyptischen Kultur* 12(1985), 255–302. A study of the orientation of the eighteenth dynasty temple, with references to earlier temples on the site that date to Predynastic times; the first evidence is discussed of a temple named for a stellar deity and actually aligned toward the rising of that star (and toward the winter solstice sunrise).

Wells, R. A. "The 5th Dynasty Sun Temples at Abu Ghurab as Old Kingdom Star Clocks: Examples of Applied Ancient Egyptian Astronomy." *Beiheft zu Studien zur Altägyptischen Kultur, Akten des Vierten Internationalen Ägyptologen Kongresses München 1985* 4(1990), 95–104. A discussion of the use of the sun temples as star clocks.

Wells, R. A. "The Mythology of Nut and the Birth of Ra." *Studien zur Altägyptischen Kultur* 19(1992), 305–321. The correlation study that demonstrated an astronomical connection to the Nut cosmogony.

Wells, R. A. "Origin of the Hour and the Gates of the Duat." *Studien zur Altägyptischen Kultur* 20(1993):305–326. A study of the series of axial-rising stars in front of the fifth dynasty sun temples and the manner in which the *Book of Gates* might have arisen.

Wells, R. A. "Re and the Calendars." In *Revolutions in Time: Studies in Egyptian Calendrics*, edited by A. J. Spalinger. San Antonio, 1994. A detailed discussion of the origin and evolution of the Predynastic and dynastic lunar and civil calendars; the other chapters are concerned with complex discussions of the fixing of feasts in the lunar calendar or with the intricacies of the operation of ancient Near Eastern lunar calendars.

RONALD A. WELLS

**ASWAN,** a town on the eastern bank of the Nile, at the foot of the First Cataract (24°05′N, 32°54′E). The modern name of Aswan is derived from Greek *Syene* and, ultimately, from Egyptian *swnw*, meaning "to trade." Archaeological work there has been limited, and such monuments as exist, or have been noted, are of the later historical phases. The earliest settlement was on the large island of Elephantine (in the Nile River); the island's name in Egyptian, *3bw*, derives from the word for "elephant" and "ivory," and perhaps indicates an ivory-trading center. In Predynastic times, Elephantine may have been a trading center outside the Upper Egyptian kingdom; but it and the cataract soon came to mark the southern frontier of Egypt. The town site on Elephantine came to be dominated by temples to the local patron deity, Khnum, and his associates, Satet and Anuket. Khnum was a ram-headed creator god, who was believed to control the Nile from a cave beneath the island of Bigga.

The region of Aswan was important as a major source of granite, and quarries were located on both sides of the river, the principal ones being south of the present-day town. There was also much quarrying of granite from the smaller islands in the river; that may have served the dual function of providing granite while clearing the river channels, thereby easing passage through the cataract.

From the early Old Kingdom onward, Aswan had an important role as defender of the southern frontier and the starting point for many military and trading expeditions into Nubia. Some expeditions went by river and began at the head of the cataract, near Shellal. Others went by the desert road on the western bank, beginning at the Rock of Offerings (Gebel Tingar) and regaining the river in the region of Tomas. As a result of the quarrying and the military and trading expeditions, many hundreds of rock inscriptions were found throughout the Aswan region. These have provided important historical and prosopographical information.

Many of the New Kingdom temples were later built over, or destroyed, but sufficient monuments survived to indicate that Aswan and Elephantine continued to hold military, economic, and religious importance. Following the end of the New Kingdom and the abandonment of the viceregal domain of Kush, Aswan again became a guardian of the southern frontier. Excavations have demonstrated that the office of viceroy persisted through the Third Intermediate Period, and perhaps into the Late period, but the office was often attached to a prophetship of Khnum. While it is unlikely that Egyptian control extended far south of Aswan, there is some evidence for some administrative, and probably economic, control over the northern part of Lower Nubia. That region was known as the Dodekaschoenos in Ptolemaic and Roman times (extending as far as Maharaqqa) and may actually date back to the twenty-sixth dynasty, if not earlier.

The religious importance of the Aswan region increased considerably in the later historical phases, with the Ptolemaic expansion of the cult center of the goddess Isis on the island of Philae. With the Roman conquest of Egypt, peace was made with the Kushite kingdom of Meroë, establishing the frontier at *Hiera Sykaminos* (present-day Maharraqa). Two centuries of prosperity appear to have followed. In the reign of the Roman emperor Domitian (r. 81–96 CE), the satirist Juvenal was reputedly exiled, as prefect of the garrison, to Aswan, after attacking an imperial favorite. The temples of Philae continued to flourish in the second and third centuries CE, but the problems of the later empire, notably incursions by the Blemmyes of the Eastern Desert, forced Diocletian to withdraw his frontier to Aswan in 298 CE. When the edict of Theodosius (391 CE) closed the temples of the empire in 391 CE, it was not enforced at Philae, but later attempts to close the temples led to conflict between the Roman authorities and the Nubians. A treaty drawn up in 453 CE by the Roman general Maximinus permitted the temples to remain open so that the Blemmyes could take the image of Isis on its annual pilgrimage to bless the crops in Nubia. By the time that the emperor Justinian and the empress Theodora sent their Christianizing missions, there was no objection to the closing of the temples and their conversion into a church (c. 535–538 CE).

A few visible ancient monuments survive in present-day Aswan. The most significant is the temple of Isis, which dates from the reigns of Ptolemy III (r. 246–222 BCE) and Ptolemy IV (r. 222–205 BCE), standing at the southern edge of the town; its inscriptions have been published by Edda Bresciani (1978). Close by are the remains of the Byzantine town wall, which incorporates blocks from Roman temples. A small temple built in the reign of Domitian was found in 1921.

Elephantine itself has been the focus of excavations for many years, stimulated by the discovery of an important group of Aramaic papyri in the last decade of the nineteenth century. An excavation on behalf of the Berlin Museum (1904–1907) acquired further materials from the

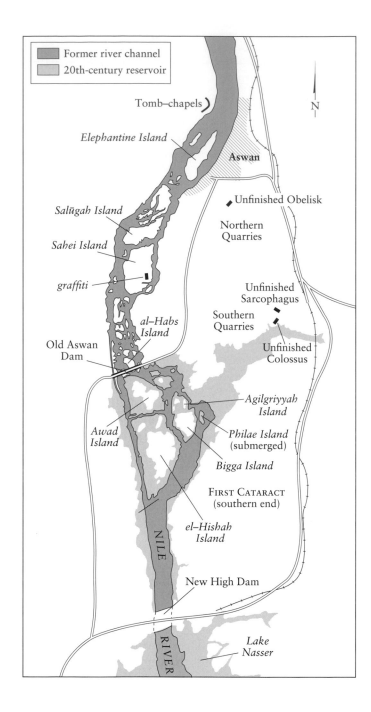

ASWAN. *Map of Aswan, Philae, and vicinity.*

"Aramaic town," and it is now known that there was a Jewish community and temple on the island from the First Persian Occupation (525–405 BCE) onward. French excavations under the direction of Charles Clermont-Ganneau (1907–1909) in the temple of Khnum uncovered the burials of the sacred rams and the temple of Satet. Later excavations by Egypt's Department of Antiquities, conducted by Labib Habachi, revealed a complex of temples dedicated to the local official Heqa-ib, who lived in

the sixth dynasty; his tomb is on the western bank of the Nile at Qubbet el-Hawa. In the twelfth dynasty he seems to have become the center of a local cult, and statues of dignitaries of that period were found in the chapel.

Regular excavation has been conducted since 1969 under the auspices of the German and Swiss Archaeological Institutes. Although in its present state the temple of Khnum dates from the Macedonian (Alexander IV) to the Roman periods, it lies over a Ramessid building, and

ASWAN. *The obelisk at the eastern granite quarries.* (Photography by the Egyptian Expedition, The Metropolitan Museum of Art.)

some blocks from many earlier structures have been re-used, notably in the quay. One of the most important structures associated with the temple is the Nilometer—in its present form there, Roman; Elephantine was one of the key sites for measuring the height of the Nile flood and calculating the strength of the inundation. At Elephantine, the ancient Greek astronomer Eratosthenes (c. 275–195 BCE), during the reign of Ptolemy III, made observations from which he calculated the circumference of the earth. Small temples, built by Thutmose III and Amenhotpe III, were drawn by the early Egyptological expeditions but the temples were destroyed around 1820.

The temple of Satet occupies a site which had been sacred since prehistoric times; the original shrine, a niche in the rock, has been excavated far beneath the eighteenth dynasty temple. Older remains included relief decoration from Middle Kingdom structures and extensive levels of the ancient townsite, which were cleared back to the original circular enclosure wall.

On the western bank of the Nile, there are several groups of rock-cut tombs from all periods. The principal group is at Qubbet el-Hawa, and some of the tombs are on an imposing scale, with porticoed entrances and many burial shafts. Yet their decoration is neither extensive nor particularly remarkable for either content or artistic interest (thus frequently described as "provincial"). The most notable features are the autobiographical inscriptions of tomb owners who recounted their journeys into Nubia. The tomb of Harkhuf has a lengthy text recording several expeditions in the sixth dynasty, including the text of a letter from the youthful pharaoh Pepy II (r. 2300–2206 BCE), which told Harkhuf to ensure the safe delivery of a pygmy to the royal residence. The tomb of Sirenput II, an important local official of the reigns of Senwosret II (r. 1897–1877 BCE) and Senwosret III (1878–1843 BCE), is the largest and most finely decorated of the tombs.

The Aswan region was the major source of granite for building and sculpture. The principal quarries were on islands in the Nile and on the eastern bank, to the south of the present-day town. There are still unfinished monuments lying in some of these quarries; that closest to the Nile contains the Unfinished Obelisk, a monolith intended to stand 41.75 meters (125 feet), but a flaw necessitated reduction of its size to around 32.1 meters (100 feet). If completed, it would have equaled the largest surviving obelisk, originally at Karnak (now in Rome, outside the church of Saint John Lateran); it may have been intended as its pair, but it was abandoned. The Southern Quarries also contain a number of unfinished monuments and inscriptions.

South of Elephantine, the First Cataract of the Nile was a formidable obstacle to navigation, although inscriptions record the clearing of channels, notably in the reign of Senwosret III. The island of Seheil had a chapel dedicated to the goddess Anuket, and the rocks there were covered with more than 250 inscriptions of officials. The southernmost point of the cataract is marked by the islands of Konosso, Philae, and Bigga. Konosso (now mostly beneath the reservoir) had inscriptions of military campaigns into Nubia. On Bigga stood the fortress of Senmet, referred to in texts of the Middle Kingdom. The rocks carry inscriptions recording the *sed*-festivals of Ramesses II and the Nubian campaign of Psamtik II. Bigga became a cult center of the deity Osiris, perhaps as early as the eighteenth dynasty, achieving its zenith in the Ptolemaic and Roman eras; the temple, which was erected and dedicated during the reigns of Ptolemy XII Auletes (r. 80–58 BCE) and the emperor Augustus (r. 27 BCE–14 CE), marked the site of the burial of the left leg of the god. The rites there were of a funeral nature completely different from those of the neighboring island of Philae, where the focus of joyful worship was the goddess Isis. The earliest monumental evidence from Philae was discovered when the temple was dismantled for transfer to Agilkia; building blocks from the Ramessid and from the twenty-fifth dynasty were excavated from the foundations of the later structures. Temples had been developed from the twenty-sixth dynasty onward and became a major pilgrimage center in Roman times. On the mainland, opposite Philae, was the Roman *castrum* ("military base"), built close to the site of the Egyptian port from which military expeditions left for Nubia.

One of the major features of the Aswan region is the large number of inscriptions (*graffiti*) carved on the rocks. These include the records of quarrying, the military expeditions, and the personal records of local officials—officials of the viceregal administration on their way into Nubia—as well as royal and private votives to local deities. Such inscriptions can be found on many rocks in the town, particularly those facing the temple of Khnum. Several important inscriptions may be seen along the ancient

military road leading south from the town, and major concentrations of inscriptions are to be found on Gebel Tingar and the island of Seheil. Gebel Tingar is on the western bank of the river, just beyond the mausoleum of the Aga Khan; it marked the beginning of a desert road into Nubia. More than 250 inscriptions on Seheil date from the Middle and New Kingdoms. Many of the viceroys and their staffs left inscriptions as they went on their inspection tours of Nubia, and many (particularly Ramessid) were made by local priestly officials and their families. Most of the inscriptions have been copied by such early Egyptologists as Auguste Mariette, Jacques de Morgan, and W. M. Flinders Petrie, some more recently by Labib Habachi. One of the most important of the Seheil texts is the pseudepigraphic Famine Stela, which purports to be from the Old Kingdom reign of Djoser but is actually from Ptolemaic times: it reports a dream of King Djoser, in which the god Khnum appears to him, telling him how to end the seven years of famine that Egypt has endured; in gratitude, Djoser donates the land immediately south of Aswan to the god's temple. The motive for the text was the increasing economic power of the temple and the priesthood of Isis on Philae, so through that text the priesthood of the ancient temple of Khnum attempted to establish a prior claim on the land controlled by their much newer neighbor.

## BIBLIOGRAPHY

Bresciani, Edda. *Assuan. Tempio tolemaico di Isi*. Pisa, 1978.
Junge, F. *Elephantine XI. Funde und Bauteile 1–7. Kampagne, 1969–1976*. Deutches Archäologisches Institut, Abteilung Kairo, 49. Mainz, 1987.

ROBERT MORKOT

**ASYUT,** a site located 410 kilometers (250 miles) south of Cairo, on the western side of the Nile (27°11′N, 31°10′E). Asyut is renowned for an extensive ancient necropolis situated on a steep elevation (known locally as Istabl Antar) of the western hills that delimit the Nile Valley. Preserving the Old Egyptian toponym *Saut* (*s3wty*) the Arabic place name Asyut designates a large provincial capital. The ancient town is buried, presumably, under the present-day city and the surrounding cultivation.

Situated in the thirteenth Upper Egyptian nome (province), Asyut had the gods Wepwawet; Anubis, and Hereret for protective deities; represented in canine form or with canine heads, they explain the name Lycopolis ("city of the dog") that was current in Ptolemaic and Roman times. Temples of Wepwawet and Osiris once existed, but their locations are unknown. Among the other deities worshiped at Asyut were Amun-Re, Hathor, Ptah, and Thoth.

Although Asyut was inhabited from at least the Old

Kingdom through the Roman period, it is most famous for its tombs of the First Intermediate Period and of the twelfth dynasty. Three of those burials, belonging to *it(.i)ib(.i)* and two persons named Khety, contain the most important inscriptions of the so-called Herakleopolitan period (ninth and tenth dynasties), a subset of the First Intermediate Period, which was a time of rivalry between a northern court at Herakleopolis and a southern counterpart seated at Thebes. A fourth tomb, belonging to a twelfth dynasty official, Hapidjefa I, contained an inscribed legal contract, detailing his provisions for his mortuary cult (A. J. Spalinger, in *Journal of the American Oriental Society* 105 [1985], 7–20).

The archaeological importance of Asyut lies not only in the historical information of the tomb inscriptions but also in the exquisite quality of the tomb reliefs, hieroglyphs, wall paintings, decorated coffins, and wooden sculptures; this material indicates that the arts flourished at least at Asyut and perhaps elsewhere in Herakleopolitan territory, no doubt because of its access to the great Memphite ateliers. The Asyut material further demonstrates the serious mistake in assessing First Intermediate Period art using as evidence only the better-dated, but much more provincial, monuments from Theban territories.

Asyut and the neighboring sites of Durunka and Rifeh have never received the comprehensive study that they richly deserve. Archaeological work at all three sites would add invaluable information about the First Intermediate Period and the twelfth dynasty. The British philologist Francis Llewellyn Griffith copied several tomb inscriptions at Asyut and Rifeh, on behalf of the Egypt Exploration Fund (now Society) in London, and published both a discussion of the site and a hand-copy of the three Herakleopolitan inscriptions. Several other missions worked at Asyut, with more modest results, and did not achieve a comprehensive archaeological, architectural, or epigraphic survey. The motivation appears to have been to collect the coffins and wooden sculpture for which the site is famous. The only architectural plans of the tombs are those published in the fourth volume of the monumental early eighteenth-century *Description de l'Égypte*. The best archaeological report was published in 1911 by Émile Chassinat and Charles Palanque, who had worked at Asyut from 1903 to 1904 for the Institut Français d'Archéologie Orientale in Cairo; this material is largely divided between the Egyptian Museum, Cairo, and the Louvre in Paris. David G. Hogarth, who had been sent to Asyut by the British Museum in 1906 and 1907, excavated portions of the necropolis and sent many monuments to London; his notes are unpublished. An Italian team under Ernesto Schiaparelli worked at Asyut periodically from 1905 to 1913; with the exception of one article

(G. Marro, in *Annales de l'Université de Grenoble* 32, pt. 2 [1921], 15–48), the results are also unpublished but many of the finds from Schiaparelli's expedition are now in the Museo Egizio, Turin. Ahmed Bey Kamal, who was an agent for both the Egyptian Antiquities Service and for the Egyptian collector Sayyid Bey Khashaba, was a frequent visitor to the site; Kamal's publications are little more than checklists and inaccurate textual copies (Kamal, in *Annales du Service des Antiquités de l'Egypte* 12 (1912), 128–142; 16 (1916), 65–114), and Khashaba's collection has been dispersed widely. Since the 1960s, military occupation of Istabl Antar has made access difficult, and in the 1990s Islamist activity in the region of Asyut has made on-site research unwise.

The tombs are in ruinous condition. The façades of many of the smaller, unrecorded burials have collapsed and filled in the entrance passageways. Portions of the biographical inscription in the cavernous tomb (number 3) of *it(.i)ib(.i)* are visible, but they are in poor condition. The fine painted-plaster alteration of the original text, which is incised on the limestone walls of the tomb, is in an extremely fragile state. Only tomb 4, which belongs to one of the two persons named Khety, is well preserved; the extensive biography on the northern wall and the large well-rendered relief of warriors on the southern wall have made this tomb the most famous of the three Herakleopolitan burials.

The order of the three Herakleopolitan tombs is perplexing. Although the generally accepted line is 5, 3, 4, Diana Magee has demonstrated that Griffith's original sequence of 3, 4, 5 may be accurate. Khety of tomb 5, who is traditionally regarded as the first of the three officials, may have been the last buried.

Alone among all known Herakleopolitan provincial officials, *it(.i)ib(.i)* and the two Khetys had close connections with the royal court, but the nature or their ties is not completely clear. The revised biography in the burial of *it(.i)ib(.i)* has led to at least two interpretations. Either *it(.i)ib(.i)* once enjoyed the favor of the king and then lost it or else he or his immediate family sought to disguise his loyalties after Thebes was victorious. Neither scenario is necessarily accurate. As a child, the Khety of tomb 5 was brought up as a royal ward at the Herakleopolitan court. In the long tomb 4 inscription, Khety the overseer of priests and a nomarch (provincial civil administrator) detailed his loyal service and apparently close relationship with King Merikare, the best known of the obscure eighteen Herakleopolitan monarchs. That Khety's fidelity is conspicuous. No other private Herakleopolitan tomb has a cartouche or any mention of the reigning king, much less a record of conscientious duty, perhaps indicating that the Herakleopolitan sovereigns were unpopular in their own kingdom. The revision of *it(.i)ib(.i)* biography, for example, may have been occasioned by vacillating loyalty.

Royal ancestry may also explain the connection between the court and the Asyut region. In the Western Desert at Dara, northwest of Asyut, is a small ruined pyramid that probably belonged to a king Khui (R. Weill, *Dara*, Cairo, 1958). Although that name cannot be associated with any monarch of the Old, Middle, or New Kingdoms, it may well denote one of the eighteen Herakleopolitan sovereigns whose names are mostly unknown.

Many late Demotic papyri have been found at Asyut and in neighboring areas. Asyut lies in the center of many important ancient Coptic sites such as Deir Durunka, Ganadlah, Deir Rifeh, and Wadi Sarga. The neo-Platonist philosopher Plotinus was born in Asyut.

## BIBLIOGRAPHY

Beinlich, Horst. "Assiut." In *Lexikon der Ägyptologie*, 1: 489–495. Wiesbaden, 1975. Good general summary with excellent bibliography; perhaps the best introduction to the site.

Brunner, Hellmut. *Die Texte aus den Gräbern der Herakleopolitenzeit von Siut mit übersetzung und Erlauterungen* Ägyptologische Forschungen, 5. Glückstadt, 1937. A re-edition with corrections and commentary on Griffith's (1889) standard edition of the Herakleopolitan texts at Asyut; has valuable historical reconstruction.

Chassinat, Émile, and Charles Palanque. *Une campagne de fouilles dans la nécropole d'Assiout*. Mémoires publiés par les Membres de l'Institut Français d'Archéologie Orientale du Caire, 24. Cairo, 1911. The best report of any archaeological work at Asyut. A remarkable work for its time, not only because of the fine photographs of several wooden sculptures and coffins but also because of its pioneering attention to hieroglyphic palaeography; the copies of the hieroglyphic inscriptions are quite accurate.

Edel, Elmar. *Die Inschriften am Eingang des Grabes des "Tefib" (Siut Grab III) nach der Description de l'Égypte: Ein Wiederherstellungsversuch*. Abhandlungen für die Kunde des Morgenlandes, 39.1. Wiesbaden, 1970. This and the following work are important for their historical and architectural discussions.

Edel, Elmar. *Die Inschriften der Grabfronten der Siut-Gräber in Mittelägypten aus der Herakleopolitenzeit: Eine Wiederherstellung nach den Zeichnungen der Description de l'Égypte*. Abhandlungen der Rheinisch-Westfälischen Akademie der Wissenschaften, 71. Opladen, 1984.

Griffith, Francis Ll. "The Inscriptions of Siût and Dêr Rîfeh." *The Babylonian and Oriental Record* 3 (1989), 121–129, 164–168, 174–184, 244–252. Excellent summary of both Griffith's and some earlier work at Asyut.

Griffith, Francis Ll. *The Inscriptions of Siût and Dêr Rîfeh*. London, 1889. The standard edition of the inscriptions from the three Herakleopolitan tombs (nos. 3, 4, and 5) and the only publication on some of the tombs at Rifeh.

Magee, Diana. "Asyût to the End of the Middle Kingdom: A Historical and Cultural Study." Ph.D. diss., University of Oxford, 1988. A landmark work, but very difficult to obtain; the finest recent study of the archaeological material from Asyut. In particular, it has an important catalog and discussion of the coffin types found at Asyut, an interesting critique of the chronology of the three Herakleopolitan officials, and an extensive bibliography.

Porter, Bertha, and Rosalind L. B. Moss. *Topographical Bibliography of Ancient Egyptian Hieroglyphic Texts, Reliefs, and Paintings*, vol. 4: *Lower and Middle Egypt (Delta and Cairo to Asyût)*. Oxford, 1934. Although out-of-date and sometimes inaccurate, this important volume is the standard bibliographical reference for early publications of specific monuments found at Asyut and related sites.

Spanel, Donald B. "The Herakleopolitan Tombs of Kheti I, *Jt(.j)jb(.j)*, and Kheti II at Asyut." *Orientalia* n.s. 58 (1989), 301–314. A summary of both earlier work at the site and the current condition of the tombs; contains the only published photographs of some of the Herakleopolitan inscriptions and a paleographical study. Extensive bibliography in the footnotes.

Thompson, H. Herbert, ed. *A Family Archive from Siut, from Papyri in the British Museum, Including an Account of a Trial before the Laocritae in the Year B. C. 170*. Oxford, 1934. Excellent publication of some of the Demotic papyri found near Asyut.

DONALD B. SPANEL

**ATELIERS.** *See* Artists and Artisans.

**ATEN.** The word *Aten*, which signifies the disk of the sun, is a term that first appears in the Middle Kingdom. In texts of the New Kingdom's eighteenth dynasty, *Aten* is frequently used to mean "throne" or "place" of the sun god. Because the Egyptians tended to personify certain expressions, the word *Aten* was written with the hieroglyphic sign for "god." Through metonymy, Aten was eventually conceived as a direct manifestation of the sun god, as Jan Assmann (1975) has pointed out.

Aten was particularly favored during the New Kingdom reigns of Thutmose IV (1419–1410 BCE) and Amenhotpe III (1410–1382 BCE). Nevertheless, for the actual origin of the deity Aten, sole credit must be given to Amenhotpe IV (later Akhenaten, 1382–1365 BCE), who initiated the first historic appearance of that god by formulating a didactic name for him. In the early years of Amenhotpe IV's reign, the sun god Re-Horakhty, traditionally pictured with a hawk's head, was identical with Aten and was worshiped as a deity. The ruler's pronounced affinity with the newly created god revealed itself in the construction of an enormous temple east of the Great Temple of Amun at Karnak in the third year of his reign. The structure was adorned in a novel "expressionistic" style that broke with previous tradition and soon influenced the representation of all figures. This new style of art introduced by Amenhotpe IV reflected a concomitant religious upheaval. First he replaced the state god Amun with the god Aten, who was newly interpreted in iconography and nomenclature. The hawk-headed figure of Re-Horakhty-Aten was abandoned in favor of the solar disk, now pictured as an orb emitting rays that ended in human hands giving "life" to the nose of both the king and the great royal wife, Nefertiti. Now interpreted as a sole ruler, the Aten received a royal titulary, inscribed like royal names in two oval cartouches. The Aten's didactic name meant "the living One, Re-Harakhty who rejoices on the horizon, in his name (=identity) which is Illumination (=Shu, god of the space between earth and sky and of the light that fills that space) which is from the solar orb." This designation reflects radically new theological positions. Contrary to the traditional concept of a god, these names meant that Re and the sun gods Khepri, Horakhty, and Atum should no longer be accepted as manifestations of the sun. The perception of the new deity was not so much the sun disk, but rather the light radiating from the sun; to make this distinction, his name should be more correctly pronounced "Yati(n)."

In addition to possessing royal names, the Aten now celebrated his own royal jubilees, as described by Jocelyn Gohary in *Akhenaten's Sed-Festival,* London, 1990. Thus, the ideology of kingship and the realm of religious cult were blurred, as noted by Silverman (1995). Aten was the king of kings: he needed no goddess as a companion like other Egyptian deities; no enemy existed that could be of danger to him; he was the light that permeated the world, giving life everywhere.

Although it was customary for gods to commune verbally with the pharaoh, Aten remained silent. He had Amenhotpe IV to function as his herald and his prophet. Even though Aten had ascended to the top of the pantheon, most of the old gods retained their positions at first. This situation soon changed, however, and the gods of the dead, like Osiris and Sokar, were the first to vanish from religious life.

Step by step, the king pursued his reformation. At the beginning of the sixth year of his reign, Amenhotpe IV founded a new capital city in the desert valley of Tell el-Amarna in Middle Egypt. Fourteen unique stelae cut out of rocks in the manner of holy shrines marked the boundaries of the new residence he called Akhetaten ("horizon of Aten"). On these stelae the king explained why he chose this site: on this virgin ground to which no one could lay claim, the new city of Aten was to be erected. Here Aten could be worshiped without consideration of other deities.

Two major temples were built for Aten at Akhetaten. The great temple was an open, unroofed structure covering an area of about 800 by 300 meters (2500 by 950 feet) at the northern end of the city. The other temple was a smaller building of similar design. Both were strewn with offering tables. The first court of the small temple contained a massive mud-brick altar; these monuments may have been the first structures erected in the new city. Around the time of the founding of Akhetaten, Amenhotpe IV changed his royal titulary to reflect the Aten's reign. More remarkably, he altered his birth name from Amenhotpe, which may be translated "Amun is content,"

ATEN. *Akhenaten, accompanied by his wife Nefertiti and his six daughters, making offerings to the Aten.* In the Amarna period, the god is typically represented by an image of the sun's disk, from which extend lifegiving rays ending in human hands.

to Akhenaten, meaning "he who is beneficial to the Aten" or "illuminated manifestation of Aten." The king then proceeded to emphasize Aten's singular status above all other gods through excessively preferential treatment. In a continuing attempt to redefine and consolidate his doctrine of Aten, he ultimately suppressed all other deities. The new creed could indeed be summed up by the formula "There is no god but Aten, and Akhenaten is his prophet," as Erik Hornung has stated in *Conception of God: The One and the Many,* London, 1982, p. 248. Even though this belief was not born of the people, the king forced it on his subjects. Formerly polytheistic Egypt had always tolerated foreign gods and religions, but now the king would allow no rivals to Aten.

A hymn, the "Sun Hymn of Akhenaten," offers some theological insight into the newly evolved image of the god. This literary masterpiece, perhaps composed by the king himself, is inscribed in thirteen long lines on the walls of the tomb of the courtier Ay, who later succeeded King Tutankhamun on the throne. The essential part of the poem is a hymn of praise for Aten as the creator and preserver of the world. Parts of the text recur in *Psalm* 104 of Hebrew scriptures. Since the names of other gods are not mentioned, there are no allusions to mythical concepts. The themes of night and death, elaborated with allusions to godlike beings in all other religious texts of Egypt, are cited only briefly in this hymn, as signifying the absence of Aten. The great hymn to Aten abounds with descriptions of nature. It indicates the position of the king in the new religion. It is to him alone that the god has revealed itself: "There is no other who knows you." Only the ruler knew the demands and commandments of his god. In this setting, be became the sole intermediary between the people and Aten, a deity who remained distant and incomprehensible to the populace.

The king's family shared this exclusive privilege. The dearth of myths in the new religion was filled with the ruler's family history. The great royal wife Nefertiti, almost an equal to the king, claimed her position in cult and state. It is therefore not surprising that the faithful of the Amarna period prayed in front of private cult stelae that contained a representation of the royal "holy" family. Surely no home in Akhetaten would be without such a monument as an official place of worship.

In about the regnal Year 9, the name of the god Aten was changed once more. All mention of Horakhty and Shu disappeared. The divine name Horakhty was replaced by the more neutral one "Ruler of the Horizon." With this change, the ancient and venerable manifestation of the sun god, the hawk form, was replaced definitively, and a purer form of monotheism was introduced. The god was henceforth named "the Living One, Sun, Ruler of the Horizon, who rejoices on the horizon in his name, which is Sunlight, which comes from the disk."

The essence of the Amarna religion, which inaugurated theocracy and systematic monotheism, revolves around two central themes: the light and the king. Probably after the final alteration of Aten's name, the ruler ordered that all the other god's temples in the country be closed. To extinguish the memory of them completely, a veritable persecution commenced. Armies of stonemasons swarmed all over the land as far as Nubia, above all to hack away the image and name of the despised Amun.

Other gods were persecuted as well; even the plural "gods" was avoided. When this persecution started, the Amarna period was already at the beginning of its end, and just before or soon after the king's death, the worship of the old gods was restored. Akhetaten was abandoned as a capital, and Aten disappeared from the Egyptian pantheon. In the aftermath of the Amarna period, there was an attempt to expunge the memory of the king, his queen Nefertiti, and all those associated with this heresy—by erasing references to them and destroying their monuments.

[See also Hymns, article on Solar Hymns.]

## BIBLIOGRAPHY

Allen, James P. "The Natural Philosophy of Akhenaten." In *Religion and Philosophy in Ancient Egypt*, James P. Allen, et al., pp. 89–101. Yale Egyptological Studies, 3. New Haven, 1989. The author contests the religious character of the king's concept of nature.

Assmann, Jan. "Aton." In *Lexikon der Ägyptologie*, 1:526–540. Wiesbaden, 1975.

Assmann, Jan. "Akhanyati's Theology of Light and Time." *Proceedings of the Israel Academy of Sciences and Humanities* 4 (1992), 143–176. Important publication about the Amarna religion.

Hornung, Erik. "The Rediscovery of Akhenaten and His Place in Religion." *Journal of American Research Center in Egypt* 29 (1992), 43–49. Historic-scientific summary concerning the rediscovery of the royal religious founder.

Murnane, William J. *Texts from the Amarna Period in Egypt.* Writings from the Ancient World, Society of Biblical Literature, 5. Atlanta, 1994. Contains the complete inscriptive documents of the Amarna period in translation.

Redford, Donald B. "The Sun-disc in Akhenaten's Program: Its Worship and Its Antecedents, I'," *Journal of the American Research Center in Egypt* 13 (1976), 47–61; 17 (1982), 21–38. Description of the origin and development of God Aten.

Silverman, David P. "The Nature of Egyptian Kingship." In *Ancient Egyptian Kingship*, edited by David O' Connor and David Silverman, pp. 79–92. Leiden, 1995.

Tobin, Arieh. "Amarna and Biblical Religion." *Pharaonic Egypt: The Bible and Christianity*, edited by Sarah Israelit-Groll, pp. 231–277. Jerusalem, 1985. About the influence of the Amarna religion on Israel.

HERMANN A. SCHLÖGL

**ATUM** is one of the main creator and sun gods, with Re, Horakhty, and Khepri. His name, derived from the verb *tem*, has either a positive meaning, "the accomplished one"—or a negative one, "the one who did not come to being yet." He is known from numerous textual and iconographic sources. Atum is considered to be the primeval, self-made god of the Heliopolitan cosmogony; he then created, by masturbating, the first couplet of gods, Shu and Tefnut. This act associates Atum's hand with various goddesses responsible for sexual pleasure and fertility, such as Hathor and Nebet-Hetepet.

Memphite theology (as recorded on the stela of Shabaqa of the twenty-fifth dynasty) holds that the creation occurred differently: the gods came out of Atum's mouth, and humans from his eyes. In another cosmogony, the Hermopolitan theology, Atum appears to have been created by the Eight Gods (Ogdoad). The *Book of Going Forth by Day* (*Book of the Dead*) presents Atum as the god who would continue to exist after the destruction of the world.

Atum's most frequent epithets are "Lord of Heliopolis" and "Lord of the Two Lands." The first refers to the main center of his cult, and the second stresses the king's association with him. In the Pyramid Texts, the body of Atum is literally identified with that of the ruler, an association that Egyptian artists also made when they represented Atum, in two dimensions, as a male wearing the royal double crown of Lower and Upper Egypt. The only iconographic detail that distinguishes god from king is the shape of his beard. Representations of Atum in the round are far less numerous than those of any other god of simi-

**ATUM**. *Writing on leaves of an* ished *tree is Atum, from the Ramesseum, Western Thebes.* (Photo by Karol Myśliwiec)

lar importance, and we may speculate that statues showing a king as "Lord of the Two Lands" may also have been viewed as incarnations of Atum. The largest of the rare statues to show Atum himself is a group depicting King Horemheb of the eighteenth dynasty kneeling in front of the seated god; it was found in the "cache" of the Luxor temple in 1989.

Atum's solar associations are with the sunset and the nightly journey of the sun, when he appears with a ram's head or, sometimes, as a tired old man walking with a stick. His solar aspect also has royal associations as "Lord of Heliopolis." From the New Kingdom onward, he is often depicted on temple walls as the god inscribing royal names on the leaves of the sacred tree (*ished*). In some reliefs, mostly of Lower Egyptian origin—for example, on the shrine of Ramesses II from Pithom—Atum is the god crowning the king. Another episode of the mythicized "coronation cycle" portrays Atum as a representative of Lower Egypt and a counterpart of an Upper Egyptian god, leading the king toward the main deity. The importance of Atum in the new year feast confirming the king's rule is described in the Brooklyn Papyrus, which dates from the Late period.

Atum has anthropomorphic, zoomorphic, and composite forms. In the first, he most frequently wears the royal double crown; other attributes, either alone or in combination, include the solar disk and a long tripartite wig. Various animals are associated with Atum, and some of them also functioned as hieroglyphic signs used in the notation of his name. For example, the beetle (or scarab) appears in the god's name from the late New Kingdom until the Roman period, and the ape hieroglyph functions similarly in inscriptions of the Greco-Roman period. In these periods, particularly in the region of Heliopolis, Atum as a solar god was identified with an ape-bowman shooting at his enemies. The ichneumon, devourer of snakes, was associated with Atum in a similar way; benign snakes were, however, another holy animal of the solar god. Numerous small bronze coffins containing mummified eels, bearing a figure of the fish on the top of the box and an inscription incised on it, attest to yet another zoomorphic incarnation of Atum.

Although the cult of Atum existed throughout Egypt, its principal centers were in the Nile Delta. Atum was the god of Heliopolis, where he had a special sanctuary, and he was the main deity of Per-Tem ("house of Atum"), the biblical Pithom in the eastern Delta. He was associated with a number of other gods, especially other forms of the solar deity. Various syncretistic versions that combine the names, epithets, functions, and iconography of Re, Horakhty, Khepri, and Atum (and sometimes other solar and nonsolar gods) became popular after the Amarna period, particularly during the Third Intermediate Period.

## BIBLIOGRAPHY

Goyon, Jean-Claude. *Confirmation du pouvoir royal au Nouvel an Brooklyn Museum Papyrus 47.218.50 I.* Bibliothèque d'Étude, 52. Cairo, 1972. Excellent translation into French and a general study of an Egyptian text of the Late period, concerning a royal feast in which Atum played a particularly important role.

Myśliwiec, Karol. *Die heiligen Tiere des Atum:* vol. 1, *Studien zum Gott Atum,* Hildesheimer Ägyptologische Beiträge, 5. Hildesheim, 1978. First part of the monograph on god Atum. The author describes the zoomorphic representations of the god.

Myśliwiec, Karol. *Name. Epitheta. Ikonographie:* vol. 2, *Studien zum Gott Atum,* Hildesheimer Ägyptologische Beiträge, 8. Hildesheim, 1979. A juxtaposition of the various writings of the god's name, his epithets and iconographic forms.

KAROL MYŚLIWIEC

**AUTOBIOGRAPHIES.** *See* Biographies.

**AVARIS.** *See* Dab'a, Tell ed-.

**AY** (r. 1346–1343 BCE), fourteenth king of the eighteenth dynasty, New Kingdom. Ay was the successor of Tutankhamun and was responsible for his burial. He was not part of the main royal line but is conjectured to have been a son of Yuya and Tuya, and some claim he was the father of Nefertiti. Ay certainly rose to prominence under Akhenaten, under whom he carried the titles "Overseer of All of His Majesty's Horses," "Fan-bearer on the Right of the King," and "Royal Scribe." The extent to which he was responsible for conceiving or implementing any part of Akhenaten's program is unknowable, but Ay was close enough to Akhenaten to merit a decorated tomb at Tell el-Amarna (tomb 25).

Ay is shown as a fan-bearer to Tutankhamun in a piece of gold leaf found in an unknown tomb in the Valley of the Kings. Here he is given his principal priestly title, "God's Father." It has been argued that Ay may have taken on royal titles and prerogatives before the death of Tutankhamun, but there is no definite evidence for this. His position under Tutankhamun was evidently a leading one, however, and he may have played a significant role in Tutankhamun's policy of rejecting the Aten heresy and returning to the national gods of Egypt.

Ay was buried in tomb 23 in the western branch of the Valley of the Kings, and his granite sarcophagus remains in the tomb. The style of the painting is very similar to that in the tomb of Tutankhamun. He is also known from a chapel he sponsored at Akhmim. Ay was succeeded by Horemheb, whose reign concluded the eighteenth dynasty. Some have posited a possible coregency between Ay and Horemheb, but there seems little if any positive evidence for this.

## BIBLIOGRAPHY

Redford, Donald B. *Akhenaten, The Heretic King.* Princeton, 1984.

STEVE VINSON

# B

**BA.** Along with the body, the *ka* (*k₃;* "life force"), the shadow, and the name, the *ba* (Eg., *b₃*) was one of the major components in the Egyptian concept of an individual. Its closest analog in Western thought is the "soul"—a term with which *ba* is often translated—although the two concepts are not fully comparable.

In some respects the *ba* seems to have been understood from the point of view of an observer rather than that of the individual with whom it was associated, personifying the impression that individuals make on the world around them or their effect on others. This aspect of the *ba* is embodied in an abstract term, *bau* (*b₃w*), meaning something like "impressiveness," "effect," or even "reputation." The *Instructions for Merikare* summarizes its advice to the pharaoh on the proper conduct of kingship with the words "A man should do the things that are effective for his *bau*"—that which enhances his image in the eyes of others and the gods. Similarly, the king's actions against Egypt's enemies or the gods' intervention in human affairs are often called the *bau* of their agents. The *ba* itself seems to have been a property only of human beings or the gods, but the notion of *bau* is also associated with objects that would otherwise be considered inanimate. Warning against the misappropriation of grain, for example, the *Instructions of Amenemope* admonishes that "the threshing-floor of barley is greater of *bau* [i.e., has a greater effect] than an oath sworn by the throne."

Like the soul, the *ba* seems to have been essentially nonphysical. Unlike the soul, however, the *ba* could be viewed as a separate physical mode of existence of its owner, even before death. Any phenomenon in which the presence or action of a god could be detected could be viewed as the *ba* of that deity: for example, the sun as the *ba* of Re, or the Apis bull as the *ba* of Osiris. In the Late period, sacred writings are frequently called "the *ba*s of Re." One god could also be viewed as the *ba* of another. This is particularly true of Re and Osiris, who coalesced each night in the depths of the Duat (netherworld), a union through which Re received the power of rebirth and Osiris was resurrected in Re; the combined deity was occasionally called "He of two *ba*s." Like the gods, the king, too, could be present as a *ba* in another mode of existence: Old Kingdom pyramids were often called the *ba*s of their owners (for example, "The *ba* of [King] Neferirkare") and officials sometimes bore names that identi-

fied them as a *ba* of the king, such as "Izezi is His *ba*" (commemorating a pharaoh of the fifth dynasty).

Texts rarely refer to the *ba* of ordinary human beings during their lifetime. This silence has been interpreted as evidence that such individuals did not possess a *ba* before death, but the Middle Kingdom literary text known as the *Dialogue of a Man with His Ba* presents a major obstacle to that view. In this unique composition, a man living in difficult times argues with his *ba* the merits of life, even in misery, versus the uncertain nature of life after death. The text concludes with the *ba*'s advice to "Desire me here [in life] and reject the West [land of the dead], but also desire that you reach the West when your body is interred and that I alight after your death: then we will make harbor together." This passage demonstrates the existence of an individual's *ba* during life and reflects the view of the *ba* as a separate mode of existence—in this case, an alter ego with whom its owner could hold a dialogue.

The *ba* appears most often in texts that deal with life after death. In these sources it is both a mode of the deceased's new existence and a component of the deceased as in life. The Pyramid Texts of the Old Kingdom, the earliest textual source for the concept of the *ba*, inform the gods that the deceased "is a *ba* among you" and assure the deceased that "your *ba* is within you." In the Coffin Texts of the First Intermediate Period and Middle Kingdom, the deceased appears as the *ba* of various gods but also as his own *ba*, with the physical powers of a living body. The latter view is also reflected in the destiny described in the eighteenth dynasty tomb of Paheri at Elkab: "Becoming a living *ba* having control of bread, water, and air."

At the same time, however, Paheri's text also states that "your *ba* will not abandon your corpse," echoing the Coffin Texts: "my *ba* cannot be kept from my corpse." This relationship is reflected in vignettes of the New Kingdom *Book of Going Forth by Day* (*Book of the Dead*), which show the *ba* not only returning to the mummy and hovering over it but also participating in activities outside the tomb. This vision of the afterlife, which appeared in the earlier Pyramid Texts, is based on the daily solar cycle. Like the sun, the *ba* reunites each night with Osiris—embodied, in this case, in the mummy—and through that union is enabled to be reborn again each day among the living in a new, noncorporeal form of existence.

No depictions of the *ba* earlier than the New Kingdom

have been identified with certainty, although some funerary statues of the Old Kingdom have been interpreted as showing the *ba* in fully human form. The illustrations that first appear in the *Book of the Dead* depict the *ba* as a bird with a human head and occasionally other human attributes, symbolizing both its human nature and its mobility. This image was adopted by the Meroitic civilization of Sudan in statues of the deceased—essentially as human figures with the wings of a bird. Whether the angels or birds of Coptic art can be traced to the same motif is doubtful. Coptic texts adopted the Greek word *psyche* in place of the native *bai* (from *b3*) as the term for "soul," demonstrating an essential difference between the Christian concept and that of the earlier *ba*.

[*See also* Ka; Names; *and* Shadow.]

### BIBLIOGRAPHY

Frankfort, Henri. *Ancient Egyptian Religion: An Interpretation.* New York, 1948; repr., New York, 1961. Includes a good discussion of the *ba*.

Žabkar, Louis V. *A Study of the Ba Concept in Ancient Egyptian Texts.* Studies in Ancient Oriental Civilization, 34. Chicago, 1968. The primary study of the *ba* in all periods of pharaonic civilization.

JAMES P. ALLEN

**BADARI.** *See* Predynastic Period.

**BADARIAN PERIOD.** *See* Predynastic Period.

**BAKENRENEF** (c.717–711 BCE), second king of the twenty-fourth dynasty, Third Intermediate Period. He was known in Greek as Bocchoris and was the last ruler of the otherwise obscure twenty-fourth dynasty. According to Egyptian texts, he ruled into his sixth year; but in practice his power must have been greatly circumscribed by the Kushite kings of the twenty-fifth dynasty, who probably limited his rule to his native city, Sais. His last dated inscription records the burial of an Apis bull in the Serapeum at Memphis. According to Manetho, the third century BCE Greco-Egyptian historian, he was eventually captured by the Nubian king Shabaqa (r. 712–698 BCE), who had him burned alive.

As king, Bakenrenef gave an impression of failure, but he attracted a rich tradition. In the classical sources, the Greek historian Diodorus Siculus (first century BCE), probably following Hecataeus of Miletus (c.300 BCE), presented him as a brilliant lawgiver, especially in his cancellation of debts—an idea that was brought by Solon, the Greek statesman and poet, back to Athens (c.600 BCE) after his travels to Egypt. Plutarch (first century CE) referred to a judgment of his in a case involving a prostitute, and a debate raged in antiquity about the king's true nature, whether it matched his reputation. The wide range of his appeal can be gauged from the appearance of his name on several objects, perhaps of Phoenician manufacture, which have been found in sites in Italy and Sicily; these may not be contemporary with the king.

An interesting item about Bakenrenef is found in Manetho's history, which records that "in his reign report has it that a lamb spoke." Referring to an oracle, given through the medium of a sacred animal, it prophesied foreign conquest and eventual recovery. A version of that tale is also known from a Demotic papyrus of Roman date. One possible explanation of such traditions is that it was in Sais, in his time, that the Demotic script was invented; then, too, his achievements and personality must also have contributed to those traditions.

### BIBLIOGRAPHY

Gill, David, and Michael Vickers. "Bocchoris the Wise and Absolute Chronology." *Mitteilungen des Deutschen archaeologischen Instituts, Roemischer Abteilung* 103 (1996), 1–9. Discusses the posthumous reputation of the king, as well as the implications for chronology.

Ray, John D. "Pharaoh Nechepso." *Journal of Egyptian Archaeology* 60 (1974), 255–256. Discusses the tradition of lamb oracles and their transmission.

Ridgeway, David. "The Rehabilitation of Bocchoris and Its Consequences." *Journal of Egyptian Archaeology*, in press. Argues that objects found in Italy and Sicily that bear the king's name are contemporary with his reign.

JOHN D. RAY

**BANQUETS.** Information concerning banquets in ancient Egypt is scarce, with the richest source of evidence being tomb scenes. Some further evidence has been derived from literary texts, notably Wisdom Literature, which outlines the ideal behavior of guest and host. Stories and myths featuring banquets are infrequent; the tale of the deity Seth entrapping his brother Osiris is one of the few. Remains of some funerary feasts, such as those found by W. B. Emery (1962) in a second dynasty tomb and the festal wreaths found associated with Tutankhamun's funerary banquet, have provided further information concerning such feasts. There is no word in Egyptian that is clearly translated as "banquet"; the closest word in Egyptian is *ḥby* ("to be festal" or "to make a festival"), with *ḥb* translated as "feast" or "banquet." The injunction *ir hrw nfr* ("make holiday!") often implied the holding of a banquet or feast.

Banquets were frequently featured in Egyptian tomb decoration, starting in the late Old Kingdom and continuing into the New Kingdom. The Old Kingdom banqueting scenes, such as the one found in the sixth dynasty tomb of Kahif at Giza (tomb 2136), as well as the Middle Kingdom

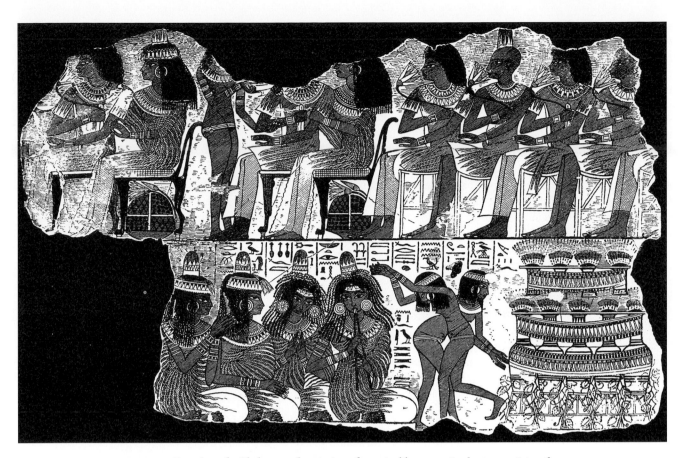

BANQUETS. *Drawing of a Theban tomb painting of a typical banquet.* In the top register, the seated guests enjoy the fragrance of lotus flowers while a female servant waits on them. The women in the bottom register are three singers, a musician playing a double-flute, and two dancers. On the right, numerous jars of wine are wreathed with lotuses. Note the cones of perfumed fat on the guests' and musicians' heads.

scenes, tended to show elaborate family gatherings; their New Kingdom equivalents show both family and friends enjoying the feast. Gargantuan banquets were a feature of *sed*-festival (jubilee), when nobles, officials, servants, and the people at large feasted below the royal balcony in the king's presence. Under Horemheb, the king treated his officials to a sumptuous feast every month. The eighteenth dynasty provided the single richest source of banqueting scenes in ancient Egypt: in later dynasties, the banquet scene appears comparatively infrequently in Egyptian sepulchers.

There has been some debate as to whether the banquets depicted in tombs are funerary banquets, akin to wakes, or a chronicle of the type of banquet that the deceased enjoyed during his lifetime, recorded in the tomb so it could be enjoyed throughout the hereafter. Banquets or feasts probably took place for celebratory or commemorative events, such as births, deaths, marriages, and other special personal celebrations. Large-scale dinner

parties might also be included in the category of banquet. Certainly, banquets were an important part of special religious festivals, such as the Valley Festival, when they were celebrated, most probably, within the tomb or its courtyard—so the activities depicted on the tomb walls were reified at least once a year. Some scholars suggest that the food put into tombs was to provide the basis for such feasts, in addition to the provisions for the afterlife depicted on the walls.

Banquets probably started in midafternoon and went on for some time thereafter. The banqueting time has tentatively been determined by the appearance of the open blossoms of the blue lotus that adorn both people and wine jars (as in Theban tombs 46, 96, 100, 155, and others). The blue lotus blooms by day and closes at sunset; thus the open blossoms indicate that the banquets started in daylight hours, and that would be true as well for banquets relating to religious festivals. Most festivals took place (or at least started) during the daytime. Certainly biblical references support an afternoon banquet—as, for example, when Joseph invited his brothers for a feast at midday (*Gn.* 43.16).

The banquet started with the hosts greeting the guests at the door (if the banquet was in a tomb, the image of the deceased provided that function). The elaborately garbed, coiffed, and bejeweled guests were then seated. Men and women were shown seated together mainly when they were related to one another. In most instances, however, they seem to be segregated, since men and women are shown on alternate panels in most New Kingdom banqueting scenes. Whether this meant they were seated in different areas of one room or in separate rooms is unclear. Seating was probably hierarchical, with the most important people placed closest to the hosts and the others arranged alongside them, according to rank. The type of seat would also depend on rank: chairs for the most favored guests, stools for the less favored, with mats, and even the bare floor for the lowest ranks. In some tomb scenes, people are shown seated before tables piled high with food (especially true for the more important guests); in other scenes, often in the same tomb, food is being passed to the guests by servants. Perhaps in addition to the seating arrangements, the amount of food provided reflected the relative importance of the guests. Generally, male servants served the men and female servants attended to the women, although female servants were sometimes shown serving the men. Once the guests were seated, servants washed the guests' hands in basins, provided them with perfumes and cones of fat (which would smell pleasant or repel insects, according to the choice of perfume burned in the fat cone), and furnished them with lotus flowers to smell and flower collars to wear. Then the food and drink were served. Entertainment was also provided. Music accompanied the meal, with musicians of both genders singing and playing harps, lutes, drums, tamborines, and clappers. There was energetic dancing, with scantily clad professional dancers, generally female, performing elaborate acrobatic combinations for the entertainment of the guests. The goddess Hathor, associated with alcohol, drunkenness, music, and dancing was often invoked during the course of a banquet and was the deity most closely associated with feasting.

Alcohol was plentiful at banquets, be it wine, beer, or *šdḥ*, a fermented pomegranate drink. Large vessels, decorated with lotus blossoms, contained the drinks and stood at the ready. Tomb scenes (e.g., Theban tombs 49 and 53) vividly record the results of overindulgence, both by men and women, with people vomiting or even passing out after an excess of alcohol. Food was no less plentiful than alcohol. A banquet was a time for excess: entire oxen were roasted, as were ducks, geese, pigeons, various other birds, and on some occasions, fish (as shown in the Mem-

phite tomb of Horemheb). Stews were also served, and there were heaps of different types of bread, fresh vegetables, and fruit. Cakes, using dates and honey as sweetening agents, were also served.

According to the ancient Greek historian Herodotus, a slightly somber note was struck at the end of the banquet. A servant carried around a model coffin, containing a wooden statue of a corpse (about one cubit or two cubits in length), to the several guests. As it was shown to each guest in turn, the servant said, "Gaze here, and drink and be merry; for when you die, you will be thus." There is no record of such an event during the feasts of pharaonic times; it was possibly a Late period practice (then again, perhaps it was told to or only occurred within the imagination of the historian).

[*See also* Intoxication.]

### BIBLIOGRAPHY

Davies, Norman de Garis. *The Tomb of Rekhmire at Thebes*. New York, 1973, reprint. One of the most elaborate New Kingdom banqueting scenes, illustrated with translated texts.

Emery, W. B. *A Funerary Repast in an Egyptian Tomb of the Archaic Period*. Leiden, 1962. Gives the menu of a funerary meal found *in situ*.

Vandier, J. *Manuel d'archéologie Egyptienne. IV: Bas Reliefs et Peintures*. Paris, 1964. Extremely useful book, which lists the tomb scenes that show banquets.

Wilkinson, J. G. *The Manners and Customs of the Ancient Egyptians*, vol. 2. London, 1854. Uses Theban tomb scenes to re-create an Egyptian banquet.

Winlock, H. E. 1941. *Materials Used at the Embalming of King Tutankhamun*. New York, 1941. Provides examples of the festal wreaths and other materials found from Tutankhamun's funerary banquet.

SALIMA IKRAM

**BARBERING.** *See* Hairstyles.

**BASKETRY, MATTING, AND CORDAGE.** Simple technologies are the sometimes unheralded vital necessities of most human societies, especially in those that produced complex technologies and monumental arts. In ancient Egypt, such seemingly mundane components of material culture as cordage, basketry, and other fiber products had their own important everyday roles on both the domestic and grand scales. Strong ropes, for example, were essential for the hobbling of farm animals, the rigging of ships, and the transport and erection of impressive stones for monuments. Baskets, which are lightweight and unbreakable, served either as versatile storage and transport containers for food and other goods or as vehicles for moving earth during construction processes. Flat plaited mats provided flooring and roofing in mudbrick homes and served as wrapping material, among numerous other uses. The often excellent preservation envi-

BASKETRY, MATTING, AND CORDAGE. *Covered basket, made of coarse fiber, palm fiber, and split reeds, eighteenth dynasty.* (The Metropolitan Museum of Art, Rogers Fund, 1912. [12.182.56B])

ronments of Egypt (dry heat) have allowed examples of such fiber crafts to survive from as early as the Neolithic period. Many specimens from dynastic times can be found in museums worldwide.

**Basketry.** In general, baskets can be categorized into at least three primary descriptive classes, based on their construction and form, each exhibiting a wide range of variation. All three types are known from ancient Egypt: coiled, twined, and plaited. In coiled construction, a basket is formed by spirally coiling a continuous foundation of tightly wrapped bundles of fibers, to create a circular or oval base and walls. The coiled foundation is bound by stitching, which intersects and binds the successive coils one to another. Twined basketry is constructed by weaving horizontal fiber elements (wefts) around a stationary vertical framework (warps). A wide variety of knots and stitches can be utilized for securing these elements. In twined basketry, one set of constructional elements is active (the wefts) while the other is passive (the warps). In all plaited basketry, constructional elements are active, and strips of material are woven into baskets by passing under and over each other usually at regular intervals. The continuous intersections of the plaited constructional elements provide a cohesive unit, so no additional stitching is usually required except, in some examples, to secure the edges. Of these three basketry classes, the coiled varieties were by far the most commonly produced in ancient Egypt.

A variety of plant fibers were exploited by the ancient Egyptians for use in the construction of baskets. The leaves of the date palm (*Phoenix dactilifera*) and the dom palm (*Hyphaene thebaica*) were commonly used, especially in plaited baskets and for wrapping and stitching the foundation elements in coiled basketry. Leaf-based fibers from palms were also used as a basic material to form the foundation bundles of coiled baskets. The halfa grasses (*Desmostachya bipinnata* and *Imperata cylindrica*), however, were a more common bundle material. Such grasses could also be twisted into cordage, which might serve as one or both sets of elements in a kind of twined basketry. Sedges (*Cyperus papyrus* and *Cyperus schimporianus*), rushes (*Juncus acutus* and *Juncus arabicus*), flax (*Linum usitatissimum*), and a woody shrub (*Coruana prateensis*) were also variously employed.

Ancient Egyptian baskets were produced in a wide variety of shapes and sizes. Oval and circular body forms were especially common. Lids were often manufactured to match, and carrying loops were occasionally attached for ease in handling. Apart from their essential functional roles, the art of basket-making also allowed a wide degree of artistic expression in terms of construction and decoration. The patterning of the various constructional elements could be manipulated, to produce not only a useful container but also an object that was aesthetically pleasing. Smooth, rounded lines and graceful reinforcement ribs, for example, can be appreciated in many surviving examples of ancient Egyptian coiled basketry.

Egyptian baskets were often decorated with ornamental or colored stitching or with plaiting incorporated into the constructional design. Geometric patterns (such as van Dyke and checkered) were very common, and animal designs were occasionally employed. Black, red, and white pigments were frequently used to color such designs through painted or dyed stitching, plaits, or threads.

It is not difficult to find evidence of the use of baskets in the daily life of the ancient Egyptians. Apart from the many surviving examples of ancient basketry, numerous artistic depictions found in tombs and on other monuments demonstrate their vast range of utility. Baskets were also prominent in several hieroglyphs: most notably, a basket with handle denoted the alphabetic phoneme "*k*"; a basket without handle could be used as the biliteral "*nb*." Words for baskets included *mndm*, *nbt*, and *dnit*.

**Matting.** In ancient Egypt, mats were constructed by the binding of plant materials with string or by plaiting. The materials used for making these mats included palm leaves, reeds such as *Phragmites communis*, rushes such as *Juncus* and *Cyperus*, halfa grass, and the cattail (*Typha australis*). The phoneme "*p*" is represented alphabetically in the hieroglyphs by a mat, and Egyptian words for mat included *p*, *ḳn*, *tm3*, and *pm3yt*.

**Cordage.** Technically defined, cordage (cords, ropes, etc.) is a flexible, linear compilation of twisted or braided fibers, capable of bearing weight. Analytically, cordage can be described in terms of its material of manufacture, its structure, and its diameter—all of which contribute to the factors of flexibility and breaking strength. In ancient Egypt, the materials primarily used in the manufacture of cordage were papyrus (*Cyperus papyrus*), esparto grass (*Stipa tenacissima*), halfa grass, flax, and fibers from the date palm and the dom palm. There are several ancient techniques for manufacturing cordage, beginning with the collection and preparation of the fibers. In the case of papyrus, it was necessary to pound the stalk flat, to prepare the fibers for twisting. Most techniques for cordage manufacture involved the twisting of fibers into linear strands. Typically, ropes were constructed of either two or three strands, which in turn could be joined together to produce cordage of even greater diameter and strength, as for example the hawsers used to moor boats.

Rope-making was depicted in about a dozen tomb scenes, including some that show the building of small papyrus boats, during which cordage was manufactured at the construction site. Other scenes demonstrate that one to three people might be involved in the actual twisting process. Although an individual working alone could clutch fibers between the toes and manually twist and join strands on the thigh or between the palms, two or three people could work as an efficient team in anchoring, twisting, and joining, with a few simple tools to assist the process. The techniques for rope-making that were depicted in various tomb scenes have seemingly persisted in the village technologies of present-day Egypt, although the date palm has become the primary source of fibers.

As in the English language, the ancient Egyptian vernacular possessed several words for cordage, which likely expressed functional or size categories (e.g., those for "string," "twine," "cable," etc.). The words *in* and *ḥr*, for example, seem to denote a type of rope used on a ship, whereas *w3w3t* and *w3t* suggest the term "cord." Other cordage words include *ʿḥ*, *ḳ3*, *nwḥ*, *stnw*, *sšnw*, and *šs*. In the writing system, depictions of cordage are found phonetically with the alphabetic character *ṯ*, which seems to represent an animal hobble. Cordage also appears to be depicted in four prominent biliterals: *w3*, *s3*, *šn*, and *šs*. Iconographically important is an oval loop of rope, the "cartouche," which encircled royal names and symbolically represented eternity.

**BIBLIOGRAPHY:**

Gourlay, Yvon J.-L. *Les sparteries de Deir el-Mćdineh. XVIIe–XXe dynasties*. 2 vols. L'Institut Français d'Archéologic Orientale. Documents de Fouille, 17.1–2. Cairo, 1981.

Lucas, Alfred. *Ancient Egyptian Materials and Industries*: 4th ed. revised by J. R. Harris. London, 1962.

Ryan, Donald P. "Old Rope: Who Cares about this Ancient Technology?" *K.M.T.: A Modern Journal of Ancient Egypt*. 4.2 (Summer, 1993), 72–80.

Ryan, Donald P., and David H. Hansen. *A Study of Ancient Egyptian Cordage in the British Museum*. British Museum Occasional Paper, 62. London, 1987.

Teeter, Emily. "Techniques and Terminology of Rope-making in Ancient Egypt." *Journal of Egyptian Archaeology* 73 (1987), 71–77.

DONALD P. RYAN

**BASTET.** *See* Feline Deities.

**BATTLE OF KADESH.** Kadesh (Tell Neby Mend) was a Hittite city on the Orontes River in what is now southern Syria. Within less than five years after the retreat of Ramesses II's forces from the field (in his fifth regnal year), official acounts of his battle with the Hittites began to appear in Egypt, circulated on papyrus and/or carved on the walls of the king's new temples. The most complete versions—found in temples at Abydos, Karnak, Luxor, Western Thebes (at Ramesses II's memorial temple, called the Ramesseum) and at Abu Simbel—consist of the literary record and the pictorial record.

**The Literary Record.** A highly rhetorical account of the battle was misnamed "Poem" in the older publications in Egyptology. The beginning of the "Poem" described the forces arrayed against Egypt and the pharaoh's advance against the city of Kadesh. The greater part then dealt with the dramatic events of the battle's first day; highlights included the pharoah's appeal to his divine father Amun, his valor in action, and his victory against great odds, despite what was described as his army's craven conduct. The remainder reports on the next day's fighting, before describing the Hittite king's appeal for a truce and the pharaoh's triumphant departure from the field of battle. The entire text, a composition independent of other Kadesh materials (from which it was separated in the temples), was also preserved in three copies on papyrus—one (dated to Ramesses II's ninth regnal year) begins as Papyrus Raifé and continues on Papyrus Sallier III; and two others are on Papyrus Chester Beatty III, *verso* 1–3.

**The Pictorial Record.** Found only on temple walls, the pictorial materials can be divided into two groups. The first is the so-called Bulletin, or Record, actually an extended commentary placed above the battle scenes. Like them, it focuses on the events of the first day, but it gives more detail about the antecedents of the battle than appears in the "Poem." The second group of materials consists of the reliefs themselves, which depict the military action in relation to two main localities (the Egyptian camp and the city of Kadesh). In this context, a number of vignettes appear that illustrate the course of the battle. They include many descriptive labels that identify assorted participants and episodes in the fighting, such as the arrival of the relief force of young fighters (*na'arn*), who appeared at the crucial moment, near the end of the first day.

**Interpretation.** Despite the wealth of detail in the various accounts, the perspective they share with other such rhetorical materials from Egypt—replete with ideological bias and the selective reporting of events—makes them problematical to use in reconstructing a full and objective account of the battle. As a result, an extensive modern literature has grown, which reflects scholarly disagreements, not only about details of what happened but even on the so-called propagandist purposes for which Ramesses II circulated these materials. The most that can be said convincingly is that the publicity given in Egypt to the Battle of Kadesh presented the young pharaoh as snatching a qualified victory out of the jaws of defeat—doubtless a useful thing—both in the battle's aftermath, when Egypt had still more land to recover from the Hittites' encroachment on its empire, and later, when enough

pressure was kept on Hatti to allow a settlement to be reached—an outcome fulfilled, at least sufficiently, the aim that Ramesses had his courtiers articulate near the end of the "Poem" (in verse 329: "There is no blame in peace when *you* make it").

[*See also* Kadesh; *and* Ramesses II.]

**BIBLIOGRAPHY**

Gaballa, G. A. *Narrative in Egyptian Art*. Mainz, 1976. An analysis of the artistic composition of the Kadesh battle reliefs.

Gardiner, Alan. *The Kadesh Inscriptions of Ramesses II*. Oxford, 1960. A handy translation, with commentary, of the Egyptian texts that detail the battle.

Kitchen, Kenneth A. *Ramesside Inscriptions, Historical and Biographical*. Oxford, 1979. A user-friendly comparative edition of the various versions of the texts published in Kuentz's comprehensive edition; the author's translation and commentary appear in supplementary volumes.

Kuentz, Charles. *La Bataille de Qadech*. Mémoires de l'Institut Français d'Archéologie Orientale, 55. Cairo, 1928–1934. The fullest documentation of sources, this edition publishes copies of both the texts and the representations (mostly in photographs) of the battle on temple walls, but no translations.

Von der Way, Thomas. *Die Textüberlieferung Ramses' II, zur Qadeš-Schlacht. Analyse und Struktur*. Hildesheimer Ägyptologische Beiträge, 22. Hildesheim, 1984. An exhaustive discussion of the literary composition of the main Kadesh Battle narratives, with some debatable conclusions resting on its "structuralist" analysis of the texts.

WILLIAM J. MURNANE

**BEARDS.** *See* Hairstyles.

**BEAUTY.** To understand the pharaonic concept of beauty, it is useful to study the ancient Egyptian words for this concept. There are two adjectives that are used to describe beautiful things or people: '*n* and *nfr*. The former is written phonetically as: *ayin* + n + the determinative consisting of an eye adorned with cosmetics. There are two variations of this hieroglyph, the eye adorned with cosmetics on the lower lid and the eye enclosed within the hieroglyph for "land." In Late Egyptian, there is even the noun '*n(w)t*, which is derived from the adjective.

The term *nfr*, usually rendered *nefer* in modern Egyptological works, is far more common than those mentioned above, and there are substantives and even verbs related to this adjective. The verbs derived from *nfr* include *snfr*, meaning "beautify or embellish." The abstract concept of "beauty" may be indicated by either *nfrw* or *nfr* and the later *bw nfr*. There are also references describing a man or woman as a *nfr* or a *nfrt*, a term that seems to have more significance than simply designating a "beautiful person." Since these terms refer to specific categories of individuals, they can reveal something of what the Egyptians regarded as beautiful. The young women called *nfrwt* are sometimes described as "never having been opened in childbirth" (as in the Westcar Papyrus). At Ramesses III's palace-temple of Medinet Habu, a list of captured foreigners includes a reference to *nfrwt* as a category between child and mature woman. Similarly, *nfrw*, the masculine version of the word, occurs in several instances when it obviously refers to "young men" or "young people." In one instance, it can even be translated as "recruits." In addition, certain cows are called the *nfrwt*.

Another method of approaching pharaonic concepts of beauty is to look at the various clichéd phrases or terms that include the adjective *nfr*. For example, the term *imntt nfrt* ("the Beautiful West") occurs often in tombs and funerary texts to describe the city of the dead. The White Crown of Upper Egypt, called the *ḥḏt* is sometimes called the *ḥḏt nfrt* and occasionally even the *nfrt*. In addition, the king is often described as the *nṯr nfr*, an epithet which is usually translated as "the Good God," although "the Beautiful God" is equally accurate. In a coregency, the term *nṯr nfr* is used to designate the younger ruler. The elder king is instead called the *nṯr ʿ3* ("Great God"). Once again, *nfr* refers, if not to a young king, then to the younger of two. This attribute of youth or agelessness is an important component both of Egyptian aesthetics and of conceptions of divinity.

The apparent connections between youth and the descriptive term *nfr* may be an important clue to understanding the ancient concept of "beauty." In Egyptian art, artists portray the ideal form as youthful and slim with narrow hips. (Anthropometric studies of pharaonic mummies have revealed that this is a fair representation of reality, at least in the case of Egyptian women. Their hip-to-shoulder proportions are not greatly different from those found on male Egyptian mummies.) Both sexes may be represented this way, yet representations of males are more likely to vary from this ideal. Age, in a representation of a woman, is depicted subtly: in a slightly drooping derriere, in subtly sagging breasts or pouching cheeks and, occasionally, in horizontal lines across the torso, indicating increasing weight. These subtle touches are usually detectable only by close examination and comparison of numerous representations. The most famous and explicit representation of youth and age in a woman's body is the depiction of the funerals of Nebamun and Ipuky, both of whom married the same woman. Since the two funerals are represented taking place simultaneously, the representations of the widow show her with bared breasts both firm and drooping and with a change in profile to suggest a sagging chin in the older version of the woman.

The same almost imperceptible clues may be used to suggest advancing age in the apparently ageless form of the ruler. For example, in studying numerous representations of Amenhotpe III and his family, it was discovered that the king's torso was depicted as being somewhat thicker than that of other men. At various periods of Egyptian history, however, wealthy tomb owners might wish to have themselves depicted as older men, to emphasize their sagacity. Tomb scenes might contain representations of aged courtiers, complete with toothless faces and heavy sagging bellies. In the Amarna period, bowing elderly court functionaries appear in many of the scenes behind the figures of the king and queen. Wrinkles, however, are rarely shown on either sex, and gray hair is hardly ever depicted. Egyptian medical documents such as the Ebers Papyrus contain "remedies" not only for wrinkles, but also for baldness and graying hair, showing that, in life as in art, the Egyptians tried to maintain the hallmarks of a youthful appearance: smooth skin and a full head of hair.

Other than the attributes of youth, however, the precise elements that made for a physically beautiful individual are more difficult to define. In the love poetry and in hymns to Hathor, goddess of beauty, some sense of what was considered physically beautiful in people may be found. In many poems, Hathor is described as "golden," and this may well be a reference to her complexion. In the eighteenth dynasty tomb of May at Thebes, it is said that her face "gleams," a reference to her solar connections.

The poet of Papyrus Chester Beatty I lists his mortal beloved's enticements rather explicitly: her scent, her hair, her eyes, and her buttocks. Another poem from the same papyrus speaks more romantically of the object of affection, describing her as "bright" of skin, her arm "more brilliant than gold," long-necked and "white-breasted," hair of "genuine lapis lazuli," and fingers like lotus blooms, and it also mentions her beautiful thighs and heavy buttocks. This paragon's other attractions are her swift walk, sweet voice, and knowledge of when to stop talking. In addition to scent, color is also an important element in other erotic poetry where the lover might desire to see the color of all his beloved's limbs or say that she showed him the "color" of her embrace. In a hymn of the twenty-fifth dynasty (recorded on stela Louvre C100), there is a description of the priestess Mutirdis, who has locks of hair black as night and dark as "wine-grapes," "brilliant" arms, firm breasts, and a complexion "like jasper."

References to male beauty are not as common, although beauty is an important factor in the story often called the *Blinding of Truth by Falsehood*. In this story, a woman desires Truth, a man more handsome than anyone else in the country; she bears his child, who looks like a young god. According to the texts left by Hatshepsut at Deir el-Bahri, when the god Amun appears in the bedroom of Queen Ahmes, mother of Hatshepsut, Ahmes is

BEAUTY. *Relief from the tomb of the vizier Ramose at Sheikh Abd el-Qurna.* (Courtesy Dieter Arnold)

awakened by his divine fragrance, a perfume that permeates the whole palace as they make love. Hatshepsut, the god-king, is described there as appearing before her subjects with skin like electrum (a light yellow gold-silver alloy) and smelling like all the perfumes of Punt. A sweet scent is indissolubly connected in the Egyptian mind with divine beauty.

Quite often the elements that constitute beauty in people are described indirectly, by analogy or simile. In a poem from Papyrus Harris 500, written around 500 BCE, the female narrator describes herself as being like a field planted with sweet-smelling herbs, much as the male protagonist of Cairo Vase 25218 says that he feels immersed in perfume when he embraces his beloved, as if he were in the land of incense. As is the case with gods, a lover's scent is part of his or her attraction. The narrator of Cairo Vase 25218 also claims to be drunk "without beer" when he kisses her. The female narrator of the Papyrus Harris 500 poem compares her beloved's voice to pomegranate wine, recalling the pomegranate tree mentioned in the poem of Papyrus Turin 1966. This amazing talking tree compares the beloved's teeth to pomegranate seeds and her breasts to the whole fruit. While it is easy to see why breasts might be compared to the fruit, it is less obvious

why a beautiful woman's teeth would be like the seeds of the fruit, unless in reference to their evenness and size.

It is not only people who may be described as "beautiful." In Papyrus Turin 1966, a sycomore fig is described as being beautiful. It has leaves greener than turquoise, branches like faience, wood the color of feldspar, and fruits as red as jasper. The beautiful jewel-like colors of the tree are an integral part of its beauty. Color is also important in nonliterary representations of ideal form. Men, for example, are almost universally depicted with red or red-brown skins. Women are shown with paler skins, although the color used by the artist varies over time: pinkish white in the Old Kingdom; yellow in the Middle Kingdom and the early New Kingdom, and shades of pink or pale orange in the later New Kingdom. (One early representation of women with pink skins is from the funerary temple of Montuhotep I at Deir el-Bahri, where his minor wives are depicted with this complexion.) Goddesses retain a yellow or "golden" complexion throughout the New Kingdom, and an effort is made to distinguish between the complexions of deities and mortals. Egyptian women are rarely depicted with the darker skin tones of a male, although in the Amarna period both sexes are occasionally depicted with the same reddish skin. The symbolism of these color variations has been explained in various ways. For example, it has been stated that upper-class women remained indoors to work, while men were out in the sun, so that a lighter-skinned woman appeared more aristocratic. Certainly, when men are depicted with newly shaved heads, their scalps are shown paler than the rest of their skin. Elderly men were occasionally shown with pale skin. Although the association of light-colored skin with lack of sun may have been to some extent true, no doubt these colors also had symbolic meaning. Red is the color of blood and heat and represents the active principle. The use of other colors for female skin tones is perhaps suggestive of youthfulness or immortality. Yellow in particular, which is used throughout Egyptian history for the skin tones of goddesses, suggests the warm gleam of gold. The love poems in speaking eloquently of the "gleaming" skin of the love object echo this idea. White, which is also occasionally used, is in some contexts interchangeable with yellow, especially in the context of solar imagery.

To the ancient Egyptians, beauty in human and nonhuman context may also have included symmetry as a necessary component. For example, in art and architecture the Egyptians favored the rectilinear geometric outline over the curved. Thus, the ideal male body may be summarized as being bounded by two triangles: the torso, consisting of broad shoulders exaggerated in two-dimensional images by frontal positioning and narrow waist, shown in three-quarter view; and the striding legs. The bodies of women were tailored to fit within a long rectangle, their shoulders narrower than the male's shoulders and the feet together or with one slightly advanced. Only in the Amarna period does the ideal body (i.e., that of the king) greatly depart from the previous athletic norm, when Akhenaten's art forms are as unconventional as his religious reforms. Whatever the reason for that pharaoh's elongated representation (Frohlich's and Marfan's syndromes have both been suggested)—his narrow shoulders, large drooping belly, massive thighs, and thin extremities seem far from the geometric perfection of the traditional royal male. His body shape is transferred almost exactly to the figure of his wife Nefertiti, in slightly less extreme form to their daughters, and occasionally in modified form to their subjects. It begets a new style and, in this case, the usual rules of determining beauty may be said to be reversed: instead of the pharaoh's body being depicted according the slim and athletic ideal of male beauty, his corporeal form is represented as the acme of perfection. Although it is often stated that all Egyptian rulers provided a model of perfect human form for their artists, still they are represented with more or less uniform bodies, with only minor variations; if the actual appearance of the royal body were truly the model by which beauty were determined, over the

course of three thousand years, there would be skinny and fat pharaohs, heavily muscled and knock-kneed pharaohs, and more courtiers who resembled them.

Among the elite who commissioned tombs, variations from the fashionable form of the time were slight, and drastic departures from the slim, youthful, and healthy "norm" are seen primarily in those of lower status. For example, pattern baldness and hernia are depicted in representations of herdsmen and other lower class males. Yet for women, age and obesity are rarely represented. A representation from Deir el-Bahri of a woman involved in the making of cloth shows someone who does not have the "ideal" shape given to the noblewomen. The most famous example of a deviation from the norm is the "Queen of Punt," who is met by Hatshepsut's expedition to the country. She is depicted as a massive, apparently obese woman, with sagging arms and a sway back. For the interpretation, the question remains, however: Is the queen the ideal of beauty in her own country, a caricature of a foreign type, or merely an artist's observation of an obvious pathology?

In the literature of ancient Egypt, the effect of beauty, and especially of beautiful women, on the story is considerable. In the Westcar Papyrus, which contains the legends of great magicians told to King Khufu by his own sorcerer, an episode motivated by the wishes of a scantily clad *nfrt* is recounted. King Sneferu has asked that he be rowed in his pleasure-boat by a crew of nubile young women dressed in fishnets and jewelry. One young oarswoman loses her amulet and refuses to go any farther until it is recovered, a task that the great sorcerer accomplishes by parting the waters of the lake. The effect of this young woman is benign compared to the destruction wrought by a beautiful wraith called Tabubu in the *Setna Khaemwase Cycle*. She convinces the protagonist to give over his house and property to her, to force his children to accede to the transaction and, finally, persuades him to have his children killed and their bodies thrown to the scavengers. Interestingly, although she is described as "beautiful, without compare," Tabubu's physical appearance is never described in specific. Similarly, in the *Story of the Two Brothers*, Bata is given a beautiful wife. Although most aspects of her appearance are not described, the scent of her hair is so entrancing that a pharaoh falls in love with her. Like Tabubu, she is evil and conspires to kill her husband after she has left him. Despite these examples, "beauty" was a much-valued quality in the literature of the pharaonic world, associated with the good and the pure, as well as the desirable.

**BIBLIOGRAPHY**

Arnold, Dorothea. *The Royal Women of Amarna*. New York, 1996.
Robins, G. *Women in Ancient Egypt*. London, 1993.

Rosalind, M., and Jac J. Janssen. *Getting Old in Ancient Egypt*. London, 1996.

Wilkinson, Richard. *Reading Egyptian Art*. London, 1992.

Wilkinson, Richard. *Symbol and Magic in Egyptian Art*. London, 1994.

LYN GREEN

**BEER.** In ancient Egypt, from Neolithic sites to the written sources of historic times, beer was known, together with bread, as a staple food. Unlike most modern commercial beers, which are clear, ancient Egyptian beer was cloudy, with suspended solids; it was rich in complex carbohydrates and sugars that provide food energy and was an important source of essential fatty acids, amino acids, minerals, and vitamins. As reflected in ritual practice, beer was always a major part of offerings to the dead and to the gods. Perhaps because of its central dietary role, beer was a key economic commodity. The values of goods were calculated in terms of beer-jar equivalents, and rations might be paid with beer. In addition, beer was an ingredient of many medications, and whether efficacious for specific ailments or not, it would have been easily digested and was an agreeable way to ingest medicinal concoctions.

Words that may refer to beer have been found in Early Dynastic sources, while the standard Old Egyptian word for beer, *ḥnḳt*, first appeared in fifth dynasty offering lists; it was used thereafter. Few specific types of beer were listed and precisely how those types, such as sweet beer, were differentiated is as yet unknown. Beer is a beverage made from fermented cereals. Fermentation results from the metabolic action of certain microorganisms (yeasts or bacteria) as they change sugars into alcohol and other by-products. Cereals, rich in starch, allow for fermentation, as the starch is converted to sugars and the sugars to alcohol. Much of the brewing process involves this conversion (see below).

The earliest evidence for Egyptian brewing comes from the Predynastic sites of Hierakonpolis and Abydos, where large conical vats set into mud-brick installations were found. The vat contents have sometimes survived as residue, consisting of coarsely broken chaff and cereal grain (identified as emmer wheat) embedded in a dark, vitreous matrix. The large amount of ash and charcoal surrounding the vats and the slight reddening of the vats' exterior walls indicate that the vats were gently heated. The combination of the cereal residue, the application of heat, and the later importance of beer in the culture suggested early brewing vessels.

Artistic representations of brewing were common. During the Old Kingdom, these were presented either as statuettes, like those found in the tomb of Ni-kau-hathor, or in tomb reliefs. By the Middle Kingdom, wooden models were popular, as well as tomb paintings, such as those

BEER. *Brewery and bakery, a wooden funerary model.* From the tomb of Meketre in Thebes, early twelfth dynasty. (The Metropolitan Museum of Art, Museum Excavations, 1919–1920; Rogers Fund supplemented by contribution of Edward S. Harkness. [20.3.12])

at Beni Hasan. Brewing scenes in New Kingdom tombs were less frequent, but a few wall paintings show beer making, for example, a scene in the tomb of Ken-amun. Artistic depictions have been the main source of evidence for the interpretation of ancient brewing methods (supplemented by observations of the modern Egyptian beer called *bouzah*). Greco-Roman descriptions have been used but are problematic, since they were dated to a much later time, when cultural influence, technologies, and ingredients had changed considerably. Nevertheless, a recipe written about the fourth century CE, by the Egyptian Zozimus of Panopolis, has frequently been quoted as a model for ancient Egyptian brewing practices.

The general consensus has been that ancient Egyptian beer was made by first preparing bread; this so-called beer bread was well leavened and lightly baked, so that the yeasts were not killed. The partially cooked loaves were then crumbled over a sieve, washed with water into a vat, and there left to ferment—through the action of yeasts derived from the bread. Some Egyptologists maintain that dates (from the date palm tree, *Phoenix dactylifera*) were a major ingredient, providing the initial source of sugars for fermentation. Others suggest that malt *(bs3)* was a beer ingredient (barley or other grain soaked, sprouted, then kiln dried). No standard view exists for the way these ingredients might have been prepared or at what stage they entered the brewing process. Archaeological data has, however, provided a different perspective on brewing in ancient Egypt. A major source of information is the residues of beer and beer precursors that were desiccated and preserved by the arid Egyptian climate. When beer residues are studied by microscopy, starch granules, yeast cells, and plant tissues are clearly visible. Starch changes its structure when prepared in different ways, and its resultant shape thus preserves a record of how the grain had been treated. Observations of the starch structure allow investigators to reconstruct the sequence of ancient Egyptian brewing steps.

The first stage of brewing was to sprout one batch of grain; this natural process produced compounds called enzymes, some of which are able to convert starch into sugars. Next, another batch of grain was well cooked in water, which dispersed the starch. The two batches of grain—the sprouted and the cooked—were then mixed. The enzymes easily attacked the cooked dispersed starch and produced large quantities of sugar. At that stage, the mixture was sieved, separating most of the chaff from the sugar-rich liquid. Then the liquid was enriched with yeast, and probably lactic acid bacteria, which fermented the sugars into alcohol. (Bread does not appear to have been an ingredient, as was originally supposed.) The reconstructed brewing method, presented above, has only a slight resemblance to modern Egyptian *bouzah* making—

but it is similar to many other domestic (nonindustrial) African brewing techniques. Ancient Egyptian brewing thus seems to belong to a known local tradition.

The majority of ancient Egyptian beer residues contained barley *(Hordeum vulgare)*, whereas only some were made entirely from emmer wheat *(Triticum dicoccum)*. Occasionally, both cereals were mixed together. Very few residues examined showed any trace of ingredients apart from cereal, yeasts, and water. No tissues from dates have yet been found; present evidence indicates that additives, including dates, were not standard for brewing, although beer may have sometimes been flavored. Residues so far studied with microscopy date to the New Kingdom. There are fewer known residues from earlier Egyptian periods, and most still await scientific investigation. A better understanding of the diversity of beers, the way brewing may have developed, and the differences in use among social classes—all require further archaeological investigation.

[*See also* Diet; *and* Intoxication.]

## BIBLIOGRAPHY

Darby, William J., Paul Ghalioungui, and Louis Grivetti. *Food: The Gift of Osiris.* London and New York, 1977. A general description of the traditional view of beer making, relying much on Greco-Roman sources.

Davies, Norman de G. *The Tomb of Ken-Amun at Thebes.* New York, 1930. Includes a description, photograph, and drawings of a rare New Kingdom brewing scene.

Dirar, H. A. *Indigenous Fermented Foods of the Sudan: A Study in African Food and Nutrition.* Wallingford, UK, 1993. Detailed descriptions of some modern, traditional African brewing methods, similar to those used by the ancient Egyptians.

Geller, J. R. "From Prehistory to History: Beer in Egypt." In *The Followers of Horus: Studies Dedicated to Michael Allen Hoffman, 1944–1990,* edited by R. Friedman and B. Adams, pp. 19–26. Oxford, 1992. A description of one of the earliest brewing installations in Egypt, at Hierakonpolis.

Helck, Wolfgang. *Das Bier im Alten Ägypten.* Berlin, 1971. Comprehensive overview of the place of beer and brewing in ancient Egyptian life; traditional description of beer making; good treatment of the documentary sources.

Samuel, Delwen. "Archaeology of Ancient Egyptian Beer." *Journal of the American Society of Brewing Chemists.* 54.1 (1996), 3–12. Fairly technical account of microscopy of beer residues; gives most detailed account of the new interpretation of ancient Egyptian brewing.

Samuel, Delwen. "Investigation of Ancient Egyptian Baking and Brewing Methods by Correlative Microscopy." *Science* 273 (1996), 488–490. The most recent publication on microscopy analysis of beer residues and their interpretation; discusses the relationship of beer and bread.

DELWEN SAMUEL

**BEES AND HONEY.** The native Egyptian honeybee (*Apis mellifera*), the smaller and more aggressive cousin of the European honeybee, was probably exploited by the

BEES AND HONEY. *Gathering honey.* A man uses a censer to blow smoke into the hives in order to stupefy the bees, while another man extracts the combs and piles them in dishes. Copy by Nina de Garis Davies of a painting in the tomb of the vizier Rekhmire at Thebes, eighteenth dynasty, time of Thutmose III to Amenhotpe II. (The Metropolitan Museum of Art, 30.4.88)

Egyptians at least as early as the Neolithic period. Honey was known to the Egyptians as *bit;* bees were called *ȝf i n bit*, "honey flies" (usually shortened to *bit*). By the first dynasty, the king was known as *nsw bity*, "He of the Reed and Bee," one of the most important components of the royal titulary, thereby associating the monarch with the heraldic emblems of Upper and Lower Egypt, respectively.

Only five scenes depicting apiculture are known from pharaonic Egypt. The earliest is from the fifth dynasty sun temple of Newoserre Any at Abu Ghurob (a fragment of a similar scene is known from the pyramid causeway of Unas at Saqqara). The scene illustrates the procedures of organized gathering, filtering, and packing honey. The eighteenth dynasty tomb of the vizier Rekhmira at Thebes

(tomb 100) depicts a man harvesting honeycomb from hives while a second holds a smoke pot to the mouths of the hives (smoke induces bees to fill their stomachs with honey and become less aggressive); elsewhere in the scene, workers pack pots with honey after having extracted it from the combs. Tomb 73, also of the eighteenth dynasty, is badly damaged, but it shows two bee-workers smoking stacked hives. Two Saite period tombs at Asasif—those of Pebes (tomb 279) and 'Ankh-her (tomb 414)—have almost identical scenes portraying a man before stacked hives, while in the register above a worker pours extracted honey into a jar (almost lost in tomb 414); these Saite reliefs are probably copies of older apicultural scenes. Ancient Egyptian beehives, as all these scenes depict, were long ceramic tubes, sealed at either end with mud or wadding and stacked horizontally in walls; a similar technique is still employed in Egypt today.

Bees and honey were important in Egyptian religion. In one myth, the tears of Re are said to become bees, while the Pyramid Texts mention that Nut could appear as a bee. The temple of Neith at Sais was called the "House of the Bee." Honey served as an offering to the gods, and that used by the cult of Min (where honey was particularly important) was provided both by professional beekeepers (*ȝftyw*) and by honey-hunters (*bityw*) who collected it from wild hives. Certain texts mention "beekeepers of Amun." Huge amounts of honey were offered by Ramesses III to the god Hapy. At Dendera, however, it was forbidden to eat honey. In the eighteenth dynasty, honey (both combs and jars) is often depicted being offered to private tomb-owners.

Besides its importance in religious rituals, honey was employed as a sweetener, utilized in baked goods, and used to prime beer and wine; it was apparently a component of some perfumes. Of the approximately nine hundred cures mentioned in medical papyri, about five hundred involve the use of honey (which has natural antibacterial properties).

Although honey was imported from Palestine, the majority was produced in Egyptian apiaries. A state-appointed "Overseer of Beekeepers of the Entire Land" is known from the Middle Kingdom, indicating widespread beekeeping. In the Ptolemaic period, large-scale apiaries—some consisting of at least five thousand hives—are known from the Faiyum; these were probably involved in migratory beekeeping, the hives being moved to fields in flower to take advantage of rich honey-flows.

### BIBLIOGRAPHY

Brewer, Douglas J., Donald B. Redford, and Susan Redford. *Domestic Plants and Animals: The Egyptian Origins.* Warminster, 1994. See pp. 125–129 for the most current treatment of Egyptian apiculture in English, though the tomb of 'Ankh-ḥer (Asasif tomb 414) is not mentioned.

Crane, Eva E. *The Archaeology of Beekeeping.* London, 1983. Written by a historian of apiculture, chapter 2 (pp. 34–43) discusses the development of apiculture in ancient Egypt (and the survival of such techniques in modern Egypt).

Kuény, Gustav. "Scènes apicoles dans l'ancienne Égypte." *Journal of Near Eastern Studies* 9 (1950):84–93. Although dated, this article is the one of the standard sources; Kuény deals with both ancient and modern apicultural practices in Egypt.

TROY LEILAND SAGRILLO

**BEETLES.** *See* Scarabs.

**BEHBEIT EL-HAGAR** (also called Behbeit el Hagara or Higara), a site in the province of Gharbieh, district of Talkha (31°02′N, 31°17′E). The ruins of a temple dedicated to the Osirian family by the last Egyptian pharaoh, Nektanebo II, (r.360–343 BCE), and by the early Ptolemies (Ptolemy II and Ptolemy III; r.282–222 BCE) remain at the site. The collapse of this temple could not have taken place after the end of the first century CE, since a Behbeit block has been found in a temple dedicated to Isis and Serapis in Rome, where it might have been placed either at the time of the temple's foundation in 43 BCE or when renovated under the emperor Domitian (r.81–96 CE). Behbeit, then, seems to have been abandoned and used as a quarry.

The site was discovered in the early eighteenth century by European travelers. Some of its inscriptions were copied and published at the end of the nineteenth century. A few decades later, Pierre Montet dug out some new blocks in the southeastern corner of the temple. In 1977, an epigraphic and photographic survey was made by Christine Favard and Dimitri Meeks. This documentation completed Montet's archives and gave the basic information on which a reconstruction has been proposed, with the help of a database, taking into account the essential iconography and texts.

According to textual information, it is fairly certain that a prior construction was undertaken by the last kings of the Saite dynasty (the twenty-sixth), with the cult of their statues being attested in place. Besides, from the New Kingdom onward, external sources mention *Per-hebite(t)*, the name of the site (*pr-hb.t*), or *Hebit*, the name of the temple. Since both names recurred in other parts of Egypt, to equate all the testimonies with the site remains to be confirmed. In any case, the first mention of *Per-hebite(t)* is not older than the reign of Amenhotpe III (1410–1372 BCE); that of *Hebit* also dates from the New Kingdom. Scholars have supposed that the site was also named *Netjery*, but this name is only certain for the foundation of Nektanebo II, and it might only describe a chapel.

In fact, the history of the site remains poorly known, since extensive excavations have never been undertaken. Nevertheless, a description of the surface ruins can be made. Within brick walls, which survived on three sides—the southern, western, and northern—and from the large and small granite blocks spread over the ground, a *dromos* can be distinguished (evidenced by a single sphinx), leading to a western façade that shows Ptolemy III making offerings to various aspects of Osiris protected by Isis. After a columned hall, the facade of the Sanctuary of Isis can be seen, where Ptolemy II is shown introduced to the goddess by Horus Behedety. A large door led to the sanctuary of Isis, well evidenced by the blocks of the southern wall. Behind the sanctuary are chapels, dedicated to the cult of various aspects of Osiris. These were identified as the Prince-(Ser) chapel, and Res-wedja chapel, the High House, the Divine-(Netjery) chapel, and the Hemag chapel. This last chapel is important as the only one decorated under Nektanebo II (who probably also built the greater part of the temple). The presence of a huge staircase, whose ruins can be seen from the columned hall, suggest that some of the Osirian chapels were located on the roof.

All the chapels were devoted through specific rites to the rebirth of Osiris as a young child or to his transformation into a falcon. In Behbeit, the cult of Osiris-Andjety, dressed as a living deity, made no allusion to his death, his permanent survival was assured through the fabrication of annual clay statues, which benefit from the exclusive cultual activity of Isis and her son Horus. This activity can be inferred from the offering scenes at the temple and the other name of *Behbeit*: "The Place Where Offerings Are Laid Down."

## BIBLIOGRAPHY

Favard-Meeks, Christine. "Un temple d'Isis à reconstruire." *Archeologia* 263 (1990), 26–33. A summary of the architectural reconstitution proposed for the temple.

Favard-Meeks, Christine. *Le temple de Behbeit el-Hagara: Essai de reconstitution et d'interpretation*, pp. 1–523. Studien zur Altägyptischen Kultur, Beiheft, 6. Hamburg, 1991, The first part of the thesis is devoted to the reconstruction of the various parts of the temple, with all the hieroglyphic texts available, translation, and commentary; the second part deals with the history of the site, based on study of the sacred names mentioned in the temple inscriptions.

Favard-Meeks, Christine. "Le site de Behbeit el-Hagara et son temple." *Dossiers d'Archéologie* 213 (1996), 82–85. The history of the site and of the cults of the temple.

Favard-Meeks, Christine. "The Temple of Behbeit el-Hagara." In *The Temple in Ancient Egypt: New Discoveries and Recent Research*, edited by Stephen Quirke, pp. 102–111. London, 1997. In English, a condensed version of the 1996 paper, with additional information on cults and rites.

Porter, Bertha, and Rosalind Moss. *Topographical Bibliography of Ancient Egyptian Hieroglyphic Texts, Reliefs and Paintings*, vol. 4: *Lower and Middle Egypt*. Oxford, 1934. Offers the basic bibliography for some of the texts copied from scattered blocks *in situ* and those in museums.

CHRISTINE FAVARD-MEEKS

**BENI HASAN,** a site located on a hillside near the eastern bank of the Nile, about 250 kilometers (155 miles) south of Cairo (27°56′N, 30°53′E). The site is a vast and important provincial necropolis containing about 930 tombs, divided into two ranges of markedly different types that span the late sixth dynasty and the twelfth dynasty (c.2200–1785 BCE). Sometimes included in the designation "Beni Hasan" is Speos Artemidos, a wadi (a dried-up bed of a Nile tributary) 3 kilometers (2 miles) south of the necropolis and the site of a beautifully decorated rock-cut temple built in honor of the lion goddess Pakhet by the eighteenth dynasty woman pharaoh Hatshepsut. In addition, many Late period, Ptolemaic, and Roman tombs pockmark the hills of the wadi.

The upper necropolis at Beni Hasan consists of about forty large rectangular or square chambers cut straight back into the hill. Here were buried the nomarchs (provincial governors) and other important civil leaders of the nome (from the Greek word *nomos,* for "province"). According to various ancient Egyptian geographical records, Beni Hasan was situated in the sixteenth Upper Egyptian nome. Inscriptions refer to the province as the "[white] oryx nome." Two ancient Egyptian toponyms used either for Beni Hasan or for nearby regions are *menat Khufu* ("that which nurtures Khufu") and *djut Heru* ("the mountain of Horus"); in the first name, the reference to Khufu, the fourth dynasty builder of the great pyramid at Giza, is not clear.

The date of the upper tombs has been debated widely. Three of the burials (nos. 2, 3, and 14) are reasonably well dated to the twelfth dynasty by their inscriptions, and many scholars regard the remaining tombs in the upper tier as contemporary. Textual, archaeological, and artistic evidence, however, has led to a redating of some of the tombs (nos. 15, 17, 27, 29, and 33) to the late eleventh dynasty or perhaps even earlier to the poorly understood era known as the First Intermediate Period. The lower cemetery contains about 890 pit tombs or L-shaped shafts sunk into the slope of the hill; these burials date from the late sixth dynasty to the first half of the twelfth dynasty. Although Beni Hasan is renowned chiefly for the wall scenes in the large tombs of the upper level—which are the most extensive, best preserved, and most significant paintings from central Egypt—the lower cemetery cannot be ignored. It has yielded a wealth of archaeological material that is invaluable for art history, architecture, social and political history, and philology.

Excavations at Beni Hasan introduced a new era of archaeological method in Egypt. The large tombs of the upper tier were recorded from 1890 to 1891 by Percy E. Newberry and George W. Fraser, who published the first excavation report in the renowned Archaeological Survey of Egypt series, established by the Egypt Exploration Fund (now Society) in London. One of their assistants was the young Howard Carter, who later discovered Tutankhamun's tomb in the Valley of the Kings at Thebes. Carter's beautiful color drawings constitute the best features of the report, which otherwise consists of overly reduced and in other respects unacceptable black-and-white line drawings of the wall paintings. Nonetheless, the publication is a cornerstone in modern epigraphy because it was a first attempt at facsimile recording.

The best preserved paintings in the upper cemetery appear in the tombs of the officials Amenemhat (tomb no. 2), Khnumhotep II (no. 3), Baqet III (no. 15), and Kheti (no. 17). The repertory of vignettes is enormous; perhaps the most popular topics belong to the genre known as "scenes of daily life" because they depict a wide variety of everyday

BENI HASAN. *Rock-cut tombs.* (Courtesy Dorothea Arnold)

activities, such as brewing, baking, butchering, cooking, wine making, hunting, fishing, fowling, harvesting, irrigating, laundering, pottery making, stone working, weaving, dancing, singing, and game playing. The tomb of Baqet III has two splendid registers of carefully detailed birds and bats. Many of those scenes may represent the material wealth and the ambience that the tomb owner hoped to enjoy in the next life—therefore, they depict not so much the actual trappings of worldly existence but an ideal, desired situation in paradise. Some pictorial elements in the tombs of Baqet III and Kheti are harder to classify: mythical animals of the desert and several unique hieroglyphs of sexual and cryptographic nature.

Other scenes and inscriptions provide tantalizing glimpses into the provincial Realpolitik. Of interest to the historian are the enormous tableaux of battles on the eastern walls of tombs 2, 3, 15, and 17. Just what conflict(s) they illustrate is not clear: either a confrontation between the rival kingdoms during the First Intermediate Period or the putative difficulties surrounding the accession of Amenemhet I at the beginning of the twelfth dynasty. The inscriptions in tombs 2, 3, and 14 contain vague references to civil strife. In tomb 3 (Khnumhotep II) is a long biographical inscription that details the division of the nome by the kings Amenemhet I and II and Khnumhotep's promotion by the second king to the office of mayor. In the same tomb, a

brightly colored and boldly executed painting shows a procession of Near Easterners, whose chief was labeled "ruler of foreign lands," a designation later applied to the groups who migrated to Egypt during the latter half of the twelfth dynasty and throughout the Second Intermediate Period. In a much later Greek historical record, those people are the Hyksos, which is simply a Greek rendering of the ancient Egyptian term. Egyptian and Greek accounts vilify the Hyksos as aggressors, and the Egyptians indeed engaged in sporadic battles with the Near Easterners during the Second Intermediate Period. Those conflicts represent a later development in Egyptian–Near Eastern relations, however, because in Khnumhotep's tomb at Beni Hasan, the "ruler of foreign lands" and his family are shown as peaceful pastoralists and traders.

According to a longstanding theory, the disappearance of the title of nomarch and the cessation of large tombs at Beni Hasan and elsewhere in Egypt during the second half of the twelfth dynasty supposedly signifies a successful royal nullification of the threat posed by those powerful provincial rulers. An important study (Franke, 1991) has convincingly demonstrated, however, the falsity of that claim, in that provincial officials did not pose a threat to the king, and the title of nomarch had been disappearing gradually since the first half of the dynasty. At Beni Hasan, for example, Amenemhat of tomb 2 was the last nomarch, and he died during the reign of Senwosret I, the second king of the dynasty. Furthermore, far from purging the nomarchs, the pharaohs promoted them to important positions at the capital to centralize provincial wealth and influence.

From 1902 through 1904, the lower necropolis was excavated by John Garstang for the University of Liverpool. The earliest of the almost 890 graves (nos. 481 and 482) are exceptional because they are cut straight back into the hillside, unlike the pit burials. The unpublished tomb 481 is important because it preserves most of its original inscriptions and raised relief. All 890 tombs are modest in size, and not one has wall paintings. Consequently, these tombs do not receive the attention accorded to the renowned tombs in the upper range. Nonetheless, the burials have yielded a wealth of archaeological material, such as pottery, coffins, wooden models of boats and servants, and other funerary equipment; these data are crucial to the determination of the date of the burials in both levels at Beni Hasan. For all its many inaccuracies, particularly in its descriptions and lists of materials, Garstang's eminently readable and still valuable report is a fine synthesis of archaeological discoveries and wider contexts, such as history, funerary practices, and religion.

Despite Newberry's and Garstang's efforts, Beni Hasan has not been completely explored, and the archaeological material has never been thoroughly analyzed. In particular, the burial shafts in the tombs of the upper range have not been completely excavated. Numerous wall paintings and inscriptions from those same burials remain unpublished. The correspondence between the many coffins from the site and the tombs in which they were deposited cannot be determined in several instances. Newberry made little, if any, effort to analyze the pottery found in the upper tombs. Furthermore, because Garstang did not record carefully the distribution of the material that he took from the lower cemetery (see *Annales du service des antiquités de l'Égypte* 5 [1904], 215–228), the current locations of many items cannot be determined. Consequently, the full significance of the lower necropolis may never be realized.

## BIBLIOGRAPHY

Franke, Detlef. "The Career of Khnumhotep III of Beni Hasan and the so-called 'Decline of the Nomarchs'." In *Middle Kingdom Studies*, edited by Stephen Quirke, pp. 51–68. New Malden, Surrey, 1991.

Garstang, John. *The Burial Customs of Ancient Egypt as Illustrated by Tombs of the Middle Kingdom. Being a Report of Excavations Made in the Necropolis of Beni Hassan during 1902–3–4.* London, 1907.

Hölzl, Christian. "The Rock-Tombs of Beni Hasan: Architecture and Sequence," pp. 279–283. *Sesto Congresso Internazionale di Egittologia: Atti.* Turin, 1992.

Junge, Friedrich. "Beni Hassan." In *Lexikon der Ägyptologie*, 1: 695–698. Wiesbaden, 1975.

Kamrin, Janice. *The Cosmos of Khnumhotep II.* London and New York, 1999.

Lapp, Günter. *Typologie der Särge und Sargkammern von der 6. bis 13. Dynastie.* Studien zur Archäologie und Geschichte Altägyptens, Deutsches Archäologisches Institut Abteilung Kairo und Ägyptologisches Institut, Universität Heidelberg, 7. Heidelberg, 1993.

Lloyd, Alan B. "The Great Inscription of Khnumhotep II at Beni Hasan." In *Studies in Pharaonic Religion and Society in Honour of J. Gwyn Griffiths*, edited by Alan B. Lloyd, pp. 21–37. Egypt Exploration Society Occasional Publications, 8. London, 1992.

Newberry, Percy E. *Beni Hasan.* 4 vols. Egypt Exploration Fund, Archaeological Survey of Egypt, 1st, 2nd, 5th, 7th Memoirs. London, 1893–1900.

Porter, Bertha, and Rosalind L. B. Moss. *Topographical Bibliography of Ancient Egyptian Hieroglyphic Texts, Reliefs, and Painting*, vol. 4: *Lower and Middle Egypt (Delta and Cairo to Asyût)* pp. 141–163. Oxford, 1934.

Schenkel, Wolfgang. *Frühmittelägyptische Studien.* Bonner Orientalistische Studien, Neue Serie, Bd. 13. Bonn, 1962.

Schulman, Alan R. "The Battle Scenes of the Middle Kingdom," *Journal of the Society for the Study of the Egyptian Antiquities* 12 (1982), 165–183.

Seidlmayer, Stephan J. *Gräberfelder aus dem Übergang vom Alten zum Mittleren Reich: Studien zur Archäologie der Ersten Zwischenzeit.* Studien zur Archäologie und Geschichte Altägyptens, Deutsches Archäologisches Institut Abteilung Kairo und Ägyptologisches Institut, Universität Heidelberg, 1. Heidelberg, 1990.

Spanel, Donald B. "Beni Hasan." In *The Dictionary of Art*, edited by J. S. Turner, vol. 3, pp. 717–718. London, 1996.

Spanel, Donald B. "Beni Hasan in the Herakleopolitan Period." Ph.D. diss., University of Toronto, 1984.

Spanel, Donald B. "Boat Models of the Herakleopolitan Period and the Eleventh Dynasty." *Studien zur Altägyptischen Kultur* 13 (1985), 243–253.

Willems, Harco O. *Chests of Life: A Study of the Typology and Conceptual Development of Middle Kingdom Standard Class Coffins.* Mededelingen en Verhandelingen van het Vooraziatisch-Egyptisch Genootschap "Ex Oriente Lux," 25. Leiden, 1988.

DONALD B. SPANEL

**BERSHEH,** village across from present-day Mallawi (province el-Minia), on the eastern side of the Nile River. Deir el-Bersheh (often called Bersheh or el-Bersheh), is a large cemetery of ancient Egypt. At its center—at the mouth of the Wadi Deir en-Nakhla, to the east of the village—were found some shaft tombs. Other cemeteries on the desert edge stretch from the mouth of the wadi to below the modern village. The administrators of the fifteenth Upper Egyptian nome (the Hare nome) whose seat was in Hermopolis (modern Ashmunein) were buried in the rock-cut necropolis behind Bersheh during the Old and Middle Kingdoms. The necropolis for the city of Hermopolis, which probably served as a cemetery for commoners as well, was accessible via a natural waterway from the city to the ferry station near the present-day town of Rairamun beri Mallawi. During the Old Kingdom, this site was used more frequently than the necropolis farther south, near Sheikh Said, which had been established by those who were sent to Hermopolis from the royal residence.

Bersheh was first explored in 1891 and 1892 by the

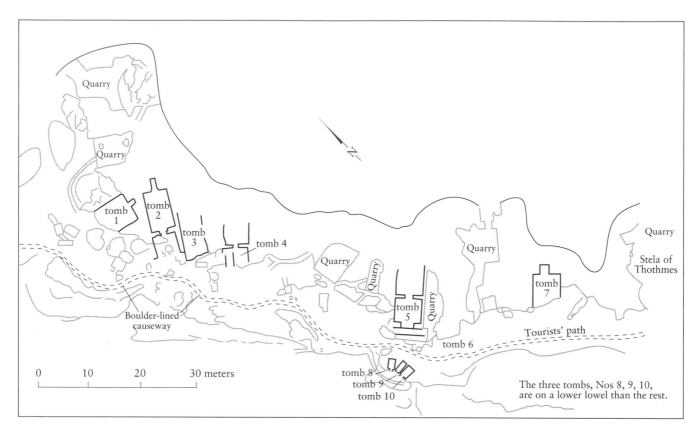

Quarry

Quarry

tomb 1

tomb 2

tomb 3

tomb 4

Quarry

Quarry

Quarry

Quarry

tomb 5

tomb 6

tomb 7

Quarry

Stela of Thothmes

Tourists' path

Boulder-lined causeway

0   10   20   30 meters

tomb 8
tomb 9
tomb 10

The three tombs, Nos 8, 9, 10, are on a lower lowel than the rest.

BERSHEH. *Plan of the tomb-chapels.*

Egypt Exploration Fund under G. W. Fraser. In subsequent years, the tombs were frequently plundered, so many objects were transported from them into various Western museums. Under Daressy and Kamal, the Egypt Exploration Fund tried to fight that development by carrying out official excavations, from 1897 to 1902. In 1915, a further exploration was undertaken by Harvard University with G. Reisner as director; the beautifully painted coffin of the nomarch Thoth-nakht (tomb 5), now in the Museum of Fine Arts, Boston, was recovered during that dig. From 1970 to 1980, the Egyptian Exploration Fund carried out several smaller digs in the flat necropolis area that was threatened by the expanding village. The shaft tombs at the mouth of the wadi have been explored anew since 1988, the old plans have been updated, and corrected copies of the texts have been produced. Among the new findings were, for example, sections of the autobiography of the nomarch Aha-nakht II, who probably also supervised the economically important quarries as "Chief of the Desert" and "Overseer of the Hunters." The new explorations have as long-term goals not only a modern archaeological description but also the creations of an art historical record and an analysis of the tomb decorations. The exploration was at first coordinated by the Depart-

ment of Egyptology of the University of Leiden (Netherlands), then by the international cooperation of the Netherlands Institute in Cairo, the Boston Museum of Fine Arts, and the University Museum at the University of Pennsylvania (under E. Brovarski, R. Freed, D. P. Silverman, H. Willems, R. van Walsem, and others).

Parallel to the work on the tombs, efforts continue to date and establish the chronology of Bersheh's decorated, box-shaped coffins that were dispersed in the various museums; they came from the tombs of the nomarchs, their administrators, and the attendant higher echelon of officials—and all contained Coffin Text spells (excerpts from the funeral spells used in the royal tombs at Memphis). A debate still surrounds the somewhat doubtful hypothesis that the Coffin Texts also contain aspects of the local theology, from the nearby Thoth temple at Hermopolis. Bersheh's very delicate coffin paintings have characteristic and extraordinary contrasting colors.

Some seventy small and plain shaft tombs were located along the southern side of the wadi. Many of those mostly uninscribed tombs have been destroyed. They were used for the burial of lower officials from Hermopolis and were dated from the Old Kingdom's fifth to sixth dynasties or from the First Intermediate Period. Other groups of shaft tombs from the Old Kingdom were located along the northern side; there was also found the rock-inscribed decree of Horus Nefer-khau (probably the pharaoh Nefer-irkare Kakai of the fifth dynasty) addressed to a Hermopolitan priestly official called Ia-ib. The best known tombs are the elaborately decorated group belonging to the nomarchs of the Middle Kingdom, situated on the northern side, high above the floor of the wadi. Those large shaft tombs consist mostly of two chambers or of a single chamber with a niche in the rear wall. The imagery is traditional in theme, depicting mostly hunting, birding, and fishing scenes, but scenes were also included of bullfighting and wrestling, as well as images of mythical animals such as the griffin. The tomb of the nomarch Thoth-hotep (tomb 2) was unusual, in that it contained an illustration of the transport of a 6-meter-high (19-foot) colossal statue—probably the king—from the calcite (Egyptian alabaster) quarries at Hatnub, using teams of laborers.

The dates and chronology of the nomarchs of Hermopolis are still under discussion, and according to some studies, the chronology of documented nomarch tombs begins with Aha-nahkt I (tomb 5), the son of a Thoth-nahkt who probably served during the Middle Kingdom reign of Montuhotep I or II of the eleventh dynasty. The nomarch title remained in the same family until the time of Senwosret III of the twelfth dynasty. Nomarchs of the Hare nome were probably still buried at Deir el-Bersheh under Amenemhet III and even later. Brovarski (1981 and 1992) mentioned a nomarch Upauaut-hotep, whose placement in the chronology cannot yet be established; that nomarch was mentioned on a seal, now at the Oriental Institute Museum, Chicago (no. 18647). The nomarchs of Hermopolis served also as high priests of the local Thoth temple. The early nomarchs enjoyed a measure of political independence, as was the case with Neheri I (tomb 4), who used military force to become involved in the succession struggle at the beginning of the twelfth dynasty; probably, he supported the later pharaoh Amenemhet I. That nomarch had his own official count of years, but later members of the family, by contrast, were subservient to the all-powerful royal court.

After the Middle Kingdom, Bersheh's cemetery seems to have been abandoned and the inhabitants of Hermopolis were buried to the west, near Tuna el-Gebel, at the beginning of the eighteenth dynasty; then, quarrying near the mouth of the wadi during the New Kingdom changed the landscape drastically. A rock stela is preserved on the northern side from Thutmose III and another stela from Amenophis III is on the south side. Both kings quarried the fossil-rich limestone on the edge of the wadi for their new additions to the Thoth temple in Hermopolis. The gallery quarries of Amenhotpe III, to the south, reach to depths of 250 meters (760 feet) in the rock. Farther along in the wadi, Demotic inscriptions were found in the quarry caves, where cartouches mention Nektanebo I of the thirtieth dynasty. The work in the quarries came to an end just before Roman times. The village of Bersheh seems to be of Roman origin, judging from the surface finds of broken pottery. During the Early Christian period, Coptic monks occupied many of the older quarry caves and the pharaonic rock-cut tombs near Bersheh, where many of their crosses and benedictions cover the "heathen" images of their predecessors.

## BIBLIOGRAPHY

Brovarski, E. "Ahanakht of Bersheh and the Hare Nome in the First Intermediate Period." *Studies in Ancient Egypt, the Aegean, and the Sudan,* edited by W. K. Simpson and W. M. Davis, pp. 14–30. Boston, 1981. On the unpublished excavations of Reisner.

Brovarski, E., et al. *Bersheh Reports I: Report of the 1990 Field Season of the Joint Expedition of the Museum of Fine Arts, Boston, University Museum, University of Pennsylvania, Leiden University.* Boston, 1992. A recent report on work in the necropolis.

Griffith, Francis, Ll., and Percy Newberry. *El Bersheh.* London, 1893–1894. The fundamental monograph.

Klemm, Rosemarie, and Dietrich D. Klemm. *Steine und Steinbrüche im Alten Ägypten,* pp. 118–124. Berlin and New York, 1993. On the stone quarries in ancient Egypt.

Terrace, Edward L. B. *Egyptian Paintings of the Middle Kingdom: The Tomb of Djehuty-Nekht.* New York, 1968. Covers the sarcophagus of Thot-nakht.

Willems, Harco. "The Nomarchs of the Hare Nome and Early Middle Kingdom History." *Phoenix: Jaarbericht van het Voorariatisch-Egyptisch Genootschap "Ex Orient Lux"* 28 (1983–1984), 80–102. On the geneaology of the nomarchs.

Willems, Harco. *The Chests of Life: A Study of the Typology and Conceptual Development of Middle Kingdom Standard Class Coffins,* pp. 68–78. Mededelingen en verhandelingen van het Voorariatischen-Egyptisch Genootschap "Ex Oriente Lux," 25. Leiden, 1988. For the geneaology of the nomarchs, see p. 71.

Willems, Harco. "Deir el-Bersheh: Preliminary Report." *Göttinger Miszellen* 110 (1989), 75–83. A recent report on work in the necropolis.

Zimmer, T. "La Moyenne Égypte: Methodes d'investigation, bibliographiques et priorités." *Bulletin Société francaise d'égyptologie: Réunions trimestrielles et communications d'archéologie* 96 (1983), 22–25. A summary of older archaeological works.

DIETER KESSLER

**BES.** The image of the deity Bes is both comic and appalling, to disarm malevolent spirits. Often represented full-faced under the more or less composite aspect of a bandy-legged gnome with a grotesque lionlike face, he might be winged, with protruding tongue, wearing a headdress of high feathers. His apotropaic (protective) power was strengthened by the musical instruments and weapons he brandished. His iconography and the very name of Bes are, respectively, attested in the New Kingdom and the twenty-first dynasty. Moreover, not until the Ptolemaic

BES. *Relief sculpture of Bes at Edfu.* (Courtesy David P. Silverman)

period is this iconography unambiguously linked in inscriptions, to the name of Bes.

Possibly, Bes was but an avatar of an ancient deity called Aha, "the fighter," who was represented on the magical ivory wands of the Middle Kingdom. Made for the protection of children, those objects often included images with an attitude and features similar to that of Bes. Even in Greco-Roman inscriptions, Bes still had names that seem derived from Aha. Several similar lionlike genii may have originally existed, but they were later confused with one another. Alternatively, this diversity reflects local or functional differences of a unique type.

The name Bes may be connected with *bs₃* ("to guard," "protect"), reflecting an obvious function of the god, or it might correspond to a rare ancient word that denoted a premature child, a weak and stunted being, perhaps related to an image of the sun or moon as it comes into being; the figure of Bes would then be the apotropaic transfiguration. The functions of Bes ranged from those of a familiar protecting genius to that of a divinity integrated in the solar cycle. A popular deity, he protected during birth, childhood, sleep, and eroticism, and his image, therefore, was put on numerous amulets and objects of everyday life, such as beds, mirrors, and toilet articles. His figure was painted on the walls of the royal palace of Amenhotpe III, as well as on those of craftsmen's houses.

Bes has been linked with Egypt's far South, not because of a Nubian origin but because of his role in the myth of the distant goddess, in which his dancing and music must convince the rebellious divinity to return to Egypt. Bes also participated in the Hathor myth as part of her entourage. There, Bes could protect the solar child, young Horus (i.e., Horpakhered, Harpocrates), thus moving from the familiar genius of popular beliefs to a guardian of the divine heir in the solar theology. That role, first clearly attested in the decoration of lotiform chalices of the twenty-second dynasty, later appeared in reliefs in the *mammisi*s (birth-houses). References to it are seen on some statuettes showing Harpocrates and his tutor together or in the presence of Bes' mask, at the top of the *cippi* (stela) of Horus standing on the crocodiles.

Associated with the child Horus, Bes gradually assumed that god's aspect and nature—as Isis' son and as an incarnation of the renewed sun—under the name of Horbes. If Bes was indeed the incarnation of a premature child, that syncretism was made possible by the myth in which Horus himself was a premature and weak newborn; that relationship was illustrated in the representations of Bes-Harpokrates, as well as in scenes where Bes appeared in the company of animals linked to the solar cycle (lions, apes, oryx, and falcons). Sharing intimately, then, in the nature of Horus, Bes sealed new alliances with several gods that have been interpreted as hypostases of Horus, such as Soped, Nefertum, Horus-Min, and Hormerty. Furthermore, the head of Bes appeared atop a series of composite figures (usually called pantheistic Bes), which incarnated the omnipotence of the solar gods. The metamorphosis of Bes to the young solar Horus may also explain the birth of Beset, who was thought to be the mother of that exceptional child.

### BIBLIOGRAPHY

Altenmüller, Hartwig. "Bes." In *Lexikon der Ägyptologie*, 1: 720–723. Wiesbaden, 1975.

Dasen, Véronique. *Dwarfs in Ancient Egypt and Greece*, pp. 55–83. Oxford, 1993.

Malaise, Michel. "Bès et les croyances solaires." *Studies in Egyptology: Presented to Miriam Lichtheim*, edited by Sarah Israelit-Groll, pp. 680–729. Jerusalem, 1990.

Meeks, Dimitri. "Le nom du dieu Bès et ses implications mythologiques." *The Intellectual Heritage of Egypt: Studies Presented to Laszlo Kakosy*. edited by Ulrich Luft, pp. 423–436. Budapest, 1992.

Romano, James, F. "The Origin of the Bes-Image." *Bulletin of the Egyptological Seminar* 2 (1980), 39–56.

Tran tam Tinh, Vincent. "Bes." *Lexicon Iconographicum Mythologiae Classicae*, edited by Hans Christoph Ackerman and Jean-Robert Gislerl, vol. 3, pp. 98–108. Zurich, 1986.

Volokhine, Youri. "Dieux, masques et hommes: à propos de l'iconographie de Bès." *Bulletin de la Société d'égypotologie de Genève* 18 (1994), 81–95.

MICHEL MALAISE
Translated from French by Paule Mertens-Fonck

**BIBLICAL TRADITION.** Ancient Egypt (Heb., *misrayim*) was given a significant place in biblical tradition. In *Genesis*, the "sons of Misraim" were the descendants of Noah and his son Ham (*Gn.* 10.6–14); the "sons of Misraim" were then divided into geographical units, such as the Patrusim (Upper Egypt) and the Naphtuhim (Lower Egypt). Abraham, the ancestral Patriarch, left the Sumerian city of Ur and went to Egypt (with his beautiful wife Sarah, who was presented his sister); but she was taken by Pharaoh's men, who brought her to the royal court, and she was married to Pharaoh—all in an attempt to keep Abraham from coming to harm. When Pharaoh discovered the deception, he graciously sent Sarah back to Abraham and they suffered no negative consequences (*Gn.* 12.10–20). Tales about the later Israelites in Egypt culminate in the story of Joseph and his brothers who moved to Egypt (*Gn.* 39–50). That move led to the era of the Israelites as slaves in Egypt, building the pyramids, and finding help from the Israelite-Egyptian Moses, who was saved as an infant from a basket in the Nile and raised in the palace by a princess, a "daughter of Pharaoh" (*Ex.* 2.1–10). The Israelites needed both Moses and divine intervention to flee from Egypt, and in their Exodus left Pharaoh's armies dead beneath the waters of the Red Sea, which returned after a divine parting made good their escape (*Ex.* 12–15). They then wandered for forty years in the desert before arriving in Canaan, the land promised to them by God.

Historical-biblical exegesis has been skeptical about the idea, commonly appearing in several biblical texts, of a united people of Israel and their predecessors being in contact with Egypt. In scholarly discussion, however, until now both *pro* and *contra* arguments have been recognized concerning critical views of the biblical material. It has become necessary to combine the literary analysis of biblical texts with the spectrum of extrabiblical information on the early conditions of a developing Israel in the region of Palestine. A general view of such development would describe the role of Egypt as a dominant factor in the time of early Israel. The only extrabiblical mention of Israel known to us, so far, is on the famous nineteenth dynasty Stela of Merenptah, which provides no information about any period of Israel's predecessors or about any kind of Exodus from Egypt.

Most of Israel's later population might actually have had its origin in its own country and the surrounding region. Only a small population—possibly those belonging to the so-called Shasu-bedouins, who came from desert regions, plus some parts of the so-called Aperu-groups, who lived in the countryside beyond the urban centers—could have been the bearers of experiences with Egypt, at least until the Ramessid era. Even these peoples could have merely laid claim to tales and memories of quasi-mythical persons—like Abraham, Isaac, Jacob, and Joseph—names with equivalencies among those used during the first half of the second millennium BCE in Syria–Palestine (see the Execration Texts, Hyksos names, Amarna Letters, toponym lists, and so forth). Such figures probably had a functional relevance and so became prototypic figures in the collective memory. No other way can be suggested by me, concerning Moses and the Exodus itself—although the name Moses is certainly Egyptian, not Hebrew. Thus we have to explain the Exodus using some historical allusions to both flight and repulsion, and they are bound together in a compound literary illustration of a spectacular event.

Moses might have been, like his predecessors and "fathers," an example of a paradigmatic image—a mediator between Near Easterners and Egyptians. There have indeed been some historical relationships enacted by well-known Semitic-Egyptian politicians, such as Bija/Beja and Ramesemperre, from the later Ramessid times in Egypt. The main function of Moses, as reflected in biblical tradition, was his role as an intercessor between his people and his God, and that cannot be checked against any information from outside the Bible.

The biblical traditions that relate the geographical, historical, cultural, and religious neighborhood of Israel and Egypt are mainly connected to a network of political correspondence during Egypt's Third Intermediate Period (1100–750 BCE), which was coterminous with the founding of the kingdoms of Israel and Judah. A very important source for identifying and interpreting biblical metaphors can be the iconography of the numerous seals and amulets that have been found in Israel. The mainstream of pre-exile Patriarchal stories should be understood as literary reactions, or answers, to the self-manifesting behavior of political power during the period of the early Israelite kingdom. In spite of the crucial problems related to the existence of a newly united kingdom, especially under King David, it may be of interest that the idea of unification in the southern state of Judah and the northern state of ancient Israel, was, to a certain extent, comparable to the important Egyptian idea of the Unification of the Two Lands. King Solomon's connections both to Phoenicia and to Egypt's twenty-first dynasty seem to have historical cultural, and religious value—and this basic period for Israel may have furthered the beginning of an international correspondence. It may well be that the beginning of biblical literary work had for background the memory of the 922 BCE secession of the southern kingdom of Judah—in looking at their political decisions, foreign affairs, and contacts.

Ancient Israel's retrospective on the past, partly preserved in the so-called Yahwistic texts, delineates the Patriarchs Abraham and Jacob as figures opposed to the bearers of actual political power. The time of the Patriarchs appears as a fictive period, offering an alternative to the politics present, mainly in the southern kingdom of Judah. A re-reading of the pre-exile *Exodus* texts is needed, because Solomon and his successors may be seen as kings, like the pharaoh who oppressed his people. Even the texts about the paradise of Eden and the original sin of Adam, as the first human being (*Gn.* 2–3), seem to offer some judgments about the dangerous influence that may originate in the home region, where official wisdom and teaching are based. It cannot be forgotten that Solomon's marriage with a "daughter of Pharaoh"—not his activities in building a palace for her near the Temple area (1 *Kgs.* 9.24)—was the special sin in the eyes of Yahwistic traditionalists. Similarly, even behind the wife of "Adam" (like King Solomon), a foreign personality appeared—the serpent of the paradise story, who possibly reflected Egyptian wisdom (the striking cobra of royalty, as used in the *uraeus* crown) or images concerning the *maat* ("truth" or "justice").

Sheshonq I, founder of the twenty-second dynasty (r. 931–910 BCE), seems to have received one of the adversaries of Solomon, Jeroboam, after his flight to Egypt. Later, Jeroboam became the first king of the northern kingdom of Israel. The reasons that led Sheshonq to mount a major campaign to Palestine are somewhat obscure (according to 1 *Kgs.* 14.26) in the fifth year of the reign of Solomon's son Rehoboam. Possibly, the pharaoh wanted to tread in the steps of his famous predecessors, with their military expeditions to Syria and Palestine during the eighteenth dynasty and the nineteenth. Possibly, Sheshonq was angry about a potentially reunited kingdom in Israel. Sheshonq then took away the treasures of Solomon's Temple and those of his palace. At Karnak, a toponym list was engraved on the southern temple wall, near the Bubastite door, and it may be regarded as attesting the king's route, although there is neither certainty nor common opinion about the real function of the list, its structure, or its tendencies. In any case, no spectacular changes occurred in the political conditions of the two kingdoms.

The prophets of Judah during the ninth and eighth centuries BCE presented themselves as great opponents to coalition with Egypt; it was the time of the twenty-fifth dynasty and the twenty-sixth—the Kushites and the Saites—in Egypt and of growing Assyrian hegemony in the Near East. Isaiah, a prophet contemporary with the Judean king, Hezekiah, did not sympathize with official politics, because he appreciated the extent of Assyrian supremacy. His speech therefore emphasized the Egyptian (Kushite) weakness, which would deprive any flight or campaign to Egypt of success and would disappoint Judeans looking for military engagement against the Assyrians. His most important argument was Israel's position as "the chosen people of God." Therefore, he promotes faithful reliance only on God to stabilize the kingdom in Jerusalem by his own power (*Is.* 30.15–17). Like the *Book of Isaiah* (especially chapters 18–20), the books of *Jeremiah* and *Ezekiel* argue against the Egyptians and their main cities in Upper and Lower Egypt, where refugees from Judah had settled (see *Jer.* 31.1–3; 46.1–26; and *Ezek.* 30–32). The reign of the "Ethiopians" (the Kushites)—Shabaqa with his campaign to Eltekeh in 701 BCE, Shabtaqa (his name was preserved in Israel as that of a Kushite tribe), and Taharqa (Tirhaka in the Bible)—accompanies the fragile history of the kingdom of Judah. For Judah, no substantial help against the Assyrians came from the Kushites.

The Saite period that followed the Kushite presented itself as an era of renaissance, and it seems to hold a certain fascination for Egypt's neighbors. The famous Joseph story, initially drafted during that time, leads us into Egypt's new era with an optimistic view of the Egyptian way of life. There, political interests had their chance to demonstrate the capacity of international relations in receiving the witness of great human experience. Israelite-Egyptian contacts during the existence of the northern kingdom of Samaria created the atmosphere in which the Joseph story may have had its origin. The Judean reception in Egypt, after the fall of Samaria in 722 BCE, led to the enlargement of the story, together with a good deal of imagination, and the fantasy of a redactor who was familiar with Egyptian titles and the way of life. The inventiveness of the author led him not only to create Egyptian-style names and titles but also to use genuine terminology (e.g., for the process of embalming, a term was used that corresponded to the activity of Egyptian women assisting in the funereal process of preparing the body).

During the later kingdom in Judah, further influence from Egypt came to the Levant—mostly, but not exclusively, by way of Phoenicia. Some traces of the phraseology of Egyptian kingship may be found in biblical narrative, as in *2 Samuel* 7 or *1 Kings* 3 and 5–15 with some elements of the so-called king's novel (or "prince's novel"), and some in Hebrew poetic literature. So the phrase "You are my son; today I have begotten you" (*Ps.* 2.7) recalls similar declarations in the inscriptions at the temple of Abydos. The beginning of Psalm 110 uses mythological elements that originated in Egyptian images of the king's dominion over his enemies. The imagery chosen in Psalm 8 leads us into Egyptian kingship as transformed by expressions that praise the role of every man. The metaphors in Psalm 104 have been long discussed as similar to the famous Amarna hymns to the sun god; those may be founded in early connections between the court of pre-Israelite Jerusalem and the Egyptian kings, but it is easier to understand it as a product of Egyptian influence via Phoenicia. A lot of words and expressions relating to architecture, trade, clothing, the cultic sphere, and daily activities found their way into Hebrew, both in the vernacular and the literary languages. The most interesting phenomenon can be seen in the borrowing and transliteration into Hebrew of foreign words whose translation was immediately based on an Egyptian title. So some curious names, such as Tahpenes, Genubat, or Goliath, may be best understood as simple titles of Egyptian origin. Titles for the Hebrew God also have their Egyptian counterparts—so the well-known Hebrew *zebaot* may be related to the Egyptian *db₃* ("he who is sitting on a throne; the enthroned one"), and Hebrew *shaddai* has a possible relation to Egyptian *šd* ("saviour").

Josiah, the great reformer on the king's throne in Jerusalem, seems to be the great tragic figure in Egyptian-Judean connections. His zeal to fulfill the laws of *Deuteronomy* led him to struggle against the Assyrians' influence in Jerusalem but prevented him from finding common interests with Egypt. He came to his death by opposing Necho II (r. 610–595 BCE) near Megiddo in 609 BCE; the detailed circumstances are not known. The second king to succeed Necho, Haaibre Apries (Hofra in the Bible), is known only in biblical texts, as "the one who attempted to lift the siege of Jerusalem" (*Jer.* 37.5–11). With the Saites on the Egyptian throne, the period of biblical association came to an end. After returning from the Babylonian Exile in 538 BCE, the renewed nation of Israel (and Judaism) had to deal mostly with internal affairs, so international contacts and foreign affairs counted for little for a time.

There are some critical aspects concerning Egypt in the later writing of biblical history. *Deuteronomy* and the priestly texts from the Babylonian Exile and from postexile times give the impression that the Hebrews' faith in the God of Israel resulted in his dominating the gods of Egypt and all pharaonic power. The main content of such biblical ideas concerning Egypt can be found in the *Exodus* formula and in several variations. Here the one God of Israel is presented as their saviour from Egypt, "the house of servitude." The early priestly texts, however, dealing with constructs of creation, seem to be influenced by Egyptian ideas of creation, including the realization of a chaotic, pre-World situation. The so-called Memphite Theology (the late eighth-century BCE commentary, written on stone)—referring to the god Ptah as creator of the world by his word alone, together with conceptions of the god Amun—most likely stands behind the biblical creation story in *Genesis*. The priestly redaction strengthens the monotheistic view of God creating light by his word (*Gn.* 1.3–5). The description of men and women as made in the image of God has parallels in Egyptian phrases relating the king to the image of their chief god. In biblical context, however, every man and woman qualified as an image of God. In that case, the longstanding contacts of the Jerusalem priesthood must be acknowledged with their Egyptian collegues of the cultic centers, such as Memphis and Heliopolis in the Nile Delta. In the view of a learned Judean priest, the Exodus would have occurred in a geographic area familiar to the author. In the time of Jeremiah, such relations were shown by the presence of Egyptian names in the Judean administration, such as Pashhur ("the son of Horus"). Some priestly families must also have had cultural exchanges in late pre-exilic times.

Since pre-Solomonic times, Egyptian wisdom entered into the Judean and Israelite cultural sphere. Egyptian teachings, especially the famous *Instructions of Amenemope*, show affinities with collections of proverbs, such as the biblical *Book of Proverbs*, where chapters 22.17 to 24.22 seem to follow an Egyptian prototype. There, and elsewhere in the Hebrew scriptures, the ideas of Egyptian wisdom and justice were represented by many Hebrew expressions. For example, the *Song of Songs* reveals metaphors and similes strongly familiar with Egyptian illustrations; despite problems in determining its date of origin, the songs in part remember some early imagery of international peace (as between King Solomon and his beloved, a royal woman from an African land). There may have been a collective memory of peace, as described by the two lovers. That imagery as a vision of humanity may have served as a kind of literary opposition against actual threats from the east, serving as a model for later times, too.

In the New Testament, the holy family of Mary, Joseph, and Jesus leaves Roman-occupied Palestine to spend time in Egypt, because the Romans' puppet-king Herod is persecuting them (*Mt.* 2.13–15). This Midrash-like story recalls that Jesus is part of the people of Israel coming back to Egypt. Then the words of the Hebrew prophet Hoseah find a genuine interpretation: "From Egypt I have called my son" (*Hos.* 11.1), which partly verifies the Messiah prophesy.

[*See also* Exodus; Islam and Ancient Egypt; Joseph; *and* Moses.]

### BIBLIOGRAPHY

Görg, Manfred. *Aegyptiaca-Biblica. Notizen und Beiträge zu den Beziehungen zwischen Ägypten und Israel.* Wiesbaden, 1991.

Görg, Manfred. *Studien zur biblisch-ägyptischen Religionsgeschichte.* Stuttgart, 1992.

Görg, Manfred. *Mythos, Glaube und Geschichte. Die Bilder des christlichen Credo und ihre Wurzeln im alten Ägypten.* 2d ed. Düsseldorf, 1993.

Görg, Manfred. *Die Beziehungen zwischen dem alten Israel und Ägypten. Von den Anfängen bis zum Exil.* Darmstadt, 1997.

Keel, Othmar. *Die Welt der altorientalischen Bildsymbolik und das Alte Testament. Am Beispiel der Psalmen.* 2d ed. Zurich, 1977. (English Translation, New York, 1978.)

Keel, Othmar. *Jahwes Entgegnung an Ijob. Eine Deutung von Ijob 38–41 vor dem Hintergrund der zeitgenössischen Bildkunst.* Göttingen, 1978.

Keel, Othmar, and Christoph Uehlinger. *Göttinnen, Götter und Gottessymbole. Neue Erkenntnisse zur Religionsgeschichte Kanaans und Israels aufgrund bislang unerschlossener ikonographischer Quellen.* 2d ed. Freiburg, 1993.

Kitchen, Kenneth A. *The Third Intermediate Period in Egypt, 1100–650 B.C.* Warminster, 1972.

Pfeifer, Gerhard. *Ägypten im Alten Testament.* Munich, 1995.

Redford, Donald B. *Egypt, Canaan and Israel in Ancient Times.* Princeton, 1992.

Römheld, Dietmar. *Wege der Weisheit. Die Lehren Amenemopes und Proverbien 22,17–24,22.* Berlin and New York, 1989.

MANFRED GÖRG

**BIOGRAPHIES.** In contrast to the autobiographies known in Western cultures, ancient Egyptian "autobiographies" are texts that characterize official persons, summarize their professional careers, or describe noteworthy episodes in their lives. Aiming at the untarnished appraisal of society and the gods' world, they present the individual in perfect harmony with the ideals and expectations of the upper class. Since Egyptian autobiographies are closely linked to the social as well as the public lifestyle of the political and administrative elites, self-representations of women are rare. Owing to its func-

tional limitations, this genre seldom touches on intellectual and emotional aspects or gives an insight into private life before the Hellenistic and Roman periods. This can be related to the role of the individual as perceived in pharaonic Egypt and in the ancient Near Eastern world in general, where identity was understood primarily as a reflection of the cultural and social context, rather than as an expression of individual values such as personality and the self. Egyptian autobiographies can appear on tomb walls, stelae, statues, rock inscriptions, and later also on temple walls and sarcophagi. In accordance with their context in the funerary cult and the limits of the available space for inscriptions, these texts tend to be condensed rather than elaborated. Distinct from other text genres in their extensive use, autobiographies occur throughout Egyptian history. With their strong focus on contemporary history and the elites' cultural values, careers, and social attitudes, they can reflect social history and, to a more limited extent, political processes. In addition, autobiographies interrelate with other genres of Egyptian literature such as royal "historiography," literary narratives, and Wisdom Texts. If seen in the broader cultural context of the ancient Near East, where the autobiographical genre never fully developed, Egyptian autobiography also provides information on the basic differences between Egyptian and Near Eastern societies.

**Characteristics of the Genre.** Egyptologists face two main problems when they apply the term autobiography to the Egyptian material: the texts' authorship and their formal and thematic organization.

The presentation of the author is a relatively late phenomenon in ancient Egyptian literature; the concept of authorship appeared at a time when Egyptian culture developed a sense of its own historical and literary heritage, in the Ramessid period. Yet even after this breakthrough, what a text thematizes is generally its protagonist rather than its author. In Egyptian autobiographies, the narrator, who is also the protagonist of the self-presentation, usually speaks in the first person; therefore, the texts are labeled "autobiographies" rather than "biographies," even though the true author remains unknown. Egyptian autobiography developed varying stylistic, formal, and thematic patterns in different historical periods. Soon after its establishment within funerary culture (at the end of the fifth dynasty), an artistic tradition evolved that can be related to specific writing skills and the tendency to formal and phraseological stereotypes. Yet some texts, especially during the Middle Kingdom, emphasize such qualities as eloquence and rhetorical sophistication. They suggest that perhaps the protagonist may have been the composer. Other representational inscriptions, in contrast, point out that they were produced at the instigation of a person different from the protagonist of the text—for example a son, spouse, or successor in office—even though they use the first person as the voice of the protagonist. These texts represent the type of the "allobiography."

Egyptian self-presentations stress the authenticity and the validity of the statements they contain; these include explicit affirmations of what is recorded and denials of any exaggeration or untruthfulness. These phrases are often accompanied by a direct address to the public, which soon became formalized as a constant element of autobiographical writing, the so-called appeal to the living. It usually includes a command to perform an offering: "Now as for all people who shall harken to this stela, who are among the living and shall say 'It is true', . . . you shall say 'Bread, beer, beef, fowl, food offerings to the owner of this stela' " (autobiography of Monthweser).

Ancient Egyptian culture never produced true "biographies"—that is, nonfictional life-stories and character studies adopting the third person, as was the case, for example, in ancient Greece and Rome. Egyptian autobiographies do not display the individual's exceptionality as a means of self-promotion only, but rather as one of seeking recognition and commemoration in present and future times. The primary intent was to secure the maintenance of the funerary cult. In later periods autobiographies, especially those of priests, temple administrators, and religious persons, were also linked to the gods' cults and enjoyed circulation in the temples.

As for the thematic structure of the texts, ancient Egyptian self-presentations include additional text units that are not directly associated with the primary topic of the praise of the individual: for example, offering formulas; curses against trespassers into the tomb and violators of the inscription; the appeal to the living; hymns, prayers, and invocations to the gods or afterlife wishes and so-called transfiguration spells, that is, spells that were thought to assist the deceased in becoming a member of the gods' sphere. Also, the autobiographical part could be reduced to only a few phrases or sentences. Thus, autobiographies are not homogeneous pieces of literature; rather, they are compositions that consist of different elements embedded into a common framework.

**Discourse Types.** Throughout its history, the Egyptian autobiography encompassed different modes of presentation and a diversity of topics. Apart from passages addressing the audience directly, the texts describe and list rather than narrate, since their primary intent was to give a complete account of the person's qualities and lifetime as well as of the situations and events surrounding it. Therefore, they often rely on repetition as a prominent stylistic device.

The general presentation of careers linked to different phases of a lifetime can, however, show a very loose narra-

tive organization. In such texts, coherence can be maintained by the chronological order of the report, which could otherwise lack any explicit sign of internal logic and cohesiveness:

> [A child born by his mother in] the time of (king) Menkaure, raised among the king's children in the royal palace, . . . , more appreciated before the king than any other child, Ptahshepses. [A boy knotting the belt in] the time of (king) Shepseskaf, raised among the king's children in the royal palace, . . . , more appreciated before the king than any other youth, Ptahshepses. (autobiography of Ptahshepses)

True narrative sequences, in contrast, pervade autobiography only sporadically, when a specific event in the owner's life was considered important enough to be included:

> Then the ruler of Qadesh let run out a mare, and she ran very quickly on her legs. She ran into the army. (But) I ran after her on my feet with my short sword and ripped her body open. I cut her tail and presented it to the king. (autobiography of Amenemheb).

Being at the interface of nonfictional historiographical and fictional narrative writing, such examples rely on both real life experiences and their simulation in order to elicit emotional reactions in the reader.

**Text Types.** There are four types of Egyptian autobiographies with varying degrees of documentation and popularity throughout time. The first, the "historical autobiography," records episodes from the life of an official and illustrates the entwinement of personal success and social recognition. The most important sign of social distinction is provided by the positive reaction—rewards, promotions, etc.—of the king, or, from the New Kingdom onward, of a god as universal arbitrator and benefactor. Flourishing especially during the Old and the New Kingdoms, this genre represents a source for historical data in different domains.

The "reflective autobiography," most common during the Old Kingdom, propagates the ethical rules of the elite. The image developed in these texts is based on the protagonist's capability to fulfill his social and moral responsibilities, especially concerning the middle and lower classes, while denying any misbehavior. Since the texts tend to formulate universal values regarding human relations, they often display a didactic or even apologetic tone.

Although this type was rather neglected during the following periods, religion offered new ideas for the reflective autobiography during the New Kingdom, for example, the correct performance of priestly functions. This development prepared the ground for a new, manneristic text type, the "confessional autobiography." In disregard of the established canons of previous autobiographical writing, these texts hypostasize the individual's change of life as a result of the king's or a god's intervention. This topic also dominates the text structure: formally and thematically, the confessions are closer to hymns than to traditional autobiographies. They appear for the first time during the reign of Akhenaten and continue in the Ramessid period.

The fourth type, the "encomiastic autobiography," was especially popular during the Middle and the early New Kingdom. These texts prefer short nominal sentences, which make the arrangement of themes and motives extremely flexible. Professional success and social status are again prominent topics, with the difference, however, that autobiography now shows a strong sense of self-initiative, whereas Old Kingdom texts stressed a total dependence on the king.

The emergence of new autobiographical types was always mirrored by cultural changes. Throughout Egyptian history, however, established text types continued to exist beyond their period of most frequent use.

**Historical Development.** The Old Kingdom saw the contemporary emergence of the historical and the reflective autobiography. They can be seen as a monarchical society's first reflections on itself, the individual, and history. The stone-built tomb, the elite's most explicit monument of success and status, granted and equipped by the king, was both the source of inspiration and the theme of autobiographical writing. In the beginning, historical autobiographies are confined to the construction of the tomb, with the king as main figure of the narrative, whereas early reflective autobiography focuses on the individual's involvement in that process, the rightful acquisition of the tomb, and the fair treatment of the workmen. Soon the practice of ethical perfection within a specific cultural situation expanded into behavioral rules of a universal nature, often expressed in formulaic prose: "I am one who speaks the good, repeats what is liked. I never spoke evil against anyone to a potentate, for I wished to stand well with the Great God. I have given bread to the hungry, clothes to the naked, and never judged between two parties in a manner depriving a son of his father's property" (autobiography of Pepinakht-Heqaib). This development strongly influenced the emergence of Wisdom Literature, the so-called Instructions, at the beginning of the Middle Kingdom.

At the same time, the historical autobiography also shifted to a stronger emphasis on the tomb owner: posthumous records of the circumstances of his death and his burial are gradually replaced by the narration of events that affected the official's life. The most famous examples of Old Kingdom historical autobiographies are the inscriptions of Herkhuf, director of many trade missions to Nubia, and Weni, high official at court, who presided over a trial involving the royal harem, commanded military campaigns against a Palestinian enemy, and directed several expeditions: "Told there were marauders among these foreigners at the 'nose of the Gazelle's-head,' I crossed in ships with these troops. I made a landing in the back of the height of the mountain range, to the north of the land of the Sand-dwellers, while half of this army was on the road. I came and caught them all and slew every marauder among them" (autobiography of Weni).

Autobiographies are the most substantial historical source for the study of the Old Kingdom. They reflect social hierarchies, political ideology, the organization of the administration, cultural and technical achievements, and Egypt's interests abroad. As a literary genre, the early historical autobiography can be considered the preliminary stage of fictional narrative literature as it emerged in the Middle Kingdom. Tales like the *Sinuhe*, the fictive, adventurous life-record of a high official who became an exile in Palestine, or the *Shipwrecked Sailor*, based on the experience of Egypt's foreign activities, explored and reshaped formal, stylistic, and thematic features of the historical autobiography.

*First Intermediate Period.* Autobiographies of the First Intermediate Period show a tendency to combine historical and reflective motifs: the presentation of a successful career is enhanced by general statements on the protagonist's blameless lifestyle. During the First Intermediate Period, the country was divided into competing principalities. The rulers of the provinces and their clientele adjusted autobiographical production to their needs: they dismissed the traditions of the former court culture, replacing the ideal of the "official" with that of the "townsman," conscious of his communal responsibilities. In this context, autobiographies frequently refer to subsistence scarcities and civil war, factors that indeed had an effect on politics at that time, but probably less than the texts suggest. To protect and nourish the population, restore and build temples, guarantee the performance of the cult, or even to be the protégé of a god became popular motifs and justified the magnates' claim to power. The texts are outstanding for their blunt communicativeness, often mixed with a passion for showing off, but also for idiosyncratic formulations and rare vocabulary, as shown in the great autobiography of Ankhtifi of Mo'alla, an Upper-Egyptian potentate who pursued an aggressive policy against his rivals: "I found the House of Khuu inundated like a marsh, abandoned by him who belonged to it, in the grip of a rebel, under the control of a wretch. I made a man embrace the slayer of his father, the slayer of his brother, so as to reestablish the nome of Edfu."

*Middle Kingdom.* With the reestablishment of the central power in the early Middle Kingdom, autobiographical discourse also changed, giving birth to a new type of self-presentation, the encomiastic autobiography. This type of text befitted the ideals and representational needs of the social class of new bureaucrats who had sustained the return to monarchy. Although loyalty to the king is again a central topic, the promoters of the restoration were aware of their part in the state's consolidation. The new autobiographical type reshaped the image of the ideal official and his position in different social and professional milieus. It stressed individual efficiency, character and firmness, and respectable parentage, as well as education and rhetorical sophistication, the last being reflected indeed in the style and lexicon of the inscriptions themselves: "I am knowing to him who lacks knowledge, one who teaches a man what is useful to him. I am a straight one in the king's house, who knows what to say in every office. I am a listener who listens to the truth, who ponders it in the heart. I am one pleasant to his lord's house, who is remembered for his good qualities" (autobiography of Intef son of Senet).

Closer to the historical tradition is a distinctive group of autobiographical inscriptions from Abydos which record pilgrimages to the cult center of Osiris, the construction of memorial chapels and stelae, the furnishing of the local temple, and participation in the religious activities of that center.

***Early New Kingdom.*** At the beginning of the New Kingdom, the historical autobiography experienced a revival. While the participation in military campaigns and expeditions triggered narrative sequences that simulate dramatic situations and events, the texts dealing with administrative operations became more specific and repetitive. Both forms of historical autobiography multiply factual details and emphasize the writer's initiative, alertness, and perseverance. The experiences of journeys abroad and military adventures offered a plethora of exceptional and exciting settings for the exploration of individuality and renown. The autobiography of Ahmose son of Ibana is a major source for the study of the liberation wars against the Hyksos and the foundation of the New Kingdom: "When the town of Avaris was besieged, I fought bravely on foot in his majesty's presence. Thereupon I was appointed to the ship 'Rising in Memphis.' Then there was fighting on the water in Pjedku of Avaris. I made a seizure and carried off a hand. When it was reported to the Royal Herald the gold of valor was given to me."

Autobiographical writing lent many of its motifs and discourse patterns to royal historiography, which also started to flourish in the New Kingdom.

***Amarna period.*** These processes, however, were abruptly interrupted when Amenhotpe IV/Akhenaten founded the new capital of Amarna and reorganized the court. Akhenaten's monotheistic doctrine excluded all gods but the sun, whose only partner was the king, and prohibited any kind of private interaction with the gods'

sphere. Previously, personal piety had great significance. Now, the king controlled both god's involvement in the world and man's fate at the mercy of divine intervention. To become part of this cycle meant to internalize the new monarchical doctrine, which, in terms of loyalty, implied unconditional devotion: as son and representative of the unique god, the king decided on the life and destruction, the success and ruin of his people. The only possible form of autobiographical writing during that time depicts the dramatic impact of the royal doctrine on life: the official acknowledges the divinity of kingship and confirms its universal dimension. By virtue of this conversion, he is able to leave his dreadful past behind and enter a new form of being: that of the chosen one, privileged through divine intervention.

Similar elements characterize a small group of texts from the Ramessid period. They show the individual in absolute dependence on a divine power and present complete devotion as the only way to live a life free from ignorance and emptiness. These confessions—on the verge between self-discovery and personal prayer—are the most extreme declarations of a growing need to communicate with the divine and to seek assistance and guidance in the power of a personal god beyond worldly interests: "I made for him [the god Amun] praises to his name, for his might is great. I made supplications before him, in the presence of the whole land, on behalf of the draftsman Nakhtamun, justified, who lay sick unto death, [in] the power of Amun, through his sin. I found the Lord of Gods coming as northwind, gentle breezes before him. He saved Amun's draftsman Nakhtamun, justified" (stela of Nebre).

***Ramessid period.*** In the later New Kingdom, the traditional autobiography that focused on the profane dimension of life loses its importance as a medium of the funerary cult. This change resulted from a basic shift from a social to a religious perspective of human existence. This new approach emphasizes a pious lifestyle and adherence to religious practices and rituals. As private documents of personal piety rose, autobiographical productivity decreased. A few autobiographical texts left by members of the clergy or the temple administration document this new religious trend.

***Third Intermediate Period.*** During the Third Intermediate Period, autobiographical production reached another climax, further developing the domain of personal devotion and religious behavior. At this stage, the genre became the monopoly of the priestly class. Now, temple statues are usually the carriers of self-presentation addressed to the public as well as to the god to whom the person was professionally attached. Although the texts deal primarily with the performance of funerary rites and the commemoration of the individual, divine worship and participation in the cult are also prominent themes.

Hymns and prayers become standard elements of the inscriptions. In accordance with the ideals of the priestly class, long lines of family succession in a specific office and family values in general become popular: "He [god Amun] provided me with a son to take office, on my entering the land of my permanence. . . . I saw my sons as great priests, son after son who issued from me. I attained the age of ninety-six, being healthy, without illness. If one desires the length of my life, one must praise god for another in my name" (inscription of Nebnetjeru). At the same time, the texts make frequent use of dedication inscriptions, which present the successor as donor of the statue and of the text. They are, therefore, "allobiographies" rather than "autobiographies."

During the following period (twenty-fifth and twenty-sixth dynasties), the social and thematic spectrum of the autobiography broadened again, combining topics found in earlier times with more recent developments. Unlike their forerunners, however, the texts now rely much on formal and phraseological elements derived from the First Intermediate Period, the Middle Kingdom, and the New Kingdom. By using these forms as models, actual political circumstances such as usurpations or foreign occupation could be handled with delicacy and put into a broader historical context.

**Late period.** During the latest phase (Persian–Roman period), the archaism and political reticence of the autobiographies can be replaced by a focus on historical details of the phases of conquest, the establishment of new governments, changes in the infrastructure of the state, political attitudes of the new rulers, etc. Yet the protagonists of the texts always seek to demonstrate perfection in their ethical and political conduct, as shown by the autobiography of Wedjahorresne, a priest of Sais, who was willing to collaborate with the Persian invaders after Egypt's defeat: "The Great Chief of all foreign lands, Cambyses, came to Egypt, and the foreign peoples of every foreign land were with him. When he had conquered this land in its entirety, they established themselves in it, and he was Great Ruler of Egypt and Great Chief of all foreign lands. His Majesty assigned to me the office of Chief Physician. He made me live at his side as companion and administrator of the palace."

Apart from these records of the officials' successful adjustments to political reality, autobiographies of the Late period also show an interest in private life, a domain that to a great extent had been disregarded so far. Now birth, marriage, family life, and fateful blows are discussed, including the dramatic circumstances of a child's death. Probably under the influence of Greek thought, the depths and cruelties of death became a central topic of the texts commissioned *post mortem* by a close relative. Social and professional success were no longer considered very effective for those dwelling in the afterlife. Rather, vivid descriptions of the pitiful and frightening existence of the dead were meant to evoke sympathy in the audience and, thus, to encourage them to perform funerary rituals. Very often, these appeals included the imperative to abhor death and enjoy life as long as possible, a topic that appeared for the first time in the New Kingdom, in so-called harpers' songs. Inscriptions like those of Petosiris or Lady Taimhotep make abundant use of these ideas and bring autobiographical writing close to fictional literature:

> Who hears my speech, his heart will grieve for it, for I am a small child snatched by force, abridged in years as an innocent one, snatched quickly as a little one, like a man carried off by sleep. I was a youngster of [ . . . ] years, when taken to the city of eternity, to the abode of the perfect souls. I therefore reached the Lord of Gods, without having had my share. I was rich in friends, all the men of my town, not one of them could protect me.

> (Allobiography of Thothrekh son of Petosiris)

## BIBLIOGRAPHY

*Text Editions*

Clère, J., and J. Vandier. *Textes de la Première Période Intermédiaire et de la XI<sup>ème</sup> Dynastie.* Bibliotheca Aegyptiaca, 10. Brussels, 1948.

Helck, W. *Historisch-biographische Texte der 2. Zwischenzeit und des frühen Neuen Reiches.* Kleine Ägyptische Texte. Wiesbaden, 1983.

Jansen-Wilkeln, K. *Ägyptische Biographien der 22. und 23. Dynastie.* Ägypten und Altes Testament, 8. Wiesbaden, 1985.

Kitchen, K. A. *Ramesside Inscriptions: Historical and Biographical.* 8 vols. Oxford, 1968–1990.

Sandman, M. *Texts from the Time of Akhenaten.* Bibliotheca Aegyptiaca, 8. Brussels, 1938.

Sethe, K. *Ägyptische Lesestücke zum Gebrauch im akademischen Unterricht: Texte des Mittleren Reiches.* Leipzig, 1928.

Sethe, K. *Urkunden des ägyptischen Altertums: Urkunden des Alten Reiches.* Leipzig, 1932–1933.

Sethe, K. *Urkunden des ägyptischen Altertums: 7 Abt.* (recto) Historisch-biographische Urkunden des Mittleren Reiches. Leipzig, 1935.

Sethe, K., and W. Helck. *Urkunden des ägyptischen Altertums: 4 Abt.* (recto) Urkunden der 18. Dynastie, Fasc. 1–22. Berlin, 1903–1958.

*Translations and Anthologies*

Kitchen, K. A. *Ramesside Inscriptions Translated and Annotated: Translations* Vol. 1. Cambridge, 1993.

Lichtheim, M. *Ancient Egyptian Literature.* 3 vols. Berkeley, 1973–1980. The source of most of the translations quoted in the present article.

Lichtheim, M. *Ancient Egyptian Autobiographies Chiefly of the Middle Kingdom.* Orbis Biblicus et Orientalis, 84. Fribourg and Göttingen, 1988.

Otto, E. *Die biographischen Inschriften der ägyptischen Spätzeit: Ihre geistesgeschichtliche und literarische Bedeutung.* Probleme der Ägyptologie, 2. Leiden, 1954.

Roccati, A. *La littérature historique sous l'Ancien Empire Égyptien.* Littératures anciennes du Proche-Orient, 11. Paris, 1982.

Schenkel, W. *Memphis Herakleopolis Theben: Die epigraphischen Zeugnisse der 7.–11. Dynastie Ägyptens.* Ägyptologische Abhandlungen, 12. Wiesbaden, 1965.

*Übersetzungen der Urkunden der 18. Dynastie.* Fasc. 1–. Berlin, 1961–.

*History*

Assmann, J. "Schrift, Tod und Identität: das Grab als Vorschule der Literatur im alten Ägypten." In *Schrift und Gedächtnis*, edited by A.

Assmann et al., pp. 64–93. Archäologie der literarischen Kommunikation, 1. Munich, 1983.

Assmann, J. "Sepulkrale Selbstthematisierung im Alten Ägypten." In *Selbstthematisierung und Selbstzeugnis: Bekenntnis und Geständnis*, edited by A. Hahn and V. Kapp, pp. 208–232. Frankfurt, 1987.

Eyre, C. "The Semna Stela: Quotation, Genre, and Functions of Literature." In *Studies in Egyptology Presented to Miriam Lichtheim*, edited by S. Israelit-Groll, vol. 1, pp. 134–165. Jerusalem, 1990.

Eyre, C. "Is Egyptian Historical Literature 'Historical' or 'Literary'?" In *Ancient Egyptian . . . Literature: History and Forms*, edited by A. Loprieno, pp. 415–433. Leiden, 1996.

Gnirs, A. "Die ägyptische Autobiographie." In *Ancient Egyptian Literature: History and Forms*, edited by A. Loprieno, pp. 191–241. Leiden, 1996.

Korostovtsev, M. A. "À propos du genre 'historique' dans la littérature de l'Ancienne Égypte." In *Fragen an die altägyptische Literatur: Studien zum Gedenken an Eberhard Otto*, edited by J. Assmann et al., pp. 315–324. Wiesbaden, 1977.

*Analytical Studies*

Edel, E. "Untersuchungen zur Phraseologie der ägyptischen Inschriften des Alten Reiches." *Mitteilungen des Deutschen Archäologischen Instituts, Abteilung Kairo* 13 (1944), 1–90.

Guksch, H. *Königsdienst: Zur Selbstdarstellung der Beamten in der 18 Dynastie*. Studien zur Archäologie und Geschichte Altägyptens, 11. Heidelberg, 1994.

Hermann, A. *Die Stelen der thebanischen Felsgräber der 18. Dynastie* Ägyptologische Forschungen, 11. Glückstadt, 1940. On text form and structure.

Janssen, J. M. A. *De traditioneele egyptische Autobiografie vóór het nieuwe Rijk*. 2 vols. Leiden, 1946.

Lichtheim, M. *Maat in Egyptian Autobiographies and Related Studies*. Orbis Biblicus et Orientalis, 120. Fribourg and Göttingen, 1992.

Rössler-Köhler, U. *Individuelle Haltungen zum ägyptischen Königtum der Spätzeit: Private Quellen und ihre Königswertung im Spannungsfeld zwischen Erwartung und Erfahrung*. Göttinger Orientforschungen, 4.21. Wiesbaden, 1991.

ANDREA M. GNIRS

**BIRDS.** Located at the northeastern corner of the African continent, Egypt is on a major migratory flyway for birds of the Palearctic region. Twice each year, during the spring and fall, since time immemorial, astonishing numbers pass through the country while on their long journey from Europe and western Asia to central and southern Africa, and then back again. Some of those travelers are drawn, in particular, to the extensive wetlands and lakes of the Nile Delta, which serve as an important wintering area for migrant waterbirds from most of the Palearctic region. Egypt is also home to a large and diverse indigenous bird population, which inhabits a wide variety of habitats.

Living close to nature along the Nile River, bordered by two inhospitable deserts, the ancient Egyptians depended on an intimate knowledge of the yearly cycles of the local fauna and flora for their livelihoods; consequently, they became exceedingly familiar with the avian world around them. Birds served significant functions in both secular and sacred spheres of life. The Egyptians surely delighted in the intrinsic beauty of those creatures and were clearly not averse to expressing that in both pictures and words. Always skilled animaliers, Egyptian artisans created many marvelous and naturalistic portraits of birds, the result of close observation. Some seventy different birds can be confidently identified in Egyptian iconography and numerous others from bone remains. Waterfowl and other tasty birds were comparatively easy to capture and made a delicious source of food, both for the tables of the aristocrats as well as those of humble station. Some birds were assigned associations with certain gods and goddesses in the pharaonic pantheon. Their images, as with falcons and vultures, could have important religious and symbolic significance, which were developed into commonly occurring decorative devices. Various species of birds, and parts of them, also figured prominently in the hieroglyphic script. The ancient Egyptians have left us with a record of their knowledge and exploitation of birds, comprising copious pictorial, textual, and osteological documentation. Taken together, this body of evidence conclusively shows that the abundance of bird life in Egypt was far greater and even more wide ranging during the time of the pharaohs than it is today. Some of the birds routinely portrayed in art and hieroglyphs have now become locally extinct or are reduced to being extremely rare visitors; for example, such are the cases of the vanished saddlebill stork (*Ephippiorhynchus senegalensis*), helmeted guineafowl (*Numida meleagris*), bald or hermit ibis (*Geronticus eremita*), and the famous sacred ibis of the Nile (*Threskiornis aethiopicus*). Today, it would take a journey up the Nile of many hundreds of kilometers, to the southern part of Sudan, to find some of these varieties. The continuing destruction of prime swampland habitat in the Nile Delta and in the Faiyum, as well as overhunting, pollution, and the encroachment by humans into vital breeding areas, have all taken their toll on Egypt's avian population.

In the time of pharaonic civilization, birds were first and foremost esteemed as articles of food and so much of the extant record relates to that theme. The decorative program of tomb-chapels, particularly in the Old and Middle Kingdoms, often had space devoted to scenes showing the procurement, maintenance, or preparation of birds, and those were customarily ducks, geese, cranes, and doves. Through these, the deceased would magically be provisioned with plump, choice fowl throughout eternity. Among the earliest representations of birds occurring in the Nile Valley are drawings scratched on rock faces, probably dating from the Amratian (Naqada I) period; they feature hunters chasing the ostrich (*Struthio camelus*) with bows and arrows. From the early Old Kingdom onward, a rich concourse of colorful avifauna was traditionally pictured inhabiting the dense stems and umbels of the papyrus swamps, as displayed on tomb-chapel

BIRDS. *Drawing of a Theban tomb painting.* It depicts the inspection of flocks of geese and their herdsmen by a high official.

and temple walls. Those compositions routinely illustrated the deceased in a papyrus raft hunting birds or other prey for sport, with various species roosting and nesting amid the lush vegetation or winging high above it. The fifth dynasty *mastaba* of a high court official named Ti (tomb 60) at Saqqara contains the first and finest of such scenes; none other has the wealth or scope of animal life portrayed that this one has. The creatures exhibited in most tomb scenes tend to be stock items, and they repeatedly occur throughout the centuries. The wetland inhabitants frequently include the kingfisher (*Alcedo atthis*), pied kingfisher (*Ceryle rudis*), Egyptian goose (*Alopochen aegyptiacus*), lapwing (*Vanellus vanellus*), sacred ibis, (*Threskiornis aethiopica*), hoopoe (*Upupa epops*), bittern (*Botaurus stellaris* or *Ixobrychus minutus*), gray heron (*Ardea cinerea*), purple gallinule (*Porphyrio porphyrio*), cormorant (*Phalacrocorax* sp.), egret (*Egretta* sp.), and dove (*Streptopelia* sp.). Some unusual birds also appear, such as the spoonbill (*Platalea leucorodia*), greater flamingo (*Phoenicopterus ruber*), sandpiper (*Tringa* sp.), avocet (*Recurvirostra avosetta*), pelican (*Pelecanus* sp.), and an occasional raptor (bird of prey). In the eighteenth dynasty, Theban tomb owners were shown in scenes going

after pintails (*Anas acuta*) and were painted hurling their throwsticks at rising flocks; the notables had unerring accuracy, knocking the ducks right out of the sky. Of all the waterfowl in Egyptian art and hieroglyphs, and those mentioned in texts, the pintail was by far the most ubiquitous, perhaps a signal of its high gastronomic appeal.

The most celebrated bird depictions to have come down from ancient Egypt are the renowned "Geese of Meidum," now in the Egyptian Museum, Cairo, which are among the masterpieces of Egyptian painting. Part of a fowling scene from the early fourth dynasty tomb of Nefermaat and his wife Atet at Meidum, this large fragment of wall painting exhibits a frieze of six geese, comprising three different species: white-fronted goose (*Anser albifrons*), bean goose (*Anser fabalis*), and red-breasted goose (*Branta ruficollis*). Owing to their striking realism and pristine state of preservation, the "Geese of Meidum" have aptly been called the first ornithological record in history. The inscriptions accompanying the encyclopedic natural history scenes on the walls of the "Chamber of the Seasons" in the fifth dynasty Solar Temple of Newoserre Any at Abu Ghurob indicate that the Egyptians were well aware of the annual migrations of birds in their land and could distinguish between resident and passage varieties. The eleventh dynasty tomb of the nomarch Baket III (tomb 15) at Beni Hasan exhibits a fascinating and informative collection of twenty-nine bird species, most of which were identified by an accompanying hieroglyphic caption. Also illustrated are three bats (of the order Chiroptera), which were drawn with much exactness, suggesting that the Egyptians classified those flying mammals along with birds. What makes that group unique is that they were not included in the decoration of the tomb-chapel to serve as food in the beyond; rather, Baket III may have been something of a bird fancier, who wished to continue to enjoy birds in the beyond. Also at the site of Beni Hasan, but in the twelfth dynasty tomb of the nomarch Khnumhotep III (tomb 3), a wall painting represents the owner under the cover of a blind, trapping waterfowl on a pond with a clap-net. Flanking the water are two small flowering acacia trees, and on their branches are nine birds. Five species can immediately be distinguished, and they are certainly among the most lovely and lifelike in all of Egyptian art: turtle dove (*Streptopelia turtur*), red-backed shrike (*Lanius collurio*), masked shrike (*Lanius nubicus*), redstart (*Phoenicurus phoenicurus*), and the hoopoe.

Many birds played a role in Egyptian religious beliefs and practices. Several raptorial (predatory) species, however, were prominent. The most notable and frequently illustrated, especially as a hieroglyph, was the distinctive falcon belonging to Horus, the powerful god of the sky, who was closely connected with kingship; if the ancient Egyptians had a national bird, this would have been it. The Horus falcon, though, was regularly used as the emblem for other deities, such as Montu and Re-Horakhty; it was principally modeled after the Lanner falcon (*Falco biarmicus*) and the peregrine falcon (*Falco peregrinus*). The griffon vulture (*Gyps fulvus*) and the huge lappet-faced vulture (*Torgos tracheliotus*) were abundantly figured too and were linked to the Upper Egyptian goddess Nekhbet, who protected the king. The two sister goddesses, Isis and Nephthys, had associations with both the kestrel (*Falco naumanni* and *Falco tinnunculus*) and the black kite (*Milvus migrans*), in their capacity as divine mourners for the dead. The barn owl (*Tyto alba*) appeared as a standard hieroglyphic sign, but only rarely appeared in art and seems to have played a minor part in religion. Precisely the same holds true for the Egyptian vulture (*Neophron percnopterus*). Among waterside birds, there was also the special relationship between the sacred ibis and the god Thoth, lord of the moon and patron of the art of writing. The god Amun, chief deity of the city of Thebes, chose as one of his manifestations the Egyptian goose. The gray heron, or *bnw*-bird (better known in the classical world as the phoenix), symbolized the god Atum when he emerged from the waters of chaos and first revealed himself on the primeval earth. As a solar creature, the *benu*-bird was identified with Re, the sun god, at the rising sun, and with Osiris, god of the underworld, at sunset. Sacred pelicans were maintained by priests in the Solar Temple of Any at Abu Ghurob, having mythological associations with the sun cult. During the late dynastic and Ptolemaic periods, the ancient Egyptians bred and mummified many millions of birds, primarily the sacred ibis and certain smaller falcons, which were then used as votive offerings at religious centers, especially at the sites of Saqqara and Tuna el-Gebel, in what was a phenomenon unique to that age; the birds were eventually interred in vast catacombs or cemeteries situated near the temples. It was believed that such prepared animals were capable of transmitting the prayers of the pious pilgrims who purchased them and who wished to petition the gods.

[*See also* Poultry.]

## BIBLIOGRAPHY

Boessneck, Joachim. *Die Tierwelt des alten Ägypten: Untersucht anhand kulturgeschichtlicher und zoologischer Quellen.* Munich, 1988. Provides authoritative information on bird life in ancient Egypt; it also includes findings from zooarchaeological investigations, including some dealing with bird mummies.

Goodman, Steven M., and Peter L. Meininger, eds. *The Birds of Egypt.* Oxford and New York, 1989. The standard work on the birds of contemporary Egypt, replacing the now largely outdated *Nicoll's Birds of Egypt* (1930).

Helck, Wolfgang, Eberhard Otto, and Wolfhart Westendorf, eds. *Lexikon der Ägyptologie.* 7 vols. Wiesbaden, 1975–1992. Massive reference work containing articles in English, French, and German on virtually every topic relating to ancient Egypt; includes important entries on all aspects of birds in pharaonic life. See especially "Vogel" by Hannes Buchberger in volume 6, cols. 1046–1051, where all the individual articles on birds in the *Lexikon* are conveniently listed.

Houlihan, Patrick F. *The Birds of Ancient Egypt.* Warminster, 1986; Cairo, 1988. The only comprehensive study of the various birds represented in Egyptian art and hieroglyphs; contains a lengthy bibliography.

Houlihan, Patrick F. *The Animal World of the Pharaohs.* London and New York, 1996. Handsomely illustrated book aimed at a general audience, with a chapter devoted to surveying the avifauna and its role in ancient Egypt; extensive bibliography.

Houlihan, Patrick F. "A Guide to the Wildlife Represented in the Great Swampland Scene in the Offering-chapel of Ti (No. 60) at Saqqara." *Göttinger Miszellen: Beiträge zur ägyptologischen Diskussion* 155 (1996), 19–53. The numerous species of birds appearing in the famous swampland scene in the *mastaba* of Ti at Saqqara, gives their Egyptian name(s), and summarizes their importance in pharaonic secular life.

Meinertzhagen, R. *Nicoll's Birds of Egypt.* 2 vols. London, 1930. Although this classic is now dated, it nevertheless remains an important source of information for the birds of modern Egypt; contains a chapter by the distinguished ornithologist R. E. Moreau on birds of Egypt in antiquity.

Wolterman, Carles. "On the Names of Birds and Hieroglyphic Sign-list G 22, G 35, and H 3." *Jaarbericht van het Voorazatisch-Egyptisch Genootschap Ex Oriente Lux* 32 (1991–1992), 119–130. Study of ancient Egyptian bird names.

PATRICK F. HOULIHAN

**BIRTH.** The Egyptian word for birth (*mswt;* in Ptolemaic times, *p'p'*) could be paraphrased "come down to the ground" (*prj hr t3*) and "come forth from the womb" (*prj m ht* or *h3j m ht*). The determinative shows the head and arms of the child protuding from the birth canal of a kneeling woman.

The Egyptians knew that infertility could be due to the mother as well as the father. Couples who did not get the child they wished for tried to influence their fate with prayers presented to a god or goddess, letters to the dead, or prescriptions of medicines and magic. If nothing helped, they could adopt a child. When a woman became pregnant she tried all types of medicine and magic to prevent a miscarriage. Some of those, plus magic spells and medicines to prevent pregnancy, have come down to us. Although most of the remedies are of doubtful origin, some of their contraceptives seem to have had the same effect as the acidic contraceptive jellies do today.

According to an Egyptian belief that dates from the beginning of the fifth century BCE through the Ptolemaic era, the semen produced in the bones of the father was kept in his testicles. With his penis, the father placed the child into the stomach (*ht*) of the mother, who was considered the receptacle for the child. In a few instances, the uterus (*hmt*) was named as the place in which the child developed. Flesh and skin were thought to be formed from the mother's milk. The heart, the site of character, mental power, and feeling, was thought to be derived from the mother.

Other means of conception were portrayed in the world of the gods. For example, the primeval god Atum swallowed his sperm, coughed, and spat out the first couple, who were Shu (*išš*, "to cough"), the god of the air, and Tefnut (*tf*, "to spit out"), the goddess of humidity; this couple then brought forth Geb, the god of the earth, and Nut, the goddess of the sky, in the natural (sexual) way. The god Seth swallowed the sperm of his rival, Horus, and brought forth the disk of the moon god Thoth from the top of his head. The primeval gods Hu ("utterance") and Sia ("perception," "knowledge") generated from the blood of the sun god Re. In a fairy tale, an unfaithful wife becomes pregnant by swallowing a splinter of one of the persea trees, which, because it embodied her husband, she had asked to be cut down.

Medical texts included many means to find out whether a woman had conceived. Besides some doubtful tests, Egyptians, for example, noticed the cessation of menstruation, the swelling of the breasts, the sensitivity to smell, nausea, and the changes in the face and eyes of a pregnant woman. Causing barley and emmer wheat to germinate by watering it daily with the urine of the woman was used as a pregnancy test (and has been proved to be reliable). Since the Old Egyptian word for barley is in the masculine gender and the word for emmer is feminine, ancient Egyptians believed that the sex of the child could be predicted by which plant sprouted first (proven unreliable).

Pregnant women used perfumed oil to massage themselves, to prevent stretch marks and ease delivery. The oil was preserved in small vessels, usually of calcite, in the shape of a pregnant woman rubbing her abdomen. Although genitals were never marked, one of those vessels showed a prominent tampon, which had the form of the so-called Isis-blood amulet, used, through analogy to the goddess Isis pregnant with Horus, to avoid the loss of blood or a miscarriage. Various mixtures were also poured into a woman's vagina to prevent miscarriage. Developing "in the egg" (*m swht*), in its mother's belly, it was cared for by a god and thus regarded as a human being, which was to be properly buried in case of miscarriage. According to Diodorus Siculus, the first-century Greek historian, an Egyptian law forbade killing a pregnant woman condemned to death before she gave birth, since the child belonged to its father.

When her time came—after nine months according to the Egyptian solar calendar—the mother gave birth to her child while squatting on the floor, squatting on two bricks, sitting in a confinement chair in her home, or, as was shown on New Kingdom ostraca, in a hut built on the roof of the house or in the garden. She was aided by other women or a midwife. To start her labor, "Lower Egyptian salt" (natron), was used as a laxative. Magical spells concerned with "separating the child from the womb of the mother" or "to speed up the birth" were thought to help. The midwife tried to ease the pains of labor with intoxicating drinks, rinsing the genitals, or applying poultices to the belly. Fumigations used to speed the delivery would have had a psychological effect, rather like the prayers to gods, magic spells, and amulets placed on her body. In the story of the birth of the three children of the sun god—the future kings of the fifth dynasty (known from the Westcar Papyrus)—the goddesses Isis and Nephthys, and the frog-headed goddess of birth Heket helped at the deliveries. They gave each child its name, cut the umbilical cord, washed the child, and placed it on a covered brick; only that story mentions a purification period of fourteen days as well as the birth of the triplets. Little is known about multiple births. The gods Osiris, Horus, Seth, Isis, and Nephthys were born on successive epagomenal days. The only sure source for the birth of twins is the stela of two architects from the eighteenth dynasty, who mention that they came forth from their mother's womb on the same day.

Although the father took part in choosing the name for the child, the mother seems to have been the one who gave it. While still in the womb, the child's lifetime and fate was decided on by the seven Hathors, by the goddess Meskhenet who helped form the child as the goddess of the birthing bricks (on which the child's fate was inscribed), as well as by Renenutet and other gods and goddesses. The placenta and umbilical cord, mentioned in a few texts, received special treatment. A person's birthday was celebrated. In the Ptolemaic period, if not earlier, it was officially registered.

Death in childbirth was always a threat to women, as well as miscarriage and the death of the infant. Studies on mummies have shown that women had two to four years shorter life expectancy than men, which was due to death in childbirth. Therefore, the Egyptians tried to protect both mother and child with magic spells and charms. Amulets, like the figures of the lion-headed dwarf Bes, whose ugliness fended off all dangerous demons, or the pregnant, hippopotamus goddess, Taweret, with a lion's feet and the back and tail of a crocodile, were worn by both men and women. Curved wands, made from hippopotamus tusk and decorated with apotropaic demons, protected mother and child by analogy to the young sun god Re. In spite of all, infant mortality was very high. To determine whether the child would live or die, a piece of its placenta, called "the mother of the human being" (*mwt rmt*), was mashed with milk and fed to the child. If the child swallowed it, the child would live. According to another test, the child would live if it cried *ny* but would die if it cried *mbi*. Small children could be buried in the house; if a child died with its mother it might be placed with her in her grave, otherwise it got its own grave. Special children's necropolises are known from ancient Egypt.

It is not known if physicians assisted at a child's birth. A late source mentions the training of midwives in the "house of life" in the Nile Delta town of Sais, where physicians also received their training. A child was suckled for as many as three years by its mother or a wetnurse. Mother's milk was kept as medicine in small vessels in the shape of a sqatting woman holding a child in her lap. A wetnurse might accompany a child as it developed. Through her milk, a relationship was formed with the child; she could be highly esteemed by her foster child and its family.

Although statuettes of pregnant women are known from prehistoric Egypt, pregnancy is depicted only three times in relief: in the sixth dynasty tomb of Ankhmahor and in the two depictions of the myth of the royal birth, best preserved in the eighteenth dynasty temples of King Amenhotpe III and of Queen Hatshepsut. According to this myth, the god Amun appeared to the queen in the shape of her own husband, to beget the future king or queen. After the builder god Khnum formed the child and its double on the potter's wheel, the queen, aided by god-desses, gave birth in a confinement chair. The child was recognized by its divine father as his own and pronounced by him as the future ruler. This myth, which proves the divine kingship, is from the New Kingdom. During the Late period and Greco-Roman times, it depicted the birth of the divine child, representing the future king, in a small temple situated adjacent to the temple of the divine triad, the so-called *mammisi*.

[*See also* Childhood; *and* Fertility.]

### BIBLIOGRAPHY

Deines, Hildegard von, Hermann Grapow, and Wolfhart Westendorf. "Übersetzung der Medizinischen Texte." *Grundriss der Medizin der Alten Ägypter* 4.1 (1958), 267–288.

Feucht, Erika. "Geburt, Kindheit, Jugend und Ausbildung im Alten Ägypten." In *Zur Sozialgeschichte der Kindheit*, edited by J. Martin and A. Nitschke, pp. 225–265. Veröffentlichungen des "Instituts für Historische Anthropologie e.V.," 4. 2. Freiburg, 1966.

Feucht, Erika. "Gattenwahl, Ehe und Nachkommenschaft im Alten Ägypten." In *Geschlechtsreife und Legitimation zur Zeugung*, edited by J. Martin and T. Nipperdey, pp. 55–84, esp. 76ff. Veröffentlichungen des "Instituts für Historische Anthropologie e.V.," 3. 1. Freiburg, 1985.

Feucht, Erika. *Das Kind im Alten Ägypten*. Frankfurt and New York, 1995.

Grapow, Hermann. "Kranker, Krankheiten und Arzt." *Grundriss der Medizin der Alten Ägypter* 3 (1956), 9–17.

Helck, Wolfgang, Eberhard Otto, and Wolfhart Westdendorf, eds. *Lexikon der Ägyptologie*. 6 vols. Wiesbaden, 1975–1986. Entries: "Adoption," "Altersangaben," "Empfängnisverhütung," "Geburt," "Geburthaus," "Geburtslegende," "Geburtstag," "Kinderlosigkeit und -wunsch," "Name," "Namengebung," and "Namensbildung."

Janssen, Rosalind M., and J. Janssen. *Growing Up in Ancient Egypt*. London, 1990.

Robins, Gay. *Women in Ancient Egypt*. London, 1993.

Strouhal, Eugen. *Life in Ancient Egypt*. Translated by Deryck Viney. Cambridge, 1992.

Watterson, Barbara. *Women in Ancient Egypt*. New York, 1991.

ERIKA FEUCHT

**BOCCHORIS.** *See* Bakenrenef.

**BOOK OF GOING FORTH BY DAY** was the principal collection of funerary literature that was used from the New Kingdom until the early Roman period. It is popularly known as the ancient Egyptian *Book of the Dead*, because its papyrus copies were often found buried with mummies. It was generally available to anyone who could copy, or afford to have copied, either the sometimes lengthy papyri documents or the briefer excerpts found on smaller sheets of papyrus or on short lengths of linen. Some of the chapters and spells from the book were also inscribed on coffins, in tombs, and even on temple walls, and individual spells known from some of those sources were associated with *shawabtis* (chapter 6), heart scarabs

BOOK OF GOING FORTH BY DAY. *The deceased before Osiris.* From a copy of the *Book of Going Forth by Day (Book of the Dead)*, in the Museo Egizo, Turin. (Scala / Art Resource)

(chapter 30), and the hypocephali (which are flat circles of linen or papyrus, sometimes covered with gesso plaster, bearing chapter 162 of the *Book of the Dead*).

Although there are hundreds of *Book of the Dead* manuscripts extant, many have not yet been published, so there is still a serious lack of accurate and useful comparative editions of the texts from the different periods. One of the first publications of the *Book of the Dead* was in 1842, by Richard Lepsius, and this was of a manuscript in the Egyptian Museum at Turin; it was a text from Ptolemaic times that had 165 chapters, and it represented the fairly standard Late period selection and ordering of the texts.

E. A. Wallis Budge, as keeper of the Egyptian Collection in the British Museum, London, was a prolific editor of its manuscripts, and he published in 1894 and 1899 a number of that museum's finest *Book of the Dead* documents, which are still useful. He also produced a text-translation-and-vocabulary set in 1898, which though readily available in more recent editions is no longer of much use, since its reprints do not have the same pagina-

tion as the 1898 edition that is generally cited in our references—and his translations were already outdated when the work was published.

In 1886, Édouard Naville published what is still the standard edition of a number of comparable texts of the New Kingdom, though it was based on the order of the published Turin manuscript of much later date (Ptolemaic); it is further flawed by its numerous inconsistencies in transcription, which make it quite unreliable. There are a number of up-to-date translations of the *Book of the Dead* spells in the same order as those early editions, but almost all of them ignore the fact that a large number of earlier manuscripts had their own arrangements of spells; because the spells discovered later were merely added to the end of the growing corpus, the original books are still not well represented. Generally omitted as well are the introductory scenes of the deceased associating with various deities, which seem to set the tone for the selection of texts that follow. The texts generally involve two gods, Re and Osiris; still, individual manuscripts can show enough texts weighted toward one or the other deity to be considered oriented toward one deity or the other—and this orientation seems to be consistent with the introductory scene of each document.

Often, some relationship exists between an individual manuscript's orientation and its conclusion, though it is not always clear that the real end of any single book has been reached. Even for the Late period examples, which list chapters 162 to 165 as additions to the original, it is not always clear whether 165 or 162 is to be the final chapter (and of course many spells can and do occur beyond these). There are 192 spells presently associated with the work, and some of these include variants that differ so greatly that originally they should have been numbered separately.

Rubrics (entries in red ink) are found in most manuscripts; these are most frequently used for titles or for additional comments about the sources of individual spells and their effectiveness, or they give specific instructions for their use. For example a number of spells were labeled as "truly excellent, proved a million times." Some were to be recited on certain days, making use of particular amulets, or with the requirement of ritual purity. In one oft-cited rubric, Prince Hordedef of the fourth dynasty is said to have discovered chapter 64 under the feet of the god at Hermopolis. The old and very interesting chapter 17 also used rubrics to present various interpretative glosses that had become attached to the sections of the original text; these show clearly that the ancients had some difficulty themselves in understanding the texts and were also not averse to providing their own not unbiased interpretations. For example, contradictory Osirian and Solar glosses were both attached to the text of chapter 17.

Two of the most interesting and important chapters of the *Book of the Dead* are 110 and 125. Chapter 110 was known already from the Coffin Texts to refer to the Elysian Fields or paradise for the ancient Egyptians; this Sekhet-ḥetepu, or Field of Offerings, is a place where an "equipped" or blessed spirit can plow, reap, eat, drink, copulate, and "do everything that is done upon earth." Chapter 125 is a new addition to the funerary literature, which includes a "judgment scene," where the heart of the deceased is weighed against the feather of truth. The deity Thoth presides and records; forty-two judges apparently represent the nomes of Egypt, though they are not consistently set forth; Ammamet is there to devour the guilty; but the vindicated always go forth to join Osiris.

What it takes to make up a complete *Book of the Dead* has not been defined. Many very short versions seem to have been complete in themselves, yet some may omit the "judgment scene" altogether, despite the fact that it seems central. These abbreviated manuscripts also lack particular spells, such as chapter 64 (variant), which is claimed to be complete enough to stand alone. Interestingly, a number of these short versions have only spells concerned with the voyage of the sun god Re.

Although many beautifully illustrated versions of the *Book of the Dead* exist on papyri, the book made for (and perhaps by) the nineteenth dynasty royal scribe Any, now in the British Museum, is certainly among the finest examples. The Greenfield Papyrus of Nesitanebetisheru, daughter of the high priest Pinedjem II of the twenty-first dynasty, at 41 meters (135 feet), is among the longest known, having almost all its chapters illustrated with large but rather basic vignettes. During that dynasty, many women had such books and some may even have been involved in their composition. If there had been great variety in earlier manuscripts, some additions and changes introduced at that time became the norm for later examples. During the Third Intermediate Period, many individuals had an abbreviated *Book of That Which Is in the Underworld* (*Amduat*) and special decrees of Amun-Re, as well, to complete their collections of guides to the beyond.

## BIBLIOGRAPHY

Allen, T. George. *The Book of the Dead or Going Forth by Day: Ideas of the Ancient Egyptians Concerning the Hereafter as Expressed in Their Own Terms.* Studies in Ancient Oriental Civilization, 37. Chicago, 1974. Translation.

Barguet, Paul. *Le Livre des Morts des anciens Égyptiens.* Paris, 1967. Translation.

Faulkner, Raymond O. *The Ancient Egyptian Book of the Dead*, rev. ed. London, 1985. Translation.

Naville, Édouard. *Das aegyptische Todtenbuch der XVIII bis XX Dynastie.* 3 vols. Berlin, 1886. Transcription of a number of New Kingdom parallel versions.

LEONARD H. LESKO

## BOOK OF THAT WHICH IS IN THE UNDERWORLD,

one of several guidebooks to the beyond (or descriptions of the afterlife) that have been associated chiefly with the New Kingdom tombs in the Valley of the Kings and the Valley of the Queens in Western Thebes. Versions of the books from the eighteenth to the twentieth dynasty have been dated through their royal owners, but there were antecedents for at least one of those books that are recognizable in the Middle Kingdom Coffin Texts. There were also abbreviated versions of the books on papyri that belonged to nobles in the eighteenth dynasty.

The *Book of That Which Is in the Underworld*, or *Amduat* (*imy-dw3t*), is the earliest and also the most detailed of the descriptions of the afterlife used in eighteenth dynasty royal tombs in the Valley of the Kings. These were all guidebooks to the beyond, intended to assist the deceased kings in their journey through the night sky as pilots for the sun god, Re. In some cases, the deceased king, who was identified with Osiris, god of the dead, was also said to become Re himself in his circuit. There is nothing specifically moral or ethical about this book, except for the presumption that the deceased is able to join the gods. Those who had copies of the *Book of Going Forth by Day* (*Book of the Dead*) to accompany the *Book of That Which Is in the Underworld* might have regarded the former as a kind of initiation or prerequisite that had to be followed up by a detailed guide to the beyond.

Several of these New Kingdom books are divided into the hours of the night, and the number of the hours in these books was regularly twelve rather than the seven found in contemporary chapters of the *Book of Going Forth by Day*, and also in the Middle Kingdom antecedents of both that work and the guidebook. A major feature of the later royal guidebooks is the combat with the serpent Apophis, who threatens to devour the sun (an etiology for eclipses), but that probably developed quite naturally from earlier serpent spells and descriptions of demons that were supposed to be encountered in the night skies. Also encountered along the way, in the fourth and fifth hour, is Sokar, the Memphite god of the dead.

The earliest royal versions of the book appear to have been huge papyrus rolls with three connecting registers that encircled the walls of burial chambers having rounded corners to preserve the unbroken scroll effect. From this we can presume that their sources were on papyri, but we cannot postulate how much earlier they were originally prepared.

The manuscripts that survive on papyri are mainly from the burials of priests and their wives. They exist in two versions; the earlier one (sometimes called the "real *Amduat*") features a long line of standing humanlike figures with the heads of different beings used to distinguish these demons from one another. The other version (the "abbreviated royal *Amduat*"), which survives mainly from the twenty-first dynasty, is an abbreviation of the eighteenth dynasty royal text; it has the same general plan of the night sky divided into hours but generally includes only the last four hours. The images in this version, as well as those in the royal tombs, are essentially stick figures like cursive hieroglyphs, which are consistent with the appearance of handwriting on papyri. At least one abbreviated version has the four hours condensed further to fit one sheet of papyrus, with enough identifying bits present but in apparent disarray.

### BIBLIOGRAPHY

Hornung, Erik. *Das Amduat: Die Schrift des verborgenen Raumes.* 3 vols. Ägyptologische Abhandlungen, 7, 13. Wiesbaden, 1963–1967. Text and translation of the *Book of That Which Is in the Underworld.*

Hornung, Erik. *Ägyptische Unterweltsbücher.* 2d ed. Zurich and Munich, 1984. Translations of New Kingdom royal funerary literature.

Hornung, Erik. *The Valley of the Kings: Horizon of Eternity,* translated from the German by David Warburton. New York, 1990. Description of funerary literature in New Kingdom royal tombs.

Sadek, Abdel-Aziz Fahmy. *Contribution à l'étude de l'Amdouat: Les variantes tardives du Livre de l'Amdouat dans les papyrus du Musée du Caire.* Orbis biblicus orientalis, 65. Freiburg and Göttingen 1985.

LEONARD H. LESKO

**BOOK OF THE DEAD.** *See* Book of Going Forth by Day.

**BREAD.** Central to the ancient Egyptian diet were beer and bread. Both were consumed at every meal, by everyone, and no meal was considered complete without them. Nutritionally, bread was a valuable source of energy—of protein, starch, and trace nutrients, and it played much the same role as beer in the Egyptian economy and in ritual. Made from a wide variety of ingredients, the most abundant constituent of bread is normally a starch-rich material, most often a cereal ground into flour. Often, only a specific species of wheat is thought best, the bread wheat (*Triticum aestivum*), yet almost any cereal is suitable. With each grain or type of flour, the structure and texture of a loaf will vary considerably; all breads are not light, risen, or spongy.

The arid climate of Egypt has preserved a rich record of organic materials, including bread loaves. Several hundred specimens survive, mostly from funerary offerings, and these are now scattered in museum collections throughout the world. Among the earliest loaves are fragments from Predynastic graves of the Badarian culture. Although a direct source of evidence about ancient Egyptian bread and baking, these loaves have been surprisingly little studied. Many different breads and cakes were named in Egyptian documents, but their distinguishing features are in fact unknown. Scholars have suggested some possibilities, for example, that *pesen*-bread was a flat round loaf. The preserved loaves show that breads of the same shape were not always made from the same materials or the same recipe and, therefore, may not have had the same name. Some surviving hand-formed conical loaves were made from emmer wheat (*Triticum dicoccum*), whereas one specimen was made largely from figs (*Ficus carica*). In contrast, various shapes and textures might be made from the same batch of dough.

Baking has usually been described from the evidence of artistic scenes. One of the most quoted examples is the relief in the fifth dynasty tomb of Ti at Saqqara. Also, Old Kingdom statuettes show baking activities, such as milling. Middle Kingdom models, such as that from Meketra's tomb, give a lively sense of a busy bakery, and several tombs at Beni Hasan contain bread-making scenes. One

BREAD. *The court bakery of Ramesses III.* Various forms of bread, including loaves shaped like animals, are shown. From the tomb of Ramesses III in the Valley of the Kings, twentieth dynasty.

example of baking in a New Kingdom wall painting was found in the Theban tomb of Nebamun.

Bread making in ancient Egypt has been misunderstood by some Egyptologists, because the distinctive nature of the ancient staple wheat, emmer, differs in some properties from most wheats grown today. This includes bread wheat *(Triticum aestivum),* with ears that easily separate into chaff and grain when threshed; its traditional processing removes the chaff from the grain through winnowing and sieving. In contrast, emmer needs a more extensive treatment; when threshed, it breaks into packets called spikelets, each of which is a thick envelope of chaff tightly surrounding two kernels. Vigorous but careful processing is needed to break the chaff apart without damaging the grain kernels, before winnowing and sieving clean the chaff from the kernels.

Research based on archaeological, ethnographic, and experimental evidence has provided information on the way the ancient Egyptians processed emmer. Whole spikelets were moistened with a little water and pounded with wooden pestles in limestone mortars. The water made the spikelets pliable, so that the chaff shredded without crushing the grain kernels inside. Although this operation was not time consuming, ancient Egyptian mortars were small and several batches of spikelets had to be processed before enough freed kernels were produced to make bread for a family. The damp mixture of freed grain kernels and broken chaff then had to be dried, probably by spreading the mass in the sunshine. This was followed by a series of winnowing steps, which removed the fine chaff, and by sieving, which removed the heavier pieces. The final fragments of chaff still had to be picked out by hand.

The clean, whole grain was then milled into flour, by the use of flat grinding stones called saddle querns. From Neolithic to Old Kingdom times, they were placed on the floor, making a laborious process. According to tomb scenes, by the Middle Kingdom the querns were raised onto platforms, called quern emplacements, and examples of some have been excavated at a few New Kingdom sites; they were much easier, more comfortable, and perhaps quicker to use. Experimental work with ancient querns has shown that no grit was needed to aid the milling process, as is sometimes suggested, and flour textures could be precisely controlled by the miller.

In ancient Egypt, baking changed with time. An excavated Old Kingdom bakery at Giza demonstrated that heavy pottery bread molds were set in rows on a bed of embers to bake the dough placed within them. In the Middle Kingdom, square hearths were used, and the pottery molds were modified into tall, narrow, almost cylindrical cones. By New Kingdom times, a new oven type was introduced, a large open-topped clay cylinder encased in thick mud bricks and mortar; then flat disks of dough, perhaps leavened, were slapped onto the pre-heated inner oven wall. When baked, they peeled off and were caught before they could fall into the embers below.

New Kingdom tombs were especially well supplied with bread, and the loaves varied widely in size, shape, and decoration. Some were formed into recognizable shapes, such as fish and human figures; others were simple shapes, such as disks and fans. The dough textures of those loaves ranged from very fine to mealy. Whole or coarsely cracked cooked grains were often added to create a texture much like modern multigrain breads. The cereal grain used for flour was almost always emmer. Added barley *(Hordeum vulgare)*, as flour of grains, is so rare that barley seems to have been accidentally mixed into dough in small amounts. Flavorings, such as coriander seeds *(Coriandrum sativum)* and dates *(Phoenix dactylifera)*, were occasionally added. Yeast was added to some recipes, but leavening was not always used.

More research is needed to determine whether different breads were available to the various social classes. It seems reasonable to suppose that bread flavored with exotic ingredients was normally accessible only to the wealthy. Until bread has been recovered from arid settlement sites, tomb loaves will continue to inform mainly on funerary practices. Numerous remains of cereal-processing equipment and baking installations at settlement sites, however, have provided some developmental evidence for the preparation of ancient Egyptian bread.

[*See also* Beer; *and* Diet.]

### BIBLIOGRAPHY

Breasted, J. H. J. *Egyptian Servant Statues.* New York, 1948. Has examples of many statuettes engaged in various baking activities, as well as Meketra's bakery/brewery model.

Darby, William J., Paul Ghalioungui, and Louis Grivetti. *Food: The Gift of Osiris.* London and New York, 1977. Provides a general overview of baking, although it relies much on Greco-Roman sources; shows a good range of ancient desiccated loaves.

Hillman, G. C. "Traditional Husbandry and Processing of Archaic Cereals in Modern Times: Part I, the Glume-wheats." *Bulletin on Sumerian Agriculture* 1 (1984), 114–152. Detailed ethnographic information on the processing of emmer wheat.

Kemp, B. J. *Ancient Egypt. Anatomy of a Civilization.* London, 1989. Includes a discussion of the administration of baking and bread as rations.

Samuel, Delwen. "Ancient Egyptian Cereal Processing: Beyond the Artistic Record." *Cambridge Archaeological Journal* 3.2 (1993), 276–283. Summary of ancient Egyptian flour production, outlining the use of archaeological, ethnographic, and experimental research.

Samuel, Delwen. "Investigation of Ancient Egyptian Baking and Brewing Methods by Correlative Microscopy." *Science* 273 (1996), 488–490. Presents the microscopy analysis of bread loaves and their interpretation; discusses the relationship of bread and beer.

Wild, Henri. "Brasserie et panification au tombeau de Ti." *Bulletin de l'Institut Français d'Archéologie Orientale* 64 (1966), 95–120, plates 9–11. A detailed and balanced consideration of artistic and documentary sources on ancient Egyptian baking; not restricted to Old Kingdom evidence.

DELWEN SAMUEL

**BREEDING.** *See* Animal Husbandry.

**BRICKS AND BRICK ARCHITECTURE.** Mud bricks and mud-brick architecture are intimately connected with the history and archaeology of ancient Egypt; the term *adobe* comes from the Egyptian word *ḏbt*, which meant "brick." Extensive use of mud brick in construction in the Nile Valley began toward the end of the Predynastic period (c.4000–3050 BCE). Wattle-and-daub construction (wickerwork plastered with mud) had been the principal method of building before this time, and remained an important building technique throughout later Egyptian history, particularly for temporary structures. While wattle-and-daub structures had a life of only a few years, some mud-brick structures from the first and second dynasties (c.3050–2687 BCE) are still well preserved.

Henri Frankfort (1941) noted that the elaborate paneled, or niched-brick, façades found in the mud-brick funerary monuments of the first and second dynasties had parallels in the temple architecture of the Protoliterate era in Mesopotamia and suggested a direct borrowing by the ancient Egyptians. While some Egyptologists have attempted to refute that, clearly, Frankfort's interpretation was correct. A long evolution of that type of construction is evident in Mesopotamia, while it appeared suddenly in Egypt at its most complex stage of development—and closest in form to that of Uruk/Jemdet Nasr temple architecture. The pattern of niched construction transplanted into Egypt is also known as palace-façade, from the assumption that the Early Dynastic period (c.3100–2686 BCE) monuments were copies of royal residences. Not until excavations at Hierakonpolis in the 1960s was a palace of that age found with such an elaborate casing. Palace-façade became an important insignia of royalty and was used as the *serekh*, which surrounded a royal name in inscriptions. The elaborate niching found on the early tombs was gradually devolved into simple forms. The last vestige of the early niched façade was the false door that became the focus of the tomb-chapel, from the beginning of the Old Kingdom onward.

While stone increasingly became the building material of choice in funerary monuments and temples for those who could afford it, mud brick remained the standard for residential structures. Mud bricks were cheap and readily available, they were made from mud from the Nile River with the addition of straw as a binder. They were made in rectangular wooden molds and could be turned out at a relatively rapid pace—an estimate of 750 per day for one man comes from ethnographic observation. Similar to construction in stone, workers were divided into gangs under the leadership of a foreman. A number of pharaonic accounts survive that detail construction organ-

BRICKS AND BRICK ARCHITECTURE. *The Shunet el-Zebib at Abydos.* This massive, Early Dynastic mud-brick enclosure, situated a little way into the desert, is thought to have served as a monumental building for royal mortuary ceremonies. (Courtesy Dieter Arnold)

ization, including the Papyrus Reisner I, which noted specifications for clay preparation, water transport, and output. The "Louvre Leather Roll" recorded the delivery of bricks by foremen and stated whether their daily quota of two thousand bricks had been met; it also recorded the transport of other building materials, including timbers and reeds. In the Bible, the *Book of Exodus* (1.11–14) recorded a similar situation, in which the Israelites made bricks under the oversight of harsh Egyptian taskmasters.

Workers in a brickfield were shown in the tomb of Rekhmire, where Egyptians, Syrians, and Nubians—under the watchful gaze of a truncheon-wielding supervisor—were all shown bearing jars of water, mixing clay and water, and making bricks with a mold. The finished bricks were shown being inventoried and transported to the construction site. Miniature brick molds have been found in foundation deposits, and they were shown in use by kings during foundation ceremonies.

Bricks were also made for special purposes. Bricks for vaults were deeply grooved by the workmen's fingers to provide "teeth" to hold mortar, and they contained additional straw to make them light. For specific state build-

ing projects, bricks could be stamped with a royal name. The use of baked brick was generally restricted to areas that would be in contact with water frequently, but it was not until the Roman period that they were used extensively in construction.

Brick sizes varied with time and use, ranging from a few centimeters square to large blocks of half a meter (16 inches) or more in length. Mortar used to join the brick courses was generally applied in round patties of the same or finer mud, usually without straw. A desert marl clay could also be used both for mortar and for bricks. The clay bricks could be combined with mud bricks and mortar, often in the same structure. The outer faces of bricks were sometimes painted; less often, they were plastered and whitewashed. Interiors could be plastered and were occasionally painted, but interior painting in domestic structures, excluding palaces, was rare in ancient Egypt. Gypsum plaster was occasionally used in dynastic times, but extensive use of lime plaster, both as mortar and for facing, did not exist in Egypt until the era of Roman rule.

There were a large number of bonding patterns used, which depended on the thickness of the wall: usually ½ brick, 1 brick, or 1½ bricks thick. Bricks laid at an angle could be used to level a course or as interior fill in a thick wall. Often, in very thick walls, only a veneer of bonded bricks was used on the wall face and the interior was filled with rubble or with headers laid one atop another. Large walls were often battered, with the base wider than the top, for added strength. Smaller edifices might be buttressed, and single walls might be built in sinusoidal fashion, for added stability.

Another type of mud-brick construction was the casemate foundation. In this type of architecture, narrow rectangular cells of brickwork were filled with rubble and capped with a layer of brick, to form a raised area for an elevated second story or temple platform. This technique appeared in the late Second Intermediate Period, but it became increasingly more popular in the Late period, particularly in association with the large temples and palaces of Lower Egypt, such as the Palace of Apries at Memphis. In order to keep the massive walls of mud brick from slumping or cracking, various bonding methods were used and additional materials, such as timber and straw—either loose or in the form of matting—were incorporated into the walls.

In Nubia, the massive mud-brick fortifications incorporated layers of reeds and timbers in the wall for added cohesion. Open ventilator shafts ran perpendicular to the wall face, to allow for the even drying of walls. An innovation in construction occurred in the walls surrounding some temple complexes of the Late period, such as the enclosure wall at Karnak temple, the Kom es-Sultan at Abydos, and the walls of Elkab. All have bricks laid in the concave pattern called "pan bedding," which helped to avoid the slumping and settling that would affect large masses of brickwork and localize collapse when it happened. Pan bedding has been suggested to represent the primeval waters of Nun, "out of which the earth was born." The symbolism of shape is likely fortuitous; a functional purpose is a more likely origin.

Bricks were also used in ancient Egyptian roofing construction. Corbelled vaults were used in first and second dynasty tombs and in true domes during the Old Kingdom. Long chambers could be roofed by inclined vaults, which have held up well. The storehouses of the Ramesseum are a good example of their longevity. Flat roofs, usually with rafters supported by one or more rows of columns, might also be covered with mud brick, as in the palace at Malqata. Floors were occasionally paved with mud brick and were sometimes laid in a herringbone pattern, which was generally restricted to high-use areas, such as courtyards. On occasion, bricks were also used as foundations for column bases and for stone construction. Specially molded bricks for torus moldings, *cavetto* cornices, and columns have been found, but they are rare.

Bricks had been stamped with royal or official names, titles, and even, on rare occasions, the name of the structure. Model bricks—with royal names and titles, in faience or in metal—were included in foundation deposits. Inscribed "magic" bricks were part of tomb equipment from the New Kingdom onward. Such bricks were placed in the four cardinal points of the burial chamber, sometimes accompanied by amuletic figures and inscribed with spells from the *Book of Going Forth by Day (Book of the Dead);* they were meant to ward off danger, which approached the deceased from every direction.

## BIBLIOGRAPHY

Fathy, Hassan. *Architecture for the Poor.* Chicago, 1973. A review of ethnographic and experimental examples of mud-brick construction by one of modern Egypt's most famous architects.

Frankfort, Henri. "The Origin of Monumental Architecture in Egypt." *The American Journal of Semitic Languages and Literatures* 58.4 (1941), 329–358. The classic study on niched-brick architecture.

Kitchen, Kenneth. A. "From the Brickfields of Egypt." *Tyndale Bulletin* 27 (1976), 137–147. Literary sources regarding bricks and brick construction.

Spencer, A. J. *Brick Architecture in Ancient Egypt.* Warminster, 1979. The principal study of the use of mud brick.

Spencer, A. J. "Mud Brick: Its Decay and Detection in Upper and Lower Egypt." In *The Unbroken Reed: Studies in the Culture and Heritage of Ancient Egypt in Honor of A. F. Shore,* edited by C. Eyre, A. Leahy, and L. M. Leahy. Warminster, 1994. A discussion of the decay and excavation of mud-brick structures in Egypt.

PETER LACOVARA

**BRONZE.** Technically, bronze is an alloy of copper and tin; in Egyptology, the term *bronze* is often used to include a wide variety of alloys—such as arsenical copper and copper with additions of lead and of nickel. Since several metals occur in nature as impurities in native copper, the determination by archaeologists of intentional alloying has been difficult, particularly with respect to the first use of bronze in ancient Egypt. Copper ores seem to have been imported into Egypt from a variety of sources, including Cyprus, the Sinai, Southwest Asia, and, possibly, Nubia. Cast copper and hammered copper objects were made in Egypt from the Predynastic period onward. From the Old Kingdom, life-size statues of Pepy I (r. 2354–2310 BCE) and his son are the earliest surviving large-scale works in hammered copper; the composition of the sculpture was analyzed at 98.20 percent copper, 1.06 percent nickel, and 0.74 percent iron.

Copper's casting ability can be improved by the addition of tin—this reduces shrinkage, inhibits porosity, lowers the firing temperature, and increases fluidity. The resulting alloy, bronze, has the advantage of being harder and stronger than copper. Despite the obvious superiority of bronze, a longtime overlap continued for the use of copper alongside bronze in Egypt from the Middle King-

BRONZE. *Inscribed New Kingdom situla vase, from Thebes.* (University of Pennsylvania Museum, Philadelphia. Neg. # S8–31568)

dom through the New Kingdom. Copper and bronze, regardless of their various respective properties, were used indiscriminately for similar objects. There seems, as well, to be some confusion in Old Egyptian terminology, with *biȝ* ("copper") being used for *ḥsmn* ("bronze").

A large furnace was discovered at the site of Kerma in Sudan, which was dated to the Second Intermediate Period. There, copper was the principal metal in use. An even larger and more elaborate foundry was discovered at the Ramessid capital of Qantir in the Nile Delta. Similar in style to the Kerma furnace, a long trench was flanked by perpendicular channels for tuyeres (a nozzle through which air is delivered). Associated with that find were crucibles, molds, tuyeres, and finished pieces, particularly

BRONZE. *Dagger with ivory handle,
from Abydos, seventeenth dynasty.*
(University of Pennsylvania Museum,
Philadelphia. Neg. # S8–41445 [detail])

trappings for horses. Both furnaces were largely for casting, rather than smelting, as most copper was imported in ingot form.

A scene in the tomb of the vizier Rekhmire at Thebes depicted the casting of a set of doors for the temple of Karnak. Simple open-face molds were used to make tools and the surfaces of vessels were raised by hammering, but elaborate sculptures were often cast in multiple-piece molds, then assembled. The casting of such pieces was produced by the lost-wax process, or *cire perdue,* wherein a model would be made in wax over a core material, usually clay, and then encased in a clay mold. The wax would be melted off as molten metal replaced it. Significant amounts of lead added to the bronze would further increase the fluidity of the molten metal, allowing a finer casting. A large number of the bronze statuettes known from the Third Intermediate Period and later were produced in that way. Multiple-piece castings were assembled through mortise-and-tenon jointing, with cold hammering rather than soldering. Wood and other materials were employed as bases, into which sculptures could be set. Many statues were also gilt and inlaid—by cold hammering, by cementing in precast settings in the surface of the bronze, or by coating the surface with a layer of gesso and applying gilding to that. The last, a largely unsuccessful technique, was nonetheless widely employed.

## BIBLIOGRAPHY

Lucas, A., and J. R. Harris. *Ancient Egyptian Materials and Industries.* 4th ed. London, 1998.

Roeder, G. *Staatliche Museen zu Berlin: Mitteilungen aus der Ägyptischen Sammlung,* vol. 6: *Ägyptische Bronzefiguren.* Berlin, 1956. The most comprehensive work on ancient Egyptian bronzes.

YVONNE J. MARKOWITZ AND PETER LACOVARA

**BRONZE STATUETTES.** As early as the second dynasty, copper was used for statuary. Although the shift from copper to bronze (a copper-tin alloy) was gradual, bronze was already in use for statuary during the Middle Kingdom. It strongly predominated in the New Kingdom and later periods when metal statuary was flourishing. Statuary made from the range of cupreous (copper and copper-alloy) materials forms a closely related group, which is considered here under the heading bronze.

**Problems of Bronze Statuary.** The study of bronze statuary poses special problems. Bronze was an extremely popular medium in the Third Intermediate Period and the Late and Ptolemaic periods. A very great number of examples therefore require analysis and organization. Archaeology has provided only limited dating assistance, because excavated bronzes tend to derive from temple deposits of statuary cleared after an extended use period. Inscriptional analyses have offered important contributions, but many bronzes are uninscribed. Stylistic analysis has been complicated, because the periods of the greatest popularity of bronze statuary were times of conscious and compounded archaism with two millennia of tradition on which to draw (Third Intermediate Period, Late period) and ones when political and stylistic relations were complicated in other new ways. Furthermore, standards for the representations of gods—the area of greatest bronze production—conservative. Compositional studies (which had been difficult to perform but have become more standard) can provide only broad suggested date ranges, based on a gradual change in alloyed metals, a criterion further obscured by the very probable practice of melting down and reusing scrap metal from earlier periods. Such technological studies and structural analyses are, however, helpful in establishing and evaluating the frauds and the modern interventions often encountered (reworkings and pastiches); these otherwise tend to be among the great numbers of Egyptian bronzes produced anciently skewing our perceptions of the range of authentic productions.

Important developments are underway that will bring new understandings. Until the 1990s, the descriptive and analytical studies of Günther Roeder (1937 and 1956) were the only significant systematic work done on Egyptian bronzes. His observations and information were typologically and technologically oriented, so only incidentally provided historical indications. Much new knowledge and more chronological refinements are promised by publication of the excavations at North Saqqara; studies of important collections, such as that by the Rijksmuseum in Leiden or that undertaken by the Musée du Louvre, which incorporates studies of a Saqqara cache, black bronzes, and Third Intermediate Period large bronze females associated with Karnak; and studies of groups of related bronzes, such as late Middle Kingdom statues, Kushite kings, kneeling kings, and statues with private inscriptions. Gradually, a full history of bronze statuary will result.

**Production and General Characteristics.** Representations of Egyptian metal statuary workshops are known but there is only sparse archaeological documentation. Still, ancient methods can be understood in large degree by the study of ancient examples and by analogy with modern methods. Metal statuary could be formed by hammering or casting. The method for most Egyptian bronze statuary was casting, using the lost-wax method—a casting mold was formed around a wax model, which could then be melted out and then replaced by molten metal. The process resulted in solid-cast statuary or elements. If the molten metal was poured around a nonrefractory core material, then hollow-cast statuary or elements were the result. The Egyptians usually did not remove core material. Statuary was either of one piece (integral) or composed of separately cast elements that were joined by a variety of methods.

Several alloys were used to make statuary throughout Egyptian history. In order of earlier to later use but with much overlapping of chronological ranges, they were: copper; possibly arsenical copper; bronze with variable tin content; and leaded bronzes. The shift from copper to bronze for statuary was gradual, owing to artisanal and economic considerations; therefore, for the early transitional period or to refer to the corpus of copper and bronze statuary as a whole, the term "cupreous" would be most accurate. Moreover, the ancient Roman writer Pliny, in his *Natural History*, noted that Roman-era bronzeworkers recommended the addition of scrap metal to a melt as an enhancing factor; that practice of melting down the copper or bronze scrap of earlier times almost certainly existed in Egypt and contributes greatly to the blurring of distinctions among alloys. Black copper or black bronze, an alloy with gold, known widely in the ancient world as early as the Middle Bronze Age, appeared frequently in high-quality statuary from Egypt's Late Middle Kingdom through the Third Intermediate Period.

Copper and bronze, which retained rich color and metallic luster longer in the dry, unpolluted air than they do today—and which might be partially or completely clad with gold or silver sheet or leaf or inlaid with other metals, stones, or glass—provided important coloristic and tonal possibilities. In contrast to Egyptian stone statuary but like wooden statuary, bronze also provided a pure and emphatic profile.

**Roles of Bronze Statuary.** Three main roles for bronze statuary can be recognized for ancient Egypt. Large bronzes—by their size, quality, and the technical complexity of their manufacture—were important images

BRONZE STATUETTES. *Thutmose III, eighteenth dynasty.* (The Metropolitan Museum of Art, 1995.21)

of a person, usually a king or a high official. Their original context is not well understood; perhaps they stood in temples or funerary chapels; small bronzes probably sometimes served similar purposes. Small royal statuary, however, was dominated by types—most significant and most numerous among them the kneeling kings—which were associated with ritual performance roles. Verified examples are rare of other types—such as seated kings or striding kings without offerings—that might have been recipients rather than performers of ritual. Small, relatively indestructible, lustrous, and conveying an important message through their clearly readable postures, such statues were probably used most distinctively in processional equipment and other types of ritual apparatus.

In addition, bronze enjoyed a great popularity in the Late and Ptolemaic periods as a medium for votive statuary, generally donated to temples by private persons. The suitability of bronze for such donations may be partly based on the ease with which fair-sized images could be produced in great numbers, because of the comparative ease of producing wax models for casting. Still, despite the great number produced, no evidence has yet been discovered for the actual replication processes or for mass production of ancient Egyptian bronzes. The popularity of bronze for votive statuary may also be related to its long association with the temple cult and, perhaps, to a perceived kinship with precious metals, which allowed it to be used as a substitute in divine statuary.

**Before the New Kingdom.** The history of Egyptian cupreous statuary begins with the large hammered copper statues from Hierakonpolis, of Pepy I of the sixth dynasty and a smaller figure (although an earlier copper statue of Khasekhemwy is referred to on the Palermo Stone). The excavators originally suggested that the Hierakonpolis statues were partially cast, but no scientific evaluation has been published. Small cast cupreous statuary that depicted male and female nonroyal persons has been ascribed to the later Old Kingdom, the First Intermediate Period, and the Middle Kingdom. Very few pieces were excavated, but stylistically they seem to span that interval, and their poses are similar to those of nonroyal wooden tomb statuary, including nude or clothed striding males, males with staffs wearing kilts or long official kilts. From the late Middle Kingdom, a large group was said to be from a single find in the Faiyum area; with other pieces attributable to that period, they form a sizeable variety of cupreous statuary. Categorized here to present the emerging roles of bronze statuary before the New Kingdom, they are: large and small statuary of royalty (a near lifesize royal male torso and head; a queen; a large striding king statuette; and a small princess of the thirteenth dynasty nursing a child), including royalty with a clear role in temple cult (a small prostrate king on an incense burner and a fairly large kneeling king statuette); large statuettes of high officials; and possible early deity representations (a nursing woman and child, which some scholars think represents Isis and Horus, and a crocodile, surely connected with the cults of Sobek, the crocodileheaded god). The Faiyum group provided verified examples of early hollow-casting, separable elements, metal inlay, and use of the black-copper or black-bronze alloy that served as a contrasting background for the inlay of other, brighter metals.

**New Kingdom.** For the New Kingdom, while textual references and likely depictions of bronze statuary (censers with kneeling statuettes of Thutmose III or perhaps processional bark statuary) were found, the number of firmly attributed statuettes remains small. Some number are probably unrecognized; still, particular temple roles for royal bronze statuary had further developed, as evidenced by an important series of kneeling statuettes of kings, including Thutmose III, Thutmose IV, an uninscribed but probable Tutankhamun, and Ramesses II. The coincidence of their appearance with the elaboration of the figural equipment of the great New Kingdom processional barks and other processional equipment depicted in reliefs suggests a possible relationship, especially since later bronze examples of statuary types restricted to baths are known. Other examples, such as a small bronze statuette of an Amarna king further emphasize the role of royal statuary as an element of cult and processional equipment. Rare examples of private and divine statuary have been identified (a small crocodile inscribed with the name of Amenhotpe III has been noted by Christiane Ziegler), and others probably exist. Genre statuary was found as part of utensils, such as mirrors and stands. *Shawabti*s of royal (Ramesses II) and nonroyal figures (as, for example, the late eighteenth dynasty milling *shawabti* of Si-Ese, now at the Brooklyn Museum of Art) were found from the New Kingdom onward into the Third Intermediate Period.

**Late Ramessid and Third Intermediate Periods.** From the late Ramessid and Third Intermediate Periods, royal statuettes or fragments thereof are known in kneeling, striding, and sphinx poses—and in a variety of sizes. Also from the Third Intermediate Period, and extending even to the twenty-sixth dynasty, came a number of large bronze statues: one of a king and the rest of high persons, especially females; Elisabeth Delange, John Taylor, and their colleagues at the Louvre and British Museum have shown that some of the females especially were connected with the cult of Amun at Karnak, and some served processional uses. A few bronze statuettes of gods are inscriptionally and a number stylistically datable to that time. The bronzes of the period show strong interest in surface decoration and coloristic effects; the large complex bronzes, most of all, testify to a very high level of technical ability.

The reasons for the particular flourishing of bronze, and indeed precious metal, statuary during the Third Intermediate Period remain obscure and are surely numerous. Moreover, our poor knowledge of the New Kingdom artifactual record may contribute to an exaggerated contrast. Nonetheless, it may be that the periods overlay of cult structure—where precious metal and bronze statuary had their most distinctive and coherent use—with political structure might have combined to influence the types and materials favored.

**Kushite Dynasty.** Considerable emphasis was placed on royal bronze statuary by the Kushite kings of the twenty-fifth dynasty. Numerous kneeling kings date to that dynasty, and a number of new ritual positions are represented by statuettes that may also date to the dynasty. The elaboration of a typology and the multiplication of ritual examples might be the extension of a process that began in the Third Intermediate Period. Kushite depictions and the existence of distinctive types of bronze processional bark statuary indicate that the dynasty gave attention to bark processions; the remains of what was conjectured to be a wooden bark in temple A at Kawa, along with bronze royal statuary scattered about the site, is however, not a convincing association.

Several examples of a type whose first certain examples were dated to the Third Intermediate Period are preserved from the Kushite period, that is, kings with arms extended and palms facing inward (as the Athens Shabako). These are often referred to as "offering bronzes," whose offering (such as a vessel) is missing or implied, although no bronzes of this type have preserved offerings, and royal bronzes seem to be generally associated with a restricted set of offerings (*nw*-pots or the goddess Maat or the *wḏꜣt*). The pose is that of royal figures shown protecting baldachin (canopy) poles on a divine processional bark or protecting and holding divine standards and emblems and the like; such statuettes, which became increasingly popular, may actually have filled that type of protective role.

The Kushite period also provided the earliest preserved example of a kneeling bronze king, offering round *nw*-pots in a fixed grouping with a god (Taharqa with Hemen, now in the Louvre). That is a rather special piece, however, without archaeological provenance uniting what seems to be an older, rather crude stone image of the falcon god Hemen with a fine bronze image of Taharqa—the god covered with gold sheet and the unifying base with silver. If not surprising, this is the first preserved physical indication that the use of bronze royal statuary extended beyond employment in ritual and processional equipment to small, simple groupings which might have been set in shrines, like those seen in the Festival Reliefs of Osorkon I. Divine bronze statuary can be attributed to the Kushite dynasty both by inscription and by style, and it provides an indicator for the major trend in bronze statuary for the rest of the Late period and the Ptolemaic era. Kushite inscribed nonroyal donations seem to be restricted to high officials of the divine adoratrices, and made on behalf of the latter.

Although they are smaller and simpler and display less interest in inlay techniques, the bronzes of the period are often very fine sculptures, with high-quality detailed castings.

**Late Period through the Ptolemaic Period.** Distinctions among these periods are difficult to make be-

cause the record is suffused with great numbers of votive bronzes, most without either inscriptions or very precise archaeological context, if any. A few indications of the situation are given here. Some large or otherwise important bronzes of private persons belong to the twenty-sixth dynasty; for example, the Brooklyn Museum's Harbes and the British Museum's Khonserdaisu, from the time of Psamtik I, and the Ephesus Museum's Ihat, from Necho II/Psamtik II.

Small, kneeling bronze kings with royal names inscribed on the statuette were made through the twenty-sixth dynasty, with the last known that of Hakoris of the twenty-ninth dynasty. Numerous other bronze kings are datable to the periods by style. In that class must be included a number of important Kushite bronzes, whose inscriptions and distinctive regalia were modified (probably at the time of Psamtik II) while the statuettes were apparently retained in use. Royal statuettes, though uninscribed, continued to be made during Ptolemaic times. At the same time, royal statuettes in various reverential positions, grouped with a deity, begin to appear.

While the private practice of donating votive bronzes had roots in earlier periods, for reasons that are poorly understood, it gained great currency in the Late and Ptolemaic periods, along with a number of other votive practices. Many important questions about the nature of religious practices, temples, and the production of votive objects have not yet been satisfactorily answered. (For bronzes, publication of the deposits of statuary found in the Egypt Exploration Society excavation of the Saqqara Sacred Animal Necropolis will be a great step forward.)

Votive statuary—comprising either individual figures or groups of figures, with the occasional inclusion of what seems to be a royal or priestly intermediary figure—generally depicted the gods and the animal manifestations of gods. Some of the statuary served also as coffins for votive animal mummies, another major votive practice of the time. Osiris seems the most popular of the subjects, but a great range of choices was displayed; some, such as statuettes of Neith or of Mahes of Leontopolis, had narrower chronological or geographical ranges. Moreover, a number of inscriptions have been dated to the Saite period, based on various criteria. Inscribed examples may name a royal or private donor (one Saite statuary corpus collected by Herman DeMeulenaere [1990], seems to record both a donor and a temple subaltern as facilitator of the donation), and they most often request that the donor be given life, indicating that one large purpose of the dona-

BRONZE STATUETTES. *The god Ptah, twenty-sixth dynasty or later.* (University of Pennsylvania Museum, Philadelphia. Neg. # S4–143063)

tions was direct request for eternal life. Some seemingly uninscribed bronzes may have been inscribed on wooden bases that are now missing.

Beyond Egypt, there were successors to the Kushite period bronzes, created by the cultures of Nubia and Sudan. Most are small and the subject matter not surprising; however, a major bronze statue of a standing, armed Meroitic king has been found on the Isle of Argo, and it has been dated to 200 BCE (by D. Wildung, *Sudan Antike Königreiche am Nil*, 1996, no. 270).

**Roman Period.** There are perhaps traditional Egyptian bronzes made in the Roman period, but they represent increasingly marginalized subjects. There are, however, also some Egyptianized Roman types, such as winged, kneeling kings who hold offering tables against their thighs.

**Archaeology.** As mentioned above, the archaeological record for bronze statuary is frustrating. Many excavations of temple sites included bronzes among the finds, but listed below in roughly chronological order are groups that either suggest a restricted date or otherwise offer important information:

- A few private statuettes from the First Intermediate Period and Middle Kingdom were traceable to tomb contexts in Middle Egypt. New Kingdom and Third Intermediate Period *shawabti*s, whether royal or private, have or clearly imply a nontemple provenance.

- A temple structure at Hierakonpolis yielded the large statues of Pepy I and the associated figure. Several large Third Intermediate Period bronzes are traceable to Karnak and chapels there.

- Deposits of Osiris statuettes at Medinet Habu were found in a number of areas, none clearly datable before the later Ptolemaic period, though the likely time of deposition may in some cases be narrowed. Some, at least, may be associated with the Gods' Wives buried there, since stone Osirises were certainly offered in their names at that site. Osiris statuettes, other gods, and king's statuettes some definitely of the twenty-fifth dynasty derived from temples constructed in the twenty-fifth dynasty at Kawa but destroyed in Meroitic times.

- Deposits from the first stage of the Heraion at Samos, which has been dated to the late eighth and first half of the seventh centuries BCE, preserved an important group of Egyptian bronzes including large statues of males and some goddesses. Other bronzes of early date are still being found. This suggests the possibility of Egyptian influence on Greek bronzes at a formative time.

- Excavations by the French near Dush in the Kharga Oasis (reported yearly in *Bulletin de l'Institut français d'archeologie orientale*) have uncovered a temple that seems to date from the mid-twenty-seventh to the early twenty-ninth dynasty and contains large deposits of bronze votive Osirises.

- A large number of bronzes came from deposits in the area of the Saqqara Sacred Animal Necropolis. Many were excavated in the nineteenth century, and the archaeological records have been difficult to reconstruct. Others derive from controlled excavations by the Egypt Exploration Society and publication of most of these is awaited; the preliminary reports by H. S. Smith promise useful segregation of the votive deposits by date and, to some extent, by purpose.

## BIBLIOGRAPHY

Bianchi, Robert S. "Egyptian Metal Statuary of the Third Intermediate Period (Circa 1070–656 B.C.), from Its Egyptian Antecedents to Its Samian Examples." In *Small Bronze Sculpture from the Ancient World*, edited by Marion True and Jerry Podany, pp. 61–84. Malibu, 1990. Focus on the Third Intermediate Period and the period of importation of Egyptian bronzes to Samos.

Davies, Sue, and Harry S. Smith. *The Sacred Animal Necropolis at North Saqqara. Falcon Complex and Catacomb*. London, forthcoming. This report deals with a significant proportion of the bronze statuary from the Sacred Animal Necropolis excavations and gives reference to the Saqqara reports.

Delange, Elisabeth, Angélique de Mantova, and John H. Taylor. "Un Bronze égyptien méconnu." *Revue du Louvre* 5 (1998), 67–75. Close art historical and technical study of a large bronze female in the Louvre, with gathering of related objects.

Delvaux, Luc. "Les Bronzes de Sais. Les dieux de Bouto et les rois des marais." In *Egyptian Religion. The Last Thousand Years*, Part 1, edited by Willy Clarysse, Antoon Schnoors, and Harco Willems, pp. 551–568. Louvain, 1998. Pieces together an early bronze find and notes other pieces that might belong iconographically.

DeMeulenaere, Herman. "Bronzes égyptiens de donation." *Bulletin des Musées Royaux d'Art et d'Histoire* 61 (1990), 63–81. Identification of a group of votive bronzes, with inscriptions that tell us something more about the votive practice.

Hill, Marsha. "A Bronze Statuette of Thutmose III," with appendix by Deborah Schorsch, "A Technological Overview." *The Metropolitan Museum of Art Journal* 37 (1997). Discussion of New Kingdom royal kneeling bronzes and their role; the appendix by the technical author includes a discussion of black copper or black bronze.

Jantzen, Ulf. *Samos VIII: Ägyptische und Orientalische Bronzen aus dem Heraion von Samos*. Bonn, 1972. Illustrates many Egyptian bronzes from Samos. For other material and discussion, see Bianchi (1990) and also Helmut Kyrieleis's contribution in the same collection.

Leahy, Anthony. "Egypt as a Bronzeworking Centre (1000–539 B.C.)." In *Bronzeworking Centres of Western Asia c. 1000–539 B.C.*, edited by John Curtis, pp. 297–309. London, 1988. Provides the larger historical and regional picture.

Müller, Maya. "Der kniende König im 1. Jahrtausend." *Bulletin de la Société d'Égyptologie, Genève*, 13 (1989), 121–130. Very condensed study that outlines the problems of bronzes depicting kneeling kings in the Late period; includes extensive references to dated material.

Ortiz, George. *In Pursuit of the Absolute: Art of the Ancient World*, nos. 33–37. London, 1996. Most of the finds from the Middle Kingdom Faiyum group are discussed and illustrated; references are given to those not in the Ortiz collection.

Roeder, Günther. *Ägyptische Bronzewerke*. Glückstadt, 1937.

Roeder, Günther. *Staatliche Muszeen zu Berlin: Mitteilungen aus der Ägyptischen Sammlung, vol. 6, Ägyptische Bronzefiguren.* Berlin, 1956. With the previous work, the basic iconographic and technological organization of the material.

Romano, James. "A Statuette of a Royal Mother and Child in The Brooklyn Museum." *Mitteilungen des Deutschen Archäologischen Instituts* 48 (1992), 131–143. Detailed study of a small royal bronze female from the pivotal late Middle Kingdom period and listing of early small statuary.

Russmann, Edna R. *The Representation of the King in the XXVth Dynasty.* Brussels and New York (Brooklyn), 1974. Includes a compilation of known Kushite bronze kings.

Russmann, Edna R. "An Egyptian Royal Statuette of the Eighth Century B.C." In *Studies in Ancient Egypt, the Aegean, and the Sudan,* edited by William Kelly Simpson and Whitney M. Davis, pp. 149–156. Boston, 1981. Observations about royal bronzes, including stylistic assessments of the known Third Intermediate Period royal bronzes, which point the way toward further identifications.

Schorsch, Deborah. "Technical Examination of Ancient Egyptian Theriomorphic Hollow Cast Bronzes—Some Case Studies." In *Conservation of Ancient Egyptian Materials,* edited by S. C. Watkins and C. E. Brown, pp. 41–50. London, 1988. Structural studies.

Taylor, John, Paul Craddock, and Fleur Shearman. "Egyptian Hollow-Cast Bronze Statuettes of the Early First Millennium B.C." *Apollo* (July 1998), pp. 9–14. Technical and archival overview of a number of large bronzes.

Thieme, Andrea. "A Brief Note Concerning the Filiation *zꜣ* Nʿ[-n-]-f-ʾlʿḥ msj ḥpt.ti." *Göttinger Miszellen* 153 (1996), 101–105. Includes listings of securely dated bronze deity and animal representations.

Vassilika, Eleni. "Egyptian Bronze Sculpture before the Late Period." In *Chief of Seers: Egyptian Studies in Memory of Cyril Aldred,* edited by Elizabeth Goring et al., pp. 291–302. London, 1997. Some suggested new datings; useful correlation of these and known pieces with compositional analyses.

Ziegler, Christiane. "Les arts du métal à la Troisième Période Intermédiaire." In *Tanis L'or des pharaons,* cat. exp., pp. 85–101. Paris, 1987. Review article; listings of Third Intermediate Period bronze statuary.

Ziegler, Christiane. "Jalons pour une histoire de l'art égyptien: la statuaire de métal au Musée du Louvre." *Revue du Louvre* 1 (1996), 29–38. Surveys bronze history through the Louvre collections, in particular. Many important dated pieces are noted, a number of ongoing investigations are signaled.

MARSHA HILL

## BROTHER-SISTER MARRIAGES. *See* Marriage and Divorce.

## BUBASTIS,

**BUBASTIS,** a site in the eastern Nile Delta, on the so-called Canal of Moses, which leads to the Tanitic branch of the Nile. The ruins of the ancient town are increasingly encroached upon by new construction in the city of Zagazig. Bubastis was the Greek transcription of the ancient Egyptian name Per Bastet or *pr Bꜣstt,* ("the house of Bastet"); it is mentioned in Hebrew scriptures as Pi-beseth (*Ezek.* 30.17). Its supraregional importance resulted from the worship of the cat-headed goddess Bastet. In the fifth century BCE, the Greek historian Herodotus wrote an account of the city and its festivals.

The political importance of Bubastis is uncertain. Belonging initially to the Heliopolitan nome (the thirteenth nome of Lower Egypt), by New Kingdom times it had acquired independence as the eighteenth nome of Lower Egypt. During the twenty-second and twenty-third dynasties, it was the capital of the northern part of Egypt under the Libyan rulers and its strategic location was, without doubt, of great importance. Situated on the trade route to Israel, it was an important base for expeditions and military operations.

The vast ruins, today encompassing about 70 hectares (175 acres), are dominated by the main temple. The site, at least 200 meters (660 feet) long and 60 meters (185 feet) wide, is littered with more than three thousand fragments of granite. The building was at one time possibly surrounded by a canal, as was reported by Herodotus. On the surface, today, is a mixed layer composed of wind-born sand, splinters of limestone, and mud that accumulated during the last two millennia; it covers the ruins of the temple with a thickness of 0.3 to 2 meters (1 to 6 feet). Since 1991, that area has been cleared to uncover the original level of the temple. The fragments indicated that much of the temple was built of limestone; in Roman times a lime kiln was located at the site. The remaining architectural features were of red granite, as was the temple's foundation. Among the finds were the Hathor capitals, some papyrus-bud columns, architraves with reliefs, cornice blocks, fragments of *uraeus*-friezes, and a palm-leaf capital. In addition, more than one hundred fragments of at least thirty statues were found.

The temple was built with three parts: to the east are the entrance and doorway, which were erected by Osorkon I and Osorkon II, with reliefs depicting the *sed*-festival; to the west are the visible remains of the construction of Nektanebo; between the two was a spacious courtyard, with an axial colonnade bounded to the north and south by a mud-brick wall.

The temple of Pepy I, located to the west of the main temple and separated by the modern road, was uncovered by Labib Habachi in 1939. The temple was surrounded by a mud-brick wall. The portal on the south was built of limestone; an inscription there identifies the founder of the temple as Pepy I. Opposite the entrance lies the sanctuary, also made of mud bricks, and passing through the entrance are a small, inner court and a hall with two rows of four pillars. Behind it were five sanctuaries. The mud-brick walls of the building are now destroyed, but the enclosure wall is clearly perceptible. Remains of later insertions show that the temple continued in use.

On the south of the ancient town is the Middle Kingdom palace, a building that covered an area of nearly 2.5

BUBASTIS. *Giant ruins of the Bastet Temple of Osorkon I and II, twenty-second dynasty.* (Courtesy Dieter Arnold)

acres, which was excavated in 1961 by Shafik Farid, Achmed es-Sawy, and Mohamed Bakr. They distinguished three strata. The latest was dated to the Ramessid era, as brought to light by vaulted tombs and *shawabti* (funerary figures). Below that, the vast palace area was located, which can now be seen. Below the palace, tombs were found that testify to an early settlement. The palace was built with four parts: (1) the roofed entrance and the reception court on the southeast; (2) an extensive domestic and administrative building, with granaries, on the southwest; (3) a festival court, main hall, and numerous small rooms on the northeast; and (4) the domestic area on the northwest, which included the house of the owner and three adjoining houses. The whole construction was of mud bricks; some limestone column bases and thresholds were also found.

Cemeteries extended to the east and west of the palace. In the eastern cemetery, dated to the Old Kingdom, numerous tombs were excavated; in some cases they contained false doors, reliefs, and inscriptions. In another cemetery, on the southwest, was found the tomb of Hori II, the viceroy of Kush under both Ramesses III and Ramesses IV. It was a family tomb with a corridor and three chambers that contained sarcophagi carved from both granite and limestone. Bubastis is also noted for some chance discoveries, such as the 1905 find called the Treasure of Zagazig, which consists of numerous cat statuettes and a silver vessel, as well as the statue of a seated woman with her son(?) on her knees, found in 1997.

### BIBLIOGRAPHY

El-Sawi, Achmed. *Excavations at Tell Basta: Report of Seasons 1967–1971 and Catalogue of Finds.* Prague, 1979.

Habachi, Labib. *Tell Basta.* Supplément aux Annales du Service des antiquités de l'Égypte, 22. Cairo, 1957.

Naville, Édouard. *Bubastis (1887–1889).* Memoir of the Egyptian Exploration Society, 8. London, 1891.

Naville, Édouard. *The Festival-Hall of Osorkon II in the Great Temple of Bubastis (1897–1889).* Memoir of the Egyptian Exploration Society, 10. London, 1892.

CHRISTIAN TIETZE

**BUHEN.** *See* Forts and Garrisons.

**BULL GODS.** The ancient Egyptian pantheon included bull, cow, and calf divinities. Alongside the forms of higher gods—human figures with bovine heads—representations of naturalistic forms show a corresponding variety, from cult figures shaped like bulls, cows, and calves to small sculptures and amulets. Bovine shapes and cult figures of bulls with changing attributes have been found on processional and district standards, on the finials of staffs, in reliefs and paintings on temple walls, on stelae, coffins, and other surfaces. The figures reflect the theological role of the bull-shaped god as a form of the sun god and the events of creation at the beginning of time.

**Origins.** Various origins have been suggested for the bull gods of Egypt. Generally, they are thought to have originated in Late Paleolithic to Neolithic times. Four categories have been distinguished: the wild bull; the herd bull; the threshing animal; and the heavenly bull, in a star group. Eberhard Otto (1923) had assumed that bulls and bull cults emerged out of the locally venerated bull gods of the Nile Delta. They were thought to be connected with Egypt's royal cattle, raised on the western edge of the Delta. Through those herds, the Apis bull became the sacred bull of the western district, where it was later venerated in a sanctuary, alongside the Sechathor cow goddess, its mother figure. From there, it may have gone to the royal city of Memphis. Similar prehistoric origins have been claimed for the bull on the district standard of the eleventh Lower Egyptian nome (province), the "black bull." There is, however, reason to posit an Upper Egyptian milieu for the wild bull—the Buchis bull of Armant, first attested in the New Kingdom; its theological name means something like "who makes the *ba* dwell within the body." There was also the Merhu bull ("the anointed one") who was identified with a daughter of an Old Kingdom queen.

Very early in dynastic times, the aggressive wild bull became the manifestation of the Egyptian king. Its subsequent butchering; the selection of the choicest parts (front shank); the sacrifice of the flesh with presentation to the god; and the eating of the flesh, whereby the bull's strength was assimilated—all were certainly very ancient components of hunting activity that were ritualized as a chief's or king's duty. On late prehistoric rock drawings near Hierakonpolis and on dynastic ceremonial palettes, the "charging bull" depicts the chief or king. In Hierakonpolis, some tombs of bovine groups were found. There is early documentation, under Horus Aha, of the royal ritual of capturing and spearing the wild bull. Since the wild bull was encountered in the mid-Delta (Chois and Buto), however, Wolfgang Helck (1987) prefers to assume a different kind of prehistoric world of eastern Mediterranean cultures—all with a common veneration of the "storm bull." At the harvest feast of the god Min, a "white bull" was used. The bull called Tjai-sepf ("the manliest of his threshing floor") is part of the title used by queens of the Old Kingdom. Both bulls must have been connected to the threshing of grain.

The heavenly bull was associated with a star group that had rows of bull heads. Their horns encompassed a star. One of the signs of the Egyptian zodiac was the front part of a bull.

Most bull gods of dynastic Egypt were initially connected with the king or queen. A bull cult that came from Egypt's own regional prehistory cannot yet be demonstrated. Perhaps the bull gods of the Delta came to the settlements of the Delta only in dynastic times, via the royal seat of Memphis, as divine protection figures for the new royal administration (in the standards and bull statues of the temple court). From the first dynasty, the "manifestation of the king" was firmly connected with the "course of the Apis bull." During the royal residence feasts in Memphis, a holy bull was led to the Nile or to its herd of cows; this yearly procession played a roll in the official cattle count (which at first took place every two years). For the Memphis court, it represented a guarantee for the annual Nile flooding and the fertility of the cattle herds, as well as a reaffirmation of the power of the kingdom.

According to the Late period Greek historian Manetho, only in the second dynasty was the Apis bull installed as a god in Memphis—with its own shrine or an external stone image of a bull in stride. The Apis god of Memphis that protected the king and the residence, however, must be sharply distinguished from the holy Apis bull of the Memphite festival procession. Like every Egyptian god, the new tutelary god of the royal seat of Memphis needed a yearly renewal process to make him effective at the enthroning of the high gods. From the Old Kingdom, the recording of the "capture of the (wild bull) Apis," the "drowning of Apis" in the Nile, or the "eating of the flesh of Apis" appears to contradict the original task of the bull of the royal seat of Memphis—ensuring the fertility of the herds. The renewal ritual of the bull god included the royal sacrifice of the bull, his ritual killing, and his transformation into Osiris, god of the dead. In the feast of Apis at Memphis, there may have been an increasing use of substitute animals. The yearly festival was repeated at Egypt's sacred places, in reduced ritualized forms, but with the help of Apis standards, staffs, and sacrificial bulls. Formal scenes of the royal Apis hunt were later added to many temples. The royal military and administrative seat at Heliopolis had its own holy bull for annual festival processions, and a protective cultic image of a bull was installed. Theologically, the Mnevis bull god of Heliopolis had many parallels with Apis as a royal god—both turned over the goddess Maat to the heavenly sun god (Atum and Re) at the first creation. Perhaps the origin for the Mnevis bull of Heliopolis was an archer with the head of a bull, derived from comparable later archers with the head of a bull, which were erected at the royal *sed*-festival.

**Theology.** In texts, the bull of the Egyptian festival procession was designated as a "holy animal," an "animal belonging to a god." From the New Kingdom, increasing theologizing of the bull gods occurred, which previous theory had considered of secondary importance. Earthly bull gods that protected the temple and the city were minor filial forms of the cosmic creator gods. In the texts, they can be the "*ba* of a high divinity"; however, if the high god wished to manifest himself in a permanent manner in a living bull, he could do so. Thus the living Memphite Apis bull became a form of the son and representative of the god Ptah; the living Mnevis bull became the son and representative of the god Re. In fact, all the bull gods could have *ba*-forms of the various primeval and high gods (the gods of the Great Ennead; the Nine Great Gods). Depending on the text, Apis was Ptah, Ptah-Sokar-Osiris, Geb-Shu, Osiris, Re, Atum, and/or Horus—or, as later texts say, "all in one." That the living holy bull is something like a "*ba* of Osiris, the god of the dead" is not stated anywhere.

The changing *ba* of the bull gods may describe various identity phases that are not possessed by the living bull but only by the bull god made manifest in the visible statue. These identities with the gods of the Great Ennead are possessed by a bull god during his yearly cyclical renewal (or the reduced cultic form repeated daily)—for example, at the annual civil new year feast, after the bull god has first become Osiris during the procession into the necropolis. The form in which the bull god was first carried to the tomb during the procession was that of the resting bull, and from the Saqqara cemetery, a portable, wooden processional bull survives. After its resurrection as Osiris, during the Osiris feast some days before the new year's festival, the god that reigned and sat upon the throne as Osiris held such syncretic names as Osiris-Apis, Osiris-Mnevis, Osiris-bull of Pharbaithos, and the like. The Osiris bull god was made visible outside the necropolis temple, in the stone cultic image of the resting bull. On new year's day, the bull was then once again presented as a "revived god," in the cultic image of the pacing bull. As a youthful god resembling Horus, it could effectively act as the tutelary (guardian) god of the city. During the procession, it accompanied Horus the king, and in a standing image it assisted in the enthronement of Horus. Only during the enthronement of the youthful city god on new year's day, however, was the holy processional bull similar to Horus in the role of the royal "city god." Only then were the Horus king and Horus-like bull god identical in phase, like "twins" at the enthronement of the bull god in Memphis. Official name-taking by several Ptolemaic kings reflects this.

The very ancient fusion of Egypt's king with the bull—with both the aggressive wild bull and the bull of fertility—allowed the bull's characteristics, his strength and sexual potency, to become part of the essence of royalty. The bull's primeval strength became an essential element of kingship. During the *sed*-festival the king became a bull

as part of his own physical and bodily renewal. The king's Horus-name is "the strong bull," from the time of the eighteenth dynasty, and the king is also the "bull of his mother." With the incorporation of the bull's strengths through the sacrifice, the king attains all the various identities. The burning of the sacrificed bull's flesh led the deities Atum and Re through his smoke in the morning and evening rituals.

Eventually, the royal characteristics from the primeval bull and their related phase identities were transferred to the gods. Since every Egyptian high god functioned as a king, theoretically the bull form could be attributed to all of them: Amun, Atum, Re, Ptah, Thoth, Shu, Osiris, Min, Seth, and others. There were cow forms, as well, for the corresponding female deities. The high gods transformed themselves during mysterious primeval divine processes (in the events of the creation of the world, as repeated in the ongoing cult), for example, on the feast days before the new year. Among the most significant original forms—alongside the bull—were the lion, crocodile, falcon, and ram. The essential characteristics of the primeval bulls were then needed for subsequent transfer to the god of heaven: the entire group of bulls were again found with this high god—the heavenly sun god Re, Amun-Re, the high Ptah-south-of his wall, and others. The earthly bull image, as youthful divinity, was in turn visible every morning, as the son of this high god, who then dwelled in the form of the bull. Thus in the cosmogony of Memphis, eight primeval bulls were used and attributed to the creator god Ptah(-Tatennen).

What relevance the numerous bull gods had for the Egyptian population is in dispute. Were the bull gods derived from early agricultural beliefs or was their origin in the renewal ritual of the king and his administration at the royal temple? Entering into the temples of Egypt by way of the royal administration, the bull gods might have been associated with the people, as perhaps is the case in Saqqara. As a rule, where bull gods were venerated, only that local population could erect its own stela, to which they became administratively and personally bound, as partakers in that feast and the ensuing cultic event. The people had no free access to the bull gods, and they could not present them with personal petitions. Priests, however, were entitled to such access, as were officials who visited the necropolis shrines on the days of processions out of the city. Despite the popularity of the Apis bull processional among the common people, even into Roman times, and its status as a tourist attraction, the people had no real emotional attachment to or faith in the individual Apis god. The Memphis Apieion was insignificant, and the court god Apis was only one of innumerable animal-shaped gods representing royalty in all the temples.

**Historical Development.** During the Old Kingdom, the bull gods, aside from the Apis bull, are mentioned mainly in titles, but they occur also in inscriptions in pyramids and coffins. During the New Kingdom, under Thutmose III, the sacred herd of Mnevis bulls of Heliopolis was mentioned for the first time. From the time of Amenhotpe III, animal tutelary gods were increasingly placed into the courts of the royal temples, and the Amun-bull-of-Egypt may have been among them. Under Amenhotpe III, the Apis bulls of Memphis were interred in sumptuous individual tombs in the necropolis of Saqqara. The entombment of the Apis bulls should not be ascribed to or confused with any popularity of the Memphis bull. The Apis god, to whom the processional bull belonged, was essential for the king's bodily renewal and his *sed*-festival; through that cyclical renewal, the king and the bull divinity were brought together. Akhenaten (Amenhotpe IV) abandoned the many royal tutelary gods, keeping only one god, Aten, in his new theology; however, in his early boundary stelae as his new capital, Akhetaten (Tell el-Amarna), he mentions a tomb to be erected for the Mnevis. Whether this was ever carried out is not known, but what was involved was not the entombment of a bull but a planned processional cult, as was customary for the monarchy, between the royal temple and the necropolis that ensured the ongoingness of *maat* ("order"). The bull-shaped tutelary gods were returned to the temple court alongside the image of the king after Akhenaten's death.

For the first time, under Ramesses II of the nineteenth dynasty, the cultic image of the Buchis bull of Armant was encountered on a stela. Not until the thirtieth dynasty was the processional bull entombed for the first time in its own tomb complex, the Bucheion near Armant. When the Buchis bull processions began to visit the places where bull images were venerated—Medinet Habu, Tod, and Medamud—is not known. Eighteenth dynasty tomb images for Thutmose, which show a bull statue, cannot be unequivocally ascribed to Buchis. Nineteenth dynasty kings had the royal temples in the necropolis expanded, including in Saqqara, at which the king entered into a phase identity with Apis; a place was also made for Osiris-Apis and, underneath that, chambers for the Apis bulls. The bulls that became gods only after death were then accessible through the cult.

In the necropolis of Heliopolis, the complex for the Osiris-Mnevis bull must have been a new building, since there the calves of the Mnevis were entombed. In Elephantine, a priest violated sacred law, using royal cattle (showing their precisely defined coloration) for prosaic tasks. Beginning in the New Kingdom, a royal necropolis temple, the Osiris shrines, and the tomb chambers of the bull required their own caretaker organization. The *sḏm-ʿš* group ("those that hear the call") comprised the organization's working staff; they cared for the living sacred animal and recorded the vital data in its stall in the city or in its area of the necropolis. They also carved out the underground vaults for the bulls. Their superiors, often royal scribes and officials, exercised mainly temporary priestly service. The caretaking organization was controlled by the clergy of the Ptah temple, and its theological requirements were set by its elders.

The cult leaders belonged to the distinguished Pastophoren group, which regularly gathered to offer burnt sacrifices at the *dromos* access, between the royal temple and the Osiris shrine. On a feast day, the replies of the god were proclaimed. The oracle god Osiris-Apis in Saqqara, personally accessible only to the Egyptian mystery bearers, became increasingly the giver of authoritative decisions for the population of Memphis. In time, the mysterious "incorporeal" oracle god of the nightly invocation was separated—even by name—from Osiris-Apis (Gr., Osoroapis). Ptolemaic rulers finally give the oracle the Greek name Sarapis.

The stelae of the initiated partakers in the burial and its personnel help explain the Apis organization. The access of non-Egyptian soldiers and merchants to the royal feasts had been restructured. In the temple handbooks, the standards of Apis, Mnevis, and Buchis appear, and they may have been carried by the army, long responsible for such insignia. The military was important in the Apis entourage and the ceremonies on mourning the deceased Apis bull. Under Amassis, the Memphis shrine of Apis (the Apieion, theologically the "birthplace" of the god) was rebuilt along with the bull's stall, and he had the mother cows ("mothers of the Apis bull"), which were equated with Isis, entombed in their own complex in Saqqara-North (they are still undiscovered as of the 1990s). The cattle skeletons known from that vicinity may belong to the many substitute bulls of the great yearly festivals. The youthful divinity, which was numbered among the children of Apis, was Kem (Gem). Statues of the young bull god Gem were found at several sites, probably in the vicinity of the cattle herds from which the sacrificial animals were taken.

The Ptolemies followed ancient Egyptian tradition, maintaining the sacred animals as well as their sumptuous funerals. Alexander the Great had set precedent for the Greek Ptolemies with his sacrifice to the Apis, not to the living bull. In the fourth century CE, the non-Christian populations of Egypt's cities still had processions of their sacred bulls, which remained economically lucrative although the imperial subsidies had long since been discontinued. The Buchis entombments were stopped under the Roman emperor Diocletian, but the date of discontinuation of the sumptuous Apis funeral ceremonies is unknown. An attempt to revive the Memphis Apis processions, under the Roman emperor Julian, was unsuccessful.

**BIBLIOGRAPHY**

Helck, Wolfgang. "Stiergotte." In *Lexikon der Ägyptologie*, 6: 14–17. Wiesbaden, 1987. For the prehistoric and early historical origins of the bull cults.

Helck, Wolfgang. *Untersuchungen zur Trinitenzeit*. Ägyptologische Abhandlungen, 45. Wiesbaden, 1987. For the conceptual world and such particulars as the Apis run and its subsequent connection to the *sed*-festival.

Hodjache, Svetlana, and Oleg Berlev. *The Egyptian Reliefs and Stelae in the Pushkin Museum of Fine Arts*. Moscow and Leningrad, 1982. On the earliest instances of stelae honoring Buchis.

Hoffman, Michael A. *The Predynastic of Hierkonpolis—An Interim Report*. Egyptian Studies Associations Publication, 11. Oxford, 1982. On the petroglyphs of the charging bull and the cattle tombs in Hierakonpolis.

Hopfner, Theodor. *Der Tierkult der Alten Ägypter*. Vienna, 1913. The citations of the ancient authors.

Jones, M. "The Temple of Apis in Memphis." *Journal of Egyptian Archeology* 76 (1990), 141–147. On the embalming station of Apis in Memphis. Distinguishes between the Apis god of the royal feast and the special form of the oracle god as sacred processional bull.

Kessler, Dieter. *Der Gott Thot-Stier*. Commemorative article for Winfried Barta, pp. 229–245. Frankfurt, 1995. On the cattle of Thoth and the Thoth bull god.

Marin, Geoffrey. *The Tomb of Hepetka*. Oxford, 1979.

Otto, Eberhard. *Beiträge zur Geschichte der Stierkulte in Ägypten*. Leipzig, 1923. Basic to the bull cults, particularly to Apis, Mnevis, and Buchis.

Smith, H. *A Visit to Ancient Egypt. Life at Memphis and Saqqara (ca. 500–30 B.C.)*. Warminister, 1974. A lively description of the living and dead Apis bull.

Vos, R. L. *The Apis Embalming Ritual: P. Vindob 3873*. Orientalia Lovaniensia Analecta, 50. Louvain, 1993. For the funeral ritual of the dead Apis bull.

DIETER KESSLER

**BURIAL PRACTICES.** Numerous tombs of various dates and styles, many containing carefully prepared bodies as well as a variety of funerary goods, reveal an ancient Egyptian belief in life after death. The decoration in some tombs, in paint or relief, includes representations of burial rites and rituals. Some texts from the body of ancient Egyptian literature relate the views of the afterlife and emphasize the need for offerings made in perpetuity. Such archaeological, artistic, and textual evidence show that the burial practices centered around three events: the construction of the tomb; the burial of the body; and the performance of cultic rituals to permit the deceased to attain the afterlife and remain there for eternity.

**Tomb Construction.** With the exception of the cenotaph (an empty, honorary monument), such as those built during the Middle Kingdom at Abydos, ancient Egyptian tombs were designed to contain at least one body. Tombs were usually built during an owner's lifetime, to be ready upon his or her death. Tombs were usually built in groups, with others of similar date and similar class, within cemeteries located in the desert. Most of the cemeteries are on the western bank of the Nile River. Tomb structures can generally be divided into three components: the superstructure; the substructure, which often includes the burial chamber; and the shaft or passage that connects the above- and below-ground structures. Originally, not all tombs had all three components, and some tombs have been partly destroyed in the centuries since they were built. Enough well-preserved tombs remain, however, to demonstrate that tomb styles change with time; tomb size and degree of embellishment also often reflect the relative wealth and status of a tomb's owner. Since the king was the most powerful member of society, royal tombs are the most elaborate known from ancient Egypt, and they often show forms different from those of nonroyal tombs.

The earliest Predynastic tombs, such as those in the Nile Delta cemetery of Merimda, consist of simple oval or round pits hollowed out of the sand, wherein the body was placed in a contracted position; sometimes mounds of sand (*tumuli*) marked the placement of those graves. More elaborate tombs, presumably owned by wealthy and high-status individuals, were developed as early as the late Predynastic, a tomb of that date at the site of Hierakonpolis included a large mud-brick chamber; its western wall was painted with scenes of ships and hunters.

Abydos, site of the burials of the first dynasty kings and those of the last two kings of the second dynasty, provides clear evidence for the elaboration of royal tomb types during the Early Dynastic period. The Early Dynastic royal tombs at Abydos consist of two structures, located some distance from each other; near the cliffs at Umm el-Gaab, where the kings' bodies were placed, lie large mud-brick underground chambers, which are supported and roofed with wooden beams. The superstructures of those tombs had offering niches on their eastern sides, with stelae placed in them. Surrounding the royal burials at Umm el-Gaab were small mud-brick tombs built for the servants of the king, some of whom were sacrificed at the death of their ruler; the Egyptians abandoned such practices before the end of the second dynasty. Closer to the Nile at Abydos, large mud-brick enclosures were built, which contained cultic buildings. Near one were buried twelve boats.

During the Old Kingdom, the elaboration of royal tomb types continued, with the construction of the most famous royal tomb type in Egypt—the pyramid. If modern visitors have attributed many other functions to them, pyramids at the simplest level represent the most visible component of an Old or Middle Kingdom royal tomb complex. The large-scale stone pyramid complexes at Giza of the fourth dynasty kings Khufu, Khafre, and Menkaure are the most well known; the main pyramid of these complexes contained the burial chamber for the king and smaller pyramids near the main pyramid contained the burials of royal wives. Elements of such pyramid complexes that emphasized the importance of cultic rituals in royal burials included a chapel built next to one side of the main pyramid, a valley temple built close to the river's edge, and a causeway that connected them. The precursors of many such pyramid-complex elements can be seen in the third dynasty Step Pyramid complex of King Djoser at Saqqara and, to some extent, even earlier at Abydos.

Around the pyramid complexes were clustered many tombs of Old Kingdom officials. These are *mastaba* tombs (from the Arabic word for "bench") and are known as early as the Early Dynastic (Archaic) cemeteries, like Saqqara; they have free-standing rectangular superstructures, constructed of mud-brick or stone, which contain one or more rooms. The burial chamber lies below ground. One interior wall of a chamber in the *mastaba* bears a false door—a carved depiction of a niched doorway. An offering table would have been placed on the floor of the *mastaba* in front of that doorway; the *ka* (*k3*), a spiritual aspect of the deceased important for his or her nourishment, would come to the false door to partake of the offerings. Some *mastaba* tombs have very ornate superstructures—the Saqqara *mastaba* of Mereruka, a vizier under the sixth dynasty king Teti, is justly famous for its large size and complex relief decoration. Texts within such *mastaba* tombs often state that they or parts of them were given to officials as gifts from the king. *Mastaba* tombs continued to be built into the twelfth dynasty, yet by the First Intermediate Period, most private tombs were of the rock-cut type.

The main chambers of many officials' tombs of the Middle and New Kingdoms are carved in the cliffs bordering the Nile Valley. The New Kingdom necropolises at Thebes include numerous rock-cut tombs with burial chambers below ground, connected by a vertical or stepped shaft. In front of some of them were courtyards that once contained trees or shrubs. Although many rock-cut tombs have no built superstructures today, the Ramessid tombs of the artisans at Deir el-Medina often included very small pyramidal superstructures. Theban superstructures were sometimes decorated with rows of funerary cones—cone-shaped objects of baked clay whose flat end was often stamped with the name and title(s) of the tomb owner. [*See* Funerary Cones.]

New Kingdom rulers had rock-cut tombs, excavated on the western bank of the Nile at Thebes, in the Valley of the Kings, where the surrounding cliffs effect a naturally occurring pyramidal peak. The tombs in the Valley of the Kings were often extended deep into the cliff face, to include numerous corridors and chambers. The lack of a man-made superstructure may reflect architects' attempts to make such royal tombs less conspicuous than the ear-

lier royal tomb complexes, and so safer from tomb robbers. (Nevertheless, only the relatively small eighteenth dynasty tomb of Tutankhamun was discovered with most of its burial goods still inside.) Since the tomb locations in the Valley of the Kings were supposed to be unknown, funerary cult offerings had to be performed elsewhere; often, they took place in separate royal mortuary temples, also built on the western bank at Thebes but close to the river's edge.

A few architectural components appeared consistently in ancient Egyptian tombs despite regional, chronological, and socioeconomic differences. All tombs contained at least one chamber for the body of the deceased, which might also contain the funerary goods, though a wealthier or more ornate tomb might have extra chambers for burial equipment. A place in the tomb or in an associated structure provided access for the living to place offerings for the deceased. The consistent inclusion of those structural elements makes clear the importance of placing the body in a protective burial chamber, surrounding the body with objects, and making offerings to the deceased.

After a tomb was constructed, it was often decorated. Tombs were decorated with flat painted scenes, with scenes carved in either raised or sunken relief, or with scenes carved in relief and then painted. In the Old and Middle Kingdoms, tomb scenes included activities of the tomb owner and his family. For example, they were shown hunting or fowling in the marshes (which might have had symbolic meaning as well). Some Old and Middle Kingdom tombs included models, small clay or wooden figures engaged in activities similar to those on the walls. By the Ramessid period, in the later New Kingdom, only scenes depicting aspects of the afterlife were used, such as tomb owners adoring various deities. Most earlier decorated tombs showed the deceased receiving offerings: in numerous Old Kingdom tombs, the tomb owner is shown seated on a chair before a small table. Upon and around the table appear all types of food offerings—bread, jars containing liquids, and cuts of meat. Processions of people carrying similar offerings also appear in many tombs.

Sometimes tomb decoration included scenes of the burial itself. The eighteenth dynasty Theban tomb of Kamose, for example, bears on one wall a painting of the funerary procession carrying the tomb owner's funerary goods to his tomb; it included weeping women throwing sand on their heads, in a gesture of mourning, and men carrying chests and pieces of furniture. Scenes in tombs also depicted rites that would have been carried out there, such as the Opening of the Mouth ceremony.

The texts that accompanied the decorative scenes in tombs ranged from short inscriptions identifying individuals and/or their actions and speech to long autobiographical texts describing the tomb owner's life. Many tomb texts pertained to offerings, with the deceased's name and a list of items following an introductory phrase that emphasized the offerings (in theory) coming from the king or a deity. Offerings were also itemized in a list, and they appeared on a wall of the tomb, frequently near the false door. Such lists itemized the names of the goods desired by the deceased, including materials for the tomb and food items, sometimes in numbers indicating the amount, in hundreds or thousands.

**Burial.** The process began with the death of the owner and the preparation of the body. In Predynastic burials, bodies were not artificially preserved; the desiccating action of the hot sand in which they were placed was often sufficient to ensure some degree of preservation. Predynastic bodies were usually placed on their left sides, with their faces looking toward the west. In ancient times, the finding of some naturally preserved bodies, caused by shifting desert sands, may have strengthened the Egyptian belief that preservation of the body was necessary for life after death. During the Early Dynastic period, the development of more ornate tomb structures and the use of coffins resulted in the separation of the body from the surrounding sand. Thus, artificial preservation of the body—mummification—became necessary.

From the Old Kingdom, a second dynasty body is known with evidence of rudimentary mummification techniques. The process was perfected in the embalmers' workshop (*w'bt; wabet*), and by the New Kingdom, the steps in mummification included removal of the brain through the nose; evisceration of the body (except for the heart, which was left in place); drying of the body with a natron (salt) mixture; and the separate drying of the internal organs. After the fourth dynasty, the lungs, liver, stomach, and intestines were each placed in a container; such canopic jars were sometimes held within a canopic chest. By the early Middle Kingdom, the four canopic jars were believed to be under the protection of the four demigods called the Sons of Horus: Imsety, Hapy, Duamutef, and Kebehsenuef. After the body was sufficiently dried, it was wrapped in yards of linen. During Greco-Roman times, the wrappings on mummies showed very ornate patterns, yet the bodies within were often poorly preserved. Amulets were sometimes included among the wrappings, to help protect the deceased. The entire mummification process lasted about seventy days. When completed, the mummy was usually placed inside a coffin, which might be rectangular or anthropomorphic (human-shaped), and might, especially in the cases of royal burials, be enclosed within a sarcophagus. Coffin styles have often provided information about the date of a burial. For example, Middle Kingdom rectangular coffins may bear simple bands of painted hieroglyphs; early New Kingdom an-

thropomorphic coffins from Thebes were often decorated with painted multicolored feathers, called a *rishi* pattern.

Scenes and inscriptions from various tombs of pharaonic times illustrate rituals (only some of which may have been performed for most burials) that took place after the preparation of the body. The mummy received food offerings in the *wabet weskhet* (*w'bt wsḫt;* "purification hall") and was then carried in procession to ritual places named for the sites of Sais and Buto. The *tekenu* (*tknw;* a priest crouched on a bier) was then pulled to the tomb; the *tekenu* procession included the canopic chest. At the tomb, offerings were presented and a bull was slaughtered. Then priests recited words of protection for the deceased, whose mummy was placed in the burial chamber.

Along with the mummy, burial goods were usually placed within tombs, and some could have been used by the owner while alive, while some were designed solely for use in the tomb and afterlife. Just as analysis of mummies provides information about nutrition and health in ancient Egypt, analysis of grave goods provides glimpses into the Egyptian view of the afterlife. The most basic burial goods found within the tombs of all the pharaonic periods were the ceramic containers for such foodstuffs and drink as bread and beer or wine. Other containers, such as vessels of stone and, especially in the New Kingdom, faience, might also be included among funerary goods. Some tombs included clothing and objects for personal adornment, such as *kohl*-jars for eye makeup and jewelry of gold and/or silver and semiprecious stones. Wooden furniture, such as chairs and the headrests used for sleeping, might be placed in a tomb. Weapons (such as daggers) and tools (such as chisels and axes) were also placed in tombs. All such objects were similar to or identical with those the deceased would have possessed while alive and suggest that in death the basic necessities of life on earth were required.

Other types of funerary equipment were manufactured solely for use in the tomb. First Intermediate Period tombs and sometimes those of later times contained small-scale statuettes, often depicted holding agricultural implements, such as picks and hoes, and sometimes inscribed with a text describing their duties. The text written on them (chapter 6 of the *Book of Going Forth by Day*) tells us that funerary figurines, or *ushabtis*, were designed to work on behalf of their owner in the afterlife. Offering tables, often inscribed with texts, were also manufactured for placement in the tomb. The presence in the tomb of many images of the deceased, which could be used as substitute bodies should the mummy be destroyed, implies the importance of the body's preservation. Although much of the funerary equipment recovered by excavation has been adversely affected by tomb robbery and decay, the types of objects that remain reflect the wealth and status of the tomb owner. For example, meat and metal were limited to high-ranking burials.

**Cultic Rituals.** Although archaeological and artistic evidence from Egyptian tombs provide some information about burial practices, knowledge remains incomplete without reference to the texts, including the inscriptions that accompany scenes of cultic activity, the funerary literature, and the autobiographical inscriptions in tombs. Such texts provide a rationale for the construction of tombs. In the most simple terms, before the New Kingdom, tombs were modeled after houses of the living; after the New Kingdom, tombs were constructed to mirror aspects of the afterlife. Texts are particularly useful for delineating the steps involved in the *funerary cult*, defined here as the ritual activities that centered around the tomb and the deceased.

The Opening of the Mouth ceremony was a burial ritual that accompanied the placement of funerary goods in a tomb—and was a necessary step in the deceased's rebirth. A few New Kingdom tombs (e.g., the Theban tomb of the eighteenth dynasty vizier under Thutmose III, Rekhmire) provided detailed texts and pictures of the rites that formed this ceremony, most components of which probably occurred at the tomb. Served by this ritual were statues, scarabs, sacred animals, temples, and, most importantly, the mummy. New Kingdom scenes show statues being dressed in various materials, purified with water, and offered sacrificed animals. Priests touched the mouth of the object undergoing the ritual with a number of items, to "open" it. A recitation of spells accompanied the actions, to render them effective. When completed, the ceremony supplied inanimate objects with the ability to perform all the functions of a living being.

Most aspects of the funerary cult were designed to continue in perpetuity, for to exist, the deceased's spirit required daily offerings of food, incense, and libations. The deceased's oldest son was responsible for making the daily offerings, and he is often shown doing so on tomb walls; by performing the rituals, the oldest son took on the mythical role of Osiris' son, Horus. Usually, however, a priest hired by the family performed the cultic activity on behalf of the eldest son, and the priest's wages included the use of the offerings after the spirit of the deceased had taken what was wanted. In the early Old Kingdom, three types of funerary priests were identified in tomb representations: the *wedpu* (*wdpw*), the *wety* (*wtj*), and the *khery-wedjeb* (*ḥrj-wḏb*). During the fifth dynasty, the *hery-khebet* (*ḥry-ḫbt;* lector-priest) appeared in texts; he was responsible for the recitation of the necessary spells for the deceased. The title *hem-ka* (*ḥm kꜣ;* "servant of the *ka*") first appeared in the Middle Kingdom; that priest, whose Old Kingdom counterpart was called the *hem-sekhen* (*ḥm sḫn*), offered the deceased such items as incense and water.

Ritual activities like the festivals of the dead provide evidence for ancient Egyptian ancestor worship, although it usually extended back only a generation or two. Festivals of the dead were held at the new year, among other days, and involved celebrating in the courtyard of the tomb with music, dance, and food. Some other evidence for ancestor worship includes letters written to the dead, which suggest that the deceased spirit could aid—or hurt—the living, and the later so-called ancestor busts that were found in the houses at Deir el-Medina. There were not, it seems, any formal rituals in the funerary cult that centered around the worship of ancestors.

Egyptian funerary literature provides information about the afterlife as the society understood it and helps to illuminate many aspects of the burial process and the funerary cult. The Pyramid Texts, called that because they were found first in an Old Kingdom royal tomb, are the oldest examples of Egyptian funerary texts. Although the earliest Pyramid Texts were discovered in the pyramid of Unas, last king of the fifth dynasty, and some were also found in queens' burials of the late sixth dynasty, yet their language and images seem to reflect an even older tradition, one perhaps first preserved orally. The restriction of the Pyramid Texts to royal burials emphasizes the differences between royal and nonroyal interment during the Old Kingdom—already visible in the monumental scale of the royal pyramid tomb versus the comparatively small nonroyal *mastaba*. The Pyramid Texts describe in part the dead king's ascension to the heavens as a god, to join the other deities. Biographical inscriptions reveal that during the Old Kingdom, nonroyal individuals did not attain an afterworld but continued to "live" in their tombs; they did not become gods, but their *ka* lived in proximity to the divine dead king. That religious belief was also represented physically, by the rows of officials' *mastaba* tombs built near and around the royal pyramids. Prior to the Middle Kingdom, however, nonroyal individuals acquired some access to texts for the afterlife. Certain Pyramid Texts and Coffin Texts began to appear in private tombs. By the eleventh dynasty, and later in the Middle Kingdom, versions of the Pyramid Texts appeared frequently on the walls of tombs of nonroyal officials and on the walls of their coffins. In addition, the Coffin Texts—the later, private version of funerary literature derived in part and edited from the Pyramid Texts—also appeared regularly. These new texts contained knowledge that the deceased required to attain the afterlife, where he or she wished to be in the company of the underworld god Osiris and to travel in the bark of the solar deity Re. Osiris' underworld, which now accompanied the heavenly afterworld seen earlier in the Pyramid Texts, was inhabited by demons and other dangers that the deceased must recognize and be able to circumvent by means of the knowledge contained in this body of information.

By the New Kingdom, another development in funerary literature took place. That set of spells, called the *Book of Going Forth by Day* (modern editors call it the *Book of the Dead*) has about two hundred spells. Some individual spells or a set are found inscribed on tomb objects, on jewelry, amulets, and architectural elements—but the largest group are found on rolls of papyrus. In the *Book of the Dead*, the deceased continued to want to see the gods Osiris and Re in the afterlife (though during the Amarna period, when the ruler Akhenaten worshiped only the solar disk called the Aten, the *Book of the Dead* spells did not refer to the underworld of Osiris, but instead contained wishes that the deceased receive offerings in the tomb and see the Aten). The afterlife that the deceased hoped to attain was, in many respects, identical to the world of the living. The afterworld was believed to contain a river, like the Nile; there were fields on either side of the river, wherein food was produced; the sun traveled through the sky of the underworld at night after it had set in the west, just as it traveled from east to west through the sky of the physical world during the day. This daily "death" of the sun lead to the placement of most cemeteries on the western bank of the Nile, as well as the placement of some burials with the heads or faces toward the west.

To reach the underworld, the deceased had to be judged free of sin. The *Book of the Dead* Spell 125 described the judgment of the dead that allowed each one to become an Osiris. The vignette accompanying that spell showed the deceased, dressed in white robes, entering before the god Osiris and the forty-two deities who served as judges. Believed to be the seat of an individual's character (and thus important enough to be left inside the mummy), his or her heart appeared on one pan of a balance-scale, with the feather of Maat, goddess of righteousness, on the other pan. A creature with the head of a crocodile waited nearby, to eat the heart if judged unworthy, and so condemned the unfortunate deceased to a permanent, second death. If the deceased was judged worthy *ma'a-kheru* (*mꜣꜥ ḫrw*; "true of voice"), he or she was allowed to enter the presence of Osiris for eternity.

When studying ancient Egyptian burial practices, the limits of the available evidence must be respected. Most Egyptians could not afford to pay for the construction of a tomb, to outfit it with funereal goods, to maintain the cult after the funeral, or to hire priests to conduct the necessary rituals; they may have been buried in simple shafts dug into the desert sand. To some degree, then, the burial practices described above were those of the wealthy and high-ranking. Women, too, remain underrepresented; most often, females appear within tombs only as wives, mothers, or daughters of the male tomb owners. High-ranking women, were, however, sometimes accorded the same or similar burial practices as men (see Erik Hornung, *Valley of the Kings*, translated by David Warburton [New York:

1990], for a discussion of royal burial practices from the Valley of the Queens tomb of Nofretari).

Within limits, the evidence shows all elements of ancient Egyptian burial practices were designed to work together, to permit the deceased to achieve spiritual immortality. The body was carefully mummified and placed in the burial chamber; should it somehow be destroyed, substitute bodies were available there in the statues and the two-dimensional depictions of the tomb owner. The priests made offerings of food, drink, and recitations for the spirit of the deceased; should the offerings not be made, they were also available in representations on tomb walls and among the burial goods. Rituals needed to be performed for the spirit of the deceased on a regular basis; if they were not, representations of the rituals on tomb walls, and written versions of the necessary spells on tomb goods and papyri, would serve as substitutes.

[*See also* Afterlife; Canopic Jars and Chests; Coffins, Sarcophagi, and Cartonnages; Funerary Figurines; Funerary Literature; Funerary Ritual; *and* Mummification.]

## BIBLIOGRAPHY

Allen, Thomas George. *The Book of the Dead, or Going Forth by Day: Ideas of the Ancient Egyptians Concerning the Hereafter as Expressed in Their Noun Terms.* Studies in Ancient Oriental Civilization, 37. Chicago, 1974. Comprehensive translation of *Book of the Dead* spells, noting origin and variants of each; not illustrated.

Andrews, Carol, ed. *The Ancient Egyptian Book of the Dead.* Translated by Raymond O. Faulkner. New York, 1985. Translation of examples of *Book of the Dead* spells; includes many illustrations of vignettes accompanying spells but no discussion of variants.

D'Auria, Sue, Peter Lacovara, and Catharine H. Roehrig. *Mummies and Magic: The Funerary Arts of Ancient Egypt.* Boston, 1988. Well-illustrated catalog of the Egyptian collection at the Museum of Fine Arts, Boston, with numerous essays on topics ranging from social aspects of death to mummification; contains chapters on all major chronological periods and an extensive bibliography.

Davies, Nina de Garis, and Alan H. Gardiner. *The Tomb of Amenemhet (No. 82).* London, 1915. Contains many illustrations of burial rituals. Gardiner's commentary, though dated, provides a good introduction to the rituals accompanying a New Kingdom burial.

Faulkner, R. O. *The Ancient Egyptian Coffin Texts.* 3 vols. Warminster, 1973–1977. Translation of the Coffin Texts, arranged by number, with commentary on translation problems.

Harris, James E., and Edward F. Wente, eds. *An X-Ray Atlas of the Royal Mummies.* Chicago, 1980. Collection of essays (each with bibliography) on such topics as health, dental health, and age at death of Egyptian kings; written on the basis of X-ray analysis.

Otto, Eberhard. *Das ägyptische Mundöffnungsritual.* 2 vols. Ägyptologische Abhandlungen, 3. Wiesbaden, 1960. Provides detailed descriptions of the rituals involved in the Opening of the Mouth ceremony, with reference to all original sources.

Quirke, Stephen. *Ancient Egyptian Religion.* London, 1992. Well-illustrated volume, with the chapter on death and the afterlife integrating archaeological and textual evidence.

Spencer, A. Jeffrey. *Death in Ancient Egypt.* New York, 1982. Comprehensive discussion of all aspects of death and the burial process, with an emphasis on archaeological evidence.

STACIE L. OLSON

BUTO. *Statue group*. On the left is Edjo, the goddess of Buto, and on the right, Ramesses II, nineteenth dynasty. (Courtesy Donald B. Redford)

**BUTO** (Ar., Tell el-Fara'în, "Mound of the Pharoahs"), located in the northern Nile Delta, 15 kilometers (about 9.5 miles) east of the Rosetta branch and 30 kilometers (about 19 miles) south of the Mediterranean coast (31°12′N, 30°45′E). The ancient mound occupies about 1 square kilometer (a half mile square). Visible structures on the surface are the temple precinct (B) and the two settlement mounds (A and C) of up to 20 meters (66 feet) above the level of cultivation. The first trial pits were dug in 1904; further excavations were undertaken during the 1960s by the Egypt Exploration Society (EES) and, since 1982, by the universities of Alexandria and Tanta and by the Egyptian Antiquities Organization. Since 1983, surveys and excavations have been carried out by the Deutsches Archäologisches Institut in Cairo.

The hieroglyphs spelling "House of Uto" (i.e., the temple of a cobra goddess named Uto) was the name of the town since the Ramessid period in the thirteenth century BCE; it gave rise to the Greek form, Buto. Before that, however, the names Pe (*p*) and Dep (*dp*) were used, and an even older name was in use during the late fourth millennium, Djebaut ("the heron"). Stressing the duality of the country, Uto was the representative of Lower Egypt but, in rituals and myths, Buto was treated as the capital of Lower Egypt—represented like Hierakonpolis, its Upper Egyptian counterpart, by "souls," believed to be the deities or former kings. A burial custom, called "Butic burial," is supposed to have its roots in the rituals of the prehistoric kings of Lower Egypt; however, despite a pictorial representation showing the subjugation of enemies, most probably at Buto, it seems doubtful that such a prehistoric kingdom ever existed. The town, which was later in the sixth Lower Egyptian nome, lost its political importance by the Old Kingdom and, apart from the Coffin Texts, is not mentioned again before the eighteenth dynasty. Finds from the New Kingdom include a Thutmose III–era stela and statuary from the time of Ramesses II, who rebuilt the temple. Finds from the twenty-sixth and the twenty-ninth dynasties included votive sculpture. In the fifth century BCE, Herodotus was impressed by the overall grandeur of the shrine. During Ptolemaic times, Buto was the capital of the nome Phthenotes, "The Land of Uto."

The prehistoric settlement (layers I and II, c.3500–3200 BCE) belonged to a distinct Lower Egyptian culture, called Buto-Ma'âdi culture, which now is represented by about a dozen localities in the Nile Delta, where the culture reached its apex, as well as in the Faiyum. The most outstanding of the artifacts are some fingerlike clay objects, locally manufactured, but most likely influenced by personal contacts with people from the Uruk culture of Mesopotamia or its colonies in northern Syria. They may best be compared with clay nails from western Asia that were associated with architecture and used to form mosaic patterns. The local architecture, however, to which the objects must have been applied, has never been identified from excavations at Buto.

The later, so-called transitional layer (IIIa) showed remarkable cultural change, from the Lower Egyptian Predynastic to the Upper Egyptian culture of Naqada (which has been interpreted as a gradual cultural superposition by assimilation). This shift, recognized for the first time in Egyptian archaeology at Buto, has been dated to the time of Naqada IId (c.3300–3200 BCE).

Layer V, probably mid-second dynasty, yielded a building of extraordinary ground plan. It still showed remains of plaster and colored-wall decoration; its function was most probably nonsecular, either cultic or palatial.

### BIBLIOGRAPHY

von der Way, Thomas. *Untersuchungen zur Spätvor-und Frühgeschichte Unterägyptens. Studien zur Archäologie und Geschichte Altägyptens,* 8. Heidelberg, 1993.

von der Way, Thomas. *Tell el-Fara'în-Buto,* vol. 1: *Ergebnisse zum frühen Kontext Kampagnen der Jahre 1983–1989.* Archäologische Veröffentlichungen, Deutsches Archäologisches Institut Abteilung Kairo, 83. Mainz, 1997.

THOMAS VON DER WAY

**BYBLOS,** present-day Jebail, ancient seaport on the Lebanese coast, about 40 kilometers (25 miles) north of Beirut. An important commercial port during the Bronze Age and Iron Age, Byblos (known in Egyptian as *kbny* or *kpny;* in Akkadian as *gubla;* in Canaanite as *gublu;* and in Hebrew as *gebal*) was an eastern Mediterranean transshipment point for timber, oil, resins, and wine, and it was a shipbuilding center as well. The ancient Greek name of the town, *Bublos* (from which comes the English word Bible), meant "papyrus scroll" and was so called because the residents obtained papyrus from Egypt and shipped it to the Aegean world. First settled during Neolithic times, the town had nearly continuous occupation until it was abandoned after the seventh-century CE Moslem conquest.

Egypt had maintained a special commercial and political relationship with Byblos during most of the third and second millennia BCE, and Egyptian kings had sent valuable gifts to the temples and rulers of Byblos to sustain that relationship. For example, more stone vessels, statuary, reliefs, and other large objects inscribed with Egyptian royal names are known from Byblos than from any other site in the Near East; nearly 20 percent of the Amarna Letters from the fourteenth century BCE came from Byblos. The Egyptians linked the town's principal goddess, Baalat Gebal, with their own goddess Hathor, whom they often referred to as "Hathor, Lady of Byblos."

Byblos was first excavated by Ernest Renan in 1860, then by Pierre Montet from 1921 to 1924, and by Maurice Dunand starting in 1928 and continuing into the 1970s. The nearly continuous occupation and rebuilding at the site for more than five thousand years and the antiquated field techniques and recording methods used by the excavators make it difficult to reconstruct the cultural history at the site.

Egyptian trade with Byblos may have started as early as the Naqada II period, when Byblos served as a conduit for trade between the sites of Uruk in Mesopotamia and Buto in the western Nile Delta, but regular contact is first attested in the Early Dynastic period. Such contacts were suggested by the discovery at Byblos of various small Egyptian objects, including a fragment of a breccia vessel, on which was inscribed the name of Khasekhemwy, the last king of the second dynasty. Egypt developed especially close ties with Byblos during the Old Kingdom, when the town appeared as *kbny* in Egyptian texts. The Old Kingdom rulers named on calcite (Egyptian alabaster) vessels found at Byblos include Khufu, Khafre, and Menkaure of the fourth dynasty; Sahure, Neferirkare Kakai, Newoserre Any, Izezi, and Unas of the fifth dynasty; and Teti, Pepy I, Merenre Antyemsaf, and Pepy II of the sixth dynasty. Egyptian architectural influence is apparent in Byblos in the construction and decoration of the Balaat

BYBLOS. *General view of Byblos.* (Courtesy Donald B. Redford)

Gebal temple. Toward the end of the third millennium BCE, when Egypt went into political disarray, Byblos suffered much destruction. A literary text perhaps composed or set in this period (*Instructions of an Egyptian Sage*) lamented that ships no longer went to Byblos.

Egypt restored contacts with Byblos in the eleventh dynasty and expanded them substantially in the twelfth. The *Story of Sinuhe* reported that following the death of Amenemhet I, Sinuhe first went to Byblos (henceforth normally written as *kpny*) after fleeing Egypt. A collection of 105 scarabs, found by Pierre Montet, with other Egyptian and Near Eastern objects in a large jar beneath the Syrian temple (part of the Balaat Gebal temple complex) attests to early twelfth dynasty relations. Small objects containing the names of Senwosret III and Amenemhet III are also known from Byblos. In addition, the "Asiatics [i.e., Near Easterners] of Byblos" are mentioned in the Berlin group of Execration Texts from the middle of the twelfth dynasty, while the "clans of Byblos" are mentioned on the Brussels clay figurines of the early thirteenth dynasty. In the twelfth and early thirteenth dynasties, the local rulers of Byblos frequently wrote in the hieroglyphic script—on scarabs, stelae, and reliefs—and even took the Egyptian title *ḥȝty-ʿ* ("mayor"), suggesting that Egypt dominated the town politically during that period. Valu-

able Egyptian gifts, including an obsidian jar inscribed with the name of Amenemhet III and an obsidian box containing the name of Amenemhet IV, were found in tombs 1 and 2, respectively, in Byblos' Middle Bronze Age royal cemetery. A relief fragment with a depiction of a local ruler, Yantin, and a cartouche of Neferhotpe I (1747–1736 BCE) of the thirteenth dynasty provide an important chronological link between Egypt and the Near East. Egypt's relations with Byblos evidently continued until the late eighteenth century BCE, after which contact probably ended, not to begin again until the New Kingdom, early in the eighteenth dynasty. Among the Egyptian finds of the New Kingdom at Byblos are a fragmentary relief (possibly from an Egyptian temple of Hathor, Lady of Byblos) and numerous scarabs inscribed with the name of Thutmose III; scarabs naming Amenhotpe II and III (and the latter's principal queen, Tiye); and a fragmentary stela, doorway blocks, and several calcite (Egyptian alabaster) vessels naming Ramesses II (two vase fragments come from the tomb of Ahiram). The Annals of Thutmose III report that during his eighth campaign, he had his troops construct ships in the vicinity of Byblos, then drag them overland to the Euphrates River.

The Byblian ruler Rib-Hadda was the sender of at least sixty-seven cuneiform tablets that were found in the

Amarna Letters, the diplomatic archive at Amarna. Letters 68 to 95 probably date to the reign of Amenhotpe III, whereas letters 101 to 138 and 362 were composed during the reign of Amenhotpe IV (Akhenaten). Throughout those documents, Rib-Hadda professed his loyalty to the king while bitterly complaining in the earlier group of letters about the hostile actions of his enemy, Abdi-Ashirta of Amurru, and in the later group of letters about the activities of Abdi-Ashirta's son, Aziru. Rib-Haddi's successor, Ili-Rapiḥ, continued the complaints about Aziru in letters 139 and 140. The Byblian letters reflected the weakening of Egyptian authority in the northern Levant during the Amarna era.

Egypt's decline as an international power at the end of the New Kingdom was clearly depicted in the Report of Wenamun, in which an Egyptian priest recorded the dismal reception he received from the prince of Byblos, Zekerbaal. That trade between Phoenicia and the Nile Valley continued, despite the change in political relations between the two administrations, is evident from the mention in the Wenamun text (lines 1,58–2,2) of seventy ships in the harbors of Byblos and Sidon that were trading with Smendes (1076–1050 BCE), the first king of the twenty-first dynasty. Byblos also appeared in a list of Syrian cities in the late New Kingdom *Instructions of Amenemope.*

Direct Egyptian-Byblian relations during the early first millennium BCE are attested by a fragmentary statue of Sheshonq (reinscribed in Phoenician with a dedication by the local ruler, Abibaal), which was purchased at Jebail, and by a fragmentary statue of Osorkon I (reinscribed by Abibaal's successor, Elibaal), also probably from Byblos. Those objects, as well as a few other fragments of Egyptian royal statues (including one of Osorkon II) from the excavations at Byblos, document its contact with Egypt during the early twenty-second dynasty. No archaeological or textual evidence is known for close relations between Egypt and Byblos after that.

[*See also* Wenamun.]

## BIBLIOGRAPHY

Ben-Tor, Daphna. "The Absolute Date of the Montet Jar Scarabs." In *Ancient Egyptian and Mediterranean Studies in Memory of William A. Ward*, edited by Leonard H. Lesko, pp. 1–17. Providence, 1998. Redates the scarabs found in the Montet Jar to the early twelfth dynasty, in accordance with Ward's latest views.

Chéhab, Maurice. "Noms de personnalités égyptiennes découverts au Liban." *Bulletin du Musée de Beyrouth* 22 (1969), 1–47. Presents a useful catalog of important inscribed Egyptian materials from Lebanon, including Byblos.

Dunand, Maurice. *Fouilles de Byblos.* 5 vols. Paris, 1937–1958. Final report on Dunand's excavations at Byblos.

Helck, Wolfgang. "Byblos." In *Lexikon der Ägyptologie*, 1: 889–891. Wiesbaden, 1975.

Joukowsky, Martha Sharp. "Byblos." In *The Oxford Encyclopedia of the Ancient Near East*, edited by Eric M. Meyers, vol. 1, pp. 390–394. New York, 1993. A summary of the archaeology and history of the site.

Kitchen, Kenneth A. "Byblos, Egypt, and Mari in the Early Second Millennium B.C." *Orientalia* 36 (1967), 39–54. Discusses the early thirteenth dynasty relief, showing the Byblian ruler Yantin and the name of King Neferhotpe.

Montet, Pierre. *Byblos et l'Égypte: Quatre campagnes de fouilles à Gebeil 1921–1924.* Paris, 1929. Final report on Montet's excavations at Byblos.

Moorey, P. R. S. "From Gulf to Delta in the Fourth Millennium: The Syrian Connection." *Eretz-Israel* 21 (1990), 68*–69*. Discusses possible prehistoric connections between Mesopotamia and Egypt via Syria and Byblos.

Saghieh, Muntaha. *Byblos in the Third Millennium B.C.: A Reconstruction of the Stratigraphy and a Study of the Cultural Connections.* Warminster, 1983. Sets the Egyptian finds of the third millennium BCE from Byblos in their stratigraphic setting.

Tufnell, Olga, and William A. Ward. "Relations between Byblos, Egypt, and Mesopotamia at the End of the Third Millennium B.C." *Syria* 43 (1966), 165–241. Detailed study of the contents of the Montet Jar at Byblos; dates the deposit to the Herakleopolitan period (a dating later abandoned).

JAMES M. WEINSTEIN

# C

CALCITE. Egyptologists today correctly use the term *calcite* when referring to lithic materials that were historically called travertine, alabaster, Egyptian alabaster, or Oriental alabaster. Geologically, calcite is a mineral composed of hexagonal crystals of calcium carbonate ($CaCO_3$). As used by geologists, the term *alabaster* refers to a fine-grained, massive variety of rock gypsum, consisting largely of the mineral gypsum (hydrous calcium sulfate, $CaSO_4 \cdot 2H_2O$), which is a secondary mineral formed by the hydration of anhydrite ($CaSO_4$) in a zone of weathering. Ironically, *alabastrites* was the original, ancient Greek and Latin name used for "Egyptian travertine" (a limestone), but that had been forgotten when alabaster acquired its modern definition in the 1500s. Another term sometimes used for Egyptian travertine is *calcite-alabaster*, which is both inappropriate and self-contradictory. Many Egyptologists now call travertine by the term calcite, to avoid confusion with the well-known and very different-looking Italian travertine, from Tivoli, Italy (the Romans' *tivertino*, the Latin word for "travertine"). From the Old Kingdom onward, the Egyptians called travertine *šs*, but during the Old Kingdom it was also occasionally referred to as *biȝt*. [See Limestone.]

Egyptian travertine (calcite) occurs in two varieties: (1) a nonbanded to faintly banded, tan to brownish-yellow, coarse-grained, translucent form; and (2) the strikingly banded form with interlayering of the first-mentioned variety with a white, fine-grained, opaque form. With prolonged exposure to sunlight, the brown and yellow colors become white. An example of this weathering phenomenon may be seen at the Mosque of Muhammad Ali (built from 1824 to 1848 CE) in Cairo's Citadel. Both the interior and exterior surfaces of this building were clad with banded travertine (calcite), but now the outside surface has become nearly white whereas the inside surface is still brightly colored.

Travertine (calcite) occurs as fracture-and-cavity fillings in the limestone deposits that border the Nile Valley between Esna in the south and Cairo in the north, and nine ancient quarries are known for this rock. The locations, from south to north, and the dates for these sites are the following: one site near Wadi Asyut (New Kingdom); four sites near the Tell el-Amarna ruins at Hatnub (Old Kingdom through Roman period), both in and near Wadi el-Zebeida (Middle and New Kingdoms), and in Wadi Barshawi (possibly Middle Kingdom); one site at el-Qawatir near the city of el-Minya (possibly Old through New Kingdoms); one site in Wadi Umm Argub near the Wadis Muwathil and Sannur (Late period); one site in Wadi Araba near Wadi Askhar el-Qibli (Roman); and one site in Wadi el-Garawi near the city of Helwan (Old Kingdom). Banded travertine was obtained from all those quarries, but the nonbanded variety may have come only from Hatnub. (*Hatnub* is an ancient Egyptian word meaning "golden house," and it may have been applied to that quarry because of the uniform golden-brown color of its rock.)

As a relatively soft mineral (number 3 on the Mohs Hardness Scale), calcite is easily worked with bronze, copper, and other metal or stone tools. Its translucency, pleasing colors, and ability to take a fine polish made it a popular decorative stone in Egypt from early dynastic times onward. Because of the difficulty of obtaining large pieces, it was mainly employed for small objects, such as statuettes, *shawabti*s, offering tables, vases, bowls, dishes, canopic jars, and unguent jars. The unguent jars are the *alabastra* of classical Greece, originally ceramic and only later carved from Egyptian travertine (calcite), hence the Greco-Roman name *alabastrites* for this rock.

Occasionally, calcite was used for paving stones and wall linings in temples as, for example, in the fourth dynasty valley temple of Khafre at Giza and the nineteenth dynasty sanctuary in the temple of Ramesses II at Abydos, respectively. Although large travertine (calcite) objects are less common than small ones, many are known; these include sarcophagi, life-size and colossal statues, *naoi*, embalming beds, whole shrines, and other objects. One mode of transport for such articles was shown in a detailed painting on the wall of the twelfth dynasty tomb of Djehutihotpe (or Thuthotpe) at Bersheh, where a colossal statue of that nobleman is pulled on a sledge by 172 men. Some notable examples of large objects are the following: (1) the sarcophagus of King Sety I from his tomb in the Valley of the Kings at Thebes, now in Sir John Soane's Museum, London; (2) two huge blocks at Karnak temple in Luxor—one a Late period offering stand or kiosk foundation in the Great Court and the other, possibly, a statue pedestal of uncertain age in the Central Court; (3) the colossal statue of the god Sobek with the eighteenth dynasty King Amenhotpe III from Dahamsha, now in the Luxor

Museum; (4) the colossal statue of King Sety I from Karnak temple, now in the Egyptian Museum, Cairo; and (5) two bark shrines, one by the eighteenth dynasty kings Amenhotpe I/Thutmose I, and one by the twelfth dynasty king Senwosret I, now in the open-air museum at Karnak temple. Numerous other examples may be found in Alfred Lucas, *Ancient Egyptian Materials and Industries* (1962).

### BIBLIOGRAPHY

Aston, Barbara G. *Ancient Egyptian Stone Vessels: Materials and Forms.* Studien zur Archäologie und Geschichte Altägyptens, 5. Heidelberg, 1994. Discusses the use of travertine (calcite) for small vessels.

Aston, Barbara G., James A. Harrell, and Ian M. E. Shaw. "Stone." In *Ancient Egyptian Materials and Technologies*, edited by Ian M. E. Shaw and Paul T. Nicholson. London, 1999. Offers an up-to-date summary of the petrology, uses, and sources of travertine (calcite) in ancient Egypt.

Harrell, James A. "Misuse of the Term 'Alabaster' in Egyptology." *Göttinger Miszellen* 119 (1990), 37–42. Describes the nomenclatural problems related to travertine (calcite) and gives a detailed petrological description of the rock.

Klemm, Rosmarie, and Dietrich D. Klemm. *Steine und Steinbrüche im Alten Ägypten.* Berlin, 1993. Presents the most complete description of Egyptian travertine quarries and, although written in German, is still useful for its maps and bibliography.

Lucas, Alfred. *Ancient Egyptian Materials and Industries*, 4th ed., rev. & ed. by J. R. Harris. London, 1962.

Shaw, Ian M. E. "The 1986 Survey of Hatnub." In *Amarna Reports IV*, edited by Barry J. Kemp, pp. 160–167. London, 1987. See also Shaw's 1986 paper in *Amarna Reports III*. These papers describe the results of recent archaeological work at Hatnub and provide references to earlier surveys.

JAMES A. HARRELL

**CALENDARS.** Pharaonic Egypt's calendrical system was both straightforward and simple. From the first dynasty onward, the Egyptian year was divided into three seasons, based on the agricultural rhythm of the Nile Valley: (1) *ȝht*, inundation; (2) *prt*, emergence (of crops); and (3) *šmw*, harvest. These seasons consisted of four months apiece, each containing thirty days. Hence, the basic year of the Egyptians comprised a regular number of days (360) as well as an orderly number of months (12). Such a system had to have five additional days added to it, the epagomenals ("days above the year"), which neatly fixed the annual rotation of the sun to a set integer of 365; there were no intercalary days in that native year.

The calendrical order was most advantageous to Egyptologists' cumulative reckoning of such large-scale time elements as dynasties and epochs. Mainly from hypothetical reasoning, it is assumed that the Nile year was created by the early Egyptian state in order to regularize its economic stability (tax collecting through a census placed on cattle) as well as to record its kings' reigns. Modern scholars, therefore, call this 365-day year the civil calendar, to indicate the original purpose of its reckoning. The number of months, as well as their names, were based on an older, lunar calendar. In this earlier system, it is unclear whether the Egyptians intercalated an extra month (the thirteenth), every three years or so, to bring the calendar into accord with the seasons. Although the extant data neither support nor reject that, traces of the lunar calendar exist in the presence of some feast days, which were determined by the moon's cycle rather than permanently fixed on a day (or days) within the civil calendar.

Some ancient Egyptian festivals were therefore determined by the moon, and quite a number of significant religious events were solely set to a specific lunar day, such as the new moon. For example, the Valley Feast took place within the tenth Egyptian civil month but was not permanently set on a predetermined day within that month. Similarly, the funerary event of Wagy seems to have taken place on day eighteen of lunar month two, although a civil calendar counterpart always occurred on day eighteen of the first civil month. For the most part, Egyptian religious festivals became civil calendar–based since a change had been made from lunar time to the civil calendar when it came into being.

The regnal years of the kings were also reorganized so that they coincided with civil calendar years. In Predynastic times, a lunar calendar must have been the basis for the regnal year. In the Old Kingdom, as the Palermo Stone clearly indicates, the regnal year counts were originally labeled by names of auspicious or important events that occurred within a civil calendar year of 365 days, among which one can single out building projects of a religious nature. After the second dynasty, the regnal years also became orderly, since they were referred to, on a regular basis, by the biennial cattle census that took place throughout Egypt. Eventually, probably by the sixth dynasty, the biennial census was replaced by an annual one. From that time on, all regnal years were rationalized so that the king's year in office was nothing more than an integer that was counted every civil calendar year. The causes for such change included the importance of the centralized state apparatus and the necessity to establish a workable and relatively easy method of counting. Egyptian regnal years were dependent upon a 365-day civil calendar year, not a lunar year, and they operated independently of whether the anniversary of a pharaoh's accession caused a change in the year count (as in the New Kingdom) or whether the presence of subsequent new year's days effected such a change. In the Middle Kingdom (unlike the New Kingdom), counting of regnal years was reckoned from the first day of the civil calendar year to the next, excluding the opening year, which almost always began within a civil calendar year.

Although later sources, mainly of Greco-Roman times, put great emphasis on the star the Egyptians called Sothis (our Sirius), as being connected with an enormous cycle of 1,460 Egyptian civil years, that lengthy period seems not to have been employed by them for any historical reckoning. Nonetheless, the commencement of a year was intimately associated with the goddess Sothis (identified with the goddess Isis), especially if an ideal, rather than a real, beginning was to be stressed. Such was the case because the reappearance of the star Sothis at dawn, after a disappearance of seventy days (its heliacal rising, *prt spdt*), was originally linked with the inauguration of the year at a time when the Nile waters had crested. Owing to this connection, scholars argue that the first day of the just-created civil year (new year's day) began at the exact time of *prt spdt*. In many extant festival calendars, as well as a few other sources, Sothis' heliacal rising was given great prominence although it did not interrupt the mundane flow of time, since the astronomical event occurred independently of the way the civil calendar operated.

Research has obviated the need to claim that the Egyptians invented a second lunar calendar, somewhat later than their civil calendar. From our knowledge of the festival system, it appears that most religious celebrations were only on the civil calendar. Those festivals that were lunar-based seem to have been organized around specific lunar occurrences (such as the new moon) that could be seen with the naked eye, but they were nevertheless based partly on the civil calendar. It was understood that the lunar occurrence was fixed within a given civil month and that no independent lunar year was operating alongside the established civil calendar. Therefore, all administrative work, such as daily accounts and the like, were set by the civil calendar; lunar-based events appear to have been restricted solely to the cultic sphere.

The names of the twelve civil months betray their origins, since it is evident that they are mere copies of the original names of their twelve lunar-month counterparts. The first, Thoth, was named after the god of the moon, who was also the reckoner of time. The third, Athyr, overtly indicates that it was named after the goddess Hathor, whose festival took place on day one of the following civil month. Khoiak, the designation for civil month four, was similarly borrowed from a major religious event that occurred at the crucial change of season—from the first season, *ꜣḥt*, to the second, *prt*—the festival held on day one of the fifth month. In this case, the first day of *peret* served as a second new year's day, on which the rejuvenation of the subsistence-based agricultural society of Predynastic Egypt was predicated. A similar change from the second season to the third can be observed with the name of month eight, Renenutet. Then, the goddess of the harvest Renenutet bequeathed her name to the final civil month, *šmw*, in recognition of the festival for the gathering of grain, which took place at the beginning of the ninth month. In some cases, for historical reasons, the designations of the civil months were changed. For example, Menchet ("clothing"), civil month number two, was altered to Paophi in honor of the important Theban festival of Opet, which occurred at that time. In similar fashion, Phamenoth, civil month seven, reflected the festival of the deified Amenhotpe I. Yet the final civil month revealed its origins in the rebirth of the sun god Re, for that is what its name, Mesore, actually meant. Earlier, the designation was Wep-renpet ("the opener of the year"), called after the most important festival in the year, that of new year's day, on the first day of Thoth, the first month.

A careful comparison of the month names has determined that at least some of the older designations were based on key religious festivals; however, they seem always to have occurred on or about day one of the following civil month. The clear case of Athyr, mentioned above, provides an excellent example of this. Although the civil month was the third in the year, its religious counterpart, the feast of Hathor, began with the following civil month. Insofar as the civil months postdate the original lunar calendar months in which the key feasts were first celebrated, any attempt to equate a month name with the eponymous feast name must consider this. Even at the inception of the newly created civil calendar, such a shunting of festival dates must have occurred—an alteration partially explained by the original lunar year of only 354 days, and the new civil year of 365 days. The difference of nineteen days (called the lunar-solar epact) explains the lack of equivalence and provides a reason for the observance of the festival of the moon god Thoth on day nineteen of the first civil month. (In a similar lack of concurrence, present-day Easter and Passover continue to be celebrated on old lunar dates that have no fixed Western calendar dates.)

The various festival calendars of the Egyptians reflected the civil calendar insofar as they located their celebrations within the civil year. Quite often a clear separation was made between the "festivals of heaven," which occurred more than once a year, and the "seasonal festivals," which took place annually. By the nineteenth dynasty, the first group merely comprised the various celebrations in honor of lunar days (e.g., day 1, 2, 6, 15, and the like). In contrast, the second group reflected the developed theological outlook of the various temples, wherein the crucial religious manifestations took place once a year. Note that the dichotomy was not merely one of celestial phenomena versus earthly ones, since the heliacal rising of Sothis was placed under the "seasonal festivals." The festival calendars are very important to us because they reveal, in precise fashion, just which days were of crucial importance to the Egyptians and how they were celebrated.

Other segments of time from ancient Egypt also are known. A week was in reality ten days, with the standard holidays at the end (day ten) and the day following. Hour measurements were known, too, but they were of irregular length, roughly identical to the "seasonal hours" of Hellenistic and Roman times. There are Egyptian words for small segments of time other than the hour, but no precise designations for the "half-hour," the "quarter hour," or the "minute." Such a lack of specificity was mainly the result of the relatively simple timekeeping used in the Nile Valley; pharaonic civilization had no need for precise time intervals such as seconds or minutes. The Egyptian hours appear to have been based always on groupings of stars. In the First Intermediate Period, if not earlier, a system of decanal stars was invented, by which there were twelve night hours. These twelve intervals were determined by sight, and they depended on the sighting of various star groups that cannot be identified. As each star group rose, it designated a specific hour of the night sky for ten days (hence each is called a "decan" and the method a decanal system). The decan-hour stars would then move on one integer, for 120 days, or 12 "weeks." At first, the system depended on naked-eye viewing at the eastern horizon; later, in the Middle Kingdom, a more refined method of observation was used, in which the crossing of the star groups across a meridian determined the nightly hours. From the New Kingdom onward, the Egyptians preferred to work out nocturnal timekeeping by the transit of stars across various reference points on a man's body (head, neck, etc.) as he faced south and was checked by a second man who faced him. All such attempts to work out an effective hour system for the night were affected by various difficulties.

Research on such star clocks has confirmed their usefulness; nevertheless, by modern standards such timekeeping was limited by the lack of a coordinate system for the heavens. Only during the Ptolemaic dynasty was a zodiacal system introduced to Egypt, one that had as its basis the division of the Sun's annual path along the ecliptic. This system was based on a "degree" system—originally of Babylonian origin—into which each star group occupied thirty "degrees," there being twelve star groups in all ($30 \times 12 = 360$ degrees, as used today, to describe a complete circle).

The beginning of the Egyptian day was at "dawn," probably in morning twilight (although that is contested by some researchers); the actual dawn, when the Sun first rises in the east, is also a possibility. The inscriptional material is ambiguous. The crucial point is that the Egyptians' calendrical perspective was fixed toward morning sightings directed at the eastern horizon. A lunar month began on the day when the waning crescent moon could not be sighted on the eastern horizon. (The Egyptian month was therefore regulated in a different tradition than either the Babylonian or the Greek, in which months were based on the evening sighting of the first lunar crescent in west). Since the absence of any lunar crescent indicates that the Egyptian system depended on the eastern, morning sighting, the Egyptian lunar epoch occurred about one day earlier than those cultures that regarded the day as commencing with the first western, evening sighting.

The Old Egyptian names for the lunar days are useful to survey for a linguistic connection. The first day, that of no lunar crescent visibility, was connected to the Egyptian word for "new," whereas the "crescent" gave its name to the second day, and the third day was called "arrival," indicating actual visibility (the first crescent might be delayed by atmospheric anomalies, so that it would turn up on day three). There was a "second arrival" on day sixteen, heralding the completion of the full moon (from day fifteen, the Egyptian "half month"), with "first quarter" and "last quarter" (called "parts") the terms for day seven and day twenty-three, respectively. Finally, day thirty was associated with the god Min, owing to his virility; in this case, it is clear that the association with Min indicated procreation. Theologically, the following day was considered the "moon in the womb," with its appearance— birth—occurring on day two of the following lunar month.

For the Ptolemaic period, a few extant sources from Egypt indicate that a regular correlation was drawn between lunar months and their civil calendar counterparts. Papyrus Carlsberg 9, in particular, supplies us with a full (though not complete) listing of such equivalences; from the text, a relatively simple, albeit artificial, cycle was introduced to Egypt, in which 25 Egyptian years (of 365 days apiece) were equated with 309 lunar months, the latter consisting of 16 years of 12 months and 9 of 13 months ($365 \times 25 = 9{,}125$ days; 309 lunar months with those parameters yield 9,124.95 days). Such a cycle eliminates the need for an actual lunar sighting. Originally thought to be a native Egyptian creation, reinterpretations have placed its sophisticated workings outside the Nile Valley. Other scholarly arguments have connected this Demotic papyrus with the Macedonian calendar—in use for the duration of the Greek domination over Egypt—although serious questions remain concerning the exact extent of its use. One difficulty in textual interpretation is that the columns of odd lunar–civil calendar equivalences were not presented, if those sections merely repeated the integers in the even columns, as some believe, then the entries in Papyrus Carlsberg 9 are still incomplete. Some Egyptologists see the inauguration of this cycle (c.357 BCE) being based on the nonvisibility of the lunar crescent. Classicists interested in Ptolemaic Egypt prefer to understand the system as one developed for equating Egyptian days and months with the Macedonian calendar, and one extremely fragmentary Greek papyrus reveals that such an equivalence was made (Papyrus Rylands 586); however, the extant pieces are not sufficient to draw any firm conclusions regarding its origins.

[*See also* Astronomy; Festival Calendars; *and* Festivals.]

### BIBLIOGRAPHY

Altenmüller, Hartwig. "Feste." In *Lexikon der Ägyptologie*, 1: 172–191. Wiesbaden, 1975. Very detailed study of all Egyptian festival calendars and their connection to the various religious celebrations of the Egyptians.

Clagett, Marshall. *Ancient Egyptian Science*, vol. 2: *Calendars, Clocks and Astronomy*. Philadelphia, 1995. A useful, though surprisingly incomplete and already dated study by a very competant non-Egyptologist.

Gardiner, Alan. "The Problem of the Month Names." *Revue de l'égyptologie* 10 (1955), 9–31. Discusses problems of Richard Parker's analyses regarding Egyptian civil months.

Gryzbek, Erhard. *Du calendrier macédonian au calendrier ptolémaique: Problemes de chronologie hellenistique*. Schweizensche Bieträg zur Altertumswissenschaft, 20. Basel, 1990. A refreshing look at the Macedonian-Egyptian calendar, although somewhat limited by the author's presuppositions.

Ingham, M. F. "The Length of the Sothic Cycle." *Journal of Egyptian Archaeology* 55 (1969), 36–40. A useful study of the time it takes the star Sothis (Sirius) to return to its exact spot in the sky.

Koenen, Ludwig. *Eine agonistische Inschrift aus Ägypten und frühptolemäische Königsfeste*. Beiträge zur klassichen Philologie, 56. Meisenheim am Glan, 1977. An attempt to revise Alan Samuel's Macedonian-Egyptian calendars; also based on Papyrus Carlsberg 9.

Krauss, Rolf. *Sothis-und Monddaten: Studien zur astronomischen und technichischen Chronologie Altägyptens*. Hildesheimer ägyptologische Beiträg, 20. Hildelsheim, 1985. The first major attempt to present Egyptian calendrics and chronology from a mature point of view since Richard Parker's works.

Leitz, Christian. *Studien zur ägyptischen Astronomie*. Ägyptologische Abhandlungen, 49. Wiesbaden, 1989. An idiosyncratic study on Egyptian calendrics and astronomy that tends to claim modern scientific exactitude for the ancient Egyptians.

Leitz, Christian. *Altägyptische Sternuhren*. Orientalia Lovaniensia analecta, 62. Leuven, 1995. A controversial study of the Egyptian decanal star system that attempts to identify various star groups ("constellations") of the Egyptians.

Luft, Ulrich. *Die chronologische Fixierung des ägyptischen Mittleren Reiches nach dem Tempelarchiv von Illahun*. Sitzungsberichte der Österreichischen Akademie der Wissenschaften, 598. Vienna, 1992. An up-to-date analysis of the Middle Kingdom temple archive from Illahun and its importance for festival dating.

Neugebauer, Otto, and Richard A. Parker. *Egyptian Astronomical Texts*. 3 vols. Brown Egyptological Studies, 3. London and Providence, 1960–1969. The basic compendium on Egyptian astronomy by two great scholars in the field.

Parker, Richard A. *The Calendars of Ancient Egypt*. Studies in Ancient Oriental Civilization, 26. Chicago, 1950. The seminal study, though now dated, on Egyptian calendrics by the major English-speaking scholar in the field.

Parker, Richard A. "The Problem of the Month Names: A Reply." *Revue de l'égyptologie* 11 (1957), 85–101. A relatively successful rebuttal of Alan Gardiner's attempt to jettison the 1950 study.

Samuel, Alan Edouard. *Ptolemaic Chronology*. Munchener Beiträge zur Papyrusforschung und antiken Rechtsgeschichte, 43. Munich, 1962. Originally a revolutionary work concerned with the Macedonian calendar in Egypt; Samuel was the first classicist to employ the Demotic evidence from Papyrus Carlsberg 9 to resolve the problem.

Schott, Siegfried. *Altägyptische Festdaten*. Wiesbaden, 1950. A useful compendium of Egyptian festivals (mainly Theban) with a lengthy introduction concerning ancient Egyptian timekeeping and calendrics.

Spalinger, Anthony J. *Three Studies on Egyptian Feasts and their Chronological Implications*. Baltimore, 1992. A new Egyptian festival calendar and the various calendrical results that its study reveals.

Spalinger, Anthony J., ed. *Revolutions in Time: Studies in Ancient Egyptian Calendrics*. San Antonio, 1994. A collection of four studies concerned with the interrelated aspects of dating, various time epochs, festivals, and the lunar–civil calendar interrelationship.

ANTHONY J. SPALINGER

**CALENDARS OF LUCKY AND UNLUCKY DAYS.** *See* Horoscopes.

**CANAAN,** a geographical term (Eg., *kn'n;* Akk., *ki-na-aḥ-nu;* Heb., *kn'n*) for the area broadly encompassing the Eastern Mediterranean lands that are to the west of the Jordan River, Phoenicia, and part of southern Syria during the second millennium BCE. The term *Canaan* is frequently used in the scholarly literature as a conventional reference for that region during the entire Bronze Age (occasionally referred to as the Canaanite period), although no certain mention of Canaan or Canaanites has survived in any texts of the third millennium BCE. There are few references to Canaan outside the Bible in the first millennium BCE, although in that period the Phoenicians along the Lebanese coast continued to think of themselves as living in the land of Canaan. The etymology of the word *Canaan* is uncertain: one suggestion is to derive the name from a Semitic root meaning "to bend"; another relates it to a Hurrian word meaning "blue cloth."

Canaan first appears in Near Eastern texts in the fifteenth century BCE in the autobiography of Idrimi, a ruler of the north Syrian kingdom of Alalakh. The earliest reference to Canaanites is on an eighteenth-century BCE cuneiform tablet from Mari on the Euphrates River in Syria. New Kingdom Egyptian texts contain more than a dozen references to Canaan. Canaan was the name that the Egyptians applied to the territory of the Near East (Western Asia) that was under their control, and for which they often had to contend with the empires of Mitanni and the Hittites. Ramessid period documents refer to both Canaan and "the (town of) Canaan (*p3 kn'n*)": the latter was an appellation for Gaza, the administrative headquarters of the Egyptian empire in Canaan. It is not always clear whether the mention of "Canaan" in a particular text (especially a topographical list) refers to the land of Canaan or to the town of Gaza.

The oldest reference to Canaan in Egyptian texts is in the annals recording Amenhotpe II's (1454–1419 BCE) campaign of his seventh regnal year to the land of Retenu; the booty list from that campaign included 640 Canaanite prisoners. "The (town of) Canaan" (i.e., Gaza) appears in Sety I's (1321–1304 BCE) campaign report for his first regnal year in the hypostyle hall at Karnak. There is also a mention in the famous Israel Stela from regnal Year 5 of Merenptah (1237–1226 BCE) of the plundering of "the Canaan": that citation is thought by most scholars to be a reference to Egypt's Near Eastern province, but by a few as another mention of Gaza. Papyrus Anastasi I (line 27.1) from the reign of Ramesses II mentions the "end of the land of Canaan" (i.e., the route leading eastward across Sinai to Gaza). Papyrus Anastasi III A (lines 5–6) and its duplicate, Papyrus Anastasi IV (line 16.4), belonging to the reign of Sety II (1221–1215 BCE), mention Canaanite slaves from Kharu. The land of Canaan shows up in two cuneiform letters sent by Ramesses II (1304–1237 BCE) to his Hittite contemporary, Hattusili III, at the Hittite capital Hattusha (present-day Bogazkoy). The latest pharaonic period reference to Canaan is on a Middle Kingdom statuette reinscribed in the Third Intermediate Period for Pediese, son of a Near Easterner named 'Apy, who evidently was a messenger of "[the] Canaan and Philistia."

Canaan appears on eleven cuneiform tablets (Letters 8, 14, 30, 109–110, 131, 137, 148, 151, 162, 367) and the Canaanites on one (Letter 9), from the diplomatic archive found at Tell el-Amarna. Letter 8 is notable for the Babylonian king Burnaburiash's acknowledgment to Amenhotpe IV that "Canaan is your country," while in Letter 30 the kings of Canaan are addressed as the "servants" of the king of Egypt.

Middle and Late Bronze Age Canaan was divided politically and territorially into perhaps several dozen small city-states of varying size and importance. Each city-state normally consisted of an urban capital as well as a number of smaller towns and villages and the supporting agricultural land. Generally independent, and not infrequently feuding with one another, the city-states occasionally banded together (especially in the Late Bronze Age) to oppose Egyptian and other foreign conquerors; perhaps the best-recorded case of such cooperation is that of the towns that gathered at Megiddo to oppose Thutmose III's Near Eastern campaign of regnal Year 22.

Egyptian contacts with Canaan in the early twelfth dynasty apparently focused on sites along the Levantine coast (especially Byblos). Later on, in the twelfth and continuing into the thirteenth dynasties, Egypt's foreign interests expanded considerably: the Execration Texts of the period mentioned many of the principal towns of both northern and southern Canaan.

The fifteenth dynasty (c.1664–1555 BCE) was the one time in antiquity when a line of kings of Canaanite origin ruled in Egypt. The capital of those sovereigns, whose non-Egyptian names included Sheshy, Khayan, and Apophis, was established at Avaris (i.e., Tell ed-Dab'a) in the eastern Nile Delta. The origins of those Canaanite rulers is to be sought in the movement of Near Easterners into the Delta during the late twelfth and early thirteenth dynasties. The political and military connections of the Hyksos kings with the Canaanite city-states of the late Middle Bronze Age is unclear and much debated: some scholars feel that a Hyksos "empire" included much of southern Canaan, while others deny Hyksos control over any part of the Levant.

During the Late Bronze Age, the Egyptian military, political, and economic activity in the Near East was focused on the major Canaanite towns that lay along the principal routes (e.g., Gaza, Gezer, Megiddo, Hazor), had ports to facilitate maritime trade and/or Egyptian naval activity (e.g., Joppa, Acco, Byblos, Tyre), and/or could support Egyptian political and military control of Canaan (e.g., Gaza and Beth Shan in Palestine, Kumidi and Sumur in Lebanon). The annals of the New Kingdom pharaohs repeatedly mentioned such towns, often as military adversaries of the Egyptians. There is substantial archaeological and textual evidence from the nineteenth and early twentieth dynasties (Late Bronze IIB–Iron IA periods) of Egyptian garrisons or administrative centers in Canaan, especially in the Gaza region, as well as at sites such as Tel Mor, Joppa, Megiddo, Beth Shan, and Kumidi. Finally, in the first millennium BCE, Egypt's relations with Canaan were largely of a commercial and political nature, the occasional Egyptian military forays into the region (most notably that of Sheshonq I in the late tenth century BCE) usually had only short-term consequences for the region.

[*See also* Byblos; Gaza; Jerusalem; Joppa; Megiddo; *and* Syria-Palestine.]

## BIBLIOGRAPHY

Ahituv, Shmuel. *Canaanite Toponyms in Ancient Egyptian Documents.* Jerusalem, 1984. Study of Near Eastern place-names in Egyptian texts; includes the area stretching from Palestine to southern Phoenicia and eastward to the Damascus region.

Lemche, Niels Peter. *The Canaanites and Their Land: The Tradition of the Canaanites.* Journal for the Study of the Old Testament, Supplement Series, vol. 110. Sheffield, 1991. Offers a controversial interpretation of the history and geography of Canaan and the Canaanites during the second and first millennia BCE.

Moran, William L. *The Amarna Letters.* Baltimore, 1992. Translations of all the letters in the Amarna archive.

Na'aman, Nadav. "The Canaanites and Their Land: A Rejoinder." *Ugarit-Forschungen* 26 (1994), 397–418. Responds to Lemche's 1991 book; analyzes the references to Canaan in the second millennium BCE.

Na'aman, Nadav. "The Network of Canaanite Late Bronze Kingdoms and the City of Ashdod." *Ugarit-Forschungen* 29 (1997), 599–626. Study of the Canaanite city-state system in the Late Bronze Age.

Redford, Donald B. *Egypt, Canaan, and Israel in Ancient Times*. Princeton, 1992. History of Egyptian relations with the land of Canaan, focusing on the textual sources.

Schmitz, Philip C. "Canaan." In *The Anchor Bible Dictionary*, edited by David Noel Freedman, vol. 1, pp. 828–831. New York, 1992. Survey of the ancient references to Canaan, focusing on the biblical sources.

Steindorff, Georg. "The Statuette of an Egyptian Commissioner in Syria." *Journal of Egyptian Archaeology* 25 (1939), 30–33. Initial publication on the statuette of the envoy Pediese.

Ward, William A. "Egyptian Relations with Canaan." In *The Anchor Bible Dictionary*, edited by David Noel Freedman, vol. 2, pp. 399–408. New York, 1992. A good, basic history of Egyptian connections with Canaan in dynastic times.

JAMES M. WEINSTEIN

**CANINES.** The ancient Egyptians were well acquainted with several species of carnivorous animals belonging to the family Canidae: the Cape hunting dog (*Lycaon pictus*); the domestic dog (*Canis familiaris*), called *ṯsm* and *iwiw* or *iw* (probably onomatopoetic, "howler"); the common or golden jackal (*Canis aureus* subsp. *lupaster*), *wnš* and *sᴣb*; the striped hyena (*Hyaena hyaena*), *ḥtt*; and the red fox (*Vulpes vulpes* subsp. *aegyptiaca*), *wᴣs* and *wsr*. There is an abundance of pictorial, textual, and zooarcheological evidence indicating that some of these beasts were accorded important roles in sacred and secular life during pharaonic times. In spite of repeated assertions to the contrary, however, there is a dearth of firm proof that the ancient Egyptians were familiar with the common wolf (*Canis lupus*), since it apparently never lived in their country. This error can be traced back to the Greeks, who mistakenly identified Wepwawet—the local canine god of the town of Asyut (also known as Lykopolis)—as a wolf. Therefore, most references to "wolves" in literature on ancient and modern Egypt are actually to jackals.

Cape hunting dogs are prominently represented as heraldic figures in the carved decoration on a small number of ceremonial or votive schist palettes dating from the Late Predynastic period (Naqada III). Here they are depicted surrounding their prey, just as these pack-hunting wild dogs do in nature. This species does not appear in the faunal repertory of artisans during the dynastic period, and it had probably become locally extinct or rare quite soon after the rise of the first dynasty. Nowadays, the Cape hunting dog lives mostly on the sub-Saharan savannas.

The progenitor of the domestic dog, and ancestor of every breed, was the common wolf, whose domestication is thought to have begun at least twelve thousand years ago in western Asia. As much the faithful companion in antiquity as today, the dog was always regarded by the ancient Egyptians as the pet *par excellence*, the subject of special attention and heartfelt affection. There are innumerable images of this household animal in Egyptian iconography. Dogs are featured in the company of monarchs, aristocrats, and humble laborers alike, as both pets and workers. The oldest securely dated appearance of the dog from Egypt occurs on a ceramic bowl from the Amratian period (Naqada I), now in the Pushkin State Museum of Fine Arts, Moscow. Its white-on-red painted design illustrates a bowman holding four dogs on leashes that are clearly a type of greyhound. This sleek and sinewy hunting hound, possessing pointed ears and a short curled tail, becomes the most commonly portrayed "breed" of dog throughout the Old Kingdom. Scholars have seen a strong resemblance between this type and the modern Sudanese Basenji. Other varieties of the dog already existed during the Predynastic period: one was a robust mastiff hound, with drooping ears and a comparatively straight tail. Beginning in the Middle Kingdom, more "breeds" become recognizable. From osteological and pictorial evidence, we know that a small, short-legged dog with erect ears, somewhat resembling the Dachshund, had developed by that time. Another was a robust, Boxer-like hound with pricked ears. With the coming of the eighteenth dynasty, the renowned Saluki makes its appearance in Egyptian art, regularly portrayed at the side of royalty and well-to-do citizens. Foreign dogs, too, were highly prized in ancient Egypt; they were imported from Libya, Nubia, Punt, and possibly the Near East and western Asia. Antef II of the eleventh dynasty was so proud of his pack of five exotic dogs that he had them recorded near his feet on the lower part of a funerary stela from his Theban tomb-chapel, now in the Egyptian Museum, Cairo; these Libyan dogs are named "Oryx," "Hound," "Black One," "*Khenfet-kettle*," and "Tekenru."

From its earliest appearances in Egypt, the domestic dog was utilized primarily for the hunt, originally a means of obtaining essential food but later a sport for kings and aristocrats. It is in this capacity that dogs are ubiquitously encountered in scenes on tomb-chapel walls and elsewhere, running down and dispatching desert game for their owners. However, the dog filled many other roles in ancient Egypt. They were almost certainly trained to aid herders and farmers in guarding flocks and crops from marauding wild animals. When not at their masters' sides viewing activities on the estates, venturing out on hunting expeditions, accompanying the sovereign into battle or war, assisting in the policing of the deserts, and serving as trusted watchdogs, dogs are routinely pictured in compositions as favored pets, wearing collars and sitting, ever alert, under their owners' chairs. These dogs are sometimes named in hieroglyphic captions, a sign of their special status; examples include "Brave One," "Lively One," "Exultation," "The Tail is as a Lion's," "Good Watcher," "He is a Shepherd," and "Reliable One." Otherwise, animals in pharaonic Egypt were rarely given names. A pair of wide leather dog collars (now in the Egyptian Museum,

CANINES. *A peasant sitting in a portable seat holds a young puppy, which he is feeding in a most curious mouth-to-mouth fashion.* Perhaps he is attempting to wean the dog with milk placed on his tongue. From the tomb-chapel of the vizier Kagemni at Saqqara, sixth dynasty. (© Patrick Francis Houlihan)

Cairo) were included in the eighteenth dynasty tomb of the courtier Maiherperi in the Valley of the Kings (tomb 36); one bears the name "She of the Town [Thebes]."

Some beloved dogs were honored with a fine burial in wooden coffins of their own. One royal watchdog so pleased a pharaoh of the fifth or sixth dynasty that it was rewarded with the construction of a tomb at Giza (tomb 2188). The death of other dogs was hastened so they could follow and serve humans in the beyond. This was particularly true during the Predynastic and Early Dynastic periods, although some later instances are known. Dogs were mummified by the hundreds of thousands, especially in the Late and Greco-Roman periods, and were interred in cemeteries at Saqqara, Asyut, Abydos, and other locations around the country as creatures sacred to the canine funerary gods Anubis, Wepwawet, and Khentamenti. Classical writers, such as Herodotus (II, 67) and Strabo (XVII, 1, 40), also mention the interment of dogs in Egypt at this time.

The first representation of a jackal in Egyptian iconography is a fine figure executed in schist, found at el-Ahaiwa and dating from the Gerzean period (Naqada II), and now in the Phoebe Hearst Museum of Anthropology, Berkeley, California. This portrait is also thought to be one of the earliest images of an Egyptian deity in animal form. Jackals are a customary member of the community of fauna portrayed in desert hunting scenes. Especially during the Old Kingdom, they are occasionally displayed being savagely attacked by packs of domestic hounds as they flee. Which animal(s) served as the prototype for the gracile black canine, sacred to Anubis, has been the subject of perennial disagreement among scholars (this same creature was linked with a number of other deities, too). Nevertheless, there can be little doubt that the beast was principally fashioned after the common or golden jackal, but its form seems to have been influenced by other species as well, notably by the long, bushy tail of a fox. Always depicted entirely black, a color of resurrection and rebirth, Anubis was responsible for embalming the dead and protected burials in his role as lord and sentinel of the necropolis. The most deftly executed and famous likeness of the Anubis jackal to have come down to us from ancient Egypt is the recumbent statue on top of a gilded shrine from the tomb of Tutankhamun in the Valley of the Kings, now in the Egyptian Museum, Cairo. The animal cemeteries associated with the cult centers where Anubis and the other canine funerary gods were worshiped usually contain only dog mummies. This may suggest that the Egyptians did not always clearly distinguish between dog and jackal, but it is more likely that domestic dogs were more readily obtainable and easier to propagate in captivity for sale to pious pilgrims as votive offerings.

The striped hyena was likewise a stock item in Egyptian desert hunting compositions from an early age. Hyenas are routinely portrayed in these scenes bloodied by the tomb-owners' arrows, at bay, or fleeing from packs of hounds in hot pursuit, or even captured alive, slung on a pole and carried by huntsmen. Hyena meat seems to have been highly regarded in ancient Egypt, especially under the Old Kingdom. This beast was a standard feature of the traditional file of desert game presented to the deceased in the decoration of tomb-chapels, intended as food for eternity, where it is often labeled "young hyena." A handful of images from the fifth and sixth dynasties illustrate striped hyenas being forcibly fed, fattening them up prior to slaughter. These were not domestic animals, but captured from the wild and kept until needed. Certainly the most unusual instance of hyena hunting comes from a wall painting in the eighteenth dynasty Theban tomb of Amenemhab (tomb 85), which depicts the deceased doing battle with a giant, menacing female striped hyena. That the Egyptians knew the scavenging and opportunist feeding behavior of this carnivore is revealed by the fact that, at the close of the twentieth dynasty, when the Egyptian countryside was in the grip of a terrible famine, one year was appropriately dubbed "the year of the hyenas."

Last, the red fox can sporadically be recognized amid the diverse wildlife in scenes of the desert chase, beginning in the early fourth dynasty. It has been argued that a standard hieroglyph having the phonetic value *ms* (Gardiner F 31) is comprised of three foxes' skins tied together. Foxes also make a humorous appearance on "satirical" papyri and figured ostraca during the nineteenth and twentieth dynasties, where these legendary enemies of the farmyard are rendered feeding and shepherding their usual prey. Like the hyena, this species apparently had little religious significance for the ancient Egyptians.

## BIBLIOGRAPHY

Baines, John. "Symbolic Roles of Canine Figures on Early Monuments." *Archéo-Nil: Bulletin de la société pour l'étude des cultures prépharaoniques de la vallée du Nil* 3 (1993), 57–73. Offers an interesting discussion of the possible symbolic significance of certain canine figures on Egyptian monuments of the Late Predynastic period (Naqada III); contains a useful bibliography.

Boessneck, Joachim. *Die Tierwelt des alten Ägypten: Untersucht anhand kulturgeschichtlicher und zoologischer Quellen.* Munich, 1988. An authoritative discussion of canines in ancient Egypt, including zooarcheological findings.

Helck, Wolfgang, Eberhard Otto, and Wolfhart Westendorf, eds. *Lexikon der Ägyptologie.* 7 vols. Wiesbaden, 1975–1992. Massive reference work containing articles in English, French, and German on virtually every topic relating to ancient Egypt; with important entries on all aspects of canines in pharaonic life and religion.

Houlihan, Patrick F. *The Animal World of the Pharaohs.* London and New York, 1996. A handsomely illustrated book for a general audience devotes considerable space to surveying the various canines in ancient Egypt; extensive bibliography.

Osborn, Dale J., and Ibrahim Helmy. *The Contemporary Land Mammals of Egypt (Including Sinai).* Fieldiana Zoology, new series, 5. Chicago, 1980. The standard work on the land mammals of modern Egypt, but now out of print.

Osborn, Dale J. with Jana Osbornová. *The Mammals of Ancient Egypt.* Warminster, 1998. Provides a good survey of the canines recognizable in Egyptian iconography.

Paton, David. *Animals of Ancient Egypt.* Princeton and London, 1925. Contains some useful information on canines, but is largely out of date.

Tooley, Angela M. J. "Coffin of a Dog from Beni Hasan." *Journal of Egyptian Archaeology* 74 (1988), 207–211. Good survey of the evidence for the burial of pet dogs in ancient Egypt through the Middle Kingdom.

PATRICK F. HOULIHAN

## CANOPIC JARS AND CHESTS.

Items intended as containers for the internal organs removed during the process of mummification are generally termed *canopic*. They principally comprise jars and chests but also miniature coffins and masks. The actual term *canopic* derives from a case of mistaken identity: one form of visceral container was a human-headed jar. According to writers of the Classical period, the Greek hero, Kanopos, helmsman for Menelaeus, was worshiped at Canopus in the form of just such a jar. Early Egyptologists saw a connection between that object and the quite separate visceral jars and began calling them "canopic." The name has stuck and has been extended by scholars to refer to all kinds of receptacles intended to hold viscera removed for mummification in ancient Egypt.

From the end of the Old Kingdom, the four basic organs removed became associated with a specific deity, (each called a *genius*): (1) the liver was identified with the genius Imsety, one of the four sons of Horus, who could claim protection from the goddess Isis; (2) for the lungs, the pairing was the genius Hapy and the goddess Nephthys; (3) for the stomach, the third son Duamutef and the goddess Neith; (4) for the intestines, the fourth son Kebehsenuef and Selket. These genii are usually identifiable from the middle of the New Kingdom by their heads: Imsety having a human visage; Hapy that of a baboon; Duamutef that of a jackal; and Kebehsenuef that of a hawk.

The earliest canopic installations placed the desiccated and wrapped visceral bundles directly into a chest or a specially built cavity in the wall. Although such potential canopic niches have been alleged to occur at the cemetery of Saqqara in tombs of the second dynasty, the first clear examples are dated to the fourth dynasty reign of Sneferu (c.2649–2609 BCE), where a number of tombs at Meidum contain niches whose size and position (corresponding to later canopic usage) point to their being canopic. An actual chest was provided for Sneferu's wife, Hetepheres, carved from a block of translucent calcite (Egyptian alabaster) and divided into four square compartments, each of which contained a mass that almost certainly was part of her internal organs, immersed in a weak solution of natron.

During the fourth dynasty, it became firmly established that canopic receptacles should be placed at the southern (foot) end of the corpse, most often slightly offset to the southeast. Normally, such receptacles were cubical niches in the chamber wall or cuttings in the floor. The earliest identifiable kingly example was constructed in the paving blocks to the southeast of the sarcophagus of Khafre, in the second pyramid of Giza. (Suggestions that the South Tomb of Djoser and later subsidiary pyramids had canopic roles were shown to be wrong.) The niches and rock-cuttings within burial chambers may have held wooden boxes; by the end of the dynasty, the organs were sometimes placed inside simple stone or pottery jars, with flat or domed lids. The earliest such canopic jars came from the fourth dynasty tomb of Queen Meresankh III at Giza, during the reign of Menkaure (c.2551–2523).

Early chests were normally cut from soft stones or into the fabric of the wall or floor of the burial chamber. From the beginning of the sixth dynasty, however, granite examples begin to be found in royal tombs, sunk in floor pits southeast of the foot of the sarcophagus. Fragments of a canopic jar and its complete contents were recovered from the tomb of Pepy I (r. 2354–2310 BCE). The wrapped viscera had been soaked in resin and had solidified in the shape of the interior of the jar.

During the First Intermediate Period, a number of innovations appeared; most important, canopic jars started to have human-headed lids instead of flat or domed lids. In parallel, the wrapped bundles of viscera were adorned occasionally, with cartonnage masks, again with human faces. During that period, human heads and faces seem to represent the dead, rather than the genius who was invoked on the jar and/or the chest. Previously, any inscriptions had been restricted to the name and title of the deceased, but wooden canopic chests now followed the design of contemporary coffins: strings of text were run around the upper part and on occasion displayed vertical complements. The close link between the design of the canopic chest and either the coffin or the sarcophagus was maintained in most cases until the latter part of the New Kingdom.

By the end of the Middle Kingdom, a basic ideal pattern for canopic equipment had been achieved. A stone outer chest would reflect the design of the stone sarcophagus; the inner, of wood, that of the coffin. The texts of the wooden chest would call on each of the four tutelary goddesses to wrap her protective arms about her particular genius, and would proclaim the deceased's honor before her and the genius. Within the wooden chest would be four human-lidded jars, one per genius, with texts repeating the sentiments expressed on the chest. A typical example of such a text, from the Imsety (liver) canopic jar of the thirteenth dynasty king Awibre Hor, ran as follows:

> Isis, extend your protection about Imsety who is in you,
> O honoured before Imsety, the King of Upper and
> Lower Egypt, Awibre [Hor].

Not all burials could conform to that ideal, but the existence of the pattern for canopic jars and chests was confirmed by the appearance of painted representations of the jars, complete with texts, on the inner lid of one chest whose size showed that it had contained only simple bundles of viscera—the chest of King Sobkemsaf (II).

During the seventeenth dynasty, the period that saw the definitive replacement of the traditional rectangular coffin by one of human form, a new decoration was initiated for the canopic chest, centering on a recumbent figure of the jackal god Anubis. Early examples imitated the latest group of rectangular coffins, with a background painted in black varnish; later ones were decorated on a ground of plain or yellowish gesso. Those chests also have exaggerated vaulted lids, with raised end pieces which were characteristic of late rectangular coffins.

Early in the eighteenth dynasty, canopic chest decoration was changed again, to focus on images of the four goddesses and their genii. The form of the chests also

CANOPIC JARS AND CHESTS. *Set of limestone canopic jars from Giza, twenty-sixth dynasty.* (University of Pennsylvania Museum, Philadelphia. Neg. # S4–143069)

evolved from simple boxes with flat or vaulted lids to those that imitated the form of *naos* shrines. Usually mounted on a sledge, the upper part of the box had a flaring *cavetto* cornice, while the lid was rounded at the front and sloped down to the rear. The color schemes followed those on contemporary wooden coffins and sarcophagi: beginning with a white background, shifting to yellow/gold on black, and then to polychrome on yellow at the very end of the eighteenth dynasty.

Initially, canopic jars followed Middle Kingdom patterns, but as the New Kingdom progressed, more and more sets of lids included animal and bird heads, replacing the uniformly human faces used on earlier jars. That change resulted from New Kingdom modification of the iconography of three of the four canopic genii. That also marked a definitive shift from the jar embodying the dead person to embodying the relevant genius. (The distinction had been blurred for some considerable time, but the change in the mode of representing the genii resolved this confusion.) Various materials were used to make canopic

jars during the eighteenth dynasty, including calcite, limestone, pottery, wood, and cartonnage.

Until the late eighteenth dynasty, the placing of masks on visceral bundles was a cheap alternative to using jars; however, some particularly rich eighteenth dynasty burials have both—a fine example being the canopic material from the burial of Tjuiu, the mother-in-law of Amenhotpe III (r. 1410–1372 BCE). She was equipped with a *naos*-form chest, black varnished, with texts and divine images richly gilded on raised gesso. Within the chest lay four human-lidded calcite jars, having long texts filled with black pigment. Inside, the visceral bundles had been shaped into mummies; over the "head" of each was placed a gilded cartonnage mask; in all those cases, human heads were used.

Before the New Kingdom, royal canopic equipment had broadly followed contemporary private practices in their basic forms, but from the reign of Amenhotpe II (r. 1454–1419 BCE) there was a marked divergence. The earliest royal chests of the eighteenth dynasty, that of

Queen Hatshepsut (r. 1502–1482 BCE) and that made for Thutmose I by Thutmose III (r. 1504–1452 BCE) were simple *naos*-form boxes, ornamented by simple texts and distinguished from private examples only by being made of stone (quartzite) rather than wood. Amenhotpe II, however, had an elaborate calcite confection prepared for himself, with the jars carved within the matrix of the box and raised figures of the protective goddesses enfolding each of the corners; the jar stoppers represented the king. Such a pattern, further elaborated, was followed by the kings until the early part of the nineteenth dynasty.

The Amarna interlude toward the end of the eighteenth dynasty, when Aten was worshiped, is but little represented in the canopic record. The most impressive items are the four jars found accompanying the mummy in the Valley of the Kings, tomb 55. Their fine human heads seem to have been made for one of Akhenaten's daughters; the jars once belonged to the king's junior wife, Kiya. Although erased before final use, their texts were successfully read as giving the names and titles of the king, those of the Aten, and those of the deceased. The traditional gods and goddesses of burial had no place in Akhenaten's religion. Akhenaten (r. 1372–1355 BCE) used a chest in the general pattern of his predecessors, but with the hawk, the earliest embodiment of his god, replacing the protective goddesses at the corners. Those divine ladies reappear in the equipment of Tutankhamun (r. 1355–1346 BCE), where they not only enfold the corners of the stone chest but also, as gilded wooden statuettes, stand guard around a great gilded wooden shrine that enclosed it. Within the chest—a solid block bored with four cylindrical compartments and topped with carved heads of the king—lay four solid gold miniature coffins, each holding a package of viscera. The later (fragmentary) calcite chests of Horemheb, (r. 1343–1315 BCE), Sety I, (r. 1314–1304 BCE), and Ramesses II (r. 1304–1237 BCE)—the last two from the nineteenth dynasty—are similar in pattern, but added wings to the arms of the goddesses and, for Ramesses II, glass inlay. By the end of the nineteenth dynasty reign of Ramesses II, uniformly human lids seem to have been replaced definitively by the faunal forms of the genii. Private jars showed considerable variation, some being made of faience; and some were replaced altogether by wooden or stone miniature coffins, which usually showed the faunal heads of the genii.

Royal calcite chests were changed under Merenptah (r.1237–1226 BCE), in that they no longer displayed corner goddesses; they were then replaced by four separate jars early in the twentieth dynasty. How the jars were housed is unclear, but they do not seem to have been put in a stone chest. The one extant royal example, that of Ramesses IV (r. 1166–1160 BCE), is very large. Large canopic jars are also found in the Ramessid burials of the sacred Apis and Mnevis bulls at Saqqara and Heliopolis.

From the beginning of the twenty-first dynasty, if not somewhat earlier, most mummies had their viscera returned to the body cavity after embalmment. The canopic jar had become so fundamental to the funerary outfit, however, that high status individuals still used them, even though they were empty. By the twenty-second dynasty, they were superseded by solid dummies—an extreme example of that triumph of form over function was reached when dummy packets of viscera were placed inside the silver canopic coffinettes of Sheshonq II (c.910 BCE). Twenty-first dynasty jars broadly followed Middle and New Kingdom prototypes in their texts, with the exception of some unique examples belonging to Smendes (r. 1081–1055 BCE). In contrast, the texts on jars of the twenty-second to twenty-third dynasties tended to be rather simple, frequently resorting to the minimalist approach of merely naming the dead person and the genius. Form varied considerably, as did decoration, which was often in bright polychrome during the twenty-third dynasty. Although not uncommon, canopic equipment is found in a minority of Third Intermediate Period burials. The dummy jars were often placed within chests of the *naos* form, although decorated in ways different from those of the New Kingdom; about the beginning of the Third Intermediate Period, a recumbent jackal of Anubis was affixed to the lid of the chest. Kings generally had wooden canopic chests, with the exception of Sheshonq I, who had a calcite box, the design of which was derived directly from those of the eighteenth dynasty kings.

The number of canopic jars increased considerably at the end of the twenty-fifth dynasty and during the following Saite period. Also, formulations were used in the texts. Rather than merely differing in the deities invoked, the actual wording on each was somewhat distinctive. The two jars of Apries of the twenty-sixth dynasty (r. 589–570 BCE) are interesting in that neither seems to have been used in his burial. (One was used a century or so later to contain a mummified hawk; the other found its way into an Etruscan tomb in Italy.) Jar shapes were also changed in Saite times becoming somewhat rotund. Earlier jars usually had their widest points at their shoulders; with Saite jars, the greatest width tended to be lower. Such jars all bear the usual faunal genius heads. There appears to have been a brief reversion to uniformly human heads during the early twenty-seventh dynasty (First Persian Occupation), to judge from the tomb of Iufa (found at Abusir in 1996); his jars also have a nonstandard textual decoration. Unfortunately, there is insufficient material to judge properly the trends of that epoch.

Canopic material from the end of the Late period is rare, but it seems to follow Saite practice. A few Ptolemaic jars are known, yet they were superseded by small but tall shrinelike chests, brightly painted, including images of the genii, and topped by a three-dimensional hawk figure squatting on its haunches in the "Archaic" pose. In shape, the boxes were very similar to some *ushabti* boxes of the same time span.

The point at which canopic equipment disappeared is unclear, but it seems to have been well before the end of Ptolemaic times in Egypt.

[*See also* Four Sons of Horus; *and* Mummification.]

### BIBLIOGRAPHY

Brovarski, E. J. *Canopic Jars.* Corpus antiquitatum aegyptia carum, 1. Mainz, 1978. A catalog of the museum's comprehensive holdings.

D'Auria, Sue, et al. *Mummies and Magic: The Funerary Arts of Ancient Egypt.* Boston, 1988. A fundamental work on Egyptian funerary material, which places the jars in their context in the tomb.

Dobrowlolska, K. "Génèse et évolution des boîtes à vases-canopes." *Études et Travaux* 4 (1970), 73–85.

Dodson, Aidan. *The Canopic Equipment of the Kings of Egypt.* London, 1994.

Dodson, Aidan. "A Canopic Jar of Ramesses IV and the Royal Canopic Equipment of the Ramesside Period." *Göttinger Miszellen* 152 (1996), 11–17.

Dodson, Aidan. *The Coffins and Canopic Equipment from the Tomb of Tutankhamun.* Oxford, forthcoming.

Ikram, Salima, and Aidan Dodson. *The Mummy in Ancient Egypt.* London and New York, 1998. A chapter describes and illustrates the evolution of all types of canopic material.

Lucas, Alfred. "The Canopic Vases from the 'Tomb of Queen Tiyi'." *Annales du service des antiquités de l'Égypte* 31 (1931), 120–122. The examination of the contents of the canopic jars from tomb 55 in the Valley of the Kings.

Lüscher, Barbara. *Untersuchungen zu ägyptischen Kanopenkästen. Vom Alten Reich bis zum Ende der Zweiten Zwischenzeit.* Hildesheimer ägyptologische Beiträge, 31. Hildesheim, 1990. A comprehensive study of canopic chests from the Old Kingdom through to the Second Intermediate Period.

Martin, Karl. "Kanopen II." In *Lexikon der Ägyptologie,* 3: 316–319. Weisbaden, 1980.

Martin, Karl. "Kanopenkasten." In *Lexikon der Ägyptologie,* 3:319–320. Weisbaden, 1980.

Reisner, George Andrew. "The Dated Canopic Jars of the Gizeh Museum." *Zeitschrift für Ägyptische Sprache und Altertumskunde* 37 (1899), 61–72. Although old, still an important analysis of the development of canopic jars, as illustrated by the Cairo collection.

Reisner, George Andrew. *Canopics.* Cairo, 1967. This extensively illustrated catalog of the Cairo Museum's Egyptian holdings was completed around the turn of the twentieth century but not published for some seventy years. It did not include all items held in 1900, yet none of the items missing or subsequently acquired was added prior to publication; however, it comprises the best corpus of material extant.

Sethe, Kurt. "Zur Geschichte der Einbalsamierung bei den Ägyptern, und einiger damit verbundener Bräuche." *Sitzungsberichte des Preussische Akademie des Wissenschaften. Sitzungsberichte. Philosophische-Historische Klasse. Berlin 1934.* Jahrgang (1934), 211–239; 1*–16*. The fundamental discussion and classification of the texts inscribed upon canopic jars and chests.

AIDAN DODSON

**CAPTIONS.** Hieroglyphs are a kind of pictorial art. Over thousands of years they did not lose any of their original pictorial character and they also retained their character as symbols. In paintings and reliefs, depiction and writing are closely related and complement each other. For example, the illustration, generally larger than the caption, can serve as the caption's determinative. In the composition of a flat painting, the writing serves an autonomous function. Horizontal and vertical lines subdivide registers and large wall areas or serve as borders for painted scenes. Thus, it is difficult to differentiate between the concepts "caption" and "inscription." In a broader sense, captions are any lines of hieroglyphs on pictures—that is, in reliefs and paintings—in which the direction of the writing is oriented toward persons and objects and in which the text does not extend beyond the picture. Even ritual scenes in Greco-Roman temples can be said to have captions, although there the writing follows fixed, definite patterns—as in royal and divine framing columns and spells—and shapes the scenes. The texts accompanying the figures (personifications, priests, etc.) of the processions that are depicted on basement and stairs, usually also arranged according to a definite pattern, are also called "captions." Secondary pictorial captions also appear, mostly as Hieratic inscriptions by visitors, or they supplement older captions to adapt them to new cult conditions.

For the purposes of this article, a narrower definition of *caption* will be used: texts integrated into a picture that, through changes in the direction of the writing—right and left, horizontal and vertical—harmonize completely with both the composition and the orientation of the figures. In some cases, these texts are also "reversed" or "retrograded," without necessarily following a definite, fixed pattern. Through time, the picture and writing were integrated and the size of the caption developed, according to both historical conditions and aesthetic influences. The range runs from a sparing use of a few hieroglyphs—mostly names and indications of rank or title—to the narrative captions arranged in large blocks—in Ramessid historical pictures—and from the lavish use of captions (prompted by *horror vacui*) in the large *mastaba*s of the fifth and sixth dynasties to the speeches by gardeners and overseers that serve as divisions between the registers in the tomb of Petosiris.

In most cases, the captions enhance the appeal of a work, in terms of content and form, if they are integrated into the composition and harmonize with it. Occasionally, however, captions can seriously jeopardize the autonomy of a picture and even overshadow it. Their unlimited placement may serve to foreshorten the depth of the background, so that it may become nothing more than a two-dimensional surface for the caption. The viewer experiences the background as alternately revealing an indeterminate three-dimensional depth and a two-dimensional flatness. To this tension do the Ramessid historical pictures owe their uniqueness.

The use of captions together with pictures has an amazingly long tradition; for example, the names of the prisoners that appear on the Libyan relief in the temple of Sahure, which are also depicted in the temples of Unas and Pepy II, are still noted in the temple of Taharqa in Kawa in the twenty-fifth dynasty. The captions do not, however, necessarily lend a picture greater authenticity and historicity; for example, the famine reliefs from the Unas causeway lost some of their originality when the block with the relief depicting starving bedouins was discovered in the temple of Sahure. Captions can also diverge in content from their pictorial setting, as in the myth of the god-king's birth or in the depiction of the Battle of Kadesh, particularly when they are intended for a literate as well as an illiterate public. From the third dynasty until Meroitic times captions can be found in reliefs and paintings, on the walls of tombs and temples, less frequently on coffins, and also on the stelae and stelae chapels of the twelfth dynasty.

The transition from captions as text integrated into a picture to illustrations as pictures integrated into a text was fluid. Captions had multiple functions: as headings, they explained pictures; they identified persons by name, occupation, and title; they identified objects by name, number, material, and dimensions. They also supplemented a picture with information and immortalized its meaning. The immortalization of the name of a person was of special importance.

In the mid-fifth dynasty, captions took on a new function—that of recording direct speech. In most cases, the dialogues are written directly next to the human figures on the same level as their heads, similar to the speech balloons in present-day comic strips. The group of captions that Adolf Erman labeled "speeches, calls, and songs" appeared as early as the "world chamber" of the sun temple of Newoserre Any and in tombs in the scenes of everyday life—and they were used until the end of the pharaonic era. Apart from such mural paintings, these captions are mentioned only very rarely; the most detail about them can be found in tomb inscriptions of the seventh century BCE, in which the conversation among the workers is characterized as "quarreling" (*sḫwn*) and "loud praises" (*sḏꜣm ꜥꜣ*), and the visitor is supposed to hear that, as well as the "singing of the musicians" and the "lamenting of the mourners." The dialogues, singing, and lamenting are thus presumed to be audible, at least for the literate elite.

Although some passages from the Coffin Texts are interpreted as substantiating that captions allude to the hereafter, the scenes of daily life were depicted iconographically. Mostly, the speeches and calls were concerned with matters of this world and did not allude to resurrection. During the Old Kingdom, the Beautiful West was considered the dwelling place of the dead and thus a continuation of this world. Since the tomb represents a symbolic extension of this world into the hereafter, the deceased took this world with him into the next in the form of mural paintings and tomb furnishings. Even when the notions about the hereafter changed at the end of the Old Kingdom, the tradition of the calls continued in the paintings.

At their most plentiful, in the fifth and sixth dynasties, the speeches and calls contained commands to animals, onomatopoeic drover calls, and interjections (e.g., "gee," "run"); names, even affectionate ones, for cattle (e.g., "friend," "brother"); or exhortations to work (e.g., "Let's get to work, servant girls!"); terms of address by the workers for the overseer (e.g., "prince," "patron") and for each other (e.g., "my dear," "comrade," "he who is with me," "bird catcher," "herdsman"), as well as mocking and bantering terms (e.g., "loudmouth," "chatterbox") and even terms of abuse (e.g., "thief," "whoremaster," "blockhead," "shitter"). Among these captions, dialogues occur very frequently, mostly in the form of exhortations to work, to hurry up, and as commands and compliant answers, often couched in idioms found only here ("I do [this] so you will praise it," "I do what you praise"), which take the place of the usual "yes, sir!" or "upon my life." A certain question-and-answer play is typical for depictions of the grain harvest and asks for the most hardworking man; an individual or a chorus then answers: "I am the one!" This play occurs in numerous variations and was also applied to other types of work; it was still in use in the tombs of the Middle Kingdom. The captions also frequently refer to human weaknesses and needs, for example the recurring calls for beer during the harvest ("Bring me beer, I am cutting *bšꜣ* malt") or for Sokar beer among the metal workers. These calls are often accompanied by apotropaic gestures—warding off evil—as for example in the depiction of the birth of a calf or that of wading across a canal ("Your arm above the water!"). Several variations have been found of a longer incantation to ward off a crocodile, addressed by its cover name *šj*. Since calls and incantations often use the same or similar phrasing, it may be assumed that the artist drew upon a repertory of phrases. Even individual figures and their titles are probably taken from a repertory—for example the "foreman of the fishermen" is often depicted with his outstretched arm resting on a stick. The titles and refrains of songs in captions bear witness to the general fondness for singing, for example, while hauling in the fishing nets or while harvesting. These songs are so straightforward and plain that if it were not for the depiction of the flute player, they could easily be taken for simple calls; among them are true work songs whose rhythm supports the work—such as the thresher's song, which accompanies the animals in their circular walk with its frequent repetitions of "Thresh!"— as well as more artistic songs. In the scenes of daily life, the "Herdsman's Song," which is known to occur eight times next to a flock of sheep, alludes to the world of the gods; the song of the sedan bearers, also found eight times, is dedicated to the lord of the tomb.

Liveliness, naiveté, seriousness, and humor are all characteristic of the speeches and calls of the fifth and sixth dynasties. Figures may exchange mocking remarks and banter together, but these are never directed at the lord of the tomb. Such remarks take aim at human short-comings—laziness, bragging, self-praise, and indulgence in eating and drinking. In this way, despite their generally standardized nature, the captions create a lifelike atmosphere and relieve the pathos of the paintings in the tombs. The figures of the workers are in various postures and contortions, with the clothing, hairstyles, and injuries typical of their trade. Thus they serve as a contrast to the lord of the tomb, who stands or sits calmly, in timeless, flawless repose. The calls in the captions also serve as a foil to the formulaic, official inscriptions dictated by decorum. It is hard to tell to what extent these calls, aside from their use of the demonstrative pronoun $p_3$, $t_3$, $n_3$, reflect the language of the common people. The use of the demonstrative pronoun, however, can be connected to the "always saying $p_3$" or the "speech of the $hwrw$," from which the lord of the tomb refrains. Captions often contain technical terms and reflect communication among skilled workers, but they were shaped by the presence of the lord of the tomb, so they are by no means a true picture of reality. Captions are concerned with a practical purpose and, for that reason, are an invaluable source for cultural history studies. They depict the richness and depth of life, show wit and humor, and serve to delight the lord of the tomb—and for that reason can be compared to the balloons in present-day comic strips. In contrast to the satires on various trades during the Middle Kingdom, these captions depict everyday life as tranquil.

Scenes depicting banquets and funeral repasts are also accompanied by captions, among them songs and calls connected with musical and dance performances. Songs accompanied by the harp are typical of festivals; their style is more refined than that of songs for everyday use. Quite often, these festival songs allude to the world of the gods and are dedicated to the lord of the tomb. According to Altenmüller (1998), the Hathor songs and the "Song of $sn$-$ntrw$" call on the lord of the tomb to return to this world. Due to their brevity, they are often very difficult to translate.

Very little such material is known from the First Intermediate Period; in Mo'alla, captions elucidate crude situations that are not entirely without originality. Occasionally, calls can be found written on stelae, as for example the one labeled Cairo JE 91095, which came originally from Herakleopolis. In Middle Kingdom provincial tombs, the tradition of the speeches and calls was continued but not to the same extent as it had been during the Old Kingdom. At Meir, there is a recognizable local tradition. The tombs at Beni Hasan are less lavishly furnished. The categories "human weaknesses," "exhortations to work," and "mocking replies" are still represented among the captions. Among the pure art songs, there is the song to the beef cattle imported from the Near East; another is the song to the field goddess Sechet, sung during the hauling in of the fishing net at Bersheh. Calls of dedication appear on coffins and, during the eleventh dynasty, dog names also appear in captions.

During the New Kingdom, the tradition of the calls was continued at first, but from the mid-eighteenth dynasty they became less frequent. On the whole, they became more like eulogies and were well-phrased and longer than before. Nevertheless, there are calls in their typical forms, as well as some terms of abuse (e.g., "You old geezer, you bald-pated peasant" in a mocking reply to a braggart) and "antiphonal" songs ($hn$ $n$ $wsb$) during work in the fields. (A paraphrase of the threshing song in Paheri's tomb at Elkab and its variant in the tomb of Setau inspired Bertolt Brecht to write the poem "Address of a Peasant to his Ox [after an Egyptian peasant song, 1400 B.C.E.].")

Although most of the calls focus on providing for the lord of the tomb or simply report on the completion of the work assigned, the genre did not fall into oblivion. For example, the longest substantiated conversation comes from the tomb of Eje in Amarna and comments on the praises heaped upon him from the common man's point of view. The original intention, "to listen to the way the ordinary people speak," was thus turned into an instrument of propaganda. Even in the Ramessid era, lively and witty calls are found in unexpected places, as in a conversation in the gold house in the Theban tomb of Paser (tomb 106) where the wish for a vacation is expressed. The cheers exchanged during banquets and the songs of the musicians form a group of their own; they are often of great poetic beauty. On the whole in the Ramessid era, captions became much less frequent as tombs became much more funereal.

On temple reliefs, captions also contain direct speech, as with the questions asked by the Puntites in the depictions of an expedition into Punt, the address of the bearers to the myrrh trees they had brought with them, or the dialogues between the butchers in the temple of Hatshepsut. In the captions accompanying Ramessid historical pictures, however, narrative style predominates and the captions are arranged in vertical lines and blocks. Topographic information may occasionally be found, such as the names of fortresses and wells. The depiction of the Battle of Kadesh is accompanied by mocking labels, for example, the picture of a man being held upside down and said to have almost drowned in the Orontes: "the miserable prince of Aleppo, who is held by his soldiers after His Majesty had thrown him into the water."

In the Theban tombs of the twenty-fifth and twenty-sixth dynasties, captions were mostly imitations that followed the patterns of the eighteenth dynasty. For example, a wall with butchery scenes from the temple of Hatshepsut was copied, including its captions, and from there made its way into others' tombs. Occasionally captions based on the pattern of the Old Kingdom were also used. The tradition continues even in Nubian Kawa. Later, the reliefs from the thirtieth dynasty from Heliopolis and Buto and the neo-Memphite reliefs of the twenty-sixth dynasty used headings in the style of the Old Kingdom. The end point of this development is represented by the idyllic scenes in the tomb of Petosiris, where tranquil and poetic calls form the setting for the thoughtful rule and social sensitivity of the lord of the tomb; they are closely related to the (auto)biographical texts but are very different from the serious language of the Old Kingdom.

## BIBLIOGRAPHY

Altenmüller, Hartwig. *Die Wanddarstellungen im Grab des Mehu in Saqqara.* Archäologische Veröffentlichungen, 42. Mainz, 1998. The numerous calls and songs in this tomb are discussed together with their variants.

Bryan, Betsy M. "The Disjunction of Text and Image in Egyptian Art." In *Studies in Honor of William Kelly Simpson*, edited by Peter Der Manuelian, pp. 161–168. Boston, 1996.

Der Manuelian, Peter. *Living in the Past: Studies in Archaism of the Egyptian Twenty-Sixth Dynasty.* Studies in Egyptology. London and New York, 1994.

Fischer, Henry George. *Egyptian Studies II: The Orientation of Hieroglyphs, I. Reversals.* New York, 1977.

Guglielmi, Waltraud. "Reden, Rufe und Lieder auf altägyptischen Darstellungen der Landwirtschaft, Viehzucht, des Fisch- und Vogelfangs vom Mittleren Reich bis zur Spätzeit." *Tübinger Ägyptologische Beiträge*, 1. Wiesbaden, 1973.

Guglielmi, Waltraud. "Reden und Rufe." In *Lexikon der Ägyptologie*, 5:193–195. Wiesbaden, 1984.

Junker, Hermann. "Zu einigen Reden und Rufen auf den Grabbildern des Alten Reiches." *Sitzungsberichte der Akademie der Wissenschaften in Wien*, 221. Vienna and Leipzig, 1943.

Kuhlmann, Klaus, and W. Schenkel. "Das Grab des Ibi, Theben, No. 36, I." *Archäologische Veröffentlichungen*, 15. Mainz, 1983.

Montet, Pierre. *Les Scènes de la vie privée dans les tombeaux égyptiens de l'Ancien Empire.* Strasbourg, 1925.

Moussa, Ahmed M., and Hartwig Altenmüller. "Das Grab des Nianchnum und Chnumhotep." *Archäologische Veröffentlichungen*, 21. Mainz, 1977.

Vandier, Jacques. *Manuel d'archéologie égyptienne VI, Bas-Reliefs et peintures.* Scènes de la vie agricole à l'Ancien et au Moyen Empire. Paris, 1978.

Van Walsem, René. "The Interpretation of Iconographic Programmes in the Old Kingdom Elite Tombs of the Memphite Area: Methodological and Theoretical (Re)considerations." In *Proceedings of the Seventh International Congress of Egyptologists*, edited by C. J. Eyre, pp. 1205–1213. Orientalia Lovaniensia Analecta, 82. Leuven, 1998.

WALTRAUD GUGLIELMI
Translated from German by Sabine H. Seiler
and Martha Goldstein

**CARCHEMISH.** *See* Mesopotamia.

**CARNELIAN.** *See* Gems.

**CARTER, HOWARD** (1874–1939), British Egyptologist and artist. Born in London, Howard Carter was the youngest son of Samuel John Carter and Martha Joyce (née Sands). He received no formal education, but, as a member of the artistically gifted Carter family, he was trained to draw and to paint in watercolor. With the encouragement of the Amherst family of Didlington Hall in Norfolk, Carter was engaged in 1891 by the Egypt Exploration Fund to work as an artist with Percy E. Newberry; in January of 1892, he was assigned to work with William Matthew Flinders Petrie at Tell el-Amarna. There, Carter received his initiation into excavation under the guidance of the best Egyptological excavator of the time—a testing experience.

From 1894 to 1899, Carter worked with Edouard Naville on the temple of Queen Hatshepsut at Deir el-Bahri. His principal task was to record the fine relief carvings in the temple, and he was responsible for drawing the plates in the six volumes of Naville's *The Temple of Deir el Bahari* (1896–1908), a work that set new standards for the recording of Egyptian monuments. Carter also acted as Naville's deputy in all works at Deir el-Bahri; in consequence, he was appointed, in 1899, the first Chief Inspector for Upper Egypt by Gaston Maspero, Director General of the Antiquities Service. He supervised many excavations at Thebes, including those of Theodore Davis in the Valley of the Kings.

In late 1904, Carter was transferred to the Lower Egyptian inspectorate, but an unfortunate fracas at the cemetery site of Saqqara in January 1905, involving French visitors to the Serapeum, ultimately led to his resignation from the Antiquities Service in November 1905. For three years, Carter lived a hand-to-mouth existence in Egypt until, in late 1908, the fifth Earl of Carnarvon engaged him as his professional assistant, on the recommendation of Maspero. Carter introduced discipline and systematic recording to Carnarvon's excavations, and their significant results were published in *Five Years' Exploration at Thebes* (1912), the major archaeological content of which can be credited to Carter.

In 1914, Carnarvon took over the concession to work in the Valley of the Kings, but the onset of World War I delayed the start of serious work until 1917. Until the spring of 1922, Carter worked there with little success. Then, returning in the following October, he discovered the steps leading down to the tomb of King Tutankhamun on 4 November. The opening and clearing of this rich

CARTER, HOWARD. *Photograph of Howard Carter, at left.* (University of Pennsylvania Museum, Philadelphia. Neg. # S4–141437)

royal burial occupied Carter until 1932. His attention to the conservation and recording of the tomb's contents was meticulous. A popular account of the work in three volumes, *The Tomb of Tut.ankh.Amen* (1923–1933), was prepared by Carter with the help of Arthur Mace and others. For the remaining years of his life, Carter suffered from poor health and was unable to prepare a scientific report on his great discovery. His papers are preserved in the Griffith Institute, Oxford, England. A bibliography of Carter's principal publications is included in T. G. H. James, *Howard Carter: The Path to Tutankhamun* (1992).

### BIBLIOGRAPHY
James, T. G. H. *Howard Carter: The Path to Tutankhamun.* London, 1992. A full biography, based on all known records.
Reeves, N., and John H. Taylor. *Howard Carter before Tutankhamun.* London, 1992. A well-illustrated and well-documented catalog to a British Museum exhibition.
Winstone, H. V. F. *Howard Carter and the Discovery of the Tomb of Tutankhamun.* London, 1991. A biography concentrating on Carter's major discovery.

T. G. H. JAMES

**CARTOGRAPHY,** the study of maps and their construction, especially as graphic representations of spatial relationships—the distribution of places, objects, or other features. In the context of ancient Egypt, cartography includes four general categories of maps: topographical, architectural, mythological, and cosmological. Ancient Egyptian maps share the following characteristics: (1) they are more pictorial than planimetric; (2) they show nonperspective, bird's-eye views, with features drawn on a flat background, in either profile or plan views and with either a constant or a variable orientation; and (3) when actual areas are represented, as in the case of topographic and architectural maps, they are not drawn at constant scale—instead, precise measurements are written where they are deemed important.

**Topographical Maps.** A topographical map is one that depicts the natural or cultural features of a portion of Earth's surface (especially with respect to its contours, heights, and depths). The earliest representations of topography in Egypt date from the Naqada I (Amratian) and Naqada II (Gerzean) phases of late Predynastic times (c.4000–3000 BCE). Painted on pottery, they show either real or imaginary landscapes with rivers and hills. An especially good example is a Naqada II vessel in the Petrie Museum of London's University College. On it, were painted several intertwining river channels and the pyramid-shaped hills in the adjacent desert. Beside the river are antelopes and cranes (or flamingos), with a line of birds in flight; on the river is a boat from which fishermen are thrusting spears or punting poles into the water.

During the New Kingdom, elaborate narrative scenes describing royal exploits in battle were carved in relief on the walls of temples. The best-known example, and the only one to include a map, was Ramesses II's depiction of the Battle of Kadesh, which occurred about 1285 BCE, near the present-day city of Homs in western Syria. That relief shows the king triumphant in his struggle against the Hittite king Muwatallis. The map includes the meandering River Orontes and, at its confluence with a tributary, the fortress town of Kadesh; also shown are the dispositions of the Egyptian and Hittite forces. Good examples of that relief may be seen on the northern side of the pylon at Luxor temple, on the eastern side of the first and second pylons of the Ramesseum, and on the northern wall of the first, or pillared, hall at Abu Simbel.

Given the importance of land surveys for the generation of tax revenues in ancient Egypt, land-survey, or cadastral, maps might be expected. In fact, the oldest surviving example is on a papyrus dating from the reign of Ptolemy II (285–246 BCE); it comes from the cartonnage of a mummy buried at Ghoran, in the Faiyum, and is now in Paris in the Institut Papyrologique (Lille number 1). Drawn on the papyrus is a plot of land that is subdivided by numerous canals and dikes. Cadastral maps of that type may have existed in earlier periods, as evidenced by the Rhind Mathematical Papyrus from Thebes that is now in the British Museum (number EA 10057) in London. Written in the fifteenth dynasty (c.1600 BCE) but claiming to be a copy of a twelfth dynasty manuscript (c.1991–1786 BCE), it includes diagrams of fields accompanying exercises for calculating land areas.

The map of greatest topographical interest to survive from ancient Egypt, and the only one of a known geographic area, is on a papyrus from Deir el-Medina in Thebes and is now in the Egyptian Museum (numbers 1879, 1899, and 1969) in Turin. Probably made about 1160 BCE by the well-known Scribe-of-the-Tomb Amennakhte, son of Ipuy, the map was prepared for Ramesses IV's quarrying expedition to the Wadi Hammamat, in the Eastern Desert. That expedition was to obtain blocks of *bekhen*-stone (a graywacke sandstone) to be used for statues of the king. The fragmentary remains of one of those statues can be seen on the northern side of the eighth pylon of the Karnak temple in Luxor. The map shows a 15-kilometer (10-mile) stretch of the Wadi Ham-

mamat and has depictions of (1) that wadi's confluence with the wadis Atalla and el-Sid; (2) the surrounding hills; (3) the *bekhen*-stone quarry; and (4) the gold mine and the settlement at Bir Umm Fawakhir. The map also includes numerous annotations that identify the features shown on the map, the destinations of the wadi routes, the distance between the quarry and mine, the location of gold deposits in the hills, and the sizes of the stone blocks quarried. The top of the map was faced toward the south, the source of the Nile River. Besides being a topographic map of surprisingly modern aspect, the papyrus in Turin is a geologic map—the earliest one known—because it accurately shows the areal distribution of the different rock types (with black and pink hills) and the lithologically diverse wadi gravels (with brown, green, and white dots); it also contains information on quarrying and mining.

**Architectural Plans.** Many architectural plans survive from the Old Kingdom onward, but the most elaborate and sophisticated have been dated to the New Kingdom. Easily the most impressive is one painted on a wall in the eighteenth dynasty tomb of Meryre I, at Tell el-Amarna. The plan shows—in detail—the buildings and gardens of King Akhenaten's palace grounds. In a limestone quarry of the same age, at nearby Sheikh Said (now destroyed), a temple plan drawn on the wall probably represented another structure at Tell el-Amarna.

Other notable examples of architectural plans are of tombs. One was drawn on a limestone ostracon, and it shows what is probably Ramesses IX's tomb in the Valley of the Kings at Thebes; it was found nearby and is now in Cairo in the Egyptian Museum (number CG 25184). Another, more elaborate, tomb plan was drawn on papyrus and comes from Deir el-Medina; it is now in the Egyptian Museum (number 1885) in Turin. That plan's author was the same Amennakhte who made the topographical Wadi Hammamat map. The plan shows Ramesses IV's tomb, also in the Valley of the Kings and, like that of Ramesses IX's, it depicts the corridors and chambers with only a rough approximation of their true shapes and relative sizes. Ramesses IV's plan differs, however, in that it was richly colored and annotated, showing his tomb lying beneath a mountain.

At a number of sites, garden plans were a common motif in New Kingdom tomb paintings. Good examples may be seen in the eighteenth dynasty private tombs at Thebes, such as that of the vizier Rekhmire. Those and others elsewhere typically show a rectangular or T-shaped pool, surrounded by a grove of trees, often of many species; drawings of birds, fish, and people commonly populate the gardens.

**Mythological and Cosmological Maps.** Included under the rubric of mythological maps are various depictions of the netherworld. For example, from the twelfth

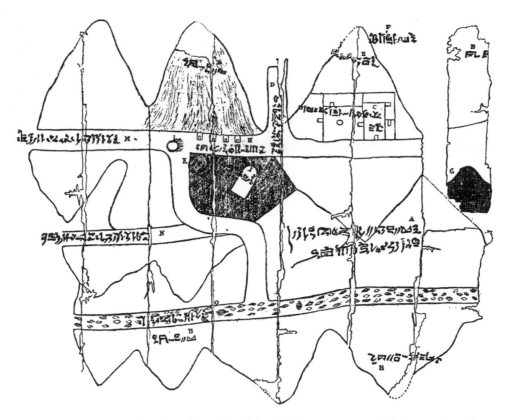

CARTOGRAPHY. *Drawing of a portion of the Turin Papyrus map, which depicts the Wadi Hammamat and documents a quarrying expedition.* It was found at Deir el-Medina.

dynasty tombs at Bersheh, the floors of some wooden coffins have painted maps, showing the land and water routes across the netherworld on which the deceased may travel. Such maps are associated with spells in the ancient *Book of the Two Ways.* One such coffin is now in the Egyptian Museum (CG 28083) in Cairo. Another, based on a spell in the New Kingdom's *Book of Going Forth by Day (Book of the Dead)* shows the ideal plot of land, with fields and canals, to be worked by the deceased in the afterlife. Such a map may also be seen on the Nebseny Papyrus in the British Museum (number 9900) in London.

Cosmological maps were formulaic depictions of the Egyptian universe. A particularly fine example was carved on the lid of a thirtieth dynasty limestone sarcophagus from Saqqara, which is now in The Metropolitan Museum of Art (number 14.7.1), New York; it shows the arched figure of the sky goddess Nut above Shu, the god of air and sunlight, as well as Geb, the god of earth. The space between Shu and Geb is occupied by a circular, nontopographical map of Egypt and the surrounding regions. An inner ring names the nomes (provinces), and an outer ring identifies the peoples and nations that bordered Egypt.

## BIBLIOGRAPHY

Arnold, Dieter. *Building in Egypt: Pharaonic Stone Masonry.* New York and Oxford, 1991. Describes and illustrates numerous ancient plans for temples and tombs, including the one for a Tell el-Amarna temple in the Sheikh Said quarry.

Badawy, Alexander. *A History of Egyptian Architecture.* 3 vols. Berkeley, 1966–1968. Shows many examples of ancient plans, from the Old to the New Kingdom, for temples, palaces, houses, tombs, and gardens; includes in volume 3 the Tell el-Amarna palace grounds in Meryre I's tomb.

Harrell, James A., and V. Max Brown. "The Oldest Surviving Topographical Map from Ancient Egypt (Turin Papyri 1879, 1899 and 1969)." *Journal of the American Research Center in Egypt* 29 (1992), 81–105. Offers the latest interpretation of the Wadi Hammamat map, including translations of all annotations and a new reconstruction of the map fragments; also has a comprehensive bibliography.

Shore, A. F. "Egyptian Cartography." In *The History of Cartography,* vol. 1, edited by J. B. Harley and D. Woodward, pp. 117–129. Chicago, 1987. Presents a comprehensive survey of all facets of ancient Egyptian cartography; includes an extensive bibliography and illustrations of some of the examples cited in this article.

JAMES A. HARRELL

**CARTONNAGE.** *See* Coffins, Sarcophagi, and Cartonnages.

**CARTOUCHE.** *See* Titulary.

**CATTLE.** Two viable hypotheses have been proposed to explain the origins of Egyptian cattle: (1) they were introduced to ancient Egypt from the Near East and the Levant; or (2) they arose from the indigenous aurochsen (*Bos primigenius*) of North Africa. Early dates for Near Eastern tamed (Mureybit, Syria, c.8000 BCE) and domesticated cattle (Turkey and Iran, c.6200 BCE) have been used to support the first view, but excavations of early Holocene occupations in Egypt's Western Desert suggest that tamed indigenous cattle may have been present in the western Sahara as early as 8000 BCE. That second position, however, remains hotly debated. The earliest undisputed evidence for domesticated cattle in Egypt is from Merimde and the Faiyum (c.5000 BCE). Nevertheless, as early as 12,500 BCE, a special human/cattle relationship existed in the Nile Valley. At Tushka, in Egyptian Nubia, horn cores of wild cattle were found directly over two human burials, and a horn core was found near the skull of a third burial; those horn cores appear to have been grave markers.

Ruminants (cud-chewing animals) such as cattle are valuable to humans because they are able to transform otherwise unusable plants into edible products. In ancient Egypt, grasslands generally occurred in areas where agriculture was impractical but where enough moisture existed to support a nutrient-rich flora, such as the uncultivated areas of the Nile Delta and along the borders of the agricultural lands beyond the reach of irrigation. The productivity of grazing lands, however, would have varied from year to year, owing to the vagaries of ancient Egypt's rainfall, the reluctance to irrigate fields not devoted to cash or food crops, and the planting/fallow schedule of given plots. Consequently, a grazing strategy evolved that would acceptably counter the local constraints—a mixed system of penned animal raising and range herding became established throughout ancient Egypt.

Based on textual evidence, the majority of Egyptian cattle was herded and range fed. Texts described many large herds, so overgrazing was undoubtedly a problem. The great numbers of cattle recorded as attached to temple and personal estates were not, however, an unnecessary overindulgence, because large herds do make evolutionary sense under certain conditions. Primarily,

CATTLE. *Depiction on a relief from the tomb of Nefer at Saqqara.* (Courtesy David P. Silverman)

large herds are a means of ensuring the survival of at least some cattle after natural disasters, such as drought or disease, providing both an emergency food source and enough stock to propogate new herds. Therefore, evidence suggests that the Egyptian preference for large herd sizes actually represents an adaptive response to the region's environmental uncertainties.

**Egyptian Breeds.** Some Saharan Neolithic rock art and some later Egyptian tomb scenes provide interesting clues to the development of cattle breeds after their initial introduction. While the rock art usually depicts animals with long horns of varying morphology—including a lyriform type and a type with horns pointed forward—short-horned and polled animals appear more frequently in later tomb scenes, with the polled being more common than the short-horned cattle. Long-horned cattle (*ngiw*), on the basis of artistic scenes, were the oldest domestic cattle breed in Egypt. The *ngiw* were often used in religious sacrifices, as well as for meat, and long-horned castrates (oxen) appear to have been the working animals of choice. The short-horned *wnḏw* has been dated to the fifth dynasty, but it does not appear to have been a popular breed until the Hyksos period. Textual evidence suggests that a short-horned bovid was imported into Egypt from Syria, but a genetic relationship between the Syrian cattle and the Egyptian short-horns has not been substantiated. Perhaps the Egyptian short-horned cattle were derived from the long-horned forms; early domesticated cattle, for example, tended to have long horns, with short-horned types generally appearing later, as the more advanced form of the domesticated species. A hornless breed became increasingly more prominent in the art of Egypt's later periods, and because they were never depicted as draft animals, seem to have been highly valued. The zebu, or brahma, was introduced into Egypt during the New Kingdom. The colors of the Egyptian cattle, based on painted scenes, included black, brown, brown and white, black and white, white spotted with black, and pure white. (Table 1 lists Egyptian terms related to cattle.)

**Cattle Care.** Egyptian herdsmen were obviously aware of fundamental breeding practices, because certain bulls were kept for breeding purposes, and the herdsmen understood how to assist the cows in calving. Although cattle care was primarily in the hands of herdsmen, a section of the Kahun (gynecological) Papyrus, which deals with diseases of cattle, makes it evident that some physicians also possessed veterinary skills. For example, many priests of the goddess Sekhmet were medical physicians (*swnw*) but also "knew cattle." The job of herdsmen was also to see that food for the cattle was plentiful and properly balanced. With the exception of certain chosen animals, cattle were allowed to graze in open fields whenever pos-

TABLE 1. *Egyptian Names for Cattle (after Faulkner 1962)*

| | |
|---|---|
| bull | *wšh* |
| | *k3* |
| | *ih* |
| | *id* |
| cow | *iht* |
| | *idt* |
| | *ḥmt* |
| milk cow | *iryt* |
| | *mhit* |
| | *mn 't* |
| ox | *tpiw* |
| | *iw3* |
| yoke oxen | *nḥbw* |
| plow ox | *sk3* |
| long-horned cattle | *ng3w* |
| short-horned cattle | *wnḏw* |
| dappled cow(?) | *s3 bt* |
| bred for offering | *iw3* |
| sacred cattle | *ṯntt* |

sible. Large numbers of free-ranging cattle or small herds allowed to graze together required some means of identification. One means, inferred from the excavation of a twenty-sixth dynasty animal cemetery, was to etch or mark the horns of the cattle. Branding (*3bw*), however, was a more effective means of identification and was probably practiced on the large estates that belonged to the crown and the temples. Branding scenes are known from several Theban tombs (Nebamun and Neferhotep), and the Varzy Papyrus tells of a man apparently involved in cattle stealing, who placed his own brand over the brand of the true owner.

By dynastic times, the Nile Valley was heavily cultivated, so open range was becoming more limited. The tethering of cattle by means of ropes fixed to pierced stones, trees, or stumps became more common. Judging from tomb scenes, one method of adding important proteins and amino acids to the cattle diet was by hand-feeding them fresh green produce and bread dough, important supplements in the dry season or anytime when green grasses were not available; dried grasses are not adequate suppliers of several important minerals and proteins.

Although grain or bread dough served as a healthy supplement to range-fed cattle, to grain feed all of Egypt's vast herds would not have been economically feasible, because it would have put cattle in direct competition with humans for the same foodstuffs. Consequently, during the unproductive dry season of each year, evidence suggests that at least some cattle herds were driven to better pasture in the marshlands of the northern Delta.

The earliest evidence for the use of cattle as providers of milk comes from fourth-millennium BCE Egypt and Mesopotamia. Cows being milked and nursing calves were frequently depicted throughout the dynastic period, and artists even showed regard for the cows' feelings; in many scenes, the cow was shown looking back or shedding tears at the removal of her milk while her calf was denied its meal. Excavations at Amarna recovered a series of sticks that were thought to be a muzzle that prevented a calf from drinking its mother's milk. Similar finds elsewhere suggest that muzzling was a common means of preserving some of the cows' milk for human use.

If an animal was to be raised for meat, the taste and quality of the beef could be altered by regulating its feeding habits, exercise, and quality of life. For example, the *iwʿ* bulls—which were exceedingly fat, sat low on their haunches, and had pendulous bellies—seem to have been fattened and nurtured for a special purpose, probably sacrificial offerings. Sacrificial bulls were depicted in reliefs on Akhenaten's *rwd-mnw* temple at Thebes and in the *sed*-festival (jubilee) reliefs of Ramesses II at Luxor temple. Their everted horns were indicative of the *ngỉw* breed, but their particular lifestyle gave them a distinctly obese form. Their flavor certainly would have differed from that of range-fed cattle or of oxen toughened by hard labor.

**Cattle Cults.** Certain chosen cattle were important in ancient Egyptian religion. The Apis bull, for example, was famous throughout the ancient world. The earliest written reference to the Apis is on the Palermo Stone, which dates to the second dynasty reign of Khasekhemwy. The Greco-Egyptian historian Manetho, also attributed the Apis to a second dynasty king. Apis personified the god Ptah of Memphis and, after death, was assimilated into the god Osiris. Only one bull among Egypt's thousands was chosen to be an Apis at any one time; at its death, the search began for its replacement. To be an Apis, the animal had to meet certain criteria: it had to have a saddle-marked back (evidently the same pale saddle-patch so common in wild cattle) and a colored patch on the tongue and forehead. From various tomb scenes, the Apis was known not to be a particular breed—only the special markings were the distinct selective criteria.

In addition to Apis, several other bulls were worshiped in similar ways at other localities. The Mnevis bull was associated with the god Re-Atum of Heliopolis; it also possessed special markings to demonstrate its authenticity, although the exact nature of the marks is not certain. The Buchis bull was believed to be a manifestation of the god Montu of Armant (ancient Hermonthis); it could be recognized as authentic by its long hairs, which grew backward, contrary to the nature of other animals (and it was reported to change color every hour).

Cattle worship was not limited to bulls. One notable example is the deity Hathor, who also took on several personalities in her role as a cow goddess. In the Nile Delta, she was equated with the sky; in Thebes, she was a mortuary goddess. She was also a goddess of dance, music, and love.

[*See also* Animal Husbandry.]

**BIBLIOGRAPHY**

Darby, W., P. Ghalioungui, and L. Grivetti. *Food: The Gift of Osiris.* 2 vols. London, 1977. Decent reference for domestic plants and animals in Egypt (but some citations are incorrect and several species identifications in tomb scenes are in error).

Faulkner, R. *A Concise Dictionary of Middle Egyptian.* Oxford, 1962.

Gautier, A. "Archaeozoology of the Bir Kiseiba Region, Eastern Sahara." In *Cattle Keepers of the Eastern Sahara*, edited by F. Wendorf, R. Schild, and A. Close, pp. 49–72. Dallas, 1984. Speculations concerning very early cattle domestication in Egypt's Western Desert; domestication is here based on environmental needs rather than on the morphological criteria of animal bones, leaving the result suspect.

Smith, H. "Animal Domestication and Animal Cults in Dynastic Egypt." In *The Domestication and Exploitation of Plants and Animals*, edited by P. Ucko and G. Dimbleby, pp. 307–314. London, 1969. Discusses the different breeds (or forms) of Egyptian cattle.

Vandier, J. *Manuel d'archéologie égyptienne*, vol. 6: *Scènes de la vie agricole.* Paris, 1978. A review of agricultural scenes, mostly from the Saqqara area, many of which present domesticated cattle in detail.

Wendorf, F., R. Schild, and A. Close. *Cattle-Keepers of the Eastern Sahara: The Neolithic of Bir Kiseiba.* Dallas, 1984. Composed mostly of site reports, but speculates on the Neolithic nomadic lifestyle of the Western Desert peoples, depicting them as pasturalists.

DOUGLAS J. BREWER

**CENOTAPHS.** The term *cenotaph* is a Greek word that means "empty tomb," but in Egyptology it denotes a symbolic structure that has specific associations with the afterlife of the deceased. Applied to a range of ancient Egyptian funerary and cult structures, cenotaphs include both royal and private tombs devoid of actual burial, as well as other buildings of a mortuary nature.

It is important to recognize that there is no single word in ancient Egyptian that corresponds with the meaning of "cenotaph." The various structures to which the term is applied appear to have embodied different religious concepts and functions in the context of Egyptian funerary practice. The term has often been loosely applied, without full explanation of the specific functions of the various structures so identified. In many cases, the simple designation "cenotaph" does not fully indicate the complex religious notions inherent in such mortuary structures.

The overview of the evidence presented here includes two major groups of structures. The first consists of tombs that did not contain the actual interment of a body, but which through other contents or specific features are identifiable as having a symbolic function for the afterlife of the deceased. The second group is composed of mortuary buildings where a funerary/offering cult was maintained, although the actual burial of the deceased was elsewhere. The primary concept involved in structures of both types is that of providing necessary housing and support for the *ka* of the deceased. Symbolic royal tombs often contain statues associated with the *ka* of a deceased king, while mortuary chapels of both kings and private individuals were focused on the afterlife associations of the deceased and on the maintenance of the *ka*. Under this heading examples are also discussed of symbolic god's tombs (divine cenotaphs), as well examples of tombs that have been identified as cenotaphs, but for which that designation now appears to be incorrect.

**Royal Tombs.** A variety of royal tombs and mortuary complexes from the Early Dynastic period through the New Kingdom have been identified as cenotaphs. In some cases the word is warranted, particularly where a symbolic tomb exists without an actual burial. In many cases, however, empty or unused royal tombs do not appear to have been purposefully designed as cenotaphs.

***Early dynastic tombs at Abydos and Saqqara.*** One of the longest scholarly debates relating to the issue of royal cenotaphs has concerned the identification of the royal tombs of the Early Dynastic kings at Abydos. In 1899–1900, W. M. Flinders Petrie (following earlier work of E. Amélineau) excavated the royal cemetery of the Early Dynastic period at Abydos (Umm el-Qa'ab), where he recorded subterranean tombs of all of the kings of the first dynasty as well as two kings of the second. Although Petrie initially identified these tombs as the actual burial places of these pharaohs, later work from 1936 to 1956 by W. Emery at north Saqqara revealed a large elite cemetery of the Early Dynastic period containing numerous mudbrick *mastaba* tombs. Sealings and inscribed objects with royal names, as well as the proximity of the site to the royal capital of Memphis, led Emery to suggest that the Saqqara tombs were the true royal burial places. The Abydos tombs, then, were to be identified as cenotaphs or symbolic tombs built in the south for religious purposes.

More recent excavation of the royal cemetery at Abydos, combined with more critical analysis of the evidence, leaves little doubt that the Abydos tombs were in fact the actual burial places of the kings of the first dynasty. Kemp (1966, 1967) has shown that the scale of the Abydos complexes (which include a subterranean tomb with associated funerary enclosure at the desert edge) is substantially greater than that of the Saqqara *mastaba*s. Although Emery had originally raised the possibility that brick mound-like architectural elements contained within the Saqqara *mastaba*s were the precursors to the royal pyramid, recent

discussion by Kaiser (1969), Dreyer (1991) and O'Connor (1991) has further shown how closely the Abydos mortuary complexes precede the elements contained in the third dynasty pyramid complex of Djoser at Saqqara, as well as later pyramids. The excavations of G. Dreyer have provided considerable new evidence on the form and contents of the royal tombs at Abydos and support the claim that the cemetery is an actual royal burial ground with roots in the Predynastic period, rather than a series of symbolic tombs.

At Saqqara, on the other hand, the same royal names occur on objects in different *mastaba*s, making it likely that these represent the burials of more than one high-ranking individual from any particular reign. The Saqqara Early Dynastic *mastaba*s are most likely the burials of contemporary elite and members of the extended royal family. The combination of this evidence suggests strongly that the notion of the royal cenotaph has been mistakenly applied to the Early Dynastic tombs at Abydos and Saqqara.

***Multiple and unused burial places.*** The issue of royal cenotaphs has also emerged in instances where kings possessed more than one viable burial place; the Early Dynastic tombs at Abydos and Saqqara are an example. Some kings of later periods, however, did possess multiple tombs, and in such cases, the question of actual versus symbolic tomb has become an issue. Multiple burial places are attested for a number of kings, including Sneferu, Amenemhet I, Senwosret III, Amenemhet III, Ahmose, and others. In most cases, the occurrence of multiple tombs can be explained primarily through factors such as construction problems (for example, under Sneferu and Amenemhet III) which led to abandonment of a site, or political shifts (Amenemhet I) which produced more than one royal burial monument. In some instances a completed monument was not used for the actual burial but was the site of an active mortuary cult; such structures might be understood as de facto "cenotaphs," though not purposefully designed as symbolic empty tombs.

Most unused or empty burial places may, however, have other explanations. At Saqqara, the unfinished pyramid of Sekhemkhet contained a sealed but empty alabaster sarcophagus. In the fourth dynasty secondary tomb of Hetepheres at Giza, the tomb was sealed without burial of the queen's body. Factors other than construction of a symbolic empty tomb seem likely in these two instances, and probably others.

***Royal ka-tombs.*** More specifically identified as symbolic tombs are secondary tombs built within or adjacent to the actual burial monument of a king. This phenomenon emerges quite early in the Step Pyramid complex of King Djoser of the third dynasty at Saqqara, where the complex includes a second royal tomb, the "South Tomb." The South Tomb at Saqqara is a subterranean structure which includes a stone burial vault and employs a form and decoration similar to that of the actual tomb beneath the pyramid. This vault is likely to have contained a royal statue burial or some other related symbolic interment. Without specific textual descriptions of the concepts associated with this tomb, its precise symbolic role is somewhat ambiguous. Most likely, however, the South Tomb was employed for the symbolic burial of the king's *ka* or double. In subsequent pyramids of the Old Kingdom, a satellite or "*ka*-pyramid," generally situated on the southeastern side, represents the continuation of the South Tomb concept. In the satellite pyramid of Khafre (fourth dynasty) at Giza, a deconstructed wooden "divine booth" provides evidence for the use of the satellite pyramid for the burial of a royal *ka*-statue.

One of the most significant examples of a royal tomb that had a symbolic function and hence has been understood as a "cenotaph" is the so-called Bab el-Hosan in the courtyard of the eleventh dynasty mortuary complex of Montuhotep II at Deir el-Bahri. The tomb, located by H. Carter in 1912, was a large subterranean structure consisting of a sloping passage leading down to a rock-cut burial chamber. In the burial chamber was found a wooden sarcophagus which contained a painted limestone statue of the king, dressed in a *heb-sed* robe and wearing the Red Crown. This statue had been wrapped in linen and purposefully buried in the tomb along with offerings.

Several possibilities have been raised regarding the function of the Bab el-Hosan. The purposeful wrapping and burial of a statue of the king in a secondary tomb would appear to be the physical expression of specific symbolic or religious concepts. It has been suggested that the Bab el-Hosan is an "Osiris-tomb," *ka*-tomb, or a royal *shawabti* burial, or that it is connected with the king's *sed*-festival. Although the nature of the evidence makes it difficult to discriminate among these various possibilities, it is probable that one or more of these concepts are expressed. The purposeful burial of a statue of the king in its own tomb strongly suggests that the statue was conceived as a physical substitute for the actual body of the king, which was buried elsewhere in the mortuary complex. An association with the king's *ka* or possible needs or activities of that *ka* in the afterlife is likely to pertain to this tomb. The Bab el-Hosan therefore parallels similar concepts in *ka*-tombs and *ka*-pyramids of the Old and Middle kingdoms.

The concept of the *ka*-burial of kings and royalty continues into the later Middle Kingdom and is attested explicitly in the layout of the interior of the pyramid of Amenemhet III at Dahshur, where burial chambers for the king and queens are paired with southern "*ka*-tombs." The concept of the royal *ka*-burial is continued in an attenuated manner in the tomb of the thirteenth dynasty king Awibre Hor at Dahshur, where, apparently because of limits of size, a wooden *ka*-statue is included within the actual tomb.

***Royal mortuary complexes at Abydos.*** At Abydos, a number of possible "cenotaph" complexes of kings of the Middle Kingdom and later have been identified. A mortuary complex of Senwosret III (named "Enduring-are-the-Places-of-Khakaure-maa-kheru-in-Abydos") at South Abydos consists of a large subterranean tomb with attached funerary temple, as well as a town that housed the priests and administrators connected with the cult and royal mortuary foundation (Wegner, 1995, 1996). Since Senwosret III also built a pyramid complex at Dahshur near Memphis, it was long believed that the Abydos complex was a "cenotaph." Its major function would in this case be that of symbolic tomb built at the holy city of Abydos in order to associate the deceased king with the god Osiris. Recent work at Abydos and Dahshur, however, suggests that the Abydos complex was conceived and built as a fully functional burial place for Senwosret III. The king's pyramid at Dahshur was never used for a burial, while the Abydos tomb was used for a royal interment. This makes it probable that the king was buried at Abydos, and the complex therefore may not be accurately identified as a cenotaph.

Later monuments at south Abydos—a mortuary complex of King Ahmose I of the eighteenth dynasty and an offering chapel/pyramid for his grandmother, Queen Tetisheri—have been identified as cenotaphs. The Ahmose complex includes a pyramid, mortuary temple, and underground tomb (Harvey, 1994). The complex has been thought to be a cenotaph because a body identified as that of Ahmose was found in the Deir el-Bahri royal mummy cache and some form of the cult of Ahmose is attested in Western Thebes. However, whether the complex was intentionally designed as a symbolic cenotaph (rather than a viable burial place) is questionable. Like that of Senwosret III, it may have been intended as a functional funerary complex for the king, but may have become a de facto cenotaph if the king was buried in Thebes. More specifically allied with the concept of cenotaph is an offering chapel, which probably had a pyramidal superstructure and was dedicated to Queen Tetisheri at south Abydos. It contained an inscribed stela which describes the building as a votive chapel and also says that the queen's tomb (i.e., her actual burial place) was at Thebes.

Although use of the term "cenotaph" oversimplifies the manifold religious concepts inherent in these monuments, it is possible these structures of Ahmose and Tetisheri could have functioned primarily as commemorative

CENOTAPHS. *Middle Kingdom cenotaphs at Abydos.* (Courtesy David P. Silverman)

or votive mortuary cult structures which associated their deceased owners with Osiris, the main god of Abydos.

**Mortuary Cult Buildings without Tombs.** Another group of buildings that have been identified as cenotaphs includes structures that maintained a mortuary or offering cult but were not associated with any actual burial (Simpson, 1974, 1979). Such votive cult buildings are attested for both royalty and private individuals. They were often constructed in proximity to an important temple or cult site, such as that of Osiris at Abydos.

*Royal* **ka-*chapels*.** Royal mortuary chapels were built at a number of important religious centers beginning in the Old Kingdom (Abydos, Dendera, Bubastis, Ezbet Rushdi, and others). These structures designated by the Egyptian term *ḥwt-k₃* ("ka chapel") are dedicatory or votive cult structures which associated the king with various gods. They housed statuary and were the sites of royal mortuary/offering cults. At Abydos, for example, remains of a number of such buildings indicate that the main Osiris temple was surrounded by a cluster of royal *ka* chapels. The function of these chapels falls within the general rubric of "cenotaph" in that one of their major functions was to maintain a mortuary/offering cult, even though they possessed no attached tomb and the king's burial place was elsewhere. The tradition of royal mortuary chapels continued through the New Kingdom. Known examples at Abydos include buildings of Amenhotpe I, Thutmose III, Thutmose IV, Ay, Sethnakhte, Ramesses III, and Psamtik I.

*Private mortuary chapels.* In the nonroyal sphere, the term "cenotaph" has most commonly been applied to offering chapels with a commemorative/mortuary function that were dedicated or built by private people. These buildings represent the nonroyal equivalent of the *ka* chapel. The best documented example of a nonroyal cenotaph occurs again at Abydos, where clusters of votive offering chapels were built directly behind the precinct of the Osiris temple, associated with an area designated *rwd n nṯrꜥ₃* ("Terrace of the Great God") in stelae of the Middle Kingdom. These votive chapels were situated adjacent to the temple and in proximity to a processional route which led from the Osiris temple out to the symbolic tomb of Osiris in the old Predynastic and Early Dynastic royal cemetery at Umm el-Qaꜥab. The practice of private chapel construction at Abydos is first attested during the early Middle Kingdom (eleventh dynasty). It became extremely popular during the Middle Kingdom and continued through the New Kingdom.

The private cenotaphs at Abydos include structures of a number of different types. Besides actual underground burials with accompanying offering chapels, there are also empty tombs with associated offering chapels, and votive offering chapels which possessed neither a real nor symbolic burial for the dedicator (O'Connor, 1985). The basic plan of all of these chapels consists of a one- or two-room brick structure which could contain one or more offering stelae, statuary, and an offering slab where an offering cult would be maintained by priests. Some of the larger votive chapels were set inside a courtyard and could be fronted by trees. The major role of the private cenotaphs at Abydos was connected with a desire for religious and afterlife association with the important funerary deity Osiris. These structures are described in contemporary stelae by the term *m'ḥ't*. As discussed by Simpson (1974), these private chapels were intended to allow the deceased an eternal association with Osiris, as well as participation in the offering cult associated with his main temple. Votive chapels that lack a real burial may be called "cenotaphs" insofar as they have an explicit mortuary function but do not serve as the actual burial place.

The construction of such votive mortuary chapels in the region of the Osiris temple at Abydos has been linked with the development of the pilgrimage to Abydos, a popular theme in tomb decoration beginning in the Middle Kingdom. This event is indicative of the importance of visiting or associating oneself with the main cult center of Osiris. Most people never actually undertook such a pilgrimage, but many of sufficient wealth appear to have expressed a desire for eternal association with Osiris through building commemorative chapels or "cenotaphs" there. Although Abydos is the best-known site for such nonroyal cenotaphs, the practice was widespread throughout Egypt, especially during the Middle Kingdom. Many other religious centers (e.g., Dendera, Asyut, Elephantine, and Gebel el-Silsila) possessed zones where private dedicatory or votive chapels were established.

**Symbolic Tombs of Deities.** Another type of cult structure that can be classified as a cenotaph is the symbolic god's tomb. This type of structure is best known in connection with the god Osiris, and symbolic "Osiris-tombs" were constructed at a number of sites; documented examples occur at Abydos, Giza, Karnak, and the island of Biga to the south of Philae. Symbolic burial places of other gods also seem to have existed at other locales.

The Osireion at Abydos is the best preserved example of such a god's tomb. Situated immediately to the west of the temple of Sety I (nineteenth dynasty), the Osireion was substantially built by Sety and completed with additions in the reign of Merenptah. It is a massive underground complex, the core of which is a symbolic tomb for the deceased god-king Osiris. The symbolic tomb is situated on a raised central area which is surrounded by water channels. In its central section, the architecture of the Osireion employs monolithic construction techniques that copy Old Kingdom architecture (i.e., an archaizing style). Attached to its core are sections decorated with texts and scenes employing New Kingdom royal funerary texts, including sections of the *Book of Gates* and *Book of Caverns* as well as the *Book of Going Forth by Day* (*Book of the Dead*). The tomb represents a symbolic burial place of Osiris and incorporates aspects of the royal afterlife. The Osireion's role as a symbolic tomb warrants its inclusion within the range of structures identified as cenotaphs.

**BIBLIOGRAPHY**

Altenmüller, Hartwig. "Doppelbestattung." In *Lexikon der Ägyptologie*, 1:1128–1130.

Arnold, Dieter. *Der Pyramidenbezirk des Königs Amenemhat III in Dahschur*. Mainz, 1987.

Badawy, Alexander. *A History of Egyptian Architecture*. Los Angeles, 1966.

Dreyer, Günther. "Umm el-Gaab Excavation Reports." *Mitteilungen der Deutschen Archäologischen Instituts, Abteilung Kairo* (1986, 1990, 1991, 1993).

Emery, Walter. *Great Tombs of the First Dynasty*. 3 vols. Cairo and London, 1949–1958.

Harvey, Stephen. "Monuments of Ahmose at Abydos." *Egyptian Archaeology* 4 (1994), 3–5.

Kaiser, Werner. "Zu den Königlichen Talbezirken in Abydos und zur Baugeschichte des Djoser-Grabmals." *Mitteilungen der Deutschen Archäologischen Instituts, Abteilung Kairo* 25 (1969), 1–22.

Kemp, Barry. "Abydos and the Royal Tombs of the First Dynasty." *Journal of Egyptian Archaeology* 52 (1966), 13–22.

Kemp, Barry. "The Egyptian First Dynasty Royal Cemetery." *Antiquity* 41 (1967), 22–32.

Lehner, Mark. *The Complete Pyramids*. London, 1997.

O'Connor, David. "The 'Cenotaphs' of the Middle Kingdom at Abydos." *Mélanges Gamal Eddin Mokhtar* (Cairo, 1985), 161–177.

O'Connor, David. "Boat Graves and Pyramid Origins." *Expedition* 33 (1991), 5–17.

Petrie, W. M. Flinders. *The Royal Tombs of the First Dynasty*. Parts I and II. London, 1900, 1901.

Simpson, William K. *The Terrace of the Great God at Abydos*. Pennsylvania-Yale Publications, 5. Philadelphia and New Haven, 1974.

Simpson, William K. "Kenotaph." In *Lexikon der Ägyptologie*, 3:387–391. Wiesbaden, 1979.

Wegner, Josef. "Old and New Excavations at the Abydene Complex of Senwosret III." *KMT* 6 (1995), 59–71.

Wegner, Josef. "The Mortuary Complex of Senwosret III: A Study of Middle Kingdom State Activity and the Cult of Osiris at Abydos." Ph.D. diss., University of Pennsylvania, 1996.

JOSEF W. WEGNER

**CERAMICS.** Knowledge about ancient Egyptian pottery has derived from various sources, ancient and modern. Scattered tomb and temple representations, tomb models, stelae, ostraca, and some texts have provided valuable contemporary testimony on ancient Egyptian ceramic production, technology, terminology, end-products, and functions. Occasional potmarks, incised before or after firing or painted on a vessel, indicate vessel capacity, the potter or workshop that produced the pot, or ownership of the pot. Archaeological remains of potters' workshops, kilns, and equipment afford further insights into production methods. The most copious source of data, however, is the ancient ceramics. Vast amounts of mostly broken pottery—potsherds—comprise the single largest category of material culture recovered from most Egyptian sites. Archaeologists may process literally millions of potsherds during field investigations. Town sites and living contexts yield mainly sherd material; whole pots occur most often in mortuary contexts. The modern scientific study of ancient ceramics helps illuminate raw material sources, production methods and technologies, dates of manufacture, pot functions, stylistic changes, and distribution and trade networks. Ethnoarchaeological research into modern traditional potters, and experimental archaeological investigations such as reconstructing potters' wheels and kilns or using cookpots, furnish additional data for understanding ancient ceramics in context.

Enormous quantities of pottery were used for countless activities by all classes of Egyptian society, which therefore supported large numbers of professional potters. Such potters were men according to tomb scenes, texts, and models and they generally ranked low on the Egyptian social scale. The craft was passed from father to son, although family members probably assisted with production. Where potting was a household rather than a workshop industry, or possibly where pottery was hand made, women may have predominated as potters. Some artisans doubtless worked alone, but most potters were likely organized into individual or nucleated workshops of varying size. Small villages or hamlets probably had a single potter at most; larger villages one or more; and towns and cities would have had potters and workshops in considerable numbers. Palaces, temples, and private and public estates likely had their own potters and workshops, established in close proximity to other craftsmen and subordinates such as carpenters, metal craftsmen, bakers, beermakers, and butchers.

Local, regional, or centralized patterns of ceramic production, specialization, or distribution may occasionally be inferred from archaeological remains. The interrelationships among such variables were complex, however, and varied both geographically and temporally. The evidence for their reconstruction is usually limited and problematic, the parameters of discussion are generally underinvestigated, and understanding of the issues involved is often inadequate. In a few notable instances, archaeologists can document probable cases of centralized ceramic production. Such centralization likely reflected government monopoly—control or regulation over particular commodities—in this case the pot, its contents, or both. Colin Hope (1987, 1989), for example, has shown that blue painted and polychrome wares were manufactured only in the main palace centers of the New Kingdom, especially Thebes and Amarna. R. F. Friedman (1994) documented a shift from the production of regionally diverse utilitarian wares in the Predynastic period, during Naqada I, to a single, standardized, technologically superior, chaff-tempered "rough ware" during Naqada II. She attributed that shift to a new centralized control of economic necessities based at Hierakonpolis.

Particular potters or workshops may have specialized in specific fabrics or forms, or both. J. Bourriau (1981) suggested an early and ongoing division of potters working exclusively with marl clays. Temple workshops may have concentrated on manufacturing ritual vessels for temple and funerary use; other workshops may have specialized in fine wares, utilitarian wares, or mortuary vessels. Hope (1987, 1989) also made a case for centralized specialization of fabric and form in eighteenth dynasty amphora production; he noted that from the middle to the end of the dynasty, amphorae were made consistently from one basic marl clay type and that they exhibited remarkable uniformity of surface treatment, morphology, and dimensions. As the amphorae were used primarily for storing and transporting wine, and to a lesser extent beer, Hope inferred that they were manufactured for industrial needs in the Nile Delta and in the Faiyum (the centers of viticulture in ancient Egypt), filled with wine, and then distributed throughout Egypt. Once the original contents were gone, the vessels were reused for various commodities, thus complicating the archaeological record.

**Function.** Pottery was an essential, dominantly utilitarian element in Egyptian society, used copiously in all spheres of Egyptian life at all social levels. It was employed in innumerable domestic and agricultural tasks, especially the processing, preparation, serving, and storage of food and drink for people and animals. Pottery also played a key role in ancient industry and trade: ceramic vessels were used to hold, process, and store commodities, as well as transport them over short and long distances, by land and water. On occasion, the pot rather than the contents was a desired commodity. Public ceremonies, religious and funerary rituals, and magical rites all used ceramics for various purposes. Miniature pottery was made in great quantity for foundation deposits that were placed under the corners of royal buildings. Magic bowls were inscribed with letters to the dead or with execration texts. Pots were "ritually killed," by piercing a hole through them, usually near the base. Ceramic bowls were used to burn incense; stereotyped hs-vases were used for pouring libations and for purification ceremonies associated with funerary and temple rituals. The "breaking of

CERAMICS. *Predynastic pottery vessels.* (University of Pennsylvania Museum, Philadelphia. Neg. # S8–41452)

the pots" was a regular feature of New Kingdom funeral ceremonies, during which several large jars were ritually broken at the tomb entrance.

One of the most archaeologically visible uses of pottery in ancient Egypt was for mortuary purposes. Pottery held offerings to the dead that were presented as part of the funerary cult. Most burials included quantities of ceramics left for use in an afterlife that the Egyptians regarded as an extension of life on earth. The exact burial assemblage changed with time, location, and social status, but might include a variety of fine and utilitarian domestic wares, libation vessels, "soul houses," miniature pots, canopic jars, and *ushabti* or *shawabti* holders. During various periods of Egypt's history, adults or infants were buried in large pots or ceramic basins. Significantly, specialized funerary ceramic forms existed as early as the Neolithic, and certain types of vessels came to be used almost exclusively in tombs, an important distinction for the archaeologist.

Even broken pottery was a useful cultural resource: sherds were recycled for ostraca or for rubbing tools, or they were ground into grog and used as temper (a clay binder) by potters.

**Origins.** Two early ceramic traditions are well documented in Egypt: an older, more southern, sub-Saharan African tradition; and a later, northern tradition, likely derived from the Near East. The earliest Egyptian pottery comes from the eastern Sahara of Upper Egypt and was dated to the mid-tenth to early ninth millennia BP. Along with some contemporaneous ceramics from the Khartoum region, they comprise the earliest known pottery of North Africa. This early African pottery was well made from local clays; its careful forming and firing suggest a prior, undocumented period of development. The simple, but varied, pottery was extensively decorated with an assortment of motifs that were formed by combing, rocker-stamp impressions, incisions, and cord-and-wand impressions. The eastern Sahara pottery was rare; and this, along with its high quality, has suggested a cultural role outside of everyday life.

The early southern pottery was apparently associated with semisedentary or nomadic transhumant societies. The eastern Sahara groups were then herding domesticated cattle, but no obvious causal relationship exists between potmaking and cattle domestication. Otherwise, in that region, there appears to be no association of pottery with either plant or animal domestication. In the pristine African context, food production and ceramic technology developed independently—and pottery generally appeared two thousand to three thousand years after the first plant or animal domestication. There does, however, appear to be an association between the quantity of pottery at a site and its inferred degree of sedentism, and it has been suggested that pottery production perhaps stimulated sedentism, rather than vice versa.

The first known pottery in the lower Nile Valley was dated to the seventh millennium BP, when utilitarian pottery appeared in sites of the Faiyum and Delta. The poorly made, generally unaesthetic northern pottery compares poorly to its southern counterparts. It may have entered Egypt from the northeast, since in the second half of the seventh millennium before present, a suite of Near Eastern domesticates appeared in the Faiyum (emmer wheat, flax, sheep/goats). These domesticates were accompanied by ceramic vessels, some found in basin-shaped hearths that were surrounded by fuel and contained fish and other bones.

**Raw Materials.** The basic raw materials of ancient Egyptian pottery production were clay, water to make the clay plastic for shaping, aplastic tempering materials to improve clay characteristics and performance, and fuel to fire the shaped clay into a permanently hard and durable object. All four factors were readily available to the potter: water from the Nile; miscellaneous, easily accessible tempers from a variety of sources; fuel from straw, chaff, dung, or other combustibles; and various clays from numerous locations.

Egyptian potters favored two major clay types for ceramic production: Nile alluvial clays and marl clays. Nile alluvial clays were deposited on the river's floodplain and used for ceramic production at all times; they are characterized by significant amounts of silica, finely disseminated hydroxides of iron, mica, and organic matter. Typically fired at temperatures from 600° to 800°C, when oxidized, Nile silts produced clay fabrics in varying shades of red and brown (measuring between 2 and 3 on the Mohs Scale of Hardness). Egyptian marl clays had formed among the calcareous shales, mudstones, and limestones along the river valley, between Esna in the south and Cairo in the north, as well as in the western oases; they contain significant amounts of calcium carbonate (because it reacts with dilute solutions of hydrochloric acid, its presence is easily ascertained by scientists), as well as finely disseminated oxides of iron in smaller quantities than the calcium carbonate and generally less silica than the Nile silt clays. For ceramic production, they were usually fired to higher temperatures (800°–1050°C) for longer periods than the Nile silts and produced harder clay fabrics (measuring between 3 and 4 on the Mohs Scale of Hardness). Oxidized marl fabrics are usually pale red or pale-to-light greenish grey. They were used from Naqada II times onward. Other naturally occurring local clays were exploited less often by Egyptian potters. For example, Egyptian kaolin clays occurred in the Aswan region of the Nile and contained finely disseminated hydroxides of iron but no calcium carbonate; these clays fired to a light red or to red in an oxidizing atmosphere and were used *only* beginning in the Late period. Pliocene clays, found in spots between Esna and Cairo and in the oases, are not yet known to have been used in antiquity. Some secondary deposits of naturally mixed clays also occurred in various locations along the Nile floodplain, and although unverified, a number of these were likely utilized in antiquity. The Nile silt clays could have been collected from myriad locations, including river banks, canal spoil banks, irrigation ditches, and fields. The other clays would have been mined in more limited and specific locations. Our knowledge of specific ancient clay sources is as yet poor.

All naturally occurring clays contain mineral grains; many also contain rock fragments, organics, or other inclusions. Potters often remove some of the natural inclusions during clay processing; they may also introduce additives to improve the clay's performance. For example, they may render a sticky clay less plastic and more workable, reduce shrinkage during firing, alter porosity, improve resistance to thermal shock, or increase fabric hardness. Aplastic and organic inclusions deliberately added to clay by potters are often called temper; in ancient Egypt, tempers included silica sand, various mineral grains and rock fragments, grog (finely ground or crushed sherds), calcium carbonate (such as shell bits or crushed calcite), ashes, and organics such as bits of straw, chaff, or dung. Purposely added temper sometimes can, and sometimes cannot, be distinguished by archaeologists from natural inclusions in fired fabrics.

**Clay Preparation and Vessel Forming.** After collection, raw clay must usually be prepared for use. Impurities must be removed, generally by drying, crushing, sieving, and then slaking the dry clay—placing it in a vat or pit and adding water. After slaking, further water is added for soaking, and the clay-water mixture is thoroughly stirred, to place the clay particles into uniform suspension (thereby creating a slip). A number of Egyptian tomb paintings show this stirring process, accomplished by the potter or an assistant treading the clay-water mixture with his feet. The clean slip is then separated out by sieving, settling, or levigation. The finest clay fractions are obtained through levigation, a process in which the clay slip flows slowly through a long, shallow trough leading to a vat or pit; the coarser and heavier particles sink and are trapped in the trough, by baffles or low walls placed along its bottom, while the finer material rises and travels along into the vat or pit. Once the slip has been sieved, settled, or levigated, temper may be added and the mixture brought to a workable state. The temper may be stirred into the liquid clay slip, which is then drained into beds, pits, or containers, to be rendered solid through evaporation. Alternatively, it may be kneaded into solid clay made appropriately plastic by the addition of water. The resulting clay body may be used immediately or stored; if stored, it must be kneaded again just prior to shaping.

Kneading and wedging remove air bubbles that might cause cracking during firing; this process is the final preparation of the clay body prior to forming and is always done immediately before pots are shaped. Any impurities remaining in the clay can be removed, and additional temper added if desired. At that point, different clay types may have been kneaded together if Egyptian potters wished to mix clays.

The prepared clay body was then ready to be shaped into pots. Shaping was accomplished by one or more of three forming techniques: hand-building, molding, and rotation (centrifugal force). In general, forming technology in Egypt became more sophisticated over time, although improved technology did not necessarily result in higher quality or more aesthetically pleasing pots; for example, some extraordinarily high-quality pottery—Predynastic black-topped red ware and Kerma pottery—was achieved with very simple techniques. The history of Egyptian ceramic technology is one of enlarging the technical repertory, not substituting advanced for simpler methods; and earlier technology remained in use side by side with later advances. Although the general outlines of technical evolution are clear, the details and exact timing often are not, since pictorial testimony is limited and not always clear; archaeological evidence of workshops and equipment is scattered, sporadic, and incomplete; and the inference of technological details and developments from traces left on fired pots is often inconclusive.

Hand-building and centrifugal force were definitely used for shaping by Predynastic potters, as in all probability was a primitive type of molding or pressing. All three processes continued in use throughout Egyptian history. Hand-forming techniques included pinching, drawing, coiling, slab-building or segmental-modeling, and paddle-and-anvil. Molding might have been convex or concave

and was accomplished by pressing or paddling the clay over or into some kind of core, hump, mold, or cavity in the ground; this technique was widely practiced throughout dynastic times, especially the ubiquitous bread molds, with their characteristic smooth interiors and rough exteriors. D. Arnold (1993) thought it was also used to form Meydum ware bowl bodies in the fourth and fifth dynasties, although those from the sixth dynasty were wheel made. More advanced concave molding techniques—using carefully fashioned, more sophisticated molds—do not seem to have occurred prior to the New Kingdom; comparable convex molds are known only for the production of Saite marl clay pilgrim flasks. The earliest documented use in Egypt of centrifugal force in potting was dated to Naqada II, and from then onward it becomes of steadily increasing importance in Egyptian ceramic technology.

The initial recognition of the existence of centrifugal force and its value for pottery production in the Predynastic was a major breakthrough for Egyptian potters. From that time on, manipulation of centrifugal force developed along an increasingly effective and sophisticated technical continuum that harnessed increasing amounts of force over longer periods of time and culminated in the most efficient potter's wheel known to the ancient Egyptians: the kick wheel. The kick wheel is first attested in the temple of Hibis at the time of Darius I of the twenty-seventh dynasty (First Persian Occupation), and was called a "true" potters wheel by Rice (1987) that "combines rotary motion and pivoting with centrifugal force, producing more-or-less continuous high-speed rotation." The kick wheel is a heavy and fairly complex mechanism, generally associated with large-scale workshop production.

Exactly when and how the initial Egyptian discovery of the value of centrifugal force for potting took place is unknown, but it likely occurred as potters experimented with convenient ways to rotate pots for shaping and finishing. Centrifugal force comes into being as soon as an object spins. Many rudimentary turntables produced only disjointed, discontinuous rotation and little centrifugal force. Others, however, such as a curved sherd or bowl, might achieve intermittent spinning, sometimes at quite high speeds. On occasion, the vessel itself might be the source of the centrifugal force, as in the case of a round-bottomed pot spun in a circular depression on a board. These or similar procedures might generate enough centrifugal force or speed to enable the potter's hands to remain stationary for a period of time while shaping the pot as its walls moved. Thus began a long development that went from unpivoted turntables or turning devices, to pivoted tournettes or slow simple wheels, to fast simple wheels, to the kick wheel. Pottery went from partial formation by centrifugal force to complete construction by centrifugal force—the latter are called thrown pots. Our knowledge of that technological journey has been constrained by limited evidence: some sporadic depictions and representations, rare archaeological finds, and surviving traces of manufacturing on the pottery. Depictions and representations must be carefully interpreted. Far more research is needed on both the creation and the temporal and geographic ranges of manufacture marks, especially those on sherds associated with production techniques. Nevertheless, the overall technical direction is clear, so particular methods may be known with reasonable certainty.

The first signs of forceful rotation, most likely achieved with unpivoted turntables, are present on rims and shoulders of Naqada II vessels. Centrifugal force was used from that time on to form the rims, necks, and shoulders of some vessels. Such composite vessels, with handmade bodies and turned rims and necks, continued to be made throughout pharaonic times. The next major development in the harnessing of centrifugal force was the invention of a pivoted tournette or slow simple wheel. Arnold (1981) reserved the term "wheel" for pivoted turning devices. The first known depiction of such a device is in the fifth dynasty tomb of Ti. Several variants of the slow simple wheel are also known; such instruments made it easier for the potters to better control the centrifugal force and keep their pot centered, although the force of rotation was insufficient to keep the wheel spinning independently for any length of time, requiring the potter to work mostly with one hand. Wheelmade pottery increased in the sixth dynasty and spread rapidly, especially in the First Intermediate Period. By the eleventh dynasty and the twelfth, wheelmade pots comprise the majority of all pottery found. An extra-low simple wheel with a very broad wheel head is attested in the First Intermediate Period and early Middle Kingdom; it continues in use well into the New Kingdom. In the late Middle Kingdom, another advance was made—a new type of simple wheel with a tall central axis; generating greater centrifugal force, perhaps because it was weighted at the edge of its wide platform, it is called a fast, or powerful, simple wheel. It was used into the Ptolemaic and Roman periods. Sometime in the thirteenth dynasty another new wheel construction was developed that permitted the production of pots from Memphite marl C clay, which had previously been considered inappropriate for wheel use. Vessel throwing marks suggest that New Kingdom wheels provided more even rotation than did Middle Kingdom wheels, permitting the application of even greater amounts of centrifugal force. Not until the eighteenth dynasty, however, is there evidence for potters turning wheels with their feet or for an assistant who helped turn the wheel. The introduction of the kick wheel during or prior to the Persian period, with its powerful application of sustained centrifugal force, seems to have resulted in greater vessel angularity and imitation of metal prototypes.

Handmade and, to a lesser extent, mold-made pottery were labor intensive and enormously time consuming. The wheel, especially the fast wheel, enabled the potter to make more pots in less time with less effort. This potential for increased output permitted a primitive form of ceramic mass production that had profound implications for the craft and for those sectors of society—industrial, agricultural, and redistributive—that used large numbers of pots. It may also have been a factor in abetting uniformity of ceramic style.

**Drying, Finishing, and Decorating.** After shaping, the pot was dried to a leather-hard stage, when handles and spouts were usually attached. The pot might also be returned to the wheel at this time for secondary shaping or finishing, and several drying phases often occurred in pot production.

Surface modification or finishing of the pot involved manipulating the clay body from which the vessel was made. It changed the texture, altered the surface appearance, and enhanced the esthetic character of the pot, using techniques such as scraping, smoothing, polishing, burnishing, appliqué, incising, impressing, and carving. The shape and proportions of the vessel might be fine tuned by scraping or cutting away some excess clay. Burnishing and polishing were both done at the leather-hard stage, making the vessel less porous and imparting an aesthetically pleasing glossy finish to the clay surface or the slip. Burnishing involved rubbing the surface of the pot with a hard, smooth object, such as a pebble; polishing involved rubbing it with a yielding tool, such as a piece of cloth. Further decorative modifications to the pot might also be undertaken at the leather-hard stage. These included "cutting out" windows or other patterns in the vessel walls, with a knife or its equivalent; adding applied, molded, or modeled elements—ranging from simple knobs or flat buttons to human or animal body parts to Bes or Hathor deity faces; and incising or impressing various decorative or other patterns into the clay. All these techniques were used in Egyptian pottery of particular times, regions, or both, but none is especially common. Incised decoration was used on some of the earliest Egyptian pottery ever produced: Merimde level 1 pottery exhibits its incised herringbone patterns and other simple designs. In general, however, incising and impressing were decorative techniques more characteristic of Nubian than Egyptian pottery. Rope impressions often appear on Egyptian vessels. Generally, more utilitarian than decorative, they derived from the potter's practice of tying rope or string around the vessel walls as a support for the unfired pot while it dried. Sometimes such impressions were removed in finishing, sometimes not. When found on small vessels, which would not have required drying support, the rope impressions may be considered decorative.

Another method of finishing and decorating pottery, commonly employed in Egypt, was the application of a coating to all or part of a pot's surface. Such a coating was most often applied before firing at the leather-hard stage, but it might also have been added during or after firing; slips and washes of varying colors were used for this purpose. *Slips* are pigments plus water plus clay. A *wash* is sometimes defined as pigment (predominantly red ocher) plus water, but sometimes specifically as a post-firing coating. Wet smoothing helps blur the signs of manufacturing and also applies a thin coat of water and clay, sometimes called a self-slip, on the surface of the pot. Practically speaking, it is very difficult to distinguish pre-firing slips from pre-firing washes, or to identify the presence of a self-slip. The application of colored washes and slips to the external surface of a vessel, without additional decoration, was common in every period of Egyptian history and remained basically the same from first dynasty times to the Arab conquest of the seventh century CE. A *glaze* is a surface coating of glass melted in place and fused onto the vessel surface during firing; glazing does not occur in Egypt prior to very late Roman or even early Arab (Islamic) times.

Lastly, painted patterns and designs of various types and colors were used on pottery in all periods of Egyptian history. Painted decorative motifs were only relatively common, however, during the Predynastic, New Kingdom, and Coptic eras. Painting may be applied either before or after firing. Arnold (1981) identified a total of eight painted styles for Egyptian ceramics. Where analyzed, all paint pigments were based on minerals, with the exception of soot (carbon-black from burned material), sometimes used for black. The most unusual paint used by the ancient Egyptians was a cobalt-based blue used only during the New Kingdom—then lost until the early 1800s.

**Firing.** The most critical stage of pottery production is firing, since it creates a permanent change in the clay's state; it turns it into a stonelike material. Different clays had different firing as well as forming characteristics—attributes about which the ancient Egyptians were well aware. Drying clay loses water, so it shrinks; firing clay continues the process and renders the loss of plasticity irreversible. If heated too rapidly, fired too long, or not long enough, an unuseable or inferior product (e.g., cracked, warped, bubbled surface) resulted. Firing takes place in either an *oxidizing atmosphere*, containing free oxygen that produces bright, clear colors, or in a *reducing atmosphere*, containing gases that take free oxygen away from the clay and result in dull or smudged colors, or even completely grey wares. Some black or dark vessels are

however created by smoking during or after firing, rather than in a reducing atmosphere. In reality, it is rare for primitive (uncontrolled) firing conditions to achieve a completely oxidizing *or* reducing atmosphere, although an overall oxidizing atmosphere is most common. Controlled firing is achieved by regulated kilns of various types.

Extensive studies of ancient Egyptian firing technology suggest a tripartite type classification: (1) open, or bonfire firings, where fuel and vessels were intermixed without any associated installations, such as pits or walls; (2) firing structures, incorporating pits or walls or both, but with no separation between fuel and vessels; and (3) updraft kilns, structures where a fire was usually placed directly below the vessels and separated from them by a perforated floor, through which hot gasses passed up and around the vessels, to escape from a vent in the roof or gaps in the material (sherds or tiles) that covered an open top. Type 1, which would leave few if any archaeological traces, was the earliest, followed by type 2, first known from the Predynastic era, then type 3 during the Old Kingdom and First Intermediate Period. All three types coexisted for most of the pharaonic period. Types 2 and 3 are known archaeologically: type 2 has been found at predynastic sites; type 3 at sites ranging widely in date. Type 3 is also known from ceramic tomb models, small-scale sculptures that show various human endeavors. The other major kiln variety, downdraft, is unknown from ancient Egypt.

Arnold (1981) divided true updraft kilns from Egypt into three main types: a simple chimney kiln; a two-story kiln, as known from models; and, most sophisticated of all, a conical or slightly biconical kiln. Most known kilns were circular in plan, although a number of horseshoe-shaped examples are also attested. All were loaded from an open top, with pots stacked on a perforated brick floor that was supported on a central wall or pillar in the middle of the firing chamber. That basic kiln design remained essentially unchanged until after 600 BCE. In Ptolemaic and Roman times, when Egypt became integrated into the Hellenistic world, Egypt's ceramic production became more industrial. More substantial kilns were introduced, along with other foreign influences, since Egypt then shared in the general culture of the entire eastern Mediterranean.

**Scientific Study.** Once largely ignored or relegated to secondary importance, since the 1970s the study of ceramics in Egyptian archaeology has gained prominence with the founding of the International Group for the Study of Egyptian Ceramics. Now a recognized and increasingly sophisticated branch of Egyptology, ceramology involves the study, classification, and analysis of ceramics and ceramic attributes from diverse perspectives. The study of archaeological ceramics has progressed through three broad phases: an art-historical phase, focused on admiring the artistry and techniques of individual pots; a typological phase, concentrated on delineating chronological and regional ceramic distributions; and a contextual phase—which extended ceramic studies beyond simple description and classification—characterized mainly by a diverse and rich approach that includes technology studies, ethnoarchaeological and experimental archaeology investigations, as well as examinations of the mechanisms of stylistic change and ceramic contexts.

Traditional ceramic analyses focused on applying art-historical analytical techniques to painted ceramic motifs (particularly in Predynastic pottery); they used form and ware typologies to develop relative chronologies for archaeological strata, to identify trade and exchange patterns, and to establish pot function and owner status. The Sequence Date System, originated by the pioneering Egyptologist William Matthew Flinders Petrie, formed the basis of our understanding of the Predynastic: it was based on just such a ceramic typology, one derived from seriation. Relative chronologies have also helped establish which ceramics can function as horizon markers for the archaeologist, those that securely link finds to particular time periods and, sometimes, locations. Such horizon markers include Ripple Ware for the Badarian, Petrie's Decorated Ware for Naqada II, the so-called Meidum bowls for the Old Kingdom, Tell el-Yehudiyyah Ware for the Second Intermediate Period, the blue-painted ware for palace centers in the New Kingdom, mortaria bowls for the Persian and Hellenistic periods, *terra sigillata* for the Roman era, and so forth. Typologies continue to be important to Egyptological research, and they are both more scientific and more sophisticated than ever before. Shape description and classification of whole pots, for example, are now based on vessel proportions as defined by the vessel index (the relationship of maximum width to maximum height of the body, excluding the neck and foot) and the location of the point of maximum diameter.

The analysis and classification of Egyptian pottery fabrics is now a very active branch of study. A framework for and a working classification of fabrics was drafted at a conference in Vienna in 1980 by Do. Arnold, M. Bietak, J. Bourriau, H. and J. Jacquet, and H.-Å. Nordström. This visual ceramic classification system, named the Vienna System after the city sponsoring the conference, defined the main classes of Egyptian fabrics and suggested subdivisions; it provided a starting point and a nomenclature guide for field descriptions and the classification of ceramic fabrics. As a work in progress, it is intended to be modified according to the dictates of new discoveries, further field testing, and updated analyses. Although archaeologists at many excavations continue to use their own analytical systems for pottery, most relate those classifications to the Vienna System, which provides a commonly understood point of reference for fabric discussion, much as the Wentworth System does for grain size, the Mohs Scale for hardness, and the Munsell Charts for color.

The Vienna System defined *fabric* as a group designation, that includes all significant physical and chemical properties of the clay and the nonplastic inclusions in a fired ceramic material, as well as all its relevant technological features in a finished product. Diagnostic features identified for Vienna System fabrics included groundmass, aplastic mineral inclusions, crushed-sherd inclusions, organic inclusions, shell inclusions, the colors of both fracture and surface, firing, hardness, transverse strength, and porosity. The basic division in the Vienna System is between the fine ferruginous (iron-rich) Nile silt clays and the calcareous (calcium carbonate–rich) marl clays. Five main subdivisions of silt are distinguished: Nile silt fabrics, A to E, with two subtypes of B; five classes of marl fabrics, A to E, with four subtypes of A and three of C. In addition, the system distinguishes non-Egyptian fabrics, including Nubian, Aegean, Cypriote, and Palestinian. Today, a few mixed clays are also being integrated into the classification.

A number of detailed, often highly sophisticated scientific analyses have become available to illuminate numerous aspects of the ceramic record, with more analyses being developed. Some vessels can be dated by the carbon-14 analysis of organic inclusions in low-fired pottery or by thermoluminescence. Provenience can be established through compositional studies that rely on physical (petrographic), mineralogical (X-ray diffraction), and chemical (X-ray fluorescence spectroscopy, instrumental neutron-activation analysis, optical-emission spectroscopy, atomic-absorption spectroscopy, and inductively coupled plasma-emission spectroscopy) analyses. Pot function can be examined through residue analysis, accomplished by gas chromatography or by protein-residue (plant and animal) analysis. Forming technology can be investigated through radiographic or xeroradiographic examination. Firing temperature can be determined through Mössbauer spectroscopy, electron-spin resonance, and X-ray diffraction.

One final note, a caution, must be sounded. The terminology used among ceramologists has yet to become consistent, so some may use different terms for the same thing and the same terms for differing things. For example, *wash*, may be defined as a pigment and water mixture or as a post-firing coating. *Turning* may signify either forming on some kind of wheel or trimming using a fast wheel. *Temper* sometimes refers to material added by the potter and, sometimes, to all inclusions in a clay or fabric. *Wheelmade* may mean different things to different archaeologists. Care must be taken, therefore, in reading reports to understand how researchers are using terminology and/or defining their terms.

[*See also* Vessels.]

### BIBLIOGRAPHY

Arnold, Do., ed. *Studien zur Altägyptischen Keramik.* Mainz, 1981. Written before the development of the Vienna System but an important collection of articles on various aspects of Egyptian pottery.

Arnold, Do., and J. Bourriau, eds. *An Introduction to Ancient Egyptian Pottery.* Deutsches Archäologisches Institut, Abteilung Kairo, Sonderscrift 17. Mainz, 1993. Includes major work by Arnold on the techniques and traditions of pottery manufacture, as well as the most complete explanation and description to date by Bourriau and Nordström of the Vienna System; has useful appendices by Nicholson on firing and Rose on turning.

Bourriau, J. *Umm El-Ga'ab: Pottery from the Nile Valley before the Arab Conquest.* Cambridge, 1981. An exhibition catalog, presenting material in chronological order, including additional essays on topics such as production technology, decoration, trade, and methods of analysis.

*Bulletin de Liaison du Groupe International d'Étude de la Céramique Égyptienne* 1–20 (1975–1997). This journal series provides rapid publication for the summaries of ceramic finds from current excavation, the results of other ceramic research, and the relevant papers presented at professional conferences; also a listing of recent publications relating to Egyptian pottery.

*Cahiers de la Céramique Égyptienne* 1–5 (1987–1997). Provides a journal forum for publishing detailed and lengthy results of research on ceramics; volumes are sometimes organized around regions (North Sinai) or themes/workshops (Ateliers de Potiers et Productions Céramiques en Égypte).

Close, Angela E. "Few and Far Between: Early Ceramics in North Africa." In *The Emergence of Pottery: Technology and Innovation in Ancient Societies*, edited by W. K. Barnett and J. W. Hooper, pp. 23–37. Washington, D.C., 1995. Discusses the earliest known appearances of pottery in North Africa.

Friedman, R. F. "Predynastic Settlement Ceramics of Upper Egypt: A Comparative Study of the Ceramics of Hierakonpolis, Nagada and Hemamieh." Ph.D. diss., Department of Near Eastern Studies, University of California, Berkeley, 1994. An extended analysis of the pottery from three Upper Egyptian Predynastic sites and what it can tell us of sociopolitical developments at the time.

Holthoer, R. *New Kingdom Pharaonic Sites: The Pottery.* Lund, 1977. Provides an early but thorough treatment of New Kingdom ceramics and the ancient Egyptian depictions and models of ceramic technology.

Hope, Colin A. *Egyptian Pottery.* Shire Egyptology, 5. Aylesbury, 1987. A good, short, popular introduction to and overview of Egyptian ceramics.

Hope, Colin A. *Pottery of the Egyptian New Kingdom: Three Studies.* Victoria, 1989. Results of research into eighteenth dynasty pottery from Malqata, Ramessid pottery, and New Kingdom amphorae.

Rice, Prudence M. *Pottery Analysis: A Sourcebook.* Chicago, 1987. A masterly, comprehensive volume dealing with all aspects of ceramic production, study, and analysis.

Rye, Owen S. *Pottery Technology: Principles and Reconstruction.* Washington, D.C., 1981. An invaluable manual that outlines processes of ceramic technology, then identifies archaeological features useful for reconstructing that technology.

CAROL A. REDMOUNT

**CEREMONIAL MACE HEADS.** In Predynastic cultures, maces were a popular type of weapon; later they were a symbol of authority. As the preserved examples show, the shafts were made variously of horn, bone, ivory, and wood. Two types of heads were known: the conical, probably originating in the Khartoum Neolithic and soon characteristic for Naqada I; and the pear-shaped, originating from southwestern Asia and characteristic for Naqada II. During Naqada III, the pear-shaped type became a symbol of power held by local chiefs and early rulers. Toward the end of the Predynastic period, ceremonial mace heads were decorated with elaborate scenes. Five specimens were preserved in the Main Deposit of the Hierakonpolis temple: four large ones of limestone (20–30 centimeters/10–15 inches in height and diameter), and a small one of ivory. In addition, numerous examples (often huge) of undecorated conical and pear-shaped mace heads have been found there, which may have been given as votive offerings to the god Horus or put on display in the courtyard as a symbol of the donor's power.

The partially preserved King "Scorpion" mace head is probably the oldest. In its upper register are five standards (the *h3st*, sign of foreign countries; Seth's animal, Min's emblem, Seth's animal again, and the jackal of Wepwawet), and under each is a suspended lapwing (*rhyt*, symbol of Lower Egypt). On a separate fragment appear three standards, one with a falcon on a half-moon, with suspended bows (a symbol of Nubia). In the center register is the king, wearing the White Crown and a tunic with a bull's tail, holding a hoe. Before his face are a rosette and a scorpion. In front of the ruler is a man with a basket; behind him is the fragment of a figure holding a plant, and above him, two standard-bearers. Behind the pharaoh are two fan-bearers. Farther on, the scene is divided into three registers; the figures are turned to the left. In the upper register appear two clumps of plants, a man with a staff, and figures in palanquins; in the second, three clumps of plants and four women dancing were above boats and the remains of a *heb-sed* kiosk. The lowest register is separated by a band depicting water, and a similar one divides the frieze into two: on the left appear fragments of a *pr-nw* shrine and a man; on the right are two men and behind them are a palm inside a fence and part of a boat. This mace head has aroused considerable controversy. It has been speculated that the ruler is depicted during work involving irrigation and the opening of a canal, or at the foundation of a temple in Hierakonpolis or Buto, or at the foundation of Memphis, or during the ritual tilling of the fields. The whole has been read variously as a reference to taking possession of Lower Egypt, to the conquest of Nubia, or to domination by the ruler and the celebration of his *sed*-festival (the *heb-sed*).

On the Narmer mace head, the bearded pharaoh, wearing the Red Crown and a cloak (and holding *nh3h3*) is sit-

CEREMONIAL MACE HEADS. *Reconstruction of the King "Scorpion" mace head.* (Courtesy Krzystof M. Cialowicz)

ting in a kiosk set on a dais composed of nine steps. Above him is a predatory bird with outspread wings, and below the throne are fan-bearers. Royal officials in two lower registers (priest/vizier/scribe; sandal-bearer), identical to those on the Narmer Palette, are followed by servants who may be carrying a palanquin. Before the pharaoh are three registers. In the upper are two horned animals in a frame and four standard-bearers. The center register is opened by a figure in a palanquin, followed by three men between signs made of three vertical half-moons, known from scenes depicting the *heb-sed* race. Below and behind is a large hieroglyph of a captive, with numerals for 120,000. The third register depicts a bull and a goat, with the numbers 400,000 and 1,422,000. The rest of the representation is separated off by vertical lines. In the upper part is a sanctuary, or *pr-nw* shrine, with a long-legged bird on the roof and a low fence with a forked rod and a vessel on a stand inside. Below, in an obvious depression, are three dead horned animals. The figures have been var-

iously interpreted. The bird above the ruler has been seen as the Horus falcon, or the Nekhbet vulture. The animals in the frame may be a cow and a calf, a pair familiar from later funerary rituals, or the oldest known depiction of Apis. The figure in the palanquin has been identified variously as the Lower Egyptian princess Neithhotep, a partner for the holy wedding, the chief of the defeated people, the oldest representation of *rpw.t*, or the figure of a god. The men may be dancing slaves, participants in a ritual race, or prisoners brought to the ruler by the person in the palanquin. The bird on the roof of the shrine has been said to be an ibis, and the sanctuary to be one devoted to Thoth; or a heron, and the location Buto. The scenes as a whole were generally associated with the *heb-sed*, sometimes with the ritual "Appearance of the King of Lower Egypt," or with the subjugation of hostile areas of the Nile Delta.

The King's mace head has a badly damaged relief; the pharaoh, wearing a robe and the Red Crown, is sitting in a kiosk. Before him, a falcon is held in a human hand, as on the Narmer Palette, a rope leading to the fragmentary figure of a prisoner. Some have argued that this artifact is connected with those discussed above, and that all come from the Narmer period; others, though without foundation, have reconstructed the illegible signs in front of the ruler's face as the rosette and scorpion and postulate that it belongs to a ruler of that name.

The Bearer mace head contains two partially preserved friezes with the fragments of three figures. The first, in the upper register, wears a short kilt and carries an animal skin. The next two persons have garments reaching to mid-calf. In the lower frieze can be seen men with pig-tails, wearing short kilts and holding vessels and a skin.

The last example is a fragment of an ivory mace head. It is decorated with three bands showing bearded slaves, bound by the neck, with their arms tied behind their backs.

The subject matter of ceremonial mace heads is concerned with triumph and the *heb-sed* rite. On the King "Scorpion" and King's mace heads, both kinds of scenes occur. Other artifacts are monothematic: on the Narmer mace head the *heb-sed* is dominant, and on the ivory head there is only a triumph. The large stone heads may have been put on display on high poles in the temple courtyard in Hierakonpolis (according to representations); therefore, the themes used to decorate them may have emphasized the power of the ruler and its perseverance, constantly reinforced during the *heb-sed*.

Most symbols known from the mace heads (throne, cloak, standards, boats, prisoners, dancing women) also occur on the oldest preserved scenes—the Turin linen and Hierakonpolis painting. Others (*pr-nw* shrine, falcon with human arm leading prisoner) appear on slightly earlier or contemporary objects (palettes, knife-handles, or burners), which proves the early introduction of important symbols known in pharaonic art.

## BIBLIOGRAPHY

Adams, Barbara. *Ancient Hierakonpolis. With Supplement.* Warminster, 1974. A catalog of the artifacts from Hierakonpolis found in the collections of the University College Petrie Musuem.

Baines, John. "Origins of Egyptian Kingship." In *Ancient Egyptian Kingship*, edited by David O'Connor and David Silverman, pp. 95–156. Leiden and New York, 1995.

Ciałowicz, Krzysztof M. *Les têtes de massues des périodes prédynastique et archaïque dans la vallée du Nil.* Zeszyty Naukowe UJ. Prace Archeologiczne, 41. Warsaw, 1987. Typology of mace heads and a discussion of ceremonial heads.

Ciałowicz, Krzysztof M. "Remarques sur la tête de massue du roi Scorpion." In *Studies in Ancient Art and Civilization*, edited by J. Sliwa. Krakow, 1997. A new reconstruction of the King "Scorpion" mace head.

Hoffman, Michael A. *Egypt before the Pharaohs.* 2d ed. London, 1991. Predynastic Egypt in the perspective of archeological discoveries.

Kemp, Barry. *Ancient Egypt: Anatomy of a Civilisation.* London and New York, 1989. An original approach to the origins of the Egyptian state.

Millet, N. B. "The Narmer Macehead and Related Objects." *Journal of the American Research Center in Egypt* 27 (1990), 53–59. An attempt at a new interpretation of certain decorated artifacts.

Vercoutter Jean. *L'Egypte et la vallée du Nil.* vol. 1: *Des origines à la fin de l'Ancien Empire.* Paris, 1992. A compendium on the beginnings of Egyptian civilization, taking into account the development of art.

KRZYSZTOF M. CIAŁOWICZ

**C-GROUP.** Originally known as Group C, the C-Group was one of a number of similar terms first coined by the American archaeologist George A. Reisner in 1907 to designate a Nubian grave type located during his excavations in Cemetery 7 at Shellal, immediately upstream of the First Cataract of the Nile River. The C-Group was characterized by graves with the deceased orientated east–west, laid on its right side, head to the east, facing north. Accompanying the body were beads, and closely associated with the graves were black-and-red polished pottery and a unique incised ware of local Nubian production that remains one of the most distinctive features of the C-Group cultural assemblage. The form of the grave monument was another distinctive feature, a tumulus constructed of concentric rings of small upright stone slabs.

Research, especially on the ceramics by Manfred Bietak (1987), refined the chronology of the C-Group, which has been divided into phases I, II, and III, with the first two also subdivided into a and b. The C-Group was contemporary with Egypt's Old Kingdom and lasted into the New Kingdom's early eighteenth dynasty, approximately seven hundred years. The C-Group culture is still largely known from its mortuary remains; the people, at least in the earlier phases, are thought to have been pastoralists, with flocks principally of sheep and goats but also including cattle, which were frequently depicted on the locally made pottery. The early C-Group population probably occupied temporary camp sites, which have left little trace in the archaeological record. A more settled lifestyle gradually developed, associated with some reliance on agriculture, and hunting and fishing probably remained important. In the larger centers, an abundance of wealth derived from trade led both to increased social differentiation and to political development toward statehood. The most substantial of the few permanent settlements known from that phase, at Wadi es Sebua, is a village of over 100 stone-built, circular and subrectangular houses, bounded by a thick defensive wall. Archaeologically the C-Group is attested from Kubanniya, a little to the north of the First Cataract, to the Batn el-Hagar, the inhospitable region in present-day Sudan immediately upstream of the Second Cataract.

Although there are some similarities between the C-Group and the preceding culture in that same Nubian area—the A-Group—a long period of abandonment of

Lower Nubia appears to have separated them. It has been suggested that the C-Group moved into the region, probably from the south or perhaps from the west, forced by climatic deterioration to leave their homelands in what was becoming the Sahara. All the evidence for the early C-Group is confined to the western bank of the Nile. The close similarities with the Kerma culture (that was at the time based in the Northern Dongola Reach) has suggested that those two groups shared a common origin. The C-Group's artifactual material and grave types have also been found in association with materials characteristic of the Kerma culture, at least as far upstream as the region of present-day Dongola.

The C-Group were a nonliterate people. To learn about their history, the ancient Egyptian sources were consulted, which contain a wealth of information recorded by traders and military expeditions that operated to the south of Elephantine; later, records were kept by administrators. The northern part of this area was known to the ancient Egyptians as Wawat; farther upstream, was Irtjet, Setju, and Yam. Today, many scholars believe that the first three were in Lower Nubia—the area occupied by the C-Group—whereas David O'Connor (1991), in particular, is of the opinion that Wawat occupied the whole of Lower Nubia, with Irtjet and Setju much farther upstream, and Yam south of the Fifth Cataract. Clearly, the presence of the C-Group cultural assemblage cannot be equated with ancient political boundaries.

The annals of the merchant Horkhuf have indicated that Wawat, Irtjet and Setju were on occasion independent entities; at other times, they formed part of a single political unit under one ruler. Although the rulers of those states were in a position to tax or otherwise hinder Egyptian trading ventures—testifying to their power—still, they were forced to acknowledge the military might of their southern neighbor, Yam. Horkhuf has informed us that on his return from the south he was escorted, presumably through Lower Nubia, by soldiers provided by the king of Yam. Under the pharaoh Pepy II (c.2300–2206 BCE), the Egyptians mounted a campaign against Wawat and Irtjet, and the rulers of those areas subsequently traveled to the pharaoh in Memphis, to pay homage.

Egypt's definitive solution to the problem of interference with the southern trade was the conquest of virtually the whole of the region occupied by the C-Group, during the reigns of the twelfth dynasty pharaohs Amenemhet I and Senwosret I (1991–1928 BCE). The C-Group elite thus lost its position as middlemen in any trade along the Nile Valley, and that loss of wealth was reflected in the greater rarity of Egyptian objects imported at that time—although the area lay under direct Egyptian control. The new middlemen in the African trade were the rulers of the kingdom of Kush to the south of the C-Group, the successors to the rulers of Irtjet and Setju, or of Yam.

The C-Group people had been warlike, and for a long time had served as mercenaries in the armies of the pharaohs. The conquest of Wawat by the Egyptians was thus no easy matter, and hostilities were extended for some time—for about one hundred years. More than ten extremely powerful fortresses were built by the Egyptians at strategic points along the Nile Valley particularly at the Second Cataract of the Nile. Their function may have been mainly to protect the trade routes down the Nile, although a few of the fortresses appear to be situated near major C-Group population centers and may have been located at least partly to keep those populations under surveillance.

During the Second Intermediate Period, Egyptian control of the C-Group lapsed but the political vacuum was rapidly filled by an advance of the Kushites from the south, who brought with them their distinctive Kerma Classique culture, which was overlain on that of the indigenous population. It was during the Kushite domination that C-Group culture, as an independent entity, became increasingly adulterated. It disappeared forever with the New Kingdom occupation of Nubia.

[*See also* Kerma; Kush; *and* Nubia.]

## BIBLIOGRAPHY

Adams, William Y. *Nubia: Corridor to Africa*. London, 1977. Discussion of the C-Group is found on pp. 142–162.

Bietak, Manfred. *Studien zur Chronologie der Nubischen C-Gruppe*. Denkschrift der Österreichischen Akademie der Wissenschaften in Wien, Phil.-hist. Klasse, 97. Vienna, 1968. Of fundamental importance for our understanding of the chronology and internal development of the C-Group.

Bietak, Manfred. "Ceramics of the C-Group Culture." *Meroitica* 5 (1979), 107–127. A detailed analysis of some of the finest products of the C-Group, its incised ceramics.

Bietak, Manfred. "The C-Group and Pan-Grave Culture in Nubia." In *Nubian Culture Past and Present*, edited by T. Hägg, Stockholm, 1987. pp. 113–128.

O'Connor, David. "Early States along the Nubian Nile." In *Egypt and Africa*, edited by W. V. Davies, pp. 145–165. London, 1991. One of several articles by this author on the location of the areas recorded by Egyptian sources upstream of Aswan; includes discussions of their political organization and level of development.

Reisner, George A. *The Archaeological Survey Report for 1907–1908*. Cairo, 1910.

Sauneron, Serge. "Un village nubien fortifié sur la rive orientale de Ouadi es- Sébouʿ." *Bulletin de l'Institut français d'archéologie orientale* 63 (1965), 161–167. A description of one of the few known C-Group settlements.

Säve-Söderbergh, T., ed. *Middle Nubian Sites*. The Scandinavian Joint Expedition to Sudanese Nubia, vol. 4.1. Partille, 1989. A general introduction to the C-Group is to be found on pp. 6–14.

Trigger, Bruce G. *Nubia under the Pharaohs*. London, 1976. A detailed account of Egyptian activities south of Aswan and of the cultures, including the C-Group, with which they came into contact.

DEREK A. WELSBY

**CHALCEDONY.** *See* Gems.

CHAMPOLLION, JEAN-FRANÇOIS. *Portrait of Champollion.* (Courtesy David P. Silverman)

**CHAMPOLLION, JEAN-FRANÇOIS** (1790–1832), Egyptologist and the first person to decipher hieroglyphs. Born in Figeac (Lot), France, he was educated by his older brother, Jacques-Joseph Champollion-Figeac (1778–1867), an archaeologist and historian, whose interests in ancient Egypt may be gauged by his request to accompany Napoleon Bonaparte's military expedition to Egypt in 1799. Scholars are in agreement that the younger Champollion could not have successfully deciphered the hieroglyphs without Jacques-Joseph, a modest, but nevertheless accomplished classical scholar who never stood in his younger brother's limelight after the posthumous editing of some of his brother's works (see below).

At the age of sixteen, the precocious Jean-François had delivered an address before the Academy at Grenoble, France, in which he had maintained that links existed between Coptic, the language of the Christian Egyptians, and the hieroglyphs. He continued his studies at the Collège de France, under such luminaries as Baron Antoine-Isaac Silvestre de Sacy (1758–1838), who is regarded as the first modern scholar to be able to read, in however a rudimentary fashion, the hieroglyhphs. In 1802, de Sacy had recognized and translated three names in the Demotic text on the Rosetta Stone that had been found in northern Egypt, near the city of Rosetta.

In 1809, Champollion was appointed to his first academic post, in history and politics, at the University of Grenoble. Nine years later, he was made chair of history and geography at the same university, during which time he visited Egyptian collections in Italian museums. He was appointed curator of the Egyptian collections at the Musée du Louvre, Paris, in 1826; in 1828 and 1829, he traveled to Egypt at the head of a scientific mission, which included Ippolito Baldessare Rosellini (1800–1843), Italy's first Egyptologist. (The results of that mission were being prepared for publication at the time of Champollion's death and were posthumously published.) In 1831, Champollion was appointed to the first chair of Egyptian history and archaeology, which was created especially for him at the Collège de France. He had married Rosine Blanc, to whom a daughter, Zoraïde Chéronnet-Champollion (1824–1889) was born. He died of a stroke in Paris on 4 March 1832 and was buried there in Père Lachaise cemetery.

Called the "Founder and Father of Egyptology," Champollion was a polymath whose command of languages was so prodigious that by 1808 he was able to equate fifteen Demotic signs on the Rosetta Stone with their corresponding signs in Coptic. Within a decade, he had begun the successful translation of the hieroglyphs on the Rosetta Stone. In 1822, his now famous *Lettre à M. Dacier*, although flawed by six incorrectly identified signs, nevertheless marked a turning point in the decipherment of hieroglyphs. Heretofore, many reputable scholars were still incorrectly maintaining that the hieroglyphs were signs that had to be "interpreted" rather than understood as a language conforming to strictly formulated rules of grammar and syntax. Champollion built upon that foundation and in 1824 published his *Précis du système hiéroglyphique des anciens égyptiens*, which contained a listing of 450 words and/or hieroglyphic groupings. It was followed by his *Panthéon égyptien* (1925), as well as his Egyptian grammar (1836–1841) and dictionary (1841–1843)—the last two edited posthumously by his brother Jacques.

The modern mind recoils when considering that Champollion's decipherment of the hieroglyphs was based, in no small part, on the language of the Rosetta Stone, written in what is popularly termed the Ptolemaic version of ancient Egyptian, with its more than seven thousand individual signs. His fame endures as the one person responsible for the decipherment, despite an occasional protest by supporters of his English rival, Thomas Young (1773–1829).

[*See also* Decipherment; *and* Rosetta Stone.]

### BIBLIOGRAPHY

Andrews, Carol. *The Rosetta Stone*. London, 1981.

Dawson, Warren R., and Eric P. Uphill. *Who Was Who in Egyptology*, 3d ed., rev. by M. L. Bierbrier. London, 1995.

Galeries nationales du Grand Palais. *Naissance de l'écriture: Cunéiformes et hiéroglyphes*, pp. 370–375. Paris, 1982.

ROBERT STEVEN BIANCHI

**CHENOBOSKION.** *See* Nag Hammadi.

**CHEOPS.** *See* Khufu.

**CHEPHREN.** *See* Khafre.

**CHILDHOOD.** The Egyptians had two terms for child/children: *ms/ms.w* and *ḥrd/ḥrd.w*. Both boys and girls were welcome in ancient Egypt, though a first-born son was preferred. The first century BCE historian Diodoros Siculus (80.3 ff.) informs us that no child, not even the child of a slave, was looked on as a bastard, because the father was regarded as the creator and the mother as the source of nourishment. The execution of a condemned pregnant woman could be delayed until her confinement ended. Exposure of a child was considered monstrous. The Greek authors Strabo and Diodoros marveled at this because in Greece poor families abandoned unwanted children, especially girls. If a couple remained childless, they could adopt a child. In its mother's womb the child was regarded as a living being developing under the protection of a god or goddess. In the sun hymn of Amarna, the god Aten is described as he "who makes seed grow in women, who creates people from sperm, who feeds the son in his mother's womb, who soothes him to still his tears." The child was thought to belong to both parents. Formed by the father's *ka*, the father transmitted to his child part of his *ba*-soul and part of his *akh* power. According to the Pyramid Texts, the Coffin Texts, and the *Book of Going Forth by Day* (*Book of the Dead*), the heart, the site of a person's character, feeling, and intellect came from the mother. A belief from the Persian, preserved through the Ptolemaic period and also known among central African tribes, held that the semen went from the father's bones into the bones of the child; and in the Jumilhac Papyrus (third century BCE), we read that the bones were formed by the semen, while the flesh and skin of the child came from the mother. In filiations, Egyptians often preface the name of the father with the phrase "made by" and the mother's with "born to."

The birth of a child was attended by the female members of the household. The existence of midwives in ancient Egypt is not certain. Some deities were associated with pregnancy and childbirth; in the Westcar Papyrus, births are attended by Meskhenet (the personification of the birthing stool), Heket (a birth goddess), Isis, and Nephthys. Taweret, a hippopotamus goddess, protected the pregnant woman, while the bandy-legged dwarf god Bes protected women in childbirth and young children; he was also associated with fertility.

The mother or a nurse breast-fed the child for as many as three years. The Egyptian wet-nurse came to live in the child's home. The Egyptians believed that a relationship between the child and its nurse was established through the milk, and a king acquired the gifts of a goddess when suckled by her. In noble families the nurse might remain with a child while it grew up, becoming its teacher. Royal children had many nurses, often from noble families, and their children grew up with the princes and princesses. These nurses were highly esteemed: Thutmose III married the daughter of his nurse, and Ay, husband of the nurse of Queen Nefertiti, became king after the last male offspring of the royal family had died. Male instructors were also called "nurse" (*mn't*, written with the breast as a determinative). According to later contracts written in Greek, a child was sent to live with the nurse. This seems to be a Greek fashion, since according to the only contract between an Egyptian and a nurse from the same period, the nurse came to live in the child's father's house. From the Old Kingdom on, reliefs and statuettes show simple women nursing their children, holding them in their laps.

In spite of all this, children were threatened by all kinds of diseases. With prayers, amulets, magic spells, and medicines—many of them belonging to a dubious pharmacopeia—parents tried to protect their children. They lamented desperately if they died. The sage Ani says: "When death comes, he steals the infant who is in his mother's arms, just like him who has reached old age." When small children died they might be buried under the floor of their parents' house, in special children's cemeteries, in their own tombs in a cemetery for adults, or together with one or both parents; the last indicates the close relationship between parents and children.

The Egyptians seem to have registered birthdays from an early time. An official, Sobek-hu, mentions the twenty-seventh year of Amenemhet II as the year of his birth, and some officials of the eighteenth dynasty have their ages noted at their death. According to Ramesses IV, the living counted the days and months of their lifetime. An exact age to the day is preserved from the twenty-first dynasty, and an exact birthday from the twenty-sixth. During the Ptolemaic period, registers of births and deaths were kept in the House of Life. Texts from Deir el-Medina seem to indicate that a workman could take a day off to celebrate his own birthday or that of a family member. An invitation from a man to the birthday celebration of his son survives from the Ptolemaic period.

The child received its name at birth. The name could be chosen by the father, the mother, or both parents. It might refer to a king, a god, or a feast during which the child was born. The child could be named after another family member or after an animal, or it might simply get a number: First, Second, etc. Sometimes the name was composed of the words the mother uttered during her labor, imploring the help of or giving thanks to a god or goddess. A name like "They placed him in front of the god

NN," known from the Late period, may indicate exposure in a temple; a name like "May (the god) Khonsu kill them" points to opposition against foreign rulers. During the Old Kingdom, a child had a "big" (*rn 'i*) or "beautiful" (*rn nfr*) name, composed with the name of a king, a second name composed with the name of a god, and a pet name. The "big" name was given up in the sixth dynasty. In the Middle Kingdom it is replaced by a "name by which he is named," which disappeared in the New Kingdom but is revived in the Third Intermediate Period. A "name of his mother" is always placed at the beginning in lists.

A baby was carried in a sling at its mother's breast, seldom on the back. Older infants rode astride the hip of a mother, elder sister, or servant. During the Old Kingdom, the status "child" was expressed in art by nakedness; in the Middle and New Kingdoms, children were depicted either nude or clothed. The sex of girls was sometimes indicated by small breasts and a marked pubis. Garments, some of which have survived, protected them against the cold. Small animals made of clay or wood, dolls with movable limbs, balls, and tops were common toys for children. Boys in images often carry a bird hanging down by its wings, while girls may hold a chicken or duckling nestled in their palms in front of their chests. Boys usually suck the middle finger, but girls very seldom do. Their hair is shaved, except for a sidelock or a braided plait with the end rolled up; this plait was first worn only by boys, but from the fifth dynasty on also by girls. The gods Horus, Khons, and Ihy were depicted as child gods with a sidelock or plait. This hairstyle was also worn by Iwenmutef "Pillar of his mother" the priest, formerly a god representing the eldest son in the royal cult and later in the cult of the dead. The hair of girls was either totally shaven or worn in a pigtail, which became the fashion for girl dancers. During the New Kingdom, the sidelock became broader for girls as well as for boys. A wide sidelock became the fashion for the royal children and the high priest of Memphis, who was often a prince.

The close relationship between parents and children is expressed through all periods. During the Old Kingdom, children are represented with their parents inspecting activities on the estate. In the New Kingdom, we can see the whole family on a pleasure trip in a papyrus skiff, hunting birds and catching fish. An elder son goes hunting in the desert with his father. Children are present at the festival of the deified king Amenhotpe I and at the Valley festival when families visit their deceased in the necropolis. They dance with the musicians when a noble receives the gold of honor, or at the festival of the goddess Bastet. They participate at the burial of a parent or relative: the youngest is carried in a sling, toddlers hold onto their mother or an elder sister, and young girls mourn along with the wailing women. With their parents, they adore the gods.

Children were considered to be ignorant, innocent, and without sin. "Nobody is born wise," the sage Ptahhotep states, and in the Insinger Papyrus we read that humans live for ten years before they can tell life from death. The scribe Djehutimose, who fell ill on an official mission, writes to his colleagues to take the little boy to the god Amun and to pray for his recovery. According to Egyptian belief, as the Greek historian Plutarch related, innocent children were closer to the gods and had prophetic gifts: children told Isis where she could find the coffin of her murdered husband. Other authors wrote that during a procession of the bull god Apis, children started to give oracles. As in life, so were children close to their parents in the hereafter. From the Old Kingdom on, they can be seen taking the funerary meal with their parents, thus being provided for in eternity, and in New Kingdom representations they accompany their parents on a boat ride on the river of the hereafter.

Children grew up close to their mother, who cared for them while they were small and while they went to school. Nefertiti, as we read on a boundary stela from the city of Tell el-Amarna, was under the guidance of the king, Akhenaten, and their children, the princesses Meritaten and Meketaten, "will reach maturity under the guidance of their mother." A father was not only obliged to nurture his children, he was also supposed to protect them from physical and psychic difficulties, he needed to know about the disposition of his child and help him in time of need; but if a son opposed his father, he could be rejected.

When the children of nobles accompanied their parents to inspect their estate, they learned by seeing and listening. From the fifth dynasty on, youths intended to become high functionaries were educated at residential schools, or together with the royal children at the palace, to become loyal followers of the future king. From the end of the sixth dynasty, boys coming from the lower class could attain high office. They were educated by an official who was called their (mental) father. The first mention of a school is around 2000 BCE. The didactic method was to listen, obey, and learn the teaching of the master by heart (to memorize). But the sage Khety teaches his son "A good son, whom the god gives, is one who adds to that which his teacher told him."

Student ostraca in the Hieratic script, corrected in red ink, show that besides learning how to write, school pupils were taught conjugation, orthography, literary style, grammar, geography, astronomy, mathematics, geometry, and sometimes even foreign languages like Babylonian, Cretan, or Nubian. Behavior was important: the ideal was the "silent one," the one who could listen well. The boys were instructed in behavior toward superiors and subordinates, as well as in table manners. Laziness was punished by beating. That students sometimes had their feet locked in the stocks is recorded. Besides mental training, upper-class youths had physical training, such as swimming, shooting, or running. Old and Middle Kingdom tomb walls show naked boys high-jumping, wrestling, whirling around holding one another's hands, balancing, or throwing sticks. Two boys try to force each other's forearm down; teams try to pull each other down. They were also trained in dancing and music.

Except in a few depictions, the sexes play apart. Girls are always shown dressed. They learn how to dance, to play music, and to sing, but they also take part in acrobatic games or juggling with balls. Girls grew up near their mothers. Letters from middle-class women from the workmen's village at Deir el-Medina suggest that women too could learn how to read and write, possibly from their fathers or brothers. Princesses had male instructors (called "nurse"). Daughters of noble families probably also had home instructors perhaps the nurses with which some are depicted. Poorer girls learned what they would need when they married by helping their mothers in the household, with poultry and small livestock, or gleaning in the fields. We see bigger girls carrying their younger siblings around. Some might go to work for a noblewoman; scenes show them preparing the bed, caring for their mistress in the confinement hut, or serving and dancing at the meals of the rich. Boys helped with the cattle in the fields, shooed away birds from the crops, climbed palm trees at harvest time, and helped pick grapes or press them. Little boys accompanied their fathers to work. They are depicted at the shipyard, playing and trying to help their father.

Boys who went into the army had to leave their parents at an early age; they began with odd jobs in the camp, such as looking after the animals. We can see boys and girls in market scenes and in processions, carrying goods. In the tomb of the vizier Rekhmire, there is a record of children of slaves being taxed according to the work they could do. Diodoros Siculus wrote that boys who had not yet reached maturity worked in the mines, carrying blocks through low galleries; possibly these were children of slaves working with their parents. Papyri from the Greco-Roman period mention children being rented out to work by their fathers or widowed mothers. The kind of labor the children had to do depended on their masters and mistresses. According to the Egyptian principle of *maat* (justice) monuments only show us children at lighter work. A New Kingdom letter in which a mother complains that her daughter has to work, although she is still a child, may indicate that the mother had rented her daughter out for service under the condition that she should only do light work. The statement that she was exchanged for a servant might indicate that she had to do the work of an adult.

We do not know whether any initiation rites marked the end of childhood. After a ceremony in which a band was knotted around the head (*ts mdḥ*), a boy took over adult responsibilities, thus ending his childhood. According to texts from the Old Kingdom, Horus set out to avenge his father, and officials took over their first officer, after that ceremony. Ptolemaic texts speak of the deity, Horus ascending the throne after having gone through the *ts mdḥ*. Old Kingdom scenes showing boys trying to escape from an enclosure while others—carrying a sort of scepter and accompanied by a man in a lion's mask—run away after dancing girls, might be interpreted as initiation rites if not as some kind of game. Whether circumcision was practiced as an initiation is not known either. From prehistory, some men depicted partially nude and some mummies may show circumcision, but others do not. According to a few representations and texts, small boys as well as adult men were circumcised. Whether a Coffin Text refers to circumcised boys *and* girls is not clear. Texts that clearly mention circumcision of girls date to the Greek period; one of them says that a certain girl had to be circumcised according to Egyptian custom as she had reached the age of marriage.

Children were supposed to love and honor their parents and look after them when they were ill or old. Although it was mainly the duty of the eldest son to bury his parents, care for their funerary cult, and keep their names alive, the other children—boys as well as girls—were obliged to do the same. Children who did not look after their parents could be disinherited.

Orphans and widows of the lower class must have led a miserable life if there was no male relative to look after them. From the First Intermediate Period onward, nobles boast of having taken care of the widow and her child. According to other texts, the lot of orphans was put into the hands of a god, which suggests a kind of orphanage in the temple. Often enough, however they were left to fend for themselves, and older ones might have led a vagrant life.

From the Early Dynastic period, male child gods were venerated. Most important of these is Horus, the son of Isis, later known as Harsiese. As a child with his finger at his mouth, he is depicted in the first dynasty and is documented in many Late period terracottas as Harpocrates. Then too, as Harendotes, he is the avenger of his father, who was murdered by his brother Seth. Horus, the fatherless child, was borne and brought up by his mother Isis hidden in the papyrus thickets of the Nile Delta at Khemmis. Because he had been guarded by his mother from the threat of his uncle Seth, from illness, and from wild animals, he became a savior god and was later assimilated to (Pa)Shed, the savior. From the Middle Kingdom on, he was associated with the child gods Nefertum and

Ihy. Nefertum appears as a newborn child on a lotus flower in the primeval flood and symbolizes the renewal of the sun and the beginning of the world. The musician Ihy, son of Horus of Edfu and Hathor of Dendera, was born in the so-called *mammisi* (birth-house) and enthroned as the follower of his father. He and Nefertum in turn were assimilated with Harsomtus. Khons, the son of Amun and Mut, symbolized the renewal of the moon. Neper personified the new-grown grain and was venerated as the son of the harvest goddess Renenutet. Neferhotep, son of Hathor, symbolized the duration of kingship. In the Late period, even Heka, the god of magic, was worshiped as a child and assimilated to different divine couples.

[*See also* Birth; Education; *and* Family.]

**BIBLIOGRAPHY**

Feucht, Erika. *Das Kind im Alten Ägypten.* Frankfurt and New York, 1995.

Janssen, Rosalind M., and Jac. J. Janssen. *Growing Up in Ancient Egypt.* London, 1990.

Robins, Gay. *Women in Ancient Egypt.* London, 1993.

ERIKA FEUCHT

**CHRONOLOGY AND PERIODIZATION.** The structure of Egyptian history remains, as always, its chronology. Unlike the other cultures which surrounded the Nile Valley and remained, for all practical purposes, in a preliterate stage, pharaonic civilization developed writing in Early Dynastic times and so was able to systematize its complex society around key historical and chronological events. During the first dynasty and the second, for example, a rudimentary system of calendrics was developed with the interconnected system of regnal-year dating (counting the years of a king's reign). Although little is known from sources of that period, the Egyptians worked with a relatively efficient method of time demarcation that included separate names or designations for the pharaoh's years in office; however, it does not seem that any overt reckoning based on dynasties or ruling houses (families) was then in operation.

Our present historical schema of dividing the history of Egypt into periods called "Kingdoms" (Old, Middle, and New) is a modern one; it is based on the Egyptian eras of political unity and effective internal pacification. Developed by Egyptologists in the nineteenth century, this division depended on a wealth of textual and pictorial data that emanated from economically and politically viable epochs, not all of which fit neatly into separate dynasties. Moreover, since the earliest dynasties—in particular the first two—were barely known at that time, the collective unity of the "Old Kingdom" was set from the third to the sixth dynasty. Similarly, as the second phase of pharaonic unity occurred within the eleventh dynasty (under Nebhepetre Montuhotep I), rather than at the end of one, the term "Middle Kingdom" came to encompass a period that did not properly coincide with a break between ruling houses. The same may be said for the end of that era of stability; in the eighteenth century BCE, the ruling house of the thirteenth dynasty was pushed out of the north, where a rival kingdom was based. In that case, the designation "Middle Kingdom" ends at a time in which the legitimate rulers were faced with an effective new dynasty, not with the total demise of their own.

The Egyptians, although witnessing and understanding their periods of social harmony and strength as well as those of civil war, disunity, and relative weakness, nonetheless did not arrange their own schema of history to reflect that inherent dichotomy. In fact, the present-day detailed listing of various dynasties—from the presumed foundation of the unified state in the first dynasty (the joining of the Two Lands) to the very end—was developed over a long time period. It began with Manetho, an Egyptian priest from the Nile Delta, who wrote in Greek for the Ptolemies, his foreign overlords (c.280 BCE); his king lists formed the basis of the Classical era's understanding of Nile Valley history and remains the basis for ours. Although the records concerning the various ruling houses with which Manetho worked reflected, to no small degree, the inherent political segmentation of ancient Egypt, it can be shown that many of his divisions were not based on sources contemporary with those dynasties. For Egyptologists, the major outline of Early Dynastic history remains the fifth dynasty Palermo Stone, as well as additional fragments that may belong to another stela.

The Palermo Stone covers, in a very schematic fashion, the regnal years of the pharaohs, which were set within their civil calendar (of 365 days/annum). Although Predynastic rulers were included, they are mere names. Only for the pharaohs of the first two dynasties (the so-called Archaic Age or Early Dynastic period) is there evidence that connects a king's year with a specific event. Usually religious in import, these early regnal years appear to be brief designations of the most important event that occurred within the given year; full reigns with integers from one onward were not the rule. Later, however, there was a growing attempt to simplify matters, and it is not surprising that the expanding bureaucratic state of ancient Egypt began to develop a more consistent means of counting regnal years. Certainly by the third dynasty the state had brought into its apparatus the concept of a census of cattle, one that took place on a regular biennial basis. The cattle "counts" appear on the lower portions of the entries on the Palermo Stone, and they coincide with the establishment of the expansive economic unity of the third dynasty and onward. Although difficult to determine with total accuracy, this system became annual in the

sixth dynasty, thereby forming the basis of the regularized and simple system of official state bookkeeping and records. Unfortunately, the Palermo Stone breaks off in the mid-fifth dynasty, so other sources were used to document this change.

The Palermo Stone, as well as various fragments that may belong to it, have been augmented by the publication of a second, rather detailed list of such "annals." Dated to the late fifth dynasty and the sixth, this list follows the same counting style as the earlier record. Significantly, all of these early lists do not provide demarcations that coincide with Manetho's account. Except for the obvious break between the Predynastic monarchs and the dynastic, the compilers of such lists felt their kingdom to be a unity, one which began with the unification of Egypt and the first dynasty and then proceeded onward; the only sharp division is that between these rulers of the Double Crown—the pharaohs over all Egypt—and their predecessors, who may have worn either the Red Crown of Lower Egypt or the White Crown of Upper Egypt.

The division into dynasties with which Manetho worked holds well if such ruling houses as the twelfth or the eighteenth dynasties are considered. As many scholars have seen, problems arise when there are attempts to analyze in detail the reasons for those divisions. Manetho's dynasties reflect a lengthy historiographic tradition, in which the geographical location of a ruling lineage mattered, with respect to its origins. Manetho's Dynasty 18, for example, was said to be Theban (Diospolite), which corresponded perfectly with their origins although the pharaohs of the age had their capital in the North, at Memphis. His Dynasty 15 is said to be that of the Hyksos, foreign overlords from the Levant who eventually ruled the Nile Delta and a sizable portion of Middle Egypt. One major problem with Manetho as a late source—and it is an intractable one—is that the text is mainly preserved in excerpts drawn up by later chronographers; what is preserved is a mere summation of a relatively detailed work in which a few specific events associated with the pharaohs are recorded. By and large, what matters are the dynasties, the names of the kings, and their lengths of reign. Even with the additional problems of textual corruption over the centuries, Manetho presents a very confused arrangement of dynasties when he covers Egypt's periods of disunity. Egyptologists call those Intermediate Periods, and they are labeled First, Second, and Third. The First Intermediate Period followed the Old Kingdom. It corresponds to the time when the old Memphite line had ended but before a new lineage or ruling house had taken over the whole Nile Valley; the exact beginning and end of that period of social upheaval did not coincide either with the commencement or the end of a dynasty. The Second Intermediate Period was placed after the Middle

Kingdom but before the New Kingdom. Its precise beginning is unclear, but modern scholars consider the collapse of the unity under a feeble thirteenth dynasty to provide the demarcation between the Middle Kingdom and the ensuing era of disunity. The Third Intermediate Period refers to the time after the New Kingdom but before the reunification of Egypt under the Saite monarchs of the twenty-sixth dynasty.

These convenient designations of Egypt's national success and failure are purely modern schematic terms and must not be considered to reflect ancient usage. To take a good example: in the First Intermediate Period, two rival houses of Thebes and Herakleopolis waxed and waned in their attempts to consolidate their own power over all of the Nile Valley. In the North, the Herakleopolitans are considered by Manetho to have ruled in Dynasties 9 and 10, although that tradition is now considered to be partly false; specifically, those Northern monarchs ruled from one house rather than two. Another case is worth stressing: the problem of the Second Intermediate Period. Sources from that time allow us to reconstruct a complicated series of events that are summarized here: A growing feebleness of the national dynasty (the thirteenth) eventually led to the establishment of a rival power in the Delta (the fourteenth dynasty). Not long thereafter, the North was taken over by Near Easterners, who had settled in the eastern Delta (the Hyksos of the fifteenth dynasty). When they eventually seized the old capital, Memphis, it is probable that remnants of the ruling house of the thirteenth dynasty fled to Thebes in the South and established a rump state there (the end of the thirteenth dynasty). The sixteenth dynasty included various local potentates, probably of a military nature, who were ruled by the various Hyksos pharaohs of the fifteenth dynasty, while at the same time a new Theban dynasty emerged (the seventeenth), one that eventually began a successful counterattack upon the North. This brief account of Second Intermediate Period history is barely reflected in the standard native Egyptian accounts of their past that are king lists or annals. Manetho was confused over his Dynasties 12 and 14. The valuable Turin Canon was prepared in the nineteenth dynasty as a detailed papyrus of the pharaohs and their reigns and appears to connect all of the native rulers of Dynasty 12 with those of Dynasty 17. Although the Hyksos kings were treated separately from the Egyptian kings, problems still occur among the other numerous pharaohs on this list. Long series of royal names, often called king lists, also help in the reconstruction of the historical aspect of this foreign domination; however, they ignore the foreign rulers of the North, preferring to include some (but by no means all) pharaohs of the Second Intermediate Period.

In many ways, the Turin Canon provides a more exact basis for historical periodization than any other native source, Manetho included. The twelfth dynasty is explicitly indicated, although its location is given (the Northern capital of Itjtawy) rather than a dynasty number. The kings who followed after that dynasty were noted, as well as the earlier Theban state of the eleventh dynasty. A useful totaling up of reigns is given, such as from the first dynasty to the fifth or from the first to the eighth, the latter clearly indicating a time in which unity prevailed. Hence, the Turin Canon can be conceived as a precursor to Manetho, as well as to the modern scholarly divisions called "Kingdoms." Yet the chronological divisions called "Intermediate Periods" remain outside that ancient detailed list of pharaohs and regnal years. Since the divisions of ruling houses were mainly based on geographical locations, any disunity or conflicting states within Egypt was avoided. For that reason, the Turin Canon reads as if none of the dynasties overlapped but instead occurred in a purely sequential fashion. The document assumes as well the existence of a Memphite monarchy from the first dynasty onward (until the eighth dynasty), and thus it provides a false impression of the earliest phase of pharaonic unity. Nevertheless, the Turin Canon records, in the native language, a useful parallel to Manetho; for example, the various gods and demigods of Predynastic Egypt were included, thereby paralleling Manetho's records of early divine rulers and later "heroes."

The king lists have also been useful in reconstructing the various royal lines, but these documents do nothing more than place the names one after another. Found mainly in temples, these royal lists were drawn up for reasons other than presenting all the known pharaohs (or at least the presumed legitimate ones); in addition, no regnal years were given. The best-known king lists are located at the Karnak temple in Thebes, in the holy cult area of Abydos, and at the royal cemetery of Saqqara. The Karnak list indicates those rulers who had a statue of themselves set up within the precinct walls of the Great Temple of Amun at Karnak. The pharaoh who oversaw the work, Thutmose III, laid great stress on the cult of those royal ancestors, so such king lists should be considered in a very different light than those solely connected to royal lineages or to the chronological arrangement of the pharaohs. That is to say, the religious or cultic interests of the commissioner of the list—in this case Thutmose III—lay at the basis of the rows of cartouches carved into the temple walls. Not surprisingly, those rulers who were not associated with the Great Temple of Amun are not represented in the Karnak list (e.g., the Herakleopolitans of the ninth and tenth dynasties or the Hyksos).

If such epoch-names as the Old, Middle, and New Kingdoms are useful today, it is because they reflect an expansive and economically stable Egyptian state. At the same time, we can develop an exact chronology for these three main eras of pharaonic success, since many inscriptions deal with chronological matters. Through astronomical correlations, the Middle and New Kingdoms can be placed on a relatively secure chronological base, and independent of each other. The New Kingdom has been dated by two major occurrences of lunar and civil calendar equivalences (dated to the reigns of Thutmose III and Ramesses II), wherein a specific day in the civil calendar was equated with a day from the lunar calendar. In addition, there is a useful record of the heliacal rising of the star Sothis (Sirius) set within the reign of Thutmose III, and from that a possible exact date for the event can be determined. Other similar astronomical occurrences, albeit of a more contentious nature, have also aided in reconstructing a tight chronological outline for the New Kingdom. Nevertheless, it was mainly the Turin Canon, Manetho's works, the king lists, and an important series of dated monuments and texts that helped establish a relatively accurate arrangement of the pharaohs and their regnal years. The main points of contention remain concentrated on the interpretation of the astronomical data. For example, within the New Kingdom, the beginnings of the reigns of Thutmose III and Ramesses II are disputed, with various modern chronologies set into a schema of three choices. (The consensus places the commencement of the reigns of Thutmose III at 1479 BCE and that of Ramesses II at 1279 BCE, although some prefer 1504 BCE and 1304, respectively.)

Dates for the Middle Kingdom, interestingly enough, have to be reconstructed independent from the New Kingdom. Papyri archives from a temple at Illahun have provided another date for the heliacal rising of Sothis in Year 7 of Senwosret III. Even this seemingly exact point is disputed, if only owing to the location from which Sothis was sighted: if it was seen in the South at Elephantine then the date would compute earlier than if it was seen at Heliopolis in the North—the choice is either 1872 or 1830 BCE.

For the Old Kingdom, no firm bases exist for a fixed point in time; the same may be said for the Intermediate Periods. Except for the Palermo Stone, which ends in the mid-fifth dynasty, and the list that goes into the sixth dynasty, no evidence yet provides a relatively tight or exact chronology from the first dynasty to the eighth. Therefore, the count has been back from the twelfth dynasty, using the evidence from the Turin Canon; the procedure ultimately contends with the First Intermediate Period's two rival houses—Herakleopolis (ninth and tenth dynasties) and Thebes (eleventh dynasty)—and their rivalry for control. Then, too, the effective end of the old Memphite monarchy (the eighth dynasty) is also impossible to determine, owing to the scarcity of contemporary dateable sources. Therefore, the chronology earlier than the eleventh dynasty is approximate at best, and the presumed unification of Egypt by Menes at the beginning of the first dynasty is still disputed (within a range of about one hundred years—c.3050–2950 BCE—the best but nevertheless a highly unsatisfactory solution).

Scholars are still unsure of the exact dates of any phase of Egyptian civilization, except those of the Saite period, the twenty-sixth dynasty, 664–525 BCE. For that period, the wealth of native plus foreign sources (in particular Greek but also Assyrian and Babylonian) has resolved the problem. For the earlier phases of Egyptian history, such is not the case. Attempted synchronisms of the New Kingdom with Babylon and the Hittites has not yielded precise dates. Even the astronomical events cited earlier provide, at best, an interval in time rather than a specific point. Lunar–civil calendar correlations yield an interval within fifty years; Sothic datings also vary and depend on knowing the place of this star's sighting. Finally, no useful synchronisms exist for Egypt and her neighbors before the New Kingdom. The dates offered by scholars, with regard to Egyptian civilization, remain approximate, and they become even more so as they refer to earlier time.

[*See also* Time.]

## BIBLIOGRAPHY

Gardiner, Alan H. "Regnal Years and Civil Calendar in Pharaonic Egypt." *Journal of Egyptian Archaeology* 31 (1945), 11–28. The standard study connected to pharaonic regnal years.

Helck, Wolfgang. "Anmerkungen zum Turiner Königspapyrus." *Studien zur altägyptischen Kultur* 19 (1992), 151–216. The most recent analysis of the intricacies of the Turin Canon.

Kitchen, Kenneth K. "The Basics of Egyptian Chronology in Relation to the Bronze Age." In *High, Middle or Low*, edited by Paul Åström, pp. 37–55. Studies in Mediterranean Archaeology and Literature, 56. Gothenburg, 1987. A useful study of the parameters of Egyptian exact dating.

Malek, Jaromir. "The Original Version of the Royal Canon of Turin." *Journal of Egyptian Archaeology* 68 (1982), 93–106. The best study of the problems associated with the Turin Canon.

Malek, Jaromir. "The Special Features of the Saqqara King-List." *Journal of the Society for the Study of Egyptian Antiquities* 12 (1982), 22–28. A neat analysis of one king list.

Malek, Jaromir. "A Chronological Scheme and Terminology for the Early Part of Egyptian History. A Contribution to a Discussion." *Discussions in Egyptology* 15 (1989), 37–50. A further analysis of the difficulties connected with the modern terminology of the Old Kingdom and the related dynasties.

Malek, Jaromir. "La division de l'histoire de l'égypte et l'égyptologie moderne." *Bulletin de la société française d'égyptologie* 138 (1997), 6–17. A very expert analysis of the situation of the Old Kingdom and the inherent difficulties in connecting the history to the so-called dynasties.

Redford, Donald B. *Pharaonic King-Lists, Annals and Day Books.* Mississauga, 1986. A valuable and detailed study of the parameters of Egyptian chronology and historiography; calendric matters are avoided.

Spalinger, Anthony J. "Dated Texts of the Old Kingdom." *Studien zur altägyptischen Kultur* 21 (1994), 277–319. A discussion of the problem of regnal year dates from the third to the sixth dynasty.

Von Beckerath, Jürgen. *Chronologie der ägyptischen Neuen Reiches.* Hildesheim, 1994. The most recent study of exact chronology for the New Kingdom.

ANTHONY J. SPALINGER

**CIRCUMCISION.** *See* Hygiene.

**CITIES.** The emergence of cities in ancient Egypt was linked to the development of agriculture and the emergence of the state as the unifying and predominant form of political organization. By 3500 BCE, towns and cities consisted of large regional capitals linked to the capitals of smaller administrative districts. Since Greek times, the provinces are known as nomes, ruled by nomarchs. During the New Kingdom, the Egyptian word for "city" was *niwt*, a term that, in the earliest texts of the first dynasty, referred to "settlement." The term for a "town" or large village is *dmi*, as known from the fifth dynasty. The term for "village," with an etymology related to "household," is *wḥyt*. The domain of Thebes as a city included the town of Western Thebes and smaller villages belonging to the town. The term *grgt*, used since the third dynasty, referred to settlements associated with agricultural estates and those established for a special purpose. There are also the two terms *ḥwt* and *pr*, both often used to mean "house," that designated an estate or a domain, including a planned settlement, agricultural land, and other nearby resources; these served as sources of revenue to the royal palace (as an institution), the cult of a god, the cult of the king, or, in some circumstances, the cult of a high official.

Knowledge about Egyptian cities (and settlements in general) is limited. Settlements and cities were located on the floodplain, with a preference for proximity to the Nile, in order to receive goods by boat. Since the preferred building material was local Nile mud, throughout pharaonic times, shifts in the course of the Nile, aggradation (the build-up of the floodplain by the annual deposition of silt), and the impact of high Nile floods has led to the destruction, obliteration, and/or burial of riverside settlements. In addition, instead of settlements, archaeological investigations since the nineteenth century have focused on temples and tombs, with their rich and spectacular art, sculpture, and architecture. Memphis, the quintessential capital of Egypt, on the western bank of the Nile only 20 kilometers (13 miles) south of the center of modern Cairo, is almost completely obliterated; however, recent investigations using new techniques of subsurface prospecting are beginning to piece together the complex history of the city. They show that the site was moved eastward in re-sponse to invasions by sand dunes and a shift in the course of the Nile. The capital city of Thebes (which at times rivaled Memphis in its power), situated in the area now occupied by Luxor, remains unknown except for the data from its temples and monuments, and from some limited excavations. During the Middle Kingdom, Thebes created a mound of some 1000 by 500 meters (3,200 by 1,600 feet). The city was laid on a grid plan and was surrounded by a wall about 6 meters (20 feet) thick. The Middle Kingdom temple town seems to have been leveled at the beginning of the New Kingdom, to accommodate the creation of the Great Temple complex of Karnak, with a new residential area and suburbs that probably spread as far as 8 kilometers (5 miles) from the city center.

Situated at a fairly safe distance from the vagaries of high Nile floods, a village of workers at Deir el-Medina, on the western bank of the Nile opposite Thebes, provides a glimpse at the organization of a specialized village—and possibly a useful, albeit distorted, view of village life. Another workers' village was discovered at Illahun on the eastern end of the twelfth dynasty pyramid complex of Senwosret. The town was later occupied by officials in charge of this king's mortuary cult. A third workers' village, found at Tell el-Amarna, was associated with the new city of Akhetaten founded by the heretic king Akhenaten. Built by Akhenaten in Middle Egypt, on the edge of the desert to the east of the Nile, it provides the clearest indication of the plan and construction of a royal capital city. The new city was associated with a new religious ideology that was antithetical to the main Theban dogma, associated with the worship of Amon. Inasmuch as the city was a result of deliberate planning and the seat of a new ideology, how representative it is as an example of Egyptian national capitals is difficult to ascertain. Most likely, it is representative of the formula of a royal city—with a palace, separate administrative and religious complexes, residential quarters, suburbs, and a village for workmen.

Tell ed-Dabʿa, a town in the northeastern Nile Delta, was the residential site of Egyptianized Canaanites and Delta elite administrators. The town was possibly established on the site of an earlier estate, at the beginning of the twelfth dynasty, as a royal estate of Amenemhet I. The town, which became the capital city of Egypt under the Near Eastern Hyksos dynasty, from 1585 to 1532 BCE, perhaps owed its prominence to trade with the coastal Levant and the administration of mining activities in the Sinai. Later, during the Ramessid era, the new capital of Piramesse was relocated to the vicinity of Avaris, the Hyksos capital. During the Third Intermediate Period, another castle was established at Tanis, about 20 kilometers (13 miles) north of Piramesse. Sais, one of the earliest prominent settlements of the Delta, and situated on one of the western branches of the Nile (currently the Rosetta branch), became a powerful capital during the Late period. Under the Ptolemies, the port city of Alexandria—founded by Alexander the Great on the Mediterranean, northwest of Sais—became Egypt's capital until the Arab invasion of the seventh century CE, when al-Fustat, the precursor to medieval Cairo, was founded on the Nile. Today, Cairo is a metropolitan conglomerate that has sprawled to encompass all previous settlements founded by Islamic rulers, as well as many of the older villages in its vicinity. Cairo has also expanded to include some new settlements in the desert, to its east and north.

The cities of ancient Egypt—their locations, functions, and organizations—are related to various dynamics that shaped the course of Egyptian civilization, including both internal and external forces. The earliest towns and settlements were related to trade, cult centers, and the emergence of administrative districts. For example, Maadi was related to trade with the Near East; the prosperity and prominence of Hierakonpolis was probably a result of trade with Nubia; Naqada might originally have been a political-religious center; Buto was perhaps a religious center transformed through maritime trade to a trade center, then to a capital of a polity. Other towns might have developed as defensive settlements.

The rise of the Egyptian managerial and governing elite was associated with religious ideology, ritual, and mythology. The ideology was predicated upon a principle that linked the chief—afterwards the king—to a mortuary cult. The cult developed with the rise of kings and a religious creed, which linked the king to a family of gods and to a deceased god-king, who had been the first king of Egypt. Royal cemeteries served as the material manifestation of the divine ancestry of the king and were thus associated with centers of royal power. In Predynastic times, the emergence of social stratification was marked by the establishment of special burial grounds for the elite adjacent to their towns. Thus a royal necropolis at Saqqara was associated with the first national capital of Egypt at Memphis. The Pyramid of Pepy I in the necropolis at Saqqara (*mn-nfr*, meaning "established and beautiful") gave its name to a royal city, which was called in Greek Memphis, in Arabic, Menf. The location of Memphis—near the apex of the Nile Delta, intermediate between the capitals of southern Egypt and the Delta—represented the role of kingship, establishing a central focus for the emerging nation-state that unified both regions. The position of Memphis also provided the king with a strategic control of the Delta and southern Egypt, at least as far south as Abydos. The possibility thus existed for developing additional centers of power (administrative, religious, or defensive) in outlying regions, either by the ruling sovereign (to consolidate his power) or by his opponents.

Abydos—situated to the north of Naqada and Hierakonpolis, where towns were established as capitals of powerful Predynastic polities in Upper Egypt—was probably the center of operations. It was the locus of a proto-national power that commanded parts of the Delta two centuries before the emergence of the first dynasty. A royal necropolis of the kings of this transitional stage (c.3300–3000 BCE) remained as a significant religious establishment well after the emergence of Memphis and its necropolis. It is also now agreed (but not conclusively established) that the kings of the first dynasty were buried at Abydos; their officials and nobles were buried at Saqqara. By the second dynasty, kings were buried at Saqqara, at a location now under the temple of Unas; however, the last two kings of the second dynasty, Peribsen and Khasekhemwy, were buried at Abydos. Following the First Intermediate Period, a time when centralized government collapsed, the reunification of Egypt was achieved by a family from Upper Egypt who established their dynastic rule at Thebes. Situated beyond the reach of the kings of the Delta (when the unity of Egypt came unglued) or from foreign invaders at the fringes of the Delta (as during the New Kingdom), Thebes proved to be a center of considerable power. During the New Kingdom's eighteenth dynasty, Thebes rivaled Memphis as an administrative and religious center.

Religion was always an important element of (theocratic) Egyptian kingship. The pharaohs were supported by a religious establishment that maintained the mortuary cults and the ceremonies central to the legitimization of their divine rule. Religion was also used for economic and political advantage, and it was used at times to undermine the rule of certain kings. During the New Kingdom, the establishment of Akhetaten as a center of a new religion might well have represented a threat to the power of the Theban priests, who had benefitted immensely from land donations and tax reduction. Akhenaten's reign and religion were, however, short-lived, and his city was abandoned. Also during the New Kingdom, Egypt was drawn to military conflicts with its Near Eastern neighbors. Although Memphis and Thebes remained the important religious and administrative centers, it became necessary to establish a frontier capital on the eastern edge of the Delta. The erosion of Egypt's centralized power—as a result of a series of wars and internal conflicts between rival religious and regional powers—not only led, during the Third Intermediate Period, to a split between Upper Egypt (ruled by the high priests of Amun at Thebes) and the Delta (ruled by northern kings at Tanis) but also, during the Late period, to its subdivision into several kingdoms. During the Late period, Egypt's last nationalist pharaohs managed to rule from the western edge of the Delta, from one of the religious centers at Sais.

With Egypt's conquest by the Macedonian, Alexander the Great, his port city of Alexandria was established to link Egypt with Greece and the Hellenistic world—a period that lasted almost a thousand years before the Arab bearers of Islam took Egypt in 643 CE. Alexandria was then neglected by them in favor of settlements on the eastern bank of the Nile, about 15 kilometers (10 miles) northeast of the ancient capital of Memphis; the new capitals, from Al-Fustat to Al-Qahira (Cairo), were located in a position that linked them via a land-bridge to the power base of the caliphs in the Arabian Peninsula.

**The Earliest Urban Centers.** Until c.5000 BCE, the inhabitants of the Nile Valley were foragers who practiced fishing, fowling, hunting, and collecting wild plants. The first known farming community then occupied a site at the edge of the floodplain of the Nile Delta at Merimda Beni Salama, some 25 kilometers (15 miles) to the northwest of Cairo. The village was large, about 180,000 square meters (1.9 million square feet), and was populated for a thousand years, until about 4000 BCE, when clusters of semisubterranean huts were built from mud, with walls and floors mud-plastered. (The earliest dwellings had been windbreaks and various light constructions.) Merimde had residential areas interspersed with workshops and public areas. The orientation of huts in rows suggests the emergence of some organizational order, but there is no indication of elite areas or any pronounced hierarchical organization. Although initial estimates of occupants were around 16,000, investigations of several Predynastic settlements and comparisons with later urban settlements suggest a more likely size of 1,300 to 2,000 persons, if the whole area was simultaneously occupied.

By 3500 BCE, a settlement at Maadi, about 15 kilometers (10 miles) to the south of Cairo, was established as a trade center. The site shows evidence of huts, storage magazines, silos, and cellars. Maadi was the end of an overland trade route to Palestine and was probably occupied by middlemen from the Levant, as indicated by the house and grave patterns. Trade items included copper and bitumen from southwest Asia, and artifacts that show affinities with Upper Egypt suggest that Maadi was a trade link between Upper Egypt and the Levant. The size of the settlement was similar to that of Merimde Beni Salama. At about the same time in the Nile Valley, the two towns of Hierakonpolis and Naqada became much larger than the neighboring villages. Hierakonpolis consisted of an area of about 50,000 square meters (536,000 square feet), comparable in area to South Town in the Naqada region. Investigations of Hierakonpolis revealed that occupied areas shifted in a northeasterly direction, suggesting that older areas were abandoned and used for disposal. The inhabited area of the town was probably

between 50,000 and 100,000 square meters, with perhaps no more than 1,500 to 2,000 persons. Prehistoric sites in the Nile Valley varied in size from as little as 16 square meters (170 square feet) to as much as 30,000 square meters (321,600 square feet). The largest sites probably represent repeated occupations, with lateral displacement through time. By contrast, the towns of Predynastic Egypt were the result of permanent occupation with a vertical build-up of deposits, a pattern also seen in the Predynastic villages at Naqada.

Before the emergence of South Town in the Naqada region, the area was dotted with small villages and hamlets, on the desert margin, at the edge of the floodplain. Dating to about 3800 BCE, the villages, spaced about two kilometers (1.3 miles) apart, consisted of flimsy huts of wattle and daub. By 3600 BCE, one of those villages developed into a town. No other villages at the edge of the desert are known from that time. Some of the rural population was incorporated into the emerging urban center, and a low Nile flood level caused some shifting of village communities closer to the river. South Town probably developed into an urban settlement because of its association with a religious cult and a shrine; if the custodians of the shrine were also involved in mediating community conflicts, the shrine became a center for solidarity among the villages, which were probably organized by kin-related lineages and clans. The custodians may also have been responsible for overseeing food exchanges and trade transactions among the villages, as well as between the villagers and the nomads of the Eastern Desert. The desert dwellers provided the Naqadans with desirable minerals and rocks from the Red Sea Hills, some of which included the much coveted gold and copper. Naqada established trade with Hierakonpolis, as well, where the development of an urban center was probably most related to its trade with Nubia and the Near East via Maadi; boats were used for river transport and donkeys were used for overland travel.

From 3500 to 3300 BCE, a decline in the Nile flood discharge and an increase in the demands for trade goods by expanding urban dwellers led to the integration of neighboring communities into large political units—territorial chiefdoms and petty kingdoms—as well as sporadic warfare. Fortified walled cities soon emerged, such as those depicted on the Libyan Palette. Each became associated with a mascot, or a territorial standard (similar to symbols, totems, or signifiers of tribal and ethnic groups). The political unrest and conflict did not lead to the emergence of city-states, as in Mesopotamia, perhaps because of the linear arrangement and limitations of the Nile floodplain. Instead, the course of Nile Valley urbanization followed a political transformation that led by about 3200 BCE, to the emergence of some subnational unity and, by 3000 BCE, to the unification of all the administrative districts under a single theocratic dynasty.

The kings of Egypt's first dynasty established their capital at Memphis, on the Nile, and by consolidating their power diminished the possibility of the rise of rival urban centers. A royal ideology was developed that bonded all the districts to the person of the king, rather than to any given territory. Some of the most powerful local deities were included in a cosmogony that removed them from their local political districts, to be embedded in an Egyptian cosmic space. The king was identified with a falcon god, Horus, who was the emblem for both Hierakonpolis and Behdet (which perhaps reflected their mutual affinity as trade partners). Horus, as the living king, was regarded as the son of the deity Osiris, who was regarded as the "real" first king of Egypt. Osiris was worshiped at Leopolis, Heliopolis, Memphis, Herakleopolis, Hermopolis, Busiris, and Abydos. The sanctuary at Busiris (Djedu) is mentioned in invocations formulae found in Old Kingdom courtiers' tombs. The cult center of Osiris at Abydos (Ibdju) is one of the oldest sanctuaries of the god and the most important. The wife of Osiris was Isis. Seth, a deity from Upper Egypt (Naqada), was amalgamated into the brother of Osiris. His wife, Nephthys, was Isis' sister. These divine personages were linked to a creator god Atum from Heliopolis in the Delta, in later times, the creator god was substituted by, or amalgamated with, Re (a sun god), Ptah, and Amun. Amalgamations and substitutions also affected Horus and Osiris. Various local gods and goddesses were introduced into religious rituals, ceremonies, and syntheses, and some became cosmic deities. (For example, Hathor—who might have been the "original" mother of Horus—was replaced with Isis.) Neith, the goddess of the city of Sais, became the "Lady of Lower Egypt"; Nekhbet of the city of Nekheb became the "Lady of Upper Egypt"; thus the two goddesses were called the "Two Mighty Ones," the tutelary goddesses of unified Egypt.

The association of kingship with a royal cosmogonic ideology created a theocratic conjunction of palace, temple, and tomb. The royal residence was associated with restricted cemeteries and temples. Temples, following a standardized plan, signaled the centralized authority of the king. The largest temples were associated with the royal capitals at Memphis, Thebes, Piramesse, and for a short time, Akhetaten (Tell el-Amarna). A major temple also existed at Heliopolis, the center of the royal cosmogony. At Karnak in Thebes, the temple of Amun-Re covered an area of some 30,000 square meters (321,000 square feet). Small temples were in the range of 1,000 to 1,500 square meters (10,720 to 16,080 square feet), whereas village temples were in the range of 150 to 200 square meters (1,608 to 2,144 square feet), with a national total of approximately two thousand temples. Some fourteen hundred villages then existed in ancient Egypt (compared with 956 in Egypt following the mid-seventh-century Arab conquest to 1,785 during the reign of Mohammed Ali Pasha, at the beginning of the nineteenth century).

**The Urban Population.** Egypt had some seventeen cities and twenty-four towns in an administrative network that linked them to the national capital. The urban population of Egypt may be estimated at 100,000 to 200,000 persons. The populations of provincial capitals and towns were fairly small, ranging from 1,400 to 3,000 persons. Kahun, Edfu, Hierakonpolis, and Abydos, would have been populated by 2,200, 1,800, 1,400, and 900 inhabitants, respectively. As the national capital during the New Kingdom, the population of Tell el-Amarna was about 20,000 to 30,000 persons. The populations of the older capitals, Memphis and Thebes, probably reached 30,000 to 40,000 at their peaks of occupation. (Population estimates for the cities of Mesopotamia include the following: 24,000 for Ur in the late fourth millennium; 34,000 in the third millennium.)

Egyptian towns and cities were not urban in the modern sense, perhaps similar to today's provincial Egyptian towns, which have an unmistakable rural aspect to them. The towns consisted not only of urban dwellers but also of rural people, such as farmers and herdsmen (who went out to the countryside daily), as well as the artisans, scribes, priests, tax-collectors, servants, guards, soldiers, entertainers, and shopkeepers. The kings, the nobles, and the temples possessed estates that employed a variety of personnel. Citizens not dependent on a great lord or an institution lived either in cities or on their own farms outside the cities. In New Kingdom Egypt, towns commanded a district (sp't); that included, in addition to the major town, some satellite towns and villages and a rural hinterland supervised by a town mayor and a supervisor of the fields, who was assisted by a councilor of the rural district. The district was in charge of the local temples and the collection of revenues, as well as the general maintenance of the basin irrigation system, accounting, the registration of land claims, and other economic and legal transactions. Cities and towns had not only palaces, mansions, and temples but also the humble dwellings of the functionaries and peasants and workshops, granaries, storage magazines, shops, and local markets—all the institutions of residential urban life.

**Cities and Power.** Regardless of their size, towns and cities were centers of power. In towns, the ruling elite (which included the priests, not just nobles) provided the fabric of the state ideology, as well the administration of major economic and legal affairs. Taxes were collected and transmitted to the royal house. Taxes were imposed on agricultural products, nonagricultural products, individuals, and officials. A vizier—sometimes two viziers, one for Upper Egypt and another for Lower Egypt—oversaw the collection taxes in the districts. The transport of taxes and all goods depended on donkeys and on Nile boats.

*A royal capital.* Of all the capitals of ancient Egypt, the archaeology of Tell el-Amarna provides the best information about the structure and organization of Egypt's principal seat of power. The city district was some 16 by 13 kilometers (10 by 8 miles), as marked by boundary stelae. The central part of the city was at the waterfront. The city commanded a large cultivable area that could support as many as 25,000 farmers and 15,000 nonfarming inhabitants. The actual population of Akhetaten was perhaps closer to 20,000—but with offerings, tribute, and taxes from distant lands, a much large population could have been supported. Tell el-Amarna comprised three cities: northern, southern, and central, with the king's house as its center. The North City contained a riverside palace, with massive fortified walls, perhaps the principal royal residence. Storehouses, barracks, and other buildings filled the courtyard space between the palace and the wall. A road, the royal avenue, connected the three cities. Across the road from the palace in the North City, were the residences of the court and high officials. Warehouses, granaries, and administrative offices extended to the north of the North City, which nestled under a cliff that was both imposing and well defended.

To the south of the North City stood a palace for the eldest princess. Beyond this palace was the Northern Suburb, consisting of private houses; it was bordered on the south by the Central City, with a prominent Great Palace, intended for royal receptions, public occasions, and religious display. The Great Palace was adjacent to two temples, one of which was the Great Temple of Aten. To its south stretched a residential suburb with a large stone temple; the residential areas consisted of interconnected "villages." The plans of the houses were uniform, consisting of domestic areas, granaries, animal byres, gardens, shrines, and workshops. The households were not secluded townhouses but were practically farm houses serving as centers for the storage, handling, and processing of farm products.

*A pyramid town.* Settlements existed where priests and others were responsible for the rituals and observances related to the mortuary cult of the king. One of the Middle Kingdom pyramid towns is Illahun (Kahun), at the eastern end of the pyramid complex of Senwosret II, on the southeastern edge of the Faiyum Depression. The town is at the edge of the desert, adjacent to the valley temple of the pyramid, a large square settlement, some 384 meters (1,200 feet) on the north and 335 meters (1,000 feet) on the west; it consists of a main part separated from the rest of the town by a thick wall, with no evidence of fortification. The town consisted of houses, perhaps a temple and an administrative center, with storage buildings and granaries. The large houses included a residential area, a portico, a garden, a granary, and workshops. The small houses—two hundred and twenty are still recognizable—are far more common than the large houses, with a ratio of about 20:1. The population was not likely to have exceeded 3,000 persons and was perhaps closer to 2,000. Estimates of the capacity of the granaries suggests that 5,000 to 9,000 persons could have been supported. The town was probably an administrative center; in addition to its responsibility for maintaining the cult observances, it also engaged in economic transactions, supported (occasionally or regularly) a dependent population in nearby villages, and/or supplied revenues to other officials or to the royal house.

*Fortress towns.* Clear examples of Egyptian fortress towns are known from Nubia, and they date to Middle Kingdom times. The Egyptian state had assumed a strategy to control the exploitation and flow of goods from Nubia; military activities by Egyptian kings in Nubia were conducted as early as the first dynasty. Following the First Intermediate Period, when centralized government in Egypt collapsed, Middle Kingdom Egypt reestablished control of Nubia by a series of campaigns and fortresses established to maintain Egyptian rule. Forts were built on flat land and on hills. One of the largest is the fortress excavated at Buhen, about 250 kilometers (160 miles) south of Aswan. The fortress was built on an Old Kingdom site and consisted of an inner citadel, measuring 150 by 138 meters (450 by 420 feet), which overlooked the Nile. The citadel was surrounded by a mud-brick enclosure wall 5 meters (15 feet) thick and 8 to 9 meters (18 feet) high. Residential areas surrounded the citadel and were adjacent to a temple. Fortresses commonly included towers, crenellations, bastions, and ditches. During the New Kingdom, the fortresses in Nubia were developed into towns, with temples and residential areas beyond the fortress.

[*See also articles on individual cities.*]

**BIBLIOGRAPHY**

Bietak, M. "Urban Archaeology and the 'Town Problem' in Ancient Egypt." In *Egyptology and the Social Sciences*, edited by K. Weeks, pp. 95–144. Cairo, 1979.

Butzer, K. *Early Hydraulic Civilization of Egypt.* Chicago, 1976.

Hart, G. *A Dictionary of Egyptian Gods and Goddesses.* London, 1986.

Hassan, F. A. "The Predynastic of Egypt." *Journal of World Prehistory* 2 (1988), 135–185.

Hassan, F. A. "Town and Village in Ancient Egypt: Ecology, Society and Urbanization." In *The Archaeology of Africa*, edited by T. Shaw, P. Sinclair, B. Andah, and A. Okpoko, pp. 551–569. London, 1993.

Jeffreys, D. *The Survey of Memphis*, pt. 1, *The Archaeological Report*. London, 1985.

Kemp, B. "The Character of the South Suburb at Tell el 'Amarna." *Mitteilungen Der Deutschen Orient-Gesellschaft Zu Berlin* 113 (1981), 81–97.

Kemp, B. "The Amarna Workmen's Village in Retrospect." *Journal of Egyptian Archaeology* 73 (1987), 21–50.

Kemp, B. *Ancient Egypt, Anatomy of a Civilization*. London, 1989.

Kemp, B., and S. Garfi. *A Survey of the Ancient City of El 'Amarna*. London, 1993.

Moret, A. *The Nile and Egyptian Civilization*. London, 1927. Reissued 1972.

O'Connor, D. "The Geography of Settlements in Ancient Egypt." In *Man, Settlement and Urbanism*, edited by P. Ucko, R. Tringham, and G. W. Dimbleby, pp. 681–698. London, 1972.

O'Connor, D. "The Social and Economic Organization of Ancient Egyptian Temples." In *Civilizations of the Ancient Near East*, edited by J. M. Sasson, pp. 319–329. New York, 1995.

Redford, D., S. Orle, and S. Shubert. "East Karnak Excavations, 1987–1989." *Journal of the American Research Center in Egypt* 28 (1991), 75–106.

Shaw, I. "The Settled World." In *Ancient Egypt*, edited by D. P. Silverman, pp. 68–79. London, 1997.

Storey, G. R. "The Population of Ancient Rome." *Antiquity* (1997), 966–978.

Trigger, B. G., B. J. Kemp, D. O'Connor, and A. B. Lloyd. *Ancient Egypt: A Social History*. Cambridge, 1983.

Troy, Lana. *Resource Management and Ideological Manifestation: The Towns and Cities of Ancient Egypt*. In press.

FEKRI HASSAN

**CLEANLINESS.** *See* Hygiene.

**CLEOPATRA VII** (69–30 BCE), sixteenth ruler of the Ptolemaic dynasty, Greco-Roman period, ruled 51–31 BCE. Despite the racist insinuations of Strabo (c.64/63 BCE–21 CE), who denigrated her lineage in the service of Roman imperial propaganda, careful study of the ancient inscriptional evidence proves beyond a shadow of a doubt that Cleopatra VII was born to Ptolemy XII Auletes (80–57 BCE, ruled 55–51 BCE) and Cleopatra, both parents being Macedonian Greeks. Cleopatra VII, called the Great, may have briefly shared the throne with her mother from 57 to 55 BCE, during the interval of her father's exile to Rome. In March of 51 BCE, she became coregent, at the age of seventeen, with Ptolemy XIII, her six-year-old brother, although at least one ancient Egyptian monument, dated to her first regnal year, described her as Egypt's sole monarch. In 48 BCE, the pursuit into Egypt by Roman general Julius Caesar of his rival, the Roman general Pompey, occasioned the death of Ptolemy XIII, by drowning, in a sea battle against Caesar. The younger brother Ptolemy XIV Philopator I was thereby elevated to the position of Cleopatra's coregent in 47 BCE.

Cleopatra's involvement with Julius Caesar began in 48 BCE and soon blossomed into an equal partnership, based on shared political objectives. To that end, she accompanied Caesar to Rome, was installed in opulent surroundings, and was presented as Venus (the mythological ancestress of the Roman race), an act in accord with Caesar's own imperial ambitions but perceived as sacrilegious by conservative Romans. In 47 BCE, she bore Caesar a son, Caesarion by name. His lineage was later denied by agents of Octavian, who became the emperor Augustus (r.27 BCE–14 CE), whose agenda it was to promote his own cause at the expense of Caesar's heir, whom they assassinated after entering Egypt in 30 BCE.

The assassination of Julius Caesar in Rome, in 44 BCE, had forced the return of Cleopatra VII to Egypt, at which time she murdered her brother and coregent Ptolemy XIV with a lethal dose of poison. In 41 BCE, she courted the assistance of Caesar's heir Mark Antony, who wed her in 37 BCE. She bore him three children—a set of fraternal twins and a second daughter, Cleopatra Selene. Together, she and Antony continued to implement her dream of world domination, eliminating all opposition at home, including that of her sister Arsinoe IV, whose murder they occasioned at Ephesus. On 2 September 31 BCE, Cleopatra and Antony challenged the might of Rome at Actium, in the ancient world's last sea battle. Recent excavations at Actium and a critical reassessment of the pertinent ancient texts suggest that Cleopatra's flight from that encounter was not due to cowardice but is rather to be attributed to a planned maneuver effecting her successful escape.

Realizing that her principles would be compromised if she effected a rapprochement with Augustus, and unwilling to subject herself to the humiliation of a Roman triumph, Cleopatra VII nobly chose ritual suicide rather than life as a captive. She took her own life on 12 August 30 BCE, eleven days after the ritual suicide of Antony. The means of her death remain unknown, although theories range from the bite of one or more serpents to poison, either ingested or pricked into the bloodstream with a pin. Her three children by Anthony survived her death, the twins being brought to Rome to be raised and the second daughter, Cleopatra Selene, eventually marrying Juba II, the king of Mauretania.

Hardly a beauty, as Cleopatra's coin portraits reveal, the ancient sources are, however, unanimous in their assessment of her intellect and political acumen. She was the only member of her Macedonian Greek dynasty who knew the hieroglyphs. Furthermore, she based the external trappings of her monarchy on the precedents provided by famous ancient Egyptian female monarchs, Hatshepsut among them, as were clearly demonstrated in her representations and the accompanying inscriptions at the temple of Hathor at Dendera. From both a Hellenistic Greek and an ancient Egyptian perspective, Cleopatra VII was a heroine, one who dared to assert her Greco-Egyptian legacy, openly consorting with and challenging the might of Rome. She lost. As a result, the triumphant Romans put their own spin on the legend of Cleopatra VII, casting calumny on all aspects of her character. They impugned her lineage and portrayed her as a vacuous sex kitten. The people of Egypt held a contrary view and honored the memory of this illustrious monarch. As late as 393 CE, Egyptians were still caring for her statues, such as the one on the island of Philae in the Nile, which was covered once again in gold at that time. So forceful was the impact of her real reputation in the region that subsequent queens of note, Xenobia of Palmyra (Syria) above all, were (in their biographies) cast in the mold of Cleopatra VII—so much so that it is difficult to discern their individuality.

### BIBLIOGRAPHY

Bianchi, Robert Steven, et al. *Cleopatra's Egypt: Age of the Ptolemies.* Brooklyn, 1988.

Murray, William M, and Photios M. Petsas. *Octavian's Campsite Memorial for the Actian War.* Transactions of the American Philological Association, 79. 4. Philadelphia, 1989.

Pomeroy, Sarah B. *Women in Hellenistic Egypt: From Alexander to Cleopatra.* New York, 1984.

Ricketts, Linda. "The Administration of Late Ptolemaic Egypt." In *Life in a Multi-Cultural Society: Egypt from Cambyses to Constantine and Beyond,* edited by Janet H. Johnson, pp. 275–281. Studies in Ancient Oriental Civilization, 51. Chicago, 1992.

Thissen, H.-J. "Kleopatra VII." In *Lexikon der Ägyptologie,* 3: 452–454. Wiesbaden, 1980.

ROBERT STEVEN BIANCHI

# CLOTHING AND PERSONAL ADORNMENT.

In general, clothing of pharaonic Egypt has escaped the close study that was applied to European costume of more recent millennia. This lack is gradually being rectified by textile specialists, but many misconceptions and gaps in knowledge are still obvious. One of the chief problems in the interpretation of artistic evidence is the extreme stylization of personal appearance in ancient Egyptian sculpture, painting, and relief. People, especially those of the upper classes, are often shown in clothing that is archaic, or at least entirely unlike the actual garments found in tombs. For example, women's dresses almost always appear to hug the body, revealing the line of hip and pubic area; by contrast, surviving ancient dresses tend to be loose. Artists were also anxious to "code" representations so that the subject's age, status, and function were immediately apparent. To this end, they relied on visual clichés of nudity versus clothing, elaboration versus simplicity, and archaic versus contemporary. Upper-class Egyptians are usually represented in their finest clothing, even when it is not suitable for the task at hand. For example, in the New Kingdom, a tomb owner might be shown plowing and harvesting in elaborate court clothing. This was a convention designed to indicate the subject's status and wealth. In addition, the artistic treatment of clothing was often influenced by the desire to create harmonious patterns of regular curving or straight lines; thus, folds or creases in garments were sometimes represented as if they were geometrically perfect pleats.

**Clothing as an Indicator of Social Status and Profession.** In Egyptian art, generally speaking, the more elaborate is the clothing, the higher is the social status of the wearer. Restrictive, bulky, or elaborate clothing was the hallmark of the supervisory class. Scribes are often depicted in ornate garments, the neatness of which would have been difficult to maintain, especially in the heat of summer; however, their pleated, enveloping garments are badges of rank and function, just as certain grades of priests might wear leopard skins over their shoulders.

Servants, entertainers, and those involved in vigorous activities are often shown naked, or wearing only a girdle (belt) or loincloth. For example, laborers of the Old Kingdom might wear only a sash around the waist or a loincloth. Boatmen and acrobats, to name just two professions, also wore loincloths. The sailors would have worn an additional, outer loincloth made of soft leather, with slashes for coolness; a square patch was left beneath the buttocks. Various types of leather, including gazelle skin, were used to make these garments. Clothing of pierced leather has been excavated in Nubia (where pierced leather girdles were worn by women until very recently), and it has been suggested that this type of garment was imported into Egypt with Nubian soldiers. In pharaonic times there is, however, little evidence that these garments were worn by women, though it is possible that some acrobats, such as the young woman depicted on a Turin ostracon, are meant to be wearing a leather rather than a cloth wrap. More frequently, girdles (i.e., bands of beads around the hips) were worn by dancing girls and female musicians. Dancers might also wear bead dresses, similar in construction to beaded shrouds, with the beads arranged in a pattern of large, open squares. The dress worn by the dancers is intended to accentuate rather than conceal their nudity, and to maximize their erotic potential.

**Royal Clothing.** With the exception of certain garments worn only by a pharaoh, there are relatively few distinctions between royal and nonroyal clothing, except in the subtleties of folds and knots (Simpson 1988). By the New Kingdom, both kings and queens are sometimes shown wearing relatively contemporary clothing. Queens begin to appear in the draped gowns popular in the New Kingdom by the reign of Amenhotpe II, while kings in similar male garments do not occur in art until the reign of Amenhotpe III. Kings are far less likely to be depicted on temples in "private" garb, however elaborate this might be. Small objects of furniture and representations of the king from the tombs of high officials comprise the great majority of images of the king dressed in the elaborate clothes of a commoner. Some of the best examples of royal persons in upper-class fashion come from the tomb of Tutankhamun. On the small golden shrine, on the back of the throne, on lamps, buckles, and other small items, the king and queen can be glimpsed in the flowing, draped garments popular at the end of the eighteenth dynasty. The queen wears variations on the wrapped gown, while the king wears a variety of garments, including a calf-length kilt.

Official artistic representations of the king make it clear that some garments were reserved for certain rituals. During the king's *sed*-festival (the jubilee), for example, he was required to wear an enveloping cloak. An ivory statuette from Abydos shows the cloak as being decorated with a pattern of very large diamond shapes, a detail not visible in other representations. These patterns could have been rendered in beads, tapestry work, or painting; examples of all of these decorative techniques have survived in garments from Tutankhamun's tomb. The tomb also contained imitation leopard skins, perhaps for his use as *sem*-priest. The kingly wardrobe also contained beaded aprons, belts, and tails, to be worn during various offering ceremonies and rituals.

**Clothing for Children.** Egyptian artists represented both slaves and children without clothes, but they are easily distinguished because children are often shown wearing jewelry and may have their heads shaved, except for the sidelock of youth. The artistic convention of nudity seems to have been an indicator that the person represented had not yet reached puberty; however, we should not regard this as a reflection of reality. Children certainly must have worn clothing at least part of the time—probably smaller versions of the garments worn by adults, as shown by surviving examples. In New Kingdom tomb paintings, children, especially young girls, are shown in long, elaborate gowns like their mothers. It is not certain whether this is meant to indicate that these are nubile daughters, as seems most likely. The daughters of Akhenaten and Nefertiti, for example, are depicted wearing adult pleated gowns from their earliest appearances on the monuments of their parents, although they may still be shown as naked children elsewhere. The representation of nubile naked girls on the handles of ointment spoons, mirrors, and similar objects was intended to be erotic, rather than a reference to age.

**Undergarments.** We do not know if women wore anything analogous to a brassiere, although such a garment might have existed. In the laundry lists there are mentions of sashes and bands, the uses of which we do not know. The British Museum contains a very simple garment consisting of a square of material, with a fringe on the bottom, which has been folded in half and sewn up both sides, leaving a keyhole neckopening. Miriam Stead in *Egyptian Life* (British Museum Series, Cambridge, 1986) has suggested that this was worn as an undergarment. A triangular loincloth was the basic item of underclothing, worn by all classes and both sexes. It was put on much as a diaper might be, with the base of the triangle across the back and the long end pulled between the legs and tied in front. These cloths, both laundered and previously worn, were sometimes included among the burial goods in both royal and private tombs.

**Men's Garments.** The garment worn by Egyptian men of all classes and throughout every time period was a wraparound skirt, usually called a "kilt" by modern scholars. It consisted of a rectangular piece of linen wrapped around the body and tied at the waist with a knot or fastened with a sort of buckle. The resultant garment went from the waist to the knee or below. The style could be varied with a squared end, a rounded end, pleating, or a starched piece forming an apron. Aprons might be rectangular, pointed, or bifurcated, or might consist of a large triangular piece of fabric, often elaborately pleated. Men certainly also wore cloaks, although these are not shown often in art. At the beginning of the Old Kingdom, King Narmer is shown in an archaic form of dress, consisting of the usual kilt with the rectangle of cloth made longer than usual, so that the ends could be pulled across the torso and knotted on one shoulder. A popular form of garb in the Old Kingdom was a kilt with a large triangular apron of stiffened fabric attached. Both kilt and apron might be covered in horizontal pleats.

In the Middle Kingdom, men began to wear longer and more voluminous outfits which stretched from the diaphragm to mid-calf. Some representations show a pattern of squares decorating these garments; the squares depicted are the creases left by the folding of the fabric for storage. By the end of this period, the "bag tunic" had been introduced. This was virtually identical to the women's long tunic discussed below: a rectangle of cloth folded and sewn up the side to form a sleeveless garment. Upper-class men might also be shown wearing fringed or unfringed cloaks wrapped tightly around their bodies.

It was in the New Kingdom that the great revolution in men's clothing came about. Male attire became more and more ornate, involving layers of draped or pleated garments, with additional pleating on aprons or sashes and sleeves. Men still wore kilts, but often with a "bag tunic" and elaborately draped cloak or shawl. The "sash-kilt," introduced at this time, consists of a length of linen

CLOTHING AND PERSONAL ADORNMENT. *Examples of New Kingdom clothing.* Clockwise from top left: shawl, child's shirt, sandals, child's sandals, kerchief. All from Thebes. (The Metropolitan Museum of Art. 30.3.11; 25.3.215; 10.184.la-b; 36.3.234a-b; 09.184.219)

wrapped around the hips and tied so that the ends hang decoratively in front, forming a sort of apron. It was generally worn over other clothing, especially the bag tunic. Certain older forms of clothing were still worn, including a type of kilt that wraps from the chest to mid-calf; this is the official garment of the vizier of Thebes in the New Kingdom. As is evident from the tomb paintings, fashionable men's clothing of the later New Kingdom often exceeded women's in complexity. A wealthy man might be shown wearing a long or short sash kilt with voluminous pleating, and a bag tunic with pleated sleeves.

**Women's Clothing.** Of the various styles of women's costume depicted in Egyptian art, the type of dress often referred to by modern scholars as the "sheath dress" is ubiquitous from the Old Kingdom to Ptolemaic times. Over those millennia, however, the symbolism of the dress changed. In earlier periods, it was worn by women of all classes, including queens and goddesses. The dress

was long and tubular, with shoulder straps. The straps were sometimes represented as if they went between the breasts; however, elsewhere they were depicted as quite broad and covering both breasts. The dress was also represented as if it were quite form-fitting, revealing the outlines of the hip and legs, but the real examples that have been excavated are much looser. The extant versions of those gowns usually have long sleeves, although one actually found on a mummy was sleeveless. That example is a "false dress," which forms part of the mummy wrappings; the limbs, and even fingers and toes, of this woman were individually wrapped to preserve the natural shape of the body, and the "dress" (front part only) was sewn on to complete the illusion. Other mummies have been found with these imitation garments, but the dresses on those bodies have long sleeves. The construction of these dresses was also discussed by Rita E. Freed in the 1982 catalog of the Boston Museum of Fine Arts' exhibition called "Egypt's Golden Age." In her opinion, these dresses were probably made by folding a single piece of linen in half and stitching up the side, then sewing on shoulder straps at the bustline to hold it in place. Yet the textile expert Gillian Vogelsang-Eastwood (1992, 1993) believes that the type of dress most often seen in tomb reliefs and paintings should be distinguished from the V-necked dresses found in tombs, and that it is to be interpreted as a wraparound garment, the straps of which are independent of the rest of the garment.

Goddesses in paintings and reliefs from all Egyptian periods continue to wear patterned sheath dresses of this type. The patterns are probably overdresses made of beads, like those believed to have been worn by dancers; however, it is certainly possible that the colored dresses were constructed of patterned fabric. The patterns and bright colors of the cloth could be achieved by painting or embroidery, or by tapestry weave. Bead overdresses that have survived are made of faience, usually strung in a large, roughly diamond-shaped net pattern. Although similar dresses are worn by "servant figures" in Middle Kingdom tombs, by the eighteenth dynasty only deities are represented wearing patterned dresses. In the New Kingdom, both male and female divinities are shown in brightly colored archaic dress.

From the early Old Kingdom onward, women frequently wore a dress consisting of a rectangle of fabric wrapped once around the body, with an additional half-turn to bring the corner up to be tied with its fellow at the shoulder. This dress may have become the breast-baring garment worn by widows at funerals and by professional mourners. These "mourning dresses" are tied below the breasts and are shown with gray streaks, representing the ashes that mourners smeared on themselves. The single-shouldered wraparound is used as a everyday garment, until it develops into the elegant eighteenth dynasty draped party gowns worn by queens and commoners alike.

This wrapped gown with sleeves became popular around 1350 BCE. It is one of the types of ancient Egyptian women's garments that were created by draping a large rectangle of linen around the body. This garment is essentially a rectangle of linen, with a self-fringe along one of the short sides. It was often made of diaphanous linen of the highest quality, but because it was wound twice around the body, it was not as revealing as might be expected. It was wrapped around the body and self-tied in front, leaving one shoulder bare. Judging from ancient depictions on statues and in tomb paintings, this garment seems to have been reserved for special occasions, such as parties and banquets. A few actual examples of this garment have been found. A piece formerly identified as the "shawl" of an eleventh dynasty princess in the Royal On-

tario Museum (906.18.41) may have been a dress of this kind. In the collection of the Metropolitan Museum of Art in New York, there are a number of eighteenth dynasty fringed robes of this type. Their fringes, as in all extant fringed garments from ancient Egypt, are formed from the loose threads at the edge at the fabric. The fact that these garments from the tomb of Senenmut's parents have survived in several thicknesses and weights of linen may reflect either seasonal wear or distinctions between "everyday" and "best." Vogelsang-Eastwood (1992, 1993) believes that there were not one but many versions of the complex wraparound dress, made from one or two lengths of cloth. In all cases, the garment consisted of a large rectangle of linen, with a fringe along one side. It might be draped over one or both of the wearer's shoulders and held in place with a self-knot or a sash. Examples of this type of gown are shown on statues of Nefertiti, on a few depictions of Tutankhamun's queen, and in numerous tomb paintings of the New Kingdom.

Another type of woman's gown worn in the New Kingdom seems to be a combination of the sleeveless sheath or short-sleeved tunic and a fringed, draped cloak or long shawl that covers one shoulder. The sheath/tunic is usually regarded as a variation on the "bag-tunic." Yet Vogelsang-Eastwood (1992, 1993) interprets the construction and wearing of these New Kingdom gowns quite differently. She believes it to have developed from the draped gowns of the eighteenth dynasty. This gown was especially popular in the Ramessid period, worn by queens and women of rank in reliefs and tomb paintings, while goddesses were shown in the archaic sheath dress. From the New Kingdom onward, depictions of goddesses and mortal women were kept distinct by skin color (yellow for goddesses) as well as by costume.

**Seasonal Variations in Clothing.** In art, there are few indicators of the changes in seasons and the variations in clothing these necessitated. The temperature of dry desert air drops quickly in the evening, and warmer clothing was undoubtedly necessary for night as well. Certainly, shawls and cloaks were worn by both sexes. The Museo Egizio in Turin has a great portion of the wardrobe of a man called Kha, which was found around 1900. Among the thinner garments was found a heavy-weight "bag-tunic" with tapestry bands along its side and neckhole; presumably, it was for winter wear. Although Kha's New Kingdom wardrobe may not be typical of all Egyptian periods, it does indicate that different types of garments were created for different seasons or travel to other climates. Samples of wool were found in burials from the earliest pharaonic periods, but until the Coptic period few woolen garments are attested. The exceptions are the woolen cloaks depicted in a few tombs. Presumably wool was not used for other types of garments because it was not suitable for creating the pleating effects that were popular in elite clothing.

**Materials.** During pharaonic times, the primary fabric for clothing was linen. It was woven in numerous weights, from "royal," through "fine thin," "thin cloth," and "smooth [ordinary] cloth." Spinning and weaving were recognized as specific professions, and Tayet (Tait) was the patron deity of clothmaking. Artistic evidence suggests that in the Old and Middle Kingdoms the professions of spinning and weaving were dominated by women, but by the later New Kingdom, males are shown weaving at the vertical and mat looms, which were probably introduced, along with new techniques of tapestry weaving, from the Egyptian empire. Women are depicted only using the older horizontal ground loom. Men are also shown beating flax stems or twining spun thread; both sexes are depicted spinning thread. The differentiation of labor and tools along gender lines may represent changes in both society and technology over time, but these distinctions appear in artistic representations that may not reflect reality. Both types of looms continued in use throughout Egyptian history; the horizontal loom presumably was used by those weaving at home, and the vertical loom in temple and palace ateliers, where larger bolts of cloth might be made.

In a satirical passage in the Sallier Papyrus, the author writes that the launderer's whole body is weak from washing and bleaching clothes. The strenuous regime for cleaning linen clothing called for rolling the fabric into a ball, wetting it, rubbing natron (sodium carbonate and sodium bicarbonate) into the cloth, and beating it against a rock with clubs. Excess water was then wrung out by tying the cloth around a stick and twisting it. The garments were then spread out to dry and bleach. Pleating was done while the cloth was wet, using a wooden crimping board. No hot irons or heavy weights were used in the process, nor, according to some authorities, any sort of starch. (This last point is debated: Miriam Stead (1986) thinks that there must have been a fixative, but Rosalind Hall (1986) feels that one would not have been necessary.) These pleats were so much a part of upper-class costume that they formed an element of the "uniform" of prestige and wealth. Although washermen are mentioned in satires on the trades and in the *Story of the Two Brothers*, women undoubtedly did much of the washing at home.

Artists generally represented only the finest type of linen in tomb paintings and reliefs, to emphasize the wealth and high social status of the wearer. Similarly, elaborate clothing which also emphasized wealth and status was depicted. Until the eighteenth dynasty, the clothes that the deceased were shown wearing often seem to have been archaic or stylized fashions. By the reign of Thutmose IV, there was a dramatic shift in the styles of coiffure and clothing shown in the tomb paintings. The new styles of draped, crimped, and fringed linen and of braided, curled, and layered wigs became the indicators of the wealthy of both sexes.

**Footwear.** Many Egyptians would have gone barefoot much of the time; in fact, it is sometimes said that they preferred to do so. Quarrymen and other workmen, however, received sandals as part of their pay; travelers certainly needed footwear; and the rules of etiquette stated that sandals were to be removed in the presence of one of superior rank. Footwear was thus another indicator of wealth and rank. Examples of sandals made from woven grass or reeds, rawhide, or leather have survived. In the Metropolitan Museum of Art in New York, there is a pair of rawhide sandals consisting of a sole of thick hide, cut to the approximate size and shape of each foot. Two loops of hide project upward on either side of the ankle and a third loop passes upward between the first two toes. A leather strap that passes behind the heel and over the instep runs through the loops. In the New Kingdom, upturned toes were fashionable; occasionally the toe was even attached to the strap. Solid gold sandals were found on the body of at least one pharaoh, but these were probably intended only for funerary use. In the Middle Kingdom, model sandals or painted wooden reproductions of them were put in coffins with the mummy. The most expensive and ornate kind of footwear worn by the living were those of leather, which might be decorated with painting, gilding, or beading. Tutankhamun owned a pair of sandals with the figures of the enemies of Egypt painted on the soles, so that he could crush his enemies with every step.

**Personal Adornment.** Since most clothing was probably white (or off-white), color might be added to an outfit with jewelry of various types. Beads might also be sewn onto a garment or worn as a separate overdress. The patterns of beaded garments are generally geometric rather than floral or representational. Jewelry, however, often had a symbolic or apotropaic value and thus contained hieroglyphs and images of various deities. Both sexes and all classes of society wore necklaces, bracelets, armlets, anklets, and, from the eighteenth dynasty onward, earrings. Excavations at the workmen's village at Tell el-Amarna have uncovered many thousands of small disc-shaped beads of blue faience, obviously the most popular material for jewelry at the time; these were probably arranged in simple strands, unlike the elaborate imitation floral collars depicted in art. Examples of the collars, composed of faience beads shaped like flower petals, leaves, and fruit, have also been found. Anklets and bracelets came in various types, from single-piece bangles to flexible bands composed of rows of beads. Anklets were more commonly worn by women, and some have a small claw-shaped pendant at the back. Bead belts or girdles were also commonly worn by women, especially dancers; however, these were worn under diaphanous clothing, or as the only garment. Men, including the king, were shown with belts that might be beaded. By the early eighteenth dynasty, there are the first representations of upper-class Egyptians wearing earrings, and by the time of Tutankhamun the fashion was obviously universal. During the late eighteenth dynasty, earrings of many varieties were widely represented, although they were much more commonly worn by women.

[*See also* Amulets; Jewelry; Leather; *and* Weaving, Looms, and Textiles.]

### BIBLIOGRAPHY

Barber, Elizabeth Wayland. *Women's Work: The First 20,000 Years.* New York and London, 1994. A popular version of *Prehistoric Textiles: The Development of Cloth in the Neolithic and Bronze Ages* (Princeton, 1991), the author's earlier scholarly work on ancient textiles.

*Egypt's Golden Age: the Art of Living in the New Kingdom, 1558–1085 B.C.* A Catalogue of the Exhibition held 2/3–5/2/82, Boston Museum of Fine Arts. Boston, 1982. The catalog of this exhibit (which contained objects from dozens of museums) includes some excellent summaries and examples of ancient Egyptian clothing and textiles.

Green, L. "Seeing through Ancient Egyptian Clothes." *KMT: A Modern Journal of Ancient Egypt* 6.4 (Winter 1995–1996), 28–40, 76–77. A general article, lavishly illustrated, on Egyptian clothing and textiles.

Hall, Rosalind. *Egyptian Textiles.* Shire Egyptology Series, 4. Princes Risborough, Bucks, England, 1986. A most useful book on ancient Egyptian fabric and clothing, and one that provides much information on how clothes were to be worn.

Hayes, William C. *The Scepter of Egypt: A Background for the Study of Egyptian Antiquities in the Metropolitan Museum of Art.* Pt. 2: *The Hyksos Period and the New Kingdom (1675–1080 B.C.)* Cambridge, Mass., 1959. A most useful book, with references to fabric and clothing throughout.

Janssen, Rosalind. "Ancient Egyptian Erotic Fashion: Fishnet Dresses." *KMT: A Modern Journal of Ancient Egypt* 6.4 (Winter 1995–1996), 41–47. This article describes the reconstruction of the dress in the Petrie Museum collection and proposes an interpretation for the specialized uses for garments of this type.

Robins, Gay. "Problems in Interpreting Egyptian Art." *Discussions in Egyptology* 17 (1990), 46. Discusses the issues behind the manner in which women's clothes were treated in ancient Egyptian art.

Simpson, W. K. "A Protocol of Dress: The Royal and Private Fold of the Kilt." *Journal of Egyptian Archaelogy* 74 (1988), 203–204.

Vandier, Jacques. *Manuel d'archéologie égyptienne,* vol. 3, Les Grandes Époques: La Statuaire. Paris, 1958. An important book that offers several sections on clothing.

Vogelsang-Eastwood, Gillian. *Patterns for Ancient Egyptian Clothing.* Leiden, 1992. Offers practical suggestions on how to make and drape ancient Egyptian clothing.

Vogelsang-Eastwood, Gillian. *Pharaonic Egyptian Clothing.* Leiden, 1993. Destined to be the major sourcebook for studies of ancient Egyptian clothing and textiles.

LYN GREEN

# COFFINS, SARCOPHAGI, AND CARTONNAGES.

The distinction between the three terms for containers to protect a mummified corpse is conventional. Coffins may be made of wood, metal, or pottery; sarcophagi are usually understood to be objects made of stone; and cartonnages are made of several layers of linen pasted together and covered by a thin layer of plaster.

The most important cemeteries of the ancient Egyptians lie on the western side of the Nile, the side of sunset and of the world of the dead; this explains several characteristics of the Egyptian tomb and its decoration. The deceased lies on the left side, with the head facing north so that it may look toward the east, where the bereaved approach bearing offerings. The eastern face of the coffin and the coffin chamber is therefore reserved primarily for the offering motif, while the western face displays scenes showing the burial and the tomb equipment. A pair of eyes is painted on the eastern side of the coffin, through which the deceased can watch the offerings, gaze on the rising sun, and participate in the diurnal journal of the sun god. The desire of the deceased to leave the coffin chamber freely and return at any time is made possible with the help of the false door façade which is often used to decorate the long, narrow sides of the coffin; this can be reduced to a simple false door on the eastern face alone, near the pair of eyes. Another essential idea is that of protection, ensured by the coffin itself and the preservation of the corpse; the repulsion of dark forces is guaranteed through apotropaic gods, which are listed in vertical lines on the coffin.

The Egyptian word for coffin is *ḳrsw;* the same root, whose meaning is unclear, forms the basis for the words for "tomb" and "tomb equipment." The coffin is also sometimes euphemistically called "Master of Life." Inner coffins are distinguished as *wt šri* or *wsḫt*, and outer ones as *wt ʿȝ* or *ḏbȝ*.

**Old Kingdom and Middle Kingdom.** The question of whether the royal tombs of the Old Kingdom were situated in Saqqara or in Abydos is still unanswered. Therefore, the first clearly established royal coffins date from the third dynasty. Stone coffins (sarcophagi) of kings from the Old Kingdom and the Middle Kingdom have been preserved. Some are very plain in form—a simple rectangular coffin with a flat cover—and some are more elaborate in design, with vaulted lids and crosspieces. The royal sarcophagi are sparsely decorated, the main motif being the false-door façade along the perimeter of the coffin. Bands of hieroglyphs are rare. These sarcophagi are notable for their precious materials, such as calcite (Egyptian alabaster), granite, or quartzite. They seem to have had little influence on the decoration of the coffins and coffin chambers of nonroyal individuals, perhaps because the king was able to equip his tomb with all the objects necessary

COFFINS, SARCOPHAGI, AND CARTONNAGES. *Coffin of Nephthys, twelfth dynasty.* This wooden outer coffin belonged to the noble family that governed Meir, one of the provinces of Upper Egypt. (Metropolitan Museum of Art, Rogers Fund, 1911. [11.150.15])

in the underworld. Private people were more limited, for financial reasons and no doubt by decorum, so they sought other ways of ensuring access to these desired objects, which were then painted on the coffin and on the interior walls of the tomb. By Predynastic times, the Egyptians enshrouded corpses in mats or furs and enclosed them in pots, baskets, or clay coffins. In some areas a wooden scaffold was constructed around the body; this may be considered a precursor to the later coffins. At this time, the dead were usually buried in a crouching position—a practice clearly maintained in the first wooden coffins, which are only long enough to accommodate a flexed body. By the second and third dynasties, however, coffins display some of the typical characteristics of the later stone and wooden coffins—they have vaulted lids with crosspieces and are decorated with false doors.

Coffins and coffin walls are decorated from an early date. The main motifs are initially the false door and false-door façade, which first appear on wooden coffins of the second and third dynasties, and later on royal and private sarcophagi of the Old Kingdom. A new phase in development took place in the transition from the fifth to the sixth dynasty, when Unas was the first king to decorate the interior walls of the tomb chamber in his pyramid with Pyramid Texts and false-door façades. As a consequence of this innovation, private individuals of that period also began to decorate the interiors of their subterranean tomb chambers, but they developed their own elements of decoration. In Giza, the walls were decorated with scenes of offering, agriculture, boating, music, and other activities, similar to the decorations in the above-ground tombs. During the Old Kingdom, typical friezes show containers and vessels, first on the walls of the

tomb, while the coffins remain relatively plain and devoid of decoration. At most, coffins have a pair of eyes and a horizontal band of hieroglyphs on the outside; and on the inside, a false door, list of offerings, and bands of hieroglyphs.

During the Middle Kingdom, the traditions of Giza and Saqqara developed into the Upper and Lower Egyptian styles. The Lower Egyptian style extends from the Nile Delta to Thebes, while the Upper Egyptian reaches south from Asyut. Development of burial practices among private individuals during the Old Kingdom was led by the highest officials of the kingdom, and at the beginning of the Middle Kingdom we find decorated tomb walls exclusively in the tombs of the highest officials of the Theban eleventh dynasty. During the subsequent period, mostly wooden coffins were decorated. Because the tombs of nobles were conspicuous, they were often prey to tomb thieves, so very few of their wooden coffins remain. The few preserved examples show, however, that while the decoration of these coffins is elaborate, they are in other respects basically the same as those of lower officials.

***Lower Egyptian and Upper Egyptian styles.*** The Lower Egyptian style, also known as "standard class coffins," is relatively homogeneous compared to the variable Upper Egyptian style. In the eleventh dynasty, the coffin is positioned in a north/south direction, allowing the deceased within to observe ceremonies at the offering site above ground. The interior eastern wall of the coffin is often decorated with a painted false door through which the dead can step out to the offering site. The pair of eyes painted on the outside is intended to enable him to see the activities at the offering site. Osiris is mentioned in the offering spell on the outer eastern side, followed by a plea for offerings to the dead. On the inside are painted offerings and a list of offerings, in lieu of a depiction of the offering ceremony. The western side of the coffin is decorated with the burial scene, where the god Anubis is included in horizontal bands of hieroglyphs, followed by a plea in which the dead expresses desire for a beautiful burial. During the eleventh dynasty, the frieze of objects is shown on the western side and on the narrow sides of the coffin. The objects shown are mostly those which the dead person carried in life, such as jewelry, rods, weapons, and clothing. Coffin Text spells, originally written on papyri, were copied onto the interior sides of the Lower Egyptian style coffins and are generally not restricted to a specific side of the coffin. Such specific references, however, do occur, for example in a group of coffins from Asyut with Coffin Text Spells 589–606. The most significant innovation of the twelfth dynasty is the transfer of friezes of objects onto the east side of the coffin and the addition of vertical lines on the exterior sides. During this period more objects are shown in the friezes, and even entirely new classes of objects, such as amulets or royal attributes.

The Upper Egyptian style exhibits strong local characteristics, although they are more difficult to date. All coffins of this style are decorated mostly on the exterior sides and have freely rendered representations of the human figures, in contrast to the Lower Egyptian style. Cities and towns such as Asyut, Akhmim, Thebes, and Gebelein develop their own distinctive styles. The coffins from Akhmim are decorated in a very simple fashion: the main motif is the food offering; below the offering spell on the east side, which asks for the habitual offering to the dead, a pair of eyes is shown to the right and a list of offerings to the left.

In Asyut, almost all coffins have vertical as well as horizontal bands of hieroglyphs on the exterior sides. In general, bands of hieroglyphs from this period consist of a single line; in Asyut, however, we find two or three lines. In addition to the offering spell, the lines often contain Coffin Text Spells 30, 31, 32, 345, and 609. Coffins from Asyut are easily recognized by these characteristics. Salve containers, offerings, weapons, fabrics, and other objects are painted in the rectangles between the vertical and the horizontal lines. On each narrow side of the coffin appear images of two children of Horus.

Sarcophagi in Thebes from the eleventh dynasty are decorated in an especially beautiful and careful manner. Most notable is a scene showing a cow being milked while the calf next to it receives no milk; this scene is sometimes also set in a papyrus thicket. Often a female tomb owner is shown holding a mirror while being attended by her maids. On Gebelein coffins, the most noticeable difference is the representation of scenes from the burial ritual. The deceased is shown resting on a stretcher surrounded by maids. Scenes depicting the brewing of beer also seem to be popular in this location.

*Other styles.* In addition to the Upper and Lower Egyptian styles, there exist two other Middle Kingdom types, both richly decorated. One of these appears only in Asyut. It is characterized by interior paintings whose arrangement is in contrast to the standard style. Here we find a theme of food offerings on the western side, while the frieze of objects is on the eastern side. The objects of the frieze are usually arranged in horizontal registers, but in Asyut the longitudinal side of the coffin is divided into laterally arranged rectangles within which the objects are painted. The second type is represented only by four coffins originating from Thebes, Gebelein, and Aswan. They too are decorated on the inside and are exceptional because they all contain the same group of Coffin Text spells, whose significance—and this is rare for this period—is emphasized with ornamental designs.

Aside from the types and styles described above, there is the court style, which was reserved primarily for members of the royal family. Court coffins are decorated exclusively with bands of hieroglyphs, in a very simple style. On some coffins the corners and bands of hieroglyphs are embellished with gold leaf. The thirteenth dynasty coffins from Thebes whose outer sides are painted in black constitute another separate group. Horizontal and vertical bands of hieroglyphs are painted on the black ground; these hieroglyphs are mutilated in a characteristic fashion, in which only the upper bodies of all birds and snakes are shown.

*Anthropomorphic forms.* The main coffin shapes used in Egypt are rectangular and anthropomorphic. In the Old and Middle Kingdoms, the body is usually placed in a rectangular coffin; there are, however, attempts to wrap the body itself and to imitate its outline. This development leads to the anthropomorphic (or "anthropoid") coffin. Early on, the body is wrapped in strips of linen soaked in various solutions for preservation. Representations of the face and other body parts are then painted onto these strips. Another technique is modeling of the body—or in some cases, only the head—in gypsum. This may have been the origin of the custom of creating separate cartonnage masks which were then placed on the corpse. The next phase in development occurs in the twelfth dynasty, when we find the first indications of separate anthropomorphic coffins into which the body is laid. These become more frequent during the transition to the thirteenth dynasty. They are placed, like the mummy, into a rectangular coffin, lying on the left side so that the dead can look through the pair of eyes painted onto the outer coffin. In the seventeenth dynasty the anthropomorphic coffin is separated from the rectangular coffin and becomes the

COFFINS, SARCOPHAGI, AND CARTONNAGES. *Drawing of a ḳrsw-type coffin from the Third Intermediate Period.* It is now in the Ashmolean Museum, Oxford. (Courtesy Günther Lapp and Andrzej Niwinski)

sole container for the body. The lids of these coffins are decorated with a feather pattern and are called *rishi,* from the Arabic word for "feather." They mostly originate from Thebes and are also used for kings.

**Eighteenth Dynasty through Greco-Roman Times.** The elaboration of coffin styles continued during the New Kingdom. Single coffins, particularly those made of cheap materials like pottery or reeds, indicate the low social status of the owner, although exceptions—richly equipped mummies buried in single cartonnage or wooden coffins—are known. Double, triple, or quadruple sets of coffins, one placed inside the next, are typical of middle-class and upper-class burials. These coffin ensembles utilize various combinations of materials and shapes: one cartonnage and two anthropomorphic wooden coffins, anthropoid coffins in rectangular sarcophagi; or cartonnages in stone sarcophagi. The materials for stone sarcophagi include quartzite, used in most royal sarcophagi of the eighteenth dynasty; red granite, typical in the Ramessid era; gray or black granite and basalt, from the twenty-sixth dynasty to Ptolemaic times; Egyptian alabaster (calcite), employed in the sarcophagus of Sety I; green serpentine; and limestone. The finest wooden coffins are made of cedar, and others of sycamore or acacia. Solid gold and silver were reserved for kings, while gilding or silvering of a coffin or its parts may indicate the owner's relationship with the king's or high priest's family. In all periods, coffins vary in quality of execution, having originated from various workshops. Even the best of these produced both custom-made coffins, on which the name and titles of the owner were inscribed during the making, and less expensive anonymous coffins.

Many wooden coffins, and some stone sarcophagi as well, bear evidence of usurpation. In some cases the coffin of an earlier pharoah was usurped as a powerful amulet; for example, the coffin of Thutmose I was reused for Pinudjem I, and the sarcophagus of Merenptah for Psusennes I. In most instances, however, usurpation was clandestine, perhaps because wood was in short supply; craftsmen employed in the coffin workshops arranged the changes. To adapt a coffin for a new possessor, craftsmen had to alter the names and titles of the first owner, and sometimes the general appearance of the anthropoid lid; for example, the characteristic traits of a twenty-first dynasty man's coffin (striped wig, ears, beard, and clenched hands) could easily be changed into those typical for a woman's coffin (monochrome wig, earrings instead of ears, lack of beard, and open hands). Gilded coffins were tempting to robbers, and the surface of many has been chipped off. The coffins belonging to King Pinudjem I, his sister, and his wife were damaged in this way, but some gilded figures and texts were left untouched, perhaps for religious reasons.

***Theological meaning.*** Cartonnages or inner mummiform coffins represented the deceased person during the burial ceremony of the Opening of the Mouth, often depicted in tomb paintings and funerary papyri. In these the coffin is shown in a vertical position, which explains the solid foot-boards of anthropomorphic coffins and cartonnages. When positioned horizontally, the mummy-shaped container resembles the dead Osiris awaiting resurrection. The figures of Isis and Nephthys are often represented on both extremities of the coffin, behind the head and under the feet, evoking the ritual of the Lamentations of Isis and Nephthys over their dead brother. These figures also recall a vignette in chapter 151 of the *Book of Going Forth by Day* (*Book of the Dead*), entitled "Spell for the mysterious head" (i.e., the mummy mask). The iconography and text of Spell 151 relate to the burial assemblage, and the mask accompanied by wig and collar is the most representative decorative element of anthropomorphic mummy containers.

The frieze of cobras and the feathers of justice of the goddess Maat on the upper edges of some coffin-cases, squatting divine figures (often armed with knives), and the judgment scene are typical elements of the figural decoration of coffins and sarcophagi. They evoke the Hall of Maat—the Double Truth—where the fate of the deceased in eternity is decided: the coffin thus plays the role of the Hall of Maat. After the judgment, the deceased took on the role of Osiris, the king of the underworld. Royal coffin lids reflect this idea in portraying the deceased as Osiris, with his typical scepters held in crossed hands. On private coffins, carved or painted representations of hands crossed on the breast have the same function. The coffin or sarcophagus, being a "residence" of the deceased identified with Osiris, was a theological counterpart of the Osirian kingdom.

The iconographic repertoire painted on the interior of mummy containers is also to be understood in cosmological terms. The deceased is placed between the figure of a *ḏd*-pillar (often painted on the bottom of the case, inside or outside) and that of the goddess Nut, represented on the lid, and thus between earth/underworld and sky, a position corresponding to that of Shu in the scene of creation. The coffin is thus cast in the role of the universe. In the twenty-first dynasty, this is corroborated by cosmological compositions placed on both shoulders of the coffin cases, representing the lower, Osirian part and the upper, solar part of the created world. The fourth dimension is alluded to by numerous scenes of the eternal solar circuit, scenes from the *Book of That Which Is in the Underworld* (*Amduat*), figures of the "goddesses of hours," or the Uroboros—the serpent biting its own tail. Numerous cosmogonic symbols (scarabs, *bnw*-birds, lotus flowers, etc.) made the coffin a symbol of the primeval hill on which the Creation took place; the deceased was identified with the solar creator god. The word for the inner coffin; *wšt*, means "egg," which evokes associations with the Creation myth of the cosmic egg.

Finally, according to another theological conception, the mummy container decorated with the principal figure of Nut and inscribed with a prayer to her played the role of the sky, which swallowed the sun every evening, became pregnant, and gave birth to it at the next dawn; this created a mythic model of the future rebirth of the deceased.

***Historical development.*** The different workshops undoubtedly varied in their respect for tradition and interest in novelty, so various forms of mummy containers often existed contemporaneously. This is particularly true for the intermediate periods of Egyptian history; by contrast, periods of political stability are characterized by more standardized shapes, colors, and iconography of coffins throughout the country.

*Eighteenth dynasty.* The *rishi*-coffins and rectangular chest-coffins, still decorated with the motifs of the Middle Kingdom tradition, were used sporadically until the reign of Thutmose III, but meanwhile a new type of anthropoid coffin spread in Thebes to become the most characteristic form of the early eighteenth dynasty. These wooden coffins—called "white" because of their predominant ground color—reproduce, in a sense, the mummy that in previous periods had been provided with a cartonnage mask and collar. An inscribed vertical band is painted in the middle of the lid and descends to the edge of the feet, and four transverse bands are painted on both sides of the lid and case of the coffin, in imitation of mummy bandages. Texts on these bands contain the common formulae *ḥtp-di-nsw* ("a gift that the king gives"), *ḏd-mdw-in* ("words said by the king"), and *imȝhy ḥr* ("revered before"), evoking the names of Osiris, Anubis, and the Sons of Horus. Figures of these mythical protectors of embalming and burial are sometimes painted in the panels between the texts, but the most typical iconography of the "white" coffins shows various burial motifs: the transport of a mummy, mourners, offering rituals, and so on. On the lid, at breast level, a figure of a protecting goddess (Nekhbet or Nut) is usually painted.

Once political conditions stabilized, Theban carpenters quickly mastered the technique of constructing and shaping mummiform coffins. The finest examples of their craftsmanship are the atypically large (over 3 meters/10 feet high) cedarwood coffins made for the queens Ahmose-Nefertari, Ahhotep, and Meritamun. These coffins accurately render the shape of the upper body, with portrait mask and arms crossed on the breast, while the gilded pattern of feathers covering the lower mummiform part reveals a link with the *rishi*-coffins. This type of adornment was in use for royal tomb equipment until the end of the eighteenth dynasty, including Tutankhamun's coffins, and probably also in the Ramessid era and twenty-first dynasty (e.g., the silver inner coffin of Psusennes I).

The complete nested set of Tutankhamun's coffins suggests what other royal burial equipment in the New Kingdom probably comprised. The mummy, provided with a golden mask and golden inscribed bands imitating bandages lay in three mummiform coffins; the innermost is made of solid gold, and the other two of wood covered with sheet gold. Figures and hieroglyphs impressed in the gold are inlaid with colored paste, glass, and semiprecious stones such as lapis lazuli and carnelian. In the New Kingdom, a set of anthropomorphic coffins was laid into a rectangular or cartouche-shaped stone sarcophagus, which in turn was surrounded by several chapel-like wooden structures, gilded and covered with religious texts and motifs. Of these funerary ensembles, only that of Tutankhamun survives intact; only the stone sarcophagi remain of others. Their iconographic repertoire comprises figures of Nut on the top and under the lid, Nephthys and Isis at the head and foot ends, and Anubis and the Sons of Horus on the walls of the case. Inscribed bands envelope the lid and case. Sarcophagi after the Amarna period also have figures of four winged goddesses carved at the corners of the case.

In the nonroyal sphere, from the reign of Thutmose III a new color scheme predominates in wooden coffins: figures and texts are gilded or painted in yellow on a black ground. The iconographic repertoire of these "black" coffins is constant: a winged figure on the lid, the Four Sons of Horus, and Thoth and Anubis on the walls of the case. This type of coffin is also attested outside Thebes, in Memphis and the Faiyum. The richest ensembles of "black" coffins—such as those of Yuya and Tuyu, Amenhotpe III's parents-in-law—comprised several objects: the cartonnage mask and collar; the "network" of bandage imitations lying on the mummy; two or three anthropomorphic coffins; and an outer rectangular coffin, shaped like a chapel and set on runners, which served for transport during burial.

*Nineteenth and twentieth dynasties.* In the post-Amarna period, there developed a new type influenced by the coloring of royal coffins. These "yellow" wooden coffins are attested from Thebes and Memphis. Figures and texts are painted in red and light and dark blues on a yellow ground; the yellow varnish that covers the exterior makes the blue appear green. In the coffin ensembles (e.g., that belonging to Sennedjem), the outer receptacle is still a chapel-like rectangular case on runners; the one or two inner coffins are anthropoid, with carved forearms crossed on the breast. On men's coffins, the hands are clenched and hold sculpted amulets, while those of women are open and lie flat on the breast. The mummy is covered with a wooden or cartonnage "false lid" or "mummy board," usually imitating the shape of the lid. These mummy covers consist of two pieces: the upper one represents the face, collar, and the crossed arms, while the lower piece, often made in openwork technique, imitates the network of mummy bandages, with figural scenes filling the panels between the bands.

In the early nineteenth dynasty a new type of mummy cover and lid was used. It represents the deceased as a living person, dressed in festive garments, with the hands either placed on the thighs (men's coffins) or pressed to the breast and holding a decorative plant (women); the naked feet are also sculpted below the costume. The wigs of men are of either the Ramessid duplex type or of the traditional tripartite, vertically striped type; women's wigs are richly ornamented with curls and plaits. Both the male "Osirian" lid and the "living effigy" type were also

fashioned in stone for the anthropomorphic sarcophagi of high officials. The innermost coffins of some royal sarcophagi are anthropomorphic (e.g., the alabaster case of Sety I), but others are cartouche-shaped.

In the twentieth dynasty, the royal sarcophagi were buried in crypts cut into the floor of the burial chamber and were covered with massive granite lids. Osirian effigies of the kings sculpted in high relief decorate the exterior of the lid, while the goddess Nut is sculpted on the lid's underside. Besides the traditional repertory, there appear scenes and texts from royal funerary books. The repertory of nonroyal coffins is enriched with vignettes and texts from the *Book of Going Forth by Day* (e.g., chapter 17) and with solar motifs (bark of Re, scarab, etc.). In most instances, however, only the traditional scheme is used, continuing the repertory of the "black" coffins. This pattern is repeated on pottery coffins of the lower classes discovered in the eastern Nile Delta, at Tanis and Tell el-Yehudiyya.

*Twenty-first dynasty.* Only anthropomorphic coffins are known from this period, mostly from Thebes, similar in form and coloring to Ramessid examples. Only wooden mummy covers are yet attested; these are made in one piece and are usually of the "Osirian" type. The last decade of Ramesses XI's reign brought revolutionary changes in iconography. The old motifs (e.g., the Four Sons of Horus, Isis and Nephthys as mourners, or the Nut figure on the lid) are never entirely abandoned, but a great number of new scenes are introduced. New motifs derive from the *Book of Going Forth by Day* (e.g., the vignettes from chapters 30, 59/63, 81, 87, 125–126, 148, 186), as well as from newly created compositions. The latter focus on cosmological deities such as Geb and Nut or the Serpent on *tnṯ3t* scenes that illustrate the god's activities during the journey through the underworld, the revivication of a mummy, the triumph over the Apophis serpent, the Osirian myth, and the eternal circuit of the sun. Each scene includes both solar and Osirian elements, illustrating the solar-Osirian unity as the theological principle of the period. This extensive repertoire is supplemented by numerous offering scenes covering every surface of the coffin except the exterior of the bottom. Texts comprising rather simple formulae are of secondary importance. Most of the figures are represented in small scale in an attempt to fill all empty spaces.

In the late twenty-first dynasty new iconography appeared on coffins as a consequence of the royal status gained by the high priest Menkheperre. This includes excerpts from the *Book of That Which is in the Underworld* and some other elements of royal iconography (e.g., scenes of the *sed*-festival). The pattern for an ensemble of royal mummy containers is furnished by the tomb of Psusennes I at Tanis. A two-piece golden mummy cover

COFFINS, SARCOPHAGI, AND CARTONNAGES. *Inner lid to a coffin from the twenty-first dynasty.* It is now in the Egyptian Museum, Cairo. (Photo by Andrzej Niwinski)

lay on the king's mummy, deposited in the innermost anthropomorphic coffin made of silver. This was placed in a reused Ramessid anthropomorphic granite sarcophagus, which was enclosed in another sarcophagus, rectangular in form, that had belonged to King Merenptah.

*Third Intermediate Period (twenty-second to twenty-fifth dynasties).* The early years of Libyan rule in Egypt exerted no visible impact on coffins, and the "yellow" type persisted in Thebes until the reign of Osorkon I. The frequent usurpation of these wooden coffins suggests illicit dealings. This may have influenced the introduction, under Osorkon I, of one-piece anthropomorphic cartonnage mummy containers. The multicolored, varnished decoration on a white or yellow ground utilizes such motifs as a winged, ram-headed vulture, a falcon with spread wings (both surmounted with solar disks), the sacred emblem of

Abydos, and the Apis bull with a mummy on its back (painted on the only wooden piece, the foot-board).

The political chaos of the middle and late Libyan period generated multilineal development of forms and decoration schemes. Richly painted one- or two-piece cartonnages (the latter also decorated inside) coexisted with variously shaped and decorated wooden coffins, originating from different workshops. First, there are coffins of traditional anthropoid form, with a case deep enough for the mummy, and covered with a flat or convex lid. Second, there are mummy-shaped coffins consisting of two equal parts, a shallow lower case and an upper lid, joined at the level of the mummy lying inside; a rectangular pedestal under the feet served as a base for the coffin in vertical position; and the back of the lower part projects slightly (the so-called dorsal pillar). A third type is the rectangular coffin reproducing the *ḳrsw* form, with vaulted roof and four posts in the corners. A richly varied iconography accompanies this plurality of forms.

This complexity increased in the turbulent times of the eighth and seventh centuries BCE, when a trend toward archaizing revived motifs of the Middle and New Kingdoms. In this troubled period, a scarcity of skilled craftsmen resulted in the widespread production of crude coffins, particularly in Middle Egypt and the Memphite region.

During the period of stability in the reign of Taharqa, however, coffins became more uniform. The inner coffin of a typical ensemble of this time is of the mummiform type with a pedestal; the "dorsal pillar" has a large *ḏd*-column depicted on it. On the lid, below the winged Nut figure on the breast, appear scenes of the judgment and the mummy on its bier. On both sides of the lid are small figures of protective deities. The inside of the coffin contains excerpts from the *Book of Going Forth by Day*, often accompanied by the figure of Nut. The outer coffin of the typical twenty-fifth dynasty ensemble is of *ḳrsw* form, decorated with solar scenes on its vaulted roof and the Four Sons of Horus on the side walls. A sculpture of a recumbent Anubis is placed on the roof, while small figures of falcons surmount the posts. Little royal material of the period is known; kings in Tanis were buried in usurped stone sarcophagi, but the falcon-headed silver coffin of Sheshonq is remarkable.

*Late period (twenty-sixth dynasty and later).* During the Saite period, the highest officials used rectangular and anthropomorphic stone sarcophagi. The former resemble the royal sarcophagi of the New Kingdom, with effigies of the deceased sculpted in high relief on the lids. The latter, usually of gray granite or basalt, are in general form and decoration replicas of the wooden "pedestal" coffins, though with a preponderant lid. Wooden coffins of this period have similar shapes. The flat lower part of the coffin serves merely as a support, not a container, for the mummy, because it is now covered with much more convex lid. Figural representations become less numerous, replaced partly or totally by long texts—excerpts from the "Saite version" of the *Book of Going Forth by Day*—written on the lid in vertical columns. Some wooden coffins of the Saite or post-Saite periods have carved decoration.

Innovations include the gilded cartonnage mask and painted coverings, consisting of several pieces, regularly laid on mummies. Figures of bound enemies now appear under the feet of the mummy on a separate cartonnage piece. The "bulging" coffin was prevalent in the Late period, alongside other types. The stone sarcophagi of the archaizing twenty-ninth and thirtieth dynasties used for inspiration not only royal compositions of the New Kingdom but even the much earlier Pyramid Texts. Types of

coffins and a "new generation" of complete cartonnages appeared, reproducing very old patterns.

At the present stage of research, exact dating of this late funerary material is risky. On the other hand, well-dated burials of the Roman period have been excavated in various spots in Egypt, including Thebes, the Faiyum, and Marina el-Alamein. These discoveries reveal the variety of mummy containers then in use: wooden coffins resembling the old *ḳrsw* form, with vaulted roof and corner posts; wooden anthropoid coffins with hands and portrait masks made of plaster and attached to the lid (these first two types of coffins have painted decoration with traditional iconography and hieroglyphic inscriptions); cartonnages "living effigies" of the deceased, in Roman dress; and mummies, bandaged in characteristic manner following a rhomboid pattern, and provided with portraits painted in encaustic on wooden panels (the so-called Faiyum portraits).

## BIBLIOGRAPHY

*Catalogs*

The series *Catalogue générale des antiquités égyptiennes du Musée du Caire* presents the world's most important collection of Egyptian coffins and sarcophagi. Relevant volumes include the following:

Chassinat, Émile. *La seconde trouvaille de Deir el-Bahari (sarcophages)*. Vol. 1, fasc. 1. Leipzig, 1909.

Daressy, Georges. *Cercueils des cachettes royales*. Cairo, 1909.

Edgar, C. C. *Graeco-Egyptian Coffins, Masks, and Portraits*. Cairo, 1905.

Gauthier, Henri. *Cercueils anthropoides des prêtres de Montou*. 2 vols. Cairo, 1913.

Maspero, Gaston, and Henri Gauthier. *Sarcophages des époques Persanes et Ptolémaïque*. 2 vols. Cairo, 1914, 1939.

Moret, Alexandre. *Sarcophages de l'époque Bubastite à l'époque Saite*. 2 vols. Cairo, 1913.

Niwiński, Andrzej. *La seconde trouvaille de Deir el-Bahari (sarcophages)*. Vol. 1, fasc. 2. Cairo, 1996.

*General Works*

Andrews, Carol. "Coffins and Sarcophagi." In *Egyptian Mummies*, pp. 42–51. London, 1984. Short introduction with numerous illustrations; besides coffins, outlines mummies, funerals, and tombs.

Brovarski, Edward. "Sarkophag." In *Lexikon der Ägyptologie*, 5: 474–485. Excellent outline of history of stone sarcophagi, with rich reference to the literature.

Buhl, Marie-Louise. *The Late Egyptian Anthropoid Stone Sarcophagi*. Copenhagen, 1959. A nearly complete collection of source material.

Donadoni-Roveri, Anna Maria. *I sarcofagi egizi dalle origini alla fine dell' Antico Regno*. Rome, 1969.

Egner, Roswitha, and Elfriede Haslauer. *Särge der Dritten Zwischenheit I*. Corpus Antiquitatum Aegyptiacarum, Kunsthistorische Museum Wien. Mainz, 1994.

Hayes, William. *Royal Sarcophagi of the XVIII Dynasty*. Princeton, 1935. One of the most important studies.

Hoffmeier, J. K. "The Coffins of the Middle Kingdom: The Residence and the Regions." In *Middle Kingdom Studies*, edited by Stephen Quirke. Kent, 1991.

Lapp, Günther. *Typologie der Särge von der 6. bis 13. Dynastie*. Studien zur Archäologie und Geschichte Altägyptens, 7. Heidelberg, 1993.

Lapp, Günther. "Die Entwicklung der Särge von der 6. bis 13. Dynastie." In *The World of the Coffin Texts*, edited by Harco Willems. Leiden, 1996.

Niwiński, Andrzej. "Sarg NR-SpZt." In *Lexikon der Ägyptologie*, 5: 434–468. A survey of history and decoration of coffins and cartonnages from the New Kingdom to the Roman period, with ample bibliography.

Niwiński, Andrzej. "Zur Datierung und Herkunft der altägyptischen Särge." *Bibliotheca Orientalis* 42 (1985), 494–508. A supplement to Verner, 1982.

Niwiński, Andrzej. *21st Dynasty Coffins from Thebes: Chronological and Typological Studies.* Mainz, 1988.

Niwiński, Andrzej. "Coffins from the Tomb of Iurudef—a Reconsideration: The Problem of Some Crude Coffins from the Memphite Area and Middle Egypt." *Bibliotheca Orientalis* 53 (1996), 324–363. A critical review presenting an alternative view of the dating and interpretation of coffins excavated in 1985 in Saqqara, published in Raven, 1991.

Polz, Daniel, and Hubert Roeder. "Särge (Kat. Nr 70–82)." In *Liebighaus-Museum Alter Plastik: Ägyptische Bildwerke*, vol. 3: *Skulptur, Malerei, Papyri und Särge*, pp. 302–389. Frankfurt am Main, 1993.

Raven, Maarten J. *The Tomb of Iurudef, a Memphite Official in the Reign of Ramesses II.* Leiden and London, 1991. Includes a chapter by J. Taylor on coffins from secondary burials in the tomb, which the author maintains should be dated to the late twentieth and twenty-first dynasty; cf. Niwiński, 1996.

Taylor, John H. *Egyptian Coffins.* Shire Egyptology, 11. Aylesbury, 1989.

van Walsem, René. *The Coffin of Djedmuthiufankh in the National Museum of Antiquities at Leiden.* Leiden, 1997. First part of a recent study of the early twenty-second dynasty coffin type, with imitation leather mummy braces on the coffin lid.

Verner, Miroslav. *Altägyptische Särge in den Museeun und Sammlungen der Tchechoslowakei.* Corpus Antiquitatum Aegyptiacarum. Prague, 1982.

Willems, Harco. *Chests of Life.* Leiden, 1988.

GÜNTHER LAPP AND
ANDRZEJ NIWIŃSKI

**COFFIN TEXTS.** Perhaps the most misleading term used to designate a corpus of ancient Egyptian funerary literature is the Coffin Texts. The term applies first to religious spells or chapters inked or scratched onto the insides of more than two hundred Middle Kingdom coffins from various sites. The edition of these spells published as *The Egyptian Coffin Texts* (1935–1961) includes only some of those texts: it excludes those that had been found in Old Kingdom pyramids, and previously edited as *Pyramid Texts* by Kurt Sethe (1908–1922), and those that were simply lists of offerings. Related texts that are included in the corpus of Coffin Texts are found on papyri, in tombs, and on mummy masks, canopic chests, biers, statues, and stelae. The group is unified by two features: first, by its position temporally between the Old Kingdom Pyramid Texts and the New Kingdom *Book of Going Forth by Day* (*Book of the Dead*); and second, by the fact that these texts were generally the earliest known to have been used for nonroyal men and women, usually high officials and their wives. The Coffin Texts come from sites throughout Egypt, including Kom el-Hisn, Saqqara, Dashur, el-Lisht, Herakleopolis, Beni Hasan, Bersheh, Qau, Meir, Akhmim, Siut, Abydos, Dendera, Thebes, Gebelein, and Aswan.

The manuscripts with Coffin Texts vary a great deal in their selection of texts and the quantity used. Sometimes very abbreviated versions of spells were deemed sufficient to stand in for the whole. In a few cases, more or less complete versions of small separate books were included; occasionally, different versions of the same book are found on the same document or on an accompanying document—for example, inner and outer coffins can contain variants of the same group. Some of these books are generally associated with a particular site, such as the *Book of Two Ways*, which is found essentially complete on most of the coffins from Bersheh, with only a small portion of its spells found elsewhere.

The *Book of Two Ways* is especially interesting because its two basic variants are centered on Osiris in one case and on Re in the other. Which was the earlier makes a real difference, and attempts have been made to show priority based on the contents, the variants, the coffins' owners, and the different styles of the coffins. The dates of the coffins, however, are still uncertain, and even if they could be clearly arranged chronologically, the sources from which their texts were drawn are still totally lacking. Moreover, some individuals in the Middle Kingdom obviously had both variants copied on their coffins in any case. If the contents and variants are the principal criteria used, it still seems that, based on apparent additions to the text—some of which amount to duplication—the Re version should have been the later development. This also fits in remarkably well with what has been termed the "democratization of the hereafter," which apparently accompanied the social changes around the First Intermediate Period. The nonroyal elite seem first to have been able to join, or become, Osiris, which should have been a royal prerogative originally; the next step was to join and even become Re, which had been the more recent royal goal.

A second significant group of texts within the Coffin Texts involves the Field of Hetep, which is often described as a paradise or Elysian Fields because of its verdant fields, lush orchards, and ample water supply. It is clear that some of the Coffin Text references emphasize that this is a place to work at producing what would become "offerings" for Osiris (a play on the word *ḥtp*, which also means "peace" or "rest" and is often personified as a god). Merely "living and rotting" beside Osiris must surely have been presented as a less desirable goal than sailing in the sun's bark.

These and most other groups of spells involve knowledge that the deceased should have about the afterlife. Very little in them would have been considered useful for a living person. Obviously, the geography of the day and night skies and the demons to be encountered at various locations had to be identified to be passed safely, and the deceased would also have to learn all the ship's parts to be a successful sailor on the solar bark.

Coffin Texts include hymns, prayers, descriptions of the afterlife, ascension texts, transformations, serpent spells, and offering lists—generally the same types of material found in the Pyramid Texts and the *Book of Going Forth by Day*. In fact, the Middle Kingdom coffins contain many spells that are close variants of those found in both these earlier and later collections, which interestingly have almost nothing else in common with each other. The descriptions revolve principally around three deities: the sun god, Re, whom the deceased joins or must guide in his daily circuit; the god of the dead, Osiris, with whom the deceased identifies himself, or herself and who died and rose from the dead to thrive in the west in a tomb equivalent to a mansion of eternity, living on abundant offerings; and the goddess Nut, who as mother of Osiris represents both the sky through which Re passes at night and the tomb—or, more specifically, the coffin/womb—from which Osiris is reborn.

There are a great many other mythological allusions in the Coffin Texts, as well as explanations that are at times both contradictory and syncretistic. The Coffin Texts, like the Pyramid Texts, illustrate how little dogma there was in Egyptian religion generally. Differing explanations occur, often side by side, sometimes made to fit together somewhat logically but more often presented as alternative possibilities.

Unlike the Pyramid Texts, which are generally confined to fewer than a dozen manuscripts and half as many variants, there are now more than 250 manuscripts of Coffin Texts, and often dozens of variants. While the number of variants is quite useful for establishing correct readings, the fact that so few of the documents can be dated precisely has made attempts at producing stemmata questionable. The need for some clear ordering is easy to see, but dating by stylistic features is also rather subjective. It seems that in one group or the other within the Coffin Texts an order can be established, but in another group the order might appear different. This is undoubtedly the result of our not having any of the original sources on papyri for any of these texts. The large number of spells (1,185) as well as the diffusion of these texts to the coffins of nomarchs, generals, scribes, and some important wives throughout Upper Egypt, are perhaps the most compelling features of this intermediate corpus of funerary literature.

[*See also* Funerary Literature.]

**BIBLIOGRAPHY**

Buck, Adriaan de. *The Egyptian Coffin Texts.* 8 vols. Oriental Institute Publications, 34, 49, 64, 67, 73, 81, and 87. Chicago, 1935–1961. The standard edition of the transcribed texts.

Faulkner, Raymond O. *The Ancient Egyptian Coffin Texts.* 3 vols. Warminster, 1973–1978. Translation of the de Buck edition.

Lesko, Leonard H. *The Ancient Egyptian Book of Two Ways.* Near Eastern Studies, 17. Berkeley, 1972.

Lesko, Leonard H. *Index of the Spells on Egyptian Middle Kingdom Coffins and Related Documents.* Berkeley, 1979. Arrangement of the spells on the individual documents, including parallels to the Pyramid Texts.

Willems, Harco, ed. *The World of the Coffin Texts: Proceedings of the Symposium Held on the Occasion of the 100th Birthday of Adriaan de Buck.* Egyptologische Uitgaven, 9. Leiden, 1996.

LEONARD H. LESKO

**COINAGE.** In essence, there was no money as we know it in pharaonic Egypt. For most of its history, the Egyptian economic structure was essentially homogeneous, with little private enterprise and a population that, for the most part, had marginal economic status. Given these circumstances, there was little pressure for the development of a system of coinage before the Ptolemaic and Roman periods.

This picture changed somewhat in the Late period with the advent of foreign mercenaries in the armies of the pharaoh. With soldiers drawn from Greece, Syria, Israel, Persia, and other areas of the ancient Near East came the institution of coined money and the expectation of payment in that medium. By the sixth century BCE, Phoenician shekels, Persian (Achaemenid) darics, and Greek drachms (drachmas) were circulating among the mercenaries. It is highly doubtful, however, that these coins were considered of any intrinsic value by native Egyptians, other than the artisans who worked in gold and silver. To the metalworkers, such coins were desirable as a source of bullion—an interpretation attested by a number of coin hoards that predate the conquest of Alexander the Great. These hoards contain a mixture of lumps of silver and silver coins from cities throughout the Greek world. The coins do not seem to have been specially selected, nor do the hoarders seem to have had a preference for coins of a particular type. Thus, beyond their value as metal, coins appear to have played next to no role in the Egyptian economy of the sixth and fifth centuries BCE.

A statement by Diodorus Siculus, the first-century BCE historian, that King Hakoris (392–380 BCE) of the twenty-ninth dynasty offered to pay Athenian and Spartan mercenaries in coin refers to what may have been the earliest use of coined money in Egypt. Even if true, the statement sheds no light on what coins Hakoris intended to use as payment. Later in the fourth century BCE, in the reign of

Tachos (362–361 BCE), coins based on the "Athenian" gold unit and struck on the Persian standard with Egyptian motifs were introduced. Although they are undoubtedly Egyptian, their dates remain a matter of controversy. One type of gold coin shows a horse on the obverse and the hieroglyphs *nfr* ("good") and *nb* ("gold") on the reverse. A number of modern studies say that these coins are extremely rare and that their circulation was quite limited; however, there are approximately twenty-eight known specimens of this unit—by the standards of ancient coinage not profoundly rare. Additionally, there are some small silver coins that have an image of the god Bes. Finally, a series of poorly executed tetradrachms that bear the Demotic legend "Artaxerxes Pharaoh" is believed to have been struck by the Persian king Artaxerxes III shortly after his conquest of Egypt in 342 BCE, a practice followed by the thirty-first dynasty satraps Sabakes and Mazakes. Dies of Athenian tetradrachms found in the Nile Delta have also been attributed to the reign of Artaxerxes. The presence of Egyptian motifs and writing on these coins of the fourth century BCE raises questions about their intended purpose and has led one scholar to assert that this money was intended to be used in Egypt by Egyptians. Yet there is little other evidence for Egyptian coinage or local mints dating to this period that can help to substantiate such a claim. It may be safest to say that coinage does not appear to have had any meaningful presence in the Egyptian economy before the conquest by Alexander the Great.

The coin types instituted by Alexander and his successors, the Ptolemies, were purely Greek in style and inscription. Like Greek coins, they were struck in gold and silver and were based on the denominations of the Greek drachm, a coin whose average weight was a little more than four grams. Gold and silver coins like octodrachms, didrachms, and hemidrachms are known from a number of Ptolemaic reigns. The Ptolemaic penchant for very large denominations in their precious metal coinage was not unique in the Hellenistic world, but the broad and unprecedented range of multiples of the tetradrachm was. The standard silver coin of the Ptolemaic period, however, was the tetradrachm, an imitation of the Athenian tetradrachm, a coin which had virtually become the international currency of the Mediterranean world in the fourth century BCE.

There were inherent problems encountered by the new rulers in the introduction of coin currency into Egypt. The silver standard used in the Greek world was based on a 10:1 ratio of silver to gold. Although gold had always been readily available from the south of Egypt and Nubia, and copper was also plentiful in Egypt, silver had always come from abroad. Consequently, the value of silver in pharaonic Egypt had always been very high, its ratio to gold at the time of Alexander's conquest being approximately 2:1. To produce a viable silver coinage, the Ptolemies had to import all of the silver needed for minting coins and were thus completely subject to the fluctuations of the silver market abroad.

One attempt to remedy this situation, at least partially, was to create a "closed" coinage system within Egypt, something that the Ptolemies seem to have done over the course of their rule, perhaps by accident. The first step in this direction was the straightforward reduction of the weight of the Egyptian tetradrachm by Ptolemy I, as early as 310 BCE. He applied reduced weights to gold coins as well by the time of his assumption of the royal title in 305. By the end of the reign of Ptolemy II, the average weight of the Egyptian tetradrachm was approximately 14.2 grams—nearly 3 grams lighter than the standard Athenian issue. In the reign of the same king, if not earlier, it seems to have become policy to allow only the Ptolemaic coinage to circulate in Egypt. All foreign currency was to be confiscated and handed over to the royal mints to be melted down and reissued. Given the lighter weights of the Ptolemaic silver coins, the reduction in their manufacture as silver shortages became more frequent, and the debasement of Egyptian silver coinage (for the most part, later in the Ptolemaic period) ultimately resulted in coins that had little appeal to merchants outside Egypt.

A second problem encountered in establishing a coined currency was that values in pharaonic Egypt had traditionally been based on weights in copper. For Ptolemaic coinage ever to gain acceptance beyond Alexandria, there would have to be a substantial coinage in copper or bronze, the metals to which native traders were accustomed. The introduction in the reign of Ptolemy II of bronze coins in multiple weight groups, the minting of which continued throughout the Ptolemaic period, may well have been an attempt to address this situation. Three of these weight groups feature very large coins, and it is perhaps no accident that the weight of the coins of the largest group corresponds almost exactly to the ancient Egyptian copper standard weight, the deben, at approximately 96 grams. Such large bronze coins were only sporadically known elsewhere in the Mediterranean world. The ratio of bronze to silver in Egypt fluctuated between 500:1 and 400:1, usually nearer the higher figure. It has been stated that at the time of the conquest of Egypt by Augustus in 30 BCE, the official ratio was 480:1. Thus, in the Ptolemaic period there appears to have been a move in the direction of a dual currency in Egypt: a silver-based currency used for foreign trade, and a copper standard for internal trade. Certain factors, however—the low frequency of counterfeit or cast coins, evidence from documents that most native people continued to trade in kind, and the low incidence of Ptolemaic coins found in Egypt outside of Alexandria—underscore the reality that coin currency of the Ptolemies was not a highly successful economic institution among native Egyptians.

The principal sources for the currency of the early Ptolemies were the mints in Alexandria in Egypt and those in Tyre and Sidon in Phoenicia. Some coins came from Cyprus, but it was not until the loss of Phoenicia and Coele-Syria shortly after the death of Ptolemy IV that Cyprus became a principal supplier of Ptolemaic coinage, a role that its mints played from 200 to 80 BCE.

Gold and silver coins of the Ptolemaic period typically show a profile bust on the obverse (front). Modeled on a very popular coin type, minted by Greek rulers in the Near East—the so-called Hellenistic ruler portrait-coin—such coins bear an image of the ruler under whom they were minted or of a distinguished ancestor, as well as motifs that connect him with important family members, heroes, and even gods. Such coins were often used to publicize claims to legitimacy, political prowess, or military success. After the initial coinage of Alexander, which shows him wearing an elephant-skin headdress, the particularly distinctive feature of Ptolemaic period coinage is the repeated use of the bust of Ptolemy I on the obverse throughout the period. There were, of course, variations: Ptolemy II, for example, minted coins with the jugate (paired) busts of his parents, Ptolemy I and Berenike I; he struck another series with the jugate busts of himself and his sister-wife Arsinoe II. Some tetradrachms and octodrachms have jugate busts on both obverse and reverse. He commemorated the death of Arsinoe with the issue of gold and silver coins that have her veiled head on the obverse. Ptolemy III authorized a silver and gold coinage struck in honor of his wife Berenike. Ptolemy IV minted coins honoring his father, showing him with the radiate crown of Helios, the aegis of Zeus, or the trident of Poseidon on the obverse. The legendary Cleopatra VII struck several series of silver coins, apparently at the mint in Askalon, with her portrait on the obverse. On the reverse (back), Ptolemaic coins have an extremely limited number of motifs. Most (more than 95 percent) show a single cornucopia (on gold coins) or a single eagle or pair of eagles astride a thunderbolt (on silver and bronze coins). Scholars have attempted to use the portrait coins to identify portraits of Ptolemaic rulers known from other media, such as cameos, seals, and sculpture. Some have seen in the bust of an obese ruler an image of Ptolemy VIII, who had the nickname Physkon ("pot-belly") assigned to him by ancient writers, but this interpretation remains controversial. The coins of Cleopatra, however, attest clearly to her legendary nose.

Our knowledge of Ptolemaic bronze coinage is more problematic. Very little is securely known about the dates and means of its manufacture. The motifs and legends used on bronze coins from any given reign appear largely to follow those of the contemporary gold and silver coinage. The most frequently used image for the obverse is the head of Ptolemy I with a large beard and the horns of a ram, both attributes of the god Zeus-Ammon. The most common icon found on the reverse is an eagle astride a thunderbolt. Interesting variations are encountered: one example from a series of bronze coins dating to the reign of Cleopatra VII depicts her as Aphrodite, holding her son Caesarion in the guise of Eros or Cupid. She also struck a great many bronze eighty- and forty-drachm portrait pieces at Alexandria.

Following the conquest of Egypt by the Roman emperor Augustus (r. 27 BCE–14 CE), his special treatment of the country had a profound and lasting impact on Egyptian coinage until the reign of Diocletian. There was no minting of silver until the reign of Tiberius, who first followed the debased system of coinage in use in the reign of Cleopatra, beginning with coins that are 46 percent fine. By the reign of Nero, such coins are only 17 percent fine. Tiberius also took steps to continue the closed coinage system of later Ptolemaic policy to ensure that Egypt would remain economically isolated from the rest of the empire. The coins struck in Egypt by the Roman rulers were of markedly inferior quality. There seems to have been virtually no movement of coins into or out of the country during this period. It was not until the end of the third century CE and the currency reforms of Diocletian (intended to standardize the currency of the Roman Empire) that debased Roman coins seem to have been present in Egypt. They have been found, however, in far fewer numbers than Alexandrian coins. Between the reigns of Augustus and Diocletian, the mint output at Alexandria fluctuated dramatically, the highest periods of production corresponding to the months immediately preceding tax collection.

The motifs on the obverse of coins from Roman Egypt were borrowed from purely pharaonic sources as well as from Ptolemaic and Roman coinage: imperial portraits and busts of deified emperors, as well as those of empresses. By the second century CE, images of Greek and hybrid Greco-Egyptian gods appear commonly alongside those of traditional Egyptian gods like Ptah and Khnum. From as early as the reign of Augustus, the reverses show a variety of stock types as well as a growing interest in specifically Egyptian motifs like sphinxes, hippopotami, crocodiles, ibises, and the lighthouse at Pharos, none of which are found on Ptolemaic coins. A series of coins called "nome coins" was produced at Alexandria, with personifications of the nome gods and their attributes as common motifs. Although seemingly connected with the nomes, there is no evidence that these were distributed in the nome capitals. Despite the fact that the special coinage re-created by the Romans was highly imaginative and prolific in its choice and range of motifs, it was no more successful than that of the Ptolemies. Contemporary documents attest to the far more common practice of trading in kind (wine, oil, and beer) outside of Alexandria before the economic reforms of Diocletian. The native Egyptians seemed to have eschewed using coins for anything other than the payment of taxes.

[*See also* Prices and Payment; *and* Weights and Measures.]

### BIBLIOGRAPHY

Christiansen, E. *The Roman Coins of Alexandria: Quantitative Studies: Nero, Trajan, Septimius Severus.* Copenhagen, 1988. A comprehensive survey of coins originating from the mint at Alexandria during the reigns of three Roman emperors.

Daumas, F. "Le problème de la monnaie dans l'Égypte antique avant Alexandre." *Mélanges de l'école française de Rome: Antiquité* 89 (1977), 426–442. An important study of the sporadic attempts at coinage in Egypt before Alexander the Great.

Haatvedt, R. A. *Coins from Karanis: The University of Michigan Excavations 1924–1935.* Ann Arbor, 1964. A useful overview of Ptolemaic and Roman coins found at a single site in Egypt.

Kromann, A. and O. Mørkholm. *Sylloge nummorum Graecorum: The Royal Collection of Coins and Medals, Danish National Museum.* Vol. 8: *The Ptolemies.* Copenhagen, 1977.

Svrounos, I. N. *Ta nomismati tou kratous Ptolemaion.* Athens, 1904–1908. This work remains the most comprehensive study of Ptolemaic coinage to date, still useful though outdated.

PAUL F. O'ROURKE

**COLOR SYMBOLISM.** The use of color in art and its symbolic value depended on the range of pigments available; for example, a blue pigment was introduced in ancient Egypt about 2550 BCE. Much color use—whether in visual or written materials—was ultimately based on natural colors, but it was schematic, used to indicate the class of object depicted rather than its relationship to a specific object at a specific time. In addition to natural coloring, there were nonrealistic uses of color, as, for example, the skin color of some gods. Color choices were also, in many instances, governed by systems of patterning. Both the realistic and the nonrealistic uses of color carried symbolic meaning.

In Old Egyptian, basic color terminology was more restricted than the range of colors actually used in art: Old Egyptian had four basic color terms—*km*, *ḥd*, *dšr*, and *w3d*. Other terms were secondary. Although color terms rarely translate exactly from one language to another, the general range of those terms is not in doubt. *Km* corresponds to "black" and had been used as a pigment from prehistoric times. In dynastic times, it was considered the color of the fertile soil of *kmt* ("the Black Land"), one of

the names for Egypt; it therefore carried connotations of fertility and regeneration. It was also the color of the underworld, where the sun was regenerated each night. The deity Osiris, ruler of the underworld, was referred to in texts as *kmjj* ("the black one"), which not only alluded to his role in the underworld but also to his resurrection after he was murdered. Black stones were used in statuary to evoke the regenerative qualities of Osiris and the underworld. During some periods, coffins were given a black ground as a reference to the underworld, to Osiris, and to the renewal of the deceased.

The term for "white" was *ḥd*. Like black, it was also a pigment from prehistoric times. White was associated with purity, so it was the color of the clothes worn by ritual specialists. The notion of purity may have underlain the use of white calcite for temple floors. The word *ḥd* also meant the metal "silver," and it could incorporate the notion of "light"; thus the sun was said to "whiten" the land at dawn.

The term *w3d* seems to have had its focus in "green" (as the term for "malachite," a green mineral), but it may also have included "blue." Green had been used as a pigment from prehistoric times. The term *w3d* was written with a hieroglyph that represented a green papyrus stem and umbel; it also carried connotations of fresh vegetation, vigor, and regeneration—giving it very positive and beneficial symbolism. For example, the deity Osiris was frequently shown with green skin, to signify his resurrection, and in the twenty-sixth dynasty, coffin faces were often painted green to identify the deceased with Osiris and to guarantee rebirth. In the *Book of Going Forth by Day* (*Book of the Dead*), chapters 159 and 160 are for making a *w3d*-amulet of green feldspar, although the known amulets show that a variety of materials were used, ranging in color from green to light blue. Such amulets were included in funerary furnishings to ensure the regeneration of the deceased.

The most valued of the green stones was *mfk3t* ("turquoise"), which was mined in the Sinai. This stone was connected to the deity Hathor, who was called "Lady of Turquoise," as well as to the sun at dawn, whose disk or rays might be described as turquoise and whose rising was said "to flood the land with turquoise." Because the color turquoise was associated with the rebirth of the sun, it promised rebirth in a funerary context, so turquoise-colored faience wares were often used as items of funerary equipment.

There was no basic color term in Old Egyptian for "blue," and there was no blue pigment until about 2550 BCE, with the introduction of one, based on grinding lapis lazuli (Lat., "azure stone"), a deep blue stone flecked with golden impurities. Blue was therefore not part of the original system of color symbolism found in texts, although it became the most prestigious paint color, owing in part to its initial rarity. Because lapis lazuli had to be imported, it was a very prestigious material, which may provide one of the reasons for the high value placed on the color blue in art. In Old Egyptian, "lapis lazuli" was called *ḥsbḏ*, and the term was then extended to mean, secondarily, the color "blue." The stone, and by extension its rich blue color, was associated with the night sky—often rendered in dark blue paint with yellow stars—and with the primordial waters, out of which the new sun was born each day; the rising sun was sometimes called the "child of lapis lazuli." From the post-Amarna period, the deity Amun-Re was normally given blue skin, to symbolize both his role as the creator god who came out of the primordial waters and his nightly regeneration as he passed through the primordial waters in the underworld. Items of funerary equipment made of blue faience were to harness the regenerative properties of the color.

The last basic color term was *dšr*, written with a hieroglyph that represented a flamingo; it is a warm color, with its focus in red, but it also included yellow and orange, for which there were no basic terms. Red was a pigment used from the earliest prehistoric times. It was considered a very potent color, hot and dangerous, but also life-giving and protective. It is both the color of blood, a substance that relates to life and death, and of fire, which may be beneficial or destructive. It is also a color frequently given to the sun, which may be red at its rising or at its setting, and which can overwhelm with its heat or warm to bring life. In contrast to *kmt* (the fertile "Black Land"), the term *dšrt* ("the red land") referred to the desert, which was inimical to human life and agriculture; it was the domain of the god Seth, who represented chaos, who both threatened the order of the world and helped maintain it by protecting the sun god in his nightly passage through the underworld. The dangerous, uncontrolled aspects of red connected the color to notions of anger, as in the expression *dšr jb* ("red of heart"), meaning "furious" or "raging."

In texts, rubrics (Lat., "red pigments") were often used to emphasize headings, but red ink was also sometimes used to write the names of dangerous entities. For example, in calendars of lucky and unlucky days, the lucky days were written in black and the unlucky ones in red. In execration rituals, red ink was used for the names and figures of enemies, and in many religious and magical texts, the names of dangerous beings, such as Seth and Apophis, were written in red. By contrast, the name of Re is written in black, even in rubrics.

Stones such as rosey or golden quartzite and red granite had solar significance, because of their colors, and they could be used to invoke the regenerative properties of the solar cycle. Royal statuary made of such stones stressed the solar aspect of the kingship. In jewelry, the most frequently occurring red stones were *ḥnmt* ("red jasper"), mostly used for beads and amulets, and *ḥrst* ("carnelian"), mostly used for inlay. Chapter 156 of the *Book of Going Forth by Day* contains the recitation and instructions for activating an Isis-knot amulet of red jasper. The recitation begins: "You have your blood, O Isis. You have your power," showing the connection between blood, power, and the color red. In Greco-Roman times, *ḥrst* acquired the meaning of "sadness" or "sorrow," perhaps because of an increasing emphasis on the negative aspects of red. The stone was unlikely to have carried such negative connotations earlier, because of its popularity as a jewelry component. In the Middle and New Kingdoms, the most frequent combination of stones in inlaid jewelry consisted of lapis lazuli, turquoise, and carnelian. By analogy with the positive symbolism attached to the first two, it seems reasonable to assume that the red carnelian was then valued for its life-giving potential and for its apotropaic (safeguarding) properties. Wearers thereby might harness the potentially dangerous powers of red for their own protection and benefit.

Although yellow occurred as a pigment from prehistoric times, there was no basic color term for it in Old Egyptian, unless it was included in *dšr*. Like red, it was used as a color for the sun disk and so carries solar significance. In art, yellow pigment was often used to represent the metal "gold" (*nbw*), and gold, too, was closely associated with the sun god, who was said "to be made of gold" and "to flood the Two Lands with gold." In the eighteenth dynasty, black-ground coffins were decorated in yellow or gold, symbolizing the nightly renewal of the sun in the underworld, from which it rose each morning.

According to texts, gold was not only associated with the sun but also was the flesh of the gods. Re's bones were said to be of silver, his flesh of gold, and his hair of true lapis lazuli. The divine snake (in the *Story of the Shipwrecked Sailor*) had a body covered with gold and eyebrows of true lapis lazuli. Descriptions of divine cult statues indicate that they were fashioned from precious metals and stones. One of the very few surviving cult statues is made of solid silver, originally overlaid with gold; the hair is inlaid with lapis lazuli. Those three minerals were considered to be solidified celestial light, and they were fitted to form the bodies of deities.

Although the painted images of deities in temple reliefs and elsewhere were often shown with blue hair, their skin color seldom indicated gold flesh. Most male deities were represented with reddish-brown skin; most female deities with yellow skin, similar to the colors used to differentiate human figures. Nevertheless, other colors, such as the green skin of Osiris, also occurred. Osiris was occasionally shown with black skin, to refer to the renewing properties of Egypt's black soil and the underworld. The jackal that represented the deities Wepwawet and Anubis was also shown in black (although the majority of jackals are sandy-colored), to signify the funerary role of those gods and their connection with the underworld. The reference of black to fertility also makes it a suitable color for the ithyphallic figures of Min and Amun-Re (-Kamutef).

Black skin was given to some royal images, to signify the king's renewal and transformation. Although throughout his funerary temple at Deir el-Bahri, the eleventh dynasty king Nebhepetre Montuhotep I was regularly shown in relief and in statuary with reddish-brown skin, one statue found ritually buried shows the king with black skin, to symbolize his renewal in the afterlife and possibly his identification with Osiris. A fragment of relief, on which the king is suckled by the Hathor cow, shows him with black skin, to portray the transformation caused by the divine milk. The eighteenth dynasty king, Amenhotpe II, erected a statue group at Deir el-Bahri to illustrate the same theme. There, however, the image of the king being suckled had the normal reddish-brown skin—but in a second royal image, the transformation of the king was symbolized by his black skin, as he stood beneath the head of the Hathor cow.

The association of black with the underworld and its transformatory powers explains the black statues of the king that were buried in the royal tomb of Tutankhamun and in other New Kingdom royal tombs. For similar reasons, the faces on nonroyal coffins were, during some periods, also painted black. The most common color for coffin faces, however, apart from "natural" red (male) and yellow (female) was gold, which both showed the owner of the coffin as successfully transformed into a divine being and also linked the deceased with the sun god, whose endless cycle he or she hoped to join.

From the eighteenth dynasty onward, figures of Amun-Re were depicted as blue. The color referred both to the primordial waters of lapis lazuli and to the blue of the sky across which the sun travels. The lapis lazuli blue skin set the god apart from the other deities, emphasizing his status as "king of the gods": the most important god was given a body of the most precious stone. Perhaps a lapis lazuli cult statue of the god once existed.

Goddesses show far less variation in skin color than gods, usually being depicted with the yellow skin also given to human women. When male deities are shown with a reddish-brown skin, they have the color normally given to human men. Thus, the gender distinction encoded for human figures was transferred at times to the divine world. The symbolism inherent in the skin colors used for some deities and royal figures suggest that the colors given to human skin—although initially seeming to be naturalistic—might also be symbolic. Male and female skin colors were most probably not uniform among the entire population of Egypt, with pigmentation being darker in the South (closer to sub-Saharan Africans) and lighter in the North (closer to Mediterranean Near Easterners). A woman from the South would probably have had darker skin than a man from the North. Thus, the colorations used for skin tones in the art must have been schematic (or symbolic) rather than realistic; the clear gender distinction encoded in that scheme may have been based on elite ideals relating to male and female roles, in which women's responsibilities kept them indoors, so that they spent less time in the sun than men. Nevertheless, the significance of the two colors may be even deeper, marking some as yet unknown but fundamental difference between men and women in the Egyptian worldview.

The choice of the single red-brown color to represent the Egyptian man, rather than a more realistic range of shades, should also be considered within a wider symbolic scheme that included the representation of foreigners. The foreign men to the north and west of Egypt were depicted by yellow skin (similar to that of traditional Egyptian women); men to the south of Egypt were given black skin. Although undoubtedly some Egyptians' skin pigmentation differed little from that of Egypt's neighbors, in the Egyptian worldview foreigners had to be plainly distinguished. Thus Egyptian men had to be marked by a common skin color that contrasted with images of non-Egyptian men. That Egyptian women shared their skin color with some foreign men scarcely mattered, since the Egyptian male is primary and formed the reference point in these two color schemes—contrasting in one with non-Egyptian males and in the other with Egyptian females. Within the scheme of Egyptian/non-Egyptian skin color, black was not desirable for ordinary humans, because it marked out figures as foreign, as enemies of Egypt, and ultimately as representatives of chaos; black thereby contrasted with its positive meaning elsewhere. This example helps demonstrate the importance of context for reading color symbolism.

The color that regularly embodied both positive and negative meanings was red. While the potency of red undoubtedly derived from the power inherent in its dangerous aspects, again it was the context that determined, in any given case, whether the color had a positive or a negative significance.

[*See also* Beauty; *and* Gems.]

### BIBLIOGRAPHY

Aufrère, Sydney. *L'univers minéral dans la pensée égyptienne.* Cairo, 1991. Mainly devoted to exploring the symbolism of metals, stones, and their colors.

Baines, John. "Color Terminology and Color Classification: Ancient Egyptian Color Terminology and Polychromy." *American Anthropologist* 87 (1985), 282–297. Fundamental article on ancient Egyptian color terminology and color usage in Egyptian art.

Baines, John. "Colour Use and the Distribution of Relief and Painting in the Temple of Sety I at Abydos." In *Colour and Painting in Ancient Egypt*, edited by W. V. Davies. London, forthcoming. Explores color use and meaning in the temple of Sety I at Abydos, with comments on color symbolism in temples in general.

Dolińska, Monika. "Red and Blue Figures of Amun." *Varia Aegyptiaca* 6 (1990), 3–7. Discusses the significance of Amun figures having blue skin.

Fischer, H. G. "Varia Aegyptiaca. 1. Yellow-skinned Representations of Men in the Old Kingdom." *Journal of the American Research Center in Egypt* 2 (1963), 17–22. Studies Old Kingdom representations of male officials with yellow skin and suggests that in mature figures it symbolizes the successful bureaucrat who sits in his office all day out of the sun; in youthful figures that represent statues, both dark- and light-skinned figures alternate as part of a patterning system.

Griffiths, J. G. "The Symbolism of Red in Egyptian Religion." In *Ex Orbe Religionum. Studia Geo Widengren, XXIV Mense Apr. MCMLXXII quo die lustra tredecim feliciter explevit oblata ab collegis, discipulis, amicis, collegae magistro amico congratulantibus*. Studies in the History of Religions, 21–22. Leiden, 1972. Considers positive as well as negative examples of the use of the color red.

Kees, Hermann. "Farbensymbolik in ägyptischen religiösen Texten." *Nachrichten der Akademie der Wissenschaften in Göttingen, phil.-hist. Klasse* 11 (1943), 413–479. Fundamental text on color symbolism in Egyptian religious texts.

Kozloff, Arielle, and Betsy M. Bryan, et al. *Egypt's Dazzling Sun: Amenhotep III and His World*. Cleveland, 1992. Reference is made to the symbolic meanings of both the colored stones and the glazes used in statuary.

Manniche, Lise. "The Complexion of Queen Ahmosi Nefertere." *Acta Orientalia* 40 (1970), 11–19. Suggests that the black images of the queen embody the concept of regeneration, as the fertile ancestress of the royal line of the eighteenth dynasty.

Pinch, Geraldine. "Red Things: The Symbolism of Colour in Magic." In *Colour and Painting in Ancient Egypt*, edited by W. V. Davies. London, forthcoming.

Wilkinson, Richard. *Symbol and Magic in Egyptian Art*. London, 1994. Chapter 6 is devoted to a discussion of color symbolism.

GAY ROBINS

**CONSANGUINOUS MARRIAGES.** *See* Marriage and Divorce.

**CONTENDINGS OF HORUS AND SETH** is the name usually assigned to the composition given in pages 1 through 16 of Papyrus Chester Beatty I, a document of twentieth dynasty date, which undoubtedly originated in a scribe's private collection. The proper title may be derived from the *incipit*: "[Here beginneth] the trial of Horus against Seth." The piece thus purports to be a court transcript, and as such the papyrus abounds in direct speech in the form of the verbatim declarations of the litigants and the responses of the judge and jury. Except in the conclusion, direct speech is in Late Egyptian vernacular. The colophon is brief and does not name either author or copyist.

The *Contendings* treats that portion of the Horus–Seth myth in which the fighting has temporarily ceased, and the two contenders for the office of Osiris (who is now in the underworld) have brought their dispute before the Ennead, presided over by Re-Horakhty. Although in form an undifferentiated whole of sixteen papyrus pages in length, the narrative is divisible into fourteen episodes (in each of which Seth is discomfited), followed by a conclusion. The first five take place in court and involve, *inter alia*, the disposition of various members of the court, the advice of Banebdjed and the letter of Neith, and the insult to Re-Horakhty perpetrated by Baba the monkey god. Episodes six through ten find the court in recess, and the rival litigants reduced once again to acts of physical combat. This "central" section includes material of very ancient origin, some of it reaching back to the Old Kingdom and beyond: the hippopotamus incident, the blinding of Horus and the decapitation of Isis, and the homosexual attack on Horus by Seth. The final four episodes transfer the auditor back to the court setting, where the litigation continues under the guise of an exchange of invectives in epistolary form between Re and Osiris. The conclusion rather perfunctorily disposes of the candidates by giving Horus the verdict and crowning him successor to his father.

In the entire corpus of ancient Egyptian belletristics, the *Contendings of Horus and Seth* is a singular work in its robust, even crude characterization of the gods and its picaresque ambience. Although the context may be quite different, one is reminded of other seemingly irreverent satire from epic to miracle plays. It stands outside the logonomic parameters of the cult per se, and rather at the level of receptors conditioned by profane social norms. The characterization is particularly noteworthy: Horus appears as a physically weak but clever Puck-like figure, Seth as a strong-man buffoon of limited intelligence, Re-Horakhty as a prejudiced, sulky judge, and Osiris an articulate curmudgeon with an acid tongue. The text is sensitive to etiology (cf., the punishment of Nemty, the cow-head replacement for Isis, or the fate of Seth in the sky), and it even plays on inherent contradictions in the myth in a sophisticated manner—note the mutually exclusive relationship of Seth to Horus, now uncle and now elder brother, or the antipathy of the solar cult to Osiris.

The *Contendings* as a narrative smacks slightly of a pastiche shoddily put together. There are corrections on pages 4, 6, 8, 11, 12, and 14, although the calligraphy is superior. The venues of the court are clearly secondary additions; some statements of the members of the court are out of position; and one episode, although referred to, is not included. The text does not, however, represent an arbitrary sequence of individual incidents, even though each incident is self-contained; rather, the sequence anticipates that reflected twelve hundred years later in Plutarch's *De Iside et Osiride,* and it must indicate the rudiments of a canonical order. The notion that the *Contendings* arose out of an identifiable historical event, or that it reflects a social situation in a specific locality, must remain moot, if not downright unlikely.

### BIBLIOGRAPHY

Gardiner, A. H. *The Library of A. Chester Beatty. The Chester Beatty Papyri,* no. 1. Oxford, 1931.

Griffiths, J. G. *The Conflict of Horus and Seth.* Liverpool, 1959.

Griffiths, J. G. *Plutarch's De Iside et Osiride.* Cardiff, 1970.

Lichtheim, Miriam. *Ancient Egyptian Literature,* vol. 2, pp. 214–223. Berkeley, 1976.

Loprieno, A. *Topos und Mimesis: zum Auslander in der Aegyptischen Literatur.* Wiesbaden, 1988.

Loprieno, A., ed. *Ancient Egyptian Literature, History and Forms.* Leiden, 1996.

Oden, R. A., Jr. " 'The Contendings of Horus and Seth' (Chester Beatty Papyrus, no. 1): A Structural Interpretation." *History of Religions* 18.4 (1979), 352–372.

Spiegel, J. *Die Erzaehlung vom Streite des Horus und Seth in Pap. Beatty I als Literaturwerk.* Gluckstadt, 1937.

Westendorf, W. "Ein neuer Fall der 'homosezuallen Episode' zwischen Horus und Seth?" *Goettinger Miszellen* 97 (1987), 71–78.

DONALD B. REDFORD

**COPPER.** The use of copper (*hmti*) in Egypt dates back to the Badarian period, since jewelry (pins, beads, bracelets, and rings) and tools (harpoon tips, chisels, and knives) have been found in graves of the period. Metallic copper can be found in nature as native copper; as such, it only requires hammering to shape it into form. How much of Egypt's early copper was worked from native metal rather than smelted from ores remains unresolved. The principal copper-bearing ores found in Egypt were azurite, chrysocolla, and malachite. Malachite had been commonly used as early as the Predynastic period for a green pigment, so copper might easily have been smelted from it; the temperature required to smelt copper, 800°C, is well within the range of the early ovens and kilns that were used to bake bread and ceramics. Yet some Early Dynastic and A-Group copper objects have been analyzed and found to contain significant amounts of gold and silver, which indicate instead the use of native copper.

Deposits of copper were found in the Eastern Desert that were worked in antiquity, and an Old Kingdom smelting facility was discovered in the area of Buhen. Nonetheless, those sources were minor in comparison to the vast quantities of copper that came from the Sinai, where rock inscriptions around Wadi Maghara of kings of the Early Dynastic and Old Kingdoms attest to the antiquity of working those deposits. A large, rambling temple dedicated to Hathor "Mistress of Turquoise" is situated at Serabit el-Khadim. Inscriptions and stelae were left there by mining expeditions from the Middle Kingdom to the Ramessid period. A vast amount of copper was extracted from the Sinai—one slag heap alone at Wadi Nasb is thought to have yielded more than 100,000 tons. Additional mines were situated at Timna in the Negev. Yet these were still not enough to fill Egypt's needs, so considerable amounts were also imported from Syria and Cyprus. Copper was imported in the form of cast ingots, in an "oxhide" shape; they were depicted as such in tomb paintings and were discovered in shipwrecks.

Copper objects from the Early Dynastic period and the Old Kingdom tended to be formed from flat ingots or from sheets of metal, by cutting, folding, raising, and hammering. For joining, welding and soldering were not used on copper objects; instead, the joins were made by cold hammering or with rivets. Copper objects were also cast, with molten copper poured into stone or ceramic molds. For knives and axes, the cutting edges were hardened by hammering. Small examples of cast copper sculpture are known from the Early Dynastic period and the Old Kingdom, but the large statues of Pepy I and Merenre were made from sheet copper, hammered into shape over wooden forms. A head and torso of Amenemhet III is the earliest large-scale cast sculpture known in copper. Also from the late Middle Kingdom, a number of patinated copper objects are known, called in Egyptian texts *hmty km* ("black copper"); their color was achieved by adding small amounts of gold, silver, and arsenic to the copper.

By the New Kingdom, although copper was eventually replaced by bronze for most of its uses, it remained the most important standard of currency, the *deben.* The value of copper to silver (another standard of value) was 1:100, however that ratio seems to have fluctuated at times.

### BIBLIOGRAPHY

Giumliar-Mair, A. "Black Copper is not Niello." *Egyptian Archaeology* (1998), 35–36.

Maddin, R. ed. *The Beginning of the Use of Metals and Alloys.* Cambridge, Mass., 1988. A discussion of copper working and early metallurgy in ancient societies.

Rothenberg, B. *Were These King Solomon's Mines? Excavations in the Timna Valley.* New York, 1973. An account of mines and mining in the Negev.

PETER LACOVARA

**COPTIC LITERATURE.** Literature in Coptic, the latest phase of the ancient Egyptian language, has had a long and diverse history, closely linked with the rise and dominance of Christianity in Egypt. The category of "Coptic literature" traditionally takes into consideration not only original compositions in the Coptic language but also translations into Coptic from other languages (mostly

Greek) and works known only from translations of (now lost) Coptic originals into other languages (mostly Arabic and Ethiopic). Literature by Egyptian Christian writers in Arabic, from the time after active composition in Coptic had died out, is sometimes added to this category but is more often treated separately as "Copto-Arabic" literature. The varying uses of the term "Coptic" as an ethnic, cultural, or religious indicator can lead to some confusion. For the purposes of the present essay, "Coptic" is used only with respect to language, and the survey will focus on literature available in Coptic, whether original or in translation, but will also take into account later Christian Arabic literature from Egypt.

Coptic literature may be further subdivided by the various dialects of Coptic. Although Sahidic is often described as the standard "literary" dialect of Coptic, practically all other dialects of Coptic preserve at least some literary remains. The Fayyumic, Lycopolitan, Akhmimic, Subakhmimic, Oxyrhynchite, and (especially in later periods), Bohairic dialects are all well represented by literary texts, while important individual works are known in many other Coptic dialects and subdialects. Dialects are significant in the study of Coptic literature in that they can often help to identify the point of origin or date of a particular work. In general, however, it is safe to say that the bulk of Coptic literature survives in the Sahidic dialect, though often tinged with regional variations, and the works discussed below should be assumed to be in Sahidic Coptic unless otherwise stated.

**History.** The earliest texts in a form of Coptic are the least typical of what was ultimately to become Coptic literature. Texts written in what is known as "Old Coptic" were pagan in origin and magical or divinatory in nature. Although its writers used (for the most part) the alphabet found in later Coptic, Old Coptic did not have the regular script system, the extensive adopted Greek vocabulary, and, perhaps most important, the Christian associations of Coptic. Although ease of writing and full vocalization were important reasons for the transition from the complex Demotic script to the simpler Coptic alphabet, the break with the earlier pagan associations of Egyptian writing was an important reason for the ultimate transition to Coptic. Not surprisingly, then, the earliest literature in Coptic consisted of texts associated with Christianity; initially, most were translations from Greek. The association of the Coptic language and Christianity also paralleled a development that had a direct impact on Coptic literature—the introduction of the codex. The rise of the codex (a collection of individual sheets bound together into a book) and the decline of the scroll in Egypt had some connection with the dominance of Christianity. Thus, most Coptic literature originally appeared on papyrus, parchment, or (after the Muslim conquest) of the seventh century CE paper codices, although the survival of such codices intact to the present is relatively uncommon. Scrolls were still used for some Coptic magical texts, and single, unbound leaves were used for short literary texts or excerpts of longer works (again, often for magical purposes). Shorter Coptic literary works or excerpts were also copied out onto ostraca and writing boards, most often as school texts or again as magical amulets. The great majority of Coptic literary texts are known from codices or fragments thereof.

The Bible in Coptic was translated from the Greek—from the Septuagint and the New Testament. It was perhaps the earliest work of literature in Coptic and remained the most important. The initial translation of the Bible into Coptic had most probably taken place by the early fourth century CE, and this translation is likely to have been in the Sahidic dialect. Very early manuscripts of portions of the Bible are known in Sahidic Coptic, but comparably early manuscripts of biblical books are also known in other dialects (notably Bohairic, Fayyumic, Oxyrhynchite, and the archaic P dialect). In general, the books of the New Testament (especially the gospels) are more commonly encountered in Coptic than are those of the Septuagint, although both *Psalms* and *Proverbs* are widely attested in Coptic in some very early manuscripts. Coptic translations of the Bible are sometimes useful for understanding their sources: editors of the Septuagint and Greek New Testament frequently cite the Coptic versions in their critical notes. The early Coptic translations of the Bible were significant for all Coptic literature to come, in that they served as essential reference points for the grammar, orthography, and vocabulary of the respective dialects of Coptic. Moreover, the individual biblical books are easily the best-attested works of literature in Coptic—many more Coptic biblical manuscripts have survived than of any other work—and they were frequently quoted and alluded to in other works.

Biblical apocrypha and pseudepigrapha, again often translated from Greek originals, are well represented in Coptic, in some cases providing unique witnesses to otherwise unknown works. Important compositions relating to Hebrew scriptures are especially well attested in Coptic, including the *Wisdom of Solomon* and the *Testaments* of Abraham, Isaac, and Jacob. Coptic literature was especially rich in apocryphal works relating to the New Testament. A wide range of gospels (including those of Thomas, Nicodemus, and Bartholomew, the *Epistula Apostolorum,* and the *Protevangelium of James*), writings on the life of Jesus (including the Abgar Letter) and his family, and apostolic acts (including the *Acts* of Paul, Peter, John, and Andrew) are known in Coptic, which is sometimes the only version to survive. Apocalyptic works, especially, seem to have captured the imagination of the

Coptic-literate audience, since both translated and original apocalypses (including the *Ascension of Isaiah* and the *Apocalypses* of Elijah, Sophonias, and Paul) are well represented in Coptic. The *Apocalypse of Paul*, in particular, derived at least some of its inspiration from the ancient Egyptian images of gods and demons visible to its author on pharaonic ruins. Although these extrabiblical works were not accorded as much authority as those of the canonical Bible, they were still popular with Coptic-literate audiences. The important early Christian collection of the Apostolic Fathers was available in Coptic, as were certain works by such early church fathers as Clement of Alexandria and Hippolytus of Rome.

A substantial body of early Coptic literary texts (mostly translations from Greek) is known from two finds of papyrus codices from the fourth to fifth centuries CE, which attest to a wide range of religious belief in Egypt in this period. In particular, the Nag Hammadi codices contain works of Gnostic, Hermetic, and Christian influences, while the Medinet Madi codices are Manichaean in nature. The Nag Hammadi codices are better known, more thoroughly published, and more extensive than the Medinet Madi codices: the Nag Hammadi find consists of thirteen volumes containing fifty-one works (some in multiple copies). The contents of the Nag Hammadi codices range from the important early Christian *Gospel of Thomas,* to a portion of the Hermetic tractate *Asclepius,* to widely divergent works of different schools of Gnostic thought, and even a translation of a scrap of Plato's *Republic* into Coptic. Other important works from the Nag Hammadi codices include the *Hypostasis of the Archons,* the *Apocryphon of John,* the *Three Steles of Seth,* the *Teaching of Sylvanus, Thunder: Perfect Mind, Acts of Peter and the Twelve Apostles,* and *Second Treatise of the Great Seth.* The eight Medinet Maadi codices contain a more limited selection of works—Manichaean homilies and psalms, and a long work known as the *Kephalaia.* Both the Nag Hammadi and Medinet Maadi codices are important for a number of reasons. They represent very early manuscripts, with a unique set of dialect features, of texts that are, in most cases, unattested elsewhere. Indeed, the Nag Hammadi and Medinet Maadi codices provide the bulk of the evidence for the Subakhmimic dialect of Coptic. However, the chance survival of these two major collections of early Coptic manuscripts may give a somewhat skewed picture of early Coptic literature, since the traditions they represent were, for the most part, well outside the mainstream of Egyptian Christianity. Aside from the Nag Hammadi codices, Gnostic texts are known in Egypt from other contemporary manuscripts, the most important of which are the extensive *Pistis Sophia* and the *Book of Jeu.* Roughly contemporary Manichaean texts have also been found in considerable numbers in excavations at the site of Kellis.

Many of the Gnostic, Manichaean, and Hermetic texts known in Coptic show influences of pre-Christian Egyptian religious traditions. Manichaeism, Hermeticism and the different branches of Gnosticism represented in these texts did not last long beyond the fifth century in Egypt.

The mainstream of early Coptic literature includes the many works that recorded and perpetuated early monasticism in Egypt. This is not entirely a coincidence, given the important role of monasticism in the development and dissemination of Coptic literature. Although most of the early "classics" of Egyptian monasticism—the *Apophthegmata Patrum,* the *Lausiac History,* the *Historia monachorum,* and Athanasius' *Life of Antony*—were originally written in Greek, most were available in Coptic and commemorated the Coptic-speaking pioneers of Egyptian monasticism. The extraordinary interest on the part of the early Christian world in the solitary monks of Egypt led to extensive documentation and interpretation of these monks by both Egyptian and non-Egyptian authors. The literature describing Egyptian monasticism spread throughout the Christian world—both east and west—and went on to influence monastic practice in Europe. The early Egyptian writers on monasticism, such as Athanasius, reached a wider audience through their use of Greek, but their works were also a profound source of inspiration within Egypt, where they were available in Greek originals and Coptic translations. The *Apophthegmata Patrum* in particular was popular in its Coptic translation and provided models for later compositions in Coptic. Nonmonastic literature of the early church in Egypt, including works by Athanasius, Peter of Alexandria, Hierakas, and others, also exerted a major influence on the writings that were to come.

Much early Coptic literature came from the founder of community-based monasticism in Egypt, Pachomius, and his followers. Based on his military experience, Pachomius developed monastic communities governed by rules in a group of monasteries in southern Egypt and, in doing so, generated a substantial amount of literature. Perhaps Pachomius's best-known composition in modern times is his monastic rule, the first of its kind in Egypt and, via the Latin translation by Jerome, an important influence on early monasticism in Europe. Pachomius's monastic rule was a collection of short instructions on the practical aspects of the monastic life that was intended to secure both the smooth functioning of the monastery and the spiritual well-being of its inhabitants. Some scholars have found parallels between the style of Pachomius's rule and earlier Egyptian wisdom texts. Pachomius also wrote a number of instructions and a cryptic series of letters, most if not all of which were originally written in Coptic, although a substantial portion of the literature about Pachomius was written in Greek. Indeed, Pachomius and his rule-based monasticism proved a compelling subject for other writers; in addition to various shorter writings and the letter of Bishop Ammon, different versions of lives of Pachomius exist in Greek, as well as in Sahidic and Bohairic. Pachomius's successors Theodore and Horsiesios left behind a number of Coptic letters and instructions, while the work of his follower Carour is known from an enigmatic *Apocalypse* in Coptic.

Pachomius's impact on monasticism in Egypt was great, but he did little to shape the use of Coptic as a vehicle for literary expression. This was left to another important figure in early Egyptian monasticism, Shenoute, a near contemporary of Pachomius and also from southern Egypt. Shenoute was head of the White Monastery (at Atripe near modern Sohag), which ultimately housed thousands of monks in separate men's and women's communities. The running of these communities and their interactions with the outside world formed the basis for Shenoute's extraordinary literary output in Coptic: he was perhaps the most prolific writer of Coptic literature ever. His voluminous writings were ultimately collected together in a series of "Canons" (writings addressed to members of the community) and "Discourses" (writings directed outside the community); it is by these designations that Shenoute's work is known today among scholars. Stephen Emmel has reconstructed Shenoute's literary corpus from the substantial but scattered remains of the library of the White Monastery, as well as from texts originating elsewhere. Shenoute was an extremely important figure to contemporary and later Christians in Egypt, but he went unrecorded by writers in Greek on Egyptian Christianity—presumably a result of the fact that he wrote in Coptic rather than Greek. His use of Coptic as a literary language was unprecedented: these are highly complex compositions making careful use of the particular features of Coptic grammar (the circumstantial and second tense especially) to rhetorical effect. He is one of the first authors to make conscious use of literary form and style in Coptic; the complexity of his writings also makes them among the most difficult of Coptic literary texts. Shenoute used an intricate set of scriptural citations and allusions, along with an array of metaphors drawn from the world around him. His writings presented and shaped his interactions with both the monks under his charge and the nonmonastic people of his region. He describes conflicts with local pagans and officials, as well as conflicts within his own communities, particularly with the women under his authority. Shenoute saw pagans and heretics as real threats to his monastery, but he also saw disobedience within the community as a danger both to his authority and to the salvation of the individuals under his charge. His assertive and frequently combative personality comes through in his writings with striking vividness. In contrast, Shenoute's successor Besa seems almost drab and colorless; aside from a few letters of his own, he is known primarily for his biography of Shenoute.

Indeed, the volume and quality of Shenoute's output often overshadows that of other writers in Coptic. Although no one ever reached the same level of output and style as Shenoute, many other writers and their works in Coptic are known. Some caution must be used in making identifications of authors; writings were often incorrectly attributed, either intentionally or inadvertently, by the scribes who copied them. Nevertheless, the list of authors of securely attributed works is extensive. After Shenoute and Besa, some of the most important authors of the fifth century CE were Paul of Tamma, Paphnute (who wrote a history of the monks of Upper Egypt), Makarius of Tkow (author of an encomium on Dioscorus of Alexandria) and Timotheus II, who wrote a number of encomia on various subjects. Early sixth-century authors include Theodosius of Alexandria and Damian, while Constantine of Siut and Rufus of Shotep were prominent in the later sixth to early seventh century. Pisentius of Coptos was an author of the early seventh century, known for his homily on Onnophrios but perhaps better known from the biographical accounts of his life by his followers. Pisentius is one of the very few writers of Coptic literature for whom we also have documentary evidence: an extensive corpus of letters addressed to him during his stay in western Thebes. The Muslim conquest of Egypt in 641 CE is reflected in certain Coptic biographical and apocalyptic works, but it seems to have had little immediate impact on the production of original literature in Coptic. Patriarch Benjamin I and his follower Agathon, Samuel and Isaac of Qalamun, and John and Menas of Nikiou are among the writers known from the post-conquest seventh century, when they wrote saints' lives, homilies, and even histories. The seventh and eighth centuries have been described by Tito Orlandi as the "Period of the Cycles"—a time when scribes devoted much attention to the compilation of collections of related works centering on events in the past. Writers continued to produce literature in Coptic through the eighth and ninth centuries and even later, but few works can be securely attributed to individual authors after the early ninth century.

**Genres.** Authors of Coptic literature worked within a number of genres. There was some fluidity between different categories of composition, and, in general, genre in Coptic literature is a subject that has yet to be fully examined by modern scholars. Sermons, homilies, encomia, panegyrics, pastoral letters, hagiographies, and martyrdoms are all genres used by Coptic authors to communicate with their audiences—quite often in a form that was intended to be read aloud on an appropriate occasion. Within these genres, writers covered a wide range of subject matter. Original Coptic literary works sometimes commented on contemporary history or local politics, but they more often concentrated on church or monastic affairs. Biblical texts and their interpretation were frequently the subject of sermons and homilies; when delivered aloud, such exegetical work allowed the author to help shape his audience's understanding of the Bible. Very frequently, the lives of saints were the subjects of sermons, homilies, and encomia—the life of the saint being used to make specific points or highlight certain themes of concern to the writer. But just as often, writers dealt specifically with the lives of saints in the context of biographies and martyrdoms.

Biographies of holy men and women formed an important part of Coptic literature, and many of these are likely to be original Coptic compositions. Although they were sometimes about saints of the near or distant past, most lives were written (or purported to be written) by an associate or follower of the subject. Most Coptic saints' lives were intended to be read aloud, especially on specific holy days; thus, the writer often addresses his audience directly to point out the relevance or importance of specific incidents. Some saints' lives contain information about contemporary political history; Isaac's life of Samuel of Kalamun, for example, describes events relating to the Muslim conquest of Egypt. Others are demonstrably ahistorical, such as the Pambo's life of Hilaria, a legendary daughter of the Byzantine emperor Zeno who disguised herself as a man and ran off to a monastery in Egypt. In most, such as Besa's life of Shenoute or the biographies of Pisentius of Coptos, the words and deeds of the subject are the main focus. A series of episodes presents edifying events from the subject's life, often claiming the eyewitness authority of the writer, in a progression toward a suitable deathbed scene. Although the biographical data presented cannot always be taken literally, the incidental details of those lives often provide a vivid picture of attitudes and perceptions in Late Antique Egypt. Thus, Bishop Pisentius's conversations with a revived mummy in the Bohairic life cannot be taken seriously as factual, but the descriptions in that episode give unique insight into Christian understandings of ancient Egyptian funerary practices and beliefs. Similarly, the accounts of Moses of Balliana's ongoing battle with a demon named Bes are clearly invented for dramatic effect, but they tell much about Christian perceptions of the ancient pagan religions of Egypt. These lives can also provide useful incidental details about daily life in Late Antique Egypt; Besa's life of Shenoute gives much specific information about the organization of Shenoute's White Monastery and unparalleled estimates of the numbers of men and women living there. Collections of lives, either of related individuals or more encyclopedic compilations (such as the *Synaxary*

and the *History of the Patriarchs of Alexandria*), were not uncommon in Coptic, but they assumed greater importance in later Arabic Christian literature from Egypt.

The martyrdom in Coptic is a subset of saints' lives that was a genre unto itself. Coptic martyrdoms form a substantial portion of Coptic literature; Greek originals of some can be identified, but the great majority of these texts were originally composed in Coptic. Nearly all are set either during the Decian or Diocletianic persecution of Christians in the mid-to-late third century CE—events that held a powerful fascination for later Egyptian Christians. Coptic martyrdoms often follow a set format. A general account of the life of a persecution-era Christian sets the stage for a specific scene of the Christian's refusal to sacrifice to pagan gods, followed by a confrontation with a pagan official. This encounter in turn leads to an escalating series of tortures, climaxing in the ultimate martyrdom of the unyielding Christian, and concluding with some sort of miraculous story involving the martyr's remains. Many Coptic martyrdoms are attributed to persecution-era authors (several to Julius of Aqfahs, who is also a participant in the narrative), but the majority seem to have been written long after the period in which they are set. In many cases, martyrdoms appear to have been written to promote the cult of a local martyr as a pilgrimage site. Striking similarities between certain accounts of different martyrs suggest that some martyrdoms were written to order, with local names and details inserted into a stock story. To modern readers, Coptic martyrdoms often seem overly repetitive and gratuitously gruesome, but their popularity and frequency suggest that their intended audience saw them in a very different light.

Beyond these standard genres, other literary forms existed in Coptic. There was some historical writing in Coptic, although most, such as the Coptic and Arabic histories of the patriarchs of Alexandria, might be more precisely classed as collections of biographies. The seventh-century writer John of Nikiou wrote a world history in Coptic, but this work survives only in an Ethiopic version of an Arabic translation of John's Coptic original. Regional histories and surveys of churches and monasteries did not become common until after the Muslim conquest, and these were mostly written in Arabic. A Coptic fragment from Deir el-Balaizah, preserving a chronology of the Ptolemies, suggests a more general interest in historiography among Coptic writers. Historical romances were not especially common in Coptic, but the few fragmentary examples (concerning Alexander the Great and Cambyses) are of great interest to scholars.

Far more common than either of these genres were the hymns and liturgical texts that made up such an important part of worship among Christians in Egypt. Complex services and series of hymns reflecting a fully developed liturgical calendar served (and, to some extent, continue to serve) the ceremonial needs of the Christian populations of Egypt. Coptic hymns were a particularly important part of Coptic literature, offering their writers considerable range for literary expression within an accepted framework. Alphabetic acrostic hymns were common in Coptic; although these may seem contrived to modern readers, to their authors they offered opportunity for verbal dexterity within a format of symbolic significance. Beyond formal hymns, rhymed, rhythmic poetry intended for singing is known from a number of manuscripts. Such poems or songs were often on biblical themes or dealt with historical legends.

A variety of nondocumentary genres outside the traditional modern boundaries of "literature" are known in Coptic; these are sometimes categorized as "subliterary" by scholars, though it is probable that such distinctions would not have been so clear to their authors. Magical texts are well represented in Coptic—most of an eminently practical nature. One finds healing spells, curses, erotic magic, spells to obtain power and wealth, and less specific spells. Much Coptic magical literature survives either in the form of anthologies of spells or in the form of the artifacts of magical practice—copies of individual spells that have been put to practical use. Coptic magic often adapted more traditionally "literary" texts (especially prayers and biblical texts) for magical use. The Coptic version of the legendary letter of Abgar of Edessa to Jesus (and, more frequently, the reply attributed to Jesus) was a highly popular example of such literary adaptation for magical purposes. Coptic magical literature often appealed to Jesus and other Christian figures, but frequently alongside invocations of pagan deities and spirits. Oracular questions, similar in form to much earlier examples in Demotic and even Hieratic, are well attested in Coptic; many are addressed to Saint Colluthos. The boundaries between magic and medicine were not rigidly defined, and a number of magico-medical or medical treatises exist in Coptic. Likewise, other categories of text have parallels with Coptic magical literature, such as alchemical works and what are often known as "farmers' almanacs," complex sets of calendrical and meteorological omens designed to aid in agricultural practice. The little scientific and technological literature that has survived in Coptic is entirely oriented toward practical use. Scholastic texts tended to concentrate on language acquisition and frequently made use of literary texts for this purpose, but they also included extensive mathematical works. Coptic epigraphic texts, such as monumental inscriptions, funerary epitaphs, and graffiti, are often literary in form or cite known literary works, even if they are not usually classified as literature.

Finally, the extensive corpus of documentary texts in Coptic—letters, legal documents, accounts, and lists—should be noted. Although documentary texts are by their very nature nonliterary, they frequently invoke and use phrases from Coptic literature, especially the Bible. Conversely, the characteristic phrasing and formulas of documentary texts are sometimes used in consciously literary works to lend verisimilitude to a fictional letter or legal document in a narrative. Even more frequently, a consciously literary production is conveyed in the form of a letter (as in the writings of Pachomius, Shenoute, and many others). The original holograph of such literary letters may have been a sort of documentary text, but content and form, as well as subsequent recopying and editing, place them firmly in the realm of Coptic literature.

**Libraries.** Much of the surviving Coptic literature comes from monastic libraries; this is not particularly surprising, since monasteries were the primary centers for production and distribution of books. The contents of a particular monastic library can provide useful information about the regional distribution of books and the discursive archive of a particular community. One of the most extensive monastic libraries was surely that of the Shenoute's White Monastery, which survived well beyond his death and amassed an enormous collection of his works as well as those of other authors. Sadly, the White Monastery library suffered the fate of many such collections—the individual volumes were split up and their contents dispersed by early collectors—and it is only in recent years that scholars have managed to get a clear idea of what this library contained. A few monastic libraries have been found largely intact; a collection of more than fifty volumes containing many otherwise unknown works came from a monastery at Hamouli in the Faiyum and is now preserved mostly in the Pierpont Morgan Library in New York. The extensive libraries of the various monasteries of the Wadi Natrun attest to a diverse literature in the Bohairic dialect of Coptic, with liturgical texts and hymns predominating. The contents of monastic libraries now lost can sometimes be guessed at through surviving catalogs and book lists. The monastic context of the production of much of Coptic literature remains an important factor in the study of such material. The scribal colophons on manuscripts often give important clues to the context in which specific literary manuscripts were produced, in addition to valuable information about the scribes themselves and the historical milieu in which they worked.

**Later Coptic Works.** Literature in Coptic was directly affected by the gradual replacement of Coptic by Arabic as Egypt's language of daily life and, eventually, literature. The Muslim conquest of Egypt in 641 CE seems to have had little direct impact on Coptic initially; Arabic replaced Greek as the language of administration in Egypt, but

Coptic literature continued to flourish and Coptic remained a major language of business and private communications. When Arabic began to replace Coptic in Egypt is difficult to show precisely. Arabic papyri are known in significant numbers from the eighth century, but the real transition does not seem to have taken place until the tenth and eleventh centuries. By that point, documentary texts in Coptic more or less disappeared, but new literary texts continued to be composed and, more frequently, older texts were recopied. There seems to have been major activity in the collection and copying of Coptic literature in the ninth through eleventh centuries; the majority of Coptic literary manuscripts to survive come from this period and preserve, in many cases, the sole examples of a particular work. There also seems to have been a conscious effort to preserve Coptic literature during this period, in the face of its decline as a spoken language.

Christian writers in Egypt adapted quickly to the use of Arabic over Coptic as a literary language; transitional devices such as Coptic transliterated into Arabic characters and vice versa were relatively short-lived. Much of the earliest Egyptian Christian Arabic literature was made up of translations from Coptic originals, but new compositions in Arabic soon became common. Important Copto-Arabic authors include Severus of Ashmunein, Cyril Ibn Laqlaq, Christodulos, and Athanasius of Qus. As the knowledge of Coptic began to decline, there was a conscious attempt to preserve it through grammars and word lists in Arabic. The shift to Arabic also gave Egyptian Christians access to a range of literature from throughout the Near East and ensured that Egyptian writings could be similarly transmitted without additional translation. A very late (fourteenth-century) poem in Sahidic Coptic, known as the *Triadon,* seems in part intended to encourage the continued use of Coptic; but the very form of the sole surviving manuscript of this poem, with its facing Arabic version, shows the ultimate direction of Christian literature in Egypt (and may indeed suggest that the Arabic was the original and the Coptic a translation). As far as can be determined, literary composition in the Coptic language had effectively ended by the fourteenth century, in the time of the *Triadon.* Although Coptic continued (and continues to this day) to be used as a liturgical language, this use of Coptic has not involved any significant composition of new texts.

Literary composition in Coptic made a very brief reappearance in the seventeenth century, when European scholars began a systematic study of the language. Athanasius Kircher, whose publications on Coptic were of great importance for the early study of the language in Europe, contributed a short poem in Coptic to Jean-Jacques Bouchard's *Panglossia,* in memory of the eminent French antiquarian Nicolas Claude Fabri de Peiresc.

Kircher's poem in honor of Peiresc is recognizable as Coptic from its script and vocabulary, but it is otherwise a grammatical oddity and remains an isolated, artificial effort. Since Kircher's time, Coptic communities within and outside Egypt have made sporadic attempts to revive the Coptic language and, in the process, have produced compositions in Coptic. It remains to be seen, however, whether these attempted revivals of Coptic will ultimately lead to a new literature in the Coptic language.

## BIBLIOGRAPHY

Atiya, Aziz S., ed. *The Coptic Encyclopedia.* 8 vols. New York, 1991. Important reference for the study of Coptic literature; note particularly the article "Literature, Coptic," by Tito Orlandi, and the articles devoted to individual authors and literary works.

Behlmer, Heike. "Ancient Egyptian Survivals in Coptic Literature: An Overview." In *Ancient Egyptian Literature: History and Forms,* edited by Antonio Loprieno, pp. 567–590. Probleme der Ägyptologie, 10. Leiden, 1996. Important survey of pharaonic Egyptian influences on Coptic literature.

Cannuyer, Christian. *Les coptes. Fils d'Abraham.* Turnhout, 1990. Historical and cultural survey that includes a substantial anthology of Coptic literature in translation.

Depuydt, Leo. *Catalogue of Coptic Manuscripts in the Pierpont Morgan Library.* Corpus of Illuminated Manuscripts, 4–5, Oriental series 1. Leuven, 1993. Major collection of Coptic literary manuscripts; includes descriptions of the library of manuscripts from the monastery at Hamouli.

Drescher, James. *Three Coptic Legends: Hilaria, Archellites, the Seven Sleepers.* Supplément aux Annales du Service des Antiquités de l'Égypte, 4. Cairo, 1947. Text and English translation of three characteristic Coptic literary works.

Emmel, Stephen Lewis. "Shenute's Literary Corpus." Ph.D. diss., Yale University, 1993. Major study of the works of Shenoute.

Graf, Georg. *Geschichte der Christlichen Arabischen Literatur.* 5 vols. Studi e Testi, vols. 118, 133, 146, 147, 172. Vatican City, 1944–1953. Comprehensive survey of Arabic-language Christian literature, including material from Egypt.

Hasitzka, Monika R. M. *Neue Texte und Dokumentation zum Koptisch-Unterricht.* 2 vols. Mitteilungen aus der Papyrussammlung der Österreichischen Nationalbibliothek (Papyrus Erzherzog Rainer), new series, 18. Vienna, 1990. Corpus of Coptic school texts, with useful commentary and references.

Krause, Martin. "Koptische Literatur." In *Lexikon der Ägyptologie,* 3: 649–728. Wiesbaden, 1979. Essential survey article.

Kuhn, K. H., and W. J. Tait, eds. *Thirteen Coptic Acrostic Hymns from Manuscript M574 of the Pierpont Morgan Library.* Oxford, 1996. Recent edition of a group of Coptic hymns, with English translation.

Layton, Bentley. *Catalogue of Coptic Literary Manuscripts in the British Library Acquired since the Year 1906.* London, 1987. Catalog of a major collection of Coptic literary manuscripts.

Layton, Bentley. *The Gnostic Scriptures.* Garden City, N. Y., 1987. Translations of the major Coptic Gnostic texts.

Meyer, Marvin, and Richard Smith. *Ancient Christian Magic: Coptic Texts of Ritual Power.* San Francisco, 1994. Corpus of Coptic magical texts, in translation, with commentary.

Orlandi, Tito. "Coptic Literature." In *The Roots of Egyptian Christianity,* edited by Birger A. Pearson and James E. Goehring, pp. 51–81. Studies in Antiquity and Christianity. Philadelphia, 1986. Important survey by one of the world's authorities on Coptic literature (see also his articles in *The Coptic Encyclopedia,* 1991, cited above).

Reymond, E. A. E., and J. W. B. Barns. *Four Martyrdoms from the Pierpont Morgan Library Coptic Codices.* Oxford, 1974. Text and English translation of four representative Coptic martyrdoms, with useful introduction.

Veilleux, Armand. *Pachomian Koinonia.* 3 vols. Cistercian Studies Series, 46–48. Kalamazoo, Mich., 1981–1982. English translation of the works of Pachomius and his followers.

Winlock, H. E., and W. E. Crum. *The Monastery of Epiphanius at Thebes, Part I.* Publications of The Metropolitan Museum of Art Egyptian Expedition, 3. New York, 1926. Crum's essay on the literary environment of the Theban monks remains an important survey.

Young, Dwight Wayne. *Coptic Manuscripts from the White Monastery: Works of Shenute.* Mitteilungen aus der Papyrussammlung der Österreichischen Nationalbibliothek (Papyrus Erzherzog Rainer), new series, 22. Vienna, 1993. A sampling of Shenoute's work, with English translation.

TERRY G. WILFONG

**COPTS,** term commonly used for the Egyptian people in Late Antiquity and for the Christian population of Egypt from the Arab conquest of 640–641 CE to the present. The adjective Coptic is variously applied, not without controversy, to a language and its literature, a church, a historical period, and an entire culture.

**Terminology.** The modern words *Copt* and *Coptic*, to describe the inhabitants of Egypt, come from an Arabic truncated borrowing (*qubt/qibt*) of the Greek for "Egyptian," *Aigyptios* (usually said to be itself derived from the Egyptian name of Memphis, *Ḥt-k₃-Ptḥ*). There is no connection to the place name Coptos. Originally, no specifically religious or linguistic reference was implied, nor was reference made to any subdivision within the Egyptian population. The people of Egypt at the time of the Arab conquest referred to the language that we call "Coptic" simply as "Egyptian," in both the Greek and Egyptian languages. Because the postconquest population of Egypt was largely monophysite Christian, Renaissance and later writers were led to apply the term *Coptic* to the surviving minority Christian church in early modern Egypt, as well as to the language that by that time was essentially a liturgical rather than a living tongue. From that usage has come the application of the term by modern writers to other domains, which include literature, art, religion, and the whole range of studies concerning that culture in history.

Language and script are the least problematic of the extended uses, for there is no other suitable term to distinguish the Coptic writing system (which was used as early as the third century CE) from other, earlier, means of representing the Egyptian language. Moreover, Coptic is as deliberately shaped a writing system as any other in Egyptian history, and it represents a conscious attempt to create a language and script that would give Egyptian as much power and flexibility as Greek. A separate name for it is thus well justified.

Difficulties arise in moving from language to literature, for much that survives in Coptic was translated from other languages (especially Greek), and much that was written in Coptic or once existed in it now survives only in translation (particularly Arabic). Nonetheless, practicality suggests that Coptic literature, as a concept, is unobjectionable, as long as its close ties to the eastern Mediterranean literature of late antiquity and the early Middle Ages are kept in perspective.

Many scholars find it difficult to accept the widely found extension of the term *Coptic* to art, archaeology, history, and even to the church in the period before the Arab conquest; the reason is that Egypt was a largely bilingual society (with minority use of other languages). Moreover, Egypt was a complex society that had been strongly imprinted with the metropolitan culture of the Eastern (Greek) Roman world. Hence, most of those objects or phenomena now called "Coptic" are in fact simply characteristic of that bicultural local version of an international society (even the concept "bicultural" is difficult to apply, since it tends to suggest a clearer division than actually existed). Unfortunately, no other terminology has so far found universal acceptance, although Late Roman, Late Antique, and Early Byzantine have all found adherents—but not with consistently used meanings. Despite the consequent ambiguity, however, they are better descriptions for both history and art than is "Coptic." (Part of what is usually considered Late Roman or Late Antique [284–395 CE] is treated in the article Roman Occupation; however, this article will, with partial overlap, cover the period from the Roman emperor Constantine [who ruled Egypt from 324 to 337 CE] to the Arab conquest of 641 CE. Consequently, for its purposes, Late Antique is used here to cover the period from 284 to 641 CE.)

The use of the term *Copts* to refer to the people of Egypt in preconquest times is also common but misleading, particularly because they are usually contrasted with Greeks or Romans. To the population of Late Antique Egypt, however, Greek and Egyptian were not opposites; a Greek-speaking resident of Egypt was as likely to display pride in Egyptian origin as an Egyptian-speaking person. Although many writers have claimed that the monophysite church of the period, after the Council of Chalcedon (451 CE), represented an Egyptian (i.e., "Coptic") nationalistic movement, the evidence supports the contrary view: both Chalcedonian and monophysite churches operated in the Greek language at the highest levels and contained speakers of both the Greek and Egyptian languages, and there is no significant evidence of hostility to the use of Greek in either body until quite late in the period. Although there is a sense of the monophysite church being beleaguered by the outside world, Egypt nonetheless remained connected to Christian currents in other parts of the Roman Empire, especially Syria, until after the Arab conquest.

**Political History.** Constantine's defeat of Licinius in 324 CE gave him control of the eastern part of the Roman Empire, including Egypt. After the foundation of Constantinople (330 CE, now Istanbul, Turkey), Constantine directed Egypt's wheat taxes to the "new Rome," rather than to the old, and Egypt's fate thereafter lay firmly and unsurprisingly with the Greek part of the empire. The effective split of the Roman Empire into Eastern and Western after 395 CE reduced further Egypt's connection to the West, although in ecclesiastical politics Alexandrian connections to Rome remained strong until the middle of the fifth century. From 324 until 617 CE, Egypt enjoyed three centuries largely free from external threat and internal revolt. The dramas of imperial succession were played out elsewhere. Internal political turbulence, however, was common and was often closely connected with religious developments. The volatility of the Alexandrian population, often commented on in Hellenistic and Roman times, continued to be widely remarked.

In the fourth century and into the fifth, both pagan–Christian strife and the conflict between Christian groups were frequently recorded. For example, one of the accusations against Athanasius by his enemies was his violent handling of Meletian and Arian clergy, and his exiles and returns to Alexandria were sometimes accompanied by turmoil. Ammianus Marcellinus described violence in Alexandria during the emperor Julian's reign, when pagans felt free to attack Christians, but the destruction of the Serapeum by a Christian mob three decades later, in 391 CE, was not much different in kind. The murder of the philosopher Hypatia in 415 CE, although hardly a momentous political event, was emblematic.

Byzantine Roman rule over Egypt was temporarily ended in 617–619 CE by a Persian invasion, leading to a decade of Persian rule before the restoration of Roman government in 629. That invasion was said to have been accompanied by widespread massacres and devastation, but only scanty details of the decade of Persian rule are known. A decade later, the Arab commander Amr led a small force into Egypt in late 639. Although he initially made rapid headway, it was only after substantial reinforcements that he was able to defeat the Romans in a pitched battle at Heliopolis (July 640), to take the fortress at Babylon (Old Cairo) by siege, and finally to negotiate the surrender of Alexandria by the Chalcedonian patriarch Cyrus (late 641, effective in September 642). A substantial exodus of officials and the upper classes followed, although the Byzantine general Manuel recaptured the city briefly, in 645, before the final Arab takeover in 646.

**Religious History.** Egyptian Christianity included diverse strains of thought and practice from relatively early in its history, but not until the fourth century was there a growth of major divisions and considerable conflict. The earliest history of Christianity in Egypt is poorly known, despite the traditional claim of Saint Mark as its founder. Ironically, the destruction of Egypt's Jewish population in Trajan's regime (r. 98–117 CE) wiped out an important matrix for the church's growth. Only in the third century do the bishops of Alexandria start to be more than names. Theologically, Egypt was marked from the beginning by a strongly Platonist strain, which owed much to the Jewish writer Philo of Alexandria; it also surfaced in Christian authors, such as Valentinus, Clement, Origen, and Didymus. Although Clement and Origen polemicized against the so-called Gnostics, both men shared much of their intellectual background. At the same time, however, the more materialistic and less *logos*-centered "Asiatic" (Near Eastern) theology also had its supporters. The city of Alexandria included much theological diversity in the third century, and the bishop was not yet invested with as dominant a role as was later the case; nonetheless, Origen's activity was centered in the catechetical school, not in an independent institution.

"Gnostics" have been a major center of scholarly interest since the late 1940s, owing above all to the discovery of the so-called Nag Hammadi library, a group of thirteen fourth-century codices that have a large number of compositions not belonging to the Christian biblical canon. Of diverse origin and contents, but consistently distant in outlook from the main lines of the organized church, its texts—translated from Greek into Coptic—have evoked an equally wide variety of views. It remains unclear whether the codices point to the existence of any organized body for whom they were important or whether they were simply part of the library of Christians who saw themselves as members of the catholic church.

A somewhat different situation obtained with the Manichaeans, whose dualistic philosophy ultimately resulted in a definitive break with Christianity. Yet many groups in the fourth century seem to have regarded themselves as true Christian churches, using much of the same vocabulary for institutions and offices. Recent finds at Kellis (today's Ismant el-Kharab, Dakhleh Oasis), coupled with earlier discoveries in the Faiyum, as well as the Cologne Mani Codex, have greatly expanded the body of fourth-century Manichaean textual material.

The last major imperial persecution of Egyptian Christians was that under Diocletian (r. 284–305 CE). During it, a group of bishops led by Meletius of Lykopolis broke with the authority of the bishop of Alexandria, Peter. This split is often ascribed to diverging views over the appropriate treatment of those who had denied the Christian faith during the persecution, but it has also been argued that it focused rather on the Alexandrian bishop's claims to universal power over the Egyptian church. The Meletian movement had a long afterlife, although probably with small numbers in later centuries. Athanasius tried, with considerable success, to treat the Meletians as heretics along with the Arians, but there is no evidence that they were doctrinally distinct from the orthodox church in any way. The conflict with the Arians, which intersected with imperial politics throughout the century, formed the main action of Athanasius's long (328–373 CE) reign as bishop of Alexandria. He suffered five periods of exile, two abroad (335–337 and 339–346) and three largely in hiding in Egypt (356–362, 362–364, and 365–366). Although mainly successful in molding the Egyptian church into a united and centrally controlled body, he fared poorly for the most part on the larger political scene, and his weak successors did no better. It was not until under the emperor Theodosius (r.379–395 CE) that an orthodox successor was able to get a firm grip on the see of Alexandria. Yet throughout this period, Egypt remained a major force in the church at large, despite feeling a beleaguered bastion of Athanasian orthodoxy much of the time.

A major crisis at the start of the fifth century brought to a head a controversy over doctrines called Origenist, more by acknowledgment of their theological ancestry than because they were all drawn directly from the third-century theologian Origen. The bishop of Alexandria, Theophilus, who has been described as a purely political man, first supported an Origenist, anti-anthropomorphite view. Soon, pressure from monks produced an about-face in 402, entailing the exile of the four Origenist monks called the Tall Brothers, and thereafter he had a determinedly anti-Origenist stance.

The highwater mark of Alexandrian influence in the church came with the patriarchate of Cyril (412–444), who used the first Council of Ephesus in 431 to depose Nestorius, the patriarch of Constantinople (428–431). The council was fought on the use of the term *theotokos* ("God-bearer") for the Virgin Mary, which Nestorius opposed. Apart from the emotional evocation of devotion to the Virgin, the controversy involved important Christological differences, with Cyril's position stressing Christ's identity as God, his divinity. That position was characteristic of the long Platonist tendency of Alexandrian theology to stress the divine *logos* against the humanity of Christ, but the term *theotokos* was used by both sides in the dispute for divergent purposes.

Cyril's successor Dioscorus I (444–458) tried a similar coup at the second Council of Ephesus in 449, removing bishops Flavianus of Constantinople and Domnus of Antioch from office; that time, however, the papal delegates were left unheard and unhappy, and Pope Leo denounced the council as a "Robber Synod," as it has been known ever since. The new emperor, Marcian, convoked a new council at Chalcedon in 451, and at that time Dioscorus was not in control. Leo's *Tome* held the day doctrinally, and Constantinople gained politically by achieving virtual parity with Rome. Dioscorus was condemned, both for his refusal to accept the Chalcedonian formula of the hypostatic union of two natures in one and for the arbitrariness of his exercise of power in his own see. From that point on, there were usually two contending bishops of Alexandria, one supporting the Chalcedonian formulations, most typically with imperial support, and the other maintaining Dioscorus's monophysite position.

The period from Chalcedon to the accession of Damianus in 578 was formative for the ultimate character of the Egyptian church. Some emperors (especially Anastasius, r.491–518) were of monophysite sympathies, or at least neutral; but at other periods there was severe pressure for conformity to Chalcedonian views. One result was Egyptian closeness to the Syrian monophysite church, which was more consistently pressed by the emperors; another was a much diminished likelihood that theological works in Greek but written elsewhere would circulate in Egypt or be translated into Coptic. The long and complex relationship of the Egyptian church with that of Syria led at times (particularly when the Syrian monophysites were themselves under imperial pressure to conform to Chalcedon) to the flight of Syrian clergy to Egypt. Severus of Antioch (c.465–538), for example, spent the last twenty years of his life in Egypt and had substantial influence. A generation later, Jacob Baradaios rebuilt the hierarchy of the church after the reign of Justinian (r. 527–565). The monophysite patriarch Damianus (in office 578–605) was also of Syrian origin; his period saw a substantial renewal of the Egyptian church.

The last Chalcedonian patriarch of Alexandria before the Arab conquest, Cyrus, led a concerted effort to enforce conformity to the imperial, pro-Chalcedonian, will. Around the turn of the twentieth century, it was shown to be false that claims that the Egyptians, as a result of his persecution, welcomed the Arabs. If anything, it was Cyprus's weak conduct of the defense of Egypt that led to its fall—but the memory of Cyrus unquestionably was execrated in the monophysite church, perhaps beyond his actual deserts.

By the start of the fourth century, the structure of the Egyptian church was already largely formed, but how much earlier it is hard to say. Egypt had by that time some seventy-two bishops, and by 357 CE the total, including the Libyan coast as far as Cyrenaica, amounted to about one hundred. The earliest bishops were largely members of the higher socioeconomic strata, and the increased tendency over time to draw bishops from the ranks of monks did not eliminate the bias in favor of those with an education and those of prosperous background. The clergy seemed on the whole to have been largely part-time practicioners, earning much of its keep from secular property holdings or occupations. Many were ordained only in mature years, the office passing down family lines, and no training process is known to have existed.

There were no archbishops other than that of Alexandria, and thus no intermediate regional centers of official power; neither did episcopal synods play a significant role in Egypt. The absolute dominance of bishops within their sees was thus repeated in the control of the bishop of Alexandria over the entire country, cemented firmly by Athanasius and administered by a curia about which little is known. The church of Egypt was by the standards of the period unusually hierarchical. Its other distinctive characteristic, which plays a determinative role in Coptic literature, is the importance of monasticism. Monasticism was the invention of Egyptian Christianity, and Egypt provided the fundamental exemplars of both eremitic asceticism, in Antony, and of cenobitic monasticism, in Pachomius. The literature about the Egyptian monks, much of it written by admiring travelers, was widely diffused throughout the Mediterranean and had an enormous impact. Within Egypt itself, the prestige of the ascetic life was great, and monks acquired influence and patronage, to some extent in competition with bishops; but as more bishops were drawn from the monasteries, the two spheres became closely intertwined. Shenoute, who is discussed as a writer in the section below, was important as a mentor of the clergy and the laity, not only as an abbot and writer.

**Language, Literature, and Texts.** Coptic Egyptian is a product of a bilingual society, using Greek characters and a large quantity of Greek vocabulary, along with new Egyptian formations consciously designed to provide equivalents for Greek words. Puristic features and learned terms in the Greek testify to the high educational level of those responsible for the formation of Coptic into a literary instrument. Not surprisingly, Coptic literature is closely linked to the wider world of Christian writing in other languages and, even when (as in Shenoute's works) displaying hostility to Hellenic (i.e., pagan) culture, bears the marks of Greek education. In fact, the major figures of Egyptian Christianity, who were discussed above, wrote mainly in Greek, not in Coptic.

The earliest true Coptic writing (third century) was apparently the translation of the Bible, and other Christian theological works were also translated relatively early, including some from non-Egyptian authors, such as Meliton of Sardis, John Chrysostom, and the Cappadocian fathers (Basil, Gregory of Nyssa, and Gregory of Nazianzus). The known works from those authors in Coptic translation are, in the main, sermons and ascetic works, reflecting the interests of the monasteries; most of their major standard works are not known to have been translated into Coptic. A vast amount of post-conquest manuscripts of literature in Coptic is purported to be translations from the major patristic authors—but in fact it is late composition and falsely ascribed to them.

When the first original (i.e., not translated from Greek) literary work in Coptic was written is not known; even whether Antony's letters were originally written in Greek or Coptic is unknown. The earliest documented Coptic literature is the body of letters and rules from Pachomius and his successors, although these were perhaps not seen as literature by their authors. In Egypt, the monasteries always played an important role in Coptic literature and what survives today may offer a distorted picture of the ancient reality, because most of it survived in monasteries. If part of a library belonging to a cultivated urban layman of the sixth century came to light, it might give a different picture. As things stand, we do not even know if there was any secular literature in Coptic. Large numbers of private letters in Coptic that deal extensively with worldly matters have been preserved on papyrus and clay, but those, too, come disproportionately from monastic sites. The importance of the monasteries to the survival of Christianity in Egypt after the Arab conquest no doubt reflected, in part, the significance of monastic institutions before the Arabs, but this may also have led to a distorted image of preconquest culture.

Original writing in Coptic reached maturity with Shenoute (c.348–454), the abbot of the White Monastery at Atripe (Sohag; across from Akhmim, the ancient Panopolis) and Coptic's greatest author. He was the first to try to place Coptic on the same level as the other major theological languages, but he did so drawing on the rhetorical modes and genres of Greek culture. His writing, much of it sermons and other moral discourses, is generally regarded as difficult, no doubt because of its ambitious nature.

The split between the Chalcedonian and monophysite parts of the Egyptian church after 451 CE had substantial consequences for literature. Shenoute's successor Besa wrote a life of his great predecessor, in a style (sometimes called "plerophoric") composed of a series of vignettes combining miraculous episodes and dogmatic position-taking, aimed at validating an anti-Chalcedonian view and in general a depreciation of theological subtlety. Besa also composed letters and catecheses. The genre of plerophoric works flourished during this period in Egypt and Syria, the great monophysite bastions. Also from this period comes the composition of the *Ecclesiastical History*, part of which (books 1–7, down to Diocletian) was drawn from Eusebius of Caesarea's great fourth-century work on

COPTS. *Coptic textile.* Bottom of woolen skirt with elaborate angle band and knee roundels, from the Faiyum. (University of Pennsylvania Museum, Philadelphia. Neg. # S8–31706)

the subject. The remaining five books, running from the Diocletianic persecutions down to the time of writing, presented an Egyptian view of controversies over the nearly two hundred years in question. Like Eusebius, this work lists the writings of the major figures in its drama (Athanasius, Theophilus, Cyril, John Chrysostom, and Timothy Aelurus).

In the last part of the sixth century, the renewal of Damianus' period also had a significant impact on Coptic literature. Although no one author of that period stands out in the way Shenoute did in his time, the expressiveness of the language fostered by Shenoute's legacy was joined to a straightforward style, to produce many works of quality. The single most important author was perhaps Constantine of Siut, whose encomia and homilies drew on the Athanasian tradition but also reflected a knowledge of Syrian thought.

**Art and Archaeology.** Of all the areas of Late Antique Egyptian culture commonly called "Coptic," art has posed the most severe problems, in considerable part because the historical context of many of the surviving works was unknown. Neither artists nor patrons were known, and chronology has been controversial at best. Some of this art is earlier than previously thought; some does not come from Christian contexts; in general, the art is the product of commissions from the multilayered culture of the bilingual upper classes of late antique Egypt. As with literature, our information comes disproportionately from the monasteries, many of which have survived to some degree either through preservation in use (although with constant alteration) or through burial by the sand and then modern excavation. Both cenobitic monasteries (like Bawit, Phoibammon at Thebes, and Saqqara) and laura-type ascetic settlements (like Kellia, Esna, and Naqlun) have been excavated—the first group showing, as one would expect, a centralized and organized form with many communal facilities, the second consisting largely of individual hermitages. These latter are, however, often relatively spacious, with separate rooms for prayer, and they reflect the prosperous social background of many of the ascetics.

Urban settlements are, by comparison, scarcely known,

although there have been a few excavations. Cemeteries, which were wherever possible located in the desert, have survived better; an outstanding example is that at Bagawat (near Kharga, ancient Hibis, in the Great Oasis), where the decoration has survived in many tombs. It was mainly painting over plastered mud brick, a medium widely used even in major buildings, such as churches, where stone was scarce or expensive. Sculpture in stone was, however, used in many important places, as (for example) in the extensive remains from the monastery of Apollo at Bawit. Carved stone grave stelae were also in continuous use in large numbers. Painting was of great importance, for scenes from the Bible and of the saints, both on the walls of churches and for icons. Perhaps the best-known aspect of Coptic art, however, is the textiles—mainly in wool and linen—which drew on long Egyptian traditions and often used old artistic motifs, although with new significance. Most of the textiles—of a stylized and intricate design, have come into museums and collections through the antiquities trade, and they thus lack archaeological contexts.

Generally, the artists of Byzantine-era Egypt worked with stylistic means and figural repertories inherited from earlier periods; even mythological scenes and decorative programs retained the pagan gods until quite late in antiquity, sometimes reusing motifs for new purposes to suit Christianity; most famous is the transformation of Isis nursing Horus into the Virgin Mary nursing Jesus. Because classical culture remained part of the heritage of educated people in Late Antique Egypt distinguishing "Christian" art from "pagan" is difficult or impossible, except where explicitly religious uses are involved. The patrons who paid for most of the buildings and art during the Byzantine era were mainly Greek-speaking or bilingual; even the monasteries contained mainly bilingual communities. Moreover, until the seventh century, Egypt remained linked to artistic and architectural currents in the rest of the empire. Once again, therefore, the use of the term Coptic is inappropriate for Egypt's broader cultural phenomena in late antiquity. Until some new discoveries yield a better understanding of the cities and villages of those times—especially of the last two centuries of Roman rule, it will be impossible to say how far the dominant imprint of the monasteries on the Christian, Egyptian-speaking culture of those centuries results from the pattern of text and artifact survival, as opposed to how far it represents the actual character of the larger society.

[See also Coptic Literature; Grammar, article on Coptic; Roman Occupation; and Scripts, article on Coptic.]

### BIBLIOGRAPHY

Attiya, Aziz S., ed. *The Coptic Encyclopedia.* New York, 1991. The principal reference work on everything that can be referred to as Coptic, with articles written by a large number of scholars; the quality is very uneven.

Bagnall, Roger S. *Egypt in Late Antiquity.* Princeton, 1993. Offers a comprehensive discussion of Egyptian society, economy, and culture in the period from the accession of Diocletian to the middle of the fifth century.

Brakke, David. *Athanasius and the Politics of Asceticism.* Oxford, 1995. A study of Athanasius' attempt to make monks and anchorites a part of his struggle to unify the Egyptian church.

Butler, Alfred J. *The Arab Conquest of Egypt and the Last Thirty Years of the Roman Dominion.* 2d ed., edited by P. M. Fraser. Oxford, 1978. The standard work on this subject, with full citation of sources; Fraser's addendum is largely bibliographic.

Camplani, Alberto, ed. *L'Egitto Cristiano: Aspetti e problemi in età tardo-antica.* Studia Ephemeridis Augustinianum, 56. Rome, 1997. Excellent survey articles by seven scholars on theology, literature, monasticism, church institutions, papyrology, and art.

Clark, Elizabeth A. *The Origenist Controversy: The Cultural Construction of an Early Christian Debate.* Princeton, 1992. Describes the pivotal theological and ecclesiastical controversy of the Egyptian church at the end of the fourth and start of the fifth century CE.

Falck, Martin von. Ägypten, *Schätze aus dem Wüstensand: Kunst und Kultur der Christen am Nil.* Wiesbaden, 1996. Extensive and wide-ranging exhibition catalog, with introductory essays on the culture of late antique Egypt, monasticism, churches, and art.

Haas, Christopher. *Alexandria in Late Antiquity: Topography and Social Conflict.* Baltimore, 1996. A social description focused on religious communities and their conflicts.

MacCoull, Leslie S. B. *Dioscorus of Aphrodito: His Life and his World.* Berkeley, 1988. A study of the career and culture of the bilingual poet and notary of the sixth century.

Martin, Annick. *Athanase d'Alexandrie et l'Église d'Égypte au IVe siècle (328–373).* Collection de l'École Française de Rome, 216. Rome, 1996. An exhaustive treatment of the great bishop's career, set in a broad context of the history of the period.

Pearson, Birger A., and James E. Goehring, eds. *The Roots of Egyptian Christianity.* Philadelphia, 1986. A collection of high-quality essays, each providing a synthesis for an aspect of the subject.

Thomas, Thelma. "Greeks or Copts?: Documentary and Other Evidence for Artistic Patronage During the Late Roman and Early Byzantine Periods at Herakleopolis Magna and Oxyrhynchos, Egypt." In *Life in a Multi-cultural Society: Egypt from Cambyses to Constantine and Beyond,* edited by Janet H. Johnson, pp. 317–322. Studies in Ancient Oriental Civilization, 51. Chicago, 1992. Important article on the social context of "Coptic" art.

Walters, C. C. *Monastic Archaeology in Egypt.* Warminster, 1974. A useful survey, although no longer up-to-date.

Wipszycka, Ewa. *Études sur le christianisme dans l'Égypte de l'antiquité tardive.* Studia Ephemeridis Augustinianum, 52. Rome, 1996. Eighteen important and original studies on church institutions, monasticism, the persecutions, and the social context of Egyptian Christianity, drawing on papyri as well as literary sources.

ROGER S. BAGNALL

**COREGENCY.** Occasionally throughout the history of ancient Egypt it became politically expedient to recognize two persons simultaneously as pharaoh. Usually this arrangement conformed to the Egyptian ideal of the "staff of old age," whereby an elder functionary was assisted by a younger man whom he trained to succeed him in office.

In a coregency, the father elevated his heir apparent to full kingship, to ensure a smooth transition and to transfer to the junior partner those duties (such as military leadership) that the senior partner found too taxing. Such partnerships regularly operated in a wide variety of circumstances, and they occurred not only between fathers and sons but also among siblings or other members of the royal family (notably during the Ptolemaic dynasty). In some cases, the "junior" partner was actually the elder of the pair (as with Queen Hatshepsut and the young Thutmose III).

Coregencies play a significant role in the scholarly literature of Egyptology, because their very existence is often in question. Suggestive evidence is often unclear, and even after strenuous debates on methodology, facts may be interpreted in more than one way. Coregencies are thus most securely identified in Ptolemaic and Roman times, when they are attested not only in narrative histories but also by double dates on contemporary business documents—typically in the form "regnal year X of King A, which is (*nty iw*) regnal year Y of King B." The relative sparsity of such records in earlier periods makes it more difficult to determine whether coregencies took place. In the eighteenth dynasty, for example, Hatshepsut's coregency with Thutmose III is beyond question because the latter's progress from regent to coregent was indicated with tolerable clarity in a number of contemporary sources; moreover, the two kings' partnership is attested by numerous representations that show both rulers acting together, as well as by jointly dated records—"single-dated" documents which imply that Hatshepsut should have reigned alongside her nephew from the death of their predecessor. Thutmose II (e.g., "regnal year 12 . . . under the Person of the Good God Maatkare [Hatshepsut], given life, [and of] . . . Menkheperre [Thutmose III]"; see Obsomer 1995, pp. 57–59). In this case, though, the facts are exceptionally clear and the circumstances unusual. In other situations, the evidence is so much more indirect or ambiguous that an element of doubt remains even where the probablity of a coregency seems high. These more debatable instances, in chronological order, are discussed below.

**Old Kingdom.** Several coregencies in the fourth dynasty (Khafre and Menkaure), fifth dynasty (Neferirkare Kakai and Newoserre Any), and sixth dynasty (Merenre Antyemsaf and Pepy II, Pepy II and Antyemsaf II) have been suggested because those kings' names were suggestively juxtaposed on cylinder seals and/or sealings (Kaplony 1977, pp. 286–293). Even when the reigns are indisputably contiguous, though, it may be more likely that these references are to periods and/or functions within the careers of officials who owned these artifacts. Further evidence for a coregency of Pepy I and Merenre Antyemsaf rests on the assumption that two royal statues,

found together at Hierakonpolis in Upper Egypt, belonged to these kings and were designed to be displayed together: even if this were so (and if the smaller statue could be identified securely as Merenre Antyemsaf's), however, the reasons behind this pairing remain obscure.

**Middle Kingdom.** Ending the First Intermediate Period, Montuhotep I of the eleventh dynasty united the Two Lands in 2040 BCE.

***Montuhotep III and Amenemhet I.*** Neither the presence of each king's name (in two distinct styles) on different sides of a stone vessel, nor the existence of a titulary for Amenemhet I earlier than the one he used through most of his reign, is regarded as convincing proof that they were coregents.

***Amenemhet I and Senwosret I.*** Doubts about this coregency, long regarded as certain, have mounted in recent years. What has been regarded as a double date, equating the senior ruler's thirtieth regnal year with his son's tenth (on Cairo Museum stela CG 20514), consists of two separate and uncoordinated labels, each located in an upper corner of the tablet, which can be read literally as "thirty years" and "ten years" (i.e., as periods of time rather than dates, although similarly abbreviated writings of "regnal year" are found later). Also, an assumed dateline of Amenemhet I that seemingly includes the names of both kings (on Louvre stela C 1) has been reattributed to Senwosret I alone (Obsomer 1993), although neither the new reading nor the inferences drawn from it seem absolutely certain. Evidence from the royal cemetery at Lisht, indicating that Senwosret I did not begin work on his own pyramid before completing that of his father during the first decade of his reign suggests a coregency but can be explained without one. Also ambiguous is a passage in the *Instructions of Amenemhet I* (W. Helck, *Kleine Ägyptische Texte* edition [Wiesbaden, 1986], VIII.a–c) that speaks of an attack on the old king as having occurred "before I had sat down with you, before the court had heard that I was bequeathing to you": it is unclear whether this attack ended in the king's murder (cf. W. D. Waddell, *Manetho* [Cambridge, 1940], pp. 67–71 [fragments 35–37], though attributed there to Amenemhet II), or whether it was a failed coup that preceded the coregency. The issue is further clouded by a recent proposal to redate the work itself to the eighteenth dynasty (Grimal 1995), though here too the case falls short of disproving the conventional twelfth dynasty date. Such inconclusiveness overall makes it unwise to exclude this coregency at present.

***Senwosret I and Amenemhet II.*** Dates that appear in each of the upper corners of a stela (Leiden V 4: regnal Year 44 of Senwosret I and his son's regnal Year 2) are interpreted as "dating" the monument to the same year of a coregency. They might also refer to separate dates important to the stela's owner, although their nature is not made clear by the text.

***Amenemhet II and Senwosret II.*** Here there is a genuine double date, with Amenemhet II's regnal Year 35 "corresponding to" (*ḥft*) regnal Year 3 of his son. Although it can be argued that the coordination is between two identical activities, occurring at separate times, it still seems more likely on grammatical grounds that the equivalence is between the datelines themselves—that is, in a coregency.

***Senwosret II and Senwosret III and/or Senwosret III and Amenemhet III.*** An entry in one of the Illahun papyri records the nineteenth year of an unnamed king of the twelfth dynasty followed by the first year of another. Following the Turin Canon of Kings (which can be interpreted as giving nineteen years to Senwosret II), this item was attributed to Senwosret II and Senwosret III, allowing them only the shortest coregency or none at all. Later scholarship, noting that contemporary records indicated only eight years for Senwosret II and nineteen for Senwosret III, set aside the Turin data (as erroneous or out of order) and reattributed the Illahun dates to Senwosret III and Amenemhet III. Although this "short" reign for Senwosret III (instead of the thirty-plus years suggested by the Turin Canon) excluded all but the slightest overlap between him and his successor, contemporary materals made a suggestive case for a coregency with Amenemhet III; along with a variety of objects inscribed with the names of both kings, there is a text from the Faiyum, ostensibly a speech by the senior monarch that recognizes his son as king. In a time frame compatible with only a short coregency (or none), this is ambiguous evidence. Joint namings might be commemorative, and the speech could be the younger ruler's propaganda on his own behalf—a doubt not lessened by this composition's later reuse by Hatshepsut in her fictitious claim to have been crowned by her father, Thutmose I. Between 1992 and 1994, however, there appeared fresh evidence that revives a "long" reign of thirty-nine years for Senwosret III (Wegner 1996), which strengthen the case for a long coregency with Amenemhet III (starting in his father's twentieth regnal year.

***Late twelfth dynasty.*** There are no dated monuments that even suggest a coregency in this period. Although the temple at Medinet Madi in the Faiyum is decorated in the names of both Amenemhet III and Amenemhet IV, this might mean only that the son finished what his father had begun; and a commemorative impulse might also lie behind other monuments that coordinate their names. The same probably applies to the association of Sobekneferu's name with Amenemhet III on a few monuments.

**Eighteenth Dynasty.** Ending the Second Intermediate Period, the New Kingdom dynasties were founded by Ahmose (r. 1569–1545 BCE).

***Ahmose and Amenhotpe I.*** King Ahmose's wife, Ahmose-Nofretari, held the title "king's mother" before her husband's death; however, it need not follow that their son Amenhotpe I was already reigning as coregent, since the queen's new rank might have been awarded formally, to establish her position in the hierarchy late in her husband's reign, if it did not refer to another prince elevated to titular "kingship" before he died and Amenhotpe I became heir apparent.

***Hatshepsut and Thutmose III.*** This undisputed coregency is discussed in the introductory section of the article.

***Thutmose III and Amenhotpe II.*** A coregency seems likely because the dates of the elder king's death and the younger king's accession feast are separated by four months in the civil calendar. Supporting evidence includes the juxtaposition of both king's names and images throughout the temple of Amada in Nubia, as well as the relative frequency with which they are shown together on private monuments. Based on information from a mid-eighteenth dynasty account papyrus, the coregency lasted no more than two years and ten months.

***Amenhotpe II and Thutmose IV.*** The case for a coregency is weak, given the inconclusiveness of attempts to identify both kings as senior and junior rulers on a statue from Karnak and to relate each one's claims to have celebrated a *sed*-festival (thirty-year jubilee).

***Amenhotpe III and Amenhotpe IV (Akhenaten).*** Speculation as to how the elder king might have foreshadowed or even promoted his son's religious revolution has helped make this the most hotly debated case of all. Proposed models have ranged from a long coregency (ten years according to Kitchen 1962; twelve for Aldred 1988) to short (e.g., two years at most, in Murnane 1977) to none at all (e.g., Redford 1967). There are no double dates: graffiti from Dahshur, discovered and attributed to the time of Amenhotpe III/IV, belong instead to Thutmose III. Proofs for a coregency have thus been sought indirectly—in "evidence" that the senior monarch dwelt at Tell el-Amarna, his son's preferred residence, between the latter's fifth and twelfth regnal years, or that officials and activities associated with one ruler overlapped significantly into the other's reign. Not one of these arguments has been able to withstand close scrutiny: some parts of the puzzle cannot be reconciled with a coregency without special pleading, while others (though compatible with a coregency) fall short of proof and can be explained without one. This ambiguity in much of the evidence has kept the issue alive. The most recent of the serious arguments in favor of a long coregency (Johnson 1990), while it calls attention to intriguing parallels between both the artistic styles and religious programs current during Amenhotpe III's final decade and his son's first twelve years on the throne, also falls victim to the temptation, endemic among scholars who have wrestled with this problem, to coax more specificity out of the evidence than is there (cf. Romano 1990).

In sum, I believe that the Scottish verdict of "not proven" still stands in this case.

***Akhenaten and Smenkhkare (and/or Nefernefruaten).*** As in the previous case, all too much of the evidence can be described as suggestive but ambiguous. Even so, a block from Tell el-Amarna (found out of context) shows the lower halves of two pharaohs, one standing behind the other, before Akhenaten's god—reasonable grounds for assuming a coregency, but between which two kings? This is bound to remain doubtful as long as uncertainties persist regarding the number, identity, and sequence of Akhenaten's immediate successors, a debate which will go on for some time to come (see most recently, Gabolde 1999).

**Late Eighteenth and Early Nineteenth Dynasties.** Coregencies are likely neither between Tutankhamun and Ay nor between Horemheb and Ramesses I; claims for these rest on an association of their names that can just as easily have been commemorative. The case for a joint reign of Ramesses I with his son Sety I, while somewhat stronger, partakes of the same uncertainties.

***Sety I and Ramesses II.*** It is Ramesses II who claims that his father made him coregent "that I [may see] his beauty while I am [still] alive." Since plausible data pointing to their joint rule can be detected in the younger king's earlier monuments, this coregency has been reckoned as certain. Recent investigation, however, raises enough questions about the interpretation of the evidence to put the matter once more in doubt.

**Later New Kingdom, Third Intermediate Period, and Late Period.** Many of the alleged coregencies rest on evidence that can be construed as commemorative or inconclusive (Sethnakhte and Ramesses III: kings of the twenty-first, twenty-second, and twenty-fifth dynasties). Periods of joint rule are not rare during the Third Intermediate Period, but most should be viewed as reflecting mutual recognition among kings who reigned over different parts of Egypt. True coregencies between rulers of the same line (Osorkon III and Takelot III in the twenty-third dynasty, or Nektanebo I and Tachos in the thirtieth) can be demonstrated on the basis of dated records.

**Ptolemaic and Roman Periods.** The numerous coregencies among rulers of the Ptolemaic dynasty, as well as the fewer instances among Roman emperors, are attested primarily in narrative histories. They are also confirmed in Egyptian records (dated documents and, to some extent, decoration on the monuments).

## BIBLIOGRAPHY

Aldred, Cyril. *Akhenaten, King of Egypt.* New York, 1988. Contains the author's final statement of his case for a coregency of twelve years between Amenhotpe III and Akhenaten.

Beckerath, Jürgen von. "Mitregentschaft." In *Lexikon der Ägyptologie,* 4: 155–161. Wiesbaden, 1982. An extended encyclopedia entry that includes some references not found in Murnane's 1977 book-length study of coregencies, listed below.

Brand, Peter. "Studies in the Monuments of Sety I." Ph.D. diss., University of Toronto, 1997. Advances strong grounds for doubting a coregency of Sety I with Ramesses II.

Campbell, Edward Fay. *A Chronology of the Amarna Letters, with Special Reference to the Coregency of Amenhotep III and Akhenaten.* Baltimore, 1964. A solid study with conclusions (leaning toward a negative assessment) that fall short of being completely convincing.

Delia, Robert. "A New Look at Some Old Dates: A Re-Examination of the Twelfth Dynasty Double Dated Inscriptions." *Bulletin of the Egyptological Seminar* 1 (1979), 15–28. Argues that these entries do not indicate the correspondence of regnal years in the reigns of coregents.

Delia, Robert. "Doubts about Double Dates and Coregencies." *Bulletin of the Egyptological Seminar* 1 (1982), 55–69. Reply to Murnane's 1981 rebuttal, listed below.

Gabolde, Marc. *D'Akhenaten à Toutankhamon.* Lyons, 1999. Especially valuable for its insights on the later Amarna period.

Grimal, Nicolas. "Corégence et association au trône: l'*Enseignement d'Amenemhat Ier,*" *Bulletin de l'Institut français d' archéologie Orientale* 95 (1995), 273–280. Questions the relevance of this composition for the debate on the coregency of Amenemhet I and Senwosret I, suggesting that the work dates to the eighteenth dynasty instead of the Middle Kingdom.

Johnson, W. Raymond. "Images of Amenhotep III in Thebes: Styles and Intentions." In *The Art of Amenhotep III: Art Historical Analysis,* edited by Lawrence Berman, pp. 26–46. Cleveland, 1990. Argues for a long coregency of Amenhotpe III and Akhenaten based on artistic and religious motifs.

Kaplony, P. *Rollsiegel des Alten Reichs,* vol. 1. Monumenta Aegyptiaca, 2. Brussels, 1977. Publishes documents that might (or might not) reflect coregencies during the Old Kingdom.

Kitchen, Kenneth A. *Suppiluliuma and the Amarna Pharaohs: A Study in Relative Chronology.* Liverpool, 1962. Makes a case for a coregency of Amenhotep III with Akhenaten lasting about a decade.

Murnane, William J. *Ancient Egyptian Coregencies.* Studies in Ancient Oriental Civilization, 40. Chicago, 1977. A critical study of the evidence for coregencies and how they worked, due to be reissued in a revised new edition.

Murnane, William J. "In Defense of the Middle Kingdom Double Dates." *Bulletin of the Egyptological Seminar* (New York) 3 (1981), 73–82. Rebuttal to Delia's 1979 article, listed above.

Murnane, William J. "The Kingship of the Nineteenth Dynasty: A Study in the Resiliency of an Institution." In *Ancient Egyptian Kingship,* edited by David O'Connor and David Silverman, pp. 185–215. Probleme der Ägyptologie, 9. Leiden and New York, 1995. Touches on issues relevant to the situation of Ramesses II early in his reign.

Obsomer, Claude. "La date de Nésou-Montue." *Révue d' Égyptologie* 44 (1993), 103–140. Republishes this document advancing cogent arguments against interpreting it as proof of a coregency between Amenemhet I and Senwosret I.

Obsomer, Claude. *Sésostris Ier: Étude chronologique du règne.* Connaissance de l'Egypte Ancienne, 5. Brussels, 1995. A study of the period that includes strong objections to this king's alleged coregency with his father.

Posener, Georges. *Littérature et politique dans l'Égypte de la XIIe dynastie.* Paris, 1956. A well-reasoned analysis of Middle Kingdom literary works, asigning a political subtext to most of them; while details of this case have come under attack recently, this book is still a classic and remains the starting point for any serious consideration of "propaganda" in the twelfth dynasty.

Redford, Donald B. *History and Chronology of the Eighteenth Dynasty of Egypt: Seven Studies.* Toronto, 1967. Chapters 3 to 6 are devoted, respectively, to coregencies of the early eighteenth dynasty: Hatshepsut and Thutmose III, Amenhotpe III and Akhenaten, and Akhenaten and Smenkhkare.

Romano, James F. "A Second Look at 'Images of Amenhotep III at Thebes: Styles and Intentions' by W. Raymond Johnson." In *The Art of Amenhotep III: Art Historical Analysis,* edited by Lawrence M. Berman, pp. 47–54. Cleveland, 1990. Rebuttal of Johnson's 1990 article above.

Schaeffer, Alicia. "Zur Entstehung des Mitregentschaft als Legitimationsprinzip von Herrschaft." *Zeitschrift für Ägyptische Sprache und Alterumskunde* 113 (1986), 44–55. Argues for the origins of the institution of coregency in the First Intermediate Period.

Seele, Keith C. *The Coregency of Ramses II with Seti I and the Date of the Great Hypostyle Hall at Karnak.* Studies in Ancient Oriental Civilization, 19. Chicago, 1940. Based mostly on styles of decoration in contemporary buildings, makes the case for a coregency in which the junior partner did not use an independent system of his own regnal years.

Simpson, William Kelly. "The Single-Dated Monuments of Sesostris I: An Aspect of the Institution of Coregency in the Twelfth Dynasty." *Journal of Near Eastern Studies* 15 (1956), 214–219. Uses the datelines as the springboard for a stimulating discussion of the interactions of senior and junior partners in the Middle Kingdom coregencies, as they were conventionally understood when this article was written.

Wegner, Josef W. "The Nature and Chronology of the Senwosret III–Amenemhat III Regnal Succession: Some Considerations Based on New Evidence from the Mortuary Temple of Senwosret III at Abydos." *Journal of Near Eastern Studies* 55 (1996), 249–279.

WILLIAM J. MURNANE

**CORRESPONDENCE.** During the Old and Middle Kingdoms, the prevalent terms for *letters* were *mḏ't* ("papyrus document") and *sš* ("writing"). By the New Kingdom, the customary word for a "letter" had become *š't,* derived from the verb "cut"; literally meaning "piece," this reflects the practice of cutting off a sheet from a papyrus roll for the purpose of writing a letter. For royal and official letters of the New Kingdom the term *wḥ'* ("directive," "rescript," or "inquiry") conveyed the notion of the writer's authority, whereas a letter sent to the king was called *wsty* ("report"). Throughout pharaonic times, letters from the king were "royal decrees," which also designated formal edicts emanating from the palace. Yet administrative orders from the vizier were not called "decrees."

Expressions having to do with the writing of letters reflect the situation in which the writer dictated the letter to a scribe. Thus, in addressing the recipient, the verb "say" commonly appears at the beginning of communications. Just as a person might employ a scribe to write a letter from dictation, so it was frequently assumed that the recipient would have the communication read aloud by a secretary. If there was no third party to recite the letter, a literate recipient would still read it aloud. The oral aspect of reading is also indicated by the frequent use of the verb "hear" in reference to the addressee's taking note of a let-

ter's contents. In a very few instances, which are not beyond dispute, the verb "see" may have referred to visual reading of a communication. Evidence indicates that the fifth dynasty King Izezi was literate, and a letter of Amenhotpe II to his viceroy of Nubia is expressly stated to have been made by the king's own hands. Since princes received a scribal education at court, it is probable that most pharaohs were literate, although the king generally made use of a "pharaoh's letter-writer," his secretary.

Some sort of messenger service was available for the transmission of official correspondence. Dispatch-carriers might be entrusted with a number of letters to be delivered to various destinations, and occasionally such a courier might even carry a private letter. Generally, however, private correspondence was transmitted informally. Frequently a trusted retainer or acquaintance simply hand-delivered the letter. Sometimes replies to letters were requested to be sent by the hand of anyone who happened to be coming in the right direction. External addresses on letters, when present, do not usually indicate the location of the addressee. There was no general postal system in the modern sense.

Once received and read, a letter might be retained by the recipient for future reference. In New Kingdom letters written on papyrus, the addressee is often urged to preserve the letter so that it might be used as evidence or authorization at some later date. The handwriting of a letter-writer occasionally served to demonstrate a letter's authenticity. Official letters were frequently copied into journals maintained by state and temple administrative units.

The epistolary conventions and formulas of letters from the Old and Middle Kingdoms generally exhibit more awareness of the relative social status of writer and addressee than do New Kingdom letters. In older letters, a superior recipient is commonly referred to as "lord," while the inferior writer, who may call himself "servant of the estate" in the salutation, often refers to himself in the body of the letter by using a third person expression equivalent to "your humble servant." Although in the formulaic introduction of New Kingdom letters a superior recipient might still be called "lord," formal expressions indicating relative status are generally lacking in the body of the letter, where first and second person pronouns are used for writer and addressee regardless of social status. When writer and addressee are of equal status, the writer may refer to himself politely as "your brother" in older letters.

The invocation formulas of the Old and Middle Kingdoms tend to be more tightly phrased than in the New Kingdom, when writers employ a freer style that reflects an intimate relationship between a person and the deities, whose blessings are invoked on behalf of the recipient.

Such invocations, however, are generally absent in letters from a superior to an inferior. During the Ramessid period, often lengthy appeals to local deities for the addressee's well-being reflect the increase in personal piety that characterized the religion of that age.

**Sources.** There are various sources for correspondence, the originals of which were invariably written in the cursive Hieratic script. Longer letters have been preserved on papyrus, which could be conveniently folded and tied with a string, to which a mud seal was applied to ensure the confidentiality of the contents. Papyrus letters were provided with simple external addresses and were easily transportable. Some royal letters were considered to be so important to the recipient as expressions of honor that they were carved in stone in hieroglyphs on the tomb or stela of a high official. Such permanent copies from Old Kingdom tombs preserve the format of the original papyrus letters.

Many letters, generally brief, were written on flakes of limestone or potsherds, called "ostraca." Some of these letters are copies or drafts of letters that were written on papyrus, but many short communications on ostraca were themselves hand-delivered. There was no way of sealing them to ensure the confidentiality of the message. The addressee was indicated by either naming the recipient at the beginning of the communication or simply telling the letter-carrier to deliver it to a particular individual.

Many papyrus letters are palimpsest; that is, the papyrus on which the letter was written had been cut off from a previously inscribed roll and the earlier text erased to provide a blank sheet. This common practice, as well as the use of limestone flakes or potsherds, indicates that although new papyrus was not exorbitantly expensive, the cost and availability of a papyrus roll must have figured in the choice of writing material.

**Groups of Letters.** Although many letters stand isolated in content and provenience, there are several groups of letters from specific locations that are worthy of note. The Hekanakhte Letters, found discarded in a Theban tomb of the early Middle Kingdom, relate to the affairs of a mortuary priest who was also a gentleman farmer. These letters reveal his concern for members of his household, especially as regards their food rations, and the economics involved in renting land for the cultivation of emmer wheat and barley. Hekanakhte appears as a miserly individual who is seeking to accumulate fluid capital that could ultimately be used for his burial expenses, according to Baer (1963).

From the second half of the twelfth dynasty come the Semna Dispatches, which were copied on a papyrus roll found in Western Thebes. These letters relate to the movement and activities of Nubians in the vicinity of the western Semna fort in Nubia. Of similar date are letters from the valley temple and the adjoining pyramid town of the deceased king Senwosret II at Illahun. While the letters from the valley temple deal largely with temple affairs, those from the pyramid town are more varied and often personal, covering such matters as farming, rations, household affairs, shipping, conscripts, fishing, weaving, and the education of a slave.

Among the subjects treated in a group of letters involving a scribe Ahmose, who was active during the reign of Hatshepsut, are the building of a house and litigation over a maidservant. Two fragmentary letters from an unguent preparator living at Tell el-Amarna provide important evidence for a commoner's ability to pray to the god Aten directly, without the intermediation of Akhenaten. They also contain the earliest occurrence of epistolary formulas that were subsequently in vogue during the Ramessid period.

Several letters of the standard-bearer Maisety treat interference with a god's personnel, improper arrest of laborers, and mobilization of prisoners in the reign of Sety I. Nine letters involving the family of Ramesses II and its entourage at the Nile Delta capital of Piramesse shed light on the activity of princes. In one of them, the term "general" is applied to Ramesses II, expressing his human nature rather than the divine nature generally stressed in more formal inscriptions. Among several letters that were discovered pasted together, there is a missive of Ramesses IX reprimanding the high priest of Amun-Ramessesnakhte for providing inferior galena (a blue-gray mineral) for the king's eye-paint. The same high priest penned a letter of congratulation to Nubian troops for routing nomads who had been creating trouble for gold-washing teams in the Eastern Desert. In speaking of this action, the high priest by convention attributes the victory to the king's energetic arm, even though the king was not actually involved. These letters are important for evaluating the relationship of the king to the high priest in a period of declining royal authority.

From the Ramessid workmen's village of Deir el-Medina, the residence of the families of artisans employed in the excavation and decoration of the royal tombs, and from the royal necropolis of Western Thebes, derive many letters, mainly ostraca. Some of those documents are concerned with the progress of work on the royal tomb and with administrative matters relating to the crew's wages and supplies; others deal with more personal affairs, including illness, death, marital problems, disputes, consumer needs, and transactions. The communications on ostraca tend to be brief and usually lack the epistolary formulas found at the beginning of more formal letters.

Because of Deir el-Medina's vulnerability to attacks by marauding Libyans at the end of the twentieth dynasty, the community moved within the fortified enclosure of Ramesses III's mortuary temple at Medinet Habu. From this period there exist more than fifty papyri that constitute a corpus now known as the Late Ramessid Letters. Most were written or received by the aging necropolis scribe Dhutmose, whose various activities included the collection of taxes in grain to supply the workmen, the preparation of materials for warfare in Nubia, and his own dangerous trip into Nubia. These letters are among the liveliest documents from ancient Egypt; although they are partly official, they also abound in expressions of concern for the well-being of Dhutmose and the men and women of his family and community. Through the exchange of letters one can trace the course of events in the last years of Ramesses XI's reign, when southern Egypt was under the military control of a general who assumed the function of high priest of Amun. In what was probably the final year of Ramesses XI's reign, General Piankh conducted a military campaign against a former viceroy of Nubia. In one of his letters, sent from Nubia to Dhutmose, occur these treasonous words: "Regarding Pharaoh, how will he ever reach this land (Nubia)? Regarding Pharaoh, whose superior is he after all?" The subject matter of this letter is the political assassination of two policemen. In the Late Ramessid Letters, Piankh is first and foremost a general, whose military activities entirely overshadow his secondary role as high priest of Amun; this supports the view that the downfall of the New Kingdom was due more to the military strength of generals, who commanded Libyan mercenaries, than to the power of the Amun priesthood.

The latest extant letters of pharaonic times are from the succeeding twenty-first dynasty, whose kings and high priests were of Libyan origin. These, written mostly by priests, concern such matters as fugitive servants, horses and warriors, fowlers, and the illness of the high priest of Amun, who bore the Libyan name Masahert.

**Model Letters.** An important instrument in the education of Egyptian scribes was the model letter. The earliest of these is a composition in epistolary form, known as *Kmyt*, which was composed in the early Middle Kingdom and often copied by students in the New Kingdom. The most significant corpus of model letters is on papyri of the Ramessid period. Today referred to under the rubric "Late Egyptian Miscellanies," some of these papyri were anciently called "instructions in letter-writing" and contained model letters composed for educational purposes. The student is exhorted to be assiduous in his studies and to avoid dissipation. Many model letters elevated the profession of scribe by describing the pleasant life of a bureaucrat—refined in his attire, esteemed by society, and wealthy in his villa estate; by contrast, other occupations were denigrated. Other letters were concocted to acquaint the student with unusual vocabulary. Also included in the Miscellanies are original letters that the teacher apparently extracted from his files to serve as models.

The letters in the Miscellanies provide a mass of information on state and temple administration, economics, and society. Particularly important are references to agricultural matters, such as the demarcation of fields, tenant farmers, and the collection and transport of the harvest tax. These Miscellanies inform us that the scribe was not taxed but rather saw to the assessment and collection of revenues for the state and temples. Included in this corpus are complaints about excessive taxation, the illegal seizure of people by unauthorized individuals, and the corvée, whereby people were conscripted to perform agricultural labor or work on building projects.

Apart from the Miscellanies, there exist two literary letters. The longest is Papyrus Anastasi I, composed early in Ramesses II's reign and frequently copied on ostraca by student scribes. This lengthy epistle includes such matters as the rhetoric of composition, engineering problems, calculations of supplies for the army, and the geography of the Near East. The writer employs sarcasm and irony as means of improving the quality of the student's mind beyond rote memorization of facts. The epistolary form was also used to frame the fictional narrative of Papyrus Pushkin 127, which describes the tribulations of a wandering priestly outcast of Heliopolis at the end of the New Kingdom.

**Letters to the Dead.** As early as the late Old Kingdom, we find the practice of writing letters to the dead. These documents were often written on pottery vessels that were deposited in the deceased's tomb-chapel. Offerings in the vessels served to placate the dead person's spirit (*3ḥ*). Other letters to the dead were inscribed on such materials as linen, papyrus, or limestone flakes. In these letters, a number of which were written by or addressed to female relatives, the writer complains about unfortunate circumstances that he or she believes were caused by the dead relative or by some other individual in the beyond. In the latter case, the writer implores the spirit of the deceased relative to take legal action against the dead offender in the netherworld tribunal, composed of spirits of the dead and presided over by the great god.

Although letters to the dead possess a legalistic flavor, the writer's emotions often intrude. In one such letter, on a stela of the First Intermediate Period, the writer explains how carefully he has performed ritual spells on his dead wife's behalf and expresses his hope to see her in a dream contending and interceding on his behalf—the earliest evidence for the incubation of dreams in ancient Egypt. In a long letter to the dead from the nineteenth dynasty, the writer stresses how devoted and faithful he has been to his wife both before and after her death. Another such letter from the twenty-first dynasty, addressed by the grieving Butehamon to his dead wife, expresses the common fate of all beings—gods, kings, and the rest of humanity; it states, "There is no one who shall stay alive, for we shall all follow you [the dead wife]." In general, letters to the dead reflect the high esteem that women enjoyed in ancient Egypt.

**Letters Involving Women.** Prior to the New Kingdom, few letters have survived that involve a female writer or addressee. In the several Middle Kingdom examples of such letters, appropriate epistolary greetings are directed to the female recipient, and in an Illahun letter from a woman to her lord about the weaving of clothing, she employs the same epistolary formulas that men use and even complains about the lord's neglectfulness. In the Ramessid period, when introductory formulas and prayers to gods on the recipient's behalf became more common, it is noticeable that letters addressed to chantresses in the time of Ramesses II utilize extended greetings. Model letters even existed in the Miscellanies for female writers, and these also contain introductions with intercessions on behalf of the recipient.

Approximately 14 percent of the Deir el-Medina letters involve women either as writers or recipients. Men tended to write to women twice as often as the reverse; and one-fourth of the letters are between family members. Communications to or from women deal with transactions, complaints about the recipient's conduct, family matters, and errands of various sorts. Absent from letters sent by women of Deir el-Medina are petitions to higher authorities, such as men might write to the vizier. Elsewhere, however, women of high status communicated in writing to higher authorities, including the king—as is evident from a letter addressed to Sety II by a lady in charge of women weavers at the harem of Miwer in the Faiyum area.

Particularly difficult to resolve is the question of female literacy. There is some meager evidence that a very small percentage of women were literate; and given the generally favorable status of ancient Egyptian women, it is possible that some of the Deir el-Medina women were capable of penning a short letter. In the Late Ramessid Letters, the authority wielded by some of the ladies does suggest that they may have been literate. It has been argued that one letter of this archive is in the distinctive handwriting of the chantress of Amun-Henuttawy and that certain linguistic features of this letter indicate feminine authorship. In general, however, letters involving women as writer or recipient resemble letters involving men.

**Conclusion.** In addition to many diverse subjects treated in correspondence, letters have contributed significantly to our understanding of the history of the Egyptian language. Perhaps more than any other type of document, they reflect the living colloquial language as it evolved; this is particularly true of genuine letters, whereas model and literary letters tended to retain older features of the language.

## BIBLIOGRAPHY

Baer, Klaus. "An Eleventh Dynasty Farmer's Letters to His Family." *Journal of the American Oriental Society* 83 (1963), 1–19. Discusses the economic aspects of the Hekanakhte Letters.

Baines, John, and C. J. Eyre. "Four Notes on Literacy." *Göttinger Miszellen* 61 (1983), 65–96. Treats literacy in the population, including kings and women, and the literacy rate at Deir el-Medina.

Bakir, Abd el-Mohsen. *Egyptian Epistolography from the Eighteenth to the Twenty-first Dynasty.* Bibliothèque d'Étude, 48. Cairo, 1970. Offers a comprehensive discussion of epistolary style and formulas during the New Kingdom.

Caminos, Ricardo A. *Late-Egyptian Miscellanies.* Brown Egyptological Studies, 1. London, 1954. Provides translations of New Kingdom model letters, with commentary.

Caminos, Ricardo. *A Tale of Woe: From a Hieratic Papyrus in the A. S. Pushkin Museum of Fine Arts in Moscow.* Oxford, 1977. Publication of the literary letter on Papyrus Pushkin 127.

James, T. G. H. *The Ḥekanakhte Papers, and Other Early Middle Kingdom Documents.* Publications of The Metropolitan Museum of Art, Egyptian Expedition, 19. New York, 1962. The basic publication of the Hekanakhte Letters.

Janssen, Jac J. "A Notable Lady." *Wepwawet: Research Papers in Egyptology* 2 (1986), 30–31. Discusses the literacy of a late Ramessid lady, Henuttawy, who performed administrative duties on her husband's behalf.

Janssen, Jac J. "On Style in Egyptian Handwriting." *Journal of Egyptian Archaeology* 73 (1987), 161–167. Analyzes the handwriting of individual scribes of the Late Ramessid Letters and suggests that the women of Deir el-Medina may have inscribed their own letters on ostraca.

Janssen, Jac J. *Late Ramesside Letters and Communication.* Hieratic Papyri in the British Museum, 6. London, 1991. Publication of recent additions to the corpus of Late Ramessid Letters.

Sweeney, Deborah. "Intercessory Prayer in Ancient Egypt and the Bible." In *Pharaonic Egypt: The Bible and Christianity*, edited by Sarah Israelit-Groll, pp. 213–230. Jerusalem, 1985. Considers the introductory formulas of Ramessid letters as they relate to prayer.

Sweeney, Deborah. "Women's Correspondence from Deir el-Medineh." In *Sesto Congresso Internazionale di Egittologia: Atti*, vol. 2, pp. 523–529. Turin, 1993. Includes a cautious appraisal of the problem of female literacy at Deir el-Medina.

Sweeney, Deborah. "Women and Language in the Ramesside Period." In *Abstracts of Papers: Seventh International Congress of Egyptologists, Cambridge. 3–9 September 1995*, edited by Christopher Eyre, pp. 180–181. Oxford, 1995. Suggests that the letter of Henuttawy exhibits peculiarities of language that identify the writer as female.

Wente, Edward F. *Late Ramesside Letters.* Studies in Ancient Oriental Civilization, 33. Chicago, 1967. Provides a discussion of the chronology of the Late Ramessid Letters, translations, and commentary.

Wente, Edward F. *Letters from Ancient Egypt.* Writings from the Ancient World, 1. Atlanta, 1990. After an introduction treating the writing of letters and their transmission, provides translations of many real letters from the fifth dynasty through the twenty-first, as well as those of Kemit, the Papyrus Anastasi I, and some letters to the dead; comprehensive bibliography.

EDWARD F. WENTE

**COSMETICS.** *See* Toiletries and Cosmetics.

**COSMOGONIES.** *See* Myths, *article on* Creation Myths.

**COSTUME.** *See* Clothing and Personal Adornment.

**CREATION MYTHS.** *See* Myths, *article on* Creation Myths.

**CRETE.** Sporadic contacts, perhaps indirect, between Egypt and Crete go back into the third millennium BCE. The first truly sustained contact, however, began with the rise of the Minoan palaces early in the second millennium BCE, continuing then through the end of the Late Bronze Age (c.1150 BCE).

Old Kingdom objects, primarily stone vessels, have been found at a number of sites on Crete, as have Second Intermediate Period objects, such as a calcite (Egyptian alabaster) lid with the cartouche of the Hyksos king Khyan that was uncovered at Knossos. In the Nile Delta region of Egypt, fresco wall paintings were discovered at the Hyksos capital of Avaris (present-day Tell ed-Dab'a), with scenes of bull-leaping, are similar to those more commonly found on Minoan Crete. Debate currently rages as to whether those paintings date to the Hyksos period or to the Egyptian reoccupation of the city during the New Kingdom, early in the eighteenth dynasty.

Certainly, contacts between Minoan Crete and Egypt flourished during the eighteenth dynasty. For example, numerous New Kingdom Egyptian objects have been found on Crete, and a number of Minoan ceramic vessels have been found from that time in Egypt, indicating that trade and contact were ongoing (albeit, perhaps, sometimes indirectly via Canaanite merchants). In addition, wall paintings and inscriptions record visits from "Keftiu" (usually identified as Crete and the Minoans), primarily during the time of Hatshepsut and Thutmose III. The Keftiu were depicted as bringing *inw* (usually translated as "tribute" but with a secondary meaning of "gifts") to the pharaoh and were most likely representations of actual commercial missions or diplomatic embassies between Minoan Crete and New Kingdom Egypt. While precise depictions were replaced by less precise portrayals of Mi-

noan wall paintings after the time of Thutmose III, the inscriptions continued and only become stereotyped during the nineteenth and twentieth dynasties.

Perhaps the most important of all those inscriptions was that found at Kom el-Hetan, dating from the time of Amenhotpe III, which not only mentioned Keftiu but listed Knossos, Phaistos, Kydonia, and Lyktos, among other Aegean place names. Objects with the cartouche of Amenhotpe III and his wife Queen Tiye have been found at several such Minoan sites, and they may indicate a connection to the list at Kom el-Hetan. Perhaps an official Egyptian embassy was sent to the Aegean by Amenhotpe III, of which the Kom el-Hetan list and some scarabs are the only remaining extant evidence—but the hypothesis remains to be proven.

The Keftiu frequently shared their place in Egyptian inscriptions with "Tanaja" (the Mycenaean Greek mainland) and the "Isles in the Midst of the Great Green" (the Cycladic Islands), indicating that the Minoans on Crete were not the only peoples from the Bronze Age Aegean with whom the New Kingdom Egyptians were in contact. After the fourteenth century BCE, Minoan-Egyptian contacts seem to have declined in favor of Mycenaean-Egyptian contacts, probably reflecting a sociopolitical change in the Bronze Age Aegean, rather than a conscious decision on the part of the Egyptians. Contact between Egypt and Crete resumed again in the first millennium BCE.

[*See also* Mediterranean Area.]

### BIBLIOGRAPHY

Cline, Eric H. *Sailing the Wine-Dark Sea: International Trade and the Late Bronze Age Aegean.* Oxford, 1994. An overview of the international trade in the Mediterranean during the second millennium BCE; catalog of Egyptian objects in Crete and chapter on Egypt are particularly relevant.

Kemp, Barry J., and Robert S. Merrillees. *Minoan Pottery in Second Millennium Egypt.* Mainz, 1980. Discussion of exports from Crete found in second millennium BCE contexts in Egypt.

Pendlebury, John D. S. *Aegyptiaca: A Catalogue of Egyptian Objects in the Aegean Area.* Cambridge, 1930. Original catalog of Egyptian objects found in Crete and elsewhere in the Bronze Age Aegean; now updated by Cline (1994).

Pendlebury, John D. S. "Egypt and the Aegean in the Late Bronze Age." *Journal of Egyptian Archaeology* 16 (1930), 75–92. Original discussion of Egyptian contacts with Crete and other areas in the Bronze Age Aegean; now updated by Cline (1994).

ERIC H. CLINE

**CRIME AND PUNISHMENT.** Crimes are offenses that are considered to affect the whole community, not only their individual victims. Unlike civil actions, in which the plaintiff seeks compensation for the damage he has suffered, criminal prosecutions demand the punishment of the guilty. The transgressions that are classified as crimes by a society can thus be recognized by the penalties they bring on, such as loss of freedom, mutilation, or death.

**Sources.** Our information about crimes and criminal procedure in pharaonic Egypt derives mainly from official records rather than from private documents. Three genres are especially informative: decrees on behalf of temples and funerary cults that describe the means by which the decree will be enforced; records of the Great Prison from the late Middle Kingdom; and papyri documenting actual criminal investigations of the late New Kingdom. No criminal law code has been preserved, and it is doubtful that such a thing existed.

Documents concerning crime most often survived when inscribed on stone. Decrees on behalf of temples, for example, were often carved on stelae, both to commemorate the generous piety of the donor king and so that the temple's privileges would not be conveniently forgotten by the next generation of civil servants. The few surviving texts on papyrus also concern politically important criminal cases and may have been stored separately from or more carefully than records concerning common criminals. These latter were probably housed in the prisons or in government offices in the cities; only one such document has survived. The accidents of preservation have thus favored texts dealing with crimes against the state rather than crimes against individuals, such as murder, rape, or theft.

Nevertheless, the almost complete lack of evidence concerning prosecutions for crimes against individuals remains puzzling. There is no doubt that such incidents occurred, since they are alluded to in both private and official documents, but only a handful of such texts include any reference to investigation or punishment. It has been suggested that prosecutions for violence against individuals are missing from our sources because, in fact, this was not classified as a crime; but the few references to persons punished for assault suggests that *this* at least was criminal.

**Old Kingdom.** In contrast to later periods, the Old Kingdom appears to have had established law courts staffed with permanent, specialized officials who were empowered to deal with criminal cases. The numerous legal titles—such as "overseer of the court" and "master of the secrets of judgments in the court"—form the bulk of the preserved evidence about the court system. The top office, "overseer of the six courts," was held by the vizier himself (the location and function of the "the six courts" is not known). In general, however, the agents of the legal system were not of high status, although some "overseers of the court" also held the important title "overseer of works," perhaps because convicted criminals could be sent on to the department of works. The courts were not closely associated with the temples, except in that a number of legal officers served in the cults of the minor deities Heket and Ha, who may have been the patron gods of the legal profession. The common title "prophet of Maat" is thought to have been administrative rather than religious.

What little we know about the operation of the courts in criminal matters derives mainly from such decrees as that of Neferirkare on behalf of the temple of Abydos. The text proclaims that anyone who interferes with the priests or cultivators of the god's fields shall be sent to the court, where his property will be seized and he himself will be assigned to the stone quarries. The text specifies that no distinction is to be made for rank:

> Every official, every king's acquaintance, and every *ḥry-wdb* who will act following this that my majesty decreed shall be taken to court. His house, fields, people, and everything in his possession, shall be confiscated and given to [ . . . ]

Further punishments administered by the court included beatings and imprisonment.

A different type of criminal investigation is described in the famous autobiography of Weni of the sixth dynasty. The alleged offense is not named, but since it involved the queen, it was clearly both important and politically sensitive. In what appears to have been an unusual arrangement for the time, Weni and one other colleague conducted a secret investigation, the result of which is not reported. Similar investigations would take place under similar circumstances in the New Kingdom, most notably in the case of the Harem Conspiracy (see below).

### Middle Kingdom and New Kingdom

*Crimes and punishments.* Literary texts reflect an aversion to capital punishment in general and suggest that this sentence was reserved for rebellion, the ultimate attack on the established order. The author of the *Instructions for Merikare* advises moderate punishment in general:

> Do not kill; it is not useful to you. Punish with beatings and with detention so that the land will be well founded. Except for the rebel whose plan is discovered. (Papyrus Leningrad 1116A, 48–50)

King Piya of the twenty-fifth dynasty boasted on his triumphal stela that no one had been killed in the Southern nomes (provinces) except, again, the rebels who cursed god and who were executed. Finally, the notorious King Khufu (Cheops) of legend, in Papyrus Westcar, proposes that the magician Djedi use a prisoner for a magic display involving decapitation, at which the magician uttered the rebuke, "But not to a human, Sovereign! . . . It is not permitted to do thus to the noble cattle!" (Papyrus Westcar 8, 16–17).

The execution of rebels, on the other hand, was a religious duty. Indeed, execution did not go far enough; the rebel was to be annihilated altogether. "Expel him, kill [him], obliterate his name, [destroy] his associates, banish the memory of him and of his supporters who love him," is the advice given in the *Instructions for Merikare*. As Anthony Leahy (1984) and Harco Willems (1990) have shown, rebels were identified with the opponents of the goddess Maat and, in particular, with the gods Seth and Apophis, the enemies of the legitimate ruler deities Osiris and Re. Just as in myth, the enemies of Osiris were destroyed by fire, so too human rebels against the king and the gods were executed on a brazier or in a furnace, perhaps on the altar of the god they had offended. Burning was the extreme punishment for an Egyptian because it destroyed the body and with it the hope of an afterlife: the victim ceased to exist.

The most conspicuous act of rebellion was, of course, an attempt on the life of the king, such as the conspiracy to assassinate Ramesses III and place one of his sons on the throne. The plot appears to have been hatched by women of the harem, including the mother of the pretender; harem officials carried their messages outside to relatives in high government office in the treasury, the temples, and the army. Whether they succeeded in murdering the king is not clear; at any rate, they failed in their ultimate aim of securing the throne, and either Ramesses III or his lawful successor, Ramesses IV, ordered their arrest and trial. The sentences passed on the guilty are recorded in the Judicial Papyrus of Turin. Twenty-four conspirators were found guilty and sentenced, but their fate—almost certainly execution—is not specified. Ten others, including the probable pretender to the throne, were allowed to take their own lives. The record does not indicate to what they owed this concession; the two groups appear to have been equally culpable and of equally high rank, and both included active conspirators as well as others who merely knew of the conspiracy and failed to report it. Each of the accused is called a "great enemy" (*ḥrw ʿȝ*). Some of the names have been changed—one, for example, to "Re hates him"—as a further step toward the obliteration of the criminal's identity. Once the leaders of the conspiracy had been duly punished, Ramesses IV issued a general amnesty to fugitives and prisoners, which was explicitly said to include rebels.

The practice of burning rebels alive is better documented in the Third Intermediate Period. In a number of cases, the method of execution is the brazier. The *Chronicles of Prince Osorkon* of the twenty-second dynasty relate that the Theban rebels against Amun-Re were punished by Prince Osorkon, their real opponent, with death, "each one being burned in the place of [his] crime." The word "braziers" appears twice in the broken passages preceding this statement. A similar incident is described in the fictional *Instructions of Ankhsheshonqy*. The background to the *Instructions* is a plot to assassinate the king, which was overheard by a loyal servant and reported to his majesty. The latter, after reproaching the ringleader for his disloyalty and ingratitude, ordered an altar of earth to be built at the door of the palace; on it, the ringleader, his kin, and his coconspirators were burned on the brazier. Ankhsheshonqy himself was imprisoned because he had heard about the plot and failed to reveal it, although he had earnestly tried to dissuade the ringleader from his purpose. Nor was he released with the other prisoners on the anniversary of the king's accession—a reference to a practice of general amnesties issued on important state occasions, which may go back to the Middle Kingdom.

Political opponents, as a variety of rebels, might also be banished or, like Sinuhe, go into self-imposed exile. We are most likely to hear of them when they are magnanimously recalled. Thus, the Banishment Stela of the twenty-first dynasty records that Prince Menkheperre, the high priest of Amun, asked Amun-Re to pardon the rival claimants to his office who had been banished to the Kharga Oasis some years before and to forbid the practice of banishment for the future.

The idea of rebellion extended also to crimes against religious foundations; royal inscriptions and decrees on behalf of temples used the vocabulary of insurrection and capital punishment, though not always in the same text. For example, the word "rebel" was applied to anyone who might conscript staff of the temple of Min at Coptos, in violation of an exemption decree issued by Pepy II. Six hundred years later, a priest of Min who had stolen a cult object was called "a rebel and enemy of his god." He was punished with loss of office and income, removal of his offerings from the temple, and perhaps debaptism; death was not mentioned explicitly.

A few texts of the pharaonic period specify burning alive as the penalty for cultic offenses. A decree usurped by the thirteenth dynasty king Neferhotpe, for example, names burning as the penalty for trespass on a protected area of the Abydos necropolis. Actual executions on the brazier or furnace are described by Senwosret I in his inscription at Tod; the temple had been wrecked by vandals who were arrested, placed on the brazier, and burned as "enemies." Execution for cultic thefts could also be carried out by impalement rather than burning. The Nauri Decree, which generally sets lighter penalties (see below), specifies the death penalty for two crimes: sale of temple livestock, and the transferring of an animal from the offering-list of Osiris to some other list. Both offenses have to do with the alienation of sacrificial animals. The offender was to be executed by impalement, and his wife, children, and property were forfeit to the temple. Similarly, a New Kingdom exemption decree of unknown provenance announced that theft of sacred property or people would be punished with impalement next to the protected temple. The Great Tomb Robberies are also in this category of desecration of a sacred site.

Crimes against the state, other than treason or cultic crimes, are sometimes identified as "worthy of death," although not explicitly called rebellion. The Horemheb Decree announces that false rulings by judges are "great crimes [worthy] of death" (*bt3 ʿ3 n mwt*), but it does not specify the means of execution. Similarly, in the *Instructions of Amenompe*, falsifying official documents is called a "hostility [worthy] of death." Finally, in a Deir el-Medina legal document, a woman who stole copper is called "worthy of death." Her case was referred to the vizier, so we do not know how she was actually punished. Possibly, the expression "worthy of death" is not to be taken literally.

For persons of the official class, the most serious punishment short of death was loss of property, office, status, and sometimes also identity, whereby an erstwhile official was reduced to the status of a laborer in the fields of a temple or, in the worst cases, in the granite quarries or in the gold mines of Kush. The criminal's descendants shared in his ruin, since the office and property were lost to the family forever; if the offender himself had escaped, his relatives might be sent to prison in his stead. In the New Kingdom, mutilation of the ears and nose of the criminal could be added to other penalties. The crimes that incurred mutilation were similar to the capital offenses listed above but were not characterized as rebellion. In the Nauri Decree, those who move the boundaries of fields belonging to the temple of Osiris lose their ears and nose and become cultivators for the temple, as do those caught in the act of stealing animals. The families of the latter group were also handed over to the temple.

For other property crimes against the temple of Osiris, the Nauri Decree sets yet different penalties—beatings, open wounds, and multiple restitutions, in various combinations. Theft of property other than animals was punished by one hundred blows and a fine of one hundred times the value of the stolen goods. Temporary requisitioning of staff for corvée or agricultural work in another district drew two hundred blows, five "flowing wounds" (precise meaning unclear), and restitution of the lost work time, even if the staff or vessel had been used for official business and not for the borrower's own purposes. These penalties are much harsher than those for theft from private persons, which are thought to be threefold restitution of the stolen property with no accompanying physical punishment.

Punishment in the form of incarceration with hard labor is well documented, most notably by the Middle Kingdom records of the Great Prison at Thebes. This and other prisons were not only places of confinement but also workhouses or labor camps with links to the "Office of Provider-of-People," or labor bureau. Some of its inmates were there for life, including those who had been convicted of running away to avoid compulsory labor on state projects. In one exceptional case, this penalty extended to the whole family; he was "given to the plow-lands together with his people forever [as ordered by] the court."

Shorter sentences for various crimes are known, especially from the New Kingdom. A school text mentions the possibly fictional case of a sailor sentenced to twenty-three days in a local prison (*itḥ*), where he was made to cultivate public lands. Hard labor is also named in two of the three documented cases of punishment for assault on an individual. One offender was set to cut stone in the Theban necropolis and the other, a policeman, is said to be "in the compulsory labor since he hit with a stick and he was like every enemy of Re," a characterization which again associates myth, rebellion, and crime. Neither case happens to mention a prison, but this may have been understood to be the setting for the penal labor.

Finally, prisons also served as a places of detention for criminals awaiting a harsher penalty. If the lawbreaker eluded the authorities, his family members were sometimes imprisoned in his stead. The wives and children of those who evaded compulsory labor were held in the law court, rather than in the prison, and they were released when the fugitive was captured or, perhaps, when the government had given up hope of catching him. In other cases, the family evidently had to serve out the entire sentence of the offender.

The mildest form of punishment was a beating, usually specified as "one hundred blows with a stick." A beating is often named in oaths as the sanction for perjury or for default on a contract, but it was seldom actually carried out. Occasionally, however, the local court did administer a beating to a litigant who ignored several verdicts against him, gave false testimony, or brought what appears to be a false accusation. The common element of these offenses appears to have been contempt of court. Yet if the literary texts are to be taken at face value, officials, tax collectors, and schoolteachers frequently beat their subordinates without recourse to a court; it is thus impossible in many cases to tell whether the offense that provoked the blows was considered a crime.

Except for the few cases of assault mentioned above, crimes against individuals are poorly documented. Theft appears to have been a tort rather than a crime; it was privately prosecuted, and the penalty was three times the value of the stolen goods. Adultery was not a matter for the courts but probably led to private acts of revenge; the status of rape is unclear.

Murder appears to have been a capital offense, however, at least in later periods. On the Banishment Stela, the god Amun-Re agreed that he would in the future kill (or have killed) those who were found guilty of murder; and a stela from Napata of the seventh or sixth century BCE records that Amun ordered the death by fire of some priests who murdered or plotted to murder an innocent man (Cairo JE 48865). The Petition of Petiese contains a suggestion that Petiese the elder should have caused the murderers of his grandchildren to be brought and placed on the brazier; the suggestion was not followed, however, and no action was taken against the offenders.

***Criminal procedure.*** Egypt during the Middle and New Kingdoms, like many other ancient societies, lacked institutions that are associated with criminal procedure today, such as police, public prosecutors, and professional judges. Instead, the official class as a whole was responsible for reporting crime to the office of the vizier; the latter then conducted the investigation, examination, and punishment. In routine cases, he may simply have ratified the decisions of lower officials.

Reporting crime was every official's duty and not only the business of police. The *medjay*, who are usually described as police, were in fact more like a military guard who protected areas such as the Valley of the Kings against physical threat. They were not concerned with crime control in the wider sense, although they might apprehend some criminals, especially burglars, in the course of their duties. Another group of officials, the *3tw*, had some investigative role, but their duties are not well documented and they do not play a major role in the known cases. Instead, as early as the First Intermediate Period, persons of the official class were required to report wrongdoing to their superiors and, in some cases, to confiscate the suspect's property until higher authorities arrived to deal with the offender (Edict of King Demedjibtawy for Idy). In the New Kingdom tomb-builders' community of Deir el-Medina, all workmen from scribes to stonecutters swore an oath of office not to commit crimes in the royal necropolis and also to report the crimes of others. The oath, administered to the work gang *en masse* by outside officials, read in part, "I will not hear a matter, I will not see a theft in the great and noble places and conceal it." At least one workman named the oath as an introduction to charges against his colleagues. Laconic references to the oath of office from other parts of Egypt suggest that all civil servants were sworn to report crimes committed in their sphere of work.

Failure to report crime was itself a crime and was punished almost as heavily as the original offense. Those who knew of the Harem Conspiracy against Ramesses III but did not reveal the plot were executed along with the others. In contrast, King Demedjibtawy's decree, protecting the funerary cult of Idy, threatened any chief who failed to take action against criminals with loss of office and property, a lesser punishment than the execution and loss of burial rights suffered by the thieves and vandals.

Reports of crime passed up the chain of authority to the office of the vizier or, in exceptional cases, to the king, who sent agents to investigate. In New Kingdom texts from Thebes, those agents are sometimes identified as "officials of the Place of Examination"; suspects and witnesses were interrogated at this Place of Examination and could be imprisoned there for several days if necessary. The "great officials of the Place of Examination," who handled the Harem Conspiracy investigation by order of the king, included two overseers of the treasury, standard-bearers, and royal butlers—that is, high-ranking officials close to the king. Generally, however, the officials are not identified, nor do is it known how they conducted their examinations.

The only criminal hearings that are described in detail are the Great Tomb Robbery investigations of the late twentieth dynasty. The robberies were a series of assaults on the tombs and temples of Western Thebes by various gangs of thieves. Over the years, a number of large-scale investigations were launched to punish the criminals and recover their loot, and the records of these unique proceedings have largely survived. The proceedings were carried out by the country's highest officials, including the vizier and the high priest of Amun. Interrogations were conducted under torture described as "twisting the hands and feet." The suspects were confronted with contradictions in their story, and confederates were brought together to accuse one another; one of the defendants was even ferried over to the Valley of the Kings, to see whether he could point out the tomb he admitted to robbing (he could not). Although some of the officials were as anxious to cover up the scandals as to expose them, dozens of thieves were found guilty and imprisoned until word should be received from the pharaoh about their fate. We know from other sources that some were executed, but not by what means; a few suspects were acquitted and released.

Although the Great Tomb Robbery investigations were in some ways unique, in other ways they appear to have conformed to standard criminal procedures. The vizier seems to have been personally involved in most criminal investigations, and probably in all cases involving individuals of the official class; the Harem Conspiracy trials, from which the king deliberately distanced himself, form a notable exception to this rule. There is also reason to believe that only the king could authorize capital punishment. Again, the Harem Conspiracy provides a counterexample: the pharaoh explicitly placed full responsibility for the executions on the examining officials and declared himself blameless—a curious stance for one whose role was to battle the enemies of the state—and most likely because the defendants included members of the royal family.

One group of cases that does not follow the pattern described above is that of the fugitives from compulsory labor, whose fate was recorded in the late Middle Kingdom records of the Great Prison. When a peasant failed to appear for duty or was discovered to have fled from his work, action was first taken against his family. The relatives were held as security for his return by order of a council or court (ḏꜣḏꜣt), which was either a local body or one attached to the Great Prison. The facts of the case were entered into the register of the Great Prison and, evidently, also forwarded to some higher authority. When the runaway was captured or turned himself in, or perhaps while he was still at large but all of the facts in the case were known, this higher authority pronounced his sentence. The family was then released, the case was checked off in the prison register, and the case was declared closed by a scribe of the vizier. The identity of this higher authority who made the final decision and the means by which he reached its verdict are not specified, but the fact that a scribe of the vizier had the last word on the case suggests that it was the office of the vizier that decided a fugitive's fate or, at least, confirmed the decision of the council or court. If this is so, then it would appear that the office of the vizier had exclusive jurisdiction over all criminal cases, whether they involved peasants or officials.

[See also Law; and Tomb Robbery Papyri.]

**BIBLIOGRAPHY**

Capart, J., A. H. Gardiner, and B. Van de Walle. "New Light on the Ramesside Tomb-Robberies." *Journal of Egyptian Archaeology* 22 (1936), 169–193.

Eyre, C. J. "Crime and Adultery in Ancient Egypt." *Journal of Egyptian Archaeology* 70 (1984), 92–105.

Gordicke, H. *Königliche Dokumente aus dem alten Reich.* Wiesbaden, 1967.

Hayes, William C. *A Papyrus of the Late Middle Kingdom in the Brooklyn Museum [Papyrus Brooklyn 35.1446].* Brooklyn, 1955.

Leahy, Anthony. "Death by Fire in Ancient Egypt." *Journal of the Economic and Social History of the Orient* 27 (1984), 199–206.

Lorton, David. "The Treatment of Criminals in Ancient Egypt through the New Kingdom." *Journal of the Economic and Social History of the Orient* 20 (1977), 2–64.

McDowell, A. G. *Jurisdiction in the Workmen's Community of Deir el-Medina.* Egyptologische Uitgaven, 5. Leiden, 1991.

Peet, T. Eric. *The Great Tomb Robberies of the Twentieth Egyptian Dynasty.* Oxford, 1930, 1977.

Smith, H. S. "A Note on Amnesty." *Journal of Egyptian Archaeology* 54 (1968), 209–214.

Strudwick, Nigel. *The Administration of Egypt in the Old Kingdom.* London, 1985.

Willems, Harco. "Crime, Cult and Capital Punishment (Moʿalla Inscription 8)." *Journal of Egyptian Archaeology* 76 (1990), 27–54.

A. G. MCDOWELL

**CROCODILES.** The Nile crocodile (*Crocodilus niloticus*) was called *msḥ* in Old Egyptian and was referred to by some twenty other words; it belongs to the order Crocodilia and can reach a length of some 6 meters (20 feet). The crocodile played a meaningful role not only in secular aspects of ancient Egypt but also in mythology, magic, and metaphor (imagery). Its mythical-magical names were Chentekhtai, Nephoros, Petesukhos, Maga, Wenti, but most often Soknopaios and Sobek (Grk., Sukhos). It was worshiped as a god (the crocodile-headed god), Sobek, from the marshes of the Nile Delta to the sandbanks of Gebel es-Silsila, around Lake Qarun in the Faiyum, as well as near Thebes; it was also associated with the great gods Re, Geb, Seth, and Osiris. In the Pyramid Texts, this dangerous aquatic reptile was recognized by its "wrinkled or rough face," its form—a combination of jackal and snake—and its color, designated by *mfkꜣt* ("turquoise-green").

In ancient Egypt, the crocodile not only inhabited the entire length of the Nile but also was found in canals and pools, as well as in Lake Moeris, in the Faiyum. It rested there on sandbanks, baking in the sun. Today, the crocodile's range is smaller and it lives in and around southern, sub-Saharan African waters. In ancient Egypt, it was both hunted and worshiped because of its extreme strength. In the region south of Khartoum, often far from the banks of the Nile, near waterholes or animal herds, it may unexpectedly rise from the water with a meters-long leap to crush its victim.

The crocodile is usually a part of Nile scenes or papyrus swamp landscapes, showing its preferred territory. From the Old Kingdom until Roman times, it is shown in the midst of shoals of fish—its main food—of which the Nile was proverbially full until the 1960s to 1970s construction of the Sadd el-Ali (the Aswan High Dam). Several ancient tomb scenes showed the predator grabbing a baby hippopotamus as it emerged from its mother during birth. The adult hippopotamus, capable of biting a crocodile in half, is its only enemy besides humans. Other ancient tomb scenes showed crocodile-mating; its sexual potency inspired the Pyramid Text, Spell 510, according to which the king changed into a crocodile before robbing husbands of their wives.

The writers and travelers of the ancient world, including Plutarch, Pliny, and Aelianus, observed the daily habits of the crocodile, reporting that it settled itself on an east-facing sandbank "with idle feet" when the sun rose, with wide-open "fearsome jaws"; in the afternoon, it turned westward, and in the evening entered the water. The crocodile is usually silent, nevertheless, it was accorded the honor of inclusion among the animal musicians of the Turin Satirical Papyrus. If the animal is

CROCODILES. *Crocodile toy with a movable jaw.*

frightened or wounded, a gruesome roar or piercing scream may escape it.

The ancient Egyptians came into conflict with the crocodile when it was necessary to drive herds across a ford in the Nile. Although a magical spell was spoken at the same time, crocodiles were not affected; nor were magical gestures and entreating verses as effective as frightening cries by the herder. At special risk were swimmers or those whose jobs took them onto or into the Nile: sailors, water carriers, fishermen, boat builders, launderers, and the many marsh workers. A later magical custom to ward off crocodiles was documented by the Horus Stela: if water was poured over them and this "magic water" drunk, one was believed to be protected. In the *Instructions of Khety*, as published by Hellmut Brunner, a despondent schoolboy was threatened with having to live like the launderer among the crocodiles and hippopotami.

Not only were the tooth-studded jaws of the reptile feared but also its tail, a blow from which may smash the backbone of its victim. Only the adult hippopotamus was safe from the crocodile. Camels, donkeys, cattle, horses, and even water birds—except for the trochilos (*Pluvianus aegyptiacus*), which sits on the crocodile's nose and picks off vermin—were dragged into the depths. According to the Theban cosmogony, the Golden Age would be characterized by "no crocodiles thieving" (and "no snakes biting"). Only for the lover was the crocodile "as harmless as a mouse" when he "enters the waters" to hurry to his beloved. According to Athanasius (fourth-century CE patriarch of Alexandria), Saint Anthony (the Great; 251–356 CE) was able to control the reptile with prayer. The thousands of crocodile bodies that were placed in ancient temples and caverns, however, prove that it was possible to master them; they were overcome by means of harpoons.

Attempts were made to tame crocodiles caught young, although those were not successful. When the Egyptians filled the moats around the fort at Sile with crocodiles, as the second-century BCE Greek historian Diodorus Siculus recorded, they were probably as well protected as we are today by defensive weapons. The menacing character of the crocodile was utilized in stories to protect the Hermetic writings; there, the reptile was called a "dragon," who even interfered with cosmic events, since he slobbered upon the water on which the sun god traversed the sky.

As a nocturnal being, the crocodile played a significant part in mythical and magical contexts, as well as in imagery; there, it served as "the symbol of all maliciousness." It was said, the name of "the man who is tired of life" reeks more "than the stench of crocodiles." Nevertheless, the crocodile was used as a man's name from the Old Kingdom onward and was the emblem for the sixth Upper Egyptian nome (province).

[*See also* Amphibians and Reptiles.]

**BIBLIOGRAPHY**

Brunner-Traut, Emma. *Altägyptische Tiergeschichte und Fabel*. Darmstadt, 1977.

Posener, Georges. *Festschrift für Siegfried Schott*. Wiesbaden, 1968.

EMMA BRUNNER-TRAUT
Translated from German by Julia Harvey

**CROWNS** played a dominant role in the composition of the royal and the divine image: kings and gods were never represented without them, because they indicated important aspects of both royalty and divinity. In this discussion, general features of the crowns' shapes and functions will be outlined first, followed by a description of the main types of royal and divine headdresses.

**Form and Composition.** Egyptian crowns were worn by kings, queens, and princesses, as well as by gods, in representations and texts. Apart from circlets and kerchiefs, no real-life examples have survived, and their actual size and material remain uncertain. As in most cultures, crowns mark the wearer as distinct from the average human being. This is usually achieved by optically "enhancing" the wearer, making him or her appear taller, and by using precious materials, such as gold, silver, and gemstones. Egyptian crowns are generally represented as very tall, sometimes so tall that they could hardly have been worn, and indeed such elements as high feathers are represented in token form at a much smaller scale on some surviving royal headdresses. This fact emphasizes the emblematic significance of items of regalia, which functioned virtually as "hieroglyphs," with their combinations forming "sentences" that could be read and altered by varying their constituent elements. This view is supported by cases of posthumously altered headdresses in representations of royal personae.

Royal regalia, and in particular crowns, often link their wearer with the superhuman sphere, and the height of Egyptian crowns itself points toward the heavenly or divine; thus, the crown of Queen Hatshepsut can be stated to "pierce the sky" during her coronation before the god Amun. Bestowed on the ruler by the gods in texts and representations, crowns symbolize the connection of earthly and divine rule: most crowns can be said to belong to the sun god Re or some other deity. Adornment with precious materials (or their colors), in particular the shimmer of gold and silver, provides a further link with gods who are associated with radiance. Solar or stellar disks can be added to a crown-type, as well as one or more cobra-form *uraeus* snakes, which represent the fire and blinding radiance issuing from the sun god's "eye," the solar disk, to consume potential enemies. Crowns themselves are often equated with the eyes of Re or Horus.

Normally, a single *uraeus* adorns the forehead of the ruler; in the Early Dynastic period and Old Kingdom it appears exclusively with kerchiefs (e.g., the *nms*) and headbands, never with the tall crowns. From the sixth dynasty onward, royal women too may wear a *uraeus*. A few *uraei* of gold, some of them inlaid, survive from Middle and New Kingdom tombs. The distinctive shape of the *uraeus*, like that of crowns in general, at different periods can be an important factor in dating uninscribed representations. A double *uraeus*—one usually wearing the Red Crown and the other the White Crown—is attested for royal women from the reign of Ahmose on. A variation is the (sometimes double) *uraeus* augmented by a vulture head, referring to the goddesses Wadjit and Nekhbet of the two halves of the country, or—on a deceased king—to Isis and Nephthys as the two mourners of Osiris. Among the gods, only Montu and the Abydos fetish representing Osiris are shown wearing the double *uraeus*. Attached to the plain Kushite cap, it is distinctive of rulers of the twenty-fifth dynasty and their Napatean and Meroitic successors. Depending on the context, the *uraeus* can also bear the head of a gazelle (especially for subsidiary royal women) or an ibis. Ptolemaic queens may even wear a triple *uraeus*. A further increase in the number of cobras is attested from the reign of Amenhotpe III on, when a *kalathos* of *uraei* as a crown base is attested. Akhenaten is the first king to display a circlet of *uraei*, also worn by gods, around some of his crowns. The radiance conveyed by disks and *uraei* likens the wearer to the gods, and the increase of their number on crowns occurs during periods of intensified solar cult, developing in particular during the Amarna period.

Many Egyptian crowns contain elements of plant or animal origin, including feathers (of falcon or ostrich) and horns (of ram, cattle, or gazelle). These features associate the wearer with the qualities of the specific god who was manifest in a given animal. Thus, the curved ram's horn, a symbol of Amun, which occurs at the side of royal headdresses from the time of Amenhotpe I, identifies the ruler with this god and imbues him with divine qualities.

Plant ornaments are confined mostly to the crowns of queens and princesses, and seem to evoke beauty and youth or rejuvenation. Exceptions are the central element of the *atef*-crown and the occasional presence of the *ished*-fruit on the same crown, and the "wire" or "curl" of the Red Crown.

**Religious and Political Significance.** The large number of crowns attested for a single ruler—the coronation of Hatshepsut shows nine different types, and the same number of basic headdresses is attested in depictions from the Old Kingdom on—reflects different aspects of kingship. Of the ten royal crowns enumerated for Ptolemy V in the Decree of Memphis on the Rosetta Stone (196 BCE), the Double Crown—a combination of the White and Red Crowns of Upper and Lower Egypt—is said to be the diadem worn during the coronation ceremony in the temple of Memphis. Attested from the Middle Kingdom onward, the titles "Foremost of the Secrets of the Two Crown [-goddesse]s" (i.e., the Double Crown; *ḥrj-sšt₃ n W₃dty*) and "Priest of the Two Great of Magic," both applied to the "Keeper of the Royal Diadem," support the dominant role of the Double Crown in symbolizing terrestrial political rule.

The political and religious significance of crowns for the image of the king can be inferred from the fact that different headdresses were favored in different periods. Thus, some types of crowns do not appear in the Amarna period. Akhenaten's queen Nefertiti wore crowns confined to the king in other periods, such as the cap crown, and new crown types were invented for her, apparently to symbolize her expanded role.

Some texts suggest a metaphorical use of the royal crowns to embody the office of kingship, or even the political or geographical notion of the kingdom, similar to the European medieval concept of the *corona regni* (royal crown). Thus, in Medinet Habu the captured princes beg the Egyptian king for air so that they may "serve his diadem" (*w₃dty*)—that is, the Double Crown.

Egyptian crown forms were adopted in the iconography of kings and gods in neighboring cultures, notably in the Levant and Nubia. The crowns of the Lower Nubian Ballana culture maintained many Egyptian features until the fifth century CE.

**Crowns in the Funerary Sphere.** Funerary literature from the period of the Pyramid and Coffin Texts on gives crowns an important role in the rites of passage that transform the deceased into an inhabitant of the sky. Endowing him with divine attributes such as radiance, they both liken him to the gods of the sky and impart to him authority over them. They symbolize ascent to the sky and rebirth, as is shown by representations of crowns in the object-friezes on coffins and beneath the bier, and by the practice of placing crown-amulets on mummies. This symbolism relates to the range of meaning of the Egyptian term *ḫ'w*, which can be rendered "arisings" and "manifestations" as well as "crowns." The same root is

CROWNS. (left) *The White Crown of Upper Egypt;* (middle) *The Red Crown of Lower Egypt;* (right) *The Double Crown.*

used in the term for accession to the throne. Crowns were also used in the temple ritual evoking the rebirth of deities, and crown models are known to have been kept in temple crypts.

**Crown Types.** The forms of crowns are most usefully discussed in three groups: royal crowns, restricted to kings; royal women's crowns; and divine crowns, depicted on images of gods.

*Royal crowns.* There are ten basic types of royal headdresses. The most prominent are the White Crown and the Red Crown, the oldest crowns of the king, attested from the Predynastic period onward. They were generally associated with the kingship of the Two Lands, and as such were worn by King Narmer, supposedly the first ruler of the unified country. The White Crown, most commonly called *ḥḏt* ("The White, Bright One"), adorned the king as ruler of Upper Egypt; the Red Crown, most commonly called *dšrt* ("The Red One") and *nt* (interpreted from the Middle Kingdom as referring to the goddess Neith), marked him as ruler of Lower Egypt. Their material has been proposed to be fabric or leather, supplemented in the case of the Red Crown by a "wire" ending in a spiral (Eg. *h3bt, ḥm3tt*). Both crowns are mentioned in the Pyramid Texts, where their luminous color is associated with the light of celestial bodies. From the time of Thutmose IV, they can be combined with the striped cloth called *nemes*, and from the nineteenth dynasty on they are rarely depicted alone. They were worshiped as manifestations of the tutelary goddesses of the Two Lands, Nekhbet and Wadjit, and were glorified in hymns. They were also known as "The Two Great of Magic" (*wrty ḥk3w*).

The complementary character of the White and Red Crowns finds expression in their combination as the Double Crown, most commonly *(p3) sḥmty* ("The Two Powerful Ones"). This crown primarily symbolizes kingship over the entire country; it also occurs as an attribute of gods associated either with kingship, like Horus, or with cosmic rule, like Atum. Worn atop the vulture cap, it also forms part of the headdress of the goddess Mut. It

appears in representations from the first dynasty onward (ivory label of Den, c.3000 BCE; BM 32.650), and in the Pyramid Texts. From the Middle Kingdom on, the Double Crown may replace the Red Crown in complementary representations of the Upper and Lower Egyptian crowns.

The Double Feathers Crown, principally called *šwty* ("The Two Feathers"), may have a pair of ostrich or falcon feathers. As a royal crown, this type is attested from the reign of Sneferu in the fourth dynasty onward; the divine (ostrich) Double Feathers, apparently those of the god Anedjti, are first attested in the sixth dynasty Pyramid Texts. The feathers also adorn gods such as Amun, Min, and Montu. Like many other crowns, the Double Feathers— usually combined with ram horns—may be adorned with additional *uraei* and disks from the New Kingdom on. Some texts suggest that this crown held a special position within the rites surrounding the ruler's accession to the throne, complementing the role of the Double Crown at his coronation. In the religious literature, the *šwty* appears mostly in conjunction with the *atef*-crown, as an integral part of which the feathers are perceived.

The earliest depiction of the *atef*-crown dates to the reign of Sahure (fifth dynasty); it consists of a central element, similar in shape to the White Crown, which is woven from plant stems and flanked by two ostrich feathers. Generally worn on top of a wig adorned with the simple circlet and horns, it may from the New Kingdom onward, also have disks and *uraei*. The meaning of the word *atef* (*3tf*), which occurs from the Coffin Texts on, is disputed; it may mean "his might" or "his terror." This crown is associated particularly with the gods Osiris and Herishef, the latter embodying the united gods Re and Osiris, the rulers of the sky and netherworld, day and night. According to chapter 175 of the *Book of Going Forth by Day* (*Book of the Dead*), it is bestowed by the sun god. The *atef* can also be worn by Horus and Re in their various forms. From the time of Thutmose III on, an *ished*-fruit, from the mythic tree that stands on the horizon at sunrise, can replace the solar disk normally surmounting the *atef*. This symbolism of solar renewal, and related fertility, appears to complement that of the *nemes* (*nms*; see below).

The triple *atef*, Egyptian *hmhm* ("The Roaring One"), occurs first under Akhenaten and may have replaced the traditional *atef* during the Amarna period. Common in representations of the solar child emerging from the lotus flower in the morning, it may identify the king with the sun god at sunrise.

The *nemes*, attested from the time of Djoser in the early third dynasty, is worn almost exclusively by the king in representations. Its use on the standards representing the royal *ka* underlines its significance for kingship. From the eighteenth dynasty, it is shown mostly in combination with other crowns (see below). It appears to be represented by the term *nws* in the Pyramid Texts and is associated with Re-Khepri at sunrise. Another close link is with Horus, who is said in the Coffin Texts to bestow it on his father Osiris in order to bring about the latter's rebirth. The king wears the *nemes* when represented as a sphinx or falcon; it seems to express the royal "Horus" and "Son of Re" names.

Closely connected with the *nemes* is the *khat* or *afnet* (*ḥȝt* or *ˤfnt*), which it appears to complement. These two kerchiefs generally appear together in the object friezes as well as on the pairs of royal wooden statues found guarding the entrances to the burial chambers of several New Kingdom royal tombs. Remnants of a *khat* were found on the mummy of Tutankhamun. Its dominant representation in funerary contexts has been interpreted to convey a particularly strong symbolism of rejuvenation, and it appears to represent the nocturnal side of the solar cycle, complementing the solar symbolism of the *nemes*. Like the latter, it is used in representations of the royal *ka*. The name *afnet* is attested beginning in the Pyramid Texts, where it is worn in particular by the maternal Semat-cow, who is associated with Nekhbet. The earliest certain representation dates to the reign of Djoser; the headdress on an ivory label of King Den from Abydos (BM 55.586) may also represent a *khat*. It is typical of Isis and Nephthys as mourners of Osiris, and of the four goddesses protecting the sarcophagus of the deceased king.

The *seshed*-circlet (*sšd* or *mḏḥ*) is attested from the reign of Sneferu on. At this early time it is always combined with the *atef*-crown or the Double Feathers. Its primary function is to bear the *uraeus*. A few examples survive of golden or silver circlets, usually inlaid with semiprecious stones or colored glass; one is from the tomb of Tutankhamun, where it was placed on top of the bandages covering his head. It is always shown worn around a short wig; when combined with the Amun-crown (see below), the *seshed* may be tied directly onto the crown base. Textual evidence for the terms *sšd* ("luminous") and *mḏḥ* can be found in the Pyramid Texts as well as in the later funerary literature, where they denote the radiant appearance of stellar gods, Thoth, and the deceased. Like the *nemes*, the circlet appears in conjunction with the transfiguration of Osiris.

The Cap Crown is attested from the Old Kingdom but not until the twenty-fifth dynasty is the term *sdn* used for the so-called Kushite cap with two *uraei*. The crown term *ḫprš* (see below) first appears in the Second Intermediate Period determined with the symbol of the cap, suggesting its derivation.) The cap appears either without decoration, with horizontal lines, or with circlets, and is worn with a *uraeus*. Colored representations are blue or gold. The only surviving cap, on the mummy of Tutankhamun, is of white linen, embroidered with gold and faience beads. Its use in representations of the cult has led to its being interpreted as the headdress of the royal or divine son. During the Amarna period, it can be worn by the queen, often complementing the Blue Crown. A similarly shaped blue cap is worn by the god Ptah.

The Blue Crown (*ḫprš*) is attested in texts from the Second Intermediate Period onward. It may have evolved from the cap crown. It is typically decorated with circlets. The earliest distinctive representation is from the reign of Kamose. The contexts in which it is depicted suggest that it came to be the quintessential crown of the living ruler, which could incorporate the symbolism of other headdresses. It is closely related to the *nemes*, which appears to mark a deceased king when both headdresses are shown together.

The Amun Crown, a flat base like that of the Red Crown augmented by a pair of tall feathers, is the typical crown of the god Amun, but it can also be worn by a king. It appears to associate the ruler with Amun and to legitimate his rule under the god's protection. First attested during the reign of Nebhepetre Montuhotep I, when Amun became the dominant deity of the pantheon, this crown may have been called *ḥnw*. Its base alone is worn occasionally by kings, and more commonly by queens, of the eighteenth dynasty. The Amun crown can be adorned with horns, disks, and *uraei*.

There are numerous combinations of royal and divine crowns and their elements. Most common is the combination of *nemes* and Double Crown, which probably expresses the two most prominent royal titles, "Son of Re" and "Lord of the Two Lands." The combination of *atef* and *nemes*, which appears from the time of Thutmose I, is almost as widespread. Representing the two typical insignia of the god Herishef from the New Kingdom on, it may symbolize the combined royal aspects of the Son of Re and (Son of) Osiris.

In the Greco-Roman period the composite crowns became increasingly elaborate, and more and more types evolved.

***Crowns of royal women.*** The oldest and most common headdress of royal women is the vulture cap, which associated the wearer with the goddesses Nekhbet (of Upper Egypt) and later Mut, and thus emphasized the maternal role of the queen. The cow horns, usually combined with a solar disk and a *uraei-kalathos* as well as the tripartite Hathor wig, worn by queens from the late eighteenth dynasty onward, associate them with Hathor, the goddess who combined maturity and beauty with the dangers of the raging solar eye. The use of the *uraeus* for women may have originated in an association with the Lower Egyptian Wadjit, the solar eye; from the Middle Kingdom on it designates a royal daughter. The double *uraeus* may refer to the two aspects of the solar eye, regenerative and destructive. The Double Feathers (falcon or ostrich), representing the two horizons and thus also the two solar eyes, are attested for queens from the thirteenth dynasty onward; goddesses wear them only beginning in the late eighteenth dynasty, when they may be augmented by a solar disk. The platform crown, most commonly forming a base for the feathers, appears in the early eighteenth dynasty and may evoke the papyrus thicket of Khemmis. From the time of Amenhotpe III onward, the same crown is augmented by a pair of gazelle horns and is known as Isis-Sothis feather crown. Royal women below the rank of queen are often distinguished by gazelle heads on their headdresses.

***Divine crowns.*** Every divinity has a particular set of iconographic features that distinguish him or her in various functions. A god often wears a specific symbol on the head, and this is frequently the only sure means of identifying the deity represented. The most common divine headdresses are cow horns and solar disk for the leading goddesses of the pantheon, such as Hathor and Isis, emphasizing their maternal role; they may also wear tall feather crowns augmented by the same attributes, which appear to relate to their cosmic, luminous nature, like the Isis-Sothis crown discussed under queens' crowns. Gods associated with the cosmos, such as Re, mostly wear solar or stellar disks; royal gods, such as Horus, bear the Double Crown. The White Crown with a pair of ostrich feathers adorns Osiris; the Red Crown is associated primarily with Neith and Geb. From the Third Intermediate Period onward, especially youthful gods, such as Harpocrates, can be shown wearing almost any type of royal crown, while beginning in the New Kingdom, a single solar or stellar disk or a lunar crescent may denote a "divinized" king.

[*See also* Insignias.]

## BIBLIOGRAPHY

Abubakr, Abd el-Monem J. *Untersuchungen über die altägyptischen Kronen.* Glückstadt, 1937. Very brief but wide-ranging study of Egyptian crowns, now quite outdated, but remaining the most-cited work on the subject.

Collier, Sandra A. "The Crowns of Pharaoh: Their Development and Significance in Ancient Egyptian Kingship." Ph.D. diss., University of California, 1996. The only study of the symbolism of most crowns available in English; coverage is rather uneven. Many plates and tables present the formal development of crowns through Egyptian history.

Davies, W. Vivian. "The Origin of the Blue Crown." *Journal of Egyptian Archaeology* 68 (1982), 69–76. Derives the form of the Blue Crown, to which he attributes a symbolism of legitimate succession, from the simple Cap Crown.

Eaton-Krauss, Marianne. "The *KHAT* Headdress to the End of the Amarna Period." *Studien zur Altägyptischen Kultur* 5 (1977), 21–39. Development and symbolism of this headdress; complementary character of the *nemes.*

Ertman, Earl L. "The Cap-crown of Nefertiti: Its Function and Probable Origin." *Journal of the American Research Center in Egypt* 13 (1976), 63–66. Implications of Nefertiti's use of this crown for the political role of the queen during the Amarna period; proposes that the Cap indicated the royal or divine son.

Ertman, Earl L. "The Search for the Significance and Origin of Nefertiti's Tall Blue Crown." In *Sesto Congresso Internazionale di Egittologia,* vol. 1, pp. 189–193. Turin, 1992. Holds that this crown was invented specifically to underline Nefertiti's status as equal to that of the king.

Ertman, Earl L. "From Two to Many: The Symbolism of Additional Uraei Worn by Nefertity and Akhenaten." *Journal of the Society for the Study of Egyptian Antiquities* 23 (1993), 42–50. Discusses the double *uraeus* worn by queens from the eighteenth dynasty on and argues that the White and Red Crowns found on the two heads were aligned with south and north, allowing one to reconstruct the position of a statue or relief within its original setting. The *uraeus*-circlet and *kalathos* are also discussed.

Goebs, Katja. "Some Cosmic Aspects of the Royal Crowns." In *Proceedings of the Seventh International Congress of Egyptologists, Cambridge, 3–9 September 1995,* edited by C. Eyre, pp. 447–460. Louvain, 1998. Explores the luminous nature of the royal crowns, and their role in the transfiguration of the king and private persons after death, as described in funerary literature.

Habachi, Labib. *Features of the Deification of Ramesses II.* Glückstadt, 1969. Describes iconographic elements, including headdresses, that indicate the divinized state of a ruler.

Johnson, Sally B. *The Cobra Goddess of Ancient Egypt: Predynastic, Early Dynastic, and Old Kingdom Periods.* London, 1990. Traces, mostly in photographs and line drawings, the formal development of the *uraeus.*

Russmann, Edna R. "Vulture and Cobra at the King's Brow." In *Chief of Seers: Egyptian Studies in Memory of Cyril Aldred,* edited by E. Goring et al., pp. 266–284. London, 1997. Explains the *uraeus* with one cobra and one vulture head on representations of the king in funerary contexts as referring to the goddesses Isis and Nephthys.

Török, Laszlo. *The Royal Crowns of Kush: A Study in Middle Nile Valley Regalia and Iconography in the 1st Millennia B.C. and A.D.* Oxford, 1987. Study of the crowns of the Nubian rulers, including those of the Egyptian twenty-fifth (Kushite) dynasty. (Reviewed by E. Kormysheva, "The Royal Crowns of Kush: An Extended Review," *Beiträge zur Sudanforschung* 5 [1992], 55–71.)

Troy, Lana. *Patterns of Queenship in Ancient Egyptian Myth and History.* Uppsala, 1986. See especially pages 115–130, on the function of the cobra and vulture and the *šwty*-feathers in the ideology and regalia of Egyptian queens.

Vassilika, Eleni. *Ptolemaic Philae.* Leuven, 1989. Contains a comprehensive survey of all crown types employed in the decoration of the temples of Philae; gives a very good impression of the forms and usage of the elaborate composite crowns of the Greco-Roman period.

KATJA GOEBS

**CULTS.** [*This entry surveys various types of cults in ancient Egypt, with reference to their organization, and to the types of priests, services, prayers, offerings, and sources of documentation associated with them. It comprises five articles:*

*For related discussions, see* Priesthood; *and* Religion.]

## An Overview

For the ancient Egyptians, religion did not consist of a set of theological principles to which they gave assent, nor was it based on the content of particular writings deemed canonical. Religion consisted rather in what people did to interact with their gods. These actions are termed "cult," and when used in this fashion, "cult" is roughly synonymous with "ritual." There is no specific word for "ritual" in the Egyptian language; they variously referred to it as *irt ḫt,* "doing things," *irw,* "things done," or *nt-ꜥ,* "regular procedure (lit. that pertaining to prescription)."

The focus of Egyptian ritual was entities referred to with the substantive *nṯr.* Since the Ptolemaic period, *nṯr* has been translated as "god" (*theos*). While entities labeled as *nṯr* and "god" share several characteristics, the Egyptians applied the term to people and things which we would hesitate to call gods. In a recent article, Dimitri Meeks has suggested that the common feature shared by all entities called *nṯr* by the Egyptians is that they are the beneficiaries of ritual. These beings can be divided into several classes. First are those beings who existed originally as gods; ritual serves to preserve their existence as gods through providing them with sustenance. Second are entities who become *nṯr* through undergoing a ritual. This category can be further subdivided into those who undergo ritual, and hence become *nṯr,* during their lifetimes, and those who become *nṯr* after death. Examples of the former include the king and special animals who were thought to be manifestations of the gods. Individuals who become *nṯr* after death include common people, special "heroized" individuals, and mummified animals.

While this definition of *nṯr* may be overly reductionistic, it provides a useful framework.

To conduct the cult of the gods, the Egyptians constructed temples, which they called *ḥwt-nṯr,* "the house of the god." Frequently several gods were worshiped in a single temple. In order to conduct the rituals, a temple needed to control an extensive network of land, livestock, and personnel; all the elements necessary for the business of the temple were referred to as *r-pr,* or "temple estate." The earliest Egyptian temples seem to have been built of perishable materials. Only temples dedicated to the funerary needs of the dead kings survive from the Old Kingdom, but a few nonroyal temples from the Middle Kingdom remain. Beginning with the New Kingdom, and continuing until the end of the Greco-Roman period, the enormous stone temples and their reliefs are our main source of evidence for the cult which went on within their walls.

An Egyptian temple employed a large number of priests and servants. Technically, only the king, the only living person in Egypt who possessed the status of *nṯr,* could officiate in the cult before the gods. He was considered to be the high priest of all the gods and goddesses of Egypt. In actual practice, the king delegated this responsibility to the priesthoods of the various gods throughout Egypt. Many priestly appointments came directly from the king, but some could be made by local administrators. Frequently, priestly offices could be inherited.

There were two main classes of priests. The higher class was the *ḥm-nṯr* ("god's servant"), who functioned in the cult before the god's statue. The Greeks translated *ḥm-nṯr* as "prophet," an equation which derived from the priests' role in interpreting oracles. The lower class was the *wꜥb,* or "pure ones." They served as carriers of the god's bark, pourers of water for libations during the temple service, as overseers of craftsmen, artisans, or scribes, or as craftsmen themselves, making such sacred objects as the gods' sandals. There was also a third title, the *it-nṯr,* or "god's father." It has been suggested that the title "god's father" was given to senior *wꜥb*-priests who had reached the level of prophet but were not yet formally inducted into that office. One of their functions seems to have been to walk in front of the god's image in processions and sprinkle water to purify the path.

Priests were divided into four groups, called *sꜣw wnwt* ("gangs of the service"), to which the Greeks gave the name *phyles.* Each phyle served one lunar month in rotation, so that during the year each gang served for a total of three months, with three months off between months of service. This free time allowed individuals to hold priesthoods in several temples. The chief priests of a temple were designated by ordinal numbers, and the high priest of the temple was called the *ḥm-nṯr tpy,* or "first

CULTS: AN OVERVIEW. *Wall painting of a ritual pilgrimage to Abydos, the holy town of Osiris, eighteenth dynasty, reign of Tutankhamen.* It is now in the Museo Egizio, Turin. (Mimatallah / Art Resource, NY)

prophet"; the next senior priest was the second prophet, followed by third and fourth prophets. The high priests of some gods bore special titles: the high priest of Ptah was called "he who is great at directing the crafts," that of Re was "he who is great at seeing," that of Thoth was "the arbitrator between the two," and that of Khnum was "the modeler of limbs." These titles derive from the various spheres of influence or mythological roles of these gods.

In addition to these classes of priests, there were also priestly specialists. The *ḥry-ḥb* ("he who carries the festival roll") was responsible for reading the hymns and spells which accompanied many rituals. The *sš n pr ʿnḥ* ("scribe of the house of life") was responsible for copying the papyri used in temple and funerary ritual. Women also participated in the temple priesthood. During the Old Kingdom, women of high social station could hold the office of priestess (*ḥm.t nṯr*) of Hathor, or of Neith. Women rarely served as priestesses in the cult of a god. Prior to the New Kingdom, the priesthood was not viewed as a full-time occupation, but with introduction of a professional class of priests, women no longer were able to hold priestly titles. They then served mainly as musicians, singers, and dancers in the temple. Later, however, they could hold titles associated with deities: at Thebes the "Divine Adoratress" held a prominent position from the Middle Kingdom.

The main purpose of the temple and its priests was to carry out the cult for the gods. The successful performance of the cult was thought to be absolutely vital to Egypt's continued existence and prosperity. At the time of creation, the Egyptians believed, a small space of order had appeared in the midst of chaos. It is within this space of order that life was possible. In order to keep chaos from encroaching on the created world, it was necessary to perform the cult of the gods. This cult took two main forms: those rituals conducted on a daily basis, and rituals carried out during particular festivals.

The focus of temple ritual was the statue of the god,

called *ḥm* ("image"). This was usually a small (one estimate is that they averaged about 50 centimeters/22 inches tall) statue of the divinity, kept in a *naos* or bark shrine in the chapel of the temple. Since most temples housed more than one god, they also contained more than one cult statue. These statues could be made of wood, stone, or precious metals. After a cult statue had been completed by the craftsman, it underwent a ritual called the "Opening of the Mouth" which transformed it into a vehicle through which the god could manifest itself and in which the divine *b₃* and *k₃* could take up residence. The statues themselves were not the object of worship; they were simply one means through which the gods received worship and offerings and made themselves manifest in the world.

The daily temple ritual took essentially the same form in every temple in Egypt. It derived from the ritual for the sun god Re at Heliopolis, and represented the rebirth of the sun each morning. Later, elements of Osirian belief were incorporated into the ritual, and it also came to symbolize the restoration and revivification of the dismembered body of Osiris. For the purposes of the ritual, the cult-statue was identified as both Re and Osiris. Our information regarding the sequence of events of the daily temple ritual comes from two main sources: temple reliefs depicting the king performing the various rituals of the ceremony, and papyri listing the rituals and the hymns which accompany them. Analysis of these various sources has allowed scholars to reconstruct the likely sequence of events of this ritual. Because the sources do not agree as to the order of events, scholarly reconstructions differ.

Before dawn, two priests filled containers with water from the sacred well of the temple and replenished all the libation vessels. Priests were busy in the temple kitchens preparing offerings for the gods. The main officiating priest, a *ḥm-nṯr*, went to the *pr-dw₃t* ("house of the morning") where he was ceremonially purified, dressed, given a light meal, and prepared to conduct the morning ceremony. The priest approached the shrine containing the god's image, and as the sun rose the bolt was drawn back and the door opened. Since only the king was able to confront the god, the officiating priest declared that "it is the king who has sent me to see the god." Once the doors to the shrine had been opened, the priest prostrated himself before the image, and a ritual purification of the chapel with water and incense took place in preparation for removing the image from its shrine. At this point, the statue was presented a small figure of the goddess Maat, which symbolized the proper order established for the world at creation. The image was then removed from its shrine, and the clothing and ointment that had been placed on it the previous day were removed. The image was then placed on a pile of clean sand and the shrine was purified

with water and incense. Next, green and black eye paint were applied to the image and it was anointed with several oils. The god was dressed in four colored cloths: white, green, blue, and red. The white and red cloths protected the god against his enemies, the blue hid his face, and the green ensured his health. The god was presented with various objects, such as his crowns, scepter, crook, flail, and *wsḫ*-collar. Next the god's face was anointed, sand was scattered around the chapel, the cult image was replaced in the shrine, and the door bolt was thrown and sealed. Finally, the priest performed the final purifications and exited the sanctuary, dragging a broom behind him to obliterate his footprints.

At some point during the morning ritual, the offering ritual would take place. The purpose of this ritual was to provide the god with his "breakfast." Some reconstructions of the ritual have it occurring before the final purification of the chapel in preparation for replacing the statue in the shrine, while others would have the offering ritual take place before the undressing and dressing of the statue. In this ritual, the offerings prepared that morning by the priests were presented to the god. Although an enormous meal was prepared for the god, consisting of meat, bread, cakes, beer, milk, honey, vegetables, and fruit, only a small part of this repast was actually placed before the statue. An offering formula listing the various items of the offering was recited by the priest, and incense was burned and libations made to purify and sanctify the offerings. Since the god did not actually consume the offerings, but simply partook of their essence, they could be shared with the other deities in the temple. The offerings were also used in the ritual of the royal ancestors, in which the king made offerings to all his predecessors in office, often depicted in the form of a list of their names. After this ritual, the offerings could then be made to the statues of other individuals found in the temple; finally, they became the property of the priests, who received a share based on their rank in the priestly hierarchy. This reuse of the offerings until they were finally consumed by the priests, called the "reversion of offerings" (*wḏb ḫt*), was one way in which the priests were compensated.

This morning ritual was the main one of the day, but less elaborate ceremonies were also held at noon and in the evening. During these rituals, the doors of the sanctuary housing the god's statue were not opened. These rituals consisted primarily of pouring water libations and burning incense before the shrines of the gods. In addition to these offering rituals, certain apotropaic dramatic rituals were conducted in the temples throughout the day and night in order to repel the threats to existence, frequently thought of in terms of Seth, the murderer of Osiris, or Apophis, the serpent who tried to stop the daily voyage of Re and thereby bring an end to creation. Hymns were sung during the twelve hours of the day and night to protect Re from Apophis and to keep the solar bark moving along on its voyage. Images of enemies were created from wax or clay and then destroyed, thereby bringing about their destruction through magic.

In addition to their daily rituals, temples also celebrated a number of festivals (*ḥbw*) throughout the year. For example, during the reign of Thutmose III, the temple of Amun-Re at Karnak celebrated fifty-four festival days, and Ramesses III's temple at Medinet Habu celebrated sixty festival days. Festivals could last from one to twenty-seven days, and involved large expenditures of food and drink for those participating in or observing the festival. Records from the village of Deir el-Medina indicate that workers were frequently given days off for festivals. During one festival of Sokar, 3,694 loaves of bread, 410 cakes, and 905 jars of beer were distributed. Important festivals included New Year's Day, the festival of Osiris at Abydos—during which the "mysteries" of this god were celebratcd—the festival of Hathor, during which the goddess would visit the royal cult complex (as did Sokar during his festival), and the festival of the Coronation of the Sacred Falcon at Edfu. The Beautiful Festival of the Valley was an important occasion during which Amun-Re traveled from Karnak to the temple at Deir el-Bahri and visited the royal cult complexes on the west bank of the Nile, particularly that of the reigning king. This was also an occasion for people to visit the tombs of their relatives, where they observed an all-night vigil and shared a feast with their deceased relatives.

The focus of a festival was the gods in their bark shrines. Egyptian gods always traveled in boats—in real boats when traveling by water, or in bark shrines carried over land on the shoulders of priests. Festivals could involve the procession of the god in his boat within the temple, or the god could leave the temple to visit another deity. These shrines were carried along processional avenues, often lined with sphinxes. At intervals, small altars were built which were essentially open-ended buildings containing a station on which the priests could rest the bark. When the porters rested, priests performed fumigations and libations and sang hymns to the god in its boat.

Such festivals and processions provided the general population with access to the gods, since the farthest most people were admitted into the temples was the open forecourt. It is usually thought that the shrine in the bark containing the god's image was closed during the procession, hiding the image from onlookers. Dirk van der Plaas (1989) has argued otherwise, suggesting that the doors of the bark shrine were open during such travels, since numerous texts describe the desire of people to see the image of a god. It was believed that beholding the image during a procession could heal an individual of illness.

It was also during festival processions that people could approach the gods seeking an oracle. The first clear evidence for oracles occurs in the New Kingdom. John Baines (1987), however, has argued that evidence for the existence of oracles occurs much earlier, perhaps as early as the First Intermediate Period, and earlier examples may exist. During processions, people could approach the god with a yes-or-no question written on small flakes of limestone or on ostraca, which would be placed before the god. Surviving examples of such questions include "Is it he who has stolen this mat?" "Shall Seti be appointed as priest?" and "Is this calf good so that I may accept it?" The movement of the bark-shrine as it was carried on the shoulders of the priests indicated the answer: forward for affirmative, backward for negative.

**Private Cults.** The temple was not the only place where the Egyptians worshipped their gods. The New Kingdom sites of Amarna and Deir el-Medina preserve evidence of public chapels which would have contained either a small cult statue or, more commonly, a stela with an image of the god. Here private individuals served as lay priests. Some homes were also equipped with areas set aside for worship. Upper-class homes at Amarna had domestic shrines containing statues of Akhenaten and his family, or stelae showing the royal family venerating the Aten. Many houses of the workmen at Deir el-Medina contained household shrines, which consisted of a wall niche which could be accompanied by an offering table or libation trough. These niches can be found in any room, including the kitchen. Deities particularly popular in such shrines were Meretseger, Renenutet, Sobek, Amun, Taweret, and Hathor. Deceased relatives were frequently worshipped in the home, in the form of *3ḫ iḳr n rꜥ* ("able spirit of Re") stelae or small anthropoid busts ranging in height between 10 and 25 centimeters. We are ill informed about the nature of the cult practiced at such public and domestic chapels and private shrines, but the worship of the gods undoubtedly involved making offerings of food, libations, and incense. Such shrines would have served as places where people could make specific requests of their gods in prayer.

**Royal Cults.** The king, by virtue of his status as *nṯr*, received a cult both while living and after his death. The study of ancient Egyptian kingship has been beset with confusion: on the one hand, the king of Egypt was labeled a god, but on the other hand, numerous texts describe the king in a very ungodlikc fashion. A further confusion may arise from applying Western notions about the characteristics of a god to the Egyptian king. In ancient Egypt, the king acquired and maintained his "divinity" as a result of specific kingship rituals.

The primary kingship ritual was the coronation, which transformed the king into a *nṯr* by means of his union with the royal $k_3$. According to Lanny Bell (1997, p. 140), the $k_3$ personified "inherited life force," and the royal $k_3$ was "the immortal creative spirit of divine kingship." All previous kings of Egypt had possessed the royal $k_3$, and at his coronation the king became divine when he became "one with the royal $ka$ [$k_3$], when his human form [was] overtaken by this immortal element, which flows through his whole being and dwells in it" (Bell 1985, p. 258). Since his status as $ntr$ depended on his union with the royal $k_3$, there were rituals intended to reinforce this relationship during the king's reign. Every year, the Opet festival was held at the temple of Amun-Re at Karnak during the fourth month of the inundation season, during which the king had his union with the royal $k_3$ renewed and his right to rule reconfirmed. After roughly thirty years of rule, the king celebrated his first $sed$-festival, which served both to reconfirm his relationship to the royal $k_3$ and to restore his flagging vitality.

Just as the cult statue was the receptacle of the divine $b_3$, the king, as the receptacle of the royal $k_3$, could also receive a cult. This practice became especially prominent in the New Kingdom, beginning with the reign of Amenhotpe III. The cult was patterned after the daily temple ritual of the gods. Kings erected statues of themselves, sometimes colossal, for the purpose of receiving offerings; perhaps the most famous monument dedicated to the cult of the living king is the temple of Ramesses II at Abu Simbel. The image of the living king, representing the royal $k_3$, could be shown traveling in a bark carried on the shoulders of priests, just as the gods traveled during their festivals. There are even depictions of a king making offerings to his deified self. The king is worshipping not himself, but the concept of deified kingship as represented in the royal $k_3$, which he embodies.

The worship of the divine king continued after his death. From the beginning of Egyptian history, royal burials included a place where the dead ruler's spirit could receive offerings of food and drink. The royal pyramid establishments introduced by the fourth dynasty kings included a temple complex situated on the east side of the pyramid for the cult for the deceased king, represented by a statue. Beginning with the pyramid of King Userkaf of the fifth dynasty, a false door stela became the focal point for offerings to the spirit of the deceased king. The kings of the eighteenth dynasty instituted a new form of royal burial, building rock-cut tombs in the Valley of the Kings at Thebes. Nearby, along the west bank of the Nile across the river from Karnak, the kings built structures which Egyptologists have called "mortuary temples," although the propriety of the term has recently been called into question by Gerhard Haeny. Here the spirit of the deceased king continued to receive offerings, frequently in the company of Amun and Re-Horakhty. Temples known as "houses of millions of years" were built by the New Kingdom kings as places where a royal cult could be carried out both before and after their deaths. Worship of deceased kings was not limited to state-run temples: the tomb builders at Deir el-Medina built shrines to the deified Amenhotpe I and his mother Ahmose Nefertari, who were revered as the founders and patrons of the city, and during the Middle Kingdom, Egyptian miners in the Sinai carried out a cult for the long-deceased Sneferu.

**Funerary Cults.** Not only kings attained divine status after death. A deceased person was transformed into a $ntr$ through the rituals of mummification and interment, which included the Opening of the Mouth ceremony. This ritual could be performed on the mummy or on a statue of the deceased, and through the use of spells and gestures it served to animate the image and enable the $k_3$ of the deceased to consume the offerings brought to it. The dead, like the gods, needed daily sustenance, provided by means of the offering ritual. Egyptian tombs were equipped with an area in which offerings could be made for the deceased. In Old Kingdom *mastaba*s, this area began as an offering niche on the south end of the east side of the *mastaba* and later evolved into an elaborate offering chapel inside the *mastaba*. A chamber inside the *mastaba* enclosed a $k_3$-statue of the deceased and served as another focal point of offerings. After the Old Kingdom, $k_3$-statues could be set up in separate $k_3$-chapels near the temples of the gods. Rock-cut tombs included an aboveground chapel, which contained a stela of the deceased, giving his name and titles and showing him either before a table of offerings or receiving offerings from family members. Offerings were deposited on offering tables before these stelae.

The Offering ritual included the recitation of the offering formula, known as the $htp$-$di$-$nswt$ ("an offering which the king gives"). Since in Egyptian theology only the king was able to make offerings to the gods, every time an offering was made, the offerer claimed that it had been made by the king to a god and was then passed along to the deceased, or that the king and a god were jointly making an offering to the deceased. This formula listed the typical items of a funerary offering. The offering itself was called $prt$-$r$-$hrw$ ("going forth at the voice"), referring to the role of recitation in providing the deceased with sustenance. Even if no offerings had been brought to the tomb, simply by reciting the formula a visitor was able magically to provide the dead with food and drink. A typical example of the offering formula from the Middle Kingdom is the following: "An offering which the king gives (and) Osiris, Lord of Busiris, the great god, lord of Abydos, so that he may make invocation offerings (consisting of) oxen, fowl, bread, clothing, alabaster, (and) every good and pure thing which a god lives on, (including) offerings, provisions, and divine offerings for all the gods, to the *k3* of the revered one, the overseer of the house, Montu-hotep, deceased" (Papyrus Berlin 9). The offering formula frequently stressed that the deceased was to receive the same offerings as the gods did in their daily cult. In order to ensure a continual supply of offerings at the tomb, an Egyptian would establish a funerary foundation prior to his death in which an individual (or individuals) was given land in exchange for an agreement to carry out faithfully the cult of the deceased. These individuals, the *ka*-priests (*ḥm-k3*), were responsible for providing for the funeral, burial, and continued offering cult. Frequently the eldest son of the deceased fulfilled this role. The establishment of funerary foundations was common during the Old and Middle Kingdoms, but was replaced during the New Kingdom by the statue foundation, in which a statue of the deceased would be dedicated to a temple, and the deceased through his statue would participate in the daily offerings and festivals there.

For the vast majority of Egyptians, offerings to the dead were made largely by family members, or by those under contract to carry out such offerings. For a few individuals who had been particularly prominent during life, their funerary cults took on a wider currency and began to resemble those of gods. People would visit their shrines to make offerings in hope of receiving blessings or favors. The cult at the tomb of Isi, a nomarch of Edfu during the early sixth dynasty, continued for six centuries after his death. A large temple was built at Elephantine during the Middle Kingdom to honor the sixth dynasty nomarch Hekaib. The worship of these divinized individuals was primarily a local affair, but some expanded and became national. Imhotep, the chief architect of the third dynasty king Djoser, was worshipped as a healing god of wisdom during the Greco-Roman period, and even provided with a divine lineage—he was said to have been the son of Khereduankh, his real mother, and the god Ptah. Amenhotep son of Hapu, a prominent official under the eighteenth dynasty king Amenhotpe III, was also worshipped during the Ptolemaic period as a god of wisdom and healing.

**Animal Cults.** No other aspect of Egyptian religion elicited more derision from Classical-era authors than did the worship of animals, for which evidence dates back to the fourth millennium BCE. Predynastic burials of animals such as gazelles, dogs, cattle, monkeys, and rams have been found at such sites as Badari, Naqada, Maadi, and Heliopolis. Erik Hornung has observed that "the care with which these animals were buried and provided with grave goods is evidence for a cult of sacred animals" (1982, p. 101). The earliest mention of the Apis bull dates from the reign of King Aha of the first dynasty. The cult of animals received particular emphasis beginning with the twenty-

sixth dynasty, perhaps as part of a resurgence of Egyptian nationalism.

The complexity of Egyptian animal cults escaped the Greco-Roman critics. The Egyptians rarely (if ever) worshipped animals *as* gods, but rather as *manifestations* of the gods. Animals functioned much as did cult statues, and were simply one vehicle through which the gods could make their will manifest, and through which the faithful could demonstrate their devotion to the gods. There were three types of sacred animal honored in ancient Egypt. One type is the temple animals, which performed the same function as the cult statues in the temples; they could visit other deities in their temples and could give oracles. These animals lived in or near a temple and were distinguished by special markings. For example, the Apis bull, who lived at Memphis, had to be a black bull with a white triangle on its forehead, a crescent moon on its chest and another on its flanks, and double hairs (black and white) in its tail. The Apis bull was thought to be the *b3* (manifestation) of Ptah. At certain times of day the bull was released into a courtyard where worshippers would gather to see him and receive oracles. Apparently, people could put yes-or-no questions to the bull, and the answer was received when the bull entered into one of two stables. When the bull died, there was a time of general mourning and elaborate embalming. The Apis bull was buried in an enormous stone sarcophagus in the Serapeum at Saqqara, and then the search for the next bull began. Other examples of this type of temple animal are the Mnevis bull at Heliopolis, which was the manifestation of Atum-Re; the Buchis bull at Hermonthis, who represented Montu and was especially important during the reign of Nektanebo II; the ram of Mendes (Osiris-Re); and the ram of Elephantine (Khnum).

The second category was animals of the same species as the temple animal. Large numbers of these animals could be kept near a temple. For example, at Saqqara there was an extensive complex of buildings dedicated to the priestly care of large flocks of ibises (who represented Thoth) and falcons (Horus). It is from such flocks and herds that the enormous number of animal burials found in Egypt derive. Sacred animal necropolises throughout Egypt contain literally millions of mummified animal burials. In addition to the ibis necropolis at Saqqara, there are necropolises for cats at Bubastis; rams at Elephantine; crocodiles, snakes, falcons, and ibises at Kom Ombo; and ibises and falcons at Abydos. These burials were frequently paid for by pilgrims during visits to the temples at festivals or when seeking divine blessings. The mummified animal corpse served as a votive offering for the god, and the devotee hoped to earn the goodwill of the deity by providing for the burial of one of its sacred animals; an inscription on a jar containing an ibis mummy preserved a prayer asking Thoth to be benevolent toward the woman who had embalmed his sacred animal. Major differences between the temple animal and the animals kept in large numbers are that there was only one temple animal at a time; the temple animal received a cult, while these animals did not; and the mortuary services for the temple animals were much more elaborate. The third type of sacred animal comprises members of the same species as the temple animal which were kept in private homes as representatives of the gods. For example, snakes, cats, or dogs were often kept in cages and buried at their death. This practice is analogous to the construction of household shrines to allow for domestic worship.

## BIBLIOGRAPHY

Assmann, Jan. "Semiosis and Interpretation in Ancient Egyptian Ritual." In *Interpretation in Religion,* edited by Shlomo Biderman and Ben-Ami Scharfstein, pp. 87–109. New York, 1992. An important theoretical discussion of relationship and interplay between the actions of ritual, their symbolic meaning, and the words recited during the ritual.

Baines, John. "Practical Religion and Piety." *Journal of Egyptian Archaeology* 73 (1987), 79–98.

Bell, Lanny. "Luxor Temple and the Cult of the Royal *Ka.*" *Journal of Near Eastern Studies* 44 (1985), 251–294. A groundbreaking study of the Opet festival and its relationship to divine kingship. A popular treatment of the same topic is Bell, 1997.

Bell, Lanny. "The New Kingdom 'Divine' Temple: The Example of Luxor." In *Temples of Ancient Egypt,* edited by Byron Shafer. Ithaca, 1997.

Černý, J. "Egyptian Oracles." In *A Saite Oracle Papyrus from Thebes,* by Richard A. Parker, pp. 35–48. Providence, R.I., 1962. A summary treatment of the practice of receiving oracles in ancient Egypt, with particular attention to New Kingdom evidence; several important texts are translated. In this article Černý establishes the correspondence between the forward/yes and backward/no response of the bark shrine.

David, Rosalie. *A Guide to Religious Ritual at Abydos.* London, 1981. A discussion of the rituals carried out at a particular temple, based primarily on a close study of its reliefs. A particularly good discussion of the daily cult and the ritual of the royal ancestors, utilizing comparative material from other sources.

Donadoni, Sergio, ed. *The Egyptians.* A translation of *L'Uomo egiziano,* by Robert Bianchi, Anna Lisa Crone, Charles Lambert, and Thomas Ritter. Chicago, 1997. A collection of articles on aspects of ancient Egyptian society; those on priests, the dead, and the pharaoh are particularly relevant to cults and worship.

Fairman, H. W. "Worship and Festivals in an Egyptian Temple." *Bulletin of the John Rylands Library* 37 (1954), 165–203. Important survey of the architecture, rituals, and festivals of the temple of Horus at Edfu.

Fairman, H. W. "The Kingship Rituals of Egypt." In *Myth, Ritual, and Kingship,* edited by S. H. Hooke, pp. 74–104. Oxford, 1958. Although old, still one of the best concise discussions of the rituals associated with Egyptian kingship.

Friedman, Florence Dunn. "Aspects of Domestic Life and Religion." In *Pharaoh's Workers: The Villagers of Deir el-Medina,* edited by Leonard H. Lesko, pp. 95–117. Ithaca, 1994. A survey of the evidence for the use of "bed-altars" and household shrines at Deir el-Medina, with particular attention to ancestor worship.

Hornung, Erik. *Conceptions of God in Ancient Egypt: The One and the Many.* Translated by John Baines. Ithaca, 1982.

Manniche, Lise. *Music and Musicians in Ancient Egypt.* London, 1991. Note chap. 4, "Music for the Gods," on the role of music and hymns in temple ritual.

Meeks, Dimitri. "Notion de 'dieu' et structure du panthéon dans l'Égypte ancienne." *Revue de l'Histoire des Religions* 205 (1988), 425–446.

Meeks, Dimitri, and Christine Favard-Meeks. *Daily Life of the Egyptian Gods.* Translated from by G. M. Goshgarian. Ithaca, 1996. Draws extensively from less-known Egyptian texts on the characteristics of the gods and their worship. Part two, by Favard-Meeks, deals particularly with cults and festivals of gods and kings.

Moret, Alexandre. *Le rituel du culte divin journalier.* Paris, 1902. Still the only publication and translation of the papyri relating to the events of the daily temple ritual.

O'Connor, David, and David P. Silverman, eds. *Ancient Egyptian Kingship.* Probleme der Ägyptologie, 9. Leiden, 1995. Most recent treatment of the subject; its particular value comes from articles that focus on kingship at various periods.

Quirke, Stephen, ed. *The Temple in Ancient Egypt.* London, 1997. Proceedings of a symposium held at the British Museum. A discussion of recent work by archaeologists and philologists.

Robins, Gay. *Women in Ancient Egypt.* Cambridge, Mass. 1993. Of particular interest is chap. 8, "Women and Temple Ritual."

Sadek, Ashraf Iskander. *Popular Religion in Egypt during the New Kingdom.* Hildesheimer Ägyptologische Beiträge, 27. Hildesheim, 1987. A comprehensive discussion of evidence for the private religious practices of the average Egyptian.

Sauneron, Serge. *The Priests of Ancient Egypt.* Translated by Ann Morrisett. New York, 1969. An overview of the function and requirements of the priesthood in ancient Egypt.

Shafer, Byron E., ed. *Temples of Ancient Egypt.* Ithaca, 1997. An excellent summary of the architecture and function of the different types of temples in use throughout Egyptian history.

Spencer, A. J. *Death in Ancient Egypt.* Middlesex, 1982. Popular overview of all aspects of Egyptian funerary practices, including tomb architecture, mummification, and burial rituals.

van der Plaas, Dirk. "Voir Dieu: Quelques observations au sujet de la fonction des sens dans le culte et la dévotion de l'Égypte ancienne." *Bulletin de la Société Français d'Égyptologie* 115 (1989), 4–35.

Wildung, Dietrich. *Egyptian Saints: Deification in Pharaonic Egypt.* New York, 1977. Overview of divine kingship and the cults of the deified mortals Imhotep and Amenhotep, son of Hapu.

STEPHEN E. THOMPSON

## Royal Cults

The cult of the king is one of the most prominent features of ancient Egyptian society. Physically, the importance of royal cult is visible in the numerous great monuments still standing today, such as the great pyramid complexes of the Old and Middle Kingdoms or the mortuary temples on the west bank of the Nile at Thebes. The characteristics of royal cult, as attested by the buildings themselves and evidence for associated cult practices, derived from the central religious and political role of the king. The Egyptian pharaoh was a sacred individual. Although mortal, he was understood to be related to the gods through a multilayered mythology which is articulated in scenes and texts on royal cult buildings and in the decoration of royal tombs. The king was the son of Re, the sun god. He was a manifestation of Horus, the falcon god and son of Osiris. From the time of the Middle Kingdom, increasing emphasis was placed on his relationship with the syncretic deity Amun-Re, and the king was described as the son of Amun, king of the gods. The king was the intermediary between mankind and the divine, responsible for sustaining the balance of the universe through maintaining *maat*, or divine order, in his earthly activities. In death, the king was held to become a fully divine being. Central to the royal afterlife was the king's assimilation with Osiris and the sun god Re. These divine associations provided the basis for the development of cults of both living and deceased kings.

**Royal Funerary Cults.** Early evidence for the development of the royal funerary cult occurs in the mortuary buildings of Early Dynastic kings at Abydos. Burial places of the kings of the first and second dynasties have associated "valley enclosures." The full repertory of functions of these structures remains a matter of debate; however, evidence for long-term presentation of offerings in the enclosures of Khasekhemwy and Peribsen suggests the existence of a mortuary cult for the deceased king. The third dynasty Step Pyramid of Djoser at Saqqara is the first fully articulated funerary monument where concepts of the king's divinity and the associated funerary cult can be analyzed in detail. The Step Pyramid includes numerous architectural elements designed to perpetuate the role of the king in the afterlife. Symbolic components of the royal palace, both above ground and below the pyramid itself, provide a palace complex from which the king could rule for eternity. Elements associated with celebration of the *heb-sed* (festival of rejuvenation of the kingship) express the desire to maintain the king's rulership in the netherworld. Integrated into this architectural setting was a full offering cult, which was housed in a mortuary temple positioned on the north side of the Step Pyramid. This assemblage of architectural elements alongside a sustained offering cult for the king presents a concrete statement on the importance of kingship and its divine associations in both living world and afterlife.

With the fourth dynasty, the royal pyramid complex increased in size. The tremendous scale and physical investment required for the pyramid complexes of Sneferu, Khufu, and Khafre is testimony to the central importance of the pharaoh and his cult during this period. It has been suggested that a significant proportion of the activities of the central government during the Old Kingdom were focused on the construction of the royal funerary complex. Thus, royal cult became a driving force in the political and economic growth of the Old Kingdom state.

Royal pyramid complexes from the fourth, fifth, and sixth dynasties typically are situated on an east–west axis and include two main cult buildings: the mortuary temple, situated on the east side of the pyramid, and a valley temple at the edge of the Nile floodplain. The mortuary temple was the location of the funerary offering cult, which was maintained by rotating teams of priests. The valley temple was decorated with scenes and statuary expressing the king's association with a wide variety of deities; it appears to have been a building used especially in linking the royal cult with other temples through periodic festivals and processions. Beginning with the reign of Unas in the late fifth dynasty, a major source of information on royal funerary cult is the Pyramid Texts, which are inscribed on the walls of the burial compartments of kings. The Pyramid Texts present a complex series of spells and religious statements intended to aid in the king's entrance into the netherworld: his transfiguration in the image of Osiris and his association with Re. Parts of the Pyramid Texts record embalming and burial rituals; other parts are written versions of the offering formulae and records of the offering ritual itself.

During the Middle Kingdom the tradition of royal pyramid construction continued, but with changes in emphasis. The first royal mortuary complex of the period, the eleventh dynasty burial complex of Montuhotpe I, represents a departure from the pyramid complexes of the Old Kingdom in its emphasis on veneration of the newly important state god of Thebes, Amun-Re. The cult of the king is given legitimacy through the king's association with that deity. The sanctuary of the Montuhotpe I complex focuses principally on the Theban triad (Amun, Mut, and Khonsu) but integrates a statue cult for the king. The link between king and god was emphasized in ritual form by the annual Valley festival, called the "Beautiful Festival of the Valley," in which the image of Amun was borne on his traveling bark to the west and visited the king's funerary temple.

Although later royal funerary complexes of the Middle Kingdom attempted to return to the Old Kingdom model, there were significant changes in conceptions of kingship which had restructured ideas on the nature of the king's role. These changes are reflected in the design and decoration of royal cult buildings. Royal funerary temples of the later Middle Kingdom appear to place increasing emphasis on veneration of the gods, with the king's cult appended and legitimized through his association with the gods. Late in the twelfth dynasty, the term "mansion of millions of years" appears in reference to the funerary temple of Amenemhet III at Hawara. This term can be understood to denote royal cult buildings in which the king's cult was important but subordinated to the cult of major deities.

Trends in royal cult structures of the Middle Kingdom set the stage for the New Kingdom, when the mansion of millions of years became the standard type of royal cult building. On the west bank of Thebes, the rulers of the eighteenth, nineteenth, and twentieth dynasties erected a series of great temples, of which the best preserved today are the Ramesseum (Ramesses II) and Medinet Habu (Ramesses III). These New Kingdom royal cult buildings were associated with the burial places of the rulers in the Valley of the Kings. They were surrounded by precincts which included storerooms and housing for priests and officials who ran the economic foundations that sustained the temple cult. Although many of these royal cults were supported by economic foundations set up at the time of the temples' construction, they were also considered part of the domain of Amun and were connected administratively with the great temple of Amun at Karnak. The temples were constructed first as buildings dedicated to Amun-Re, and the cult of the king was mediated by his divine associations with that deity. The Beautiful Festival of the Valley, which had emerged in the Middle Kingdom, continued as the most important ritual link between the royal funerary temples and the main cult place of Amun.

The construction of mansions of millions of years was not limited to Thebes. The temple of Sety I at Abydos is one in which royal cult is linked with Egypt's principal gods, especially Osiris. Insofar as Osiris was understood to be a deceased king of Egypt reborn to rulership in the netherworld, the Sety temple was also a temple to the institution of kingship itself as embodied in Osiris.

**Cult of Royal Ancestors.** In addition to incorporating the cult of the king, Osiris, and other gods, the Sety temple at Abydos illustrates a royal cult of another nature: veneration of royal ancestors through cult activity mandated by a living king. This practice is attested during the Old and Middle Kingdoms but becomes especially visible during the New Kingdom. Veneration of royal predecessors could be established through patronage of existing temples, as is illustrated by activity at Karnak, or the dedications of Senwosret III within the funerary temple of Montuhotpe I. It might also be articulated within a newly founded cult building, as occurred in that of Sety I at Abydos.

**Royal Cult in Gods' Temples.** In addition to monuments specifically created for the cult of a king, provisions for royal cult were regularly made in gods' temples throughout Egypt. Kings of all periods would have expressed their association with the gods by dedicating statuary and votive objects. In many of the large state temples, the cults of god and king became inextricably linked. Sites such as the temple of Horus at Hierakonpolis or the temple of Montu at Medamud include considerable remains of royal dedicatory material, and many gods' temples no doubt maintained subsidiary royal cults. Provisions for royal cult in a god's temple may have been as simple as a king's statue which received a portion of the daily offerings. In many of the larger state temples, however, entire ancillary buildings were created linking royal cult with god's cult. Sites such as Bubastis, Dendera, Hierakonpolis, Abydos, and Tell ed-Dabʿa preserve remains of structures that can be identified as royal "*ka*-chapels"— buildings in which a royal offering cult was maintained and the link between the king and local god was expressed. Other royal structures within gods' temples were intended to emphasize overtly the king's divine connections. From the New Kingdom on, chapels decorated with scenes of the divine birth of the pharaoh were erected in the temple precinct of Amun at Karnak. This type of structure is a precursor to the large and complex *mammisi*, or divine birth houses, at sites such as the Hathor temple at Dendera.

**Cult of the Living King.** The fact that the king was a sacred being engendered by the gods provided the basis for the development of the cult of living kings. This type of royal cult was more significant in certain periods, and emphasis on the divine associations of the living pharaoh may have been linked with political and economic as well as religious trends. One context in which the cult of living kings may have been emphasized was periods of coregency. During the Middle and New Kingdoms, evidence suggests that the coronation of a king's successor could occur before the death of the elder ruler. In this case, the senior ruler may have been projected into a fully divine role, perhaps conceptualized as a living Osiris and venerated as a god before death.

The most important development in the cult of the living king, however, occurred during the New Kingdom, when there is evidence for greater emphasis on the divine birth of the ruler. The key concept in the divine birth is that a pharaoh was engendered by the seed of the god Amun himself. Cult activity focused on the divinity of the ruling monarch may possibly have been linked to a need to legitimize claims to the throne by such rulers as Hatshepsut in the early eighteenth dynasty. It continued to be expressed, however, through the remainder of the New Kingdom and may be understood partially as a means of contributing to royal power and legitimacy over an increasingly complex governmental system. The Luxor temple is the greatest surviving monument dedicated to this concept. The building had roots in the Middle Kingdom but underwent its major construction during the reign of Amenhotpe III, with significant additions during the Ramessid period. The building can best be understood as a cult place of the living king and his divine associations with the Theban triad. The Luxor temple was the focal point of the great Opet festival, in which the image of Amun journeyed from his sanctuary at Karnak and the living king participated in rituals celebrating his divine origins.

The period characterized by the greatest emphasis on the divine authority of the pharaoh was the Amarna period of the late eighteenth dynasty. The reign of Akhenaten (successor of Amenhotpe III) witnessed the emergence of a royal religion focused on the supreme power of the sun disk or Aten. The religious program of Akhenaten emphasized the indispensable role of the king as the sole intermediary between mankind and the life-giving force of the Aten. Direct worship of the Aten was limited to Akhenaten himself, while the king and royal family were the intended object of worship by the populace at large. Household cults at Amarna included offering stelae depicting the royal family. Such veneration of the king within the domestic sphere represents an emphasis on divinity of the living king not seen in other periods. Following the Amarna period, royal cult buildings—such as the temples of Ramesses II at Abu Simbel—were erected during the ruler's lifetime and presented the royal cult as an inseparable part of the divine order.

**Royal Cult at the Popular Level.** Aside from royal cult within the established context of mortuary buildings and gods' temples, the veneration of deceased kings could develop in a more spontaneous fashion in the framework of popular cult. In such cases, the royal cult displays many similarities with the cult of local deities. An example of such a popular royal cult is the veneration of Amenhotpe I by the community of royal tomb builders at Deir el-Medina. During the eighteenth through twentieth dynasties, Amenhotpe I was venerated for his role in the early establishment of the community. He became a patron deity of the town, and his cult was celebrated at the popular level during periodic festivals and processions. During such events the populace was able to interact with a statue of the king carried by priests, particularly through the mechanism of oracles. Similar royal cults are attested in the Sinai, where Sneferu emerged as a local patron deity, and in the Second Cataract region, where Senwosret III was venerated locally as a god. This type of popular royal cult contrasts with the more formal structure of royal worship maintained in state-established temples, which were generally off limits to the community at large. Formal royal cult temples could, however, conduct similar processions in which royal images were carried in procession and were subject to popular venera-

tion. The mortuary temple of King Ahmose at Abydos is one documented example of a royal cult building where a statue of the king was carried by priests during festivals and gave oracles.

**Cult and Ritual.** Like other cults in temples throughout Egypt, the most important element of ritual in royal cult buildings was the daily offering ritual. This was essentially a statue cult in which the priests were responsible for ritual interaction with a cult image, which thereby was imbued with the elements necessary to make it a suitable abode for the *ka* of the king. Elements of the offering cult are presented in the Pyramid Texts. The most detailed records are those that document in scenes and texts the steps involved in the daily temple ritual. These are recorded in detail in the nineteenth dynasty temple of Sety I at Abydos and in the Ptolemaic period temple of Horus and Edfu. The daily temple ritual involved a series of ritual acts accompanied by spells and offering formulae uttered by the priests. These rituals included the awakening, cleansing, anointing, and dressing of the cult image. The spirit of the king would be invited through the burning of incense before the face of the cult image. Following the summoning of the spirit, libations and food offerings would be presented. After completion of the offering presentation, the shrine would be closed and the floor swept clean. The daily temple ritual was repeated three times daily, and in large royal cult temples it was certainly enacted for multiple images and subsidiary cults within the temple. The daily cycle of the offering ritual was punctuated by periodic festivals and statue processions in which a royal cult image was taken to nearby gods' temples. This type of activity provided for interaction between surrounding community and royal cult.

**Cult Personnel.** Royal cults from the time of the Old Kingdom were maintained by large, complex organizations of priests and officials. Old Kingdom papyri excavated in the pyramid complexes at Abusir are an important source of information on the administrative and economic aspects of royal cults in the late Old Kingdom. These documents record a system of five phyles (groups of priestly personnel responsible for running the cult) which rotated on a monthly basis. Temple personnel were organized into priests (principally *ḥmw-nṯr*, "god's servants") and a group of royal cult officials (termed *ḥnṯyw-s*). Also detailed in the Abusir records are the complex arrangements for supply of the mortuary cult, which depended on income from estates owned by the temple as well as on material distributed from other major temples in the Memphis region. For the Middle Kingdom, temple archives of the valley temple of Senwosret II at Illahun provide evidence on cult organization in a twelfth dynasty royal funerary temple. For the New Kingdom, extensive scenes and texts in the Theban royal temples are important evidence on the organization of the royal cult. The temple of Ramesses III at Medinet Habu is decorated with an extensive list detailing the festivals and offerings. Material from administrative records as well as scenes and texts in private tombs provide detail on the complex organization that surrounded royal funerary temples during the New Kingdom. The "reversion of offerings" was an important aspect of the royal cult, as it was in temples throughout Egypt. The offerings presented in the king's temple were redistributed to the priesthood and their dependents, and in many cases to secondary cults such as nonroyal chapels. The reversion of offerings was administered through contracts which defined the amount of offerings due to various people.

### BIBLIOGRAPHY

Bell, L. "Aspects of the Cult of the Deifies Tutankhamun." In *Mélanges Gamal Eddin Mokhtar*, vol. 1, pp. 31–60. Bibliothèque d'Études, 97. Cairo, 1985.

Bell, L. "Luxor Temple and the Cult of the Royal Ka." *Journal of Near Eastern Studies* 44 (1985), 251–294.

Bjorkman, G. "Kings at Karnak: A Study of the Treatment of Royal Predecessors in the Early New Kingdom." *Boreas* 2 (1972).

Bleeker, C. J. *Egyptian Festivals: Enactments of Religious Renewal.* Leiden, 1967.

Faulkner, R. O. *The Ancient Egyptian Pyramid Texts.* Oxford, 1969.

Habachi, L. "King Nebhepetre Mentuhotep: His Monuments, Place in History, Deification and Unusual Representation in the Form of Gods." *Mitteilungen Deutsches Archäologisches Institut Kairo* 19, 16–52.

Harring, B. J. *Divine Households: Administrative and Economic Aspects of the New Kingdom Royal Memorial Temples in Western Thebes.* Leiden, 1997.

O'Connor, D., and D. Silverman (eds.). *Ancient Egyptian Kingship.* Leiden, 1995.

Redford, D. B. *Akhenaten: The Heretic King.* Princeton, 1984.

JOSEF W. WEGNER

## Private Cults

It is obvious from discoveries in prehistoric cemeteries that belief in magic, life after death, and the presence of sacred power in animals (clan divinities) existed long before political unification and the arts of civilization flourished in Egypt. The large female figures and numerous images of hills, fields, water, and herds in the early pot paintings suggest, to prehistorians like Fekri Hassan, the veneration of a goddess associated with the cycles of nature, including death and resurrection. Private cults that focused on sacred trees, on impressive places (like the Peak of the West at Thebes) believed to be inhabited by divine force, or on deities helpful with plentiful harvests and human fertility continued to flourish throughout the country after prehistoric times, but it is the funerary rituals that are the best documented over the long history of ancient Egypt.

**Funerary Rituals of the Historic Period.** Euphemisms in texts and lack of portrayal in art show the Egyptians' distaste for death. To mitigate death they established elaborate procedures. The wrapping of the body, resembling the reassembling of Osiris's corpse, symbolized the overcoming of death, a transfiguration to a new body. Placement in the coffin was putting the deceased into the arms of the sky goddess Nut, to be born anew. Pouring of water, for its life-giving as well as purification qualities, was part of every ritual. The corpse, whether first desiccated or not, would have been washed (in the Tent of Purification) and then anointed and wrapped in the embalmer's shop. Seven sacred oils used for anointing the body are known already in the first dynasty. Last rites before interment were performed by the officiating *sem*-priest, who libated and burned incense and then carried out the Opening of the Mouth ritual to renew faculties: "opening" the mouth, nose, eyes, and ears by ritually presenting tools such as the adz to the orifices (originally on the statue of the deceased, and later on the mummy itself), while an ox was slaughtered and its foreleg and heart presented to the image as part of the revivification process. Offerings were also presented to the deceased, and then the body and the statue were transported to the burial site. An accompanying liturgy of prayers or spells was read by the lector-priest (*ḥry-ḥb*), who was distinguished by wearing a leopard-skin across one shoulder. At the funeral and afterward, the invocation of offerings, known as "the boon which the king gives," called for the sustenance of the dead. Music and acrobatic—perhaps ecstatic—dancing were as much a part of the funeral at the tomb door as was the shrieking of mourners. The *ḥnr* or musical troop of the goddess Hathor perhaps both announced the goddess who would receive the deceased in the netherworld and also reawakened the dead, or even sexually charged the atmosphere, since the deceased needed to be reborn in the afterlife. Incense was burned and floral tributes, as well as furniture and foodstuffs, were deposited in the tomb, which was seen as a dwelling for the dead. A wealthy funeral might include a pilgrimage to Abydos and the great shrine of Osiris, lord of the dead, where many people left cenotaphs or stelae commemorating themselves, understanding that they could hope for eternal life in the god's realm. The judgment rendered by his divine tribunal, with the heart of the deceased weighed against the feather of truth, seems to be a development of the eighteenth dynasty.

The maintenance of the identity and personality of the deceased required a funerary cult at the tomb, which was ensured by endowments for mortuary priests. Such *ka*-servants would bring bread and beer regularly to the tomb; illumination and prayers were probably also part of their duties. However, the supplies of early burials in time were replaced by models and then just lists of commodities needed by the deceased. This menu became a sacred text itself. Survival was possible for the worthy dead in two destinations: the sun's boat in the original solar cult, and the fields of the Osirian cult. Both demanded justification, which involved wisdom (knowing secret names of many entities of the netherworld) and passing an examination before forty-two judges in Osiris's tribunal. For this, magical spells, such as the religious literature on Middle Kingdom coffins and the later funerary papyri, were furnished in the burial.

**Religion and the Commoner in the Old and Middle Kingdoms.** With the establishment of the Egyptian state (c. 3050 BCE), the theology was organized to support the king, giving him a divine genealogy and making him identical with the great falcon god Horus. Only the king was represented in literature and art as having direct access to the gods. The idea of the king as sole worshipper must lie behind the *ḥtp di nsw* formulas on commoners' monuments, on which a person's fortune in life and death depended: "a boon which the king gives of a thousand of bread, a thousand of beer, of oxen and fowl, of ointments and cloth." Although the dead king (and later also queen) of the Old Kingdom was laid in the pyramid accompanied by the power of sacred texts containing very old hymns and rituals, the Old Kingdom nobles had nothing comparable and were able to have an afterlife only as a dependent *akh*.

Not until after the fourth dynasty, when the royal power began to decline, are commoners found holding divine offices in major cults; the goddess Hathor's is best documented, with hundreds of priestesses and numerous male overseers of priests. The collapse of the centralized government in the First Intermediate Period allowed for the stealing and divulging of magic spells (as Ipuwer describes in horror) that were once the exclusive knowledge of royalty. Texts on Middle Kingdom coffins utilize much of the Pyramid Texts, giving their nonroyal owners divine status once deceased and promising an eternity spent with the gods. At least two autobiographical texts of elite commoners describe their participation in the pageants and rites of Osiris at Abydos, and the *Instructions for Merikare* speaks of the sun god's sympathy for humans in distress. In a literary tale, the nobleman Sinuhe credits the mercy of a god for his survival and prosperity in Syria after his flight from Egypt. Thus, Middle Kingdom people interacted with deities as never before.

**Developments in New Kingdom Religion.** Nonroyal Egyptians continued to borrow what were once prerogatives of royalty, and the eighteenth dynasty tombs of the elite contain paintings of the once-royal hippo hunt rite, a metaphor for the victory of Osiris's avenging son Horus over Seth. Also beginning in the eighteenth dynasty, scenes depict the deceased worshipping a god directly, showing no royal intermediary. Now almost everyone had access to the divine. The cheaper papyrus scrolls containing the *Book of Going Forth by Day*, the so-called *Book of the Dead*, put immortality even closer at hand for larger numbers of people. This was the principal collection of funerary literature used by commoners in the New Kingdom and continuing into the early Roman period. While copies vary in length, some being quite short, there are 192 spells presently associated with the work which provided a deceased person with an aid to gaining eternal life. In the twenty-first dynasty, another text, the *Book of That Which Is in the Underworld* (*Amduat*) was added, and toward the end of Egypt's history, the *Book of Breathings* was also deposited with the dead.

**Temples and Votives.** There is more evidence for the laity's access to temples in the New Kingdom than has been generally realized: the spacious open courtyards of Luxor Temple, and even the hypostyle hall at Karnak, bear inscriptions which indicate that members of the public were able to assemble and praise pharaoh and experience the manifestation of the king of the gods himself. A shrine built under Sety II (nineteenth dynasty) just outside the hypostyle hall was a "place of honoring and praying to all the gods." A chapel of the Hearing Ear was built against the north exterior wall of Karnak under Ramesses II, where people could come to pray to listening deities. Indeed, engravings of ears are found on many exterior temple walls, and an image of Ptah Who Hears Prayers exists in the passage of Ramesses III's High Gate at the Medinet Habu temple, which facilitated people's access to the great gods within.

The Egyptians' desire for progeny motivated many votives offered to helpful deities. Pottery fertility figurines have been found in private houses of the Middle Kingdom and, by the New Kingdom, at shrines within many temples and at local community shrines. Excavations at the eighteenth dynasty royal temples of Deir el-Bahri (which included major chapels of Hathor, a promoter of sex and fertility) reveal votive items so uniform as to suggest mass production. Visitors to temples would pray, offer perishables like food, flowers, and beverages as their sacrifice, and then leave a purchased nonperishable votive in the form of a pottery cow, miniature Hathor-mask pillar, jewelry, or a painted cloth showing the goddess and containing a brief text into which the donor's name could be inserted. Such votives suggest female devotees, but men also made appeals for progeny and dedicated wooden and stone phalli to ensure their virility and fertility.

**Deification of Mortals.** Even with their huge pantheon, the Egyptians embraced foreign deities and also elevated mortals to divine status when warranted. Probably no one could have a statue of himself placed within the great temples of the land without royal favor. Imhotep, the architect who served King Djoser of the third dynasty (c.2687–2668) and designed for him the first pyramid, was revered by later generations as a sage; by the New Kingdom he was being called "the son of Ptah" and had become something of a patron saint of artisans. During the last dynasties, he became known as a healer— an attribute of a number of major deities—and was identified by the Greeks with Asclepios. Ptolemaic temples in Egypt often had sanatoriums on their premises where the afflicted in mind or body could come to spend the night and, in dreaming, be approached and helped by the resident deity of the temple. Other early sages became divinities, as did certain famous kings. Amenemhet III (1843–1797) was worshiped in the Faiyum two thousand years after his death, and scarabs bearing the name of Thutmose III, the great empire-builder, were made for centuries after his death, showing that the power of his name really was potent magic. Great queens like Ahmose Nefertari, and her son, Amenhotpe I, enjoyed cults for centuries after their deaths.

A royal scribe who served Amenhotpe III of the eighteenth dynasty as counselor and architect was Amenhotep, son of Hapu, born in the Delta town of Athribis during the reign of Thutmose III. This courtier was so highly regarded by the king that he was allowed to set up statues in Karnak near the Tenth Pylon, where he exhorts people to come to him for the transmission of their requests both to the king of the gods and to the living king. Thus, during his lifetime Amenhotep was introduced to the Egyptian public as someone in direct communication with the divinities, and something of a saint. Five hundred years after his death, his cult still flourished at Karnak, and by the twenty-sixth dynasty he was being credited as a divine physician. Under the reign of Ptolemy VI, Amenhotep, son of Hapu, was referred to as "the great god" and had an oracle at Deir el-Bahri. Both he and Imhotep were given cults at the temple Ptolemy VIII built at Qasr el-Aguz, attracting large numbers of votive statues, offering tables, and texts on ostraca. Seen as a healer and the granter of progeny, Amenhotep's original identity as a wise man was not forgotten either. A colossal statue in front of the magnificent First Pylon at Karnak temple commemorates him a millennium later as a great scholar of Amenhotpe III's reign. In the Hellenistic period, moral didactic texts were attributed to him.

**Oracles.** New Kingdom Egyptians generally saw their gods' interest extending to them as individuals, and this encouraged the use of oracles. Direct appeals to the opinion of the deity for a decision in a matter were utilized by ordinary people, sometimes when the findings of the local tribunal did not please the claimant. At the tomb-builders' community of Deir el-Medina, the oracle of prominence

was the deified king Amenhotpe I, who had many feasts during the year when his statue was carried in procession. He might then be called on to resolve disputes concerning property rights and the guilt or innocence of accused persons in matters of theft. Questions could be put orally or in writing and were presented before the image of the god when it was carried by his priests. An affirmative response seems to have been expressed by a downward movement of the front carriers, and a negative by a withdrawal away from the petitioner. The findings of the local tribunal could be overturned at such occasions.

**Interactions with the Dead.** Similarly, the Egyptians believed that the dead were still part of the population and could be of assistance or cause problems. Thus, families looked after the tombs of their relatives, and at home a statue bust of an ancestor of the family received prayers and oblations from the lady of the house, judging from artistic portrayals in the New Kingdom. Such busts are also found in shrines and tombs, and a rectangular stone stela showing a deceased person seated and holding a lotus before a table of offerings identifies the portrayed as an Able Spirit of Re (*akh iqr n R'*). These were dedicated by living relatives and apparently also used for imploring the deceased by those who also brought offerings to seek cooperation. Such stelae are found throughout Egypt but seem to be a phenomenon of the late eighteenth through twentieth dynasties; letters to the dead are found from all periods, often written on a bowl that had contained an offering at the tomb. Many are attempts to inform a deceased relative about a family crisis for which intercession is sought. In other cases, the dead person is suspected of causing the problems of the living and is asked to desist from this malign intervention.

**Personal Religious Practice and Private Cults.** The royal artisans' community unearthed at Deir el-Medina, dating to the New Kingdom, reveals many signs of personal religious practice and private cults. Numerous chapels to various deities are scattered about the outskirts of the community. Artisans naturally responded to the god Ptah, patron of craftsmen, and he had a small temple here, but so did foreign gods from Canaan and deities associated with the southern boundary of Egypt, at the First Cataract of the Nile. Local deities—such as Meretseger, a cobra goddess who inhabited the thousand-foot peak overlooking the village, and the alleged founder of the village, Amenhotpe I, and his mother, Ahmose Nefertari— were popular here too.

Thus both national and local deities were worshiped by ordinary people who built their own chapels, carved the cult statues, and filled the roles of clergy. Mostly *wab*-priests are attested, with only certain families being eligible to fill the role. A few men held the superior office of a *ḥm-nṯr* (prophet) in the local cult, carrying fans rather than the poles of the divine bark shrine. Some literate men could easily have served as lectors, reading a liturgy; women participated by singing hymns and playing musical accompaniment. Were daily services maintained here, or only festivals celebrated? The nature of the community makes the latter seem more likely. Some chapels had benches that seated twelve: seven seats on one side, five on the other. Ash from cooking as well as libation basins and animal pens suggest that here were gathering places for family groups or guilds to assemble to mark special events. There would have been numerous holy days when everyone was freed of work duty, and a joyous festival replete with eating, drinking, and dancing was enjoyed by all. But personal celebrations of one's own god were also observed: "Pray by yourself with a loving heart, whose every word is hidden" (*Instructions of Anii* [*Any*]). At home, certain deities protective of women, childbirth, and the young were given homage (Taweret and Bes in particular). Deities were not regarded as remote from ordinary people, at least not after the First Intermediate Period.

So religious were the workers on the royal tombs that fifty small shrines to various deities were maintained near the encampment where they spent the nights of their workweek at the royal tomb. Stelae of the Ramessid period reflect expressions of faith, gratitude for divine favor, and petitions in adversity. Some workmen have left pious testimonials to the power of the gods to affect a person's life for good and evil. Afflictions were understood as divine punishment meted out to those who had transgressed. Mercy is attributed to the god who is omnipresent and caring and may be called on in distress. Even the greatest gods were inclined to aid the deserving, as the painter Neb-Re recorded in a hymn of thanksgiving that Amun himself had saved the draftsman Nakht-Amun. A votive stela of Nefer-abu contains a long penitential hymn to the patron god of craftsmen, Ptah, which describes a failing and eventual salvation. Universalism is another feature of the hymns beginning in the reign of Amenhotpe III and continuing into the following dynasty.

It is not known how people were selected to serve in temples. That the vast majority of the clergy were the *wab*-priests who were lay people is obvious. The intermittent one-month service of these people, who were organized in phyles, demanded that they observe rituals of cleanliness and abstinence. Shaven bodies, including the head, were required during the time of temple service. Washing of the body and chewing natron to cleanse the mouth were also demanded before one could come in contact with the deity. Women also did such temple service, as is clear from a letter dated to the twelfth dynasty in which a woman explains her absence from her job as due to her month of temple service as a *wab*-priestess.

A vast proportion of personal names in ancient Egypt were theophorous and expressed faith: Amun is Strong, My God is a Mountain for Me. Herodotus described the Egyptians of the Late period whom he encountered as the most pious of all nations.

## BIBLIOGRAPHY

Englund, Gertie, ed. *The Religion of the Ancient Egyptians: Cognitive Structures and Popular Expressions.* Uppsala Studies in Ancient Mediterranean and Near Eastern Civilizations, 20. Uppsala, 1989. Seven authors examine various topics; the chapter on "Divine Access" by Jorgen Podemann Sorensen is particularly useful.

Hassan, Fekri. "Primeval Goddess to Divine King: The Mythogenesis of Power in the Early Egyptian State." In *Followers of Horus: Studies Dedicated to Michael Allen Hoffman,* edited by R. Friedman and B. Adams, pp. 307–320. Oxford, 1992.

Hassan, Fekri. "The Earliest Goddesses of Egypt: Divine Mothers and Cosmic Bodies." In *Ancient Goddesses: The Myths and the Evidence,* edited by L. Goodison and C. Morris, pp. 98–112. Madison, 1999.

Lesko, Leonard H., ed. *Pharaoh's Workers: The Villagers of Deir el-Medina.* Ithaca, 1994. Of particular relevance to this topic are chapters by Florence Friedman, "Aspects of Domestic Life and Religion," and Joris Borghouts, "Magical Practices among the Villagers," as well as the editor's introduction to their section.

Lichtheim, Miriam. *Ancient Egyptian Literature.* 3 vols. Berkeley, 1975–1980. Vol. 2, on the New Kingdom, contains many translations of private religious texts.

*Mummies and Magic: The Funerary Arts of Ancient Egypt.* Catalogue, Museum of Fine Arts. Boston, 1988. Particularly see the chapter by H. Te Velde on "Funerary Mythology," pp. 27–37.

Pinch, Geraldine. *Magic in Ancient Egypt.* Austin, 1994. A popularly written but thorough survey.

Pinch, Geraldine. *Votive Offerings to Hathor.* Oxford, 1993. Contains an enormous amount of material pertinent to private cults.

Sadek, Ashraf Iskander. *Popular Religion in Egypt during the New Kingdom.* Hildesheim Ägyptologische Beiträge, 27. Hildesheim, 1987. A thorough discussion of the private chapels at Deir el-Medina.

Shafer, Byron E., ed. *Religion in Ancient Egypt: Gods, Myths and Personal Practice.* Ithaca, 1990. Chap. 3, by John Baines, "Society, Morality and Religious Practice," is most relevant to this topic.

Shafer, Byron E., ed. *Temples of Ancient Egypt.* Ithaca, 1997. See particularly chap. 4 by Lanny Bell on "The New Kingdom 'Divine' Temple: The Example of Luxor."

Simpson, William Kelly, ed. *Religion and Philosophy in Ancient Egypt.* Yale Egyptological Studies, 3. New Haven, 1989. See especially Jan Assman, "Death and Initiation in the Funerary Religion of Ancient Egypt," pp. 135–159.

Teeter, Emily. "Popular Worship in Ancient Egypt." *K.M.T.: A Modern Journal of Ancient Egypt* 4.2 (1993), 28–37.

Wente, Edward. *Letters from Ancient Egypt.* Society for Biblical Literature Writings from the Ancient World, 1. Atlanta, 1990. The 355 texts translated here provide numerous insights into life and thought processes in ancient Egypt. Among them are thirteen letters to the dead.

Wildung, Dietrich. *Egyptian Saints: Deification in Pharaonic Egypt.* New York, 1977.

Williams, Ronald. "Piety and Ethics in the Ramessid Age." *Journal of the Society for the Study of Egyptian Antiquities* 8.4 (1978), 131–137.

BARBARA S. LESKO

## Divine Cults

The gods of ancient Egypt were considered to have much in common with humans: they needed food, clothing, entertainment, and recreation. These basic requirements were met by a series of performative actions and utterances that were formalized into cult actions and liturgy. These preestablished actions served the needs of the gods, and their special repetitive nature established a routine through which humans and the divine routinely and predictably interacted.

Documentation for divine cult comes from many different types of sources. These include representations of deities and brief references to gods and their festivals, recorded on ivory labels and carvings from the first dynasty and the annals on the Palermo Stone. Later and more complete information is given by the reliefs that adorn the walls of temples (especially the eastern interior wall of the hypostyle hall of the temple of Amun at Karnak, the chapels of the temple of Sety I at Abydos, and the sanctuaries of the temples of Horus at Edfu and of Hathor at Dendera). These are especially rich sources because they depict the individual acts that made up the divine service. Types and amounts of offerings employed in the cult are listed in calendars and so-called menus carved on temple walls. Biographical inscriptions record the duties that priests and priestesses performed for the god. Papyri, such as the Papyrus Berlin 3055, contain lengthy records of the liturgies and actions that were performed before the god. Although these records date to the New Kingdom or later, there is little reason to assume that the basic services performed for the god were significantly different in earlier, less well-documented eras.

A conventional anthropological model suggests that divine cults originated in the worship of local deities whose veneration eventually spread throughout the country, but this does not fit the Egyptian situation. Textual evidence indicates that the cult centers of many Egyptian deities were unrelated to a god's earliest attested place of origin. For example, Khnum, whose main cult center developed at Elephantine, first had a cult in Memphis and Abydos; Amun, who was so closely associated with Thebes, gained that geographic association only in the early New Kingdom after he supplanted and eclipsed the veneration of Montu, who had previously been associated with Thebes. Alongside these gods who gained their cult centers secondarily are purely local gods whose cult centers are in the same location as their first attestation.

Divine cults can be traced well back into the Early Dynastic period. The cult of Neith, perhaps at Sais, is mentioned on an ivory label of the first dynasty, and that of a baboon deity called Hedjwer, to whom votive offerings were left, is attested from a label of Semerkhet of the first dynasty. The Palermo Stone records festivals of the second dynasty that may be associated with early divine cults. Among the deities for whom early cults can be documented are Satet at Elephantine, Khentyamentiu at Abydos, Ptah at Memphis, and Horus at Nekhen (Hierakonpolis). The cults of certain gods were, for unknown reasons, subject to fluctuation in popularity. For example, the cult of Hathor was especially prevalent during the Old Kingdom, the cult of Amun became important only during the New Kingdom, and that devoted to Isis was not significant until the Ptolemaic period.

There were innumerable divine cults celebrated throughout Egypt, Nubia, and Egypt's foreign outposts. Although specific areas were associated with certain gods (Amun with Thebes, Re with Heliopolis, Satet and Khnum with Elephantine), the cult of a single god was not restricted to a particular area, and there were multiple cult centers for a single god throughout Egypt. For example, Hathor had temples in Dendera, Thebes, Nubia, Sinai, and elsewhere. In addition, a deity might have several temples in one area, as documented by the many shrines of Amun in his various aspects in Eastern and Western Thebes. These cult centers could be linked by divine ritual; for example, during the annual festival of the marriage of Hathor and Horus, the goddess of Dendera traveled to Edfu. In similar way, Amun of Karnak traveled to the Luxor temple, and Amun of the Luxor temple on the eastern bank of the Nile traveled to cult centers at Deir el-Bahri and Medinet Habu on the western bank.

Divine cults played an important role in the Egyptian economy. Great numbers of people were involved in the fulfillment of ritual, from those who served as priests, to those who built and maintained the shrines, wove the fabric offerings, and grew and prepared the food offerings. The economic structure of the divine cult paralleled that of the state's, in that the offerings given to the divine image during the thrice-daily offering service (see below) reverted to the temple workers as a part of their compensation.

The cult actions were executed by men and women of various ranks who were arranged in a hierarchical structure. These posts include the *wab* (*w'b;* the "pure one"), a part-time priest who served in the temple on a rotational basis one month a season, hence three months a year. There were innumerable *wab*-priests, and the majority of workers in the divine cult were probably these lowest-level priests. They permeated the entire society, since they held other, nonpriestly positions outside the period of their rotation. The lector-priest (*ḥry-ḥbt*) was responsible for the recitation of prayers during the rituals and thus had to be literate. The "prophets" (*ḥm-nṯr*) were, at least in Thebes, divided into four ranks, the fourth prophet of Amun being the equivalent of the high priest. These men,

CULTS: DIVINE CULTS. *Menat-necklace.* Necklaces of this type were dedicated to the goddess Hathor. This one is made of faience, glass, and bronze, and is from the eighteenth dynasty, reign of Amenhotep III. (The Metropolitan Museum of Art, Rogers Fund, 1911. [11.215.450])

whose range of duties is not entirely clear, evidently also served as the administrators of the vast temple domains of the divine cult. Other ranks of lesser priests, known from later period texts, include the *stoalists* (a Greek term), perhaps to be equated with the ranks of the *ḥm-nṯr* (the "pastophores"), who carried sacred objects in the divine cult, and the ranks of water-carriers (*wꜣḥ mw*).

The method and means of priestly appointment is not entirely understood. It is unclear, for example, whether the highest-ranking priests of a regional temple were appointed by a central administration (perhaps located at the largest or most influential cult center), or whether appointments were handled on a purely local level, or

through a combination of the two means. Clearly inheritance was a major factor, since genealogies indicate that a son often held the same priestly title as his father. The appointment of Nebwenenef as high priest of Amun was, according to his autobiography, made directly by Ramesses II, and in the Restoration Decree of Tutankhamun, that king claims that he personally appointed both *wab*-priests and prophets. Other priests were confirmed by oracles. Our imperfect understanding stems in part from the facts that few regional records have survived, and that most of the records extant come from Thebes, one of the greatest metropolitan centers.

**Activities.** The divine cult enacted in temples consisted of adoration of the god and making offerings to the divine being. In theory, the divine cult actions were performed by the king, who was the highest priest of all the cults and who bore the title "Lord of [ritual] Action" (*nb iírt ḫt*). In actual terms, a priest acted on behalf of the king, declaring to the god "It is the king who sends me." The god, in the form of a statue, dwelled in a shrine (or *naos*) within the temple sanctuary. Our best description of what a cult statue looked like is preserved in the Restoration Decree of Tutankhamun: "his holy image being of electrum, lapis lazuli, turquoise and every precious stone." As attested by the well-preserved example at Edfu, the shrine in which the god dwelled had a pyramidal roofline and its base was carved with lotus and papyrus plants, thereby equating it with the place of creation. The shrine was equipped with double wooden doors and was closed with a sealed cord.

The daily cult was enacted three times a day, roughly coinciding with the interval of meals, in each of the numerous temples, large and small, throughout the Nile Valley. The cult actions were closely patterned on the established rhythms of human needs transferred to the world of the gods. Various versions and sequences of the cult activities are attested, and often the exact sequence is not clear because of the ambiguous order in which the scenes on temple walls can be read. Generally, the offerant first purified the *naos* and the surroundings of the god with incense. The seals of the divine shrine were broken, an act likened to "opening the doors of heaven to see the god." The priest then prostrated himself, "kissing the earth" before the face of the god. Praises of the god were recited as the priest began the ritual purification of the cult image. In some temples, a pile of clean sand was poured on the ground in imitation of the mound of creation. After the priest intoned prayers for "laying hands upon the god," the statue of the god was removed from the shrine and placed on the mound of sand, symbolizing the rebirth of the god. The unguents and garments that had been applied in the previous service were removed and the statue was cleansed with incense and ointments. Pieces of red, green, blue, and white fabric were purified with natron and presented to the god. A broad collar was placed on the statue and again purified with incense and libations. A crown, scepters, and amulets in the form of an Eye of Horus and the goddess Maat were arrayed on the statue. Food offerings were presented to the god and a prayer intoned to encourage the god to partake of the meal. The statue was clothed in special *nms*-cloth, adored four times, and finally wrapped in a length of pure linen. The priest then closed the doors of the shrine and backed from the room, wiping away his footprints with a broom.

The temple-based divine cults probably showed little variation in cult activity from deity to deity; all gods were served by forms of the daily offering service. Yet there was more diversity in cult practice in the smaller localized cults, which, though possibly supported by state patronage, were outside the formalized context of the temple. The type of worship enacted by the nonelite tended to focus either on simple adoration of the god or on establishing an understanding under which the worshiper prayed and sacrificed or left food, drink, or votive offerings to the god; this was a means of obtaining divine intercession against sickness or infertility, or to secure wealth or guidance. Such worship may not have been executed on a regular basis, but only when an individual required divine intercession.

The best documentation for such informal divine cults are shrines to various deities, votive objects made of clay, wood, or bronze, and graffiti and more formal texts. Divine cult rituals performed outside the temple context can be traced to the Early Dynastic period by means of ivory, stone, and faience figurines of men, women, and animals excavated at the temple of Satet at Elephantine. These offerings were found in the temple precinct, where they had apparently been left by those who came to worship and, presumably, to petition the goddess for her help.

This practice is well attested by the New Kingdom cult of Hathor at Deir el-Bahri. That cult demonstrates the permeability of classification in Egyptian religion. Although it was dedicated to Hathor and hence is classified as a divine cult, it had decidedly funerary overtones; not only was Hathor associated with the Western Hills (the cemetery), but in addition, life after death was a constant concern of the Egyptians. Their veneration of gods during their lifetime was often in association with the hope for a happy afterlife.

The cult of Hathor at Deir el-Bahri indicates that there was considerable variety of type in cult activities. A series of shrines dedicated to the goddess date from the eleventh dynasty into the Ptolemaic period. The center of her worship was at the Montuhotep temple and also at the eighteenth dynasty chapel of the mortuary temple of Thutmose III. There, recovered from the ruins, were Hathor masks, faience figurines of eyes and ears, *menat*s, sistra, plaques molded with the image of a cow, and linen shirts or pieces of fabric painted with scenes of Hathor.

These small-scale cults, like the more formalized ones, appear to have employed priests. The biography of a certain Ameniminet relates that "I am the *is*-priest of the goddess [Hathor]. Anyone with petitions, speak . . . to my ear, then I will repeat them to my mistress in exchange for offerings [consisting of beer and oil]." These offerings were given directly to the priest, circumventing the official practice of presenting the offering to god briefly before it reverted to the temple staff.

Nothing is known about the rituals that may have been enacted in conjunction with the manufacture and deposi-

CULTS: DIVINE CULTS. *Late period aegis, most likely of Mut, Isis, or Hathor.* An aegis was a cult object, usually featuring the head of a female deity over a large collar. It was associated with protection, and, as such, was often placed on temple equipment. This one is bronze, with glass inlays. (University of Pennsylvania Museum, Philadelphia. Neg. # S8–134396)

tion of the votive objects; nor is it known if the votives were somehow consecrated by a priest before they were left in the shrine, nor whether priests were employed by the shrines to maintain the offerings.

**Cults of Deified Kings.** Although in theory all kings were venerated after their deaths through their mortuary cults, a few kings were worshiped in a deified state during their own lifetime. The king was venerated in his form of the royal *ka* or in his association with an aspect of Amun or Re. The cult of the living king focused on a statue of the pharaoh. Sacred boats that bore these images of the deified king in ritual processions are attested from Nubian and Egyptian temples.

Stelae and temple reliefs show the king and members of the community offering and adoring the statue of the deified king. Among the statues that have been identified as the focus of the divine cult of a king are those before the first and second pylons of the Luxor temple, the four colossal statues of Ramesses II on the facade of Abu Simbel, and the statue of Ramesses II within the sanctuary of that temple. Some stelae, such as that of Rahotep, a contemporary of Ramesses II, have the depiction of ears alongside an image of the divine statue, suggesting that the royal cult could involve the hearing of petitions. So too, the temple of "Ramesses II Who Hears Petitions," situated to the east of the temple of Amun at Karnak, was a place of public supplication based on worship of the divine king. Although little is known about the staff of such cults, the base of the cult statue of Ramesses II at the Luxor temple depicts *iwenmutef*-priests who officiated in the divine cult.

Few kings were honored with a cult during their lifetime; the cults of Sneferu, Senwosret III, Amenemhet III, Amenhotpe III, Tutankhamun, Sety I, Ramesses II, and Ramesses III are the best documented. Little is known about the rituals that were enacted in their honor, but certainly the creation of such a cult bolstered the prestige of the king during his lifetime. Ironically, most of the kings who created a divine cult for themselves were all long-reigning, powerful kings, rather than ephemeral rulers who might have profited more from such artificial status.

Other royal cults were activated only long after the death of the king, such as the cult of Amenhotpe I in Western Thebes. Most of our information about this cult involves the role of the king as a community oracle. As attested by paintings from private tombs and from petitions, a statue of the god-king, often in the company of his mother Ahmose-Nefertari, was dragged on a sledge in community processions. In the course of the procession, questions were put to the statue for adjudication. A similar role was played by Montuhotep and by Amenhotpe III and Tiye. Such attestations suggest that a major focus of the royal divine cults was to make the king more approachable to the populace.

**Cults of Deified Individuals.** A few private individuals elevated to the status of gods were the recipients of cults after their death. The best attested are the architects Imhotep (designer of the Step Pyramid, third dynasty) and Amenhotep, son of Hapu (architect of Amenhotpe III, eighteenth dynasty). Temples or shrines to both those men, or to them together, were situated throughout Thebes, as well as at Aswan, Dendera, Armant, Aswan, Saqqara, and Memphis. Other individuals so honored include Hekaib (governor of Aswan, sixth dynasty) and Isi, a sixth dynasty vizier who, as late as the thirteenth dynasty was referred to as a "living god." As with the divine cults, the object of these cults was also viewed as an intercessor who could make the needs of an individual known to the gods. An inscription on the base of a statue of Amenhotep, son of Hapu, is particularly explicit about the function of the cult:

O people of Karnak who wish to see Amun, come to me! I will transmit your request because I am the herald of this god. . . . I will transmit your word to Amun in Karnak. Give me an offering and pour a libation for me, because I am an intermediary nominated by the king to hear requests of the suppliant, to report to him the desires of Egypt.

As indicated by the text, the cult of these deified individuals apparently consisted of offerings to the memory and honor of the deceased in hope that the cult figure would obtain assistance from the gods.

The cult of deceased individuals became more common in the Late and Ptolemaic periods. Examples include Djedhor (thirtieth dynasty), who was deified as a form of Thoth, and Petosiris of Tuna el-Gebel, who was closely associated with Imhotep and Amenhotpe. From the thirtieth dynasty, individuals who drowned were accorded cults and were the subject of popular veneration. The divinity of such people was apparently based on the analogy of their drowning with the dispersal in the Nile of the body parts of Osiris. Among the best-known recipients of this cult are Pedesi and Pihor, who were buried at the Temple of Dendur and who are shown in that temple receiving offerings from the Roman emperor Augustus.

## BIBLIOGRAPHY

Barta, Winfried. "Kult." In *Lexikon der Ägyptologie*, 3: 839–848. Wiesbaden, 1980.

David, Rosalie. *A Guide to Religious Ritual at Abydos*. rev. ed. Warminster, 1981. Discussion of the ritual scenes in the temple of Sety, including their sequence and significance; has a handy condensation of the drawings of the original (now out of print) publication of the Abydos temple.

Dreyer, Günter. *Der Tempel der Satet: Die Funde der Frühzeit und des Alten Reiches*. Elephantine, 8. Mainz, 1986. Excavation report that details the votive objects recovered from the Early Dynastic and Old Kingdom temple of Satet at Aswan.

Habachi, Labib. *Features of the Deification of Ramesses II*. Glückstadt, 1969.

Habachi, Labib. *The Sanctuary of Heqaib*. Elephantine, 4. Mainz, 1985. The fundamental publication of the cult shrine of Hekaib (Heqaib), who was deified.

Hornung, Erik. *Conceptions of God in Ancient Egypt: The One and the Many*. Translated from German by John Baines. Ithaca, 1982. The standard work for the theory of Egyptian religion.

Moret, Alexandre. *Le rituel du culte divin journalier en égypte, après les papyrus de Berlin et les textes du temple de Seti 1er à Abydos*. Paris, 1902. Compilation of the hieroglyphic texts (with translations) that comprise the daily offering service.

Nelson, Harold H. "Certain Reliefs at Karnak and Medinet Habu and the Ritual of Amenophis I." *Journal of Near Eastern Studies* 8 (1949), 201–232, 310–345. A study of the divine cult and its actions as documented by Theban sources of the New Kingdom.

Nelson, Harold. "The Rite of 'Bringing of the Food' as Portrayed in Temple Reliefs." *Journal of Egyptian Archaeology* 35 (1949), 82–86. A study of the act of sweeping the footprints from the sanctuary floor.

Pinch, Geraldine. *Votive Offerings to Hathor*. Oxford, 1993. A study of informal cults, with valuable considerations of their form and function.

Rowe, Alan. "Newly Identified Monuments in the Egyptian Museum Showing the Deification of the Dead together with Brief Details of Similar Objects Elsewhere." *Annales du Service des Antiquités Égyptiennes* 40 (1940), 1–67. A study of the deification of royal and nonroyal individuals; one of the few sources for the cult of the drowned ones.

Sauneron, Serge. *The Priests of Ancient Egypt.* Translated from French by Ann Morrissett. New York, 1960. Basic work on priests and their duties.

Silverman, David P. "The Nature of Egyptian Kingship." In *Ancient Egyptian Kingship*, edited by David O'Connor and David P. Silverman, pp. 49–91. Leiden, 1995. Discusses the cults of the living king.

Teeter, Emily. "Popular Religion in Ancient Egypt." *KMT Magazine: A Modern Journal of Ancient Egypt* 4.2 (1993), 28–37. Discussion of informal divine cults unrelated to the state temples.

Wildung, Dietrich. *Egyptian Saints: Deification in Pharaonic Egypt.* New York, 1977. A condensation based on his work *Imhotep und Amenhotep* (Munich and Berlin, 1977), which deals with the deification of Amenhotpe and Imhotep.

EMILY TEETER

## Animal Cults

Like all early societies, the Egyptians lived their lives surrounded by animals. They depended on them for their livelihood, and they could not afford to be sentimental about them. At the same time, they were aware that animals possessed some qualities that were similar to those of humans and others that differed in important ways. This ambiguity aroused their curiosity. In addition, the Egyptians were often averse to making hard-and-fast distinctions in their view of reality. The living and the dead, for example, were often thought of as part of the same continuum, and the same to an extent was true of gods and human beings. It was therefore natural that the Egyptians would regard animals as part of a seamless world in which clues to the divine nature could be found.

Not all animals fell into the category of the potentially sacred. Most beasts of burden were regarded as unsuitable, though the donkey can be given religious associations that were disruptive or hostile to divine order. The ant was not recognized as sacred and seems to be absent from the hieroglyphic script. The horse, which in many societies was given heroic status, was highly valued, but it arrived too late in Egyptian history, when the canon of the sacred was already fixed. (It is true that the Syrian goddess Astarte could be shown riding a horse, but she too was borrowed.) The same is true of exotic animals such as elephants. Another late arrival was the camel, which also had the misfortune to be a beast of burden. However, most other animals were considered to reflect the world of the gods in some way. Occasionally they appear as divine mascots; for example, the gazelle accompanies the goddess Anoukis. But normally it is the animal itself that is thought of as conveying the divinity to which it is assigned; hence the falcon can be an image of Horus and in late texts can even be described as his soul ($b_3$), while the cat and the ichneumon are seen as embodiments of the gods Bastet and Atum, respectively. An interesting offshoot of this association is the use of animal heads on top of human figures to represent gods. Some gods can be shown this way as an option—for example, the occasional representation of Osiris with the head of a hare, which may be a lunar symbol. Other gods, such as Thoth and Sokar, are invariably shown as hybrids of this type. It is possible that the Egyptians conceived of such a head as a mask that served to hide the true form of the god, which was inexpressible. Whatever the explanation, the prominence of animals in the iconography is beyond doubt.

Since the animal and human worlds were thought to be parallel, it is not surprising to find the animal equivalent of the pharaoh. This is the Apis bull of Memphis, which is attested as early as the first dynasty. The principal titles of the Apis are of significance: he is *nswt n iw' nb ntry* ("king of every divine animal"), which emphasizes his preeminence; he is also *whm n Pth* ("repetition (?) of Ptah"). The word *whm* refers to the particular incarnation of the god that was thought to be present in his animal, and in some respects it is close to the Hindu concept of the avatar. It may also convey the notion of a herald or mouthpiece. On death, the Apis was thought to merge into the god Osiris, and the compound *Wsir-Hp* (Osiris-Apis or Osorapis) was used to signify the entire procession of historical animals that had gone to their divine destiny. The worst crime that could be ascribed to the Persian conqueror Cambyses was the (untrue) allegation that he had murdered the Apis. At Memphis, the theologians of the later period provided the bull with a mother: Isis, mother of the Apis, who had her own sacred cow. There was even a cult of children of the Apis, known from papyrus contracts of Ptolemaic date.

The complexity of Egyptian religion combined with the facts of geographical rivalry to make sure that the Apis was not unique. At Heliopolis there was the Mnevis (*Mr-wr*), a jet-black bull that was the *whm* of Atum; at Armant in the South, there was Buchis, a white bull with a black head, which was taken to be the *whm* of various solar deities. The splendor of the Buchis bull's temple and catacomb shows that, at least in the Late period, the Buchis was a serious rival to the Apis. There were other sacred bulls, notably in the Delta, and there was also the ram of Mendes. Edfu had the cult of a royal falcon. All these animals were singular and were succeeded by another only when they died. Most of them had elaborate rituals of enthronement and public display which were adapted from royal ceremonial. Many of them were thought to have oracular powers, doubtless because of their close associations with the divine.

Below this stage in the hierarchy were animals that functioned in small groups, like faunal aristocracies. The best known example is the sacred baboons of Memphis; Ptolemaic texts from the Sacred Animal Necropolis at Saqqara confirm that a colony of these animals was kept in the temple of Ptah "under his *moringa*-tree" in the valley. From time to time this colony was replenished with monkeys brought either from Ethiopia or from the royal zoo in Alexandria. There may have been a dozen or more in the colony at any one time. They had their own names, and the dates of their births were recorded when possible. One of the baboons would be singled out as oracular, and was given the name *Ḏd-ḥr-pȝ-ꜥn* ("the face of the baboon has spoken"). When an animal died, it was mummified and placed in a special catacomb hewn out of the rock at North Saqqara. A short obituary was written across the front of the niche where it was buried. A similar colony sacred to Thoth seems to have existed at Hermopolis in Middle Egypt, but it is uncertain how far back this practice extended. The lions of Leontopolis, in the Nile Delta, may have been a similar group.

The next step was to extend the concept of divinity to animals *en masse*, and there are signs even in the New Kingdom that this was beginning to happen. In the Cairo Museum there is a sarcophagus of a cat that may have belonged to Prince Thutmose, the short-lived elder brother of Akhenaten. The cat is depicted as a mummy and is termed *Wsir tȝ mit* ("Osiris the she-cat"). There is a jar in Munich with a Hieratic inscription recording that it contained the body of an ibis, which the dedicator had found in a canal of Ramesses I. It had presumably drowned and therefore had been claimed by the gods. In later times, the custom of burying animals found by chance may have become the norm, as suggested by the fifth-century BCE Greek historian Herodotus. This is confirmed by a Demotic text from Saqqara that records the burial of a falcon found dead at the entrance to some temple outbuildings; it was still sacred, whether in its right place or out of it.

By the Late period, reverence for cats and ibises, which could be kept in hundreds or even thousands, became commonplace. The true situation can be seen from the lists compiled by Dieter Kessler of sites and their associated animal cults. There were several major centers of worship for ibises, falcons, crocodiles, monkeys, ichneumons, cats, and most other animals, and there were many lesser centers as well. Theologically, these represent a straightforward extension of the notion of divinity resident within an animal, but there are several interesting ramifications. At Saqqara, the lunar and solar connotations of falcons and ibises were developed into a con-

trasting system, and the ibis god Thoth also acquired the epithet "Three Times Great."

In general, however, these extended cults were treated in a more reticent way. Ibises, for example, were not named individually, and on death were merely thought to merge into a collective entity known as Osiris the Ibis (*Wsir pȝ ḥb*). Nevertheless, when dead and awaiting burial, they might be referred to openly as "gods" (*nṯrw*). With a few exceptions, their burials are uninscribed, and no obituaries survive. The underground catacombs, however, are extensive, as they needed to be. One figure suggests an ibis population at North Saqqara of sixty thousand, and the late Ptolemaic-era Prinz-Joachim Ostraca from Kom Ombo reveal a burial rate of several hundred a month. Ibis mummies could be stacked in chapels known as "houses of waiting" (*ꜥwy.w n ḥrr*), since the catacombs would be opened only on ceremonial occasions for mass burials. In the case of ibises, the final total could run into millions, as at Saqqara and at Tuna el-Gebel, west of Hermopolis.

The driving force behind these enormous cults was that they paid. They were expensive to run, but they attracted worshipers and pilgrims in the thousands, in some cases from outside Egypt, as can be seen from hieroglyphic dedications on bronze votive statues. This mass appeal is evident in the large numbers of oracular questions and responses that survive. Oracles were a mechanism for decision-making, important or otherwise, and in a sense they occupied the niche nowadays filled by personal therapists and professional advisors. In addition, they were tangible and accessible in the way that conventional cults were not. They could interpret pilgrims' dreams. The same was true of the cults of the deified men Imhotep and Amenhotep, son of Hapu, which developed along similar lines. These gods listened: one of the epithets of the baboons at Saqqara was "The Hearing Ear." A moving prayer to the deified Buchis, inscribed on a pebble from his temple at Armant, shows this well: "Come to me Osiris-Buchis, my great lord. . . . I am your servant, and call upon you. I never weary of calling. Cares are heavy upon me, and I am small against them all. . . . Do not weary of calling upon [a] god. Has he his hour of dying, when he will not hear?"

The care offered by animal cults could be more than psychological. George Hughes has published a Demotic papyrus of Ptolemaic date, probably from the principal ibis cult at Hermopolis. This is a plea to the god of the temple by two children who have been thrown out of their home by a cruel father or stepfather. They are reduced to sleeping in holes in walls and begging for food. This plea is essentially a request to be taken into care, and in practice the various animal cults offered a variety of solutions to social problems, such as asylum for political refugees,

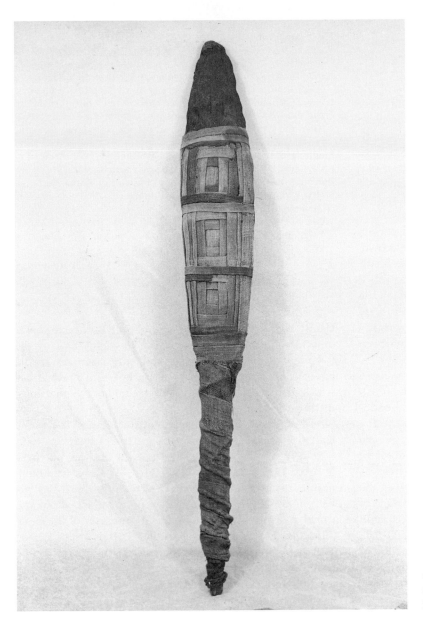

CULTS: ANIMAL CULTS. *Crocodile mummy.*
(University of Pennsylvania Museum, Philadelphia.
Neg. # S4–141201)

self-sale (in which a person would do menial work for the temple in exchange for maintenance), and forms of refuge for debtors and persons in similar difficulties. Perhaps the founding of Alexandria and the removal of the court from Egypt proper increased feelings of alienation among the native Egyptians; whatever the explanation, these cults filled a social need.

Another interesting discovery has come from the dedications on the temple furniture found in the falcon galleries at Saqqara. Some of these items were extremely costly, and most were offered to the cult of a young ibis deity, otherwise unknown, named Thutmose. (Whether this is linked to the earlier prince of the same name is still un-

known.) Many of these dedications were by women from the nearby township of Abusir, and in one case the occasion was a personal festival, perhaps a marriage. The cult of Thutmose was clearly a favorite with these women, some of whom had considerable wealth to spare. Perhaps they too felt excluded from more conventional worship.

We know something about the organization of these cults. There were the usual *wab*-priests and prophets (*ḥmw-ntr*), but the more menial caretakers or animal feeders were known as servants (*sḏmw-ꜥš* or *sḏmw*). Jobs of this sort ran in families, and a similar arrangement can be found among the masons (*byw* or *byw mnḫ*) who excavated and maintained the catacombs. These operated in teams, and it was not uncommon for such teams to be seconded from one cult to another. A similar, but probably more important, body was the stonecutters, workmen who made and installed the huge sarcophagi of the Serapeum and the nearby Mothers of the Apis. Some of the former at least had minor priestly titles, and all were attached to the cult of the appropriately named Ptah "great of strength" (*ꜣ pḥty*). From the mid-Ptolemaic period's Archive of Ḥor, all the animal cults at Saqqara were known to be subordinate to the Serapeum; however, in a major crisis, authority could be referred to the temple of Ptah in Memphis, which had the power to enforce reforms and punish abuse.

Self-regulation had its limits. In the Ptolemaic period, animal cults received an annual subsidy from the crown, known in Greek as *syntaxis*. In return for this, each cult had to accept a royal inspector (*epistates*), whose job it was to keep an eye on the administrative head of the temple, the *mr-šn* or *lesonis,* who was normally an Egyptian. In addition, rights such as asylum were rigorously controlled, and major building projects seem to have been subject to the royal purse-strings.

Proving a negative is difficult, but the sudden collapse of most animal cults after the Roman conquest in 30 BCE makes it likely that the new conquerors abolished the subsidy. The notion of animal worship was anathema to the Romans, especially when it was conducted by people whom they regarded as Hellenes, and they would not have been interested to know that Hermes Trismegistos was originally an ibis. However, traditional cults such as the Buchis were allowed to continue in reduced form. One of the last stelae from the Bucheum at Armant was dedicated by the Roman Emperor Constantius II (r. 337–361 CE), who was a declared Christian. Animal worship dwindled along the Nile, although the occasional Coptic icon showing a saint such as Christopher with a dog's head shows that vague folk memories persisted for centuries.

[*See also* Bull Gods; *and* Feline Deities.]

### BIBLIOGRAPHY

Gabra, Sami. *Chez les derniers adorateurs du Trismégiste.* Cairo, 1971. Account of excavations in the animal necropolis at Hermopolis in Middle Egypt.

Hughes, G. R. "The Cruel Father: A Demotic Papyrus in the Library of G. Michaelides." In *Studies in Honor of John A. Wilson,* pp. 43–54. Chicago, 1969. Insight into the social role played by animal cults.

Insley Green, Christine. *The Temple Furniture from the Sacred Animal Necropolis, North Saqqâra 1964–1976.* London, 1987. Evidence for wealthy dedications and the use of such practice by women.

Kessler, Dieter. *Die heiligen Tiere und der König.* Wiesbaden, 1989. Comprehensive lists of sites with associated animal cults.

Malek, Jaromir. *The Cat in Ancient Egypt.* London, 1993. Covers domestic as well as sacred aspects of a popular animal.

Martin, G. T. *The Sacred Animal Necropolis at North Saqqâra.* London, 1981. Final report on the southern sector of this important site.

Meeks, D., and C. Favard-Meeks. *Daily Life of the Egyptian Gods.* London, 1996. Covers rituals in sacred animal cults, pp. 129–140.

Mond, R. L., and O. H. Myers. *The Bucheum.* 3 vols. London, 1934. Full publication of a prominent Upper Egyptian cult.

Preisigke, F., and W. Spiegelberg. *Die Prinz-Joachim Ostraka.* Strasbourg, 1914. Information on mass burials of sacred birds.

Ray, J. D. *The Archive of Ḥor.* London, 1976. Demotic evidence for administration of an animal cult, and for the ideology behind it.

Ray, J. D. *Demotic, Hieroglyphic and Greek Inscriptions from the Sacred Animal Necropolis, North Saqqâra.* London, forthcoming. Publishes the texts from the falcon and baboon catacombs, including genealogical lists of workforce.

Smith, H. S. *A Visit to Ancient Egypt.* Warminster, 1974. Account of the Egypt Exploration Society's work at North Saqqâra.

Wildung, Dietrich. *Egyptian Saints: Deification in Pharaonic Egypt.* New York, 1977. Treatment of two popular cults that have much in common with animal worship.

Wildung, Dietrich, and Günter Grimm. *Götter Pharaonen.* Mainz, 1978. Exhibition catalog; number 28 is the cat sarcophagus of Prince Thutmose.

JOHN D. RAY

**CURSES.** In modern times, popular myths about pharaonic Egypt often focus on the use of curses. During the twentieth century, the press and entertainment media have concentrated on supposed curses against individuals who seek hidden burial places in the land of the pharaohs, disturb them, and desecrate the tombs. In these recent interpretations, such blasphemous activities inevitably lead to a dire fate for the defilers and can often haunt their families and friends as well. The most famous of these updated maledictions is "The Curse of King Tutankhamun." It surfaced shortly after the death of Lord Carnarvon on 6 May 1923, and was reported throughout the world. Carnarvon was the financial supporter of the expedition led by the discoverer of the tomb, Howard Carter. This tragic incident occurred less than one year after the tomb of that pharaoh had been opened. Although the tomb contained no hieroglyphic text that resembled the supposed curse that the media issued, the public apparently preferred to accept what they read about the curse in the newspapers and journals, rather than to listen to scholars. In the beginning, only one death was attributed to the curse, but soon the death of anyone even remotely connected with the tomb was ascribed to the same cause. Books focused on it; films were made about it, and interest in it surfaces every so often, despite frequent published refutations. Although Howard Carter lived more than seventeen years after discovering the tomb, his longevity is never referred to. What should be perhaps of more interest is that the ancient Egyptians did in fact employ various types of curses and threats, and some of them were specifically aimed at trespassers who attempted to violate the tomb.

The presumed efficacy of these curses derived in part from a belief in the power of the written and spoken word, and this form of magic (*ḥkꜣ*) was a divine property accessible to the pharaoh as well as to humankind. Traditionally, the antagonist could take the form of a being, either human or spiritual, living or dead. Fear of the known or the unknown could be controlled through the use of this *ḥkȝ*. The first step was to identify the foe, an act that exerted some power over it, and this was often accompanied by a description of any potential or actual action. Then the consequence for such deeds could follow. Sometimes a statement of protection against a hostile act would accompany the identification of it.

Though recorded in both hieroglyphs and Hieratic, curses clearly also had a spoken aspect, and occasionally a spell included directions for its recitation. Certain spells in mortuary literature (for example, BD 151 regarding magical bricks) and some inked on other types of papyri (for example, a letter to the dead) could function as curses, and texts on tomb façades or clay figurines could also have the same role. The execration texts, which represent extensions of this practice, are lists of the names of hostile individuals and foreign enemies that appear on figures or pottery. The ritual destruction of these items was thought to render such antagonists harmless. This practice, a form of sympathetic magic, took place at various levels of Egyptian society.

To deal with potential or actual afflictions, the Egyptians also made use of spoken and written incantations. These would address the entity that they thought was responsible for such ills and threaten it with destruction. "The Magical Spells for Mother and Child," for instance, warn that any foe intending to take an action against the child would be met with resistance and repelled. Though not always explicitly expressed, similar intentions can be inferred by the existence of amuletic objects such as magical wands. These artifacts, which were used especially for newborn children, could carry the same protection, even if their surfaces omitted the traditional text and had only the associated iconography. Both royal and nonroyal individuals used magical bricks in their tombs to safeguard them against demons that might come against the deceased from each of the four cardinal points. These inscribed objects generally occur with accompanying images and were meant to be apotropaic devices to threaten potential antagonists. Such objects were also part of the funerary equipment of Tutankhamun, and might be identified more properly as the real curse in the tomb of that pharaoh.

Slightly different were the letters to the dead, entreaties to the *akh*s, residents of the netherworld who often were deceased relatives of the sender. Those who were still among the living would write to these spirits requesting aid in time of need. The *akh*s were assumed to have some control over events that were taking place (or would occur) in this world, and, in order to ensure that they responded positively, the sender would often threaten to deprive them of their offerings and thus jeopardize their eternal existence.

The ancient Egyptians spent considerable time and effort preparing for their afterlife. Since the tomb was an essential element in the plans for their eternal survival, they considered it important to protect it in the best manner possible. One of the means that they used to secure their final resting places was a curse. They believed that a threat could safeguard the structure from a variety of attacks against the construction itself, its purity, its contents, the mummy, and the accompanying imagery, iconography, and texts. Among the many types of hostility that the ancient Egyptians specified were any sort of damage to the tomb, theft, disrespect or vilification of the owner, and sacrilege. Old Kingdom tomb owners were especially preoccupied with fears that an impure individual might enter the chapel and thereby defile the sacred area. Traditionally, such blasphemers are referred to as those who had not purified themselves, or those who had eaten a forbidden food before entering the chapel. At least one example, however, also places adulterers in this category. Negative connotations regarding sexual activities before entering a holy place such as a temple are documented later in the mortuary literature.

Many messages to potential enemies were carved on stone and inscribed as part of the tomb owner's biographical statement, such as those referred to above. Examples can be found from most periods of Egyptian history, although those from the earlier times are more common. Inscriptions with similar communications can occur in the form of graffiti at quarries, but they can also be inscribed on stelae, offering tables, temple walls, and papyri. During different time periods, there were certain preferences in terms of the style of the curse, the type of individual addressed, the reaction to the hostility, or the medium on which the message was placed. For example, it appears that biographical maledictions in private tombs were more popular in the Old and Middle Kingdoms than in the New Kingdom. The Egyptians also incorporated threats in their legacies. Often, especially in the Third Intermediate Period and later, wills inscribed on papyri would contain a malediction to ensure the desired distribution of willed property to the appropriate beneficiary.

Curses inscribed on the walls of temples date primarily from the New Kingdom and later, but even in earlier times royalty had threats inscribed as punishments to violators (see, for example, the temple inscription of Senwosret I at Tod). The pharaohs used not only the walls of temples but also stelae and other types of inscriptions (see, for example, the Nauri Decree of Sety I) to record their warnings.

The terminology in the first part of the curse often appears to have parallels in legal or juridical texts, and the same observation seems to be even more valid in the statements that follow. Some of the threats against the hostility are expressed in terms of judgment, sentencing, or punishment; in the later periods, the offender can be exposed to sexual penalties, some including bestiality.

[*See also* Execration Texts.]

### BIBLIOGRAPHY

Assmann, Jan. "When Justice Fails: Jurisdiction and Imprecation in Ancient Egypt and the Near East." *Journal of the Egyptological Association 78* (1992), 149–162.

Assmann, Jan. "Inscriptional Violence and the Art of Cursing: A Study of Performative Writing." *Stanford Literature Review* 9.1 (1993), 43–65.

Morschauser, Scott. *Threat-Formula in Ancient Egypt: A Study of the History, Structure and Use of Threats and Curses in Ancient Egypt.* Baltimore, 1991. A complete list of the different types of curses, with many examples and comprehensive analysis.

Nordh, Katarina. *Aspects of Ancient Egyptian Curses and Blessings: Conceptual Background and Transmission.* Boreas: Uppsala Studies in Ancient Mediterranean and Near Eastern Civilizations, 26. Uppsala, 1996. The most recent analysis of the subject; also discusses religious, sociological, and cultural aspects.

Silverman, David P. "The Curse of the Curse of the Pharaohs." *Expedition 29* (1988), 57–63. A popular account of the curse of the pharaohs, with a select bibliography of both popular and scholarly works.

Silverman, David P. "The Curse of Hezi." *Journal of the American Research Center in Egypt* 37 (2000), in press. A discussion of an Old Kingdom curse with the earliest reference to adultery.

Sottas, H. *La preservation de la propriété funéraire dans l'ancienne Égypte.* Paris, 1913. A standard monograph on the subject.

Willems, Harco. "Crime, Cult, and Capital Punishment (Mo'alla Inscription 8)." *Journal of the Egyptological Association* 76 (1990), 27–53. In reviewing this inscription the author includes a discussion of the threats against desecrators.

DAVID P. SILVERMAN

**CYNOPOLIS.** *See* Asyut.

**CYPRUS.** The Egyptian name for Cyprus during the New Kingdom is still debated, but it was most likely *'ir3s,* probably to be equated with the name Alashiya in Akkadian, the *lingua franca* of the Bronze Age. A second term, *'isy,* favored by some scholars as Cyprus, may well have been a reference to Aššuwa, located in northwestern Anatolia. Correspondence from the king of Alashiya written in Akkadian on clay tablets were found among the Amarna Letters of Amenhotpe III and Akhenaten (e.g., EA 33–35, 37–39); analysis of the clay from those tablets indicates that they probably originated in Cyprus.

In one of the Amarna Letters (EA 35), the king of Alashiya apologized to the pharaoh for the small amount of copper he had sent—only 500 *talents* (alt.: *shekels*)—and blamed the low output on an incidence of plague ("the hand of Nergal") in his land. Cyprus seems to have been an especially valuable source of copper during the Bronze Age, and it served as an international clearinghouse for goods from Syria-Palestine, Anatolia, and the Aegean. Commercial exchanges between Egypt and Cyprus seem to have been common throughout at least the latter half of the second millennium BCE, if not earlier as well.

Cypriot pottery, ranging from White Slip milkbowls to Base Ring jugs and juglets, has been found in New Kingdom contexts in Egypt. In turn, Egyptian imports, ranging from pottery and stone objects to silver rings and scarabs, are known from Cypriot trading ports, such as Hala Sultan Tekke and Enkomi. Many of the commercial exchanges between Egypt and Cyprus were no doubt conducted by merchants, but it is not always clear whether such merchants were acting on their own or on behalf of the crown. The Amarna Letters indicate that a fair amount of "gift giving"—the exchange of goods on an elite or royal level—took place during the eighteenth dynasty, and finds on Cyprus of objects with the cartouches of Amenhotpe III, Queen Tiye, Akhenaten, and Horemheb may confirm the existence of trade and contact at the highest levels of society.

The importation of Cypriot pottery came to a sudden halt in Egypt some time before the end of the New Kingdom, at approximately the same time as the cessation of Mycenaean pottery into Egypt. Such a drastic interruption of international trade might be connected to the appearance of the Sea Peoples (c.1200 BCE); however, the Hittites were known to have fought several naval battles with Alashiya at the end of the thirteenth century BCE, and perhaps those military actions were enough to disrupt the economy of Cyprus and its international trade links. Although contacts between Egypt and Cyprus did resume during the first millennium BCE, the days of high commerce and international royal transactions had essentially come to an end with the fall of the New Kingdom in Egypt and the end of the Late Bronze Age across the Mediterranean.

[*See also* Mediterranean Area.]

### BIBLIOGRAPHY

Cline, Eric H. *Sailing the Wine-Dark Sea: International Trade and the Late Bronze Age Aegean.* Oxford, 1994. An overview of the international trade in the Mediterranean during the second millennium BCE; chapters on Egypt, Cyprus, and trade goods are particularly relevant.

Jacobsson, Inga. *Aegyptiaca from Late Bronze Age Cyprus.* Jonsered, 1994. A catalog and discussion of all Egyptian objects found on Cyprus from second millennium BCE contexts.

Knapp, A. Bernard. *Near Eastern and Aegean Texts from the Third to the First Millennia BC: Sources for the History of Cyprus,* vol. 2. Altamont, N. Y., 1996. Compilation, with translations, of all mentions Cyprus in texts dating from the Bronze Age; particularly relevant is the section on Egyptian mentions of Cyprus.

Moran, William L. *The Amarna Letters.* Baltimore, 1992. Recent translation into English of the Amarna Letters of Amenhotpe III and Akhenaten, including letters to and from Alashiya (Cyprus).

ERIC H. CLINE

# D

DAB'A, TELL ED-, site to the north of Markaz Faqus, in the eastern Nile Delta, has been identified with Avaris, capital of the Hyksos (c.1640–1530 BCE) and with the southern part of Piramesse, the Delta residence of Ramesses II and his successors. Some also argue that the site was identical with the biblical town Raamses/Ramesse. The Pelusiac branch of the Nile once passed to the west of the site, which was protected on its east by the huge swamps and lakes of what is today the Bahr el-Baqar drain. Situated between the two water systems, the town controlled the access path into the northeastern Delta—an important strategic position.

Excavations there were started in 1885 by Édouard Naville. From 1941 to 1942, Labib Habachi worked there for the Egyptian Antiquities Service and first suggested an identification with Avaris. From 1951 to 1954, Shehata Adam partly excavated the twelfth dynasty site of 'Ezbet Rushdi. From 1966 to 1969 and from 1975 onward, the site has been under survey and excavation with more than forty-five fieldwork and study campaigns by the Austrian Archaeological Institute in Cairo.

The site was founded at the beginning of the twelfth dynasty, under Amenemhet I, with a planned settlement. Probably in the Herakleopolitan period there had existed the estate of a king Khety, as mentioned on a stela found by Shehata Adam (1959). Soon afterward, another settlement began on the southeastern bank of the Pelusiac at 'Ezbet Rushdi es-Saghira. A memorial temple for Amenemhet I, the founder of the twelfth dynasty, was constructed in the fifth year of his reign by Senwosret III. That temple was abandoned by the second half of the eighteenth century BCE, during the time of the thirteenth dynasty.

A community of Canaanites (carriers of the Syrian-Palestinian Middle Bronze Age culture IIA) settled there in the late twelfth dynasty, which led to a considerable enlargement of the town. The majority of the settlers seemed to have been soldiers, to judge from the offerings in their tombs; probably they were also employed as sailors, shipbuilders, and craftsmen by the Egyptian crown. Their tombs, arranged in cemeteries, can be found in the midst of the settlement. At the beginning of that settlement, the Syrian "middle-room" and the "broad-room" house could be found among the architectural features; later, only Egyptian house architecture was used there.

During the thirteenth dynasty, a palatial quarter for officials was constructed. Their function was to supervise trade and expeditions abroad. They were in Egypt's service but were of Near Eastern origin. Their cemetery was found attached to the palace. It was arranged in the Delta tradition of the old royal cemeteries of Buto and Sais. In front of each tomb a tree had been planted, and each tomb was covered by a chapel. Donkey sacrifices in front of the entrances displayed, however, Near Eastern burial traditions, and the weaponry from the tombs was of Near Eastern type. According to a scarab, found in one of the plundered tombs, some of the officials were titled "Overseers of the Foreign Countries" and "Expedition Leaders." One of the tombs had a pyramidal superstructure; in its adjoining chapel, the remains of a colossal limestone statue of an official in Near Eastern dress and coiffure were found. The statue was mutilated by hammer blows, perhaps the result of inner political turbulence during this period, especially since the palace was abandoned soon afterward. (Another such statue appeared on the antiquities market and may have come from the same cemetery.) The statues of Queen Nofru-Sobek and King Hornedjheryotef of the late twelfth and early thirteenth dynasties, found by Labib Habachi, were probably only transported to this site during the Hyksos period, along with numerous other royal statuary.

The settlement size increased steadily. During the second half of the eighteenth century BCE, an influx of Syrian-Palestinian Middle Bronze Age elements is noticable. Among the settlement pottery, the percentage of Middle Bronze Age IIA-types, the majority imports, increased from about 20 to 40 percent. Soon afterward, epidemics seemed to have decimated the town. The eastern suburbs were abandoned and in the excavated quarters emergency burials were found, some with multiple interments in shallow pits.

A sacred precinct was constructed in the Eastern town; it consisted of two temples of Near Eastern type and mortuary chapels of Egyptian type, with adjoining cemeteries. In front of the main temple, oak tree pits were identified. Possibly the cult is to be associated with the Canaanite godess Ashera, in syncretism with the Egyptian godess Hathor, who was not only established in the Near East but also had an association with the mortuary cult. Because of two fragments of door jambs with the names of King

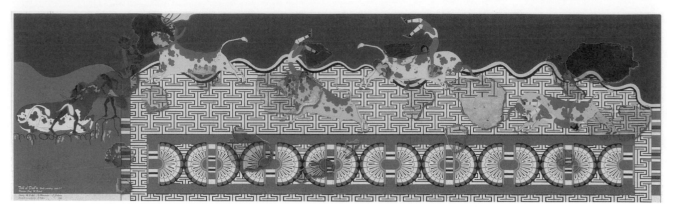

DAB'A, TELL ED-. *Minoan taureador frieze against a maze background from the royal residence of the early eighteenth dynasty.* (Reconstruction by Manfred Bietak, Nanno Marinatos, and Clairy Palyvou)

Nehesy of the fourteenth dynasty, this precinct should be associated with him. Unfortunately both stone fragments were found in secondary positions; by the scattering of his monuments, the evidence indicates that Nehesy or his unknown father separated from the reigning thirteenth dynasty and established a small kingdom in the northeastern Delta, with the capital in Avaris, as the name of the settlement became. The Egyptian storm god Seth was then introduced as the dynasty's god, with every reason to believe that he is actually the Syrian (Canaanite) storm god Hadad/Baal-Saphon, because a cylinder seal with his representation is known from the palace of the early thirteenth dynasty. Since the seal was locally made, the cult of that god was probably already established in the eastern Delta, and it is understandable why the later Hyksos chose Seth as their chief god—the local variant of Seth was actually a god from their own Canaanite pantheon.

Of special interest is the development of the settlement. At first an egalitarian pattern prevailed, which gave way to social differentiation. Bigger houses became surrounded by smaller houses on the same plots. Then with the beginning of the Hyksos period (fourteenth to seventeenth dynasties) the town expanded considerably, with a gradual internal density. During the Hyksos period, some new settlements and cemeteries were also found at the eastern edge of the Delta. Such a development can only be explained by a population influx, probably from the southern Levant, but perhaps some Egyptianized Canaanites who had settled previously in other areas of Egypt came to the eastern Delta, contributing to a "homeland" for the Hyksos rule in Egypt.

The mortuary practices found at the site before the Hyksos era display some Near Eastern features. Tombs were arranged either in small cemeteries within the settlement or in small groups within courtyards or even within houses. Normally chambers were constructed of mud bricks, covered by vaults. The vaulting technique has no real parallels in Egypt. In late Hyksos times, Egyptian vaults were introduced. Infants in their first or second year were buried within amphorae that had been imported as wine or oil containers from the Levant. Particularly interesting are burials of female servants in front of tomb entrances—all between eleven and sixteen years of age. In two cases, it was possible to prove that they were interred at the same time as their masters. This custom is so far unknown in the Levant and occured only briefly at the site. Another feature was the burial of pairs of donkeys, yet in Canaan, donkeys have been found only singly (with the exception of Tell el-'Ajjul). That custom seems to have originated from northern Syria, where donkey sacrifices in pairs at tomb entrances are attested. Typical for this Canaanite population living in the northeastern Nile Delta were burials with such weapons as daggers, battle axes, and sometimes spears (which end in the middle of the Hyksos period).

Ceramic materials show that in Hyksos times practically all imports from the Levant came from the southern Palestine region. Almost all imports were amphorae, which contained wine or olive oil. Imports of Cypriot pottery also increased with the beginning of the Hyksos era and flourished in some parts of the town toward the end of Hyksos times. An increasingly isolationist tendency can be seen in the site's internal trade, since almost no Upper Egyptian, or Middle Egyptian wares of the Memphite area were found from that time.

Toward the end of the Hyksos period, at the western edge of Avaris, along the eastern bank of the Pelusiac branch of the Nile, a huge citadel was constructed on as yet unused land. Along the river was built a buttressed enclosure wall of mud bricks, 5.25 meters (16 feet) wide, which was enlarged later to 8.4 meters (25 feet). It is unclear so far whether that is the town wall or the citadel's enclosure. Behind those walls a stratum of gardens with tree pits and traces of a vinyard were discovered—a reminder of the second stela of King Kamose, who threatened the Hyksos with uprooting the trees of Apophis' garden and drinking wine pressed from his vinyards. The stela mentions also the frightened wives of the Hyksos peeping down from the towers of Avaris. Other archaeological features of the citadel include the substructure of a huge building enclosed by another buttressed wall from the north; its stone blocks have royal inscriptions of the Hyksos, which can be seen as evidence that it was a royal citadel.

After the conquest of Avaris by Ahmose (c.1530 BCE), the major part of the town was abandoned and the citadel was destroyed. There alone was evidence of violence found. When a cleaning operation was carried out before the construction of new palatial quarters, bodies, most probably those of soldiers, were buried in pits without any offerings. One type of burial is in orderly fashion, with bodies in extended supine position; another type is of skeletons lying face down, often in multiple burials. Some multiple burials have dismembered bodies, and some of the skeletons show traces of severe injuries. Of special interest was a round pit with two bodies, and on top of them were some hundred broken pots and pieces of limestone.

In the New Kingdom, a new palace compound was constructed in the early eighteenth dynasty, mainly of brick materials taken from the Hyksos citadel. It consisted of two main elements: a platform construction with an access ramp cut through the fortification walls along the riverside, to serve as a probable base for a raised small fortress; and a big palace building with thick walls, storage magazines, corridors, and bathrooms. The two buildings so resemble the so-called Southern and Northern Palace of the late seventeenth dynasty at Deir el-Ballas that a similar function seems likely. Deir el-Ballas was probably the campaign residence of Sekenenre and Ahmose during their war against the Hyksos. It was abandoned at the beginning of the eighteenth dynasty, just at the moment that Avaris was taken. A new residence seems to have been constructed at that time, most probably by the same king for his final campaigns against the Hyksos in the southern Palestine region. Evidence for a military presence included numerous arrow tips and Kerma household pottery. Without doubt, Nubian archers had been stationed there, probably recruited from prisoners of war during campaigns in the south against the kingdom of Kush.

The site's biggest surprise was the numerous fragments of wall plaster with Minoan wall paintings that were genuine in technique and style. They were partly in dumps east of the platform and partly *in situ;* half were also *in situ* at the northern entrance of the palace. The motifs included bull hunting, bull grappling, bull leaping, floor acrobatics, hunting scenes, and felines such as lions and leopards chasing fallow deer and goats, as well as a lion devouring a bull—all showing the Minoan ideal of nature's hierarchy. The style is quite naturalistic. Some fragments depict the typical craggy landscape of Crete. The half-rosette frieze and the maze motif suggest a direct connection to the court of Knossos. Representations of a full-scale emblematic griffin and, probably, lions and leopards are similar to those in the throne rooms of Knossos and those of the Mycenean palaces, although they were later than the paintings at Tell ed-Dab'a. Nevertheless, at Knossos similar motifs must have already existed in an early phase. Such discoveries are reminders of *niello* inlaid Aegean motifs on an axe and on a dagger of Ahmose, as well as the unexpected title of the mother of Ahmose as ḥnwt idbw h3w-nbwt ("Mistress of the Shores of Haunebut"), the toponym identified in the past with the Aegean. In the future, a better understanding may be effected in the light of such finds.

In the early eighteenth dynasty, the New Kingdom rulers quickly took advantage of their free access to the eastern Mediterranean. While the ceramic imports (mainly containers of wine and olive oil) at the end of the Hyksos period were those of southern Palestine and Cyprus, the pottery from the citadel shows a much wider range of trading partners. The citadel was probably not long in use as a royal residence, but its area was settled at least until the time of Amenophis II and perhaps continued until the time of Piramesse, when restorations were done at the platform building. Also a temple must have been constructed at that time, to the northeast, as a huge mudbrick enclosure wall was found there.

From the twenty-first dynasty onward, the site, as the southern part of Piramesse, served as a quarry for building materials, especially stone blocks and monumental statues used for the new residences at Tanis, Bubastis, Leontopolis (Tell el-Muqdam), and elsewhere. Along with the monuments, the cults of Piramesse were to some extent also transferred to the new sites, so it is not surprising that in the thirtieth dynasty some secondary cults of the gods of Ramesses II appeared independently in Tanis and Bubastis. This explains why in the Bible the town of Raamses/Ramesse was located at Tanis and to the east of Bubastis in the Wadi Tumilat. Without knowing the original position of Avaris or Piramesse, the identity of those two towns (and their association with the biblical town of Raamses/Ramesse) were kept in memory until Manetho's history of Egypt, according to the first-century Roman historian Josephus, became known and was reinterpreted.

**BIBLIOGRAPHY**

Adam, Shehata. "Report on the Excavations of the Department of Antiquitites at Ezbet Rushdi." *Annales du Service des Antiquités de l'Égypte* 56 (1959), 207–226.

Bietak, Manfred. *Tell el-Dab'a*, vols. 2 and 5. Vienna, 1975 and 1991.

Bietak, Manfred. "Avaris and Piramesse, Archaeological Exploration in the Eastern Nile Delta." Ninth Mortimer Wheeler Archaeological Lecture. *Proceedings of the British Academy* 65 (1979), 225–290. Oxford, 1981 and 1986.

Bietak, Manfred. "Egypt and Canaan during the Middle Bronze Age." *Bulletin of the American Schools of Oriental Research* 282 (1991), 28–72.

Bietak, Manfred. *Avaris, The Capital of the Hyksos—Recent Excavations at Tell el-Dab'a*. The Raymond and Beverly Sackler Foundation Distinguished Lecture in Egyptology, no. 1, British Museum Publications. London, 1996.

Boessneck, Joachim. *Tell el-Dab'a*, vols. 3 and 7. Vienna 1976 and 1992. On the osteology at the site.

Habachi, Labib. "Khata'na–Qantir: Importance." *Annales du Service des Antiquités de l'Égypte* 52 (1954), 443–559.

Habachi, Labib. *Tell el-Dab'a I and Qantir or Avaris and Piramesse*. Edited by E. Engel and P. Jánosi. Vienna, forthcoming.

Winkler, Eike-Meinrad, and Harald Wilfing. *Tell el-Dab'a*, vol. 6. Vienna, 1991. Provides an anthropological perspective on the finds.

MANFRED BIETAK

**DAHSHUR,** a site about 50 kilometers (40 miles) south of Cairo (29°40'N, 31°15'E). The present-day name derives from Coptic by way of Greek *tachsour;* the ancient Egyptian was probably *Wnt Snfrw.* Dahshur was the southernmost necropolis of the ancient residence city of Egypt—later Memphis—in the first Lower Egyptian nome (province). Although two calcite (Egyptian alabaster) sarcophagi come from Dahshur's third dynasty necropolis, its great period began in the fourth dynasty with the reign of Sneferu (c.2649–2609 BCE). After his fifteenth year of reign, he established his residence there, called "Sneferu is appearing," and he successively constructed two large stone pyramids. His southern pyramid was the first to be attempted as geometrically true. The development from the stepped pyramid to a true pyramid was neither logical nor obvious; it required an intellectual understanding of a pure architectural form, which also reflected the developing philosophy of Egypt's newly centralized state. For that reason and for the development of the cult installations around the pyramids, Dahshur is of historic importance. When the South Pyramid had reached a height of about 50 meters (160 feet), dangerous cracks appeared in the outer casing, the corridors, and the chambers—as the clay layers that formed the foundations subsided under the pressure of the mass. As a result of an additional coating of limestone around the four sides of the pyramid, fresh cracks emerged. The corridor leading from the northern side of the pyramid to the funerary apartments became too ruined to be used further; therefore, a new corridor was constructed from the west to the upper funerary chamber. Yet this corridor and the funerary chamber were also affected by the subsidence. Even the decrease of the angle of inclination, at half of its actual height, to reduce the planned height of 160 meters (500 feet) to 104 meters (330 feet) could not save the monument. This alteration of the incline angle determined the form and gave the pyramid its name—Bent Pyramid or Rhomboidal Pyramid. It had finally to be abandoned, and Sneferu began in his fifteenth year of counting (which is the twenty-ninth regnal year) a new pyramid farther to the north, the third of his reign.

Called the North Pyramid or Red Pyramid, because of the reddish hue of the local core stones, this new pyramid was constructed on a solid foundation and was the first successfully completed true pyramid, some 104 meters (330 feet) high, with three chambers, one beyond the other, each with a nearly 15-meter- (50-foot- ) high corbelled roof. The Red Pyramid contained the royal burial: some human remains were still present in 1957, when it was excavated. Both pyramids were surrounded by cult installations; those of the Red Pyramid were hastily completed in brickwork after the death of Sneferu. Excavations by the German Institute of Archaeology have revealed the foundations of a funerary temple, at the eastern side of the Red Pyramid, with two statue chapels, an open court, and an offering chapel with a false door. The funerary installations of the South Pyramid were never abandoned but were completed with two tall royal stelae, a large cult pyramid to the south, and a causeway leading to a valley temple halfway to the pyramid. The cultic orientation of this temple and its six chapels, containing life-size statues of the king, had been faced toward the North Pyramid—indicating that it was built at the same time as the North Pyramid. To the east of the two stone pyramids extend large *mastaba* tombs of the family and descendants of Sneferu. To the north, a depression marks another uncompleted pyramid of the Old Kingdom, probably the pyramid of Menkauhor of the fifth dynasty, as mentioned in a sixth dynasty exemption decree of Pepy I.

On the edge of the cultivation three kings of the Middle Kingdom built their pyramids cased with white limestone, and these were surrounded by large precincts that have the cult installations and the tombs of their wives, daughters, and high officials. These burials of the queens and princesses had acquired a particular fame at the end of the nineteenth century, as the provenance of remarkable jewelry and precious objects, the so-called treasure of Dahshur (now in the Cairo Museum). The twelfth dynasty pyramid of Amenemhet II, built from white limestone, has nearly disappeared, owing to stone quarrying in the Arab Middle Ages. Farther to the north, Senwosret (Sesostris) III, also during the twelfth dynasty, built his large

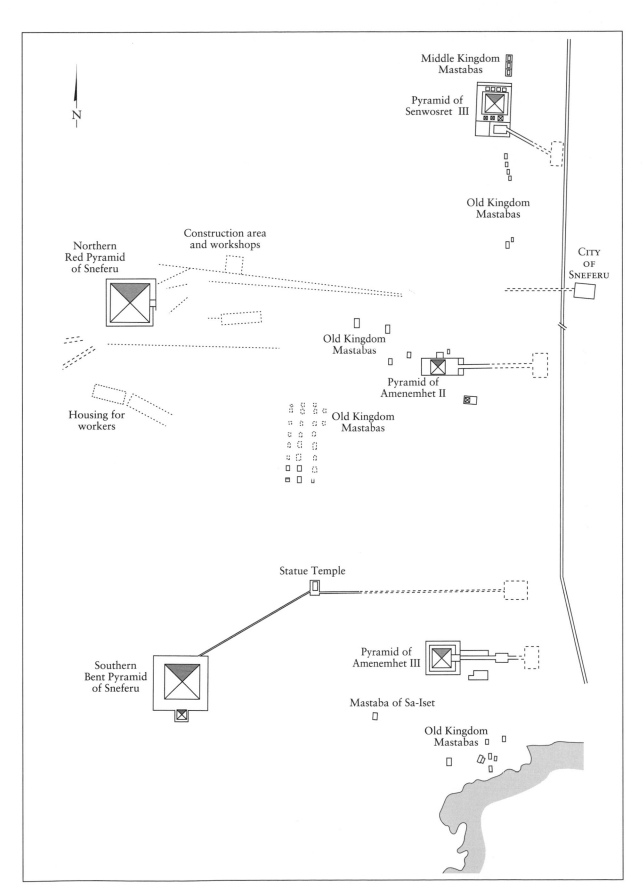

Middle Kingdom
Mastabas

Pyramid of
Senwosret III

Old Kingdom
Mastabas

Construction area
and workshops

Northern
Red Pyramid
of Sneferu

CITY
OF
SNEFERU

Old Kingdom
Mastabas

Pyramid of
Amenemhet II

Housing for
workers

Old Kingdom
Mastabas

Statue Temple

Southern
Bent Pyramid
of Sneferu

Pyramid of
Amenemhet III

Mastaba of Sa-Iset

Old Kingdom
Mastabas

DAHSHUR. *Plan of Dahshur.*

pyramid precinct, oriented north–south, with a paneled enclosure wall that resembled the precinct of Djoser of the third dynasty. The pyramid of Amenemhet III at Dahshur South suffered the same construction destiny as the Bent Pyramid; built on the same clayey strata as that fourth dynasty pyramid, it also suffered from subsidence and was abandoned for the king's burial but was still used for queens' burials. For security reasons, the entrances to these Middle Kingdom pyramids were moved from the north to other sides. Inside, the corridors and funerary apartments became real labyrinths, with staircases, blind corridors, and several additional chambers. The burial chambers had vaulted white-painted granite roofs, and they contained magnificent sarcophagi of pink granite, decorated with paneled enclosure walls.

Several small pyramid precincts of kings from the thirteenth dynasty and later, among them the pyramid of Imeni Qemau, still await excavation. The pyramid towns and residences that are known from royal decrees and inscriptions have not yet been discovered but are now probably covered by gardens and cultivated land. Dahshur was often visited in the nineteenth century by Egyptologists. In 1837, John Shea Perring surveyed both pyramids of Sneferu; Karl Richard Lepsius then prepared the plan of the area from 1842 to 1843. In 1894 and 1895, Jacques de Morgan excavated the Middle Kingdom pyramids, finding the jewelry. Modern systematic excavations started with Ahmed Fakhry in 1951 at the Bent Pyramid. They have been continued by the German Institute of Archaeology under Rainer Stadelmann at the Red Pyramid and at the *mastaba* tombs. Dieter Arnold worked for the same institution and later for the Metropolitan Museum of Art, New York, at the twelfth dynasty pyramids of Senwosret III (r. 1878–1843 BCE) and Amenemhet III (r. 1843–1797 BCE).

## BIBLIOGRAPHY

Arnold, Dieter. *Der Pyramidenbezirk des Königs Amenemhet III. in Dahschur.* Mainz, 1987.

Edwards, I.E.S. *The Pyramids of Egypt.* Rev. ed. Harmondsworth, 1986.

Fakhry, Ahmed. *The Monuments of Sneferu at Dahshur.* 2 vols. Cairo, 1959.

Lehner, Mark. *The Complete Pyramids.* London, 1997.

Stadelmann, Rainer. *Die Ägyptischen Pyramiden.* 3d enl. ed. Mainz, 1997.

RAINER STADELMANN

**DANCE.** Moments of joy and leisure are evoked by dancing, as was the case in ancient Egypt. Some texts show that teachers warned their pupils against dance, considering it a mere amusement and, therefore, a loss of time. "One who dances in the desert" is a lazy and neglectful person, they admonished. Scenes of banquets with young dancing girls were represented in New Kingdom tombs at Thebes, where the impression made was that they were only concerned with entertainment in a mundane sense. Scrutiny revealed, however, that this was only the superficial aspect of such scenes, which have become rightly famous for their artistic achievement.

The Egyptian language does not have a generic word *dance*, which can cover all aspects of this concept, no matter what type of dancing or movement is involved. Instead, Egyptian had, from the very beginning, two or three words usually translated as "dance," without further precision. The most common and ancient word is *ib3*, which frequently includes a game piece in its hieroglyphic orthography, suggesting that there might be some resemblance between the movement of the game piece and the dancer: "caper" may be a proper translation. Another common word, but of obscure etymology, is *ḥbi*, usually considered an acrobatic dance. In the *rwi* ("run away"?) dance, performers bear, in most cases, clappers ending with animals heads. Other terms have even less clear meanings. A *ksks* ("twist"?) dance seems to have been practiced mostly by non-Egyptians or even by animals. The *ṯrf* dance of the Old Kingdom was, in most cases, performed by a pair of men. Contrary to the commonly expressed opinion, its relationship to the later *ṯrf* remains questionable; in its only known representation, it is not associated with dance but with music, in a rather static way. After the New Kingdom, many new terms appeared, adding little to our understanding. The growing vocabulary may give the impression that each word was related to a specific dance but, unfortunately, pictorial evidence has failed to confirm that view.

The problems related to the *ṯrf* activity and a closer examination of scenes in which dances are represented raise the question of their relationship to musical instruments in general. In tombs, where wall scenes are displayed in superimposed registers, bands of musicians and groups of dancers are usually shown in different registers, giving the impression that their respective activities may not be too closely associated. Even when they are represented in the same register, some element frequently interferes with the scene to separate them from each other. People painted in direct contact with dancers are, as a rule, clapping their hands, using sticks of various forms as clappers, or playing tambourines, drums, sistra, *menat*-necklaces, or any form of percussion intended to beat out tempo and rhythm. Only occasionally were wind or stringed instrument players closely associated with dancers in the same scene.

In most instances, dances were performed either by men or by women, but in separate groups. Within a single group, a movement could be executed solo, by a couple, or by several persons; however, all dancers were part of the whole, as in a modern ballet, in which different danc-

DANCE. *Priestesses and dancing girls.* Copy of a wall painting from the tomb of Intefoker at Thebes, twelfth dynasty, reign of Senwosret I. (The Metropolitan Museum of Art, 30.4.160)

ers onstage execute different movements but all are part of the same choreography.

The oldest dances known from ancient Egypt are those related to different phases in funerals. In some Old Kingdom tombs, just after mummification was completed, dances were first performed by a specialized group, the ladies of "the acacia house." The members of that institution were concerned with the appeasement of the dangerous lion goddess Sekhmet and the rejuvenation of the dead. The ladies mourned the dead but also celebrated the regenerated body. The appeasement of Sekhmet was probably related to successful mummification—the victory over demons endangering the rebirth of the deceased. After that, dancers were involved in what is called the "offering table" dance, which invited the dead, born to a new life, to his first meal. Variations on this topic do not always include the ladies of "the acacia house," since there are portrayals of other groups of women and even men. A range of dance scenes, especially during the Old Kingdom, have been loosely associated with the dead sitting at a table. Another group of dance performers, the *ḫnrt*, apparently specializing in childbirth ceremonies, might also have been associated with funerals in helping the deceased enter a new life. On its way to the grave, the

funeral equipment and the statues of the dead were again followed by dancers. Some Middle Kingdom tomb scenes in Beni Hasan gave a special emphasis to that episode; they show groups of acrobats executing complicated figures, some looking more like circus performances than dancers. Beni Hasan princes were very fond of acrobatic or wrestling games and perhaps they wished to introduce a personal touch in their funerals. That kind of scene was also used later on in the New Kingdom, but it was depicted in a less vivid manner. As was already the case with the old *ṯrf* dance, a special kind or variant of funeral dance was performed in honor of the goddess Hathor, known from Middle and New Kingdom tombs. It was characterized by leaping or skipping and was meant to celebrate the coming of the goddess. Hathor could represent the comely aspect of the dangerous Sekhmet, but she was also the goddess who met the dead at the entrance of the underworld. She helped them enter it and is the main agent of rebirth. An appeal to her was recited or sung, accompanied by the clapping of hands and sticks or by the rustling of the *menat*-necklace beads.

As part of the funerary procession the dances required no other setting. Such was not always the case for the *mww*-dancers, known from the Old Kingdom until the end of the New Kingdom. In the less sophisticated scenes, their dance, performed when the procession reached the tomb, differed only from the others by their special head-dresses. Woven of papyrus stalks, their "caps" identified them as marsh dwellers and, more precisely, as ferrymen. Their role was to ferry the dead across the waters leading to the netherworld, a travel patterned on a fictitious journey through the Nile Delta, from Memphis to Sais, then to Buto and back. In more complex settings, the *mww*-dancers were part of a scene that included lightly built chapels, pools surrounded by trees, and religious symbols—a scene that endeavored to re-create, on a small scale and near the tomb, the sacred precincts of the cities mentioned above.

Although they were depicted as dancing at the entrance of the tomb, *mww*-dancers should not be confused with the dwarfs dancing "at the entrance of the shaft," as texts usually put it. Dwarfs as dancers were known from the Old Kingdom and were much prized because of their rarity. King Pepy II (c.2300 BCE) warmly congratulated the noble Horkhuf for bringing back a dwarf for "god's dances" from an expedition abroad. In the Pyramid Texts, the dead king was identified, once, with such a dwarf. In the few scenes in which they were portrayed, the dwarfs appeared alone, discretely mixed in with children or adults. The dances performed by them at the entrance of the tomb were mentioned in texts only, from the Middle Kingdom onward. These were clearly farewell dances, where the departure of the dead was associated with the departure of the sun for its night journey into the underworld; like the sun that appears each morning as a newborn child, the dead would rejuvenate during their own journeys. The dwarf, who hardly exceeds a youth in height, was considered a representative of the sun, never growing old. Dwarfs also danced at funerals of the sacred bulls, Apis and Mnevis, who were closely related, respectively, to the rebirth of Osiris and the sun god. A magic spell from the New Kingdom also linked the solar dwarf to the baboon, a well-known sun dancer.

From numerous representations in tombs and from short texts that comment on them, funeral dances are better known any others; but this does not mean that dances were performed mainly for such sad events. Many of the dance scenes from the Old and Middle Kingdoms, for example, appear at first glance, to be set in the context of daily life. Their very presence in tombs, however, and their many details in that setting have suggested an unquestionable religious significance. The dividing line between both aspects of the same activity—the sacred and the profane—is especially true for banquet scenes painted in New Kingdom tombs at the Theban necropolis. These scenes brought together the ritual and domestic sides of a family feast, where musicians and dancers were present.

The scenes gave special emphasis to the banquet, where food was much less important than wine. Richly dressed guests were attended by youths pouring out wine in cups. As musicians sang "make-merry" songs, guests made "long life" toasts and drank until drunkenness descended—a condition that allowed them to communicate with Hathor, "the lady of drunkenness." Offerings were even made to gods of the necropolis or to gods like the ferocious Sekhmet, to satisfy them and to keep malevolent beings at a distance. All was done to enjoy the present day, to forget how short life is. The New Kingdom scenes differ from the "offering table" dances of the Old and Middle Kingdoms. The religious element is still present, however, in those banquet scenes.

As the wise Anii recommended in his teaching, celebrate in due time the feast of one's own god by a banquet to which family and other relatives are invited. During the feast, he said, make offerings, play music, dance, and drink until drunkenness. Anii's text provided the clue to the banquet scenes; in some, a girl dancing alone was represented among musicians, thus complying with the wise man's advice. In most cases the girl, in a curious attitude, bowed and hid her face behind her arm. The female musicians, near her, were generally lute players. They were represented with a bent knee, striking the ground with the tip of the foot. They were not dancing but just beating out the rhythm. Their stance, however, was similar to the ideogram that depicts, after the New Kingdom, the supposed *tnf* lute-dancer, so the question remains, was *tnf* really a dancer, as generally accepted in past years? He might have been a musician with specific attributions in religious rites, those related to the appeasement of Sekhmet and similar deities.

The link between the old "offering table" dance and the dances in New Kingdom banquet scenes might be less tenuous than has usually been supposed. A Middle Kingdom stela (Louvre C 17) shows a scene halfway between both representations. Guests were sitting at tables and wine was absent, but the harp player and the dancing girl shown were heralding what was usually seen in banquets. All the dance scenes pictured in tombs showed moments of sadness or moments of joy, because dance was the hinge of both. It might end the one and pave the way for the other. It might be performed for the pleasure of the living or for the dead, auguring a good event to come—their rebirth. Always with a religious background, the only difference in such dance was the schedule: the moment of the death was unpredictable but family feasts, in all probability, were intended to coincide with religious events that were turning points in a cycle.

Notwithstanding some remarkable exceptions, dancing scenes disappeared from tombs after the end of the New Kingdom. That was probably due to changes of habits in tomb decoration and did not mean that dances ceased to be practiced during funerals. Mortuary texts of the Late period confirmed that dances were still an important part of these ceremonies. In contrast, dancing scenes in temples were depicted only from the New Kingdom onward; this may be explained by the circumstance that temples prior to the New Kingdom are scarcely known to us. The dances pictured in temples concern both royal and divine ceremonies; their role was, ultimately, not really any different from those already discussed.

The king was, from a dogmatic point of view, the representative of the gods on earth; they bestowed on him the power to govern, to preserve cosmic order by performing their rites in temples. These activities supposed that the king was, at any moment, at the peak of his ability. When the king grew old, the jubilee ceremony, the so-called *sed*-festival, was intended to restore his declining vigor. From reliefs preserved in the tomb of Kharuef (reign of Amenhotpe III, c.1410 BCE), at crucial moments, festival dances were performed. Dances performed during religious ceremonies related to turning points in the year can also be considered moments of renewal. The variations of dances performed on those occasions were mostly explained by their religious context and by the way they had to conform to or reflect the local mythology of the god to whom they were addressed. The factor they have in common is that perhaps all ceremonies of this kind reached their climax in the popular rejoicing that focused on a solemn procession of the sacred barks, since most of the important dance scenes showed that kind of procession.

During the Valley festival at Thebes, the god Amun left his temple at Karnak to visit the tombs on the western bank, after crossing the Nile River on his bark. While transported overland, the bark was escorted not only by priests but also by musicians and dancers. That visit, paid to private tombs on the new moon of the tenth month of the year, was surely related to the banquets discussed above. The families were probably awaiting the procession in the court of the tombs, preparing the banquet, and rejoicing when it passed by. Eventually the procession reached the sanctuary of Hathor, situated in the Deir el-Bahri valley, where the deity was honored as a child-giving goddess and protectress of the dead. A vigil called "the inebriation feast" was important on this occasion. During the Opet festival, the bark of Amun was accompanied by much the same retinue as during the Valley festival. For that occasion, when the flow of the Nile was at its highest, the god traveled from Karnak to Luxor temple (called the "Southern Opet") to meet his wife, the goddess Mut. Some clues indicate that this feast was considered a sacred marriage, which would result in giving birth every year to a reborn or rejuvenated king. The procession was identified with the journey of the sun in its bark, in the

company of Hathor in her role of sky and love goddess. Acrobatic dances executed by groups of women were the most characteristic feature of the processions, even if such figures were performed for other occasions; in addition, dark and exotic dancers—perhaps Nubians—jumped and weaved to the beat of drums. During the feasts of Min, the god of fertility and regeneration, dancers specially attached to his cult took part in ceremonies and processions. Dancing monkeys were also pictured, at least during the Late period, although they had been used for entertainment long before. In Egyptian mythology, monkeys were supposed to have executed farewell and greeting dances to the setting and the rising sun; they announced that the god was to be born again during his night journey, and they rejoiced at his rebirth in the morning. These trained animals were consecrated to Thoth, the god of science and writing. The priests of Min danced with monkeys and had, as their inscriptions tell us, knowledge of the sacred books. In ancient Egypt, writing was considered a major tool for the preservation of life.

In all those ceremonies, as in the funeral rites, dances announced or celebrated rebirth in all its possible aspects. That was especially important for new year's feasts. In most temples, during the last five days of the year, music was played and dances were performed to appease Sekhmet and to protect the country from attacks of her disease-bearing and deadly demons. They swarmed around, marking the agony of the year; dancing was intended to protect against this dreadful possibility. The new year was marked by the coming of the Nile flood. At the southern border of Egypt, joyful and noisy feasts were organized to greet the first manifestations of "the new water," as it was called. The coming of the flood was thought to be nothing more than the return to Egypt of the angry and dangerous Sekhmet—to be transformed by music and dancing into the mild Hathor. With the flood, she fertilized Egypt for the year to come, providing wealth, ease, and comfort. All kinds of performers were involved: acrobats, foreigners with their exotic dances, and even the trained monkeys. The god Shu, who brought back "the distant one," danced and welcomed the goddess, his wife, for the promising harvests she was bringing with her.

In ancient Egypt, dance was a time marker. It evidenced the moment of radical change, when something ends and something else begins. It protected from the dangers of what was dying and celebrated what was to be born anew.

[*See also* Music.]

## BIBLIOGRAPHY

Altenmüaller, Hartwig. "Zur Frage der MWW." *Studien zur Altägyptische Kultur* 2 (1975), 1–37. An extensive study on the *mww*-dancers and their ritual significance.

Assmann, Jan. *Stein und Zeit. Mensch und Gesellschaft im Alten Ägyp-

*ten.* Munich, 1991. Chapter 8 (pp. 200–237) is devoted to banquet scenes and their ethic and religious significance.

Brunner-Traut, Emma. *Der Tanz im Alten Ägypten.* 3d ed. Glückstadt, 1992. Chronological analysis of dance scenes and texts concerning dance in general; this edition reproduces that of 1938, augmented by the 1986 article on dance, "Tanz," published by the same author in *Lexikon der Ägyptologie.*

Burkard, Günter. "Der in der Wüste tanzt." In *Wege öffnen. Festschrift für Rolf Gundlach,* edited by M. Schade-Busch, pp. 23–29. Wiesbaden, 1996. Remarks on dance as amusement and a sign of laziness.

Daumas, François. "Les propylées du temple d'Hathor à Philae et le culte de la déesse." *Zeitschrift für ägyptische Sprache und Altertumskunde* 95 (1968), 1–17. Studies the texts of a Hathor temple that mentioned hymns and dances for this goddess during the new year's feast.

Edel, Elmar. *Das Akazienhaus und seine Rolle in den Begräbnisriten des alten Ägyptens.* Munich, 1970. A study of the "acacia house" and its ladies as dance performers in funerary rites.

El-Aguizy, Ola. "Dwarfs and Pygmies in Ancient Egypt." *Annales du Service des Antiquités de l'Égypte* 71 (1987), 53–60. Summarizes the religious and mythological roles of dwarfs, with comments on dancing dwarfs.

Gardiner, Alan H. "A Didactic Passage Re-examined." *Journal of Egyptian Archaeology* 45 (1959), 12–15. Comments on a literary text that mentioned music and dance in relation with family feasts; the text was, in some ways, a description of banquet scenes depicted in tombs.

Green, Lynda. "Egyptian Words for Dancers and Dancing." *Egyptological Miscellanies. A Tribute to Professor R. J. Williams,* edited by J. K. Hoffmeier and E. S. Meltzer, pp. 29–38. The Ancient World, 6. Chicago, 1983. A handy survey of the dance vocabulary.

Nord, Del. "The Term *ḫnr:* 'Harem' or 'Musical Performers'?" *Studies in Ancient Egypt, the Aegean, and the Sudan: Essays in Honor of Dows Dunham,* edited by W. K. Simpson and W. M. Davis, pp. 137–145. Boston, 1981. Stresses the existence of a specialized group of musician-dancers frequently represented or mentioned on tombs of the Old and Middle Kingdom.

Quaegebeur, Jan, and Agnès Rammant-Peeters, "Le pyramidion d'un "danseur en chef" de Bastet." *Studia Paulo Naster Oblata,* vol. 2: *Orientalia Antiqua,* edited by J. Quaegebeur, pp. 179–205. Leuven, 1982. A study (pp. 193–205) examining the role of the *ṯrf* musician and his possible dancing activities.

Van Lepp, Jonathan. "The Role of Dance in Funerary Ritual in the Old Kingdom." *Akten des vierten Internationalen Ägyptologen Kongresses,* vol. 3, edited by S. Schoske, pp. 385–394. Beihefte Studien zur Altägyptischen Kultur. Hamburg, 1989. Summarizes the ritual context of some funeral dances shown on Old Kingdom tombs.

Wild, Henri. "*Les danses sacrées de l'Égypte ancienne.*" In *Les danses sacrées: Sources Orientales,* vol. 6, pp. 33–117. Paris, 1963. The basic study on the subject; although limited to sacred dances, treats almost all aspects of the topic.

DIMITRI MEEKS

**DARA.** *See* Asyut.


**DEATH.** *See* Afterlife.


**DECIPHERMENT.** In Hadrian's Gateway on the island of Philae, at ancient Egypt's southern border, is the last known hieroglyphic inscription, dated precisely to August 24 CE by the accompanying Demotic text. Demotic itself, the third and most cursive of the Egyptian scripts, survived at least until December 452 CE; the latest dated Demotic text is also on Philae. For the next thirteen and one-half centuries, ancient Egypt was silent, for the art of reading her scripts was lost. The language itself, Old Egyptian, survived written in Greek letters, supplemented by seven borrowed Demotic signs, in a form called "Coptic," the script and language of the Christian descendants of the ancient Egyptians. Coptic vocabulary consists of a mix of Old Egyptian and Greek words. Of even greater importance for decipherment, early Coptic primers were written in Arabic, so a knowledge of Arabic grants access to the latest form of the ancient Egyptian language.

The Rosetta Stone's inscription has been popularly held as the key to decipherment, but in fact it was only of limited use. Even without it, an understanding of ancient Egypt's scripts would eventually have been achieved, though a little delayed. Named from its find-place in the western Nile Delta, the Rosetta Stone was discovered in mid-July 1799 by a French officer with Napoleon's expedition to Egypt called Bouchard or Boussard. It was surrendered to Britain in 1801 by the terms of the Capitulation of Alexandria and reached England the following year. Copies of its texts were distributed to centers of scholarship throughout Europe before it entered the Egyptian Collection of the British Museum in London.

The Rosetta Stone is an inscribed slab of granitoid stone, over a meter (nearly 4 feet) in height though missing about two-thirds of its first inscribed section. Its inscription is bilingual, written in three scripts (14 lines of hieroglyphs, 32 lines of Demotic, and 54 lines of Greek) but only two languages, Egyptian and Greek. The Greek could easily be read, and it proved to be a copy of a decree passed by a general council of Egyptian priests meeting at Memphis on 27 March 196 BCE to celebrate the first anniversary of the coronation of King Ptolemy V Epiphanes, who, like all the Ptolemaic rulers of Egypt, was a Macedonian Greek. The text is little more than a catalog of priestly privileges and a list of the reciprocal honors bestowed on Ptolemy V by the Egyptian temples, but it ends with the information that the decree is to be inscribed in the sacred, the native, and the Greek characters. In other words, the Greek section is a translation of the two sections written in hieroglyphs and Demotic.

First attempts at decipherment concentrated on the Demotic section, not just because it was virtually complete but also because it was thought that Demotic represented an alphabetic script and would therefore be easy to decode. That hieroglyphs were of an enigmatic, esoteric, symbolic nature was a long-held tradition, formulated as early as the writings of Diodorus Siculus in the first century BCE. Moreover, during the early centuries of the current era, hieroglyphs were adopted by the Neoplatonist philosophers as a divinely inspired script that symbolically embodied all human wisdom, giving rise to a body of Hermetic writings and a genre of literature devoted to their explanation. The *Hieroglyphika* of Horapollo, probably compiled in the fourth or fifth century CE, is one of the best-known works on the subject. It comprises 189 chapters; each deals with a particular hieroglyph by first describing it and then explaining its meaning, the relationship between form and meaning always being allegorical.

Unfortunately, tracts such as these were among the first works on the subject to be discovered during the European Renaissance, and they encouraged the incorrect view of later scholars—that hieroglyphs were purely symbolic and contained in their signs the lost lore of ancient Egypt. The wildly incorrect translations and erroneous conclusions that could result from such a false premise are probably best illustrated by the work of the German priest Athanasius Kircher in the mid-seventeenth century.

At first, scholars working on the Demotic section of the Rosetta Stone met with great success. Like the Greek section, it began with a dating not only by the ruler's name but also by a list of the Greek-named priests and priestesses who held office during that particular year, the so-called eponymous priesthoods. In 1802, the French scholar A. I. Silvestre de Sacy first read successfully the Demotic groups for the names "Ptolemy" and "Alexander." Later in the same year, his pupil, the Swedish diplomat and orientalist Johan Åkerblad, was able to add the remaining non-Egyptian names. As non-Egyptian, they were spelled phonetically with alphabetic signs, and this strengthened the misapprehension that Demotic consisted only of alphabetic signs. Even when Åkerblad went on to identify correctly several individual Demotic words apart from names (such as "Greek," "temple," and the pronouns "him" and "his") and to correlate them with their Coptic equivalents (thus demonstrating that Coptic was the language of the ancient Egyptians), by ill luck these words too were written alphabetically.

Consequently, no further advances were made until the second decade of the nineteenth century, when the English polymath Thomas Young turned his attention to the task of decipherment. His manuscript notebooks with the results of his work on the Rosetta Stone's Egyptian sections, carried out during his summer holidays at Worthing on the southern coast of England between 1814 and 1818, are in the British Library's Manuscripts Department in London. Young's outstanding mathematical aptitude enabled him to distinguish the Demotic groups for a whole series of words other than personal names.

Young's method was to find a word in the Greek text that occurred a number of times, and then to identify a group of Demotic signs that occurred an approximately equal number of times. He decided a group found in nearly every line must be Demotic for "and." After this, the most frequently occurring groups were the words for "king," "Ptolemy" (already identified), and "Egypt." Even so, all Young could do was write above groups of Demotic signs, which were spaced throughout the section, their translatable Greek equivalents. Before long, his Greek-Demotic vocabulary amounted to eighty-six Demotic words, which he had translated correctly but had in almost every instance transliterated incorrectly.

Young's notebooks make it clear that he drew on texts other than the Rosetta Stone's for his researches—in particular, those on papyri written in Hieratic and linear hieroglyphs, as well as in Demotic. He had already accepted the mixed nature of the Demotic script, in which some signs had a phonetic value and others were ideograms that expressed an idea or denoted the object depicted. When he reached the momentous conclusion that Demotic and hieroglyphs were closely related, he realized that Demotic was ultimately derived from hieroglyphs through the intermediate stage of Hieratic. Then he had within his grasp the proof that hieroglyphs could not be an essentially symbolic script.

When Young turned to the hieroglyphic section of the Rosetta Stone, he soon demonstrated that many Demotic and hieroglyphic signs were equivalents. He also demonstrated the fact, long suspected but unproved, that the elongated ovals called "cartouches" contained the royal name—in that instance, "Ptolemy," in short and longer versions. His reasoning was that if the name was expressed phonetically in Demotic, the hieroglyphs must express it phonetically too. He used that premise to analyze the name "Berenice" (a Ptolemaic queen) in an inscription from the temple at Karnak. Its writing also confirmed an earlier supposition that a certain hieroglyphic group attached to what were evidently female names denoted a feminine ending.

Young had now conjectured quite correctly the phonetic values of seven hieroglyphic signs (and one partially correctly), but he was still convinced that the phonetic principle was applicable to the hieroglyphic script only in certain cases, notably the rendering of foreign names. The results of his work were published in 1819 in the *Supplement to the Encyclopaedia Britannica* (4th edition) and were undoubtedly known to the French scholar Jean-François Champollion, although two years later Champollion still clung to the mistaken belief that hieroglyphs were symbolic, as proved by his 1821 article *De l'écriture des anciens Égyptiens*.

Like Young, Champollion approached hieroglyphic decipherment through the name "Ptolemy," and he made the same deductions by a remarkably similar procedure. Consequently, there has always been speculation that initially, at least, he relied on Young's findings without ever acknowledging them. Among Young's documentation in the British Library is a letter written to him by the French scholar Silvestre de Sacy, warning the Englishman lest Champollion appropriate his ideas and claim them as his own. Nevertheless, even if Young's results did point in the right direction (although Champollion never admitted it in print), it took the Frenchman to prove that the hieroglyphic script operated on a phonetic principle.

Champollion realized he needed a pair of known names having several hieroglyphs in common. The sound values thus far allotted could then be tested and further identifications made. For that purpose, the Rosetta Stone had reached the end of its usefulness, but in 1821 a new stimulus was provided by the inscription on an obelisk that had been excavated on Philae in 1815 by W. J. Bankes and in 1819 brought to Kingston Lacey in Dorset, England. The obelisk's hieroglyphic inscription contained two different cartouches, one of them like those on the Rosetta Stone; a Greek text on the obelisk's plinth named a King Ptolemy and a Queen Cleopatra. Bankes distributed to interested scholars lithographed copies of both texts, helpfully annotated with suggested identifications of the names. Champollion was then able to prove the sound values of the signs common to the two cartouches and to work out the sound values of the remaining signs.

Writing the cartouche from the Rosetta Stone that is thought to contain the shorter version of the name "Ptolemy" above the signs from the Bankes's obelisk inscription that are believed to write the name "Cleopatra," and numbering the signs, produces the following: The symbols at A1 and B5 in Figure 1 are identical and must represent *p;* A4 and B2, also identical, must represent *l.* Thus, B1 can only be *k* (in Greek, the name is "Kleopatra"). Substituting these sound values in Cleopatra's cartouche provides the sequence K L 3 4 P 6 7 8 9 (B10 and B11 are known to represent a feminine ending). From their position, B3 and B4 were assumed to be the equivalent of *e* and *o* (this only holds good for the phonetic writing of foreign words: B3 is actually *i,* and B4, *wa*). In other writings of "Cleopatra," B7 is sometimes replaced by B10, itself identical with A2, so the sound represented must be essentially *t* (B7 actually represents *d*). B6 and B9 can only have the phonetic value *a,* leaving B8 to represent *r.* Applying these values to the cartouche of Ptolemy results in P T O L 5 6 7. The Greek form of "Ptolemy" is *Ptolemaios,* so A7 must represent *s,* leaving A5 to represent *m,* and A6 a vowel in which the sound *i* predominates (A6 actually has the phonetic value *y*).

Champollion knew his identifications were correct when he was able to read such cartouches as "Autocrator," "Caesar," "Alexander," and "Tiberius," although those names were also foreign and of late date. Nevertheless, in his epoch-making *Lettre à M. Dacier relative à l'alphabète des hiéroglyphes phonétiques,* published late in 1822, Champollion made the final breakthrough when he announced that the phonetic system was of far wider application than to the writing of names, that it could, moreover, be extended back into dynastic times. Earlier in 1822, he had received copies of inscriptions from various temples, including Abu Simbel in Nubia, where the same name (with variations) constantly appeared in a cartouche. In its simplest form, the last two signs were known from Greco-Roman cartouches to represent *s.* The first sign was a sun disc, in Coptic *re;* so supplying this sound value produced the sequence *re* + unknown sign + *s* + *s,* which at once suggested to him the name of the

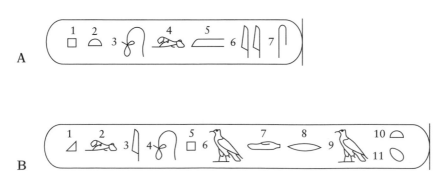

DECIPHERMENT. Figure 1 (A) *the cartouche from the Rosetta Stone containing the shorter version of the name Ptolemy;* (B) *the cartouche from the Bankes obelisk containing the name Cleopatra.*

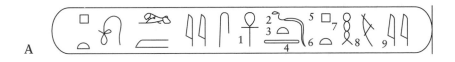

DECIPHERMENT. Figure 2 (A) *the cartouche from the Rosetta Stone containing the name Ptolemy, followed by the expression "living forever, beloved of Ptah"*; (B) *the corresponding cartouche from the Bankes obelisk.*

famous nineteenth-dynasty pharaoh Ramesses. In another cartouche with the same unknown sign (to which the sound value *m* was now allotted) Young had already identified the initial hieroglyph of an ibis as signifying the god Thoth. This could only be the name "Thothmes" (the eighteenth-dynasty king Thutmose). Final proof came from the Rosetta Stone itself, where the unknown sign appears, again in conjunction with *s*, as part of the hieroglyphic group corresponding to the Greek for "birthday": the Coptic word for "to give birth to" is *mise*. In fact, the unknown sign is a biliteral with phonetic value *mes*, the two *s* signs being phonetic complements.

Progress was still difficult: nearly two-thirds of the hieroglyphic section of the Rosetta Stone was missing, and there was a linguistic gulf between the fossilized form of the language written in the hieroglyphic script and that embodied in the Demotic. In the hieroglyphic, the word "king" was *nsw bity* ("He of the Reed and Hornet") an ancient title dating back to the very beginning of the dynastic period, three thousand years before. Demotic used the term "pharaoh" from *pr ʿȝ*, literally "great house" or "palace," extended to refer to its resident only since the New Kingdom, about 1450 BCE. In the hieroglyphic section, "Greeks" were designated by the term *ḫȝw-nbw*, "(Aegean) islanders"; in Demotic, they were *wynn* ("Ionians"), because it was the eastern Greeks with whom the Egyptians in the Late period had most contact. Best illustrating the way the language embodied in the two scripts had undergone change was the rendering for the words "stela of hard stone": in hieroglyphs, *ʿḥ ʿ* ("stela") *nty* ("of") *ʿȝt* ("stone") *rwḏ* ("hard"); in Demotic, *wyti* ("stela") *iny* ("stone") *ḏry* ("hard").

Even the supposition that the signs at the end of the longer form of the cartouche of Ptolemy represented the epithet "Living Forever, Beloved of Ptah," as in the Greek, needed to be proved (see Figure 2). In Coptic, the word "living" was *onkh*, presumed to be derived from the ancient Egyptian word *ankh*, written with the T-shaped cross and loop (Fig. 2, sign 1). Of the remaining signs, 2 was also the initial sign in the hieroglyphic group known from Greek to mean "called" or "nicknamed," in Coptic a word beginning with *dj*. Since sign 3 was known to have the phonetic value *t*, the word meaning "ever" was surmised to have the sound value *djet* (sign 4 is an unpronounced determinative). Application of the known values *p* and *t* to signs 5 and 6 suggested that sign 7 must be a form of *h*, thus producing the name of the god Ptah. Hence, sign 8 in both writings must mean "beloved," in Coptic, *mere*. The sound value *mer* allotted to both these forms is indeed correct. The signs at the end of the Rosetta Stone example, with phonetic value *y*, represent a participial ending.

Decipherment of the ancient Egyptian scripts based on Champollion's principles has stood the test of time—some two centuries—and its essential correctness has been repeatedly confirmed by new evidence.

[*See also* Champollion, Jean-François; *and* Rosetta Stone.]

**BIBLIOGRAPHY**

Champollion, J.-F. *Précis du système hiéroglyphique des anciens Égyptiens.* 2d ed. Paris, 1828.

Davies, W. V. *Reading the Past: Egyptian Hieroglyphs.* London, 1987. Contains a good condensed account of decipherment.

Pope, Maurice. *The Story of Decipherment from Egyptian Hieroglyphic to Linear B.* London, 1975. One of the fullest accounts of the history of decipherment, with good references to primary sources.

Ray, John. "The Name of the First." *Journal of Ancient Chronology Forum* 4 (1990–1991), 49–53.

C. A. R. ANDREWS

**DEFORMITY.** Egyptian reliefs, wall paintings, and ostraca depict kings and tomb owners using the conventional image of a well-formed, healthy human body with a young face. In scenes with servants, however, a body afflicted by a deformity may occasionally be shown. An exception to the rule is the naturalistic style of the Amarna period, which presented the king, Akhenaten, with deformed features. John F. Nunn (1996) expressed the view that abnormal forms might have been artistic conventions, too; obesity could have indicated high social status, and all dwarfs were shown with short limbs.

If the Egyptian sense of individualization is taken into account, as was inherent in their afterlife beliefs, abnormal forms may be considered an accentuation of individual identity, especially in commoners. Most of the deformities depicted really existed, then as now, and have been found in mummies and skeletons. They could not have escaped the attention of ancient Egyptian artists. Many examples are known in reliefs and paintings of specific individuals who were characterized by their features, attributes, activities, names, and titles. For deformities, only iconographic and palaeopathological sources have been used. Egyptian medical texts do not deal with them, perhaps because there were no means to treat them.

For clarity, recorded deformities were divide into those which affected (1) the whole body, (2) the head, (3) the face, (4) the spine and thorax, (5) the belly, and (6) the extremities.

**The Body.** The form of the body was affected in systemic disorders, such as aberrant growth caused by chondrodystrophy, a genetically transmitted disorder; there, enchondral ossification afflicts the bones of the face, pelvis, and extremities, which become short, broad, and deformed. Bones of the cranial vault and trunk remain normal but the stature of such adult males is only about 125 to 130 centimeters (47 to 51 inches), adult females only 115 to 120 centimeters (45 to 47 inches).

Depictions of chondrodystrophic dwarfism are abundant in Egypt, especially from the Old Kingdom. V. Dasen (1993) has collected as many as 207 instances; and Kenneth R. Weeks (1970) described nine skeletal finds. Two more were discovered in the fourth-to-sixth dynasty cemeteries at Giza by Zahi Hawass. One was Perenakh, in whose tomb were found not only his skeletal remains but also his funerary statue, allowing assessment as to how accurately his deformity was reproduced. The second was a female who died in childbirth, delivering a normal (nonchondrodystrophic) baby whose head could not pass throught her small and deformed birth canal.

Chondrodystrophy did not disqualify people from moving into higher levels of society or even to attain significant offices, as the nobleman Seneb attests. Their short hands were usually dexterous and their well-developed brains indicated intelligence. Thus, they might be employed as jewelers, servants, attendants, or wardrobe officials. In some depictions, they care for the pets of their masters or perform music and dance. Some gods, such as Bes, the protector of homes and childbirth, and the late form of the god of craftsmen and artists, Ptah (Pataikos), were depicted as chondrodystrophic dwarfs, especially in the form of protective amulets. No other types of dwarfism are yet known from ancient Egypt—not ethnic (Central African) or pathological (pituitary, thyroid, etc.); nor are instances of oversize growth (gigantism).

The conventional ideal image of King Akhenaten was replaced in his third regnal year by acromegalic features (long protruding chin, long fingers) and feminine proportions and traits. This abrupt change has sometimes been explained as a hypophysal disorder (acromegaly, or Fröhlich's syndrome, also called dystrophia adiposogenitalis), caused usually by the pressure of a pituitary tumor. J. Worth Estes (1989, p. 50) pointed to the occurrence of gynecomastia in the putative father and two half-brothers of Akhenaten; he conjectured that they might have shared genes for it, but the relationship is by no means certain. The endocrinologist Charles Edmonds has suggested (Nunn 1996) Klinefelter's syndrome for Akhenaten, a chromosomal abnormality with a doubling of the female X strand alongside the male Y chromosome (XXY, instead of the normal XY). Marfqu's syndrome has also been suggested. The alternative view is that it was an artistic convention, exaggerating certain features of the actually normal body of the king. As Joyce Filer (1995, p. 36) suggested, it could also have been an expression of Akhenaten's religious doctrine; because his sole god Aten was considered father and mother of all beings, the king might therefore have been depicted as male and female simultaneously.

None of the hypotheses may be checked by examining the king's mummy, because the only extant male royal mummy of the period, found in Theban tomb number 55, is too young (20–25 years) to be in harmony with the seventeen-year duration of his reign.

Obesity might be considered a physiological feature that older wealthy people might have added to depictions to indicate an elite social position. In the relief showing the Queen of Punt, however, in the temple of Hatshepsut at Thebes, her obesity is so exaggerated that the fat tissue forms thick folds and lobes that hang like grapes on her arms, belly, hips (steatopygia), and legs. The belly weight caused a hyperlordosis of her spine. Such deformities had a pathological cause: either lipodystrophy, or neurolipomatosis (Dercum's disease), a painful disorder in which fat accumulates as multiple lipomas or neurolipomas. Scenes with the contrasting condition, emaciation in people afflicted with hunger, are known from the reliefs

DEFORMITY. *Eighteenth dynasty calcite (Egyptian alabaster) vessel in the shape of a dwarf carrying a jar.* The dwarf was probably a servant in a noble household or a royal residence. (The Metropolitan Museum of Art, gift of J. Pierpont Morgan, 1917. [17.190.1963])

nial growth occasionally seen in Egyptian skulls? Or, again, was it some symbolism important to Akhenaten and the Amarna period?

An enlarged skull with signs of increased intracranial pressure was published by Douglas E. Derry (*Journal of Anatomy and Physiology* 47 [1912/13], pp. 436–458) in a thirty-year-old male from the cemetery of Roman date at Shurafa near Helwan. It probably caused his left hemiplegia, since his left upper and lower limb bones were thinner than the right ones. He could have survived only by being cared for. Such finds are rare, because children so afflicted usually die at a young age, and the thin bones of their cranial vaults do not survive.

**The Face.** Deformities of the facial skeleton are known only from rare finds and not from depictions. Cleft palate (usually combined with hare lip in living humans) was present in an adult female from Nubia (now in the Natural History Museum, London) and in two other adult female skulls of the twenty-fifth dynasty and Roman period. In another adult woman from a cemetery south of Asyut, the premaxillary portion of the upper jaw is missing. In the Christian period series from Sayala in Nubia, a skull was found with a swollen middle region of the upper jaw, the result of a developmental defect, a cyst of the nasopalatinal ductus. Finds of larger inborn anomalies cannot be expected, because they led quickly to the death of the afflicted infants.

Deformities of the chondrodystrophic face (broad saddle of the nose deeply inserted under the protruding glabella, small cheeks and jaws) and those called acromegalic features (broad, long and high lower jaw) are known, but the typical features of the leprous or syphilitic face have not, however, been found in the remains of ancient Egyptians or in their depictions.

**The Spine and Thorax.** Curved spine is known from pictures, mummies, and skeletons. It can be an exaggerated, kyphotic, fluently arched bend of the spine's thoracic vertebrae, sometimes combined with a scoliotic deviation and a deformity of the thorax. The causes for it include the following: Scheuerman's disease; lowering of the intervertebral discs in old age; severe osteoporosis, bad body posture, and intensive vertebral osteophytosis; ankylosing spondylitis; rachitis, or other less common spinal diseases.

An angular humpback is the result of the compressive fracture of a vertebra. Single or more vertebrae, usually not adjoining, are in an osteoporotic spine or in a spine with cancers (metastases of carcinoma). If a few adjoining vertebrae (usually two to four) are involved, spinal tuberculosis (Pott's disease) should be taken into account; the typical place for it is the lower thoracic spine or the thoracolumbar transition. Some ten statuettes and reliefs depict this condition, and a few are from the Predy-

on the walls of the Unas causeway at Saqqara and recently found on blocks that fell off the causeway of Sahure at Abusir. They show emaciated bodies with protruding ribs and may have been portrayals of desert nomads. Similarly emaciated bodies can be found in old individuals leaning on a walking stick and in the ideogram or determinative for seniority.

**The Head.** The Egyptians did not belong to those cultures that caused artificial deformation of the heads of their children during the nursing period. Yet statues and drawings of Akhenaten's daughters exist in which their heads are drawn up and backwards into protruding round occiputs. It has been considered a foreign custom, perhaps introduced to Egypt by Akhenaten's queen, Nefertiti. Her supposed Mitannian origin has however, been rejected in favor of Egyptian ancestry. Was it then an artistic exaggeration of the less common, but normal type of cra-

nastic period. The same deformity has been found in seven mummies, including that of the priest Nesparehan of the twenty-first dynasty, the skeletized ones of Huyankh found at Abusir from the Middle Kingdom, and that of the son of Sety I, Pa-Ramessu, from Abu Ghurob.

More than thirty cases have been detected of chronic tubercular infection in skeletons, in which the course of the disease can be followed. It results in abscess cavities in vertebral bodies, which later fuse into one large one. Following evacuation of the tubercular pus down along the psoas muscle, a pathological fracture imparts a wedge shape to the affected vertebral body and an angular humping of the spine. The tuberculosis process destroys also the intervertebral discs between the affected bodies.

A coincidence of two skeletons with Pott's disease, found in two nearby graves at the Predynastic site of Adaima near Esna, was accompanied in both cases by pottery representations of the same deformity, a rare case of congruence of the skeletal and iconographic evidence (E. Crubézy and T. Janin, *Papers on Paleopathology Presented at the 20th Annual Meeting* in Toronto, 1993). The diagnosis of tuberculosis was provable in the mummy of a five-year-old child (1000–600 BCE) from the tomb of Nebwenef by Michael R. Zimmerman (*Bulletin of the New York Academy of Medicine* 55 [1979], 604–608). Tubercular infection of the lungs was shown histologically, and Mycobacterium tuberculosis was demonstrated in a destroyed lumbar vertebra, along with hemorrhage in the trachea.

This oft-mentioned occurrence of tubercular deformation of the spine, as well as about five cases in which tuberculosis was suspected in other anatomical locations, signifies the extent of that disease in ancient Egypt and Nubia. Future research, based on DNA determinations in suspect finds, could reveal the prevalence of tuberculosis with respect to the social status of those infected, as well as other quantifiable factors.

**The Belly.** In a few tombs, scenes (with numbers in the sixth dynasty tomb of Mehu at Saqqara) show servants and workmen with a protruding formation in the umbilical region, suggesting umbilical hernia. Knowledge of that condition is reflected in Papyrus Ebers (Case 864), which refers to swelling "above the umbilicus" apparent when the patient coughs. Yet inguinal hernia has not yet been discerned. Cases of scrotal hernia might have manifest themselves by swelling of the scrotum, known, for example, in the sixth dynasty tomb of Ankhmahor at Saqqara.

This last diagnosis is, however, not unequivocal, since similarly enlarged scrotums could contain hydrocele, an effusion of tissue fluid into the tunica vaginalis, which surrounds the testicles. Both possibilities were taken into account by Grafton Elliot Smith in his *Royal Mummies* (Cairo, 1912, p. 91), after finding an enlarged but empty scrotum in the mummy of Ramesses V.

A swollen scrotum, with an enlarged penis and swollen abdomen, shown in the reliefs from the same tomb were attributed by P. Ghalioungui (1963, pp. 89–90) to the parasitic disease schistosomiasis. It might instead be an expression of filariasis, as suggested by Edmund Tapp and K. Wildsmith in *The Mummy's Tale* (edited by A. R. David and E. Tapp, London, 1992), who found tissue, perhaps from the scrotum of the mummy of Natsef-Amun at the Leeds Museum, permeated by *Filaria bancrofti* worms. In no picture or mummy, however, has the typically swollen legs that often accompany this disease, yet been found.

**The Extremities.** Club foot (talipes equinovarus) that touches the ground not by the sole but by toes, combined with a shorter and thinner leg, is a characteristic feature of two different conditions. It can be inborn (often combined with the anomalous inward rotation, shape, and size of the foot) or it can be the result of poliomyelitis experienced in childhood. This is the case of the mummy of King Siptah, whose left foot was considered at first to be a club foot but later a result of poliomyelitis or an inborn defect of the spine. Similarly, the stela of the door-keeper Ruma of the nineteenth dynasty (now in the Copenhagen Museum) depicts the same condition, which was more probably the result of poliomyelitis than a club foot. Through the depiction of very long, thin fingers, the condition called arachnodactyly has been observed in a statue from the Old Kingdom (see Westendorf 1992, p. 251).

## BIBLIOGRAPHY

David, A. R., and E. Tapp, eds. *The Mummy's Tale.* London, 1992.

Dasen, V. *Dwarfs in Ancient Egypt and Greece.* Oxford, 1993. An up-to-date listing of iconographic evidence for dwarfs.

Estes, J. Worth. *The Medical Skills of Ancient Egypt.* Canton, Mass., 1989. Deals with healers, diseases, surgery, and medicines of ancient Egypt and is written by a modern medical specialist.

Filer, Joyce. *Disease.* London, 1995. Descriptions of common diseases of the ancient Egyptians; discusses treats deformities in detail.

Ghalioungui, P. *Magic and Medical Science in Ancient Egypt.* London, 1963. A survey of the Ancient Egyptian medical profession; deals with diseases described in the medical papyri and some known from iconography.

Ghalioungui, P., and Z. el Dawakhly. *Health and Healing in Ancient Egypt.* Cairo, 1965. Well-illustrated book based mostly on pictorial evidence, with a chapter on diseases and deformities.

Manchester, K. *The Archaeology of Disease.* Bradford, 1983. A survey of paleopathology, dealing with the deformations of congenital and infectious diseases.

Nunn, John F. *Ancient Egyptian Medicine.* London, 1996. Survey of the different aspects of Egyptian medicine, written by a medical doctor who is also an Egyptologist.

Weeks, Kenneth R. "The Anatomical Knowledge of the Ancient Egyptians and Representation of the Human Figure in Egyptian Art." Ph.D. diss., Yale University, 1970. Analysis based on linguistic evidence, medical texts, iconographic sources, and skeletal finds.

Westendorf, Wolfhart. *Erwachen der Heilkunst: die Medizin im Alten Ägypten.* Zurich, 1992. A general survey of Egyptian medicine based primarily on textual sources.

EUGEN STROUHAL

**DEIFICATION.** *See* Divinity.

**DEIR DURUNKA.** *See* Asyut.

**DEIR EL-BAHRI,** a valley on the western bank of the Nile River, near Thebes, an archaeological site of tombs and temples. The first terraced temple to be excavated was by Auguste Mariette, Édouard Naville, and Herbert Winlock; it was Middle Kingdom and reconstructed by Emile Baraize. Since 1961, the reconstruction has gone on through the Polish Center of Mediterranean Archaeology in Cairo, on behalf of the Egyptian authorities. In 1962, while clearing a heap of debris to the south of the New Kingdom Hatshepsut temple, the Polish team discovered the remnants of a second terraced temple, one built by Thutmose III. The site was cleared by 1967, uncovering thousands of fragmentary reliefs and sculptures. Destroyed at the end of the New Kingdom, that temple was then used as a quarry.

The first monument built at the site was a Middle Kingdom terraced temple, now in ruins, of Nebhepetre Montuhotep I of the eleventh dynasty; it consisted of a central, altarlike element that rose above the ambulatory; all was surrounded by a portico. Under the main structure, a cenotaph for the king was found, containing an empty sarcophagus and a now-famous statue of Montuhotep I swathed in linen. The entrance to the corridor leading to the sarcophagus was located in the temple's courtyard. Behind the main structure, a court was located, which lay before a columned hall and sanctuary. From that court, a long, sloping passage led to the rock-cut tomb of the king, a granite chamber with an empty calcite (Egyptian alabaster) shrine for a sarcophagus.

Six tombs with shrines for royal ladies were constructed on the western side of the ambulatory, and their finely carved sarcophagi were found there. Another tomb was discovered in the southwestern corner of the colonnaded hall, with an empty calcite sarcophagus that belonged to Queen Tem. The courtiers of the king set their own tombs on either side of a large causeway that led to the temple. The most important of those tombs belonged to the viziers Dagi and Khety. Below Khety's, a tomb was found that contained the bodies of sixty slain soldiers of Montuhotep I.

During the New Kingdom, the procession of the Valley festival gained importance, and Amenhotpe I built a brick

DEIR EL-BAHRI. *The mortuary temples of Nebhepetre Montuhotep I* (foreground) *and Hatshepsut* (background). (Courtesy Dorothea Arnold)

shrine to the north of the terraced temple, probably as a bark-chapel. That building was dismantled when the temple of Hatshepsut was being constructed, since it occupied the entire northern half of the site; her temple followed the lines of the older edifice, but it was larger and more complex. The terraced building, with its three levels of porticoes, was partly hewn in the cliff, and it was provided with long ramps that led from level to level. In the courtyard in front of the temple, trees were planted and papyrus reeds grew in small pools. A long processional alley leading to the temple was lined with sphinxes, while other sphinxes and statues of the queen decorated the temple. The walls were covered with polychrome reliefs, the most famous depicting the divine birth of the queen, the expedition to Punt, and the transportation of two obelisks from Aswan to Karnak. The temple of Hatshepsut was still used in the Ptolemaic period, and another sanctuary, built behind the older one, was hewn for the healing gods Imouthes, Amenothes, and Opet. Still later, a Coptic monastery of Saint Phoebamon was founded in the upper part of the temple at the end of the sixth century, surviving about one hundred years.

### BIBLIOGRAPHY

Arnold, Dieter. *Der Temple des Königs Mentuhotep von Deir el-Bahari*, vol. 1. Archäologische Veröffentlichungen, Deutsches Archäologisches Institut, Abteilung Kairo, 8. Mainz, 1974.

Arnold, Dieter. *The Temple of Mentuhotep at Deir el-Bahari*. Publications of The Metropolitan Museum of Art, Egyptian Expedition, 21. New York, 1979.

Godlewski, Wlodzimierz. *Le monastère de St. Phoibammon*. Deir el-Bahari, 5. Warsaw, 1986.

Laskowska-Kusztal, Ewa. *Le santuaire ptolémaique de Deir el-Bahari*. Deir el-Bahari, 3. Warsaw, 1984.

Lipinska, Jadwiga. *The Temple of Tuthmosis III: Architecture*. Deir el-Bahari, 2. Warsaw, 1977.

Lipinska, Jadwiga. *The Temple of Tuthmosis III: Statuary and Votive Monuments*. Deir el-Bahari, 4. Warsaw, 1984.

Naville, Édouard. *The Temple of Deir el-Bahari*. Vols. 1–6. London, 1895–1908.

Naville, Édouard. *The XIth Dynasty Temple at Deir el-Bahari*. 3 vols. London, 1907–1913.

Winlock, Herbert. *Excavations at Deir el-Bahri, 1911–1933*. New York, 1942.

JADWIGA LIPINSKA

**DEIR EL-MEDINA** (Ar., "monastery of the town"), the modern name of an archaeological site located in a desert valley, on the western bank of the Nile River, opposite Luxor (25°44′N, 32°36′E). The site is chiefly known for the remains of a settlement that was founded in the early eighteenth dynasty (second half of the sixteenth century BCE), to house the workmen who constructed and decorated the royal tombs in the Valley of the Kings and in the Valley of the Queens. The settlement was inhabited by the necropolis workmen and their families until the end of the twentieth dynasty (shortly after 1100 BCE). During the Ramessid era, the number of workmen was normally between forty and seventy. The lower parts of the stone walls of the houses in the village were well preserved, and the cemeteries to the west and northwest of the settlement include some of the finest decorated private tombs of Thebes. From that same period are the remains of the small temples (dedicated to the goddess Hathor, the deified King Amenhotep I, and Queen Ahmose-Nefertari) and the minor cult chapels to the north of the ancient village, as well as a group of huts that were on the mountain pass, between Deir el-Medina and the Valley of the Kings.

Excavations of Deir el-Medina have been carried out since the beginning of the twentieth century by Ernesto Schiaparelli (Egyptian Museum, Turin), Georg Möller (Berlin Museum), and Émile Baraize (Egyptian Antiquities Organization); they were followed by the extensive site-clearing expeditions (of the settlement, cemeteries, and chapels) of Bernard Bruyère (French Institute, Cairo) from 1922 to 1940 and from 1945 to 1951. A wealth of objects and inscriptions was found among the remains of the village and its surroundings (including the Valley of the Kings). The most important find comprises several thousand Hieratic texts—written on pottery, on limestone fragments (ostraca) and on papyrus; these include letters, lists, accounts, reports on work and deliveries, and legal records, as well as a large number of literary and magical texts. Together, they constitute the most important source of information about the social, economic and legal history of the New Kingdom. They provide information on all aspects of the daily life of the inhabitants and on the organization of the necropolis workforce. Many publications have been devoted to the houses, tombs, and chapels; to the objects found in them (statues, stelae, offering tables, burial equipment, and objects of daily use); and to the texts (hieroglyphic inscriptions, Hieratic ostraca and papyri, and graffiti). The publication and study of the vast corpus of nonliterary texts relating to the necropolis workmen was the lifework of Jaroslav Černý. Because of the vast amount of material, however, Černý was unable to complete his work before his death in 1970 and many texts remain unpublished to this day.

In the Late period, Deir el-Medina was used as a cemetery. Ptolemy IV and later kings built a temple, dedicated to the goddess Hathor, to the north of the village, on the site formerly occupied by the Ramessid temples and chapels. Among the remains of one of the houses next to the temple, Schiaparelli found two jars, containing fifty-three Greek and Demotic papyri from the second century BCE that were related to a family of priests officiating in the Hathor temple. Other archaeological remains in the vicinity are a Middle Kingdom tomb, the tombs of the

Saite princesses Ankhnesneferibre and Nitokris, and the Coptic monastery (built within the Ptolemaic temple precinct) that gave the site its present name.

[*See also* Theban Necropolis.]

### BIBLIOGRAPHY

Bierbrier, Morris. *The Tomb-builders of the Pharaohs.* London, 1982. General introduction to the life and work of the people living in Deir el-Medina during the Ramessid period, with a chapter on the later history and rediscovery of the site.

Černý, Jaroslav. *A Community of Workmen at Thebes in the Ramesside Period.* Bibliothèque d'Étude, 50. Cairo, 1973. Standard work on the royal necropolis as an institution and its personnel.

Haring, Ben. "A Systematic Bibliography on Deir el-Medîna." In *Village Voices: Proceedings of the Symposium "Texts from Deir el-Medîna and their Interpretation": Leiden, May 31–June 1, 1991,* edited by R. J. Demarée and A. Egberts, pp. 111–140. CNWS Publications, 13. Leiden, 1992. An updated bibliography and a database of nonliterary texts from Deir el-Medina are being prepared by the Deir el-Medina Database project (Leiden University). Available in a preliminary form on the World Wide Web (http://www.leidenuniv.nl/nino/dmd/dmd.html).

Porter, Bertha, and Rosalind L. B. Moss. *Topographical Bibliography of Ancient Egyptian Hieroglyphic Texts, Reliefs, and Paintings,* vol. 1, *The Theban Necropolis, part II: Royal Tombs and Smaller Cemeteries.* 2d ed. Oxford, 1964. Brief description and bibliography of the archaeological remains at Deir el-Medina from all periods, in chapter 9, pp. 685–749.

Montserrat, D., and L. Meskell. "Mortuary Archaeology and Religious Landscape at Graeco-Roman Deir el-Medina." *Journal of Egyptian Archaeology* 83 (1997), 179–197.

Valbelle, Dominique. *"Les ouvriers de la Tombe": Deir el-Médineh à l'époque ramesside.* Bibliothèque d'Étude, 96. Cairo, 1985. Standard work dealing with various aspects of the workmen's settlement and its documentation.

Zonhoven, L. J. "A Systematic Bibliography on Deir el-Medina." In *Gleanings from Deir el-Medîna,* edited by R. J. Demarée and Jac. J. Janssen, pp. 245–298. Egyptologische Uitgaven, 1. Leiden, 1982.

BEN HARING

**DEITIES.** Mankind began settling in the Nile Valley long before the dawn of our era and well before the beginning of the pharaonic society that the modern public associates with ancient Egypt. The seeds of the civilization that was to develop and many of the concepts that appeared in the time of the pharaohs, therefore, clearly came into being well into the distant past. Some of the ideas were generated before the establishment of any settlements along the banks of the river Nile. Archaeological evidence from the earliest periods suggests that the environment in which mankind lived played a very influential role in the religious ideology that would be recorded much later. At first, these beliefs were private and focused only on the personal level, but as people became more settled in particular areas and oriented more toward structured groups, they adapted doctrines to reflect the requirements of a larger society. The doctrines of an earlier era did not necessarily disappear; in fact, some clearly survived the initial transition to the society and can be seen in the development of local cults and such practices as ancestor worship. Eventually these succumbed to change and adaptation when the even more settled organization of the state emerged. Once the country became united under a single ruler, it eventually favored the establishment of a national religion to which the local beliefs would have to become secondary. A king could, however, bring to national prominence a deity known primarily in the area from which the pharaoh came, but even when that did not happen, the local cults could persist. For example, the god Ptah had national significance during the pharaonic period and was especially prominent in the creation texts, but his original connection with Memphis never ceased to be recognized, and his status as a god in that region was maintained.

**The Environment and Early Beliefs.** Some traditions can be traced back to the early stages of the development of the state such as the falcon god Horus, whose image appears along with the names of the earliest kings on early dynastic monuments, and then it becomes a standard element in the royal titulary. He also maintains an important role in several creation myths. Other animals, such as cattle, also figure prominently in pharaonic religion, and they appear to have an even longer history. Artisans created sculptures, reliefs, and paintings of cow-goddesses such as Hathor, who was known on a national level throughout dynastic times and was an important deity to whom the Egyptians built and dedicated temples. Other goddesses whom they associated with cattle, such as Bat and Mehetweret, were perhaps less well known, and their popularity did not remain constant. Images of these goddesses could take the form of a complete bovine or composite human/bovine. The latter type, occasionally accompanied by stars, appears during the Early Dynastic period. The head of a human female with bovine ears and horns in frontal view appears in raised relief, two times at the top of each side of the Narmer Palette. The repetition of the image four times, as well as its placement at the pinnacle of the composition, imply that this deity was particularly influential. Reinforcement for this conclusion might be seen in the inclusion of the image on a work whose main scenes appear to commemorate perhaps Egypt's earliest king uniting the legendary two lands of Upper and Lower Egypt.

The prominence of the human/bovine divine emblem at the beginning stages of recorded Egyptian history suggests that it may have been a focus of reverence and veneration even earlier. Archaeological evidence indicates that cattle were apparently quite important as a source of milk, blood, and perhaps also meat in pre-pharaonic cultures that developed in the southern part of Egypt, near modern Sudan. These benefits, as well as certain characteristics of cattle, may have led early mankind to hold these animals in high esteem. The recent excavations by the American and Polish expeditions in the Sahara Desert, about 100 kilometers (60 miles) west of Abu Simbel, have unearthed sacrificial burials of cattle bones as early as five thousand years before any pharaoh walked the earth. Such findings, as well as their recent discovery of the burial of a completely intact cow, suggest that practices originating in earlier African cultures may well represent the root of the later ideology that appears in the historic periods of the riverine society out of which pharaonic culture emerges.

While the flora and fauna in the environment helped shape the form that their deities took, the varying elements of the physical world were the significant factors affecting the underlying concepts of the gods and goddesses. The world around early mankind provided memorable experiences that shaped the beliefs of these individuals. Their universe could sometimes be most hostile, yet at other times quite gentle and beneficent, and they had to find ways of coping with and surviving in it. Certain elements of nature such as the sky brought forth the crop-supporting rain and the warm, life-sustaining rays of the sun, but from it also emanated chaotic windstorms, damaging torrential downpours, and lethal, parching heat. Likewise, later, when the Egyptians settled along the Nile; the river became to them a source of sustenance in the form of its life-giving water and the fertile soil it left after its yearly flooding. It too, however, could become the bearer of disaster in the form of an inundation that was either too high, resulting in devastating floods, or too low, leading to droughts.

Early individuals certainly observed and experienced the effects of these phenomena, but their struggles for survival took precedence over their contemplation of the causes and results of such forces of nature. As time progressed these peoples accumulated both knowledge and experience, and they soon acquired the necessary skills to thrive in their environment. Only then did they have the opportunity to contemplate their own role within their physical world and how they related to it. In other words, they no longer simply reacted to the elements of their environment, but stepped back to observe them and recognize the dynamics occurring before them. At these early stages of cultural development, however, the cognitive processes functioned primarily on a personal level. It is possible to suggest a simple model of how these events might have happened. An early human might one day notice that the light of the new day also brought warmth as well as a renewal of energy. Repetition of these feelings day after day might cause the individual to associate the initial perceptions of security with elements of the physical environment. In a subsequent move, he or she might then attribute the consequences to the disk of the sun as it reappeared at the eastern horizon. Some people might respond similarly to the same stimuli, while others react differently. Whatever their sentiments, they may have communicated them among each other as they came together once society came into being. Through these processes, they developed the basic concepts underlying the inner workings of the universe. That these very elements were critical at this point in history seems to be suggested by the many deities, appearing later in the recorded Egyptian pantheon, that focus on the environment.

Explicating the "behavior" of the universe was in a way a means of controlling it. Attributing some logic to the manner in which all of the physical elements functioned allowed early man to begin to predict what would or could happen rather than to react after it happened. In time, increased observations would result not only in refined knowledge of the world, but also in more elaborate explanations for its existence and interactions among its components. A theoretical universe was envisioned, and its relationship to the real world and mankind's role in both were explained through the use of myth. It is likely that attributing animal imagery, characteristics, and traits to the elements of the physical world was also part of this process. Such associations may well have happened through the ancient Egyptians' keen sense of observation. An often-cited example is the falcon, an animal that the Egyptians associated early on with the sun. It has been suggested that this creature's ability to fly so high that it appears to merge into the disk of the sun may well underlie its relationship to the solar deity Re.

Such a correlation allowed the Egyptians to link a conceptual element, heat and light, with a less abstract one, the solar disk, and then a concrete one, the falcon. By making further attributions with human traits, the mystical, enigmatic, and indefinable became recognizable, approachable, and tangible. This transcendence was facilitated through the allocation of special space for communing with the conceptualized deity. These specialized areas, which would later give rise to temples, were places where some form of the divinity could be approached, venerated, supplicated to, or worshiped. To visualize it in concrete form, the Egyptians used a fetish, a statue, or other type of related symbol or image, and in these locations appropriate ritual could take place. Eventually the structures became quite elaborate and were understood as residences for the god. The Egyptians used particular decorative programs of carvings and paintings and employed architectural elements of specific forms to reflect cosmic symbolism.

**Gods, Goddesses, and the Stories of Creation.** Most of the deities that comprise the pantheon of ancient Egypt

can be thought of as relating to the environment in some
way. The question has often been asked whether the Egyptians viewed each god as a distinct element of the cosmos,
or as integral components held together by a single universal force. Scholars have debated such questions over
the last century and have proposed many arguments to
support their conclusions. It is clear that a hierarchy
among the deities existed and that it reflected societal divisions among mankind. For example, just as there was a
king on earth, there was a king of the gods. For much of

the historical period Re, or his composite form Amun-Re,
had this role. Another divine king was Osiris, whose realm
was limited to the afterlife, but the two were connected in
many ways, some of which are reflected in the funerary
texts written on papyri and recorded on coffins, tombs,
vessels, and amulets. Osiris's son Horus resembles the
crown prince, and the relationship between the two—as
well as the events of their lives—mirror the transfer of
power involved with inherited kingship. Some gods had
bureaucratic positions, such as Thoth, the scribe and mes-

senger of the gods, while others, such as Montu, were related to the military.

To be sure, associations such as these came well after the early beliefs that focused on the forces of the universe confronting early man. Cosmic powers, however, continued as part of Egyptian ideology into the historical period. The Egyptian concept of primeval gods appears to reflect these doctrines. This group would consist either of several gods or a series of divine couples that represent the aspects of the universe prior to creation. The Egyptians associated creator gods with different geographic areas, and separate myths and creation theologies were set around the major religious centers such as Heliopolis, Hermopolis, and Memphis. In Heliopolis, which was linked with the center of the solar cult in the North, Atum functioned as the primary deity, and the Ennead was completed by his eight children: Shu, Tefnut, Geb, Nut, Osiris, Isis, Seth, and Nephthys. Atum is the progenitor, and he singlehandedly creates the elemental components of the universe. He begets air and moisture, as a matched pair, and this couple in turn creates earth and sky, the chthonic and celestial elements, who in turn are responsible for the last two pairs. Further elaboration of this mythology involves the conflict between the two brothers, Horus and Seth, and the battles between Horus, the son of Isis and Osiris, and his uncle Seth. The relationship of this doctrine and ancient Egyptian kingship is clear, and the derivation of it rests, at least in part, on the ostensible need for the legitimization of the royal genealogy.

Hermopolis, the local association of another version of creation, is a site in Middle Egypt. There prevailed the god Thoth, who was associated with wisdom, writing, and the moon. Eight gods grouped into four couples comprise the Hermopolitan mythology, which focuses on the ordering of the chaotic universe at the time of creation. Traditionally, Amun and his female counterpart Amaunet refer to hiddenness, and they are called in early texts the source of the other gods. They are paired with primeval waters, Nun and Naunet. Kuk and Kauket, representing darkness, and Heh and Hauhet, endlessness, make up the last two pairs. These in turn generate other divinities, and already in the Coffin Texts, passages relate that the deities of this cosmogony are associated with that of Heliopolis.

Memphis in the North is one of the earliest religious centers, and it retains its importance throughout most of Egyptian history. Its story of creation, however, derives from an ancient inscription, recorded in the eighth century BCE under the reign of King Shabaqa, that purports to be a copy of a much earlier original. Recent scholarship, however, disputes that attestation in the text and dates the document to the Late period, thereby suggesting that it represents the latest of the theologies of this type. Ptah, a deity associated with Memphis from early times, is the primary focus in this version. He is a god who is capable of creating with his heart and tongue, and this ability refers to the concepts of intellectual activity (thought) and its result (speech). Ptah also creates Atum in this myth, and through this action the Memphite theology is linked to that from Heliopolis. Many of the deities involved in these ideologies were of national renown during historic times, but their associations with a particular area may reflect their role as local deities at an earlier period.

Other gods and goddesses also became prominent figures or featured players in the stories of creation, as well as in the related narratives that became associated with them. For instance, the deity Nefertum, known both in the funerary texts as well in the local cult of Memphis, is symbolized as the lotus blossom, the first form of life that appears from the primeval mound after waters of chaos recede.

In all levels of the divine hierarchy and throughout Egyptian society there existed the unifying concept of balance and harmony. The creation myths describe the earliest periods in the memory of humankind as pure chaos. Out of it derived some form of harmony, and this calmed state made possible the existence of the world as the Egyptians knew it. The gods are responsible for maintaining the order and presenting it to the king who in turn reinforces the system. Humankind must live according to its rules and regulations; no one is exempt. So important was the concept of order and balance in the universe that it was deified as a goddess, Maat.

**Divine Unions.** It is not unusual for a deity to be amalgamated, that is to say, syncretized, with one or more divinities, such as Re-Atum, Khnum-Re, Ptah-Sokar-Osiris, and Amun-Re-Horakhty. In these divine links, one god was combined with another, or became an extension of another, and the elements of each would become unified in the composite without the loss of their original identity. Other less bound associations would include the series of couplets generally made up of a god and a goddess. Often the two divinities are a reflection of the elements of the environment, perceived as dual opposing components, such as light and darkness, air and moisture, and other "dualities" that figure prominently in the creation myths referred to above. Although not as common, same-sex pairs exist, as with the sisters Isis and Nephthys. The Egyptians also formed triads of deities, which groupings consist generally of two elemental gods and goddesses along with their offspring. Often these sets of divinities become associated with specific geographic areas. Ptah and Sekhmet, long linked with Memphis, add a son, Nefertum, in the New Kingdom, but other kinship groups, such as Osiris, Isis, and Horus, are attested as a group much earlier. Three deities also form a trinity, and this phenomenon, derived perhaps because of political considerations, was more common after the eighteenth dynasty. Such associations linked not only primary deities like Amun, Re, and Ptah, but also their cult places, Thebes, Heliopolis, and Memphis.

**Categories of Egyptian Deities.** Several different terms for the classification of Egyptian gods have been used in the sections above, such as creator, local, and national. While some of these designations and others are of modern derivation, it is not unreasonable to assume that the Egyptians themselves would have sought some means of differentiating among the hundreds of deities that comprised their pantheon. In fact, the phrases "local gods" and "district gods" are referred to in both the Pyramid Texts and biographical inscriptions. In addition, the names of several gods derive directly from the city of their provenance, as with the goddess Nekhbet of Nekehb.

Modern publications often refer to the gods of the afterlife, and in fact the ancient Egyptians understood that many of the supreme beings they venerated functioned primarily in that domain. Such a reference could be made iconographically in statuary or relief, in which case the representation would situate the deity within an environment, clearly not that of the contemporaneous world. The Judgment of the Dead scene would be a good illustration of this process. There the god Osiris, whose visible body parts appear either green or black, presides over a court composed of animals as well as composite and fantastical creatures. The genre of text in which the god would appear, or the accompanying descriptive phrases might also help to categorize him or her. Funerary literature like the Pyramid Texts, the Coffin Texts, and the *Book of Going Forth by Day* (*Book of the Dead*) focus on these deities. Phrases such as "who is in the netherworld" might designate a specific god, perhaps Horus, in one text, or it might refer to a group of demons to be avoided in a particular area of the underworld in another inscription. This category of deities was perhaps the most populated of all, and because so much funerary material has survived into modern times, we are aware of the many gods and goddesses who played a role in this environment. The mortuary temples of the pharaoh and the tombs focus on Osiris, the king of the underworld, but Isis, Horus, Re, Anubis, and Thoth figure prominently as well. Those associated with embalming, in addition to Anubis—i.e., Nephthys, Selket, Neith; and the four sons of Horus: Imsety, Hapy, Duamutef, and Kebehsenuef—also belong to this classification. Other spirits of the netherworld included demons, demigods, and personifications of the underworld. In addition, major deities like Ptah and Hathor also took part in the afterlife, but their role was not as significant as that of others. Their presence, however, indicates that the Egyptians imagined their gods as functioning in more than one capacity, and they assigned many roles to them. Re, for example, was instrumental not only as a funerary deity, but as a national one as well; likewise, Hathor appears in the context of the afterlife, was a state deity, had an international role, and also was the focus of local cults.

The Egyptians did not treat each god in the same way throughout the country. With the local, district, or domestic deities the relationship was more personal, and access was more direct and less formal. Other divinities that maintained more prominent positions in the pantheon, however, were worshiped at more of a distance. The formalized rituals were more uniform, since these gods and goddesses were worshiped all over Egypt. Temples were dedicated to these national divinities, and services, rituals, and festivals were held in their honor on a statewide basis. The temples of Luxor and Karnak were built in honor of Amun-Re, the king of the gods, and during certain holidays the image of the god would be brought forth from the shrine for view and worship by the people. Further access occurred when the priests transported the image to other temples along a prescribed route. Hathor, Isis, and Ptah are among other state deities to have been held in such repute.

The type of temple, the texts and decoration therein, as well as the associated documents help to distinguish the roles of the major gods and allow us to identify the many categories into which they were classified. A sense of the popularity of a divinity, the manner in which it was approached, and the type of group to which it belonged can also be seen by looking carefully at figurines, hymns, and prayers. Amulets represented a sign of devotion to and respect for a particular god, but they could also become a means of protection, benefit, and advantage. Deities associated with the more personal aspects of the individual are often rendered in the form of an amulet to be worn or carried. In amulets to be used in the afterlife, funerary deities predominate. Amulets used by the living with their magical properties were frequently used as personal adornments, and their use can be traced back to the earliest periods. Most of the early amulets took the form of animals, and these can be seen as symbols of particular deities. Particularly popular were the frog and hippopotamus, associated with fertility, over which, along with childbirth, the goddesses Heqet and Taweret would later have influence. Another of the minor deities, Bes, also important at birth, was particularly popular in the New Kingdom. Not much later, the repertoire of deities would increase and include many of the major figures, such as Sekhmet, Isis, Sobek, or Khnum, as well as minor ones like Heh, Horpakhered, and Imhotep. These tiny figures were thought to offer the wearer the protection or power of the divinity represented. It is clear from the great variety of deities depicted in amulets, from the many different forms of votive figurines, and the numerous deities addressed in prayers that the Egyptians eventually considered most of their gods and goddesses as capable of performing the role of a personal god.

Certain members of the pantheon had roles beyond the borders of Egypt, for during different periods, the pharaohs had extended the country's influence over foreign areas. Moreover, settlements outside Egypt would require access to native deities. Hathor was worshiped in the Sinai and at Byblos, and she along with Horus, Amun, Re, and others had cults in Nubia. Certain of Egypt's gods were assigned to border areas, like Ash, who is associated with the Western Desert and sometimes Libya. Especially in the New Kingdom and later, foreign deities made appearances on Egyptian monuments and were mentioned in texts. Reshef, Ba'al, Hauron, Astarte, and Anat are some of those from western Asia who figure prominently in the iconography and inscriptions; Dedwen appears to derive from Nubia.

Part of the concept of kingship included the doctrine of the pharaoh's deification after death, but this process was extended occasionally to lesser members of society as well. Perhaps the most famous of nonroyal individuals to receive such status was Imhotep, the high priest of Re during the third dynasty. Reputed to be the architect of the Step Pyramid, this vizier of King Djoser was, according to later sources, a great sage and the author of some of the earliest Wisdom Literature. Although he achieved cult status, as did other writers of similar works, such as Ptahhotep, Hordjedef, and Kagemni, only Imhotep was worshiped as a god, but not until the Late period. A cult for the deified late Old Kingdom official Heqaib was established after his death, and several centuries later people still visited the sanctuary. Amenhotep, son of Hapu, the director of works for Amenhotpe III, was accorded the honor of having a funerary temple dedicated to him in Western Thebes in an area reserved for pharaonic mortuary temples. Apparently a cult to him, especially in regard to medicine, developed later.

A king, however, was thought to achieve divinity routinely after death, and worship was in theory expected to occur through the mortuary cult in the funerary temple forever. Just how long the cult would actually last was determined by the length and quality of a particular ruler's reign, as well as political, sociological, and economic conditions during the king's life and after. Some officials of the Middle Kingdom held titles in the priesthood of kings who died in the Old Kingdom, a situation that indicates that cults could survive several centuries. Some cults, for example that of Amenhotpe I, existed beyond the mortuary temple. He became known as a personal god and often, along with his mother Ahmose-Nefertari, was accepted as a patron deity of Western Thebes and the village

of Deir el-Medina. He could be approached for aid with other deities, and an oracle associated with him helped resolve legal issues.

While earlier evidence exists for the concept of the deification of a pharaoh prior to his death, it is not displayed so obviously until the eighteenth-dynasty reign of Hatshepsut. The reliefs depicting her divine birth occur, however, in her mortuary temple. Later, those of Amenhotpe III were carved on the walls of the state temple built for Amun at Luxor. He promoted the concept further by establishing cults at several locations dedicated to his living divine form. This idea promoted the conception of the king less as a superhuman hero whose divinity after death was assured than as a divine living being. His son and successor, Amenhotpe IV, was iconoclastic in both his conception of the divinity of the king and the manner in which he expressed it. This enigmatic figure changed his name to Akhenaten, abolished the many gods of the ancient pantheon in favor of a single preeminent one, the Aten, and moved the capital to Amarna, an area with no preexisting deity. Many scholars see in these and other moves a major step in the evolution toward monotheism, but others recognize rather a radical sociopolitical experiment to raise the level of kingship to a status more equal with the godhead. Other interpretations exist as well, but whichever is correct, to the Egyptians the concept was not acceptable. The changes were shortlived, and the orthodoxy was quickly reestablished. Eventually, with traditional religious ideas restored, Ramesses II of the nineteenth dynasty adapted the concepts of divine kingship developed in the preceding dynasty. He had many representations of his divine living image created, and in several inscriptions referred to his own deified state. The people, however, probably had at all times both an official and a personal view in regard to these ideas, and they expressed them for example in letters where the monarch is described in very human rather than divine terms.

[See also Bull Gods; Contendings of Horus and Seth; Cults, articles on Divine Cults and Animal Cults; Demons; Feline Deities; Four Sons of Horus; Myths; and articles on individual deities.]

## BIBLIOGRAPHY

Englund, Gertie, ed. *The Religion of the Ancient Egyptians: Cognitive Structures and Popular Expressions.* Uppsala, 1989. A useful group of essays.

Forman, Werner, and Stephen Quirke. *Hieroglyphs and the Afterlife in Ancient Egypt.* Norman, Okla., 1996. A useful source with a short glossary of deities.

Frankfort, Henri. *Before Philosophy.* Baltimore, 1948. One of the earliest attempts to deal with the concepts underlying the religion of the historic periods.

Frankfort, Henri. *Kingship and the Gods.* Chicago, 1948. A standard on the subject, but recent scholarship differs on many points.

Hornung, Erik. *Conceptions of God in Ancient Egypt: The One and the*

*Many.* Translated by John Baines. Ithaca, 1982. An excellent treatment of the subject with updated footnotes and references by the translator.

Morenz, Sigfried. *Egyptian Religion.* Translated by Ann E. Keep. London, 1960. A good standard book on religion.

Quirke, Stephen. *Ancient Egyptian Religion.* London, 1992. A concise and informative treatment.

Silverman, David P. "Divinities and Deities in Ancient Egypt." In *Religion in Ancient Egypt,* edited by Byron Shafer. Ithaca, 1991. A detailed treatment of the subject with many notes and further references. The two other chapters in the book are also useful.

Silverman, David P. "The Nature of Egyptian Kingship." In *Ancient Egyptian Kingship,* edited by David O'Connor and David P. Silverman. Leiden, 1995. Focuses on the relationship between the king and the gods and the concept of divine kingship. The essays of D. Redford and J. Baines in the same volume also deal to some extent with this topic.

DAVID P. SILVERMAN

**DEMONS.** From an ancient Egyptian point of view, any being, whether supernatural, human, or material, which was involved in a ritual at some time, whether occasional or incidental, was a "god." The performance of a ritual did not necessarily require a temple, and thus demons were part of the "god" category. There is no Egyptian term, however, that corresponds even approximately to our word "demon." Demons are usually classified by Egyptologists as "minor divinities," a category that is hard to define. A temple reveals the theological and political importance of a deity but it does not show the real degree of the god's popularity. The importance of a divinity is a matter of subjective interpretation. For example, the hippopotamus goddess Taweret began her career anonymously during the Middle Kingdom among the fantastic animals figured on magic wands. During the New Kingdom, she acquired a name and became a renowned and revered goddess in temples and with priests. The lion-masked dwarf Bes had a similar origin and destiny. He also became an important god, although there is little evidence of his temples and priests. Many demons were not associated with temples or priests but were nonetheless greatly feared and respected.

The fact that demons were subordinates to a superior authority defined them most appropriately. They were not autonomous and performed tasks on command, usually in a specific sphere, while the greater gods were more universal in character. The specificity of demons concerned their actions, their behavior, and their location. Some demons were attached to a person, place, or building, and these demons remained there. When a demon was freed from his specific bonds of subordination, he became a greater god. This "promotion" was not the result of a conscious decision by an authority; rather, it evolved over centuries from a historical process that involved Egyptian society as a whole.

Demons had a protective-aggressive role: they were aggressive and hostile because they had to protect something or someone. Even evil, cosmic enemies had something to protect. In their passive role, demons repelled whatever threatened the object of their protection; in their dynamic role, they were sent to punish those who transgressed the principles that organized the created world, which had been established by the gods themselves. The dual nature of demons made them either dangerous or beneficial to humans. Demons were distinguished from genies through this aggressive-protective aspect. Though assigned to specific tasks and usually subordinated to another deity, genies were not, by their very nature, involved in protective-aggressive activity. This was true, for example, of numerous genies concerned with economic production. Other deities, either subordinate or dangerous, were assistants to the creator god; they personified different aspects of his creative power and his comprehensive, divine authority. As assistants, they were incorporated in the insignia of royal power on crowns and scepters. They were considered "auxiliaries" to creative power and divine or royal authority outside the categories of "demon" or "genie."

Demons in the ancient world were also differentiated by their origins or the type of their subordination. Some demons were emanations of human beings, either dead or alive; they were evoked for an individual by divine decision, either permanently or occasionally. Divine subordinates, though used by gods for their personal purposes, were sometimes invoked by humans for their own protection. Cosmic enemies represented a specific case of "subordination" which involved the survival of the created world.

From the beginning of life, the ancient Egyptian was surrounded or assisted by powers which affected his destiny in many ways. Demons of fate were present at his side all his life and accompanied him after death, as witnesses before the Tribunal of Osiris. Such is the case of Shai ("Destiny") and his female companion Renenet ("Nurse"), or the spirit of the birth-stool, Meskhenet. Shai and Renenet represented a given span of life that could be lengthened or shortened by good or bad deeds. Meskhenet was the personal share or stock of capabilities given to each person at his birth, a kind of life-program to be respected. The righteous man came before Osiris without having modified his personal Meskhenet. These demons were not passive attendants who simply executed a god's will or checked human actions. They were generally positive protectors who acted like "guardian angels" to repel what threatened their charges. Demons of fate also dispensed advice. Unfortunately, protector demons were not always able to shield the ancient Egyptian from bad demons. A child who died was usually not considered the

DEMONS. *Fragment of the* Book of That Which Is in the Underworld (Amduat) *papyrus with representations of the demons of the underworld.* The papyrus belonged to the twenty-first dynasty princess Entiuny, and was found on her mummy, folded eight times and placed across her knees. From the tomb of Queen Meritamun at Deir el-Bahri. (The Metropolitan Museum of Art, Museum Excavations, 1928–1929 and Rogers Fund, 1930 [30.3.32])

victim of a decision carried out by Shai and Renenet. A demon called Shepeset ("Noble Lady") seems to have had a more personal relationship with those she was supposed to assist. Each month of the year had its Shepeset, who was a kind of fairy godmother for all born in the month under her protection. The Seven Hathors, also known as the "old ladies," played a role akin to that of European witches. They were supposed to state, at the moment of birth, all the events (usually bad ones) that one would have to face during life. Once their words had been pronounced, it was impossible to avoid the bad fortune they promised. Magic spells were recited to close the mouths of these Hathors and prevent them from foretelling the

future. Other spells, however, ask for their help in desperate situations.

Protective personal demons probably belong to ancient traditions. Fantastic animals represented on magic wands of the Middle Kingdom were the ancestors of some of the above-mentioned creatures. The hippopotamus holding a knife with its feet later became the major goddess Taweret. She was the patroness of childbirth and motherhood, chasing away demons dangerous to the vulnerable mother and her child. Many of these features were shared by Bes. Both Taweret and Bes—or, at least, hippopotami and Bes-like demons—recur later on in birth scenes. They protected not only human children but also the young

Horus and his mother Isis when they were hidden in the Nile Delta marshes. There the young Horus was subject to sickness, stung by scorpions, and hunted by demons sent by Seth, the murderer of his father; that is why his image is represented on stelae from the end of the New Kingdom, the so-called Horus *cippi*, which are engraved with magic spells against fever, crocodiles, and venomous animals.

People were also surrounded by petty domestic demons that resided practically everywhere: in water, doors, bolts, pots, and so on. Some of these had very little power and could be used, after divine approval, by humans themselves for their own purposes. Incubi that "sat" inside a person were also known. Some demons teased humans, apparently just for fun. Peasants usually attributed to them all kinds of mishaps—bad weather, sick cattle, or domestic conflicts.

Once dead, a human could trouble those still alive, so surviving relatives occasionally wrote letters to complain to the dead and try to calm them. A deceased human might even become a dangerous demonic power, not only as an evil soul escaped from the tomb but also as a physical entity. It could attack sinners or those disturbing the tomb, but also any other person without apparent reason. As a ghost, it could haunt homes, perhaps to obtain the reconstruction of the ruined tomb. Little tablets inscribed with the names of supposedly demonic dead persons were buried to prevent them from coming back from the grave. A tale tells how a dead man, wishing to have news about his survivors, asked Osiris to sculpt for him an earth-man, a kind of semi-live "golem." This humanlike being was sent out to the world of the living to report on the situation and punish those behaving badly to the dead one's family.

Gangs of demons were responsible for many troubles and misfortunes. Most of the main deities had such troops at their service. They could be used against both men and other gods, though the latter had demon bodyguards. These demon troops bear names like *khatyu* ("fighters"), *habyu* ("emissaries"), *wepwetyu* ("messengers"), or *shemayu* ("wanderers"), which reveal a good deal about their basic nature. They are very anciently known: the *khatyu* were mentioned in the Pyramid Texts from the Old Kingdom, the first known Egyptian corpus of religious texts. There is no important religious or magical text that does not mention them in some way, to invoke them or to avert them. All these troops are known under the more generic term *sheseru* ("arrows"). Because the groups usually have seven members, or a multiple of seven, they were also called the "seven arrows." Their superiors were often dangerous goddesses like Sekhmet, Bastet, and Nekhbet, or the sphinx god Totoes. *Sheseru* is also the name of the seven Decan stars that are closest

to the sun. Emissary demons, arrows, and Decans were identified. All these demons could punish sinners, but they could act simply out of malice to strike any person they found in their path. They occasioned inexplicable illness. Magic spells written on a papyrus strip, simply folded or wrapped inside a little container and worn on a necklace, were considered effectual in keeping them at a distance. In medical documents, spells may be added to recipes to improve the treatment or to protect the patient from demonic influence.

The relationship of demons with astronomic cycles made them most active during specific periods: for instance, when the Decan they belonged to culminated, or at a time corresponding to a baleful mythological event. The last five days of the year—those which were "over the year" because they did not fit in the ideal year of 360 (30 × 12) days—were considered especially dangerous because their departure from the ideal pattern introduced chaotic elements in the organized world. During that period, demons, unbound and uncontrolled, spread over the earth. In all the temples of Egypt, priests recited litanies to dangerous goddesses and their demonic servants, to appease them and calm their wrath.

Demons that protected a person or a place were similar to the emissaries, but their behavior was more static and defensive. The arrow demons were related to the Decans of the southern sky, where the new year star (Sirius) rose and whence came the Nile flood. In contrast, the troop of demons protecting Osiris was connected with the northern sky, the realm of the dead. The underworld was full of evil demons, especially in the spaces between the living world and the Hall of Osiris, which gave access to the green fields of paradise. They guarded the gates, channels, crossings, and so on, which the dead had to pass to reach the hall. Unable to avoid them, the deceased had to persuade them to let him pass. He usually had to answer questions posed by the demons, who only let pass those who could prove that during life they had learned enough about the underworld to be allowed to travel in it. Living persons might meet these demons, too, at least in pictures—but even these images were dangerous. In pharaonic times, visitors to the Osireion of Abydos were frightened by the underworld demons painted on the walls and left inscriptions asking the sun god to protect them from these *khatyu*.

The demons created to protect the sun god against cosmic enemies might be invoked to protect Osiris, the dead, or even a temple. Emissaries and guardian demons were depicted as having human bodies with animal heads. What usually distinguished them from other deities were the long knives they bear in each hand, hence the name "knife-bearers" or "butchers" sometimes given to them.

Each temple was supposed to be an ordering of the

world, and the same held true for Egypt. Once the world was created, the original unorganized and chaotic element was cast out to its margin. A demon called Apophis was supposed to dwell in this element, endlessly fighting to reconquer the space of which the chaotic element was deprived. Every day he attacked the sun in his bark, and after every defeat he returned, a permanent threat to the world. Many rituals were performed to protect the sun bark, to prevent the victory of the chaos demon, or to destroy his evil eye. Similarly, the territories around Egypt were supposed to shelter Seth and his allied demons, who were striving to reconquer Egypt. Here again rituals were used to keep them at a distance. The world, Egypt, gods, and men were bound to be threatened or attacked by demons wanting to gain power over them. Other demons were invoked to repel them, keeping the world in order and people and gods at peace.

[*See also* Fantastic Animals.]

### BIBLIOGRAPHY

Borghouts, J. F. "The Evil Eye of Apopis." *The Journal of Egyptian Archaeology* 59 (1973), 114–150. A thorough study of the rite intended to destroy the eye of Apophis, with remarks on various malevolent beings.

Borghouts, J. F. *Ancient Egyptian Magical Texts.* Leiden, 1978. A good, handy translation of major magical spells, many of which were used against different kinds of demons.

Cauville, Sylvie. "À propos des 77 génies de Pharbaïthos." *Bulletin de l'Institut français d'archéologie orientale* 90 (1990), 115–133. A history of the evolution of one troop of protective demons.

De Meulenaere, Herman. "Meskhenet à Abydos." In *Religion und Philosophie im Alten Ägypten*, edited by U. Verhoeven and E. Grafe, pp. 243–251. Orientalia Lovaniensia Analecta, 39. Leuven, 1991. A brief commentary on Meskhenet with the recent bibliography.

Edwards, I. E. S., ed. *Oracular Amuletic Decrees of the Late New Kingdom.* London, 1960. Complete study of a particular kind of protective amulet, with magic spells inscribed on papyrus strips, intended to protect against various demons.

Germond, Philippe. *Sekhmet et la protection du monde.* Agyptiaca Helvetica, 9. Geneva, 1981. Study of the litany addressed to Sekhmet to ask her to protect the world from demons at the end of each year.

Goyon, Jean-Claude. *Les dieux-gardiens et la genèse des temples.* Bibliothèque d'étude, 93. Cairo, 1985. An analysis of the main temple protecting demon troops.

Kakosy, Laszlo. "Decans in Late-Egyptian Religion." *Oikumene* 3 (1982), 163–191. A detailed study of Decans as demons and their mythological context.

Meeks, Dimitri. "Génies, Anges, Démons en Égypte." In *Génies, Anges et Démons.* edited by P. Garelli, pp. 19–84. Sources Orientales, 8. Paris, 1971. A general overview of the demons and genies in Egypt.

Meeks, Dimitri, and Christine Favard-Meeks. *Daily Life of the Egyptian Gods.* Translated from French by G. M. Goshgarian. Ithaca, 1996. An overview of the gods' community and the myths and rites attached to their different activities.

Pantalacci, Laure. "Compagnie de gardiens au temple d'el-Qal'a." In *Ägyptologische Tempeltagung*, edited by D. Kurth, pp. 187–198. Wiesbaden, 1995. A study of an original troop of temple protective demons.

Posener, Georges. "Les 'afarit dans l'ancienne Égypte." *Mitteilungen des Deutschen Archäologischen Instituts, Abteilung Kairo* 37 (1981), 393–401. An insight into the world of petty disturbing demons.

Quaegebeur, Jan. *Le dieu égyptien Shaï dans la religion et l'onomastique.* Orientalia Lovaniensia Analecta, 2. Leuven, 1975. The basic study on Shai, the fate demon, with many comments on related demons, male and female.

Thompson, Herbert. "Two Demotic Self-Dedications." *Journal of Egyptian Archaeology* 26 (1941), 68–78. Studies a category of petitions addressed to gods by humans wishing to become their servants, with their families and descent. In exchange, they ask gods to protect them from various forms of supernatural beings.

DIMITRI MEEKS

**DEMOTIC LITERATURE.** Literary texts written in the Egyptian Demotic script survive from a period of about six centuries, with the earliest material from the fourth century BCE. These are the Saqqara Demotic Papyri, excavated during the 1960s and 1970s in the Sacred Animal Necropolis, part of the necropolis at Memphis. They include narrative texts, but no fragments of Wisdom Literature. The latest material comprises texts on magic from the third century CE, all found at Thebes (but a wide range of texts had been copied or written down in the previous century). A large proportion of known texts have been dated to the first and second centuries CE; hundreds of them, even if some are very fragmentary, are known from temple contexts in the Faiyum. Most were associated with the community of priests at Dime and that at Tebtunis. Before that, from Ptolemaic times, there are only a small number. A coherent picture of the development of Demotic literature is therefore difficult to establish.

From the early Roman period, many types of text are known. Wisdom Literature and narratives, including mythological and cosmological narratives, are probably the best-represented types. A few other texts might have as good a claim as these to belong among literary works, or belles-lettres. The *Harpist's Song* (or *Poème Satirique*) is a metrical work in which abuse is poured upon an unfortunate harpist. Another metrical text, Papyrus Carlsberg 69, rejoices in good eating and drunkeness, and it invokes the goddess Bastet. If "literature" is understood in a wider sense, then scientific, magical, and religious material might also be taken into account. Scientific papyri include mathematical, astronomical, and medical texts. Examples are known of astrological handbooks and manuals for the interpretation of dreams and omens. Although magic plays a role in several types of text, the substantial surviving papyri generally referred to as the Demotic magical papyri—dealing with spells and divination—all date from the very end of the history of Demotic literature. There is, as well, a wide and complex variety of funerary literature in Demotic.

From the Demotic Wisdom Literature, two substantial and well-preserved texts survive along with two shorter texts and a number of small fragments. The Insinger Papyrus, one of the two major works, became damaged after its modern discovery, and lacks the first five of its twenty-five sections, as well as any introductory matter that it may once have had. Apart from this chief manuscript, a number of other more fragmentary copies of the text survive. This might suggest that the text was something of a classic, at least in Roman times. Of the second major work, the *Instructions of Ankhsheshonqy*, which was somewhat shorter, only one manuscript survives. Like some earlier Egyptian instructional texts, *Ankhsheshonqy* has an introductory narrative section, part of which is preserved. (A variant version of part of that narrative, in very different wording, is preserved in Copenhagen, with no indication that it was ever accompanied by the Wisdom material.) Whereas the Insinger Papyrus is organized in a highly elaborate and systematic fashion, *Ankhsheshonqy* at best includes some groupings of material—and often it is difficult to detect any connected thread of thought.

As a whole, the Demotic Wisdom texts display considerable similarities. In form, there are significant changes from the earlier Egyptian instructional tradition. Complex metrical structures are no longer used; the texts are generally agreed to be written in prose; and they are largely constructed of separate maxims, which the manuscripts lay out with each on a separate line. In content, the Demotic material has much in common with earlier Egyptian Wisdom Literature. The emphasis on certain topics, however, differs from that in earlier material; some scholars have stressed that the Egyptian texts need to be seen in the context of the Wisdom Literature throughout the whole of the ancient Near East, especially in a period when influences passed from culture to culture.

The Demotic texts address the individual. In *Ankhsheshonqy*, the narrative introduction specifically presents the text as advice from a father to his son—dealing with finding his proper place in society, with not acting or speaking out of turn. A contrast is made between the behavior of the wise man and that of the fool. The Insinger Papyrus is more concerned than other texts with fate and the uncertainties of life, whereas *Ankhsheshonqy* has a proverbial flavor, and concentrates on pragmatic self-interest. The similarities among the Demotic material are far greater than any differences.

Demotic narrative texts form a body of literature that shares many features of language, form, and subject matter. From the early Roman period, with no parallel in earlier Egyptian literature, are the "cycles" of stories—a series of stories that involve the same character or set of characters, and which have certain themes in common. Only two such cycles have so far been securely identified. One is the *Setna Khaemwase Cycle*, with the plots in the surviving texts all following a remarkably similar pattern, as far as judgment can be made from the fragmentary condition.

The other is the *Inaros–Petuabastis Cycle*, which deals with the fortunes of the very extensive "family" of a military leader and hero named Inaros. The first two texts of the cycle that came to light involve a king Petuabastis (there were several Late period kings of this name in Egypt), who is depicted as maintaining an unhappily precarious authority over an Egypt effectively divided into a number of separate princedoms. Some details suggest a historical setting in the seventh century BCE, but there are also echoes of other periods from the eighth to the sixth century, and even later. In these two texts, as in most but not all of the others known, Inaros himself is already dead, and it is difficult to see a consistent historical original for the figure of Inaros; his death is an event that must have provided some sense of a chronological sequence in the stories, but it is not yet apparent that the individual texts make any reference to one another, as each seems to be designed with a separate, independent plot.

The first text of the cycle to come to light, edited by Krall at the end of the nineteenth century, was "The Struggle for the Armor of Inaros" (preserved upon the Krall Papyrus in Vienna). The beginning of the papyrus is damaged, but a fragmentary parallel to the first surviving pages has recently been identified in Copenhagen. The plot is set in motion by a council of the gods, where it is decided to instigate strife in Egypt. Demons are sent down to earth to put a determination to fight in the hearts of two heroes, one belonging to the family of Inaros, the other to an opposing faction. The cause of the ensuing series of battles and duels is a dispute over the possession of the splendid armor of the dead Inaros. Many have argued that a number of ideas for the plot of this text and those of others belonging to the cycle have been adopted as a result of some kind of knowledge of Greek epic (not just knowledge of the two Homeric epics, the *Iliad* and the *Odyssey*), although this is not universally accepted. Preserved on the Spiegelberg Papyrus of the first century BCE is "The Struggle for the Priesthood of Amun." The greater part of this papyrus is housed at Strasbourg, and there are a number of fragments elsewhere. Several fragmentary examples of other manuscripts of the text are among collections with material from Tebtunis. Among Demotic narratives—and indeed among Demotic literature as a whole—this text is the one of which we have most evidence for multiple copies. Like "The Struggle for the Armor of Inaros," the text involves duels between heroes, often preceded by taunts and boasting. The dispute in this text, however, concerns the very Egyptian idea of the contested succession to a priestly office and to the enjoyment of its income. The son of King Petuabastis has taken possession of the office of "First Prophet of Amun" at Thebes. A young priest of Horus, from Buto in the Delta, goes to Thebes and comes before the king to lay claim to the priesthood, assisted by thirteen "herdsmen" (this term places them as outsiders, as ferocious warriors). They do not appear to play a role in any other texts of the cycle. After seizing and occupying the sacred bark of the god Amun, they capture in turn the king's son and his chief ally and imprison them on the boat. Amun has revealed to the king in an oracular response that the only hero who can overcome the "herdsmen" is Pamu, a member of the family of Inaros. He is part of a faction that bears a grudge against the king and his son, because they had not been invited to a festival. Pamu agrees to come to Thebes, but the very end of the story is lost, and the precise outcome unclear. The text perhaps involves some serious reflections on Egyptian religious and political institutions, which certainly would be hard to comprehend for anyone unfamiliar with the culture.

The story about the "Egyptians and Amazons" is preserved in two similar copies (housed at Vienna), probably of a late second century CE date. The hero Petekhons, a member of the family of Inaros, leads an Egyptian military expedition into the Near East. They encroach upon the territory of Serpot, "the pharaoh of the land of women" (the term *Amazon* is not used), and her army of women. Serpot sends her sister to spy on the Egyptian encampment. The queen then inspects her warriors and delivers a speech of encouragement, after which the women inflict a great slaughter upon the Egyptians and their allies. Next day, Petekhons and Serpot fight in single combat. Unlike the tragic encounter of Achilles with Penthesilea, this duel ends with a truce. The two proceed to fall in love, and that leads to an alliance.

Among the plentiful material of the early Roman period, the *Setna Khaemwase Cycle* and the *Inaros-Petuabastis Cycle* seem to predominate (although it should be mentioned that their early discovery and well-preserved texts concentrated scholarly attention). Some fragmentary material is known for many individual texts, which do not seem to belong to any cycle; these involve quite different characters or sets of characters, set in a wide range of historical periods. Their themes may be seen as having some resemblance to the magical and heroic preoccupations of the two cycles discussed above.

In assessing the nature of Demotic narratives in earlier periods, there is only questionable evidence that any text existed directly relating to (and involving the same characters as) the cycles. From Ptolemaic times comes the *Demotic Chronicle*, preserved on a single papyrus (housed in the Bibliothèque Nationale in Paris). The longest text on this papyrus is hardly a narrative; it comprises a series of obscure oracular statements, which are each given an interpretation and serve to reflect on the stature or deficiencies of the Egyptian kings who had reigned from the late fifth century BCE onward. The opposite side of the same papyrus (the *verso*) preserves, among other material, the beginning of a story concerning King Amasis of the twenty-sixth dynasty: to the dismay of his courtiers, the king insists upon drinking a large quantity of wine and, therefore, the next morning suffers a terrible hangover. For relief, he demands to be told a story. Before the manuscript breaks off, a priest begins to relate a tale which was probably about to take a ribald turn. Whether or not the story eventually came to point a moral is uncertain.

The Saqqara Demotic papyri, plausibly the earliest examples of Demotic narrative, include several fragmentary mythological texts: one is an otherwise unknown episode of a Horus and Seth text, much in the New Kingdom style of the *Contendings of Horus and Seth* (including the manner in which the character of Seth is depicted). The text relating the story about Nanefersakhmet includes elements of romance and surprise meetings; it tells of the tribulations suffered by a priest cheated of his priesthood and the wanderings of characters who had to go into hiding. There are many individual details that are paralleled in later, Roman-era material, but the plot seems very different.

In the 1940s, the Demotic narratives seemed to Egyptologists very remote from the stories expressed in Late Egyptian language, written in Hieratic script, and preserved from the New Kingdom. At that time, the latest Hieratic story known was the *Misfortunes of Wenamun*, from about 1000 BCE, and the earliest Demotic was from the third century BCE; it could then even be suggested that narrative as a genre needed to be reinvented in Ptolemaic times. New material has changed scholarly perceptions. A wider range of textual types is now known, making the two narrative cycles from the Roman period less predominant. Evidence for Demotic narratives now extends back into the fourth century BCE. Hieratic manuscripts (of scientific and Wisdom texts, as well as narratives) have been discovered or published, which begin to bridge the chronological gap between the New Kingdom and Ptolemaic times. Demotic narratives, in their use of prose, their exploitation of the story within a story, their high proportion of direct speech, and their shadowing of the style of oral literature, can be seen as belonging to the same tradition as the stories of the New Kingdom. Just how this tradition operated, however, remains a topic of investigation and debate. The apparent flowering of Demotic literature in early Roman times can be understood as part of a general and deliberate program in Egyptian priestly circles, an attempt to keep traditional Egyptian culture alive in written form during a time of cultural change. Such a context surely did not obtain for earlier stages of Egyptian literature.

[*See also* Ankhsheshonqy; *and* Setna Khaemwase Cycle.]

**BIBLIOGRAPHY**

Betz, Hans Dieter, ed. *The Greek Magical Papyri in Translation, Including the Demotic Spells.* Chicago, 1986.

Depauw, Mark. *A Companion to Demotic Studies.* Papyrologica Bruxellensia, 28. Bruxelles, 1997. Includes a survey of Demotic literature, pp. 85–121, with the most up-to-date bibliography of text editions and of studies.

Kitchen, K. A. *The Third Intermediate Period in Egypt.* 2d ed. Warminster, 1986. See "Notes on the background of the story-cycle of Petubastis," pp. 455–461. The story "Naneferkasokar and the Babylonians" is *not* now believed to belong to the cycle.

Lichtheim, Miriam. *Ancient Egyptian Literature: A Book of Readings,* vol. 3: *The Late Period.* Berkeley, 1980. Includes English translations of a selection of texts, with introduction and notes.

Lichtheim, Miriam. *Late Egyptian Wisdom Literature in the International Context: A Study of Demotic Instruction.* Orbis Biblicus et Orientalis, 52. Göttingen, 1983. Includes translations.

Posener, G. "Literature." In *The Legacy of Egypt,* 2d ed., edited by J. R. Harris, pp. 220–256. Oxford, 1971.

Tait, W. J. "Demotic Literature and Egyptian Society." In *Life in a Multi-cultural Society: Egypt from Cambyses to Constantine and Beyond,* edited by J. H. Johnson, pp. 303–310. Studies in Ancient Oriental Civilization, 51. Chicago, 1992.

Tait, W. J. "Egyptian Fiction in Demotic and Greek." In *Greek Fiction: The Greek Novel in Context,* edited by J. R. Morgan and R. Stoneman, pp. 203–222. London, 1994. A survey and basic bibliography of narrative texts.

JOHN TAIT

**DENDERA,** a site important from the Predynastic period onward, owing to its location at the crossroad of the Eastern Desert and the Red Sea (32°10′N, 26°08′E). Dendera was the capital of the sixth nome of Upper Egypt and is famous for the magnificent temple of Hathor—the goddess's most important temple—surrounded by various sanctuaries and protected by a brick enclosure some 280 meters (930 feet) in length.

An archaeological survey of the enclosure was undertaken by William M. Flinders Petrie in 1897 and 1898. More systematic excavations were conducted from 1915 to 1918 by Clarence S. Fisher in the Predynastic sector and in the necropolis of the First Intermediate Period and the eleventh dynasty, as well as in the Ptolemaic and Roman tombs. The western section of the necropolis, with large *mastaba*s of the sixth dynasty could not be explored (especially the *mastaba* of Idu). There are few sources from Dendera during the New Kingdom and the Late period; most of the objects found, approximately 450 pieces from the Old and the Middle Kingdoms, are housed in museum collections at Chicago, Philadelphia, and Cairo. A topographical survey of the enclosure and the necropolis was carried out by the Institut français d'archéologie orientale du Caire (IFAO). Inside the enclosure, the monuments include the following:

- temple of Hathor
- domain of Isis
- Sacred lake, chapel of the barge, wells
- *mammisi* of Nectanebo I
- Roman *mammisi*
- north gate and Roman fountains
- chapel of Montuhotep
- chapel of Thoth's oracle
- sanatorium
- Coptic basilica

The initial epigraphic studies were begun in 1865, by J. Duemichen, Auguste Mariette, Heinrich Brugsch, Émile Chassinat, and François Daumas. Publication is in process by S. Cauville of the work on the pronaos, the exterior of the temple of Hathor, and the large gates. The work on the sacred foundation, centered on the heliacal rise of the star Sirius under Ramesses II and the "re-foundation" under Ptolemy Auletes (80–58 BCE), was published in 1992 by S. Cauville, as "Le temple d'Isis à Dendera," in the *Bulletin de la Société française d'Égyptologie*. Astronomical research has shown that the famous "Zodiac of Dendera" was first conceived in 50 BCE; it also mentions the position of various planets, as well as the solar and lunar eclipses.

The crypts that form the foundation of the temple of Hathor are in the name of Ptolemy Auletes, and they were decorated from 54 to 51 BCE. The remainder of the *naos*, with anepigraphic cartouches, was decorated during the joint reigns of Cleopatra and her brothers; the names of the great queen and of her son appear only on the rear wall of the temple. The dedications engraved on the exterior of Hathor's temple describe the dimensions of each chamber. The plan of the temple of Hathor is similar to that of Edfu; it has a sanctuary, sacred chapels, and large liturgical halls next to cult rooms designed for the storage of fabrics, salves, and food supplies that were required for daily rituals or for various feasts. The originality of the architecture resides in the majesty of the crypts, cut into the thick walls on three levels. Those below ground held statues of deities, whose dimensions varied from 22.5 centimeters (about 9 inches) to 2.10 meters (about 6 feet).

The most ancient deities at Dendera are Hathor and Harsomtus, the ones to whom the most beautiful celebrations were dedicated. In the Ptolemaic period, the sacred pantheon was centered on Hathor and on Isis (who had his own domain located in the southern section of the enclosure). Horus was the father of Harsomtus, brought into the world by Hathor in the *mammisi* (birth house); Osiris was the father of Harsiesis (Eg., Hor-sa-iset), guarded by Isis. Hathor was presented in four readily identifiable forms, in name, in epithet, and in iconographic components. Those two triads (Hathor-Horus-Harsomtus and Isis-Osiris-Harsiesis) were the center of sacred circles chosen to express theological subtleties or to express the function of a particular temple hall. Hathor was the "efflux" of the eye of Re, who was transformed upon contact with sand into a beautiful woman, called "Gold of the Gods." Dendera was created for Hathor as a substitute for Heliopolis, which was the ancient cult center for Re, her fa-

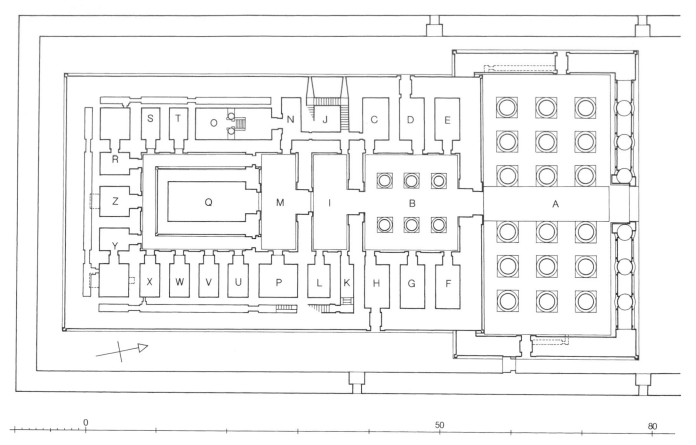

DENDERA. *Plan of the Hathor temple at Dendera, built by the Roman emperor Tiberus.* (From Dieter Arnold, *Temples of the Last Pharaohs.* New York, 1999)

ther. Re-Horakhty, together with Ptah of Memphis, enthroned Hathor as queen of the divine universe.

The chapels to Osiris, located on the roof of the temple to Hathor, were partially decorated from 50 BCE onward; they were inaugurated on 28 December 47 BCE, on the occasion of the extremely rare conjunction of the full moon at zenith and the festive twenty-sixth day of the month of Khoiak, when Hathor is resurrected. The six chapels are the most beautiful complex in all Egypt for her resurrection; each chapel is used in turn on the days between the twelfth and the twenty-sixth; the number 6 also symbolized the astral rebirth of the deity in the form of the moon. Throughout the year, the most secret of the chapels was considered the sacred tomb of Osiris, where a barley statuette made during the Khoiak ceremonies was kept.

Each culture creates its own guarantee and permanence of divine life; in this way, the *mammisis* was placed at the center of the celebration of the divine birth to Hathor of the heir and the chapel of the bark was erected on the shore of the sacred lake, to serve as a theater during the annual boat procession, which celebrated the return of the goddess to Nubia.

## BIBLIOGRAPHY

Aubourg, É. "La date de conception du zodiaque du temple d'Hathor à Dendera." *Bulletin de l'Institut français d'archéologie Orientale* 95 (1995), 1–10.

Cauville, Sylvie. *Dendera: Les guides archéologiques de l'IFAO.* Cairo, 1990.

Cauville, Sylvie. *Dendera: Les chapelles osiriennes.* Bibliothèque d'étude, 117–119. Cairo, 1997.

Cauville, Sylvie. *Le zodiaque d'Osiris.* Louvain, 1997.

Cauville, Sylvie. *Dendara I: Traduction.* Louvain, 1998.

Cauville, Sylvie. *Dendara II: Traduction.* Louvain, 1999.

Daumas, François. *Les Mammisis des temples égyptiens.* Paris, 1958.

Daumas, François. *Dendara et le Temple d'Hathor.* Cairo, 1969.

Fischer, Henry G. *Dendera in the Third Millennium B.C., Down to the Theban Domination of Thebes.* Locust Valley, New York, 1968.

Quaegebeur, J. "Cléopâtre VII et le temple de Dendara." *Göttinger Miszellen* 120 (1991), 49–72.

Slater, Ray A. *The Archaeology of Denderah in the First Intermediate Period.* Ph.D. diss., University of Pennsylvania, 1974.

Waitkus, Wolfgang. *Die Texte in den unteren Krypten des Hathortempels von Dendera.* Wiesbaden, 1997.

SYLVIE CAUVILLE
Translated from French by Elizabeth Schwaiger

**DENTAL CARE.** Since ancient Egypt ranges from the Predynastic period through the Greco-Roman period, it is an ambitious task to characterize dental health throughout this vast period of time. The literature concerned with dentistry and dental health during that three thousand year span is fragmentary. Therefore, the study of dental health in ancient Egypt has been based on two principal sources: (1) the direct examination of teeth and skulls and (2) written records from medical papyri and tomb inscriptions. The problem is that conclusions have often been based on a small number of samples or even on single mummies, usually from museum collections. Many of these mummies date from the later periods, particularly the Greco-Roman period, whereas fewer examples date from the Old, Middle, or New Kingdoms. Hence, overgeneralization may exist for the discussion of dental health in ancient Egypt. Nevertheless, the most significant dental disease identified was attrition, wear that resulted in the reduction of the protective enamel. The teeth were rapidly worn down throughout life by the chewing of a coarse diet, made even more abrasive by the sand of the Nile Valley or from the flour produced by millstones made of sandstone. In time, this wear became so extensive that the enamel and dentine were eroded and the pulp chambers were exposed. Once the living tissue inside the tooth died, empty root canals became a source of chronic infection and abscesses.

The second major dental problem was periodontal, disease of the supporting tissue. Periodontal disease is often associated with plaque or calculus (tartar) deposits on the teeth at the gumline that may lead to deep periodontal pockets, loss of the bony support of teeth, and therefore loose teeth. Severe periodontitis may ultimately lead to infection, abscesses, and loss of teeth. The teeth of Ramesses II are excellent examples of the effects of old age, with periodontal disease (loss of bony support), dental attrition, and root abscesses. James H. Breasted (1930) examined a twelfth dynasty mandible (lower jaw) that had

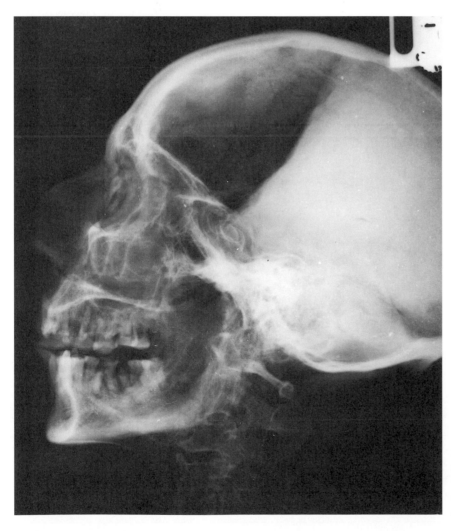

DENTAL CARE. *Lateral X-ray of the mummy of Ramesses II.* Note the extreme wear of the teeth, with resulting exposure of the pulp chambers and periapical abscesses. (Courtesy James E. Harris)

two circular openings at the apex of the right first molar root tip and concluded that a dental surgeon had drained these root abscesses through a hollow reed.

Dental caries (cavities) were infrequently seen in ancient Egypt. Caries were attributed in the Papyrus Anastasi IV to a worm. The ancient kings, queens, and nobles did not have extensive dental decay; where it was observed, the decay tended to be the pit-and-fissure variety (top of the tooth) rather than interproximal (decay between the teeth). Two major environmental factors reduced the amount of dental decay. The first was the absence from the diet of refined carbohydrates, such as sugar. The second was the extreme attrition (wear) mentioned earlier, because the wear occurred not only on the occlusal surface (top of the teeth) but also between the teeth (interproximally). Extensive wear provides a difficult environment for both plaque and decay. (It has been suggested that the increase in caries in ancient Egypt was due to the availability of honey among the more affluent population.)

A brief comment should be offered here on dental occlusion or malocclusion and facial types. In general, perhaps owing to extreme wear, the dentition of the ancient Egyptians exhibited normal molar relationships with only moderate dental crowding. The faces of the queens of the New Kingdom (early eighteenth dynasty), however, resemble many modern European, African, and American faces, with maxillary (upper jaw) prognathism (protrusion). This condition may be either hereditary or environmental, the latter resulting from thumb sucking or other oral habits. Queen Ahmose Nefertiry of the eighteenth dynasty is an excellent example of this type of occlusion.

There has been considerable controversy concerning the role of a dental profession in ancient Egypt. F. Filce Leek, an English dentist has been the most quoted proponent of the view that there is not a sufficient body of evidence to indicate that there were dental specialists ("The Practice of Dentistry in Ancient Egypt," *Journal of Egyptian Archaeology* 53 [1967], 51–58). In contrast, Paul Ghalioungui, in *The House of Life: Magic and Medical Science in Ancient Egypt* (Amsterdam, 1973), and Kent Weeks (1980) in his chapter "Ancient Egyptian Dentistry" in *An X-Ray Atlas of the Royal Mummies*, conclude that there were dental specialists.

Hesy-Re (third dynasty) was the earliest person to carry the title of physician, and he called himself "Chief of Dentists" (*wr ibḥ swnw*). There are many medical papyri, such as the famous Ebers Papyrus (Eb. 739, 740, and 743), that prescribe medicines to relieve dental pain and even describe how to fix loose teeth. According to Ghalioungui (1973): "resin, chrysocall or Nubian earth" was recommended for stopping or filling teeth. Harris, Iskander, and Farid (1975) reported the discovery of an Old Kingdom dental bridge, from the fourth dynasty, c.2500 BCE. This bridge replaced two upper front teeth (a maxillary lateral and central incisor). The bridge consisted of prepared extracted teeth, drilled with very fine holes, and fixed with gold wire to the patient's remaining teeth. Two teeth bound by gold wire were also found in an Old Kingdom burial site, and silver bridge was found in a skull at Tura el-Asmant from the Ptolemaic period. These finds add support to Paul Ghalioungui and Zeinab el Dawakhly in their *Health and Healing in Ancient Egypt* (Cairo, 1963), when, speaking of Egypt's specialization of medicine, they observed: "Men-kau-Re-ank who was called a maker of teeth (*iry-ibḥ*), to distinguish him from Niankh-Sekhmet who figures on the same stele as a "tooth physician" (*ibḥ swnw*").

Kent Weeks (1980) listed six Egyptian dentists known to us, but only one, Psammetik-seneb of the twenty-sixth dynasty, was not from the Old Kingdom. Weeks speculated that the specialty of dentistry may have peaked in the Old Kingdom (c.2400–2000 BCE); nevertheless, the Greek historian Herodotus noted the existence of dentists during the Greco-Roman period in Egypt. On the whole, the evidence indicates that professional dental specialists existed in ancient Egypt; however, the extent of their knowledge for diagnosis, treatment, and restoration requires further examination of both the biologic and written records.

[*See also* Hygiene.]

**BIBLIOGRAPHY**

Breasted, J. H., trans. *The Edwin Smith Surgical Papyrus.* 2 vols. The University of Chicago. Oriental Institute Publications, 3–4. Chicago, 1930. Provides evidence of surgical drainage of dental abscesses.

Ebbell, E., trans. *The Papyrus Ebers. The Greatest Egyptian Medical Documents.* Copenhagen, 1937. Chapter 89 deals with dental concerns.

Harris, James E. "Dental Health in Ancient Egypt." In *Mummies, Disease and Ancient Cultures,* edited by Eve Cockburn, Aidan Cockburn, and Theodore A. Reymond, 2d ed. Cambridge, 1998. Contains an extensive bibliography.

Harris, James E., Zaki Iskander, and S. Farid. "Restorative Dentistry in Ancient Egypt: An Archaeologic Fact." *Journal of the Michigan Dental Association* 57 (1975), 401–404. Detailed description of the only true bridge found in an Old Kingdom tomb.

Hoffman-Axthelm, W. E. "Is the Practice of Dentistry in Ancient Egypt an Archaeological Fact?" *Bulletin of the History of Dentistry* 29.2 (1979), 71–77.

Iskander, Zaki, and James E. Harris. "A Skull with Silver Bridge to Splint or Replace a Central Incisor." *Annales du service des antiquiés de l'Égypte* 62 (1975), 85–90.

Nunn, John F. *Ancient Egyptian Medicine.* Oklahoma, 1996. An excellent review of medical history, with a brief section on dentistry.

Piccione, P. A. *Comprehensive Bibliographical Database of Ancient Egyptian Medicine and Medical Practice.* Chicago, 1996. Includes practically every medical and dental publication relating to ancient Egypt.

Weeks, Kent R. "Ancient Egyptian Dentistry." In *An X-Ray Atlas of The*

*Royal Mummies,* edited by James E. Harris and Edward F. Wente. Chicago, 1980. Probably the most authoritative review of the dental profession in ancient Egypt.

JAMES E. HARRIS

**DESERT ENVIRONMENTS.** The Nile Valley is the lifeline between two of the world's driest deserts; it is maintained by an exotic river that derives its waters from tropical East Africa. The Nile floodplain provides a long, narrow oasis, and the ancient Egyptians were vividly aware of the stark contrast between the "Red Land" of the desert uplands and the "Black Land" of its seasonally inundated alluvium. In terms of aridity and lack of vegetation, the Egyptian deserts rival Death Valley in the United States; only the Atacama Desert of Chile is drier. Rainfall in an "average" year decreases rapidly from 200 millimeters (8 inches) on the northwest coast of the Nile Delta to 30 millimeters (1 inch) near Cairo; most of the Western Desert (Libyan Desert) statistically receives less than 5 millimeters (0.2 inch) equivalent to a modest shower every few generations. The Eastern Desert or more mountainous Red Sea Hills may receive 50 millimeters (2 inches) in places, but even when collected in wadis or in larger, dry river courses, flood events occur there only once or twice a century.

The potential concentration of occasional rainwater in wadis, in local depressions, or in shallow aquifers is critical to the regional distribution of vegetation and game. In the north, the desert shrub cover thickens from the Faiyum Depression toward the shores of the Mediterranean Sea. To the south, the Libyan Desert is essentially lifeless, with the exception of some scattered, spring-fed oases. Occasional rains are a little more frequent in the highland areas, making possible the ephemeral blooming of a sparse cover of grasses. In the Red Sea Hills, there are scattered thorn trees, with some shrubs and grasses along many of the wadis; otherwise there is barren desert. As a consequence, very small groups of pastoralists move through the wadis of the Eastern Desert, while for millennia sedentary populations have persisted in several oases of the Western Desert. Yet, until at least the 1920s, southern Sahara pastoral families and their cattle sporadically visited the Gilf Kebir highlands of southwest Egypt.

Although the eastern Sahara is parched Red Land, small numbers of resourceful people and their hardy animals have managed to use its occasional opportunities to advantage—complementing the caravans of traders and camels that once traversed this forbidding desert, moving from one watering place to another. The Sahara was and is no more a barrier than the oceans, one that could and can be crossed by experienced pastoralists and mer-

chants. The Sahara became a wasteland only in the last three or four millennia, since in late prehistoric times, the environmental conditions were modestly wetter; for those skilled in surviving the desert, the Sahara was then a world of opportunity. Consequently, the prehistory of the Nile Valley was actively interlinked with that of the eastern Sahara.

The first clue that the prehistoric Red Land had not always been barren was provided by the rock engravings and paintings found deep within the desert; they first came to public attention during the 1920s and 1930s, depicting game animals now found in the Sahel, as well as livestock and peoples that were ethnographically distinctive. Systematic archaeological work began in the 1970s, and it has enhanced these once ambiguous impressions. A substantial and complex archaeological record is now linked with a robust body of geo-archaeological data that documents the environmental change. Precisely because desert resources are and were localized and point-specific, the overall picture is composed of a collage of micro-studies—all of which differ in detail.

Today, occasional summer rains of southerly, monsoonal origin rarely stray north of the Tropic of Cancer; the winter showers, of northerly origin in the westerlies, very seldom penetrate south of the Tropic of Cancer. In areas of mountainous topography, however, occasional rains of both kinds may overlap. Whether water is collected and stored in a deep or a shallow aquifer is important, as is whether surface runoff is a major component. Such factors will affect the threshold conditions when water becomes available at or near the surface, as well as the persistence of that water for months, years, or even centuries. Similarly, the presence of animals and fish depends on a cyclic evolution, from smaller to larger life forms, at the point when water first becomes available until it finally gives out. Points of water surrounded by a complex biota will support more people than those with limited biotic diversity; whether an optimal association will develop, with the capacity to support repeated and protracted human settlement, will depend on the constellation of environmental variables and the predictability and productivity of resources.

In sum, the Egyptian deserts are very different, discontinuous environmental mosaics from the dependable, riverine oasis that forms the Nile corridor. At times, overall, some degree of co-variance occurred in environmental trends, but not sufficiently to allow normative inferences. Equally important to the region is that the productivity of the desert oases was never great—certainly not when compared with the Nile floodplain—and that their resources were ecologically fragile. Yet the Red Land was never a void, and the emergence of Egyptian civilization in the Nile Valley was based on both the human experience and the cultural roots of the diverse prehistoric adaptations to the desert.

**Floodplain Margins.** Representations of animals and, more occasionally, vegetation are fairly common until Middle Kingdom times; these include tomb paintings and carved tomb reliefs. Tombs were usually located on the desert edge and rock engravings were placed on cliffs bordering the Nile Valley, mainly in southern Egypt. There are also a variety of art pieces with such portrayals—slate palettes, ivory carvings, and the decorations on pottery, primarily those from late Predynastic and Early Dynastic times. Such representations are to some degree equivocal as to their ecological interpretations. Do they provide an authentic record of locally familiar biota or are they mainly symbolic? Do they attempt to represent "nature" in such areas, or are they an elite contrivance similar to the hunting enclosures stocked with game captured elsewhere? Do they reflect desert environments rather than the riverine oasis watered by the Nile? No categorical answer is possible, but independent evidence as well as a number of ecological arguments suggest that such representations are informative.

The artistic record of the fourth millennium BCE suggests a fauna in and around the Nile floodplain that resembles the present-day dry savanna fauna of central Sudan, as known during the 1800s. There are numerous representations of such floodplain-dependent life forms as the elephant, giraffe, and hartebeest, with less frequent wild cattle, cheetah or leopard, rhinoceros, and possibly fallow deer. Semidesert "runners," such as the oryx and gazelle, also are common, as are the "climbers" of dry rocky environments, the ibex and Barbary sheep. Desert-edge species include the lion, jackal, hyena, and ostrich. During Old Kingdom times, the large savanna forms were no longer shown, while lions and Barbary sheep became rare. The main animals shown were the large and small antilopines—oryx, gazelle, addax, and hartebeest (in that order of frequency)—while ibex representations remained fairly common. For the Middle and New Kingdoms, there was a further shift to showing desert-adapted forms—with gazelle the most common, oryx and ibex declining, hartebeest increasing, and addax no longer shown.

From the animal portrayals, then, a progressive aridification of the environment beyond the floodplain is suggested, in conjunction with partial or complete elimination of small populations of the larger animals—the elephant, giraffe, and lion—by hunting. That this array of game and predators was once present in the region is plausible from the consistent depiction of diagnostic features in the representations. Further, elephant bone has been recovered from the Faiyum Neolithic, and leopard skeletons have been found in a prehistoric cave in the Red Sea Hills. Addax and oryx were still hunted in the coastal

steppes of Egypt in the 1890s. Barbary sheep only became extinct in the Eastern Desert in historical times; and ibex is still present there but very rare. Hartebeest and gazelle were standard forms in Paleolithic times, verified in the Faiyum Neolithic and at el-Omari, with gazelle still present in the coastal areas and in Sudan. The high probability is that the animals shown were directly familiar to the artists and, in fact, all had established names in the Old or Middle Egyptian language.

The question of the local versus the regional presence of the animals depicted is more difficult to answer. Egypt's trade and diplomatic contacts with the Sudan increased during the Old Kingdom and, more important, by the fifth dynasty the animals are shown being hunted within fenced enclosures. Therefore, the animals shown on Old Kingdom reliefs would probably not have been familiar to the average floodplain farmer. By that time, the animals were probably trapped in the Red Sea Hills or on the coastal steppes, at some distance from the Nile Valley, and herded to elite private game parks. Since that is consistent with the ecological adaptations of the animals depicted, it implies that the simplification of the recorded faunal assemblage was due more to hunting pressures than to progressive aridification.

The relatively sparse representations of desert vegetation nonetheless argue for a parallel deterioration of desert productivity. The fifth dynasty sun temple of Newoserre Any at Abusir attempted to show the course of the seasons for the floodplain and for the adjacent desert, depicting a range of wild animals giving birth—gazelle, addax, oryx, wild cattle, ostrich, and cheetah. The animal scenes have a gently undulating surface, stippled to suggest sand, which supports an elaborate flora that, significantly, is labeled "plants of the Western Desert." The tree types, as conventionally drawn in ancient Egypt, include acacia and sycomore fig. Although that fig is a floodplain genus, demanding considerable water, thick roots of both types of tree were found in a wadi fill under a twelfth dynasty building at Armant; found in 1.6 meters (4.5 feet) of fill, resting on Badarian potsherds, the trees grew before the Predynastic fill was cut into them. The lower vegetation tier shows a variety of shrubs, some suggesting succulents, as well as distinctive bunchgrasses. The last probably represent halfa grass, today common on desert-edge sand surfaces, but halfa was also recorded at Neolithic el-Omari, together with acacia, tamarisk, and several chenopods.

The Newoserre Any reliefs, confirmed by other evidence, provide an authentic representation of the edge of the Western Desert as explicitly perceived by Egyptians c.2500 BCE. Other reliefs in fifth and twelfth dynasty private tombs show animal enclosures on a similar rolling sandy surface, highlighted by red stipples, although

Middle Kingdom counterparts are devoid of vegetation. This would argue that the small wadis of the Western Desert margin once had scattered trees, with a groundcover of halfa grass and semidesert forbs and shrubs, much of which is vestigially preserved in the larger wadis of the Eastern Desert even today. What modest vegetation existed had apparently disappeared by the Middle Kingdom, much like the bulk of the desert fauna. Yet a tree root dated c.1150 BCE, under drift sand near the Neolithic site at Merimde, suggests that degradation of the Western Desert edge to its current barren condition was not abrupt. Yet the evidence for floodplain fodder plants that were cut for the domesticated livestock of the desert-edge Predynastic Naqada peoples cautions against the assumption that the desert edge provided substantial grazing resources.

**Climatic Fluctuations.** The geological record confirms some minor climatic fluctuations on the margins of the Nile Valley. In the South, in Egyptian Nubia, medium-sized eastern-bank wadis were periodically active, with repeated flood events from about 10,000 to 7800 BCE, when a conspicuous fossil red soil developed; such wadi activity took place when the floodplain was dry. Since the Nile flood rose in midsummer, and the river in Nubia receded into its channel by mid-October, the local desert rains came during the winter half of the year and were not monsoonal. Subsequent soil formation, with abundant snail shells, implies a protracted period of weathering with fairly frequent gentle rains. Some large wadis debouch on the edge of the floodplain east of Kom Ombo. They were quite active during that time span, and the sandy composition and bedding indicate repeated strong floods. Abundant vegetation is indicated by proliferations of snail shells and common calcareous root casts (vertical and horizontal) that record some shrub and tree vegetation. These thick accumulations were terminated by the same red soil that developed in Nubia. A later episode of wadi activation records strong but sporadic periods of rain, which eroded slope materials, but with little organic evidence. By 3100 BCE, this had ended, prior to occupation of late prehistoric surface sites.

Nonetheless, beyond the floodplain margin, opposite Qena, tree roots of tamarisk and acacia on the desert are extensive in a level with six dates of 5570 to 3650 BCE. Well into the desert, north of Qena, sites within a colluvium dated 5280 to 3970 BCE have charcoal of acacia and two other thorny, tropical trees. Earlier deposits near Qena began to accumulate before 8700 BCE. A last pulse of activity in the great Wadi Qena deposited clays on the channel floor in Islamic times (eleventh century CE)—an episode that was recorded in various smaller eastern-bank wadis, by more modest sandy fills, in part spreading out over Roman ruins.

From the margins of the Holocene lakes of the Faiyum there is fragmentary evidence of what appears to have been a complex sequence of modest, local climatic changes. Between 4000 and 1700 BCE, there were various episodes of colluvial deposition, minor gullying, and the brief development of semidesert soils. Earlier, about 5900 to 5700 BCE, there was a stronger pulse of stream activity. Possibly, some sort of groundcover inhibited dune movement for much, but not all of the time, from before 7000 to 1700 BCE. The Faiyum evidence indicates the possible amplitude of these late prehistoric to early historical climatic fluctuations and cautions against assumptions of extended duration.

A further perspective is provided by the Tree Shelter and Sodmein Cave, both near Quseir, in an area decidedly affected by winter rains today. Adjacent torrential alluviation before 7100 BCE points to sporadic, very heavy rains. Then, until 3600 BCE, stream deposition was less torrential, suggesting more frequent but less intense rains, apparently closing with humic soil formation. Thereafter, hyperarid conditions like those of today prevailed, and there was no more mobilization of rock on the valley slopes. Alluviation was unusually rapid about 7000 BCE and again about 5950 to 5250 BCE. Cave deposits of the latter age include at least six genera of trees, with acacia, tamarisk, and wild olive among them.

The sum of this geological and botanical evidence implies that from somewhat before 7000 to about 3500 BCE, the desert margins of the Nile Valley and the Red Sea Hills were at times wetter than today, with some tree growth typical along the wadi floors. Since then, the adjacent deserts have been hyperarid, but with brief episodes of higher rainfall continuing until perhaps 1700 BCE. The thinning of the wadi tree stands and the reduction of biotic diversity has therefore not been entirely a result of human impact. The fifth dynasty desert reliefs are substantially younger than the termination of the modest "wet phase" of mid-Predynastic times, however, which suggests that the former vegetation of the desert margins was also degraded by human use, just as the riverine and desert fauna was progressively eliminated by hunting during dynastic times.

**Late Prehistory and the Libyan Desert.** The wadis that occasionally spilled out onto the edge of the floodplain emphasize the effect of concentrating a little water in and along a stream channel—most important where igneous or metamorphic rocks of low porosity act almost like an impervious cover. Even if floods only wash down such a channel once in fifty years or more, water collects and is stored in the gravelly sands below the stream bed, accessible to the deep-rooted trees and shrubs adapted to an arid environment. This water concentration effect is magnified in the Libyan Desert, where there are no linear channels, and water instead collects in central points or in deep and extensive aquifers, especially in porous sandstones and at the base of dune sands. In a dry climate, aquifers provide an additional advantage—that they collect water during wet intervals to store for millennia—later emerging in wells or springs.

The ecological opportunities provided by the Libyan Desert for plants, animals, and people during late prehistoric times were made possible by only modest climatic changes. The Libyan Desert has many shallow depressions—essentially hollows in a fairly flat but undulating surface—that are almost undiscernible to the human eye. Created over long time spans by wind erosion, others formed between dunes or where a dry valley was blocked by an encroaching dune. Surface runoff from a single heavy rain on a rock surface can form a sheet of standing water that may persist for months. If the frequency of good rains increases to several times a decade, clays and silts accumulate in the depression and seal the floor against water percolation into the soil, so that waters remain for years, with moisture retention in the subsoil allowing colonization by reeds. If persistent enough, such a mud pan or ephemeral playa lake may acquire a ring of shrubs and trees, which attract insects, waterfowl, animals, herders, and their flocks.

Sandstones or thick sand covers absorb and retain groundwater, and recurrent heavy rains every few years can recharge small or large aquifers to raise the water table by tens of meters, until a deep and persistent lake may form. Such groundwater may initially be brackish or saline from accumulated minerals, but as the volume of water in the aquifer expands, the calcium, magnesium, and sodium salts are diluted and the lake may turn fresh. Microorganisms and mollusca will be introduced by visiting birds that carry traces of mud and leave wastes with spores, seeds, and more. A diversified biotic community evolves in and around such a micro-oasis, with a ring of aquatic plants screening out blowing sand but trapping wind-borne dust. As the freshwater lake first deepens and then eventually shrinks, its water chemistry is transformed, becoming a salt lake and then a dry, salt flat. The Selima Oasis in northwestern Sudan is a prime example of such a groundwater lake. The aquifer was recharged before 9000 BCE, and by 8200 BCE, a shallow brackish water body was transformed into a deeper freshwater lake. It was a modest salt lake from 2500 to 2000 BCE, and it finally remained a salt flat, although residual savanna trees survived in the area for another millennium.

From a dozen or so key locations of the Libyan Desert broad parallels become apparent in the environmental response to climatic change, with first a weak pulse of wetter conditions (c.8000–7600 BCE), followed by three stronger peaks (7300–6300, 5800–5200, and 4500–3400 BCE). This composite picture, which parallels that of the Nile Valley margins and the Red Sea Hills, nonetheless masks a lack of synchroneity in detail between centers. At Bir Kiseiba, improved water conditions are apparent two thousand years before the Kharga Oasis. Optimal moisture conditions at Selima, Nabta Playa, Kiseiba, Kharga, and the Tibesti Mountains of Libya were dated to about 7000 BCE, while those of the Gilf Kebir, the Great Sand Sea, and the Dahkla Oasis were delayed until about 4500 BCE. Nabta Playa was last abandoned in 4700 BCE, twenty-five hundred years before the Gilf Kebir. Modest later improvements of moisture, evidenced by tamarisk trees fixing dune sands, are apparent on the northern foothills of the Tibesti (1600–350 BCE and 90–640 CE) and in the Siwa Oasis (1210–1110 BCE and 65 BCE–560 CE). There are similar shifts in the time spans of the largest array of Sudanese tree types and game animals.

These discordances probably reflect the different thresholds at which surface waters became available or reliable through geohydrological conditions, as well as a complex interplay of augmented monsoonal and westerly rains. Groundwaters can be dated by the radiocarbon dating technique. Histograms of dated fossil water for the region show nonsynchronic patterns of short-term recharge in the northerly and southerly aquifers. In fact, the viable oases of the Libyan Desert today draw on fossil waters.

Until about 5000 BCE, the mobile peoples of the eastern Sahara were hunter-gatherers (despite the mainly unaccepted claims for domesticated cattle at Nabta Playa two millennia earlier, but sheep or goats may have been present a little earlier in places). Both the stone tools and the economy that are sometimes labeled Early Neolithic in the Libyan Desert were Epi-Paleolithic. A pastoral Neolithic, with some bifacial tools, was only established near Kharga and Dakhla Oases about 5500 BCE. These are the two oases that remained important throughout historical times, and the ones that show the closest archaeological affinities with the emerging Neolithic of the Nile Valley. Elsewhere, the northern Libyan Desert was only lightly and sporadically utilized by small groups after 3500 BCE, and the Libyan invaders of Old Kingdom Egypt probably came from the coastal semidesert.

The late prehistory and changing environments of the Libyan Desert remain of paramount interest for emerging desert adaptations in Africa, as well as for the incorporation of livestock into nomadic economies. Still, the sum of all the late prehistoric oases will have supported hundreds, not thousands, of people at the best of times—and they never formed a demographic reservoir that later drained into the Nile Valley. Occupation was seasonal or episodic, and whatever the patterns of periodic movements to better watered areas, they probably ran north and south, from and to better watered areas in the Sahel.

[*See also* Eastern Desert and Red Sea; Geography; Land and Soil; *and* Western Desert.]

### BIBLIOGRAPHY

Banks, Kimball M. *Climates, Cultures and Cattle: The Holocene Archaeology of the Eastern Sahara.* Dallas, 1984. A good presentation, with primary data on Nabta Playa.

Butzer, Karl W. "Wüste, Wüstentiere" (Desert and Desert Animals, English text). In *Lexikon der Ägyptologie*, 4:1291–1297. Wiesbaden, 1986.

Butzer, Karl W. "Late Quaternary Problems of the Egyptian Nile: Stratigraphy, Environments, Prehistory." *Paleorient* 23.2 (1998), 151–173.

Friedman, Renée, and Barbara Adams, eds. *The Followers of Horus.* Oxford, 1992. A diverse and useful collection, with several papers on rock art.

Haynes, C. Vance, C. H. Eyles, L. A. Pavlish, J. C. Ritchie, and M. Rybak. "Holocene Palaeoecology of the Eastern Sahara: Selima Oasis." *Quaternary Science Reviews* 8 (1989), 109–136.

Keding, Birgit. "Prehistoric Investigations in the Wadi Howar Region." *Kush* 17 (1997), 37–46.

Kröpelin, Stefan. "Palaeoclimatic Evidence from Early to Mid-Holocene Playas in the Gilf Kebir (Southwest Egypt)." *Palaeoecology of Africa* 18 (1987), 189–208.

Kuper, Rudolph, ed. *Forschungen zur Umweltgeschichte der Ostsahara.* Acta Praehistorica, 2. Cologne, 1989. A major compendium of recent research, mainly in German.

Moeyersons, Jan, P. M. Vermeersch, H. Beekman, and P. Van Peer. "Holocene Environmental Changes in the Gebel Umm Hamad, Eastern Desert, Egypt." *Geomorphology* 26 (1999), 297–312.

Neumann, Katharina. "Holocene Vegetation of the Eastern Sahara." *African Archaeological Review* 7 (1989), 97–116.

Pachur, Hans-Joachim and S. Kröpelin. "Wadi Howar: Paleoclimatic Evidence from an Extinct River System in the Southeastern Sahara." *Science* 237 (1987), 298–300.

Pachur, H. J., H. P. Roper, S. Kröpelin, and M. Goschin. "Late Quaternary Hydrography of the Eastern Sahara." *Berliner Geowissenschaftliche Abhandlungen* (A) 75.2 (1987), 331–384.

KARL W. BUTZER

**DESERTS.** *See* Eastern Desert and Red Sea; Geography; Land and Soil; *and* Western Desert.

**DESTRUCTION OF MANKIND.** The *Destruction of Mankind* is actually the initial portion of a longer composition known to modern scholars as the *Book of the Heavenly Cow.* The text of the *Destruction of Mankind*, which accompanies a depiction of the celestial cow, appears in the tombs of Sety I, Ramesses II, and Ramesses III in the Valley of the Kings. On the outermost shrine that encompassed the sarcophagus of Tutankhamun, there is an earlier representation of the heavenly cow, but the accompanying text omits the *Destruction* section. The *Destruction* story may be the oldest preserved narrative myth from ancient Egypt; there is an allusion to its existence in the *Instructions for Merikare,* composed toward the end of the First Intermediate Period. The role of the god Shu and the eight infinity deities in uplifting the sky also bears some relationship to the cosmogony of the Shu-spells in the *Coffin Texts* of the early Middle Kingdom.

The Destruction begins with the situation in which the sun god Re is reigning on earth over deities and people. During his old age, however, humans plot rebellion against him. Following the advice of the divine council, Re sends out his eye in the form of the goddess Hathor, who proceeds to decimate humanity. When Hathor returns, very pleased with her bloody mission, Re experiences a change of heart. In a ruse to deter the goddess from further slaughter, he orders red ocher to be added to beer, which is then poured out during the night in great abundance over the areas where Hathor would continue to slay people. Thinking the reddened beer is blood, Hathor becomes so drunk that she can no longer recognize mankind and desists from her mission.

Following that *Destruction* episode, Re, weary and fearful of another attack, withdraws from earth, placing himself on the back of the sky goddess Nut, in the form of a cow supported by the god Shu and eight infinity deities. The remainder of the text of the *Book of the Heavenly Cow* is complex; it provides numerous etiologies based on wordplay—which explain the origins of deities, places, and customs—and it contains instructions on how the celestial cow is to be drawn on the wall. The representation of the heavenly cow and the sun god voyaging along its belly may have given rise to the narrative myth explaining the way that earth and sky became related following mankind's rebellion. The rebellion itself may be a reflection of the political instability and social turmoil that existed during the First Intermediate Period, when the prestige of the institution of kingship suffered. The presence of the myth of the *Destruction of Mankind* in the context of the royal tomb can be related to the fact that at the king's death, his reign on earth ceased, as did Re's in the story; moreover, the pharaoh ascended to heaven to be amalgamated with the sun god, a concept commonly expressed in texts treating the king's passing.

### BIBLIOGRAPHY

Allen, James P. *Genesis in Egypt: The Philosophy of Ancient Egyptian Creation Accounts.* Yale Egyptological Studies, 2. New Haven, 1988. Relates the depiction of the celestial cow, uplifted by Shu and the eight infinity gods, to the Shu-spells in the Coffin Texts.

Assmann, Jan. "Die Verborgenheit des Mythos in Ägypten." *Göttinger Miszellen* 25 (1977), 7–43. Regards the myth of the heavenly cow as an explanation of the depiction of the cow, rather than vice versa.

Hornung, Erik. *Der ägyptische Mythos von der Himmelskuh: Eine Ätio-*

*logie der Unvollkommenen.* Orbis Biblicus et Orientalis, 46. Freiburg and Göttingen, 1982. The basic publication of the entire *Book of the Heavenly Cow,* with translation and commentary.

Lichtheim, Miriam. *Ancient Egyptian Literature, A Book of Readings.* vol. 2. Berkeley, 1976. Includes a translation of the *Destruction of Mankind.*

Piankoff, Alexandre. *The Shrines of Tut-Ankh-Amon,* edited by N. Rambova. New York, 1962. Provides a translation of the entire *Book of the Heavenly Cow.*

EDWARD F. WENTE

**DIET.** Sources of information for the study of food and diet in ancient Egypt are the artistic, written, and archaeological records, which include physical remains of food from domestic and funerary contexts, found at the sites of Tell el-Amarna, Malqata, Deir el-Medina, Illahun, and several tombs. These sources are supplemented by ethnohistorical accounts, ethnography, experimental archaeology, and the scientific testing of ancient materials.

The two staples of the ancient Egyptian diet were bread and beer, eaten by the entire population. They were augmented by various other foods: meat (including domesticated animals and wild game, poultry, and fish), vegetables, pulses and legumes (peas, beans, lentils), fruits, dairy products, grains, oils, butter, eggs, honey, and other sweets. Egyptian diet changed through time; first, from climatic and environmental changes and second, from trade. In the lush environment of the Predynastic period, when many wild species lived in and around the Nile River, hunting was the main source of meat. Hunted animals included antelope, gazelle, hippopotamus, crocodile, pig, ostrich, waterfowl, fish (riverine and marine), small game, hyena, wild ass, sheep, goats, and wild cattle. The variety and number of hunted animals decreased during dynastic times, owing to a combination of factors: animal domestication and the competition for resources from herd animals, environmental changes causing species to die out or migrate, and overhunting. The hunting of large mammals became more a sport for the wealthy than a serious way of acquiring food, but the poor continued to hunt small game, avifauna, and fish to augment their diet. Since the poor would have owned few domesticated animals (if any), they would have nurtured them for their valuable byproducts (milk, cheese, eggs) in preference to slaughtering them.

The Egyptians' main domesticates were those of the region: sheep, goats, cattle, donkeys, pigs, and poultry (see below). During the Old Kingdom, the Egyptians attempted to domesticate some other wild species, mainly antelopes (a group of ruminants that include oryx, bubalis, and ibex), and also the hyena (genus *Hyaena*). Moderate success attended antelope domestication, since those animals appeared repeatedly in the artistic record as food offerings; they were also found in the archaeozoological record. Antelopes were probably bred in captivity, rather than being fully domesticated—with *domestication* defined as the controlled selective breeding of animals. The majority of evidence for the domestication of the hyena comes from Old Kingdom *mastaba* tombs at Saqqara (the tombs of Kagemni and Mereruka), which contain scenes of hyenas being force-fed, in association with other force-fed animals, some of which were clearly domesticates. Still unclear is whether the hyenas were to be eaten or to be used for hunting instead of dogs (which is doubtful, since hyenas are primarily scavengers). The scarcity of hyena bones from settlement sites and the paucity of textual references would argue against their being commonly eaten.

The most important food animals were cattle (genus *Bos*), and the ovicaprines (the sheep and goats, *Ovis* and *Capra*). The majority of meat offerings found in tombs are of cattle and, in addition to meat, fat, and bone marrow, the cows provided milk (from which cream, butter, and cheese were made). Beef came from either oxen—castrated male cattle—or bulls. The oxen became fatter than the cows or bulls fed on the same diet and, therefore were more economical; that also helped spare the life of milk-producing cows. Almost the whole animal would be consumed, including most of the internal organs. Sheep and goats were the second most important domesticated meat source, and they were cheaper to raise than cattle, so small farmers and peasants kept them for their milk and meat. Sheep were especially important in ancient Egypt, since their rump fat was used in cooking, food preservation, medicines, perfumes, and unguents.

Pigs (genus *Sus*) were also common food animals of ancient Egypt, although it was long thought by Egyptologists that they were a taboo meat. Herodotus, the fifth-century BCE Greek traveler and historian was largely responsible for that belief; he had reported that the Egyptians never touched pigs or ate them, since they were identified with Seth and Typhonic forces. An Egyptian who accidentally touched a pig, he wrote, would have to plunge into the Nile for purification, and "swineherds [!]" were so shunned by other Egyptians that they had to live apart. Most early Egyptologists relied on the work of Herodotus, therefore his so-called reports of Egyptian diet and taboo have, until recently, formed much of the basis of Egyptological thought. In addition, the paucity of pigs in the artistic record (only nine representations from tombs) and the repeated identification of pigs with Typhonic forces (e.g., the *Contendings of Horus and Seth,* the *Book of Going Forth by Day* [*Book of the Dead,* chapters 112 and 125]) have served to support the idea that pigs were taboo. The Near Eastern and Egyptian pork taboo may actually stem from considerations of health, rather than from philosophy or sentiment. Animals can become taboo if they have offensive habits or smells, transmit diseases, or are impractical to rear. Pigs are pungent and have a tendency (necessary for their sweat glands) to wallow in mud and in their own excrement, which they sometimes eat. Pork spoils faster than most other meats unless consumed or preserved immediately. Pigs can also transmit trichinosis to humans, a disease caused by parasitic worms in the intestine and muscles, which results in diarrhea, pain, stiffness, swelling, sweating, insomnia, and even death. Such factors might contribute to pork being a less than desirable consumable, even if not taboo.

Other evidence contradicts the idea of a pork taboo. In Ramesses III's temple at Medinet Habu, list number 45 mentions pigs as offerings for a feast of the god Nefertum; Amenhotpe III gave one thousand pigs and one thousand piglets to the temple of Ptah at Memphis; and the Nauri decree states that pigs were bred in the Abydos temple domains of Sety I. The third dynasty (c.2687–2632 BCE) biography of Methen mentions pigs, and the title "Overseer of Swine" existed in the time of Senwosret I (r. 1971–1928 BCE). Pigs as food also featured in Deir el-Medina texts and in medical texts. In Early Dynastic sites, pig bones were found more frequently than the bones of cattle, sheep, or goats, especially in Lower Egypt at Maadi, Merimda Beni Salama, Buto, and Helwan. At the Nile Delta site of Kom el-Hisn, the bones of domestic pigs comprised the largest number of animal bones found. Pig bones have also been recovered from Armant, Tukh, Abydos, and Malqata. As Barry Kemp reported in the *Amarna Reports* I (London, 1984), the workmen's village at Tell el-Amarna has yielded pig bones scored with butchery marks, pigpens, and evidence of pork processing. Pigs are easily bred for food, since they reproduce quickly, require little herding, and forage in fields and in human debris. They were probably regarded as a cheap, low-status food. Thus, the absence of pigs from important funerary contexts might be due to elitism, an economic snobbery, or their cultural association with the god Seth. Perhaps the pig was taboo only in certain situations (e.g., funerary contexts), or for certain people (e.g., priests), or perhaps for all people at specific times of the year (holy/unholy days, feasts, etc.), or perhaps there was an evolving avoidance with time.

Herodotus had reported in the fifth century BCE that fish were taboo for priests in ancient Egypt; Diodorus Siculus, the first-century BCE writer, extended this ban to everyone. The fish taboo might actually derive from the Egyptian belief that fish had consumed the penis of the dismembered god Osiris and, therefore, in deference to the god, fish were forbidden food. Generally, the Oxyrhynchus fish (*Mormyrus*) was named as the offender, although sometimes the *Barbus bynni* (a carp-like fish) or

even mullets (*Mugil*) were considered responsible. Possibly this taboo dated only to the eighth century BCE, when Piya's victory stela spoke of the taboo nature of fish, or to Greco-Roman times, rather than to the earlier pharaonic period. Fish appear continuously in the artistic and literary records (in offerings, taxes, and payments), as well as in the archaeozoological record. A cooked fish was featured in the funerary repast of the Early Dynastic period tomb 3477 at Saqqara, dried fish have been found in other tombs as offerings, and miniature *Shilby* were used as votives at Mendis. Of the more than fifty-six species of riverine and marine fish available to the ancient Egyptians, most if not all were probably caught (by net, harpoon, or angling) and consumed.

Egyptian bird life (avifauna) was rich and varied. It was not restricted to the species indigenous to the Nile Valley but was expanded by the migration paths of several species who stopped over between Europe and Africa. The diet of ancient Egypt might have included partridges, quails, pigeons, doves, and various aquatic birds, including many species of ducks and geese. Several examples of cooked and preserved birds have been recovered from funerary contexts (e.g., Kha, Senenmut, and the Valley of the Kings). The eggs of several birds also formed a significant part of the diet; jars filled with duck eggs have been found in New Kingdom tombs and ostrich eggs were especially prized and carefully consumed, leaving the shell to be used for beads or vessels. In the Late period, eggs were placed in tombs, sometimes mummified, as food offerings for the deceased and as symbols of rebirth.

Chicken (*Gallus domesticus*), the most common form of poultry today, was not indigenous to ancient Egypt but was originally a jungle fowl from Southeast Asia. It probably arrived in Egypt by way of India and Syria, in the fifth or fourth century BCE. A pre-Ptolemaic representation of what can be interpreted as a chicken is an ink drawing on a small ostracon found by Howard Carter in Thebes. To date, however, no chicken bones have been found in any Egyptian site before Greco-Roman times.

The Egyptians ate some small animals, such as mice (genus *Mus*) and hedgehogs (family Erinaceidae). Mouse bones have been found in the stomachs of human mummies, and there are several textual allusions to the eating of mice. Oil of mouse was a common ingredient in medicinal recipes, and it was possibly used in food. Perhaps the Egyptians, like the Romans, force-fed mice on special foods (such as nuts and raisins) and then cooked them. In Old Kingdom *mastaba* tombs, hedgehogs were shown in art as food offerings, probably prepared, coated with clay, and baked in the fire; when they were ready, the clay coating would be cracked open, removing the prickly spines of the hedgehog with it, leaving the tender flesh.

Cereal crops were the basis for the most commonly

consumed items in ancient Egypt—bread and beer. Since Neolithic times, these grains were the major crops in the Nile Valley. They were used as a measure of wealth, to estimate, allocate, and pay taxes, and as payment of wages. Evidence of cereal use, in the form of grinding stones and sickles, came both from settlement and funerary contexts, and the remains of cereals were found in the intestines and stomachs of mummies. Examination has shown that emmer wheat (*Triticum dicoccum*) and barley (*Hordeum distichum* and *Hordeum vulgare*) were the commonly cultivated grains in the pharaonic period and that both were used for bread and beer.

Bread was the food available to all Egyptians regardless of rank, forming the basis of any meal. It was the first item listed in offering texts. Egyptian workers were often paid in bread and beer or in measures of grain. Bread was generally made of emmer wheat, although barley was occasionally used, as was lotus-seed flour and tiger-nut flour for special loaves. After harvesting, the grain was winnowed, sieved, and stored in granaries until needed. To make flour, it was ground and pounded in a saddle quern. Often, grit from the quern mixed into the grain, making it easier to grind but also producing a gritty bread that was hard on the teeth (as attested by the tooth wear on most Egyptian mummies; excessively worn teeth are common in Egyptian mummies, and the exposed pulp cavity became a breeding ground for infections that caused abscesses). The ground flour was kneaded with water or milk and salt. Although it is still unclear as to when yeast was first used in dough, this would be the point in the process at which it was added; alternatively, natural airborne yeasts might have been used to make the bread rise, as was documented by Mark Lehner at Giza (see "Rediscovering Egypt's Bread Baking Technology," *National Geographic*, January 1995, pp. 32–35). The dough was shaped into loaves—round, oval, or triangular—or placed in molds and baked inside an oven.

Beer, the other important product of cereal grains, followed bread in the standard funerary offering formula. Several jars containing beer have been found in Egyptian tombs of all periods. Beer and bread making were generally performed at the same locations. Egyptian beer was thick, rather like gruel, and highly nutritious, thus an important part of the diet. Both bread and beer were made in the home, while the excess was used for trade.

Wine pressed from grapes was also used in ancient Egypt, but it was for the wealthy and elite. Most vineyards were located in the Nile Delta and at the oases. Wine containers (amphorae) have been found as tomb offerings and in settlement sites, such as Tell el-Amarna and Malqata. Vintages (type and year of production) were marked on the jar or on the bung, with the name of the vineyard owner and the vineyard of origin. The quality of wine was also sometimes on the label: "good," "very good," or "very very good" was found on the jars from Malqata, Tell el-Amarna, and tomb 62 in the Valley of the Kings. The date of production was important, since Egyptian wine was not particularly long-lasting and had to be consumed well within a year of production. In Greco-Roman and Coptic times, that was less important; the amphorae were by then rendered more impermeable, with coats of resin on their interiors, a Greco-Roman innovation.

Other alcoholic beverages included date wine, made from the fruit of *Phoenix dactylifera*, the date palm tree. Palm wine, made from the fermented sap of the same tree, was obtained by incising the top of the tree at the base of the fronds. There was also fig wine, made from *Ficus carica*. Some debate exists as to whether the ancient Egyptian word *shedeh* meant pomegranate wine or pomegranate juice (genus *Punica*). Alcoholic beverages of many sorts formed an important part of the Egyptian diet; a few Theban tombs of the New Kindom show in tomb art the unfortunate results of overindulgence on the part of banqueters (e.g., Djeserkaraseneb, tomb 38).

A large portion of the Egyptian diet was composed of fruits, vegetables, and their byproducts. Those were more readily available than meat to the average Egyptian and, consequently, the main source of nourishment after bread and beer. Long-shooted green onions (scallions, genus *Allium*) were the most common accompaniment to bread. According to Herodotus, the pyramids were constructed by workers whose staple foods were onions, garlic (also *Allium*), and radishes (genus *Raphanus*). Garlic, eaten plain or used to flavor food, has been found in tombs, notably that of Tutankhamun. Both onions and garlic were also used extensively in medicinals—to treat blood disorders, colds, and stomach complaints. Archaeological evidence shows that another *Allium*, the leek, was most probably grown in ancient Egypt, although perhaps only from the late New Kingdom onward.

Other vegetables were lettuce (genus *Lactuca*), celery (genus *Apium*), cucumber (genus *Cucumis*), and perhaps a type of Old World squash (genus *Cucurbita*). Egyptian lettuce resembled romaine (cos) lettuce, with elongated leaves; it was noted as an aphrodisiac and was sacred to the ithyphallic fertility god Min. Lettuce seeds were used to make lettuce oil. Celery was known in New Kingdom times and was eaten raw and used as a flavoring in stews. When the cucumber first arrived in ancient Egypt is as yet unknown; some seeds have been tentatively identified as cucumber from New Kingdom archaeological contexts. Vegetables resembling cucumbers are also depicted in art, on offering tables, although they may actually be gourds, squash, or even a form of melon, all of which existed in ancient Egypt. Egyptian terms for these plants do nothing to clarify the situation; the remarks of classical authors

DIET. *Women at a banquet*. The tables on the left are piled with a large variety of foods. Drawing of an eighteenth dynasty painting from the tomb of Nebamun at Dra Abul Naga, now in the British Museum.

on this subject only serve to intensify the confusion. Although turnips (genus *Brassica*) were consumed in Greco-Roman times—in boiled, stewed, fried, and pickled forms—some debate exists on their use before this period.

Aquatic plants played a large role in the Egyptian diet. The tubers of sedges (family Cyperaceae), including papyrus, are very rich in carbohydrates, protein, and fats; they were eaten raw, boiled, roasted, or ground into flour. Cyperus-grass tubers (tiger-nuts) have been found in tombs and in the intestines of mummies from Neolithic times onward. They were the basis for an Egyptian dessert made of tiger-nut flour and honey, the recipe for which appears in Rekhmire's tomb (Theban tomb 100). The seeds of lotus and similar flowering aquatic plants were also eaten raw, dried, or ground up for flour; the roots and stem were edible as well and a cheap source of good nutrition.

Legumes provided a large proportion of protein for commoners and included lentils, peas, fava beans, lupines, lobia, and chickpeas. Evidence for them is varied and, in some cases, disputed for pharaonic times but not for Greco-Roman times. Models as well as real examples of chickpeas, lobia, and lentils have been found in tombs (e.g., Valley of the Kings tomb 62), and significant textual evidence exists for the presence of all these legumes in pharaonic Egypt. Peas were cultivated only from the Middle Kingdom onward, but lentils were grown from Neolithic times throughout the Near East and Egypt.

The most common fruit in ancient Egypt was the date, eaten fresh, dried, baked, in beer, and cooked. Other fruits were figs (the sycomore fig, *Ficus sycomorus*, which is small and not overly sweet, as well as regular figs), grapes (and raisins), *dom* palm nuts (eaten raw or steeped to make a juice), persea (genus *Mimusops*), and *nabk* berries (genus *Zizyphus*), which grew wild and were a frequent funerary offering; their flesh might also have been used as flour. Melons (native to Asia and sub-Saharan Africa) may also have been eaten in Egypt; some seeds have allegedly been found in tombs and other excavated sites. The New Kingdom was a time of great change in the Egyptian diet, owing to increased contact through trade and warfare with other regions. New plants were introduced then and cultivated in Egypt, such as pomegranates, probably introduced by Thutmose III. Apricots (genus *Prunus*) might have been grown in New Kingdom times or might have been imported. The apple (genus *Malus*) in ancient Egypt is uncertain, although it might have been imported and grown on a small scale (in palace orchards, perhaps) during the Ramessid period. Other fruit trees (such as pear, quince, plum, and peach) were only introduced in Greco-Roman times. Nuts (such as filberts, walnuts, pinenuts, and pistachios) were also introduced in Greco-Roman times; although almonds were in the New Kingdom tomb 62 in the Valley of the Kings and in the tomb of Kha, the archaeobotanical evidence suggests that they were imported rather than grown in Egypt.

Olives (genus *Olea*) were present in Egypt and were eaten raw or pickled in brine. To date, however, olive oil, ubiquitous in Greco-Roman times, is not known from pharaonic times. Vegetable oils were commonly produced and used in cooking in ancient Egypt. In addition to lettuce-seed and radish-seed oil, there was oil from safflower (*Carthamus tinctorius*), from the New Kingdom onward; *ben* oil, made from the pods of the *Moringa aptera* tree; balanos oil, made from the *Balanites aegyptiaca* nut; and oil from sesame seeds (*Sesamum indicum*), common from the New Kingdom onward. Animal fat (*aadj*) was also used for cooking. Fat jars have been recovered from settlement sites, such as Deir el-Medina, Malqata, and Tell el-Amarna.

Honey was the main sweetening ingredient in ancient Egypt. Bees were bred in special pottery hives, and their honey was collected (after smoking out the bees), as was the beeswax; both were used for many medicinal and practical purposes. Honey was a precious commodity, available only to the wealthy; the poor used dates or did without. The other sweetener in ancient Egypt was carob, from the leguminous tree *Ceratonia siliqua*. The carob pod was the basis for the ancient Egyptian hieroglyph for sweet (*nedjem*).

The methods of cooking employed by the Egyptians were stewing, boiling, grilling, frying, and roasting. Spices and herbs were used to flavor their foods, and if some of those were indigenous to Egypt, others were obtained by trade. Dill (*Anethum graveolens*), fenugreek (*Trigonella*), parsley (*Petroselinum sativus*), thyme (*Thymus*), coriander (*Coriandrum*), white and black cumin (*Nigella sativa*), fennel (*Foeniculum*), marjoram (*Origanum*), and possibly mint (*Mentha*) were all native to Egypt. Cinnamon and peppercorns were imported from Southeast Asia and the East Indies and available to wealthy Egyptians by New Kingdom times. Excess food was preserved by drying or salting. Thus dates and raisins were kept, as were meat, fish, and poultry that were dried and salted, to be used in lean times or during travel.

Limited evidence is available about meal times. Probably, the wealthy would have eaten two if not three times a day: a light meal in the early morning, followed by a large lunch, and an evening dinner. Peasants would probably have eaten a simple breakfast of beer, bread, and onions, with their main meal being late in the afternoon. Bread and beer were consumed by all levels of society, probably as a basis for all meals, while wine was drunk by the wealthy or on special occasions. Meat of some type would have been available to most of the population at least once or twice a week. Beef was expensive and therefore consumed frequently only by the royal family, the nobility, the wealthy, the resident priests in temples where animals were sacrificed, and by butchers. Beef would have been available to the poor only on feast days, when the meat of sacrificed animals was distributed to them. Private individuals only slaughtered an ox for some grand event or when the meat was to be preserved. Mutton and pork would have been available to more people than was beef, since artisans and people of moderate wealth reared their own sheep, goats, and pigs (the ancient Egyptian "small cattle") in their own compounds or on small pieces of land. Some evidence indicates that meat was sold, generally from the temple surplus. Poultry, wild or domestic, and fish, would have been affordable for all but the poorest, since birds and fish were easily available by hunting and fishing. The major protein sources for the lower levels of society, therefore, came from legumes, eggs, and cheese, as well as the beer and bread. Everyone's diet was augmented by vegetables and fruits. The finest type of dessert bread, cakes, and wine were prepared only for the wealthy.

Osteological (skeletal) evidence indicates that most ancient Egyptians, unlike many Nubians, had balanced diets. Human skeletal remains show relatively few examples of lines of arrested growth (Harris lines) formed; there is also little evidence of anemia or other diet-related abnormalities.

[See also Agriculture; Animal Husbandry; Beer; Bees and Honey; Bread; Cattle; Fish; Fruits; Oils and Fats; Poultry; Vegetables; and Wine.]

## BIBLIOGRAPHY

Blackman, A. M. "The King of Egypt's Grace Before Meat." *Journal of Egyptian Archaeology* 31(1945), 57–73. Interesting discussion of meal times and types, amongst other things.

Brewer, D. J., and R. F. Friedman. *Fish and Fishing in Ancient Egypt.* Warminster, 1989. List of fish found in ancient Egypt, including ways of catching them.

Crawford, D. J. "Food: Tradition and Change in Hellenistic Egypt." *World Archaeology* 11 (1979–1980), 136–146. Discussion of possible innovations in Egyptian diet during Hellenistic times.

Darby, W., et al. *Food: The Gift of Osiris.* 2 vols. London, 1977. Covers all types of food consumed by the ancient Egyptians.

Dixon, D. M. "A Note on Cereals in Ancient Egypt." In *The Domestica-*

*tion and Exploitation of Plants and Animals*, edited by P. J. Ucko and G. W. Dimbleby. London, 1969. A discussion on the types of cereals available to the ancient Egyptians.

Emery, W. B. *A Funerary Repast in an Egyptian Tomb of the Archaic Period*. Leiden, 1962. Lists and discusses a set of funerary offerings from the Archaic (Early Dynastic) period.

Geller, J. "From Prehistory to History: Beer in Egypt." In *The Followers of Horus*, edited by R. Friedman and B. Adams, pp. 19–26. Oxford, 1992. Presents the history of beer consumption in Egypt.

Hecker, H. M. "A Zooarchaeological Inquiry into Pork Consumption in Egypt from Prehistoric to New Kingdom Times." *Journal of the American Research Center in Egypt* 19 (1982), 59–71. An overview of the pork taboo and the archaeological evidence.

Houlihan, P. F., and S. M. Goodman. *The Birds of Ancient Egypt*. Warminster, 1986. A comprehensive list of avifauna in ancient Egypt.

Ikram, S. "Food for Eternity I, II." *KMT: A Modern Journal of Egyptology* 5.1 (1994), 25–33; 5.2 (1994), 53–60, 75–76. Popular articles dealing with the foods of ancient Egypt and how they were prepared.

Ikram, Salima. *Choice Cuts: Meat Production in Ancient Egypt*. Leuven, 1996. Discusses types of meats available, how animals were slaughtered, and how the meat was preserved; section also on meat consumption.

Lesko, L. L. *King Tut's Wine Cellar*. Berkeley, 1977. Discusses wine and vintages, using the Tutankhamun material as a basis.

Miller, R. "Counting Calories in Egyptian Ration Texts." *Journal of the Economic and Social History of the Orient* 34 (1991), 257–269. Interesting article calculates grain rations and caloric intake.

Nicholson, P., and I. Shaw (eds.). *Ancient Egyptian Materials and Technology*. Cambridge, forthcoming. Useful chapters deal with wine, beer, meat, and plants.

Nunn, John F. *Ancient Egyptian Medicine*. London, 1996. Excellent book on diseases, including those related to diet.

Poo, Mu-chou. *Wine and Wine Offering in the Religion of Ancient Egypt*. London, 1995. Covers wine production and the role of wine in diet and religion.

Samuel, D. "Their Staff of Life." In *Amarna Reports*, 5, by B. J. Kemp, pp. 253–290. London, 1989. Clear discussion of bread-making.

Samuel, D. "Archaeology of Ancient Egyptian Beer." *Journal of the American Society of Brewing Chemists* 54.1 (1996), 3–12. Good description of brewing and Egyptian beer.

SALIMA IKRAM

**DIODOROS.** *See* Ancient Historians.

**DIORITE AND RELATED ROCKS.** Geologically, diorite is a dark-gray or greenish igneous rock, consisting chiefly of feldspar and hornblende. Egyptologists, however, misapplied the name diorite to rocks from Chephren's quarry, 65 kilometers (40 miles) northwest of Abu Simbel on the Nile. This quarry is named after the fourth dynasty king Khafre (Chephren, in its Greek form), who used the rock for six statues found in his valley temple at Giza (the site is also sometimes called the Tushka or Gebel el-Asr quarry). The so-called Chephren's diorite is misnamed and actually comprises two varieties of the metamorphic rock called gneiss: the first is a greenish-black

and light-gray banded gabbro gneiss, which was used primarily for royal statuary during the fourth, fifth, and sixth dynasties, as well as in the twelfth; the second is a light-colored anorthosite gneiss, with greenish-black streaks and patches in a light-gray matrix, which was used primarily for small vessels in the late Predynastic period and in the first through sixth dynasties. In ancient Egypt, this gneiss was called *mntt*. In bright sunlight, the rock has a bluish glow that probably attracted quarrying, because of its iridescence (this quality is not seen under the indoor lighting of museums, however).

A true diorite was also used in ancient Egypt, the exceptionally coarse-grained, pegmatitic rock from Wadi Umm Shegilat in the Eastern Desert. This rock consists of greenish-black crystals of hornblende, up to several centimeters in length, set in a light-gray to pale-pink matrix of plagioclase feldspar. It was widely employed for small vessels and occasionally for animal figurines from the late Predynastic period through the Old Kingdom. Such objects are commonly misidentified in the older Egyptological literature as composed of porphyry. The same diorite quarry was used by the Romans during the first two centuries CE. They exported it from Egypt and used it for small columns, basins, pedestals, wall tiles, and pavement tiles. Partially worked materials in the quarry were all dated to the Roman period—stone blocks with saw marks that are not found in any other Egyptian quarry. The extreme coarse grain of the diorite there may have caused the Romans to use saws in shaping the blocks, rather than chisels and picks, as was done in other quarries. The Wadi Umm Shegilat quarry was rediscovered about 1950, but the rock it supplied has long been known from both Roman and later buildings outside Egypt, especially those in Italy, where it is called *granito della colonna* ("granite of the column"), after one particular pillar in the Basilica of Saint Prassede in Rome. The Roman and earlier Egyptian names for this rock (true diorite) are unknown.

Other igneous rocks with compositions similar to and gradational with that of diorite were worked by the Romans in the Eastern Desert. These include (1) quartz diorite, from quarries in Wadi Umm Balad, near Mons Porphyrites (Ar., Gebel Dokhan), and in both Wadi Barud and Wadi Fatiri el-Bayda, near Mons Claudianus; (2) gabbro, from quarries in Wadi Umm Wikala, near Wadi Semna, and in Wadi Maghrabiya; and (3) granodiorite, from a quarry at Bir Umm Fawakhir, near Wadi Hammamat and Wadi el-Sid. Yet another granodiorite was quarried from the early dynastic through Roman times—the so-called but misnamed black granite, from Aswan.

## BIBLIOGRAPHY

Aston, Barbara G. *Ancient Egyptian Stone Vessels: Materials and Forms*. Studien zur Archäologie und Geschichte Altägyptens, 5.

DIORITE AND RELATED ROCKS. *Anorthosite gneiss statue of a scribe, eighteenth dynasty.* This statue came from Buhen in Nubia. (University of Pennsylvania Museum, Philadelphia. Neg. # S5–23177)

Heidelberg, 1994. Discusses the use of gneiss and diorite for small vessels.

Aston, Barbara G., James A. Harrell, and Ian M. E. Shaw. "Stone." In *Ancient Egyptian Materials and Technologies,* edited by Ian M. E. Shaw and Paul T. Nicholson. London, 1999. Offers an up-to-date summary of the petrology, uses, and sources of all igneous and metamorphic rocks used in ancient Egypt.

Brown, V. Max, and James A. Harrell. "Topographical and Petrological Survey of Ancient Roman Quarries in the Eastern Desert of Egypt." In *The Study of Marble and Other Stones Used in Antiquity— ASMOSIA III, Athens,* edited by Yannis Maniatis, Norman Herz, and Yannis Bassiakos, pp. 221–234. London, 1995. Provides a comprehensive survey of Roman quarries in the Eastern Desert.

Harrell, James A., and V. Max Brown. "Chephren's Quarry in the Nubian Desert of Egypt." *Nubica* 3.1 (1994), 43–57. Describes the results of a recent survey of Chephren's (Khafre's) quarry, with emphasis on the rocks it supplied; gives a complete bibliography of all the earlier work at the site.

JAMES A. HARRELL

**DIPLOMATIC MARRIAGES.** *See* Marriage and Divorce.

**DISEASE.** Many of the diseases prevalent in Egypt in ancient times still occur there today. The ever-changing pattern of disease in the world is, however, reflected in important differences between pharaonic times and the present. Many conditions well known today were unknown in ancient Egypt: for example, syphilis, leprosy, and bubonic plague probably did not appear until after the pharaonic era, and cancer was very rare. A difficult problem for identification is the incidence of diseases that are today unknown or much modified. Fortunately, the special geography, climate, and literary legacy of Egypt have enabled an unparalleled insight into the state of disease among ancient Egyptians.

**Sources of Information.** The study of the pattern of disease in pharaonic times depends on three main sources: human remains, artistic portrayals, and the accounts of disease in the medical papyri. Data from those sources do not greatly overlap, and each has serious limitations.

*Human remains.* The locations of tombs and burial grounds, as well as the hot, dry climate of Egypt favored excellent preservation of human remains. Simple burial in hot sand often resulted in desiccation proceeding faster than putrefaction. Then, too, the process of mummification frequently resulted in the good preservation of organs left in the body; however, the brain was sometimes removed and discarded, and the liver, lungs, stomach, and intestines were often removed and placed in canopic jars, where their state of preservation has usually been poor. The overenthusiastic use of resin, pitch, and cosmetic packing in the mummification process tended to cause severe damage to soft tissue, as did the attentions of tomb robbers.

Scientific paleopathology was pioneered by Marc Armand Ruffer, professor of bacteriology in Cairo from 1896 to 1917. Today, the objective has become the extraction of maximal information with minimal destruction of irreplaceable material. Simple radiography has been supplemented with the more informative, computerized tomography, which can be undertaken without opening a mummy cartonnage. Fiber-optic endoscopy allows the sampling of tissues, which can be examined by light microscopy and by electron microscopy, in both the transmission and scanning modes. Studies of antibodies require only very small samples of tissue and have enormous potential for population-based studies.

The recovery and replication of DNA (deoxyribonucleic acid) has provided the possibility of determining individual genetic profiles, sex determinations, kinship studies, genetic diseases, and, perhaps, the identification of ethnic groups. The DNA from bacteria, viruses, and parasites may also be sampled from infected individuals, and skeletal remains are a very important resource for this and for population-based studies.

In ancient Egypt, the average life expectancy was thirty to thirty-six years, although some people lived much longer, even into or beyond their eighties, notably Pepy II

and Ramesses II. Known burials for those over the age of sixty are rare, but those that exist show the expected changes of aging, including osteoarthritis, arteriosclerosis, and calcification in major blood vessels. Texts describe the ravages of age in explicit terms.

*Representations of the body.* Male tomb owners and important people were usually portrayed in exuberant good health. Women were generally shown as tall, slender, and beautiful, with graceful poise. For servants and occasionally for the tomb owner, the canon of proportions might be set aside in favor of what appears to be realistic portrayal of disability. There are, however, important caveats in the interpretation of such representations. For example, special conventions may have applied to certain conditions or diseases, particularly dwarfism, blindness, and obesity; then, too, the highly atypical artistic style of the Amarna period has created a special problem.

*Medical papyri.* Injuries are very well described, particularly in the glosses of the Edwin Smith Papyrus. However, the medical (as opposed to surgical) papyri usually assumed that the diagnosis was already made and merely identified the disease by a name—one usually unknown outside the medical papyri and thus difficult to translate. The medical papyri tell us nothing of the prevalence or the epidemiology of diseases.

**Parasitic Diseases.** Parasites enter the human body through the ingestion of water or foods or by contact with the soil, infected people, or substances. Some are acquired through insect bites or the bites of other animals. Undoubtedly, parasitic diseases were prevalent and probably a major cause of ill health and early demise for ancient Egyptians.

Microscopic identification of the eggs of schistosomiasis (also called bilharziasis) and the detection of the schistosome's antigen have indicated schistosomiasis in bodies from Predynastic times to the Roman era. Evidence of the disease in the medical papyri is, however, less secure. Recent opinion has veered away from translating the 'ꜣ'-disease as "hematuria (blood in the urine) caused by schistosomiasis." No text links 'ꜣ' directly to the bladder, and it is not certain that "voiding of much blood" (*wsšt snf 'šꜣ*) necessarily refers to urine. Perhaps schistosomiasis and hematuria were so common that they were considered normal (as they were later in some locales). A calcified Guinea-worm (*Dracunculus medinensis*) was found in the abdominal wall of mummy number 1770 of the Manchester Museum Mummy Project. Parts of filarial worms were found in a Leeds Museum mummy, Natsef-Amun. Adult worms of some species can block the lymph system, causing swelling and thickening of the skin (as in elephantiasis). Although in tomb paintings there are many representations of the enlarged male external genitalia of servants, the typical swollen legs of elephantiasis are almost never portrayed. Larval forms of strongyliodiasis have been found in the intestinal wall of the mummy Asru of the Manchester Museum Mummy Project. The ancient Egyptians were probably unaware of their existence, and there is no obvious mention in the medical papyri. A roundworm egg was found in the mummy PUM II, and tapeworm eggs were in the mummy ROM I (Nakht), who was also infected with *Trichinella*. A hydatid cyst was also found. The papyri contain unequivocal references to intestinal infestation by parasitic worms, with *ḥrrt* and perhaps *ḏdft* being general terms for worms; *pnd* and *ḥf3t* probably refer to particular species, but precise identification is difficult. Other Old Egyptian words (*ḥsbt, btw, s3, sp,* and *fnt*) also carrying the worm determinative may have only metaphorical meaning. The *Para* Sight™-F test for the plasmodial antigen of malaria has demonstrated many cases of malarial infection with *Plasmodium falciparum* in a series of naturally desiccated bodies from the Predynastic period and embalmed mummies from the New Kingdom, twenty-fifth dynasty, and the Nubian Ballana period (350–550 CE). No gross pathological changes are to be expected in malaria-infected mummies, and the medical papyri are silent on malaria's characteristic recurrent bouts of fever and chills.

**Bacterial and Viral Infections.** Bacteria and viruses have not yet been identified in mummies or in ancient skeletons, so we must infer the existence of infections from the appearance of the mummies and DNA studies, with some additional clues from the medical papyri and the tomb illustrations.

*Tuberculosis.* Dan Morse and colleagues reviewed thirty-one cases (from the Predynastic to the twenty-first dynasty), mostly with gross pathological appearances highly suggestive of bone tuberculosis, a bacterial infection. The best authenticated case showed classic spinal tuberculosis (Pott's disease), with the collapse of a thoracic vertebra, angular kyphosis (hump back), and tuberculous suppuration tracking downward toward the right groin (apsoas abscess). There are many tomb scenes portraying hump-backed servants, but from them it is difficult to distinguish between Pott's disease, porter's hump, ankylosin spondylitis, and bad posture. Andreas Nerlich and colleagues have detected DNA of *Mycobacterium tuberculosis* in a New Kingdom mummy's lung with the appearance of tuberculosis. Dan Morse has also described another possible case of pulmonary tuberculosis.

*Leprosy.* No unequivocal case of a mummy or skeleton from pharaonic times has presented the appearance of leprosy, a bacterial infection. The earliest case is from a sixth-century CE Coptic Christian burial at el-Bigha in Nubia. It has been suggested that "Khonsu's tumor ('3t nt ḥnsw)," as mentioned in the Ebers Papyrus might be nodular leprosy, but there are alternative interpretations.

*Tetanus.* Evidence of tetanus, a bacterial infection, is not to be expected in human remains. Yet Case 7 of the Edwin Smith Papyrus, describes lockjaw and distortion of the face, suggesting tetanus.

*Plague.* No mummy has shown signs of bubonic plague, a bacterial infection, and the medical papyri are silent on the subject. There is some evidence, however, that bubonic plague reached Egypt only after the Moslem era began.

*Sepsis and abscesses.* Sepsis (a toxic state of infection that enters the bloodstream) must have been common in ancient Egypt, but there is no convincing evidence in mummies. There are, however, highly suggestive descriptions of sepsis and abscesses (pus-filled swellings) in the medical papyri. The words for "pus" (*ryt* and *wḥdw*) are strongly supported by context, although *wḥdw* undoubtedly has other important meanings. A graphic account of an infected wound is given in the Edwin Smith Papyrus, Case 41.

*Osteomyelitis.* Nontuberculous osteomyelitis, a bacterial infection, is surprisingly rare in the skeletal remains of ancient Egyptians. There are many healed fractures in which the bone shows no signs of such infection.

*Poliomyelitis.* Evidence for this viral infection comes largely from the Stela of Roma, where a man is portrayed with a grossly wasted and shortened leg, strongly suggesting poliomyelitis contracted in childhood, before the completion of the growth of his leg bones; an equinus deformity of the foot thereby compensates for the shortened leg. An alternative diagnosis would be an equinus variety of club foot. The mummy of the nineteenth dynasty pharaoh Siptah, usually diagnosed as suffering from club foot, has other abnormalities—actually suggesting the possibility of poliomyelitis. No mention of this disease exists in the medical papyri.

*Smallpox.* Diagnosis of this viral infection rests upon the appearance of the skin of well-preserved mummies. If correct, the most distinguished victim would be Ramesses V. Nothing in the medical papyri can be related to smallpox.

**Cancer and Other Tumors.** Untreated cancer often produces large tumors before death, which would be conspicuous in mummies. Yet tumors are extremely rare in both mummies and skeletons of pharaonic times. In part, this may be due to relatively early deaths, but an additional factor might be low levels of carcinogens.

The malignant tumors known from ancient Egypt include multiple erosions of a skull from the Old Kingdom, attributed to carcinoma of the nasopharynx, with widely scattered secondaries. Benign tumors include the celebrated osteochondroma of the femur in a skeleton from the fifth dynasty found in Giza; the cystadenoma of the ovary in the Granville mummy (Irty-senu), now in the British Museum; and the usual skeletal reaction to meningiomata in two skulls, one from the twentieth and one from the twenty-first dynasty. In the medical papyri, evidence of cancer is very uncertain. Khonsu's tumors were mentioned above, in relation to leprosy, and they might refer as well to cancer. The Ebers Papyrus, paragraph 813, refers to an "eating" (*wnmt*) of the uterus, which might also be construed as cancer.

**Diseases of Internal Organs.** There are major difficulties in the detection and identification of most diseases of the internal organs. The problems arise in both paleopathology and in the interpretation of the medical papyri.

*Cardiovascular system.* Atherosclerosis and the calcification of large arteries are common in the mummies of older persons, including the kings. Otherwise, our limited knowledge of their circulatory disorders must be gleaned from the medical papyri. The Ebers Papyrus, paragraph 855, is largely composed of a series of misplaced glosses, explaining terms used to describe pathological states of the heart. The link between the heart and the peripheral pulse was apparently understood, and heart failure may be the subject of a misplaced gloss (Ebers, paragraph 855e):

As to: "the heart (*ib*) weakens (*'md*)," it means the heart (*ḥзty*) does not speak, or it means the vessels (*mtw*) of the heart (*ḥзty*) are dumb.

Elsewhere in the Ebers Papyrus, there are hints of congestive cardiac failure, disordered rhythms of the heart, and possibly ischemic heart disease, with anginal pain radiating into the arm.

*Lungs.* Sand pneumoconiosis was found in the course of the Manchester Museum Mummy Project. Evidence for pulmonary tuberculosis is considered above. Paragraph 305 of the Ebers Papyrus announces the "Beginning of the remedies to drive out cough (*sryt*)," and paragraph 190 of the Ebers Papyrus describes what may be production of purulent sputum.

*Gastrointestinal system.* Paleopathology has shed little light on ancient diseases of the stomach and bowels. Although there remains uncertainty in the translation of *r-ib* as "stomach" (as in the Ebers Papyrus, paragraphs 188–208), much attention was devoted to its obstruction (*šn'*). The ancient Greek historian Herodotus noted that the Egyptians were obsessed with their bowels, and much of their pharmacopeia was devoted to facilitating bowel movements, with aperients "to drive out feces (*ḥs*)" and "to evacuate (*fgn* or *wsš*)," often with the unmistakable ideogram for defecation.

There are also many remedies to "cool or refresh (*sḳb*) the anus (*pḥwt*)" and to "drive out heat (*ṯзw*)," suggesting an infection, possibly fungal or one related to schistosomiasis. The Ebers Papyrus, paragraph 161, specifically refers to "the vessels (*mtw*) of the anus," which may mean hemorrhoids.

*Urinary system.* Stones in the kidney or bladder are very rare in mummies. The urinary section of the Ebers Papyrus (paragraphs 261–283) includes consideration of urine that is "plentiful" or "frequent" (*šз*). The former interpretation might refer to diabetes (with polyuria) and the latter to cystitis (with frequency of micturition). Paragraph 265 is "another [remedy] to eliminate obstruction (*šn'*) of heat (*ṯзw*) in the bladder, when he suffers retention (*ḥdbw*) of urine." Since heat suggests inflammation, obstruction and retention must mean outflow obstruction, caused perhaps by urethral stricture or an enlarged prostate gland. Reference has been made above to the difficulty in translating '*з*' as hematuria, the cardinal sign of schistosomiasis.

DISEASE. Table 1. *Important Medical Papyri*

| Title | Location | Approximate date of copy | Contents |
|---|---|---|---|
| Kahun (gynecology) | University College, London | 1820 BCE | gynecological |
| Ramesseum III, IV, V* | Oxford | 1700 BCE | gynecological, ophthalmic and pediatric |
| Edwin Smith | New York | 1550 BCE | surgical, mainly trauma |
| Ebers | Leipzig | 1500 BCE | general, mainly medical |
| Hearst* | California | 1450 BCE | general medical |
| London* | British Museum | 1300 BCE | mainly magical |
| Carlsberg VIII | Copenhagen | 1300 BCE | gynecological |
| Chester Beatty VI* | British Museum | 1200 BCE | rectal diseases |
| Berlin* | Berlin | 1200 BCE | general medical |
| Brooklyn snake* | Brooklyn Museum | 300 BCE | snake bite |
| London | British Museum | 250 CE | general medical |
| *and* Leiden | Leiden | 250 CE | *and* magical |
| Crocodilopolis | Vienna | 150 CE | general |

*No translation into English is available.

*Nervous system.* Although the ancient Egyptians did not understand the function of the brain, there are excellent descriptions of the neurological consequences of spinal injuries, as in the Edwin Smith Papyrus, Cases 31–33. There is also a possible reference to facial-nerve paralysis (Bell's palsy) in the Berlin Papyrus, paragraph 76. The Ebers Papyrus, paragraph 250, probably refers to migraine:

> Another [remedy] for suffering (*mrt*) in half the head (*gs-tp*). The skull of a catfish (*n'r*), fried in oil. Anoint the head therewith.

**Diseases of Women.** There is disappointingly little mention of gynecological disorders in the Kahun Papyrus, the so-called gynecological papyrus, which is much concerned with pregnancy tests and contraception. The Ebers Papyrus, paragraphs 783–839, contains a wide range of prescriptions for diseases of women.

*Problems relating to birth.* Prolapse of the uterus is known from human remains, and the Ebers Papyrus, paragraph 789, relates, "to cause the uterus (*mwt rmt*) of a woman to go down (*h3*) to its place (*st*)." The Kahun Papyrus, Case 34, refers to "a woman whose urine is in an irksome (*ḳsn*) place (*st*)," suggesting a fistula between the bladder and the vagina, which has also been observed in human remains.

*Other pathology.* The ovarian cyst of the Granville mummy was mentioned above. Amenorrhea was clearly defined in the Ebers Papyrus, paragraph 833, as "a woman who has spent many years without her menstruation (*ḥsmn*) coming." Excessive bleeding (menorrhagia) was not clearly defined, but there were remedies mentioned "to draw out (*itḥ*) the blood of a woman." The *h3'w* of the uterus (in the Kahun Papyrus, Cases 3, 7, and 10) has been variously translated as "discharges," "excrementa," and "defluxions." The context and the treatment gave no clues to the meaning. There were many remedies for "cooling the uterus" and "driving out heat," but the pathology remains unclear.

*The breast.* Remedies for the breast are embedded within the gynecological section of the Ebers Papyrus. Paragraph 808 mentions "the beginning of remedies to prevent the breasts going down," presumably referring to sagging. Reference to more serious disorders, such as tumors or those related to lactation, are difficult to discern.

**Disorders of Other Parts of the Body**

*Hernias and hydroceles.* The mummy of Ramesses V (of the twentieth dynasty) has a bulky but empty scrotum, which might indicate an inguinal hernia or possibly a hydrocele. Several tomb paintings and reliefs show servants with protuberances that resemble umbilical hernias. A marsh fowler in the tomb of Ankh-ma-hor shows a scrotal swelling that might be a large inguinal hernia or a hy-drocele. An abdominal swelling (*'3t*) "which comes forth when he coughs" was described in paragraph 864 of the Ebers Papyrus.

*Locomotor system.* Skeletal remains show many fractures, often well united. The bony changes of wear and tear have also been widely reported. Ankylosing spondylitis (fusion of the spine) has been well documented from Predynastic to Coptic times. A series of remedies to strengthen, soften, relieve pain, and soothe the *mtw* which seems to refer to the "muscular system," was described in paragraphs 627–694 of the Ebers Papyrus. There has been a remarkable lack of reports on nontuberculous infections, on gout, and on rickets.

*Eye diseases.* There is virtually no paleopathological evidence of eye disease, but there are many representations of blindness in ancient Egypt, particularly of harpists. The best source of information is from the papyri, particularly paragraphs 336–431 of the Ebers Papyrus. The Egyptian word for "blindness" (*špt*) is well attested, but most of the causes remain unclear. The *š3rw* disease of the eyes was treated with liver, suggesting the possibility of night blindness. Although cooked or even raw liver, applied locally, would be ineffective for a condition caused by vitamin A deficiency, the Kahun Papyrus, Case 1, recommends raw liver by mouth for "a woman who cannot see."

The Ebers Papyrus refers to a wide range of eye diseases that cannot be identified with any certainty, but *kkw* ("darkness") and *h3ty* ("cloudiness") might refer either to opacities in the cornea or in the lens (cataract); *dfdft* ("drip") may well mean excessive tearing (lacrymation), from a variety of causes. Perhaps *nh3t* (in paragraphs 350, 383, and 407) is "trachoma," since the adjective *nh3* has various meanings, including "uneven" and "terrible." Paragraph 424 describes troublesome eyelashes, growing inward to irritate the cornea, and *pdst* ("pellet") of the eye might be either a sty or a Meibomian cyst in paragraph 355.

*Ears and nose.* Deafness was well understood. The mummy PUM II had a perforated eardrum, suggesting a middle ear infection. Rather unclear diseases of the ears were also mentioned in paragraphs 764–770 of the Ebers Papyrus and in the Berlin Papyrus, paragraphs 70–71 and 200–203. Remedies for the nose are offered in paragraphs 761 and 418 of the Ebers Papyrus; *rš* and *ḥnt* are thought to mean "coryza" or "catarrh." Paragraph 762 provides a remedy for the unknown *ni3*-disease of the nose.

*Skin.* Mummies have shown a few examples of skin diseases (as reviewed in Brothwell and Sandison, 1967), but paragraphs 708–721 of the Ebers Papyrus, paragraphs 150–154 of the Hearst Papyrus, and the *verso* of the Edwin Smith Papyrus (Cases 21, 3–8) list remedies for skin complaints that are difficult to identify and which may belong to the realm of beauty care. Concerns about skin problems are remarkable for the omissions rather than for the discussions.

**Teeth.** The wearing down of teeth (called attrition) was almost universal—caused by the chewing of hard particulate matter in food. Attrition resulted partly from the grinding of grain with stones and partly from the contamination of grains with wind-blown sand after the harvest and during its processing to separate grains from chaff. There was gradual improvement in these matters in the Late period. Caries (cavities) were extremely rare until the first millennium BCE, probably from the absence of sugars in the diet; their incidence increased during the Ptolemaic era, as attrition declined. Caries reached high levels in the early Christian era, probably owing to dietary changes. Dental abscesses were quite common, arising from caries or through the tooth pulp that became exposed by attrition. Periodontal (gum) disease was widespread, as well, leading to loss of alveolar supporting bone, thus loosening the teeth.

[*See also* Deformity; Magic, *article on* Magic and Medicine; *and* Medicine .]

### BIBLIOGRAPHY

Breasted, James H. *The Edwin Smith Surgical Papyrus.* 2 vols. Chicago, 1930. Facsimile reproduction, hieroglyphic transcription, English translation, and exhaustive analysis of the Edwin Smith Papyrus; an outstanding work, essential for the understanding of ancient Egyptian expertise in the management of trauma.

Brothwell, Don R., and B. Chiarelli, eds. *Population Biology of the Ancient Egyptians.* London, 1973. A collection of thirty-four papers, many from a symposium held in 1969 and published in the first two volumes of the *Journal of Human Evolution.* The work is a valuable source of information on the general health of the ancient Egyptians.

Brothwell, Don R., and A. T. Sandison, eds. *Diseases in Antiquity.* Springfield, 1967. A collection of fifty-seven papers, dealing with a very wide range of diseases in antiquity; particularly useful for comparing Egypt with other ancient civilizations.

Cockburn, Aidan, and Eve Cockburn, eds. *Mummies, Disease, and Ancient Cultures.* Cambridge, 1980. A collection of twenty papers, focused on findings in mummies that are mainly but not exclusively from Egypt.

Cockburn, Aidan, et al. "Autopsy of an Egyptian Mummy." *Science* 187 (1975), 1115–1160. A multidisciplinary account of the examination of the mummy PUM II.

David, A. Rosalie, ed. *The Manchester Museum Mummy Project: Multidisciplinary Research on Ancient Egyptian Mummified Remains.* Manchester, 1979. A multidisciplinary paleopathological investigation of a group of seventeen mummies, from the Middle Kingdom to Greco-Roman times.

David, A. Rosalie, ed. *Science in Egyptology.* Manchester, 1986. Fifty-six papers from symposia held in 1979 and 1984; mainly concerned with new noninvasive technology in the study of ancient Egyptian human remains.

David, A. Rosalie, and E. Tapp, eds. *The Mummy's Tale: The Scientific and Medical Investigation of Natsef-Amun, Priest in the Temple of Karnak.* London, 1992. An account of the exhaustive study of the Leeds Mummy.

Davies, Vivian W., and Roxie Walker, eds. *Biological Anthropology and the Study of Ancient Egypt.* London, 1993. Twenty illustrated papers relating to biology and disease in ancient Egypt, based on a symposium held in 1990.

Deelder, A. M., et al. "Detection of Schistosome Antigen in Mummies." *Lancet* 335 (1990), 724–725. Reports the presence of schistosome circulating anodic antigen in two mummies of the Predynastic period (BM 32753) and the New Kingdom (Nakht-ROM I).

Filer, Joyce. *Disease.* London, 1995. Although constrained in length, this book contains much valuable information and new insight, based on the author's extensive fieldwork experience.

Grapow, Hermann, H. von Deines, and W. Westendorf. *Grundriss der Medizin der alten Ägypter.* 9 vols. Berlin, 1954–1973. A comprehensive study of ancient Egyptian medicine, including hieroglyphic transcription, translation into German, and detailed analysis of the medical papyri, with an Egyptian-German dictionary; essential source material for the serious student.

Miller, Robert L., et al. "Diagnosis of 'Plasmodium falciparum' Infections in Mummies Using the Rapid Manual *Para*Sight™-F Test." *Transactions of the Royal Society of Tropical Medicine and Hygiene* 88 (1994), 31–32. A valuable account of a new approach to the epidemiology of malaria in ancient Egypt.

Millet, N. B., et al. "Autopsy of an Egyptian Mummy (Nakht–Rom I)." *Canadian Medical Association Journal* 117 (1977), 461–476. A multidisciplinary collection of nine articles on various aspects of the detailed examination of Nakht (Middle Kingdom).

Morse, Dan, D. R. Brothwell, and P. J. Ucko. "Tuberculosis in Ancient Egypt." *American Review of Respiratory Diseases* 90 (1964), 524–541. A critical review of sixteen previously reported and fifteen new cases that resemble tuberculosis, from ancient Egypt's Predynastic to Late periods.

Nerlich, Andreas G., C. J. Hass, A. Zink, U. Szeimies, and H. G. Hagedorn. "Molecular Evidence for Tuberculosis in an Ancient Egyptian Mummy." *Lancet* 350 (1997), 1404. The first detection in an Egyptian mummy of DNA from the bacterium causing pulmonary tuberculosis.

Nunn, John F. *Ancient Egyptian Medicine.* London, 1996. A systematic account of medical papyri, medical science, disease, rational and magical treatment, and the medical profession—with three hundred references, including many relevant to this encyclopedia article.

Sauneron, Serge. *Un traité égyptien d'ophiologie.* Cairo, 1989. The first translation and analysis of a new papyrus concerned with snake bite and its rational treatment.

Smith, Grafton E. *The Royal Mummies.* Cairo, 1912. The classical and most comprehensive account of the autopsy of fifty royal mummies.

Westendorf, Wolfhart. *Erwachen der Heilkunst: die Medizin im alten Ägypten.* Zurich, 1992. An excellent but concise overview of ancient Egyptian medicine.

JOHN F. NUNN

**DIVINITY.** In considering the confrontation between the two opposing concepts of the "unity" and "multiplicity" of the divine in ancient Egypt, we must begin with some of the intellectual modes of thought in that culture. To begin with, Egyptian religious philosophy did not employ abstraction but used a concrete vocabulary. It defined from the external and the global a reality—here, a divinity—with the aid of images that complete and correct each other. As a consequence, this mode of thinking is a stranger to the principle of contradiction and postulates simple identities. In ancient Egypt, the principle of "identity" had far wider application than in our culture, resulting in what Henri Frankfort called a "multiplicity of approaches." Facts do not exclude one another, but are added in layers, doing justice to the multiple facets of reality. This art of combining rests on the capacity of an entity to manifest itself in different forms: one divinity may be taken for the manifestation of another. Finally, thought and utterance are seen as creative. In the Memphite doctrine, the operative mode of the creator god is thought, which resides in the heart, which in turn is informed by the senses—and thought is executed in language. This results in a creation, through the word of the elements of the world, which the god Ptah named after having perceived and thought them—an intellectual concept without precedent, completed by the creative value of the image. The image of the gods is an extension of reality that goes beyond representation. On the one hand, there is a plurality of meanings of images and objects; on the other, the performative character of word and image.

**Concept of God.** The hieroglyph for "god" has been described as a "staff wrapped in cloth"—"whose extremity projects like a flap or a streamer." Hornung (1986) specified that the "cult drape or curtain," is doubtless a secondary form, and that the original model was rather a stick wrapped in bands or ribbons and thus charged with strength or power. This hieroglyph then suggests the veneration of inanimate objects or a representation of a cult object whose derivatives were drapes and other streamers. At the same time, there is evidence of the veneration of divinities in the form of animal figures perched on a staff. Several centuries later, the anthropomorphic forms of gods appear in depictions.

The application of etymology to comprehend the Egyptian notion of "god" (*ntr*) produces hypotheses that are sometimes seductive but rarely convincing. It is more interesting to study the use of the word *ntr*. The plural may refer to a limited group of gods at a specific location or region, or gathered into a particular theology, or to the totality of all Egyptian gods. The dual form was applied exclusively to divine pairs, such as Horus and Seth, "the two masters," or to "the two ladies"—Isis and Nephthys or Nekhbet and Ouadjet—to designate the titular divinities of Upper and Lower Egypt. Important to an understanding of divinity is the use of the singular without reference to a particular god. The absolute form is found in the names of persons, in titles, and in Wisdom texts. Names including the word *ntr* indicate a relationship between a person and a particular individual divinity to which the person giving the name to his child alludes. In the ecclesiastic title "servant of god," the use of the word

*ntr* is so generic that it can also be applied to a goddess; it is used in a vague sense to designate certain specific divinities. In the Wisdom texts, we find a preference for the indefinite word *ntr* instead of the names of individual gods. The reason for this is that the Wisdom texts were written for professional purposes, usually to instruct a son or a successor; far from being treatises that pose axioms and definitions, these texts are meant as practical advice for students. They contain descriptions of specific situations and detail the preparations necessary for entering into contact with a god, whose identity will depend on the locality where the apprentice official finds himself established. Thus, the word *ntr* in the Wisdom texts is by no means to be interpreted as the unique God of monotheism; rather, this is the god that the student will encounter in his professional life.

Aside from this pragmatic polytheism, from the middle of the second millennium BCE onward the priestly elite made a genuine attempt to define *divinity*. The god Amun could be described both in his immanence as "prodigious in transformations" and also in his transcendence in a manner that recalls great monotheisms: unknown, distant, and unapproachable, Amun is "he who hides from the gods, his appearance is unknown, he is farther than the highest heaven" (Leyde Papyrus, end of the eighteenth dynasty). Derchain (1981) has shown that the sun hymns studied by Assmann, according to whom a "crisis in the polytheistic philosophy of life" occurred in the Ramessid era, were written according to a body of century-old archival texts. They did not constitute an "intangible canon" and became a reservoir from which the theologians drew to transform the initial concepts, by correlating and modifying expressions. The text engenders knowledge and allows one to move from familiar expressions to the formulation of a new conceptual apparatus in relation with history. Every divine quality remains open to new interpretation, which retroactively redefines the known qualities, making more severe the uncertainty with regard to the ultimate nature of the god.

Transcendent in his demi-urgic pre-existence, Amun is immanent in his manifestations. The paradox is important: it expresses the passage from non-time to time.

**Multiplicity of the Divine.** Are the gods alone at the heart of the divine sphere? More precisely, is there a diversity of the divine—and what kinds of divinities are encountered among the Egyptian gods, the god-king, and the sacred animals?

From the first dynasties onward a cult developed based on the images of living kings and their predecessors. Ancestry and the veneration of the reigning king were used to reinforce the monarchy. In the Sinai during the twelfth dynasty, Senwosret II surrounded his statue with those of Montuhotep I, Montuhotep II, and Amenemhet I; in another depiction, an expedition leader offers pieces of turquoise to Amenemhet II wearing the crown of Soped, the god of the Arabian borderlands. These are revealing instances of commemorating royal deeds—note the divine nature which the turquoise confers on the king.

In the New Kingdom, the Akhmenu at Karnak is the building with the most complete ensemble of ancestral kings ever assembled by a living king: sixty-one. Thutmose III brings to them "the offering given by the king," and they participate in processions inside the building as do the statues of the gods. The Great Sphinx at Giza, probably sculpted in the image of Khafre and restored by Thutmose IV, is given the name Harmakhis ("Horus-in-the-horizon") Khepre-Re-Atum, a manifestation of its divine character and of the influence of the clergy of Heliopolis. The solar aspect of the sovereign, beginning with Amenhotpe III, leads to the veneration of the living king in colossi erected at either side of the temple entrance, in which the spirits that inhabit the king are incarnated; they carry the name of the king linked to that of Re: "Amenhotpe-sun-of-sovereigns," "Ramesses-beloved-of-Atum." Ramesses II, who established a cult to his own likeness, becomes of necessity a servant of his own image for the perpetual cult, thus engendering a functional dislocation in the person of the king. During the reign of Ramesses II, the image of the sovereign wearing the *atef*-crown merged with the dyads consisting of the principal Egyptian gods. The statue sometimes carries a name: "Living-image-of-Ramesses-beloved-of-Amun"—that is to say, image of himself. He is even identified (by osmosis, as it were) with Re-Horakhty in a relief above the entrance door to the temple of Abu Simbel, showing a falcon-headed figure crowned with the sun disk and holding a scepter (*wsr*) in one hand and the feather of Maat in the other, a rebus of the crown name of the king: User-Maat-Re (*Wsr-m3't-r'*). On the one hand, the efficacy expected of the king is comparable to that of Re, the luminous god who repels the enemies of Egypt into the shadows; the king and Re collaborate in the magical protection of the lands of Nubia. On the other hand, the king, who is not the god, is the sign of the efficacy of the god's power, which requires royal intermediation to be actualized.

It must be understood that the "divinized" kings who created a cult of their deified images differ from the gods, in whom this dislocation between being and image does not exist. In this respect, kings can be likened to the sacred animals—not the species protected by a taboo, but the unique animals, chosen for veneration, which succeed their deceased predecessors in the same manner as royalty does. Enthroned, sometimes given grand funerals and rituals of passage like kings, they are equally depositories of the divine presence: the animal's body is the receptacle of divinity. In the end, however, the divinity of kings and animals alike derived from the gods and is therefore not original. If kings and sacred animals can be compared to gods, the resemblance lies only in the identity of their situations: both preside over the destinies of a world, but the worlds in question are not the same. Mortal kings and sacred animals are not confused with a god who is perpetually present, despite intermittency.

The representations of Egyptian gods and their names confirm the multiplicity of the divine nature. Anthropomorphic, zoomorphic, composite, the gods change form among many bodies, heads, and attributes; there is no canon of divine representation. With the exception of the iconography of Anubis as a dog and that of Taweret in a body composite of hippopotamus, lion, and crocodile, Egyptian divinities are "rich in manifestations" and "of numerous faces," so the inscribed name frequently provides the only means of recognizing Isis or Hathor. The numerous forms of the gods are limited, though: Thoth never takes the form of a tree or a snake. The boundaries of the individuality of gods prevents infinite actualization and forbids certain manifestations so as to prevent a progression toward complete pantheism. This process of creating divine representations correlates with an "anthropomorphization of powers" (Hornung 1986) during the first dynasties, contemporaneous with the end of the practice of forming kings' names from animal names. Man passes from a world in which he does not live in opposition to nature—a universe that shares power with the animal, which was the highest referent of strength—into a world where man submits the universe to his capacity for organization.

The multiplicity of names for a divinity is another fundamental characteristic. Litanies are sung to Osiris under all his names. On the architraves of the first hypostyle hall at Edfu, the "Powerful Ones" taking the form of Hathor receive as many epithets as there are days in the year and, the astronomical calendar being divided in two parts, each epithet has two variants. The gods are "rich in names" and these are innumerable, as in the case of Amun, "whose number [of names] is unknown." The names of the gods are open repertories, even if certain names—such as the "secret name"—enjoy an exceptional status, which protects one who retains it from any annexation of his power; by contrast, the formula "I know you, knowing your name," protects the traveler in the underworld from demons. The multiple epithets of a god whom one invokes, far from being exclusive to that god, are transferable to other gods. The notion of identity is not limited by strict outlines and reveals itself as an expandable concept. A god may even leave his own "body" and temporarily inhabit that of another god.

Finally, a major question of the history of religion, and one not limited to ancient Egypt, is that of why and how a god from one location moves from his place of origin to other places. How do the specific attributes of an ancient god from one place change, allowing the accretion of new attributes and a new ubiquity for the god?

In local theologies surrounding the god of Athribis in the Nile Delta, a double effort at synthesis is made; this effort aims to unify the multiple local traditions in the sphere of the principal gods of the nome (province) and to give to the cult of these gods a sense of belonging to the mainstream of the "national" religion. The goal is to inform the idiosyncrasy and thought spread throughout Egypt. With time, this reveals itself not as the irreducible expression of a single protohistoric cult, but rather as a continuous speculative effort to express the power of local divinities, across temporal evolution and alongside other local divinities. In the act of adoration, power is concentrated in the chosen god whom one addresses, and any other gods become insignificant. In this sense, the god to whom one speaks is the "first"—hence the term "henotheism," to describe the veneration of one god at a time, who is nevertheless not unique.

Ancient Egyptian theologians utilized the legend of the dismembered god Osiris to unify Egypt. Through the expedient word plays conflating geographic terms and parts of the human body, any nome might become a place where the divine body of Osiris, torn apart by Seth, and dispersed across Egypt, might be restored. This egalitarian and unifying point of view undoubtedly explains the extraordinary prevalence of Osirian mythology in Ptolemaic temples, one characteristic of which is to manifest Egyptian "nationalism."

In addition to these pan-Egyptian theological reflections, an anthropomorphic concept of the structure of the world led the Egyptians to assimilate deceased persons with deities responsible for cows, milk, grain, or clothing, or otherwise connected to production. The domains of human activity are also personified; the spirit of fishing in a duck-headed body; Renenutet, the harvest goddess; or Hedjhotep and Tait, the spirits of weaving. There are gods of the administrative regions of Egypt, the forty-two nomes, as well as of other aspects of the physical world: Heb and Sekhet, the spirits of the marshes; Hapy, the spirit of water for agriculture; Ou, the arable soil of the nome; Mer, the canal or the portion of the Nile that crosses it; Pehu, the fringes or green parts of the marsh, refuge for fish and birds; Wadj-ur, the "Very-green," that is the ocean; and the four spirits of the winds. These geographical personifications, derived from a taxonomy of the physical world, frequently appear on the base of temples, close to the fertile soil. This peopling of the invisible enabled Egyptians to enter into dialogue with the forces of nature and to tame them. Guilty of abusing nature, they asked for its consent to take from it what it contains.

**Nontranscendence of the Divine.** The immanence of gods is especially noticeable in *The Contendings of Horus and Seth*, a long account of the succession conflict between Horus, son and rightful successor of Osiris, and Seth, Osiris' brother and a counter-claimant. Their rivalry for the royal role of Osiris is fought out in front of the tribunal of the Ennead, which, in its enlarged form, consists of some thirty divine members who are lazy, fickle, and prone to human frailties. This anthropomorphism also characterizes the gods as having an appetite for power and all its attendant vices, a viewpoint that extends to their physical aspect. The gods of this account are equipped with human bodies, although free of human weaknesses and limitations. The visibility of these bodies is the first hint that they lack complete transcendence: Thoth places on his head a disk of gold taken from the forehead of Seth. The battle equipment—Seth's "scepter of four thousand five hundred *nemes*," Horus's "knife of sixteen *debens*"—demonstrates that the use of arms is an expression of the energy of the gods. The abilities of the gods, while exceptional, once again bring them closer to mankind, since they are described in terms of a human body: longevity, in a process that has lasted eighty years; the ubiquity of their adventures on Earth, from fields, woods, and mountains to the depths of the oceans and the sky; reversible wounds, without bleeding or scars, and short-lived amputations; tirelessness; and even triumph over death (the decapitated Isis reappears intact in a subsequent episode)—with the exception of Osiris. Finally, the appearance of the gods is a finely drawn evocation of human bodies that are not directly described. Horus and Seth are "mysterious in form," and Horus appears in his veil of light on the day of coronation. Yet this heroic attenuation still makes reference to the human body: hands, semen, eyes, head, and the infirmity of Horus are mentioned. It makes reference to human behaviors and reactions: speech and tears, the greediness and brutality of Seth, the fury and weariness of Horus, the subtle intelligence of Isis, and the inertia of the creator god. The human body of a god is at times replaced by that of an animal—the hippopotamus for Seth, and the kite for Isis—as the god attempts to be elusive. The human body is also liable to metamorphosis through aging, as when Isis, "young girl of beautiful body," changes into "a bent old woman" to aid the just cause of her son Horus through her deceptions; or through transsubstantiation, when Isis turns into a statue of flint, or when the dead god Osiris "feeds on gold and precious stones."

The immanence expressed in the likening of gods to man is revealing, with regard to the divisions of the divine—that is to say, its fragmentation. The ontological approach to the problem of the one and the many in the cosmogony texts that elaborate on the Pyramid Texts provides a good insight into the struggles attendant on the hereditary transfer of the royal function. The "enemy brothers" Horus and Seth, in reality nephew and uncle embroiled in eternal conflict, reflect the "complementary duality of the world and the necessity for constant confrontation" (Hornung 1986). Ancient Egyptians held a negative view with regard to the natural course of human life, which took place in a world that was originally uninhabitable and could be made harmonious only through tireless efforts. There is no doubt that hereditary monarchy was the order intended by the gods, in order to establish *maat*, the correct order of the world. This myth was therefore a meditation on the relationships between force and right through the medium of the divine antagonists, Horus and Seth.

Two aspects of divine fragmentation include (1) the ancient formulation of the trinity of gods and (2) the underlying proto-arithmetic thought in constituting the Ennead of Heliopolis. The triad of Amun-Re-Ptah appears on the trumpets of the funeral equipment of Tutankhamun, but the *Hymn of Leyde* to Amun (end of the eighteenth dynasty) is the first known textual formulation of the trinity of these three gods: "All gods are three . . . His name is hidden as Amon. He is Re (before men). His body is Ptah. Their cities on Earth remain for ever: Thebes, Heliopolis and Memphis, for all eternity." The plural "all gods" is followed by a singular pronoun that carries a specific name, and the cult sites remain distinct. Yet the text does not say that "god reveals himself in three forms," as is emphasized by Hornung (1986). In effect, there is no text in which the unique god is designated by the name of "god." Undoubtedly, Egyptian thinkers came close to remaking the traditional religion, but they were not yet ready to unify that which appeared irreconcilable—the various manifestations of a unique sun god—in order to go beyond the models inherited from ancient times.

The Heliopolitan cosmogony, behind its genealogical presentation composed of three generations, contains the elements of a proto-arithmetic. When the autogenous demi-urge forms Shu and Tefnut, each of the gods becomes one-third of the universe: "When he (Atum) begat Shu and Tefnut, when he was One and became Three." This reasoning by means of dividing the unity applies to subsequent generations, when Geb and Nut, the issue of Shu and Tefnut, and then their four children, Osiris, Isis, Seth, and Nephthys, each become one-fifth and one-ninth part of the world, respectively. The mathematical sequence 1–3–5–9 governs the first increments of the world. The multiplicity is seen, by giving preference to fractions with a numerator of one, as the decomposition of a sum, and thus the choice is made for an arithmetic of identity. The Egyptians were surely aware of the exponential sequence 1–2–4–8, etc., as the unlimited incremental law of the universe. After the demi-urge, Shu and Tefnut, Geb and Nut, and their four children, "it was their children who created the crowd of forms existing in this world in the shape of children and grandchildren" (Bremner Rhind Papyrus). This sequence that doubles at each stage is an instrument indicative of the dynamic future, that of a universe in expansion. And yet, the ancient Egyptians preferred—in order to verify that their national state conformed to the initial intentions of the creator god—to use their knowledge of fractions to imagine the following result: Atum, uncreated and without beginning, takes Osiris with him into a distant future where nothing changes (*Book of Going Forth by Day* [*Book of the Dead*], chapter 125), that is, to the original point of departure.

All these are indications that the religious universe of Egypt is unlike the Cartesian system, wherein God is uniquely transcendent. The "absolute" was not a necessary attribute of the divine, even though Egyptian thinkers were able to perceive their gods as transcendent and to express this at certain stages of their history.

[*See also* Cults, *the overview article and articles on royal, private, divine, and animal cults;* Deities; Demons; Kingship; Monotheism; Religion; *and articles on individual deities.*]

## BIBLIOGRAPHY

Assmann, Jan. *Re und Amun: Die Krise des polytheistischen Weltbilds im Ägypten der 18.–20. Dynastic.* Orbis Biblicus et Orientalis, 51. Freiburg and Göttingen, 1983.

Bonnet, Hans. *Reallexikon der Ägyptischen Religionsgeschichte.* Berlin, 1952.

Caquot, André. "Les découvertes de Ras Shamra." *Académie des Inscriptions et Belles-Letres* 19 (1983), 3–12. The author investigates whether Israelite monotheism may not in fact be a reformation of the ancient religion of Ugarit.

Derchain, Philippe. "Divinité: Le problème du divin et des dieux dans l'Égypte ancienne." In *Dictionnaire des mythologies,* edited by Y. Bonnefoy, pp. 324–330. Paris, 1981.

Derchain, Philippe. "Encore le monothéisme." *Chronique d'Égypte* 63.125 (1988), 77–85.

Frankfort, Henri. *Ancient Egyptian Religion: An Interpretation.* New York, 1948.

Hornung, Erik. *Les dieux de l'Égypte: Le Un et le Multiple.* Monaco, 1986. An excellent synthesis.

Meeks, Dimitri. *Génies, anges et démons en Égypte.* Sources orientales, 8. Paris, 1971.

Meeks, Dimitri. "Zoomorphie et image des dieux dans l'Égypte ancienne." In *Corps des dieux,* (*Le temps de la réflexion,* 7), edited by C. Malamoud and J.-P. Vernant, pp. 171–191. Paris, 1986.

Meeks, Dimitri. "Notion de 'dieu' et structure de panthéon dans l'Égypte ancienne." *Revue de l'histoire des religions* 205 (1988), 425–446.

Meeks, Dimitri, and Christine Favard-Meeks. *La vie quotidienne des dieux égyptiens.* Paris, 1993. This work in two parts describes the daily tribulations of an agitated and querulous divine community (D. Meeks) as well as the fascinating rituals of the monarchy and the gods (C. Favard-Meeks).

Morenz, Siegfried. *La religion égyptienne. Essai d'interprétation.* Bibliothèque historique, Collection les religions de l'humanité, 1. Paris, 1962.

Pritchard, James B. *Ancient Near Eastern Texts Relating to the Old Testament*. 2d ed. Princeton, 1955. Contains translations of numerous important Egyptian texts.

Sauneron, Serge, and Jean Yoyotte. "La naissance du monde selon l'Égypte ancienne." In *La naissance du monde*, Collection Sources orientales, 1, pp. 17–91. Paris, 1959.

Traunecker, Claude. *Les dieux de l'Égypte. Que sais-je?*, no. 1194. Paris, 1992.

Van der Leeuw, G. *La religion dans son essence et ses manifestations*. Paris, 1970. This summary of religious sciences is intended for prehistorians, experts in the history of religion and liturgy, and anthropologists. Although quite old, the work is still a valuable reference book owing to its interesting and original approach to the phenomenon of religion.

Yoyotte, Jean. "La pensée préphilosophique en Égypte." In *Histoire de la philosophie*, vol. 1: *Encyclopédie de la Pléiade*, edited by B. Parain, pp. 1–23. Paris, 1969.

MARIE-ANGE BONHÊME
Translated from French by Elizabeth Schwaiger

**DIVORCE.** *See* Marriage and Divorce.

**DJOSER.** *See* Old Kingdom, *article on* Third Dynasty.

**DOMESTICATION.** *See* Animal Husbandry.

**DONKEYS.** *See* Equines.

**DOOMED PRINCE.** The "Tale of the Doomed Prince" is preserved solely on the *verso* of the Hieratic Papyrus Harris 500 (BM 10060), inscribed in the reign of Sety I or Ramesses II. The story, the end of which is lost, is written in Late Egyptian and was probably composed in the late eighteenth dynasty, just before the collapse of the kingdom of Mitanni. The simple narrative style and the consistent motivation of the characters put this work in the genre of fairy tale.

The story begins with the birth of a crown prince to the Egyptian king. At his birth, the Hathor goddesses determine his fate: death by a snake, a crocodile, or a dog. Initially, the child lives a protected existence, but he is given a young hound for a pet, and eventually, accompanied by his dog, he leaves his home on a journey to the Near East. Although the reader knows of the prince's royal background, his true identity is not revealed to the princes with whom he competes for the hand of the daughter of the king of Naharin (Mitanni). They have been told by the prince that he is the son of a chariot warrior, and he has

fled Egypt because of his stepmother. After considerable reluctance, the Mitannian king sanctions the marriage of his daughter to the Egyptian hero, who has won the competition. The prince, still claiming to be the son of a chariot warrior, informs his new wife of his three fates, and she becomes protective of him. Although she kills the snake, both the crocodile and the hound remain. When the dog states that he is the lad's fate, the prince flees into a lake, only to be seized by the crocodile, which had been engaged in fighting with a water spirit. The crocodile soon releases the hero, thus leaving the dog to be his fate. Here the tale breaks off, giving rise to opposing interpretations. Some have suggested a tragic ending, but the fairy-tale nature of the story suggests that the conclusion was a happy one, with the hero revealing his true identity and succeeding to the throne of Egypt.

"The Doomed Prince" is important for its treatment of the concept of fate in ancient Egypt. It is the prophecy's imprecision regarding the manner of the prince's death that makes fate seem less inexorable than in neighboring Near Eastern cultures. From other New Kingdom texts we know that the fated span of one's life might be altered by requesting of a god a longer life than was initially predetermined. The flexibility of fate thus removes "The Doomed Prince" from being a tragedy and allows for a resolution that is less strictly predetermined. Indeed, there is a deity superior to the fate-decreeing Hathors, and it is the piety of the hero toward his god, as well as his good qualities, that governs the eventual outcome, overriding the destinies given at his birth. It is quite likely that the dog did not kill the young prince, since the sun god is the ultimate arbiter of an individual's destiny.

**BIBLIOGRAPHY**

Gardiner, Alan H. *Late-Egyptian Stories*. Bibliotheca Aegyptiaca, 1 Brussels, 1932. Offers a convenient transcription of the Hieratic text of "The Doomed Prince."

Lichtheim, Miriam. *Ancient Egyptian Literature, a Book of Readings*. vol. 2. Berkeley, 1976. Provides a translation of "The Doomed Prince," with bibliographical references.

Möller, Georg. *Hieratische Lesestücke für den akademischen Gebrauch*. 2d rev. ed. Leipzig, 1927. Presents a facsimile copy of the Hieratic text of "The Doomed Prince."

Posener, G. "On the Tale of the Doomed Prince." *The Journal of Egyptian Archaeology* 39 (1953), 107. Suggests a happy ending for the story and some mythological connotations.

Simpson, William Kelly, ed. *The Literature of Ancient Egypt*. New ed. New Haven, 1973. Provides a translation of "The Doomed Prince," with comments on the tale's treatment of fate.

EDWARD F. WENTE

**DRA ABUL NAGA,** area of Western Thebes that extends along the gebel front in a northeasterly direction from the point at which the gebel cuts into the Deir el-

Bahri bay to the wadi leading to the Valley of the Kings. The site's cemetery includes both royal and nonroyal burials from the Second Intermediate Period into the Saite period. Exploration in Dra Abul Naga in the early to mid-nineteenth century yielded a considerable amount of the funeral furniture of several seventeenth dynasty kings, some of which is reported to have come from intact tombs. Known items belong to Antef V (tomb reportedly discovered by villagers in 1827; coffin now in the British Museum), Antef VI (coffin and canopic chest discovered in a cache in Dra Abul Naga sometime between 1845 and 1849; both now in the Louvre), and Sobekemsaf I (canopic chest now in Leiden). Other seventeenth dynasty kings who were probably buried in Dra Abul Naga include Sekenenre Ta'o, whose coffin and mummy were discovered in the Deir el-Bahri cache in 1881, and Kamose, whose intact coffin was discovered buried in debris in Dra Abul Naga by Auguste Mariette's workmen in 1857. Presumably Ahmose, first king of the eighteenth dynasty, was also originally buried in Dra Abul Naga, but his coffin and mummy were, along with those of Sekenenre Ta'o, discovered in the Deir el-Bahri cache. It seems possible that Ahmose's successor Amenhotpe I was likewise buried in Dra Abul Naga, but with the reign of Thutmose I, Dra Abul Naga was abandoned as a royal cemetery in favor of the Valley of the Kings on the other side of the mountainous ridge.

Dra Abul Naga continued in use as a noble and private cemetery throughout the New Kingdom. Although none of the decorated tombs in the area is currently accessible, a number of them are of considerable importance, including the tomb of Nebamun, scribe and royal physician under Amenhotpe II (?), and the tomb of Kenamun, mayor of Thebes, whose tomb is best known for the illustration of the arrival of Syrian ships in port and their encounter with Egyptian merchants and traders. Also important are the Ramessid tombs of Bakenchons and Nebwenenef, both first prophets of Amun under Ramesses II, and Tjaynufer, a third prophet of Amun who probably lived under Ramesses III.

Aside from the rock-cut tombs of the area, excavations in the 1990s carried out by the German Archaeological Institute revealed a previously unknown cemetery in the plain at the north end of Dra Abul Naga. These tombs are of a type previously unknown in Thebes: free-standing structures typically consisting of a mud-brick enclosure wall, an entry structure, a mud-brick wall enclosing a small courtyard (in most cases a simple doorway, but in a few examples consisting of a massive pylon), and an enclosed chapel appended to the rear of the enclosure wall. The actual tomb was dug in the courtyard, marked off by the enclosure wall. Grave structures of this type appear to have been in use from the end of the seventeenth dynasty until the reign of Thutmose III of the eighteenth dynasty. Interspersed among these relatively elaborate structures are other graves that appear never to have had superstructures. The apparent conclusion is that this was a cemetery in which both elite and lower-class Egyptians were buried; possibly the lower-class graves were placed near the elite tombs so that their chapels could be used by family members of the lower-class deceased.

### BIBLIOGRAPHY

Polz, Daniel. "The Location of the Tomb of Amenhotep I: A Reconsideration." In *Valley of the Sun Kings: New Explorations in the Tombs of the Pharaohs*, edited by R. H. Wilkinson, pp. 8–21. Tucson, 1995.

Winlock, H. E. "The Tombs of the Kings of the Seventeenth Dynasty at Thebes." *Journal of Egyptian Archaeology* 10 (1924), 217–277.

STEVE VINSON

**DRAMA.** The topic of drama in ancient Egypt is a complex and somewhat controversial one. Many have categorically claimed either its existence or its nonexistence. A judicious assessment of the evidence, or lack thereof, indicates that a more qualified position allows greater insight into this question.

There is no archeological or textual evidence for theaters as we know them in pharaonic Egypt. There do not appear to be specific words in the Egyptian language for technical terms like "drama," "play," or "actor." Thus, the claim for the presence in Egypt of secular drama, as we know it, seems to have no supporting evidence to date.

There are a number of religious texts from papyri and temples that have been labeled "dramatic texts" by some modern scholars in their search for drama in religious rituals. These texts, for the most part, focus on certain acts performed by the god(s) at the beginning of time, at "the first occasion," and are believed to contain material for commemorative reenactments of incipient cosmic events for the purpose of maintaining life and the order of the cosmos. Their content is based on myth, and their purpose is to reenact, not to instruct or to reflect. In no way do they attempt to explain human behavior, good or bad.

Studies of such texts by modern scholars have provoked some interesting discussions, most of which founder on the rocks of semantics. The majority of those who have looked into the question of the origins of drama in ancient Egypt have begun their discussions with somewhat subjective and personal definitions of drama and its essential elements; they have then proceeded to manipulate the details of the so-called Egyptian dramatic texts to prove their points. Many of these studies led to the coining of terms like "dramatic ritual," "liturgical drama," "sacred drama," and the like—rhetorical niceties that offer nothing by way of an answer to the question. Furthermore, in the case of most specific "dramatic" rituals, even

DRAMA. *Relief in the Temple of Horus at Edfu, depicting the drama of the "Triumph of Horus," which was performed in the temple.* (Courtesy Dieter Arnold)

in the so-called Osirian mysteries celebrated at Abydos and the rituals conducted in the Edfu temple in which Horus triumphs over Seth/Apophis and the forces of chaos, what we encounter is fundamentally different from anything that we today would regard as drama. Additionally, the majority of the texts identified as "dramatic texts" are hopelessly fragmentary and often abbreviated—perhaps intentionally so. Therefore, what one can say about such texts as drama is usually limited to conjecture.

These objections, however, can best serve as caveats to underscore the difficulties encountered in attempting to address the question of drama in ancient Egypt. There is no denying that a number of Egyptian rituals can be viewed as dramatizations of certain events in the lives of the Egyptian gods. To what degree these dramatizations were "staged" is difficult to say.

Many of the texts identified as "dramatic" contain elements that point to their oral components. The oral nature of Egyptian religious texts is well known. Many texts and sections of texts are framed by labels like $r_3$ or $\underline{d}d$ $mdw$ $in$ . . . , "Utterance" and "Words to be recited by . . . ," respectively. Do such oral markers indicate that texts so labeled are to be dramatically enacted as well as recited? If one simply answers yes, as a number of Egyptologists have done, then one may well argue that virtually all religious texts are dramatic texts by definition, an all-inclusive definition that seems to beg the question.

It has generally been argued by the proponents of Egyptian drama that the actors in these plays were members of the priesthood under the direction of a lector-priest. They have postulated dramatic reenactments both inside and outside the temple proper. In certain rituals depicted on the walls of Egyptian temples, scholars have claimed to find not only dramatic texts but reliefs as well that depict various stages of what they perceive as drama; one of these rituals belongs to the Osirian Khoiak festival. Unfortunately, the evidence for the ritual is found piecemeal in a number of temples and papyri, and the sources for the evidence are also scattered over a broad time span. An assessment of the dramatic elements of this ritual, thus, relies on the reconstruction of the ritual from its various components and their locations, a process that is largely hypothetical. A second ritual is that of the so-called Triumph of Horus over his enemies, found in the Ptolemaic temple at Edfu. The texts and reliefs of this ritual, found on a single wall, form a connected series that has been seen by some as a play. The texts and reliefs involve a number of different deities, and the sequence of the texts does move forward in storyline form. One editor has even argued that certain elements within the texts comprise stage directions. Despite the fact that this ritual is self-contained within a single temple, in order to see it as drama, primitive or otherwise, we are faced with the problem of a hypothetical reconstruction and evaluation of what may only possibly be dramatic elements.

An examination of two texts, both of which form part of the so-called mysteries of Osiris celebrated at Abydos, reveals several important pieces of information and may serve as better evidence for dramatic elements in Egyptian rituals. Both papyri have been dated to the Ptolemaic period. The first text, from a papyrus in Berlin, contains a ritual to be performed in the Abydos temple on the twenty-fifth day of the fourth month of Akhet, or Inundation. The ritual involves strophic addresses to the god Osiris by the goddesses Isis and Nephthys. The colophon states that at the completion of the ritual, the temple where it was read is to be "made holy, not seen [and] not heard by anyone except the chief lector-priest and a *sem*-priest." It then states that "two women beautiful in body are to be brought and made to sit on the ground in the first doorway of the Hall of Appearances, the names of Isis and Nephthys written on their upper arms." After receiving certain offerings, they are required to sit with "their faces bowed down." The reading of the text is to be conducted twice on that day, at the third hour and at the eighth hour, apparently by the lector-priest.

In the second text, the Bremner-Rhind Papyrus in the British Museum, similar but expanded instructions are given at the beginning of the text. The text is said to contain the ritual of the Two Kites—i.e., Isis and Nephthys—which is celebrated in the temple of Osiris Kentyamentiu in the fourth month of Akhet, from the twenty-second to the twenty-sixth day. The instructions then state that "the entire temple shall be made holy [and] there shall be brought in two women pure in body, virgins, the hair of their bodies removed, their heads adorned with wigs . . . tambourines in their hands, their names inscribed on their upper arms, namely Isis and Nephthys. They shall sing from the stanzas of this book in the presence of this god." The alternations between first person singular and plural in the text seem to indicate shifts between solos sung by Isis and duets sung by the two goddesses.

The instructions in these two texts contain important differences. The two women mentioned in the first text are required to possess physical beauty, to sit in a specific place in the temple, to have the names of the goddesses Isis and Nephthys written on their arms, and to sit with their faces bowed down. These are their only requirements, and no further specific roles are assigned to them. The text specifically states that it is to be read, apparently by the lector-priest despite the fact that the title of the text is "The evocation of ritual recitations which is made by the Two sisters." In the second text, the women are required to be ritually pure and virgins, to undergo depilation, to wear wigs, and to have the names of Isis and Nephthys written on their upper arms. The text also explicitly states that it is they who are to sing the ritual. Thus, the women in the second text take on active roles as the sisters of Osiris, whereas in the first text their role appears to be passive, almost that of players in a tableau. These differences in instructions may simply indicate variant forms of the same ritual.

Beyond the descriptions and instructions encountered in texts like the two discussed above, we have little other information about the nature of the reenactment of these rituals. They both contain clear elements that we would associate with dramatic performance, namely song and role-playing. Despite the presence of such elements of dramatic expression in Egyptian ritual, at this point we can discuss them only as such. The question of the existence of an independent genre of drama in ancient Egypt, and what its individual components may have been, remains to be answered.

## BIBLIOGRAPHY

Altenmüller, H. "Zur Lesung und Deutung des Dramatischen Ramesseumspapyrus." *Journal Ex Oriente Lux* 19 (1964–1965), 421–442. A reappraisal of the Dramatic Ramesseum Papyrus published by Sethe in 1928 and the article by Helck mentioned below. Interspersed are remarks about the nature of Egyptian drama.

Drioton, E. *Le Théâtre égyptien.* Editions de la Revue du Caire, 1942. Reprinted in *Pages d'Egyptologie* (Cairo, 1957), pp. 217–330. The fundamental study by a scholar who dedicated much time to the research and discussion of the topic of drama; thought-provoking but problematic.

Fairman, H. W. *The Triumph of Horus.* London, 1974. A study of a single ritual in the Ptolemaic temple of Horus at Edfu; interesting but highly conjectural.

Faulkner, R. O. "The Lamentations of Isis and Nephthys." *Mélanges Maspero* I: *Mémoires de l'Institut Français d'Archéologie Orientale du Caire* 66:337–348.

Faulkner, R. O. "The Bremner-Rhind Papyrus-I." *Journal of Egyptian Archaeology* 22 (1936), 121–140.

Helck, W. "Bemerkungen zum Ritual des Dramatischen Ramesseums-papyrus." *Orientalia* 23 (1954), 383–411. A reappraisal of the Dramatic Ramesseum Papyrus published by Sethe in 1928.

Mikhail, L. B. "The Egyptological Approach to Drama in Ancient Egypt, I." *Göttinger Miszellen* 75 (1984), 19–26. An assessment of the history of the discussion of the topic, as are the following.

Mikhail, L. B. "The Egyptological Approach to Drama in Ancient Egypt, II." *Göttinger Miszellen* 77 (1984), 25–33.

Mikhail, L. B. "The Egyptological Approach to Drama in Ancient Egypt, III." *Göttinger Miszellen* 78 (1984), 69–77.

Mikhail, L. B. "The Egyptological Approach to Drama in Ancient Egypt, IV." *Göttinger Miszellen* 79 (1984), 19–27. A comparative analysis of other dramatic forms from ancient and some non-Western cultures.

PAUL F. O'ROURKE

**DREAM BOOKS.** Long associated with pharaonic Egypt though the tale of Joseph (*Gn.* 40–41), the interpretation of dreams was an indigenous practice long antedating the biblical story. In late dynastic Egypt, prophetic dreams were actively sought by the medium of "incubation," in which the dreamer slept within a sacred precinct, but such attempts to evoke meaningful dreams can be traced at least as early as the First Intermediate Period (c.2206–2041 BCE), when a letter written to a deceased wife asks: "Please become a spirit for me [before] my eyes so that I may see you in a dream fighting on my behalf." The Letters to the Dead from the Old through the New Kingdoms request information and assistance that were probably to be visualized through dreams. In contrast, the Execration Texts of the Old and Middle Kingdoms include sections designed to combat "every evil dream in every evil sleep," and elaborate rituals were devised to protect the sleeper from nightly terrors sent by personal enemies or demons. As in the Joseph tale, dreams might influence the pharaonic court: both Thutmose IV of the eighteenth dynasty (1419–1410 BCE) and the Nubian ruler Tanutamun of the twenty-fifth dynasty (664–656 BCE) ascribed their ascendancy to the intervention of inspired dreams, while the overthrow of the last native pharaoh (thirtieth dynasty, r. 360–343 BCE) was popularly recounted in the "Dream of Nektanebo (II)."

It was in Egypt that the oldest extant manual of dream interpretation was found, the *Chester Beatty Dream Book* (Papyrus British Museum 10683 *recto*), probably composed in the twelfth dynasty (c.1991–1786 BCE). The surviving manuscript of that ancient reference work was copied early in the reign of Ramesses II (c.1304–1237 BCE) and was the property of senior scribes at the royal workmen's village of Deir el-Medina. The book comprises eleven columns laid out in tabular form, each preceded by the vertically written heading, "If a man see himself in a dream." While ancient Egyptian, like some Western languages, invariably uses the masculine gender to denote generic reference to persons, the *Dream Book* interpretations are explicitly limited to male readers, as internal references to wives and penises make clear; the dreams of females are not considered. The horizontal lines of the columns briefly detail the dream image, indicate whether it is favorable or unfavorable, and conclude with a prognostication for the dreamer. The text is arranged in discrete units, with good dreams listed before bad ones (highlighted by red ink), and a concluding incantation to avert any evil results. Within the "good" and "bad" sec-

DREAM BOOKS. *Limestone statuette of a woman sleeping on a bed with a headrest, eighteenth dynasty.* (The Metropolitan Museum of Art, Rogers Fund, 1915. [15.2.8])

tions, dream imagery is listed in fairly random arrangement. The entire pattern was repeated twice, once for "followers" of the deity Horus, and again for those associated with the god Seth, in a section now largely lost. This division corresponds to the two personality types recognized in Egyptian Wisdom Literature: the ideal, restrained man of Horus and the intemperate man of Seth.

The explanation of dream imagery in the papyrus seems to be motivated by a variety of principles, including wordplay (paronomasia), contemporary symbolism, and contraries. A pun underlies the interpretation of column 2, line 21 in the papyrus: "If a man see himself in a dream: Eating the flesh of a donkey. Good. It means his promotion." Similarly, in column 3, line 3, the vision of white bread foretells the occurrence of "something [at which his face] will light up." Because language was considered to be divinely inspired and not merely the chance product of linguistic history, such puns were believed to express inherently meaningful links between individual words and concepts.

Symbolic interpretations are common and may be coupled with wordplay or ironic reversals. In the example noted above (column 2, line 21), the destruction of the donkey, a symbol of Seth, necessarily entails the advancement of a partisan of his opponent Horus. Images of mourning suggest not loss, but personal freedom and inherited wealth. Thus, in column 3, line 2, a vision of oneself in mourning indicates a favorable increase of property, while the rending of one's clothing is good, for it signifies release from all ills (column 4, line 12). Dreaming of the burial of an old man is a harbinger of prosperity (column 6, line 1). A knowledge of execration ritual provides the rationale for the unfavorable vision of broken pottery as a symbol of fighting (column 10, line 9). Other symbols are readily comprehensible: "Binding malefic people at night" is good, for it means "taking away the speech of his enemies" (column 4, line 5); and "crossing in a ferryboat" foretells a favorable extrication from all quarrels (column 4, line 6); consuming the flesh of a crocodile presages "living off the property of a bureaucrat" (column 2, line 22); and the principle of contraries presumably explains why "seeing himself dead" foretells "a long life before him" (column 4, line 13).

Sexual symbolism abounds, and seeing one's penis enlarged is good, for "it means an increase of his property" (column 2, line 11). The image of a woman's vulva, however, ensures "the ultimate in misery against him" (col-

umn 9, line 9). Oedipal copulating with one's mother is favorable, indicating "cleaving to him by his relatives" (column 3, line 7). The statement that copulation with a man's sister presages "the transferal to him of property" (column 3, line 8) anticipates an economic reality later practiced in the Roman era, when brother-sister marriage safeguarded family holdings.

The recording of dreams continued throughout later Egyptian history, and "dream diaries" are well attested in Demotic and Greek during the Ptolemaic era, when dream-interpreters openly advertised along the pilgrimage routes of the Serapeum in Memphis. The records of the priest Hor, attached to a nearby shrine of Thoth, detail many prophetic dreams concerning state and temple matters, and several of these prophecies were presented to the court of Ptolemy VI. More private concerns appear in dream records recovered from the Serapeum itself; in these, the recluse Apollonios and his colleagues note imagined conversations, sexual escapades, and fantastic images. From the Roman period (second century CE), several Demotic dream books are preserved that continue the imagery and approximate format of the Chester Beatty example, but with greater thematic organization and the first mention of women's dreams.

## BIBLIOGRAPHY

Gardiner, Alan. *Chester Beatty Gift*. 2 vols. Facsimiles of Egyptian Hieratic Papyri in the British Museum, 3. London, 1945.

Lewis, Naphtali. *The Interpretation of Dreams and Portents*. Toronto, 1976.

Ray, John D. *The Archive of Hor*. London, 1976.

Ritner, Robert K. "O. Gardiner 363: A Spell Against Night Terrors." *Journal of the American Research Center in Egypt* 27 (1990), 25–41.

Ritner, Robert K. "Dream Oracles." In *The Context of Scripture*, edited by William Hallo and Lawson Younger. Leiden, 1997.

Sauneron, Serge. "Les songes et leurs interprétation dans l'Égypte ancienne." In *Sources Orientales*, vol. 2, pp. 17–61. Paris, 1959.

Tait, W. John. *Papyri from Tebtunis in Egyptian and in Greek*. London, 1977.

Vernus, Pascal. "Traumdeutung (und Traumbuch)." In *Lexikon der Ägyptologie*, 6:747–749. Wiesbaden, 1986.

Volten, Aksel. *Demotische Traumdeutung*. Copenhagen, 1942.

Wilcken, Ulrich. *Urkunden der Ptolemäerzeit*. Berlin, 1927.

ROBERT K. RITNER

**DUAMUTEF.** *See* Four Sons of Horus.

**DWARVES.** *See* Deformity.

# E

**EARLY DYNASTIC PERIOD.** Egypt's Early Dynastic period (c.3050–2686 BCE), also called the Archaic, was a brief era in the long span of pharaonic history, but it was during those few centuries that many elements of what we now think of as "ancient Egyptian civilization" first appeared. The evidence suggests that the Nile Valley and Delta were first brought under the rule of a single pharaoh and the control of the national state administration in the Early Dynastic period. It was also during that period that the Egyptians developed a written language capable of expressing virtually the entire spoken language of Egypt, in a form that made this writing system an indispensable administrative tool. Another crucial development of this era was the shift of the centers of Egypt's central government from the South to the North. Before the Early Dynastic period, the largest and most important communities, such as Hierakonpolis and Naqada, were all in the South, in Upper Egypt. By 3000 BCE, the centers of power were in the North, in Lower Egypt, and the demographic center of the country also shifted, as Memphis (near modern Cairo) became the national capital and the Nile Delta became the agricultural heartland of the country. A simple geographic shift may seem unimportant in Egypt's long history, but the northward shift was an early and powerful demonstration of the effects of Egypt's increasingly important interactions with its neighbors, as the Mediterranean world began to affect Egypt's political history and, to a lesser degree, its culture. Another major development of the Early Dynastic period was the development of the national religious and political ideology and the economy, which served as the basic principles on which state and society were organized for most of pharaonic times.

**Chronology.** Most Egyptologists identify the Early Dynastic period with (in modern terminology) the first and second dynasties, but there is reasonable evidence that a Dynasty "0"—referring to the transition between the Predynastic and the Early Dynastic period—should actually be included in the Early Dynastic period. The third dynasty, as well, has often been included in the Early Dynastic period, but some see it as a part of the early Old Kingdom period. In this article, the Early Dynastic period is considered to have encompassed Dynasty "0," the first, and the second. The dates ascribed to all three dynasties are based largely on fragmentary texts written many centuries after the Early Dynastic period. Radiocarbon dates, however, roughly agree with the textual chronology, although there are some disparities. The bulk of the evidence suggests that what we label the Early Dynastic period was the interval between about 3100 and 2700 BCE.

**Origins of the Early Dynastic State.** Almost all the developments in the Early Dynastic period had deep roots in the Predynastic period (c.4000–3050 BCE). The evolution of Egyptian civilization was a long and complex pattern of change, and terms such as "Predynastic" and "Early Dynastic" only roughly divide the continuum of cultural change undergone in Egypt.

The cultural changes that the term "Early Dynastic" was intended to describe can perhaps be best understood by way of comparison with the Predynastic. At about 3500 BCE, the evidence suggests that nearly all Egyptians were basically Neolithic farmers who lived in insubstantial houses of mud bricks or mud and straw, arranged in small communities that appear to have had little to do with one another except for some modest trade in stone tools and a few other commodities. Every extended family probably made almost all its own goods and did all the work necessary for its own survival, and almost every extended family made more or less the same goods and performed the same activities as every other family. They made crude pottery, bows and arrows, stone tools, thatched mud-brick huts, baskets and fabrics, and not much else. Their lives probably did not encompass much beyond the ordinary events of subsistence farmers everywhere—birth, marriage, death, and the incessant demands of extracting a reliable living by cultivating a few crops, herding some sheep, goats, and/or cattle, and supplementing their diet through hunting, fishing, and foraging. By 3000 BCE, and rapidly increasing thereafter, major cultural changes were underway. Like their Predynastic ancestors, the great mass of Egyptians still lived as illiterate peasants in small villages—but there are signs that they were becoming citizens of a national state. One of the earliest indications of the rise of the Egyptian state is in the humble form of pottery styles. The Predynastic peoples of the North of Egypt had significantly different styles of pottery and architecture from those in the South. Yet by about 3000 BCE, styles of architecture, pottery, and other artifacts were beginning to show great similarity throughout Egypt, from the Mediterranean to the Nubian frontier to the oases of the Western Desert.

The processes by which Egypt was changed from a Neolithic society to one of the first and most powerful states of antiquity have been debated by scholars for more than a century; many surmise that Egypt was politically unified through warfare. The Narmer Palette, for example, is particularly intriguing in this context. Found at Hierakonpolis in Upper Egypt, the Narmer Palette probably dates to about 3200 to 3000 BCE—precisely the period in which Egypt first became a unified, powerful, wealthy, and literate state. Even if we knew nothing else about this era, the headless bodies, military-style flags, and mythical ferocious beasts incised so beautifully on this stone slate would suggest that the ancient Egyptians were no strangers to bloody warfare. Some scholars think the Narmer Palette was made to commemorate the initial formation of the Egyptian state by means of the Southern armies' conquest of the cities of the Delta, others, however, think that it commemorates later events that had nothing to do with the political unification of Egypt. Yet the Narmer Palette is engraved with various symbols conveying ideas that we know from later texts were at the very heart of the ancient Egyptians' idea of the nature of their state—for example, the symbols in the shape of crowns. When the Narmer Palette was made, these symbols may have referred to the political unification of small Southern polities. Most scholars think they were references to the political unity of "the Two Lands"—that is, Northern and Southern Egypt. The crowns of Upper and Lower Egypt (the White Crown and Red Crown, respectively) were depicted throughout the history of pharaonic Egypt, often in association with texts that clearly indicate this meaning. Another symbol on the Narmer Palette that may relate to the unification of Egypt is the bull that is shown apparently battering towns: this stylized depiction of architecture and the image of a bull as a symbol of the pharaoh's power may be an evocation of military attacks on fortified settlements. What the Narmer Palette and similar artifacts "mean" will always be ambiguous. What is certain, however, is that between 4000 and 3000 BCE, Egypt became a powerful integrated state, and most of the primary elements of pharaonic civilization first appeared.

Many ideas about the factors that produced Egyptian civilization have been argued. Donald Redford (1989), for example, has suggested that Near Eastern cultures of Southwest Asia may have influenced these first Egyptian states. He has documented the apparent presence of Semitic elements in early written Egyptian and, on the basis of this and other evidence, has suggested that the initial confrontation between these cultures may have occurred in the eastern Nile Delta. Redford notes that traditional interpretations of Egypt's Early Dynastic history argue a kind of "*Drang nach Norden*," with the forces of political unification and expansion moving up the Nile Valley, engulfing the Delta, and expanding into Southwest Asia, but that "there is one element that is particularly difficult to accommodate within this south–north sweep of Egyptian political evolution, and that is the clear evidence in Gerzean and later sites of artifacts and artifact (and architectural) styles that are Syro-Palestinian and Irano-Mesopotamian in origin" (1989, p. 1). Redford also observes that for years scholars have debated what kinds of contacts these elements reflect, and he sees in these debates "a tendency toward an Egyptian view of the world, in which all things are in balance, and thus to postulate *a priori* an early and independent Delta polity opposing an independent Valley polity, and the eventual union of these" (1989, p. 2, also see Frankfort, 1956, pp. 15–23).

Whatever the influence of foreign cultures and internal factors in creating the Early Dynastic state, we do have some evidence about its history. Dynasty "0," that time between the end of the Predynastic and the beginning of the Early Dynastic, is known from only a few excavations. Succeeding dynasties, however, are known from texts and other evidence.

**The First Dynasty.** Many of the central elements of ancient Egyptian civilization, such as techniques of tomb construction, theology, and the national political administrative system, were present in embryonic form in Upper Egypt before 3200 BCE, but between about 3200 and 2700 BCE these elements achieved the basic form in which they were to persist for about three thousand years. With the Early Dynastic period, Egypt moved into the historical era; from about 3100 BCE onward, there are at least a few texts to aid in interpreting the archaeological data, but these texts are few and fragmentary. The later writings about this period may record as much legendary information as historiographical data, but some record the names of mothers, wives, and other people, not just the names and exploits of kings. To complement these texts, there is much spectacular archaeological data. Many tombs of the first and second dynasties were found at Abydos, Tarkhan, Helwan, and Saqqara; although most had been looted in antiquity, when they were excavated they still contained rich stores of grave goods, from food to tools to precious stones.

If we correlate the various Early Dynastic king lists, it seems that the first dynasty consisted of eight pharaohs, all of whom were probably buried at Abydos. After Narmer, Aha is the first known king, but Aha may have been the same person as Narmer, may have established Memphis as the permanent capital of Egypt, instituting the cults of the crocodile god Sobek (of the Faiyum) and

EARLY DYNASTIC PERIOD. *Figure from the Early Dynastic (Archaic) period, in the Brooklyn Museum of Art.* (Courtesy Stephen Phillips)

the Apis bull (of Memphis) as major religious institutions. The Egyptians—at least until Akhenaten's time (c.1350 BCE)—saw no conflict in a profusion of different gods or the combination of the attributes of several gods in one. Religion provided the connective tissue for all early states, and state religions provided efficient methods to get the population to pay taxes, serve in wars, and in general act as citizens of a nation: people acted in these socially constructive ways out of a sense of duty, not out of coercion. This is not to suggest that Aha or other Egyptian pharaohs cynically manipulated their subjects by inventing a religion; Aha, for example, almost certainly did not coldly calculate the costs/benefits ratio of raising the status of Sobek and the Apis bull in a cynical ploy to solidify his power. He probably genuinely believed in these gods.

If the fragmentary texts—and some inventive speculations based on these texts—are to be believed, Aha promoted the socioeconomic and political integration of the Nile Delta and Valley. It was an integrative process that probably began centuries earlier, in part perhaps by his marrying Neithhotep, who appears to have been the daughter of Delta royalty. He apparently also sent military expeditions to Nubia and Libya, while expanding trade with Syria-Palestine. Aha's political strategy was in some ways a model for every subsequent pharaoh: to legitimize his rule and unite the country, he associated himself with the gods and invoked their power and blessings, he used strategic marriage as a political tactic to maintain national solidarity, and he confronted his neighbors with both military might and trade relationships. In so doing, he enriched his state, defused possible invasions, and brought glory to himself.

Aha also either initiated or continued an important tradition, one where even in death the pharaoh served the needs of the state. Aha's tomb and cenotaph (a monument to the king that recorded his death but did not contain his body) emphasized the integration and unification of "the Two Lands." Aha and most of the Early Dynastic pharaohs appear to have been buried at Abydos. The contemporary tombs at Saqqara were probably those of high government officials or provincial rulers.

After Aha's death (perhaps about 3100 BCE), there may have been some struggles in the line of succession, as there are gaps in the king lists. Ancient Egyptian texts suggest that after two or three others had succeeded Aha, a king named Djer ruled Egypt. Djer built a tomb at Abydos (in the South) and a temple at Memphis (in the North), apparently to express in architecture the principle of the integration of the Two Lands. The great wealth of the tombs of the time of Djer suggests a prosperous era, and as Nicolas Grimal notes (1992, p. 50), Djer is the first pharaoh who appears to have considered the importance of the mortuary needs of his subordinates; near Djer's tomb are the tombs of what are likely members of his royal court. Grimal suggests that there is no evidence that those royals were killed at the pharaoh's death in order to be entombed *en masse*, but the situation is ambiguous. This is an interesting point because both ritual murder or the suicide of a king's court were common in such other ancient cultures as Mesopotamia, China, and Mesoamerica. As efficient as such ritual murder-suicide arrangements were in protecting the king against court intrigues, poisoning, or other forms of assassination, they were extremely expensive in terms of the loss of some of the most knowledgeable members of the royal family and bureaucracy, as well as much wealth. Marxist scholars have asserted that "religion is the opiate of the masses," in the sense that religion can be used to keep a population docile and reasonably content with the premise that their nasty, brutish, short lives on earth will be followed by life in an eternal paradise. There are also clear advantages to a royal bureaucracy in which the elites, not just the king, could aspire to a rich eternal afterlife. They would thus have a stake in maintaining the royalty, amassing wealth, and remaining faithful to the ancient gods. Djer's mortuary complex may reflect the first formal recognition of the nobility's aspirations for eternal life, but some Egyptologists suspect that his mortuary complex reflects instead the ritual killing of nobles at Djer's death.

Little is known of Wadji (Djet), who followed Djer. The successor, Den, however, had a glorious reign of about fifty years, during which he seems (based on a few scanty texts) to have successfully dealt with problems that would face nearly every pharaoh for the next twenty-five hundred years. One particularly important and continuing problem was balancing the power of the pharaoh against that of royal officials and the provincial rulers and elites, while at the same time keeping the country under a unified administration. This delicate balancing act must have given many pharaohs sleepless nights and made them suspicious of intrigues. Den seems to have taken active steps to limit the power of his subordinates, and he created the post of "Chancellor of the King of Lower Egypt" to help him maintain the unity of the state. The tomb of this official, named Hemaka, was large and lavishly furnished—a sign of the growing importance of bureaucratic functionaries in the Egyptian state.

There is some evidence that Den used a tactic that was employed by most pharaohs, in that he promoted the national religion by building temples and celebrating public rituals in honor of Atum, Apis, and other gods. Many of the pharaohs manipulated the state religion for political purposes, for example, by elevating the importance in the national religion of particular regional gods. Den also confronted another problem faced by all pharaohs: dealing with Egypt's neighbors. Den, for example, in his very first year as pharaoh, invaded Syria-Palestine and brought back, among other spoils of war, many women to stock his harem. An ivory label or small plaque found at Abydos shows King Den in battle, beating a Near Eastern–looking enemy on the head with a mace, the whole composition entitled "The First Occasion of Smiting the East" (Quirke and Spencer 1992, fig. 21). Although the figure of the enemy appears to be parrying the king's blow, it is not clear whether the king actually fought hand to hand in this fashion. This may simply represent the king's power as exercised through his soldiers.

Then, too, the figure of the warrior-king is a primary icon of all ancient societies. One of the more intractable questions about human history is why organized warfare is such an ancient and enduring part of our past. Den may well have had what for him were reasonable motives for his battles in Palestine. If later Egyptian history is any guide, Syrian-Palestinian groups, Nubians, and Libyans continually threatened Egypt's frontiers, probably in small hit-and-run attacks aimed at looting rather than conquest. Egypt probably did not have a permanent standing army until very late in its history, so foreigners along the borders could usually overpower local defenses, especially when the power of the central Egyptian government had weakened. In primitive warfare, the adage "the best defense is a good offense" is particularly true. Egyptian military expeditions could save the country much grief by periodically invading its neighbors and dispersing their troop concentrations.

Frequent military excursions were also a means to get

material goods. When we look at the foreign commodities found in tombs and listed in texts, it is clear that the vast bulk of these items were not things that Egypt needed in any practical sense. Numerous texts record leopard and panther skins, ebony, cedar, turquoise, giraffes, monkeys, ostrich eggs, ivory, incense, gold, copper, and other exotic goods that had great symbolic importance but not much to do with the provisions of everyday life. Similarly, the capture of foreign women to stock a pharaoh's harem seems to have been a common military goal; that there was a shortage of Egyptian nubilia, which had to be supplemented by women captured abroad for harem duty, is not realistic. War prisoners captured and used as slaves were certainly numerous in some periods and of considerable economic value, but there is no evidence that they met some urgent labor requirements that could not be filled by locals. Many anthropologists would contend that this kind of cost-benefit analysis of Egyptian warfare is beside the point: these people did not live with a capitalistic, money-based economy, so these seemingly "worthless" exotic goods had enormous intrinsic value—they validated the power of the pharaoh and helped distinguish the elites from the common folk. Moreover, the pharaoh could only demonstrate his worthiness in traditional ways, and one of these was military exploits. Regardless of the personal motives of Den and his successors, Egypt, like all ancient states, appears to have been intrinsically expansionistic—an excellent evolutionary strategy for any organism, whether it be a biological population or sociopolitical organization.

Enedjib, Den's successor, apparently reigned only briefly, but he is the first pharaoh known to use the title "Lord of the Two Lands," in the sense of uniting the gods Horus and Seth. As noted above, this title implies the reconciliation of these two potent, competing Egyptian deities. Horus's association with order and Seth's association with disorder, and their melding in the person of the pharaoh, are at the center of one of the many major ancient Egyptian concepts that we will probably never fully understand. "Disorder" was not necessarily and intrinsically bad—if it could be visited on Egypt's enemies (Grimal 1992, p. 48). We'll never know how often the disorder of an actual violent confrontation between the Delta and the Valley occurred in early Egyptian times, but from Enedjib onward pharaohs took names that involved the reconciliation of the Two Lands. They took as one of their titles a phrase that means "He of the Two Ladies"—a reference to the protection of the king by the cobra goddess Wadjyt of the community at Buto in the northern Delta and Lower Egypt and the vulture goddess Nekhbet of Hierakonpolis and Upper Egypt.

**The Second Dynasty.** The kings of the second dynasty are poorly known, as are the reasons why a change of dynastic families occurred. The third-century BCE Greco-Egyptian historian Manetho reports the change but gives no explanation. During the second dynasty, some pharaohs may have been buried not at Abydos in the South as their predecessors apparently were, but at Saqqara, although the evidence is uncertain. Saqqara's increased importance was tied to the rise of the nearby city of Memphis as the capital of a united Egypt.

In the second dynasty, bronze vessels are known to have been made in Egypt for the first time. The appearance of bronze has been used as a major mark of cultural development, and the term "Bronze Age" is applied across the whole of the ancient Near East. The use of bronze for tools and other artifacts, however, may not have been that revolutionary, since flint knives and sickles continued to be the primary agricultural tools until the Late period. Nevertheless, the spread of bronze artifacts across the Mediterranean region from Southwest Asia probably reflects growing interactions among countries.

There is some evidence that during the reigns of the second dynasty's early kings the political relationships between Upper and Lower Egypt had deteriorated (Grimal 1992, pp. 52–59). A ruler named Peribsen rose to power in about 2734 BCE, but he may have ruled only Upper Egypt; he appointed a "Chancellor of the King of Upper Egypt," and seals bearing Peribsen's name have been found as far south as Elephantine. Peribsen also chose Seth, the god of disorder as his tutelary deity—the god he hoped would instruct and protect him—instead of Horus, the traditional Early Dynastic choice.

Peribsen's successor, Khasekhem ("the powerful [Horus] is crowned"), was born at Hierakonpolis in the South; at the time of his coronation, he had incised on stone statues of himself and on stone vessels several texts that commemorated victories over the North. The bases of these statues were decorated with a tableau of dead and disarticulated bodies, presumably depicting the fate of rebels and enemy war casualties. Khasekhem's victory over the North may have been the reason that he "later changed his name to Khasekhemwy: 'the Two Powers are crowned', placing both Horus and Seth over the *serekh*. . . . At the same time he chose 'the Two Mistresses are at peace through him'" (Grimal 1992, p. 56).

Khasekhemwy retained a primary interest in Southern Egypt, where he built large tombs and temples at Elkab, Abydos, and Hierakonpolis. His huge mud-brick "forts" at Hierakonpolis and Abydos were probably temple enclosures, not defensive fortifications, but they remain to this day very impressive building projects. Khasekhemwy's apparent reunification of Egypt, however, seems to have been quickly followed by another shift northward of Egypt's political center. Throughout pharaonic history, there were oscillations in the geographic center of political, economic, and religious power, but after Khase-khemwy, Memphis and Lower Egypt dominated the country for many centuries. Throughout much of the rest of the pharaonic era, ancient Egyptians thought of their country as balanced, like a weighing scale at Memphis—so the Memphite nome (province) was known as Mekhattawy ("balance of the Two Lands"). The national state fractured into two parts, on a few occasions, in later periods; but throughout the rest of pharaonic history, the union of the Two Lands was perceived as the only legitimate form of the state.

[*See also* Khasekhemwy; Menes; *and* Narmer.]

### BIBLIOGRAPHY

Adams, B. and K. M. Cialowicz. *Protodynastic Egypt.* Shire Egyptology, Princes Risborough, 1988.

Frankfort, H. *The Birth of Civilization in the Near East.* Garden City, N.Y., 1956.

Grimal, N. *A History of Ancient Egypt.* Translated by I. Shaw. Oxford, 1992.

Quirke, S., and J. Spencer, eds. *The British Museum Book of Ancient Egypt.* New York, 1992.

Redford, Donald B. "Prolegomena to Archaeological Investigations of Mendes." Manuscript, on file with the author. Seattle, 1989.

Rice, M. *Egypt's Making: The Origins of Ancient Egypt 5000–2000 B.C.* London and New York, 1991.

Spencer, A. J. *Early Egypt: The Rise of Civilisation in the Nile Valley.* London, 1993.

ROBERT J. WENKE

**EASTERN DESERT AND RED SEA,** region to the east of the Nile River. Today, the Eastern Desert is called the Arabian Desert, and it lies between the Nile Valley and the Red Sea, covering some 21 percent of present-day Egypt. It consists of a high mountain range of ancient volcanic rock—Precambrian hard rock, formed approximately three billion years ago—which runs the length of the Red Sea. It has wide, high plateaus with accumulations of rubble from eroded sandstone and limestone. The topography is the result of faults and elevating shifts that occurred during the formation of the Red Sea basin, some twenty to thirty million years ago. The Eastern Desert's climate is similar today to climatic conditions in pharaonic times. The desert began to dry out about 3500 BCE, and its northern half is nearly devoid of vegetation as a result of the arid climate. Higher humidity to the south creates slightly increased precipitation in that area, so shrubs and trees are found in some of the desert valleys.

The "Eastern Desert" of pharaonic times included the eastern reaches of the Nile Delta, the Wadi Tumilat that led to the Red Sea, and the western parts of the Sinai. Sopdu was the deity of the Eastern Desert regions; however, his significance was actually negligible in the Eastern Desert (in the area between the Cairo–Suez line and the southern border of Egypt). There, in the southern part of the Eastern Desert, Min or Amun-Min (phallically represented) was the dominant deity.

**Ancient Settlements.** The Eastern Desert was more densely populated in prehistoric times and in the early historic period than it was in pharaonic times, because of slightly higher than present-day precipitation in the region. Proof includes the numerous rock drawings in the Eastern Desert, which are, however, limited to the desert's southern region; to the north, we find evidence of only sporadic travel through the desert. The rock drawings are concentrated in the wide reaches of the Wadi Hammamat between Coptos and Quseir; in the Wadi Qena; near the continuously settled Laqiya Oasis to the southeast of Coptos; around wells, such as Bir Menih; throughout the Wadi Barramiya near Edfu; in regions close to Aswan; and at Quseir on the Red Sea. The earliest drawings, dated to the Naqada I period, show Nile Valley and desert-border fauna that retreated from the region soon after 3500 BCE—elephant, giraffe, rhinoceros, and ostrich, as well as indigenous desert wildlife, such as ibex, gazelle, and antelope. Images of people wearing the typical Libyan penis pouch, and others with ornamental wigs (the so-called Dirwa people), can be dated to about 3500 BCE. The many representations of boats flying standards and groups of people wearing feather ornaments were originally thought to be a new population that moved into the area from the Red Sea, across the Wadi Hammamat; more likely, those images and the many cattle drawings are indications of local contact with the population in the Nile Valley during the Naqada II period. By and large, that type of rock drawing came to an end at the close of the Old Kingdom. Later, some horse and camel drawings were dated to Roman and Arab times.

Then as now, desert nomads traveled to water sources and across the coastal regions of the southern part of the Eastern Desert. In pharaonic expedition reports, those people were referred to collectively as "Medjay." Today's Bedja and Ma'aza tribes are assumed to be descendants of the pharaonic Medja; yet the similarity in the tribal names may be coincidental. There is no documented continuity of settlement, since during the fourth and fifth centuries, nomadic groups called the "Blemmyes," had penetrated into that region. Members of the Medjay groups were used by the Egyptians as scouts and workers, organized under their own chiefs on pharaonic expeditions. Some Nubian groups to the south, along the Red Sea—the names of regions such as Kebeh and Mu-qed were handed down—would have profited from coastal navigation and exchange trade with Egypt.

**Historical Overview.** Aside from its significance as a transit route to the Red Sea, the Eastern Desert was primarily a supply source of special rocks and ores. Late

EASTERN DESERT AND RED SEA. *View of the Wadi Hammamat.* (Courtesy Donald B. Redford)

prehistoric and early historic stone vessels and smaller objects in breccia, porphyry, serpentine, and steatite (a soapstone) were fashioned from accumulations of rock shingle found in the Eastern Desert. Gold was most likely found and extracted initially as placer gold, from the bottom of the wadis. The Horus names of Early Dynastic rulers were then inscribed in the Wadi el-Qash (by King Narmer) and in the Wadi Barramiya, farther south, near Edfu (by King Wadji). The many expedition inscriptions, beginning with the fourth dynasty, document "state" interest in the special harder rock deposits because of cult significance; for example, greywacke from the Wadi Hammamat to the southeast of Coptos, as well as ore and gold extraction. In the Wadi Mueilha, halfway between Edfu and the Red Sea, numerous graffiti were found from the Old Kingdom and the First Intermediate Period. Some have suggested that this was an Early Dynastic mining site for native tin dioxide (cassiterite). The Old Kingdom inscriptions in the Wadi Barramiya and at the well of Bir Dunqash, east of Edfu, often refer to the same persons and may be linked to pharaonic mines. A unique fourth dynasty stone dam across the Wadi Gerrawi, 11 kilometers (7 miles) southeast of Helwan, presumably blocked floodwater from the Nile Valley. The first ancient Egyptian

expeditions to the land of Punt, located in the approximate region of present-day Eritrea, probably followed the natural desert route from Coptos through the Wadi Hammamat to the Red Sea; it is less certain whether the southern Sinai was also made accessible from that point.

The many large and small limestone quarries in the Eastern Desert, worked from the Old Kingdom onward, were all located near the Nile Valley and were less well documented, owing to the absence of rock inscriptions. The most important sandstone quarries of the Eastern Desert were near Gebel es-Silsila, north of Aswan, and in the areas near Edfu and Elkab. The granite and granodiorite quarries southeast of Aswan were used in early times for royal palaces. Calcite (also called Egyptian or Oriental alabaster) had been quarried since the Early Dynastic period; during the Old Kingdom, the center of calcite quarrying was to the east of el-Minya, near Hebenu (the sixteenth nome of Upper Egypt), and called by the Romans, Alabastronpolis. The quarry at Hatnub, 18 kilometers (12 miles) southeast of the Amarna plain, was the richest and most documented of Egypt's quarries; it was worked continuously from the fourth dynasty into the New Kingdom, and nearby were the Ramessid-era calcite quarries at Bersheh. Other pharaonic calcite veins were farther away in the Eastern Desert; for example, in the Wadi Gerrawi near Helwan, in the Wadi Sannur near Beni Suef (Late period), and near Asyut.

During the Middle Kingdom, under Amenemhet I, the village of Menat-Khufu ("Khufu's wetnurse") near Beni Hasan, in Central Egypt, became the administrative center for the northern area of the Eastern Desert. The official called the "Supervisor of the Eastern Desert" controlled the area from the southern Sinai to the Wadi Hammamat; this arrangement was based less on convenient routes than on the fact that Central Egypt, with its large calcite and sandstone quarries, could provide the necessary workers, expertise, and transport for quarry work. A bedouin donkey caravan of women, children, and soldiers transporting galena (lead ore, used for black eye makeup) to the Nile Valley, and probably to the royal palace, was portrayed on the grave of Khnumhotep II, an administrator of the Eastern Desert, near Beni Hasan. The caravan leader was accompanied by an Egyptian official, but the weapons and musical instruments identify the group as either from Canaan or Transjordan. Quite possibly, a small tribe worked for the Egyptians in the galena mines on the Red Sea. The quarries in the Wadi Hammamat region (the Egyptian names translate to "Upper Rohana Mountains" and "Bechen Stone Mountains") were developed at the end of the eleventh dynasty and during the twelfth on a very large scale, spreading out from Coptos. Amethyst (a violet variety of quartz) was extracted in the Wadi el-Hudi, 35 kilometers (20 miles) southeast of Aswan; the local expedition inscriptions span the period from the end of the eleventh dynasty to the thirteenth. Court officials with titles such as "Treasurer of Gold," "Administrator of the Southern Districts," "Administrator of the Southern Narrow Doorway," and so on, were given responsibility for oversight. Work groups in the thousands were common; most workers were probably bedouins, hired from their chiefs, accompanied by hunters, soldiers, and interpreters, all led by top officials, such as a vizier. On those expeditions "miracles" occurred, such as the discovery of wells that were unknown even to natives of the region or the sighting of a pregnant gazelle resting on a rich rock deposit. Galena was extracted at Gebel el-Zeit on the Red Sea coast, from the time of Amenemhet III (r. 1843–1797 BCE) to the time of Ramesses III (r. 1198–1166 BCE), with the most active quarrying during the Second Intermediate Period.

During the New Kingdom, the larger quarry area of the Wadi Hammamat and its gold deposits were administered from Thebes. The "Coptos gold" was mentioned on the famous site plan of the Ramessid-era Mine Papyrus, which included the location of the gold-panning site and the gold-worker village, near a rock-cut temple of Amun, at Bir Umm Fawakhir. The center of gold mining was in the Wadi Sid; more than sixty ancient gold mines have been documented in the Eastern Desert, especially in the Wadi Semna, the Wadi Hammamat, and the southern regions (Wadi Barramiya, Dunqash, Wadi el-Hudi, and others). Bir Umm Fawakhir was the site of the Min shrine, important to travelers on their way to the Red Sea. Green diorite was mined, as well as graywacke (a sandstone) and granite and, especially in the Wadi Atalla, serpentine. Softer stone (such as steatite, a soapstone) was used for the small pharaonic scarabs, amulets, and figurines.

The "desert of Coptos" was carefully controlled and monitored by Nubian soldiers and scouts. Ramessid-era account papyri, on deliveries to the Amun temple at Thebes, mention "galena in elephant husk," as well as acacia wood, spice or aromatic plants, and ivory objects, which were probably traded at the Red Sea ports. The southern desert areas, especially the gold deposits in the Wadi Barramiya and in the Wadi Mia across from Edfu, were controlled by the viceroy of Nubia, who brought along Nubian experts. Sety I (r. 1314–1304 BCE) had a stone temple to Amun (temple of Kanais) erected in the Wadi Mia, next to a well and gold-panning site, from which the earnings were taken to Abydos, to the pharaoh's new funerary temple. Later, the site had an important Min shrine (Paneion) for travelers to the Red Sea.

From 600 BCE onward, the activities of the Saite pharaohs were only sporadically documented. Amasis (r. 569–526 BCE) restored an older Min shrine in the Wadi Hammamat and in Wadi Barramiya; the cult site in Wadi Hammamat, described as a rock-cut temple of Nektanebo I (r. 380–363 BCE), served as a Pan shrine for later Roman travelers. Stelae from the twenty-sixth dynasty were located in the Wadi Gasus, near the harbor. During the First Persian Occupation of 525 to 405 BCE, economic contacts between the Nile Valley and Persia were maintained, in part across the Wadi Hammamat and at the Egyptian harbors on the Red Sea; Darius I (r. 521–486 BCE) renewed graywacke quarrying in the Wadi Hammamat on a large scale.

Under Ptolemy II (r. 282–246 BCE), sea trade with Arabia and more distant regions, collectively called "India," was intensified. The southern port of Berenice (also called Troglodytike, with the temple of Ptolemy VII) was built, and foreign trade was conducted by boat along the coast to Suez (Arsinoe); north of Berenice were Nechesia harbor (Mersa Mubarak?), Leukos Limen (Quseir, with a Ptolemaic temple), Philoteras (Mersa Gawasis), and Myos Hormos (island of Abu Sha'r). All harbors had been linked by road to the Nile Valley, however, travelers began to use those connections more frequently only in Roman times. Near Philoteras harbor, smaller galena deposits had been found in Ptolemaic times, close to Aenum in the Wadi Gasus, while amethyst mines had been located near Abu

Diyaba. Southwest of Berenice, a road led to a small Ptolemaic station in the desert near el-Abraq (Shenshef). In Ptolemaic and Roman times, at Gebel Sikeit (Mons Smaragdus) and at Gebel Zabara, green beryl (emerald) was mined.

In Roman times, the Eastern Desert routes were reinforced with wall-enclosed outposts and way-stations. The supervision of Egypt's earnings from the numerous mines and from pearl fishing was carried out in the time of Augustus (r. 30 BCE–14 CE) by specialists, such as the "Archimetallarch of Emerald, Topaz, and Pearls." The Greek god Pan, equated with the Egyptian god Min, was the overseer of travelers through the Eastern Desert; many shrines to Pan (Paneion) were built along the main routes and, in a wadi behind Akhmim, "Pan-who-goes-into-the-mountains" or "Pan-who-is-with-the-expeditions" was honored. Mining in the imperial porphyry quarries of Mons Porphyrites (imperial red porphyry and smaller deposits of green porphyry) and in the granite and quartzdiorite quarries of Mons Claudianus was begun in the Augustinian era and was continued into the fifth century CE. The last dated inscriptions from the stone quarries in Wadi Hammamat were from the middle of the third century CE. The deities Zeus, Helios, and Sarapis were revered by the nonindigenous mine workers—many slaves and prisoners—and by the guards, soldiers, and supply workers.

**Roads.** In the northern region of the Eastern Desert, the pharaonic roads cannot be accurately traced; and the road running parallel to the Red Sea coast cannot be mapped. Findings of some Ramessid-era stelae near Nag' 'Alalma have led to the inference that a road may have existed connecting el-Saff/Atfih, north of Beni Suef and past the Antonius monastery, to Zaafarana on the Red Sea. An often presumed route from the Central Egyptian villages of the eastern bank of the Nile—especially from the Beni Hasan region to the Red Sea and, also, in a southeasterly direction over the Wadi Qena to the Wadi Hammamat—is unconfirmed. The first confirmed road is the Via Nova Hadriana, built in 130 BCE by the Roman emperor Hadrian from his newly founded city Antinoöpolis (today's Sheik Abade), in Central Egypt, to the Red Sea and then farther along the coast to the southern Berenice.

The most important ancient road link from the Nile Valley to the Red Sea ran from Coptos to Thebes during the New Kingdom. The Wadi Hammamat was reached after passing the Laqeita Oasis, and caravans then traveled through the Wadi Atalla and the Wadi Gasus to the harbor of Mersa Gawasis (Eg., Sauu) south of present-day Hurghada. The harbor was mentioned in inscriptions only in the Middle Kingdom (after Senwosret I), but was probably older, and was the departure point for trade via the Red Sea with the southern land of Punt. Prefabricated boat components were built on the wharfs of Coptos, transported to the coast by huge donkey caravans of up to three thousand men, then assembled there. The harbor was still active in the New Kingdom, where a "fort of (pharaoh) Merenptah" was probably located to control the traffic of goods. Philoteras, 2 kilometers (1.2 miles) to the south, was the Ptolemaic era's successor to the pharaonic-era harbor.

The southern route from Edfu, or from Elkab across the Wadi Abbad and the Wadi Barramiya, to the Red Sea was surely traveled in pharaonic times; however, it was only verified at the time of the foundation of the Ptolemaic harbor of Berenice. In Roman times, the same route, from Edfu (Apollonopolis) over Contra-Apollonopolis and the Wadi Abbad, was expanded at Falacro to join the main route from Coptos to Berenice. In Ptolemaic times, a new road led from Coptos to Berenice (a five-to-six-day journey). It left Coptos harbor in the direction of Phoinicon (the Laqeita Oasis); there it turned southeast and passed Didyme, Aphrodite, Compasi, Jovis, Aristonis, Falacro, Apollonos, Cabalsi, Vetus Hydreuma, and Novum Hydreuma before reaching Berenice harbor. The road from Coptos to Quseir (Gr., Leukos Limen) on the Red Sea was a three-and-a-half-day journey through the Laqeita Oasis, Qusur el-Banat with a Roman shrine to Pan/Min, el-Bueib (with a Roman Pan shrine), Mweih, through the Wadi Hammamat, and on to Zerqa and Sayala.

The road from Qena (Kaineopolis) to Philoteras (Mersa Gawasis) on the Red Sea passed through the stations of el-'Aras, Abu Qreiya, the Wadi Gidami, the Wadi Semna (with a Pan shrine) and, probably, through the settlement of Aenum in the Wadi Gasus (with a temple of Ptolemy VI), then on to Philoteras. The road from Qena to Myos Hormos (island of Abu Sha'r) crossed the fortified stations of el-'Aras, el-Hetah, Saqia, Der el-Atrash, and Qattar, went past the Mons Porphyrites region either on to Myos Hormos or on to the nearby water source at Fons Tadnos. An alternative road forked off from the northern route at el-'Aras and continued to Myos Hormos, through Abu Zawal; it then passed Mons Claudianus and the road station, with Sarapis temple, in the Wadi Sidris.

[*See also* Sinai.]

**BIBLIOGRAPHY**

Bernand, André. *De Koptos a Kosseir.* Leiden, 1972. Research history and collection of Greek and Latin inscriptions from the Eastern Desert.

Castel, Georges, et al. *Gebel el-Zeit,* vol. 1: *Les mines de Galène.* Cairo, 1989.

Goyon, Georges. *Nouvelles inscriptions rupestres du Wadi Hammamat.* Paris, 1957.

Helck, Wolfgang. "Eine Briefsammlung aus der Verwaltung des Amuntempels," *Journal of the American Research Center in Egypt* 6 (1967), 135–151.

Hume, William F. *The Geology of Egypt, 1925–37*. Classic work on the geology of the Eastern Desert.

Klemm, Rosemarie, and Dietrich Klemm. "Pharaonischer Goldbergbau im Wadi Sid und der Turiner Minenpapyrus." *Akten des vierten. Internationalen Ägyptologen Kongresses, München, 1985*, vol. 2, 73–87. Studien zur altägyptischen Kultur Beiheffe, 1–4. Hamburg, 1988. Newest proposal on the location of gold deposits in the Turin Mine Papyrus.

Klemm, Rosemarie, and Dietrich Klemm. *Steine und Steinbrüche im Alten Ägypten*. Berlin and New York, 1992. The nomenclature for the rock formation and numerous antique quarry areas are systematically presented.

Meredith, David. *Tabula Imperii Romani: Coptos*. Oxford, 1958. Map of the southern part of the Eastern Desert; summarizes research on the Roman and Ptolemaic paths and roads.

Porter, Bertha, and Rosalind Moss. *Topographical Bibliography of Ancient Egyptian Hieroglyphic Texts, Reliefs, and Paintings VII: Nubia, the Deserts, and Outside Egypt*. Oxford, 1951.

Rothe, Russell D., and George R. Rapp. "Trace-Element Analysis of Egyptian Eastern Desert Tin and its Importance to Egyptian Archaeology." *Proceedings of the Egyptian-Italian Seminar on Geosciences and Archaeology in Mediterranean Countries*, edited by Abdel Aziz A. Hussein, et al., pp. 229–244. Cairo, 1995.

Rothe, Russell D., et al. "New Hieroglyphic Evidence for Pharaonic Activity in the Eastern Desert of Egypt." *Journal of the American Research Center in Egypt* 33 (1996), 77–104.

Sadek, Ashraf I. *The Amethyst Mining Inscriptions of Wadi el Hudi*. Warminster, 1980–1985.

Sayed, Abd el Moneim. "Discovery of the Site of the 12th Dynasty Port at Wadi Gawasis on the Red Sea shore." *Revue de l'Égyptologie* 29 (1977), 138–178.

Seyfried, Karl-Josef. *Beiträge zu den Expeditionen des Mittleren reiches in die Ost-Wüste*. Hildesheim, 1981. Evaluates the inscriptions of the Wadi el-Hudi.

Whitecomb, Donald, and Janet Johnson. *Quseir el-Qadim 1978: Preliminary Report*. Cairo, 1979; and *Quseir el-Qadim 1980: Preliminary Report*. Malibu, 1982. Recent excavations have revealed little evidence for the Ptolemaic period; Quseir began to flourish after the Roman period.

Winkler, Hans A. *Rock-Drawings of Southern Upper Egypt*. London, 1938–1939. The first collection and chronological classification of the rock drawings.

DIETER KESSLER
Translated from German by Elizabeth Schwaiger

**ECONOMY.** [*This entry surveys various aspects of the economy of ancient Egypt, with reference to its structure, supervision, and chronological development, to the products involved and the nature and conditions of the labor force, and to sources of documentation. It comprises four articles:*

An Overview
Royal Sector
Private Sector
Temple Economy

*For related discussions, see the composite article* Administration.]

## An Overview

One cannot understand the economy of pharaonic Egypt without first analyzing the original documents, which demonstrate the close relationship between the emergence of the state and its economic organization under a new ideology that integrates the king with cosmic and earthly cycles. The Narmer documents display the basis for this system.

In this article, emphasis is given to the dominant traits of the pharaonic economy and the vital role of rural production (agriculture and animal husbandry) that led to the organization of the domains under the supervision of the temples and high officials of state, who acted as delegates for and under the control of royal authority.

**Origins.** Economy, power, and ideology are the three factors that together determined the birth of the Egyptian state, its monarchic expression, and its divine role in the Egypt of the fourth millennium BCE (Menu 1996a).

Toward the end of the Neolithic, two fundamentally different cultures coexisted in Egypt: in the North, a sedentary society of agriculturalists, cattle-herders, and traders carried out their activities within the political framework of an egalitarian and community-oriented society; in the South, hierarchically organized principalities flourished with plentiful natural resources and evolved an elaborate symbolic universe, producing objects of art of great esthetic value (Hoffman 1979; Midant-Reynes 1992).

The cultural and artistic amalgamation, followed by territorial unification to the benefit of the South, was accompanied in Upper Egypt by the adoption of an economy of production, succeeding one that had been largely exploitative of the abundant Nile fauna and flora. Hunting scenes, as well as scenes depicting animal and plant domestication, are often represented on predynastic objects (carved elephant tusks, knife sheaths, combs, vases, and palettes) and so linked to the crucial and deliberate shifts from hunting to husbandry, from gathering to farming, with their attendant rites and techniques, with a concomitant impulse to control arable lands. So when Narmer ascended to the throne, Egypt was already unified and controlled commercial routes within a federal or confederate political structure under the "shepherd's crook" of a single ruler; several kings in succession thus constituted Dynasty "0," which was based in Hierakonpolis in the South.

**Documents.** According to this view of agricultural exploitation by conquest, a group of royal documents, consisting of graywacke palettes and mace heads, is particularly important with regard to the origins and development of the divine monarchy and the state; these are the Battlefield Palette (British Museum), the Bull Palette (Louvre), the Scorpion mace head and the mace head of Narmer (Ashmolean Museum), and finally, the Narmer

Palette (Cairo Museum). These documents give evidence for a fundamental shift from a political authority shared with tribal or territorial gods (indicated by nome standards) to one linked to a unique and divine authority, suggested by four standard-bearers (Menu 1996b).

***The Battlefield Palette (recto).*** The king, in the shape of a lion, overwhelms his adversaries, some of whom are being attacked by predatory birds. Two standards with human arms and surmounted by a falcon and an ibis head (respectively, Horus and Thoth), bind the arms of two prisoners behind their backs while they walk toward the king-lion.

***The Bull Palette.*** Five standards in succession are surmounted by two canine shapes (each on a different support), followed by an ibis (Thoth), a falcon (Horus), and two stylized thunderbolts (emblems of the god Min). At the other end of these poles are hands, which hold a rope that binds enemies, while the king, in the shape of a bull, crushes another adversary. Only the king, in the shape of lion or bull, can put the enemy to death; the role of the standard-bearers is to capture them and to bring them to the king. Throughout pharaonic history, the sovereign is often identified with lion or bull in his epithets.

***The Scorpion mace head.*** This mace head belongs to Narmer, and "Scorpion" may express a title indicating the nurturing role of the king (Baumgartel 1966). It is not necessary to postulate the existence of two "Scorpion" kings: the only King "Scorpion" whose name is in the *serekh* is separated from Narmer by several kings (among them Iry-Hor, Crocodile?, Ka). Moreover, the simultaneous appearance of four human standard-bearers (an innovation of great importance, see below), on the Scorpion mace head, on the Narmer mace head, and on the Narmer Palette leads one to assume that these three objects date from the same period. This conclusion is reinforced by the fact that the two mace heads were discovered side by side in the Early Dynastic period and discovered in the "Main Deposit" of the temple of Hierakonpolis (Quibell 1900). In short, the Scorpion and Narmer mace heads represent the two branches of the economic order attributed to Narmer: the organization of agriculture and animal husbandry (Menu 1996a).

The Scorpion mace head presents, in its preserved section, some ten standards bearing the following recognizable emblems: the three hills of the god Ha (god of the Western Desert), the Seth animal, the lightning bolts of Min, two canine figures, and one falcon (Horus) on a bark. Below the flags, bows and lapwings, symbolizing defeated enemies, are hung from strings. For the first time, opposite the king crowned in a white miter, the group of four standard-bearers appear, of whom only two are preserved; the others can be reconstructed, owing to the Narmer mace head and the Narmer Palette. These are no longer animated standards but human beings, marching in procession, either approaching the king or preceding him. On the Narmer mace head where the king is seated, wrapped in the ceremonial mantle and wearing the Red Crown, there are four individuals who surmount the scene and walk toward the king: the dog Khentyamentiu ("Foremost-of-the-Westerners"), guardian of the necropolis and also the personification of the king deified after death; the *nḥn*-object, or the royal placenta (Posener 1965), and the falcon of the South, followed by the falcon of the North (or vice versa). On the Narmer Palette, preceding the king in a marching posture, covered in royal insignia and wearing the Red Crown, the falcon of the South is followed by the falcon of the North (or vice versa), followed by the dog Khentyamentiu, and the royal placenta. From this one may conclude that on the Scorpion mace head, two falcons are needed at the head of the procession.

***The Narmer Palette and mace head.*** On these documents the standards have disappeared; the predominant (and apparently exclusive) role is now given to the four standard-bearers. The poles surmounted by a divine emblem (whose number increases from two to five, then to ten or more) are succeeded by four standard-bearers, human figures holding high the royal symbols of life and duration (from the egg to postmortem deification), as well as the dual kingship (conceived functionally before it was adapted to the territorial duality, see below), expressed by the two succeeding falcons. The affirmation of the preeminence of royal, personal, and divine might in its earthly and cosmic manifestations supplant the representation of the hypostases of tribal or territorial gods, auxiliary to royal victory.

**Ideology of Kingship.** The documents of Narmer contain the founding principles of the pharaonic regime.

***Royal divinity and political alternation.*** The king, integrated into the cosmic and terrestrial energies, becomes a solar and Horus god, incarnating time and space along two axes: the path of the sun from east to west (for the king, from egg to deification), and the course of the Nile from south to north (for the king, the dual kingship). The celestial position of the king at the four cardinal points is indicated on the Narmer Palette by the bovine figures (representing the goddess Bat), who appear in pairs at the top of each side of the palette. The king thus replaces the local gods, who are not in evidence as such but remain in reserve for the kingdom, and are the object of a first redistribution of lands (see below); the alternation between king-god (the unique sovereign) and god-kings (local gods represented by the nomarchs during the Intermediate periods) is the survival mechanism of the regime and guarantees, often at the cost of bloody battles, the emergence of a new royal line.

***Functional duality of royal power.*** On the documents of Narmer, the king wears the Red Crown in scenes that are more or less static (counting cattle, receiving homage from defeated chiefs, and even preliminaries to land surveys; see below), and the White Crown whenever he is shown in a dynamic stance (opening the land for seeding and slaying enemies). In Ptolemaic temples, the Red Crown is associated with the *ḥḳ3*-scepter (government and rites), and the White Crown with the *sḥm*-scepter (power and domination) (Derchain 1990).

With government (*ḥḳ3*), rites, and the construction of sacred monuments, the king brings *maat* ("order") to his country, along with victory, prosperity, equilibrium, truth, and justice. By exercising might or power (*sḥm*), through combat but also through his dominion over the earth and the underground, the king repels *isft*, that is, enemies, adversity, injustice, misery, and barrenness.

During the reign of Narmer (possibly from the construction of Memphis onward), the crowns serve as a symbol of territorial duality; the White Crown is associated with power over Upper Egypt, and the Red Crown indicates sovereignty over Lower Egypt.

***Economic organization.*** By placing himself on a level with the gods, the king presents himself as the guarantor of the fertility of the land and the fecundity of livestock. Thus the king possesses divine powers to confer well-being on the people. He imposes his superiority as victorious warrior, but he also orchestrates feasts that generate prosperity and organizes the country.

On the Scorpion mace head, the central scenes evoke the appropriation of the soil by the king with agrarian goals (seeding, harvest, and planting a tree); they are accompanied by fertility rites (presentation to divinities and dances). The river is used for navigation (a ship can be discerned) and for the improvement of land by planting. On the lower part there are traces of the two primordial sanctuaries of the South and of the North, which gives the document universal meaning. The Scorpion mace head records on its base acts of the monarchy that render the territory agriculturally valuable. Fertility is ensured through the knowledge of techniques, but also through ritual. The initial and symbolic gesture of the king finds its realization in the work of others (defeated chiefs and their people).

The Narmer mace head parallels the Scorpion mace head and focuses on animal husbandry by depicting a possible effort to domesticate antelopes, which are seen running in an oval space, along with cows and calves in shelters, and countless other beasts (Menu 1996a and 1998b). Here again, homage to chiefs and foreign gods is accompanied by ritual fecundity dances (recalling the "Hathor dances" seen on Gerzean vases). This is a ceremonial balance sheet in whose creation the king, sur-rounded by his dignitaries and a wader, calculates the inventory. The census reveals 400,000 cattle, 1,422,000 head of small cattle (sheep and goats), and 120,000 men (the people under the authority of the king).

It thus falls to Narmer to negotiate the shift from an economy that is still based on hunting and gathering to one that is agricultural. In this he has two important objectives: on the one hand the organization of agriculture and animal husbandry and the redistribution of conquered land, and on the other hand, the subjugation of the peoples who are most knowledgeable in methods of farming and husbandry, as well as those who possess the secrets of fertility and fecundity.

The king guarantees the subsistence and protection of his people, who in turn owe him obeisance and work. This "contract" is outlined in the Pyramid Texts (Faulkner 1969); in paragraphs 1587–1606, Egypt is assimilated with the Eye of Horus, which the god has reconstituted with his own hands after Seth's attacks. Then the king addresses the land, in exactly in the same terms, passing in recognition of the cause from the mythological realm, where he is Horus incarnate, to the political realm where he exercises his restorative powers. The king has reconstructed the physical integrity of Egypt, in symbiosis with his own existence identified with that of the creative sun (allusion to the foundation documents of Narmer). He has founded domains and constructed towns; in exchange, he can demand total obedience from his subjects, as well as all the fruits of their labor. The sovereign's role as nurturer is proclaimed throughout pharaonic history: he is the provider of Egypt, he gives it an overabundance of provisions (Grimal 1986), coming from its own land and its neighbors, be they vassals or conquered territories.

***Ownership of land.*** The soil of Egypt is the exclusive property of the king. The four standard-bearers of the Narmer documents are the markers of Egyptian territory. The four royal symbols carried by Narmer's standard-bearers are linked to the delimitation of an idealized rectangular territory: the east, the rising sun, the Eastern Desert, and the Red Sea, symbolized by the royal placenta; the west, the setting sun, and the Libyan mountain chain, revealed in the figure of the dog, Khentyamentiu; the southern border (the First Cataract of the Nile), and the northern border (the Nile Delta), identified with the falcon of the South and the falcon of the North, dual champions of the monarchy of Horus.

From the time of Narmer, temples of local gods received lands which they could exploit. The importance of temples was already great during the Early Dynastic period (Williams 1988). By inscribing his name on the colossi of Min, Narmer confirmed a process, described above, by which royal authority imposed itself over that of the gods—in this case, Min of Coptos, the god of fecundity. The rectangle on the upper left-hand side of the Narmer Palette (*recto*) tells us that the land was surveyed with agricultural purpose, in legal documents relating to lands; later, the rectangle would signify a field or an ensemble of fields. The land was measured with the help of an illustrated instrument (not *ḏbꜣ*-floats or sandals, but some kind of compass; Menu 1996a and 1998b) and surveyed for the purpose of agricultural production. The surveying and redistribution of lands by an authority invested with supreme power is a fundamental component of political constitution.

**Agricultural Domains and the Beneficiary System.** It fell to the king, owner of Egypt's soil, to create domains (for example, Sneferu, fourth dynasty), and place them under the temple administration, and, in later periods, under high officials (fifth and sixth dynasties). Priests and high dignitaries were given them as benefits with ownership of use, but the king retained direct ownership. From earliest times, a careful distinction was made between the ownership of land, a royal prerogative, and the right to gain income from land.

All the beneficiaries drew income from the land, and could, in turn, hand over portions of their rights over the soil. This progressive division went hand in hand with various degrees of authority, always reserving exclusive ownership to the king. Though it seemed meaningless during some periods, this system continued to be the basis for the geographic and legal redistribution of lands throughout the history of Egypt (Menu 1998b). At the beginning only two choices were possible for the king: the foundation of domains on virgin land, newly acquired or taken by him; and the concession of rights that could revert to royal authority, and were in part leasable.

In the edict "Coptos A," the pharaoh Pepy I conceded a funerary domain to the god Min, that is, to the temple of Coptos, which translated into a transfer of authority over this parcel of land. No longer would requisitions be made on this property, nor would the right of passage be exercised, nor would royal taxes be collected. In short, the domain became the responsibility of the temple, freed from all obligations to the royal administration. The temple thus gained authority over the domain that had become deeded land, whose income was in part given to the queen mother, Iput, so that she could dispose of it during her lifetime and then it would be given to her estate. The king, however, remained owner of the deeded domain in theory. He conferred upon the temple authority over a parcel of soil, but this was not irreversible, because the only thing that had really been deeded was the income from the domain. The other "edicts" of the Old Kingdom followed this legal pattern. The principle of donation would persist without change throughout pharaonic history. According to the donation stelae of the Late period, the king (or his representative) "gives" (deeds) land to a god (or his representative) in order to assign the income to a third beneficiary, who in turn can install a manager or overseer.

The system of tenancies arose from the same principle on a different level. The king gave his faithful servants (or valiant warriors) plots of land, whose title they then held temporarily. While the state (the king) remained owner of the soil, the tenant who worked his fields paid rent, in recognition of the eminent right of the state (or of the concession-holder) to a benefit. With time, the tenures became transferable or deedable (and became after two or three generations *nmḥw*-fields), but they could always (and at any moment) return to the central administration by various mechanisms. Thus, the Stela of Appanage (Menu 1998b) records the creation of a land deed by the royal family through the repurchase of rights from the titleholders of the tenures that formed the newly created domain.

Deeded lands were divided into three principal categories: deeded land, long-term lease, and tenures. The tenures could be regrouped and given as deeded land or lent on the basis of a long-term lease, which was usually accompanied by one or two provisions for dividing the rights linked to a parcel of land. In each of the three categories, short-term gains could be realized. The exploitation of the land could furthermore be entrusted to managers and the fields worked by farmers; the farmers were remunerated in the form of salaries or a small tenure (on average, several hundred square meters). At each level of the division of a property, a transaction could take place in the transfer of an established right.

The absence of any ground rights over any portion of the soil is described as follows by Akhenaten: "It [the territory defined for constructing Amarna] does not belong to a god, it does not belong to a goddess . . . it does not belong to anyone who may do something. One know not what . . . I noticed that it was abandoned" (Murnane and van Siclen 1993). This is a *res derelicta* (a case of dereliction) where the king could exercise his ownership.

The mechanism of property severances was extremely sophisticated in ancient Egypt. All extant private transactions are concerned with a nonphysical good, that is a right to the income from land, possessed in any way—that is, as a benefit, "donation," tenure, or long-term lease (Menu 1998a). Hence, the price of land in ancient Egypt was low (Baer 1962), and represented the transfer of rights allowing for the earning of income.

Turin Papyri 2118 and 2120, dating from the reign of Psamtik I, mention several degrees in the hierarchy of deeded land, characterized by a diversified and remarkably precise terminology. Like the inscriptions of Mes (in the reign of Ramesses II), the partitioning is the preamble to the transfer of tenures; it does not outline the ownership of the fields, but rather the right to gain personal income from them. A papyrus from a later period (Louvre Papyrus E 10935, dating from the reign of Amasis) gives a marvelous explanation of the distinction made between the "body" of the fields (that is, their physical reality), their legal use within the domain of the temple of Amun, and the negotiable rights: "eleven *arouras* (2735 square meters/29,430 square feet) of high lands, *nmḥw*-fields (tenures) located in the domain of Amun of the district of Coptos to the west, and which are part of the body of twenty-two *arouras* of fields that are in the "Milk-Farm-of-Amun" (Malinine 1953).

Through his universal right over the land, the king imposed the supremacy of the state economy. However at the heart of the local units that the state economy covered, as in the urban societies that grew around the provincial temples, an important place was given to private initiative.

[*See also* Administration; Agriculture; Animal Husbandry; Coinage; Irrigation; Prices and Payment; Seafaring; Slaves; Storage; Taxation; Technology and Engineering; Trade and Markets; Transportation; Weights and Measures; *and* Work Force.]

### BIBLIOGRAPHY

Baer, Klaus. "The Low Price of Land in Ancient Egypt." *Journal of the American Research Center in Egypt* 1 (1962), 25–45.

Baumgartel, Elise "Scorpion and Rosette and the Fragments of the Large Hierakonpolis Mace Head." *Zeitschrift für Ägyptische Sprache und Altertumskunde* 93 (1966), 9–13.

van den Boorn, G. P. F. *The Duties of the Vizier.* London and New York, 1988.

Derchain, Philippe. "L'*Atelier des Orfevres* à Dendara et les origines de l'Alchimie." *Chronique d'Égypte* 65 (1990), 219–242.

Faulkner, Raymond O. *The Ancient Egyptian Pyramid Texts.* Oxford, 1969.

Gaballa, G. A. *The Tomb-Chapel of Mose.* Warminster, 1977.

Goedicke, Hans. *Königliche Dokumente aus dem alten Reiche.* Wiesbaden, 1967.

Grimal, Nicolas C. *Les termes de la propagande royal égyptienne, de la XIXe dynastie à la conquête d'Alexandre.* Paris, 1986.

Helck, Wolfgang. *Materialien zur Wirtschaftsgeschichte des Neuen Reiches.* 6 vols. Wiesbaden, 1961–1970. A first-rate work that provides an exhaustive presentation of the texts relating to the economy of the New Kingdom and commentaries.

Hoffman, Michael A. *Egypt before the Pharaohs.* Austin, 1979.

Jacquet-Gordon, Helen. *Les noms des domaines funéraires sous l'Ancien Empire égyptien.* Cairo, 1962.

Janssen, Jac J. "Prolegomena to the Study of Egypt's Economic History during the New Kingdom." *Studien zur Altägyptischen Kultur* 3 (1975), 127–185.

Malinine, Michel. *Choix de textes juridiques en hiératique "anormal" et en démotique.* Paris, 1953.

Meeks, Dimitri. *Le grand texte des donations au temple d'Edfou.* Cairo, 1972.

Menu, Bernadette. "Naissance du pouvoir pharaonique." *Egypte pharaonique: pouvoir, société. Méditerranées* 6/7 (1996), 17–59.

Menu, B. "Enseignes et porte-étendards." *Bulletin de l'Institut Français d'Archéologie Orientale* 96 (1996), 339–342.

Menu, B. "L'émergence et la symbolique du pouvoir pharaonique, de la palette de Narmer aux Textes des Pyramides." *Méditerranées* 13 (1997), 29–40. These articles present a new explanation for the emergence of royal power in correlation with a completely revised interpretation of the Narmer documents on the basis of fundamental observations.

Menu, Bernadette. "Le prix de l'utile en Egypte au 1er millénaire av. J.-C." *Prix et formation des prix dans les économies antiques. Entretiens d'Archéologie et d'Histoire* (1997), 245–275.

Menu, B. *Recherches sur l'histoire juridique, économique et sociale de l'ancienne Egypte.* Vol. 1, Versailles, 1982. Vol. 2, Cairo, 1998.

Midant-Reynes, Béatrix. *Préhistoire de l'Egypte. Des premiers hommes aux premiers pharaons.* Paris, 1992.

Murnane, William J., and van Siclen, Charles C. *The Boundary Stelae of Akhenaten.* London and New York, 1993.

Müller-Wollerman, R. "Bemerkungen zu den sogenannten Tributen." *Göttinger Miszellen* 66 (1983), 81–93.

Posener, Georges. "L'enseigne appelée 'Khons'." *Revue d'Egyptologie* 17 (1965), 193–195. Establishes the *nekhen* reading of the object that is the royal placenta.

Quibell, J. E. *Hierakonpolis* I. London, 1900.

Warburton, David. *State and Economy in Ancient Egypt.* Freiburg, 1997.

Williams, Bruce. "Narmer and the Coptos Colossi." *Journal of the American Research Center in Egypt* 25 (1988), 35–59.

BERNADETTE M. MENU
Translated from French by Elizabeth Schwaiger

## Royal Sector

Given the absolute, divine, totalitarian, and paternalistic features of the pharaonic monarchy, as well as its origins, which were substantially linked to the formation of the state, the royal sector emerged as the dominant sector of the pharaonic economy. The sovereign was assisted by the central administration, as shown by the Narmer documents, where the king is already surrounded by his relatives and scribes. The purpose of royal power was to exploit the resources of the primary sector (agriculture, animal husbandry, mines, and quarries), but also to regulate the flow of goods, to control the organization of labor and the movement of manpower, and to oversee imports and exports.

During the periods when royal power was in decline, the temples and their representatives became substitutes for the sovereign. A completely different phenomenon consisted of conferring privileges on the temples, during the imperial epochs, by the king, who maintained his authority by exercising tight control over the deeded lands. In this manner, the Decree of Nauri (reign of Sety I) reveals the imperial intent (in evidence throughout the Ramessid period) of organizing the economy through the temples. The temples had, as a result of the general increase in wealth, become intermediaries between the central and local administrations.

**Redistribution.** Any centralized economic system involves considerable redistribution: local taxes are paid on income; in return, benefits are received in the form of services from the state (for example, education of children, protection of goods, and individuals), from the region (for example, organization of cultural activities), from the province (for example, road maintenance), and from the municipality (for example, household waste disposal). The pharaonic state functioned in much the same manner: a large portion of the surplus from agriculture (the most important economic sector) was collected and reassigned to various other needs—offerings, rations, and salaries. A number of deductions made it possible to redistribute the wealth or to use it directly for state projects.

The central administration, under the management of the vizier, replenished the treasury with revenues from merchandise (*inw*), or with deductions on products from labor, or on the work itself (*b3kw*), or with periodic taxes (*ḥtri*) with occasional levies on goods, especially livestock (*tp-ḏrt*). Expenditures and income were balanced according to a provisionary budget based on estimated harvests, closely linked to the height of the Nile flood.

The various running expenses were quantified with the help of "money" in the broadest sense (that is, an instrument of evaluation, exchange, and saving); this currency was flexible, thanks to the institution of tables of equivalence, principally between the units of weight for various metals and the measures used for several types of cereal. With regard to the accounts of the Middle Kingdom, one can even think in terms of an era where loaves of bread were a form of currency, and gave rise to complex conversion systems. This was when symbolic currency was invented. The different (and vast) quantities of bread listed in the accounts were not real amounts of bread used for each operation, but a metaphor used for the purpose of putting the exchange in writing (Menu 1982).

**Taxation.** Within the framework of the temples, the production of cereals created an elaborate taxation system. Text A from the Wilbour Papyrus, dating from the reign of Ramesses V, records the income from farming gained by the sharecroppers and their landowners (that is, individuals to whom land had been granted or deeded). This income was then subject to taxation by the central administration. There were two kinds of revenue: the revenue arising from the net product of the large temple domains (but also from other institutions whose lands are much smaller); and the revenue from rents and interest paid by individuals to these temples and institutions.

The domains of temples of lesser or medium importance were generally administered by the priest who maintained the cult, while those of the large sanctuaries were divided into agricultural departments (*rmnyt*), consisting of fields which were not necessarily adjacent.

These agricultural departments were administrative units which were at the same time "under the authority" (*r-ḥt*) of an important individual and "in the hand" (*m-ḏrt*) of a manager, the *rwḏw*.

The person in charge of all agricultural departments was usually a high dignitary or a state official, and a relative of the pharaoh. He received the *rmnyt* from the temple, and his stipend was a portion of the harvest. Indeed, the total mentioned in the Wilbour Papyrus (the net product submitted for tax), represents half of the yield from the earth, which was on average ten bags of cereal per *aroura*.

The managers who held the *rmnyt* "in their hand" and who effectively ran the domains, were remunerated with small fields that they exploited as tenant farmers for their own profit, in exchange for payment to the temple of a fixed amount for the use of this land. This became clear in another type of domain, which was divided into tenures, allotted to the same *rwḏw*, and whose rents (from the fixed amount of the lease or rent) were set aside for the temples. The farmers were remunerated like the managers, with leases for small productive parcels or with rations, depending on the temple to which they belonged.

The temple received the income (fixed amount) from the leaseholders of its domain, as well as interest for the rental of services it provided. The agricultural departments divided into tenures were called *rmnyt pš* ("department of distribution").

The temples practiced a mutual system of rental of services, in conjunction with their requirements for agricultural manpower. One temple could rent (or lend) a farm-worker to another temple. The price of the loan was recorded twice, because of the two types of corresponding entries that were carried out at both temples. Entry A, the price paid by the temple loaning the worker, was always equal to 7.5 percent of the net income from the cultivated field, and was indicated after the net income of the field; it was then subtracted by the fiscal authorities at the stage of tax collection. Entry B showed how the temple that lent one of its farmers to another temple received rent, which was then taxable income.

The management of the temples was closely controlled by the king. The principal administrators were usually high officials of state. The temples were subject to taxes and the state kept close control over them to ensure optimal agricultural productivity.

**Composition of Income.** The pharaoh could confer on an institution (usually a temple) the right to collect certain types of income in his stead. This process of jurisdiction—the composition of income—is indicated in the Wilbour Papyrus (collection by the temple of fixed amounts usually due to the state) and confirmed in Papyrus Harris I and in the stela of Sheshonq I.

***Papyrus Harris I.*** Most of this 42-meter (138-foot) document consists of a speech by Ramesses II that lists his generous grants to gods and their temples during his reign. The inventory in four sections is for the three large temples—Thebes, Heliopolis, and Memphis—with the fourth section devoted to the combined total of all secondary temples of Egypt. Complementary lists, followed by a recapitulating list, provide proof of and account for Ramesses II's donations and include lands, personnel, dishes, precious stones and metals, cereal, livestock, ships, fabrics, and various products. The royal donations have three functions: donations for operation, for reserves, and for offerings, in the form of specific transfers and annual interest. The whole donation is expressed in terms of a universality of goods, the *ìmyt-pr* (Menu 1982). The amounts of gold allotted to temples are impressive (close to 8 tons) and are largely in support of a general policy of building reserves. Cereal was used for both consumption and payment, its total in royal payments to the temples reaching the fantastic amount of a billion and a half liters. Arable land and dependent personnel total close to 30,000 hectares (74,100 acres) and more than one hundred thousand people. After listing the many advantages granted to the temples, the king addresses the gods to ask for the rewards he expects, on the basis of a law of immanent remuneration (this is not a case of reciprocity), and of a possible transfer of a positive life balance to the account of a relative (at this juncture, the heir to the throne, the future Ramesses IV).

Papyrus Harris I (Grandet 1994; Menu 1998) outlines the main economic structures within which the temples played a leading role as autonomous sites for production, consumption, savings, and investment, even though their land endowments and the majority of their income originated from royal generosity. This document emphasizes the fundamental split between the king, who maintained the overlordship, and the temples, which had practical ownership. The treasury made deductions from production, but the king could give any temple some of the income generated in his domain (for example, the fixed amount paid for the tenures) and held by a different cult institution, or by the royal domain itself. This is a process similar to that of rental income. Other examples come from the Theban lists of temples dedicated to Amun: "Goods [in] deductions and products [of people and] of temporary personnel . . . which King User-Maat-Re-Mery-Amun, life, prosperity, health, the great god [Ramesses III], has given to their treasuries, stores and granaries as their annual dues" (12a, 1); "Silver in [various] goods, considered as products of the people, given for the Divine Satisfaction: 3,606 *deben* and one *kite*" (12b, 2), "Heqat-measures of grain of the farmers' products: 309,950 sacks" (12b, 3). It is important to note that the transfer of offerings for the benefit of priestly and funeral personnel allowed for immediate distribution of production surplus prior to the allocation of private surplus.

***The stela of Sheshonq I.*** The stela Cairo JE 66285 (Blackman 1941; Menu 1982) records an act of endowment through which King Psusennes created a new cult institution, the Divine Offering (literally, the "Divine Satisfaction") of Osiris Nemrod, who would found the twenty-second dynasty. He allocated to this institution various goods, revenues, and services for its operation. The income from the deeded lands, as well as the services, was deducted in advance by the king from the temple of Osiris at Abydos by means of two judicial procedures: the rent (that is, the income from the deeded land), and transfer of services as income from labor. The payment of ten *deben* of silver to the temple of Osiris enabled the Divine Offering of Osiris Nemrod to collect income from one hundred *arouras* of *nmḥw*-fields (that is, the tenures), consisting of fixed amounts, usually owing to the temple of Osiris (the latter naturally retained practical ownership of these fields). In the same way, the payment of six and two-thirds *kite* of silver to the temple of Osiris for each worker partially assigned to the Divine Satisfaction of Nemrod represents the beginning of a right to utilize a portion of the services provided by each worker who remained a dependent of the temple of Osiris.

**Endowments for Various Goods.** Papyrus Harris I lists a considerable quantity of products and objects (aside from merchandise for consumption and replaceable goods) for the enrichment of the temples, both as reserves and as investments. The stela of Sheshonq I describes how a new foundation was established. The stela Cairo JE 36 861 confirms this process (Meeks 1979).

**Labor.** Field labor and enormous construction works required abundant manpower. From the early periods onward, the king procured this in two ways: from prisoners of war, and through requisitions and forced service (corvée) from the entire rural population.

Through rites and the construction of sacred monuments, the king ensured *maat* for his subjects, a principle of prosperity based on the fruits of the labor of the population, which the king gathered and presented to the gods. As the earliest documents and scenes in temples relate, this is a cyclic schema, a marriage of cosmic and earthly processes, far removed from a single principle of reciprocity.

Gigantic projects—the Great Pyramid of Khufu or the excavation of the double *speos* at Abu Simbel, for example—represent an ideology whose practical and immediate consequence was direct employment. In all such efforts—the creation or maintenance of agricultural domains, the organization of expeditions to mines and quarries, the realization of large building projects, or the development of the artisans' class—the central administration, directed by the vizier, acting on behalf of the king, controlled the movements of the population and the use of manpower, through the intermediary of the "Office of the Vizier" and the "Office of Manpower" (Menu 1982, 1998).

Mobility, organization, imports, and vast displacements of manpower, after times of war and in response to specific technological requirements, were all part of the the economic mechanism and of the execution of large-scale programs. Important texts from the Middle Kingdom, such as Papyrus Reisner I–IV (Simpson 1963–1986), or Papyrus Brooklyn 35 1446 (Hayes 1955), reveals how tight state control was over collective labor. This is documented from the Old Kingdom onward in titles such as "Director of Fields" and "Director of Works of the King," which were often held by the vizier himself.

The organization and utilization of labor are characterized in pharaonic Egypt by two features: great flexibility, and the absence of discrimination among the working population, be they Egyptian or foreign. The terms *'ȝm* and *'ȝmt* ("Asian") are synonyms of *ḥm* and *bȝk* ("slaves"). The words *bȝk* and *ḥm* are interchangeable and could be rendered in more generous terms such as "dependent" and "servant" because they reflect jurisdiction and hierarchy more than the deprivation of liberty. A vizier may call himself a *bȝk* ("servant") of the pharaoh, who is himself the *ḥm-f* ("his [own] servant")—that is, he depends on no one. The *ḥmw* and the *bȝkw* appear in the administrative or economic texts as the driving forces of the production apparatus. Negotiable boundaries existed between forced labor (theoretically, slavery or servitude; practically, compulsory service and various forms of conscripted service) and the type of labor that is more or less freely given in exchange (functionaries, salaried work, assignments, the hiring out of services, and the sale of manpower). A craftsman could alternate between exercising his talents and performing more servile tasks; as a *smdt* the holder of a rented farm could be assigned as defendant to a temple; or as a farmer who sold his services as a domestic servant; or as a debtor who discharged his debt by entering into service with his creditor. Legally, the *ḥmw* and the *bȝkw* are free men (they may start a family, work under contract, and own possessions); economically, they are considered capital that can produce quantifiable and tradable services within a given legal framework. By the same token, arable land is also considered to be capital, capable of producing quantifiable and negotiable agricultural income within a given legal framework. Indeed, private transactions for labor and services are legally identifiable: hiring out of labor, sale of manpower, hiring out of services, or transfer of services (Menu 1998). The system of conscription, applicable to the entire working population, excludes by definition the necessity for slavery. Papyrus Harris I (77, 6) mentions the practice of branding prisoners of war with the name of the pharaoh, turning them into *ḥmw*. Slavery could simply be a means of enrollment, a preliminary step in a series of jobs in the various jurisdictions enumerated above.

**Trade.** In an essentially agricultural country such as ancient Egypt, trade was essentially the reciprocal flow of products and provisions. Foreign trade (often over long distances and, most likely, controlled by the state through the collection of tribute, commercial trade, and levying of duties) satisfied the need for commodities, merchandise, and various goods that were not produced on Egyptian soil (Grimal and Menu 1998). Imperial edicts declared that the submission of foreign peoples served the purpose of increasing Egypt's wealth. During the eighteenth and nineteenth dynasties, when political power was shared among a mosaic of cities and autonomous small states, Egypt did not hide a sometimes uneasy economic interdependence between the merchant elite (Phoenicians and Syro-Persians) and the landed Egyptian aristocracy. The economic relationship between Egypt and Nubia was quite different. Nubia was a province exploited as a colony.

With domestic trade, one must differentiate between local and regional trade. Both existed in a market economy founded on production surpluses and on the increase of value through individual labor.

[*See also* Administration, *article on* State Administration; Taxation; Wilbour Papyrus; *and* Work Force.]

**BIBLIOGRAPHY**

Blackman, Aylward M. "The Stela of Shoshenk, Great Chief of the Meshwesh." *Journal of Egyptian Archaeology* 27 (1941), 83–93.

Bleiberg, Edward. "The King's Privy Purse during the New Kingdom." *Journal of the American Research Center in Egypt* 21 (1984), 155–167.

Bleiberg, Edward. "The Redistributive Economy in New Kingdom Egypt." *Journal of the American Research Center in Egypt* 25 (1988), 157–168.

Boorn, G. P. F. van den. *The Duties of the Vizier.* London and New York, 1988.

Černý, Jaroslav. *A Community of Workmen at Thebes in the Ramesside Period.* Cairo, 1973.

Gardiner, Alan H. *The Wilbour Papyrus.* 4 vols. Oxford, 1941–1952.

Grandet, Pierre. *Le Papyrus Harris I.* 2 vols. Cairo, 1994.

Grimal, N., and B. Menu. *Le commerce en Égypte ancienne.* Cairo, 1998.

Hayes, William C. *A Papyrus of the Late Middle Kingdom in the Brooklyn Museum.* Brooklyn, 1955.

Janssen, Jac. J. "The Role of the Temple in the Egyptian Economy during the New Kingdom." In *State and Temple Economy in the Ancient Near East*, vol. 2, pp. 505–515. Orientalia Lovaniensia Analecta, 6. Louvain, 1979.

Katary, Sally L. D. *Land Tenure in the Ramesside Period.* London and New York, 1989.

Meeks, Dimitri. "Une fondation memphite de Taharqa." In *Hommages à Serge Sauneron*, vol. 1, pp. 221–259. Cairo, 1979.

Menu, Bernadette. *Le régime juridique des terres et du personnel attaché à la terre dans le Papyrus Wilbour.* Lille, 1970.

Menu, Bernadette. *Recherches sur l'histoire juridique, économique et sociale de l'ancienne Égypte.* Vol. 1, Versailles, 1982. Vol. 2, Cairo, 1998.

Müller-Wollerman, R. "Warenaustausch im Ägypten des Alten Reiches." *Journal of the Economic and Social History of the Orient* 29 (1985), 121–168.

Posener-Kriéger, Paule. *Les archives du temple funéraire de Néferirkaré-Kakaï.* 2 vols. Cairo, 1976. This important administrative and accounting archive from an Old Kingdom temple comprises tables that inventory goods and services, and accounts registering the flow of merchandise between the residence and the royal temples.

Redford, Donald B. *Pharaonic King-Lists, Annals and Day-Books.* Mississauga, Ont., 1986.

Simpson, William Kelly. *Papyrus Reisner I, II, III, IV.* 4 vols. Boston, 1963–1986. Remarkable documents on building sites: cross-referenced accounts record the presence of workers, transport of labor, distribution of tools, rations, and salaries. Provides evidence of complex notions of production and expenditure units within teams of laborers.

BERNADETTE M. MENU
Translated from French by Elizabeth Schwaiger

## Private Sector

Whether the economic systems of ancient societies were primitive or modern is debatable. What is certain is that explanations based on external and all-encompassing models (capitalism, Marxism, and their by-products) are doomed to failure. There have been many attempts to explain the pharaonic economy by applying systems of thought as diametrically opposed as those of Polanyi and Keynes. The best way of understanding the economic reality of ancient Egypt is through observation of the facts and analysis based on appropriate intellectual tools: legal and economic terminology, frameworks, and concepts.

Though the state played an important role in the pharaonic economy, it does not necessarily follow that private transactions did not exist. On the contrary, they played an important role, both inside and outside the state system.

**Transactions and Products.** Land, animals, and labor belonged to the state. However, individuals using fields and livestock, could complete transfers on the rights that they held, subject to certain restrictions. Animals, often used within the state or national system, could be subject to private appropriation.

The holding of land resulted in the division of rights to an estate. In most cases, this led to "tenures" (*nmḥw*-fields). Depending on the level at which the transaction took place, the buyer either acquired the tenure itself, as documented in the Appanage Stela, or simply the right to farm, for example in exchange for the transfer of a cow, as mentioned in Papyrus Berlin 9784 (Gardiner 1906).

In the Late period, cattle could be the object of three types of transactions: bills of sale, leasing contracts, and contracts related to the rental of yokes for tilling. In the first type, either the cow itself was sold (which occurs rarely, Papyrus Rylands 8), or else the cattle farmer in effect sold the labor and food used to fatten the animal—for example, Papyrus Michigan 3525A; C and B (Cruz-Uribe 1985) register successive transactions relating to the same cow. In the second instance, the cow is part of a herd in a temple that has been trusted to cattlemen, two of whom become associates in order to share the calves and the milk (Papyrus IFAO 902; Menu 1998). According to the Papyrus Loeb 41, two soldiers purchase a cow in order to share in the profits. The third type of contract (rental of yokes for tilling, Hughes 1952) also occurred in relation to a temple. (It should however be noted that only the temples had archives.)

Therefore, the cattle trade existed only in connection with the temple, which was partly responsible for breeding, and, on an individual basis, probably through a trader. With donkeys, the Deir el-Medina archives indicate the same division between animals belonging to the state that are used without cost by the workers, and those acquired by them on an individual basis. Services of dependents could also be the object of transactions between individuals. [*See the* Royal Sector *article in this entry.*]

**Transactions in Personal Property.** This relates to objects such as houses, private animals, tools, dishes, and textiles.

As far back as the Old Kingdom, sales of houses, tombs, or elements of architecture occurred (Menu 1985); however, it is doubtful that the land for building them ever became the object of private appropriation, given the pharaoh's universal mastery and the royal right to property on land that in theory derived from it. In the Late period, Aramaic documents from Elephantine stipulate that on the occasion of the sale of a house, only the building is transferred, not the land (Menu 1997).

Any heifer or calf born in a cattleman's private stable became his private property (*nmḥw*). It is probable that private appropriation of cattle was the result of a share (per head of cattle) given to keepers of large herds as a form of payment.

Furniture or funerary components (that is, beds, baskets, fabrics, clothes, and copper or bronze dishes, as well as other personal property) were often exchanged between workers at Deir el-Medina (Janssen 1975). Prices are given, and expressed in copper *deben* (*dbn*) or cereal *khar* (*ḫ3r*).

The state provided tools to work gangs, using strict bookkeeping methods on work sites. The Papyrus Reisner (Middle Kingdom) and New Kingdom documents from Deir el-Medina record loans (symbolized by pebbles left on the site by the user), and even thefts, which were severely punished. Workers even owned their own home-made tools, with which they liked to be buried. A set square and lead wire were found with the worker Sennedjem in his tomb, for example.

**Food.** Cereals, oil, and dates were part of rations and salaries. In fact, ancient Egyptians made clear distinctions between rations that were part of their sustenance and those given as payment. These involved either immediately edible food, or that which could be processed into edible food, or that which could be exchanged (barley for dates, for example), thus serving (like the weighed metal units) as a form of money.

**Compensation.** The terminology used to signify compensation in commercial transactions evolved through the ages. The words most commonly used are *isw*, *db3w*, and *swnt*. In the Old Kingdom, *isw* meant "compensation" or "benefits," regardless of legal status: revenues earmarked for wages of funeral priests and priestesses; salaries paid out to workers by the master of a work (that is, the building of a tomb); exchange (that is, a small house for a piece of cloth); and sale and purchase, as in *r-isw*, ("to buy" or "to bring as compensation"). The word *db3w* seems to refer to payments (Menu 1985). In the Middle Kingdom, a more specific term is used. *Swnw* refers to "price," in transactions defined as sales (*swnt*). Finally, in the New Kingdom, certain expressions become more common: *in r-db3*, signifying "to bring against payment" or "to buy," *di* (or *rdi*) *r db3* "to give against payment" or "to sell."

**Money.** The disadvantages of bartering became apparent early on. In effect, this process requires a dual adjustment: each partner is asked make an offer, while at the same time requesting something. However, the reason one falls back on a term to complete a transaction lies in the possibility of agreeing on the units of value, accepted not only by the two parties to the contract (initially, more often than not an oral one), but also by the community at large. This intermediate means took the form of a product (cereal or oil), desired because it could be ingested or hoarded, which could be kept for future purchases (silver, copper, or bronze). Since grain was more readily available than silver (or even more common metals), metal rings and ingots (*šnʿty* or *sniw*, *dbn*, or *kdt*) soon served as units of accounts, not appearing on the market but constituting commonly accepted references.

Distinct from metallic currency (or coinage), "money" denotes an exchange term, a means of evaluation, and a savings mechanism. In pharaonic Egypt, these three functions were fulfilled via a system comprised mainly of metal weights and measures of cereal: this can be considered money in its broadest sense, and consists of units convertible according to established tables of equivalence, which are often referred to in legal acts (Parker 1962).

In the Ramessid period, the silver *sniw* (or *šnʿty*) always weighed 7.6 grams, the *dbn*, 91 grams, and the *kdt* (one-tenth of the *dbn*), 9.1 grams. The ratio of silver to copper stood at approximately one to sixty; one *sniw* was worth about five copper *dbn*; one *hn* (about 0.5 liter) of oil was worth about one sixth silver *sniw* or five copper *dbn*; and one *h3r* of cereal (about 76 liters) was usually worth around two copper *dbn*, with the *h3r* being subdivided into *ipt* (one-fourth of a *h3r*). The Deir el-Medina documents also had lists of types of solid objects and lists of methods of payment (Janssen 1975; Menu 1982). In the Late period, transfers of debts were a common occurrence.

One of the advantages of the "monetary system" of pharaonic Egypt was its flexibility and its surprising fluidity. Comparative assessments were carried out between the two main cereals grown in Egypt: barley and wheat. These different currencies would eventually generate various forms of financial credit. No wonder this system was operational for nearly two thousand years (Menu 1974).

**Exchange Networks.** The state controlled the principal exchange networks through various methods: attribution and reversion of donations to cultal institutions and their priests and dependants, tax collection, the creation of stocks, and distribution of rations and salaries. In agriculture, production surpluses were used for different ends: central stockpiling, increase of donations in temples and on funeral altars, with additional income for managers, controllers, and farmers.

On construction sites (at Deir el-Medina, for example), a two-tiered system of distribution can be observed (Menu 1974). The first tier consists of supplies (tools, containers, and donkeys for transport) and raw materials (water, wood, gypsum, pigments, glue, and textile fibers for the manufacture of lamp wicks); this is a straightforward system, wholly administered by the state and existing outside the laws of the marketplace. The other tier consists of rations and salaries, which were capable of generating, on behalf of their beneficiaries, surpluses used for the acquisition of various goods. Workers received consumables (meat, fish, vegetables, clothing, or sandals) and salaries (mostly in oil and cereals), with surpluses serving as cash reserves.

The state was also forced to intervene to control seasonal variations leading to speculation and, therefore, inflation. Papyrus Louvre E 3.226 (Megally 1977) is an example of state regulation of distribution networks and flow of basic goods. This document, dating from the reign of Thutmose III (eighteenth dynasty), reflects an intricate accounting system as a result of the centralized government procedures of the granary and treasury. Two teams of *bnriw* (date-collectors) receive throughout the year quantities of barley collected through state taxes, and supply to the granary and treasury corresponding amounts of dates, also throughout the year. A $ḫ3r$ of barley is always equivalent to a $ḫ3r$ of dates, and balances calculated periodically over up to twenty months indicate equal amounts of barley expenses and date revenues. Seven periods are recorded, covering eight years, from the twenty-eighth to the thirty-fifth year of the reign of Thutmose III. The origin of grains, as well as that of dates, is recorded on sheets of papyrus. Ripening takes place at different times in the year: the barley harvest takes place in the summer, whereas the gathering of dates occurs in November. Vargyas has shown that because date flour was complementary to cereal flour in the common diet, self-regulation between the demand and supply of the two products discouraged speculation, thereby stabilizing price fluctuations. Demand could suddenly increase for barley just as it could for dates. In the spring, barley was too expensive, and its price increased according to demand. Then it fell in May, with the harvest making cereal cheaper. Therefore, price changes stemmed from seasonal changes in demand rather than natural inclination. It is likely that the granary and treasury took advantage of these dips to spread out the fluctuations of supply and demand for these two products. The central government thus prevented speculation and inflation by building up annual reserves, as opposed to seasonal ones, and by distributing stocks of grain ($it$), dates ($bnr$), and date flour ($bni$), to dispose of them according to need. In addition to state-controlled networks of distribution, the management of supply and demand could have a strong effect on prices, thereby suggesting that state intervention stabilized the effects of a market economy.

**Market Economy.** Supply and demand are terms used to define a market economy. Supply comes from production surpluses realized at the state or governing level in the primary (farming and animal husbandry) and secondary (crafts) sectors. Demand implies needs and that means exist to meet them. Remuneration allowed certain people to build up surpluses of rations and salaries in order to acquire various goods and services.

The calculation of a salary took into account the increased value of a finished product due to specialized work. Ostracon IFAO 764, of the twentieth dynasty (Janssen 1975; Warburton 1984–1985), mentions a sum of one $dbn$ paid out for decorative work on a lot of forty *shawabti*s. Papyrus Louvre E. 3168 (Malinine and Pirenne 1950), dating from the reign of Taharqa (twenty-fifth dynasty), registers an agreement whereby a woman sells an unspecified amount of weaving thread to a *choachyte*. It is of great interest to analyze the price paid by the *choachyte*, for it involves an exchange value of 2.25 silver $ḳdt$ corresponding to the merchandise delivered (weaving thread) and 1.5 measures of grain "to pay for the work" of the spinner, possibly a monthly wage. In other words,

a distinction is made between the exchange value of the product and remuneration for the work. Unfortunately, we cannot determine the cost of the raw material, but the contract is clear about the finished product: it stipulates that thread is to be used for weaving and that it has been prepared for this purpose.

**Prices.** As has been noted above, prices, arrived at in principle by adjusting the offer to the demand, were noticeably affected by state intervention. The available figures are not continuous enough to determine what rules were followed. But fluctuations in the price of grain, often showing substantial increases (Černy 1934, 1954; Janssen 1975), can certainly be explained by the interplay between the two sectors, royal (or state) and private, with price stability attributable mainly to the authority of a strong monarchy, capable of investing large amounts to correct certain negative effects of market flow.

**Places of Commerce.** The locations of markets are not known, and there is insufficient information on how markets developed. However, scenes depicted on the walls of tombs from the Old to the New Kingdom show that markets did exist. Texts mention commercial transactions carried out by merchants (*šwtiw*) from state-administered properties and temples. These representatives acted as agents or salesmen (Grimal and Menu 1998), going from property to property to make deals for crafts, farm products (Menu 1982), and completing transactions on behalf of their superiors. We cannot tell whether they received a salary or a commission for their services.

[*See also* Coinage; Prices and Payment; Trade and Markets; *and* Weights and Measures.]

## BIBLIOGRAPHY

Černy, Jaroslav. "Fluctuations in Grain Prices during the Twentieth Dynasty." *Archiv Orientalni* 6 (1934), 173–178.

Černy, Jaroslav. "Prices and Wages in Egypt in the Ramesside Period." *Cahiers d'Histoire Mondiale* 1 (1954), 903–921.

Cruz-Uribe, Eugene. *Saite and Persian Cattle Documents*. Chico, 1985.

Gardiner, Alan H. "Four Papyri of the 18th Dynasty from Kahun." *Zeitschrift für Ägyptische Sprache und Altertumskunde* 43 (1906), 27–47.

Griffith, Francis Llewellyn. *Hieratic Papyri from Kahun and Gurob*. London, 1898.

Griffith, Francis Llewellyn. *Catalogue of the Demotic Papyri in the John Rylands Library*. Manchester, 1909.

Grimal, Nicolas, and Bernadette Menu, eds. *Le commerce en Egypte ancienne*. Cairo, 1998.

Hughes, George Robert. *Saite Demotic Land Leases*. Chicago, 1952.

James, T. G. H. *The Hekanakhte Papers and Other Early Middle Kingdom Documents*. New York, 1962.

Janssen, Jac. J. *Commodity Prices from the Ramesside Period*. Leiden, 1975.

Janssen, Jac. J. "Debts and Credit." *Journal of Egyptian Archaeology* 80 (1994), 125–136.

Malinine, Michel. *Choix de textes juridiques en hiératique anormal et en démotique*. Paris, 1953.

Malinine, Michel, and Jacques Pirenne. *Documents juridiques égyptiens* (*Archives d'Histoire du Droit Oriental*, 5). Brussels, 1950.

Megally, Mounir. *Recherches sur l'économie, l'administration et la comptabilité égyptiennes à la XVIIIe dynastie, d'après Papyrus E. 3226 du Louvre.* Cairo, 1977.

Menu, Bernadette. "Quelques principes d'organisation du travail d'après les textes du Moyen Empire égyptien." *Le droit égyptien ancien* (1974), 115–137.

Menu, Bernadette. *Recherches sur l'histoire juridique, économique, et sociale de l'ancienne Egypte.* Vol. 1, Versailles, 1982. Vol. 2, Cairo, 1998.

Menu, Bernadette. "Ventes de maisons sous l'Ancien Empire égyptien." *Mélanges offerts à Jean Vercoutter* (1985), 249–262.

Menu, Bernadette. "Le prix de l'utile en Egypte au 1er millénaire av. J.-C." *Prix et formation des prix dans les économies antiques. Entretiens d'Archéologie et d'Histoire* (1997), 245–275.

Parker, Richard A. *A Saite Oracle Papyrus from Thebes in the Brooklyn Museum* [Papyrus Brooklyn 47.218.3]. Providence, 1962.

Simpson, William Kelly. *Papyrus Reisner, I, II, III, IV.* Boston, 1963–1986.

Valbelle, Dominique. *Catalogue des poids à inscription hiératiques de Deir el-Médineh.* Cairo, 1977.

Vargyas, Peter. "L'économie de la Mésopotamie et les tablettes astronomiques." *Méditerranées* 17 (1988).

Warburton, David A. "Some Remarks on the Manufacture and Sale of Shabtis." *Mélanges H. Wild, Bulletin de la Société d'Égyptologie de Genève* 9/10 (1984–1985), 345–355.

BERNADETTE M. MENU

## Temple Economy

Pharaoh, the preeminent high priest of all the temples of Egypt, was also, by both natural and legal right, the owner of all their lands. The Egyptian temple economy rested chiefly on these two fundamental ideas: as master and leader of the cult, the king also ensured the material upkeep of the sanctuaries. He bestowed gifts and exemptions in place of intervening more directly in temple administration. For almost three thousand years, the temples remained nearly independent economic units that were nevertheless closely linked to the crown. A state within the state during times when the temples had strong political power (such as the theocratic state in Thebes at the end of the New Kingdom), the temples were major landholders, at all times the second-most important economic power in ancient Egypt. Such interdependence between the temples and the state inevitably led to conflicts, as with the royal loss of power to the temples about 1000 BCE or with the unique status of sanctuaries during Greek and Roman rule.

**Sources.** The study of the economy of ancient Egypt is a new discipline. The sources are difficult to access, and direct sources—actual economic documents—are rare; indirect sources are numerous but difficult to interpret. Indirect sources include the following:

- archeological findings from the excavations of urban sites and the economic annexes of temples and palaces

- information derived indirectly from funerary texts on tombs, stelae, and other private documents with references to offerings or to the specific economic function of a dignitary
- allusions to economic facts in literary texts

These indirect sources can be interpreted only with the help of the less commonly found direct sources. The latter present difficulties in decipherment because they were always written in Hieratic and expressed in an administrative style. The bulk of these documents consists of papyrus rolls from temple archives, fiscal and land registers, and records of exemptions. Offerings, in contrast, were inscribed principally on stelae.

Only for the latest periods (second half of the first millennium BCE) do we have access to complete archives for a few areas. For preceding periods, the best-known documents are the Wilbour Papyrus, a scroll longer than 10 meters (32 feet), from the time of Ramesses V, and the Harris Papyrus.

**Types of Temples.** Little is known about the distribution in time and space of the different types of temples in ancient Egypt. From Predynastic times, divine temples were erected in the Nile Valley, often modest sanctuaries maintained by the local inhabitants. Some of the temples stagnated or decayed, while others, such as the temple of the goddess Neith at Sais (in the Nile Delta), expanded in influence and size through the centuries. During the Old Kingdom, a specific type of sanctuary flourished in the Memphis–Heliopolis region: the solar temples, which were very closely linked with the crown.

Royal funerary temples, an element of Egyptian history from the very beginning and usually associated with the pyramid of a sovereign, quickly became important economic units. Parts of the archives of the temple of Neferirkare Kakai (third king of the fifth dynasty) at Abusir, south of Memphis, have been recovered. The Abusir Papyri offer rare evidence of the functioning of this type of temple. Little is known about the funerary temples of the Middle Kingdom, but those of the New Kingdom are well represented in the Theban area by the temples of Hatshepsut at Deir el-Bahri and of Sety I at Buhen, and by the Ramesseum of Ramesses II. Storage facilities and offices are frequently identifiable in their ruins. Some temples can be considered both divine and royal, because the divinity they housed "incarnated" an aspect of royal power. Examples include the temples of Horus at Edfu (Upper Egypt), Neith at Sais (Delta) and, above all, Amun at Karnak and Luxor.

**Relations between Temple and State.** Aside from modest primitive sanctuaries maintained locally, the upkeep and management of temples was one of the main responsibilities of the state from the time of the Old Kingdom. Most important, each temple needed land to supply the necessary goods for daily offerings. During the Middle Kingdom, the sovereign or his delegates visited the local sanctuaries to evaluate at first hand what would be required for each temple. In the case of the Old Kingdom funerary temple of Neferirkare Kakai, the central administration provided direct aid in economically difficult times to supplement the supplies needed by the sanctuary.

Kings influenced the management of the temples until the end of the New Kingdom mainly through donations of land. Royal decrees of such acts were displayed on large stelae at the entrance to the building. Other decrees, however, are known only through allusions to them on contemporary monuments or through copies on papyrus. The Harris Papyrus (for Year 32 of Ramesses III) indicates that the king allotted 300,000 hectares to the main sanctuaries of the country; of this total, 240,000 hectares were assigned to the Amun temple at Thebes, another large area went to maintain the king's own funerary temple at Medinet Habu. Although these tracts seem enormous, unfortunately we have no comparable data from earlier periods.

Some land donations to temples specified not only the extent of the area and the legal status of the lands but also the use to which they must be put: the production of grain, flax for royal linen, various types of cloth, herds, and the like.

The rulers showered various benefits on these religious properties. From the Old Kingdom, tax exemption and exemptions from labor appear in the first known decree (fourth dynasty, reign of Shepseskaf). Several documents are known from the Middle Kingdom; one stipulates that a portion of the territory assigned to the temple of Wepwawet at Abydos may not be used as a cemetery. The temple of Sety I, also at Abydos, benefited from revenues in gold (*Decree of Kanais*); the rules for mining precious metals are outlined in detail, as well as the punishment to be inflicted for disobeying these. In fact, in all periods such decrees are framed and presented as truly judicial acts.

**Temple Organization and Economic Management.** The daily offerings and the celebration of the various festivals varied in number according to the importance of each temple. Archaeological remains and indirect sources (particularly texts on privilege) grant an overview of the temple's various agencies as an economic unity. In addition, tomb scenes in *mastaba*s of the Old Kingdom and Theban burials of the New Kingdom frequently show temple officials and other workers performing their duties.

The management and administration of the temple were housed close to the cult building, generally within the enclosure. The treasury and the scribe's office were adjacent to the archive, in which bookkeeping scrolls were kept; some that were found include the Abusir Papyrus, the Wilbour Papyrus, and the Prachov and Reinhardt scrolls.

The products destined for offering—bread, beer, poultry, meat, fruit, vegetables, flowers, fine fabrics, and dishes, or "all the beautiful and pure things through which a god lives," according to the consecrated formula—were kept in storerooms: the "granary of the divine offerings" was one of the most important rooms or buildings. Geese, ducks, and other birds were kept in the lower courtyards and in aviaries (in Karnak the birds could travel between the aviary and the sacred lake through a narrow passage). The storerooms were situated closer to the cult sites than were the slaughterhouses. A separate place was reserved for food offerings; it included or was adjacent to a room where the offerings were kept. Over time, the butchering site, brewery, and bakery were separated from the area dedicated to the cult and to consecrating the offering. An economic system was established to deliver the quantities of offerings regularly required for rituals and festivals; for that purpose, the temple functioned like any other estate. The poultry were usually raised within the temple grounds, while cattle were kept in fields allocated to the temple. Agriculture was the basis of the religious estate's prosperity. During the earliest periods, some temples had only tiny parcels of land. Through time, the pharaohs more and more often established land use intended as much for their own worldly maintenance as for their funerary cult. There seems to have been a gradual shift in economic power from mortuary temple to divine sanctuary, beginning with the rise of solar temples. In the New Kingdom, that trend became even more pronounced. Exploiting ever greater areas of land, the temples constituted an important economic force and thus acquired political power on which the crown could rely. The result was an increase in royal donations, as the king attempted to conciliate the powerful clergy, and this led to an imbalance between the two. The growth of the estate of Amun at Thebes at the end of the New Kingdom is particularly revealing with regard to this evolution. By granting crown lands accompanied by tax and labor exemptions, the state favored the rise to power of the so-called king-priests, who instituted a veritable theocratic state.

Moreover, texts reveal that among the temple lands, a certain category (the *iḥt* fields) were reserved for the cultivation of the divine offering. A statute specified the supply of grain to the temple to which those fields belonged, regardless of how distant that temple was. Certain sensitive "marsh" crops required careful irrigation, such as cucumbers, which were highly valued by the Egyptians and were grown in the low-lying lands near the Nile, rich in alluvium. Most agriculture, however, concentrated on grain—

barley (*it*) and, to a lesser degree, emmer wheat (*bdt*). These two crops were central to the Egyptian diet in both baking and brewing, since beer was made with fermented barley. Hence, they were the basic unit of value measurement: taxes, calculated on the basis of farmed area, were measured in sacks (*h3r*) of these two commodities.

**Temple Workers.** Various administrators ran the economic sector (*pr*) of the temple. The high priest was the chief executive officer, or at least the person responsible to the pharaoh with regard to management; however, not all important posts were necessarily occupied by clergy. For example, Amenemhet, the owner of the eighteenth dynasty Theban tomb 82, accumulated duties linked to an accounting for grain from the estate of Amun at Thebes without having held priestly office. The rank and previous experience of the managers of temple troops, granaries, or works varied greatly. High-ranking military men occupied such posts, as did magistrates, viziers, and other dignitaries. An army of scribes controlled temple and worker administration, since land surveys before and after the harvest, and the calculation, collection, and registration of taxes, called for a large staff. Laundrymen, potters, cooks, shepherds, cowherds, guardians of the sacred herds, beekeepers, and fishermen were also regularly employed.

The crops depended on the rhythms of nature. The preparation of the soil, the maintenance of the various irrigation systems, and the seeding and harvesting took place only when the land was not flooded. When the fields were inundated, the farmers were employed elsewhere—in the mines and quarries, on military expeditions, or in construction. Whether the work in the fields was assigned to regular or seasonal workers, to free men or slaves, varied from era to era. Beginning in the Old Kingdom, the state employed men—peasants and, above all, soldiers—who were free but who submitted to forced labor for a certain period, sometimes on the temple agricultural lands. By the New Kingdom, slavery in the strict sense was mostly the fate of prisoners of war; assigned to serve a temple, they were literally "purified," thus achieving the status of freed men. At the end of the Ramessid period there seems to have been a shortage of peasant labor, and there is evidence of the "kidnapping" of agricultural workers from large estates. The kings tried to alleviate this shortage by dispatching to the estate of Amun at Thebes, in particular, repeat offenders and captives as field laborers.

The consequence of these continuing interventions and direct exploitations was the progressive and effective replacement called land lease. Several documents are known that registered land leased even to women.

**Economic and Social Consequences.** Divine offerings presented in temples to the deity reverted to the clergy; it often provided the source of support for a great number of individuals in the great New Kingdom funerary or divine temples of Thebes. According to the quotas proportionate to their rank, the servants or prophets of god, the pure priests, ritualists, and other clerics were allowed to help themselves directly from the hall of offerings. Temples also supported beneficiaries who were not strictly part of the priestly circle, since other functionaries of high rank were also partly paid—at the temple of Neferirkare Kakai in the Old Kingdom and in the New Kingdom, state employees at Deir el-Medina. To the growing economic weight of the sanctuary was added the ever more important social role of the clergy. In the eighteenth dynasty, the Decree of Horemheb gave priests the same prerogatives on sacred lands—especially with regard to exercising justice—that had previously been reserved to royal officers.

While royal intervention increasingly focused on decrees of donation and immunity, the temples' relations with private individuals evolved. From the New Kingdom onward, private individuals began giving land donations to the sanctuaries: since the tax levied by the temple on cultivated fields was smaller than the tax due the crown, Egyptians preferred giving lands that they continued to manage on behalf of the gods. This situation, which developed rapidly in the Late period, resulted in a new division of economic forces by Ptolemaic and Roman times.

**Conclusion.** The temple administrations were traditionally focused on their treasuries; however, in some Late period Egyptian temples, engraved on the walls are treasury lists of foreign tribute, consisting of precious materials, as if temple treasuries served as the storage warehouse for items delivered to the king. Even if this notion of tribute conceals the reality of an often commercial exchange, the fact that such tribute existed reveals an interesting role for Late period temples. Then, too, as a result of private donations, a powerful indigenous priestly caste had developed—one with which the non-Egyptian pharaohs had to deal. The scope of religious construction in Late period times is not sufficiently explained by royal decree alone; in fact, local interests and indigenous economic power had taken over to a large degree. In this light, the change in tone is understandable of the royal edicts (decrees at Canopus, Raphia, Rosetta, and Philae): the kings no longer bestowed lands and exemptions on a specific sanctuary but on all temples of the country as a whole—thus recognizing the clergy as not only spiritual but also economic leaders and managers of the local population.

[*See also* Administration, *article on* Temple Administration.]

## BIBLIOGRAPHY

Gardiner, Alan H. *The Wilbour Papyrus.* 4 vols. Oxford, 1941–1952. Outstanding publication of the most important economic papyrus and the founding study of the most work undertaken on the ancient Egyptian economy.

Gasse, Annie. *Données nouvelles administratives et sacerdotales sur l'organisation du domaine d'Amon—XXᵉ–XXIᵉ dynasties à la lumière des papyrus Prachov, Reinhardt et Grundbuch (avec édition princeps des papyrus Louvre AF 6345 et 6346–7).* Cairo, 1988. Study of a rare group of "economic" papyri.

Grandet, Pierre. *Le Papyrus Harris* I (BM 9999). 2 vols. Cairo, 1994. Important publication (with a very complete bibliography) on this document.

Helck, Wolfgang. *Wirtschaftsgeschichte des Alten Ägypten im 3. und 2. Jahrtausend vor Chr.* Leiden, 1975. The first (and still unique) synthesis on the economy of pharaonic Egypt.

Lipinski, Edward, ed. *State and Temple Economy in the Ancient Near East.* 2 vols. Louvain, 1979. Material from an international conference held in 1978; still a relevant work.

Meeks, Dimitri. *Le grand texte des donations au temple d'Edfou.* Cairo, 1972. Study of an important offering text from the Ptolemaic period; presentation of different units of measure.

Menu, Bernadette. *Le régime juridique des terres et du personnel attaché à la terre dans le Papyrus Wilbour.* Lille, 1970. Study that emphasizes the intervention of the state in temple economy.

Posener-Kriéger, Paule. *Les archives du temple funéraire de Néferirkarê-Kakaï.* 2 vols. Cairo, 1976. Study and commentary of the papyri edited by Posemer-Kriéger and Jean-Louis de Cenival in *Hieratic Papyri in the British Museum*, 5th series, London, 1968.

Vleeming, Sven P. *Papyrus Reinhardt, An Egyptian Land List from the Tenth Century B.C.* Berlin, 1993. Fundamental study of one of the main papyri on the ancient Egyptian economy.

ANNIE GASSE

**EDFU,** modern Idfu, a site on the western bank of the Nile River (28°58′N, 32°52′E). The ancient Egyptian name was Djebat (*Dbȝt*), probably derived from the root that means "to adorn," whence *djebat*, which means "robing chamber (for a god or king)"; the name is not attested in the Old Kingdom, however, as the site then was called *Behdet* (*Bḥdt*). Edfu owes its importance to the Horus temple and the *mammisi*. In addition, the ancient site, located between the Ptolemaic-era temple and the Muslim cemetery, has yielded as its main discovery the necropolis of the Old Kingdom (which was used into the Middle Kingdom) with *mastaba* tombs and numerous stelae from the sixth dynasty to the thirteenth. There is also a Greco-Roman and Byzantine complex, with baths, homes, and other structures. French excavations lasted there from 1914 to 1933; then French-Polish excavations lasted from 1934 to 1939.

From remote antiquity, the city of Edfu was focused on the cult of Horus of Behdet, and a shrine had existed there even in prehistoric times. Remains of the Ramessid-era temple are in evidence on the eastern side of the forecourt, and blocks with painted reliefs of Taharqa and Psamtik II have come to light in the peristyle court, where they were reused as flooring in the Ptolemaic-era temple. The Horus temple texts have been published in their entirety, and the construction and descriptions of different sections of that temple were recorded in the dedication texts. It took from 237 to 57 BCE to build and decorate the Horus temple—the largest temple still standing in Egypt. The construction history may be tabulated as follows:

*Naos*: 23 August 237 BCE, laying of first stone. 17 August 212 BCE, start hypostyle decoration. Completed in 206 BCE. Consecration on 10 September 142 BCE. Length 53 meters (160 feet), width 33 meters (100 feet).

*Pronaos*: 2 July 140 BCE, laying of first stone. 5 September 124 BCE, completion of ceiling. Decoration from 122 to 116 BCE.
Length 19 meters (60 feet), width 40 meters (135 feet).

*Completion of temple*: 7 February 70 BCE, consecration. 5 December 57 BCE, placement of large doors.
The temple's length was 137 meters (425 feet); the width was 47 meters (155 feet).

The sanctuary of the Horus temple was surrounded by chapels consecrated to Horus, Horus-Re, Osiris, Khonsoi, Min, and Mehyt. Radiating from this religious center are the public spaces (the entrance hall, *wabet* [*w'bt*] or "purification room," and the stairs) and the cult areas (the laboratory, treasury, Nile chamber, and the offerings hall). The hypostyle hall was the space of exaltation for the power of Horus. The *pronaos* provided the visualization of the primordial place from which sprang the creation; it is a scaled-down image of the Egyptian territory, with all nome (province) capitals represented. The courtyard was a mythic space (the snake of origin was slain there), one of ceremony or the celebration of both Hathor and Sokar. In the passage separating the temple from the enclosure wall, engravings tell the great myths: that of the genesis of the temple, the Horus myth, the rite of net hunting, and the feast on the first day of the month called Tybi. On the exterior wall, the important registry text of the endowment of Edfu was recorded. The pylon records the glory of Horus, based on the transfer of power to Horus from Osiris and Re.

Some forty feasts and festivals marked each Egyptian ceremonial year. The principal ones were described in the temple texts that were published by M. Alliot in *Le culte d'Horus à Edfou au temps des Ptolémées* (Cairo, 1949 and 1954). Some of the feasts important at Edfu were the following:

- the new year celebration, during which the divine statues recharged themselves with the sun's energy;
- the crowning of the falcon, which took place on the

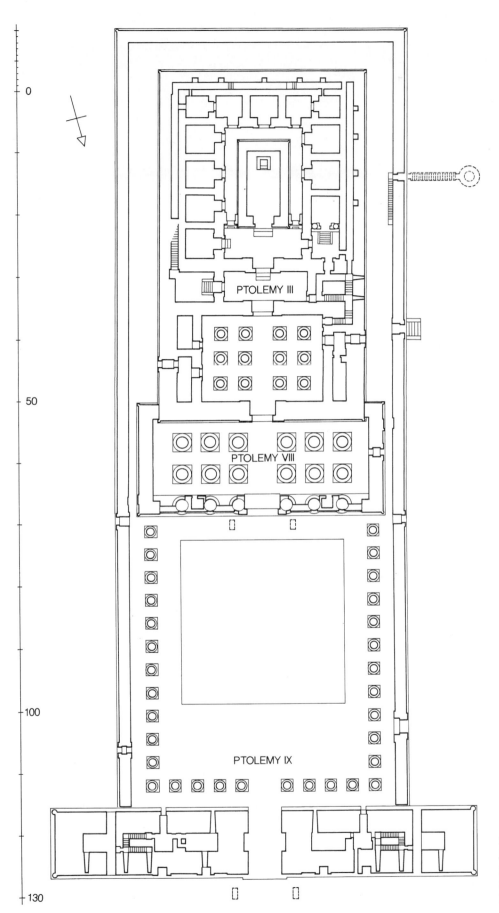

PTOLEMY III

PTOLEMY VIII

PTOLEMY IX

0

50

100

130

EDFU. *Plan of the Horus temple at Edfu, built under Ptolemy XII.* (From Dieter Arnold, *Temples of the Last Pharaohs.* New York, 1999.)

EDFU. *The pylon of the Horus temple at Edfu.* The reliefs feature scenes of Ptolemy XII smiting foreigners. (Courtesy David P. Silverman)

first of Tybi, immediately following the birth of Osiris that had been celebrated in the last days of the month of Khoiak (it symbolized the renewal of the power of Horus with his sacred animal acting as an intermediary);

• the victory celebration on the twenty-first of the following month, Mechir, which reenacted the struggle between Horus and Seth; and

• the sacred marriage in the month of Epiphi, which was the mystical union of Hathor of Dendera and Horus of Edfu.

The Horus temple at Edfu was a royal jubilee (*sed*-festival) temple of Heliopolitan inspiration, and the influence of Edfu extended into the South from Elephantine to Thebes. Numerous divinities of the Tanite nome had been exported to Edfu, hence Edfu had a relationship with Heliopolis, Dendera, and Mesen/Sile. The twinning with Dendera was due to the coupling of Horus and Hathor. Heliopolitan doctrines informed the theology as a whole, with the Horus temple intended as a replica of the Great Temple of Heliopolis. Edfu was considered the Mesen of the South, the counterpart to the guardian city of the eastern marshes of the Nile Delta, where Horus of Mesen reigned.

**BIBLIOGRAPHY**

Alliot, M. *Le culte d'Horus à Edfou au temps des Ptolémées*, Cairo, 1949, 1954.

Cauville, S. *Edfou, Les guides archéologiques de l'IFAO.* Cairo, 1984.

Cauville, S. *Essai sur la théologie du temple d'Horus à Edfou.* Cairo, 1987.

Fairman, H. W. *The Triumph of Horus: An Ancient Egyptian Drama.* London, 1974.

Finnestad, R. B. *Image of the World and Symbol of the Creator: On the Cosmological and Iconological Values of the Temples of Edfu.* Wiesbaden, 1985.

Kurth, D. *Die Dekoration der Säulen im Pronaos des Tempels von Edfu.* Wiesbaden, 1983.

Kurth, D. *Treffpunkt der Götter.* Zurich and Munich, 1994.

Kurth, D. *Die Inschriften des Tempels von Edfu. Übersetzung. Edfou VIII.* Wiesbaden, 1998.

SYLVIE CAUVILLE
Translated from French by Elizabeth Schwaiger

**EDUCATION.** Ancient Egyptian education, as described in this article, was restricted to male members of the upper class; it entailed mastery of the writing system and acquaintance with a stock of religious and literary texts. Parallel to learning those texts came inculcation with moral and cultural values. Education, therefore, was a privilege in Egyptian society provided to those intended for supervisory roles in administration, building projects, temple cults, and other professional capacities. (Excluded, thereby, were females, as well as slaves, either Egyptian or foreign.) During the New Kingdom, children of neighboring rulers were sent to an institution at the Egyptian court called *k3p*, where they were educated along with youths of the middle and higher echelons of Egyptian society. Egyptian education, at least in that period, became an international affair and acquired an overt political dimension.

Education was an indispensable prerequisite for starting a career as a scribe in administration or as a priest in a temple cult. During the Old Kingdom, the social elite who ran those institutions comprised an estimated 1 percent of the population, the literate sector of society. By late New Kingdom times, literacy may have expanded to about 5 percent, but it dropped after that. The principles underlying the selection or exclusion of new members are not easy to discern, but the system seems to have been largely self-regenerating, except in a few periods such as the twelfth dynasty. Next to nothing is known about education among the illiterate majority, but knowledge seems to have been transmitted among craftsmen from father to son.

**Terminology.** The general term for "education" throughout pharaonic time was *sb3yt*, the basic meaning of which is "teaching" with a derived connotation of "punishment"; educators apparently used a stick on recalcitrant students. The standard term for "instruction" and "teaching" in both its written and oral forms was also *sb3yt*. Most of the Wisdom Texts contain the word *sb3yt* in their titles, and in New Kingdom and Demotic instructions we encounter such derivations as *sb3y.t-š'.t* ("instruction in letter form") and *sb3y.t-mtrt* ("instruction [based on the teacher's own] experience"). In the Late period, Demotic uses *mtrt* ("testimony") as well. The distinction between *sb3yt* and *mtrt* may have resembled that between "theory of education" and "practice of education."

**Methods.** Students had to learn to write whole words, not single signs. In pre-Demotic times, they started with cursive hieroglyphs and went on to Hieratic; the latter is even more cursive than the former and may roughly be compared to modern cursive. In Greco-Roman times, Hieratic was still a necessary qualification of temple priests, although by the sixth century BCE, Demotic had replaced that type of script for business purposes. There is no evidence that scribes in training studied monumental hieroglyphs; these were the domain of painters and stonemasons, who nevertheless also acquired a certain degree of literacy.

Writing and copying texts often implied memorizing them, or, as a rather idealistic Ramessid instruction commands, "Apply yourself to writing by day, while you read by night" (Papyrus Sallier I, *recto* 3,6). The apprentice scribe was expected to know the classics of literature by heart, and also a vast number of religious texts, although his repertory of religious texts may have depended on his specific job in the administration, outside the temple cult. Rote learning was done by singing the texts aloud, since silent reading was unknown in ancient Egypt until Roman times.

Beginners were generally assumed to have been given flakes of limestone or potsherds (ostraca) for writing exercises, and they were allowed to use papyrus as soon as they had acquired mastery of the Hieratic script. This assumption is borne out by the fact that handwriting on ostraca tends to be clumsier than that on papyri. The economic factor may have been decisive: papyrus was expensive, whereas ostraca were readily available.

**Subjects.** Among the subjects of general knowledge covered by the curriculum of scribal apprentices, at least from the New Kingdom onward, were the following: epistolary formulas and letter-writing; grammar, orthography, and rhetoric; foreign languages; onomastics; geography; and mathematics and geometry. These are discussed in detail below.

*Epistolary formulas and letter-writing.* A letter normally consisted of three sections: the initial address, its content, and the final address, sometimes including a farewell to the addressee. The introduction contained certain polite formulas commending the recipient to the care of a god or gods. A composition from the early Middle Kingdom served as a model for letter-writing. The *Instructions of Khety* quotes the very end of that text. From the Middle to the New Kingdom, it was copied in cursive hieroglyphs written in vertical columns; it starts with an elaborate introduction composed of formulas that betray their place of composition as the Memphis region. The Satirical Letter of Papyrus Anastasi I emphasizes the importance in a standard letter of certain stylistic features.

*Grammar, orthography, and rhetoric.* Schoolboy exercises display orthographic mistakes that can only be accounted for by the assumption that the apprentices were taught to write single words and even whole sentences, but not single signs. The Egyptian term for "hieroglyphs" (*mdw-ntr*) may be taken as corroborative evidence for this feature of education, since it literally means "god's words," not "god's signs," even though there was the separate term *tit* for "sign, image, picture, representation."

There is strong evidence that students were taught grammatical paradigms in a standardized way. This practice betrays a certain awareness of basic linguistic elements. An example from the Ramessid era:

> I being . . . ;
> he being . . . ;

you (masc.) being . . . ;
we being . . . ;
they being . . . (twice);
you (fem.) being . . . (Ostraca Petrie 28)

Many more of these exercises survive from Demotic schools. Judging from the variety of lexical as well as syntactic paradigms, it seems a reasonable guess that there existed a sort of precursor to modern language tools. (Greek influence may also have contributed here.)

Rhetoric was held in high esteem and is a constant topic in instructional literature. How the "rules of proper speech" were taught remains unknown, but according to Ptahhotep, eloquence was not restricted to members of the elite. Even female slaves were sometimes credited with the gift of fine speech: "Good speech is more hidden than greenstone, yet may be found among maids at the grindstones." In literary fiction at least, even the king may be stirred by the fine speech of an eloquent peasant.

The Egyptian language of pharaonic times developed through four phases—Old, Middle, and Late Egyptian, and finally Demotic. From the New Kingdom onward, scribes were well aware of their own language's history. Old texts were sometimes translated from an earlier variety into that of the copyist; we have samples of exercises rendering single sentences in both Middle and Late Egyptian. In the Late period, even long compositions of religious character were copied, transferring a sort of earlier, classical Egyptian into an advanced stage of Late Egyptian.

***Foreign languages.*** Expeditions, war, and trade implied contact with neighboring countries at all times. Such relations necessitated mastery of foreign languages, such as Nubian and Libyan. In the New Kingdom, an ever-increasing number of loan words, especially Semitic, can be seen rendered in the so-called syllabic orthography of the Egyptian script. Ramessid school texts make ample use of them; the Satirical Letter of Papyrus Anastasi I bears extensive witness to this. Not only were single words borrowed from the Levant; even whole compositions from Canaanite culture were translated into Egyptian. As the famous Amarna Letters show, the ancient site of Akhetaten (Tell el-Amarna) must have housed a place where Akkadian was read and taught—a Near Eastern language indispensable for the maintenance of foreign relations.

Trade with the Aegean, and with Crete in particular, involved language barriers. A wooden tablet of the eighteenth dynasty entitled "To make [proper] names of Keftiu (i.e., Crete)" is evidence of the study of the language that was written in Linear A (Late Minoan I). The fact that this list of foreign names is accompanied by an excerpt of the *Prophecy of Neferty*, a much-copied classic of Middle King-

dom literature, suggests that it was used as a school exercise.

There are occasional allusions to foreigners being taught Egyptian (in the epilogue to the *Instructions of Anii*), but these do not imply the existence of school-like institutions for such instruction.

***Onomastics.*** In a technique similar to and perhaps inspired by Babylonian practice, Egyptian scribes showed a strong tendency toward organizing their knowledge in word lists. These lists, or onomastica, are arranged in subject sections—for example, Egyptian toponyms from south to north, classes of people, professions, titles, or animals. Specimens of these catalogs from the late New Kingdom and the Middle Kingdom confine themselves to naming the items belonging to a specific section, but the onomastica of Roman times had much to say about their entries, supplying real commentaries on them. These Late period onomastica derived from temple schools and were destined for priests; those of earlier times remained silent as to their place of composition.

From the first and second centuries CE, there are fragments of lists that organize their entries in alphabetic order. Lists of this kind may have been drawn on when a scribe was composing a literary text of marked didactic import, such as the Satirical Letter. Much of a typical Late period onomasticon's material was based on a Ramessid-era school text: the geography and topography of Syria and Palestine, the parts of an Egyptian soldier's equipment, including a chariot, and so on. Other lists drawn up for school purposes contained indigenous or foreign proper names and those of past Egyptian kings.

***Geography.*** The onomastica may be taken as evidence that scribes were supposed to know at least the most important place names of Egypt and its neighbors, as well as their locations. Officials who were involved in foreign affairs, trade, or military campaigns also needed such additional knowledge.

***Mathematics and geometry.*** Bookkeeping was one of a scribe's primary occupations, so the four basic arithmetic operations formed another subject of his education. These calculations were supplemented by various problems of geometry, examples of which are found in mathematical manuscripts both in Hieratic and in Demotic. To what extent these manuscripts were objects of study in schools remains a matter of debate, but the Moscow Mathematical Papyrus of the late Middle Kingdom is a reasonable school candidate; its instructions directly address the potential user in the second person. Invented problems served as models for future calculations. Abstract formulas, like those used by the Greek mathematicians, are sometimes implicit in the texts, but they are never formulated explicitly.

**Ethics and Moral Virtues.** The term *sb3y.t* denotes not

only "punishment" and "education" but also "instruction, teaching" in written form. These texts are directed from a father to his son or children, royal or otherwise; *sbꜣy.t* instructions cover a wide range of subjects. Generally speaking, their topics may be summarized as follows (not all of these occur in every text):

- Conventions of behavior in different social situations and relationships
- Acting and speaking in solidarity toward one's subordinates
- Loyalty to the king
- Worship of the god or gods

These and further topics can be subsumed under a key term of ancient Egyptian culture: *maat*.

"Instructions" of this sort, mostly written and transmitted in school, were also copied as separate chapters, or from beginning to end, sometimes even including a colophon. Those so-called instructions in letter-form may have been studied by the student in private, outside the classroom. Their title does not denote a literary genre to which they were intended to belong, but rather implies a sort of transfer between master and pupil.

Most instructions were created as single, self-contained treatises. In the early twelfth dynasty, however, there seems to have existed a distinct set of three texts, which were taught in sequence and which thus form a complete curriculum: the *Instructions of Khety*, the *Instructions of a Man for His Son*, and the *Loyalist Instruction*. Arranging the texts in this order, we get a triptychon that starts with the introduction of the future scribe into the residence school (*Instructions of Khety*). The inculcation of loyalty and the teaching of *maat* in its two aspects of speaking and doing follow (*Instructions of a Man for His Son*). The last section of the *Loyalist Instruction* marks the end of the curriculum. The speaker, at that point, leaves the scene by mentioning his own funerary cult, which involves preparing his children to take up office in the administration. Several cross-references distributed through the text trio render their arrangement in the way proposed here very plausible.

**Schools and Private Tuition.** The first literary attestations of schools, in the sense of an architectural complex exclusively serving the needs of education, date from the First Intermediate Period and the early twelfth dynasty (probably to be located in the residence of Itjtawy; see the *Instructions of Khety*). Even from the New Kingdom we have only scanty references to schools—for example, at or near the Deir el-Bahri temple complex, the Ramesseum, the Mut complex within the Karnak temple, and the village of Deir el-Medina. It is especially the last-named site that has supplied innumerable copies of literary texts reproduced in class. The location of the Rames-

seum and Deir el-Medina schools, however, cannot be determined exactly, and recently their existence has even been doubted. The plentiful scribal and painter's exercises on ostraca found in the forecourt of one of Senenmut's tombs in Western Thebes (tomb 71) attest to education on the spot, during its excavation and decoration.

The Egyptian word for "school," *ꜥt-sbꜣyt* (Coptic, *ansebe*), literally means "room of instruction." It is still unknown whether students of different levels were taught simultaneously in a single class; the existence of several classes representing different levels of education is not supported by the evidence. Types of schools may have varied, both inside and outside the temple, but their curriculum certainly depended on the function that future scribes or priests were supposed to fulfill. The institution at Deir el-Medina was probably located outside the sacred precincts and outside the village proper as well; its curriculum did not include the education of priests.

Students were introduced to the basics of writing by professional scribes, some of whom even held the title "teacher" (*sbꜣ*) or "overseer of teachers" (*imy-r sbꜣw*). Despite these specific titles, teaching was not their main occupation.

Instruction in class lasted for about four years and was followed by individual teaching or on-the-job training. Apprentices were now credited the title "assistant" (*ẖry-ꜥ*, literally "being under the hand/guidance of someone") and sometimes also that of "scribe" (*sš*). During this stage of education, some students developed a rather familiar relationship with their masters, as documented by some Ramessid private monuments mentioning and depicting former teachers as if they belonged to the student's family. Cases are known where fathers and even grandfathers instructed their own sons. Deir el-Medina has also produced evidence of an otherwise unknown sort of individual training: during the twentieth dynasty, the scribe Amennakht, son of Ipuy, cared for the eldest son of his colleague Hori, while Hori in turn cared for the son of Amennakht; the reason for this educational exchange remains obscure.

Usually teaching was given by the master in the pupil's presence, but once again Deir el-Medina—which may not be representative—supplies evidence for another kind of contact. This was teaching by correspondence. As already mentioned, "instructions-by-letter" imply silent study outside school. In addition to this, a student could have been expected to make copies, presumably of literary texts, at home. After he had finished one or more chapters, these copies were sent to the master for correction.

There was no compulsory school attendance for all children, and we cannot say if its place was sometimes taken by private tuition alone. During the Old Kingdom, this system seems to have prevailed, if indeed it was not the only form of instruction. It was comparable to the much later Roman model of individual education (of a *famulus* or "son" by an experienced official). This system constitutes the background of Ptahhotep's famous teaching. Since most of the administration in the Old Kingdom was situated in Memphis, it is a reasonable guess that children of provincial governors were sent there to be educated.

No definite proof of examinations in any form are yet known. Some stylistic features in the Moscow Mathematical Papyrus point in this direction, however, as when the teacher says, "Do it this way!" or "Let me know its volume!" and so on. If the student had finished his exercise correctly, he was rewarded by the teacher's comment: "You have found it correctly!" It should be stressed that Egyptian students and apprentices were not spoiled by praise; on the contrary, the relevant texts teem with reproaches and admonitions.

**Access to Knowledge and Education.** In principle, any male Egyptian was allowed to receive as much education as he needed to accomplish his job properly. Women were excluded from scribal education, although from internal evidence in Deir el-Medina documents, it can be deduced that a few women must have been literate or at least semiliterate. They could have achieved this only by autodidactic means. Pictorial evidence for female scribes, showing women in collocation with scribal equipment in eighteenth dynasty tombs, does not stand up to close examination. The scenes follow a specific iconographic convention, and scribal tools always refer to the ladies' husbands, who are sitting next to them.

**BIBLIOGRAPHY**

Baines, John R., and Christopher J. Eyre. "Four Notes on Literacy." *Göttinger Miszellen* 61 (1983), 65–96.

Bickel, S., and Mathieu, B. "L'Écrivain Amennakht et son *Enseignement.*" *Bulletin de l'Institut français d'archéologie orientale* 93 (1993), 31–51.

Brunner, Hellmut. *Altägyptische Erziehung.* Wiesbaden, 1992.

Fischer-Elfert, Hans-W. *Die Lehre eines Mannes für seinen Sohn. Eine Etappe auf dem »Gottesweg« des loyalen und solidarischen Beamten des frühen Mittleren Reiches.* Wiesbaden, 1999.

Janssen, Jac J., and Rosalind M. Janssen. *Growing Up in Ancient Egypt.* London, 1990.

Kaplony-Heckel, U. "Schüler und Schulwesen in der ägyptischen Spätzeit." *Studien zur Altägyptischen Kultur* 1 (1974), 227–246.

Williams, Ronald J. "Scribal Training in Ancient Egypt." *Journal of the American Oriental Society* 92 (1972), 214–221.

HANS-W. FISCHER-ELFERT

**EDUCATIONAL INSTITUTIONS.** Among the major educational institutions worldwide that offer doctoral programs in Egyptology are many that have had long-standing programs with some varying emphasis on lan-

guage, archaeology, and art history. There are also older institutions that are known for one specialization or another within the broader field, and some more recent programs with more or less breadth essentially at the undergraduate and master's level.

Unlike the largest university departments in history or classics, which have sufficient faculty specialists to be assured of adequate coverage of every decade or author, Egyptology departments, programs, institutes, and seminars over the years have benefited greatly from generalists who were familiar with and could teach many if not all phases of one of the oldest and longest-lived languages that can be studied, a history that spans thirty-five hundred years or more, a culture with seemingly unlimited archaeological resources, with exceptional art and artifacts, and with well-documented religious beliefs and practices. Generally one or two, and rarely three or four individuals at a given time have maintained the outstanding centers of Egyptological instruction. Traditionally, almost all university professors have been specialists in their own right, often providing required introductions to the other aspects of Egyptology, but in some cases an institution has become closely identified with the specialty of one scholar and has attracted primarily philologists or archaeologists, or even aspiring Demotists, Coptologists, Nubiologists, and so on.

**France.** One of the world's oldest centers for Egyptological study is the Collège de France, where a chair in Egyptian history and archaeology was established for Jean-François Champollion in 1831, within a few years of the acceptance of his decipherment of Egyptian hieroglyphs, but only a year before he died. Champollion had held a chair in history and geography at Grenoble from 1818 and would have achieved most of his success while there. His student in Egyptology, Ippolito Rosellini, accompanied him on his major epigraphic survey of Egypt in 1828–1829 and was certainly Italy's first modern Egyptologist, though the chair he held at Pisa since 1824 was a professorship of Oriental languages.

Champollion's successors at the Collège included Charles Lenormant (1848); Oliver Charles de Rougé (1860); Gaston Maspero (1874); and Alexandre Moret (1923). More recently, there was Etienne Drioton, appointed in 1957 after he had been professor of Egyptian philology and Coptic at the Catholic Institute since 1919; George Posener, who was professor of Egyptian philology and archaeology from 1961 to 1978; Jean Leclant, who has been active in all aspects of Egyptology; and Jean Yoyotte, who has held the chair most recently.

Before Gaston Maspero became professor at the Collège de France, he had been appointed professor of Egyptology at the École des Hautes Études in 1869. E. Grébaut, who had lectured at the École from 1876 to 1878 and had succeeded Maspero as director of the Egyptian Antiquities Service, returned to teach ancient history at the Sorbonne from 1892 to 1915. E. Lefébure, who was appointed lecturer in Egyptology at Lyons in 1880, succeeded Grébaut at the École in 1885. Emile Amelineau, who had excavated at Abydos in 1894–1898, was primarily a Coptologist and became professor of the history of religions at the École. The renowned Alexandre Moret was director at the École from 1899 to 1938. P. Guieysse was associated with the École from 1880 to 1918 and was succeeded as professor of Egyptian philology by Henri Sottas (1918–1927). From 1928 to 1945 Raymond Weill was director of the École in history and Egyptian archaeology. G. Lefebvre was director of studies at the École Pratique des Hautes Études with the chair in Egyptian philology from 1928 to 1948; he was succeeded by J. J. Clére in 1949. M. Malinine, who was professor of Coptic at the Institut Catholique from 1936 to 1948, was directeur d'Études at the École Pratique from 1952 to 1970. P. Montet was professor at Strasbourg from 1928 to 1964.

Currently, Egyptology is taught at many institutions in France. Among the best-known professors are J. C. Goyon, director of the Institut d'Égyptologie at Lyon; Dominique Valbelle, director of the Institut de Papyrologie et d'Égyptologie at Lille; G. Godron and J. C. Grenier, professors at Montpellier; Nicolas Grimal, director of the Centre de Recherches Égyptologiques at the Sorbonne; Pascal Vernus, director at the École Pratique (fourth section, history and philology); and Annie Gasse, professor of Egyptian at the Institut Catholique.

**Germany.** In 1846, Karl Richard Lepsius became professor of Egyptology at Berlin University, the first in a long line of distinguished scholars who made Germany the world's center for Egyptology. Germany's prominence was due in part to its scholars' success in systematizing Egyptian grammar and later producing the first comprehensive dictionary of the language. Lepsius died in 1884, and his student Adolf Erman assumed the professorship, which he held until 1923. In this period scholars came from all over to study in the Berlin school. Erman taught a wide range of subjects, and his student and successor (from 1923 to 1934), Kurt Sethe, was more narrowly philological. The Berlin school included appointments in papyrology (U. Wilcken, 1917–1931), and art (H. Schaffer, from 1907). Hermann Grapow, known for his work on the Wörterbuch and the medical texts, became honorable professor in 1928 and was ordinarius professor from 1937 to 1945. Fritz Hintze, who worked on the Wörterbuch before the war, returned as lecturer in 1947, was made professor in 1951, and was ordinarius professor from 1957 to 1980. He founded an Institute for Egyptology to cover the Sudan, and his successors Steffen Wenig and Erika Endesfelder have continued in that tradition. At the Ägyptol-

ogisches Seminar of the Freien Universität Berlin, Gerhard Fecht has been succeeded by Jürgen Osing as ordinarius professor.

Among the other old Egyptology positions in Germany, H. Brugsch was professor at Göttingen in 1867 and founded the great *Zeitschrift für Ägyptische Sprache und Altertumskunde* in 1863. J. Duemichen was professor at Strasbourg from 1872 to 1894, and W. Spiegelberg went there in 1898. Spiegelberg went to Heidelberg in 1918, and from there to Munich from 1923 to 1930. K. A. Wiedemann was professor at Bonn from 1891 to 1928. Hans Bonnet was professor of Egyptology at Bonn from 1928 to 1955, and he was followed by E. Edel, who has been succeeded by U. Rössler-Köhler. G. Seyffarth had been professor of archaeology at Leipzig already in 1830, but got off to a bad start with respect to the the Egyptian language by refusing to accept Champollion's decipherment. G. Steindorff was much more successful at Leipzig from 1893 to 1938. The Coptologist Johannes Leipoldt, who was lecturer at Leipzig then Halle in 1906, became professor at Kiel in 1909, at Münster in 1914, and at Leipzig from 1916 to 1954. A. Scharff was professor at Munich from 1932 to 1950. Kurt Sethe, who was at Göttingen from 1900 to 1923, was succeeded by Herman Kees in 1924. Siegfried Schott was professor at Heidelberg in 1952, but in 1956 succeeded Kees at Göttingen, from which he retired in 1965. His successor, W. Westendorf, has now been succeeded by F. Junge. Eberhard Otto, who was professor at Heidelberg from 1955 to 1974, was succeeded by J. Assmann. At Tübingen professor Helmut Brunner was succeeded by Wolfgang Schenkel as ordinarius and institutsdirektor. At Köln P. Derchain was succeeded by H. J. Thissen. At Hamburg W. Helck was succeeded by H. Atenmüller. Elke Blumenthal is ordinarius professor at Leipzig, R. Gundlach is at Mainz, and at Marburg Günther Burkard succeeded professor Ursula Kaplony-Heckel, but has now become ordinarius at Munich. Erhart Graefe is ordinarius and institutsdirektor at Münster, and Erich Winter is ordinarius at Trier. Erich Lüddeckens was succeeded by K. T. Zauzich at Würzburg. While all of the German Egyptological centers are well staffed, some, such as Heidelberg, Tübingen, Göttingen, and Berlin, are indeed exceptional.

**Italy.** In Turin, the Egyptian Museum has a wonderful collection of objects and papyri and this of course has had its effect on the university. Francesco Rossi who became assistant in the Egyptian Museum in 1865, was appointed extraordinarius professor in 1876, and was ordinarius from 1906 to 1909. Giulio Farina, who was director of the museum from 1939 to 1943, was also appointed professor at the university. More recently, Silvio Curto, who was director of the Museum, was professor in the department of archaeological science as well. The ordinarius professorships in Italy now are at Pisa, with professor Edda Bresciani working in Demotic and excavating in the Faiyum, and at Rome (where G. Botti was appointed from 1956 to 1960 after teaching Egyptology at Florence from 1942 to 1956), with professor Alessandro Roccati, successor to Sergio Donadoni, interested in both philology and in archaeology, and at Bologna with professor Sergio Pernigotti in the Institute of Ancient History. The universities at Milan, Naples, and Florence also have some Egyptology, and the Pontifical Biblical Institute in Rome has had a long tradition including A. Mallon from 1913, É. Suys from 1929, and A. Massart from 1948 to 1985.

**Egyptology in the United Kingdom.** While the British Isles produced a number of fine Egyptologists who worked more or less independently during much of the nineteenth century—scholars such as Thomas Young, Edward Hincks, John Gardner Wilkinson, and Samuel Birch being exceptionally noteworthy—it was Amelia Edwards, "the first woman Egyptologist," who was primarily responsible for founding the Egypt Exploration Fund, which sponsored the important archaeological work of Edouard Naville and W.M.F. Petrie. Amelia Edwards also established the first chair of Egyptology in England at University College, London, in 1892. Petrie was the first to hold the Edwards Chair and began University College's long and distinguished history of fieldwork and teaching of Egyptian archaeology. F. L. Griffith began his career as assistant to Petrie at University College from 1892 to 1896, and Petrie's student Margaret Murray became junior lecturer in 1898. She continued teaching there till 1935, two years after Petrie retired and S. R. K. Glanville became Edwards Professor. Petrie and his successors worked at numerous sites throughout Egypt, and later W. B. Emery and G. T. Martin had remarkable success at their important concessions at Saqqara. With the recent appointments of professors F. Hassan and W. Tait there should be a very good balance between archaeology and philology.

F. L. Griffith became lecturer in Egyptology at Manchester University in 1896, then reader at Oxford in 1901, and eventually professor there in 1924. The Brunner Chair in Egyptology at Liverpool University first held by P. Newberry in 1906 was filled by T. E. Peet in 1920. When Griffith became professor emeritus at Oxford in 1933, Peet was appointed professor designate but died suddenly the following year, and Battiscomb Gunn began his sixteen-year career as professor of Egyptology at Oxford. In Gunn's time Oxford thrived with Sir Alan Gardiner's enormous contributions to scholarship and his considerable involvement in its Egyptology program. With J. Černý's appointment as professor, philology was further enhanced and Late Egyptian Hieratic specifically became a central focus. Emphases have changed with the more re-

cent appointments of John Barnes and currently John Baines, with Mark Smith as reader, but the program continues to be highly productive.

Egyptian language as well as the social sciences aspects of Egyptology continue to be taught to large numbers of students at Liverpool. With H. W. Fairman, K. Kitchen, and A. F. Shore as professors the University became known for Late period studies, Ptolemaic hieroglyphs, Ramessid texts, and Coptic. Again, emphases change, but the program continues to be well balanced with the appointments of C. Eyre and M. Collier.

S. R. K. Glanville left London to become Herbert Thompson Professor of Egyptology at Cambridge University (1946–1956). Because of W. E. Crum's enormous contributions to Coptic studies, England had considerable influence in this field as well, and M. Plumley's subsequent appointment as professor at Cambridge was a significant recognition of the importance of the field. Following Plumley's retirement, however, his two successors there, Barry Kemp and John Ray, as readers, are doing outstanding work in both archaeology and philology, with emphasis on Demotic.

Durham University's School of Oriental Studies also has had an Egyptological presence, with J. R. Harris as professor and Dr. K. Kuhn as reader in Coptic.

**Egyptology Elsewhere in Europe.** At the University of Vienna, the philologist Simon Reinisch, who was professor from 1868 to 1903, was clearly interested in Egyptology, but Jakob Krall, who worked with Demotic and Coptic, was the first Egyptology appointment as extraordinarius professor in 1890, ordinarius in 1897, and as professor in 1899. After Krall's death in 1905, Hermann Junker, who had worked in the field for many years, became assistant professor in 1909 and professor in 1912. He founded Vienna's Institute of Egyptology and African Studies in 1923, served as director of the German Archaeological Institute in Cairo, and was professor of Egyptology at Cairo University from 1933 to 1939. Gertrude Thausing succeeded him as professor, and she in turn was followed by Manfred Bietak, who has moved toward archaeology and has made spectacular finds at Tell ed-Dab'a.

In the Netherlands, Egyptology developed out of two sources: the Museum of Antiquities in Leiden and various faculties of theology. Willem Pleyte had worked at the Museum in Leiden since 1869, but it was Pieter Boeser, his successor as keeper, who was the first to occupy a university position in Egyptology as university lecturer (1910–1925). Boeser was succeeded by H. P. Blok and then by A. De Buck (1929–1949), who later became the first ordinarius professor (1949–1969). He was succeeded by A. Klasens as extraordinarius professor (1961–1978), then by J. J. Janssen, again as ordinarius (1980–1985). Since 1986 the chair has been held by Joris Borghouts, who, with several assistants, maintains a very active teaching program, with special interests in philology and Deir el-Medina studies. W. Brede Kristensen occupied a chair in ancient religions at Leiden from 1901 to 1937, and from 1969 to 1998 Leiden also had a chair in Greco-Egyptian law occupied by P. W. Pestman. Since 1985, H. D. Schneider has been extraordinarius professor in Museum Archaeology of Egyptian Objects.

At Amsterdam, extraordinary chairs of Egyptology were occupied by J. M. A. Janssen (1962–1963) and by J. Zandee (1963–1979). Zandee's principal position was with Utrecht University in the faculty of theology. Others active in Egyptology with positions in ancient religions were C. J. Bleeker (1946-1969) and then M. Heerma van Voss (1969–1979) at Amsterdam; G. Leeuw, H. Te Velde, and now J. van Dijk in Groningen; and D. van der Plas since 1989 at Nijmegen.

In Belgium, Jean Capart had appointments as conservator at the Musees Royaux du Cinquantenaire since 1900. Guiding his queen on a tour of Egypt in 1923 resulted in her establishing the Fondation Égyptologique Reine Élisabeth, with Capart as first director. He became chief curator and director of the Museum as well as professor at Liege. M. Werbrouk, A. Mekhitarian, and more recently H. de Meulenaere succeeded Capart as directors of the fondation, which also publishes the *Chronique d'Égypte*.

The Coptologist L. Lefort became professor and director of the Oriental Institute of the University of Louvain early in the twentieth century. His student Jozef Vergote taught Coptic and Ancient Egyptian at Louvain from 1938 and was professor from 1943 to 1978, when he was succeeded by Jan Quaegebeur, a very productive young scholar who died unexpectedly in 1995; Quaegebeur has been replaced by Harco Willems. C. Vandersleyen held the chair at Louvain-la-Nueve and still directs the Center for Egyptian Archaeology there. H. de Meulenaere had the chair at Ghent, which once belonged to Louis Speleers, and he is now the director of the Fondation; and M. Malaise, successor to B. van de Walle (1929–1972), is professor at Liege.

In Switzerland, the University of Basel created a chair for professor Ursula Schweitzer in 1950, and her successor, Erik Hornung, has succeeded in turning the Ägyptologisches Seminar der Universität into one of the foremost centers for Egyptological teaching. There are also Egyptology programs at Geneva University under Ordinarius Professor M. Valloggia and at Zurich under Professor P. Kaplony.

At the University of Copenhagen, the linguist Valdemar Schmidt was appointed professor (1882–1921) and was succeeded by his student H. O. Lange, who had been chief librarian since 1901. Lange founded Copenhagen's Institute of Egyptology in 1924, and after his death in 1943 was succeeded by his student C. Sander-Hansen, who was chair from 1946 to 1963. Wolja Ericksen, who had taught at Mainz (1948–1953), became lecturer in Coptic at Copenhagen in 1953 and was professor of Egyptology from 1963 to 1966. H. J. Polotsky was there in 1967–1968, and J. R. Harris, J. Osing, and P. Frandsen have maintained the teaching program more recently.

In Sweden, Uppsala has long had an Institution for Egyptologi at the Gustavianum, and for many years professor Torgny Säve-Söderbergh held the chair, which passed at his retirement to Rostislav Holthoer assisted by Gertie Englund.

In Norway, J. Lieblein was appointed professor of Egyptology at the University of Christiana (Oslo) in 1867, but this position has not survived.

At Prague in the Czech Republic, Frantisek Lexa, who had studied with Adolf Erman and W. Spiegelberg, became extraordinarius professor at Charles University in 1922 and professor in 1927. Jaroslav Černý was lecturer there from 1929 to 1946, before going to University College, London. Lexa then became director of the Czechoslovak Institute of Egyptology in 1958. Zbynék Žába, who had become reader in 1954 and negotiated the institute, became professor of Egyptology in 1959 and director of the institute in 1960 when Lexa died. After Žába's death in 1971, E. Strouhal became director and the institute continues now under the direction of professor Miroslav Verner.

In Poland, the emphasis had been largely on archaeology, particularly because of the efforts of the very influential Kazimierz Michalowski who was named professor at Warsaw in 1933, and was ordinarius from 1939 to 1973. Tadeusz Andrzejewski held the Egyptian philology position at Warsaw between 1951 and 1961, and was succeeded by Elzbieta Dabrowska-Smektala. Professor Jadwiga Lipinska worked for the Egyptian department of Warsaw's Archaeological Institute for many years, and Karol Mysliewiec is now professor, with Andrzej Niwinski and Zbigniew Szafranski as assistant professors.

Budapest continues to have Egyptology well represented with the courses taught by professors L. Kakosy and U. Luft, who have done fieldwork in Egypt.

At Saint Petersburg in the former Soviet Union professors Oleg Berlev and Alla Elanskaya have positions at the Institute of Oriental Studies of the Academy of Sciences.

In Spain, Professor Padro i Parcerisa is with the Centre d'Egiptologia in the Department of Prehistory at the University of Barcelona.

**Egyptology in North America.** While Charles E. Wilbour, who studied at Paris and Berlin, is often called "America's first Egyptologist," and with the help of two of his children has made considerable contributions to Egyptology in the United States, he himself neither taught nor published. James H. Breasted, a philologist and historian who received his doctorate from Berlin, became the first assistant (1895), then instructor in Egyptology and Semitics at the University of Chicago (1896), and was promoted to professor there in 1905. George Reisner also studied at Berlin, became instructor in Semitics at Harvard University in 1896, excavated in Egypt for Phoebe A. Hearst and the University of California, became assistant professor of Semitic archaeology at Harvard in 1905, and became professor of Egyptology there in 1914, but that position did not survive his retirement in 1942.

At the University of Chicago, Breasted trained many students, raised considerable funds, mainly from John D. Rockefeller, and built up an outstanding research center in the Oriental Institute, as well as two expedition houses in Egypt, one of which survives at Luxor, with ideal facilities for careful epigraphic work. His students succeeded him, John A. Wilson for Old and Middle Egyptian language and history, William F. Edgerton for later stages of Egyptian. They were later joined by Keith Seele, another Berlin and Chicago–trained philologist who later became quite involved with the salvage effort in Nubia. When the three of them retired in the mid 1960s, George Hughes, after many years with the Epigraphic Survey in Egypt, returned to Chicago to teach Demotic (replacing Edgerton), and the next generation brought E. F. Wente back from Chicago House in Luxor, Klaus Baer back from the University of California, Berkeley, and, following Hughes' retirement, Janet Johnson to continue the Demotic tradition. More recently, Lanny Bell and Peter Dorman also returned from Chicago House to teach language and history courses, and Robert Ritner returned to Chicago from Yale as associate professor. To teach Egyptian archaeology, Chicago had Henri Frankfort, Helene Kantor, and more recently Mark Lehner.

The University of California, Berkeley, had George Reisner as director of the Hearst Egyptian Expedition from 1899 to 1905, but did not have a real academic appointment in Egyptology until Henry Lutz, who had trained in Semitics at Yale, became assistant professor of Assyriology and Egyptology in 1921. Becoming full professor in 1929, Lutz served until 1954, and was followed by Klaus Baer who came as lecturer in 1959 and became associate professor before returning to Chicago in 1965. William F. Edgerton after his retirement from Chicago filled in for one year, when Leonard H. Lesko came as acting instructor of Egyptology in 1966, along with Akhmed Fakhry as visiting professor of Egyptian Archaeology. Lesko became professor of Egyptology in 1977, had teaching assistants for some language courses, and obtained a second regular position in Egyptian Archaeology in the

Department of Near Eastern Studies before he left to accept the Wilbour Chair at Brown University. Cathleen Keller currently has the philology position and Carol Redmount teaches Egyptian archaeology.

Yale University has offered courses in Egyptology since Ludlow Bull, a Yale undergraduate with a doctorate from Chicago, became lecturer in 1925 and professor in 1936. William Kelly Simpson, who was curator at the Museum of Fine Arts in Boston for a number of years, has now been professor of Egyptology at Yale for many years. Simpson has trained a number of Egyptologists, has had assistants (Robert Ritner and now John Darnell) and distinguished visiting professors, and oversees epigraphic and archaeological work.

After developing a fine museum collection and maintaining active fieldwork in Egypt for many years, the University of Pennsylvania brought Battiscomb Gunn to the United States to serve as curator from 1931 to 1934. In 1934 he returned to England to become professor at Oxford. His successors at the museum were two established philologists from Germany: Hermann Ranke, who came in 1938 and was the first to hold a joint teaching position; and Rudolph Anthes, who was appointed in 1950 (through 1962) and produced Penn's first doctorate in Egyptology, Henry Fischer. Then W. K. Simpson, A. Fakhry, and J. Černý had visiting appointments, while David O'Connor became teaching curator in 1964. David Silverman came in 1977 and also became curator. When O'Connor left in 1995 to become L. A. Wallace Professor at New York University's Institute of Fine Arts, Professor Silverman became curator in charge.

In 1948, Theodora Wilbour left Brown University half of her estate to endow a chair professorship and a department of Egyptology in memory of her father, Charles Edwin Wilbour. Richard A. Parker, who was then director of the Epigraphic Survey of the University of Chicago in Luxor, became the first Wilbour Professor. He hired Ricardo Caminos as assistant professor in 1952 and brought distinguished visiting professors to Providence for many years. Their doctoral graduate Caroline Peck was added to the teaching staff, but that position was not continued when Caminos became Wilbour Professor in 1972 following Parker's retirement. Totally involved with his research, Caminos did very little teaching and retired in 1979. Leonard H. Lesko left his professorship at Berkeley to become Wilbour Professor in 1982, now has Leo Depuydt as associate professor, and several adjuncts and visitors (Edward Brovarski, Lanny Bell, and Florence Friedman) to round out the teaching program.

New York University's Institute of Fine Arts had Bernard Bothmer, who was on the curatorial staff at the Brooklyn Museum of Art since 1956, as lecturer from 1960, and appointed him as professor in 1979. He was

Lila Acheson Wallace Professor of Egyptian Art there from 1982 until his death in 1993. He was succeeded in 1995 by David O'Connor, who came from the teaching/curatorial position at the University of Pennsylvania's museum.

The University of California at Los Angeles' commitment to Egyptology began with the appointment of John B. Callender in 1968; he became professor of Egyptian and Coptic in 1986. Following Callender's premature death, Antonio Loprieno was appointed to the philology position, and an archaeology position has also been added.

There has been some interest in Egyptology at Johns Hopkins University dating to the professorship of William F. Albright from 1929 to 1958. More recently, a chair endowed by Alexander Badawy was filled by Betsy Bryan, and Richard Jasnow also has a regular position there.

Nathaniel Reich, who had been lecturer at Prague, became professor of Egyptology at Dropsie College in Philadephia in 1925; he died in 1943. The position no longer exists.

Louis V. Žabkar, who trained in Egyptology at Chicago, taught history at Loyola University in Chicago before becoming professor of Egyptology at Brandeis University in Waltham, Massachusetts. He indeed produced a number of successful doctoral students there, but the position has not been continued.

Other recently established centers of Egyptological training in the United States with at least two faculty members include Memphis State University, Pennsylvania State University, the University of Michigan, and Emory University in Atlanta.

The Department of Near Eastern Studies of the University of Toronto had S. A. B. Mercer appointed as professor of Semitic Languages and Egyptology from 1924 to 1946. Ronald Williams began teaching Egyptian in 1946 and served as professor from 1957 to 1982. Donald Redford joined him as a historian with considerable interest in archaeology, and he inaugurated an era of multiple expeditions. With Redford's move to Pennsylvania State University, Ronald Leprohon is now professor with several assistants.

**Egyptology Elsewhere.** In Cairo, Ahmed Kamal, who had studied with Brugsch and worked for the Antiquities Service and the Egyptian Museum for thirty years, was nominated to be director of the School of Egyptology that he helped establish, but on Kamal's death in 1923, Vladimir Golenischeff was appointed professor of Egyptology; he served from 1924 to 1929. Girgis Mattha, who had studied at Paris and Oxford, became lecturer at Cairo University in 1937 (P. Jouguet was professor from 1937 to 1949), and later Mattha became director of the Institute of Archaeology, a post he held from 1950 to 1965. Golen-

ischeff's students included the distinguished Egyptian Egyptologists Ahmed Fakhry, who became professor of Egyptian history at the University in 1952 till 1965; Labib Habachi of the Antiquities Services; and the archaeologist Abdel-Moneim Abu Bakr, who went on to become professor at the University of Alexandria and then Cairo in 1954. Vikentiev and Hermann Junker also taught at the Cairo Institute, and their student Abel el-Mohsen Bakir became professor of Egyptian Philology in Cairo (1954–1968). More recently, the Cairo Institute's faculty of archaeology has included professors Sayed Tawfik, Gaballa Ali Gaballa, Ali Radwan, Mohamed Abd el-Halim Nur-el-Din, Mohamed Moursi, Faiza Haikal, and Tohfa Handoussa.

In Jerusalem, Hebrew University appointed Hans Jacob Polotsky as instructor in Egyptology in 1934; he served as professor of Egyptology and Semitic linguistics from 1951 to 1972. His student and successor, Professor Sarah Israelit-Groll recently retired, and Professor Irene Shirun-Grumach and the senior lecturer Orly Goldwasser teach Egyptology in the Department of Ancient Near Eastern Studies. A. Shisha-Halevy is there in linguistics and Abraham Malamat in history. Egyptology also continues to be studied at Tel Aviv University.

There is a Programa de Estudios de Egiptologia in Buenos Aires under the direction of Perla Fuscaldo. This program traces its origins to Abraham Rosenvasser, a self-taught Egyptologist who held many different positions in ancient history departments in Argentina between 1939 and his death in 1983.

In Australia, professor Naguib Kanawati and senior lecturer Boyo Ockinga have developed a fine teaching and research center for Egyptology in the School of History at Macquarie University in New South Wales.

The Department of Classics and Ancient History at the University of Auckland, New Zealand, has senior lecturer Anthony Spalinger offering both undergraduate and graduate courses in Egyptian language and history.

In Japan, at Waseda University's Egyptian Culture Center, professors of Egyptian architecture and archaeology, under the direction of Professor Yasutada Watanabe, maintain a very active program of fieldwork.

In China, the Institute for the History of Ancient Civilizations of North-East Normal University in Changchun has brought a number of visiting scholars to teach Egyptology.

[*See also* Archaeological and Research Institutions; *and* Museums.]

LEONARD H. LESKO

**EGYPTIAN BLUE.** *See* Faience.

**EGYPTOLOGY.** Egyptology in its modern form, along with archaeology, decipherment, and critical biblical studies, grew out of the seventeenth- and eighteenth-century movement in European intellectual history known as the Enlightenment—the movement of Locke, Newton, Leibniz, Humboldt, Goethe, Descartes, Spinoza, Franklin, and Jefferson. It was the Enlightenment that transformed the already ancient fascination with Egypt and its past into a systematic recording, tabulation, and analysis of data and an exploration and application of methodologies informed primarily by a secular-rationalist model of knowledge. The first fruits of this activity were the compilation and publication of the magnificent *Description de l'Égypte* and the decipherment of the ancient Egyptian scripts and language. The Egyptian expedition of Napoleon, the Enlightenment despot *par excellence* and would-be new Alexander, resulted in the publication of the *Description*, the discovery of the Rosetta Stone, and the inception of the organized study of Egypt on a vast scale.

The ancient Egyptians had been interested in their own past and made efforts to chronicle and systematize it as it grew increasingly longer, a process which gave rise to the king-list tradition and ultimately to Manetho's *Aegyptiaca* (third century BCE). The best-known ancient Egyptian "Egyptologist" or antiquarian is the high priest of Ptah, Prince Khaemwaset, son of Ramesses II in the thirteenth century BCE, a restorer and scholar of ancient monuments, remembered in later ages as a sage and wonder-worker. There are, however, many other indications of ancient Egyptian antiquarian study. The various phases of "archaism" in ancient Egyptian art and architecture reflect the study, and sometimes the rediscovery and revival, of materials belonging to earlier periods. This is also true of texts; the Pyramid Texts of the late Old Kingdom were copied and redacted through Greco-Roman times. Highly educated scribes of the entire era of hieroglyphic literacy studied the classical Egyptian language. A number of texts contain parallel versions in classical and later forms of Egyptian, including but not limited to bilingual (sometimes called "trilingual") decrees such as the Rosetta Stone and the Canopus Decree.

Egypt occupies a prominent place in classical literature as early as Homer. The accounts relating to Egypt in Herodotus, Diodorus Siculus, Strabo, and Plutarch were available in the predecipherment period, although they had to await the revival of Greek learning in the late High Middle Ages and Renaissance. A number of eminent Greek thinkers and authors, including Pythagoras, Solon, Thales, and Plato, are credited with traveling or even studying in Egypt. These claims have been treated with skepticism by many modern scholars, though there seems to be more receptivity to the credibility of these traditions in the past couple of decades. There have been several reasons for the adoption of a "hermeneutic of suspicion" when dealing with classical writers on Egypt: the language barrier, the question of the authors' informants and their reliability, and the presence of obviously secondary material and misinterpretations of known Egyptian material. Methodologically, scholars have been reluctant to accept the veracity of classical statements without corroborative Egyptian evidence, and they have tended to jettison the classical authors once native materials in Egyptian became available. Many Egyptologists found native materials markedly different from the presentations by the classical writers, though some of these judgments were made prematurely on the basis of a rudimentary knowledge of Egyptian and a very limited selection of materials. In particular, it has been common to regard interpretive statements by classical authors, especially any with metaphorical or allegorical content, as purely Greek elaborations out of keeping with the Egyptian "character." This attitude has, however, been moderated somewhat in recent scholarship, and some of the glosses in Egyptian mortuary texts ("As for ———, it means ———," etc.) can be cited as native precedents. Regarding ancient Egyptian writing, the prevailing tendency has been to emphasize the revolutionary nature of the phonetically based decipherment and to regard classical and Late Antique statements on hieroglyphs as wrongheaded symbolic obfuscation concealing kernels of accurate knowledge. In the second half of the twentieth century, scholars have shown greater willingness to explore Egyptian and classical sources for suggestive correlations and to look for the connections and affinities rather than the disjunctions between the two corpora. (Important relevant works include those of B. H. Stricker, L. Kákosy, L. V. Žabkar, J. Hani, T. DuQuesne, and H. Jackson.) Thus, Horapollo, the fourth to fifth century CE Greek grammarian of Egypt, who does preserve some traditions of identifiably genuine Egyptian origin, can be regarded as the last gasp of native hieroglyphic scholarship, and Plotinus (third-century CE Egyptian-born Roman) on hieroglyphs can be understood to say something meaningful about the system. With regard to Plotinus himself, some scholars no longer regard it as a geographical accident that he was born in Middle Egypt and are willing to explore his affinities with Egyptian thought. The existence of authors such as Manetho and Horapollo, the material relating to Egyptian religion provided by Plutarch (first-century CE Greek) and Apuleius (second-century CE Roman), and the intimate interrelationship between the Egyptian and Greek Isis materials are only some of the indications that a cultural apartheid such as that envisaged by many scholars simply does not account for what is attested. One Greek scholar who may well have had unusually expert knowledge of Egypt is Eratosthenes (third-century BCE Greek), though many modern scholars do not consider the king list ascribed to him to be his authentic work. This king list includes translations of the royal names that incorporate accurate renditions of words and hieroglyphs. Eratosthenes was librarian of Alexandria, and his experiment to calculate the circumference of the earth shows that he traveled as far as Aswan.

The figure of Thoth, Egyptian god of wisdom and writing and author of sacred books, was the focus of a religious synthesis in late antiquity that gave rise to a body of writings in Greek known as the Corpus Hermeticum. Thoth was equated with Greek Hermes, Roman Mercurius, and (according to the Persian-Jewish author Artapanus) biblical Moses. A number of scholars have proposed Egyptian analogues and antecedents for materials and concepts in the Hermetica. Thoth-Hermes and the Hermetica provide a bridge from late antiquity to Renaissance Europe, when they—and Greek texts as a whole— were rediscovered and translated by Italian scholars such as Marsilio Ficino, Pico della Mirandola, and Giordano Bruno.

In medieval times, the main source of information about Egypt available to European scholars was the Bible. Then the large-scale encounter between Europe and the Middle East began, with the Crusades (eleventh to thirteenth centuries CE), which opened up an exotic realm to European experience and imagination. This was an indubitable factor in the genesis of European fascination with the ancient Near East, including Egypt, but for a long time the primary motivations for visiting the Near East remained crusading and religious pilgrimage (which were often identical). The Crusades brought Europeans face to face with the Arabs' civilization and language and (along with the Muslim occupation of Spain) began the process by which Greek learning reentered western Europe. Greek literature would dramatically increase the available materials dealing with Egypt and foment much new interest, while travel to the Middle East—including Egypt—would take on a much more scholarly and antiquarian cast. Both these tendencies would emerge strongly in the Renaissance.

Along with the development (or revival) of humanistic philosophy, the Renaissance was characterized by the flowering of an interest in antiquity focusing on but not limited to the classical civilizations. This interest was far from merely academic, but was predicated on the premise that the wisdom and accomplishments of the "ancients" can serve as a model for present endeavors, and as an incentive for excellence. This movement was fueled by the obelisks and other Egyptian and Egyptianized monuments in Rome itself. Renaissance scholarship subsumed the classical texts' Egyptian content and was intrigued by Egypt for its own sake, attaching considerable impor-

tance to Egyptian religion. In a sense, the Renaissance was picking up where the classical world left off, as Egyptian deities and mysteries had been among the most popular in the Roman Empire. There has been a tendency to regard the Egyptianizing elements of Renaissance (and subsequently Enlightenment) culture as more façade than substance, but some recent scholarship has questioned this position.

Although all of Father Athanasius Kircher's life fell within the seventeenth century, he straddled the cusp between the Renaissance and the Enlightenment. This learned Jesuit, who is often unfairly ridiculed for his unsuccessful attempts to read hieroglyphs, made signal contributions to Egyptian studies, as well as to other fields, such as Sinology and geography. Iversen (1971) rightly regards Kircher as "the father of modern Egyptology." He was the first European scholar to write a grammar of Coptic, which he recognized as a form of the ancient Egyptian language. He also produced legible copies of hieroglyphic inscriptions, as did his older contemporary G. Hoerwart von Hohenburg, author of *Thesaurus Hieroglyphicorum*. The rigorous exploration and description of the Great Pyramid by John Greaves, published in *Pyramidographia* (1646), was probably the first instance of scientific archaeology in Egypt, just as Kircher's Coptic grammar was the starting point for Egyptian philology. Likewise, the study of Egyptian art can be said to begin with a pioneering exposition of an aesthetic of Egyptian sculpture in its own terms by the eighteenth-century artist Giambattista Piranesi.

The Enlightenment paved the way for the decipherment of pre-Coptic Egyptian in a number of concrete ways. Great interest in the typology and origins of writings and language, focusing on Chinese, Egyptian, and Hebrew, provided important impetus toward decipherment. In the seventeenth century, the English philosopher John Locke studied ancient Jewish coins with inscriptions in the Paleo-Hebrew alphabet; in the eighteenth century, the Phoenician/Paleo-Hebrew script was definitively deciphered, as was the script used for Palmyrene Aramaic. Cryptography, used in international intrigue, made great strides from the early work of Trithemius to the expertise of Isaac Newton's older contemporary John Wallis. The mathematical discoveries of Gottfried Wilhelm Leibniz of the seventeenth century added to the toolbox of decipherment procedures. William Warburton anticipated some of the arguments of the decipherers of Egyptian, calling for a rejection of the symbolic/Neoplatonist approach. Thus, at the beginning of the nineteenth century, Georg Friedrich Grotefend was making the first strides in the decipherment of Old Persian cuneiform, even while Sylvestre de Sacy and Johan Åkerblad achieved their initial successes in the decipherment of Demotic.

It has been normative for modern Egyptology to define itself as beginning with the decipherment of the native scripts and pre-Coptic forms of the Egyptian language, consummated though not singlehandedly achieved by J.-F. Champollion. The success of this decipherment depended on the affirmation of the essential phoneticism of Egyptian writing and the rejection of the symbolic-metaphorical-allegorical perspective; this in turn seemed to entail the rejection of much of what classical sources contain relative to Egypt. It was the culmination of a process that had gathered steam in the seventeenth century with the increasing emphasis on pure rationalism and the rise of empiricism. To some extent, the decipherers and their immediate successors were simply overwhelmed by their new-found ability to read texts in pre-Coptic Egyptian and to plunge into the deep well of primary sources. More problematic was the increasing tendency to deny profundity and insight to the Egyptians in contrast with the Greeks, a development that has been explored in Martin Bernal's controversial work (1987). Scholars' appreciation of the content of the Egyptian texts was limited by rudimentary understanding of grammar and lexicon and colored by nineteenth-century theories of "primitive" languages. Although it is dubious whether the beginning of Egyptology can be adequately defined as occurring at the turn of the nineteenth century, it remains clear that the decipherment is a watershed, separating modern Egyptology from the history, or prehistory, that preceded it.

The decipherment of pre-Coptic Egyptian was an intellectual triumph of a very high order, all the more so because the texts used, primarily of the Greco-Roman period, would strike fear into the heart of any beginning student of Middle Egyptian today. As already noted, classical authors are often blamed for propounding a stereotype of the hieroglyphs as esoteric symbols knowable only through initiation, and thus for delaying correct decipherment. In the context of Greco-Roman texts, we can see how this attitude needs to be qualified. During the period of the classical writers, knowledge of the hieroglyphs was steadily declining among the Egyptians themselves, who were using Demotic as the utilitarian script and introducing the Old Coptic alphabet. Many of the Ptolemaic and Roman hieroglyphic texts feature hundreds of new hieroglyphs and new values of hieroglyphs, based on graphic variation, phonetic change, puns, etc., and the teaching of this tradition was increasingly specialized and restricted. In light of the scribal tradition of the time, the characterization by some classical authors is far more appropriate than many modern writers have concluded.

An important aspect of the legacy of the decipherment to modern Egyptology is the philological tilt which has characterized Egyptology as an academic discipline—an emphasis that has sometimes been questioned or quali-

fied by its own practitioners. There has been a tension between philology and archaeology/art history that only in recent decades has begun to yield to an integrated or holistic view, largely following the lead of H. G. Fischer. In general, Egyptology continues to define itself by the ability to read the language; with very limited exceptions, hieroglyphic literacy has been a "litmus test" for defining who is an Egyptologist.

The rise of archaeology/decipherment-based disciplines in the first half of the nineteenth century did not merely open up new vistas of the past and extend our reliable continuum of history. It also raised questions that were ambivalent and sometimes threatening for the intellectual and ideological status quo. Like Darwinian evolution and geology, archaeology—which was especially closely linked with the latter—attempted to address the reconstruction of the past independent of Scripture, and to challenge the "biblical" reckoning of the age of the earth. The reading of royal names of the pharaonic period quickly showed that the king list given in Manetho's *Aegyptiaca* corresponded closely with the original monuments, even in Egypt's early periods, and Manetho's totals reached back to a very remote antiquity. There were several responses to the advent of this extrabiblical data. At one extreme, some rejected archaeology and "pagan" sources (though they were used and transmitted by many early Christian authorities, such as Eusebius) and considered it impious even to appeal to extrabiblical sources to affirm the truth of Scripture. At another extreme, some scholars welcomed the opportunity to cut the Bible down to size, as it were—especially the Hebrew scriptures and the Jews. Many scholars used archaeological and documentary/inscriptional discoveries to proof-text or vindicate biblical accounts. Some (like A. H. Sayce in his 1904 *Monument Facts and Higher Critical Fancies*) regarded archaeology and Near Eastern texts as providing a corrective to what were seen as the dangerous excesses of the higher critics. In both the archaeological and textual spheres, these are controversies that continue today. Excavations were sometimes undertaken in order to resolve biblical questions, and findings were often interpreted in a biblical light, as indicated by such titles of early excavation memoirs as *The Store-City of Pithom and the Route of the Exodus* or *The Land of Goshen*. The Famine Stela on the island of Sehel, copied by Charles E. Wilbour, was immediately compared with the biblical famine in the Joseph narrative and published by H. Brugsch under the title *Die biblischen sieben Jahre von Hungersnoth* (1891). The proposal (now widely accepted) that the Egyptian *Instructions of Amenompe* was a source of part of the *Book of Proverbs* met with strong resistance from some scholars. Undoubtedly, the new Near Eastern discoveries provided an ancient context and milieu for the Bible for the first time. Meanwhile, many scholars applied themselves to learning as much about ancient Egypt and its neighbors as possible without ulterior biblical concerns.

One of the main thrusts of nineteenth-century Egyptology was the compilation of copies of inscribed standing monuments by individual scholars and major expeditions, an enterprise initiated by the Napoleonic expedition. Some copyists ranged over Egypt and Nubia; others stayed in one inscription-rich area. The most celebrated were Champollion himself, Ippolito Rosellini, John Gardner Wilkinson, Robert Hay, Prisse d'Avennes, Charles E. Wilbour, and Karl Richard Lepsius. James Breasted's great work of collation and translation, *Ancient Records of Egypt,* while published after the turn of the twentieth century, is really the culmination of the nineteenth-century copying effort, and the Epigraphic Survey he initiated is one of its offspring.

The first scholarly attempt to explore the relationship between the Egyptian and Semitic languages was made by the nineteenth-century philologist Theodor Benfey when Coptic was still the only form of Egyptian known. As research on pre-Coptic Egyptian advanced, Egyptologists and linguists propounded diverse views of the relationships—if any—between Egyptian and neighboring languages. For some, Egyptian was *sui generis* or represented a primitive type of language in which the word and root were the same (thus P. Renouf, see below), a view echoed by the great American linguist William Dwight Whitney. In this approach, similarities between Egyptian and Semitic were seen as superficial, illusory, and/or the result of borrowing. For some of these scholars, Egyptian, while essentially unrelatable in a phylogenetic sense, was regarded as somehow essentially "African." (Perhaps these views of Egyptian were facilitated by the strong specialization in Chinese of a number of nineteenth-century Egyptologists, such as Charles Wycliffe Goodwin, Samuel Birch, and Renouf, linked with the then-current European stereotypes of the Chinese language. Could the major shift from "nineteenth" to "twentieth" century or "pre-Erman" to "Berlin school" Egyptology [see below] have been partly a function of a shift from the ascendancy of largely Sinological Egyptologists to others who were primarily Semitists?) For others, Egyptian became a component of phylogenetic schemes, some of them prefiguring proposals that remain part of the current linguistic discussion. For Lepsius (also a pioneer of the study of modern Nubian), Egyptian belonged to a group essentially similar to Afroasiatic; for Jens Daniel Carolus Lieblein, this itself was part of a group tentatively designated "Noahitic," much like the proposed "super-family" or "macro-family" of Nostratic.

As the decipherment ushered in modern, "scientific" Egyptology, so the work of Adolf Erman and his colleagues and students in the Berlin School, starting in the 1880s, initiated the modern, "scientific" phase of Egyptian philology. One aspect of this was a marked turn in the direction of Semitic for the perceived affinities of Egyptian. There were several fundamental reasons for this stance: (1) the identification of the native scripts as unvocalized and including in their inventory the *aleph* and the *ayin;* (2) the consequent identification of the Egyptian root as essentially similar to the Semitic root, and the pursuit of methodologically rigorous lexical/etymological comparisons; (3) the analysis of Coptic verb-classes as corresponding to types of older consonantal root; (4) the identification by Erman of the Stative ("Pseudoparticiple," "Old Perfective") form of the Egyptian verb as corresponding to the Akkadian Stative ("Permansive") and other Semitic forms; and (5) the insistence on the paradigmatic alignment of pronouns and grammatical formatives in Egyptian and Semitic. The general methodological rigor of the Berlin scholars suggested productive lines of research, yielded impressive results, and at least in some quarters enhanced the work's credibility. It did, however, become mired in nationalistic bickering, especially among English, French, and German scholars. Erman and his coworkers propounded a clear division of the ancient Egyptian language into stages, each of which required its own grammar; and the work of Kurt Sethe and others on the verbal system gave rise to the "classical" Egyptological view that the geminating and non-geminating forms correspond to the Semitic categories of perfect and imperfect. The perfect/imperfect dichotomy was powerfully influential and is still maintained at least in part by many Egyptologists, although its monolithic nature has been increasingly questioned, beginning with the work of Battiscombe Gunn in the 1920s. The strong Semitic cast assumed by Egyptian in the work of the "Berlin school" was a major target of criticism by opponents of the new approach, such as Édouard Naville and Gaston Maspero. Indeed, Maspero's emphasis on Berber comparisons actually pointed to a more balanced assessment of the place of Egyptian in what would come to be regarded in the 1930s to 1950s as Hamito-Semitic or Afroasiatic. Under the leadership of the Berlin scholars, remarkable pinnacles were reached before World War II, with Erman's grammars, Kurt Sethe's magisterial work on the Egyptian verb, and the *Wörterbuch der ägyptischen Sprache* (1926–1963), to mention only a few of the most outstanding achievements.

It is often assumed that pre-Berlin Egyptian philology was a blundering, haphazard, entirely "unscientific" enterprise. This caricature is reinforced by the often-reprinted careless works of E. A. W. Budge (who fell far short of the standards of the best of the "old school" and was blasted by his "pre-Berlin" colleague Renouf), and by the crusading denunciations of Breasted. This is a grave injustice. The best nineteenth-century Egyptian philologists were learned in many other languages, including Chinese, as Champollion and Thomas Young had been, and in the new discipline of "comparative philology" or linguistics as represented by the Grimm brothers (Jacob Ludwig Carl and Wilhelm Carl), Franz Bopp, and other architects of that field. Their work often shows an erudition and sophistication for which it is given scant credit today.

The study of language was strongly related to other emergent comparative studies in anthropology, folklore, and religion, all of which were significant in nineteenth-century Egyptology. One of the scholars most active in this research was English, Peter Le Page Renouf, who subscribed to the then-popular etymological theory of myth. With this perspective, he compared Egyptian *Wenen-Nefer* with the Hare of Native American mythology, not on a diffusionist level but on what might be called an archetypal level. Following the publication of James G. Frazer's *The Golden Bough* (1890), some Egyptologists applied his approach to Egyptian materials and became adherents of the "Myth and Ritual" school. Moving into the twentieth century, a seminal development in the study of religion was the publication of Rudolf Otto's *Das Heilige* (*The Idea of the Holy*, 1917), and the rise of the phenomenology of religion. This had a strong effect on the study of Egyptian religion, especially in the work of Dutch Egyptologists, beginning with G. van der Leeuw and continuing with A. de Buck, C. J. Bleeker, J. Zandee, M. Heerma van Voss, and Herman te Velde. Outside of the Netherlands, such major contributors to the field as Siegfried Morenz and Erik Hornung have also taken a phenomenological approach.

In general, it can be noted that a dispassionate look at the history of Egyptology refutes the accusation that Egyptologists have been (or are) isolated and disregard other fields. In language, archaeology, literature, myth, and religion, Egyptology from the beginning has been intertwined, engaged, and interactive with other disciplines and has attempted to locate itself in a "global" context—as witnessed by Baron von Bunsen's mid-nineteenth-century work *Aegyptens Stelle in der Weltgeschichte.*

Nineteenth-century Egyptian archaeology began, and continued for decades, as an unregulated and fiercely nationalistic enterprise focused on the acquisition of objects for major museums, and it was inseparable from the purchase of and other forms of prospecting for antiquities. Giovanni Belzoni, perhaps the most colorful figure of early nineteenth-century exploration, has been revealed as a more careful excavator and recorder than the stereotype would suggest. A regulatory authority was introduced in 1858, when the French scholar Auguste Mariette (who would also originate the plot for *Aida*) was appointed the first Conservator of Antiquities in a newly formed government department.

If Erman marks the turning point in philology, William Matthew Flinders Petrie marks the shift from the exclusive focus on *objets d'art*, inscriptions, and monumental remains to "dirt archaeology," introducing a new set of priorities and a methodological approach far more rigorous than other work then being done in Egypt. The use of stratigraphy and the concept of the type-series was fundamental in his approach; the type-series is exemplified by his ambitious development of the "Sequence Dating" system for Predynastic pottery. Petrie did not ignore monumental remains, but he studied them with increased precision, as in his early work on the metrology of Stonehenge and his Giza survey (undertaken initially to test claims about the measurements of the Great Pyramid). By today's standards, Petrie's work was very fast and was characterized by taking small samples of many sites, but by the standards of the times it was a major systematic endeavor. Petrie's publication program was just as remarkable: a steady stream of excavation reports publishing his materials in an orderly fashion, year in and year out. Petrie believed strongly that all archaeology is salvage archaeology and saw his excavations as a frantic race against time. In addition to transforming the archaeology of Egypt, he brought his rigorous approach to the Eastern Mediterranean region, where he began to work in an effort to follow the Hyksos (whose remains he correctly identified at Tell el-Yahudiyyeh) back to their homeland (*Hyksos and Israelite Cities*, 1906). Although Jacques de Morgan first correctly identified Predynastic remains as prehistoric, it was Petrie who placed the analysis of Predynastic materials on a rigorous footing, and prehistory remained a major theme of his life's work, culminating in his *Prehistoric Egypt* (1920) and *The Making of Egypt* (1939). At Abydos, he sorted out the site after Emile Amélineau's excavations, and he correctly identified and ordered the tombs of the rulers of the Early Dynastic period, bringing that formative epoch firmly into the history of Egypt. Important light was cast on the beginning of the Egyptian state by the excavation at Hierakonpolis by Petrie's students James E. Quibell and Frederick W. Green. Outspoken and often abrasive, Petrie cared little about the opinions of others, and his British School of Archaeology in Egypt/Egyptian Research Account had rocky relations with the Egypt Exploration Society, which became the dominant British Egyptological organization. Amelia Edwards, the author, traveler, and Egypt enthusiast, endowed the Edwards Professorship of Egyptology at the University of London, emphasizing the teaching of scientific excavation and created for Petrie as first incumbent.

The United States entered the world of Egyptology during the nineteenth century, although not until the 1890s was a regular university position in that field created there. Memphis, Tennessee, is named after Memphis, Egypt; a delegation of Memphis officials visited Egypt and took back a block from the original Memphis given to them by Mariette, a profoundly Egyptian act. George R. Gliddon, an American consul in Egypt during the pre–Civil War period, popularized Egyptology widely through his lectures and his book *Ancient Egypt* (1847), which went through many editions. A self-professed "Champollionist," he seems to have been the first American scholar to learn Egyptian. His insistence on the preservation and conservation of antiquities was remarkably forward-looking. Perhaps the dominant American in nineteenth-century Egyptology, though he kept a very modest profile, was Charles Edwin Wilbour, a New York journalist who fled to avoid indictment with the Tweed Ring of "machine" politicians. Moving first to Spain and then to Egypt, Wilbour became known as an Egyptologist, collector, and indefatigable copyist of inscriptions, which he generously made available to colleagues. His collection and library formed the nucleus of the Brooklyn Museum of Art's Egyptian Collection and Wilbour Library. In the later nineteenth century, Charles Moldenke, an adherent of the "old" (i.e., pre-Berlin) school, moved from Germany to the United States, where he rather picturesquely rebuilt his castle.

American Egyptology as an academic and institutional phenomenon, and ongoing fieldwork by American scholars, began with James Henry Breasted, generally regarded as the giant of American Egyptology. This great scholar and teacher was also responsible for a significant advancement of the place accorded to Egypt and the Near East in the human and Western heritage—what he called the "New Past." His zeal and evangelical style inspired large public audiences as well as wealthy patrons; he was an extremely effective fundraiser and publicist. As professor of Egyptology at the University of Chicago, beginning in 1896, he embarked on the expedition mentioned above, which culminated in the publication of *Ancient Records of Egypt* (1906), and he was the major force in the establishment of the Oriental Institute. A student of Erman and vigorous partisan of the Berlin school, Breasted firmly established the "new" movement as normative for the study of Egyptian language and chronology in North America. His history textbooks, especially *Ancient Times: A History of the Early World* (1915), appreciatively reviewed by Theodore Roosevelt, were extremely influential in the treatment of Egypt and its neighbors in the secondary school curriculum. Some of his other outstanding contributions were his authoritative *History of Egypt* (1905), groundbreaking and insightful studies of Egyptian religion, and consummate editions of two very difficult and important texts, the Memphite Theology and the Edwin Smith Surgical Papyrus. In works such as *The Dawn of Conscience* (1933), he insisted on the moral vision and sensitivity of the ancient Egyptians. The Oriental Institute itself and his students who carried on his work are probably his most important legacy.

The Victorian author Amelia B. Edwards, mentioned above, was a major benefactor and popularizer of Egyptology whose books, such as *A Thousand Miles Up the Nile* (1877), exerted considerable influence. During that period, other women also began to leave their mark on Egyptology. Mary Brodrick and Helen M. Tirard are known mainly for translating French and German works by Maspero, Emile Brugsch, and others into English, with revisions and addenda attesting to their own scholarship; they also wrote articles and general books. Husband-and-wife teams worked in the field, notably Annie and Edward Quibell and Winifred and Paul Brunton, a type of collaboration later immortalized by Elizabeth Peters (Barbara Mertz) in her "Peabody and Emerson" mysteries. Winifred Brunton, an artist, painted the memorable portraits in *Kings and Queens of Ancient Egypt* (1926) and *Great Ones of Ancient Egypt* (1930). The first woman Egyptologist of major stature was Petrie's student Margaret A. Murray, who wrote prodigiously on folklore, European witchcraft, and comparative mythology as well as Egyptology. Her work was often controversial; her oft-reprinted synthesis *The Splendour That Was Egypt* (1949) elaborates many of her ideas. Her *Elementary Egyptian Grammar* (1905) and *Elementary Coptic Grammar* (1911) were long popular. The title of her autobiography, *My First Hundred Years* (1963), gets one up on Petrie's *Seventy Years in Archaeology* (1931). This can only be seen as a good-natured dig, as she was extremely devoted to her mentor.

The first concession granted to women field directors in Egypt was the temple precinct of Mut (South Karnak); the archaeologists were Margaret Benson and Janet Gourlay, who published *The Temple of Mut in Asher* in 1899. As was the case in other academic fields, it was not easy for women to pursue Egyptological studies or careers in the early decades; Margaret Murray was discouraged from studying anthropology, and Kurt Sethe's hostility compelled Elise Baumgartel to study with Walter Wreszinski in Königsberg. Special mention must be made of Amice Calverly's exemplary work at Abydos and that of Gertrude Caton-Thompson in the Faiyum. Other women scholars who became active by the mid-twentieth century include Militza Matthieu, Miriam Lichtheim, Winifred Needler, and Nora Scott. An unusual and fascinating figure in the history of Egyptology is Dorothy Louise Eady, better known as Omm Sety, who moved to Egypt, worked as Selim Hassan's assistant, and made Abydos—of which she had unrivaled knowledge—her physical and spiritual home.

The participation of women in Egyptology has increased until today it can fairly be said that its practitioners comprise an indiscriminate assortment of men and women. The insights and perspectives of women's studies brought to bear on the study of Egyptian society and the understanding of Egyptian art, literature, and religion have been more significant than the existence and number of female Egyptologists. In recent years, notable work has included that of Gay Robins, Lana Troy, and Betsy Bryan; *Women's Earliest Records* (1989), edited by Barbara Lesko, was a benchmark for the study of women in the ancient Near East.

The Third Reich affected Egyptology as it did so much that happened globally during its cataclysmic twelve years (1933–1945), and so much that has happened since. Egyptology continued in German and Austrian institutions of higher learning. A contemporary reviewer noted the appearance of Wolfgang Helck's monograph *Der Einfluss der Militärführer in der 18. Ägyptischen Dynastie* (1939) as a sign of the times. In the neighboring field of Assyriology, it was possible for Erich Ebeling to include in a criticism of Benno Landsberger's work a call for the establishment of a "rein deutsche Wissenschaft" ("purely German science"); Landsberger was one of a number of eminent Near Eastern scholars who succeeded in emigrating. Among Egyptologists, Ludwig Borchardt moved to Switzerland; Georg Steindorff (who was deleted from the masthead of the *Zeitschrift für Ägyptische Sprache* during the 1930s), Bernard Bothmer, Rudolf Anthes, and Walter Federn sought refuge in the United States. Hans-Jakob Polotsky, who was to have been Sethe's successor at Göttingen, settled in Palestine, where he became founder of the "Jerusalem school" and of Israeli Egyptology. Polotsky went on to be recognized as the preeminent Egyptological linguist of the second half of the twentieth century. Raphael Giveon, whose Egyptological studies were then in the future, settled on a kibbutz.

Past the midpoint of the twentieth century, the study of the Egyptian language was dominated by Alan Gardiner, a scholar of almost unparalleled productivity, consummate standards, and powerful influence. In addition to his many Egyptological publications, Gardiner also wrote notable works in general linguistics. The three editions of his *Egyptian Grammar* (1927–1957) provided generations of students in many countries with their curriculum in Middle Egyptian. Aspects of the Gardiner paradigm were questioned by Battiscombe Gunn (*Studies in Egyptian Syntax*, 1924), Hans Jakob Polotsky (*Études de syntaxe copte*, 1944, and many other works), and Thomas William Thacker (*The Relationship of the Semitic and Egyptian Verbal Systems*, 1954), but the comprehensive and compendious nature of Gardiner's work made it difficult to supersede. Although Polotsky never produced a comprehensive grammar, his analysis of the Egyptian verbal system began to achieve increasing acceptance in the 1960s. His system, elaborated and in some ways revised by Morde-

chai Gilula, John B. Callender, Friedrich Junge, Wolfgang Schenkel, Helmut Satzinger, Antonio Loprieno, Eric Doret, Leo Depuydt, and others, became known in the 1980s as the "Standard Theory." The general trend has been to accord greater nuance and subtlety to Egyptian syntax.

One of the major aspects of the study of Egyptian religion in the mid-twentieth century, especially in the English-speaking world, was the identification of Egyptian and other ancient Near Eastern thinking as "mythopoeic thought"—defined as a mode of thought that automatically personifies its surroundings and all observable phenomena and is thus incapable of philosophical abstraction. This claim was associated especially with the post-Breasted "Chicago school" centering on John Wilson and Henri Frankfort; it was presented in its most classic form in *The Intellectual Adventure of Ancient Man* (1946), entitled *Before Philosophy* (1951) in its abridged edition. Frankfort and his colleagues were strongly influenced by the French anthropologist Lucien Lévy-Bruhl, who argued his concept of the "primitive mentality" in *La pensée sauvage* (*The Savage Mind*, 1962/1966); Lévy-Bruhl himself had second thoughts in notes that were published only after his death. The "mythopoeic" thesis—entailing that thought must be emancipated from myth before philosophical reasoning is possible—has been increasingly challenged and rejected, for example, by Lana Troy, Herman te Velde (who labels it a "superfluous fiction"), and M. Bilolo.

As was the case with religion, the vision of Egyptian political and cultural history in the post–World War II period was strongly influenced by John Wilson of Chicago, especially his forcefully argued work *The Burden of Egypt* (1951; paperback, *The Culture of Ancient Egypt*). This work regarded the post–New Kingdom period as one of decline in which Egypt lacked the cultural vigor to continue the constructive growth of its tradition or to interact creatively with its neighbors. Although Wilson eventually qualified this judgment in his autobiography, it set the tone for a devaluation of the Late period and a minimizing of the Egyptian contribution to the Greco-Roman world. Starting in the 1970s, the pendulum has been swinging in the opposite direction, and increasing attention has been lavished on all aspects of the post-Empire periods, beginning perhaps with Kenneth Kitchen's compendious and ambitious *Third Intermediate Period* (1972).

The profound and elegant exposition of the principles of Egyptian art by Heinrich Schäfer has had at least as much staying power as Gardiner's *Grammar* and has bridged the period from World War I through the 1970s in its successive incarnations (1st edition 1919, through 4th edition, 1964; English translation by John Baines with introduction by E. Brunner-Traut, 1974). Among the abundance of excellent work on Egyptian art, one may mention the studies of the canon of proportion by E. Iversen and Gay Robins and the proposals on symbolism in art by Philippe Derchain and Wolfhart Westendorf. Fischer introduced an increasingly fruitful focus on the interrelationships between hieroglyphs and representational art.

If Tutankhamun's tomb was the Egyptian discovery (or perhaps the archaeological discovery regardless of region) that most captured the public imagination in the first half of the twentieth century, the Aswan High Dam salvage campaign in Nubia has been the most influential and seminal event in Egyptology as well as Nubiology in the second half of the century. Its influence and consequences have been great and far-reaching. It appealed to the popular imagination and spread a global awareness of Egyptian monuments and culture while calling forth a global coordinated effort of unprecedented extent. Under the auspices of UNESCO, the campaign was conducted on the premise that the threatened sites and monuments are the common treasure of all humankind. Many countries sent missions to Nubia, including some in which Egyptology had been of low profile or virtually nonexistent. A number of important archaeologists who had never worked in the Nile Valley became directors of expeditions, among them William Y. Adams; this cross-fertilization brought more anthropological perspectives and new field methods into Egyptian archaeology and enriched its theoretical development as well as practice. The amount of fund-raising was prodigious, and the institutional base and infrastructure of Egyptology expanded. Some major discoveries, such as the A-Group cemetery at Qustul, provided important new material and sometimes gave rise to controversy. The autonomy of ancient Nubian studies received important impetus. It is to some extent the expansion initiated in that era that has more recently become the victim of the belt-tightening, downsizing, and changed priorities of the late twentieth century. Despite this, the intervening decades have seen the flowering of Egyptology in many countries, including Japan, Spain, Argentina, and China.

Afrocentrism or Pan-Africanism is a perspective—some would say an ideology—that has had considerable appeal among African Americans and African intellectuals. It is one of the most truly grassroots and most controversial approaches to ancient Egypt. It comprises two strands which have converged: one in America, beginning with G. G. M. James (*Stolen Legacy*, 1954), and one in Africa, starting with the work of the Senegalese physicist Cheik Anta Diop (e.g., *The African Origin of Civilization; Myth or Reality?*, 1974). Afrocentrism has gained a wide following in the African-American community on all levels of education and is especially identified with authors such as Molefi Keti Asante, Ivan Van Sertima, Maulana

Karenga, and Legrand H. Clegg III. In Africa, Diop's work has been continued and broadened by Théophile Obenga. According to the Afrocentrists, ancient Egypt was a black African civilization, and the ancient Egyptian *Kmt* ("the Black Land") refers not to the soil but to the inhabitants. Cultural parallels throughout Africa (many already noted by mainstream scholarship) are taken to demonstrate the black African nature of Egypt, and Egypt is held to have originated much if not all of the cultural legacy of the classical world. These points are, according to Afrocentrists, the subject of a wide cover-up by "establishment" scholars, against whom considerable hostility is sometimes expressed. Afrocentrist claims have recently received a detailed and sympathetic discussion by Martin Bernal in his controversial work, *Black Athena,* and in the late 1980s and 1990s Afrocentric issues are being addressed by mainstream Egyptologists. American Afrocentrism arose in a context of the African-American community's attempt to arrive at a positive self-definition in the face of second-class status and cultural contempt, and African Afrocentrism arose in an analogous process in the wake of colonialism. Martin Bernal is compelling, however, when he warns against the tendency to expose ulterior motives for minority paradigms while assuming that the dominant Eurocentric paradigm is objective. It is undeniable that scholarly and normative views of ancient Egypt have been strongly affected by racist and colonialist stereotyping. Many scholars have even denied that the Kushite twenty-fifth dynasty was of black African origin, and many of the classical works of Egyptology contain statements that are insensitive, to say the least. Ivan Van Sertima insists that Kushites colonized Mexico, and Théophile Obenga and others attempt to remove Egyptian from the Afroasiatic language family, providing many etymologies claimed to link Egyptian with "sub-Saharan" or "Negro-African" languages, such as Wolof. One partial by-product of Afrocentrism has been the increased appreciation of Nubia as an autonomous high civilization. Another interesting development is the adoption of ancient Egyptian *maat* as an ethic for the African-American community. The first generally acknowledged major African Egyptologist outside Egypt and Sudan, M. Bilolo, teaches at a center in Zaire named after Cheik Anta Diop.

Another approach to ancient Egypt that has considerable popular appeal can be described as metaphysical or esoteric; Egyptologists generally include in this category revisionist approaches to the age and construction of Egyptian monuments. Egyptologists often label these approaches with the rather unflattering terms "Egyptomania" and "Egyptophilia" and sometimes with the less disparaging "Egyptosophy." The unity implied by this label is less than it appears at first glance, as it encompasses a spectrum ranging from the Rosicrucian Order to "ancient astronaut" enthusiasts. Mainstream Egyptologists generally reject these approaches because, as they see it, they depend on data and claims of verification outside of "scientific" methodologies; they use materials that are inauthentic or wrongly interpreted; they bypass established Egyptology and have not "done their homework." For their part, proponents of esoteric approaches often regard themselves as transmitting or discovering the authentic wisdom of ancient Egypt and accuse Egyptologists of refusing to recognize its true nature or of knowingly concealing it. Egyptosophists generally regard established Egyptology as an exclusivist in-group that ignores them because they lack specialist credentials and that dismisses their evidence without a fair examination, and they often explicitly reject the rationalist Enlightenment paradigm. The frequently polemical nature of communications on both sides has made constructive dialogue difficult.

Ancient Egypt has continued to figure prominently in the symbolism and teachings of secret societies and mystical orders of initiates such as the Masons, the Rosicrucians, the Golden Dawn, and the orders initiated by Aleister Crowley; it also looms large in the lore of groups devoted to esoteric studies, such as the Theosophical Society. On one level, this is a continuation of Renaissance Hermeticism and its further Enlightenment developments. The Rosicrucians consider Akhenaten a founder of their tradition and maintain an Egyptian Museum in California; the Egyptologist Max Guilmot is a member of the Order and has written a rather devotional pamphlet on initiation in ancient Egypt as well as purely academic Egyptological publications. The monuments at Giza, especially the Great Pyramid and Great Sphinx, have been the focus of much Egyptosophical attention. Of the many claims made for numerological and prophetic interpretations of the Great Pyramid, the most celebrated have been those of Charles Piazzi Smyth, Astronomer Royal of Scotland, whose claims Petrie first went to Egypt to test. The American trance clairvoyant Edgar Cayce gave a number of "readings" on the history of the Giza monuments and a "hall of records" under the Sphinx; the foundation administered by his descendants has lavishly subsidized archaeology at Giza. Peter Tompkins and Livio Stecchini have revived the numerological approach to Great Pyramid measurements with a focus on correspondences with the measurements of the planet Earth. The mathematician and modern-day Hermetic philosopher R. A. Schwaller de Lubicz, along with his wife Isha, his stepdaughter Lucie Lamy, and the Egyptologist Alexandre Varille, propounded what became known as the "symbolist" approach to ancient Egypt. Schwaller spent years taking meticulous measurements of the Luxor Temple and its decoration; he interpreted it as an allegorical mapping of the human being as microcosm progressing through different stages of development, in accordance with an intricate numerical system. He expounded this in *Le temple de l'homme* (*The Temple of Man* 1957/1998) and many other works; the major advocate and popularizer of Schwaller's work today is John Anthony West. During the 1990s a major controversy has erupted over a geological examination of the Great Sphinx by Robert Schoch and Thomas Dobecki, who went to Egypt at West's invitation and published findings indicating that the Sphinx amphitheater and body are heavily eroded by precipitation and hence millennia older than generally recognized. Another geologist, David Coxhill, has recently concurred in this assessment, which has been dismissed by most Egyptologists. At least as controversial has been the related proposal by Egyptian-born Belgian engineer Robert Bauval that the Giza pyramids map the stars in Orion's belt. As part of the "New Age" pursuit of global spirituality and self-improvement, there are some who follow a highly personal vision of ancient Egyptian religion as a spiritual path. Indeed, the Egyptian religion has devoted adherents totally outside of the "New Age" community, Omm Sety having been one of them.

As John Baines has noted in a penetrating article on "restricted knowledge, hierarchy and decorum" in ancient Egypt and Egyptology, the scholarly understanding of ancient Egypt's religion has shifted to a strong consideration, and in some cases general acceptance, of features that several decades ago were the sole domain of the Egyptosophist. It can be debated how much of this is due to the Egyptosophists, but in any case it provides common ground for discussion.

Fieldwork (often with improved methodology and technology), new data, interdisciplinary cross-fertilization, and shifting and deepening theoretical perspectives have been converging to focus on a number of themes and frontiers in current Egyptology. One important frontier is the emergence of the Egyptian state, illuminated especially by discoveries at Hierakonpolis and Abydos; in the same breath one can perhaps mention the Neolithic "megalithic" site at Nabta Playa. [*See* Astronomy.] The focus on the late periods has continued along with fieldwork in the Delta and Sinai, and the remarkable underwater discoveries in Ptolemaic Alexandria, which have sparked a media outpouring on Cleopatra. Foreign relations have been highlighted by discoveries in southern Israel and the Nile Delta, including the Aegean frescoes at Tell ed-Dab'a, and by textual studies, and they have been the subject of scholarly syntheses such as Donald Redford's *Egypt, Canaan and Israel in Ancient Times* (1992). The understanding of Egypt under the Persians, Ptolemies, and Romans as a "multicultural society" has arisen in the context of the debate on "multiculturalism" in American education and society. In the realm of language and writing, grammarians have been engaged in a reassessment and sometimes attempted supersession of Polotsky's "Standard Theory," while scholars of writing systems have been focusing increasingly on the semiotic and esthetic aspects of the Egyptian scripts. Dynasty "0" discoveries at Abydos have raised the possibility that Egyptian writing may have been the earliest, after all. Thanks partly to the work of Foster and the inclusion of Egyptian selections in the *Norton Anthology of World Literature* and other standard educational resources, ancient Egyptian literature is more widely appreciated and has begun to enter the "canon." The interpretation of Egyptian literature and art have begun to reflect the poststructuralist school of criticism. In the study of Egyptian religion, "mysteries" (*sšt3, št3*) and "initiation" (*bsi*) are now well accepted, and some scholars entertain the possibility that mortuary text materials had a this-worldly application or ritual performance (a proposal first made by Walter Federn for the "Transformation Spells"). Recognition of the existence of ancient Egyptian mysticism has moved from the fringe to the mainstream, and comparisons with South and East Asian materials have been presented in scholarly literature. The word "philosophy" is now applied to Egyptian thought (J. P. Allen, M. Bilolo). More fundamentally, the seriousness and sophistication of Egyptian spirituality, theology, and cosmology are widely discussed. The expansion of public interest and of amateur Egyptology is shown by the rise of organizations such as the Society for the Study of Egyptian Antiquities, local chapters of ARCE (American Research Center in Egypt), and kindred groups in Britain, Australia, Spain, Japan, and elsewhere, and by the emergence of publications such as *KMT: A Modern Journal of Ancient Egypt.*

Should this survey then end on a note of ebullient optimism, a vision of Egyptology advancing from strength to strength? Alas, that would be naïve and Pollyana-ish. What can euphemistically be termed retrenching or downsizing in institutions of higher learning has converged with the reassessment of priorities away from humanities and in favor of "professional" and commercially oriented programs. This syndrome has resulted in a shrinkage of the academic Egyptological establishment, a paucity of positions, a decrease in job security for the positions that exist, the merger and abolition of departments, and the failure to fill positions of retirees. The very restricted job market is a disincentive to enrollment in Egyptological and cognate degree programs, as is the decrease in the size and breadth of faculties. More and more Egyptologists are working in other fields. Are we looking at the prospect of Egyptology in the twenty-first century making a full circle to the nineteenth century, once more becoming a largely amateur field, many of whose practitioners will need to pursue it as a hobby? Will this tend to restrict

substantive involvement in Egyptology to the wealthy? Will the critical mass of Egyptology, and some other fields as well, need to survive outside the university? If the universities had to preserve human knowledge in the face of some global threat, would they any longer be able to do so?

Can we affirm of Egyptology what Stephen Vincent Benét's Daniel Webster demands that visitors to his grave say of the Union—that she "stands as she stood, rock-bottomed and copper-sheathed"? We would certainly like to think so. Time will tell.

[*See also* Afrocentrism; Ancient Historians; Archaeological and Research Institutions; Archaeology; Biblical Tradition; Decipherment; Educational Institutions; Egyptomania; Historical Sources; Historiography; Interpretation of Evidence; Islam and Ancient Egypt; Museums; Rosetta Stone; Wisdom Tradition; *and biographical articles on Carter, Champollion, Herodotus, Lepsius, Manetho, Petrie, and Plutarch.*]

## BIBLIOGRAPHY

Baines, J. "Restricted Knowledge, Hierarchy and Decorum." *Journal of the American Research Center in Egypt* 27 (1990), 1–23. A thoughtful discussion which includes reflections on non-orthodox approaches to ancient Egypt.

Baines, J., and J. Malek. *Atlas of Ancient Egypt.* New York and London, 1980. One of the most useful reference works about ancient Egypt, including sections on "The Study of Ancient Egypt" and John Gardner Wilkinson.

Bernal, M. *Black Athena: The Afroasiatic Roots of Classical Civilization,* vol. 1. London, 1987. Provocative and controversial, more reliable when dealing with the history of scholarship and ideology than when theorizing about Egyptology.

Breasted, C. *Pioneer to the Past: The Story of James Henry Breasted, Archaeologist.* New York, 1943. A very sympathetic account by one of the great scholar's sons.

Brugsch, H. *Die Ägyptologie.* Leipzig, 1897. A culminative statement of one of the greatest nineteenth-century Egyptologists, including his endorsement of the Berlin system of philology.

Budge, E. A. W. *The Mummy.* 2d ed. Reprint, New York and London, 1972. Contains an interesting selection of material from classical sources about Egyptian writing. As a whole, this work exemplifies the low end of pre-Berlin Egyptology.

Davies, W. V. *Egyptian Hieroglyphs.* Berkeley and London, 1987. A clear and concise description of ancient Egyptian language, writing, and decipherment.

Dunham, D. *Recollections of an Egyptologist.* Boston, 1972. An informal and conversational autobiography; includes reminiscences of Georg Steindorff.

DuQuesne, T. "Egypt's Image in the European Enlightenment." In *Seshat: Cross-cultural Perspectives in Poetry and Philosophy,* vol. 3, pp. 28–43. London, 1999. An extremely erudite and thorough exploration of the Egyptian legacy and its European reception, with detailed consideration of material of genuinely Egyptian origin.

Greener, L. *The Discovery of Egypt.* London, 1966. A beautifully written and literate history of the study and exploration of Egypt through the death of Mariette.

Hoens, D. J. "A Short Survey of the Study of Egyptian Religion in the Netherlands." In *Studies in Egyptian Religion Dedicated to Profes-*

sor Jan Zandee, edited by M. Heerma van Voss et al., pp. 11–27. Leiden, 1982.

Hoffman, M. A. *Egypt Before the Pharaohs*. 2nd edn. London, 1991. An engaging narrative of prehistoric archaeology in Egypt as well as the prehistory of the region itself.

Iversen, E. "The Hieroglyphic Tradition." In *The Legacy of Egypt*, edited by J. R. Harris, pp. 170–196. 2d ed. Oxford, 1971. An excellent discussion of the study of hieroglyphs and other Aegyptiaca up until the decipherment; conservative in its assessment of the Egyptian content of classical materials.

Pope, M. *The Story of Archaeological Decipherment: From Egyptian Hieroglyphs to Linear B*. New York, 1975. Contains one of the most complete generally accessible discussions of hieroglyphic scholarship during the Renaissance and Enlightenment and the decipherment of Demotic.

Wilson, J. A. *Signs and Wonders on Pharaoh*. Chicago, 1964. Focusing on but not limited to the history of American Egyptology, packed with information and documentation.

Wilson, J. A. *Thousands of Years: An Archaeologist's Search for Ancient Egypt*. New York, 1972. Autobiography of one of the most influential American Egyptologists, Breasted's student.

Wortham, J. D. *British Egyptology*. Norman, Okla., 1971. Especially informative for the earlier period of scholarship.

Yates, F. A. *Giordano Bruno and the Hermetic Tradition*. London, 1964. A landmark work in intellectual history. Note that Yates dismisses the possible authentic content of the Egyptianizing material used by Renaissance Hermeticists.

Articles about many figures in the history of Egyptology have appeared in the magazine *K.M.T.: A Modern Journal of Ancient Egypt*.

EDMUND S. MELTZER

# EGYPTOMANIA.

As a dominant power in the Mediterranean region and the Nile Valley for much of the second millennium BCE, Egypt became a strong cultural influence on its neighbors during the first millennium BCE. The extent to which ancient Egypt continues to fascinate and influence Western civilization is astounding; this fascination and its expression are known as Egyptomania.

The ancient Greeks and Romans were enthralled by the age of Egypt's pyramids, temples, and hieroglyphic inscriptions, as well as its multitude of deities—the human, animal, and human-animal combinations. Both societies even adopted elements of pharaonic culture, in particular the worship of Isis, to whom temples were built in the Greek port of Piraeus by the fourth century BCE and in Rome's seaport, Ostia, by the third century BCE. By the first century BCE, Egyptomania had become a Roman fashion: frescoes showing Nile scenes decorated houses and fantasy Egyptian pleasure gardens featured a Nile setting with Egyptian statues (genuine where possible, local copies otherwise). The Egyptian-style buildings and the animals portrayed on the mosaic floor of the first-century BCE temple of Fortuna at Praeneste (present-day Palestrina, Italy) evidence the growing mystique of Egypt in Rome.

With Egypt's conquest by the Roman Octavian in 30 BCE, the flow of Egyptian objects (including obelisks) into Rome increased dramatically. Most came from sites in Lower Egypt and represented the art of the twenty-ninth dynasty through the Ptolemaic period. Imported works of art, in turn, influenced artists in Rome, some of whom were originally from Egypt. Those artists produced Egyptian-style sculptures to meet popular demand. Although some of their creations were faithful imitations, others were awkward pastiches of Egyptianized elements. One of the best known is the first-century CE Mensa Isiaca, a silver-and-gold-inlaid bronze table top that depicts a host of Egyptian deities with imitation hieroglyphs that may have come from an Isis sanctuary. Rediscovered in 1537, the figures on the Mensa Isiaca long served as models for Western artists.

Cults of Egyptian deities, particularly Isis, were popular throughout the Roman Empire. Rome's Isaeum Campense complex, rebuilt after a fire by the emperor Domitian (r. 81–96 CE), included a *dromos*, serapeum, and obelisks, as well as a temple to Isis. That complex remained an important cult center throughout the imperial era, and its ruins became a major source in Europe for both Egyptian and Roman-Egyptianized sculptures, from the thirteenth century CE. Rome also boasted several pyramid tombs, and the proportions of Gaius Cestius' pyramid (c.12 BCE), the only one to survive, became the model for later European pyramids.

Rome's greatest Egyptomaniac was undoubtedly the emperor Hadrian (r. 117–138 CE), whose friend Antinous drowned in the Nile River during their visit to Egypt; he was later deified by Hadrian. The gardens of Hadrian's villa at Tivoli (near Rome) featured an extravagant Egyptianized section, the Canopus, which contained a miniature Nile, many statues, and at least one temple to a variety of Egyptian deities, including an Egyptianized Antinous. Made in the classical style, his statues were shown wearing an Egyptian kilt and the *nemes*-headdress. These statues became a model for Europeans depicting Egyptians throughout the Renaissance and even into post-Napoleonic times, when the distinction between Egyptian and Egyptianized sculpture was widely recognized.

In Egypt, Christianity eventually superseded the older religious cults, which were finally banned by the emperor Justinian in 553 CE. Yet the influence of Egypt—particularly the Isis cult—on Christianity cannot be denied; not only does the pose of the Madonna and Child echo figures of Isis holding her son Horus on her knee but the cult of the Virgin Mary also absorbed many of Isis' attributes and titles.

With the spread of Islam out of Arabia and the arrival of Islamic forces in 641 CE, Egypt became isolated from Europe and entered into Western ideology as an unknown, mysterious, and fabulous realm, and remained so for centuries. In Rome, a modest revival of antiquarian interest began in the thirteenth and fourteenth centuries, generated by local discoveries of Roman, Egyptian, and Roman-Egyptianized remains at some construction sites. Not until the Renaissance did a real interest in ancient Egypt begin, driven in part by the fifteenth-century rediscovery and publication of the works of ancient writers, including those of the Greek historian Herodotus. Among the most important were a group of Greek texts (probably created in Alexandria in the fourth to fifth centuries CE) that purported to be written by Hermes Mercurius Trismegistus, who was identified as a contemporary of the biblical Moses and also the Egyptian god Thoth (Hermes). The Hermetic texts, including the *Hori Apollonius Hieroglyphica,* which "explained" hieroglyphs symbolically, were of great significance to those seeking to link Christian doctrine to Egypt—then perceived as the major source of all ancient knowledge and philosophy.

In the fifteenth and early sixteenth centuries, scholars began cataloging and describing ancient monuments in Rome and throughout Italy, but the distinction between Egyptian or Egyptianized monuments and antiquities in general was not recognized until the late sixteenth to early seventeenth century, when the first books dealing specifically with Egyptian monuments in Rome were published. The hieroglyphs on the monuments were usually ignored or rendered fancifully, if at all. Most scholars then assumed that hieroglyphs were not a written language but were symbols that represented eternal truths; their attempts at translation focused on mystical, not philological, meaning. During the fifteenth and sixteenth centuries, Egyptomania became a European fashion once again, primarily in Italy. Popes Pius II (r. 1458–1464) and Sixtus V (r. 1585–1590) reerected several obelisks in Rome. Pyramids and obelisks (often confused with one another, both being called pyramids) and other Egyptian elements were used in paintings and room decorations. A spectacular example is the Borgia apartments in the Vatican, decorated for Pope Alexander VI (r. 1492–1503). Alexander's claim of descent from the Egyptian deity Osiris emphasized the broadening of outlook of the Renaissance, which made it culturally possible to recognize ancient sources for various elements of Christian thought and doctrine.

To the Renaissance Humanists seeking order in the universe, Egypt (as revealed by the Hermetic texts in particular) became not only the source of wisdom and magic, but also of many skills. Freemasonry began to develop from a craft guild to a semisecret society that traced the origins of the stone mason's craft, geometry, and architecture to Egypt. An interest in the Hermetic tradition and the Kabbalah (a Jewish mystical tradition) led to the start of Rosicrucianism, in the late sixteenth century. Athanas-

EGYPTOMANIA. *Basalt ware "Canopic Jar" by the British ceramics firm of Wedgwood & Bentley (c.1773), based in part on illustrations in Bernard Monfaucon's works.* (Courtesy of the Brooklyn Museum of Art, acc. No. 56.192.33, Emily Winthrop Miles Collection)

ius Kircher, a Jesuit living in Rome from the mid-1600s, fostered this interest through his writings on many Egyptological subjects, including occult and mystical topics. He was also among the first to try to copy hieroglyphs accurately, and he amassed a huge collection of objects that became the first museum dedicated solely to Egyptian and Egyptianized artifacts. As awareness of Egypt and its monuments spread in Europe, Egyptian architectural elements began to appear in diverse settings. Obelisks and pyramids were not uncommon as funerary monuments, and sphinxes or lions often supported a sarcophagus or a tomb. As early as 1530, two female figures similar to Hadrian's Antinous model flanked a doorway at the palace of Fontainebleau, near Paris, whose gardens included a number of female sphinxes. By the mid-1600s, Bernini was designing elaborate bases for obelisks (e.g., the elephant base for a small obelisk in the Piazza della Minerva in Rome), and pyramidal tombs on the Cestius model for various popes. In France, Louis XIV's (r. 1643–1715) finance minister, Nicolas Fouquet, was acquiring Egyptian and Egyptianized antiquities for his palace, Vaux le Vicomte, and the king included many Egyptian-style objects (mainly sphinxes and obelisks) in his gardens at Versailles, setting the style for all Europe.

The exploration of Egypt remained sporadic until the late seventeenth and early eighteenth century. The first modern map of Egypt was produced by a French Jesuit, Claude Sicard, in the 1720s. The most influential eighteenth-century travelers were Richard Pococke, an Englishman who visited Egypt in the 1730s, and Frederick Norden, a Dane who ventured as far south as Derr, in Nubia, in 1737. The publications of their travels remained for years the main sources of accurate information on Egypt. During that same period, Bernard Monfaucon's ten-volume study of antiquities was one of the first to analyze rationally the Egyptian and Egyptianized antiquities in Europe, shorn of mystical interpretations. (Johann Fischer von Erlach's more fanciful reconstructions of Egyptian monuments, however—published in French, German, and English by 1725—were also influential.)

Broadening knowledge of Egyptian art and architecture, although still drawn mainly from works in Europe, and those particularly in Rome, influenced all areas of eighteenth-century thought, from the philosophy of the Enlightenment to the Romantic movement, Neoclassicism, and Freemasonry. Architects such as Etienne-Louis Boullée saw the clean lines, pure forms, and monumentality of Egyptian monuments as expressions of the "sublime"—suitable for buildings that were intended to convey a sense of awe. To the Romantics, mystic Egypt was an ideal source of inspirational gloom. From mid-century onward, Egyptian traits began to proliferate in the decorative arts, painting, literature, the theater, architecture (domestic and funerary), and landscaping. In England, Josiah Wedgwood began producing Egyptian-style ceramic wares as early as 1768. An increased use of Egyptian decoration in Masonic lodges and of Egyptian elements in Masonic ritual also dates from that time.

Egyptian elements, however, were frequently mixed with classical or other stylistic elements. One of the first to attempt a coherent Egyptian style was the Italian interior designer Giambattista Piranesi; his *Diverse maniere d'adornare i cammini* (1769), best known for its Egyptian fireplaces that combined elements from many sources, also included drawings for two walls of the Caffé degli Inglesi in Rome, the first thoroughly Egyptianized room design that was actually executed. Other rooms soon followed throughout Europe. Architects created obelisks for gardens, public squares, and memorials, and they designed pyramid tombs, some with Greek porticos. Many were built on the Cestius model although the Giza pyramids had been well published by mid-century.

In the late 1700s, Egyptian themes became increasingly popular in literature and on the stage, particularly in opera, a popularity that was to last through the nineteenth century. Some works, including the play by Tobias von Gebler, *Thamos, König in Ägypten* (with incidental music by Wolfgang Amadeus Mozart [K345], written 1773–1780) and Mozart's opera *Die Zauberflöte* (*The Magic Flute,* 1791) were steeped in the symbolic traditions of Freemasonry. Other operas, such as *Nephté* (Paris, 1789) and *La Morte di Cleopatra* (Bologna, 1792) used Egypt for their exotic settings.

When Napoleon Bonaparte led his French troops and band of scholars (the *savants*) to Egypt in 1798, interest in things Egyptian was already high. Baron Dominique-Vivant Denon's *Voyages dans la Basse et la Haute Egypte pendant les campagnes du général Bonaparte* (1802) and the expedition's multivolume *Description de l'Egypte,* which began to appear in 1809, supplied relatively accurate information for the first time on many aspects of Egyptian history and civilization. A full-fledged Egyptian revival was soon underway, but not without some political overtones. For the French, the Egyptian style represented France's rediscovery of and triumph over Egypt; for the English, it signified their conquest of Egypt and the French.

During the nineteenth century, the first of the scientific Egyptologists undertook serious exploration. Champollion deciphered hieroglyphs in 1822, proving that they could be read like any other language. With this contribution began the demystification of Egyptian civilization. The objects brought home by the Royal Prussian Expedition (1842–1845) led by Karl Lepsius and by Belzoni, Drovetti, and Salt, among others, formed the basis of museum collections and placed before the public a wide range of ancient Egyptian artifacts from all eras. Publications such as Lepsius's twelve-volume *Denkmäler aus Ägypten und Äthiopien* (1849–1859), Owen Jones's *Grammar of Ornament* (1856), and Prisse D'Avennes's two-volume *L'Histoire de l'Art Egyptien, d'après les Monuments*

EGYPTOMANIA. *Antwerp Zoo's Elephant House (1855–1856), with readable hieroglyphic inscriptions created for the building.* (Photograph by M. E. McKercher)

(1878–1879) exerted a wide influence on all areas of the arts well into the twentieth century. Prints made from the David Roberts paintings of his 1838 visit to Egypt continue to define Egyptian monuments for many.

The various international expositions of the nineteenth century, created to vaunt the achievements of participating countries, also fostered Egyptomania by including a variety of "ancient Egyptian" monuments (and sometimes actual artifacts) among their exhibits. In 1854, the Egyptian Court, designed by the English architect, Owen Jones and the Egyptologist Joseph Bonomi Jr., for the Crystal Palace Exposition in London, attempted to reproduce Egyptian monuments, design, and color accurately. Middle Kingdom jewelry discovered by the Egyptologist Auguste Mariette and displayed in the 1867 Temple Egyptien, which he designed for the Exposition Universel in Paris, inspired many jewelers. The inscriptions on the obelisks at the 1893 International Columbian Exposition in Chicago lauded both Ramesses II and U.S. President Grover Cleveland.

The nineteenth century's last Egyptomania binge occurred in the 1870s and 1880s, spurred by the opening of the Suez Canal in 1869; the opera *Aida* (story by Auguste Mariette, music by Giuseppe Verdi) written to celebrate the opening of the Cairo Opera House in 1869 but first performed in 1871; and by the erection in New York (1869) and London (1878) of actual ancient obelisks. While full-blown Egyptomania declined by the turn of the century, it never really disappeared, but strongly influenced Art Nouveau and Art Deco and remained one of the many themes in Western culture.

Egyptian motifs were particularly evident in nineteenth-century furniture, interior design, and the decorative arts. The products and publications of Charles Percier and Pierre-François-Léonard Fontaine in France and those of Thomas Hope (whose London house incorporated Egyptian designs into both furniture and decor), George Smith, and Charles Tatham in England helped popularize Egyptian styles worldwide. The basic furniture forms of the period, however, tended to be still classically inspired and were often based on pre-Napoleonic design and cabenetry sources; yet candelabra, clocks, statuettes, and jewelry all developed Egyptian manifestations. Wedgwood's Egyptian-style china may be the best known ceramic ware, but porcelain factories throughout Europe produced Egyptianized coffee sets and other goods. The Sèvres porcelain factory's Egyptian dessert service is perhaps the most elaborate, with each plate featuring a different scene from Denon's 1802 book, while the extraordinary centerpiece also drew on the *Description de l'Egypt's* preliminary drawings of temples at Philae, Edfu, Dendera, and Luxor. The first set (1808) was presented to Russia's Tsar Alexander I. The second set (1811–1812), made for and rejected by France's Empress Josephine, was later given to the Duke of Wellington and is now in Apsley House, London.

A vogue for Egyptian jewelry for both women and men began in the 1850s and continued well into the twentieth century. Jewelry design incorporated many Egyptian-style elements; scarabs and cartouches became particularly popular. Sphinx supports, lotus friezes, and other Egyptian elements appeared on all manner of furniture from 1865 onward. Mantelpiece sets with an Egyptian-style clock and pair of vases or obelisks were popular, as were statues, jardinieres, and other ornaments by noted manufacturers.

Throughout the nineteenth century, authors, composers, and stage designers acknowledged Egypt's growing appeal. Karl Friedrich Schinkel's 1816 sets for Mozart's *Die Zauberflöte*, with their mix of fact and fantasy, evoked mystic Egypt and influenced stage design for decades. Gioachino Rossini's 1818 opera *Mosè in Egitto* and its 1827 version for the Paris Opera were popular, as were the many productions of *Die Zauberflöte*, although operatic Egyptomania perhaps peaked with Verdi's *Aida*. While some stage works, such as *Aida*, strove for a measure of archaeological or historical accuracy, others merely capitalized on the appeal of exotic, mysterious Egypt. In her 1890 portrayal of Cleopatra, for example, Sarah Bernhardt was explicitly a seductress. One of the earliest novels to be set in ancient Egypt was Thomas Moore's *The Epicurean* (1825), but later authors also saw the possibility of Egyptian themes. The historical novels of Théophile Gauthier and Georg Ebers were reprinted well into the twentieth century. Characterizing Egypt as a land of dark magic gained popularity, as reflected in Arthur Conan Doyle's *Lot No. 249* (1892), whose reanimated, malevolent mummy later became a Hollywood staple.

Architecturally, early nineteenth-century Egyptomania was generally confined to the exteriors of buildings and to pylon gateways of varying archaeological accuracy. The cast-iron gate to Tsarskoye Selo in Saint Petersburg, built for Tsar Alexander I from 1827 to 1830, for example, is based on pylons that were shown in the *Description de l'Egypte*. Commercial buildings also made use of exotic Egyptian elements to attract customers. William Bullock's Egyptian Hall on Piccadilly Circus, London (1812), with its *cavetto* cornices, sphinxes, torus moldings, and pylon-shaped window frames and doors influenced later buildings in England. Appropriately, in 1821–1822, it housed London's first major exhibition of genuine Egyptian antiquities. In an entirely different style is the decoration of a building on the Place du Caire, Paris (1828), whose façade combines Moorish windows, engaged Hathor columns, and a frieze of Egyptian figures.

The Industrial Revolution drew on Egypt's connotations of stability and durability to allay public fears of new technologies. Egyptian battered walls and the shape of obelisks were functionally well suited as supports for new suspension bridges, constructed in Europe as early as the 1820s, and for the walls of pumping stations and reservoirs, including the massive walls of the Croton Reservoir in New York (1837–1842). Railway stations and factories, too, were built in the Egyptian style. A notable example is the Temple Mill, Leeds (1842), a flax-spinning mill based closely on the temples of Dendera and Antaeopolis in the *Description de l'Egypte;* the Egyptian theme was chosen because of the association of linen with ancient Egypt.

The Egyptian style was also appropriate for educational buildings, including libraries, museums (the Berlin Neues Museum, 1843–1855), universities (the Medical School, University of Virginia in Richmond, 1844), and zoos (the Antwerp Zoo's Elephant House, 1855–1856). Egyptian forms were used for prisons and courts in the United States, where the somber, heavy lines were intended to invoke the sublime nature of "the Law" and inspire criminals to reform. Two outstanding examples were the New Jersey State Penitentiary at Trenton (1832–1836), and the New York City Halls of Justice and House of Detention (1835–1838), known as "The Tombs," both designed by John Haviland and based in part on the *Description de l'Egypte*.

In the funerary Egyptomania of the nineteenth century, a new development in Europe and America was the garden cemetery. Designed as a place of repose for the dead and of reflection for the living, such cemeteries commonly featured pylon gateways and Egyptianized mausoleums. Père Lachaise cemetery in Paris (resting place of many members of the Napoleonic Expedition) is among the earliest examples; Highgate Cemetery in London (1839) and Mount Auburn Cemetery in Cambridge, Massachusetts (1831) are among the most spectacular. Egyptian motifs, with connotations of the ability to defy time, were felt to be particularly appropriate, although some Christians questioned the use of pagan symbols for their burials. Egyptian motifs were also used throughout the century on synagogues, churches, and lodges of fraternal orders.

Nineteenth-century painters increasingly used archaeologically accurate details in their depictions of biblical or historical scenes. Two widely reproduced examples are John Martin's enormous apocalyptic paintings and Sir Edward John Poynter's *Israel in Egypt* (1867), in which

Israelite slaves drag an oversized version of a stone lion (one on view in the British Museum) past a hodgepodge of carefully rendered pyramids and temples. Orientalists such as Jean-Léon Gérôme painted "re-creations" of ancient life in Egypt (usually including voluptuous nude or semiclad female figures), while the Symbolists painted Nilotic elements as part of their eclectic, occult, and poetic expression. Painters as varied as the Pre-Raphaelites, Paul Gauguin, and André Derain also used ancient Egypt for inspiration. Despite the flood of accurate data, objects, and drawings, however, most artists, designers, and writers did not adopt archaeological accuracy as their primary goal. They continued to draw on other sources— including contemporary and historic Egyptomania, particularly Piranesi and Monfaucon. The Bible, images and accounts of Cleopatra (the most often portrayed figure from ancient Egypt), and even modern novels, such as Théophile Gauthier's *Le Roman de la Momie* (1858), proved fertile sources for creative minds.

Nineteenth-century Egyptomania was essentially the preserve of the well-to-do, since only they could afford the finely crafted Egyptianized furniture and decorative arts. As mass production increased, a wider array of affordable products became available. The English designer Christopher Dresser (1834–1904) was one of the first to create designs for the mass-produced objects and furniture market; he based several furniture designs on Egyptian prototypes, while his decorative wares were produced in a range of materials and sizes to serve both the wealthy and the middle class.

In the twentieth century, a number of factors fostered a greater knowledge and appreciation of ancient Egypt and its art. Archaeological discoveries, exhibitions of Egyptian art, better education, and an enhanced Western respect for non-Western art have all led to the democratization of Egyptomania. Contrary to popular belief, however, twentieth-century Egyptomania did not begin with the 1922 discovery of Tutankhamun's tomb. It continued on from the turn of the century, spurred in part by existing trends, archaeological discoveries, and an increase in tourism to Egypt. Artists in all fields were inspired by Egyptian themes, from painters such as Pablo Picasso, Henri Matisse, and Amadeo Modigliani to Diaghilev's experimental dance company, Les Ballets Russes, to the modern dancer Martha Graham, who was re-creating Egyptian dances by 1920. Exotic Egypt was also represented in popular music, including the oriental foxtrot and such songs as *There's Egypt in Your Dreamy Eyes* (1905).

Egypt's greatest impact, however, was on the fledgling movie industry, whose earliest films explored the now-common Egyptian themes of biblical epics, mummies, and Cleopatra. Theda Bara's sultry Cleopatra (1917) and Cecil B. DeMille's lavishly Egyptianizing *Ten Commandments* (filmed in 1922, released in 1923) set the stage for filmmakers to come. Movie theater design reflected the exoticism of the new medium, resulting in such extravagances as the movie palaces of Europe and the Americas. Egyptian elements appear as early as 1916, and the Louxor Cinema in Paris (1920–1921) was one of the first of many wholly Egyptian-style movie palaces.

Commercially, Egyptian motifs were used to promote products as varied as sewing machines and cigarettes, whose packages were frequently decorated with fanciful scenes of ancient and modern Egypt. Legends of Cleopatra and ideas of exotic beauty made Egyptian themes naturals for selling beauty products such as soap, powder, and perfume (in pharaoh-headed crystal bottles by Baccarat). Advertisements ranged from completely Egyptian settings (with varying degrees of accuracy) to modern Western women in contemporary garb with an Egyptian theme.

While Egyptian architectural elements continue to be used, Egyptianized domestic architecture remains rare, perhaps because of Egypt's long association with death. It did flourish, however, in southern California—perhaps because of the sunny climate and the proximity of the fantasy-based Hollywood film industry. Los Angeles boasted one set of Egyptianized bungalow apartments by 1916; after the discovery Tutankhamun's tomb in 1922, Los Angeles and San Diego in particular blossomed with "Egyptian" buildings. The discovery of Tutankhamun's tomb immediately created a tidal wave of Egyptomania. As early as the spring of 1923, couturiers were showing Tut-inspired clothing. Books about Egypt were reissued, as were early 1900s decorative art objects. From 1923 to World War II, Egyptian themes appeared on every sort of product from Cartier jewelry to furniture, candy and cake tins. A few luxury passenger ships boasted sumptuous Egyptian lounges, and there was even a Scarab automobile in 1938.

The *internationale* or *arts modernes* movement (now commonly called Art Deco), showcased at the Exposition Internationale des Arts Décoratifs et Industriels Modernes (Paris, 1925), drew on existing Egyptomania and the Tutankhamun discoveries. The pure lines and stark shapes of Egyptian architecture were suddenly seen as modern, even futuristic. While many 1920s and 1930s buildings, such as Adelaide House (London, 1925) and the Chrysler Building (New York, 1930), combined clean lines with elaborate Egyptian-inspired decoration, others were less restrained; in choosing a colorful terracotta façade and elaborate Egyptianized interiors for their new offices in 1923, W. C. Reebie & Brother, a Chicago moving company, consciously combined Egypt's reputation for preservation and security with Tutankhamun's novelty.

EGYPTOMANIA. *Luxor Casino and Hotel, Las Vegas (1993), an extravagant example of late twentieth-century Egyptomania.* (Photograph by M. E. McKircher)

Hollywood and other filmmaking exploited the trend. *The Mummy,* starring Boris Karloff (1932), and its successors carried on the tradition of depicting Egypt as a land of mystery; a film such as *Cleopatra,* starring Claudette Colbert (1932), used history and literature as an excuse for extravagance and spectacle. Magicians and other entertainers, and even some period cartoons, featured Egypt or King Tut (Tutankhamun). Ancient Egypt was also used by writers as varied as Thomas Mann (*Joseph and His Brothers,* 1933–1943), Agatha Christie (*Death Comes as the End,* 1944), and Tennessee Williams (an early story, "The Vengeance of Nitocris," 1928). After World War II, the fashion for Egypt receded for a time, disappearing almost entirely from both decorative arts and architecture. Ancient Egypt was shown in Hollywood's biblical epics and in films such as *The Egyptian* (1954); *Land of the Pharaohs* (1955, inspired by the 1954 discovery of the Solar Bark at Giza); Charlton Heston's turn as Moses in *The Ten Commandments* (1956); and the Hammer Studios' *Mummy* movies. It was used in fantasy literature, which included popular 1950s and 1960s comic books of the "Mummy's Curse" variety; in advertisements for a variety of products; and in the 1960s revival of *moderne* as Art Deco.

The 1978 world museum tour of artifacts from Tutankhamun's tomb began a new wave of Egyptomania that had not peaked as of 1999. Its inception coincided with a renewed interest in early civilizations, the beginnings of New Age mysticism, and the growth of both the fantasy and science fiction genres.

Postmodernism in the 1980s made historical references in architecture acceptable once again. I. M. Pei's pyramidal entrance to the Louvre Museum in Paris (1988) is an outstanding example. The Memphis Zoo and Aquarium's 1990–1991 pylon entrance, with scenes drawn from the temple of Ramesses III at Medinet Habu, continues the tradition begun in Antwerp in 1855. More fanciful is the pyramid-shaped Luxor Casino and Hotel, built in 1993 in Las Vegas, Nevada, which is fronted by a sphinx 50 percent larger than its Giza prototype; the structure is thoroughly Egyptianized inside and out. Popular culture—1980s and 1990s television, American comic books and their more sophisticated French counterparts (often combining accurate drawings of modern and ancient Egypt with Egyptianized fantasies), and a flow of nonfiction and fiction writings—continues to influence the public's conceptions and misconceptions about ancient

Egypt. Historical accuracy, as always, remains a factor in Egyptomania, but not necessarily the main concern. Today's mass media, heirs to eighteenth- and nineteenth-century works as well as Hollywood productions, perpetuate old and new myths about ancient Egypt—its supposed descent from Atlantis; influence on it by beings from outer space; "pyramid power."

Egypt continues to be used to sell everything from cosmetics to computer technology, its reputation for wisdom and stability once again serving to reassure people about new technology. Egyptian-inspired products vary in authenticity from museum-sanctioned reproductions of antiquities to toys based on television shows or movies like *Raiders of the Lost Ark* (1981). Philip Glass's opera, *Akhenaten* (1984) balances the Bangles' rock song "Walk like an Egyptian." Television documentaries proliferate depicting all aspects of ancient Egyptian life and history—with varying degrees of accuracy. Serious books on ancient Egypt, its place in history, and its meaning to the modern world abound, as do mysteries, gothic novels, fantasies, and historical novels. Tutankhamun's mask and the Berlin Ägyptisches Museum's bust of Nefertiti have become modern icons, instantly identifiable, appearing in every imaginable context. Egyptomania has itself become a serious field of study, particularly in France, where the 1994 exhibition *L'Egyptomanie* and the symposium offered in connection with it were, themselves, examples of Egyptomania.

### BIBLIOGRAPHY

Carrott, Richard G. *The Egyptian Revival, Its Sources, Monuments and Meaning, 1808–1858*. Berkeley, Los Angeles, and London, 1978. One of the best books on architectural Egyptomania.

Curl, James Stevens. *Egyptomania. The Egyptian Revival: A Recurring Theme in the History of Taste*. Manchester, 1994. Perhaps the best overall survey in English of Egyptomania from the Ptolemaic period to the present; excellent bibliography.

Humbert, Jean-Marcel. *L'Egyptomanie dans l'Art Occidental*. Paris, 1989. A superb and lavishly illustrated volume, particularly concerning the decorative arts.

Humbert, Jean-Marcel, Michael Pantazzi, and Christiane Ziegler. *Egyptomania: Egypt in Western Art, 1730–1930*. Paris and Ottawa, 1994. The English version exhibition catalog of the most recent comprehensive Egyptomania exhibition; excellent bibliography.

Roullet, Anne. *The Egyptian and Egyptianizing Monuments of Imperial Rome*. Etudes préliminaires aux religions orientales dans l'empire romain, 20. Leiden, 1972. The most complete work on Roman Egyptomania in English.

RICHARD A. FAZZINI AND
MARY E. MCKERCHER

**EIGHTEENTH DYNASTY.** *See* New Kingdom, *articles on* Eighteenth Dynasty to the Amarna Period *and* Amarna Period and the End of the Eighteenth Dynasty.

**ELEPHANTINE,** modern name of the island in the Nile River now about 1500 meters long by 500 meters wide (5,000 by 1,650 feet), opposite the city of Aswan (24°05′N, 32°56′E). In pharaonic times, the main settlement with temples and cemeteries was on the southern side of the island, while on the eastern bank of the Nile there was only a small settlement and a trading post (*swnt*, which became the Greek *Syene*, or *Aswan* in Arabic). The huge granite rocks of the island provided an ideal and visually impressive place for a settlement in a strategic position, just north of the granite barrier of the First Cataract of the Nile. The island's modern name, Elephantine, derives from the Greek rendering of the Egyptian word for elephant (*ꜣbw*) a name that indicates a reshipment port for African ivory and other exotic goods. It became the central point for the southern trade routes from Egypt to Sudan and a base for governmental, military, and commercial expeditions. In addition, its black, gray, and red granite were quarried then and into modern times.

The base of the settlement on the southern part of the island is Neolithic, belonging to the Naqada culture. Its settlement had developed around a cluster of large monoliths that formed a grotto, which later became the sanctuary of Satet, the patron goddess of Elephantine. Originally, there were two islands divided by a swampy region that was inundated only during the annual Nile flood. The southern island had gained its importance through Satet's sanctuary and a fortress that had been founded in the second dynasty. To its northwest, there are the ruins of a granite step-pyramid monument from the third dynasty. Behind it was found an administrative building and a cemetery of the Old and Middle Kingdoms. During the First Intermediate Period, the river level sank and the swamp between the two islands was filled to form a larger island. It provided room for the growing settlement and its city walls, the temples, administrative buildings, and cemeteries, as well as a small hinterland. In the sixth dynasty, a cemetery for the elite was set on the terraces of an impressive rocky ledge to the northwest of the island, the Qubbet el-Hawa.

For the goddess Satet, permanent buildings were constructed around and above the original grotto and, from time to time, her temple was completely rebuilt. From the time of Montuhotep II (Middle Kingdom), a courtyard with a large water basin and aqueduct existed; there, the ceremonies of the Feast of the Nile Inundation took place. Above the grotto today stands the reconstructed sandstone temple of Hatshepsut, with Thutmose III, and nearby is the reconstructed limestone temple of Senwosret I. The blocks for those temples had been found incorporated into the foundations of the later temple for Satet, as built by Ptolemy VI and Ptolemy VIII alongside older blocks and fragments from buildings with the names of many earlier Egyptian rulers.

Today, the most impressive buildings towering above the settlement mound are the temple ruins of the ram god Khnum (originally the god of the fountains of the Nile River, which were—according to the mythical map of the Egyptians—located in the dangerous whirlpools of the Cataract region). Khnum became a guest in the Satet temple during the eleventh dynasty, then Satet's consort; Anuket, the goddess of Sehel island, was their daughter. Later, in the Middle Kingdom, a temple for Khnum was built on the site where ruins of his latest temples are still visible. Only a few limestone fragments of the Middle Kingdom Khnum temple have been found, and they were dated to the time of Sobekhotpe III. Khnum's temple was rebuilt on a larger scale under Thutmose III, but the pavement, the column bases, and the gates on the uppermost level of the temple site date from a complete enlargement undertaken by Nektanebo II during the thirtieth dynasty, while the decoration of the monumental gate was finished as late as the reign of Alexander IV (316–305 BCE). Ptolemaic kings and Roman emperors made additions to the temple, especially the gigantic terrace facing the river, which dates from Roman times. In its final stage, the temple measured about 123 meters (400 feet) in length, and its forecourt was filled with statues, stelae, offering tables, and obelisks.

In 1908, between the temple of Khnum and the temple of Satet, French archaeologists found the cemetery of the holy rams of Khnum.

An excavation to the west of the temple of Satet, completed by Labib Habachi in 1946, uncovered a "chapel for the *ka*," for the veneration of the long-dead official and local patron Heqaib. He had been responsible for the successful realization of royal expeditions to the South, for luxury trade goods, slaves, and cattle. Soon after his death and his burial in a rock-cut tomb on the Qubbet el-Hawa, he became venerated by a parish beyond the scope of his family members, so a chapel for the "Count Heqaib" was constructed on the island. He was worshiped as a mediator between humans and gods, and this was supported by both kings and the elite during the Middle Kingdom. The statue of Heqaib became part of the solemn procession through the streets of the town during the Festival of Sokar. In the sanctuary *temenos*, more than fifty statues of excellent quality have been found, and more than twenty-six stelae, as well as offering tables, twelve shrines, and *naoi*. Labib Habachi excavated the sanctuary built by the local governor, Sarenput I, which dates from the time of Senwosret I, with later additions into the thirteenth dynasty. The investigations of 1994 and 1995 led to the discovery of the chapels built during the eleventh dynasty, those underneath the pavement of the twelfth dynasty sanctuary.

Two smaller chapels, those of Amenhotpe III and Ramesses II had been seen in excellent condition by the French expedition in 1799, but they were destroyed in 1822, in the lime kilns, by order of the local government.

Archaeological discovery on the island started between 1906 and 1908, with a German expedition supervised by O. Rubensohn, in search of Aramaic papyri. It was soon followed by the French team of Charles Clermont-Ganneau, J. Clédat, and J. E. Gautier, from 1906 to 1910. The Aramaic papyri record the existence of a colony of Jewish mercenaries and their temple to Yahweh on the island, from about 525 BCE until at least 399 BCE. Because of conflicts with the priesthood of the temple of Khnum, the Jewish temple had been destroyed in 410 BCE, by order of the local governor. The Jewish parish soon applied to the authorities at Jerusalem and Samaria, and it gained permission to reestablish its temple.

In 1969, the German Archaeological Institute (Cairo branch), in cooperation with the Swiss Institute in Cairo, started long-term excavations on Elephantine, aiming at a systematic recording of the rediscovery of that regional town site, as well as all aspects of its more than three thousand-year history. Toward that end, excavation reports have been published regularly in *Mitteilungen des Deutschen Archäologischen Instituts, Abteilung Kairo* since 1970, volume 26.

[*See also* Aswan.]

## BIBLIOGRAPHY

Franke, Detlef. *Das Heiligtum des Heqaib auf Elephantine. Geschichte eines Provinzheiligtums im Mittleren Reich.* Heidelberg, 1994. History of the sanctuary, essay on Egyptian saints, with translation and interpretation of the major inscriptions, such as those of Sarenput I from the sanctuary and his tomb.

Habachi, Labib. *The Sanctuary of Heqaib.* Elephantine, 4. Mainz, 1985. Publication of the corpus of findings from the sanctuary.

Jaritz, Horst. *Die Terrassen vor den Tempeln von Chnum und Satet. Architektur und Deutung.* Elephantine, 3. Mainz, 1980. On the Roman terraces and Nilometers.

Kraeling, Emil G. *The Brooklyn Museum Aramaic Papyri.* New Haven, 1953. With an introduction on the history of excavations on Elephantine, including the Jewish colony.

Laskowska-Kusztal, Eva. *Die Dekorfragmente der ptolemäisch-römischen Tempel von Elephantine.* Elephantine, 15. Mainz, 1996. On the decoration of the Ptolemaic and Roman temples.

Porten, Bezalel. *Archives from Elephantine.* Berkeley, 1968. On the Aramaic papyri.

Porten, Bezalel, et al., eds. *The Elephantine Papyri in English: Three Millenia of Cross-Cultural Continuity and Change.* Leiden, 1996. Includes the Jewish colony as characterized in the Aramaic papyri.

Seidlmayer, Stephan J. "Town and State in the Early Old Kingdom. A View from Elephantine." In *Aspects of Early Egypt*, edited by Jeffrey Spencer, pp. 108–127. London, 1996. Discusses the shifting balance between residence and regions, with emphasis on the minor step pyramids.

von Pilgrim, Cornelius. *Untersuchungen in der Stadt des Mittleren Reiches und der Zweiten Zwischenzeit.* Elephantine, 18. Mainz, 1996. In-depth research concerning the growth of a Middle Kingdom city.

von Pilgrim, Cornelius. "The Town Site on the Island of Elephantine." *Egyptian Archaeology* 10 (1997), pp. 16–18. A good introduction to the excavation of the town.

Ziermann, Martin. *Befestigungsanlagen und Stadtentwicklung in der Frühzeit und im frühen Alten Reich.* Elephantine, 16. Mainz, 1993. On the Old Kingdom fortress and town.

DETLEF FRANKE

**ELEPHANTS.** For prehistoric and ancient Egypt, there are records of the presence of the African elephant (*Loxodonta africana*) on cosmetic palettes, ivory carvings, painted ceramics, and rock paintings, as well as osteological (bone) finds. The name of Elephantine Island in the Nile (*3bw*, "Elephantland") is further evidence. The dynastic era suffered increasing aridity and, above all, the transformation of the Nile Delta into a cultivated landscape. The process began with the first major efforts in Nile Valley farming and husbandry and became more prevalent after state formation in the late fourth millennium BCE. Such conditions caused elephants and other large wildlife to migrate south. The Syrian elephant, a subspecies of the Indian elephant (*Elephas maximus*), became known in Egypt for the first time during the Near Eastern campaigns of the New Kingdom. It was hunted by Thutmose I and Thutmose III near Nija on the Orontes River, and Thutmosis III is said to have killed a herd of 120 at that location—a great feat of which the king boasted on two stelae (the Armant and the Gebel Barkal). His officer, Amenemheb, wrote in his biography that the king's life was in danger on this hunt when a large bull charged him; however, he was saved when Amenemheb managed to sever the trunk (*dr.t*, "hand") of the enraged animal.

The image of an elephant among other exotic animals in the tribute scene in the vizier Rekhmire's tomb, as well as the elephant bones in Ramesses II's palace in Qantir (Piramesse), prove that the pachyderms were not only hunted but also captured alive and brought to Egypt, where they joined the royal menagerie of exotic animals, which symbolized the king's claim to power over foreign lands. While the image in the Rekhmire tomb clearly depicts a Syrian elephant, species identification is less certain when it comes to the bones found at Qantir. An ostracon from Ramesses III's tomb, however, clearly shows a Syrian elephant, which the Assyrian kings hunted along the upper Euphrates River or captured for their private zoos. The population of that species was made extinct by the seventh century CE, when the Islamic conquest provided new natural history and geographic surveys.

In the late fourth century BCE, Alexander the Great's campaigns in India brought the Indian elephant, trained for work and military uses, to the Near East, and it was used in the wars of the Diadochs. In 321 BCE, the regent Perdikkas and his troops entered Egypt to attack Ptolemy, Alexander's successor in Egypt. Indian elephants were used during the failed attempt to capture Memphis. That episode may explain the singular image of an elephant in the offering procession in the early Ptolemaic tomb of Petosiris at Tuna el-Gebel. Impressed by the war elephants in the Seleucid army, efforts began in the Egypt of Ptolemy II to train elephants for warfare, adapted to Egyptian requirements, but using the African rather than the Indian species. Initially, the animals were captured in the Meroitic kingdom (Ethiopia) and later on the Red Sea coast between Suakin and Massawa (Trogodytike). The Red Sea coast was easily accessible and offered Egypt transportation options, so it soon became the favored hunting ground. The capture and training of the elephants was handled by *mahouts* from India. After the battle of Raphia in 217 BCE during which African elephants proved less powerful than Indian elephants, the elephant troop became less and less important in the Ptolemaic army. Under Ptolemy V the experiment was abandoned.

There are no traces of the elephant in the religious realm of ancient Egypt. With the exception of elephants put on display in the New Kingdom, in dynastic times interest was focused exclusively on the ivory (*3bw*) of the tusks (*msw3, dh.t*). Ivory imports came to Egypt from the end of the Old Kingdom onward; the main importing nations were to the south (Yam, Kush, Punt, Wawat, etc.), but Libya, Syria, and Cyprus were also mentioned in New Kingdom texts.

[*See also* Ivory.]

**BIBLIOGRAPHY**

Boessneck, Joachim. *Die Tierwelt des Alten Ägypten.* Munich, 1988.

Houlihan, Patrick F. *The Animal World of the Pharaohs.* London, 1996.

Johnson, Sally B. *The Cobra Goddess of Ancient Egypt: Predynastic, Early Dynastic and Old Kingdom Periods.* London and New York, 1990.

Lloyd, Joan Barclay. *African Animals in Renaissance Literature and Art.* Oxford, 1971.

Störk, Lothar. *Die Nashörner, Verbreitungs-und kulturgeschichtliche Materialien unter besonderer Berücksichtigung der afrikanischen Arten und des altägyptischen Kulturbereiches.* Hamburg, 1977.

Zeuner, Frederick E. *Geschichte der Haustiere.* Munich, 1967.

LOTHAR STÖRK
Translated from German by Elizabeth Schwaiger

**ELKAB,** the present-day name of the ancient Egyptian town of Nekheb, situated in southern Upper Egypt (25°10′N, 32°50′E), on the eastern bank of the Nile River,

ELKAB. *The remains of the Temple of Nekhbet at Elkab.* (Courtesy Dieter Arnold)

about 15 kilometers (10 miles) north of Edfu and opposite Kom el-Ahmar (the ancient Hierakonpolis). Elkab has a massive, almost square, enclosure wall made of mud bricks, which in all probability was erected in the time of Nektanebo II (r. 360–343 BCE), the last king of the thirtieth dynasty. Not only within this enclosure but also in the alluvial plain surrounding it and in the desert area north and northeast of the town, remains of all periods—ranging from prehistory to Greco-Roman times—have been discovered. The site was explored by British archaeologists in the late nineteenth and early twentieth centuries, by Belgian expeditions from 1937 to the present, and occasionally by Egyptian teams.

The heart of the site consists of two contiguous temples. The largest of the temples is dedicated to the vulture goddess Nekhbet, the principal deity of Elkab and tutelary goddess of Upper Egypt; it was erected in sandstone by the kings of the last dynasties and shows several blocks that were taken from older constructions. The smaller temple, built in honor of the gods Sobek and Thoth, in its final stage dates to the reign of Ramesses II (r. 1304–1237 BCE). In the plain adjoining the eastern wall

of the town enclosure are the remains of two small peripteral temples (having one row of columns around the building). One of these temples dates to the time of Thutmose III (r. 1504–1452); the other to Nektanebo I or II (r. 380–363 or 360–343 BCE). Northeast of the town, in the mouth of the Wadi Hillal, a river run dry, three minor but well-preserved sanctuaries can be visited: a temple of Amenhotpe III in honor of the goddess Hathor; a Ptolemaic hemispeos (a temple built partially with stone blocks and partially hewn out of the rock) dedicated to a lion goddess, Sekhmet; and a chapel from the time of Ramesses II.

As shown by several settlements, the site of Elkab has been inhabited since prehistory. An epi-Palaeolithic industry, called the Elkabian (c.7000 BCE), was discovered by a Belgian expedition in 1968. No traces of pharaonic-era private dwellings have as yet been found; however, a Greco-Roman village encircles the front side of the temple of Nekhbet. Demotic and Greek ostraca and some objects found in the ruins of the houses provide useful information on the village's economic and social life. Elkab and its surroundings comprise several cemeteries from various periods. Close to the Greco-Roman village, an important Naqada III burial ground (c.3300 BCE) was excavated (in 1968, and from 1977 to 1979). On both sides of the northern and eastern town walls, Old Kingdom *mastaba* tombs and mud-brick tombs from the Middle Kingdom have been unearthed by British and Belgian archaeologists, respectively. The rocky hills northeast of the town also contain numerous tombs. The best preserved of these, decorated with inscriptions and funerary scenes, belong to civil, military, and religious dignitaries; they testify to the prominent role that Elkab played in pharaonic times, particularly in the early eighteenth dynasty. Some tombs of the sixth dynasty, a period previously unattested in the rock-cut necropolis, have been identified, as well as a mud-brick *mastaba* from the early Old Kingdom.

In several places along the Wadi Hillal, rocks are covered with drawings from prehistory to the later periods; hieroglyphic inscriptions are also in evidence, consisting mainly of the names and titles of local sixth dynasty priests. Some of the inscriptions have been identified with people buried in the main rock-cut necropolis.

### BIBLIOGRAPHY

Depuydt, Frans, et al. *Elkab*, vol. 4: *Topographie*. Brussels, 1989. Contains several maps and a detailed inventory (with bibliographical references) of the archeological sites of Elkab and the surrounding area.

Hendrickx, Stan. *Elkab*, vol. 5: *The Naqada III Cemetery*. Brussels, 1994. Describes the materials excavated in this Predynastic site.

Huyge, Dirk. "Bearers of the Sun." *Discovering Archaeology*. (1999), 48–58. Concerns the rock art in the mouth of the Wadi Hillal.

Limme, Luc, et al. "Elkab: Excavations in the Old Kingdom Rock Necropolis." *Egyptian Archaeology* 11 (1997), 3–6.

Vandekerckhove, Hans, and Renate Müller-Wollermann. *Elkab*, vol. 6: *Die Felsinschriften des Wadi Hilâl*. Brussels and Turnhout, 2000. Corpus (with translation and commentary) of the hieroglyphic inscriptions in the mouth of the Wadi Hillal.

LUC J. H. LIMME

**ELOQUENT PEASANT.** The almost complete text of the *Tale of the Eloquent Peasant* is known from four Middle Kingdom manuscripts, two of which also contain the *Story of Sinuhe*. The earliest are two copies from an archive of literary manuscripts of the second half of the twelfth dynasty from Thebes, and these present slightly different texts (Papyrus Berlin 3023, 3025); another copy comes from the Ramesseum Papyri from thirteenth dynasty Thebes (Papyrus Berlin 10499). Various factors suggest that the *Tale* was composed in the mid-twelfth dynasty, possibly in the reign of Senwosret II. Although the *Tale* is not attested among the texts copied by apprentice scribes in the Ramessid era, it was still familiar enough to be quoted in a local literary composition from Deir el-Medina. The *Tale* is about six hundred metrical lines long.

The *Tale of the Eloquent Peasant* begins in the manner of a folktale:

> There was once a man
> called Khunanup;
> he was a peasant of the Wadi Natrun . . .

It is set in the reign of the Herakleopolitan ruler Neb-kaure. The peasant is robbed of his goods as he goes to the capital; he appeals to the king's high steward, who tells the king that he

> has found one of the peasants,
> whose speech is truly perfect, and whose goods have
>   been stolen.
> And, look, he has come to me to appeal about it.

The king orders that the peasant's appeals should remain unanswered, in order that they will be extended and provide the king with "perfect speech" to hear.

This ironic narrative frames nine discursive petitions on the nature of *maat* (*mꜣꜥt*; "justice"), which occupy most of the composition. These pleas for "justice" address theodic issues though metaphorical extensions of the dramatic context, which present the peasant's plight as analogous to mankind's ability to question the justice of the creator god. The petitions grow in passion and desperation as they remain unanswered. They address the dichotomy between the imperfection of human society and the perfection of ideal justice in increasingly abstract terms. The peasant is eventually reduced to despair, and only then it is revealed that his pleas have been heard and recorded; they are recited to the king, judgment is passed in his favor by the high steward, and his goods are restored. Despite the prominence and force of the pleas, the narrative is the mode that determines the meaning of the whole as an allusive theodicy. The ironic structure of the plot, whereby the peasant's virtue prolongs his suffering before bringing final recompense, shows a complex sensibility.

The *Tale of the Eloquent Peasant* addresses central cultural concerns, such as the necessity for social order, rather than specific political issues. The petitions are complex fusions of various genres, including laments and eulogies. Although the *Tale* is in many respects a treatise about *maat*, it is not a didactic work about cultural norms. It is also in part a satire on bureaucracy, as well as a study in high rhetoric, allusive wit, and entertainment. The prominence of rhetoric is not to modern tastes, but the *Tale* is arguably the equal of the *Story of Sinuhe* in terms of literary sophistication.

### BIBLIOGRAPHY

Fecht, Gerhard. "Bauerngeschichte." In *Lexikon der Ägyptologie*, 1: 638–651. Wiesbaden, 1975.

Parkinson, R. B. *The Tale of the Eloquent Peasant.* Oxford, 1991. Standard edition of the text.

Parkinson, R. B. *The Tale of Sinuhe and Other Ancient Egyptian Poems 1940–1640 BC.* Oxford, 1997. Provides a recent translation of the *Eloquent Peasant*, based on the author's doctoral thesis (Oxford, 1988).

R. B. PARKINSON

**EMBALMING.** *See* Mummification.

**ENCOMIA.** The centrality of the institution of kingship within ancient Egyptian society made it imperative for the royal palace to engage in active propaganda to bolster the ruler's reputation and stature. Thus were developed royal encomia, "hymns" sung in honor of the ruling monarch. Little activity of this kind came from the Old Kingdom palace. Not much is known from the royal house itself, except for poorly preserved royal mortuary temples. The nobles' autobiographies describe the king in the vaguest of terms. One exception, from the tomb-chapel of an official named Metjetji, extols the virtue of following and obeying the king:

> Oh you living, who are upon the earth, adore the king as long as you live. Be vigilant of his work, and protect his command(s). Do as he wishes, and [it] will go well [for] the one who accomplishes what is praised. . . . The one beloved of the god [i.e., the king] will be an honored one. He will be hale under it, and his plans will go well as long as he lives.

This passage is later echoed in much longer compositions. This paucity of royal encomia cannot easily be explained, unless the kings of the Old Kingdom simply felt secure enough to do without the approval of their subjects. Was the king too remote from his subjects to feel the need to publish hymns of praise to himself at this time?

It took a catharsis like the fall of centralized power at Memphis and the difficulties of a civil war during the First Intermediate Period to force the new monarchs to reassess their predecessors' confidence. The eleventh dynasty kings, who won the civil war and reunited the country to begin the Middle Kingdom, felt the need to claim meritorious behavior in their inscriptions. The twelfth dynasty rulers—upstarts from the southernmost region of Egypt—wrested the throne away from the eleventh dynasty incumbents and elevated the art of praising the majesty of the king to a high degree.

From this period comes the *Story of Sinuhe*. Probably composed by court poets during the early twelfth dynasty, it is full of exciting adventures couched within timeless literary themes. The flow of the narrative is twice interrupted, however, by songs of praise for the new king, Senwosret I. The first of these portrays him as a fierce warrior

before whom no one could stand, while the second, recited by the royal children toward the end of the story, paints him as a forgiving monarch and a shepherd to his people. Set as they were within a thrilling tale, these varied descriptions of the ruler could not have failed to stir contemporary audiences. The twelfth dynasty palace introduced another genre of text, the so-called *Königsnovelle*, a royal tale in which the king is the protagonist; seated in the palace, the king presents an idea to the assembled courtiers, who declare their awe at his wisdom and their appreciation of his constant vigilance for their well-being. Yet another literary genre, the so-called Loyalist Instruction, clearly identifies loyalty and subservience to the king as the way to advance in society. These new compositions are long catalogs that glorify various characteristics of the king and expand the themes of the Old Kingdom text quoted earlier. A series of hymns composed in honor of Senwosret III of the late twelfth dynasty extol his defense of the country and his fierceness during battle. Because some of these hymns are written in anaphoric patterns, they must have been sung, and they were probably performed during the king's triumphal return from a military campaign. The songs' poetic style, with couplets and repeated choruses, would have ensured their success as propagandistic pieces, since a mostly illiterate population could have memorized them easily. Middle Kingdom texts praise other qualities of the king besides warlike ones. Panegyrics present the king's roles as intermediary between the gods and man, emulator of divine actions and attributes, beneficent ruler of Egypt, and provider of good inundations.

Similar themes were continued by the kings of the New Kingdom. Recalling earlier portrayals of the ruler as a fierce warrior, early eighteenth dynasty kings described themselves as "a mighty king" and "a strong ruler," who "acted with his own arms" and "seized the land by force." Coming as they did after a war of liberation that rid the country of foreign intruders, it is easy to understand the use of such phrases, which were disseminated throughout the realm on triumphal stelae set up in Egypt and abroad. This highly militaristic spirit pervaded many New Kingdom royal compositions; it should be noted, however, that although epithets applied to a specific king often arose from the events of the time, they joined the standard royal phraseology once they were seen to be effective.

A striking example of a royal encomium of the eighteenth dynasty is the so-called Poetical Stela of Thutmose III. The text consists of a speech by the god Amun-Re, hailing the king's military victories. The poetic section, framed by an epilogue and a prologue, comprises ten quatrains, each with two couplets introduced by anaphoras. Noteworthy is the layout of the poem on the stela itself: each quatrain is carved on a single line, and the anaphoric phrases are placed one below the other, occupying the beginning and middle of the line respectively. A similar format was employed by the court poet who hailed King Amenhotpe III's achievements; after praising the king's building activities, the text has Amun-Re celebrating his own benefactions toward Amenhotep III, with the first line of each stanza repeated in anaphoric pattern.

An unexpected example of a royal encomium comes from the Amarna Letters. One of the missives sent by Abimilki, prince of Tyre, to Akhenaten contains introductory stock phrases praising the Egyptian king. Of interest are the themes Abimilki chose to pursue in his homage to Akhenaten: not only are there phrases similar to the latter's hymn to the sun god Aten, but some passages also stress Akhenaten's belligerence and might. Given Akhenaten's general lack of enthusiasm for military campaigns, these sentiments indicate the effectiveness of the royal court's propaganda.

The Ramessid period produced more royal encomia. King Sety I emulated Thutmose III's and Amenhotpe III's victory poems, especially borrowing from the latter's anaphoric phrasing, where the god is said to turn to all cardinal points to do wonders for the king. Ramesses II's court composed two hymns in his honor: the first, from the temple of Abu Simbel, generally extols the king's military might, while the second is the well-known poem celebrating Ramesses II's bravery at the Battle of Kadesh. The latter was so important in the young king's propaganda program that he had the tale of his prowess carved on a number of temple walls as well as written in Hieratic script on papyrus. Victory hymns were also composed for the benefit of Merenptah and Ramesses III, IV, V, VI, and VII. The compositions in honor of the last two kings, probably coronation hymns, are noteworthy for having been written on papyrus, using thick dots—called "verse points" by modern scholars—to indicate the ends of lines, and terminal signs (actually the word for "end," or "cessation") to indicate the ends of stanzas. Both sets of markers were written in red ink to differentiate them from the rest of the text.

The New Kingdom also saw the continued use of the *Königsnovelle*. Most of these texts have a military setting, as Kamose, Thutmose III, and Ramesses II convene war councils in the respective tales of their prowess and wisdom. Each king presents a bold plan of attack to his startled generals, who begin by expressing doubt about the likelihood of success were they to follow their monarch's plan. But the plot of each tale is the same: the king browbeats his generals into submission and eventually wins the day. Another theme pursued within this genre is the royal audience (lit. "royal sitting"). The monarch sits in the audience chamber, presenting his decision to mount a trading expedition to a faraway land—for example,

Queen Hatshepsut's famous expedition to the land of Punt—or to ensure that men sent to gold mines have an adequate supply of water. Here the monarch is presented as a decisive but caring ruler, who, with the proper divine guidance, always ensures the well-being of his subjects.

Not every one of these statements should be taken at face value. Royal encomia were products of the palace and were meant to propagate the official dogma about the king. Their authorship is also open to question. The king must have participated in the process, but one suspects that the final product came from court poets. What is not in doubt, however, is the fact that these encomia succeeded in reaching the population at large, as shown by a statement praising Thutmose II—"The commoners rejoiced. . . . They gave praise to the Lord of the Two Lands and they honored this beneficent god"—and by a declaration about King Merenptah: "His victories are recounted (*sedjed*) in every land."

**BIBLIOGRAPHY**

Bleiberg, Edward. "Historical Texts as Political Propaganda during the New Kingdom." *Bulletin of the Egyptological Seminar* 7 (1985/ 86), 5–13. Presents a number of examples of propagandistic texts and the reason for their success within the ancient Egyptian context.

Condon, Virginia. *Seven Royal Hymns of the Ramesside Period: Papyrus Turin CG 54031.* Berlin, 1978. Full publication of two of the texts discussed above.

Grimal, Nicolas-Christophe. *Les Termes de la propagande royale égyptienne: De la XIXe dynastie à la conquête d'Alexandre.* Paris, 1986. An unsurpassed study of the words and phrases used by the pharaohs to propagandize themselves; excellent bibliography.

Loprieno, Antonio, ed. *Ancient Egyptian Literature: History and Forms.* Leiden, 1996. More than thirty articles, in English, French, and German, by leading experts in the field of ancient Egyptian literature; several discuss topics mentioned in this article; lengthy bibliography.

O'Connor, David, and David P. Silverman, eds. *Ancient Egyptian Kingship.* Leiden, 1995. A comprehensive discussion of various topics on kingship in pharaonic Egypt.

Spalinger, Anthony J. *Aspects of the Military Documents of the Ancient Egyptians.* New Haven, 1982. A discussion of the *Königsnovelle*; various phrases used by the court poets to introduce the action are on pages 101–114.

RONALD J. LEPROHON

**ENGINEERING.** *See* Technology and Engineering.

**ENNEADS.** *See* Myths, *article on* Creation Myths.

**EPIGRAPHY.** In its strictest sense—the study of inscriptions and, in particular, of monumental texts—epigraphy claims a broader scope for ancient Egyptian civilization because of the pictorial and decorative nature of the hieroglyphic writing system and its intimate link with architectural forms. Egyptian epigraphy is concerned with the precise recording, editing, translation, and publication of both monumental inscriptions and their accompanying scenes, in as definitive a manner as possible.

**The Hieroglyphic Writing System and Its Monumental Context.** Egyptian hieroglyphs consist, for the most part, of figures of humans, animals, natural features, and manmade objects rendered in miniature. The potential for employing them directly in conjunction with nontextual, purely representational art was realized at a very early date, as on such proto-historic documents as the Narmer Palette, and the intimate bond between text and figural depiction was consciously manipulated. Egyptian inscriptions were preferentially written from right to left—that is, the individual hieroglyphs face right, toward the beginning of the text—and that orientation automatically imposed certain artistic conventions on signs employing the human figure. Those conventionalized standards were faithfully extended to two-dimensional relief and painting and, subsequently, to three-dimensional sculpture.

Because hieroglyphic signs can be written in either direction and can be arranged in horizontal rows as well as vertical columns, the writing system lent itself perfectly to monumental decoration, which emphasizes both the symmetry of a building and its ceremonial orientation. Egyptian monumental texts usually occur in temple or tomb scenes and are thus bound to their immediate spatial context, ultimately to the function of public and ceremonial spaces. Within a pictorial context, the orientation of texts reflects their content: captions that describe the scene are oriented with the initiator of the action; the names and speeches of the participants face in the same direction as the figures to which they variously pertain; protective epithets are placed behind them; and the textual material, in general, frames and enfolds the scene. Reversals of normal sign orientation are due to contextual criteria.

The task of the epigrapher of pharaonic inscriptions, therefore, involves more than the translation of texts, so an appreciation of iconography and monumental context is essential. Ritual scenes cannot be fully understood without a translation of the accompanying texts; nor can the texts be comprehended without observance of their placement in and reference to those scenes. More often than not, the epigrapher is engaged in redacting not just an inscription but a monument, in its two-dimensional (decorative) and three-dimensional (architectural and functional) aspects.

**Historical Summary.** Epigraphy as a scientific study cannot be said to exist prior to a correct understanding of the texts that form the core of its subject. Although the ancient wonders of the Nile drew travelers to Egypt in increasing numbers in the eighteenth century, their early records of pharaonic monuments originated from a profound curiosity and an interest in unfamiliar and indecipherable ruins, rather than from an informed approach to documentation. Even the achievements of the French scholars who in 1798 accompanied Napoleon Bonaparte and his troops during his conquest of Egypt can be called epigraphy only in the sense that their efforts were scientifically motivated and planned on a grand scale. The extraordinary illustration plates in the *Description de l'Égypte* (published from 1809 to 1822), which was organized topographically from south to north, were not accompanied by translations or textual interpretation; yet they set a high standard for future epigraphic expeditions and initiated an age of wholesale documentation of monuments throughout the Nile Valley. Certain recording techniques made their appearance for the first time, in particular the use of sun and shadow conventions for indicating the visual difference between raised and sunken relief. There are some shortcomings from the modern point of view: many scenes were incompletely copied; reliance cannot be placed on the hieroglyphic signs; and strict attention was rarely paid to Egyptian artistic conventions, with human anatomy in particular influenced by the then current European Romantic ideal.

With the 1822 announcement of hieroglyphic decipherment by Jean-François Champollion, the comprehension of Egyptian monumental texts became a possibility. Champollion then led a team in Egypt from 1828 to 1829, the first to be able to understand monumental texts *in situ*. His results were published posthumously in *Monuments de l'Égypte et de la Nubie* (1834–1847) and in *Notices descriptives* (1844–1849). These works contain a wealth of information, and the hieroglyph signs are accurately rendered; they are accompanied by schematic diagrams, sketch plans, and elevations of buildings keyed to descriptions of the scenes. Additional texts were included as hand copies, notably those in the royal tombs of Thebes, and even the more important graffiti were noted. An auxiliary publication was that of Ippolito Rosellini, who accompanied Champollion, titled *I monumenti dell'Egitto e della Nubia* (1832–1844). The drawings are grouped thematically according to three categories: historical reliefs (primarily the major Ramessid battle reliefs); "civil" monuments (representations of daily life, fauna, Egyptian arts and crafts, shipping, sports, and funerary scenes); and cult scenes (depictions of temple rituals and gods).

Several artists from the early decades of the nineteenth century may be singled out as pioneers in epigraphy. Much of their fine recording, still unpublished, approaches the highest epigraphic standards and provides invaluable evidence for monuments that have since suffered irreparable damage. Robert Hay made several visits to Egypt between 1824 and 1838; Nestor l'Hote completed three trips between 1828 and 1841; and John Gardner Wilkinson, who had a knowledge of the hieroglyphic and Coptic scripts as well as extraordinary skill as a draftsman, spent a number of years in Egypt from 1821 to 1833.

With the Prussian expedition of Richard Lepsius (1842–1845), remarkable accuracy was achieved, to the extent that even today only marginal improvements are possible in many details. A chronological presentation was selected for the illustration plates, published in twelve volumes as *Denkmaeler aus Aegypten und Aethiopien* (1849–1859). For the first time by an epigraphic mission, the ancient Egyptian human figure was drawn with a keen eye to pharaonic convention, rather than a European-derived esthetic. Great care was also paid to the relative placement of texts and figures, as well as to representing the extent of damaged surfaces. The contribution of *Denkmaeler* to the field of epigraphy is enormous; it supersedes what came before and remains the primary source for monuments that have never been republished. It also ended the age of all-inclusive epigraphic surveys and, henceforth, fieldwork would concentrate, more manageably, on selected monuments.

Heinrich Brugsch's *Recueil de monuments* (1862) is a fine example of an early autographed collection of texts, often accompanied by a schematized sketch of a scene as well. The text lines are numbered, any damage is indicated by convention, and the hieroglyphs are oriented faithfully according to the original source (although long inscriptions are indiscriminately broken to fit the size of the page). Significantly, Brugsch also copied several loose blocks at Thebes that preserve the name of Akhenaten (c.1382–1365 BCE), presaging by seventy-five years an important trend in epigraphy.

Auguste Mariette devoted a slim but excellent volume, *Karnak* (1875), to inscriptions from that temple. His illustration plates include plans of the chronological development of Karnak, as well as numerous texts in which both damage and block lines are consistently noted for the first time. Areas of repair, where the name of Amun was restored after the Amarna period, are rendered in a hatched convention. Mariette's hand copies of Giza *mastabas*, *Mastabas de l'ancien empire* (1883), also mark a significant development in the thoroughness accorded a single group of related monuments. These private tombs are each documented *in toto*, with all texts and figures represented in context with their architecture, which is presented as a series of detailed plans, elevations, and measurements.

Percy Newberry's publications of the rock-cut tombs at Beni Hasan and Bersheh (1890–1894) were the first in a notable series sponsored by the Egypt Exploration Fund and devoted largely to the epigraphic recording of private tombs in Middle Egypt. The provincial paleography of those private tombs, the unusual content of the scenes, and the idiosyncratic arrangement of inscriptions and figures were systematically noted, reflecting an astonishingly high standard of objectivity and recording. One of Newberry's artists, Howard Carter, was later the chief draftsman for Édouard Naville at the temple of Hatshepsut (c.1502–1482 BCE) in Western Thebes. The illustration plates of *The Temple of Hatshepsut at Deir el-Bahari* (1894–1908) were produced from exquisite measured drawings executed in pencil, with architectural block lines systematically included and text columns carefully numbered. In the plates, large areas of intentional erasures—caused during the posthumous proscription of Hatshepsut's memory—were indicated by the use of hatching that only partially obscured the original text. Other alterations (such as changes in personal pronouns, the usurpation of cartouches, and erasures of her royal *ka* figures) were often noted, though not consistently, by Naville's team.

To Félix Guilmant belongs the credit for employing photography as a direct basis for final drawings, in his groundbreaking publication on the tomb of Ramesses IX (c.1139–1120 BCE) in the Valley of the Kings. The precision of his plates, each provided with scales and column numbering, still speaks eloquently for the value of the definitive facsimile copy and the application of photography in epigraphy.

Text corpora are essential tools for the advancement of epigraphic research, and between 1875 and 1925 three monumental projects were organized to bring together inscriptions of common funerary theme. These are Édouard Naville's *Das aegyptische Totenbuch* (1886, on the *Book of Going Forth by Day*), Kurt Sethe's *Die altaegyptische Pyramidentexte* (1908–1962, on the Pyramid Texts, with translation and commentary), and Adriaan De Buck's *The Egyptian Coffin Texts* (1935–1961). Each sets down all known parallel versions of the same spells, side by side, for purposes of comparative analysis. This felicitous pattern has been followed by Erik Hornung in his seminal studies of the New Kingdom's royal underworld books: *Das Buch der Anbetung des Re im Westen* (1975–1976, on the *Litany of Re*), *Das Buch von den Pforten des Jenseits* (1979–1980, on the *Book of Gates*), and *Texte zum Amduat* (2d edition, 1987–1994, on the *Book of That Which Is in the Underworld*).

From 1905 to 1907, the Nubian Expedition of the University of Chicago, led by James H. Breasted, undertook an extensive survey devoted to the recording of inscriptions south of the First Cataract of the Nile, using a camera for complete documentation and employing photographs printed on site to collate the hieroglyphic details at varying scales. At the temple of Sesebi, the expedition grappled with the problem of how to render accurately wholesale palimpsests—scenes initially decorated under

Akhenaten and later recarved to obliterate his memory. Starting in 1924, facsimile drawing based on photography was fully elaborated as a documentary technique by the Oriental Institute's Epigraphic Survey, founded as a mission devoted solely to the precise recording of monumental reliefs and inscriptions. At the temple of Ramesses III (c.1198–1166 BCE) at Medinet Habu, the extensive color traces were reproduced by the application of gouache on enlarged photographic prints.

The fundamental contribution of Norman and Nina de Garis Davies lies not only in the number of tombs they recorded in Middle Egypt and Western Thebes for the Egypt Exploration Fund and the Metropolitan Museum of Art from 1898 until 1937 but also in the remarkable fidelity of their work; it consists of meticulous line drawings and tempera facsimile paintings, whose magnificence and detail approach the semblance of fine color photography. Amice Calverley's exquisite paintings, included in *The Temple of Sety I at Abydos* (1933–1958), represent another superb effort to document extensive painted traces before the availability of reliable color film.

Particularly noteworthy epigraphic landmarks that postdate World War II include several outstanding publications of Theban tombs, sponsored in separate field surveys by the Deutsches Archäologisches Institut, appearing in *Archäologische Veröffentlichungen*, and by the University of Heidelberg, published in the *Theben* series. These combine consistently fine standards of recording, photography, and text translation with pertinent archaeological data. The potential for the study of as yet unpublished archival records is exemplified by the fine series on Giza *mastaba*s, produced from fieldwork undertaken by the Museum of Fine Arts, Boston, and Harvard University in the early twentieth century. Nonmonumental inscriptions such as graffiti are increasingly the subject of epigraphic study; an example is *Graffiti de la montagne thébaine* (1968–1971), edited by Jaroslav Černý.

A relatively new development in epigraphy has been the recognition of the importance of loose blocks to the recovery of monuments dismantled in antiquity. The largest effort of that kind has unfolded at Karnak, through the Akhenaten Temple Project and the Centre Franco-Égyptien d'Étude des Temples de Karnak, where tens of thousands of blocks from the vanished temples of Akhenaten have been reassembled with the help of computers on paper, using criteria of scale, textual content, and iconographic continuity. A similar project has been pursued with great success by the Polish–Egyptian Mission at the destroyed temple of Thutmose III (c.1504–1452 BCE) at Deir el-Bahri, where thousands of fragments of wall decoration, reconstructed in sections, can be accurately fitted to the scant architectural traces. Also at Karnak, blocks adorned with festival scenes of Thutmose IV

(c.1419–1410 BCE) have been physically reassembled in a virtually complete re-creation of an open court that was razed in the reign of Amenhotpe III (c.1410–1372 BCE) to make room for his Third Pylon. Nor is it necessary to work with large numbers of stones; for example, at the temple of Luxor, missing portions of the Colonnade Hall have been extensively restored, at least thematically, on the basis of a minuscule number of fragments. Such successes confirm the intimate link between the study of monumental decoration and of architecture.

**Tools of Epigraphy.** The basic tools for recording were and are paper and a pen or pencil, for copying scenes and inscriptions by hand; accuracy depends on the talents of the epigrapher and whatever mechanical measuring aids are employed. One of the earliest recording techniques was photography, the invention of which coincided with hieroglyphic decipherment; in fact, one of the first purposes envisioned for the camera was the instant documentation of Egyptian monuments without the inaccuracies introduced by the human eye and hand. Photography is the basis of facsimile recording and remains an essential component of recording scenes and texts, but it has limitations as well: successful photography requires access to the monument, correct lighting, and exact measurement to eliminate distortion. Even under the best conditions, not all details may be clear; the camera is of little assistance in badly damaged temples and tombs, where broken or abraded surfaces cast deceptive shadows. Nonetheless, photographs alone can be sufficient to provide a definitive record in rare instances, where the surface is undamaged, the text consists of simple incised signs, and there is no representational iconography connected with it.

An early method of reproduction was the use of "squeezes," a form of molding in which a mass of wet paper pulp is pressed against the surface until dry; after removal, the paper retains its shape. Latex has been used for the same purpose, and while it provides a much more detailed image of the wall, latex can be used only on highly durable, nonporous surfaces that are in good condition. The disadvantages of such methods include the stress and humidity placed on the ancient surface—good reasons for why squeezes and latex are not currently employed in the field. Moreover, it is the reverse image that is produced, with all the surface defects included, and at full scale. Such three-dimensional examples of recording are not by themselves publishable. Direct tracing of the outlines of a text is the another method of duplication, and it can be essential for curved surfaces or inaccessible areas. One-to-one reproduction is perfect for graffiti and small inscriptions, but it is often cumbersome for large monuments and wasteful of materials. One-to-one tracings of entire walls also require considerable reduction for publication. A related method, rubbing (where graphite, carbon, or chalks are rubbed on paper over a surface), is less precise in its details and cannot be used on soft or friable wall surfaces.

Large scenes are reducible in advance to a scale appropriate for publication through photographic prints, projection, or the use of gridded quadrants and measured reduction. Facsimile copies are most commonly produced from prints made to an exact scale, either by drawing directly on the print emulsion or by tracing over the photograph. The use of alternating sun and shadow lines to lend a three-dimensional sense to carved relief is more than mere convention, since it provides critical clarification in scenes involving overlapping figures or in damaged areas. The facsimile process, however, is very time-consuming and requires experience and long field training. Painted surfaces—in particular, painted tombs with no relief carving—present a special problem. Color is impossible to conventionalize in black-and-white drawings except in the most elementary fashion, and frequently there are numerous layers of information to be recorded: plaster, grid lines, corrections made to the initial draft, base colors laid on in blocks, final coats of paint, figural outlines, and interior details. In some cases, even individual brush strokes, mottling, and gradual shading of color are distinguishable. While color photography can capture most of this information in a single image, the wall surface must be completely clean, since even a superficial coating of dust will dim the image significantly. Color photography is expensive and must be strictly supervised, but excellent results are possible.

Photogrammetry, a survey technique that records contours, has occasionally been used to record deeply carved inscriptions, usually along with relief sculpture. Its practical application is extremely limited because changes of depth in raised and sunken relief inscriptions are very subtle, and contour changes are of less significance than the outlines and incised details of signs.

Computers, digital cameras, and scanners hold great promise for new epigraphic applications, or at least the revamping of old ones. Different hieroglyphic fonts are widely available for publications, and these can be applied to axonometric drawings of objects. Indexes of large textual corpora, such as the Coffin Texts (www.ccer.ggl. ruu.nl/ct/ct.html), are now accessible online for immediate use by researchers, and such resources will certainly proliferate. Digital cameras, which record images as a data file rather than as a film negative, will enhance the uses of field photography and will facilitate archival housing; the electronic scanning of both drawings and photographs has already revolutionized the production of epigraphic publications. Perhaps the most promising use of field scanning—not yet realized—is the possibility of producing a three-dimensional record of a wall surface as a digital file, with the capability of being viewed in light artificially beamed from different directions. The reader may then compare that image, in varying light, with the edited drawing of the wall, and independently judge the worth of the epigraphic effort. Recent advances in computer applications to epigraphy and related areas can be found in the series *Informatique et Égyptologie*, the published proceedings of the Computer Working Group of the International Association of Egyptologists.

**Epigraphic Methodology.** There is no single method to be prescribed for epigraphy. The approach to be attempted will depend on the condition and size of the particular monument, the logistic and financial resources of the expedition, the number of personnel and their respective talents, the time available, and the nature and scale of the publication intended. Ideally, field recording is initiated with a precise idea of how large the plates and photographs will be, and appropriate epigraphic methods are then chosen: drawings or photographs, tracings or reductions, hand copies or facsimiles, or a combination of these options.

An awareness of the conventions of Egyptian art and iconography and a knowledge of paleography are essential in both the copying and correcting processes. Raised relief is a relatively simple matter to draw, the outlines generally following the base cut of the sign. Sunken relief is more challenging, since the outline of a sign is usually beveled and has two edges—the perimeter and the base of the cut. Choosing one edge or the other results in signs that appear too wide or too narrow, respectively, while drawing both (an option that is scientifically accurate) results in confusion on both visual and paleographic grounds; the epigrapher should judiciously draw the line midway along the bevel of the cut. Graffiti are an especially knotty problem in this regard, since they may be incised with clearly cut lines, crudely scratched with a sharp tool, or roughly pecked out in the most cursory manner.

A long history of use and reuse may be read in most Egyptian monuments, not only through the benefactions recorded by successive generations of rulers but also through other changes undertaken for political or religious reasons, such as the purposeful usurpation of cartouches, the wholesale persecution of the god Amun during the reign of Akhenaten, and various kinds of later iconoclastic or superstitious erasures. The chronology of and motivations behind such alterations can often be deduced by noting the distribution of chisel strokes and their physical characteristics—and in a drawing, these features can be differentiated through artistic conventions.

In addition to the final carved or painted lines, other

features must be noted where extant: traces of earlier drafts of the scene, name erasures, evidence of restoration in antiquity, the remains of plaster or paint, architectural block lines, graffiti, and various types of damage. Other incidental data that do not intrude on these basics—features that are of interest for purposes of record or of conservation, those that would hinder the readability of these essential components—may be omitted: natural abrasion or erosion, uneven dressing of the wall, stray chisel marks, and salt deterioration. The task of the epigrapher is similar to that of an editor of a manuscript: to clarify the present condition and past history of a monumental text through a readable copy or facsimile for scholars who have no access to the original. In that task, the decision to omit certain information from a drawing for purposes of clarification may override the mandate to record as much as possible.

The most successful epigraphy is undertaken, in all its copying and correcting phases, in the field, where preliminary records can be constantly compared against the original. The process of epigraphy may be described as a constant series of subjective decisions as to what information should be included and what can be omitted. These decisions are based on numerous factors, including a close familiarity with the monument, a conceptual reconstruction of sections of the wall that may be missing or destroyed, a general understanding of the phenomena of usurpation and restoration, an ability to differentiate intentional from accidental damage, and even a knowledge of ancient methods of carving stone. Inevitably, decisions about the features to include in the final record depend on the current understanding of historical and textual problems; certain traces may be inadvertently overlooked that will prove to be of critical importance to a later generation. A necessary adjunct to the drawings is a series of photographs, to allow the reader an opportunity to make an independent judgment and to clarify the conventions chosen during the epigraphic process. Above all, consistency must be achieved in drawing conventions, and in preparing the publication the epigrapher should ensure that the translation of a text reflects its integration within a scene.

Ideally, scenes and texts are published together, but texts may legitimately be presented separately. For readability and comprehension, and where emphasis is on the text alone, hieroglyphs can be composed solely in horizontal lines, as in Kenneth Kitchen's mammoth *Ramesside Inscriptions* (1975–1990), with an arrow indicating whether the original disposition was vertical. Text can also be arranged purely according to the Western convention of left-to-right reading, and even artificially subdivided into sentences and clauses, as in Kurt Sethe and Wolfgang Helck's *Urkunden 4* series (1933–1958) on bio-

graphical and historical inscriptions of the eighteenth dynasty. Hieroglyphic fonts are easily adapted to such purpose, the primary obstacle being the enormous variety of signs available to the ancient scribe. Some of the most splendid font publications, however, are those of the Institut français d'archéologie orientale du Caire that deal with the Ptolemaic temples of Esna, Edfu, and Dendera— a period characterized by a bewildering range of individual sign variants.

Epigraphy is not a field in which progress is inevitable, and woeful inadequacies are evident even in the most recent publications. Ironically, exceptionally fine examples of epigraphic recording are to be found even in the early nineteenth-century *Description de l'Égypte;* for example, the Rosetta Stone—already recognized as offering the best chance for the decipherment of the hieroglyphic script—and the sarcophagus of Nectanebo that was found at Alexandria. The aspiring epigrapher could do worse for models than these drawings, made decades before their inscriptions could even be fathomed.

[*See also* Egyptology.]

## BIBLIOGRAPHY

Bell, Lanny D. "The Epigraphic Survey: Philosophy of Egyptian Epigraphy after Sixty Years' Practical Experience in the Field." In *Problems and Priorities in Egyptian Archaeology,* edited by Jan Assmann, Günter Burkard, and Vivian Davies, pp. 43–55. London, 1987. A fine summary of the facsimile method used by the survey, the methodological parameters behind it, and the continuing paramount need for definitive recording.

Breasted, James Henry. "The Monuments of Sudanese Nubia." *American Journal of Semitic Languages* 25 (1908), 1–110. An early field report that emphasizes the importance of collation, using photographic images, and the challenges of dealing with palimpsest inscriptions.

Breasted, James Henry. *The Oriental Institute.* University of Chicago Survey, 12. Chicago, 1933. Several important epigraphic projects are described.

Caminos, Ricardo A. "The Recording of Inscriptions and Scenes in Tombs and Temples." In *Ancient Egyptian Epigraphy and Paleography.* Metropolitan Museum of Art, pp. 3–25. New York, 1976. An excellent review of the historical development of epigraphy and a critical evaluation of various epigraphic methods.

Caminos, Ricardo A. "Epigraphy in the Field." In *Problems and Priorities in Egyptian Archaeology,* edited by Jan Assmann, Günter Burkard, and Vivian Davies, pp. 57–67. London, 1987. The problems of documenting the graffiti and rock shrines of Gebel el-Silsila are presented, as well as the urgency in documenting such vulnerable records.

Der Manuelian, Peter, and Christian Loeben. "New Light on the Recarved Sarcophagus of Hatshepsut and Thutmose I." *Journal of Egyptian Archaeology* 79 (1993), 121–155.

Desroches-Noblecourt, Christiane. *Le Petit Temple d'Abou Simbel,* vol. 2. Paris, 1968.

*The Festival Procession of Opet in the Colonnade Hall.* Reliefs and Inscriptions at Luxor Temple, vol. 1. Epigraphic Survey, Oriental Institute Publications, 112. Chicago, 1994. An example of facsimile publication combining *in situ* remains with considerable thematic restoration, based on the placement of block fragments.

Fischer, Henry G. "Archaeological Aspects of Epigraphy and Paleography." In *Ancient Egyptian Epigraphy and Paleography*, pp. 29–50. New York, 1976. An excellent review of the chronological, monumental, and social significance of hieroglyphic inscriptions.

Fischer, Henry G. *The Orientation of Hieroglyphs, Part 1: Reversals.* Egyptian Studies, 2. New York, 1977. A series of articles on the phenomenon of hieroglyphic sign reversals on private and royal monuments and the contextual reasons for them.

Lauffray, Jean. "Les 'Talatats' du IXᵉ pylône et le *Teny-menou*." *Karnak* 6 (1978–1980), 67–89. The reconstruction of an entire wall from one of Akhenaten's temples at Karnak, based entirely on remains no longer *in situ*.

Sauneron, Serge. *Esna.* 8 vols. Cairo, 1959–1982. An outstanding example of the publication of the inscriptions of an Egyptian temple; uses hieroglyphic fonts, schematic decorative context, and architectural data.

Smith, Ray W., and Donald Redford. *The Akhenaton Temple Project,* vol. 1: *The Initial Discoveries.* Warminster, 1976. Discusses an early computerized method of reconstructing the decoration of a temple that now consists only of numerous block fragments.

Traunecker, Claude. "Les Techniques d'épigraphie de terrain: principes et pratique." In *Problems and Priorities in Egyptian Archaeology,* edited by Jan Assmann, Günter Burkard, and Vivian Davies, pp. 261–298. London, 1987. An excellent discussion of methods of documentation in conjunction with the effective retrieval of architectural data.

Wilkinson, Charles, and Marsha Hill. *Egyptian Wall Paintings: The Metropolitan Museum of Art's Collection of Facsimiles.* New York, 1983. A catalog of painted facsimiles by Norman and Nina de Garis Davies held by the Metropolitan Museum; many reproduced in color, with a commentary on their epigraphic work and the techniques of the ancient Egyptian artist.

PETER DORMAN

**EPITHETS.** In the language of ancient Egypt, epithets are words or phrases, typically laudatory, which describe a deity or person. They occur alongside names and titles, from which they are frequently difficult to distinguish, and they serve similar purposes: to identify and vivify statues and images; to characterize the ideal attributes of individuals and their offices; to legitimize authority; and to perpetuate cult practices.

**Epithets of Deities.** Divine epithets display great variation. As Erik Horning (1982) noted, they are not simply honorific phrases but rather define the nature and sphere of influence of the deities they describe—hence they make the gods tangible. Each additional epithet increased the scope and variety of a deity's power, so that major gods—such as Amun-Re, Ptah, and Osiris—acquired long lists of epithets. Individual epithets, however, were not restricted to particular deities. Partly due to the overlap in the nature and attributes of gods and goddesses, the same epithets were often applied to different deities.

The largest category of gods' epithets includes those that emphasize divine authority, such as *nṯr ʿȝ* ("The Great God") or the less common *nṯr wr*, which is nearly identical, although more restricted, in meaning. Several epithets introduced by the word *nb(t)* (Lord/Mistress), also fall into this category, among the most common being "Lord/Mistress of Heaven" (*nb(t) pt*), "Lord of *maat*" (*nb mȝʿt*), and "Lord of Eternity" (*nb nḥḥ*).

Epithets also refer to more specific divine attributes. For example, as the state god of Egypt, Amun is called "Lord of the Thrones of the Two Lands" and "King of the gods"; Ptah, as a creator god, is "The One Who Bore the gods"; Thoth is "The Straight Plummet in the Scales"; and Anubis, Osiris, and other deities of the necropolis, are "Lord of the Sacred Land." Epithets of this type are extremely numerous and varied.

Another large class of epithets refers to the topography of local cults. Ptah of Memphis, for example, is called "South of His Wall." Many topographical epithets of this type were formed by combining such words as "lord" (*nb*), "foremost" (*ḫnty*), and "in" (*ḥry-ib*), with the toponym of a sanctuary; thus, Osiris is "Lord of Abydos" and Hathor is "Mistress of Dendera."

Epithets may also reflect the physical attributes and iconography of deities, including their animal forms, characteristic attire, crowns, staffs, and poses. Thoth, for example, is the "Great Ibis," Amun and Min are both "Tall of Feathers," and Ptah is "Benevolent of Appearance." Goddesses, especially when part of a local triad, may be said to be "beloved" (*mrt*) of their consorts or fathers; thus, Sekhmet is "Beloved of Ptah" and Mut is "Beloved of Amun."

**Royal Epithets.** Kings were designated by a variety of epithets, many referring to a pharaoh's divinity. When such epithets accompanied a representation of the king, they endowed it with a quasi-divine status, just as the epithets of deities empowered divine images. In some cases, the king is actually called a god, by direct association with a deity or with epithets such as "The Good God" (*nṯr nfr*). He may also be given divine attributes: "One Who Illuminates the Two Lands," "One Who Lives on *maat*," or "Lord of Eternity." Other epithets associate him less directly with the deity, using metaphors such as "image" (*tit*) or "likeness" (*mity*) of a god or goddess, a practice less common in nonroyal epithets. Akhenaten stressed his exclusive relationship with the sun god by calling himself "The Unique One of Re." Kings were also called "beloved" (*mry*) or "son" (*sȝ*) of a deity. While "love" may be reciprocal, it very rarely proceeds from the lower ranking individual to the higher; therefore, the king is usually described as the recipient of divine love, rather than one who loves the god. Hence, both *sȝ* and *mrr* represent the king as subordinate, but directly related, to the gods.

Royal epithets also refer to the role of the king and the office of kingship. The king's immortality is emphasized by the ubiquitous royal epithet *di ʿnḫ ḏt*, "Given Eternal

Life." Many epithets, such as "Lord of All Foreign Lands," "Lord of All that the Sun Disk Encircles," and "Lord of All," stress the scope of royal authority. Others refer to the pharaoh's responsibility for maintaining world order, portraying the king metaphorically as creator, priest, judge, military leader, and protector of his people. Closely related are epithets involving the individual king's personal success, such as "Enduring of Monuments," "He Who Smote the Foreign Rulers," and so on.

**Epithets of Officials.** Among the most common nonroyal epithets are honorific phrases, such as "Vindicated" (*mꜣꜥ-ḫrw*), "Venerated" (*imꜣḫ[w/y]*), and "Possessor of a Venerated State" (*nb imꜣḫ*), which usually occur in the offering formulas in tombs and on stelae. Common as a nonroyal epithet from the First Intermediate Period onward, "vindicated" refers to the successful outcome of divine judgment, although it could refer to the living (including royalty) as well as to the dead. From as early as the Old Kingdom, "venerated" refers both to respected elder persons and to the honored dead. In many cases, people are described as "venerated by" (*ḥr*) deities, particularly those associated with the afterlife.

Unlike kings, private citizens are rarely associated directly with gods or goddesses, although from the Herakleopolitan period onward, the dead were identified with Osiris. Like royal epithets, however, nonroyal epithets could stress the skills and attributes of an individual by comparing them to a god, using phrases such as "Truly Precise, like Thoth." Officials were also described as "beloved" (*mry/t*) of deities, especially those associated with local cults.

A great many epithets stressed royal favor. Officials often claimed to be "loved" (*mry*), "favored" (*imy-ib*), or "praised" (*ḥsy*) by the king, or to be "The One Who Does Everything He Praises" (*irr ḥsst.f nbt*). More specific epithets concerning royal favor refer to the officials' actions on behalf of the king, such as on military or quarrying expeditions; to their obedience; or to their ability to satisfy (*ḥtp-ib* or *mḥ-ib*) the king.

A large and diverse class of epithets includes references to personal attributes, emphasizing interaction with peers, and drawing upon the subject matter of biographical and didactic literature. Such epithets describe officials as being wise, just, generous, accurate, eloquent, modest, fair toward subordinates, and efficient in carrying out their duties.

[*See also* Names; *and* Titulary.]

### BIBLIOGRAPHY

Anthes, Rudolph. "The Original Meaning of *mꜣꜥ-ḫrw*." *Journal of Near Eastern Studies* 13 (1954), 21–51. Discusses the origins and meaning of this very common epithet, with a summary of earlier scholarship on the subject.

Barta, Winfried. *Aufbau und Bedeutung der altägyptischen Opferformel.* Glückstadt, 1968. Describes the development of the offering formula and associated epithets throughout Egyptian history, with numerous examples.

Barta, Winfried. "Königsbezeichnung." *Lexikon der Ägyptologie,* edited by Wolfgang Helck and Wolfhard Westendorf, vol. 3, cols. 477–481. Wiesbaden, 1980. Summarizes titles, epithets, and designations of the king.

Breasted, James Henry. *Ancient Records of Egypt: Historical Documents from the Earliest Times to the Persian Conquest.* 5 vols. Chicago, 1906–1907; London, 1988. English translations and brief commentaries on Egyptian royal and nonroyal documents; the renderings are often outdated, but the series remains the most thorough treatment of Egyptian historical records in English, with many examples of royal epithets (nonroyal epithets were sometimes omitted).

Christophe, Louis A. "Les divinités de *Papyrus Harris I* et leurs epithètes." *Annales du Service des Antiquités de l'Égypte* 54 (1956), 345–389. Listing of deities mentioned in the Papyrus Harris, with an inventory of all the epithets used to describe them; describes temple donations by Ramesses III and Ramesses IV and is one of the most comprehensive primary sources for divine epithets.

Doxey, Denise M. *Egyptian Non-Royal Epithets in the Middle Kingdom: A Social and Historical Analysis.* Leiden, 1998. In-depth treatment of nonroyal epithets from the Middle Kingdom, with numerous references and examples.

Hornung, Erik. *Conceptions of God in Ancient Egypt: The One and the Many.* Translated from German by John Baines, pp. 86–100. Ithaca, 1982. (Orig. pub. *Der Einer und der Vielen.* Darmstadt, 1971). This section of Hornung's larger work on the nature of Egyptian deities focuses on their epithets, notes the function of epithets, and the ways in which they were applied to various deities.

Janssen, Jozef M. A. *De Traditioneele Egyptische Autobiographie vóór het Nieuwe Rijk.* 2 vols. Leiden, 1946. Volume 1 lists epithets and other phrases that appear in nonroyal biographies from the Old and Middle Kingdoms; volume 2 provides commentary on their grammar, meaning, and development.

Kuhlman, Klaus. "Götterepitheta." In *Lexikon der Ägyptologie,* edited by Wolfgang Helck and Wolfhart Westendorf, vol. 2, cols. 683–684. Wiesbaden, 1977. Concise, accurate, and well-documented summary of the categories of divine epithets.

Lichtheim, Miriam. *Ancient Egyptian Literature: A Book of Readings.* 3 vols. Berkeley, 1973–1980. English translations of selected Egyptian stories, religious texts, and monumental inscriptions; with introduction, commentary, and bibliography. Provides examples of selected divine, royal, and nonroyal epithets.

Lichtheim, Miriam. *Ancient Egyptian Autobiographies, Chiefly of the Middle Kingdom.* Frieburg, 1988. Translation of and commentary on Old Kingdom, First Intermediate Period, and Middle Kingdom biographies, primarily from Abydene stelae.

Simpson, William Kelly. "Amor deii: *nṯr mrr rmṯ m tꜣ wꜣ* (Sh. Sai. 147–148) and the embrace." In *Fragen an die altägyptischen Literatur: Studien zum Gedenken an Eberhard Otto,* edited by Jan Assman, et al., pp. 493–498. Wiesbaden, 1977. Analysis of epithets introduced by the phrase "beloved of . . . ," which notes that such epithets typically refer to love passing from a superior to a subordinate.

DENISE M. DOXEY

**EQUINES.** Two main species of the genus *Equus* were utilized in ancient Egyptian society: the asses/donkeys (*Equus asinus*) and the caballine horses (*Equus caballus*). Both species were domesticated and are capable of producing hybrids.

Horse, *ssmt* in Middle Egyptian (derivation unknown;

and *ḥtr* in Late Egyptian) was used to describe a "team" or "yoked animal," and therefore a member of a two-horse chariot team. The horse is native to the Zagros Mountains and Iranian uplands, where it was first domesticated. Sumerian texts refer to the "donkey of the mountain" (*anše.kur.ra*), but its domestication postdates the third millennium BCE. Archaeological evidence suggests that by 1900 BCE, the horse had been introduced into Cyprus, and by 1800 BCE into the Troad, but the animal was still not fully accepted in Mesopotamia in the Middle Bronze II period. Certainly by the sixteenth century BCE, the horse had been introduced into Egypt, probably (though not certainly) during the Hyksos invasion, because horses are mentioned in the first Kamose text dealing with the expulsion of the Hyksos.

The earliest physical evidence of equines in Egypt comes from a horse burial found at the fortress at Buhen. Difficulties exist in dating the remains, owing to problems of stratigraphy. A study of the horse's dentition, however, shows that it was controlled with a bit—a practice that postdates the Middle Kingdom. Horses first appear in the artistic record at the beginning of the eighteenth dynasty, and they are well documented in the Egyptian wars of conquest of that period. Horse-drawn chariots are well known, forming a major contingent of the armies of the day—with the chariot-warrior (*snni*) becoming an important new officer class. The Karnak annals of Thutmose III lists 2,041 horses among the booty taken at the battle of Megiddo, including six stallions and numerous foals. From northern Syria, Hurrian documents of late New Kingdom times preserve prescriptive manuals that give instructions on the training and care of war horses. Military barracks, where soldiers were trained and registered, also functioned as stables that could, in some cases, house up to two hundred horses.

Besides their use in the military, horses were also utilized for hunting, again in concert with the chariot. Horseback riding was not favored by the Egyptians, in general, the animal probably being regarded as a less than dignified means of transportation. The care of horses and their use in recreation were favored by royalty to the extent that it became a recognized cliché corresponding to social reality. Both Amenhotpe II and Thutmose IV loved their horses, as did all the warrior kings of the nineteenth dynasty. While trade in horses is attested in the early Iron Age, there is no reason to question the genuine attachment of kings to their equines. The Piya Stela, which vilifies Tefnakhte for his mistreatment of horses, describes Tefnakhte's escape on horseback as an ignominious retreat. A stela of Amenhotpe III depicts prisoners of war being transported on the backs of the king's chariot team. Artistic representations of Egyptian horsemen from the late eighteenth dynasty and from Ramessid times suggest that they may be grooms, military scouts, or outriders.

Horses were not associated with Egyptian deities in any context. Yet the Syrian goddess Astarte, who enjoyed some popularity in the eighteenth dynasty and Ramessid period, was portrayed in Egyptian painting and relief on horseback in the guise of a war goddess.

The donkey (*Equus asinus*) is possibly an indigenous African domesticate. A species of wild ass (*Equus africanus*) is known to have inhabited northeast Africa, extending from Nubia to at least the southern part of the Nile Valley and also to parts of the Eastern Desert and the Western Desert. Physical remains of the wild African ass in Egypt are known from Late Paleolithic levels at several sites in the Western Desert, as well as at Kom Ombo; from Early Neolithic sites, remains are known in the Faiyum. Comparative physiological studies provide a strong indication that the wild African ass is the progenitor of the domestic donkey. By the late Predynastic period, the donkey is a domesticate and appears in the record in the Early Dynastic period.

Throughout Egyptian history, the donkey was an important beast of burden and functioned as the primary means of conveyance on trade caravans and mining expeditions. The sixth dynasty Elephantine-based official Harkhuf reported that he returned from one of his missions to Nubia with three hundred donkeys laden with all sorts of trade goods, and his near contemporary Sabni took one hundred laden asses with him when he went south to recover the body of his father. Farmers sometimes employed donkeys to tread out the grain.

There is no certain evidence for the breeding and use of mules in pharaonic Egypt. It has been suggested that they are represented in Thebes (tomb 57; time of Amenhotpe III), but others have identified the animals in question as onagers (wild asses, *Equus hemionus onager*) of Central Asia.

**BIBLIOGRAPHY**

Brewer, D., D. B. Redford, and S. Redford. *Domestic Plants and Animals: The Egyptian Origins.* Warminster, 1994.

Littauer, M. A., and J. H. Crouwel. "The Origins of the True Chariot." *Antiquity* 70 (1996), 934–939.

Pardu, D. *Les textes hippiatriques.* Paris, 1985.

Rommelaere, C. *Les chevaux du nouvel empire.* Bruxelles, 1991.

Schulman, A. R. "Representations of Horsemen and Riding in the New Kingdom." *Journal of Near Eastern Studies* 16 (1957), 263–271.

Störk, L. "Pferd." In *Lexikon der Ägyptologie*, 4: 1009–1013. Wiesbaden, 1982.

SUSAN REDFORD

**EROTICA.** Ancient Egyptian erotica are manifested in pictorial representations—figurines of clay, faience, or stone, wall paintings, papyrus and leather scrolls, ostraca, and other media—and in the texts of love poems, magic spells, tales, and treatises on subjects such as medicine, dreams, local customs, and calendars. The sources are rather scattered; most are of New Kingdom date or later, and the majority of erotic figurines and spells date to Greco-Roman times. Some information may also be gathered from classical authors writing on Egyptian matters. The subject is interlinked with sexuality and fertility, which for the Egyptians exceeded the boundaries of life on earth; it is not always easy to determine whether an object was thought to bring about fertility on earth or to assist in rebirth in the hereafter, if indeed it was not simply fashioned to amuse the owner.

In its most tangible form, erotic intent is apparent in numerous figurines dating especially to the Late and Greco-Roman periods. Such objects may be fashioned of clay or stone, or later, of blue or green faience. A common motif is sexual intercourse, with the male participant sporting a huge phallus; the figure of the woman has often broken off, leaving the group incomplete. Musical instruments are often involved in such representations—for example, an angular harp of which the phallus may seem to form a part. Larger figurines of limestone may pursue the theme of musical accompaniment to sexual intercourse, or the group of two participants may be extended to include a number of "helpers." The purpose of these figurines may be magico-religious, reflecting the life-giving activities of the goddess Isis.

The most significant erotic document from ancient Egypt is the so-called Erotic Papyrus in the Museo Egizio in Turin. It dates from the New Kingdom (c.1200 BCE) and shows an orgy in the form of a cartoon, presented on the same scroll as illustrations to satirical tales involving animals. The tales have no accompanying text, but fragments of Hieratic text remain among the twelve erotic illustrations. The participants in this orgy are male and female (at least two different men are shown, along with women who have at least three different hairstyles); there are also a number of helpers. Each scene shows a variation on the theme of sexual intercourse, and the text leaves no doubt about its nature, since it renders scraps of the conversation by the participants, concerning their activities. Among the paraphernalia at hand in the establishment are a bed and a stool with a cushion, a chariot drawn by two pubescent girls, musical instruments, a jar used as a dildo, a mirror, and cosmetics. The lotus flower (symbol of love and sexuality) and a twining plant that may be convolvulus (morning-glory) emphasize the erotic atmosphere; both plants are otherwise also found in scenes dealing with conception, birth, and rebirth. Completing the picture are a vervet monkey on the chariot and a duck's head decorating the lyre—both of these animals are exponents of female sexuality.

On this New Kingdom scroll, the motif and style of illustration are related to material found at Deir el-Medina,

the workmen's village that was the home of those engaged in excavating and decorating the tombs in the Valley of the Kings. A great many ostraca were found there, a number of which bear drawings of an erotic nature, from naked women with or without musical instruments to variations on the theme of intercourse. A rare fragment of leather, discovered at Deir el-Bahri (now in the Metropolitan Museum of Art in New York) shows an interesting fragment of an erotic occasion in which more than two persons take part. A woman kneels under a grapevine playing a harp, the sound of which arouses a man dancing or running in front of her. It appears that he carries a bundle of straps or similar objects. The feet and ankles of another kneeling woman appear at the edge of the fragment.

A wall painting excavated in one of the houses at the village of Deir el-Medina depicts a dancing musician playing the double oboe, clad in flimsy garments and with tattoos of the god Bes on her upper thighs. She performs in the shade of a convolvulus vine. Perhaps this is the physical setting of the orgy depicted on the papyrus and leather scrolls. The wall painting was situated on one of the walls of a kind of alcove, taken by some to be a bed; others see such a raised podium as a shelf for ancestral busts.

That establishments catering to the needs of the flesh existed is suggested by the discovery at Saqqara of a series of rooms that have been called "Bes chambers" because of their large-scale decoration, in relief, of the god Bes with female companions. Because of their lavish decoration, the chambers may well have had some ritual function rather than being a mere brothel. According to literary references, such places existed. One tale from the Late period relates how the goddess Isis had to seek refuge in a house full of women of different rank when she was fleeing with her son Horus. That women could be bought for money or merchandise is also evident from literary texts such as the "Story of Setne and Tabubu," or Herodotus' report on the daughter of King Khufu.

Prostitution carried out under the auspices of a temple probably existed in Egypt, at least in the later phases of its long history. Strabo, a Greek historian who traveled in Egypt around 25 BCE, mentions child prostitutes in the temple of Amun. The god Amun is indeed credited with having a "harem," and although the titles of some of his female associates hint at sexual matters, no detailed information is available.

Although explicit erotic images are perhaps less abundant in Egypt than in some other ancient civilizations, the subject was most frequently treated in symbolic fashion. The texts, however, are quite straightforward in their vocabulary. The expressions for sexual activities are extensive; there are at least fifteen words for "copulating," including the biblical "knowing."

In the world of the gods, it is related that the primeval

god, Re-Atum, created the world by masturbating and impregnating himself; there was no female in the world, and none was needed. The act was reenacted, if not in reality then at least in spirit, in temples where a priestess bore the title "Hand of the God." Amun-Re, the mighty god governing the acts and destiny of the rulers of the New Kingdom, enters the stage as father of royal offspring in an even more human fashion. In the guise of the king, he seduces the queen. Emotions come into the picture as well, for we are told:

> When smelling the divine scent, she woke up, and she smiled to him . . . he lusted after her, and he gave her his heart. He allowed her to see him in his real god's figure, having come close to her. She rejoiced at his virility, and love for him flowed through her body . . . thereupon the god did what he wished with her. She made him rejoice over her, and she kissed him. She said, "How splendid it is to see you face to face. Your divine strength engulfs me, your dew is all through my limbs." The god once more did what he wanted with her.

Although the text is mundane, the accompanying illustrations make it clear that this is literally a union made in heaven. It is the most detailed description of sexual intercourse from ancient Egypt, and an official one at that, since it was inscribed on the walls of three temples, with different queens playing the female lead.

Among ordinary human beings, erotic matters were treated as affection, as sexual attraction, or in purely legal terms. The last two are treated straightforwardly, however much modern translators attempt to vary or modify their vocabulary. Excerpts from court cases at Deir el-Medina give a vivid picture of the goings-on at that locality, where the regular ten days' absence of husbands would leave their wives ample opportunity for extramarital relationships. Tales and letters dating from the New Kingdom to the end of pharaonic times elaborate on the theme of physical pleasure in a romantic setting, but not without mentioning the punishment that befell those who were discovered in adultery.

References to sexual intercourse can be gathered from stray passages in various texts. The Demotic "Story of Setne and Tabubu" describes in a most dramatic way the advances and demands made by the beautiful Tabubu, who even persuades Setne to kill his own children before she lets him have his way with her. In love lyrics, the erotic acts are veiled in symbolic imagery. There is talk of the young man "playing with the latch," of "fluttering door hangings," and "the sky coming down in the wind," and of the prominence of "fragrance" at the moment of climax (see the passage quoted above about Amun-Re). On such occasions, intoxicating beverages were often mentioned: "He begins to feel the strong ale"; she lets him spend a "merry" day (*nefer*, meaning "laden with sexuality");

"when I kiss her and her lips are open, I rejoice even without having drunk beer"; "she lets him become drunk and does whatever he says . . . her garment is below me and the 'sister' is moving about."

Although these quotations are most discreet, it would seem that the erotic imagination of the Egyptians was vivid. The so-called Dream Books are a good example. Two have survived, one dealing with a man's dreams (c.1175 BCE) and another with those of a woman (second century CE). The erotic dreams of the man range from seeing his phallus erect to having intercourse with his mother or sister, or with an animal (jerboa, kite, or pig). The woman's dreams list a whole range of animals as partners (among others, baboon, horse, donkey, wolf, crocodile, and the more fanciful mouse, bird, and serpent), as well as a peasant, a foreigner, and another woman.

These lists alone introduce the question of whether the sexual life of the Egyptian world included intercourse with animals and homosexuality. The former was referred to by Herodotus, who was told of a he-goat having had intercourse with a woman. Since he mentions the incident in connection with the city of Mendes in the Nile Delta, where goats were sacred, this may well have been a ritual act performed in connection with the cult of the animal. A similar situation is hinted at in connection with the sacred bull at Memphis, but this bull had cows at his disposal from time to time. A curse of very ancient date was "May a donkey copulate with your wife and children!" But bestiality does not seem to have been common practice in Egypt, as far as we know.

Homosexuality was not alien to the Egyptians. The sources are not abundant, and discussion has usually focused on the case of Horus and Seth and the possible deficiencies of Akhenaten. In the Horus/Seth case, the episodes of homosexual behavior are components of the ongoing struggle for power and have little to do with the inclinations of the two deities; in the Akhenaten case, the question is raised by the iconography. Stray references in the literature are ambiguous; for example, a passage in a woman's copy of the *Book of Going Forth by Day* (*Book of the Dead*) mentions not having had intercourse with a woman in the temple (it was obviously copied from a male version, with incomplete editing). Pictorial evidence (as seen through the eyes of the male artist) suggests a certain sexual rapport between women who may be shown embracing or playing with erotic symbols. In images of the Amarna period it is sometimes difficult to distinguish males from females, and other representations may also appear to depict two persons of the same sex in an intimate situation.

Incest was by no means a common practice among ordinary Egyptians, but it is attested in myths and in royal families. Polygamy, too, was an exception rather than the rule among ordinary people; the stylized nature of Egyptian representation makes it difficult to say whether a man had two wives at the same time or in succession.

When Egyptians found their sex lives lacking and wanted to change the state of affairs, even with a view to the hereafter, they had recourse to magic and remedies—usually, a combination of the two. A Middle Kingdom Coffin Text recommends a formula, "concerning every man who knows it, he will be able to copulate on this earth at night and at day, and the hearts of women will come to him at any time he desires" (Spell 426). For impotence, a physician in the New Kingdom would recommend a poultice for the penis, consisting of leaves of Christ-thorn and acacia ground in honey. In the third century CE, acacia seeds ground with honey applied to the male member are recommended for making a woman love her husband; the same papyrus scroll has a number of formulas for manipulating women's feelings, either to win a woman's love or to separate a couple.

[*See also* Fertility; *and* Sexuality.]

### BIBLIOGRAPHY

Manniche, Lise. *Sexual Life in Ancient Egypt*. London and New York, 1987. The only existing monograph on the subject, including numerous illustrations of erotica.
Omlin, Josef A. *Der Papyrus 55001 und seine satirisch erotischen Zeichnungen und Inschriften*. Turin, 1973. A lavish publication of the Erotic Papyrus, particularly useful for its color illustrations and photographs of additional erotica.

LISE MANNICHE

**ESNA,** the site anciently termed *Iwnjt, Snj,* or *T3-Snj,* is located north of Aswan and east of the Nile, at the geophysical frontier between Egypt's limestone and sandstone formations. The archaeological remains consist primarily of the remnants of a single hypostyle hall; this is located at a depth of some 9 meters (27 feet) beneath the accumulation of silt and debris upon which the present-day town rests. According to its inscriptions, the preserved edifice was begun during the reign of Ptolemy VI (180–164 and 163–145 BCE) and completed under Decius (249–251 CE)—whose inscriptions there were the last imperial hieroglyphs known to have been sculpted in ancient Egypt. Although some of the scenes and their accompanying texts belong to ancient Egypt's traditional religious repertory, several inscriptions exhibit a cerebral playfulness that rely on both the pun and rebus for their effect, as demonstrated by the litanies of Khnum on some of the columns and the so-called cryptographic texts, consisting almost exclusively of ram and crocodile hieroglyphs. These texts were studied by Serge Sauneron (1982), whose commentaries and incisive observations about Esna became classics of their kind.

The temple at Esna is dedicated to two distinctive deities and their respective entourages in an attempt to supply order and coherence to the bewildering plurality of then-current religious doctrines. Primacy of place is accorded Khnum, the creator god, accompanied by the goddesses Nebetu and Menhit, and the child god Heka, a personification perhaps of magical powers. His counterpart is the goddess Neith, associated with her theological son, the crocodile god Khamanefer, and Tutu, the supreme emissary deity of the ancient Egyptian pantheon. So long-lived and inextricably linked with creation is Khnum, as the hieroglyphs on the southwestern rear wall demonstrate, that present-day women of the village of Esna enter the temple and circumambulate the columns seven times in hope of a fruitful pregnancy, reaffirming one of the texts carved on the walls of the temple, namely, "Khnum gives sons to whomever calls upon him and daughters to whomever entreats him."

In addition to the richness of ancient Egyptian theological thought expressed by the hieroglyphic texts, the decoration of some of the column capitals exhibits drolleries exceptional in ancient Egyptian architectural orders. The sculpture on some of the capitals—of insects, perhaps to be identified as cicadas, perched on open papyrus umbels—on the columns at the northern side of the hypostyle are unique; they attest to the creative impulses of these anonymous architects. No less interesting are the scenes of the Roman emperors: for example, some scholars maintain that the only image of Nerva (r. 96–98 CE) preserved in ancient Egyptian style is to be found among the representations at Esna; the sibling rivalry between Caracalla and his brother Geta resulted in the excision of the image of Geta on the interior western wall by Caracalla, who ordered his assassination upon becoming emperor in 212 CE; and the images inscribed for Decius may in fact be usurpations, because his agents appear to have chiseled out the names of Philip the Arab (r. 240–249 CE) and his son, replacing them with his own without altering the original figural representations.

The temple is located about 200 meters (one-eighth mile) east of the Nile River. The street that links the temple to the landing terminates in one of the few quays to have survived from ancient Egypt. Made of limestone, it was inscribed for the Roman emperor Marcus Aurelius (r. 161–180 CE) and still functions as a mooring for some of the Nile cruisers that put into Esna.

The depth of the debris and silt relative to the site and the location of the modern town have impeded intensive archaeological exploration there, although there is some evidence of Predynastic occupation in the region. Esna appears to have been functioning as a cult center at least as early as the eighteenth dynasty, which would explain why, perhaps, Thutmose III continued to be commemo-

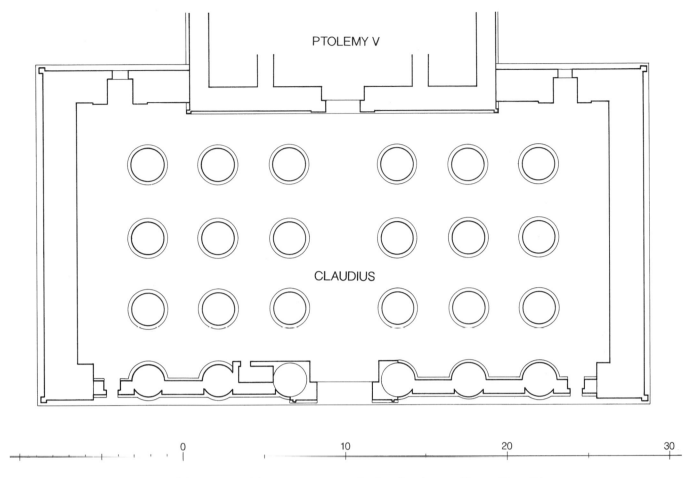

PTOLEMY V

CLAUDIUS

0        10        20        30

ESNA. *Plan of the pronaos of the Roman emperor Claudius for Khnum of Esna.* (From Dieter Arnold, *Temples of the Last Pharaohs.* New York, 1999.)

rated on the walls of Esna's Ptolemaic and Roman period temple. To the south of Esna, at Kommir, an extensive fish necropolis has been uncovered, containing numerous examples of mummified Nile perch (*Lates niloticus*), associated with the goddess Neith. Remains of an early Christian church have been cleared and partially reconstructed in the area just in front of the hypostyle hall; these remains are clear evidence of the enduring grip of Christianity on the region and should be studied in association with the Coptic monasteries of the area, Deir al-Suhada and Deir al-Fahuri and their suites of early Christian fresco decoration.

The completion in the 1990s of the Nile's locks at Esna has adversely affected the rise of the water table, with the result that ground water continues to intrude upon the site, percolating into the fabric of the temple at an accelerated and alarming rate. A major conservation effort is imperative if the temple, in its present state, is to be preserved.

## BIBLIOGRAPHY

Daress, Georges. "Remarques et notes." *Recueil de travaux relatifs à la philologie e à l'archeologie égyptienne et assyryriennes* 11 (1889), 81.

DeBono, Fernand. "Recherches préhistoriques dans la région d'Esna." *Bulletin de l'Institut français d'archéologie orientale du Caire* 69 (1971), 245–251.

Derchain-Urtel, Marie-Theresia. "Das Bildprogramm von Esna-eine Rettungsaktion." In *Religion und Philosophie im Alten Ägpten,* edited by Ursula Verhoeven and Erhart Graefe, pp. 107–121. Orientalia Lovaniensia Analecta, 39. Leuven, 1991.

Fowden, Garth. *The Egyptian Hermes: A Historical Approach to the Late Pagan Mind.* Princeton, 1993.

Kiss, Zsolt. *Études sur le portrait impérial romain en Égypte* Travaux du Centre Archéologie Méditerranéenne de l'Académie Polonaise des Sciences, 23. Warsaw, 1984.

Leroy, Jules. *Les peintures des couvents du désert d'Esna* Mémoires publiés par les membres de l'Institut français d'archéologie orientale du Caire, 94. Cairo, 1975.

Sauneron, Serge. *L'écriture figurative dans les textes d'Esna.* Esna, 8. Cairo, 1982.

ROBERT STEVEN BIANCHI

**ETHICS AND MORALITY.** Although the ancient Egyptians never dealt with ethics within a theoretical framework, their concept of correct moral conduct can be deduced from various written sources, particularly autobiographies and texts belonging to the wisdom tradition (Lichtheim, 1996). One of the difficulties in interpreting Egyptian sources, especially those intended for posterity, is that they do not always present us with what we would regard as objective truth. Statements such as "In very truth do I say all this and not as an 'office of the necropo-lis'" (from the autobiography of Ankhtifi), and assurances in inscriptions of Hatshepsut and Thutmose III that their claims are not exaggeration (e.g., Lichtheim 1976, p. 28), may not inspire confidence; nevertheless, they show that the Egyptians were aware of objective truth, and that they did not always expect to find it in an inscription. The texts tell us, however, what the ideal was perceived to be, even if this ideal was not always achieved, and the picture provided can be balanced to some extent by documents from the realm of everyday life.

**Early Sources.** Our earliest source for ethical values is autobiographies, attested from the fifth dynasty (c.2510–2374 BCE) onward, and usually addressed to succeeding generations. The official Nefer-seshem-re (c.2350 BCE) says:

> I have left my city, I have come down from my province,
> having done what is right (*maat*) for its lord, having
>   satisfied him with that which he loves,
> I spoke *maat* and I did *maat*, I spoke well and I reported
>   well. . .
> I rescued the weak from the hand of one stronger than
>   he when I was able;
> I gave bread to the hungry, clothing [to the naked], a
>   landing for the boatless.
> I buried him who had no son,
> I made a boat for him who had no boat,
> I respected my father, I pleased my mother,
> I nurtured their children. (Lichtheim 1973, p. 17)

Other contemporary texts include denials of misconduct: "Never did I take the property of any person"; "Never did I say a bad thing about anyone to the king (or) to a potentate because I desired that I might be honoured before the god"; "Never did I do anything evil against any person." The speakers identify with the generally recognized ethical values of the society of their time, hoping to obtain the approbation of the reader, but the ideals expressed in these biographies—justice, honesty, fairness, mercy, kindness, generosity—also reflect the central concept of *maat* (*mꜣꜥt*), the god-given cosmic and social order of the universe as established by the creator at creation.

**Pivotal Role of the King in the Old Kingdom.** Jan Assmann (1990, pp. 51ff.) has argued that with the unification of the country, this concept of *maat* was the governing and unifying ideology of the state, determined by the king, the focus of political unity and the god on earth. When at the start of his autobiography Nefer-seshem-re says that he left this world "having done *maat* for its lord, having satisfied him with that which he desires," he refers to the king who determines and upholds *maat:* "Heaven is at peace, the earth rejoices, for they have heard that he (the king) has put *maat* [in the place of wrong]" (Faulkner, 1969, Spells 1775–1776).

Autobiographical texts appear in Old Kingdom tombs because *maat* and the king were also central to funerary beliefs. One's fate after death depended on how one measured up to *maat*, the standard set by the king. He was the ultimate source of all funerary requirements; the traditional funerary prayer begins, "An offering which the king grants" (Assmann 1990, p. 244). Although in the course of time the king's role and the significance of *maat* in this system were to undergo some modification, the same ethical values expressed in Old Kingdom texts appear in later autobiographies. A good example from the reign of Merenptah (1237–1226 BCE) is that of An-hur-mose, high priest of the god Onuris at Thinis (Ockinga and al-Masri, 1988, pp. 37–40).

**Middle Kingdom Developments.** In the wisdom tradition of the First Intermediate Period and Middle Kingdom we find the first indications of a weakening of the dominant position of the king in statements that link *maat* more directly with the creator god. In the *Story of the Eloquent Peasant*, set in the reign of King Nebkaure of the ninth or tenth dynasty (c.2165–2040 BCE), we find the injunction "Do *maat* for the lord of *maat*"; but here the god rather than the king is meant (B1 334; Lichtheim, 1973, p. 181). In the same text, the peasant claims that his words expounding on *maat* "have issued from the mouth of Re himself" (B1 349f; Lichtheim, 1973, p. 181). A passage from the *Prophecy of Neferti* (P 51; Lichtheim, 1973, pp. 142f.) implies that it is the sun god Re who upholds *maat*, and that if disorder prevails, it is because he does not make his presence felt; this theme is also found in the *Admonitions of Ipuwer*, where one asks of the god: "Where is he today? Is he asleep?" (Lichtheim 1973, p. 160). This shift in emphasis from the king to the god is also evident in the hymn to the creator in the *Instructions for Merikare*, of whom it is said "for them (humankind) he predestined rulers, leaders to lift up the back of the weak" (P 135–136; Lichtheim, 1973, p. 106).

The new emphasis on the god can be linked with the failure of kingship at the end of the Old Kingdom. Although the king continued to have a central role in maintaining *maat* until the end of pharaonic history, he now did so as the god's representative on earth.

***Maat* in the Wisdom Tradition of the Middle Kingdom.** In the Middle Kingdom wisdom tradition we can see an attempt to reestablish the rule of *maat* after the preceding period of disorder (Assmann 1990, p. 217). It includes the genre known as "Complaints," which reflect the point of view of the scribal elite to which their authors belonged. They lament a state of affairs in which the social hierarchy has been reversed: "Behold, he who had nothing is now a possessor of riches"; "Behold, noble ladies [now travel] on rafts" (*Admonitions of Ipuwer* 7,10; 8,1; Lichtheim, 1973, p. 156). But this reversal of fortunes is a symptom of an underlying, more serious general breakdown in the order of society—in *maat*, without which society cannot function: "Behold, offices are broken into, their records stolen . . .; behold, the laws of the chamber are cast out, men walk on them in the streets, beggars tear them up in the lanes; . . . behold, the great council chamber is invaded" (*Admonitions of Ipuwer* 6,7 ff.; Lichtheim, 1973, p. 155). By lamenting the present disastrous state of affairs, these texts also give insight into expected social standards. The *Story of the Eloquent Peasant* also reaffirms the old view that proper behavior will ensure a happy afterlife: "Indeed, *maat* is for eternity, even to the necropolis it goes down, together with him who does it. He is buried and united with the earth, but his name is not obliterated from the earth. He is remembered because of goodness. It is the standard of god's word" (B1 334–342; Lichtheim, 1973, p. 181).

*Isfet:* **The Opposite of *Maat*.** Of the several terms that designate a concept diametrically opposed to *maat*, by far the most central is *isfet*, usually translated "sin" or "wrong." It appears as the antonym of *maat* as early as the Pyramid Texts (Faulkner, 1969, section 265); Khakheper-re-soneb laments, "*Maat* has been cast out while *isfet* is in the counsel chamber" (Lichtheim, 1973, p. 147); Tutankhamun "drove out *isfet* throughout the two lands, *ma'at* being established in her place" (Pritchard, 1969, p. 251). *Isfet* can be both spoken and done: "There was no *isfet* which came from my mouth, no evil thing which my arms did" (Lichtheim, 1988, p. 72); in chapter 125 of the *Book of Going Forth by Day* (*Book of the Dead*), the declaration of innocence begins, "Oh wide of movements, who comes from Heliopolis, I have not done *isfet*" (Lichtheim, 1976, p. 126).

Since *maat* also means "truth," another common antonym is *grg*, meaning "lie." In the *Book of Going Forth by Day*, chapter 126, the apes who sit at the prow of Re's bark are "ones who live from *maat*, who ingest *maat*, whose hearts are free of lies (*grg*), whose abomination is *isfet*; [the deceased asks] drive out my evil (*dwt*), remove my wrong (*isfet*)." Although *isfet* is used as an all-embracing term for "wrong," in ancient Egypt there was no concept of "general sin," a barrier between humankind and the gods which is the result of the general human condition.

**Judgment of the Dead.** Without the concept of general sin, it was theoretically possible to lead a life free of *isfet*. By teaching what behavior was compatible with *maat* and what was *isfet*, the instructions in wisdom were designed to assist one to achieve this. According to the traditional view, if people lived their lives according to the precepts of *maat* they would prosper, and society would function smoothly; transgressors were doomed to automatic failure. The king determined *maat*, and it was his task to ensure that it was upheld and *isfet* subdued. Yet even when the system functioned smoothly, there would doubtless have been cases that went against the rule, in which the unjust prospered. This will have been most obvious when the administration failed at the end of the Old Kingdom and in the First Intermediate Period; it is not surprising, therefore, that it is in a text composed after these events, the *Instructions for Merikare* (Lichtheim, 1973, pp. 97f.), that we first have evidence of the concept of a general judgment of the dead. Here the ultimate evaluation of a person takes place not in this life but in the next; consequently, although the wicked may at times prosper in this world, they will answer for their deeds in the next.

This development was to culminate in chapter 125 of the New Kingdom *Book of Going Forth by Day* (Lichtheim, 1976, pp. 124–132), which deals with the judgment before the god of the netherworld, Osiris. It includes two declarations of innocence in which the deceased denies having committed various crimes. Although the text is not a systematic treatise, it does give further insight into the ancient Egyptians' ethical values. Apart from such general statements as "I have done no injustice to people, nor have I maltreated an animal" or "I have done no wrong (*isfet*)," more specific faults are mentioned:

Crimes of a cultic nature: blasphemy, stealing from temple offerings or offerings to the dead, defiling the purity of a sacred place

Crimes of an economic nature: tampering with the grain measure, the boundaries of fields, or the plummet of the balance

Criminal acts: theft and murder

Exploitation of the weak and causing injury: depriving orphans of their property, causing pain or grief, doing injury, causing hunger

Moral and social failings: lying, committing adultery, ignoring the truth, slandering servants before their master, being aggressive, eavesdropping, losing one's temper, speaking without thinking

Chapter 125 is intended to equip the deceased to face the final judgment and, as in much of Egyptian funerary literature, appeal is made to the power of magic. Yet even if in their hour of greatest need the Egyptians were not averse to drawing on the magical power of the spoken and written word, this in no way diminishes the value of this text as a witness to their understanding of what constitutes proper moral behavior. Indeed, it is precisely because they took these moral standards seriously that they went to such lengths to avoid the consequences of not living up to them. Nor should one automatically draw the conclusion that because they appealed to magic, the Egyptians were ready to use unethical means to reach their desired goal. Chapter 30 of the *Book of Going Forth by Day*, which seeks to restrain the heart of the deceased from acting against him at the judgment (Lichtheim, 1976, p. 131) may seem to suggest this: the heart is abjured, "Do not stand up against me as a witness before the Lords of Possessions (the divine judges); do not say, regarding me 'He really did do that' concerning that which I have done." But the principle appealed to here—that accused persons cannot be forced to give evidence against themselves—is one also enshrined in present-day legal systems.

**Reality and *Maat* in the New Kingdom.** Not surprisingly, the ancient Egyptians did not always live up to the ethical standards they espoused. In the *Instructions for Merikare* there is indirect evidence for abuse of office among the royal officials who should uphold *maat:* "Make great your officials, that they keep your laws; he whose house is rich is not partial and a propertied man is one who does not lack. A poor man does not speak justly, one who says 'Would that I had!' is not upright. He is partial towards him whom he likes, favouring him who rewards (bribes) him" (P 7–9; Lichtheim, 1973, p. 100). The *Instruction to the Vizier*, recorded in the tomb of the eighteenth dynasty vizier Rekhmire, recognizes the problem of partiality on the part of officials; the king urges, "Regard one whom you know like one whom you do not know, one close to yourself like one far from your house" (Lichtheim, 1976, p. 23). But the vizier is also warned against the opposite extreme—he should not behave like an earlier vizier: "The saying is, that he impoverished his kindred in favour of strangers out of fear of that which might be said about him, (namely) that he was [partial]" (Lichtheim, 1976, pp. 22f.).

Surviving letters (Wente, 1990) and documents from the village of workers at Deir el-Medina (McDowell, 1990) also illustrate the foibles and weaknesses of the ancient Egyptians. From the end of the eighteenth dynasty (1315 BCE), evidence grows for a breakdown in standards and the spread of corruption. We find references to dishonest judges; in one prayer, Amun is "the vizier of the poor; he does not accept bribes from the guilty, he does not speak to the one who witnesses, he does not look to (favor) the one who makes promises" (Lichtheim, 1976, p. 111). We also have actual examples of corruption. A late nineteenth dynasty papyrus contains a long list of criminal charges

against a chief of workmen at Deir el-Medina; among other things, he is accused of having obtained his position by bribing the vizier, and a later vizier who punished him for other misdemeanors was himself dismissed by the king (Černý, 1929, p. 256). Another mid-twentieth dynasty papyrus records charges of large-scale embezzlement and misconduct against personnel of the temple of Khnum at Elephantine, including an unnamed priest (Peet, 1924).

Is this impression of a breakdown in moral and ethical standards a result of the destruction of the old concept of *maat*? As Brunner (1963) demonstrated, the most dramatic change in regard to *maat* was the loss of its traditional role as the mediating principle between god and humankind. Instead of a direct correlation existing between success or failure and adherence to or transgression against *maat,* in the later New Kingdom we find that success or failure depends solely upon the will of the god, whose plans are inscrutable, as we read in the *Instructions of Amenompe* (Lichtheim, 1976, pp. 146–163), which is steeped in the spirit of personal piety: "Indeed you do not know the plans of god" (22,5; 23,8). According to Amenompe, "Man is clay and straw, the god is his builder. He tears down, he builds up daily; he makes a thousand poor by his will, he makes a thousand men into chiefs" (24,13–17). It is arguable, however, whether one can go so far as to say that *maat* no longer has a place in this world (Assmann, 1990, p. 254), and that the growth in self-centered personal piety came at the expense of social coherence, leading to a growth in corruption and insecurity (Assmann, 1989, p. 80; 1990, pp. 265f.). For Amenompe, "*Maat* is a great gift of god, he gives it to whom he pleases" (22,5); *maat* is still there, but it does not operate automatically—rather, it too is subject to the will of the god. We have here a logical progression of the development, first noted in the wisdom tradition of the Middle Kingdom, whereby the god assumes an ever more direct role in human affairs; this tendency can also be traced in the institution of kingship and eventually led to the theocracy of Amun in the twenty-first dynasty.

To answer the question posed above, one needs to consider whether that which replaced the old view of *maat* was capable of doing so. The first point to note is that even if they do not often mention *maat*, the later teachings (e.g., Amenompe) and autobiographies (e.g., An-hurmose) still espouse the same ethical standards as the earlier sources and are just as interested in social cohesion. What changes is the argument in favor of these standards: in the traditional concept it is that they comply with *maat* and lead to success in this life and the next; now, it is that they are the will of the god. Success in this life is subordinated to one's relationship with the god, but the latter also determines one's fate after death. Thus at the end of Chapter 24, 13–17, Amenompe says, "Happy is he who reaches the hereafter when he is safe in the hand of god." There, at the final judgment in the "hall of double (complete) *maat*" where the eternal fate of a person is decided, *maat* still has a central role. There it is imperative that one be "safe in the hand of god," for, as Amenompe knows, "man is ever in his failure" and "there is no perfection before the god" (19, 15 and 22; Lichtheim, 1976, pp. 157, 158).

Rather than conclude that this understanding of *maat* and the will of the god was less capable of encouraging ethical behavior than the old concept that it replaced, one should look to other explanations for the apparently increased evidence for corruption in the later New Kingdom, such as a possible imbalance in our sources, or a deficiency in the administration. Rather than contributing to the breakdown of the old concept of *maat*, whereby the just prospered, the growth of personal piety simply filled the vacuum left by the failure of the old concept, which no longer tallied with everyday experience.

[*See also* Book of Going Forth by Day; Hell; Instructions for Merikare; Instructions of Amenompe; Judgment of the Dead; Maat; Paradise, *and* Piety.]

### BIBLIOGRAPHY

Assmann, Jan. *Ägypten. Theologie und Frömmigkeit einer frühen Hochkultur,* Stuttgart 1984. A stimulating interpretation of ancient Egyptian religion.

Assmann, Jan. "State and Religion in the New Kingdom." In *Religion and Philosophy in Ancient Egypt,* edited by James P. Allen et al., pp. 55–88. New Haven, 1989. An important study on developments in Egyptian religion in the New Kingdom.

Assmann, Jan. *Ma'at, Gerechtigkeit und Unsterblichkeit im Alten Ägypten,* Munich, 1990. An exhaustive study of the concept of *maat.*

Baines, John. "Restricted Knowledge, Hierarchy and Decorum." *Journal of the American Research Center in Egypt* 27 (1990), 1–23.

Brunner, Hellmut. "Der freie Wille Gottes in der ägyptischen Weisheit." In his *Les sagesses du Proche Orient ancien,* pp. 103–117. Strasbourg, 1963. Reprinted in *Das hörende Herz: Kleine Schriften zur Religions- und Geistesgeschichte Agyptens,* edited by W. Röllig, pp. 85–102. Freiburg and Göttingen, 1988. A seminal study on the change in the concept of *maat* in the New Kingdom.

Černý, Jaroslav. "Papyrus Salt 124." *Journal of Egyptian Archaeology* 15 (1929):243–58. Publication of a papyrus that provides evidence for corruption.

Edel, Elmar. "Untersuchungen zur Phraseologie der ägyptischen Inschriften des Alten Reichs." *Mitteilungen des Deutschen Instituts für Ägyptische Altertumskunde in Kairo* 13 (1929):1–90. Study of biographical texts of the Old Kingdom.

Faulkner, R. O. *The Ancient Egyptian Pyramid Texts,* Oxford, 1969. Translation of the oldest body of religious literature from Egypt.

Lichtheim, Miriam. *Ancient Egyptian Literature.* Vol. 1, *The Old and Middle Kingdoms.* Berkeley, 1973. Very good selection of sources in translation, as is the second volume.

Lichtheim, Miriam. *Ancient Egyptian Literature.* Vol. 2, *The New Kingdom.* Berkeley, 1976.

Lichtheim, Miriam. *Ancient Egyptian Autobiographies Chiefly of the Middle Kingdom.* Freiburg and Göttingen, 1988. A comprehensive collection of translations of biographies.

Lichtheim, Miriam. *Maat in Egyptian Autobiographies and Related Studies.* Orbis Biblicus et Orientalis, 120. Freiburg, 1992.

Lichtheim, Miriam. "Didactic Literature." In *Ancient Egyptian Literature: History and Forms,* edited by Antonio Loprieno, pp. 243–262. Leiden, 1996. The most recent study on didactic literature in ancient Egypt.

McDowell, A. G. *Jurisdiction in the Workmen's Community of Deir El-Medina.* Leiden, 1990. A detailed study of the administration of justice in the New Kingdom.

Ockinga, Boyo G., and Yahya al-Masri. *Two Ramesside Tombs at El Mashayikh.* Part 1. Sydney, 1988. Publication of an important biographical text of the late nineteenth dynasty.

Peet, T. Eric. "A Historical Document of Ramesside Age." *Journal of Egyptian Archaeology* 10 (1924), 116–127. Publication of a papyrus that provides evidence for corruption.

Pritchard, James B., ed. *Ancient Near Eastern Texts Relating to the Old Testament.* 3d ed. Princeton, 1969. Provides annotated translations of source material.

Wente, Edward. *Letters from Ancient Egypt.* Atlanta, 1990. Presents annotated translations of actual correspondence.

BOYO OCKINGA

## EUPHRATES RIVER. *See* Mesopotamia.

**EXECRATION TEXTS** were a class of formulas that functioned as destructive magic, designed to counteract negative influences. The performance of execration rituals centered on objects inscribed to identify the target of the magical act; they were then destroyed or otherwise symbolically neutralized. Figures made from unbaked clay were sometimes used in execration rituals. They were crudely fashioned into the shape of bound captives and inscribed with a name label on their chests, sometimes in red ink. Such figurines are attested from the end of the Old Kingdom. Several originated from the settlements of Balat and Elephantine; a set of three figurines was unearthed in the cemetery at Elephantine. Nubians and spirits of the dead were specified as targets in their inscriptions, and some personal names that lacked qualification might have referred to dead people as well. Both the spirits of the dead and foreigners—as owners of particularly dangerous magic—are attested in Egyptian magical and medical texts as mystical agents of illness. Spell 37 of the Coffin Texts attests the transfer of execration magic into the mortuary domain. The ritual instructions appended to that text advise the use of a wax figurine, inscribed with the name of the supposed foe, to be buried in the necropolis. The infrequency of archaeological examples of wax ritual objects probably underrepresents their original number, since wax is known to have been used frequently for magical purposes; yet burning the image of the victim during the ritual, thus destroying the object, was prescribed in related texts.

Small, uninscribed bound-captive figures of clay, mostly deriving from unknown contexts but attested into the Late period (747–332 BCE), might have functioned in a similar, ritual context. The same was very likely true for a series of other magical objects, such as clay balls containing human hair that are attested from the latter part of the Old Kingdom into the New Kingdom. Toward the end of the Old Kingdom, extensive execration rituals are attested as well. From the Giza cemetery, a series of four interrelated deposits are known, which include more than four hundred schematically made figurines packed in rough pottery jars. The figurines were inscribed with names, primarily those of Nubians; some have Egyptian names; and some are identified as chiefs and (probably) as military commanders. A few of the larger, tabletlike figures present a long text that lists a series of Nubian countries, appended with an early version of the "rebellion formula"; this lists evil actions, evil propaganda, and evil intentions that could become a threat to Egypt. Two large figures of the same date, but of unrecorded provenance, bear the names of Nubians and append a generalized formula directed against Nubian countries. These longer texts seem to transcend the scope of private magic, and they might accordingly stem from state ritual. In fact, it has been demonstrated from several spells of the Pyramid Texts that magic was used to counteract unloyal sentiments against the king. The focus on Nubia reflects the close contact between Egypt and Nubia during this time, since Nubian mercenaries then formed a regular component of Egyptian armies stationed near Memphis. Such mercenary troops might easily have provided the extensive name lists of the Giza deposits.

The most important find relating to execration rituals of the Middle Kingdom comes from outside the Egyptian fortress at Mirgissa in Lower Nubia. The artifacts date to the middle of the twelfth dynasty and might be contemporary with the founding of the fortress. There, a large pit was excavated that contained the remains of more than 175 pottery vessels inscribed with long execration texts; they had been broken intentionally during the ritual. This cache also contained an extensive series of other magical objects, including models of birds, ships, and parts of the human body. The remains of four inscribed limestone figures of captives were also found there that had possibly served as models for the texts on the pots. Careful analysis of the archaeological context revealed the phases of the ritual, during which even a human sacrifice occurred. Some similar limestone figures of captives were also found in the fortresses of Uronarti and Semna.

The execration texts from Mirgissa resemble the Old Kingdom prototypes in many aspects, although they were considerably expanded in scope and thoroughly systematized. There were sections devoted to Nubia, the Near East, Libya, and Egypt (the four human races according to Egyptian ideology), a section on individually named dead Egyptians, and a section on evil things, thoughts,

plans, actions, and even dreams. The sections on foreign peoples name their chiefs, countries, and allies, terminating with the "rebellion formula."

Execration texts following the same pattern are attested in a number of museum collections, although from less well-documented or even unknown contexts. For example, five large inscribed calcite (Egyptian alabaster) figures come from Helwan and are of an earlier date than the Mirgissa deposit; a series of inscribed pottery vessels are of a slightly later date than the Mirgissa find; and an important find of both large and small inscribed figures was excavated at the necropolis of Saqqara, dating to the end of the twelfth dynasty or the beginning of the thirteenth. These texts form part of a linear tradition although comparison with other texts reveals that the lists were expanded and refined in the course of time and that their content was updated. The names of foreign chiefs were changed according to the political situation, and the extensive sections on Nubia and the Near East provide crucial information, in particular on the languages spoken by their inhabitants and on their political organizations (although the identification of many toponyms remains problematic). The Nubian section covered the Nile Valley south of the Second and Third Cataracts, as well as the adjacent desert areas to the east, the country of the Medjay people. The Near Eastern section dealt with Palestine and southern Syria, touching the upper Orontes Valley to the north. In the formula, the space accorded these regions reflects their political and economic importance for Middle Kingdom Egypt and attests their close diplomatic contacts. In fact, Egyptian expeditions to those regions, to serve economic interests and to secure a political position through military means, are attested in other sources as well. The section on Libya is unusually sketchy, probably because contacts with Libya were less crucial to Egypt during that time and because the great mobility and the fluid social organization of Libyan tribes fit less easily into the Egyptian concept of "countries" headed by "chiefs."

The use of the standard formula in the Mirgissa execration ritual, as well as the overall uniformity of its basic content, proves that the texts were not tailored to meet specific crisis situations. Rather, they were characterized by the wish to forestall any potential threat from wherever it might arise and to prevent any uncooperative behavior on the part of Egypt's trade partners. This inclusive attitude was particularly clear in the sections on Egypt and on evil things. That the "rebellion formula" is set in the prospective tense throughout seems significant. Clearly, the political function of the execration rituals was to insure Egypt's internal stability and Egypt's external dominance in the most general sense.

Execration magic following the same general pattern is

attested in several religious texts from the Greco-Roman period. In the Jumilhac Papyrus, for example, the political aim of the performance is clearly stated, namely to prevent internal strife as well as to discourage attacks against Egypt from neighboring peoples—an explanation that conforms to the aims and character of earlier execration ritual.

## BIBLIOGRAPHY

Abu Bakr, Abdel Moneim, and Jürgen Osing. "Ächtungstexte aus dem Alten Reich." *Mitteilungen des Deutschen Archäologischen Instituts, Abteilung Kairo* 29 (1973), 97–133.

Assmann, Jan. "Spruch 23 der Pyramidentexte und die Ächtung der Feinde Pharaohs." *Hommages à Jean Leclant*, vol. I: *Bibliothèque d'Étude 106/1*, pp. 45–59. Cairo, 1994.

Osing, Jürgen. "Ächtungstexte aus dem Alten Reich (II)." *Mitteilungen des Deutschen Archäologischen Instituts, Abteilung Kairo* 32 (1976), 133–186.

Posener, Georges. *Princes et pays d'Asie et de la Nubie, Textes hiératiques sur des figurines d'envoûtement du Moyen Empire,* Suivis de remarques paléographiques sur les textes similaires de Berlin. Bruxelles, 1940.

Posener, Georges. *Cinq figurines d'envoûtement,* Bibliothèque d'Étude, 101, Cairo, 1987. Includes a comprehensive list of the known execration figures, with bibliography.

Redford, Donald B. *Egypt, Canaan, and Israel in Ancient Times.* Princeton, 1992. A discussion of the political situation in Palestine according to the testimony of the execration texts, on pages 87–93.

Ritner, Robert Kriech. *The Mechanics of Ancient Egyptian Magical Practice.* Studies in Ancient Oriental Civilization, 54. Chicago, 1993. Discusses execration rituals within the wider context of ancient Egyptian magic, on pages 110–190.

Sethe, Kurt. *Die Ächtung feindlicher Fürsten, Völker und Dinge auf altägyptischen Tongefässcherben des Mittleren Reiches,* Abhandlungen der Preussischen Akademie der Wissenschaften, 5. Berlin, 1926.

Vila, André. "Un dépot de textes d'envoûtement au Moyen Empire." *Journal des Savants* (1963), 135–160. Describes the archaeological context of the execration texts found near the fortress of Mirgissa in Lower Nubia, including an account of the pottery types and clay figurines, with discussion of the ritual during which the execration texts were deposited.

Wimmer, Stefan. "Neue Ächtungsfiguren aus dem Alten Reich." *Biblische Notizen* 67 (1993), 87–101.

STEPHAN J. SEIDLMAYER

**EXECUTION.** *See* Crime and Punishment.

**EXODUS.** The biblical traditions concerning the Exodus of the Israelites from Egypt are mostly preserved in the second book of the Hebrew scriptures. It recounts the memories of many events, from a time of slavery and oppression in Lower Egypt to the escape back to the homeland, after wandering for forty years in the Sinai Peninsula, under the guidance of a divinely appointed leader, Moses. Beginning with some introductory notes about the growth of the people of Israel in Egypt, the story leads to the appearance of the hero with an extraordinary past. He had been born a Hebrew, set adrift in a basket on the Nile in an effort to save him from death, and was found by an Egyptian princess who adopted him; Moses then grew up at the pharaonic court. As a young man, Moses killed an Egyptian overseer who was abusing Hebrew slaves and fled into the desert, where he learned of his own Hebrew heritage. There, he met his God, who revealed himself and chose Moses to lead Israel out of Egypt.

Moses then petitions the pharaoh, his stepbrother, to free the Israelites, but the request is denied. Moses warns the pharaoh about God's will on the matter, and soon a series of plagues descends on the Egyptians, with the last being the death of first-born sons. When the pharoah's son dies, he pretends to release the Israelites but sends his army after them. The army, is however, soon destroyed by a spectacular miracle, drowning in the Red Sea. Then for forty years, the wandering people are fed by divine provisions and at Mount Sinai, God gives Moses the Ten Commandments—the basic laws of Judaism. With that accomplished, the new generations lose their divinely inspired leader and finally enter the promised land of Canaan.

Traditional and fundamental exegeses seek interpretation of these texts primarily for their historical value. The canonical approach should not be confused with a treatment of the texts as literary works that have their own specific character and development. Biblical texts are written sources which may also be studied using the methodogical criteria of philological and linguistic research.

The *Book of Exodus*, as a text, has been the subject of many studies concerning its authorship. Longstanding critical analysis of the Hebrew grammar, vocabulary, and references has shown that there are the following: passages of Deuteronomistic and priestly origin from the Babylonian Exile and after the Exile, combined with some possibly pre-Exile material. The Exilic versions contain illustrations of the ten miraculous plagues and the spectacular crossing of the Red Sea. The central idea refers to the God of Israel dominating over foreign enemies and their gods, protecting his chosen people. The several stations of the escape route reflect an actual knowledge of the geography of the eastern Nile Delta, including names preserved in memory, such as Ramesses (Piramesse, the capital of the Ramessid kings), Pithom (*Ex.* 1.11), and possibly Pihachirot, which refers to the Delta area with the branches of the Nile. The tendency of these stories is to be seen as a view of the Babylonian Exile—so that the liberation from that Exile gains the character of a "second exodus," thus fulfilling the prophecy of the prophet Isaiah. Therefore, most of the *Exodus* account has a relatively late origin. Some possible pre-Exilic allusions to *Exodus* events offer different information from the relatively exhaustive illustrations of the priestly sources. Generally, they seem to present some genuine perspective within the genre of their specific context. So the "Song of Miriam" (*Ex.* 15.21), a hymn that possibly dates from dynastic times, celebrates the dominating God of Israel in mythological terms that may have origins from that period in the kingdom of Judah. The variants of the formula of God's leading Israel from Egypt were created not earlier than in the period of the two Hebrew kingdoms—Judah and Israel. The pre-Exile stratum of the *Exodus* tradition seems to have been written with criticism for the kingdoms of Judah and Israel concerning their problematic relations with Egypt.

The so-called Israel Stela from the fifth year of the reign of Merenptah, together with some reliefs from the temple of Karnak do not give sufficient information about details of an Exodus, because they seem to relate only to people living in the Palestine area. However, numerous textual indications from Egypt refer to the movements of bedouins—the Shasou (Eg., *Š₃sw*) in the southern Palestine region and in the Sinai Peninsula—and show some affinity to the biblical *Exodus* memories. Of great importance is the engraved illustration of the Shasou bedouins on their deportation to Egypt by Sety I, shown at the northern end of the great columned hall in the temple of Karnak. Furthermore, there were known Semitic laborers and workers in Egypt, as attested under the name "Aperu" (Eg., *'prw*). So the *Exodus* population may have consisted of Shasou and Aperu groups in not just one leave-taking but in several similar events. The memory of one or more such events may further be connected with persons of Semitic origin who entered upon a special career in Egypt. Thus representatives in politics, like the chancellor Beja or the court functionary Ramessesemperre under the Ramessids, have some features comparable to the biblical Moses, but it is not possible to identify them with the biblical leader and lawgiver. From the historical standpoint, there exists a serious possibility that several kinds of Exodus events happened both before and after the turn of the twelfth century BCE, especially with flight and repulsions. The routes of such variants may be the so-called Way of Horus or an uncontrolled way, which crossed the swampy area at Egypt's eastern border, to the south of the Ballah Sea (Heb., *yam suph?* = Eg., *p₃ ṯwf?*) into the southern parts of the Sinai.

An Egyptian view of the Exodus seems to be preserved in a story told by the Greco-Egyptian historian Manetho and referred to by the Roman-Jewish historian Josephus. There, the Exodus appeared as a repulsion of lepers under the lead of a certain Osarsiph (later named Moses), who taught contrary to Egyptian customs. Behind this story, the Egyptian experience with the monotheistic Amarna religion has been proposed; this view has even been stressed as the background to the biblical *Exodus*. So the Egyptian version should reflect an antagonism toward monotheism. The view critical to monotheism may relate to Egypt's longstanding animosity toward peoples from Near Eastern countries, such as the victorious Hyksos dynasty that ruled Egypt from its Nile Delta capital. The historical conquests by foreigners in the Delta can be seen as the fundamental background for all varieties of the Exodus idea in Egypt and perhaps in Israel/Judah.

The liturgy of the Jewish Passover (Pesach) celebrates the victorious God, who saved his people. Possibly the Hebrew term *paesaḥ* derives from the Egyptian *p₃ sḥw*, "the slaying [by God]," for the victory over his enemies and the protection of his Chosen People.

[*See also* Biblical Tradition; *and* Moses.]

## BIBLIOGRAPHY

Ahituv, Shmuel. "The Exodus—Survey of the Theories of the Last Fifty Years." In *Jerusalem Studies in Egyptology*, edited by I. Shirun-Grumach, pp. 127–132. Wiesbaden, 1998.

Assmann, Jan. *Moses the Egyptian: The Memory of Egypt in Western Monotheism*. Cambridge, Mass., 1997.

Bietak, Manfred. "Comments on the Exodus." In *Egypt, Israel and Sinai: Archaeological and Historical Relationships in the Biblical Period*, edited by A. F. Rainey, pp. 163–171. Tel Aviv, 1987.

Edelman, Diana Vikander. "The Creation of Exodus 14–15." In *Jerusalem Studies of Egyptology*, edited by I. Shirun-Grumach, pp. 137–158. Wiesbaden, 1998.

Görg, Manfred. *Die Beziehungen zwischen dem alten Israel und Ägypten*. Darmstadt, 1997.

Görg, Manfred. "Der sogenannte Exodus zwischen Erinnerung und Polemik." In *Jerusalem Studies of Egyptology*, edited by I. Shirun-Grumach, pp. 159–172. Wiesbaden, 1998.

Groll, Sarah I. "The Egyptian Background of the Exodus and the Crossing of the Reed Sea: A New Reading of Papyrus Anastasi VIII." In *Jerusalem Studies of Egyptology*, edited by I. Shirun-Grumach, pp. 173–192. Wiesbaden, 1998.

Redford, Donald B. "An Egyptological Perspective on the Exodus." In *Egypt, Israel and Sinai*, edited by A. F. Rainey, pp. 137–161. Tel Aviv, 1987.

MANFRED GÖRG

# F

**FAIENCE** is well represented in many collections of Egyptian artifacts, and yet it is commonly overlooked by visitors in the mistaken belief that it is either glass or glazed pottery. This view is unsurprising, particularly given the tendency of some collections to replace the term "faience" with an alternative, such as "glazed composition" so that a single material appears under a variety of headings in different collections. *Faience* may be defined as a nonclay ceramic with soda-lime-silicate glaze on a crushed silica body; the material is more correctly known as "Egyptian faience." The name was probably suggested through comparison by European travelers of its—frequently blue-green—glaze with those on a type of tin-glazed pottery known as faience, which was originally manufactured in Faenze, Italy, from medieval times. Since there is little chance of confusing the Egyptian material with the tin-glazed clay ceramic that is now called majolica, there seems little need to use the "Egyptian" element of the term or any of the numerous suggested alternatives.

**Glazing.** Although for faience the glaze is not complete until after firing, it is usually the glazing technique that is used as a means of subdividing the objects, glazing is treated here before the discussion of the shaping technology. Early accounts of faience production, such as that by W. M. Flinders Petrie in his *Tell el-Amarna* (London, 1894), assumed that it was glazed in the same way as pottery—namely, by applying a glaze to the exterior. This was a natural assumption, since the material seems to owe its origin to the Predynastic practice of producing objects of glazed quartz or steatite, probably in imitation of semiprecious stones, such as turquoise, lapis lazuli, and green feldspar. Such early pieces surely had applied glazes, but research since the 1960s has increasingly suggested that the earliest faience which, like glazed stone, appears during Predynastic times, may have employed a more diverse range of techniques.

The faience body material is silica, either made from sand or crushed quartz pebbles; after firing, light was reflected in a less uniform way than it would have been for an object of glazed quartz or steatite. The result, bright and often sparkling, probably made it prized as an imitation of semiprecious stones—as recognized in its ancient name, *ṯḥnt*, meaning "dazzling" or "shining." The way the transition from glazing objects of solid stone to ones of crushed silica came about is not known, although the Predynastic seems to have been a time of experimentation—and this may be the origin point for the three main glazing techniques used in pharaonic times. *Application glazing* of faience would have been similar to glazing quartz, with the object painted in a slurry or a powder of glazing mixture, made of quartz, lime, alkali, and colorant; these were simply crushed finely or fritted (see below) together, then crushed to a powder for application. The objects glazed by this means may show brush marks or drips of glaze, and the glaze may have clearly defined edges, where parts have been left uncoated to prevent it sticking to surfaces in the kiln. The body soaked up some of the glaze so that the boundary between it and the glaze is diffuse. Little interstitial glass is visible when examined under the Scanning Electron Microscope (SEM).

As well as application glazing, two other methods are known, and are believed to be present, from the Predynastic (although more work on this early material is still needed). Both are known as self-glazing techniques. The first is *efflorescence glazing*, in which the ground quartz is mixed with alkali salts, such that the carbonates, sulphates, and chlorides of either sodium or potassium are mixed with the quartz. Analytical studies, such as those by Kaczmarczyk and Hedges (1983), suggest that from Predynastic into Roman times the alkali was normally added as plant ash, rather than the mineral soda natron whose primary source is the Wadi Natrun. With firing, the salts migrate to the surface, where they form an effloresced layer that fuses to become a glaze. Examination of the body of such pieces with the SEM reveals a considerable quantity of interstitial glass, since the heating process fuses the mixture between the quartz grains. The technique is recognizable on an artifact because of the variable glaze thickness and because areas where it was in contact with the ground or other surfaces have little or no glaze.

The third glazing method is known as *cementation*, or the Qom technique (after a village in Iran where it was first observed in the 1960s). In this method, the artifact is buried in a mixture of glazing powder that contains lime, ash, silica, charcoal, and colorant; with firing, this mixture reacts with the surface of the object, leaving it with a fairly uniform overall glaze. The unreacted powder draws away from the object and does not become fused. Pieces glazed in this way do not show any marks from kiln furniture, the interface between glaze and body is well defined, and under the SEM very little interstitial glass is visible.

These three types of glazing have been recognized from the examination of ancient objects, yet Egyptian craftsmen may well have used some of them in combination. For example, a slurry of the efflorescent glazing mixture might be applied to objects where carving had cut through the original effloresced layer, as with certain decorated chalices. The three glazing techniques involve firing temperatures in the range 800–1000°C, although little evidence exists for the type of fuel used. Nicholson (1995) has unearthed charcoal that has been identified as the remains of the sycamore fig (*Ficus sycomorus*). The Roman kilns from Memphis were believed by Flinders Petrie to have been fueled with straw, but this seems improbable since straw burns so rapidly that very large quantities would have been needed (and even today straw is a valuable commodity in Egypt). Domestic rubbish, which is attested from the furnaces at Tell el-Amarna, is a much more likely source of fuel. Dung is also widely used as fuel in Egypt, and it may have been used in kilns and furnaces (but the writer has not seen it employed in this way among contemporary Egyptian potters) and it is not certainly attested from excavated kilns.

**Technology and History.** Unlike clay, which has smooth platelets that render the material highly plastic, ground quartz has angular edges, and as a result is more difficult to work. Quartz paste is thixotropic, thick at first but soft and flowing as it is deformed—although rapid deformation leads to cracking. It was assumed by modern researchers that the raw faience paste would have the properties of wet sand, making it extremely difficult to shape; however, in a series of experimental studies at the Rhode Island School of Design, Mimi Leveque has shown that if the quartz is ground very finely, it can be shaped easily, and that the grains adhere well rather than tending to crumble. This allows the material to be modeled by hand, as it was occasionally during Predynastic times, and more particularly to be roughly shaped by hand and then abraded once partly dry. Although many other crafts are represented in tomb scenes, giving at least some indication of how they were carried out, the production of faience is nowhere certainly attested. The only scene that may show it is from the tomb of Ibi (Aba) at Thebes (tomb 36) and belongs to the time of Psamtik I of the twenty-sixth dynasty. One man is shown grinding or rolling something while another is making some element of jewelry, but there is no identifying text, which severely limits the meaning of this scene. As a result, scientific and experimental studies have been invaluable in building knowledge of ancient faience manufacture.

Modeling combined with surface grinding seems to have been the preferred faience-forming method during the Predynastic and Early Dynastic periods. This view is based on the various studies of Pamela Vandiver (1982 and 1987), who examined artifacts of the period. No trace of manufacturing centers survives from that earliest developmental phase. Edgar Peltenburg in his study "Early Faience: Recent studies, Origins and Relations with Glass" (in M. Bimson and I. C. Freestone, eds., *Early Vitreous Materials*, London, 1987) reports that faience manufacture is essentially a "cold technology," more akin to stone working than to glass working or metallurgy, since the body shape is formed cold. There are however, clear links with pyrotechnology, particularly from the New Kingdom onward, and these links are of equal importance.

With the Old Kingdom, the dominant glazing technique became efflorescence and, with it, came increasingly sophisticated methods of shaping. The most notable was the forming of the tiles for the third dynasty pyramid complex of Djoser at Saqqara. The tiles were once thought to have been molded, but Vandiver's studies suggest that they were made by rolling the faience paste between two sticks that served to determine the width and thickness of the tiles, which were then cut to length. As a result, we find tiles with a very consistent width, but of varying lengths. The reverse of these tiles clearly shows that they were efflorescence glazed, since little glaze has formed where the back was ground away to leave a boss, which was then pierced for a wire attachment. Old Kingdom faience is by no means as unaccomplished as has sometimes been thought. Not only are the Djoser tiles known but also, from the fifth dynasty, a series of elaborate inlays and tablets are known from the mortuary complex of Raneferef at Abusir. Some were inlaid with white paste, as well as with gold leaf, which was then engraved. Old Kingdom faience-makers added to the blue and blue-green colors of the Predynastic, occasionally making white, black, and purple. This was also the period of the earliest faience factory evidence, as unearthed by the University of Pennsylvania Museum–Yale University–Institute of Fine Arts, New York University expedition to Abydos, under the direction of Matthew Adams. Abydos yielded a number of bowl-shaped pits lined with fired brick, which are thought to have been for firing faience; so far no traces of superstructure are known for the pits, so it is suggested that the faience was fired in lidded jars, to protect it from the direct effects of smoke and flames. Numerous fragments of misfired and broken faience were found at the site, which seems to date from the mid-Old Kingdom into the Middle Kingdom.

Vandiver (1982, 1987) believes the First Intermediate Period was the time during which the forming of faience objects around a core began, as well as the technique of marbleizing, whereby faience pastes of two colors were mixed together (neither technique is common). The mold-

FAIENCE. *Faience (Egyptian blue) head of a lioness, eighteenth dynasty, from Memphis.* (University of Pennsylvania Museum, Philadelphia. Neg. # S8–65466)

ing of faience may also have had its origins at this time, but it becomes more common during the Middle Kingdom, when vessels were sometimes shaped over a form. The use of a core to make shapes, such as the well-known hedgehog figurines, was also much more common during the Middle Kingdom, as was the widespread use of manganese as a decorative paint. In terms of glazing, cementation became popular in Egypt, although in Kerma (Sudan) there is evidence—runs or drips—of application glazing on tiles and other objects. George Reisner, in his *Excavations at Kerma IV–V* (Harvard, 1923), believed there was evidence for the wheel-throwing of faience; if correct, that would be the earliest known evidence. There is also factory evidence from Egypt, from the site of el-Lisht; this includes a kiln that may be reexcavated as part of the ongoing work of the Metropolitan Museum of Art at that site. Their excavations not only revealed a kiln, but from shaft 879 came the burial of an individual named Debeni, who held the title "Overseer of the Faience Workers." Although unclear if he was in any way connected with the nearby area identified as a faience workshop, it indicates that during the Middle Kingdom the making of faience was a recognized craft.

In the Second Intermediate Period, faience technology was developed, with marbleizing becoming more common and perhaps providing the inspiration for inlaying a faience paste of one color into a body of another color. That technique reached its peak during the New Kingdom. The Second Intermediate Period identified the further use of application glazing, following which it remained part of the Egyptian faience-maker's repertory. The New Kingdom is the period for which most is known about faience manufacture—largely the result of Flinders Petrie's work at Tell el-Amarna in 1891 and 1892, when he and Howard Carter discovered the remains of several "glass and glazing [or faience] works." From that account, faience and glass production seem to have existed side by side in the same workshops, as confirmed by Nicholson's excavations on behalf of the Egypt Exploration Society. A similar situation is thought to have existed at the Palace of Akhenaten's father, Amenhotpe III, at Malqata on Luxor's western bank.

J. Kühne noted in *Zur Kenntnis silikatischer Werkstoffe und der Technologie ihrer Herstellung im 2. Jahrtausend vor unserer Zeitrechnung* (Abhandlung der Deutschen Akademie der Wissenschaften zu Berlin, 1969) that the high proportion of interstitial glass found in some New Kingdom faience suggested its addition as ground glass. Analytical work at Oxford has, however, suggested that this interstitial glass is simply the result of the efflorescence glazing technique. The result is the same in both cases, however; the manufactured object is more durable. Thus the New Kingdom faience became suitable for small fragile objects, such as finger rings—many hundreds of which are known from Tell el-Amarna. These may have been given or sold on festival or other special occasions. Like the numerous amulets from the site, the rings were made by pressing faience paste into fired clay "open-face" molds. The shapes in the molds were probably impressions taken from originals in other materials, such as metal, wood, or even wax. Such molds (of which Petrie found some five thousand at Amarna) would have enabled the mass production of rings, amulets, and other objects. Usually the ring shank and bezel were made separately and subsequently luted together with faience paste; the two parts are sometimes of different colors—indeed bezels might even be of several colors—with inlaid hieroglyphs. During the New Kingdom, the faience worker's color palette was at its most extensive, with much use being made of yellow (not least by Amenhotpe III) and red—both then new colors—along with green, white, and the more traditional blue and blue-green. Some of those colors may be the result of adding ground glass.

Colors were used not only for monochromatic pieces or for the inlay in ring bezels but for ambitious architectural inlays. Three techniques have been recognized. The first is not really an inlay technique in the same way as the others but was used for making the well-known Amarna daisy tiles. A green tile was produced with a series of shallow circular depressions in it; after firing, the holes would be filled with yellow and white faience daisies that had been made separately; they were held in place with gypsum adhesive. The result was a joining of two pieces of faience. The other two techniques produced unified pieces. For one, a channel was cut into the main body color, then filled with faience paste of another color. The background was fairly dry, and the inlay was allowed to shrink away from it slightly; when fired, a small void became apparent around the inlay, giving a series of black lines around the inlaid pattern. For the other, the inlay paste was added early, so that the effects of differential shrinkage were less visible. Thus copper-based colors "bled" into the background color, which was usually white. After firing, this left a halo, which was used to striking effect—particularly on tiles showing foliage, where a kind of soft-focus image was achieved. The kind of glazing method used for the production of such tiles is not certain, although efflorescence is possible. Many of the tiles show three distinct layers in cross section: the glaze; a layer of very finely ground quartz; and a coarse ground quartz layer, often brownish. The fine layer helped give the object brilliance and was a technique known at least as early as the Old Kingdom, though it was rarely practiced before the Second Intermediate Period.

On the basis of his discovery of white quartz pebbles covered in glaze and sometimes adhering to pottery sherds, Petrie suggested that the floor of the furnaces at the glass and glazing workshops were covered in these pebbles and that the various glass and glazing operations were carried out in vessels that stood on them. The constant heating and cooling of the pebbles would eventually cause them to crack so that they could easily be ground up as a high-quality source of silica for use in glass or faience making, and it is likely that the fine quartz layer was made up of silica from such a source. While there is no doubting Petrie's evidence, his reconstruction should be questioned. He was quite explicit in stating that he found no furnaces for glass or glazing—only debris, from which he drew up a hypothetical outline of the process of glass and faience manufacture. Work at the Amarna site O45.1 has recently unearthed several circular kilns/furnaces, none of them with white quartz floors. The two largest of these furnaces probably served to manufacture glass but perhaps also blue frit, which might then be used as a colorant in faience. A smaller kiln may well have served for the firing of both pottery and faience, since both require a lower firing temperature than does glass. A potter's workshop is known from O45.1, along with open-face molds and fragments of raw glass and frit, strongly suggesting a link between these vitreous-material industries.

Faience and glass production are also recognized together at the important site of Qantir in the Nile Delta. As yet, no furnaces for glass or faience making were found there, although there were finds of numerous molds and waste products from both the glass and faience industry. Qantir is also the source of a series of polychrome tiles that show foreign captives—the Nine Bows, who were the traditional enemies of Egypt. They were probably parts of throne diases and other elements in the palace of Ramesses II; tiles of a similar type are known from the palace of Ramesses III at Medinet Habu. The coloring and standard of workmanship for these pieces are exceptionally high, with clothing details picked out in various colors. Qantir is also the find-spot of a faience lion some 70 centimeters (27.5 inches) high, one of the largest pieces of faience known (the other, a *was*-scepter of Amenhotpe II, had been made in sections and joined after firing). The link between the pyrotechnical industries was reinforced after the New Kingdom, and for this the chief evidence—several rectangular furnaces—came from a site excavated by Petrie at Memphis, which dated to the Roman period. The misfired vessels from the site clearly illustrate the manner in which the plates and bowls were stacked in the kilns; they were inverted and separated from one another by small cones of clay that served as setters. These would normally be removed, leaving only a small trace on the inside of the vessel but a larger mark on the stand-ring of the underside. Where vessels were misfired, they were left in place—as a result, the process can be reconstructed.

**Amulets.** As an artificial semiprecious stone, faience seems to have been regarded as a suitable substitute for actual stones. Thus the goddess Hathor was referred to as the "Lady of Turquoise" but offerings of faience artifacts were made to her at Deir el-Bahri, Serabit el-Khadim, and elsewhere. It was probably the color symbolism that had come to be more important than the material itself, and faience was by far the most common material for the production of amulets.

Even important funerary objects, whose material was specified in religious texts, might be substituted in faience. Thus the heart scarabs, which were to be made of the green *nmhf* stone (green jasper, serpentine, or basalt), were also found in faience. Heart amulets—common only after the New Kingdom—were supposed to be made in *shrt* stone (probably carnelian) but were made in numerous other stones, as well as red faience, which is known only from the New Kingdom. Color symbolism was of great importance to the Egyptians, and since faience could be used to simulate colored stones, it became an obvious choice for amulets.

**Egyptian Blue Frit.** One of the alternative names for faience deserves attention here, since it is actually a related material—to be distinguished from faience and even from glass, with which it is sometimes confused. The term *frit* should not be used to mean "faience," since it is a distinct, though compositionally related, material. Work conducted by M. S. Tite and others has distinguished two types of frit. The first is blue, with a dominant crystalline phase of copper calcium tetrasilicate, known as Egyptian blue ($CaO.CuO.4SiO_2$), in a limited matrix of glass. The second is turquoise in color, with wollastonite ($CaSiO_3$, a calcium silicate), which is crystallized from the copper-rich glass matrix. These two groups may each be coarse or fine textured, the second resulting from the grinding of the first. Unlike faience, this material is either blue or turquoise throughout; unlike glass, it is crystalline.

The mid-first-century BCE Roman architect Vitruvius, in his *De architectura*, stated that Egyptian blue (which he knew as *caeruleum*) was first manufactured at Alexandria; in fact, its origins are much earlier. Not only was it known in Greek times (as *kyanos*) but it was found in Egypt as early as the fourth dynasty. The material was used by the Egyptians both as a pigment and for molding into objects, such as figurines and even small vessels. Frit is the product of the fritting process, a reaction in which quartz, alkali, lime, and colorants (like copper) are heated together to become a crystalline mass. This process was also widely used as the first stage in the manufacture of early glass, since it allowed for the escape of gases that might otherwise cause bubbles in the molten mass. The result

was glass making as a single-stage process. Frit may thus be a material in its own right, as Egyptian blue was, or it may be from a step in the making of glass. The relationship emphasizes the special need to avoid loading the term *frit* with another meaning, namely as an alternative term for "faience."

**BIBLIOGRAPHY**

Bianchi, R. F. "Faience and Glaze." In *The Dictionary of Art*, edited by J. Turner, pp. 46–49. London, 1996.

Boyce, A. "Notes on the Manufacture and Use of Faience Rings at Amarna." In *Amarna Reports V*, edited by B. J. Kemp, pp. 160–168. London, 1989. Detailed study of the manufacture of faience rings.

Friedman, F. *Gifts of the Nile: Ancient Egyptian Faience*. London, 1998. Catalog of an exhibition devoted to faience, with essays on technology, style, chronology, and more.

Kaczmarczyk, A., and R. E. M. Hedges. *Ancient Egyptian Faience*. Warminster, 1983. The most comprehensive survey of Egyptian faience technology and chemistry, with an extensive technological appendix by Pamela Vandiver.

Kiefer, C., and A. Allibert. "Pharaonic Blue Ceramics: The Process of Self-glazing." *Archaeology* 24 (1974), 107–117.

Lucas, A., and J. R. Harris. *Ancient Egyptian Materials and Industries*. London, 1962. Despite its age, the faience chapter still contains useful material, although self-glazing is not recognized as a technique.

Nenna, M. -D., and Seif el-Din, M. "La vaiselle en faïence du Musée Gréco-Romain d'Alexandrie." *Bulletin de Correspondence Hellénique* 117 (1993), 565–598. One of relatively few recent works on late faience.

Nicholson, P. T. *Egyptian Faience and Glass*. Aylesbury, 1993. Summary of some recent views on Egyptian faience and glass.

Nicholson, P. T. "Glass making/working at Amarna: Some New Work." *Journal of Glass Studies* 37 (1995), 11–19. Discusses new evidence from the excavation of furnaces at Tell el-Amarna.

Nicholson, P. T., with E. J. Peltenburg. "Egyptian Faience." In *Ancient Egyptian Materials and Technology*, edited by P. T. Nicholson and I. Shaw. Cambridge, 1999. A new study of faience and its technology (post Lucas and Harris, 1962).

Noble, J. V. "The Technique of Egyptian Faience." *American Journal of Archaeology*, 73 (1969), 435–439.

Petrie, W. M. Flinders "The Pottery Kilns at Memphis." In *Historical Studies*, edited by E. B. Knobel, W. W. Midgeley, J. G. Milne, M. A. Murray, and W. M. F. Petrie, pp. 34–37. London, 1911. Despite its title, this paper actually deals with the faience kilns and materials at Memphis.

Stocks, D. "Derivation of Ancient Egyptian Faience Core and Glaze Materials." *Antiquity* 71 (1997), 179–182. An interesting account of the relationship between faience production and other industries.

Tite, M. S. "Egyptian Blue, Faience and Related Materials: Technological Investigations." In *Science in Archaeology*, edited by R. E. Jones and H. W. Catling, pp. 39–41. British School at Athens, 1986. One of a few recent works on Egyptian blue.

Tite, M. S., and M. Bimson. "Identification of Early Vitreous Materials." In *Recent Advances in the Conservation and Analysis of Artifacts*, edited by J. Black, pp. 81–85. London, 1987.

Tite, M. S., I. C. Freestone, and M. Bimson. "Egyptian Faience: An Investigation of the Methods of Production." *Archaeometry* 25.1 (1983), 17–27.

Vandiver, P. "Technological Change in Egyptian Faience." In *Archaeological Ceramics*, edited by J. S. Olin and A. D. Franklin, pp. 167–179. Washington, 1982.

Vandiver, P., and W. D. Kingery. "Egyptian Faience: The First High-

Tech Ceramic." In *Ceramics and Civilisation*, edited by W. D. Kingery, pp. 19–34. Columbus, 1987.

Vandiver, P., and W. D. Kingery. "Manufacture of an Eighteenth Dynasty Egyptian Faience Chalice." In *Early Vitreous Materials*, edited by M. Bimson and I. C. Freestone, pp. 79–90. London, 1987. Discusses the combination of techniques used in making such artifacts; also the assembly of faience objects.

Wulff, H. E., H. S. Wulff, and L. Koch. "Egyptian Faience: A Possible Survival in Iran." *Archaeology* 21 (1968), 98–107. On the discovery of cementation self-glazing technique, in use in Iran.

PAUL T. NICHOLSON

**FAIYUM,** region in Middle Egypt, the site of sustained human habitation for more than eight thousand years. The Faiyum region is to the west of the Nile River, roughly within the area bordered by the following sites: Kom el-Atl (29°32′N, 31°00′E) in the north; Kom Ruqaiya (29°06′N, 30°43′E) in the south; Qasr Qarun (29°25′N, 30°25′E) in the west; and Kom el-Kharaba el-Khebir (29°27′N, 31°05′E) in the east. The Faiyum is centered on Lake Moeris (Ar., Birket el-Karun), a natural body of water that is, in part, responsible for the unique character of its unusually fertile agricultural land. Although the Faiyum has a long history of human habitation and use, from prehistoric times onward, Egyptologists particularly associate it with the cultural activity of the Middle Kingdom and the Greco-Roman period.

Some of the earliest farming sites in northern Egypt are in the Faiyum, most notably the Faiyum B and Faiyum A sites that were discovered in the 1930s by Gertrude Caton-Thompson and Elinor W. Gardner. A new survey was conducted in the 1970s and 1980s by Robert Wenke and Douglas Brewer. Habitation in the area continued and seems to have grown through the Predynastic period into the Old Kingdom, but few remains are known. The rulers of the Middle Kingdom instigated major development of the Faiyum for agriculture through improvements in irrigation. Cults centering on the crocodile god Sobek became prominent features of the religious geography of the Faiyum, and parts of the region also became a resort area for the elite. The major monuments of the Middle Kingdom include the temples at Medinet el-Faiyum/Kiman Fares; Medinet Maadi and Biahmu (site of the colossi of Amenemhet III); and the pyramid and mortuary complex (later known as the Labyrinth) of Amenemhet III at Hawara. Less well-attested habitation and use of the Faiyum continued through the New Kingdom and the Third Intermediate Period. In the Late period, there was some increasing interest in the region, which foreshadowed the great changes that occurred during the Ptolemaic period.

In the reign of Ptolemy II (282–246 BCE), many new settlements were founded in the Faiyum as part of a recla-mation project, and some of these settlements grew to great prosperity during the Roman period. Religious activity in the Faiyum continued to be dominated by the cults of local crocodile gods; temples to these divinities and to the more recently introduced Hellenistic divinities were prominent features of Faiyum towns. Activity in the Faiyum reached a high point in the first and second centuries CE, but it declined in the third, and many Faiyum towns were abandoned by the fourth century CE. Of those towns and villages that remained inhabited, some became important Christian centers and a few continued to thrive even after the Muslim conquest of the mid-seventh century CE.

Greco-Roman sites in the Faiyum were known to Europeans traveling in Egypt, and they were therefore included in the itinerary of the 1799 Napoleonic Expedition. When local workmen dug for *sebakh* (decayed mud-brick, used for fertilizer) in the ruins of Greco-Roman Faiyum sites, their major papyrus finds of the 1870s and 1880s increased European scholarly interest in the region. The earliest systematic archaeological investigations of the Greco-Roman period in the Faiyum were the 1895 to 1901 surveys of Bernard P. Grenfell, David Hogarth, and Arthur S. Hunt for the Egypt Exploration Fund. Later excavations tended to concentrate on the individual town sites that are associated with papyrus finds. Greco-Roman settlement remains in the Faiyum are among the best preserved in Egypt, and large numbers of Greek, Demotic, Latin, Hieratic, and Coptic papyri, ostraca, and inscriptions have been found there. Many of the well-known Roman period mummy portraits on panels come from the Faiyum, especially from the cemeteries at Hawara and er-Rubayat. Together, the textual and artifactual remains from Faiyum sites indicate a complex combination of cultural elements that existed in the society of the Greco-Roman Faiyum.

Karanis (Ar., Kom Aushim, 29°31′N, 30°54′E) and Soknopaiou Nesos (Ar., Dimai, 29°32′N, 30°40′E) are good examples of typical Greco-Roman sites in the Faiyum; both were founded in the mid-third century BCE and are known from well-preserved archaeological remains and from myriad Greek, Demotic, and Latin documentation. Each had temples to local crocodile gods, surrounded by complex configurations of mud-brick houses and public buildings. The two sites were explored by nineteenth-century travelers and were "mined" by antiquities hunters and *sebakh*-diggers; both were excavated by the University of Michigan at the initiative of Francis W. Kelsey: Karanis from 1924 to 1935, by J. L. Starkey and Enoch E. Peterson, and Soknopaiou Nesos in 1931, by Peterson as an adjunct to the larger Karanis project. Karanis was subsequently excavated by the University of Cairo between 1966 and 1975; it became the subject of electromagnetic

FAIYUM. *Faiyum portrait from the Roman period, of encaustic on wood.* (The Metropolitan Museum of Art, Rogers Fund, 1909. [09.181.2])

investigation in 1983, by A. G. Hussain. Most material from the Michigan excavations is housed in the Kelsey Museum of Archaeology in Ann Arbor, Michigan, where new initiatives are studying the archaeological contexts of the papyri and making excavation data available electronically.

In contrast to the complex layout of streets and struc-

tures found at Karanis and Soknopaiou Nesos, the Faiyum site identified as ancient Philadelphia (Ar., Kom Darb Gerza/Kom el-Kharaba el-Khebir, 29°27′N, 31°05′E) has a regular layout plan: three main streets running north to south, crossed by eight streets running east to west, which demarcate at least twenty-seven blocks of mostly mudbrick dwellings. Philadelphia was a major town in the Faiyum region but was ultimately abandoned around the fifth century CE. The only formal excavation of the site was the 1908–1909 work by F. Zucker and P. Viereck for the Berlin Museum, which uncovered artifacts, papyri, and texts on tablets, but the site has since been the object of illegal exploration that resulted in major papyrus finds. Other important Greco-Roman sites in the Faiyum include Tebtunis (Ar., Umm el-Breigat), Theadelphia (Ar., Harit), Narmouthis (Ar., Medinet Maadi), Bacchias (Ar., Kom el-Atl), and the regional capital Arsinoe/Crocodilopolis (Ar., Kiman Fares).

## BIBLIOGRAPHY

Caton-Thompson, Gertrude, and E. W. Gardner. *The Desert Fayum.* 2 vols. London, 1934. Report on the major archaeological survey, important for the prehistory of the region.

Gallazzi, Claudio. "Tebtunis: Piecing Together 3,000 Years of History." *Egyptian Archaeology* 5 (1994), 27–29. Accessible account of ongoing work at Tebtunis.

Gazda, Elaine K. *Karanis: An Egyptian Town in Roman Times: Discoveries of the University of Michigan Expedition to Egypt (1924–1935).* Ann Arbor, 1983. Catalog of the major exhibition of Karanis objects at the Kelsey Museum; extensive bibliography and many archival photographs of the excavations.

Grenfell, Bernard P., A. S. Hunt, D. G. Hogarth, and J. G. Milne. *Fayûm Towns and their Papyri.* London, 1900; rep., 1975. Publication of papyri and artifacts from the Egypt Exploration Fund's 1895–1901 Faiyum surveys.

Lane, Mary-Ellen. *A Guide to the Antiquities of the Fayyum.* Cairo, 1985. Intended as a guide for travelers, contains much information about the region and specific sites; accessible but some inaccuracies.

Minnen, Peter van. "Deserted Villages: Two Late Antique Town Sites in Egypt." *Bulletin of the American Society of Papyrologists* 32 (1995), 41–56. Discussion of the abandonment of Karanis and Soknopaiou Nesos, with reference to recent work.

Montserrat, Dominic. "'No Papyrus and No Portraits': Hogarth, Grenfell and the First Season in the Fayum, 1895–6." *Bulletin of the American Society of Papyrologists* 33 (1996), 133–176. Publication of archival materials relating to the Egypt Exploration Fund's first survey of the Fayum, with extensive commentary.

Rathbone, Dominic. "Towards a Historical Topography of the Fayum." In *Archaeological Research in Roman Egypt,* edited by Donald M. Bailey, pp. 50–56. *Journal of Roman Archaeology,* Supplementary Series, 19. Ann Arbor, 1996.

Walker, Susan, and Morris Bierbrier. *Ancient Faces: Mummy Portraits from Roman Egypt.* London, 1997. Extensively illustrated exhibition catalog, including many Faiyum pieces and an extensive bibliography.

Wilfong, Terry G. "Kom Aushim (Karanis)," "Dimai (Soknopaiou Nesos)," "Kom el Breigat (Tebtunis)," "Medinet Madi (Narmouthis)," "Medinet el Fayum, Kom Fares, Kiman Fares (Crocodilopolis, Arsinoe)," "Kom Darb Gerza (Philadelphia)," and "Fayum:

Graeco-Roman Sites." In *The Archaeology of Ancient Egypt: An Encyclopedia*, edited by Kathryn A. Bard. New York, forthcoming. Descriptions of monuments and excavations at individual sites; includes bibliographies.

TERRY G. WILFONG

**FALSE DOOR.** The term *false door* (also *ka*-door, false-door stela, *fausse-porte*, *Scheintür*) denotes an architectural element that is found mostly in private tomb structures of the Old Kingdom (*mastaba*s and rock-cut tombs): a recessed niche, either in the western wall of the offering chamber or in the eastern tomb façade. It imitates the most important parts of an Egyptian door, but the niche offers no real entrance to any interior space. Such fictitious doors are also attested in other architectural contexts:

- mortuary temples of the pyramid complexes, as well as New Kingdom funerary temples
- private tombs of the Middle and New Kingdom
- as the so-called central-support false door, wall niche with double doors divided by a central pillar and surmounted by a round-topped lintel with latticework above it, found mostly with bark-shrines of Ramessid temples, and rarely in the middle halls of Amarna residences
- blind doors of Amarna and other residences that form a visual counterpart of the real doors

The development of the false door for the private sector is attested without major gaps, but the evidence for the feature in royal funerary temples is very scanty before the fifth dynasty. The question of their use in the fourth dynasty or earlier has been addressed variously. Stadelmann argues strongly for their existence in Khufu's pyramid temple and subsequent funerary complexes. Pursuant to Ricke's basic theory, Arnold contends that they were not used prior to the royal *mastaba* of Shepseskaf because the notion of a false door is related to that of the tomb as a dwelling—a concept that is not compatible with the idea of the Giza pyramids.

The custom probably began in the archaic period with the Helwan slab stelae. It is attested from the second and third dynasty on in Saqqara brickstone *mastaba*s (offering table stelae set up in offering niches) and reaches its fully developed canonical form during the fourth dynasty. Its importance vanishes at the end of the Old Kingdom, though in Lower Egypt the false door is retained until the twelfth dynasty.

Initially the main wall of the tomb was the eastern façade, but later the open-air offering place was moved inside the core of the *mastaba* and became a covered cult

FALSE DOOR. *False door from the offering chamber of the tomb of Perneb at Saqqara, fifth dynasty.* (The Metropolitan Museum of Art, Gift of Edward S. Harkness, 1913. [13.183.3])

chamber. At this stage, the false door is always in the western wall of the offering room. Many tombs have two false doors, for the southern and northern parts. Sometimes there is also a subsidiary one in the northern end of the façade, a remnant of the original northern part of the small, two-niched *mastaba* whose southern niche was transformed into the offering room. A few of these cult chambers have as many as five or six false doors.

Women's tombs rarely possess false doors of their own; they are usually depicted on those of their husbands. The cornice element—as a status symbol in the beginning—was used mainly for men; the first attested occurrence in a female tomb is that of Queen Nebet, wife of Unas.

The conventional type of false door is decorated on all parts with figural representations as well as standardized inscriptions: an offering-table scene on the panel; names and titles of the deceased on the jambs, upper and lower architraves (also drum); the figure of the dead sometimes on jambs or door-niche; and offering forumulae on jambs and architraves. Symmetry is a dominant factor in the arrangement of these components. Most of the decorative scenes in the offering chamber are oriented to the false door as the focus of the upper tomb complex, particularly those topics dealing with the supply of the deceased (e.g., slaughtering scenes, offering-bearers, list of oils, offering list).

Usually the inscriptions contain long sequences of titles, offering lists (already part of the early slab stelae), and the indispensable offering formula, to which are added various wishes for long life, the funeral, and a blessed existence in the necropolis or holy West. Sometimes individual texts are found: the owner's ideal biography, texts concerning the funeral equipment, or, rarely, legal texts such as a will. These features confirm the interpretation of the false door as an architectural element that condenses and concentrates the personality of the deceased forever. This memorial function is transferred to its successors, the statue-shrine and the Middle Kingdom stelae, which are of different origin from the false door despite their later syncretism.

There are two known Egyptian designations for the false door. The general word *rwt* for "door," also serves this specific use, the special application made clear by a corresponding determinative (the actual form of this example is not always reproduced). The same is true of the word *r3-pr*, normally meaning "temple," "chapel." Evidence for the latter is not attested before the second half of the fifth dynasty, so this use could be an indication that the false door underwent a semantic change, but it is doubtful that each example really means a false door. Generally, the terms designating "false door" are mentioned rather seldom in the texts, so it is difficult to deduce reliable statements.

The basic structure of false doors varies widely. Three types may be distinguished:

1. normal or conventional false door without *cavetto* cornice
2. conventional door surmounted by *cavetto* cornice
3. decorative or palace-façade door

Types 1 and 2 may be integrated into a single group, although their distinction makes good sense in considering the further evolution of the false door. The palace-façade door differs more markedly from the normal type, so it will be dealt with separately.

The conventional false door consists of several component parts which are modeled according to those of a real Egyptian door. The dimensions, proportions, and design of the special elements, as well as the number of jambs, may vary considerably. The *cavetto* cornice results from

the addition of a frieze with palm-leaf cornice. The latter feature normally occurs with a torus molding as a frame of the outer jambs; both elements originated in mud-brick architecture and constructions of wood and reed matting.

This second type first appears in the second half of the fifth dynasty, becomes increasingly common during the sixth dynasty, and finally nearly replaces the earlier type without the cornice. Until the end of that dynasty, statues of the deceased are occasionally incorporated in the false door niche and other parts as well (e.g., outer jambs); the canonical form, however admitted only representations in flat relief. Until the end of Old Kingdom, further modifications are to be found: the niche is decorated by a double-door imitation with bolts; *wd3t*-eyes may appear; the panel spreads over onto the inner jambs so that the marginal slots may be absent. Simultaneously, the proportions become less balanced.

Before the false door attained its final canonical outline, it was often built up of mud brick and wood. Otherwise, it was constructed in masonry or large stone slabs. Commonly, the composed false door was replaced by monolithic examples (inside rock-cut tombs, it was hewn out of the rock formation): limestone is the usual material, while granite is very rarely attested though sometimes imitated by red-brown paint. (Because of its preciousness, granite obviously was awarded as a royal favor.) Since the false doors were the center of the cult chamber, their careful manufacture was important.

The decorative or palace-façade paneled false door (*fausse-porte ornée*, *Prunkscheintür*) is composed of panels similar to a palace-façade, arranged in compartments which correspond to the essential components of a conventional door. Normally it has no inscriptions at all (occasionally, a name and title). Its completely different structure and function are evident in the absence of the otherwise indispensable offering table scene. The palace-façade paneling, used as front decoration in early dynastic tombs of the Negade type, is transferred to the false door: the modified cruciform chapel the of palace-façade type represents the connecting link. From the fourth dynasty on, this type is attested in some offering chapels, though the funeral cult was generally performed before the conventional type; later, in the sixth dynasty, the recessed paneling design shifts to the subterranean burial room. Although the design of multiple recessed niches probably derives from some royal prototype, the decorative false door is not restricted to high-ranking officials or members of the royal family, as has been claimed. Its intended purpose, however, remains obscure. Normally the offerings of the funeral cult took place before a conventional false door, as shown by the associated offering stones. In the case of two-niched chapels, both types may coexist, the southern one designating the main or real offering place.

In a few cases, the normal type is combined with some palace-façade elements.

Adolf Rusch in 1928 developed a system for dating which uses as a main criterion the existence or nonexistence of the *cavetto* cornice, because this element does not appear before the second half of the fifth dynasty. Thus, two main groups are established, with several subdivisions which show the special features of a certain type for a limited period. This stylistic analysis seems to provide a rather precise dating instrument. Unfortunately, the usability of this system is diminished by two major obstacles. First, Rusch does not take into consideration the modifications caused by different development processes within the individual cemeteries. Additionally, the social degree of the tomb-owner has an important influence on the tomb's execution (form, design, and size).

The idea of the false door probably originated in the combination of two concepts: the notion of the tomb as the house of the deceased person, and the offering-scene panel that shows the deceased sitting at table with bread and the conventionalized offering meal. This reflects the double function of the normal false door, which provides an imaginary passage for the deceased, a transition between the worlds of the living and the dead. At the same time, it designates the main point for the funeral repast, offered daily by the *ka*-priest. As long as people believed in the spiritual reality of such a passage between the two spheres, the original conception of the false door was preserved.

Originally the false door as an architectural element is integrated into the surrounding wall: its function as a mediator between two areas prevents any isolation. But starting in the middle of the fifth dynasty, there is movement toward detaching the monument from the wall. This is marked by the *cavetto* cornice, an element originally connected with freestanding three-dimensional buildings like shrines (e.g., for tomb statues). One early exception is the damaged example of Persen from the reign of Sahure: it probably should be reconstructed with a cornice because of the preserved torus molding. This phenomenon suggests a semantic change for the false door, which now may gradually have assumed the function of a shrine façade. The structure of the tomb provides further support: the hitherto undecorated sarcophagus chamber acquires decorative elements of its own, whereas the offering chamber is opened to the visitor. Thus, the architectural evolution reflects increasing polarization between the upper and subterranean parts of the tomb.

Probably this transition is connected with changing religious beliefs. From second half of the fifth dynasty, the god Osiris is often mentioned in offering formulae (the supposed early date of evidence in the tomb of Princess Hemetra was corrected to the later fifth dynasty): obvi-ously his importance as ruler of the dead increases considerably. The idea of an underworld region for the dead penetrates into Old Kingdom religion. Nevertheless, this assumed correspondence cannot be proved conclusively, because the interrelation between the naming of Osiris and the application of the cornice decoration is not generally attested. However, the fact that the cornice type is generally connected with owners of higher social rank suggests its association with elite religious innovation. Not before the late sixth dynasty is this type common irrespective of social status.

During the end of the Old Kingdom period, the false door undergoes the next stage in its development: decadent tendencies result in very small works of bad quality. Its further evolution is seen in stelae of First Intermediate Period tombs (mostly in Upper Egypt), which may be rectangular in shape, or in the round-topped stelae of Abydos, which clearly are cenotaphs representing the tomb structure itself. During the Middle and New Kingdoms, false doors are sometimes used in tomb architecture, but primarily for the subsidiary cult niches, where they are paralleled with stelae.

[*See also* Stelae.]

## BIBLIOGRAPHY

Arnold, Dieter. *Lexikon der ägyptischen Baukunst.* Zurich, 1994. Several informative articles concerning false door, *cavetto* cornice, recessed palace-façade paneling, etc.

Bolshakov, Andrey O. "Princess *ḤM.T-R'(W)*: The First Mention of Osiris?" *Chronique d'Égypte* 67 (1992), 203–210.

Haeny, Gerhard. "Scheintür." In *Lexikon der Ägyptologie,* 5:563–574. Wiesbaden, 1981.

Haeny, Gerhard. *Zu den Platten mit Opfertischszene aus Heluan und Giseh. Beiträge zur Ägyptischen Bauforschung und Altertumskunde* 12 (1971), 143–164. Reconstruction of original location of Helwan ceiling stelae; interpretation of Giza slab stelae (reign of Khufu) as provisional arrangement which later should be replaced by a real false door.

Hassan, Selim. *Excavations at Giza.* Vol. 5. Cairo, 1944. "The Falsedoor," pp. 85–160, offers a comprehensive description of the false door and its components.

Jánosi, Peter. "Die Entwicklung und Deutung des Totenopferraumes in den Pyramidentempeln des Alten Reiches." *Hildesheimer Ägyptologische Beiträge* 37 (1994), 143–163. Offers a theory about origin and meaning of royal false doors, which are not incorporated in funerary complexes before Shepseskaf. Conclusions concerning private false doors are contestable, as he ignores the actual interrelation between the normal false doors with and without *cavetto* cornice.

Junker, Hermann. *Giza.* 12 vols. Vienna, 1929–1955. Deals with origins and development of the false door, especially in vols. 1, 2, and 12. Special entries are to be found by detailed indexes.

Reisner, Georges Andrew. "The Position of Early Grave Stelae." In *Studies Presented to Francis Llewellyn Griffith.* pp. 324–331. London, 1932.

Ricke, Herbert. *Bemerkungen zur Baukunst des Alten Reiches.* Beiträge zur Ägyptischen Bauforschung und Altertumskunde 4, 5. 1. Zurich, 1944; Cairo, 1950. Extensive consideration of Early Dynastic and Old Kingdom architecture, presenting a general hypothesis concerning origin, meaning, and function of several building types. Basic although not uncontested interpretation of false door and stela.

Rusch, Adolf. "Die Entwicklung der Grabsteinformen im Alten Reich." *Zeitschrift für Ägyptische Sprache und Altertumskunde* 58 (1923), 101–124.

Spencer, Patricia. *The Egyptian Temple: A Lexicographical Study.* London, 1984. Analysis of ancient Egyptian terms for architectural elements.

Stadelmann, Rainer. "Scheintür oder Stelen im Totentempel des Alten Reiches." *Mitteilungen des Deutschen Archäologischen Instituts, Abteilung Kairo* 39 (1983), 237–241.

Strudwick, Nigel. "Some Remarks on the Disposition of Texts in Old Kingdom Tombs with Particular Reference to the False Door." *Göttinger Miszellen* 77 (1984), 35–49.

Strudwick, Nigel. Review of Wiebach, *Die ägyptische Scheintür.* *Bibliotheca Orientalis* 41 (1984), 630–633.

Strudwick, Nigel. *The Administration of Egypt in the Old Kingdom. The Highest Titles and Their Holders.* London, 1985. The false door as a criterion for dating is the subject of chapter 2.

Vandier, Jacques. *Manuel d'Archéologie Égyptienne.* 2 vols. Paris, 1952, 1954. Detailed description of the monuments and discussion of their origin and development with attention to offering-table panels, false doors, and stelae, vol. 1, pp. 724–774, and vol. 2, pp. 389–481.

Wiebach, Silvia. *Die ägyptische Scheintür. Morphologische Studien zur Entwicklung und Bedeutung der Hauptkultstelle in den Privat-Gräbern des Alten Reiches.* Hamburg, 1981. Studies on morphological development and ideology of the false door; account and evaluation of the various earlier theories.

SILVIA WIEBACH-KOEPKE

**FAMILY.** Ancient Egyptian has a large repertory of terms that denote various types of familial relationships. These include *h3w*, close relatives, or kindred; *ḥrw*, the people a person has to care for, family members, relatives; or the extended family household; *3bwt*, extended family household, or clan; *mhwt*, extended family, or clan; *wḥjjt*, clan; *hnw*, co-residents; and *dnjt/dnwt*, a term for family used during the eighteenth dynasty. The terms for members of the nuclear family include *mwt*, mother; *jt*, father; *z3/t*, son/daughter; and *sn/t*, brother/sister. Grandparents were specified as maternal or paternal: *mwt mwt.f/jt.f*, mother of one's mother/father; *jt mwt.f/jt.f*, father of one's mother/father. Grandchildren were specified by the sex of their parent: *z3/t z3/t.f* son/daughter of one's son/daughter. Nieces and nephews were also called *z3/t*, and cousins *sn/t*. But since *sn* can also mean "brother-in-law," and sometimes merely a member of the same generation, it often is difficult to determine the relationship between two family members.

The Egyptians usually married within the same social class. Late period archives indicate that marriage between cousins or uncle and niece was allowed, as well as between half-brothers and half-sisters with the same father but different mothers. Marriage between full brothers and sisters, rare among nonroyal Egyptians in pharaonic times, became common in the Ptolemaic period. This is often explained as a response to the increase of population and the need to keep landed property together in the family. More decisive, no doubt, was the example set by the Ptolemaic royal house; Romans living in Egypt were not allowed to marry their full siblings.

A young man of the upper class was supposed to marry when he was able to support a family. Since he finished his education around the age of twenty, this was probably about the age for him to find a wife. As in the early Judaic and the much later Islamic cultures, a woman married soon after reaching maturity, between twelve and fourteen. Thus, she was prevented from having illicit intercourse and could maximize her period of fertility. Although the marriage of an immature girl is recorded in the twenty-sixth dynasty, a man was not supposed to have intercourse with a girl before she had reached puberty. During the pharaonic period a suitor approached the father of the desired bride, or if he were dead, her mother or uncle. They signed a marriage contract, which they might keep, give to a third person, or deposit in a temple. From 536 BCE on the surviving contracts are signed by the couple themselves. Often drawn up after the couple already had children, these contracts regulate the rights of the wife and her children during the marriage and in case of divorce. Either partner could ask for a divorce and marry again. Some contracts name a sum a man had to pay (*šp n sḥm.t*) if he divorced his wife, assuming she was innocent. Others name the dowry or a sum the bride gave to her husband, which obliged him to maintain her or which he had to return in case of divorce (*ḥḏ n jr ḥm.t*). If the wife was blameless, she had a right to one-third of the husband's belongings; the other two-thirds went to her children (*sḥ n sʿnḫ*). All that a woman inherited or acquired was at her own disposal, and she could leave it to whichever of her children she preferred. Thus, it was difficult for a man to remarry. If a wife had committed "the great sin," she lost her dowry and all her rights from her husband. During the pharaonic period a man usually could afford to maintain only one wife. If he could afford it, however, he was free to have more than one official wife and to have sexual contact with dependent women of his household. The marriage contracts transmitted to us from the lower classes during the Late and Greco-Roman periods, seem to exclude second marriages without divorce or the death of one partner. The children of the first wife were the main heirs; the children of a slave woman had the same rights only if their father had adopted them.

Adultery with a married woman was forbidden in order to keep inheritance lines clear. Death penalties for both sexes or castration of the man are punishments mentioned in literary texts but not in the nonliterary records. A hundred strokes, cutting off the nose, or hard labor are

FAMILY. *Statue of Uni and Renwet, nineteenth dynasty.*
This limestone statue of Uni, the chief royal scribe of
Ramesses II, and his wife Renwet, a priestess of
Hathor, was found in the tomb of Uni's father at
Asyut. (The Metropolitan Museum of Art, Rogers
Fund, 1915. [15.2.1])

threatened, though not inflicted on, an adulterer in the
village of Deir el-Medina. During the Late period, a priest
who committed adultery had to pay a fine and leave his
community. A woman who could not state her innocence
on oath could be repudiated by her husband and lose all
her rights to him.

Among poorer people, a wife might come to live with
her husband's parents (patrilocal marriage); less often the
husband came to live with his wife's family or was received by her on periodic visits (matrilocal marriage). Because sharing a house with one's relatives resulted in all
kinds of difficulties, a man was advised to found his own
house (neolocal marriage). Literary texts, household lists,
the title "mistress of the house" for a married woman, and
the size of houses indicate that the nuclear family was the
usual situation.

Unmarried children or mostly female relatives who
could not care for themselves could be included in the
household of a male relative. Census lists of the Kahun
papyri show that in the household of a man named Snefra
were included his grandmother, mother (both probably
widowed), three aunts, and his own wife and children.
Houses of 70 square meters (230 square feet) in Deir el-
Medina and 20 to 100 square meters (66 to 328 square
feet) in Tell el-Amarna were the norm for the working
class. Well-off families lived in bigger houses. In Deir el-
Medina the houses of related families were situated in the
same square of the town. A complex of eleven living quarters, twenty-five courtyards, and a few ovens in Tell el-
Amarna has been interpreted as the compound of an extended family; this seems very doubtful, however, because
the site was inhabited for less than fifteen years.

Coffin Texts expressing the wish of the deceased to meet family members and others in the hereafter are often cited as proof for extended families. The fact that the deceased mentions not only his parents, brothers, children, and women, but also servants, friends, and colleagues, shows that this does not mean that they all lived under one roof. The same applies to the people for whom Hekanakht provides in his letters. Except for his mother, to whom he writes that the whole house is like (his) children, there is no proof that the others he mentions belonged to his family. The name of the father of one of the elder men mentioned differs from his, and three men receive provision for themselves, their wives, and their children, which proves how close the unity of the nuclear family was considered.

If a man failed, his wife and children could be prosecuted. They could be punished with him or, if he fled from his work, they were taken into custody until he returned or had to do the work for him. Persistent fleeing might lead to the entire family becoming "serfs."

The husband (*hy* or *t3j*) was advised to respect his wife (*hm.t*) in her household and to love her, but to keep her from power. Infertility was not accepted as a reason to repudiate her. Cases of adoption have been transmitted to us. On monuments from the Middle Kingdom on, a wife is usually called "mistress of the house" (*nb.t pr*); from the New Kingdom on she is "his beloved sister" (*sn.t.f mr.t.f*); on documents, married women, like their husbands, are usually titled "citizen" (*'nh.t n njw.t*). A term for a second wife seems to have been *hbsw.t*. Although the house was the main realm of a married woman, she could be well informed about her husband's external business. Reliefs of the Old Kingdom show wife and children in the company of the husband inspecting work on their estate. Documents from the workmen's village at Deir el-Medina, dating to the New Kingdom, inform us that a wife could take care of her husband's affairs during his absence. A peasant's wife helped her husband in the fields and with their cattle when needed. In the event of the early death of her husband, a mother was responsible for her children and looked after their inheritance. A queen or a nomarch's wife could rule for her son until he came of age. An eldest son or daughter, too, could look after the interests of his or her siblings in legal affairs.

As during life, a man was to care for his wife in death and in the hereafter. They were frequently buried together and depicted side by side in the tomb decoration, though the man is usually shown in the more prominant position. Sometimes they are accompanied by one or more of their children. A considerable number of tombs from the Old Kingdom, however, show the tomb owner with his children, while his wife is not mentioned. If this indicates divorce and there was no one else to see to their funerary needs, these women must have been badly off. Otherwise, a woman might have her own false door in her husband's tomb, or she might erect her own tomb where her children, but not her husband, are depicted or mentioned. During the Middle and New Kingdoms, a wife is nearly always shown at the side of her husband. Except in banquet scenes, they can be accompanied by their children at festive events. Parents can be mentioned or depicted in their son's tomb at all periods. During the Middle and New Kingdoms, they and other relatives are often included in banquet scenes. The wife, children, brothers, sisters, other relatives, friends, and colleagues follow the funerary cortège at the tomb owner's burial, as is depicted in New Kingdom tombs. Some tombs show the mummies of the couple standing upright in front of the tomb during the Opening of the Mouth ceremony. According to Theban tomb paintings, spouses went to banquets together. While men and women enjoyed themselves separately during the earlier eighteenth dynasty, they are always depicted sitting side by side from the Amarna period on.

A son to whom a father wished to hand down his office had to qualify before he was nominated by the king. With the consent of the king, the father could take his son to help him with his work as a "staff of old age," so that he could take over when his father retired or died. While the consent of the king was often only a formality, the king could deny it to break the power of mighty families (e.g., at the beginning of the Middle Kingdom and during the New Kingdom, especially during the time of Amenhotpe II and in the Amarna period), and assign qualified newcomers. Even a man coming from an unknown family could reach a high position. But, since a good education was needed to qualify, only a few men of lowly origin reached this goal, and political or priestly offices might stay in one family for many generations.

The royal family was a rather more complex matter, since the kings practiced polygamy to a far greater extent than was customary among ordinary Egyptians. This was especially true during the New Kingdom, when diplomatic marriages increased the number of denizens of the royal women's quarters. Some of this number were likely concubines rather than wives. It is not known what legal arrangements, if any, were made with the royal wives, but some appear to have had estates, along with their administrators, assigned directly to them for their support. Of the nature of the dynamics within the royal family, little is known. Royal family members were largely excluded from the bureaucracy after the fourth dynasty; in the New Kingdom, royal sons seem to have served in the military frequently, while some sons and daughters held priesthoods.

In the world of the gods, families were common. Most famous is the Ennead of Heliopolis. After Atum had created himself, he spat our Shu (air) and Tefnut (humidity). This couple begot Geb (earth) and Nut (sky), who bore four children: Osiris, Isis, Seth, and Nephthys. Isis conceived her son Horus, who became king of Egypt, by Osiris, posthumously. Common were triads: a divine couple and their child. The son of Amum and Mut in Karnak was Khonsu, the moon god. During the New Kingdom, the creator god Ptah of Memphis was associated with the lioness goddess Sakhmet, their son being Nefertem, the sun as a child rising from the lotus flower.

The ritual visit of Hathor of Dendera to Horus of Edfu—in a sacred marriage ceremony—took place in a great procession each year during the Ptolemaic era. The conception and birth of their son, the musician Ihi, is depicted in the two so-called *mammisi*s, or birth-houses, built by the last Egyptian pharaoh Nectanebo and by the Roman emperor Nero at Dendera. The child-god is identified with the king being enthroned as ruler over Egypt and the desert. This goes back to the legend of the birth of three kings of the fifth dynasty and to the depictions of the birth cycle, well preserved in the temples of Hatshepsut in Deir el-Bahri and of Amenophis III in Luxor, respectively.

[*See also* Children; Kinship; Marriage and Divorce; Royal Family; *and* Women.]

### BIBLIOGRAPHY

Allam, Shafik. "Familie, soziale Funktion" and "Familie (Struktur)." In *Lexikon der Äegyptologie*, 2: 101–114. Wiesbaden, 1977.

Bierbrier, M. L. "Terms of Relationship at Deir el-Medina." *Journal of Egyptian Archaeology* 66 (1980), 101–107.

Feucht, Erika. "Gattenwahl, Ehe und Nachkommenschaft im Alten Ägypten." In *Geschlechtsreife und Legitimation zur Zeugung*, edited by E. W. Müller, pp. 55–84. Freiburg, 1985.

Feucht, Erika. *Das Kind im Alten Ägypten*. Frankfurt and New York, 1995.

Franke, Detlef. *Altägyptische Verwandschaftsbezeichnungen im Mittleren Reich*. Hamburg, 1983.

Pestman, P. W. *Marriage and Matrimonial Property in Ancient Egypt*. Leiden, 1961.

Robins, Gay. "The Relationships Specified by Egyptian Kingship Terms of the Middle and New Kingdoms." *Chronique d'Égypte* 54. 107/108 (1979), 197–217.

Robins, Gay. *Women in Ancient Egypt*. London, 1993.

Whale, Sheila. *The Family in the Eighteenth Dynasty of Egypt*. Sydney, 1989.

ERIKA FEUCHT

**FANTASTIC ANIMALS.** A fantastic animal refers to a creature not found in nature—but a product of human imagination. Generally, the parts that form the animal's body are borrowed from various species and fitted together. The composite character of the body gives an approximate, though useful, way to define the category; yet the families observed in it are based on our modern sense of classification. For example, a sphinx, which is in most cases a human-headed lion, though fantastic in the very sense of the term, does not fit exactly in the so-called animal category, since it includes a part of the human body. If we consider only those beings with nonhuman animal parts, we still have a classification problem. Composite animals, from an Egyptological point of view, represent fantastic animals—but also demons or even gods, since no clear-cut border existed between those categories. A duck with four wings, legs, and a serpent's tail represented a constellation based on late Egyptian zodiacs; it was out of human reach, not only physically but also intellectually. The composite animal body was, in many cases, only the tentative representation of a divine, supernatural power. From an ancient Egyptian point of view, fantastic animals could be considered real, since they were often depicted as living in the wild, among antelopes and lions, in the deserts surrounding the Nile Valley. There, hunters supposedly caught a glimpse of them in the distance, though they were never supposed to have captured one.

**Origins and History.** Fantastic animals mingling in the wild with "natural" animals were pictured for the first time during the late Predynastic period (c.3100 BCE). Carved on luxury objects, and probably of royal origin, such scenes appeared on ceremonial slate palettes, ivory plaques, and ivory knife handles. Many such objects were unearthed at Hierakonpolis or from the neighborhood of Naqada, in Upper Egypt; both were among the main centers that developed the small kingdoms from which the Egyptian civilization originated. The winged, falcon-headed griffin—the "serpopard," a leopard with a long, winding neck—and most of the accompanying animals, were depicted on objects in a style usually considered to be inspired indirectly from Mesopotamian models. During the Middle Kingdom, fantastic animals appeared again on the walls of tombs of some high officials of Beni Hasan and Bersheh, in Middle Egypt. A little farther south, in Meir, also during the Middle Kingdom, the capital city, el-Kusiyeh, when written in hieroglyphs, had two serpopards back to back, their necks held by a man. Beni Hasan and el-Kusiyeh were only about 65 kilometers (40 miles) from each other. Bersheh and Beni Hasan were the starting points for the desert roads that led to the Red Sea coast, to the Sinai peninsula, and to Nubia. Beni Hasan nomarchs, who were in charge of controlling and inspecting those roads, were in contact with the nomadic populations living east of the Nile Valley. Their special interest in fantastic animals was, in all probability, motivated by their contacts with the peoples of the Eastern Desert and their beliefs about curious desert animals, beliefs that had come from a long desert tradition. Moreover, hunting in the desert was the preferred pursuit of those nomarchs. Some were very proud of their zoologi-

FANTASTIC ANIMALS. *A deceased person, holding his heart, kneels before a winged serpent and a phoenix.* The painting, on a papyrus scroll, is now in the Staatliche Museen, Berlin. (Art Resource, NY)

cal knowledge. On a wall of his tomb, Baqet III of Beni Hasan had a detailed hunting scene in which there were fantastic animals, although they were not hunted as the other animals were. On the same wall was a whole catalog of real birds, represented in color, with their names—indicating the extent and accuracy of Baqet's knowledge of the fauna. There, as in all contexts already mentioned, fantastic animals were perceived as an integral part of the natural environment.

During the Middle Kingdom, fantastic animals were also represented on so-called magic wands. Made from hippopotamus ivory (tooth) reworked into a simple curved blade, these wands include fantastic animals in a scene of a procession of demons. These figures and the few accompanying texts show plainly that the animal were considered as beings having magical and protective powers. Apparently, these objects were used mainly by the elite, many of whom came from Thebes or el-Lisht, the two prominent political centers of that time. Some were also found in Naqada, Hierakonpolis, and other cities of Middle and Upper Egypt. All those demons—and not only the fantastic animals—were connected with religious and mythological beliefs that had their origins in Middle Egypt, more or less in the same area as the tombs of the nomarchs mentioned above. Since some of the wands were also found in Palestine (at Gaza and Megiddo) and in Nubia (at Kuban and Kerma), the inhabitants of those regions also had a special attraction for the very same demons and fantastic animals. During the Middle Kingdom, in Nubia (at Kerma), animals and demons (among which were winged giraffes), strikingly similar to those depicted on magic wands, were used as inlay motifs. A study of the material shows that the Egyptian wands and

the Nubian inlays are related, on both historical and mythological grounds.

The frequency of use of fantastic animals during both the late Predynastic to Early Dynastic period and the Middle Kingdom might best be explained by the strong local powers that were probably in contact with nomadic populations of the Eastern Desert. Originating in Mesopotamia in the fourth millennium BCE, fantastic animals were probably part of the local folklore and beliefs, which then influenced the Egyptians who traveled the desert to control its roads.

Later, fantastic animals were less frequently represented in Egypt. The winged griffin alone appeared again, during the New Kingdom, at a time when Egypt was in close contact with Near Eastern populations and borrowed some religious features from them. Despite long chronological gaps in our documentation, fantastic animals were probably present during all of Egyptian history. Their images were still used as hieroglyphs even in Roman times, in the inscriptions of the temple of Esna (in Upper Egypt, second century CE).

**Role and Significance.** The oldest representations of fantastic animals were clearly, like dogs and lions, hunting animals. Hunting on the edges of the Nile Valley had, from the very beginning of Egyptian history, a religious connotation. To kill or capture wild animals beyond the valley and its civilization was, symbolically, to subdue and tame the hostile forces that threatened fertile and organized Egypt. The fantastic animals became actors in this protective hunt for the benefit of Egypt.

In the Beni Hasan and Bersheh tombs, such animals apparently played the same role, but they were not represented in hunting scenes alone. On three occasions, at least, they appeared in a daily-life context, in the company of tamed animals, like monkeys and dogs. In one scene, a winged griffin is portrayed as so similar to the dogs playing nearby that it can be distinguished only because of the wings on its back. In Beni Hasan, a lavishly colored griffin with bitch's teats bears a collar and what seems to be a leash; it accompanies a man with a dog. Its term, *sgt*, also appears in a Bersheh tomb, associated with another griffin, this one shown in the company of monkeys. This word, *saget*, was probably not the name of the animal but might have been a designation for the so-called domesticated griffin. It has been supposed that those griffins were, in fact, dogs that were disguised to look like griffins. The purpose of such a masquerade was, perhaps, to transform an ordinary hunting dog into a ferocious, ceremonial or legendary hunter. At the same time, the possession of such an animal, be it only created by magical disguise, might have enhanced the prestige of the owner. During the New Kingdom, the griffin appeared again in hunting scenes. Often it hauled the chariot in which there was a young god, whose task was to chase the desert animals that were dangerous to Egyptians.

The inclusion of fantastic animals among the demons on magic wands indicates that they probably had the same purpose. All were protective beings supposed to frighten, by their strange aspect, any kind of malevolent beings. The wands were offered to women, especially to young mothers, to protect them and their children against demons bearing sickness. Since some of those objects were also found in tombs, fantastic animals probably exerted their magic protective power in the world beyond. Before reaching the felicities of a new life, in the netherworld, the dead had to cross border zones guarded by dangerous beings. The fantastic animals portrayed on palettes, tomb paintings, and magic wands helped in this task.

Fantastic animals retained beneficial powers until pagan religion in Egypt was eclipsed by Christianity in the Roman era. Even then, their silhouettes were still used in hieroglyphic script, to write the sacred name of Osiris, an impossibility if they were representations of evil.

*Serpopard.* With a feline body, a very long neck, and a leopard head, only the serpopard among fantastic animals attacked other animals. When depicted in pairs, the two were shown with intertwined necks, as on the celebrated Narmer Palette. On magic wands, the serpopard usually has a serpent in its mouth (and infrequently wears a collar). This animal is not known to be on other documents, except in the hieroglyphs described above and in writing the name of the town of el-Kusiyeh. The term for the serpopard, in Old Egyptian, is unknown, unless the ancient name of el-Kusiyeh, *Qis*, which possibly derives from a verb meaning "to tie, to form a ligature," has some etymological connection with the supposed name of the pair of serpopards with intertwined necks. Mesopotamian serpopards also had interwoven necks. In some tombs at Beni Hasan and at Bersheh, another form, perhaps a subspecies of serpopard, was depicted. It had a feline body, but its neck and head were portrayed as a snake. This variety is termed *sedja*, which possibly means "one who travels afar."

*Griffin.* The winged specimen was the most common form of griffin in ancient Egypt; the stout feline body has a falcon head on a short neck. On early monuments, the wings are horizontal and parallel to the back of the animal, in accordance with Mesopotamian models. This species survives in the Beni Hasan tomb of Khnumhotep II, where a new one was also found, with V-shaped wings, a slender and speckled body, and a longer neck; the beak of the falcon is less apparent. Between the wings is a human head. This variant is common on magic wands, where it is frequently depicted wearing a collar and occasionally shown wearing a leash. This type is not found after this period. The stout variant reappears sporadically as an image of the war god Montu (unwinged) or as a hieroglyph in texts of the temple of Esna (winged). The Egyptian term *srf* or *sfrr* (possibly borrowed from a foreign language) was used to label figures of the animal in Beni Hasan; it also appeared in texts of different periods, once in a Middle Kingdom religious spell in the Coffin Texts. Another term, *tštš*, "one who tears to pieces," was used in the Coffin Texts and in Bersheh, to name a griffin with a stout body, short neck, and what looks like a feather crown. From the New Kingdom onward, a new winged type appeared, with a slender canine body and a vulture's or eagle's beak. It originated in a particular form of griffin, one with a Seth-animal (see below) head, depicted once on a Middle Kingdom toilet object. The relationship between the two seems established in that the New Kingdom griffin sometimes had a Seth-animal head too. The term for this creature, "the swift one," stressed its capability to run swiftly, while hauling a chariot in which the young savior god Shed, an Egyptian aspect of the Semitic god Reshef, pursued and killed dangerous animals.

*Seth animal.* Among the fantastic animals of the Beni Hasan tombs, one of them was, in all respects, identical to the animal that usually embodied the god Seth. Called *š'*, it was also represented on magic wands, on which it wore a collar, a feature known from carefully engraved hieroglyphic examples of the Seth animal in Old Kingdom inscriptions. Its general stance was that of a dog or other canine animal, but it had triangular ears, an elongated snout, and an arrow in the guise of a tail. The *š'* was known as a desert dweller, and a gang of *š'* animals was supposed to haul the solar bark.

*Related animals.* The double-headed bull, which was pictured once on both a palette and a magic wand, could be added to this group of creatures. Other composite animals became associated with the human species; if originally part of the same family, they had a different destiny. A hippopotamus with a crocodile back and tail, Taweret, though represented on magic wands, became from the New Kingdom onward a great goddess; she was worshiped in temples and was highly renowned. The same was true of the lion-masked dwarf, Bes.

[*See also* Demons.]

## BIBLIOGRAPHY

Altenmüller, Hartwig. "Ein Zaubermesser aus Tübingen." *Die Welt des Orients* 14 (1983), 30–45. Sequel and complement to the fundamental work on magic wands privately published by this author.

Altenmüller, Hartwig. "Ein Zaubermesser des Mittleren Reiches." *Studien zur altägyptischen Kultur* 13 (1986), 1–27. Contains a discussion on various fantastic animals and the significance of magic wands.

Baines, John. "Symbolic Roles of Canine Figures on Early Monuments." *Archéo-Nil* 3 (1993), 62–63. Presents some reflections on ritual aspects of hunting, as represented on early monuments.

Browarski, Edward. "Ahanakht of Bersheh and the Hare Nome in the First Intermediate Period and Middle Kingdom." *Studies in Ancient Egypt, the Aegean, and the Sudan: Essays in Honor of Dows Dunham,* edited by William Kelly Simpson and Whitney Kelly Davis, pp. 14–30. Boston, 1981. Publishes a new example of a domesticated griffin.

Griffith, Francis L., and Percy E. Newberry. *El Bersheh.* Memoir of the Archaeological Survey of Egypt, 4. London, 1893–1894. Basic publication of fantastic animals from this site.

Newberry, Percy E. *Beni Hasan.* Archaeological Survey of Egypt, 2. London, 1893. Basic publication of fantastic animals from this site.

Petrie, W. M. Flinders. *Ceremonial Slate Palettes.* British School of Egyptian Archaeology. London, 1953. Handy publication of the main decorated slate palettes of early periods.

Sauneron, Serge. "Les animaux fantastiques du désert." *Bulletin de l'Institut français d'archéologie orientale* 62 (1964), 15–18. Studies the use of fantastic animals in the Roman hieroglyphic inscriptions of Esna.

Schlichting, Robert. "Die geflügelten Giraffen der Kerma-Kultur." *Studien zur Sprache und Religion Ägyptens: Zu Ehren von Wolfhart Westendorf,* vol. 2, pp. 833–838. Göttingen, 1984. Shows some of the historical and mythological links existing between the Nubian demons and fantastic animals and those figured on Egyptian magical wands.

Smith, Harry S. "The Making of Egypt: A Review of the Influence of Susa and Sumer on Upper Egypt and Lower Nubia in the 4th millennium B.C." In *The Followers of Horus: Studies Dedicated to Micheal Allen Hoffman, 1944–1990,* edited by R. Friedman and B. Adams, pp. 235–246. London, 1992. Examines the typological and historical connections between the fantastic animals figured on Mesopotamian objects and those of early Egypt.

DIMITRI MEEKS

**FATE.** The principal Egyptian word for fate was *šзy/šзw,* which derives from the word *šз,* meaning "ordain" or "fix," generally the action of a deity. Divine predetermination is found in the *Story of Sinuhe.* The protagonist describes his flight to western Asia as a "fateful flight." Earlier in the story, Sinuhe refers to his journey in a slightly different manner: "I do not know what brought me to this country; it is as if planned (*sḥr*) by god" (Lichtheim 1975, p. 225). Clearly the ideas of a divine plan and that which has been fated are synonymous.

*Šзw* is first attested toward the end of the Old Kingdom and continues to be used down to the Late period. It appears with some regularity in texts, especially in the Wisdom Literature. From the sixth dynasty occurrence in the *Instruction of Ptahhotep,* it seems that *šзw* has to do with death, and that it is inescapable: "His time does not fail to come; one does not escape what is fated" (Lichtheim, 1975, p. 72). "Death is a kindly fate" (Lichtheim, 1975, p. 196) well reflects the pessimism of the *Admonitions of Ipuwer,* but it clearly connects *šзw* with one's demise. In fact, the writing of *šзw* is at times determined by the Hieratic sign for "death." There is textual evidence that fate was also believed to govern non-Egyptians, even enemies. Concerning the Nubian enemy Aata, Ahmose son of Ibana

reports: "His fate brought on his doom. The gods of Upper Egypt grasped him" (Lichtheim 1976, p. 13).

Apparently various aspects of one's fate, such as time and manner of death, were ordained at birth. In the *Story of Two Brothers,* Re-Horakhty, king of the gods, directs Khnum to create a wife for Bata. The seven Hathors are present, and together they proclaim, "She will die by the knife" (Lichtheim 1976, p. 207). In the story of the birth of the three children of Ruddedet in the Westcar Papyrus, Re sends Isis, Nephthys, Meshkhenet, Heket, and Khnum to assist in the birth of the triplets. The sun god announces, "Please go, deliver Ruddedet of the three children who are in her womb, who will assume this beneficent office in this whole land. They will build your temples. They will supply your altars. They will furnish your libations. They will make your offerings abundant" (Lichtheim 1976, p. 220). No indication is given here of the time and manner of death, but Re does disclose that these three will become kings, build temples, and provide for their offerings. After their delivery, it is actually Meshkhenet who declares of each one; "A King who will assume the kingship in this whole land" (Lichtheim 1976, p. 220). This latter text demonstrates that the other deities are acting on Re's behalf, and that the idea of fate goes beyond lifespan to include foretelling the kingly office they will hold. The statement in *Story of Two Brothers,* on the other hand, discloses the instrument by which death will come. A third aspect of fate is associated with the goddess Renenet. Because of her association with fertility and harvest, Renenet appears to be responsible for endowing individuals with material possessions (Miosi 1982, p. 76).

This would mean that there were three forces (or deities) associated with one's fate in the thought of the New Kingdom: *Šзw,* who is closely associated with the seven Hathors and is responsible for one's lifespan and manner of death; Meshkhenet, who decides one's status or work; and Renenet, who settles one's material fortune or misfortune. By the New Kingdom, the word for "fate" could be written with a deity determinative, as if *šзw* were personified or deified, perhaps because of its association with particular deities.

A number of critical questions regarding the Egyptian understanding of fate must be asked. Was it absolutely fixed? Could it be altered or manipulated? If so, how could it be changed? In the *Report of Wenamun,* the prince of Byblos refers to sending Egyptian envoys back to Egypt with timber "so as to beg for me from Amun fifty years of life over and above my allotted fate" (Lichtheim 1976, p. 228). This statement suggests that the Egyptians believed in a divinely ordained lifespan, and that they thought (or hoped) that Amun could extend it.

The *Story of the Doomed Prince* offers the most notable

instance of altering one's fate. At the time of his birth, the Hathors announce, "He will die through the crocodile, or the snake, or the dog." The time of death is not announced, and, untypically, three possible instruments of death are introduced. The ill-fated prince thus spends much of his life not knowing which of these entities will bring his demise. Nevertheless, he asks for a pet puppy, which his father reluctantly gives him. After years of living reclusively in hope of avoiding his fate, the prince announces: "To what purpose is my sitting here? I am committed to Fate (*šȝw*). Let me go, that I may act according to my heart, until the god does what is in his heart" (Lichtheim 1976, p. 200). So he sets off on his chariot, believing that he cannot alter his fate, and arrives in Naharin. It is not clear whether the prince thinks that by leaving Egypt he may prolong his life, but he takes his dog with him.

In Naharin he marries a princess, to whom he discloses his three deadly fates. The horrified wife wants the pet dog killed, but the prince feels this dog could not cause his death because he has raised it. A crocodile has followed him from Egypt to Naharin, but it is prevented from killing the prince by a demon or water spirit (*nḫt*). On another occasion, the wife kills a snake, which has entered the prince's bedroom. She then announces: "Look, your god has given one of your fates into your hand. He will protect [you from the others also]" (Lichtheim 1976, p. 202). This fate being averted, the prince made an offering to Pre, who has delivered him from this fate, but two fates remain.

One day while strolling with his dog, it discloses that it is his fate. The prince tries to escape by running down to the lake, only to have the crocodile snatch the dog and carry it off "to where the demon was" (Lichtheim 1976, p. 202). The crocodile returns to tell the prince that it is his fate, but offers to release him if he will help kill its nemesis, the water spirit. Unfortunately, the end of the papyrus is missing, but it is generally thought that the prince manages to avoid this final fate and lives happily ever after. The *Story of the Doomed Prince* certainly shows that one could not avoid one's fate by leaving Egypt; however, with divine intervention, life could be extended and the fated means of death perhaps changed.

It is unclear whether the calendar of lucky and unlucky days relates to one's fate. F. T. Miosi concludes, "There is no convincing grounds for positing an 'astrological' basis to the Egyptian concept of fate, destiny or whatever other term one wishes to use" (1982, p. 73). There is certainly nothing in the literature to suggest that amulets and other forms of magic had a role in altering one's fate. However, amulets may have been used in connection with unlucky days. Similarly, prophetic name formulae (e.g., *djed* + deity + *ʿnḫ.f/s* = "deity X says he/she will live") may have been used when a baby was born on an unlucky day. It is

unlikely that the use of such names was an attempt to negate one's *šȝw*, because people did not know their fate. On the other hand, a parent would know if the birthday had a bad omen and might select a name that expressed the hope that the child would live.

Thus, one's fate appears in a sense to have operated on two tracks: the *šȝw* was set by the sun god and announced at birth by the Hathors (at least in folkloristic tales); and the lucky or unlucky days were determined by mythological precedent. How these two were interrelated is uncertain, but people would not have known their ordained fate unless it was divinely revealed in some manner, whereas they would have known if they faced an ill-fated mythological omen. Prophylactic steps could be taken in the latter case, but a person could apparently do little to alter *šȝw*, as a statement in the *Story of Sinuhe* suggests: "Is there a god who does not know what he has ordained, a man who knows how it will be?" (Lichtheim 1975, p. 227).

## BIBLIOGRAPHY

Grumuch-Shirun, I. "Schicksal." In *Lexikon der Ägyptologie*, 5:598–600. Wiesbaden, 1981.

Lichtheim, Miriam. *Ancient Egyptian Literature*. 2 vols. Berkeley, 1975, 1976.

Miosi, F. T. "God, Fate and Free Will in Egyptian Wisdom Literature." In *Studies in Honour of Ronald J. Williams*, pp. 69–111. Toronto, 1982.

Morenz, S. *Untersuchungen zur Rolle des Schicksals in der ägyptischen Religion*. Berlin, 1960.

Morenz, Siegfried. *Egyptian Religion*. Ithaca, N.Y., 1969.

Ringgren, H. *Fatalistic Beliefs in Religion, Folklore, and Literature*. Stockholm, 1967.

JAMES K. HOFFMEIER

**FAUNA.** A wide variety of animals were used in ancient Egypt. The Nile Valley fauna were a source of nutrition, they inspired symbolic expression, and they served as subjects for art and literature. Today, nearly fifty species of mammals, almost five hundred species of birds, and at least 169 species of fish can be found there; in ancient times, the fauna was even more diverse. Ironicly, the domesticated species that helped provide Egypt with its legendary surpluses were, for the most part, introduced from abroad—while the indigenous fauna remained genetically wild.

By the early Neolithic period (c.5000 BCE), the deserts and the Nile Valley harbored an essentially modern fauna. Worldwide climatic change had forced savanna animals to retreat south from growing North African deserts, and during the Predynastic period, cattle, sheep, goats, and pigs, along with wheat and barley agriculture, gained the dominant role as the Nile Valley's source of nutrition. Although the desert regions would continue to harbor small populations of oryx, addax, hartebeest, and gazelle into the mid-twentieth century, the Nile Valley, altered to accommodate domesticated plants and animals, reduced the preferred habitat of native species, extirpating many and driving some to extinction. Gone were the aurochsen, hippopotamus, otter, several species of fish, a number of birds, and eventually even the marsh-dwelling papyrus plant.

Researchers have postulated that widespread changes in the environment, the ecological needs of the animals, and/or aspects of Late Paleolithic culture might have produced the impetus behind the Near Eastern and Egyptian adoption of domestic fauna and flora. It is impossible, however, to delineate the primary causes. Stimuli from many sources, no doubt, functioned together to facilitate the transformation of the Nile Valley's human population from Late Paleolithic hunter-gathers to Neolithic food producers.

The earliest datable representations of Egypt's fauna are from the early Neolithic period, when the likenesses of animals inhabiting the Nile Valley and neighboring desert regions were pecked, etched, and painted on stone surfaces along the wadis, on cliffs, and atop mountain escarpments. Representations of cattle dominate the scenes, but elephant, giraffe, hartebeest, oryx, addax, hippopotamus, ibex, gazelle, ass, Barbary sheep, lion, leopard, and other wild cats are also depicted in such detail that taxonomic identification can be readily made. Wild and domesticated animals continued to be popular artistic subjects throughout dynastic times, but they reached a peak in authenticity during the Old Kingdom. For example, twenty-three fish taxa have been identified from tomb scenes; some are so clearly defined that specific (species), as opposed to simple generic (genus), designations are possible. Old Kingdom tomb scenes also contain depictions of taxa that can no longer be found in or near the lower Nile—the moonfish, the otter, and the ibis. The relative abundance of species may also have changed with time, as a result of increased human habitation and agricultural intensification. For example, *Tilapia* is probably the most numerous food fish in the Nile today, but in a survey of the Memphis tomb depictions, *Mugils* (mullets) were the most abundantly represented fish, followed by *Tilapia* (red fish), *Clarias* (Nile catfish), *Synodontis* (schall catfish), and *Mormyrus* (elephant fish). The least frequently represented were *Lates* (Nile perch), *Citharinus* (moonfish), *Schilbe* (schilbe or Mendes fish), and *Tetraodon* (puffer fish). Interestingly, based on fish skeletons recovered from archaeological excavations, *Clarias* and *Synodontis*, not *Mugils* or *Tilapia*, were the most abundant food fish recovered (following the most popular synonymy, the genus *Oreochromis* is included within *Tilapia* spp.). Although frequency of representation in tomb scenes or frequency of archaeological recovery is by no means an accurate census of species abundance, the loss of shallow-water areas to agricultural development would have diminished prime catfish and *Tilapia* habitat. Mullets and eels, once known to migrate in great numbers as far south as Luxor, now barely reach south of Cairo.

The Nile Valley offered an excellent haven for migrating birds, and thousands of ducks, waders, and many others could be found wintering there. The Egyptians were exceptionally fond of dining on fowl, and many forms are depicted in aviaries and pens. The wild bird resources of Egypt were so large, however, that the widespread domestication of bird species may not have been as efficient or as satisfying as hunting and trapping them. Although their numbers have been dramatically reduced in modern times, even in the early twentieth century, the Faiyum Depression was noted as being extremely rich in migratory birds and a favorite site for hunters.

**Domestic Food Animals.** Given the diversity of animals in the Nile Valley, it is interesting that so few were actually domesticated. Arguably, only two domesticated species of geese (the greylag and the white-fronted goose) and perhaps the donkey, pig, aurochs (wild cow), and cat may have *some* genetic ancestry from Egypt.

The earliest undisputed appearances of domesticated cattle, sheep, and goats, come from the Neolithic site of Merimde and from the Faiyum (c.5000 BCE). Many scholars believe that the domestication of herd animals was the most important step in the exploitation of the animal world. The importance of cattle, sheep, and goats to the ancient Egyptians is based on their ability to obtain nourishment from grasses and other fibrous forage that humans cannot digest. In Egypt, grasses grew in a variety of areas and, depending on the availability of water, could be tall and lush or sparse, dry, and stunted. The productivity of grazing lands varied from year to year, owing to the vagaries of Egypt's rainfall, the reluctance to irrigate fields devoted to nontrade or nonfood crops, and the planting/fallow schedules of given plots. Consequently, a grazing strategy for herd animals evolved that acceptably countered these local constraints.

In studying present-day land and water relationships among nonmechanized farmers and herders, there exists an interesting correlation between planting and herding. Ethnographic studies suggest that when the probability of receiving sufficient water to grow a crop on a particular plot of land reached 0.90 (nine out of ten years), that land was devoted to cultivation. Land with a water ratio between 0.50 and 0.30 was characterized by chronic crop failure and was considered a high-risk area for cultivation, but excellent for pasture. Areas with ratios of 0.10 were seldom cultivated, but might be useful as pasture land. Egypt possessed lands with water ratio levels ranging from above 0.90, near the Nile, to those well below

FAUNA. *Detail from a fishing and fowling scene, eighteenth dynasty.* The copy (by Nina de Garis Davies) is of a painting in the tomb of Menna at Thebes. (The Metropolitan Museum of Art, 30.4.48)

0.10, near the desert boundaries. Thus a mixed system of cultivation, penned animal raising, and range herding proved to be an efficient strategy for capturing the most benefits from that natural environment.

The earliest Egyptian agriculturalists lived on the natural levees of the Nile or beyond the reach of the floods on the desert border; they cultivated the rich inundated lands between the levees and desert. Those areas not receiving enough water to support crops were range lands. As more land came under cultivation, less land was available for herding. Given their geography, climate, and technology, the ancient Egyptians eventually reached their limit—a point at which it became no longer profitable to expend energy for agricultural expansion. Herd animals provided the most effective means of using the otherwise unproductive lands, and they also served as insurance against crop failures.

Because Egyptian herds were large, overgrazing must have become a problem, which required seasonal grazing forays: small dispersed cattle camps and, in the driest seasons, large drives to some permanent forage and watered areas. Some evidence suggests that cattle were herded to the Nile Delta, which was not then as heavily cultivated as Upper Egypt. Although ancient drives may have crossed hundreds of kilometers, with hardships for both animals

and herdsmen, it has been documented among nonmechanized farmers that livestock productivity (in terms of weight gain, calving rate, and calf survival) is better among migratory than sedentary herds. Egyptians maximized cattle production by keeping some animals in pens or corrals and bringing the feed to the animals, as is done in present-day societies; a method of adding important nourishment was by incorporating grain and/or bread dough. If this served as a healthful supplement for the few penned animals, it could not have been done, as it was economically unfeasible, for Egypt's vast herds. Egypt's herds were large because of the cultural values attributed to cattle. The great numbers of cattle recorded as attached to personal and temple estates exemplified unnecessary overindulgence. Egypt's large herds, however, do make evolutionary sense under certain conditions: they are a means of providing an immediate food supply and they ensure the survival of at least some animals after an epidemic or an environmental disaster.

For rapid replenishment of a herd, the large-herd philosophy works well. The ancient Egyptians fully realized that a certain percentage of the herd would die each year, but in a bad year a herdsman who loses one-third of the stock is better off beginning with sixty cattle than with six. When the availability of food is threatened by catastrophe, particularly in a well-populated area such as the Nile Valley, that catastrophe will affect all agricultural products. A large herd would provide immediate food for the populace (milk, blood, and/or meat), as well as leave enough stock to propagate a new herd. A diversified herd, incorporating sheep, goats, and cattle, would have served as an additional safeguard, since each species thrives under different environmental conditions. Goats are browsers, do not compete with sheep and cattle for food, and are the most drought tolerant. Cattle and sheep are grazers, but sheep are more tolerant of drought than cattle. In an environmental crisis, the three herd animals would have different probabilities for survival, depending on the nature of the problem. Because sheep and goats reproduce rapidly, their herds can recover relatively quickly. Thus, although the Egyptian herding system would appear to be a pretentious one that overemphasized numbers, there is enough evidence to suggest that large herd sizes actually represent adaptive responses to Egypt's environmental uncertainties.

By the New Kingdom, four types of cattle were kept: a long-horned variety, a short-horned form, a hornless breed, and the zebu (brahma). There were two forms of sheep, but only one type of goat can be identified from skeletal materials and pictures. Cattle served as sources of meat, milk, and hides; the castrates (oxen) were used as draught animals. Sheep were primarily used for their meat and wool. Based on tomb scenes, Egypt possessed, in succession, two different types of sheep: to the Middle Kingdom, a hairy thin-tailed breed, with crescent-shaped, lateral horns; a later woolly breed, with a shorter fatter tail and recurved horns. As the wool of the new sheep was well suited to spinning and weaving, woolen fabrics became more prominent in the later periods. Interestingly, shears do not occur before the Third Intermediate Period, so the wool was evidently plucked or cut away from the skin with a knife. (The fat-tail sheep of modern-day Egypt was a recent introduction, not a survival from pharaonic times.)

The ancient Egyptian goat resembles goats recovered from Neolithic sites of the Near East, including Jericho, but somewhat larger in size; it was long-legged, short-haired, and had a long face with a straight nose. Scimitar-horned goats appear to have existed in Old Kingdom times, but by the Hyksos period (c.1663–1555 BCE), they had become rare. The predominant goat possessed a twisted (corkscrew) horn—and the breed can be found in Egypt today. Goats ranged in coloration from solid to piebald black and white. The modern goat of Egypt—with its convex nose, drooping ears, and long hair—is not a direct descendant of the ancient forms but is a recent introduction.

Goats were kept for their meat, skin, and perhaps milk, though less importantly for their hair. The tomb scenes depict only short-haired varieties, which would not have been good suppliers of wool; this suggests that goats were raised primarily for meat. Based on the number of goat (and sheep) bones recovered from archaeological sites, goat and mutton was a common dish for the peasant and the working class. Goatskin was used to produce a diverse number of leather objects.

According to the Greek historian Herodotus, pigs were regarded as unclean by the ancient Egyptians and the swineherd was held in the lowest regard. To the uninitiated, Herodotus' statements might indicate that pigs were therefore an uncommon or an undesirable food. Also, pigs were seldom depicted in Egyptian art or specifically mentioned in texts. Archaeologically, the pig is known as an early domestican in Egypt (c.4800 BCE) and a popular food item. The Egyptian pig was long-legged and bristly, and it resembled the wild boar more than do modern breeds. Excavations throughout Egypt have unearthed pig bones and they seem particularly abundant in areas associated with working-class or peasant-related activities. At the Amarna workmen's village, an elaborate pig-farming facility was unearthed, with individual pens for sows and their offspring. The chief role of the pig was as a source of meat and fat. Pigs are well-suited to this role because they produce two litters a year, mature within a year, and are comparatively long-lived. Their ability to adapt to different environments allows them to range freely, to root in or near the village, or to be confined to the home or sty. This versatility offers a unique advantage over other domesticants, particularly in areas of dense human populations.

**Working Animals and Pets.** The Egyptians employed a number of different animals as beasts of burden. While oxen usually served as the draught animal of agriculture, equines (horses, donkeys) played a significant role in transporting goods and later in warfare. The donkey was the principal beast of burden from at least the Predynastic at Omari. The horse, although some remains date to the Middle Kingdom, was not common in Egypt until late in the Second Intermediate Period, when it was adopted with the Near Eastern chariot for warfare. The horse, thought to have been introduced by the Hyksos, was a small Asian breed that measured less than 1.5 meters (5 feet) tall at the shoulder. Horses were never abundant in Egypt and were limited to the aristocracy and military. The camel, although its remains have been recovered as early as the first dynasty at Helwan, did not serve as a beast of burden until Roman times.

Typical household pets, such as dogs and cats, were common in Egypt. Several breeds of dogs were present, some clearly products of selective breeding, especially the greyhound and saluki type; the majority, however, were street dogs not attached to a master. Cats were part of the indigenous Egyptian fauna; in appearance, when wild, they resembled a light grey or tawny tabbie. Cats that can be considered unquestionably domesticated are not known in Egypt until the Middle Kingdom, but cat skeletons are known from the Predynastic period in a context that would suggest that they were "tamed" if not domesticated.

Although an endless variety of exotic birds and mammals (monkeys, antelopes, gazelle, ibex, and even hyenas) were tamed for religious and secular purposes—and exotic pets seem to have been fashionable for the upper class as well as given in tribute to the king—these animals remained genetically wild. Evidence from the dynastic period indicates that large numbers of wild animals were held captive in what could be described as a royal zoo or menagerie. One such example was that of Amenhotpe III, who had animals roaming freely within an enclosure 300 by 600 meters (950 by 1850 feet). The captive animals served a variety of religious and secular purposes.

Lions as well as other species of great cats were favorite companions for kings and nobles, often shown accompanying them at the hunt. The hunting of particularly dangerous animals, such as the hippopotamus and the lion, became a royal prerogative, but one that also held symbolic significance. Wall scenes that depict the king (or a noble) harpooning a hippopotamus, for example, are thought to represent the ruler's triumph over chaos.

[*See also* Amphibians and Reptiles; Animal Husbandry; Bees and Honey; Birds; Canines; Cattle; Crocodiles; Diet; Elephants; Equines; Felines; Fish; Frogs; Giraffes; Hares; Hedgehogs; Hippopotami; Hunting; Ichneumon; Insects; Milk; Monkeys and Baboons; Pigs; Poultry; Rhinoceroces; Scarabs; Scorpions; Sheep and Goats; Snakes; *and* Zoological Gardens.]

## BIBLIOGRAPHY

Brewer, Douglas J., and Renée Friedman. *Fish and Fishing in Ancient Egypt.* Warminster, 1989.

Brewer, Douglas J., Donald B. Redford, and Susan Redford. *Domesticated Plants and Animals: The Egyptian Origins.* Warminster, 1994. Brewer and Friedman (1989) and this bok are the two best sources for comparing artistic representations of Egypt's fauna to the zoological literature, for clarifying generic and specific identification of the depictions; but see also Houlihan (1986).

Clutton-Brock, Julian. "The Buhen Horse." *Journal of Archaeological Science* 1 (1974), 89–100. This work brings up the possibility that the Buhen horse stated to be of Middle Kingdom Age, might be an intrusive artifact of a later date due to wear patterns on the teeth.

Clutton-Brock, Julian. *A Natural History of Domesticated Mammals.* Austin, 1987. A standard source for introducing uninitiated readers to domesticated animals and their origins. It supersedes the classic 1963 text by Zeuner.

Houlihan, Patrick H.. *The Birds of Ancient Egypt.* Warminster, 1986.

Kemp, Barry J. *Ancient Egypt: Anatomy of a Civilization.* London, 1991. Although listed here as a source for pig-keeping, this is an excellent work for those interested in glimpsing aspects of administrating farms and herds during the Amarna period.

Janssen, Rosiland, and Jack Janssen. *Egyptian Household Animals.* Haverfordwest, 1989. Easy to read introduction to Egyptian domesticates (but lacks citations).

Osborn, Dale, and Ibrahim Helmy. *The Contemporary Land Mammals of Egypt.* Fieldiana Zoology, n.s., 5. Chicago, 1980. Best source on modern mammalian fauna of Egypt. It includes a short natural history of animals and where they are located.

Redford, Susan, and Donald B. Redford. "Graffiti and Petroglyphs Old and New from the Eastern Desert." *Journal of the American Research Center in Egypt* 26 (1989), 3–50. The only systematic treatment of the Eastern Desert's pictographs.

Winkler, Hans. *Rock Drawings of Southern Upper Egypt.* 2 vols. Oxford, 1938. One of the only comprehensive studies of Neolithic rock art.

Zeuner, Frederick E. *A History of Domesticated Animals.* New York, 1963. The classic text for those interested in the origins of animal domestication.

DOUGLAS J. BREWER

**FELINE DEITIES.** The oldest and best known of the Egyptian feline deities is the cat goddess Bastet, who is attested since the Old Kingdom. Although Bubastis was obviously the town of her origin, evidence exists to suggest that she was worshiped in various other places and associated with a number of different deities. In Memphis, Bastet was identified with the lion goddess Sekhmet.

During the Middle Kingdom Sekhmet was known primarily for her wild and warlike qualities and was generally feared, like the ferocious lioness, and Bastet came to be considered the milder, appeasing aspect of the same divinity. Likewise, Bastet was considered the mild eye of Re, as opposed to the scorching Sekhmet-eye. This position of Sekhmet and Bastet as simultaneous complements and opposites is also reflected in the association of the first with war, pestilence, and illness, and that of the second with female fertility, sexuality, and the protection of pregnant women and infants. In Heliopolis, Bastet was equated to Tefnut; she was thus acknowledged as the daughter of Atum and consequently integrated into the Heliopolitan pantheon. From Old Kingdom times, Bastet was associated with Hathor, and during the Middle Kingdom with Mut. There are also references to an association with Isis, who is occasionally pictured as a cat; in Edfu, Bastet is referred to as "the $b_3$ of Isis."

It is not always easy to distinguish the strictly feline traits from leonine traits in the representations of deities. A current suggestion is that Bastet had originally been a wild lioness, whose features in the course of time lost their ferocity and softened into those of a benevolent cat. This alleged change of character has often been ascribed to ecological and societal developments, including the gradual migration of lions from north to south and finally out of Egypt, and the increasing presence and growing popularity of the cat there. However, the proposition that mythology and religion followed zoological developments

FELINE DEITIES. *Bronze figurine of Bastet, from Merenptah's palace at Memphis, Late period.* (University of Pennsylvania, Philadelphia. Neg. # S8–68303 [detail])

Although feline deities are predominantly female, there is one divine male cat that is often encountered in religious texts (for example, in the *Book of Going Forth by Day* [*Book of the Dead*]); he is pictured cutting off the head of a snake. This scene represents the traditional theme of the sun god in the act of destroying the evil power of Apep; the tomcat is but one of the many manifestations of Re.

### BIBLIOGRAPHY

Kleinsgütl, Dagmar. *Feliden in Altägypten.* Beiträge zur Ägyptologie, 14. Vienna, 1997.

Malek, J. *The Cat in Ancient Egypt.* London, 1993.

Osborn, Dale. *The Mammals of Ancient Egypt.* Warminster, 1998.

Scandone Matthiae, Gabriela. "L'Occhio del Sole: Le divinità feline femminile dell'Egitto faraonico." *Studi epigrafici e linguistici sul Vicino Oriente antico* 10 (1993), 10–19.

Stück, L. "Katz." In *Lexikon der Ägyptologie*, 3:367–370. Wiesbaden, 1976.

ALEID DE JONG

**FELINES.** The ancient Egyptians were familiar with a number of species belonging to the family Felidae. These small to large cats included lions (*Panthera leo*), *rw*, *m3i*, and *m3i ḥz3*; leopards (*Panthera pardus*), *3bi*, *3bi šmꜥ*, *b3*, *b3 šmꜥ*, and *knmwt*; cheetahs (*Acinonyx jubatus*), *nṯr(i)t*, *3bi*, *3bi mḥ*, *b3 mḥ*, and *m3fdt* (?); servals (*Felis serval*); caracals (*Caracal caracal*), *inb*; wild cats or jungle cats (*Felis sylvestris*, *Felis chaus*); and the domestic cat (*Felis catus*), *miw* (surely onomatopoetic, "mewer") and feminine *miit*. The human–feline relationship has a very long history in Egypt, and there is a wealth of representational, textual, and zooarchaeological evidence indicating that some of these carnivores, notably the lion and household cat, considerably influenced pharaonic culture and life.

Precisely when lions became extinct in Egypt is unknown. They roamed widely the semidesert regions bordering the Nile Valley during Predynastic times and for much of the historic period, and became less common by the New Kingdom. The lion was admired for its majestic appearance, strength, and ferocity. The male was one of the most conspicuous and enduring symbols of Egyptian kingship. Already on the so-called Battlefield Palette, dating from the Late Predynastic period (Naqada III), a larger-than-life lion represents the triumphant king, devouring his defeated enemies. The link between the two is manifested through sphinxes, generally human-headed lions, the embodiment of divine royal power; the fourth dynasty Great Sphinx built by Khafre at Giza is the foremost example. This connection probably also accounts for the pharaohs' practice of keeping tame lions as palace pets; these even accompanied them into war. One first dynasty ruler was buried at Abydos with seven juvenile

is one that cannot be confirmed. Furthermore, since in the Late period Bastet appears to have regained her lioness features, it is more likely that she alternatively represents both aspects.

To a certain extent, this ambivalence of character may also be attributed to the other goddesses that are sometimes, completely or partially, pictured as felines, such as Mut, Hathor, Wadjit, Pakhet, and Tefnut. As Dale Osborn points out, the goddess Mafdet, who is often included in this list, does not belong there: she must be identified as a lynx rather than a cat.

lions. During the nineteenth dynasty, Ramesses II delighted in his pet lions; one of his favorites was named "Slayer of His Foes." Inscriptions describe this same monarch doing battle "like a ferocious lion" and "like a lion when he tasted combat."

Lions were among the characteristic fauna in desert landscape scenes during the Old and Middle Kingdoms, often seen attacking prey. Hunting them, though, appears always to have been a royal prerogative. In the eighteenth dynasty, Amenhotpe III issued a series of scarabs commemorating his killing of 102 (variant, 110) lions. The most vivid illustration of lion-hunting is preserved on the celebrated "painted box" discovered in the eighteenth dynasty tomb of Tutankhamun. From a racing horse-drawn chariot, the young king single-handedly routs a company of lions, slaying them with his superhuman abilities. Dispatching lions also showed the world how strong and mighty the ruler was. A park where such ritual hunts were staged has been identified near the temple that Amenhotpe III built at Soleb in Upper Nubia. During the New Kingdom, lions were also imported into Egypt as trade or tribute from Nubia and western Asia.

The lion was viewed as a magical guardian figure with apotropaic qualities. This symbolism is evident on royal thrones and various types of ritual furniture, which customarily incorporate protective standing lions into their design. From an early age, monumental sculptures of this noble beast were sometimes set up flanking the entrances to shrines and temples. Leonine imagery abounds in religious iconography. This species had affiliations with numerous deities in the pharaonic pantheon; the most important were lioness goddesses such as Pakhet, Tefnut, Hathor, Bastet, and Mut. Above all, there was the dangerous Sekhmet, one of the many forms of the fiery Eye (or daughter) of Re, the consort of Ptah at Memphis, who was depicted as a young woman with the head of a lioness. The male also had strong solar associations. A pair of lions placed back to back, supporting the sun disk between them, were identified with the eastern and western horizons; called "yesterday" and "tomorrow," they symbolize eternity. During the Late Dynastic and Greco-Roman periods, sacred lions were maintained in the temples of some leonine gods. At the Delta site of Leontopolis (modern Tel el-Muqdam) and at Saqqara, textual evidence suggests that these venerated creatures were mummified and received elaborate burials, but their tombs have yet to be located.

Both the leopard and the cheetah are extremely rare, perhaps even extinct, in modern Egypt. In antiquity, however, these sleek felines were certainly more abundant. Attested from the Late Predynastic period (Naqada III) onward, leopards repeatedly appear among the wildlife in desert hunting compositions on royal and private monuments. The cheetah can seldom, if ever, be positively identified in these. During the Old Kingdom, there is one depiction, on a block of limestone relief, of a tame leopard walking on a leash with its dwarf minder. Another lively vignette, in the fifth dynasty tomb-chapel of Ptahhotep II (D 64) at Saqqara, pictures a leopard and a lion being transported in strong wooden cages, fresh from the chase. In the eighteenth dynasty, Queen Hatshepsut could not have failed to impress when she arrived in the royal carrying-chair with her pair of pet cheetahs following just behind. Additional leopards and cheetahs arrived in Egypt as tribute and trade from Nubia and Punt, as captured in the Punt reliefs on Hatshepsut's mortuary temple at Deir el-Bahri, and in the eighteenth dynasty Theban tomb-chapel of the vizier Rekhmire (tomb 100). Their skins too were prized and often imported; these were traditionally worn by the *sm*-priest (or the *iwn-mwt-f* priest), the supervisor of burial rites, who performed the Opening of the Mouth ceremony.

Images of lions, leopards, and small wild cats figure in the bestiary of demons and real and imaginary animals engraved on apotropaic wands or "magic knives," fashioned from the canines of hippopotamuses during the Middle Kingdom. The felines on these objects are routinely knife-wielding or attacking serpents, helping to safeguard mothers and young children. The funerary equipment of eighteenth and nineteenth dynasty kings included wooden statuettes of striding leopards (often incorrectly called panthers). A pair of them from the tomb of Tutankhamun bear gilded figures of the pharoah standing on their backs. The leopard may have served the sovereign as a protector and guide in the netherworld. Various attempts have been made to identify the animal associated with the violent goddess Mafdet (perhaps "the Runner"). Whether it was a leopard, cheetah, or possibly a common genet (*Genetta genetta*) cannot be determined, but its Egyptian name would befit the cheetah, the world's fastest land creature.

There are only a few illustrations of the serval and caracal in Egyptian art. The former species is likely to be recognized from portraits on a series of faience plaques of the eighteenth dynasty from the temple of Hathor at Serabit el-Khadim in the southern Sinai. Servals may have been imported into Egypt from the tropical African hinterlands and may be the "cats of Miw" mentioned in a Ramessid period letter concerning the delivery of Nubian commodities. The caracal, a desert lynx, remains to this day a rare denizen of Egypt. Their realistic representations, easily identified by the long ear tufts, appear in desert hunting scenes in the fifth dynasty tomb-chapel of Nimaatre (G 2097) at Giza, and in the rock-cut tomb of the twelfth dynasty nomarch Khnumhotep III at Beni Hasan (tomb 3).

FELINES. *Statue of a cat, Saqqara, Ptolemaic period.* This hollow bronze statue served as a coffin for a mummified cat. The right ear is pierced to hold a gold ring, now lost. (The Metropolitan Museum of Art, Harris Brisbane Dick Fund, 1956. [56.16.1])

The household cat is perhaps the most frequently studied creature in Egyptian iconography. There are sound reasons for thinking that its original home was Egypt, even if conclusive evidence is still lacking. The date of its complete domestication has yet to be resolved. As ardent cat-lovers know, the most likely progenitor of the cat was the wild cat (also known as the Kaffir cat), still found along desert margins in modern Egypt. Several felines portrayed during the Old and Middle Kingdoms resemble this species; nonetheless, these may also be the jungle (or swamp) cat, a wetlands-dwelling resident of Egypt. One of these must have inspired the likeness of the fierce tomcat, probably a personification of the sun god Re, that slays the serpent god Apophis, the sun's eternal enemy, as seen in vignettes of the *Book of Going Forth by Day* (*Book of the Dead*) and other New Kingdom mythological compositions. The common cat is noticeably missing from the vast repertoire of everyday life scenes in Old Kingdom tomb-chapels of the elite, indicating to some researchers that it had yet fully to enter the company of humans. However, other specialists have doubted the reliability of the artistic record as proof of this. In any case, it is only in the eleventh dynasty that cats begin to occur in a domestic context. From its earliest appearance, in the rock-cut tomb of the nomarch Baket III at Beni Hasan (tomb 15), it is apparent that the cat was valued in ancient Egypt as a mouser.

In wall paintings and reliefs of tomb-chapels belonging to Theban notables of the eighteenth and nineteenth dynasties, we encounter the cat in its most touching role—

a beloved family pet, sometimes bejeweled, often sitting under the mistress's chair. In contrast with pet dogs, however, there is only one cat known to have received a personal name: in the eighteenth dynasty tomb-chapel of Puimre at Thebes (tomb 39), a tabby is called "The Pleasant One." Since most cat owners seem to be women, several leading Egyptologists have suggested that the cat may have had erotic connotations or was even a symbol of female sexuality. The image of a cat is known from a host of minor works of art, such as jewelry, cosmetic implements, and amulets. It was also a popular character in the topsy-turvy animal world found on limestone figured ostraca and a couple of "satirical" papyri from the nineteenth and twentieth dynasties.

Nowadays, the cat is widely known as a manifestation of the goddess Bastet, who was worshipped at the Delta site of Bubastis (modern Tell Basta), but this association came comparatively late in Egyptian history. Beginning in the Third Intermediate Period, cats became closely linked with the gentle side of the lioness goddesses. This connection prompted the thousands of votive bronze cat statuettes, as well as the tens of millions of cat mummies, offered by pious pilgrims wishing to petition these deities at their cult temples in late dynastic and Greco-Roman times. According to Diodorus Siculus (I, 84), who visited Egypt in the first century BCE, the unintentional killing of a cat brought a sentence of death.

[*See also* Feline Deities.]

## BIBLIOGRAPHY

Boessneck, Joachim. *Die Tierwelt des alten Ägypten: Untersucht anhand kulturgeschichtlicher und zoologischer Quellen.* Munich, 1988. An authoritative discussion of felines in ancient Egypt; includes zooarcheological findings.

Charron, Alain. "Des 'momies' de lions à Saqqarah." *Bulletin de la Société d'Égyptologie, Genève* 21 (1997), 5–10. Includes interesting remarks on lion cults during the Late Dynastic and Greco-Roman periods.

*Les Chats des pharaons: 4000 ans de divinité féline. Catalogue, 27 octobre 1989–25 février 1990.* Brussels, 1989. Informative catalog of a museum exhibition devoted to the domestic cat in ancient Egypt, at the Institut Royal des Sciences Naturelles de Belgique, Brussels.

Delvaux, Luc, and Eugène Warmenbol, eds. *Les divins chats d'Égypte: Un air subtil, un dangereux parfum.* Leuven, 1991. Important collection of eighteen articles relating to aspects of the common cat during pharaonic civilization, published on the occasion of the exhibition *Les chats des pharaons.* Contains an extensive bibliography.

de Wit, Constant. *Le rôle el le sens lion dans l'Égypte ancienne.* Leiden, 1951, 2d ed. rev., Luxor, 1978. Excellent in-depth study of the place of lions in sacred and secular life in ancient Egypt.

Hornung, Erik, and Elisabeth Staehelin, eds. *Skarabäen und andere Siegelamulette aus Basler Sammlungen.* Mainz, 1976. In discussing small cats, lions, and leopards on scarabs, and as scaraboids, the authors present a valuable overview of these felines in Egyptian religious beliefs, with many references.

Houlihan, Patrick F. *The Animal World of the Pharaohs.* London and New York, 1996. In this handsomely illustrated book for a general audience, considerable space is devoted to surveying the various felines in ancient Egypt; extensive bibliography.

Jordan, Paul, and John Ross. *Riddles of the Sphinx.* New York, 1998. This popular work presents much useful information on sphinxes in ancient Egypt, notably their close leonine associations.

Makek, Jaromir. *The Cat in Ancient Egypt.* London, 1993; reprint, Philadelphia, 1997. Authoritative and well-illustrated survey of the household cat in Egypt.

Osborn, Dale J., and Ibrahim Helmy. *The Contemporary Land Mammals of Egypt (Including Sinai).* Fieldiana Zoology, New Series, 5. Chicago, 1980. The standard work on the land mammals of modern Egypt.

Osborn, Dale J., with Jana Osbornová. *The Mammals of Ancient Egypt.* Warminster, 1998. Provides a fine survey of the felines recognizable in Egyptian iconography.

PATRICK F. HOULIHAN

**FERTILITY.** In the ancient Egyptian context, the concept of "fertility" is strangely elusive. There is no depiction that realizes this abstraction; it is not described, discussed, or even designated by any precise term. Its absence, however, was denoted by the words *ind* (barrenness, of women) and *mḥs* (sterility, of men).

Nonetheless, as in all other early civilizations, the concept of fertility was immanent in all aspects of life. The Nile Valley owes its fertility to the rich black silt brought downstream by the river—the womb in which the planted grain germinates and matures under proper climatic conditions. The invisible power to grow crops was visible in the dark bounty of the flooding river, which was imagined to be carried by a personification of the Nile, the androgynous deity Hapy. "Hapy" was also the name for the Nile, specifically during the annual inundation, the time when the river's water and silt were directly related to the fertility of the land. The deities connected with the end product, the harvest—for example, Nepri, god of corn, Renenwetet, goddess of the vintage, and the chthonic gods Osiris and Sokar—are, by implication, also deities of fertility.

The Egyptian pantheon included gods whose main attribute was their virility: Min is the god of vegetation and harvest, and Amun acquired this attribute through his part in the creation myth and his affinity with Min. Their main area of concern was not human fertility, but the fertility of the land. Osiris, however, was concerned with both. When the world was created, according to several versions of the Egyptian creation myth, fertility simply happened. In the Heliopolitan version, when Atum, "Lord of All," impregnated himself, the required male and female elements were already present in his own body, and his issue was the first divine pair, Shu and Tefnut. In the Memphite Theology, Atum's creation of this pair is the result of a masturbatory act, not a bizarre form of reproduction, but a solution, in sexual terms, of the transition from a unitary creator to a sexual pair. In the Hermopolitan version, four pairs of male and female elements constituted the beginning, with the implied catalyst of fertility

FERTILITY. *Depiction of the fertility god Hapy.* (Courtesy Dorothea Arnold)

to effectuate the next step, in the form of the egg that appeared on the primordial mound, with no further explanation of who was responsible for it. No goddess except Nut is recorded to have borne more than one child. As for the gods, four sons are attributed to Horus, but they were not necessarily created through the agency of a mother.

In the New Kingdom theological system of Akhenaten, predating his move to Tell el-Amarna, the king himself, as the earthly representative of the solar disk, contains both male and female principles in his body, anticipating the phrases in the solar hymn which describe how the Aten has placed the seed of men in the wombs of women.

The feminine iconography of the king in the Karnak colossi and numerous reliefs suggests that the king is not the originator of the fertile sperm—this role belongs to the Aten—but he shelters it while it matures, just as in the Heliopolitan myth Atum became the womb for his own seed. This concept emphasizes the king's direct link to the Aten, the creator god, whose power of procreation is transmitted solely via the king to ordinary humans. This interpretation may help to explain the unisexual, or feminized, aspect of the Amarna period.

Throughout Egyptian history, in the royal family the power of procreation and proof of fertility was displayed

FERTILITY. *A so-called "paddle doll," eleventh dynasty, Thebes.* Wooden figurines such as this one, graphically depicting the female body, were previously and incorrectly thought to have been children's toys. Rather, they were most likely magically connected with the sexual aspects of regeneration and rebirth. (The Metropolitan Museum of Art, Museum Excavations, 1931; Rogers Fund, 1931. [31.3.36])

in multiple offspring (in the Amarna period, there was emphasis on female children). The harem served as a repository for the royal seed, offering the promise of the renewal of divine kingship. Producing a large number of children, as is recorded by Ramesses II, among others, would have guaranteed the succession.

Among ordinary mortals, it is rarely said that a large number of children is the ideal, although it might bring respect in the afterworld. The New Kingdom *Instructions of Anii* advises that it is a good thing to have numerous children because they bring recognition. It was crucial to have children to look after their parents in old age and to arrange their burials.

The Egyptians' knowledge of the processes of conception, pregnancy, and birth implies that they held views about human and animal fertility, but they seem not to have found it necessary (or perhaps appropriate) to discuss the idea. They understood the procreative consequences of cohabitation and correctly calculated the nine months of pregnancy. They seem to have taken the powers of engendering and conceiving for granted, if only because they recorded cases to the contrary. Medical prescriptions, magic formulas, and aphrodisiacs seem to have as their ultimate aim the increase of sexual enjoyment rather than specifically securing fertility.

The numerous votive offerings presented to Hathor, goddess of love and motherhood, are not explicitly to be taken as prayers for fertility in the sense that the offerer wished for numerous children in this life. But at Thebes, where many votive offerings have been found, Hathor was also goddess of the western mountain, the gate to the afterworld. It was to her domain in the western cliffs that Amun-Re traveled from Karnak to renew his creative power in a celebration of divine marriage.

The annual cycle of the seasons was the pulse of life to the Egyptians, and its repetitiveness became synonymous with eternity. The relation of the fertile soil to the promise of eternal life was visualized in the motif combining the familiar shape of Osiris with a seed tray, a part of the burial equipment. Egyptian funeral practices express the notion of fertility in subtly sexual terms: the ministrations of Isis to awaken her deceased husband were seen as exemplifying the sexual union required to achieve rebirth.

The link between the blackness of the Nile silt and its implications for fertility were reflected in some representations of deceased royalty: black figures of Queen Ahmose Nefertari, the black seated statue of Montuhotep I, and the black image of Tutankhamun among three red images on his cartouche-shaped perfume container. The blackness symbolizes the state of the life cycle just before rebirth, before the resurrection of the individual or of the dynasty. The black unguent offered to the god Min at the temple of Edfu, and the black bitumen-smeared guardian statues from the tomb of Tutankhamun, also affirm this interpretation of the signification of blackness, which may be the only way the Egyptians knew to give visual expression to the phenomenon of fertility.

[*See also* Erotica; Hathor; Min; *and* Sexuality.]

**BIBLIOGRAPHY**

Baines, John. *Fecundity Figures: Egyptian Personification and the Iconology of a Genre.* Warminster, 1984.

"Fruchtbarkeit." In *Lexikon der Ägyptologie,* 2:336–344. Wiesbaden, 1975.

Janssen, Rorsalind M., and Jac J. Janssen. *Growing Up in Ancient Egypt.* London, 1990.

Manniche, Lise. "The Complexion of Queen Ahmosi Nefertare." *Acta Orientalis* 40 (1979), 11–19.

Manniche, Lise. *Sexual Life in Ancient Egypt.* London and New York, 1987.

LISE MANNICHE

**FESTIVAL CALENDARS.** Egyptian temple walls or doorways were inscribed with a series of detailed accounts connected with the religious activity of the residing deity or deities. These texts are called "festival calendars." Being a requisite element of the inscriptional setup, they were put into place shortly before the temple was fully operational. Usually they consist of a terse, non-narrative rendering of the key events of the Egyptian civil year as they affected the particular temple: religious celebrations, sacerdotal duties, and lists of offerings that had to be made. These texts are often crucial for reconstructing the calendrical outlook of a single priesthood and for understanding the complex economic subsistence of the priests and workers.

The most ancient festival calendar that is preserved dates from the Old Kingdom. It is written on two sides of the doorway in King Newoserre Any's funerary sun temple. Although fragments from Sahure's mortuary temple, situated in his valley complex, may be an earlier fifth dynasty example, it is Newoserre Any's lengthy account that provides us with the basic arrangement of these calendars. Generally, there is a preamble covering the construction of the temple or additions made to an existing one, the donations made by the pharaoh, often with dates, and the purpose of these offerings. Newoserre Any's text then details the festival celebrations themselves. Exact dates within the civil year are listed in conjunction with precisely described foods—for example, one haunch of beef or five bundles of vegetables. Even when the celebration is related to the moon, the calendrical organization is that of the 365-day civil year. For a lunar-based feast, such as the full moon, additional data are presented. In certain of these calendars, but not all, the estates providing the temple equipment and foods are credited. Ramesses III's extensive Medinet Habu festival calendar is the most highly itemized in this way.

Festival calendars were a continuous and characteristic aspect of most religious institutions from the Old Kingdom onward. For instance, we can reconstruct what occurred at the twelfth dynasty site of Illahun from the fragmentary temple accounts there; unfortunately, the scarcity of royal hieroglyphic records limits us in interpreting any changes over time.

These lists of religious events attempted to cover all the standard celebrations. The lunar-based "feasts of heaven" were expressly separated from the "seasonal festivals" that occurred only once a year. Thutmose III of the eighteenth dynasty left us a long but fragmentary account of additions made to his endowments at Karnak. This composition, posted in his festival temple Akhmenu, is archetypical of the more exact yet simplified approach taken by later kings. The entire calendar is drawn up as a grid, with the left-hand column containing only dates and the right-hand columns having numbers referring to headings describing foods such as oxen, bulls, and ibexes. The almost mathematical regularity of this system of horizontally and vertically ruled boxes distinguishes the New Kingdom festival calendar arrangement from that of the Old. In fact, from this king's reign there remain five other separate festival calendars: at Buto in the Nile Delta (see below); at Karnak, south of the granite sanctuary; Karnak, Pylon VI, north wing; Karnak, south wall of the temple of Akhmenu; and at Elephantine. In the latter calendar there occurs one of the few references to the key ideal New Year's Day of the helical rising of Sirius (Egyptian Sothis) set on a specific day within the Egyptian civil year. In addition, Thutmose III's Buto text, this time recorded on a freestanding stela instead on a temple wall, presents a calendar that can only be dated to an earlier time period.

It must be kept in mind that kings could often renew the offerings of past monarchs without altering the earlier or original calendar. On the other hand, they might expand or revise old calendars; and it is only from internal evidence that we can judge between these two possibilities. To take an example, the fragmentary Amenhotpe I festival calendar seems to have been recopied from the Middle Kingdom, yet some of the celebrations appear to have been current rather than anachronistic. The same may be said with regard to a very late calendar, at Esna, where the composer has added some New Kingdom references to his up-to-date calendar.

From the late New Kingdom we have a contemporary calendar of Ramesses II at Abydos, as well as the great Medinet Habu exemplar dated to the reign of Ramesses III. The latter is known to be a copy of Ramesses II's with minor additions, such as the basic daily offerings; indeed, one key festival of victory has been added later as a palimpsest over the original account. These two calendars are the most detailed cases from the New Kingdom. Others—of Thutmose IV at Karnak, Akhenaten at Thebes, or even Ramesses III and IV—do not present the awesome size of that at Medinet Habu.

By the Late period in Greco-Roman Egypt, the purpose

FESTIVAL CALENDARS. *Festival Calendar of Ptolemy VI from Kom Ombou, Ptolemaic period.* (Courtesy David P. Silverman)

of such calendars had changed. No longer do they mention the provisioning of the temple, and the endowments of the feasts are ignored. Instead, there is a detailed list of the official processional, but not the daily, feasts. These calendars could take either a fulsome or an abbreviated form, with only the day and number of celebrations cited. Dendera, Edfu, and Kom Ombu provide both versions of their calendars; Esna appears otherwise. Always the overriding emphasis is on the religious activity, not the economic substructure of the provisioning, since the entries of specific days refer solely to the travels of a local deity, his or her individual rituals, and so forth. Such festival calendars are no longer concerned with the establishment of a cult center, nor do they refer to the surplus that the priests would receive from the unused food offerings.

## BIBLIOGRAPHY

Altenmüller, Hartwig. "Feste." In *Lexikon der Ägyptologie,* 1: 172–191. Wiesbaden, 1975. The best study of all ancient Egyptian feasts and festival calendars; extremely useful.

Bedier, Shafia. "Ein Stiftungsdekret Thutmosis III." *Bulletin of the Center of Papyrological Studies* 10 (1992), 1–23. The main edition of the newly discovered festival calendar of Thutmose III from Buto.

el-Sabban, Sherif. "The Temple Calendars of Ancient Egypt." Ph.D. thesis, Liverpool University, 1992. A useful and straightforward presentation of the facts about festival calendars. The problems of dating feasts as well as religious and economic matters are not addressed.

Grimm, Alfred. *Die altägyptischen Festkalender in den Tempeln der griechisch-römischen Epoche.* Wiesbaden, 1994. The most recent survey of all of the festival calendars from the Greco-Roman period; useful for modern editions of the texts.

Luft, Ulrich. *Die chronologische Fixierung des ägyptischen Mittleren Reiches nach dem Tempelarchiv von Illahun.* Vienna, 1992. The best analysis of the Middle Kingdom temple archive and festival structure at Illahun.

Nelson, Harold H. *Work in Western Thebes 1931–33.* Oriental Institute Communications, 18. Chicago, 1934. An excellent overview of Ramesses III's mortuary calendar at Medinet Habu.

Schott, Siegfried. *Altägyptische Festdaten.* Wiesbaden, 1950. A useful compendium of virtually all of the main religious festivals listed in calendars and other texts.

Spalinger, Anthony. *Three Studies on Egyptian Feasts and Their Chronological Implications.* Baltimore, 1992. The first chapter covers the Amenhotpe I calendar from Karnak.

Spalinger, Anthony. "The Lunar System in Festival Calendars: From the New Kingdom Onwards." *Bulletin de la Société de Genève* 19 (1995), 25–40. A survey of the lunar–civil equivalencies within later festival calendars.

ANTHONY J. SPALINGER

**FESTIVAL DRAMAS.** *See* Drama.

**FESTIVALS.** Ancient Egyptian festivals were part of the official cultic religion of the Nile Valley. Many religious celebrations are known from pictorial as well as textual evidence. We possess a number of the liturgies of such events—hymns and prayers that allow us to reconstruct the arrangement and settings of the services.

It is often easy to categorize the festivals from a simple calendrical point of view. Most of them were fixed within the civil calendar so that they took place either on one set day within the year or on many. These events, labeled "annual festivals" by scholars, began with the opening of the year, New Year's Day (Wep-renpet), which heralded both the first day in the civil calendar and the idea/time when rejuvenation and rebirth took place. Seventeen days after this event, but still during the first month of the year, was the more somber feast of Wagy. Eventually associated with the festival of Thoth on day nineteen, Wagy was connected with the ingrained mortuary rituals of pharaonic Egypt. This event was celebrated by private individuals outside an official cultic setting as well as within the precincts of the major temples in Egypt. We see it as early as the fourth dynasty in the brief private feast lists that every tomb owner eventually felt it necessary to inscribe in his funerary monument. Interestingly, its original lunar basis was not discarded: in historical times, there were actually two separate Wagy feasts, one set according to the cycle of the moon and a later one firmly placed at day eighteen of the first civil month.

In the second civil month, the great New Kingdom celebration of Opet predominated. It was a rite expressly connected with the pharaoh and his father Amun(-Re). This extensive festival, also set by the moon, saw the pharaoh-to-be traveling to the temple of Luxor at Thebes in order for his father Amun to give him the powers of kingship as the living Horus falcon. By the New Kingdom, the intimate connection between Amun and pharaoh was solidified in official state religion by this festival, and its twenty-seven-day duration in the twentieth dynasty indicates how significant it had become. Before the eighteenth dynasty, however, we know nothing about this celebration, and there is little doubt that the rise of Thebes to national importance brought with it the predominance of the deity Amun, who became a state deity. The might and power of Amun were ritually bequeathed to his living son, the king. Hence, this celebration belonged to the official royal ideology of the state and, not surprisingly, witnessed the personal involvement of pharaoh, especially on his official visit to Luxor in order to be crowned.

Equal in importance to the Opet feast, but far older, was that of Choiak or Sokar, celebrated in civil month four. This event reveals the age-old importance of the god of the afterworld, Osiris, and his link with the archaic powers of Memphis, especially Sokar. Known during the Old Kingdom (unlike Opet), Sokar grew in importance owing to the early move of the capital of Egypt from the south to Memphis. It is first found in the private feast lists of the Old Kingdom, indicating that Sokar belonged to one of the oldest cult centers of the land. However, there is little doubt that the funerary deity Sokar himself predates the unification of Egypt at the beginning of the first dynasty and the foundation of Memphis as its first capital.

By the Late period, the number of days that Sokar encompassed had grown considerably beyond the original interval of six (days 25 to 30 of the fourth month). In many ways, the festival of Sokar served the duty of completing the first season of the Egyptian year (Inundation), if only because the first day of the following month was considered to open a new era. The last days of the fourth month, observed with much agony and sadness, were soon associated with the god Osiris, who was considered to be dead by the central date of the Sokar feast, day 26 in month four.

Not surprisingly, day 1 of month five had its own New Year's day of rebirth, Nehebkau, occurring just five days after the death of Osiris. The intervening days were left for the eventual rebirth of the god and later connected to the rebirth of the king as the living Horus. Nehebkau, then, paralleled the calendrical New Year of the first day of month one, and virtually the same rituals and performances took place on the two occasions.

Two other key yearly events should be mentioned. The first, the festival of the fertility god Min, not surprisingly also opened a new season; it was enacted in the ninth civil month, although set according to the moon. This is also an archaic celebration, the nature of which can be gleaned mainly from New Kingdom and later sources. The king's role was to cut the first sheaf of grain (see below), and the four corners of the universe took on significance. The Min feast saw the ritual performance of the pharaoh as life-sustainer of his people, a role that certainly reflects his original one, and the association of Min clearly indicates the fecundity and virility of rebirth. Hence, this event can be considered a third festival originally focused on birth, with the agricultural aspect predominating.

Month ten saw the famous Valley Feast, a second Theban celebration that can be traced back to the Middle Kingdom and also became quite important during the New Kingdom. From Karnak, the statues of Amun, his consort Mut, and their son Khonsu were carried across the Nile to Deir el-Bahri on the western bank. Significantly, inscriptions in the private tombs at Thebes reveal that the Feast of the Valley was an occasion for families to visit the tombs of their relatives and to venerate their dead ancestors. In many ways these private affairs parallel the present customs of modern Egypt and other cultures in which people celebrate a holiday on the grass of cemeteries in which their dead ancestors are buried.

Within the Nile Valley there were innumerable local religious sites separate from the main centers of the nation. From the extant data we can reconstruct a cultic calendar for the major deities of Egypt, such as Amun of Thebes, Hathor of Dendera, Horus of Edfu, and others. Often inscribed on the walls of the associated temples are detailed lists of the feasts, all presented in a regularized and programmatic fashion. These festival calendars were copied from the official liturgical rolls kept in the temples' archives. From these calendars we can determine whether a feast was set only within the civil calendar or according to the moon. Moreover, there were the regular lunar celebrations, one for each lunar day. The latter, the so-called seasonal festivals, were explicitly separated from the annual ones mentioned earlier.

Very rarely do we have information about a festival for a secular event; usually the data pertain to feasts within a purely cultic setting. One exception is the annual celebration established by Ramesses III to honor his victory over the Libyans (Meshwesh), who had unsuccessfully invaded Egypt during his reign. A second one was the king's coronation, the date of which would normally be included in a religious calendar. Perhaps the Heliacal Rising of Sothis (the star Sirius) can be added, insofar as there was no specific cult of the deity Sothis. This event was recognized as all-important one because the reappearance of Sothis after a period of seventy days' invisibility originally marked the emergence of the New Year and later was thought of as the ideal rebirth of the land.

One celebration that was observed over a long time span but does not appear in the festival calendars is that of the king's rejuvenation after the first thirty years of his reign. This event, the *heb-sed* festival, was a truly secular one, directly concerned with the vitality and virility of the pharaoh. The origins of the event are lost to us, although it must have been celebrated in Predynastic times. Known from extensive pictorial and inscriptional evidence, the *heb-sed* was probably originally established on a lunar basis: consider the coincidence of thirty years with the length of a month (thirty days). But it is the series of complicated events recorded that allows us to determine the exact arrangement of this key festival. The Rising of the *Djed*-Pillar, for example, symbolizes the king's role in rebirth (the pillar is an archaic symbol of Osiris). It is significant that there is a separate feast connected with the same fetish, timed to the second season, soon after the death of Osiris during the Choiak feast.

A large number of scenes depicting this event have been preserved. Key ones found in the sun temple of Newoserre Any, the tomb of Kheruef at Thebes, the temple of Amenhotpe III at Soleb in Nubia, Akhenaten's East Karnak Temple, and from later Saite times (twenty-sixth dynasty) allow us to reconstruct some of the program of events and to identify the large number of important individuals involved. Ceremonial palaces appear to have been built expressly for its duration, and the garb of the participants, including the king, reveals its age-old nature.

Behind the mere mention of a feast's name and duration were the exhaustive records connected to the celebration. Ordinarily, we possess only a fraction of the original texts that were connected to the processions, chanting, and readings, and the exact timing of the separate rituals. From the Greco-Roman period, however, the walls of the temples of Dendera, Edfu, Esna, Kom Ombo, and Philae provide additional information not included in the festival calendars, and so allow us to reconstruct the events in greater detail. Moreover, papyri rolls and fragmentary biographical texts reveal the intricate and often hidden details such as processions; morning, noon, and evening ablutions of the deity; chants; and speeches. For example, at the Min festival, the detailed program at Ramesses III's mortuary temple of Medinet Habu casts welcome light on the interesting performance of the cutting of the first sheaf of barley. Festival calendars, on the other hand, merely list in a terse fashion the date, deity, and perhaps a sentence concerning the involvement of a specific priest.

Behind these enormous records was the endowment required for the performance of the feasts. From the Old Kingdom to the New, the festival calendars contain explicit references to the offerings required by the deity or deities. This information was not trivial; the official endowment as established or renewed by a king demanded that the economic support of a feast be indicated. Once more, it is the temple of Medinet Habu that provides the most information concerning these seemingly mundane activities culminating in the religious events. The details are remarkable: exact number of bread loaves, cakes, beer containers, meat, fowl, incense, cultic charcoal, and the like are listed beside each event. The amount of grain that went into making a certain type of loaf or a specific type of beer can be determined by a specific integer that refers to the cooking or brewing undertaken (called the "cooking ratio").

Often, the introductory segments of the temple calendar include details of the provenance of such foods, although these additions might be placed next to the respective religious celebration. By listing the amount of grain (barley or emmer) that went into producing a certain number of beer jugs or loaves in conjunction with the cooking ratio, we can easily determine the exact amount of grain that was needed for these feasts. Therefore, it is relatively easy to add up the total amount of grain that was needed for the subsistence of the cult, if only for the major ceremonies celebrated in the civil year.

By means of these calculations, scholars have been

able to evaluate quantitatively exactly how wealthy a temple was and approximately how many priests were necessary for the preservation of the cult. Major festivals such as Sokar (Choiak) and Opet, not surprisingly, required a greater outlay of foods than lesser ones; the number of days each festival lasted is given in these calendars, and the duration was not brief. With regard to the anniversary of a king's accession, we learn from some of these lists that separate and additional supplies were distributed to the temple priesthood, who celebrated a holiday in recognition of this important event. Once more, by means of simple calculation, it is relatively easy to determine the approximate number of officiating personnel in a given temple such as Medinet Habu.

In addition to the almost voluminous New Kingdom data that can be gleaned from the various festival calendars, the account papyri from the Middle Kingdom temple site of Illahun help us to no small degree. In this case, although the hieroglyphic inscriptions containing such economic details are absent, the workaday records are noteworthy. Dated to the reigns of Senwosret III and Amenemhet III, the papyri from Illahun reveal the actual procedures of a middle-sized religious institution of that time. In this case, the wealth of the mortuary temple of Senwosret II is easy to calculate. As befits the era, such temples were not major land-owning corporations like Karnak in the New Kingdom. The total number of personnel probably never exceeded fifty, and their normal incomes, which can be calculated from the daily records, were relatively modest. Some of the papyri list the monthly rotas in which certain sections of the priests worked. The entire priesthood was divided into phyles, a system known from the Old Kingdom as well. Lists of festivals and the exact amount of food offered are given, with the time of delivery specified and, of course, the precise time for the ceremony noted.

From accounts such as these, it is easy to see the extent of a temple's wealth and who contributed to its upkeep. The maintenance of the cult required offerings, and since those items had to be produced, land especially was required in order to support a temple on a purely economic basis. New Kingdom festival calendars, for example, sometimes (but not always) specify the origins of foods and refer to the tenant farmers and gardeners who had to grow these supplies. Additional surveys of land-owning institutions in Egypt allow us to reconstruct the extent of agricultural territory that a certain temple owned and the revenues due to it from the agricultural laborers who leased the land from the religious corporation. It is clear that the wealth of a few key temples, such as Karnak, had increased dramatically from the Middle Kingdom. Indeed, the simple act of reversion of offerings—whereby the foods offered to the gods were subsequently redistributed (in unequal portions) to the temple hierarchy—reveals the importance of the various festivities, as well as the benefits the clergy gained from their roles within a specific temple.

One major problem associated with these celebrations remains as an outstanding question about ancient Egyptian religious thought. On the one hand, it is relatively easy to reconstruct the importance of such major celebrations as Opet or the Valley festival. The festival calendars and associated textual and pictorial evidence reveal the participation of key nonroyal figures and officials of the land as well as the officiating priests. From the Greco-Roman period, the walls of temples such as Edfu, Dendera, and the others publicly describe in detail the voyages the local gods made. The complicated myth of Horus of Edfu and his association with Hathor of Dendera indicates a more public aspect to these religious events than the terse, programmatic lists of the calendars. Such evidence is paralleled by separate descriptions and reliefs recounting the celebrations of Opet, the Valley festival, and even the *heb-sed* rites.

In many cases—and Opet is a key example—individuals not associated with the cult were involved. This can be clearly seen from data about the processions during these feasts. Such visible manifestations of the deity were rare; however, they occurred outside the temple precincts. This more public revelation of the god (or gods) frequently had further implications for the ensuing religious fervor. For example, oracles could take place with more than a few priests present. Many of these prognostications happened during the procession of the deity, and records of such decisions—auspicious or otherwise—remain to indicate how frequent these questions to the gods were. Private individuals consulted their local or regional god for a revelation. Such oracles also took place when important public decisions had to be made, such as the elevation of a private individual to the position of high priest of Amun, and in this case hieroglyphic records were publicly written on temple walls or on stone stelae. More perishable or private means, such as ostraca or papyri, were used to record a god's decision concerning private matters, such as theft. The local chapel of the deified Amenhotpe I on the west bank of Thebes, for example was often consulted by the workmen of this area to render a judgment on a contested point. Oracles usually took place on important feast days, especially those in which the god was borne outside his temple walls.

This public versus private aspect of the temple cannot be downplayed. Commencing with the mortuary temples of the first dynasties, the Old Kingdom saw an accumulation of wealth and importance of such cults. Whether associated with the king (mortuary temple) or a god (sun temple for the solar deity Re), religious entities possessed economic and social importance. Generally, however, such institutions appear to be self-centered and more forbidding to the public than actual centers of religious fervor. The same can be said for the Middle Kingdom, and the account papyri from Illahun indicate just how separate the life of a temple was from that of the town.

By the New Kingdom, the evidence indicates otherwise. Major celebrations took place that were viewed by outsiders, who looked on while the god Amun proceeded from Karnak to Luxor or crossed the Nile westward to visit Deir el-Bahri (for the Valley festival) or Medinet Habu (for the Opet festival). Oracles could be granted at these times, and the occasions were times for public and private celebrations. Similarly, when Hathor of Dendera visited Horus of Edfu, entire towns filled the streets in a carnival atmosphere.

Although this overt extramural aspect of official cults cannot be ignored, inside the temple walls more private and secret performances took place. The daily morning, noon, and evening rituals were not seen by the public. Even important nonroyal personages could rarely proceed beyond the first court. The inner chambers of the temple, roofed and dark, were kept distinct from the more sunlit public areas. Furthermore, even when the king was reinvigorated at Luxor, the mass of the townspeople had to remain outside the edifice. Permission to enter a temple and to participate in a religious ceremony was rare.

For these reasons, scholars speak of "official" or "cultic" religion in contrast to "popular" religion. The former is amply represented by the temples and their extant inscriptions and reliefs. In addition, various liturgies on papyri and other mythological tractates are preserved which enable us to imagine what the official hieroglyphic texts narrate. Thus, our material concerning ancient Egyptian festivals has a very biased point of view. Most of what remains concerns the religious celebrations connected to the major gods and goddesses of Egypt, including the pharaoh. Hence, the highest level of ancient Egyptian society, down to the major nonroyal bureaucrats, is what is reflected by these sources, among them the monumental buildings themselves. Yet the daily religious life of the average Egyptian is not revealed. The private cults did not intrude on the massive temples, nor were the somewhat tawdry and relatively inexpensive private shrines connected with the state gods.

Archaeological finds have revealed that side by side with the official cults there existed numerous personal ones. Small offering tables and votive stelae which honor a particular deity have been found in houses and courtyards. Nevertheless, we know little about the festival practices of the private Egyptian. Various records, mainly on ostraca or papyri and datable to the late New Kingdom (nineteenth and twentieth dynasties), indicate that there was a strong feeling of personal piety within pharaonic Egypt, an attitude that is not shared, for the most part, in the official records. Even the justly famous Middle Egyptian literary masterpiece, the *Story of Sinuhe*, emphasizes the protagonist's personal god, who is never named. Yet among this plethora of information, only the records of the private oracles indicate a connection to a festival.

The main temples of the land operated quite apart from the average Egyptian. Mortuary temples, which by the New Kingdom were situated on the west side of Thebes, were erected to honor the pharaoh as a god both in his lifetime and after death. This practice goes back as far as the Early Dynastic period, and there is little doubt that a separate cult for the pharaoh existed earlier. The activities of these temples were established by the king soon after he was crowned. In the Old Kingdom such temples played the predominant role within official cultic religion: witness, for example, the massive pyramids of the third through sixth dynasties. Other temples were for the most part local and small—e.g., the temple for Min or even various chapels at Abydos. With the exception of the temple of Osiris at Abydos, from the first dynasty onward, few major religious edifices were erected in the Nile Valley. Only in the fifth dynasty did a change occur, and even then it was limited to one royal lineage. Because the pharaohs of the fifth dynasty placed great emphasis upon the cult of the sun god Re, the theological father of the pharaoh at that time, they chose to honor their allegiance in a grandiose and explicit manner: each monarch attempted to erect a sun temple for Re. This practice ceased at the close of the fifth dynasty, and until the fall of the Old Kingdom, the major temple-building reverted to that of the king's own mortuary complex.

By the Middle Kingdom, minor temples were still present but somewhat greater in size than previously. This can be seen most clearly from the expansion of the temple of Satet at Elephantine. Nonetheless, although mortuary temples continued to be built, these edifices were small, self-contained economic units. Only with the rise of Thebes, and especially with the expansion of the cult of Amun during the late Second Intermediate Period, did a decided change occur. By the early eighteenth dynasty, the pharaohs reconstructed the mainly wooden temple of Amun at Karnak in stone, began to add sizable pylons to the building, and started to utilize the available free space on the temple walls for historical and religious texts and pictures. By the middle of that dynasty the burgeoning state of Egypt had at its fingertips enough resources to be able to enact a series of temple-building projects in Egypt and in Nubia as well. By the end of the Amarna period, this practice was in full swing. Therefore, it is not surprising that we find the enormous temple of Soleb in Nubia, built by Amenhotpe III, and the later numerous grotto-temples of Ramesses II in the same southern region.

Karnak, Luxor, and various temples at Memphis were

maintained by the pharaoh. Additions to the key centers of Thebes, Memphis, and even Heliopolis were effected by the nineteenth and twentieth dynasties. In Western Thebes, the mortuary temples continued to be placed along a north–south axis, but by the end of the New Kingdom alterations in the importance of the cults had evidently occurred. In the Third Intermediate Period, except at Karnak, there was a cessation of this cultic expansion. As Amun-Re had come to predominate in the south, with his high priest running this region, the other Middle and Upper Egyptian cults had diminished even further in importance. Only with a powerful dynasty such as that of the Kushite (twenty-fifth) or the Saite (twenty-sixth) was there the growth in importance of these religious corporations once more. By the twenty-sixth dynasty the major thrust of the religious cults was in the north, as befits the seat of power of that lineage, Sais.

When the Greeks and Macedonians came to dominate the Nile Valley, the local cults were left to operate their own religious ceremonies. The Ptolemaic kings, recognized as pharaohs, were worshiped as rulers and actors within edifices such as Edfu and Esna. Nevertheless, the wealth of these temples was considerably limited, especially in comparison with that of Amun-Re of Karnak many centuries earlier. Perhaps for this reason, the festival calendars avoid listing the foods and other offerings brought to the deity at specific times. In fact, they do not mention the tenant farmers or specific lands that were under the jurisdiction of the temple and which supplied their revenues to the god.

Our knowledge of religious festivals during the Ptolemaic period comes mainly from private papyrus rolls of a religious nature. They, and some funerary stelae, indicate that many of the old religious celebrations had declined, if not disappeared. Opet still remained, though considerably weakened; but the cult of Osiris was practiced throughout the land, as the famous tractate of Plutarch on Isis and Osiris bears witness.

[*See also* Festival Calendars.]

**BIBLIOGRAPHY**

Altenmüller, Hartwig. "Feste." In *Lexikon der Ägyptologie*, 1: 172–191. Wiesbaden, 1975. The best study of all ancient Egyptian feasts; extremely useful.

Kemp, Barry J. *Ancient Egypt: Anatomy of a Civilization*. London and New York, 1989. Chapters 5 and 6 cover the New Kingdom festivals at Thebes and their religious and economic importance; earlier sections deal with the growth of temples and their hierarchies before the eighteenth dynasty.

Krauss, Rolf. *Sothis-und Monddaten: Studien zur astronomischen und technischen Chronologie Altägyptens*. Hildesheim, 1985. A serious standard work concerned with the dating of the major festivals of ancient Egypt.

Luft, Ulrich. *Die chronologische Fixierung des ägyptischen Mittleren Reiches nach dem Tempelarchiv von Illahun*. Vienna, 1992. The major reference work concerned with the Middle Kingdom temple of Illahun.

Parker, Richard A. *The Calendars of Ancient Egypt*. Chicago, 1950. The classic study on ancient Egyptian timekeeping; still useful.

Quirke, Stephen. *The Administration of Egypt in the Late Middle Kingdom: The Hieratic Documents*. New Malden, Conn., 1989. A detailed analysis of the site of Illahun in the twelfth and thirteenth dynasties and the relationship of the local temple to the town.

ANTHONY J. SPALINGER

**FIFTEENTH DYNASTY** (c.1664–1555 BCE), called the Hyksos dynasty, Second Intermediate Period. Sources for the lost history of Egypt, prepared by the Egyptian historian Manetho in the third century BCE, record a Dynasty 15 group of kings that comprised six "Hyksos," who were "foreign rulers" from the Near East. An extract in a later history by Josephus, the first-century CE Roman-Jewish historian, provides two possible translations for *Hyksos*: "shepherd kings" and "captive shepherds." His second translation would apply to a people, not just to rulers, and the extract relates how they invaded from the east, during the reign of a "good king" (*tou timaiou*; otherwise interpreted as a king "Tutimaios"), and selected Salitis to be their king. He went on to found the city of Avaris in the eastern Nile Delta. On a fragment of the Ramessid king-list papyrus known as the Turin Canon, the number and title recur with six *ḥḳꜣ ḫꜣswt* ("rulers of hill-lands") covering 106 years; it preserves one king's name, Khamudy. Three other New Kingdom sources record "rulers of hill-lands," confirming the first etymology for *Hyksos* in Greek texts as a royal title, not an ethnic designation: (1) a mid-eighteenth dynasty tomb-chapel inscription of Ahmose, son of Abana, at Elkab that records the defeat of the Hyksos; (2) an inscription of Hatshepsut at Speos Artemidos, on restoring order after foreign occupation; and (3) a literary narrative attested on one Ramessid papyrus, relating origins of conflict between the Hyksos Apophis (Apepi) and a subservient Theban king, Seqenenra Taa. These three later accounts match archaeological evidence for settlement in the eastern Delta, where late Middle Kingdom sites reveal the replacement of Egyptian by Near Eastern material culture—in pottery styles, weaponry, and burial customs. The largest site is at Tell ed-Dabʿa, and from its scale and finds is now generally identified as the Hyksos capital (the *ḥwt-wʿrt* of Egyptian texts; the Greek *Avaris*). A limestone lintel from Tell ed-Dabʿa places the title *heqa khasut* ("ruler of hill-lands") before a cartouche containing the name Sekerher (perhaps Sheshy, r. 1664–1662 BCE); this is the only instance of that title and name in large-scale inscription, as opposed to those on seal-amulets of the period. Apart from scarabs and other small-scale inscriptions, period texts exclusively in Egyptian hieroglyphs provide evidence for only two other rulers, Khayan and Apepi (perhaps, respectively, Manetho's Pakhnan and Apophis). A limestone block found near Tell ed-Dab'a, names Khayan (r. 1653–1614 BCE) above the "king's son Yenenes" (recalling Manetho's Yannas; Yansas-adon, ruled perhaps 1614–1605 BCE). Three throne-names were apparently taken by Apophis (r. 1605–1565 BCE): Aauserra, Aaqenenra, and Nebkhepeshra. This recalls the three Horus-names of Nebhepetre Montuhotep at the beginning of the Middle Kingdom; war perhaps influenced such name changes. Apophis is named in the above-mentioned Ramessid tale as the opponent of the Theban king Seqenenra Taa; the skull of Taa bore the imprint of blows from a blade of Near Eastern type. Apophis was also the Hyksos in whose reign the Theban king Kamose (r. 1571–1569 BCE) besieged Avaris, according to the narrative on some stelae erected for Kamose at Karnak. The next Theban king, Ahmose (r. 1569–1545 BCE), expelled the foreigners, marking the start of the New Kingdom. (Since Manetho placed Apophis as the last Hyksos king, this leaves unexplained the Hamudi (Khamudy) named before the "foreign rulers" total in the Turin Canon.)

The Hyksos entered Egyptian texts as invading iconoclasts, which may be borne out by one deliberately erased Egyptian royal bronze found at Tell ed-Dab'a; however, the date and means of their rise to power is uncertain. The Hyksos were preceded as rulers of the eastern Delta by a group of kings (the fourteenth dynasty), of whom Nehesy is best attested, with a cult of Seth that had already been established at Tell ed-Dab'a. As the god of desert and disorder, Seth provided shared religious ground between Egypt and the settlers. The Seth cult perhaps encouraged later writers to depict the Hyksos as enemies of order, though this Delta cult continued to thrive into Ramessid times. Surviving Hyksos monuments are limited to brief, crudely incised inscriptions on older, reused blocks or statues. In material culture, the settlers appear to have remained alien. The second Kamose stela records a letter on clay from Apophis to a ruler of Kush. Besides illustrating a policy of encircling Thebes by alliance, this implies a non-Egyptian means of communication, perhaps even Near Eastern cuneiform script on clay tablets. The last Hyksos king may also have commissioned wall paintings in Tell ed-Dab'a from Minoan artists, but the dating of these is debated. The only men with Egyptian titles attested on contemporary objects that mention the Hyksos are "Aper the treasurer," on the inscription of a granodiorite offering-stand, and "Itju the scribe," on the palette from the Faiyum. Also attested are two women titled "king's daughter"; in the broken historical record, it is difficult to speculate on their biographies. As with the Rhind Mathematical Papyrus and the use of hieroglyphs, these sources indicate that the "foreign rulers" were not

hostile to Egyptian tradition; perhaps they became even more receptive by the end of their century of rule.

[*See also* Hyksos; *and* Second Intermediate Period.]

## BIBLIOGRAPHY

Bietak, Manfred. *Avaris and Piramesse: Archaeological Exploration in the Eastern Nile Delta*. London, 1986. Revised issue of a 1981 monograph first published in 1979 in *Proceedings of the British Academy* 65 (1979), 225–289. Preliminary account by the excavator of the key Hyksos site Tell ed-Dab'a.

Bietak, Manfred. "Connections between Egypt and the Minoan World." In *Egypt, the Aegean and the Levant*, edited by W. V. Davies and L. Schofield, pp. 19–28. London, 1995. Includes examples of the Minoan fresco fragments unearthed at Tell ed-Dab'a.

Habachi, Labib. *The Second Stela of Kamose*. Abhandlungen des Deutschen Archäologischen Instituts Kairo, 8. Glückstadt, 1972. The first edition of the most important Egyptian royal text on the war against the Hyksos.

Kemp, Barry J. "Old, Middle and Second Intermediate Period c.2686–1552 BC." In *The Cambridge History of Africa*, edited by J. Desmond Clark, vol. I, pp. 658–769. Cambridge, 1982. Reprinted in Bruce G. Trigger, et al., *Ancient Egypt: A Social History*. Cambridge, 1982. Represents the consensus on the history of the period (and that point of view has been presented in the encyclopedia article).

Oren, Eliezer, ed. *The Hyksos: New Historical and Archaeological Perspectives*. Philadelphia, 1997.

Redford, Donald B. "The Hyksos Invasion in History and Tradition." *Orientalia* 39 (1970), 1–51.

Ryholt, Kim S. B. *The Political Situation in Egypt during the Second Intermediate Period c.1800–1550 B.C.* Carsten Niebuhr Institute Publications, 20. Copenhagen, 1997. A wide-ranging reevaluation of the archaeological and textual sources, with comprehensive bibliography and list of sources for kings. Note that definitions of dynasties differ from those in Kemp (1982), and archaeologists have yet to review several conclusions based on specific contexts. The reappraisal, however, includes invaluable discussions of key data, such as royal scarabs and the Turin Canon.

Winlock, Herbert E. *The Rise and Fall of the Middle Kingdom in Thebes*. New York, 1947. Includes principal discussion of the burial equipment of the Theban kings of the Second Intermediate Period, with revisions of several points in his previous article on the subject in *Journal of Egyptian Archaeology* 10 (1924), 217–277.

STEPHEN G. J. QUIRKE

**FIFTH DYNASTY.** *See* Old Kingdom, *article on* Fifth Dynasty.

**FIRST INTERMEDIATE PERIOD** (c.2220–2040 BCE). As early as 1879, the time span between the end of Egypt's Old Kingdom (as marked by the great summation in the king list of the Turin Canon) and the beginning of the twelfth dynasty was called a "dark period" by the early Egyptologist Heinrich Brugsch. A certain fascination emanates from the period, because there are very few royal monuments, while the number of kings known only from king lists who left no contemporary trace is irritatingly large. As far as Upper Egypt and nonroyal monuments are concerned, many more sources are available than ever before. The label "First Intermediate Period" now characterizes the transitional time between two seemingly fixed periods—the Old Kingdom and the Middle Kingdom—acknowledging that there was no direct chronological contact between them.

From the viewpoint of political history, the limits of the period are easy to recognize: a dual rulership, with two separate dynasties, for about one hundred years. In the North, a dynasty ruled whose home town was Herakleopolis (Ar., Ihnasiya el-Medina), at the entrance to the Faiyum; in the South, another dynasty was centered at Thebes. The beginning of that schism occurred when the nomarch of Thebes, the "Great Overlord of Upper Egypt" Antef "The Great," declared himself king, chose the Horus name Sehertowy, "who pleases the Two Lands," and wrote his name in cartouche. We know him as Antef I (r. 2134–2118 BCE). He refused to tolerate the northern Herakleopolitan dynasty, and its end came in 2040 BCE, with the defeat of the northern dynasty by Nebhepetre Montuhotep I, who united Egypt under his sole kingship. Yet there are no fixed limits between the Old Kingdom and the First Intermediate Period in the fields of archaeology, art, and administration. A culture does not necessarily change simultaneously in all its subsystems to coincide with dynastic change. The rapid succession of kings did not result in rapid changes in either administration or everyday life.

The Egyptological literature offers a fund of argumentation, as well as a great number of possible dates for the correlation of dynasties, kings, personalities, and events during the First Intermediate Period. Yet every scholar must cope with the same few sources, acquiesing in obscurity; it is easy to be tempted to paint a picture that is far too coherent.

**Egyptian and Egyptological Tradition.** A certain concord occurs in the ancient Egyptian king lists tradition, concerning the period between Pepy II, fourth king of the sixth dynasty, and Nebhepetre Montuhotep I of the eleventh dynasty: it is treated in different ways, and the Saqqara list simply omitted it. For all of them, the dynasties (numbered 9 and 10 in the tradition of the third-century BCE Greco-Egyptian historian Manetho) of kings from Herakleopolis were a kind of foreign body, marking a break in the seemingly unbroken line of kingship since Teti, first king of the sixth dynasty. The king list of the Turin Canon and the *Aegyptiaca* by Manetho divided groups of kings into three sections: those ruling at Memphis (Manetho's Dynasties 6 to 8); the kings of Herakleopolis (Manetho's Dynasties 9 and 10); and the kings of Thebes (Manetho's Dynasty 11). The Turin Canon makes a break at six kings after Queen Nitocris (who reigned as the last of Dynasty 6 according to Manetho). The next

break occurs eighteen kings later, where obviously the enumeration of the Theban kings of Dynasty 11 began.

The king list at Abydos did not mention any known king of Herakleopolis or even the first Theban kings of the eleventh dynasty. Instead, it added a row of seventeen kings after the immediate successor of Pepy II. Some had rather obscure names and are not found in the archaeological record. At least Kakaure (Qaikare Aba) is known from the Turin Canon and as the owner of a modest pyramid at Saqqara inscribed with Pyramid Texts. Neferkauhor released royal decrees addressed to the "Overseer of Upper Egypt" Shemai of Coptos and his son Idi. A common hypothesis is that at least the last of the seventeen (perhaps eighteen) kings should be part of the eighth dynasty, not the ninth.

A Memphite and a Herakleopolitan line of successors descend from Pepy II, both of which left very few traces. Therefore, the bare dynastic divisions in the tradition of Manetho are difficult to reconcile with names from the archeological record or from the hieroglyphic king lists; to make them compatible with the divisions of the Turin king list, with its many serious gaps, and to relative chronology has become a puzzle for scholars to solve.

Manetho's Dynasty 7 "consisted of 70 kings of Memphis who reigned for 70 days" (according to the Roman-era historian Africanus). Most scholars interpret that as a metaphoric description for a period of confusion, to thus be eliminated as fictitious. Its mention could very well be the result of a lacuna (missing part) in Manetho's model-copy, which corresponds to the six years noted as a lacuna for his Dynasty 6, now lost. Unfortunately, most of the kings' names of the period would be in what are lacunae; the few preserved names are those of unknown kings or not very specific names, such as Akhtoy (Khety) or Neferkare. Scholars have tried to fill the gaps with names known from the archeological or inscriptional record. The six names after Nitocris are counted as the eighth dynasty, and three gaps are filled by the names of those three kings known from royal decrees found in the temple of Min at Coptos: Khay(bau?) Wadjkare, Netjeribau Neferkauhor, and Demedjibtowy Neferirkare (?). After them, kingship fell to a family originating from Herakleopolis. The founder king—styled as wicked in Manetho's tradition—with the name Akhtoy was followed by seventeen kings. According to Jaromir Malek's reconstruction of the original version of the Turin Canon, "the division of the Herakleopolitan kings into two dynasties can . . . be based on a Manethonian interpretation of the list" (*Journal of Egyptian Archaeology* 68 [1982], p. 105). Even today, the division cannot be founded on genealogical or political reasons, since it seems to be a simple transmission fault. There is no real reason to speak of two dynasties, instead of the one Herakleopolitan dynasty (that combines the ninth and tenth). Yet the rise of the Theban eleventh dynasty, with the "Great Overlord of Upper Egypt," Antef, may very well have begun after the reign of four Herakleopolitan kings. Only five kings of the Herakleopolitan dynasty are known from contemporary inscriptions (Neferkare, Nebkaure Akhtoy, Meriibre Akhtoy, Merikare, and Wahkare Akhtoy). We do not even know their sequence, but supposedly the last four ruled late in the dynasty. There are no secure traces of any of them south of Asyut; the records for Neferkare at Naga ed-Deir and Mo'alla are not beyond question.

The often romantic and dramatic picture of events, in seemingly detailed modern descriptions of the First Intermediate Period is due only to the lucky chance that the tomb of Ankhtifi and the Ramessid manuscript called the *Admonitions of Ipuwer* have survived. Until 1987, there were few attempts to deal with the First Intermediate Period from the viewpoint of archaeology. Archaeological investigations are only beginning to change our view. Famine, poverty, tomb robbing, the destruction of monuments, and regional turmoil are not exclusive to the First Intermediate Period; "that time of trouble," often conjured up, was not found in the archaeological record. Instead, scholars are having troubles with those times.

**Early First Intermediate Period.** Egyptian king lists did not account for overlapping reigns, so a choice of scenarios is possible. Some scholars like to close the gap tightly between the end of the eighth dynasty and the beginning of the eleventh dynasty. Others would prefer a considerable distance in time—of more than fifty years—between the situation described in the Coptos decrees and the rise of Antef I to kingship, leaving space for a nationwide acknowledgment of the first Herakleopolitan kings. Discussion centers around the person of Ankhtifi of Mo'alla, and six others are involved: Shemai and his son Idi from Coptos; Tjauti and Woser from Khozam; Abichu, nomarch of the nomes of Abydos, Diospolis Parva, and Dendera; and the nomarch Antef of Thebes. Royalty took part in the persons of Neferkauhor, Demedjibtowy, and Neferkare, all of whom should have reigned before the "Great Overlord of Upper Egypt," Antef I.

Ankhtifi was fighting against a coalition of rulers from Thebes and Coptos—a political constellation impossible during the eighth dynasty, as deduced from the Coptos decrees—when Coptos went with the Memphite rulers Neferkauhor and Demedjibtowy. Should we place the events described by Ankhtifi before the eighth dynasty, at the end of the sixth, or with the early Herakleopolitan kings? The available time between the end of the sixth dynasty and early in the ninth/tenth is about thirty years, and Ankhtifi's life could cover more than that period. Accordingly, Ankhtifi could have escorted the *qenbet*-council of officials of the "Overseer of Upper Egypt" from Abydos

to Mo'alla in his youth and in the sixth dynasty, while the battles with Thebes and Coptos could have happened late in the eighth dynasty or early in the ninth/tenth—at a time, when the "Overseer of Upper Egypt" resided in Coptos, or when this office had already lost its importance, and before the time of the "Great Overlord of the Theban nome" Antef. Ankhtifi's scenario seems to fit the time when his collegue Abihu ruled in the sixth, seventh, and eighth nomes, while in the tomb of Ankhtifi's contemporary Setika, at Qubbet el-Hawa near Aswan, the "House of Akhtoy" (the Herakleopolitan dynasty) is explicitly mentioned. Such considerations could support the suggestion that Ankhtifi's king Neferkare (written in "Herakleopolitan fashion," with metathesis, as Re-ka-nefer, like the names of the Herakleopolitan kings elsewhere, Re-ib-meri or Re-ka-meri) is the supposed third king of the ninth/tenth dynasty.

The prolongation of a nationwide rule for the ninth/tenth dynasty gives time for political developments. Yet events can also accelerate, and many things can happen in a relatively short time, which may never have been recorded. The ten Coptos decrees released on a single day by King Neferkauhor describe administrative acts on behalf of his son-in-law Shemai, the vizier and overseer of the first to twenty-second Upper Egyptian nomes, and Shemai's son Idi. Idi was promoted to the office of "Overseer of Upper Egypt" in the first to seventh nomes, under the supervision of his father. According to a reconstruction of events by Maha Mostafa ("Kom el-Koffar II," *Annales du service des antiquités de l'Egypte* 71 [1987], pp. 169–184), the family had to face troubles in the very same year; suddenly, we find Idi in the Wadi Hammamat carrying out an expedition to procure stone for a certain "Overseer of Upper Egypt" Tjauti-iqer, who—perhaps—was the very man buried at Khozam, about 25 kilometers (15 miles) south of Coptos. A granite false door gave his titles as "Overseer of Upper Egypt" and "One Who Fills the King's Heart [with Trust] in the Doorway of Upper Egypt, Tjauti." Tjauti controlled the important "Alamat Tal" desert road leaving the Nile Valley at Qamula, opposite Khozam, which led to a crossroad with other important roads from the South. On the way, a rock inscription was found by Tjauti: "I have made this for crossing this desert which had been block[ed?] by the ruler of another nome." Thus Tjauti's troops could reach Abydos and Thinis by land, without passing Coptos and Dendera, and control communication between the North, Thebes, and the South, as well.

Who was Tjauti's enemy "of the other nome"? If it was the Thebans, then Tjauti could not have been the partner in the Theban–Coptite coalition with which Ankhtifi was fighting. Was it the nomarch Abichu from Dendera? We do not know. Around that time, the "Great Overlord of the

Theban nome" Antef was also given the title "One Who Fills the King's Heart [with Trust] in the Doorway of Upper Egypt." Apparently, controlling the desert roads played an important part in the struggles of Tjauti, his successor (?), Woser of Khozam (a "King's Eldest Son," "Overseer of the Eastern and Western Foreign Lands," and "Overseer of Upper Egypt"), and the first Antefs of Thebes.

Tjauti might be responsible for the damage in the tomb of Shemai and Idi, which is lamented in Idi's autobiographical text at Kom el-Koffar, the cemetery of Coptos.

The last information we have about Idi is from a decree of King Demedjibtowy—that all monuments of Idi in Coptos and Upper Egypt are to be protected by royal order. Remarkably, Idi was vizier, here, not "Overseer of Upper Egypt." The conclusion is that Neferkauhor, Demedjibtowy, Shemai, Idi, and Tjauti from Khozam were close contemporaries and that a lot of political changes happened in the Coptite region at the end of the eighth dynasty and in the early ninth/tenth dynasty. The rise of the new Herakleopolitan dynasty encouraged intensive block building and a struggle for spheres of hegemony, from Elephantine to Abydos. It was a short period of very weak or nonexistent central royal power, leaving space for private enterprise, such as expeditions to the Wadi Hammamat by order of the nomarch Tjauti. The statement of a dignitary at Hawawish, the necropolis of Akhmim, seems to fit here: "I kept alive every man of this province, who requested from me, while the Great ones were dead. . . . I did not indeed do this as an order that is sent to a king's servant, but I did this out of love for Min, lord of Akhmim." The vacuum of central authority was thereby filled at the dignitaries' own initiative, motivated by respect for his city god.

The earliest part of the First Intermediate Period may be divided into two periods and networks of alliance and rivalry: Shemai and Idi, Tjauti and Woser in the fifth nome, and then Setika at Elephantine in the first nome, Ankhtifi from Mo'alla in the second and third nomes, nomarch Ini in the third nome, Antef in the fourth nome, Abichu in the sixth to eighth nomes, and finally Antef I, founder of the eleventh dynasty (r. 2134–2118 BCE), who was acknowledged in the fourth to sixth nomes. Antef gained supremacy not only by his striking force and violence but by forced agitation as well. One of Antef's generals relates that he traveled upstream and downstream "to the places where the southern and northern rulers were." Every ruler he visited rejoiced because of the perfection of his speech: rhetoric is a means of power. That recalls the admonitions on eloquent inciters in the cities, in the *Instructions for Merikare,* and the sentence: "If you are skilled in speech, you will win; the strong arm of the king is his tongue!"

**Messages and Silent Remains.** The end of the sixth dynasty passed to us in silence. Before the chronological and archaeological well-fixed group of inscriptions and tombs from the time of Wahankh Antef II and his followers, there are about three or four groups of texts that fit a gap of about one hundred years. The relative sequence of the texts has been used to determine the order of those few historical events that are known from that time. The earliest are probably the corpus of eighth dynasty royal decrees from Coptos, on behalf of Shemai and Idi, and the inscriptions from their tomb at Kom el-Koffar. The decrees speak of at least formal royal control over all Egypt, while the inscriptions of Idi hint at some trouble at Coptos. A few inscriptions that mention famine and the loss of royal authority, found in tombs from Akhmim at el-Hagarsa and Hawawish, may also fit here, or a little later.

Then come the texts from the southern Gebelein-Mo'alla region, featuring Ankhtifi of Mo'alla and the local colony of Nubian mercenaries. To the early years of the eleventh dynasty (corresponding to the mid-ninth/tenth dynasty) belong a group of stelae from Naqada (south of Coptos), showing warriors with bows, arrows, and dogs. The people of Naqada worked for a family of "Overseers of Priests" from Qus or Coptos, named Dagi, Djefai, and Akhtoy, the successors of Idi, Tjauti, and Woser—yet royalty had no place in these texts.

Knowledge of the period, if based only on texts, is narrow and biased. Autobiographical inscriptions in tombs or on stelae are few when compared to the number of tombs or stelae without them. In the cemetery of Dara, about 27 kilometers (17 miles) north of Asyut, is a monumental mud-brick *mastaba* of some 140 meters square (450 feet square) and once about 20 meters (65 feet) high. Pottery found there was dated to the early First Intermediate Period, and some inscribed fragments show the name of an unknown king, Khuy, as written in cartouche. Nothing else was found (due to inadequate exploration), so we can only imagine a local potentate with high "pharaonic" aspirations—a predecessor of the nomarchs from Asyut.

**Late First Intermediate Period.** Antef II (r. 2118–2068 BCE) described the extent of his dominion, at the end of his reign, as reaching from Elephantine to the frontier of the tenth nome (somewhere between present-day Tahta and Kom Ishkaw), and that was attested by his allies Hotpe of Elkab, Djari and Tjetji of Thebes, and Rediukhnum of Dendera. That was reflected by Antef's huge royal *saff*-type tomb at Western Thebes, which included his famous Stela with Dogs, and by the numerous stelae of his officials. From that point, in Upper Egyptian autobiographical inscriptions, the king became the obvious focus of authority for people, in contrast to the earlier inscriptions from the Akhmim region, Naga ed-Deir, Dendera, Naqada, Thebes, Gebelein, and Mo'alla. Antef II won victory fighting against the Herakleopolitan kings and their allies. From the time of the battles in the vicinity of the tenth nome and for hegemony over Abydos, information exists from both sides. There are inscriptions from two tombs at Asyut. The elite from that area were allies of the Herakleopolitan kings for more than three generations, and in the tombs of Akhtoy (no. 4) and Iti-ibi (no. 3), war with the South was described. The fleet of King Merikare intervened for the benefit of Akhtoy's rule, sailing southward to Shashotpe (present-day Shutb), where the transitional zone to the southern dominion began. Akhtoy gave thanks to his king in an elaborate hymn. Merikare was the recipient of a set of *Instructions* (known only from later copies), which described the royal duties in difficult political circumstances (*Instructions for Merikare*).

We do not know if Merikare was the last in the line of the Herakleopolitan kings. We only know that the Theban Nebhepetre Montuhotep I, at a certain point in his reign, claimed rulership for the whole of Egypt and invested a loyal governor in the nome of Herakleopolis. That marked the end of the Herakleopolitan dynasty (and the First Intermediate Period) and the beginning of the first stage of the early Middle Kingdom. From then on, Egypt was united, at least politically. There was only one ruler, and he displayed royal splendor in his mortuary complex on the impressive natural stage of Deir el-Bahri. Egypt's political and intellectual center was at Thebes for the next fifty years or so, and elite culture got a special Theban touch. To become culturally a union, it took another hundred years—from reunification to the final decades of the reign of Senwosret I of the twelfth dynasty.

**Toward a Cultural History.** While during the Old Kingdom centralizing forces prevailed, after the sixth dynasty the balance shifted to the provinces. From that point, provincial cemeteries became the most informative for history, and the development of an assimilation of cultural models of Old Kingdom court culture may be observed. Memphis and Herakleopolis have not yet yielded much on that period, although excavations continue. After Pepy II, no great royal pyramid complex was built, but the absence of a royal pyramid is not a distinctive marker for royal power. What scholars have called "weakness of royalty" may simply be absence of evidence—and this may nevertheless be a significant feature, because it is not accidental.

Provincial cemeteries and nonroyal funeral culture flourished. It was a period of change for material culture, for the diversification of local tradition, and for the evolution of social stratification—beginning in the late sixth dynasty. Networks of social dependence, not found before in the archaeological record, became clearly observable in hierarchically structured tombs and in elite necropolises having decorated rock-cut tombs but small shaft tombs in their forecourts for their dependents. The provincial elite, deprived of the level of royal authority and capital administration, developed high aspirations and responsibility. For example, to become Osiris after death—a privilege of the king and the residental elite since the end of the fifth dynasty—became attractive; everybody could become Osiris after death and accordingly each was clad like a dead pharaoh, acquired pharaonic funerary equipment (such as a mummy mask, scepters, crowns, and weapons), and needed a proper coffin, preferably inscribed with ritual texts. Demand led to the development of a special funeral industry—one both of the material and the nonmaterial world. The limitations on the art of writing and literacy were softened, more people wrote than ever before (sometimes resulting in a loss of calligraphy), and many more subjects were presented.

The men at the top of the hierarchy in their domains adapted some facets of royal ideology. That diffusion of royal prerogatives had nothing to do with "democracy," as has often been posited, but was a transference down the hierarchy of royal ideology and some of its worlds of meaning—a disentanglement of the monopolies based on royal charisma and ideology. Dignitaries, like Ankhtifi, went along with the attitude of a lesser king, only responsible to their city god. The base of power in those days was the city and its inhabitants. Being "Overseer of Priests" at the local temple allowed material income, access to knowledge, and acquaintance with the gods, which paved the way to the attractive possibility of leading other people and assembling followers, offering them in return security and prosperity for their fidelity. A system of reciprocal bonds and rewards evolved that were not, as before, confined to the court elite's unconditional obedience. An example of the patron-client relationship at work is the inscription of Hornakht from Dendera.

During this period, only the small group of royal courtiers and their household members at the residence had reasons to lament decentralization. The bulk of the nation profited from no taxation for the king. The people continued as servants for two masters: their city god and their local patron. For them, there was no place for the development of self-determination; instead basic relationships in social networks were emphasized. The few autobiographical inscriptions of the period exhibit the central role of local control over resources—goods, cattle, people, ideas—for the welfare of ruler and subjects; but the texts are ideologically biased, since chaos, hunger, and bad administration was never part of local rule. Famine might only be background for emphasizing an effective local administration and for the description of transregional trade with grain and commodities, often cloaked as charity, as gift and acquisition. Only others are insulted as egotistical, greedy, and overeager. These texts describe an intensification of normative codes and moral values not presented in detail in earlier autobiographies.

Egypt seems to have been rather introverted during this period, and the intrusion of seminomadic people from Palestine—as mentioned in the *Instructions for Merikare*—has not yet been confirmed by archaeology. Immigrants from Nubia, however, are known to have come as far north as Asyut and to have been integrated into local society. Social networks were developed beyond the nuclear family and the relationship of master and servant, the followers tied to local patrons by reciprocal bonds of security for fidelty, economic dependency, and the ideological ideal of the good shepherd. The First Intermediate Period was, therefore, not a period of decline but one of challenge. It might even be fair to view the beginnings of the Middle Kingdom as early as the time of Antef II—at least in certain cultural aspects, such as art or literature. The basic ideology of the king's men as expressed in their inscriptions are the roots of Middle Kingdom royal ideology and loyalist teachings.

**Literature.** Today's view of the First Intermediate Period is often based on repeating the maligned view invented in the late eleventh or early twelfth dynasty. This is what texts like the *Prophecies of Neferti* wanted to make their audiences believe—and we are still their victims. Other famous literary texts, such as the *Dispute of a Man and His Ba* or *The Eloquent Peasant* describe abnormal social conditions in the period, but they are of no help in reconstructing the social, mental, and political history of the First Intermediate Period. Today, no scholar should take as historical fact what those texts portray. They are stories, set within a fictitious ambiance. If the past can be considered dark, it is much easier to show the present in brilliant colors, as a royal time indeed.

The First Intermediate Period did provide a climate for innovative literary production, such as Akhtoy's tomb inscriptions, Antef II's stela with prayers to his divine parents Re and Hathor, and Montuhotep I's dialogue with his army in a fragmentary text from Deir el-Ballas, as well as the Coffin Texts and the rich trove of funerary and commemorative stelae.

[*See also* Merikare.]

**BIBLIOGRAPHY**

Darnell, Deborah, and John C. Darnell. "New Inscriptions of the Late First Intermediate Period from the Theban Western Desert and the Beginnings of the North Expansion of the Eleventh Dynasty." *Journal of Near Eastern Studies* 56 (1997), 241–258. Report on the Theban Desert Road Survey, with publication of Tjauti's graffito from the Alamat Tal road.

Fischer, Henry G. *Inscriptions from the Coptite Nome, Dynasties VI–XI.* Analecta Orientalia, 40. Roma, 1964. Includes the sources for Tjauti and Woser from Khozam, the stelae from Naqada, and Nebhepetre Montuhotep's inscription from Deir el-Ballas.

Fischer, Henry G. *Dendera in the Third Millennium B. C. Down to the Theban Domination of Upper Egypt.* Locust Valley, New York, 1968. Paradigmatic study of sources.

Fischer, Henry G. *Varia Nova.* Egyptian Studies, 3. New York, 1996. On pp. 83–90 is the publication of General Antef's stela: "Words and Weapons at Thebes."

Franke, Detlef. "Erste und Zweite Zwischenzeit—Ein Vergleich." *Zeitschrift für Ägyptische Sprache und Altertumskunde* 117 (1990), 119–129. On social and political structure, mental worlds, and kingship in the first two intermediate periods.

Kemp, Barry. *Ancient Egypt: A Social History,* edited by B. G. Trigger, et al. Cambridge, 1983. Introduction to the problems of the period viewed under various aspects (well documented but not up-to-date).

Lichtheim, Miriam. *Ancient Egyptian Autobiographies Chiefly of the Middle Kingdom.* Freiburg, 1988. Translation of the autobiographies of Ankhtifi, Akhtoy of Asyut, and others.

Müller-Wollermann, Renate. *Krisenfaktoren im ägyptischen Staat des ausgehenden Alten Reichs.* Tübingen, 1986. Evaluation of circumstances and possible causes for the fall of the Old Kingdom.

Parkinson, Richard B. *The Tale of Sinuhe and Other Ancient Egyptian Poems 1940–1640 BC.* Oxford, 1997. Up-to-date translations and commentaries on *The Eloquent Peasant, Neferti, The Dialogue of a Man and His Soul, The Dialogue of Ipuwer and the Lord of All,* and *Instructions for Merikare.*

Seidlmayer, Stephan. "Zwei Anmerkungen zur Dynastie der Herakleopoliten." *Göttinger Miszellen* 157 (1997), 81–90. Reassessment of the internal chronology of the period, including a survey of literature on the topic.

Seidlmayer, Stephan. "The First Intermediate Period." In *The Oxford Illustrated History of Ancient Egypt,* edited by Ian Shaw. Oxford, 1999.

Spanel, Donald B. "The First Intermediate Period through the Early Eighteenth Dynasty." In *Beyond the Pyramids: Egyptian Regional Art from the Museo Egizio, Turin,* edited by Gay Robins, pp. 17–22. Atlanta, 1990. Brief but excellent introduction.

Vandersleyen, Claude. *L'Égypte et la vallée du Nil,* vol. 2. Paris, 1995.

Vercoutter, Jean. *L'Égypte et la vallée du Nil,* vol. 1. Paris, 1992. Equates (not very convincingly) the six kings after Nitocris with Manetho's Dynasty 7 and the three kings before the first preserved Akhtoy to his Dynasty 8.

Willems, Harco. "A Note on the Date of the Early Middle Kingdom Cemetery at Ihnasiya al-Madina." *Göttinger Miszellen* 150 (1996), 99–109. Includes literature on the Spanish excavations in the cemetery of Herakleopolis.

DETLEF FRANKE

**FISH.** Skeletal remains and artistic representations are the main sources employed to trace the history and development of fish use in ancient Egypt. Knowledge of fish and fishing during Egypt's prehistoric period is based primarily on inferences drawn from skeletal remains, while artistic representations from tombs and temples provide the most information for the dynastic period. Certain caveats, however, apply to both types of information; problems of unequal preservation hamper skeletal studies, and rarely is the main focus of the reliefs to record the use of fish in daily life.

**Skeletal Evidence: The Prehistoric Period.** The earliest evidence of a strong reliance on fish in Egypt comes from sites identified with the Khormusan, a Paleolithic, industry (c.45,000 BCE). Khormusans hunted the wild aurochs (*Bos primigenius*) and other animals found along the Nile or on its alluvial plain, but they appear to have focused much energy on the exploitation of fish, in particular the large Nile catfish (*Clarias* spp.). The Nile catfish was also an important resource in later Paleolithic sites.

In the Wadi Kubanniya, settlements dating to c.16,000–10,500 BCE appear to have shifted seasonally to take advantage of fish resources. With the late summer flood, fish were brought into shallow pools that formed between the dunes at the edge of the alluvial plain, where they became trapped as the flood receded. Inhabitants of the region apparently moved their camps to the summits of the dunes in order to gather these fish.

Further insight concerning the role of fish in prehistoric Egypt comes from research at Lake Qarun in the Faiyum. Faunal remains provide evidence that Qarunian (epi-Paleolithic) and Faiyum Neolithic groups utilized a number of terrestrial animals but relied most heavily on the lake's fish. In fact, fish account for 74 percent of the Paleolithic faunal assemblage and 71 percent of the Neolithic. The Nile catfish, the most predominant animal recovered, accounts for 66 percent of all skeletal remains. Seasonality studies of the Nile catfish remains demonstrate that both Qarunian and Neolithic groups took fish at least twice during the year: in late spring/early summer and in late summer/early fall.

Although the shallow-water clariids (*Clarias* spp.) are the predominant type of fish recovered from Faiyum sites, increasingly greater numbers of deep-water fish species are found in later Neolithic sites, suggesting an increasingly more proficient deep-water fishing technology. This trend is particularly apparent with respect to Nile perch (*Lates niloticus*), which prefer deep, well-oxygenated waters.

The strong reliance of the Qarunians on fish also affected other aspects of their material culture. The uniqueness of Qarunian lithic artifacts, for example, has been linked to their use in fish processing, and the continued exploitation of fish in the Neolithic period may have been one reason for the relatively unimportant role of cattle, in contrast to other contemporary sites in Egypt.

In the Nile Delta, the site of Merimde has produced the most taxonomically diverse faunal assemblage recorded from Lower Egypt: twenty separate fish species have been recovered. Catfish (*Clarias, Synodontis,* and *Malapterurus*) are predominant. Evidence compiled from a number of sites in the Nile Valley suggests a developing pattern: with increasing sedentarism came an increasing reliance on fish.

**Tombs, Temples, and Texts: The Dynastic Period.** Egyptians were keen observers of nature. This is reflected in the precise depiction of fish in tomb and temple scenes, and also in the symbolic or magical powers attributed to certain fish by virtue of their observed biological behavior. For example, mullets, having traveled from the Mediterranean Sea to the First Cataract, were honored at Elephantine as heralds of the flood and as messengers of the flood god Hapy.

The mouth-brooding habits of certain species of the genus *Tilapia* were also observed and associated with creation by the creator god Atum, who took his seed into his mouth and spat out the world. This autogenesis was associated with fertility and rebirth in the next life, and the *Tilapia* in this connection becomes a favored motif in New Kingdom tomb paintings, amulets, and other minor arts, such as faience bowls decorated on the interior with *Tilapia* with a lotus bud issuing from the mouth, symbolic of new beginnings. (Following the more popular synonymy, the genus *Oreochromis* is here included within *Tilapia* spp.). The brilliant breeding colors of the *Tilapia* led

TABLE 1. *Piscine Taxa Recovered from Prehistoric Sites in Egypt*

| Site | Date (BCE) | 1 | 2 | 3 | 4 | 5 | 6 | 7 | 8 | 9 | 10 | 11 |
|---|---|---|---|---|---|---|---|---|---|---|---|---|
| **Idfu and Isna** | | | | | | | | | | | | |
| E71P101 | | | | | | x | | | | | | |
| E71P1-2 | (15,850 ± 330) | | | | | x | | | | | | |
| E71P1-3 | (15,000 ± 300) | | | x | | x | | | | | | |
| E71P1-6 | | | x | x | | x | | | | | | |
| E71P2-T2 | | | | | | x | | | | | | |
| E71K4-T4 | (10,740 ± 240) | | | | | x | | | | | | |
| E71K1 | (16,070 ± 330) | | | | x | x | | x | | | | |
| E71K3 | (15,640 ± 300) | | | | x | x | | x | | | | |
| 71K9-A | | | | | | x | | | | | | |
| 71K9-C | | | | | | x | | | | | | |
| 71P7-A | | | | | | x | | | | | | |
| 71P7-B | | | | | | x | | | | | | |
| E71K18-A | | | | | | x | | | | | | |
| E71K18-B | | | | | | x | | | | | | |
| E71K18-C | | | | | | x | | | | | | |
| E71K18-D | | | | | | x | | | | | | |
| E71K18-E | | | | | | x | | | | | | |
| E71K5 | | | | | | x | | | | | | |
| **Wadi Kubannyia** | | | | | | | | | | | | |
| E78-2 | | | | x | | x | | x | | x | | |
| E78-3 | | | | | | x | x | | | x | | |
| E78-4 | | | | | x | x | x | | | x | | |
| E78-9 | | | | | | x | | | | | | |
| E81-1 | | | | x | | x | | x | | x | | |
| E81-3 | | | | | | x | | | x | | | |
| E81-4 | | | | | x | x | | x | | x | | |
| E82-3 | | | | | x | x | x | x | | x | | |
| **Faiyum** | | | | | | | | | | | | |
| S-2 | paleolithic | | | x | x | x | x | x | x | x | x | |
| S-1 | neolithic (3910 ± 115) | | | | | x | | x | x | x | x | |
| S-3 | | | | | | | x | x | x | x | | |
| S-4 | | | | x | x | | x | x | x | x | | |
| S-5 (FS-1) | | | | x | x | x | x | x | x | x | x | |
| **Merimde (+)** | (4311 ± 50) | x | x | x | x | x | x | x | x | x | x | x |
| **Hierakonpolis** | | | | | | | | | | | | |
| HK29A | | | x | | | x | x | x | x | x | | x |

\* : x = presence of taxa
  1 = *Labeo*, 2 = *Barbus*, 3 = *Bagrus*, 4 = *Chrysichthys*, 5 = *Clariids*, 6 = *Synodontis*, 7 = *Lates*, 8 = *Tilapia*, 9 = *Tetraodon*, 10 = *Anguilla*, 11 = Mormyridae
+ = *Polypterus, Hydrocynus, Alestes, Citharinus/Distichodus, Auchenoglanis, Eutropius, Schilbe, Malapterurus, Mugil*
† = estimated date

FISH. *Depiction on a Theban wall painting.*
(Courtesy Dieter Arnold)

to its association with the sun. Called the "red fish," it was believed to accompany the solar boat as a guardian on its journey through the night; eventually, the *Tilapia* was viewed as a form of the god Horus, who kills the enemies of the sun.

The Nile catfish, which favors muddy waters, was believed to guide the solar boat through the dark river of the underworld at night. Catfish-headed demons are depicted in New Kingdom royal tombs and numerous sarcophagi assisting the god Aker to haul the solar disk on its nocturnal course. Catfish whiskers also reminded the Egyptians of the cat; according to Classical sources, the catfish became a holy manifestation of the cat-headed goddess Bastet.

The Egyptians were also aware of the peculiar habit of

*Synodontis batensoda*, which swims upside down, a characteristic depicted on several tomb scenes. In the Middle Kingdom, *Synodontis*-shaped ornaments, often made of precious metal, were popular. These were worn, usually by women, in the hair or as necklaces, possibly as a charm to protect the wearer from drowning.

As the annual Nile flood retreated, the abundance of fish caught in low-lying basins no doubt led to a connection of fish with fertility—particularly those fish that preferred to live and breed in shallow waters (i.e., *Tilapia* and *Clarias*). At the same time, an association with the chaotic flood prior to the creation of the world (couched in the imagery of the flood receding and creation emerging) also placed fish in a sphere of chaos that needed to be controlled.

In the Late period, the association of fish with certain gods and goddesses in local myths is connected to the general practice of venerating animals as manifestations of deities. For example, the goddess of Mendes province, Hatmehit, took the form of a *Schilbe;* and at Esna, the Nile perch (*Lates*) was associated with the goddess Neith, who at one point turned herself into a Nile perch to navigate the deep waters of the primeval ocean Nun. In her honor, mummified perch were offered as a token of worship.

To what extent the religious view of fish influenced their use remains unclear, but the beliefs attested in one period and place may not be valid in another. Later temple inscriptions corroborate the existence of local injunctions and provide lists of what was taboo in the different provinces of Egypt. These lists mention six fish: *Lates, Tilapia,* catfish, *Mugils, Tetraodon fahaka,* and one still unidentified fish, which may be the eel *Anguilla vulgaris.* In some places it was forbidden to eat any fish. Classical authors also provide information about fish considered holy or forbidden in local areas, such as the *phagrus* (*Hydrocynus*), *oxyrhynchus* (*Mormyrus* spp.), and *lepidotus* (*Barbus bynni*), which were participants in the Osiris myth. It was forbidden even to catch them in nets or by hook in the Oxyrhynchus district, but they were apparently fair game in neighboring areas.

### BIBLIOGRAPHY

Brewer, Douglas J. "Seasonality in the Prehistoric Faiyum Based on the Incremental Growth Structures of the Nile Catfish (Pisces: *Clarias*)." *Journal of Archaeological Science* 14 (1987), 459–472.

Brewer, Douglas J. *Fishermen, Hunters and Herders.* British Archaeological Reports, International Series, 478. London, 1989.

Brewer, Douglas J., and Renée F. Freidman. *Fish and Fishing in Ancient Egypt.* Warminster, 1989. Serves the interests of lay persons and nonspecialist scholars.

von den Driesch, Angela. *Tierknochenfunde aus Qasr el Sagha/Fayum. Mitteilungen des Deutschen Archäologischen Instituts, Abteilung Kairo* 42 (1986), 1–8.

von den Driesch, Angel N, and J. Boessneck. *Die Tierknochenfunde aus der Neolithischen Siedlung von Merimde-Benisalâma am westlichen Nildelta.* Cairo, 1985.

Wendorf, Fred, and Romald Schild. *The Prehistory of the Nile Valley.* New York, 1976.

Wendorf, Fred, and Romald Schild. *Loaves and Fishes: The Prehistory of Wadi Kubbaniya.* Dallas, 1980.

Wenke, Robert, Janet Long, and Paul Buck. "Epipaleolithic and Neolithic Subsistence and Settlement in the Fayyum Oasis of Egypt." *Journal of Field Archaeology* 15 (1988), 29–51.

DOUGLAS J. BREWER

**FLORA.** Egypt's natural flora is shaped by two basically different climatic conditions, the arid desert areas and the humid Nile Valley. There are also the Mediterranean climate along a narrow coastal strip and the oasis vegetation of the Western Desert. These vegetation zones developed by 5000 BCE; before that, the North African climate was generally humid, the Westen Desert was a savanna covered in grass and trees, and the Nile Delta would swamp with each major flood. As the climate became more and more arid, paleobotanical studies show Egypt's natural flora to have remained as it is today since the beginning of recorded history. Nevertheless, the human impact on the flora has changed it somewhat since settlement began in the Nile Valley, first as the indigenous wild flora was harvested and then as nonindigenous plants were introduced and cultivated.

Our knowledge of the flora in ancient Egypt derives from two sources: tomb paintings and substantial archaeological remains. Written records provide some additional information, although the ancient Egyptian names for many plant species are still unknown. The identification of plants depicted in paintings is often difficult, as many tomb illustrations show landscapes as a "type"—a papyrus thicket, a field, a garden, or the desert—without attention to botanical detail or accuracy. Tomb offerings are the best source of archaeological remains; these tend to be cultivated plants—fruit, vegetables, herbs, and spices—as supplies for the dead in the hereafter. The tombs also contained many objects made of organic materials, such as wood or wickerwork, and their composition provides information about the local flora as well as imported materials. Also informative are the chemical analyses of the aromatic oils included in the tomb offerings and those for the products used for mummification. The flower garlands that adorn the mummies have indicated the typical garden flora. The ancient Egyptians made careful choices as to the food or flowers they deemed both appropriate and auspicious for the dead; tomb findings, therefore, represent only some of the plants common in Egypt at any given period.

The number of known plants grown and used increases with each settlement excavation, especially those of ancient rubbish dumps. Unfired mud bricks used in construction are another important source. They were made from Nile silts or muds mixed with the chaff of straw; therefore, they contain traces of the riverbank vegetation, as well as remnants from the grain fields.

The Nile was bordered by lush vegetation. There were rushes (Juncaceae family), reeds (*Phragmites australis* and *Saccharum spontaneum*), and from the New Kingdom onward, reed-mace (*Arundo donax*), cat's tail (*Typha domingensis*), and the sedges (Cyperaceae family). The dominant Nile plant was a sedge, papyrus (*Cyperus papyrus*), which grew to a height of 5 meters (16 feet), often in an impenetrable thicket, and this economically important plant became the symbol of Lower Egypt. Egyptian esparto, or alpha, grass (*Desmostachya bipinnata*) and the composite *Ceruana pratensis* also grew on either side of the Nile but a little inland.

**Nile Plants.** The riverbank flora was put to good use. With the raw materials furnished by it a great variety of wickerwork was created, above all for household objects, such as baskets, bags, brooms, sieves, mats, and ropes. In Predynastic times the dead were buried in woven mats; in pharaonic times this practice was used only for the most impoverished, when a wooden coffin could not be purchased. Coffins created from the *Ceruana pratensis*, a plant with fragrant blossoms, are unique to the first and second dynasties; its scent was believed to keep bad spirits at bay. Its branches were also used in brooms for the same reason—since "they swept out the bad spirits."

The stalks of the rushes *Juncus rigidus* and *Juncus acutus* were used for a variety of wickerwork and writing tools. Papyrus (*mḥj.t*) was the most common and most harvested plant of the Nile vegetation. From prehistoric times, it was used to build boats for the river and to weave mats and roof coverings. Strips of papyrus stem were fashioned into baskets, boxes, and sandals and the pith—cut into strips—was stacked in crosswise layers and pressed to make papyrus sheets, a paperlike writing surface used by scribes from the first dynasty onward. The lower sections of the papyrus stalk were edible, and bundles were shown in Old Kingdom tomb paintings as offerings. The papyrus plant soon came to have a religious significance. It was a popular amulet in the shape of the *wȝḏ*-scepter, believed to safeguard the rebirth of the deceased; the same meaning was attributed to individual papyrus stalks with umbels that were carried in the burial procession. From the New Kingdom onward, papyrus umbels were often the centerpiece in flower arrangements attached to poles. Important in cult ceremony, the rustling sound of a papyrus thicket was imitated by the swinging of a sistrum. Carved in stone, papyrus became an important architectural element, above all in temple architecture; as a column, the lower section was a gathering of sheaths crowned by the umbel. From the Old Kingdom onward, tomb paintings depicted the papyrus thicket as a generic landscape, as a home to many animals; the tomb occupant was often shown on a bird hunt or pleasure boating. The intensive use of papyrus led to its depletion; today, papyrus growth has receded to small areas in the Delta, near Damietta, and in the Wadi Natrun.

The water flora in the Nile has also changed since pharaonic times. Today, the dominant plant is the water hyacinth (*Eichornia crassipes*), which floats on the water surface; although imported from North America toward the end of the nineteenth century as a decorative plant for garden ponds, it has experienced an explosive growth in the Nile. It has also become a problem, since it tends to clog the irrigation canals. In ancient Egypt, the surface of the Nile was covered in the wide leaves and flowers of both the white lotus (*Nymphaea lotus*) and the blue lotus

(*Nymphaea coerulea*). An Egyptian name for the lotus was *sšn*, although it is unclear which of the two was identified. Blue lotus flowers have an intense perfume and because they open with the rising sun and close at night, they were considered a symbol of rebirth, connected to the god Nefertum as the youthful morning sun. Lotus blossoms, papyrus umbels, and fish appear on the Nun-bowls that symbolize the primeval ocean (called Nun), believed to be the source of all life. During celebrations, guests would wear lotus blossoms in their hair or carry them in their hands to inhale the wonderful scent. The garlands that adorned the dead usually contained petals from both blue and white lotus and, sometimes, whole blossoms on their long stems fastened into the linen wrappings. As decorative flowers, lotus was always connected to the symbol of rebirth. There were also some practical reasons for valuing the lotus plant: the rhizomes were edible and the petals were used both for perfume and for medicinals, because of their slightly narcotic effect. The Indian lotus (*Nelumbo nucifera*) was probably introduced during the ancient Persian era. Its funnel-shaped leaves and flowers do not float on the water's surface but instead protrude above the water on strong rooted stems. The blossoms are white or pink, and both the seeds and the rhizomes are edible.

The water chestnut (*Trapa natans*) may well have been common in the Nile during pharaonic times. Today, it is only found in the Ethiopian stretches of the Nile. If the seeds are now a valued food staple, the only proof of this for ancient Egypt is one undated finding. Pondweed was, however, shown in numerous tomb scenes. The plant grows fully submerged in water, and only the top leaves with the spiked flowers protrude above the water. Since the illustrations are highly stylized, it is difficult to determine whether they show the smooth pondweed (*Potamogeton lucens*) or the hairy pondweed (*Potamogeton crispus*).

Trees grew along the Nile in a fairly homogenous pattern; the most common were acacia and tamarisks. The Nile acacia (*Acacia nilotica*) was called *šnd.t* in Old Egyptian and was used in many ways. The leaves and pods were used as cattle fodder, and some tomb paintings depict goats grazing on these trees. The long seed pods contain an agent useful in tanning leather and tinting linen. The characteristic shape of the pods, like pearls on a string, were also copied for jewelry, especially in gold. Acacia wood was used for boats, furniture, and coffins, and it was processed for charcoal. Its gum resin (now called gum arabic) was a binding agent for pigments and was also used to fix the linen strips that wrapped mummies. Like other parts of the acacia, the resin had medicinal uses. The white acacia (*Acacia albida*) was used with similar diversity, although it has become rare in Egypt to-

FLORA. *Sycamore trees (also called sycamore fig trees).* A few papyrus reeds are in the foreground.

day. The two types of tamarisk trees along the Nile offered materials for many purposes; both can grow in shrub or tree form, the latter with thin, flexible branches. As a tree, the anthel tamarisk (*Tamarix aphylla*) has tiny leaflets, whereas those of the Nile tamarisk (*Tamarix nilotica*), called *jsr* in Old Egyptian, are somewhat larger. The wood was processed for charcoal, and the tannin-rich bark and galls were used for both tanning and medicinal purposes.

The Egyptian willow tree (*Salix subserrata*) was called *tr.t* and had been indigenous to the borders of the Nile since prehistoric times. Since only female trees grow in Egypt, willows spread only with the help of cuttings. The tree may have originated in the Near East, then brought to Egypt by humans, not as a result of natural pollination. The salicine materials of the willow, with their anti-inflammatory and analgesic pharmacological properties (present-day salicylic acid and aspirin) were known and used by physicians. The most important tree was the sycamore fig (*Ficus sycomorus*), called *nh.t* in Old Egyptian, although it is not certain whether it was indigenous to the Nile Valley. (It is the Near Eastern, or biblical "sycamore"—unrelated to either the American or Eurasian sycamores.) It can be fertilized only by the gall-wasp (*Ceratosolen arabicus*), which is not found today in Egypt, only in areas to the south. Studies have shown that in pharaonic times, a different species of gall-wasp (*Sycophaga sycomori*) developed in the sycamore figs, which is, how-

ever, unable to effect fertilization. The only explanation is that even in prehistoric times, cuttings were used to cultivate the tree in the North; the habitat of the gall-wasp *C. arabicus* may have spread south as a result of climate change. The sycamore fig was a large and impressive tree, with a dense crown, popular for its abundant shade. This characteristic led the ancient Egyptians to regard it as a tree deity, who would offer shade and cooling water to the deceased or their souls in the form of the *ba*-bird. The fruits of the sycamore fig were small and sweetish, popular for inclusion in tomb offerings since the Predynastic period; however, the fruit is edible only if it is cut open before it ripens fully, accelerating the ripening process before the gall-wasps develop inside. In some tomb scenes, this incision is clear. The soft sycamore wood was used for furniture and coffins; its fruit, leaves, and milky fluid were used for medicinal purposes. Another indigenous fruit tree was the thornbush (*Zizyphus spina*), called *nbs* in Old Egyptian. Its small edible fruit was included in offerings as early as Predynastic times, and it was also used to make fruit bread; its hard wood was used for dowels and for bows. The carob tree (*Ceratonia siliqua*) was called *nḏm* and probably grew only on the Mediterranean coast, where it still grows to some extent. Its wood was used to make bows, and the sweetness of its pods was prized, as it still is today.

The only palm indigenous to the Nile Valley was the

FLORA. *Date palms and dom palms.*

dom palm (*Hyphaene thebaica*), characterized by the multiple forks in its trunk. The fan-shaped leaves offered raw material for weaving into mats, bags, and baskets, and its fruit is edible. Dom palm fruit was frequently included in the offerings from Predynastic times onward. It is impossible to determine whether the second type of fan palm, the argun palm (*Medemia argun*), was indigenous to ancient Egypt or whether it was merely cultivated there. According to the few findings and text sources, it was not a very common tree, and today there remain only rare examples in the Nubian desert. No consensus exists on when the cultivation of the date palm (*Phoenix dactylifera*), called *bnr*, reached Egypt. Its origins are unknown, although they are thought to have been in the area around the Persian Gulf. Findings have been dated to prehistoric el-Omari and Nabta cultures, as have palm leaves woven into mats. To date, there are no Old Kingdom findings, but evidence begins with the Middle Kingdom. Since date palms produce edible fruit only by hand pollination, the ancient Egyptians may have mastered this technique by the Middle Kingdom, thus cultivating a valuable and nutritious fruit.

*Ricinus communis* is a tree indigenous to the Nile Valley, where it usually grows to a height of 3 to 5 meters (9 to 16 feet). Numerous deposits were found of its seeds from the Predynastic period onward. They are rich in oil that was used for lamps and cosmetic purposes. The ricinus-plant, called *dgm* in Old Egyptian, was described in the medical Ebers Papyrus as an especially useful medicinal plant. Pottery from the Naqada period often shows a plant with large leaves hanging down in concentric half circles and an inflorescence that grows from the middle of the stem. This may be an illustration of the Abyssinian banana (*Ensete edule*), whose false stalk (formed of its leaves) can reach 10 meters (32 feet). Only the center of the false stalk is edible. Today, the plant no longer grows in Egypt, only in the highlands of Ethiopia.

**Desert Plants.** In contrast to the many images showing the natural vegetation along the Nile, only a few tomb scenes depict the desert flora. While these tomb paintings may feature the deceased hunting in the desert, as well as the desert animals, desert vegetation is merely indicated, usually by sketching in a few blades of grass. Nonetheless, tree growth in the more arid regions of Egypt was more abundant in ancient times than it is today; depletion began with excessive clear-cutting in pharaonic times. The tamarisks were abundant on the desert borders, and acacias grew far inland along the wadis. Two other economically useful tree species also thrived inland: *Balanites aegyptiaca* and *Moringa peregrina*. Oil was pressed from the seeds of both. Moringa oil (*b3k*) was especially popular, and domestic production was supplemented by importing more from Syria. Balanite pulp was valued as edible, and the wood of both trees was used in the manufacture of various objects. In the hot and sunny Egyptian climate, trees offered much needed shade, food, lumber, and raw materials for wickerwork, so trees came to have religious significance. The goddess Hathor appeared in the shape of a sycomore, and the deities Isis and Nut were sometimes shown in this form. The date palm symbolized the location where the youthful morning sun rose, and they were grown in the sacred grove at Buto. The acacia was especially revered at Edfu; as early as the Old Kingdom, documents show an acacia house featured in the burial ritual. The willow also played an important cult role. The dom palm was associated with the deities Min and Thoth; the *išd*, probably designating the *Balanites* as a tree of life, was linked to Thoth and Seshat.

Agricultural fields were located on either side of the Nile. Barley (*Hordeum vulgare*), called *it*, and emmer wheat (*Triticum turgidum*, subspecies *dicoccum = Triticum dicoccum*), called *bd.t*, were originally domesticated and grown in the Near East, but by 5000 BCE, the cultivation of both plants is documented for ancient Egypt. It is still unclear whether attempts to grow millet (*Sorghum bicolor*) and *Cyperus* species coincided with the introduction of cultivated grain in Upper Egypt. What is certain, however, is that the cultivation of barley and emmer spread rapidly through ancient Egypt; these grains soon became staple foods, used for baking bread and brewing beer, both served at all meals. In the absence of monetary currency, grain was also the unit of value for the exchange of goods. Surplus grain was exported, which gave Egypt political dominance over Syrian rulers, who needed to import it.

The amount of grain found among the tomb offerings is a reflection of how important it was as a staple in ancient Egypt. As a secondary benefit, these finds also help us study the weed flora present in the cultivated fields of those periods; the weeds today are the same in type and number as they were then. The most common type of weed was clover (*Medicago polymorpha*; *Melilotus* sp.; *Lotus corniculatus;* and *Scorpiurus muricatus*), the chick peas (*Vicia sativa; Vicia narbonensis; Vicia lutea*), the sweet peas (*Lathyrus marmoratus; Lathyrus hirsutus*), and the grasses *Phalaris paradoxa* and *Lolium temulentum*. When too much of the *Lolium temulentum* grows among the grain crops, the result may be a health hazard, because the grass seeds are vulnerable to infestation with the poisonous fungus *Endoconidium temulentum*, documented in materials dating from the Middle Kingdom. Cereal, above all barley, played an important cult role, and sprouting cereal was a symbol of rebirth. The cultivation of flax (*Linum usitatissimum*) was brought to Egypt from the Palestine region. Throughout pharaonic history, flax

provided linen, the material that clothed the population. Cotton (*Gossypium* sp.) came into use with the Greeks and Romans, who brought the shrubby plants from India. With the beginning of the dynastic period, ancient Egyptians began to cultivate grapevines (*Vitis vinifera*), again a plant that originated in Palestine. The grapes were consumed as fresh fruit and also used for making wine, called *irp*. The steps in cultivating barley, emmer, flax, and grapes were documented in countless Egyptian tomb paintings, from plowing the field, to sowing the seed, harvesting, and the final processing. Such detailed imagery is rare for other cultivated plants, so the only source for determining when other plants were introduced to ancient Egypt are archaeological remains; since current excavations in Egypt continue to uncover new species each season, any inventory cannot be complete.

Small fields and private gardens in ancient Egypt were used to cultivate a wide variety of legumes, many of which were first domesticated in the Near East. The lentil (*Lens culinaris*), called ʿršn, the chickling pea (*Lathyrus sativus*), and fenugreek (*Trigonella foenum graecum*) are known from Predynastic times onward. The fava or broad bean (*Vicia faba*), called *pr*, has been identified in materials from the Old Kingdom. There is Middle Kingdom evidence of the chickpea (*Cicer arietinum*), probably *hrw-bik*. The green or garden pea (*Pisum sativum*) was added in the New Kingdom. The cowpea or blackeye pea (*Vigna unguiculata*) called *iwrj.t*, was introduced to Egypt from sub-Saharan Africa, followed by the pigeon or dwarf pea (*Cajanus cajan*) in the Middle Kingdom. Finds that provide evidence of these legumes, with exception of the lentil, have been rare.

The cultivation of plants of the Cucurbitaceae family (gourds, melons, cucumbers, squash) also originated to the south of Egypt. *Cucumis melo*, the honey melon, is documented only in tomb paintings and faience models. The only kind of watermelon (*Citrullus lanatus*) grown in Egypt was the variety whose seeds, not the flesh, are edible; watermelon seeds found in excavations have been dated to the Predynastic period. The ancient Egyptians were also familiar with the gourd (*Lagenaria siceraria*).

Tomb paintings show the onion (*Allium cepa*), called *ḥḏw*, was widely cultivated as early as the Old Kingdom. Substantial remnants of onion, garlic (*Allium sativum*), and leek (*Allium porrum* or *Allium kurrath*) are, however, only known from New Kingdom finds. Few of the plants grown in fields and in gardens were indigenous to Egypt, but one was the tiger or rush nut (*Cyperus esculentus*), called *wʿḥ*, from the Predynastic period; another was lettuce (*Lactuca sativa*), called *ʿbw*, from the Old Kingdom. The rush nut, edible when cooked, was an important source of oil, which is contained in the rhizome. The cultivation of lettuce is illustrated in some Old Kingdom tombs; it was associated with Min, the deity of fertility, probably because of the milky white fluid that is expressed when the plant is cut at the base.

In addition to the date palm, the sycomore fig, and the grapevine, some more trees from foreign regions were cultivated in Egypt. The fig (*Ficus carica*), called *dȝb*, was introduced from Palestine during the Old Kingdom, the olive (*Olea europaea*) during the Middle Kingdom, and the pomegranate (*Punica granatum*), called *inhmn*, during the New Kingdom. The persea tree (*Mimusops laurifolia*), called *šwȝb*, was brought to Egypt from sub-Saharan Africa. Trees and shrubs were mostly planted in private gardens centred around a small pond, where they flourished amidst many flowers. Indigenous flower species included the white and the blue lotus, the chrysanthemum (*Chrysanthemum coronarium*), the willow herb (*Epilobium hirsutum*), the sesbania shrub (*Sebania sesban*), and the narcissus (*Narcissus tazetta*). Exotic or foreign flowers, especially flowers imported from Palestine, were very popular during the New Kingdom; documented are the common field poppy (*Papaver rhoeas*), oriental cornflower (*Centaurea depressa*), hollyhock (*Alcea ficifolia*), lily (*Lilium candidum*), delphinium (*Delphinium orientale*), and safflower (*Carthamus tinctorius*). Paintings suggest that mandrake (*Mandragora officinalis*) may have been cultivated. The henna bush (*Lawsonia inermis*) was brought to Egypt during the New Kingdom from the coastal regions of the Indian Ocean.

A new group of plants were grown in Egyptian gardens during the Roman era, including the rose (*Rosa richardii*), everlasting or immortelle (*Helichrysum stoechas*), campion (*Lychnis coelirosa*), and jasmin (*Jasminum sambac*)—brought to Rome from the Asian provinces of the empire. These flowers were not only valued for their beauty, they were also used for garlands and flower arrangements atop long staffs, the latter serving as offerings to the gods. Flowers had always been worn for adornment in Egypt during celebrations, and mummies were decorated with elaborately woven flower garlands.

Herb gardens were important and yielded crops of aromatic plants, which were used for spices, cosmetics, and medicinal purposes. Many were brought to Egypt from Palestine, including coriander (*Coriandrum sativum*), Egyptian caraway (*Cuminum cyminum*), and dill (*Anethum graveolens*). Other spices used in Egypt had originated in regions to the south. Aromatic products whose plants could not be grown in Egypt's climate, such as juniper (*Juniperus oxycedrus*) for its berries and black pepper (*Piper nigrum*) for its peppercorns, were imported. Plants with pharmaceutical properties, both imports and local, were widely used for medicinal purposes; however, only a fraction of ancient Egyptian names for those medicinal plants or herbs have been identified from the medical texts. Written sources document the prescription of

products derived from willow, acacia, tamarisk, and sycomore; from fig and pomegranate trees; from the grapevine, the date palm, and the dom palm; and from the ebony tree, juniper berries, barley, emmer wheat, and rush nuts. Some were based on incense, myrrh, and coniferous resins.

During the New Kingdom, the Palestinian method of tinting linen in various colors was adopted in Egypt. While during the Middle Kingdom linen had sometimes been dyed in red or yellow tints, using tanins and ochers, evidence suggests that new red and yellow dyes were gained from the petals of the safflower; other dyes were made from red madderroots (*Rubia tinctorium*), and blue was made either from the leaves of the woad (*Isatis tinctoria*) or indigo species. How much red and blue dyes were manufactured in Egypt or imported from Palestine as finished products is not yet known, since there have been no finds in Egypt of these dyes; what does exist are the remains of finished and decorated linen fabric, where individual dyes can be chemically analyzed and defined. Only safflower is otherwise documented because its petals were used in mummy garlands, and offerings of safflower seeds, rich in oil, were found in tombs.

Scented oils played an important role from early dynastic times, since kings would send aromatic oils in small containers made of precious stone as gifts to foreign royalty. Scented oils eventually became an important export product. In Egypt, rubbing scented oil into the skin was part of standard hygienic practice. For festivities, guests would wear small cones of scented salve on their heads, which melted during the celebration and released its scent. Yet little is known about the ingredients of these products. The base probably consisted of grease or liquid oil. The aromatic substances, immersed in a neutral oil for a length of time, allowed the aroma to be absorbed into the oil; finally the mass was pressed. The only existent images show lotus and lily blossoms used for scented oils. The aromatic lichen *Pseudevernia furfuracea*, the rhizomes of *Cyperus articulatus*, and the grass *Cymbopogon schoenanthus* may have been processed as well. Archaeological finds of the Middle Kingdom include both the lichen and rhizomes, while those of the New Kingdom include grass traces.

Since indigenous Egyptian trees yielded a fairly poor quality of wood and lumber, imports were needed on a large scale from early dynastic times for carpentry, shipbuilding, construction, and coffins. From Nubia, the black-violet, very hard wood of an ebony tree (*Dalbergia melanoxylon*) was imported. It was used primarily for the manufacture of artfully carved furniture. The main imports, however, focused on coniferous woods such as cedar (*Cedrus libani*), fir (*Abies cilicica*), cypress (*Cupressus sempervirens*), juniper (*Juniperus oxycedrus*), pines (*Pinus*, sp.), and yew (*Taxus baccata*). An Egyptian name for "coniferous wood" was ꜥš, which may have been used either for fir or cedar. Imported coniferous woods were used by carpenters in many ways: long planks were needed in tomb construction, shipbuilding, and as flag masts; shorter pieces, often deftly joined, were used for coffins, statues, and furniture. Chariots, especially the lightweight chariots used in combat, required specialty woods with elastic properties; these were imported from the Near East and from the Caucasus. An analysis of chariot remains shows elm (probably *Ulmus minor*), maple (*Acer* sp.), and a type of *Prunus* tree (plum or related fruit tree) that is difficult to define. Other imported woods were oak (*Quercus cerris*) for dowels and, from the birch family, the Eurasian hornbeam (*Ostrya carpinifolia*) for rudders. Birch bark, imported from Anatolia, was used from the Old Kingdom onward to decorate staffs, arches, chests, and chariots, a practice that became most common in the eighteenth dynasty.

With wood imports, a variety of resins and resinous products were introduced to ancient Egypt. During the Old Kingdom, coniferous resin, called *sft*, was an important component in the materials used for mummification. The same resin was prescribed by Egyptian physicians for a number of ailments. With the beginning of the New Kingdom, terebinth resin (from the terebinth, a variety of pistachio, *Pistacia terebinthus*) was imported from Palestine on a large scale. Chemical analyses of trace substances from Tell el-Amarna have shown that this resin was used mostly for incense. The gum resins for frankincense and myrrh were also imported because the trees from which they were taken, *Boswellia* and *Commiphora*, both of the Burseraceae family were not indigenous to Egypt. They grew only to the south of Egypt and in the southern region of the Arabian Peninsula. Another incense-exporting country, the land of Punt, is thought to have been located in the region now known as Somalia. Under Hatshepsut and Ramesses III of the eighteenth dynasty, naval expeditions were dispatched to Punt for the purchase of incense and myrrh.

The flora of the Nile Valley provided good living conditions throughout the time of the pharaohs. Indigenous plants and imported species provided food, building materials, clothing, cosmetics, medication, shade, and natural beauty. If some plants did not thrive in the local climate, the ancient Egyptians made use of their extensive trade relations to import what was needed. Imports were focused mainly on lumber and on resins, since the burning of incense pleased the gods.

[*See also* Flowers; Fruits; Lotus; Papyrus; *and* Vegetables.]

## BIBLIOGRAPHY

Baum, Nathalie. "Arbres et arbustes de l'Egypte Ancienne," *Orientalia Lovaniensia Analecta*, 31. Leuven, 1988.

Germer, Renate. "Flora des pharaonische Ägypten." *Deutsches Archäologisches Institut Kairo*, special edition, 11. Mainz, 1985.

Germer, Renate. "Katalog der altägyptischen Pflanzenreste der Berliner Museen." *Ägyptologische Abhandlungen*, 47. Wiesbaden, 1988.

Germer, Renate. "Die Pflanzenmaterialien aus dem Grab des Tutanchamun." *Hildesheimer Ägyptologische Beiträge*, 28. Hildesheim, 1989.

Lucas, Alfred. *Ancient Egyptian Materials and Industries*. 4th ed. London, 1989.

Manniche, Lise. *An Ancient Egyptian Herbal*. London, 1989.

Täckholm, Vivi, et al. *Flora of Egypt*. 4 vols. Cairo University, *Bulletin of the Faculty of Science*, vols. 17, 28, 30, and 36. Cairo, 1941, 1950, 1954, and 1969.

Zohary, Daniel, and Maria Hopf. *Domestication of Plants in the Old World*. 2d ed. Oxford, 1993.

RENATE GERMER
Translated by Elizabeth Schwaiger and Martha Goldstein

**FLOWERS** were an important part of daily life, whether as fresh floral decorations or as decorative elements represented in durable materials. Until the beginning of the New Kingdom, only the blossom of the water lily and the papyrus head appear to have played a role, as a model for rosette shapes. Occasionally, the chrysanthemum or camomile served the same purpose. These plants are part of the natural vegetation of the Nile countryside, flourish unaided, and could be collected as needed. In addition, the Egyptians also planted water lilies in man-made pools.

Two types of water lily grew in the Nile, mainly in its shallow branches and in the canals: the blue lotus *(Nymphaea coerulea)* and the white lotus *(Nymphaea lotus)*. Besides color, these two types are differentiated by two further characteristics, which may also be recognized in Egyptian representations; the blue lotus has pointed flowers and floating leaves with smooth edges, and the white lotus has rounded petals and leaves with toothed edges. The blue lotus also has an intense perfume. As yet, only the one Egyptian term, *sšn*, has been identified for water lily flowers. Because water lilies open in the mornings and close again at night, the Egyptians saw in them an image of rebirth or regeneration. The flowers were used to symbolize the deceased's entering into the underworld and the rebirth in the hereafter to a new life. A connection was also drawn to the sun god Re, since the youthful morning sun, in the form of the god Nefertem, emerges from a lotus flower. In the imagery of the Egyptians, an intense scent of flowers indicated the presence of a god, and thus in many tomb scenes, the deceased is shown with a lotus flower in hand, which is also often held to the nose in order to breathe in the divine perfume. At festivals, women usually wore lotus flowers in their hair; for certain special occasions—as for the fishermen's competition—men did too, as may be seen in many tombs of the Old Kingdom.

The Nun bowls, fashioned out of blue-green faience,

are decorated with lotus flowers. Together with papyrus plants, they symbolize the primeval waters Nun, from which all life springs. In pharaonic times, the papyrus (*Cyperus papyrus*) grew in thickets with ample fauna along the Nile. For the Egyptians, papyrus became the symbol of fertility and life *par excellence.* Thus the motif of papyrus stalks with their sweeping flower umbels is the most commonly used plant decoration—whether in architecture as a column or in transom windows, as the handle of a mirror, as a jewelry element, or as an amulet. In the Old Kingdom, fresh papyrus stalks with flower heads were part of the offering goods that the deceased took into the grave. They would guarantee life in the hereafter. Often, these papyrus stalks were entwined with lotus flowers, and these arrangements became the forerunners of the bouquets so often used in New Kingdom art.

The papyrus plant was the symbol of Lower Egypt, as represented on the Narmer Palette of the first dynasty. It is often designated as the plant emblem of Lower Egypt, which, when intertwined with the plant emblem of Upper Egypt, the so-called "southern lily," symbolized the unification of the two parts of the country. The botanical original of the southern plant has not yet been found. During the New Kingdom, papyrus and lotus flowers maintained their dominant position as floral decorations, decorative elements, and symbolic plants. From various representations, however, it is known that the Egyptians began planting a series of newly imported flowers alongside indigenous plants in the gardens of their houses and temples; these demanded intensive care, and above all good watering. Thus in New Kingdom tomb paintings of gardens, the flowers are being watered with the help of a *shaduf.* These scenes, the wall and floor paintings from Tell el-Amarna, and the faience wall inlays, provide information about the new flower types. For example, the cornflower (*Centaurea depressa*) and the red poppy (*Papaver rhoeas*), imported from Asia Minor or the Palestine region, can be seen for the first time. An exception is in the so-called Botanical Garden of Thutmose III in Karnak. There, foreign flowers such as arum (*Arum italicum*), dragonwort (*Dracunculus vulgaris*) and a type of iris (perhaps *Iris albicans*) are depicted; those plants, however, did not appear in other garden scenes, so they probably did not catch on in Egypt.

During the eighteenth dynasty, it became the fashion to wear large collars of faience pieces, the individual elements of which were usually made in the form of flowers, leaves, or fruits. It is possible to recognize the bloom of the cornflower, a type of camomile, the white and the blue lotus, green leaf elements, and yellow fruits. Tomb paintings show that collars of the same type, made with fresh flowers, were worn at banquets. Servant girls can be seen tying these floral decorations onto the guests. Because the floral collars are usually very schematically drawn, however, only the petals of the blue and white lotus can be recognized. At Thebes, in the nineteenth dynasty tomb of Nedjemger, "Overseer of the Garden of the Ramesseum" he is depicted inspecting the manufacture of floral collars from fresh plant material. Although it may be assumed that those floral arrangements were produced in great numbers, only a few are known preserved. In the ruins of a house at Tell el-Amarna, a single such collar was found. At least six additional collars were "buried" together in a pit outside the tomb of Tutankhamun with the remains of a banquet and the embalming materials from the burial. Presumably, guests at a last burial celebration in the tomb of this pharaoh wore these collars, three of which have survived. They show us, much better than the faience models and wall paintings, how the collars were made and which plant materials were used for them. A piece of papyrus cut into the shape of a collar served as the base and was trimmed around the throat edge with linen, with which it could also be tied around the neck. Using thin strips of a palm leaf, the individual pieces of plant material were sewn onto the papyrus in rows, one above the other: the green leaves of the persea (*Mimusops laurifolia*) the olive tree (*Olea europaea*), the Egyptian willow (*Salix subserrata*), the pomegranate (*Punica granatum*), and presumably the wild celery (*Apium graveolens*); the colorful flowerheads or petals of the cornflower (*Centaurea depressa*), the bitterweed (*Picris asplenioides*), the blue lotus (*Nymphaea coerulea*), red berries from the indigenous withania nightshade (*Withania somnifera*), and blue, disk-shaped faience beads.

At the beginning of the New Kingdom, the practice developed of providing the mummy of the deceased with a fresh garland of flowers when putting it into the tomb. Thus far, however, a floral collar has only been found on the mummy of Tutankhamun, which in its method of manufacture and the plant material used is very similar to those used at banquets; it lay on the chest area of the innermost of his three coffins. Apart from this, the Egyptians used special mummy garlands, which were made in flat strips and attached to the mummy's body in concentric semicircles; their method of manufacture was extremely simple. Green leaves were folded over strips of a palm leaf, then sewn together with thin strips of palm leaf. Inserted in with the leaves were either a few colorful petals or entire flowers on long stems. The wreath maker usually used the same types of flowers that were worked into the collars; in addition, the following flowers may be identified from garland strands: the indigenous Nile acacia (*Acacia nilotica*), the white acacia (*Acacia albida*), the sesban (*Sesbania sesban*), the hairy willow herb (*Epilobium hirsutum*), and the chrysanthemum (*Chrysanthemum coronarium*), as well as those from Asia Minor or the Palestine region, such as hollyhock *(Alcea ficifolia)*, delphinium *(Delphinium orientale)*, and safflower *(Carthamus tinctorius)*. The red petals of the safflower were also used by the Egyptians to dye linen and from the seeds they extracted a good quality edible oil. From the twentieth dynasty, mummy garlands also included the very fragrant flowers of the henna bush *(Lawsonia inermis)*, which originally came from the coastal regions of the Indian Ocean and East Africa. Mummy garlands could also consist of green leaves only, when fragrant leaves were often chosen, such as mint *(Mentha* sp.), wild celery *(Apium graveolens)*, or dill *(Anethum graveolens)*. The mummy garlands were either laid on the mummy once it had been wrapped—and into whose linen bandages lotus flowers were sometimes tucked—or on the coffin.

Only a few mummies have been found with wreath-shaped arrangements on their heads. Thus, for example, a few leaf remains were found in the hair of Amenhotpe II, and small floral garlands once hung around the royal insignia on the brows of the first and second coffins of Tutankhamun. Late *Books of Going Forth by Day (Books of the Dead)* show, for the first time, a round floral wreath as the symbol of successfully withstanding the Tribunal of the Dead before Osiris. The Egyptians not only decorated the mummies with floral wreaths but also, in many cases, parts of the accompanying burial equipment; thus the statuette of the deceased in the eighteenth dynasty tomb of Kha, divine statuettes in the tomb of Tutankhamun, and jugs that contained food and drink. Often, the floral garlands were painted directly onto the jugs. From analyzing the plant remains on mummies, we know that the Egyptians also planted flower bulbs in their gardens from the New Kingdom. Yet it was not the beautiful flowers of the plants that were found on the mummy, but only the leaves of the bulbs. Thus bulb leaves from a *Crinum* variety, which is not indigenous to Egypt, covered the eyes, nose, mouth, and mummification incision of one mummy. On the neck of Ramesses II, were the remains of narcissus bulbs *(Narcissus tazetta)*, and on the chest of a female mummy the bulbs of a type of lily.

In Greco-Roman times, the Egyptians still provided mummies with floral decorations, but those were usually made in a new way and new imported plants were found in them. Individual flowers, petals, stamens, or twigs were bound together into small bunches and joined together into compact wreaths. The new flower types included the rose *(Rosa richardii)*, the Indian lotus *(Nelumbo nucifera)*, immortelle *(Helichrysum stoechas)*, lychnis *(Lychnis coelirosa)*, jasmine *(Jasminum sambac)*, and the little marjoram bush *(Marjorana hortensis)*. Artificial flowers of copper leaf or colored wool were also added. The base for the wreaths was very often pieces of decorticated stalks of the sedge *Scirpus inclinatus*.

The flowers grown in Egypt's gardens were not only used for floral collars and mummy garlands, they were also used for large floral bouquets. The bouquets, or occasionally wreaths made in the shape of an *ankh* sign, were popular offerings to the gods, and they can often be seen in the tomb paintings. They were carried in the burial procession and were placed near the mummy when it was stood upright, in front of the tomb entrance, while the last rites were enacted. The drawings enable us to see how the bouquets were made. The central part usually consists of a few papyrus stems with large flower umbels; onto these, the same flowers, leaves, and fruits used in the collars and mummy wreaths were attached in circles, one above the other—cornflower, poppy, blue and white lotus, a kind of chrysanthemum or camomile, and the yellow fruits that are either persea or mandrake. In a few cases, the entire wreath still has a convolvulus *(Convolvulus arvensis)* vine wrapped around it or there are cos lettuce stalks worked into it. The pole bouquets of the temple and tomb decorations are also found as decorative elements on furniture and, particularly often, as the shape for ointment spoons. In a few graves, some pole bouquets have been found: in the tombs of Tutankhamun, Sennefer, Sennedjem, and Kha, but these all consist of completely different materials than those shown in the representations—they only contain the green leafy branches of the persea and the olive tree, some vine leaves, and the leafy stems of the melilot *(Melilotus indica)*. As yet there is no explanation for the differences between representations and finds.

Flowers, called *sĩj-š₃* by the Egyptians (literally "garden scent"), were not only enjoyed in the gardens or used as floral decorations but fragrant blooms such as the lotus and the lily were also turned into perfumed ointments. Flowers, especially during the New Kingdom, were of considerable economic importance. The Papyrus Harris I, for example, refers to a large number of readymade bound bouquets, in Egyptian *rnpj*, in its list of offerings for the god Amun, as well as strings of blue flowers. Because as yet the Egyptian names of only a very few flowers have been identified, hardly any details about the trade in flowers have been found in the economic texts. A few flowers, which certainly had a special symbolic meaning, were mentioned in love songs, but most of them cannot yet, with certainty, be identified botanically.

[*See also* Lotus; *and* Papyrus.]

## BIBLIOGRAPHY

Dittmar, Johanna. *Blumen und Blumensträusse als Opfergabe im alten Ägypten.* Münchner Ägyptologische Studien Heft, 43. Munich and Berlin, 1986.

Germer, Renate. *Flora des pharaonischen Ägypten.* Deutsches Archäologisches Institut, Abteilung Kairo, 11. Mainz, 1985.

Germer, Renate. *Katalog der altägyptischen Pflanzenreste der Berliner Museen.* Ägyptologische Abhandlungen, 47. Wiesbaden, 1988.

Germer, Renate. *Die Pflanzenmaterialien aus dem Grab des Tutancha-mun.* Hildesheimer Ägyptologische Beiträge, 28. Hildesheim, 1989.

Germer, Renate. "Die Blütenhalskragen aus RT 54." Miscellanea Aegyptologica. Hamburg, 1989.

Hepper, Nigel F. *Pharaoh's Flowers.* London, 1990.

Keimer, Ludwig. *Die Gartenpflanzen im Alten Ägypten,* vol. 1, Hamburg and Berlin, 1924; vol. 2, edited by Renate Germer. Deutsches Archäologisches Institut, Abteilung Kairo, 13. Mainz, 1984.

Manniche, Lise. *An Ancient Egyptian Herbal.* London, 1989.

RENATE GERMER
Translated from German by Julia Harvey

## FOREIGN ADMINISTRATION.

*See* Administration, *article on* State Administration.

## FOREIGNERS.

Egypt has always had foreigners present owing to its location at the northeastern extremity of Africa, adjacent to Asia. Egypt acts as a land bridge to Asia and, in ancient times, was surrounded by the Libyans to the west and the Nubians to the south. Foreigners arrived or traveled through Egypt since before the unification, about 3050 BCE. The Egyptians saw themselves—along with the Nubians, Libyans, and Near Easterners—as one of the four peoples of the world.

The ancient Egyptians viewed Egypt as the dominant center of the world. All other countries and their gods were subservient to Egypt and its gods. "O King, you have enclosed every god within your arms, their lands and all their possessions." This Old Kingdom Pyramid Text (Spell 455) is a reflection of a country that fought its neighbors well before its own unification. Execration Texts (ritual curses) mentioned a number of foreigners and foreign lands. During the Middle Kingdom and the New Kingdom, the Egyptians also saw all foreigners as potentially defeated. Egypt, with its king, was the land of *maat,* containing the rightful order of the world, which countered the lands of Seth (foreign lands), with their disorder. New Kingdom Egypt occasionally had a more universal world view, as found in hymns to Amun-Re and the Aten. As well, earlier indications that foreigners were more than servants to the Egyptians were present, such as in the *Story of Sinuhe,* which described Near Eastern princes as "rulers of renown." An apparent dichotomy of attitude toward foreigners existed throughout dynastic times.

There is a difference between the way foreigners were portrayed as groups and as individuals. As a member of an ethnic group, the foreigner was portrayed as an enemy of *maat,* like an animal, with strange habits and appearance. As an individual, however, the foreigner had a name and could have acted like an Egyptian. Inscriptions addressed to an internal audience portrayed the superiority of Egypt and the king over the exterior world. When ad-dressed to an external audience, such as in the Amarna Letters or a Hittite peace treaty, the letters and treaties stressed the equality of the foreigners. Both were forms of propaganda but with different audiences and aims.

Throughout Egyptian history, foreigners occupied almost all social strata and occupations. From the Old Kingdom forward, many foreigners entered Egypt as prisoners of war. From the time of King Sneferu in the Old Kingdom, there were military expeditions to Nubia to take prisoners to work in Egypt. By the end of the Old Kingdom, slavery, the most extreme version of forced labor, was in operation. By the Middle Kingdom, foreigners represented the largest portion of slaves. Often acquired in military expeditions, prisoners were frequently given to Egyptians as property. The farmer Hekanakht, for example, gave Near Eastern slaves to his wife. Many foreign slaves, however, were destined for forced labor in temples and strongholds. Evidence that a foreign slave could be freed by an individual comes from administrative texts, such as one in which Sabastet, a royal barber, freed a slave that he had captured with his own hand in order for the slave to marry his blind niece. Slaves could also be freed by adoption by their owners, or by the edict of the king. During the New Kingdom, many foreigners were acquired as slaves from foreign slave markets as well as in foreign military expeditions, but foreigners also came to Egypt voluntarily for economic reasons.

Once established in Egypt, foreigners frequently attempted to assimilate Egyptian language and culture. Foreigners took Egyptian names for themselves or gave their children Egyptian names. As in this century, name changing was seen as a prerequisite for social climbing.

**Mercenaries, Soldiers, and Foreign Rulers.** No later than the sixth dynasty of the Old Kingdom, there was a substantial number of Nubians and Libyans in the Egyptian army, including the Irtjet and the Medjay people of Nubia, based on the report of Uni. During the Old Kingdom, there were also a number of foreign interpreters who were used during military and trade expeditions. From the eleventh dynasty of the First Intermediate Period (2134–2061 BCE), there is evidence of Nubian Tjanenu mercenaries at Gebelein. The Medjay mercenaries were very important during the eleventh and twelfth dynasties of the Middle Kingdom (2061–1786 BCE). The term "Medjay," from the thirteenth dynasty (1786–c.1665 BCE), was used to describe an internal police force. Ahmose (ruled c.1569–1545 BCE), first king of the eighteenth dynasty of the New Kingdom, used his Medjay troops against allies of the Hyksos at Nefrusy near Beni Hasan.

During the thirteenth dynasty (the Second Intermediate Period), two succeeding kings, Ammenemes VI and Hornedjheritef, were each called "the Asiatic" (which may or may not refer to their Near Eastern origins), and a later king of the same dynasty, apparently a Syrian mercenary who seized the throne, was named Khendjer, the "wild boar." The Hyksos ("rulers of foreign lands") were Near Easterners from the Levant who, after gradually settling and infiltrating the northeastern Delta, took over Avaris, Memphis, and the rest of northern Egypt for more than a century. In ruling, the Hyksos adopted the Egyptian style of government rather than imposing their own. At the end of the seventeenth dynasty, just before the reunification of Egypt by Ahmose, Kamose stated that he shared Egypt with a Near Eastern ruler on one side and a Nubian on the other.

After reunification (c.1569 BCE), the Egyptian army continued to absorb an increasing number of foreign mercenaries, including Nubians, Libyans, and Mediterranean "Sea Peoples" during the New Kingdom. A fragmentary papyrus from Amarna depicted what may have been Mycenaean mercenaries. After the beginning of the Third Intermediate Period (in 1081 BCE), with the decline of the twenty-first Egyptian dynasty, the kingship was occupied by a succession of Libyans and later Nubians. Sheshonq I, a descendant of an old clan of military colonists from Herakleopolis (called the "chiefs of Ma [Meshwesh]," though he was from Bubastis in the Delta) became commander-in-chief of the armies of Egypt. He was also an advisor and was related by marriage to Psusennes II of the twenty-first dynasty before he became the first king of the twenty-second dynasty. The first king of the twenty-fourth dynasty, Tefnakhte of Sais, was also from a clan of the "chiefs of the Ma." He called himself "great chief of the Libyans and prince of the west," and he united the four great chiefs of the Ma before ascending the throne, although he ruled over only part of the Delta. The Nubian leader Piya, of Napata, invaded Egypt during the Late period and gained control over all of Egypt, thus becoming the first sub-Saharan African to rule Egypt. He and his successors of the twenty-fifth dynasty attempted to repel the increasing power of the Assyrians.

With the Assyrian conquest of Egypt, an Egyptian prince named Psamtik, who had been brought to Assyria to be educated and returned to Egypt, rid Egypt of Assyrian rule with the help of Ionian and Carian mercenaries from Asia Minor. He became the first king of the twenty-sixth dynasty of the Saite period. During this time, Egypt was a mecca for Greek mercenaries who settled there. As well, a Jewish military colony was functioning in Elephantine during this period, and Syrian and Phoenician mercenaries were available to Egypt after being uprooted by Assyrian conquests. From graffiti at Abu Simbel, it is clear that Psamtik II's army included Greeks, Carians, and Phoenicians. When Cambyses conquered Egypt in 525 BCE, Egypt was absorbed into the Achaemenid Empire (the First Persian Occupation), and was later included in the Alexandrian Empire in 332 BCE. With the end of Macedonian rule, Egypt was under Ptolemaic control and later under Roman control. During the Ptolemaic dynasty, Egypt had become increasingly multilingual and multiethnic.

**Other Vocations of Foreigners.** Over the course of Egyptian history, foreigners have acted in almost all occupations. From farmers and laborers, to bureaucrats and priests, foreigners acculturated themselves to Egypt and its mores. Frequently, they discarded their foreign names and, presumably, their foreign attire as well, although some foreigners in the military kept some of their distinguishing attire and/or body adornment. The large number of prisoners captured by the Egyptians were put to work in the palaces, temples, and funerary complexes. Captured prisoners were also used as mercenaries.

Large numbers of foreign men and women were absorbed into Egypt's social structure. In the fifth dynasty of the Old Kingdom, a Nubian seal-bearer, Seneb, and a Nubian attendant, Meri, worked in a noble's estate. During the Middle Kingdom, men and women from Punt, in Africa, worked as servants in the king's palace in the Faiyum, while Near Easterners worked at Illahun and elsewhere. During the New Kingdom, in the eighteenth dynasty, Thutmose III decided that captured foreigners should weave fine linen and thick cloth, trap animals, and work in the fields belonging to the Temple of Amun. Nubians attached to the funerary temple of Thutmose IV at Qurna worked as cooks and bakers, while captured Syrians worked as wine makers. A letter of the nineteenth dynasty tells of the Syrian Naqady, who worked as a farmer in the temple of Thoth. Near Easterners also labored at construction sites or worked in granaries. Throughout Egyptian history, large numbers of bedouin crossed into the northeastern Delta and the Wadi Tumilat to pasture their animals. Such crossings were controlled by the Egyptians.

During the New Kingdom, more specialized occupations were filled by foreigners. Near Easterners worked as shipbuilders, ship captains, coppersmiths, and goldsmiths. Perunefer, a shipyard near Memphis, had many such immigrants among its labor force. The Saint Petersburg Papyrus 1116 lists two Near Eastern naval carpenters, Aarusu and Bania. Kefia, a goldsmith and portrait sculptor, had a tomb in the Theban necropolis (tomb 140). Near Easterners were also architects: Pasbaal became chief architect in the Temple of Amun during the reign of Thutmose III (r. 1504–1452 BCE) and Tutu, whose tomb was built at Akhetaten, was labeled "overseer of all the works of the king" and "overseer of all public works"—therefore, a chief architect, as well as a treasurer, to Akhenaten. Near Eastern scribes were common, especially with regard to the treasury. At Amarna, the need for trans-

FOREIGNERS. *Statues of two kneeling captives, sixth dynasty.* These limestone statues of foreigners were ritually executed, presumably to mark some event in the history of the pyramid complex of Pepy II at Saqqara. (The Metropolitan Museum of Art, Fletcher Fund, 1947 [47.2]; The Metropolitan Museum of Art, Louis V. Bell Fund, 1964 [64.260])

lation of texts from cuneiform to Hieratic created work for bilingual scribes.

With the advent of the Ramessid period (the nineteenth and twentieth dynasties), Near Easterners played an increasingly important role in Egyptian bureaucratic life; they were approximately half of the cup bearers to the king during this time. At the end of the nineteenth dynasty, a cup bearer named Bay was elevated to chancellor (a powerful position) through the possible cooperation of Queen Tausret. Foreign cup bearers were also involved in the palace conspiracy against Ramesses III during the twentieth dynasty. Foreigners or descendants of foreigners even reached the vizierate. Late in the reign of Amenhotpe III of the eighteenth dynasty, the Near Eastern nobleman Aperel became a vizier. Paser, a vizier to Sety I and Ramesses II, had a grandfather of Hurrian origin, while the vizier Neferronpet had a Near Eastern mother.

Sons of captured or dependent foreign princes were often brought to Egypt to be educated and indoctrinated in Egyptian culture. Part nursery, part fraternity, the *kap*

functioned to cement friendships between noble Egyptians and foreigners: first, Nubians during the Middle Kingdom and during the New Kingdom, Near Easterners. Some of those foreign boys would later have a career in Egypt in the army, palace, or administration. Others would be returned to their own lands to rule, while maintaining emotional and political ties to Egypt.

Other foreigners became priests, or acted as magicians or doctors. During the eighteenth dynasty, Sarbaina was a priest of Amun, as well as Baal and Astarte, in Perunefer near Memphis. Most of the foreign magicians were Nubians, including four Nubian magicians brought back from a military expedition by Horemheb, however, a Leiden papyrus mentions Palestinian magicians who spoke with serpents. The Ebers Medical Papyrus, dated to the eighteenth dynasty, noted a cure for an eye disease known through a resident of Byblos, presumably a doctor. A chief physician named Benanath, from the House of Life, is also known to be Near Eastern.

Foreign women became weavers, maids, dancers, and

singers. Some of these foreign women may have woven non-Egyptian designs for the kings. Nubian and Libyan dancers, and Nubian and Near Eastern singers have been identified on reliefs from Thebes and Tell el-Amarna. Diplomatic marriages between foreign princesses and Egyptian kings were prevalent during the New Kingdom, but also occurred during the Old and Middle Kingdoms.

**Tourists, Traders, and Tributaries.** While there have always been foreign visitors to the Nile Valley, the evidence for them became common during the Late period when foreign graffiti were made. By Greco-Roman times, foreign graffiti covered many monuments, such as the Colossi of Memnon, and are even found inside Theban royal tombs. The Great Pyramid, before being stripped of its casing stones, contained foreign graffiti that dated to earlier than the Greco-Roman period. Greek and Roman historians also gave evidence for foreign visitors in their written accounts.

The earliest pictorial evidence for foreign trade came from the Old Kingdom Abu Sir temple reliefs of Sahure that depict foreign families, perhaps from Byblos, greeting the king from a ship. During the Middle Kingdom, Near Eastern merchants were at Tell ed-Dab'a and other Delta sites, as is known from the archaeological record. A Middle Kingdom tomb scene showing the foreign chieftain Abishai and a group of Near Easterners bearing eye paint, may represent trade, while the New Kingdom Theban tomb of Kenamun (tomb 162) depicts freight ships with Near Easterners disembarking with produce.

The New Kingdom Amarna Letters, as well as tomb and temple scenes and texts from this period present a complex of interactions that included gift-giving, trade, and tribute. The Amarna Letters reveal an international etiquette where obligation and self interest combined to form a web of relationships in which trade or tribute obligations could also include gift-giving or bribery. A number of important scenes and texts from the tombs at western Thebes portray foreigners presenting valuable items, such as vases, ivory, and metals to the king and/or his officials. Scholars are unsure whether those scenes represented trade or tribute, gift-giving or bribery. The ancient Egyptians appear to have portrayed foreigners—encompassing Nubians, Minoans, and eastern Mediterraneans, including chiefs of Mitanni, the Hittites, Lebanon, Kadesh, and Tunip—bringing "tribute" before the king or his officials, but the scenes probably represent mostly trade or gift-giving, only a few scenes actually depict obligatory deliveries. The temple walls, however, contain a number of examples of foreigners bringing tribute, especially after conquest, in which giving tribute appears to be the true act. Egyptian self-interest determined what transactions were portrayed and how they were depicted. More than one economic transaction could be portrayed at one time and the economic transactions portrayed could be more complex than what is traditionally called trade or tribute.

During the Late period, following the influx of Greek mercenaries brought in by Psamtik to defeat the Assyrians, the Greeks established trading colonies, such as Naucratis, in the Delta. An earlier trading colony at the Canopic mouth of the Nile was abandoned due to Egyptian intolerance of foreigners.

Throughout their history, the ancient Egyptians maintained an ambivalent, although primarily negative, attitude toward foreigners. The presumption that foreigners were inherently inferior and fit only to serve Egypt, and the generally negative description of foreigners, contrasts with the fact that many foreigners were able to rise to high levels in Egyptian society and government. While the Egyptians appeared to dislike foreigners as groups, they were apparently willing to enjoy or at least tolerate foreigners as individuals.

## BIBLIOGRAPHY

Barns, J.W.B. *Egyptians and Greeks.* Papyrologica Bruxellensia, 14. Brussels, 1978. Reprint of an Inaugural Lecture delivered at Oxford in 1966.

Bresciani, Edda. "Foreigners." In *The Egyptians*, edited by Sergio Donadoni, pp. 221–253. Chicago and London, 1997. The best general overview of foreigners in Egypt. Originally published as *L'Uomo egiziano*, 1990, translated into English by Robert Bianchi.

Davies, Norman de G., and R. O. Faulkner. "A Syrian Trading Venture to Egypt." *The Journal of Egyptian Archaeology* 33 (1947), 40–46.

Davies, W. Vivian, and Louise Schofield, eds. *Egypt, the Aegean and the Levant: Interconnections in the Second Millennium BC.* London, 1995. Presents new information with excellent biographies.

Fischer, Henry George. "The Nubian Mercenaries of Gebelein during the First Intermediate Period." *Kush* 9 (1961), 44–80.

Haring, Ben J. J. "Libyans in the Theban region, 20th dynasty." In *Sesto Congresso Internazionale di Egittologia. Atti,* 2, pp. 159–165. Turin, 1993.

Johnson, Janet H., ed. *Life in a Multi-Cultural Society: Egypt from Cambyses to Constantine and Beyond.* Studies in Ancient Oriental Civilization, 51. Chicago, 1995. Informative articles on Egyptian relations with foreigners living in Egypt.

Liverani, Mario. *Prestige and Interest: International Relations in the Near East ca. 1600–1100 B.C.* History of the Ancient Near East/Studies, 1. Padua, 1990. Discusses the complexities of trade and tribute, and the difference between documents intended for an internal or external audience.

Loprieno, Antonio. "Slaves." In *The Egyptians*, edited by Sergio Donadoni, pp. 185–219. Chicago and London, 1997.

Loprieno, Antonio. *Topos und Mimesis. Zum Ausländer in der ägyptischen Litteratur.* Ägyptologische Abhandlungen, 48. Wiesbaden, 1988. Discusses dual Egyptian attitude toward foreigners, as groups and individuals.

Manniche, Lise. *Music and Musicians in Ancient Egypt.* London, 1991. Discusses the evidence for foreign musicians in Egypt during the New Kingdom.

Redford, Donald. *Egypt, Canaan, and Israel in Ancient Times.* Princeton, 1992. Impressively detailed account of the relations between Egypt and Western Asia for three thousand years.

Robins, Gay. *Women in Ancient Egypt.* Cambridge, 1993. Discusses diplomatic marriages in the New Kingdom.

Ward, William A. "Foreigners Living in the Village." In *Pharaoh's Workers: The Villagers of Deir el Medina*, edited by Leonard H. Lesko, pp. 61–85. Ithaca and London, 1994. Discusses the difficulty of determining foreigners by their names; extensive notes with excellent bibliography.

ANDREW GORDON

**FOREIGN INCURSIONS.** Egypt suffered intrusions from abroad many times during its long history, from the Hyksos, the Sea Peoples, and the Libyans, Nubians, Assyrians, Persians, Greeks, and Romans. Most of these times of trouble occurred in the second half of the pharaonic period, from the seventeenth century BCE onward. Although Egypt's sea and desert frontiers gave it a degree of isolation that was sufficient to deter the small and unorganized neighbors it had during the Old and Middle Kingdoms, they did not provide enough defense to keep out the migrations of the Late Bronze Age, or the imperial armies that attacked from the Near East during the first millennium BCE. The effects of these incursions were minor in some cases, profound in others.

Before discussing their impact, we must consider the limitations of the contexts in which foreigners appear in the official Egyptian record—which is what tends to survive because it was created to last. During the formative stages of Egyptian iconography, rules for expressing the country's relationship with foreign lands were established. These centered on the pharaoh and were underpinned by a single concept: his responsibility for maintaining *maat*, or cosmic order. At the heart of this was the protection of Egypt, and it is significant in this context that Seth, god of confusion and opponent of the king in his aspect as Horus, was closely associated with foreign lands. The potential enemies of the king were divided into four groups: Near Easterners, Nubians, Libyans, and Egyptians. The inclusion of the last may seem surprising, but they too were a potential source of disorder.

The earliest and most characteristic expression of this idea is the smiting motif, in which the king raises a mace or other weapon to strike an enemy figure or figures whom he grasps by the hair. A crudely depicted prototype occurs in the predynastic painted tomb at Hierakonpolis, but the first canonical example is found on the Narmer Palette, on which the king is also shown as larger than his opponent. In early examples such as these, or on an ivory label from the tomb of the first dynasty king Den at Abydos, the act takes place in isolation. In its standard later form on temple walls, it is enacted in the presence of a deity, and may be regarded as symbolizing the sacrifice of prisoners as an act of thanksgiving on return from a successful campaign. The central position of this motif in Egyptian thought can be gauged by its continuation on pylons well into Roman times, as at Esna.

In New Kingdom and later examples, such as on the pylon of Ramesses III's mortuary temple at Medinet Habu, a "geographical list" often appears beneath the feet of the king and god. This takes the form of a series of registers in which busts of human figures with their arms bound behind them emerge from ovals with projecting buttresses. These ovals represent aerial views of fortified settlements. Inside each, the name of the place depicted is inscribed in hieroglyphs, and the figure on top is given skin coloring, hair and beard style, and costume appropriate to the locality in question. These lists are a continuation of a tradition represented by the Execration Texts of the Old to Middle Kingdoms: small plaques or model figures inscribed with a place name, then broken, burnt, and buried. The process of sympathetic magic was thought to deprive the place so treated of the ability to harm the king, and thus it protected Egypt. The temple wall lists achieve the same effect by binding the enemy figures and by placing them "beneath the king's feet," a phrase repeatedly encountered in royal texts. The same principle is exemplified by what may be the three-dimensional prototype of the geographical list—the placing of statues of captives with their arms tied behind their backs in Old Kingdom mortuary temples—or by the painting of a palace floor at Amarna with bound Near Easterners and Nubians for the king to walk on as he went about his daily business.

While these scenes and lists may sometimes form part of a particular campaign narrative, as in Sety I's decoration of the north wall of the hypostyle hall at Karnak, their purpose was not primarily historical. Their function, rather, was to show that a particular king was effectively protecting Egypt. The location of these scenes in temples shows that the intended audience was partly divine, while the frequent placing of them on pylons or exterior wall surfaces shows that they were intended to impress the people as well. Their nonhistorical nature is well illustrated by a further variant: a statue of Amenhotpe III from his mortuary temple on the west bank at Luxor has a miniature geographical list of Aegean toponyms carved on the base or podium on which the king's feet rest. Egypt certainly never exercised any suzerainty over the very distant places named, and relations at the time the statue was carved seem to have been good; it simply served to ensure that any hostile potential was nullified.

Where an actual historical event is depicted or described, Egypt is always represented as comprehensively victorious, even when the actual outcome was indecisive or a defeat. Ramesses II's transformation of his narrow escape at Qadesh into the triumphal celebration of victory encountered on the walls of the Ramesseum, or his temples of Abydos and Abu Simbel, is a case in point. Military failure was only recorded in quite extraordinary circumstances. Thus, Tutankhamun described obliquely the lack of success achieved by Akhenaten's armies in order to exemplify divine displeasure at events in Egypt itself. There is no place in Egypt's formal presentation of its foreign relations for any account that is not tendentious. Only rarely do other categories of text allow a different perspective and one closer to the diplomatic realities of foreign relations. The best example is the archive of clay tablets inscribed in cuneiform known as the Amarna Letters, which include personal correspondence between the rulers of the major kingdoms of the Near East in the fourteenth century BCE.

The second most common context in which foreigners are depicted is the "tribute scene." This is a New Kingdom motif, perhaps inspired by the greater intensity of contact with foreign lands which characterized the period. Rows of figures, usually Near Easterners or Nubians but occasionally Libyans or people from the Aegean, are shown bringing gifts of precious metal vessels, captives, cattle, or rarer animals such as giraffes, bears, or elephants, to the pharaoh or a high official acting on his behalf. Allowing for a concentration on the exotic at the expense of the mundane, such scenes provide some idea of imports into Egypt; but the scene type was devised in order to demonstrate the prestige of the king, and there is no corresponding context in which exports could be depicted. Foreigners are occasionally shown coming to Egypt for trading purposes, from the boatload of Syrians in Sahure's mortuary temple to the individual merchant setting out his stall at Thebes in the tomb of Nebamun; and it is here that we come closest to reality, which is that foreigners moved to and from Egypt with comparative ease.

The idea of a prehistoric invasion by a "dynastic race" is now discounted, as are the studies in physical anthropology that formed part of the basis for the theory. The Mesopotamian cultural elements discernible in Egypt in the late fourth millennium BCE are regarded by most as having been transmitted through trading contacts. There may well have been significant stimulus and an acceleration of development within Egypt, but there is no reason to assume that the influence came about through invasion. The first serious foreign incursions are probably to be dated to the First Intermediate Period. Firm historical evidence is lacking for the events, let alone the consequences, but the didactic and philosophical composition, the *Instructions for Merikare*, clearly refers to Near Easterners in the Nile Delta, as does the propagandist *Prophecy of Neferti*. The early Middle Kingdom rulers took the danger of renewed encroachments seriously enough to fortify the eastern Delta. It was the Middle Kingdom, too, that established the "Asiatics [Near Easterners] in Egypt" motif—the breaching of the integrity of the frontiers—as one of the standard metaphors of disorder, a sign of the world-turned-upside-down and a portent of divine anger. "Foreigners have become people (i.e., Egyptians) everywhere," laments Ipuwer. Here foreign incursions are

turned to literary advantage, but this seems to be a phenomenon peculiar to the Middle Kingdom, although in later periods such events could figure in apocalyptic literature.

In the official record, then, there is no place for reference to invasions except to describe how they were defeated, just as there is no place for mention of another recurrent disaster, famine, except to explain how it was overcome. Other sources are essential if any balanced interpretation is to be obtained. It is therefore instructive to consider two cases where accounts of incursions have come down to us from ostensibly nonofficial sources, and to compare them with other evidence, including that of archaeology. These are the Hyksos and the Persians, just over a thousand years apart. In both cases, the intruders were from societies at least as advanced materially as Egypt, but their aims differed. The Hyksos were expanding a kingdom based in the Palestine region southward into Egypt, to which they transferred their center of power. The Persians sought to add Egypt to the large number of provinces they controlled through local governors, while themselves remaining in Persia.

In the second millennium BCE, a group from the Levant—known to us as the Hyksos—seized power in the north of Egypt, built a capital at Avaris in the eastern Delta, and were recognized as overlords by kings in Upper Egypt and probably also by the kings of Kush. Their dominion lasted for perhaps a century before they were expelled by the resurgent Theban kings. The Hyksos are best known from Manetho's account as preserved by Josephus. This was written in Greek, but by an Egyptian priest of the third century BCE who had access to temple archives as well as to folk memories. It presents the Hyksos as barbarian "Asiatics," hostile to Egyptian religion, who seized Egypt through invasion and made it pay tribute. This is the tail end of a tradition that goes back to contemporary opponents of the Hyksos and is best exemplified in the stelae of Kamose. In those texts, the Hyksos king Apophis is characterized as a foreigner, an "Asiatic," and one who conspires with another foreigner, the Nubian king of Kush. He is accused of falsely arrogating royal titles to himself and denying them to a legitimate ruler such as Kamose. The Theban tradition of hostility was continued by Hatshepsut and was undoubtedly responsible for the exclusion of the Hyksos kings from all the king lists, except for the Turin Canon and that of Manetho himself. The history of these foreign kings was thus written by their victorious Egyptian opponents.

In the absence of any pro-Hyksos tradition, modification of this view of these Near Eastern rulers has had to come from archaeology, and mainly from the excavations at Tell ed-Dab'a, the site that is beyond reasonable doubt Avaris, the Hyksos capital. These have shown that, despite their occasional attempts to present themselves through hieroglyphic inscriptions as legitimate pharaohs, the material culture of the Hyksos was very much that of the Middle Bronze II period in the eastern Mediterranean. The town layout, the religious buildings, the tombs and burial practices (including horse interments and sacrificial servant burials) all remained steadfastly un-Egyptian. Coming from a sophisticated urban background, they were certainly not barbarians, but their maintenance of their own cultural traditions must have helped Kamose to demonize them as outsiders. Although scholars today incline to the view that they seized power by gradual infiltration of the eastern Delta in the late Middle Kingdom rather than by invasion, it remains possible that an invasion was the final stage in a drawn-out process which took advantage of internal divisions in Egypt. As far as their attitude to Egyptian religion is concerned, there is little evidence that they built or supported Egyptian-style temples, but neither is there good evidence for any destruction of existing structures. They chose for their capital a site sacred to the Egyptian god Seth, whom they equated with their own deity Baal. Unless this had been accompanied by veneration for other gods, however, the association of Seth with foreigners would merely have strengthened the hostile characterization of them.

The Hyksos left no written justification of themselves, and nowhere in the ancient textual record is there anything to suggest that their rule had any positive consequences. Yet they are today credited with the introduction to Egypt of the horse and chariot, and of a stronger bow and other improvements in weaponry. The superior military technology that enabled them to impose themselves on the Delta became the means of their expulsion and had a galvanizing effect, creating a desire to prevent a repetition of the humiliation and leading to the Egyptian empire of the New Kingdom. This allowed Kamose to foster a renewed sense of Egyptian identity, from which the memory of the Hyksos could only suffer. The transformation of Egyptian society included the creation of a standing army and a new military elite, but it also entailed a much greater awareness of the outside world and a more cosmopolitan culture in Egypt. It is likely that some of the cults of Near Eastern deities worshiped by Egyptians in the New Kingdom came with the Hyksos, and it is possible that the greater variety of musical instruments found in the New Kingdom should be attributed to them rather than to Egyptian soldiers returning from campaign. In both cases, however, exposure to new possibilities led to internal change. Sadly, cultural innovations were never the subject of the kinds of Egyptian texts that have come down to us.

The case of the Persians is rather different. They were the third of three great imperial powers that tried to seize control of Egypt in the mid-first millennium BCE. The Assyrians in the seventh century had marched as far south as Thebes and carried off great quantities of booty. They installed garrisons but were unable to maintain any sort of control for more than twenty years. The Babylonians at the very end of the seventh century and in the early part of the sixth were kept out on the very frontier on at least two occasions. The Persians, in contrast, conquered Egypt in 525 BCE and succeeded in keeping it as a province of their empire for nearly 125 years. The most detailed source for this invasion and its consequences, and also the purveyor of a hostile tradition, is an outsider. The Greek historian Herodotus wrote, after a visit to Egypt in the mid-fifth century BCE, some seventy-five years after the conquest and while the Persians were still in control of Egypt—fairly close in time to the events that form the subject of his narrative. He focuses particularly on the figure of the king who ordered the invasion, Cambyses, whom he presents as attacking Egyptian religious practices and institutions, but also as mad and in his derangement murdering the sacred Apis bull. He also describes the Persian's savage treatment of the body of the Egyptian pharaoh Amasis, who died six months before the invasion, on a visit to the royal necropolis at Sais. Herodotus cannot be said to be an impartial witness. He was a Greek at a time when Greek cities were in alliance with Egyptian princes against Persia. He claims to have derived much of his information from Egyptians, and especially from priests who might be expected to foster a tradition hostile to the memory of a foreign ruler who had not respected them as they felt they deserved. As a result, although he is not wholly anti-Persian—his treatment of the next ruler, Darius I, is much more sympathetic—it is currently fashionable to explain away his testimony or to minimize its value.

By an accident of survival, it is possible to compare Herodotus's account of the invasion with an Egyptian source who was actually an eyewitness and who preserves a more favorable view of Cambyses. Udjahorresne was a native of Sais, the capital at the time of the conquest, and dedicated in one of its temples a naophorous statue of himself inscribed with a long autobiographical text. It emerges from this that he had been commander of the navy under the last kings of the twenty-sixth dynasty. He must thus have had an important role in the unsuccessful defense of the country, but he says nothing of that. Instead, he begins with a discreet reference to the "great turmoil" that occurred when the great ruler of foreign lands, Cambyses, came to Egypt. Udjahorresne succeeded in getting the new king's ear and in becoming a cultural adviser to him. In that capacity, he legitimized Cambyses in Egyptian eyes by creating a proper royal titulary for him in the Egyptian format. He describes how he persuaded the king to clear the temple at Sais of squatters who were defiling it, to purify it, and to come himself to the venerable city to do obeisance to its goddess, Neith. Udjahorresne's principal motive in commemorating himself was to stress what he had done for his city and its deity, not to provide a full account of his life nor an assessment of Cambyses. It was nonetheless in his interest to make Cambyses appear to advantage and to distance him from any destruction that may have accompanied the invasion. In describing Cambyses' visit to Sais, there is no reason for him to mention the destruction of Amasis' corpse, but that does not make Herodotus' version of the visit false. Indeed, a posthumous attack on the memory of Amasis is apparent from a number of defaced statues and inscriptions with his name hacked out.

In the wider context, it is clear that Egypt was quite adversely affected, even impoverished, by the Persian invasion. The occupation of the temple at Sais, presumably by Cambyses' soldiers, is likely to have been duplicated in other towns that did not have such a powerful protector as Udjahorresne and that could not reclaim their shrines so easily. The evidence of destruction and burning at a number of temples cannot be dismissed as fortuitous. With the curious exception of the Kharga Oasis, evidence for temple-building in Egypt under the Persians is conspicuously lacking. Temple taxes seem to have been increased. Offices such as the God's Wife of Amun and perhaps the high priest of Amun were allowed to fall into abeyance at Thebes, where the sequence of decorated private tombs for high officials came to an end. Commemoration of the Apis bull burials in the Serapeum ceased after the thirty-fourth year of the reign of Darius I. Above all, little of the typically Egyptian votive and funerary equipment—statues, stelae, and sarcophagi—can be assigned to the Persian period after the very early years. This is best explained by extreme impoverishment and cultural disruption. It was certainly not, as has sometimes been argued, a period of dynamic innovation in Egyptian workshops, and the deportation of craftsmen to Persia may have played a part in this. Instead, Egyptian culture turned in on itself, emphasizing through the increasingly popular votive offering of mummified sacred animals aspects of its tradition that set it apart from its overlords and the outside world in general. There is little sign of Egyptian artisans being influenced by the art of their new rulers, although some stelae show the development of an interesting hybrid idiom. Items of clothing and a gesture of grasping one wrist with the other hand have both been called "Persian," but both seem to have developed within Egypt and without reference to foreign models. The canal stelae of Darius I and the headless statue of him found at Susa, however, show clear signs of his adoption of distinctly Egyptian elements, such as the unification motif and the geographical list, which would be consistent with

a desire to legitimize himself to his Egyptian subjects. Later kings did not follow his example, and rebellion broke out with increasing frequency. It was probably this that breathed new life into the production in Egypt of texts prophesying the end of foreign rule, or otherwise hostile to it.

The incursions of the Hyksos and the Persians were certainly the most significant in their effects on Egypt before the arrival of Alexander. The invasions of the Sea Peoples and Libyans were of a rather different order, although after the Egyptian military successes of the eighteenth and nineteenth dynasties they must have come as a great shock. The Ramessid kings were confronted by large numbers of people of uncertain background—certainly more "barbarian" than the Hyksos—seeking to force their way into the lush pastures of the Nile Delta, as Near Easterners had long been accustomed to do. None of these groups had any very strong tradition of high culture that might have been influential. The captives taken in the battles under Merenptah and Ramesses III brought an immediate benefit to Egypt in additional manpower for the army, new weapons, and new methods of fighting. The Sherden warriors would seem to have proved a particularly valuable addition to the already remarkably mixed army. The Egyptian strategy was to absorb the most useful while repelling the masses.

From the end of the New Kingdom, some Libyans became rulers of Egypt from within; but, unlike the Hyksos before them, they slowly became acculturated and were never expelled. In that sense, they were the most successful of the infiltrators. They gradually became part of the ethnic fabric of Egyptian society, adapting themselves to its artistic and architectural traditions, while retaining distinctive elements of their own political and social structures for many centuries.

Both the Hyksos conquest and that of the Libyans reversed the traditional relationship of earlier times in which the Egyptians had dominated their smaller and less well-organized neighbors. The same is true of the Nubians or Kushites, who, alone of all the invaders, came regarding and presenting themselves as legitimate heirs to the great pharaohs of the past. In the second half of the eighth century BCE they successfully established a hegemony over Egypt, especially Upper Egypt, which lasted for about seventy years and was recognized by Manetho as his twenty-fifth dynasty. Their own society was transformed by the experience. Within a generation, Egyptian-style pyramids were introduced as superstructures for the tombs of the Nubian kings in their homeland and Egyptian burial practices including mummification and *ushabti*s were adopted, as was the hieroglyphic script. The result, after their expulsion from Egypt, was the new Meroitic civilization in the south of Nubia. Their impact on

Egypt was less than is sometimes suggested and was essentially transient. They continued the archaizing tendencies already in vogue, stimulated a revival in temple construction in the south of Egypt and in Nubia, and, most distinctively, developed a new royal iconography. They made no attempt to end the political fragmentation within Egypt, and it was left to the twenty-sixth dynasty to revitalize the country in that respect.

Each of these foreign incursions will have contributed new blood and fresh ideas to ancient Egyptian society, although these may be difficult to recognize except where they influenced religious culture. Dramatic as such episodes are, it is important to remember that Egyptian society was affected just as much by nonhostile infiltration, such as that of the Greek traders and mercenaries from the seventh century BCE onward. It is also true that the daily movements of merchants and envoys ensured continuous contact with the outside world, and that there were always "foreigners" in ancient Egypt, in various stages of acculturation. Countless lives, into which we gain only the occasional glimpse, testify to the possibility of rising from humble origins to a position of authority without suffering prejudice on the grounds of being foreign.

[*See also* Achaemenids; Foreigners; Hyksos; Libya; Mesopotamia; Nubia; Persia; Sea People; Syria-Palestine; Second Intermediate Period; Third Intermediate Period; *and the composite article* Late Period.]

### BIBLIOGRAPHY

Adams, William Y. *Nubia: Corridor to Africa.* London, 1977.
Bietak, M. *Avaris, the Capital of the Hyksos: Recent Excavations at Tell ed-Dab'a.* London, 1996.
Boardman, J. *The Greeks Overseas.* Rev. ed. London, 1980.
Bresciani, Edda. "The Persian Occupation of Egypt." In *Cambridge History of Iran*, vol. 2, pp. 502–528. London, 1986.
Davies, W. Vivian, and Louise Schofield. *Egypt, the Aeagean and the Levant.* London, 1995.
Hornung, E. *Idea into Image.* New York, 1992.
Kuhrt, A., and H. Sancisi-Weerdenburg. *Achaemenid History Workshop.* 1987–1994.
Lloyd, Alan B. "The Inscription of Udjahorresnet, a Collaborator's Testament." *Journal of Egyptian Archaeology* 68 (1982), 166–180.
Mark, Samuel. *From Egypt to Mesopotamia: A Study of Predynastic Trade Routes.* Austin, 1997.
Moran, William L. *The Amarna Letters.* Baltimore and London, 1992.
Oren, Eliezer D., ed. *The Hyksos: New Historical and Archaeological Perspectives.* Philadelphia, 1997.
Redford, Donald B. *Egypt, Canaan, and Israel in Ancient Times.* Princeton, 1992.
Russmann, Edna R. *The Representation of the King in the XXVth Dynasty.* Brussels and Brooklyn, 1974.
Sandars, N. K. *The Sea Peoples: Warriors of the Ancient Mediterranean.* Rev. ed. London, 1985.
Waddell, W. G. *Manetho.* London, 1940.

ANTHONY LEAHY

**FORTS AND GARRISONS.** Written references to forts and garrisons appear in texts dating to all periods of literate ancient Egypt. They derive from a variety of sources, including literary texts, tomb biographies, monumental inscriptions, letters, onomastica, graffiti, and Greco-Roman histories. Throughout these texts appear an extensive vocabulary for a variety of fortified buildings and troops for guard duty, forts and garrisons. Images of forts also appear in most periods. Hieroglyphs may be viewed not just as the written Egyptian language, but also as pictorial representations of various kinds of fortifications, especially in the fine style of monumental inscriptions. Often they can be recognized in the schematic plan of excavated examples. Forts also appear in the decorative program of temple and tomb scenes. Caution is necessary in interpreting the historical value of these images. Sometimes, particularly when they are accompanied by specific written texts, they may be considered as historical facts. More frequently, however, they have a symbolic value to be read more as a hieroglyph representing a nonspecific fort of the region. But whether they are fact or symbol, all representations can be used in explaining architectural details and elements of fortress use and siege warfare. Moreover, clear distinctions cannot always be made between forts, towns, and temples, whether because of shared architectural elements or identical construction techniques. This is epitomized in the royal funerary temple of Ramesses III at Medinet Habu, which takes the form of a fortress. The distinction is even more difficult between forts and towns. Forts may contain towns, and towns may be fortified. Although there are exceptions, here fortifications found on a border region are considered fortresses, including examples from the Nile Valley during an Intermediate Period and an Egyptian presence in non-Egyptian territory.

**Predynastic, Early Dynastic, and Old Kingdom.** The late Predynastic and Early Dynastic evidence for forts derives from a variety of sources. Hieroglyphs such as *ḥwt*, *inb*, and *'ḥ* occur on seals, seal impressions, dockets, and labels. Models of circular towers with a ladder date to the first dynasty. Fortification imagery also appears on slate palettes, especially the Libyan (City) and the Narmer Palettes. These depict four-sided enclosures with bastions on the exterior. On the Narmer Palette a bull, symbolic of the king, is shown knocking small elements of the wall (probably bricks) to the ground in conquest.

Actual remains of forts in this period are rare. Only at Elephantine are there fragmentary architectural remains of three phases of an Archaic fortress, including short lengths of mud brick walls with curved bastions and square corner towers and a gate. Actual remains that resemble great defensive structures are the funerary enclosures at Abydos and Hierakonpolis. Other examples are the town wall at Hierakonpolis and the niched building within, possibly a palace or temple. These massive mud brick niched walls with enclosed gates (resembling the *ḥwt* hieroglyph) may be based on contemporary fortifications. The site of En Besor in southern Palestine may have been an Egyptian royal supply station, possibly with a military character, for provisioning passing caravans in the Early Dynastic period. Placed beside a perennial spring, it was a large brick structure with Egyptian pottery and sealings that reflect Egyptian administrative practices. Interpretation of this material in conjunction with contemporary Egyptian texts remains a debated issue, as to whether it was used for trading or military expeditions.

These representations continue in the Old Kingdom. Now, however, pictorial representations and written documents increase in complexity and detail. There are scenes of non-Egyptian forts under siege by Egyptians from the tombs of Khaemhasct at Saqqara of the fifth dynasty and of Inti at Deshasheh of the sixth dynasty. It has been suggested that such defensive technology would have been generally known throughout the ancient world, thus generally uniform and probably used by the Egyptians themselves. In texts, strongholds are mentioned in place names such as the "Fortress of the Bitter Lakes," implying the eastern Delta was fortified, controlling access to Egypt. Administrative titles appear, such as "Overseer of Desert Keeps and Royal Fortresses" and "Overseer of the Army and Overseer of the Way(s) of Horus," the name of the road through the northern Sinai to Palestine.

The only extant Old Kingdom fort is situated in the Western Desert at Ayin Asil, Dakhleh Oasis. Preliminary reports show that Phase I was a mud brick enclosure (170 meters squared) with massive walls and evidence of a circular bastion at the southwest corner (and presumably the other corners), as well as semicircular bastions along the wall faces. The northeast and northwest corners also have external features. The entrance is centered on the north wall, with piers flanking and projecting from it. Internal structures on the same orientation exist. Phase II (sixth dynasty) shows a "domestication" of the fort, and Phase III the filling and leveling for a large urban complex.

**First Intermediate Period and Middle Kingdom.** A wealth of textual and archaeological material remains from the First Intermediate Period and Middle Kingdom. References to forts are found in *Merikare, Neferty, The Shipwrecked Sailor,* and the *Story of Sinuhe.* The First Intermediate Period tomb biographies of Ankhtyfy at Moʻalla and King Wahankh Antef II at Thebes mention the capture of fortifications in the Nile Valley. Pictorial representations from Thebes show forts with crenellated walls and those from Beni Hasan with turreted walls, buttresses (berm?), and gates. But it is the archaeological material that gives a more accurate sense of the Egyptian use of fortresses in this period.

An entire system of fortresses was developed at the southern frontier by the early Middle Kingdom pharaohs. In the earliest phase, dating to Nebhepetre Montuhotep I, and Amenemhet I, a fortress type occurs that may have had prototypes in the First Intermediate Period's fortified townsites of Egypt proper, possibly like those to which reference is made by Ankhtyfy and Wahankh Antef II. This is exemplified by the earliest fortifications at Aniba, Ikkur, and Kubban. A variation may be found built in dry stone at Wadi el-Hudi, where the earliest graffiti date to this period. Shortly after this, in the reign of Senwosret I, a second series of fortresses was built at these sites and the fort at Buhen was built. These fortifications, each with its own history and development, were characterized by massive rectangular mud brick walls with external rectangular towers along the sides and at the corners. Buttresses abutted the exterior face of the wall and probably supported wooden battlements. These forts were built along the Nile with one wall running parallel to the river and at least one gate giving access to quays; on the remaining three sides, the walls overlooked a ditch. Buhen (about 150 meters squared), the most complex of these forts, had a mud brick-lined ditch with a counterscarp and glacis on the opposite side. A secondary defense was built between the great fortress walls and the ditch: a parapet built on the berm with semicircular bastions and tripartite loopholes pointing downward into the ditch. In the walls of the bastions, a second row of loopholes allowed the archers to shoot straight ahead or upward. The main gate spanned the ditch; it had double doors and a wooden bridge which could be withdrawn on rollers.

The third phase of the southern forts dates to the reign of Senwosret III and comprises the annexation of the entire Second Cataract region. The fortresses include Askut, Shalfak, Uronarti Semna, Kumma, and Semna South. They were characterized by an irregular outline that followed the dictates of the terrain (rectangular when flat). The walls were formed of mud brick with wooden beams to aid in stability and halfa grass matting laid at intervals to ensure drying of the mud brick. Mostly situated on rocky prominences, towers were replaced by spur walls that project at irregular intervals or follow the line of a ridge. The elaborate ditch of the previous type was unnecessary. Access to water was ensured by the presence of a stairway to the Nile, built into the rock and frequently covered. The fortress at Mirgissa at the north end of the Second Cataract region, though dating to this period of construction, not only divides the two architectural types into two regions but also contains elements of both styles. It was also the administrative center of the Nubian forts. The fortresses at Faras and Serra East may be contemporary with the Second Cataract forts, but they retain the basic design of the "plains type" of the northern Lower Nubian region. The interiors were generally orthogonally planned with regular streets, one running along the interior of the walls (the Roman *pomerium*) and others dividing the area within into identifiable units such as administrative offices, barracks and houses, storerooms, production areas, granaries and bakeries, and even an armory and garden at Mirgissa. In addition to these fortresses, a watchtower exists at Wadi el-Hudi, and a series of graffiti written by surveillance patrols were documented from the area around Buhen. Also of note are the long, heavy walls built at the First Cataract and at the Semna Cataract, the northern and southern limits of the entire Egyptian fortress system in Nubia.

The purposes of these Nubian forts were varied. They clearly had a very strong defensive nature. They were a protection for the southern trade routes and sites for local trade, with formal trading at Mirgissa and more general trading at Semna South before entering Egyptian territory. Surveillance of the local population—probably from posts like those around Buhen—was reported in documents such as the *Semna Despatches* from Thebes and possibly the fragments of papyri from Buhen and Mirgissa. Another function of the fortresses was the exploitation of natural resources; personnel mined and refined copper, amethyst, and possibly gold and transported them to the royal treasuries in Egypt proper.

The Ramesseum Papyrus includes a list of Nubian fortresses and then Egyptian towns, thereby implicitly placing the fortresses mentioned on par (perhaps administratively) with Egyptian urban centers. Although neither Wadi el-Hudi nor the watchtowers are included, most of the names can be associated with archaeological sites.

The northern border is less well documented. The "Walls of the Prince" have been variously interpreted as either a fortress by this name; or a series of fortresses along the northeast border of the Delta (the most commonly held interpretation); or a canal with dikes on one or both sides. Archaeological evidence for fortresses on this border is yet to be found. As for an Egyptian presence in Syria-Palestine during the Middle Kingdom, scholarly perspectives vary widely. Although not a frontier in the sense of the Second Cataract region, Syria-Palestine would have had similar trade and diplomatic interests for the Egyptians. Small forts, such as the one at Tel Mevorakh on the main coastal road, may be related to these interests.

**Second Intermediate Period and New Kingdom.** This period is the richest in textual and pictorial references to fortresses and garrisons. Pictorial representations occur as part of decorative programs in temples (e.g., the Hypostyle Hall at Karnak), especially on the exterior of the enclosure walls of royal funerary temples (e.g., the Ramesseum and Medinet Habu), and in several of the rock-cut temples of Nubia (e.g., Abu Simbel and Beit el-Wali).

Despite the loss of Egyptian control of the Nubian fortresses in the Second Intermediate Period, many were continuously inhabited by the former garrison families well into the period of Kerman domination of the area. In the New Kingdom, temple towns became the norm, although a fortification was built at Tombos by Thutmose I and in the time of Amenhotpe III, a fort existed at Taroy. Temple towns were fairly uniform and characterized by a thick rectangular mud brick enclosure wall with square towers flanking the gateways, at the corners, and at intervals along the perimeter. The interiors were orthogonally planned with three main types of interior buildings: a stone temple of characteristic Egyptian axial plan; complexes of long, narrow storerooms; and mud brick domestic and administrative buildings. Extramural settlements were probably also typical. Middle Kingdom sites such as Aniba and Buhen were modified to conform to this design, and new sites were built, including Aksha, Amara West, Sai, Sesebi, and Soleb. Such temple towns would have been the seats of an administration responsible for sending taxes and tribute north to Egypt as well as garrisons to protect trade and preserve the Egyptian frontier.

In the North, huge earthen embankments have traditionally been hallmarks of Hyksos "fortified camps." More recently, it has become clear that this technology was used for several purposes in Middle Bronze Age Palestine, so that it can no longer be viewed as diagnostic of fortifications alone, affecting identification of the sites of Tell el-Yahudiyya and Heliopolis in Egypt. However, sites that do have fortifications dating to the late Second Intermediate Period and early New Kingdom are Deir el-Ballas and Tell el-Dab'a, casemate platforms with thick-walled superstructures. Bietak compares one platform structure at Dab'a to the Hyksos citadel at Avaris described on the Kamose stela.

The subsequent period was marked by Egyptian raids into the Palestine region. This changed with Thutmose III, who built a siege fortress at Megiddo, "Menkheperre-Is-the-Surrounder-of-the-Asiatics" and a permanent fort, "Menkheperre-Is-the-Binder-of-the-Barbarians" in Retenu. But with Thutmose III, the Egyptian presence in Palestine changed to primarily small Egyptian garrisons posted in Palestinian cities to halt disputes among

FORTS AND GARRISONS. Table 1. *Nubian fortresses and Egyptian Towns*

| Town | Fortress |
| --- | --- |
| *Mnw n Dʒir-Styw* | The fortress of "Repressing-the-Setiu" (Semna South) |
| *Mnw n Shm-Hꜥ.k3w. rꜥ( - m 3ꜥ hrw)* | *The fortress of "Khakaure-justified-is-powerful"* (Semna) |
| *Mnw n Itnw-pdwt* | The fortress of "Warding-off-the-bows" (Kumma) |
| *Mnw n Hsf-Iwnw* | The fortress of "Repelling-the-Inw" (Uronarti) |
| *Mnw n Wꜥf-h3swt (Dr Stin)* | The fortress of "Curbing-the-countries" (Shalfak) |
| *Mnw n Dr-Styw (previously Mtiw)* | The fortress of "Removing-the-Setiu" (Askut) |
| *Mnw n Ikn* | The fortress of Iken (Mirgissa) |
| *Mnw n Bwhn* | The fortress of Buhen (Buhen and Kor as a unit) |
| *Mnw n Ink-t3wy* | The fortress of "Embracing-the-Two-Lands" (Faras or Serra East) |
| *Mnw n Hsf-Md3w* | The fortress of "Repelling-the-Medjay" (Faras or Serra East) |
| *Mnw n Mꜥ3m* | The fortress of Miam (Aniba) |
| *Mnw n B3kl* | The fortress of Baki (Ikkur and Kubban as a unit) |
| *Snmt* | Senmut (Island of Biggeh) |
| *3bw* | Abu (Elephantine) |

the cities, control troublesome peoples, provide a buffer zone between Egypt and neighboring empires, and promote Egyptian interests in trade, tribute, and communication. This is suggested by the Amarna Letters, and among the centers thought to house such garrisons were Gaza, Sharuhen, Ullaza, Sumur, Kumidi, Joppa, Yarimuta, Megiddo, Tyre, Byblos, Ugarit, and Jerusalem, where the ruler, Abdu-heda, was set upon by the Egyptian garrison, presumably because he was not providing for their upkeep. With the beginning of the nineteenth dynasty, the Egyptian presence in Palestine became more pronounced in numbers of military and administrative personnel as well as in Egyptian architectural types. At first this presence had a definite military flavor, including fortresses—especially small square towers known as "migdols," such as at Tell Mor (one each in Strata 7–8 and 5–6). Later, in the late nineteenth and twentieth dynasties, although fortresses were maintained, "residencies," often with central courtyard plans typical of large Egyptian households, appeared; these are attested at Tell el-Farʿah (South) and Tell esh-Shariʿa. Residencies with offset courtyards include those at Aphek and possibly Tell Jemmeh (Gerar), Tel Masos, and Tell Hesi. Egyptian garrisons

were probably stationed at these residencies, and the presence of Egyptian domestic pottery at Ashdod, Bethshemesh, Tell Deir ʿAlla, Lachish, Megiddo, and Tell es-Saidiyeh may also indicate garrisons. At the site of Beth Shan, the Egyptian presence in Palestine is typified through all these manifestations. Level IX (late eighteenth dynasty) produced Egyptian artifacts. Levels VIII and VII (early Ramessid) in the South sector were built in an Egyptian style with an orthogonal plan, center hall residences, a temple, a granary, and a *migdol*. In Level VI (twentieth dynasty) the "Commandant's House" and *migdol* went out of use, though the Egyptian center hall residences continued, probably including that of Ramesses-User-Khepesh, the local Egyptian governor of Beth Shan.

Connecting the eastern Delta with Palestine was the road known as the "Ways of Horus," dotted with way stations and small fortresses with wells or water basins. These are documented in the battle reliefs of Sety I from the Hypostyle Hall at Karnak and in a passage from the "Satirical Letter," Papyrus Anastasi I, 27, 2–28, 1, dating to the reign of Ramesses II. The first is virtually a map of the road between Thel and Rafa, showing fortresses of various sizes in the landscape. Each fortress and its asso-

FORTS AND GARRISONS. Table 2. *Fortresses along the "Ways of Horus"*

| Seti I battle reliefs | P. Anastasi I | Modern site |
|---|---|---|
| The fortress of Thel (Tjalu, later Sile) | Ways of Horus | Tell Abu Seify? |
| The Dwelling of the Lion | The Dwelling of Sese | Tell Hebwe? |
| The Migdol of Menma're | ——— | Tell el-Herr? |
| Buto of Sety Meneptah | Tract of Buto of Sese | Katiyeh? |
| The Castle of Menma're (called?): The . (is) his Protection | | |
| The Stronghold of Sety Meneptah (alternative name?) | In His Stronghold (is) Usima're | ——— |
| Town which (His) Majesty [built] (newly) | ——— | ——— |
| ——— | S-b-el | ——— |
| Town which His Majesty built newly at the well H-b(?)-?-t | ? = H-b-r-t | ——— |
| The Stronghold of Menma're Heir of Re (alternative name?) | ——— | ——— |
| The town of [Raphia] | R-ph | Rafa |
| ——— | K-d-t | Gaza |

ciated water feature have specific names, though not all have been preserved. The passage in Papyrus Anastasi I is a list of the various fortresses encountered on this road, though ending instead at Gaza (*Kdt*) beyond Rafa. Many of the names match those of the Sety reliefs; others vary slightly, and some supplement the earliest list.

Early work by Gardiner assigned some of the eastern Delta forts to known sites, but with more recent intensive work in the area, new information may render these correlations obsolete. Examples of early Ramessid fortresses and associated buildings have been discovered at Deir el-Balah and Haruvit. Both fortresses are characterized by mud brick walls with towers at each corner (20 meters squared and 2.4 meters thick; 50 meters squared, 4 meters thick, and at least 6 meters high, respectively). Haruvit may have had additional buttressing along the length of the walls. Deir el-Balah had an excavated water reservoir, as depicted in the Sety reliefs. Fortifications have also been found along the eastern Delta frontier, including a *migdol* at Jebel Abu-Hassa between Bitter Lakes and Suez. In addition, another route to the Egyptian Nile Valley is farther south via Maskuta (Tjekku) in the Wadi Tumilat. In Papyrus Anastasi IV, 18, 6–7, the scribe records that Shasu had been allowed to pass the fortress there, "Merenptah-Content-with-Peace," in order to water their animals.

Evidence for fortresses on the northwestern frontier begins in Ramessid documents; foundations appear in the reign of Ramesses II. In Year 5 of Merenptah's reign, Sea Peoples invaded the West Delta, probably as far as *Pr m3 Mr-n-pth Ḥtp-ḥr-m3 Ty-[ḥ]-nw m Pr-irr*, the "Castle of Merenptah Which Is in Per-Ir" (Ezbet Abu-Shawish), and were pursued to *Wp-t3*, the "Mountain of the Horns of the Earth" (Marea). Scenes on the walls of Medinet Habu depict the Meshwesh invasion of Year 5, which was defeated at the "Town of Usermare-Meriamun Repulser of Themehu," and the Year 11 invasion, which penetrated to *Ḥwt-š'*, "Castle of Sand," but was repulsed and pursued to the "Town of (Ramesses III) Which Is by the Mountain of Up-Ta." The latter parallels the invasion during the reign of Merenptah. Archaeological remains of other fortresses occur at Zawiyet Um el-Rakham as *Ḥwt-k3*, "House of the Bull" or Apis, and possibly el-Alamein. In addition, fortified wells are attested in Papyrus Harris.

**Third Intermediate and Late Periods.** Though less numerous than preceding periods, a variety of textual references are made to forts. Pictorial representation is minimal. The end of the twentieth dynasty saw the loss of both Kush and Syria-Palestine and the fragmentation of the Nile Valley into competing territories. Towns became heavily fortified, and large, inaccessible lookout stations developed. The earliest (Ramesses XI into the Third Intermediate Period) may be el-Ahaiwah, built against the crest of the hill, the main wall (140 meters long and 5 meters wide) in mud brick with supplementary timbering and buttresses at intervals. Internal architecture includes storerooms, silos, stairways, and small rooms.

In the twenty-first dynasty, Pinudjem began modifications to Medinet Habu that were to continue throughout the period, converting the fortress-shaped temple into a functional fortress. His son, Menkheperre, built fortifications at el-Hiba, Gebelein, and possibly Higazeh and Shurafa. El-Hiba was known as *Teudjoi*, "Their Walls," as well as *Iḥw*, "The Camps" and *Tehnet*, "The Rock, or Crag." As the northern limit of the Theban territory, el-Hiba was the strategic residence of the "great army commanders" and a defense against the Libyan dynasts in Herakleopolis to the north. Natural advantages were exploited and supplemented by about 600 meters of mud brick wall, built in straight sections with some slight bends. The walls measure 12.60 meters thick and are preserved to 10 meters high.

The southern frontier was probably at ElKab, leaving a buffer zone between it and the First Cataract. The enclosure wall is massive, more than 4 kilometers (2.5 miles) in perimeter, 12.10 meters thick, and built in separate lengths of undulating brickwork to provide greater stability. There were no projecting bastions, but possible thickening existed at the corners. The gateways were uniform, stone-lined and only 1 meter wide to accommodate wooden doors. Ramps provided access from the interior to the top of the walls. Closer to the First Cataract, Abu Id demonstrates the means of defense open to communities that lay south of this border: secrecy and strong physical defenses. This may have been one of the garrisons Piya (twenty-fifth dynasty) established in Upper Egypt before his conquest of the northern Nile Valley in his Year 21. His stela records his successful encounters against fortified Egyptian towns.

For the Saite period, recent excavations and restudy of previously excavated monuments have added new examples of fortresses while at the same time redefining the nature of monuments that were thought to be fortifications. The use of casemate construction, a mud brick cellular structure filled with soil and debris, had previously defined structures as storerooms or military structures. This is no longer a tenable criterion; it is now understood as an engineering technique devised to support superstructures of various types. Kemp's study of the Palace of Apries at Memphis has demonstrated that the casemates were used to support the weight of the stone pavement of the palace, and Brian Muhs has convincingly argued that the Great Mound at Naukratis was a Late period temple type.

Tell Defenneh in the eastern Delta on the Pelusiac branch of the Nile has long been considered a type site for Late period forts, in part because of the use of casemate construction. W. M. F. Petrie's interpretation of the literary evidence in conjunction with his excavations led to its identification as biblical Taphanhes, and Herodotean Daphnae and Stratopeda ("The Camps")—a palace, a Greek garrison, and a settlement of Greek mercenaries. Archaeological finds are more suggestive of a temple or palace site with associated domestic and metallurgical areas than of a fortress. The other Herodotean *stratopedon* was called the "Camp of the Tyrians." These mercenaries were settled around the temple of Hephaestus (Ptah) at Memphis, archaeologically near the Palace of Apries.

Additional evidence for Saite garrisons includes references in Herodotus, the Septuagint, Egyptian inscriptions, and corresponding material remains from some of the sites. Garrisons are attested in the written record at Elephantine, both in Herodotus and particularly in the Aramaic archive left by a Jewish garrison, and on the western Delta frontier at Marea. Memphis (Egyptian *Inb Ḥḏ*, "White Walls," and biblical Noph) was garrisoned by Assyrians in Assyrian times and by Greek mercenaries in the Saite period, and even later was a Persian garrison. Daphnae and Magdolos were particularly important fort and garrison sites in the eastern Delta, as were Pithom (*Pr-itm*) near the Red Sea and Pi-Sopdu in the Delta. Even Gaza (Herodotian Kadytis) and Carchemish (Egyptian artifacts) were garrisoned by Egyptian forces. Inscriptions from the Saqqara area in Carian, as well as a tombstone showing a typical scene of Greek prothesis, are additional evidence for a Memphite garrison of East Greek mercenaries.

Definite Saite fortresses exist at Tell Kedwa in the northern Sinai and Dorginarti on an island in the Second Cataract region of the Nubian Nile. Though different in general plan, they share the presence of extramural buildings and a late seventh-to-sixth century BCE ceramic assemblage of East Greek, Levantine, and Egyptian wares. Current excavations at Tell Kedwa have only begun to explore the Saite architecture. Excavations at Dorginarti recorded a mud brick circuit wall measuring about 8 meters thick and preserved 5 to 6 meters high. The earliest mud brick wall was crenellated, and a glacis was formed of cataract stones. The interior was divided into three main areas: the West Sector, containing the garrison quarters, storage facilities, workshops, and the main gateway; the Central Sector, containing the "Official's Residence"; and the East Sector, containing additional storage and the River Gate. The subsequent Persian occupation included a fortified tower on a platform where the former Official's Residence had been sited. The Dorginarti region was certainly a strategic zone connecting the trade routes from Kush through Egypt to the Mediterranean and the Near East.

At Tell Kedwa, the Saite fort was rebuilt after a violent conflagration. The extramural village was not rebuilt. No associated occupational debris was found to assist in dating. The north, west, and south walls were casemate construction, 13.5 meters thick, with five towers distributed evenly on each side and a moat 25 meters from the exterior. The east wall is significantly different, without towers and with a thickness of 27 meters formed by long narrow casemates. It shows building techniques that may indicate an intention to withstand erosion by water. The entire area enclosed measures 200 meters squared. A cemetery 500 meters from the fortress contained cremation burials, suggesting a garrison of Greek mercenaries for one of the occupation phases. Oren identified this site as Migdol, or "Magdolos," but identification of the eastern Delta and northern Sinai forts requires reconsideration after recent surveys and excavations.

**Roman.** A wealth of textual and archaeological material remains from the Roman period. Textual sources include ostraca, papyri, and monumental inscriptions, and the relatively vast number of these texts provides extensive, detailed information, including which military units were assigned to which duty, and often what that duty entailed. The archaeological picture is just as complex. Many forts remain unexplored, but studies and documentation have recently multiplied. A general tendency in Roman military architecture is that the Early Imperial period produced square forts without towers. Over time, forts became smaller and used ever-increasing numbers of bastions until the final form, which was architecturally adapted to the terrain. Various types seem to be represented in the Egyptian remains, and study of associated finds will disclose whether this rule is true in Egypt too. Two of the largest, most complex, and most important forts in Egypt were the now destroyed Nikopolis, 3.5 kilometers east of Alexandria, and that at Luxor.

A smaller type of fort with a distinctive plan is found throughout Egypt. It is rectangular with towers at the corners and along the lengths of the walls, generally with two flanking each gate which is centered on the walls. A colonnaded street leads directly opposite the main gate to the headquarters (*principia*). A diagnostic feature of this building is the rounded niche at the back, perhaps with symbolic or religious significance. One half of the interior area is filled with barracks (*centuriae*). The administrative building or commandant's quarters is located in one corner of the other half. Storage magazines (*horrea*) with kitchen may appear. Additional barracks or storerooms may surround the interior of the fort wall. Almost all is stone, with occasional instances of mud brick in the upper portions of walls from the interior buildings. Forts with some variation of these elements occur at Dionysias, Nag el-Hagar, Tel el-Herr, and Myos Hormos (Abu Sha'ar).

An even smaller emplacement is peculiar to the Eastern Desert, where the density of preserved fortification is particularly high. The fortified water source (*hydreuma*) is found on wadi bottoms along caravan routes and dates from the mid-first century CE, with modification in the third century. They are characterized by rectangular perimeter walls, 140 to 220 meters long, about 1.5 meters thick, and 2 to 3 meters high. Stairs lead to the parapets. The forts are primarily of dry stone construction using unworked stones; often larger worked blocks are used at the gates. Towers occur at the corners and sometimes along the length of the wall and are marked by rounded portions in the exterior face. The interiors are open with rooms around the perimeter for storage or as barracks, and a covered cistern or well is found in the center. These *hydreumata* were secure against surprise raids, but not against prolonged attack. Small towers were also part of this Eastern Desert system. They tend to be square, of stacked stone, and measure 3 to 3.5 meters per side and in height. Some may have been unmanned and used as route markers. Others were occupied by guards or used as signal stations, since they are generally within sight of one another. Access was probably by ladder.

More temporary Roman structures are the four kinds of camps: marching, practice, siege, and construction. Variations occur, but standard characteristics include either a single shallow ditch with the excavated earth forming a bank, or a stone wall when stone or sand prevented excavation of a ditch. Gates were formed by a ditch and rampart extension across the entrance (a *clavicula*) or a ditch and transverse mound (a *titulum*). The shape was often irregular, adapting to the terrain. Examples include those of Qasr Ibrim, Shellal, and Mirgissa. With the exception of the camps, most of these fortifications seem to date to the Late Empire and are either original foundations or rebuilt in the late third or early fourth century. Some were converted from an earlier temple, such as at Kysis (Dush), where the first remains may have been Ptolemaic. The fort at Luxor incorporated much of the New Kingdom temple. Others—such as at Pelusium in the northeastern Delta, Shellal near Philae, and probably Nikopolis and Babylon in Old Cairo—were built on the sites of earlier forts.

Forts existed for various reasons. In the Nile Valley, forts and garrisons existed because of local unrest. In the Eastern Desert, forts were built along five routes to protect the valuable India trade goods as well as to supervise the quarrying and transport of stone from such places as Mons Porphyrites and Mons Claudianus. Primis (Qasr Ibrim) early in the Roman period lost its role of marking the frontier in Nubia, but retained a Roman garrison in the neutral zone to prevent the Blemmys from gaining a foothold. The presence of Western Desert forts dating to the fourth and fifth centuries may have been related to the trade routes of the oases, including the Forty Days Road, as well as monitoring nomadic tribesmen, as at Primis.

**Summary.** Throughout Egyptian history, fortresses and their garrisons monitored frontiers; regulated trade, taxation, and local population movement; and catered to the Egyptian army and diplomats in transit. Within all periods a variety of fortress types existed forming an integrated system of watchtowers, temporary safe havens, and permanent enclaves. Garrison duty was viewed as a difficult task by the Egyptians. Garrison composition included Egyptians and sometimes their families (Middle Kingdom Nubia), but frequently also captured foreigners posted to a different Egyptian border. Thus, when Egyptian control lapsed, the garrisons formed communities, like the Philistine Level V at Beth Shan from the Sea Peoples garrison. In the Saite period, garrisons were composed of foreign mercenaries. Active research and field-work continue, making this a dynamic topic of study in Egyptology with the potential to expand upon our understanding of Egyptian forts and garrisons significantly.

### BIBLIOGRAPHY

*Fortress Surveys*

Badawy, Alexander. *A History of Egyptian Architecture.* 3 vols. Berkeley and Los Angeles, 1954–1968. Portions are outdated, but provides many illustrations and reconstructions as well as detailed analysis of pictorial representations.

Badawy, Alexander. "Festungsanlage." In *Lexicon der Ägyptologie.* 2: 194–203.

Clarke, Somers. "Ancient Egyptian Frontier Fortresses," *Journal of Egyptian Archaeology.* 3 (1916), 155–179. Written prior to excavations and thus often outdated, but one of the first studies of the topic; concentrates on the Nubian fortresses.

Lawrence, A. W. "Ancient Egyptian Fortresses," *Journal of Egyptian Archaeology* 51 (1965), 69–94. General survey of topic with careful consideration of the archaeological material and with particular focus on the military aspects of the architecture. Large section on the Middle Kingdom fortresses of Nubia. Site-by-site bibliography with many earlier studies and preliminary reports.

*General Works and Site Reports Published Since Above Surveys (including pertinent bibliographies)*

Adams, William Y. *Nubia, Corridor to Africa.* Princeton, 1977.

Alston, R. *Soldier and Society in Roman Egypt.* London, 1995.

Emery, Walter. *Egypt in Nubia.* London, 1965.

Emery, Walter, et al. *The Fortress of Buhen: The Archaeological Report.* London, 1979.

Giddy, Lisa. *Egyptian Oases.* Warminster, 1987.

Heidorn, Lisa A. "The Saite and Persian Period Forts at Dorginarti." In *Egypt and Africa Nubia from Prehistory to Islam,* edited by W. V. Davies, pp. 205–219. London, 1991.

James, Frances W. and Patrick E. McGovern. *The Late Bronze Egyptian Garrison at Beth Shan: A Study of Levels VII and VIII.* University Museum Monographs 85. Philadelphia, 1994.

Kemp, B. J. *Ancient Egypt: Anatomy of a Civilization.* London and New York, 1989.

Kemp, B. J. "Imperialism and Empire in New Kingdom Egypt (c. 1575–1087 BC)." In *Imperialism in the Ancient World,* edited by P. D. A. Garnsey and C. R. Whittaker, pp. 7–57. Cambridge, 1978.

Kempinski, A., and R. Reich, eds. *The Architecture of Ancient Israel.* Jerusalem, 1992.

Levy, Thomas, ed. *The Archaeology of Society in the Holy Land.* London, 1995.

Rainey, Anson F., ed. *Egypt, Israel, Sinai: Archaeological and Historical Relationships in the Biblical Period.* Tel Aviv, 1987.

Redford, Donald B. *Egypt, Canaan, and Israel in Ancient Times.* Princeton, 1992.

Redford, Donald B. "Report on the 1993 and 1997 Seasons at Tell Qedwa." *Journal of the American Research Center in Egypt* 35 (1998), 45–60.

Shaw, Ian, and Robert Jameson. "Ancient Mining in the Eastern Desert: A Preliminary Survey at Wadi el-Hudi." *Journal of Egyptian Archaeology* 79 (1993), 81–97.

Smith, Stuart Tyson. *Askut in Nubia.* London, 1995.

Snape, Steven. "Ramesses II's Forgotten Frontier." *Egyptian Archaeology* 11 (1997), 23–24.

Trigger, Bruce G. *Nubia under the Pharaohs.* London, 1976.

Trigger, B. G., B. J. Kemp, D. B. O'Connor, and A. B. Lloyd. *Ancient Egypt: A Social History.* Cambridge, 1983.

Vercoutter, Jean. *Mirgissa.* 3 vols. Paris, 1970–1976.

Welsby, Derek A. "Roman Military Installations along the Nile South of the First Cataract." *Archéologie du Nil Moyen.* Lille (forthcoming).

Ziermann, Martin. *Befestigungsanlagen und Stadtentwicklung in der Frühzeit und im frühen Alten Reich.* Elephantine, 16. Cairo, 1993.

ANN L. FOSTER

**FOUNDATION DEPOSITS.** The term *foundation deposits* designates votive offerings inserted in or beneath the foundation of a structure or in its immediate vicinity prior to the start of construction. In Egypt and Nubia, such deposits were placed under temples, royal and private tombs, palaces, forts, town walls, and other structures from earliest pharaonic times down into the Christian period. Typically they are found at the corners; beneath hypostyle halls, courts, and pylons; along the walls and main axis of temples; at the corners of free-standing tombs (*mastaba*s as well as pyramids); and in a "box-and-one" pattern of holes dug in the natural rock in front of rock-cut tombs. Foundation deposits for private tombs are similar to those from royal tombs, except that the inscribed objects often have the name and title of the tomb-owner as well as that of the king under whom the official served.

The Egyptians placed these offerings in the ground during the course of the foundation ceremony. This ceremony consisted of ten ritual events (which actually cover the period from before the ceremony to the final dedication); the third and most important one centers on the "stretching of the cord" (*pd šs*) by the king and the goddess Seshat to fix the ground plan of the future structure. A priest of the goddess and/or a high official probably substituted for the king at ceremonies conducted at all but the most important structures. The foundation ceremony is mentioned in a variety of Egyptian sources from the beginning of the historical period: the most detailed and elaborate information comes from reliefs and associated texts found in several temples of the Ptolemaic period, notably at Edfu, Dendera, Philae, and Kom Ombo.

Foundation deposits from before the Middle Kingdom are few and tend to be simple affairs—consisting principally of food offerings (especially bovine sacrifices), pottery or stone vessels (often miniature), and sometimes a grindstone—placed in small, rounded pits. Such deposits are known from Tell el-Fara'in (Buto) in the Early Dynastic period, and in the Old Kingdom from the Step Pyramid of Djoser (c.2687–2668 BCE) at Saqqara, the valley temple of Sneferu's pyramid complex at Meidum, and the Osiris temple complex at Abydos. A unique wall scene preserved in the sun temple of Neuserre (c.2470–2440 BCE) at Abusir

cause the King to ascend to Khepri when he comes into being in the eastern side of the sky.

In Spell 1333, they "spread protection of life over your father the Osiris King, since he was restored by the gods." In Spell 552, they eliminate hunger and thirst: "I will not be thirsty by reason of Shu, I will not be hungry by reason of Tefnut; Hapy, Duamutef, Kebehsenuef, and Imsety will expell this hunger which is in my belly and this thirst which is on my lips."

In the New Kingdom *Book of the Going Forth by Day* (*Book of the Dead*), the roles of the four genii in the after-life are further elaborated, as in Spell 137:

> O sons of Horus, Imsety, Hapy, Duamutef, Kebehsenuef: as you spread your protection over your father Osiris-Khenti-mentiu, so spread your protection over [the deceased], as you removed the impediment from Osiris-Khentimentiu, so he might live with the gods and drive Seth from him.

Spell 17 states:

> As for the tribunal that is behind Osiris, Imsety, Hapy, Duamu-tef, Kebehsenuef; it is these who are behind the Great Bear in the northern sky. . . . As for these seven spirits, Imsety, Hapy, Duamutef, Kebehsenuef, Maayotef, He-Who-is-under-his-Moringa-Tree, and Horus-the-Eyeless, it is they who were set by Anubis as a protection for the burial of Osiris.

Finally, in the tenth division of the *Book of Gates*, Imsety, Hapy, Duamutef, Duametef, and Kebehsenuef appear restraining the *ummti* (*wmmti*) snakes with chains. These snakes were allies of Re's enemy, the serpent Apophis. The four genii are also depicted on the western part of the astronomical ceilings found in Ramessid royal tombs.

Clearly stated to be the sons of Horus in a number of texts, their precise familial affiliations are not definitive. Apart from the aforementioned Horus of Khem, Harsiese and Horus the Elder are also cited as being their father in various texts. Isis was their mother, although a view of their having sprung from a lotus flower can be seen in the vignette that accompanies the *Book of the Going Forth by Day* judgment scene (Spell 125).

Dating from their earliest appearances in the Pyramid Texts, the Four Sons of Horus are found exclusively in mortuary contexts, and seem not to have had any cult as such; they are thus generally referred to as "genii." From the Middle Kingdom onward, however, they are ubiqui-tous within the tomb, invoked upon almost all coffins and canopic containers. In the earlier Pyramid Texts they were among the deities before whom the deceased was stated to possess "reverence" (*imзh*); such texts are normally found on the coffins' lateral textbands, with actual depic-tions added during the eighteenth dynasty. The later rep-resentations occurred on the sides of the coffin trough, with Anubis-Imywet and Anubis-Khenty-seh-netjer stand-

ing between the genii. This type of depiction recalls Spell 1092 of the Pyramid Texts, where "they flank the dead king when on the ferry to the Field of Rushes." The Four Sons likewise appear on New Kingdom sarcophagi in stone and wood, which featured less common text-formulations.

On canopic containers, where their heads functioned as lids, the Four Sons were regarded as guardians or re-incarnations in the specific organs removed during the mummification process: Imsety—the liver, Hapy—the lungs, Duamutef—the stomach, and Kebehsenuef—the intestines. There is evidence for the responsibilities of Hapy and Duamutef being switched in some cases. Other anatomical relationships existed, as is attested by Pyra-mid Text Spell 149. Hapy and Duamutef were associated with the hands; Imsety and Kebehsenuef with the feet.

The Four Sons of Horus had various other relation-ships. Geographically, Imsety was linked with the South, Hapy with the North, Duamutef the East, and Kebeh-senuef the West. In addition, Hapy and Duamutef were linked to the Delta city of Buto; Imsety and Kebehsenuef with the Upper Egyptian city of Hierakonpolis. These two ancient cities are the earliest of all Egyptian settlements. An association can be made between Imsety and the herb dill, owing to the similarity in Old Egyptian between their names. Upon both coffins and canopic containers, Imsety, Hapy, Duamutef, and Kebehsenuef are shown under the individual tutelage of the goddesses Isis, Nephthys, Neith, and Selket, respectively. These pairings are generally fixed, although variations can be found.

Until the eighteenth dynasty, the Four Sons were usu-ally depicted with human heads, although a few canopic chests of the Middle Kingdom contain images of all four gods with the heads of falcons. They were normally shown wearing the usual divine tripartite wig, but in the tomb of King Ay (tomb 23 of the West branch of the Valley of the Kings), Imsety and Hapy are each depicted with the Red Crown, Duamutef and Kebehsenuef each with the White Crown, which derived from the respective pairs' as-sociation with Egypt's North and South. Between the early eighteenth and mid-nineteenth dynasties, however, each genius gained a distinctive head: Imsety—human, Hapy—ape, Duamutef—jackal, and Kebehsenuef—fal-con. These henceforth remained standard, except during the twenty-second and twenty-third dynasties, when at least six different combinations can be found, the most common showing Duamutef and Kebehsenuef swapping heads.

From the late Third Intermediate Period onward, the presence of the four genii in mortuary contexts expanded. In addition to their presence on coffins and canopic con-tainers, faience amulets of the four were attached to shrouds or incorporated into the bead nets that came into use as body-covers. Images of the genii, often of wax, were placed in the deceased's body cavity from the time of Ramesses III (r. 1198–1166 BCE) onward. In the latter part of the twentieth dynasty, this practice was instituted in conjunction with the return of the internal organs to the abdomen, following separate mummification.

The Four Sons of Horus continued to be depicted on items of funerary equipment into Ptolemaic and Roman times; the last instances are found on stucco mummy casings of the fourth century CE.

[*See also* Canopic Jars and Chests.]

### BIBLIOGRAPHY

Drenkhahn, Rosemarie. "Kebehsenuef." In *Lexikon der Ägyptologie*, vol. 3. Wiesbaden, 1980.

Eggebrecht, Arne. "Amset," "Duamutef," and "Hapi." In *Lexikon der Ägyptologie*, vols. 1 and 2. Wiesbaden, 1975 and 1977.

Heerma van Voss, Matthieu. "Horuskinder." In *Lexikon der Ägyptologie*, vol. 3. Wiesbaden, 1980.

Munro, Peter. "Bemerkungen zum Gesaltwandel und zum Ursprung der Horus-Kinder." In *Festschrift zum 150 jährigen Bestehen des Berliner Ägyptisches Museums,* pp. 195–204. Mitteilungenaus der Ägyptischen Sammlung, 8. Berlin, 1974.

Sethe, Kurt. "Zur Geschichte der Einbalsamierung bei den Ägyptern, und einiger damit verbundener Bräuche." *Sitzungsberichte der Preussischen Akademie der Wissenschaften.* Phil. Hist. Klasse, 13. Berlin, 1934. The fundamental discussion and classification of the texts inscribed on canopic jars and chests.

AIDAN DODSON

**FOURTH DYNASTY.** *See* Old Kingdom, *article on* Fourth Dynasty.

**FROGS.** In antiquity, the Egyptian frog (*Rana mascareniensis*) was, as it remains today, an abundant resident of the country, a denizen of the Nile River and wetland areas (Eg., *ꜥbḫn* and *ḳrr*, the latter the onomatopoetic "croaker"). This species, and the now rare tree frog (*Hyla savignyi*), are extensively portrayed in Egyptian iconography. They were so well known, in fact, that the hieroglyphic sign for the number 100,000 was a diminutive tadpole (*ḥfn*). To pharaonic Egyptians, there was probably never a clear distinction between the frogs and the local toads (*Bufo regularis* or *Bufo viridis*). In the ancient representations of these creatures, it is often difficult to determine which of these amphibians was actually intended (frogs having smooth skins, with toads usually rough and warty). In the following, we use the general term "frog" without being confined to zoological exactness.

The reproductive process of the frog was a mystery to the ancient Egyptians, who were under the erroneous impression that they spontaneously self-created. This mistaken belief almost certainly stems from observing the thousands of swarming tadpoles emerging from the fertile mud each year after the waters of the Nile flood receded. For this reason, and its highly visible fecundity, the frog developed into a powerful symbol of fertility, birth, and regeneration. The four primordial male deities of Hermopolis were often shown with frogs' heads. Most importantly, however, the frog was sacred to Heket, the goddess of childbirth. Stone vessels carved in the shape of frogs were used as early as the Amratian period (Naqada I) and were included as grave goods. Votive figurines of frogs have been discovered in temple sanctuaries at several sites of the Early Dynastic period. In swamp scenes featured on tomb-chapel walls, especially during the Old and Middle Kingdoms, frogs occasionally can be seen as an element of the teeming wildlife of the papyrus thicket. In the Middle Kingdom, images of frogs, sometimes wielding knives, probably a manifestation of the goddess Heket, routinely occur on apotropaic (protective) "magical wands" and rods, which were thought to provide protection to a mother and her newborn child. Not surprisingly, the frog also had some associations with Hapy, god of the Nile inundation. Representations from Greco-Roman times depict Hapy holding a frog in his hand. Vast numbers of frogs are said to have come up from the water and covered the entire land in the biblical account of the second plague, in the *Book of Exodus*, which was divinely brought upon Egypt. Plentiful at nearly all times in Egyptian history were frog amulets in faience or stone, charms that could be worn both by the living and the dead. The popularity of this aquatic creature as a decorative motif, particularly on objects of domestic use, continued into the Roman period and beyond, as when it commonly appears on small pottery lamps.

### BIBLIOGRAPHY

Anderson, John. *Zoology of Egypt: Reptilia and Batrachia*. London, 1898. Contains much information on the frogs of Egypt.

Andrews, Carol. *Amulets of Ancient Egypt*. Austin, 1994. Excellent illustrated survey of amulets—including frogs—in pharaonic Egypt, based chiefly on those in the collections of the British Museum, London.

Droste zu Hülshoff, Vera. "Kröte." In *Lexikon der Ägyptologie*, 3: 790. Wiesbaden, 1980.

Houlihan, Patrick F. *The Animal World of the Pharaohs*. London and New York, 1996. Aimed at a general audience, this volume surveys the ancient Egyptian animal world, including frogs.

Kákosy, László. "Frosch." In *Lexikon der Ägyptologie*, 2: 334–336. Wiesbaden, 1977.

Shier, Louise A. "The Frog on Lamps from Karanis." In *Medieval and Middle Eastern Studies in Honor of Aziz Suryal Atiya*, edited by Sami A. Hanna, pp. 349–358. Leiden, 1972. Discusses the significance of the frog figured on pottery lamps from the Roman period. (This detail has been interpreted by most scholars as a symbol adopted by Christian Egyptians, alluding to the resurrection.)

PATRICK F. HOULIHAN

**FRUITS.** Along with cereal products and vegetables, fruits were an important part of human nourishment in pharaonic Egypt. The fruits were usually sweet-tasting, from trees or bushes, and eaten raw. From the Predynastic period on, they also constituted an important part of the burial goods for the care of the deceased in the hereafter, whatever his social standing. Thus fruits have been found in very simple burials but also in royal ones, such as that of Tutankhamun, which contained a wide range packed in baskets. The botanical determination of these burial goods has provided us with a good overall picture of the fruits used in ancient Egypt.

Several trees and bushes of the Nile Valley supply edible fruits. Among them is Christ's-thorn (*Zizyphus spina-christi*), whose cherry-sized, apple-flavored fruits (e.g., *nbs*) have been found in graves since Predynastic times. The flesh of the fruit was also used to make a kind of fruit bread. The tree is still common throughout Egypt. The Egyptian plum (*Balanites aegyptiaca*), in Egyptian possibly *jšd*, a tree with oval fruits of 2 to 3 centimeters (1 inch) has become rare. The flesh is sweet, and the Egyptians extracted balanos oil from the kernel. This fruit, too, was a Predynastic burial good.

Finds from the Old Kingdom onward show that the fruits of the indigenous cordia (*Cordia sinensis*) were also eaten, as well as those of the closely related species *Cordia myxa*, which is a native of India; the oldest finds of these fruits probably date to the Middle Kingdom. The Egyptians also made use of the orange-colored drupes of the grewia (*Grewia tenax*), which were found packed in baskets in the tomb of Tutankhamun, and the fruits of the *Maerua crassifolia* tree, which have a mealy taste. Two palm types with edible fruits are indigenous to Egypt, although only to Upper Egypt. The dom palm (*Hyphaene thebaica*), in Egyptian, *m3m3*, was very widespread. It has fan-shaped leaves and a forked trunk; the shiny brown fruits, called *ḳwḳw* in Egyptian, 7–8 centimeters (2–3 inches) in size, with a gingerbready sort of taste, have been found in Predynastic graves. The argun palm (*Medemia argun*), in Egyptian, *m3m3 n ḫ3nnt*, is rarer. Nowadays, only isolated instances are found, and we do not know which part of the fruit the Egyptians consumed, the dry flesh of the fruit or the seeds. Evidence for this palm species has been found dating back to the Old Kingdom.

The Egyptians did not only use the fruits of indigenous trees but as early as Predynastic times, they had begun to cultivate foreign fruit types. Economically, the most important of these was surely the date (*Phoenix dactylifera*), in Egyptian, *bnr/bnrt*. The native land of the date palm is not known botanically. The very sugary fruits can only be cultivated with the help of artificial pollination. The Egyptians produced a drink from them, called *srmt*. The second most important cultivated fruit was the sycomore fig

(*Ficus sycomorus*), one of the most common grave goods from Predynastic times on. The large tree, *nht* in Egyptian, was a popular source of shade, with its thick foliage; this is also expressed by its religious significance as a tree goddess, administering cooling water to the deceased or to his *ba*-bird. The origins of sycomore culture are unknown. The fruits form seeds that can germinate only after pollination by the gall wasp (*Ceratosolen arabicus*), which is not found in Egypt. There, another gall wasp (*Sycophaga sycomore*) develops inside the figs but does not initiate any fertilization. Thus in Egypt the tree could only be propagated vegetatively by means of cuttings. In order to accelerate the ripening of the fruit, so that this took place before the development of the gall wasps, the Egyptians notched each fruit with a knife. There is evidence from Old Kingdom for the cultivation of the common fig (*Ficus carica*), in Egyptian *d3b*, which comes from the eastern Mediterranean region.

The Egyptians adopted viticulture from Palestine during Predynastic times. "Red grapes," *j3rrt* in Egyptian, were eaten as fruit and were also made into the alcoholic drink "wine," *jrp* in Egyptian. Wine, however, was a drink for the upper classes only and was often used as an offering to the gods. The vineyards were located mainly in the Nile Delta and in the oases. Among the vegetal grave goods known since the Old Kingdom was often the fruit of the persea (*Mimusops laurifolia*) in Egyptian probably *šw3b*. Nowadays the tree grows wild only in Yemen and Ethiopia, but in pharaonic times it must have been quite widespread in Egypt. The yellow, sweet-tasting flesh of the fruit surrounds two or three large, shiny brown seeds. The fruits are about 3 centimeters (1.5 inches) in size and are almond-shaped; on the lower end is a green calyx with four to six points. Only from the eighteenth dynasty on is there any proof for the cultivation of the pomegranate in Egypt. The pomegranate (*Punica granatum*), in Egyptian *jhnm*, comes from the eastern Mediterranean region. Various types of gourds were cultivated in the Nile Valley, the origins of which are supposed to lie in regions to the south of Egypt. The elongated fruit of the cucumber (*Cucumis melo*) is depicted on offering tables from Old Kingdom times, and faience models served as burial goods; the physical remains of cucumbers have not as yet been found. The second gourd type cultivated in Egypt was a small fruiting variety of the watermelon (*Citrullus lanatus*). The flesh of this fruit is not edible, however, only the seeds; they appeared frequently in burials from Predynastic times on. In Greco-Roman times, a whole series of new fruits once again reached Egypt: the peach (*Prunus persica*), the apricot (*Prunus armeniaca*), the sour cherry (*Prunus cerasus*), and the pear (*Pyrus communis*) were cultivated, as well as the true service tree (*Sorbus domestica*) and the citron (*Citrus medica*).

The fruits found in burials and in settlement sites indicate, however, that in addition to the types mentioned here several others were also used as foodstuffs, albeit in more modest quantities. From the New Kingdom, olive trees were cultivated in Egypt (*Olea europaea*) and an olive stone has been found that dates back to the Middle Kingdom. The Egyptians imported pistachios (*Pistacia vera*) from Palestine, and from the regions to their south, the fruit of the baobab (*Adansonia digitata*). The contents of a pot from an eighteenth dynasty tomb have been identified as banana puree, but otherwise there is no proof for either the cultivation or the import of bananas for pharaonic Egypt. According to textual sources, the apple tree (*Malus sylvestris*) may have been planted during the New Kingdom, but thus far there have been no finds of this type of fruit. Furthermore, it is also unclear whether the Egyptians planted the mandrake (*Mandragora officinarum*), indigenous to Palestine, in their gardens, and perhaps even ate the fruit. The depictions of yellow egg-shaped fruits with pointy calyxes are not usually specific enough to be able to differentiate whether they are mandrake fruit or persea fruit; there have been no actual finds of mandrake fruit.

Substantial finds and texts provide information about the cultivation, medical uses, and economic significance of fruit. Above all, the texts list the deliveries of various types of fruit to the temples; the offering lists in the tombs mention the amounts of each fruit needed for the care of the deceased in the hereafter: dates, Egyptian plums, sycamore figs, figs, Christ's-thorn fruit, grapes, and wine. Tomb paintings and the reliefs on temple walls provide information about fruit cultivation and use. The representations of offering goods show the same fruits that are listed in the offering lists, including from the New Kingdom on pomegranates and yellow fruits, which are either persea or mandrake fruit. In the agricultural scenes of the tomb art, the harvesting of various fruits can be seen, most often the grape harvest and wine making.

The Egyptians planted fruit trees in agricultural estates and in their private gardens next to their houses. In the representations, they are usually growing near a pond and surrounded by flowers. Fruits trees were also cultivated in the gardens in front of the burial enclosures. The various shapes of the fruits inspired craftsmen to work them into jewelry as decorative motifs, particularly in the large faience collars. Paintings of flower garlands and of stick bouquets very often included depictions of fruit. Some vessels were made in the shape of fruits, the most popular being the pomegranate; many served as ceramic receptacles for the black eye paint, kohl. A particularly precious vessel made of silver in the shape of a pomegranate was found among the burial treasures of Tutankhamun.

[*See also* Diet.]

**BIBLIOGRAPHY**

Brewer, Douglas J., Donald B. Redford, and Susan Redford. *Domestic Plants and Animals*. Warminster, 1994.

Baum, Nathalie. *Arbres et Arbustes de l'Égypte Ancienne*, Orientalia Lovaniensia Analecta, 31. Leuven, 1988.

Germer, Renate. *Flora des pharaonischen Ägypten*, Deutsches Archäologisches Institut, Abteilung Kairo, 11. Mainz, 1985.

Germer, Renate. *Die Pflanzenmaterialien aus dem Grab des Tutanchamun*, Hildesheimer Ägyptologische Beiträge, 28. Hildesheim, 1989.

Helck, Wolfgang. *Materialien zur Wirtschaftsgeschichte des Neuen Reiches*. 5 vols., Abhandlungen der Akademie der Wissenschaften und der Literatur in Mainz. Wiesbaden, 1961–1970.

Hepper, Nigel F. *Pharaoh's Flowers*. London, 1990.

Keimer, Ludwig. *Die Gartenpflanzen im Alten Ägypten*, vol. 1, Hamburg and Berlin 1924; vol. 2, edited by Renate Germer. Deutsches Archäologisches Institut, Abteilung Kairo, 13. Mainz, 1984.

Zohary, Daniel, and Maria Hopf. *Domestication of Plants in the Old World*. 2d ed. Oxford, 1993.

RENATE GERMER
Translated from German by Julia Harvey

**FUNERARY CONES,** the cone-shaped objects of baked clay inserted as a frieze, with the circular face exposed, above the doors of Middle and New Kingdom private tombs, mainly in the Theban necropolis. During the New Kingdom, the cone's visible face bore a stamp of the owner's name and title(s), sometimes including those of a relative, or had a short supplementary text. Any number of cones belonging to one person might therefore be in existence, so the cones constitute a proof of the presence of a tomb, either extant or now lost.

The cones have been interpreted in several ways: as a means of identification of the owner of the tomb; as an ornamental memorial; as a boundary marker for the territory of the tomb; as dummy offering loaves; or as symbolic pieces of meat. The circular surface has also been interpreted in several ways: as the ends of roofing poles; as a form of visitors' cards; as a decorative element; or, most recently, as reflecting the shape of the sun disc—to thus become one vehicle for the deceased tomb owner's attainment of eternal life, by following the circuit of the sun. Possibly, the Egyptians were themselves in doubt as to the nature of the object, for they painted the cones in several colors (red, blue, white). In Egypt, colors indicated materials, and the colors mentioned encompassed substances as different as bread, meat, pottery, and the sun's red glow. As some of the texts accompanying the burial refer to solar matters, this was likely to have been one reason for the cones' existence.

The earliest known funerary cones were dated to the eleventh dynasty. Although they have no inscriptions, they have been found in context. Some are 53 centimeters (20 inches) long, but they decreased in size as the New Kingdom progressed. In the eighteenth dynasty they abounded from the reign of Thutmose I onward. In the Ramessid

FUNERARY CONES. *Inscribed, red pottery cones from the Asasif, Thebes, Late period.* (The Metropolitan Museum of Art, Museum Excavations 1912–1913; Rogers Fund, 1913. [13.180.66–74])

period, they were quite scarce compared to the number of tombs known from that time.

Funerary cones were mainly used at Thebes, although the Egyptian style tomb of the official Anu at Aniba also included cones. Yet the tomb of his more famous colleague, Penne, in the same location did not. Cones have also been found at Naga ed-Deir and at el-Deir north of Esna; the latter, in a Middle Kingdom context, but presumably intrusive, are particularly interesting in that they give the name of the locality near which they were found. It is thus unlikely that they should have been taken there from Thebes. They probably came from a tomb in the vicinity of Esna, now lost. Middle Kingdom tombs at Rizei-

qat, Armant, Naqada, and Abydos have yielded uninscribed cones.

No cones have come from the Memphis area, but some of those found at Thebes contained evidence of a Memphite connection. One belongs to Kenamun, steward of the dockyard of Memphis—but he had a tomb cut at Thebes, where the cones were found—so the reference to Memphis was purely verbal. Two seal impressions that mentioned the dockyard probably also derived from Thebes. Some other cone users had occupations that took them to various towns in Egypt, such as Heliopolis and Dendera; this distribution is also apparent from titles found in the tombs at Thebes, and there is nothing to suggest that these persons were buried elsewhere. No cones have been recovered from Tell el-Amarna (where their presumed solar symbolism might have fit in well), nor are any known from the few Theban tombs of the late eighteenth dynasty.

Funerary cones were thus largely restricted to the Theban area, and they conformed to the tradition in that part of the country. They may have been thought of as particularly suited to rock-cut tombs, and in fact most of the cones related to existing tombs have come from those with painted, not sculpted, decoration. Actually, the majority of tombs from that period were painted, so there are too many unprovenanced cones to provide significant statistics.

The Theban necropolis covers a large area, and within its various sections a pattern of distribution may be distinguished. The majority of the eighteenth dynasty tombs are at Sheik Abd-el-Qurna, so this is where most of the attributable cones would belong. In contrast, at Deir el-Medina, only one tomb has yielded a funerary cone; this is interesting, for in that locality, the solar cycle was more frequently referred to in the wall decoration than elsewhere in the necropolis. Bernard Bruyère, who excavated Deir el-Medina, suggested that *shawabti* figures somehow took over the function of the funerary cones, and he did not include the cones in his reconstruction of the Deir el-Medina tombs. Yet some tombs certainly had both cones and *shawabti* figures, so it is difficult to see a connection.

The corpus of known funerary cones is a valuable source of information on the prosopography of New Kingdom Thebes, to be compared with such objects as scarabs and seals. Cones can also be used as an indication of the number of tombs that existed in the Theban area, which far exceeded those known at present. The number of funerary cones not immediately assignable to a known tomb is more than four hundred, a figure that may be compared to the number of New Kingdom tombs in the area, about 406. The number of New Kingdom tombs for which funerary cones exist is seventy-nine, with fifty-two of these being at Sheikh Abd-el-Qurna and forty-eight dating to the eighteenth dynasty. As with other funerary items produced for the elite of ancient Egypt, funerary cones were used by both men and women.

[*See also* Funerary Figurines.]

### BIBLIOGRAPHY

Davies, Norman de Garis, and M. F. Laming Macadam. *A Corpus of Inscribed Egyptian Funerary Cones.* Oxford, 1957. The most comprehensive publication on the subject.

DeWachter, M. "Un nouveau type de cônes funéraires." *Revue de l'Égypte* 32 (1980), 140–141. About a funerary cone devoted to a woman.

Manniche, Lise. *Lost Tombs: A Study of Certain Eighteenth Dynasty Monuments in the Theban Necropolis.* London and New York, 1988.

Summarizes previous studies and relates the material to the possible number of tombs in existence in New Kingdom Thebes.

LISE MANNICHE

**FUNERARY FIGURINES.** Known as *shabti*s, *shawabti*s, and *ushebti*s, funerary figurines were small statuettes fashioned either as mummies or as living persons dressed in fine linen garb. They served as proxies for ancient Egyptian deceased by magically performing various obligatory agricultural tasks in the underworld. Over time, so many funerary figurines were produced that apart from scarabs and amulets, they are the most numerous of all ancient Egyptian antiquities. Over time they became one of the characteristic components of a proper burial.

The three terms for funerary figurines are indiscriminately and incorrectly used as synonyms. Each designation has historical limits to its usage, and the term *shawabti* is restricted geographically as well—to Deir el-Medina and other Theban areas. The appropriate spelling is found in the version of chapter 6 of the *Book of Going Forth by Day* (*Book of the Dead*) that was painted or inscribed on the figurines at some point before the eighteenth dynasty. However, because many of these statuettes lack chapter 6 and have simply the title and name of the deceased, none of the three terms applies. Hence, the designation "funerary figurines," despite its antiquarian ring, is at least accurate for all types in all periods.

Small wax prototypes appeared at Saqqara during the Herakleopolitan period and in the eleventh dynasty mortuary complex of Nebhepetre Montuhotep I at Deir el Bahri in Thebes. Shaped as humans, wrapped in linen, and deposited in coffins, these little wax figurines were miniature mummies. These earliest examples do not have chapter 6 or any other specific word for funerary figurine; however, they continue the tradition of work done on behalf of the deceased, which appears in the Old Kingdom in the form of both servant statuettes and tomb paintings and reliefs of laborers.

Throughout the Middle Kingdom, funerary figurines appeared in small numbers per burial. Usually made of stone, they were consistently mummiform and uninscribed or labeled only with the title and name of the deceased. Either in the thirteenth or the seventeenth dynasty, a simple form of chapter 6 of the *Book of the Dead* appears on sporadic examples. This text enumerates the agricultural labors to be performed—irrigation, cultivation, and sand removal. In the early version, both the spellings *shabti* and *shawabti* appear, but the latter is restricted to the strange stick figures from the Theban area. *Shawabti* does not recur until the nineteenth dynasty on no more than a few dozen figurines from Deir el-Medina and elsewhere in the Theban necropolis; hence, it is

FUNERARY FIGURINES. *Painted wooden shawabti figure of Maya, a New Kingdom official, in the coffin, nineteenth dynasty.* (University of Pennsylvania Museum, Philadelphia. Neg. #S4–143062)

probably a dialectical variant and is the least preferable of the three spellings for general reference. The etymology of *shabti* and *shawabti* is not clear.

The eighteenth dynasty was a time of great innovation, not only in the development of funerary figurines but also in all other Egyptian art. No longer made primarily of stone, funerary figurines appeared in wood, faience, terracotta, metal, and even glass, in rare examples. An expanded version of chapter 6 occurs regularly on the figurines, and *shabti* is the routine spelling. The numbers of *shabti*s per burial increase from a few to dozens and even hundreds. Still made only in mummy form, *shabti*s from the first half of the eighteenth dynasty are large and bulky. Although some terracotta and faience *shabti*s are mold made and mass produced, most figurines are hand fashioned and are of high quality.

The great innovation in funerary figurines, not only in the eighteenth dynasty but also in their entire history, happened during the reign of Thutmose IV, when crafts-men reinforced their agricultural nature—fashioning them with baskets, sacks and hoes, or mattocks held in their hands on the chest or waist. Some *shabti*s have separate models of the agricultural tools, and still others are unadorned. Once established, however, the decorative scheme of the agricultural tools became a standard feature of funerary figurines. Either at the end of the eighteenth or early in the nineteenth dynasty, figurines in the garments of the living first appeared. Finely rendered with loose folds and tight pleats, the clothing resembles the dress of the elite classes often seen elsewhere in Egyptian art. Because these raiments were inappropriate for hard labor in the fields, they perhaps had a religious significance, indicating that the deceased were reborn in the underworld and dressed in their best for all eternity.

Although many *shabti*s and most *shawabti*s of the nineteenth dynasty were carefully rendered, the majority of funerary figurines were roughly fashioned. Mold-made *shabti*s of faience or terracotta became increasingly popu-

FUNERARY FIGURINES. *Two shawabti*s. *(Left)* Blue-glazed faience *shawabti* of Queen Henutawy, probably from the Deir el-Bahri royal cache at Thebes, twenty-first dynasty. *(Right)* *Shawabti* of Paw(y) Khonsu, from Dra Abul Naga, Third Intermediate Period. (University of Pennsylvania Museum, Philadelphia. Neg. #S4–143070)

lar, and the numbers per burial expanded appreciably. Chapter 6 of the *Book of the Dead* also became elaborated; however, uninscribed figurines or those with only the title and name of the deceased are also numerous. In the twenty-first dynasty, the spelling *ushebti* occurs and is the standard word that appears in chapter 6 throughout the Ptolemaic period, when the last figurines were made. The etymology of this spelling is again uncertain; perhaps it derives from the verb *wšb* ("to answer"). The *ushebti*s of the twenty-first dynasty and the rest of the Third Intermediate Period are consistently fashioned of blue-colored faience, with details in black. In the Late period and thereafter, *ushebti*s are again rendered in faience, in pastel tones of green or blue. In the Late and Ptolemaic periods, *ushebti*s are consistently mummiform; examples in the dress of the living are exceedingly rare, if at all existent. So numerous were the figurines in each burial that in many instances there are "overseer" figurines designed to control the gangs of workers.

**BIBLIOGRAPHY**

Aubert, J.-F., and Liliane Aubert. *Statuettes Egyptiennes: Chaouabtis. Ouchebtis.* Paris, 1974.

Schneider, Hans D. *Shabtis: An Introduction to the History of Ancient Egyptian Funerary Statuettes with a Catalogue of the Collection of Shabtis in the National Museum of Antiquities at Leiden.* 3 vols. Leiden, 1977.

Spanel, Donald B. "Notes on the Terminology for Funerary Figurines." *Studien zur Altägyptischen Kultur* 13 (1986), 249–253.

Spanel, Donald B. "Two Unusual Eighteenth-Dynasty Shabtis in The Brooklyn Museum." *Bulletin of the Egyptological Seminar* 10 (1989–1990), 145–167.

Speleers, Louis. *Les figurines funéraires égyptiennes.* Brussels, 1923.

DONALD B. SPANEL

**FUNERARY LITERATURE.** The funerary literature of the ancient Egyptians includes various collections of texts associated with elite burials from almost all of Egypt's historic periods. These texts were copied in many ways on the walls of tombs, and occasionally on temple walls, as well as on various objects placed inside tombs—principally coffins and papyri. The term does not cover the biographical texts, formulaic offering texts, and texts that are essentially hymns to various deities, which may also be found in tombs. Some ritual texts are included, but others—such as the Opening of the Mouth ritual, often found in tombs—are not generally included. Some mythological and cosmogonic texts found in tombs, such as the *Book of the Heavenly Cow* or the *Birth of the Solar Disk,* are included, but the Jumilhac Papyrus and Bremner-Rhind Papyrus, which are largely mythological, are not. The emphasis of funerary literature is on eschatological works, principally those that deal with life after death in the company of the gods—that is, guidebooks to the beyond. Despite the narrowness of the topic, such works were popular in all periods of Egyptian history and represent the largest genre of texts that survive, and also the group that is represented by the largest number of copies.

The Old Kingdom's Pyramid Texts, the Middle Kingdom's Coffin Texts, and the New Kingdom's *Book of Going Forth by Day* (*Book of the Dead*), as well as certain guidebooks to the beyond, such as the *Book of That Which Is in the Underworld* (*Amduat*), the *Book of Gates,* and the *Book of Caverns,* are the principal works of this genre, and there is a certain amount of overlap among them. The Old Kingdom's Pyramid Texts include some variants found on Middle Kingdom coffins as well as on the walls of a few Saite period priests' and priestesses' tomb-chapels at Thebes that date from almost two thousand years later. The Middle Kingdom's Coffin Texts include some variants of Pyramid Texts as well as other Old Kingdom material and early versions of chapters of the *Book of Going Forth by Day.* Copies of the *Book of Going Forth by Day* are essentially papyrus documents, but many individual chapters are found on tomb walls and even on the walls of at least one royal mortuary temple; since this is the New Kingdom mortuary temple of Ramesses III at Medinet Habu, the last large and the only well-preserved pharaonic temple, such texts could also have occurred on others now lost. Some of its chapters are also found on scarabs, *shawabtis,* linen strips, and hypocephali, and in many forms these continued to be very popular well into Roman times.

In the case of the Pyramid Texts, there is a clear chronological order to the surviving documents; the burial chamber of Unas, last king of the fifth dynasty, held the earliest known copy. Earlier examples might have been on perishable materials placed in tombs that were later robbed and despoiled. Most of the funerary literature has in common the reconciliation of the two principal cults involved with death and the afterlife, and both are related to the myth of divine kingship. They come down to us first and foremost in the royal context: the Pyramid Texts within the kings' burial chambers. Considered a living king from earliest times was the divine Horus—son and avenger of his father, Osiris—who at death became Osiris, with all the mythological connections involved. In the fifth dynasty's Pyramid Texts, the king has also become the "son of Re," who at death joins his father on the sun's bark in his daytime and nighttime voyages through the sky. The cyclical nature of these cults, as well as their death and rebirth motifs, makes it possible for them to be assimilated together even if not always entirely reconciled. All three collections of texts have certain sections that show total separation, others showing some syncretism, and still others that show complete assimilation of the two deities, their cults, and their descriptions of the afterlife. What is remarkable is that these kings' texts were almost immediately used in queens' tombs, and thereafter were quickly taken over by nonroyals, then eventually made available to almost anyone.

The earliest examples of funerary literature in Old Kingdom pyramids were not all created specifically for the purpose of accompanying those royal burials. Judging from their contents, which refer to both pyramids and desert burials, and both royal and nonroyal owners, these texts indicate that they were composed from various sources dealing with death and the afterlife and were compiled by priests, generally of the Heliopolitan persuasion. The language and orthography of the texts also seem to indicate that the texts came from different time periods and perhaps from different places as well.

One interesting feature is that many if not all of the

Pyramid Texts (and the Coffin Texts, too) were written originally in the first person, and an attempt (not always successful) was made to change the pronoun references to the actual names of the intended owners. This personalization or customizing of the texts was deemed essential to ensure that the owner was fully incorporated into the texts, but the effort involved hundreds of substitutions for each document. Coffins were occasionally reused with incomplete substitution of names, which seems to indicate that some individuals were more interested in the convenience or attractiveness of a second-hand coffin than in personalized textual content.

Manuscripts of the *Book of Going Forth by Day* include not only the name of the deceased with the title of Osiris prefixed to it but also, often, his or her official title in the bureaucracy, with filiation as well. Perhaps because of individual preferences, but also to keep the books' customized appearance, they were generally written to order from beginning to end rather than produced as anonymous shelf copies with spaces left for names to be filled in later. The few drawings or paintings of the deceased in the books can hardly be considered portraits, but with the names and titles of the deceased appended, and their correct gender and proper dress for the time depicted, the purchasers would probably have been satisfied. The cost of the books probably varied considerably, based on the length and height of the scrolls and on the details of workmanship, but the proliferation of short versions, especially from the Late period, suggests that some such guide was available to almost anyone who could afford any burial expenses at all.

The *Book of Going Forth by Day* is perhaps best known for the vignettes that accompany many of its chapters. Some of these drawings, such as the judgment scene of chapter 125, are very elaborate and provide the focal point of the book even when they are not the logical heart of the work. (This vignette, without accompanying text, survives alone on a very late papyrus.) The number of vignettes is far from uniform from copy to copy. In the case of the high priest Pinedjem of the twenty-first dynasty, there is no vignette for any of the chapters following the single introductory depiction of him at the beginning of the book, while in the book of his daughter Nesitanebetisheru, almost every chapter has a rather large though sketchy drawing.

Some manuscripts seem to show that artist and scribe worked separately (even if these tasks were done by the same person), and most frequently the layout of the whole with drawings was done before the texts were added. This, of course, resulted in some dislocation of drawings, and also in the omission or abbreviation of some texts because of lack of available space. There probably were manuscripts that were carefully collated, but there were also texts that had duplications and misreadings or were otherwise garbled; presumably the latter were provided by scribes who knew that the appearance of the document was enough to satisfy a buyer who either would not or could not read it.

It is reasonably clear that some of the utterances in the Pyramid Texts contain labels that were not intended to be complete sentences or part of the text proper. Some of these may have been titles or filing entries to identify the texts, and others were there to label the deities or objects in plans or vignettes that were not depicted in these pyramid sources. It is, of course, possible that the sources (perhaps on papyri) of the Pyramid Texts had rubrics or some vignettes or both, but the Coffin Texts provide the earliest examples of real rubrics written in red; they also have the earliest vignettes, some of which continued into the *Book of Going Forth by Day*.

Today, there are editions and translations of these bodies of texts available for study, but there are problems with each of the publications of the edited versions. For the Pyramid Texts, Kurt Sethe (1908–1922) first collected the utterances from the sarcophagus and burial chamber, then worked out toward the antechamber and entrance. Since it is now clear that the texts were originally set forth to follow the funeral procession into the tomb, Sethe's numbering of the spells essentially goes backwards. The pyramid of Unas (being the earliest to have these texts) was taken as a starting point, but it had only about a third of the known texts, and the new texts found in succeeding pyramids were tacked onto the first lot with little regard to where they belonged logically. R. O. Faulkner's translation in this numerical order, though fairly literal, makes no real sense of the whole. A. Piankoff's translation of the Unas texts is closer to the proper order in proceeding from the entrance inward, but he followed the texts around each room, rather than taking the texts of opposite walls to complement each other, and his translations are in some cases a bit free.

One interesting characteristic of some of the Pyramid Texts, which also survived on some coffins, is the mutilation of most of the hieroglyphic signs representing animate objects. In some cases, these individual hieroglyphs are actually carved as two separate pieces divided by blank space, and in others, the snakes, animals, and other creatures have knives in their backs. These were two practices intended to ensure that the intact animal representations would be unable to offer any threat to the deceased person buried in proximity to them.

In editing the Coffin Texts, A. de Buck and his team had neither an established chronological order to help them, nor beginnings or endings that were consistent from one place to another, or even from one coffin to another from the same place. De Buck logically started with one fairly long sequence of spells that occurred on a comparatively large number of manuscripts. He followed this with succeeding sequences that had the best representation, until eventually he had picked up all the loose ends. Exceptions to this method were the texts on papyri included with the corpus, which were quite logically taken in order, and also the *Book of the Ways of Rosetan* (modernly known as the *Book of Two Ways*), which was recognized as a complete unit regardless of where it occurred on the coffins, though it was generally on the inside bottoms of the coffins from Bersheh. These two lots were numbered and included at the end of the whole collection, though clearly the latter at least should not have been relegated to this position, and a few spells that belonged with this group had earlier been mistakenly edited separately. Again, a reading or translation of these Coffin Text spells in numerical order has no relation to the arrangement or order of the spells on any manuscript from any of the many places where they were found. Admittedly, it is no easy task to establish an order to these spells: they occur on all six inner faces of the coffins, and in some cases they can be shown to proceed from one side to its opposite parallel wall, and in other cases from one to another contingent sides, while the tops and bottoms generally seem independent.

Among the most difficult problems to resolve in dealing with the Coffin Texts is to establish the precise chronological order of the actual manuscripts, which would probably help in producing stemmata of the texts themselves which would help us better understand the differences among them. Although much development could have taken place in papyrus versions before the texts reached what are essentially definitive versions on the coffins, until the stemmata are worked out, any changes, major or minor, can be seen as going in either direction. Of special interest in the Coffin Texts is the diversity of the texts and their layout in documents from different places, especially since they were found at so many sites throughout Egypt. The coffins from Bersheh have been studied most, but the large number from Meir, and the huge size of the coffins from Siut, make these two sites particularly attractive for further research.

It would seem that the *Book of Going Forth by Day* would have been the easiest of these collections to edit properly; however, the very early publication of one Late period papyrus established an order for the chapters that was not relevant at all to earlier manuscripts. When E. Naville published a number of parallel versions of the much earlier eighteenth dynasty manuscripts, his desire was to establish the best early text of each chapter, but when he numbered them following Richard Lepsius's publication of the Turin Papyrus, he succeeded in destroying the logical arrangement of all the early documents. When newly discovered chapters are merely tacked onto the end of a growing collection, it is clear that translations

of the chapters in numerical order keep getting further from any logical order; indeed, modern translators are in no agreement on where to end the *Book of Going Forth by Day*.

Division of the texts into units of varying size was indicated in the original manuscripts in several ways. The vertical columns of hieroglyphs that are the Pyramid Texts generally have horizontal line breaks with small squares atop and to one side of these dividing lines to turn them into "houses" (*ḥwt*) and thus to indicate textual units, which in this collection are usually termed "utterances." For the Coffin Texts written in cursive hieroglyphs without lines to divide the vertical columns, the unit (known as a "spell") could be indicated either by a bent arm in red or black, or by single or double horizontal strokes. These are often accompanied by rubrics (headings in red) which can either name a spell at its conclusion or otherwise introduce a spell in some form at its beginning. In the *Book of Going Forth by Day*, the units are likewise spells, though commonly termed "chapters" by Egyptologists and these are regularly headed by their assigned rubrics.

Of the three major collections of funerary literature, it is generally clear that these were not separate books in the Egyptian sense, though each could contain books or portions thereof. Many would say that the modern names given to these collections of funerary literature are inaccurate and should be discarded in favor of the ancient names, which survive at least in some cases. The old designation the *Book of the Dead* derives from a label in Arabic that refers to the fact that the books were commonly found with mummies. "The Beginning of the Spells for Going Forth by Day" is the way this "book" starts chapter 1 (and also chapter 17), and even though it is not clear that this describes all the spells rather than merely those at the beginning of the book, it is clear that the ancient Egyptians thought that it applied to the bulk of the work. Because chapter 163 is preceded by "Spells taken from another papyrus as additions to Going Forth by Day," it is fairly clear that in the Late period the original book of that name included the spells through chapter 161. Chapter 162 regularly follows 165 and should be considered part of that added group. It is also clear, then, that this ancient name should not properly be applied to the present entire corpus of 192 chapters.

With respect to the numbering of chapters, it can only be said that any total can be quite misleading. Many chapters have variants that are labeled "A," "B," and so on, but sometimes the variants were actually additional, newly discovered chapters given the number of the preceding identifiable chapter (e.g., chapter 41B). Sometimes the same chapter was given two different numbers, as in the case of 52B and 189; but totally different chapters can have the same numbers as well. The whole series of

W. Pleyte's chapters 166–174 have no relationship to the standard chapters with those numbers. It is also clear that many of these supposed additions actually had the titles of other works. Similarly, the rubric title of Spell I, found on perhaps three coffins of the entire Coffin Texts corpus, labels this as the "beginning of the Book of justifying a man in the necropolis." If this were indeed the title for the bulk of the texts, it is strange that no form of "judgment scene" is to be found anywhere in that corpus. It can also be pointed out that there are other books in the Coffin Texts, including the *Book of the Ways of Rosetau* (otherwise known as the *Book of Two Ways*), which is both labeled as a book and has a typical colophon at its conclusion. A similar colophon is found on one coffin after Spell 467, indicating that this *Field of Ḥetep* spell or spells may also have been considered a book.

The book of the *Field of Ḥetep* is one of the more interesting units included in both the Coffin Texts (Spells 464–468) and the *Book of Going Forth by Day* (chapter 110). Ḥetep can be singular or plural and determined by either a deity or a bookroll or offerings, which means that it can refer to the god named Ḥetep, who presides over this field, or it can mean "peace" or "offerings." There are references to the field in the Pyramid Texts, and the earliest description of the place, which seems to have been located in the western sky, presents it as a place where the deceased person lives and works for the god Osiris. The field has an abundance of water and is very productive, and in the Coffin Texts it was a sort of Elysian fields, or a paradise, where the deceased can enjoy a pleasant existence in the hereafter. The spells in the Coffin Texts that deal with the *Field of Ḥetep* are essentially different versions of the same text and vignette. On some coffins from Bersheh, the plan of the field seems to mark the starting point for the whole collection of texts. The *Book of Going Forth by Day* version, which can be much more elaborate than any version of the Coffin Texts, is for some reason found preceding the judgment scene (chapter 125) in the standard order of chapters on Late period manuscripts.

Some chapters in the *Book of Going Forth by Day* had a life of their own. One example is chapter 30, the heart spell, which is carved on stone amulets placed within the mummy's thoracic cavity before wrapping. Another is chapter 6, found on countless *shawabti*s, which were mummiform statuettes intended to act for the deceased with respect to any task that he might be called on to perform in the afterlife. In the Late period, chapter 162 was used separately under the head of the mummy to provide warmth.

Chapter 17 of the *Book of Going Forth by Day* has one of that work's most unique and interesting features—glosses. The development of these glosses can be traced fairly clearly in a large number of Middle Kingdom coffins with essentially the same material (i.e., Coffin Texts, Spell 335). This particular text has a number of rubrics, with questions about the meaning of each phrase, and it includes two or three quite different interpretations as answers to each question. These glosses indicate the difficulty that the Egyptians would have had in understanding some of the mythological and theological allusions in these texts; they also show how the proponents of different temples, gods, or religions could read and understand the same words entirely differently, entirely from their own perspectives. Some answers are strictly solar and others are Osirian, and some are less clear, but all these interpretive glosses, which may originally have been marginal notations, became part of the standard text and remained with it for the next two thousand years of Egyptian history.

Clearly, the fact that the standard text had occasionally become unintelligible would have been recognized by some scribes who could have corrected it—but apparently they did not dare to change it. For the really intractable sections of the *Book of Going Forth by Day*, most modern translators have opted to translate any available earlier parallels in the Coffin Texts, which generally make much better sense; but these were, of course, not the actual words copied for so many centuries.

The *Book of That Which Is in the Underworld* (*Amduat*) is generally a New Kingdom guidebook to the beyond that takes on significance as the principal such work in the royal tombs of the eighteenth dynasty. A portion of the work was included in the *Book of Two Ways*, which is dated at least to the early Middle Kingdom and probably earlier; and its inclusion of Sokar, the funerary god of Saqqara, the necropolis at Memphis, would seem to point to an Old Kingdom origin. Novelty, antiquity, and the illustrative nature of the work may all have helped bring it to the fore. The work itself is not a unity but has at least two and probably three or more versions. Two versions appear first in Thutmose III's tomb in the Valley of the Kings: one is the well-known painting of an enlarged papyrus roll surrounding the walls of the burial chamber, and the other comprises individually named deities in more than seven hundred boxes drawn on the walls of the antechamber to the tomb. The King's "papyrus roll" version has a cosmological plan that depicts the voyage and daily rebirth of the sun, with registers, passages with doors and keepers, and Sokar's mound—all to illustrate what was to be encountered in the afterlife journey. Shorter versions of this plan on actual papyri in different sizes belonging to the elite became fairly commonplace, especially in the twenty-first dynasty, and there are also a number of what are termed the "real" *Amduat* papyri, which have long rows of standing anthropomorphic deities.

The *Book of Gates* is the principal guidebook found in nineteenth dynasty royal tombs. The emphasis is on the gates with guardian deities, whose names must be known in order to pass them. This is an elaborate representation of what was a very old tradition, dating at least to the *Book of Two Ways* in the Coffin Texts, where there are seven gates with three keepers each, which became two different lists that survived separately as chapters 144 and 147 of the *Book of Going Forth by Day*. The Ramessid versions have twelve gates corresponding to the twelve hours of the night, which are also depicted in the star-clocks on the ceilings of the burial chambers.

The *Book of Caverns* is a later Ramessid (twentieth dynasty) underworld book that shows people in holes or caves, as well as some drowning in water or bound to stakes. As if everything before had been too easy and all the worthy deceased had succeeded in attaining their goals, this guidebook seems to be trying to show that not everyone makes it. It is certainly more threatening, and perhaps it is appropriate that it appears in very elaborate tombs just before the end of pharaonic Egypt.

The *Book of the Heavenly Cow* (its earliest version coming from Tutankhamun's tomb) begins as a mythological text, which relates how the aging sun god Re, distressed by the plotting of humans against him, takes counsel with the eldest gods and sends his eye, Hathor, to diminish the number of people on earth. Hathor was enjoying her task too much, but Re had a change of heart and provided beer as a substitute for blood to bring an end to her slaughtering. This is an etiology for the feast of Hathor and the concomitant beer-drinking, the propitiation for evildoing, and the sacrifice to ward off suffering—all are involved in this part of the text. In the next episode, Nut is the cow on whose back Re goes forth to overthrow his enemies. Riding high in the sky, Re makes Nut a multitude, and stars come into being, along with the Fields of Ḥetep and Iarru ("reeds"). Re gets Shu ("air") and the Ḥeḥ gods to support the wobbly sky goddess, providing a picturesque cosmological description. The next scene brings in Geb the earth god, snakes, and the need for magic spells as protection against them. When eventually it is said that he who knows these divine words and spells will go forth and come down from the sky, it is clear that like the other funerary books, this is a guidebook for the deceased who joins Re and who must know the heavenly topography, names, spells, and so on, as magical means for "going forth by day." The book has clear ties to the Pyramid Texts, Coffin Texts, and the *Book of Going Forth by Day;* what sets it apart is its unity, its humanized deities, and its picturesque literary style. There is also the aspect of divine punishment for the evil that people do.

Stelae are generally much better sources for information on personal piety than for funerary literature, and even instructional literature such as the *Instructions for Merikare* can provide much better ethical material. The one section of the funerary literature that provides the closest thing we have to a code of ethics or morality is the so-called Negative Confession, which is really a protestation of innocence (*Book of the Dead*, 125). As part of the judgment scene, where the heart of the deceased is weighed against the Feather of the goddess Maat (truth personified), these claims of innocence are addressed to forty-two judges—the number is presumably related to the number of nomes or districts of Upper and Lower Egypt. Of the divine judges from perhaps two dozen identifiable places, however, the vast majority are from the northern half of the country, with several locations mentioned twice. In addition to Heliopolis and Memphis as sites of major importance for the creation and compilation of funerary literature, Hermopolis and Herakleopolis may also have been particularly important for several of the books found in the Coffin Texts, and also for the *Book of Going Forth by Day*, chapters such as 64 and 175. The evils that the deceased says were not done by him or her in the Negative Confession include several generalizations such as "evil" or "wrongdoing"; many evils, such as robbery, killing, lying, cheating, stealing, doing violence, reviling the king or "god," or committing adultery; some less serious crimes, such as being ill-tempered, eavesdropping, being garrulous, inspiring terror, dissembling, gossiping, being puffed up or being loud-voiced; and some we cannot clearly understand as evils, such as wading in the water or washing the god. The practicing of homosexuality was a specified evil, though nothing was said about the mistreatment of either parents or children. Certain of the evils were specifically excepted when done in self-defense.

Of course, much of what has been said about the individuality of these collections of texts and their association with different periods is based on what has survived and how this material was published. Thus, the Pyramid Texts on Middle Kingdom coffins were omitted from the Coffin Texts publications—even when in some cases these were predominant—and these and almost all other later occurrences of the Pyramid Texts still remain unpublished.

It is clear that new discoveries could considerably change our thinking about the origins and applications of the various texts. The discovery of the tomb of Tutankhamun revealed no papyri and comparatively little of a documentary nature, but the four golden shrines that were nested to encase his sarcophagus and coffins contain excerpts from a whole cross-section of the funerary literature. Texts that we identify specifically as Pyramid Texts, Coffin Texts, and *Book of Going Forth by Day*, as well as the *Book of That Which Is in the Underworld* and the *Book of the Heavenly Cow*, all occur together on these shrines.

The distinction between royal and nonroyal texts was probably not strictly maintained at any time, although it appears to us that certain texts first used for royalty later became more proletarian and that this led the priests serving the royals to seek out and, in some cases, produce new and different texts for their patrons.

All in all, ancient Egyptian funerary literature is far from being exhaustively studied. Many documents have not been published, and most have still not been studied as logical entities. Only after these basic first steps have been taken can the interrelationships of the various texts be analyzed and perhaps understood, at least a little better.

[*See also* Book of Going Forth by Day; Book of That Which Is in the Underworld; Coffin Texts; *and* Pyramid Texts]

## BIBLIOGRAPHY

Allen, T. George. *Occurrences of Pyramid Texts, with Cross Indexes of These and Other Egyptian Mortuary Texts.* Chicago, 1950.

Allen, T. George. *The Book of the Dead: or, Going Forth by Day.* Chicago, 1974. The translation.

Buck, Adriaan de. *The Egyptian Coffin Texts.* 7 vols. Oriental Institute Publications, 34, 49, 64, 67, 73, 81, and 87. Chicago, 1935–1961. This is the standard edition of the transcribed texts.

Faulkner, Raymond O. *The Ancient Egyptian Pyramid Texts.* Oxford, 1969. Translation of Sethe's edition.

Faulkner, Raymond O. *The Ancient Egyptian Coffin Texts.* 3 vols. Warminster, 1973–1978. Translation of the de Buck edition.

Faulkner, Raymond O. *The Ancient Egyptian Book of the Dead.* Rev. ed. London, 1985. The translation.

Goyon, Jean-Claude. *Rituels funéraires de l'ancienne Égypte.* Paris, 1972.

Hornung, Erik. *Das Amduat: Die Schrift des verborgenen Raumes,* Ägy, 7 and 13. Wiesbaden, 1963–1967. Text and translation of the *Book of That Which Is in the Underworld.*

Hornung, Erik, Andreas Brodbeck, and Elisabeth Staehelin. *Das Buch von den Pforten des Jenseits.* Geneva, 1979–1980.

Hornung, Erik. *Ägyptische Unterweltsbücher.* 2d ed. Zurich, 1984. Translations of New Kingdom royal funerary literature.

Hornung, Erik. *The Valley of the Kings: Horizon of Eternity,* translated from German by David Warburton. New York, 1990. Description of funerary literature in New Kingdom royal tombs.

Lesko, Leonard H. *The Ancient Egyptian Book of Two Ways.* Near Eastern Studies, 17. Berkeley, 1972. Translation and commentary on one part of the Coffin Texts.

Lesko, Leonard H. *Index of the Spells on Egyptian Middle Kingdom Coffins and Related Documents.* Berkeley, 1979. Arrangement of the spells on the individual documents, including parallels to the Pyramid Texts.

Naville, Edouard. *Das ägyptische Todtenbuch der XVIII. bisXX. Dynastie.* 3 vols. Berlin, 1886.

Niwinski, Andrzej. *Studies on the Illustrated Theban Funerary Papyri of the 11th and 10th Centuries B.C.* Orbis biblicus et orientalis, 86. Freiburg, 1989.

Piankoff, Alexander. *Le Livre des Portes.* 3 vols. Mémoires publiés par les membres de l'Institut français d'archéologie orientale du Caire, 74–75, 90. Cairo, 1939–1962. The edited text of the *Book of Gates.*

Piankoff, Alexander. *Le Livre des Querets.* Cairo, 1946. The edited text of the *Book of Caves.*

Sadek, Abdel Aziz. *Contribution à l'étude de l'Amdouat: Les variantes tardive du Livre de l'Amdouat dans les papyrus du Musée du Caire.* Freiburg and Göttingen, 1985. Deals with the short (nonroyal) examples of *Amduat.*

Sethe, Kurt, *Altägyptischen Pyramidentexte.* 4 vols. Hildesheim, 1960. (Orig., Leipzig, 1908–1922.) The standard edition of the Pyramid Texts.

LEONARD H. LESKO

**FUNERARY RITUAL.** Rituals performed by the living for the dead were one of the principal ways that the ancient Egyptians insured their immortality after death. We know of these rituals through their depiction (or partial depiction) on tomb-chapel walls, and through ritual scripts preserved in underground portions of tombs (for example, in the Pyramid Texts) or on papyrus. Other aspects of the rituals must be deduced from administrative accounts and from references in nonmortuary texts or from the architecture of the spaces in which the rituals were performed and the placement of the texts that decorate those spaces.

There are two sets of funerary rituals, which overlap and are often difficult for Egyptologists to distinguish. "Funeral rituals" were performed only once, at the funeral of the deceased; these rituals included any ceremonies connected with the process of embalming and interment and any other rituals that required access to the sealed part of the tomb. They probably also included the processional journeys with the mummy (or a statue substitute) and various farewell gestures by the family of the deceased. The second type of rituals were performed after the funeral, either by cult functionaries maintained by a perpetual mortuary endowment or by family members or others visiting the deceased at the tomb-chapel. Ideally, many of these "mortuary cult rituals" would have been performed daily, as they were in the mortuary temples of dead kings of the Old Kingdom period. (In a royal context, the rituals may have been begun before the death of the king, to maintain his cult statues.) Other rituals seem to have been offered more rarely, on special occasions, such as festivals and on other regularly recurring dates, as given in the lists of festivals that were sometimes recorded in tomb-chapel decoration. The full set of mortuary cult rituals was probably performed for the first time at the funeral itself, although possibly some cult rituals were performed only on particular occasions or festivals and not at the funeral. Some dates may have required full repetitions of the cult ritual, while other performances may have been perfunctory. Such variations in performance are impossible to demonstrate.

It is also often difficult to determine which of the rituals depicted in funerals were repeated as part of the mortuary cult. Moreover, the types of rituals used under various circumstances probably changed with time. One funerary ritual that is particularly well attested, the Opening of the Mouth ceremony, seems constantly to have been augmented by reinterpretations and borrowings from other realms of ritual; probably, the developmental evolution of other, less well-attested, rituals was similarly complex. Our limited sources have left us with a set of rituals that is undoubtedly incomplete. Some rituals may have had a secret or particularly sacred character that prohibited their representation, whereas others may have been omitted from tomb-chapel depictions for other reasons.

In most periods, a distinction must be drawn between the rituals performed for kings and those performed for other Egyptians. The general pattern seems to be that rituals appeared first in a royal context, were then adopted by the elite, and eventually by the rest of the population. This "democratization of the afterlife," though well attested archaeologically, may not reflect actual practice; the general population possibly performed rituals that decorum forbade them to record. Given that the king and his people shared a system of beliefs about the afterlife (however those beliefs varied from period to period), the rituals performed for the king probably shared many fundamental elements with the less elaborate rituals performed for his subjects.

**Old Kingdom.** The most fundamental mortuary cult ritual is the earliest attested; this is the *ḥtp di nswt* offering formula, which begins "an offering that the king gives." (The formula is not limited to nonroyal contexts, since the king it mentions is presumably the living king, who may be asked to make offerings to his royal predecessors.) The earliest examples, from the fourth dynasty at Meidum, do not mention the king, but only the mortuary god Anubis (*ḥtp dj Jnpw*); however, the king appears very soon thereafter, although he is often joined in his gift by various gods (normally Anubis and, after the middle of the fifth dynasty, Osiris). The gifts are not limited to food offerings but extend to a good burial and admission to the realm of the spirits. The formula recorded on tomb walls often includes a list of festivals at which the offerings are to be provided. An example of such an offering formula would be that of Ankhhaf (see *British Museum Hieroglyphic Texts I²*, London, 1961, pl. 15), which reads, *ḥtp dj nswt ḥtp dj Jnpw ḫnt t3 ḏsr qrst.f m smyt jmntt prt-ḫrw n.f t ḥnqt k3w 3pdw m wp rnpt, ḏḥwtj, tp rnpt, w3g m ḥb nb rꜤ nb, n rḫ nswt zš pr-ḥḏ Ꜥnḫ ḫ3.f*, and which translates, "An offering that the king gives and an offering that Anubis, foremost of the sacred land, gives: his burial in the Western Desert and invocation offerings of bread, beer, cattle, and fowl, on the opening of the year feast, the feast of Thoth, the first of the year feast, the *wag* feast and on every festival and every day, to the king's acquaintance and scribe of the treasury Ankhhaf." This formula seems to

imply that only the king and the gods can give offerings to the dead, and that the wish that they do so is likely to benefit the deceased person for whom it is made.

The recitation of the offering formula is illustrated in tombs by a man standing with his right arm outstretched. In Old Kingdom scenes depicting the entire offering ritual, he is often accompanied by men who are offering poured water, burning incense, kneeling at an offering table, and reading the ritual from a scroll. Men reciting the formula are occasionally identified as lector-priests (*ḫrjw-ḥb*), and the men reading from the scroll are invariably so identified. Three men are shown kneeling, beating their breasts with clenched fists; the fourth dynasty representations clearly show the arms in motion, while later renderings are more static, showing the men with one fist held against the chest and another raised behind the head, with the arm bent at a right angle. These men are usually identified as embalmers (*wtw*) but may also be called lector-priests. Several of these actions may be captioned *s3ḫt* ("causing to be a spirit"), which indicates that these rituals were responsible for transforming the dead person into an *akh* (*3ḫ*), a glorified, ghostlike spirit. Another part of the ritual, not depicted but often mentioned in the caption, is the "breaking of the red jars," presumably to keep away bad influences. At the end of the ritual, a man is often depicted walking away from the cult place, dragging a broom behind him (although the caption says he is "bringing the leg"). This action removed any footprints or other traces of the ritual activity and left the offering place pristine and ready for the next repetition of the ritual. The sixth dynasty tomb-chapel of Qar shows two additional parts of the ritual, as illustrated in William Kelly Simpson's *Mastabas of Qar and Idu* (Boston, 1976, plate 25). First, a priest with little fingers outstretched in front of him is followed by a man carrying three jars on a little table. The caption tells us that he is anointing with oil, but it is unclear what is being anointed. Another man brings two strips of cloth, labelled *wnḫw*.

A fuller complement of mortuary rituals from the Old Kingdom period is the corpus of Pyramid Texts, which are first attested in the pyramid of Unas at the end of the fifth dynasty. While many of the rituals recorded there may have been considerably older, the many spells incorporating the deities Osiris and Isis had, presumably, been recently composed or adapted from older texts, since Osiris is first attested only a few decades before the reign of Unas. (Indeed, it was probably his growing ascendance and the consequent increased emphasis on the underground parts of the tomb that led to the recording of the texts on the walls of the burial chambers.) The Pyramid Texts seem to consist of both magical spells to be used by the deceased and two rituals that were probably performed at the funeral. The spells include those for the protection of the deceased and those for the transportation of the king to the realm of the gods and his rebirth in the afterlife; they are recorded in the third person, but they seem to have been adapted from spells written in the first person. The king is identified throughout as the god Osiris, and the speaker acts as his son Horus. There are two rituals carved on the walls of the burial chamber that address the king in the second person, thereby suggesting that they were performed before his mummy or a statue surrogate. The sequence on the northern wall is an offering ritual that presents the king with offerings, after first magically enabling him to partake of them by means of the Opening of the Mouth ceremony. Each ritual act (including the Opening of the Mouth sequence) was accompanied by an offering, usually of food but sometimes of ritual equipment. The southern wall shows a ritual for bringing about the dead king's resurrection.

The offering ritual, at least, was also performed as part of the mortuary cult. The offerings that accompany the addresses to the king are identical with the compartmental offering list, which dates back to the fourth dynasty, although the Opening of the Mouth sequence was omitted until the reign of Sahure. The shorter versions of such compartmental offering lists (Barta's [1963] Type A list) also found in nonroyal tombs of the Old Kingdom, suggesting that a version of the same ritual was performed in nonroyal cults. The administrative papyri found at the mortuary temple of King Neferirkare at Abusir also list the nonperishable equipment for the offering ritual in monthly inventories, including notations of damage and wear, which demonstrate that the equipment was in regular use. Such equipment also occurs archeologically, in both royal and private contexts.

At about the same time that the Pyramid Texts began to appear in royal tombs, nonroyal tombs began to depict aspects of the funeral more extensively. These scenes usually begin with one of mourning at the home of the deceased (men and women mourned separately). The coffin is then carried to a special funerary boat, called the *wrt*-boat, which was towed by an ordinary boat. Throughout these travels, the coffin was accompanied by two women called *ḏrt* (one of whom was probably the wife of the deceased), as well as the embalmer (who sometimes clapped sticks together as he walked) and the lector-priest. The boat was towed to a riverside building, with two entrances, where offerings are depicted. This building is in some sources called *tp-jbw*, which has been translated "purification tent." It may be here that the mummification of the body took place. Afterward, the coffin was carried to the desert in the hands of the mourners, with supporting poles held by formally dressed pallbearers. In some cases, this scene includes a row of vaulted shrines and palm trees that are usually associated with the Nile Delta

city of Buto. The goal of this procession was the shrinelike building called the *wʿbt*, where an offering ritual was performed. *Mww*-dancers perform outside the enclosure, often wearing tall openwork headdresses; and the wife, lector-priest, and embalmer make offerings on the altar of the *wʿbt*, often slaughtering bulls and oryxes for the occasion. Some scenes label this building not *wʿbt* but *z3w*, identifying it (symbolically) with a shrine in another Delta city, Sais. The *wʿbt* is usually the last element in these scenes. The funeral presumably moved on to the tomb after the completion of the rituals (if indeed the *wʿbt* is not itself the tomb). Scenes of the rituals at the tomb (not usually attached to the preceding processions) suggest that the last stages of the ritual took place on the roof of the *mastaba*, before the body and the *serdab* statues were lowered into the burial shaft and the *serdab* chambers.

**Middle Kingdom.** Middle Kingdom funerary texts offer fewer clues to the nature of funeral and mortuary cult rituals than do those of the previous period. The Coffin Texts consist largely of a greatly expanded number of the transportation spells of the Pyramid Texts; neither the incantations nor the ritual texts were recorded. The compartmental offering list, derived from the offering ritual, continues to appear, including the implements used in the Opening of the Mouth ceremony. In at least one Middle Kingdom tomb, the offerings were accompanied by depictions of the men who were offering them. The *Book of Two Ways*, found on coffins from Bersheh, depicts the journey to the underworld by the deceased—a journey that may have been acted out in the course of the funeral.

Although it may have taken place earlier, it has been suggested that there was a major change in the offering formula (*ḥtp dj nswt*) during this period. Whereas previously the king and various gods were jointly desired to give offerings to the deceased, the Middle Kingdom version suggests that the king was asked to make an offering to the gods, so that they might in turn supply offerings to the deceased.

The funeral itself was less often depicted in the Middle Kingdom than it was in late Old Kingdom tombs; however, the scenes resemble those known from the Old Kingdom, with the addition of some new elements, such as the figure known as the *tekenu* (*tknw*). In the Middle Kingdom, the *tekenu* appears to be a crouching figure with its limbs and torso wrapped in a striped material, which may represent an animal skin, but its head is left free. Later, in the New Kingdom, the head is sometimes also wrapped, resulting in a pear-shaped bundle; at other times, an arm as well as the head is free, or it is simply a nude human figure. All these depictions presumably represent the same thing: a human figure wrapped in a skin. In later depictions of the period, the *tekenu* can be attended by a priest of the scorpion goddess Serket, and this, together with other textual indications, seems to connect the *tekenu* with the Delta region. Its function in the funerary ritual is unknown, but it has often been suggested that it functioned as a symbolic human sacrifice. Its fetal position and its proximity in some scenes to the basin of the birth goddess Heket has also led some to suggest a connection with birth and rebirth.

The coffin was also carried differently in Middle Kingdom depictions. Rather than traveling at waist height, held on carrying poles, it was dragged on a sledge by oxen and men or, in one case, placed on a wagon. Another addition to the Middle Kingdom offering scenes is the reproduction of some of the ritual speeches spoken by the participants in the funeral. A textual account of a Middle Kingdom private funeral is to be found in the *Story of Sinhue.* It mentions an ox-drawn procession accompanied by musicians, and *mww* dancers at the door of the tomb. An offering ritual is read aloud, and then animals are sacrificed. Although brief, the text agrees with the depictions.

Royal funerary ritual during the Middle Kingdom period is less well attested than private funerals. Nevertheless, the tortuous routes of many of the pyramid entrances of the period have been connected with the complicated maps of the underworld found in nonroyal Coffin Texts; passing through the barriers may have been part of the rites. Overall, royal ritual was probably not unlike the private rituals, particularly since private individuals became identified with Osiris in the Middle Kingdom in the same way that kings and queens had been in the late Old Kingdom.

**New Kingdom.** Funerals and mortuary cult rituals of the New Kingdom are often depicted in the wall scenes of painted tombs, both in Memphis and Thebes. Episodes from the funeral are also sometimes depicted on anthropoid (human-shaped) coffins, particularly in the early New Kingdom and the Third Intermediate period. In addition, there is a new, more extensive depiction of the Opening of the Mouth ceremony, which is sometimes used in tomb-chapel decoration.

In this later period, the funeral seems to have become more elaborate, or perhaps it was just more fully represented. The order of the elements of the funeral is uncertain and may have varied. The departure of the coffin from the house and its journey across the river to the cemetery and the place of mummification were presumably among the earlier parts of the ceremony. The coffin was placed on a canopied sledge, often pulled by both oxen and male mourners; it was accompanied by a group of priests, including a *stm*-priest, wearing a leopard skin, and the *jmj-ḫnt* priest, wearing a short white robe that resembled the royal *sed*-festival (Jubilee) garment. Two women were often part of the procession. Interestingly, scenes do not include depictions of the bringing of the food and sacrificial animals that must have been part of the actual procession.

The wall scenes of the procession include the four canopic jars that held the four internal organs removed from the body (lungs, liver, stomach, and intestines). The jars were generally shown placed in a small shrine that was dragged on a sledge some distance behind the coffin; some of the men who accompanied this sledge are depicted carrying papyrus stalks. Also dragged on a sledge was the *tekenu* figure. The final (though not necessarily the last) elements of the procession were the women who wept and wailed in mourning and the men who carried the furniture and other grave goods of the deceased. The furniture-bearers were sometimes preceded by four men, each carrying a small statue (two of the statues were mummiform and wore the red crown).

After leaving the house of the deceased, the procession went aboard a special boat, which was towed by another boat or by people on a riverside towpath. The boat carried the procession to the *sḥ nṯr Jnpw*, the divine booth of Anubis—probably to be equated with the purification tent of earlier representations. Since Anubis was the god responsible for overseeing mummification, it was probably there that the body was embalmed. Afterward, the procession continued to the *j'bt wsḫt*, the broad hall of purification, which can probably be equated with the *w'bt* of the Old Kingdom. Unlike the procession to the *w'bt*, however, the procession to the *j'bt wsḫt* seems to have traveled by boat. The rituals performed there were less clearly shown than those in Old Kingdom scenes, and the building no longer seems connected with the city of Sais, which was accorded its own separate ritual. While the Old Kingdom ritual had hinted at associations with both Buto and Sais, the New Kingdom depictions included explicit ritual visits to those Delta cities, as well as to Heliopolis and the Upper Egyptian city of Abydos. Such pilgrimages may in actuality have been carried out separately, before death or afterward, using statues as substitutes for the mummy; or they may have been made symbolically to places that had been designated to represent those cities. (In the case of kings, such voyages may actually have been made, to demonstrate the death of the king and legitimize his successor's assumption of the kingship.) The voyage to the site designated as Sais was made on a boat. There, oxen joined the procession to pull the coffin on its sledge and to be sacrificed. The procession continued by land to the place designated Buto, probably within the cemetery. The coffin was either dragged on a sledge or, in the later New Kingdom, placed in a model boat and carried on the shoulders of the bearers. At the Buto site, they were received by *mww*-dancers who were only rarely depicted wearing the tall headdresses of earlier periods. The visit to Heliopolis took place by boat, and it may represent a real pilgrimage, one undertaken separately and merely added to the funeral scenes. The pilgrimage to Abydos was also undertaken separately, perhaps by a statue of the deceased. (Neither of these voyages is attested in the Old Kingdom.)

On arriving at the tomb, the mummy (or perhaps the anthropoid coffin) was removed from its box coffin and set upright to receive the blessings of the ritual. Ritual actions shown here include censing, libations, and selected episodes from the Opening of the Mouth. (The fuller sequence of the Opening of the Mouth ceremony is usually depicted separately from the funeral scenes, but it may have been carried out at this time.) Women belonging to the family of the deceased are often shown weeping and embracing the coffin during these ceremonies. Other rituals followed. These included the pulling of the (empty) sarcophagus back and forth by a *ka*-priest, who pulled it to the north, and the embalmer, who pulled it to the south. The *tekenu* on its sledge was also pulled back and forth, accompanied by some enigmatic ritual statements by the *s3-Srḳt* priest or the *jmj-ḥnt* priest. The mummy, sarcophagus, *tekenu*, and canopic chest (which held the four canopic jars) were then presented with offerings, including the sacrificed animals. The sarcophagus, mummy, and canopic chest were then probably introduced into the tomb, along with the funerary furniture. The ceremony closed with protective ritual recitations. At the same time, in other parts of the necropolis, animals were sacrificed to ensure the safety of the deceased—sacrifices that involved the mysterious *tekenu*.

Although during the New Kingdom, private funerals and mortuary cult rituals were comparatively well documented, there is very little evidence for these rituals in the royal context. The tomb of Tutankhamun contains a rare depiction of the king's funeral cortège on the eastern wall of the burial chamber. There, the king's coffin lies on a bier, covered by an open canopy decorated with garlands, banners, and royal *uraeus* snakes; the whole rests on a boat dragged on a sledge pulled by twelve men, including two shaven-headed priests. The caption tells us that the priests are chanting "Nebkheperure, come in peace! O god, may the earth protect (him)!" Adjacent to this, on the northern wall of the chamber, Tutankhamun's successor, King Ay, is shown with an adze, performing the Opening of the Mouth ceremony. These scenes, which are almost identical to those found in private tombs, suggest that Tutankhamun's funeral was not too unlike those of his wealthier subjects.

Royal mortuary cult rituals may have differed more significantly from those in the private realm. They were carried out far from the royal tombs in the Valley of the Kings, in temples built for the purpose. In such temples, the principal shrine belonged to the god Amun, while Re was worshiped in an open courtyard to the north and the king shared a cult place to the south with his ancestors. This southern shrine contained a traditional false door to serve as a cult place, but the overall architecture and decoration of the temples suggest that the rituals were less mortuary and more divine.

**Late Period.** The depiction of the funeral became rare in the Late period, although decorated tombs such as that of Petosiris at Tuna el-Gebel still contain such scenes. They differ from the New Kingdom examples only in that they often incorporated motifs from earlier periods, combining them with the later. It is not certain whether these scenes reflect the actual practices of the period or are just copied from older prototypes.

One part of the funerary ritual that was not attested in the earlier periods is the embalming ritual. Two texts of this ritual have survived, both dating from the first or early second century CE. The ritual contains both practical and religious instructions for mummification. It begins with the perfuming of the head and the body, with spells referring to the divine scent of the gods and the body's receipt of ten sacred oils. The canopic organs are removed, and again the ten oils are mentioned. The body is again anointed and partially wrapped, while spells mention the unguents and the amulets that are placed on it. While the nails of the hands and feet are gilded, spells are recited to ensure the freedom of action of the hands and feet. After a last anointing, the wrapping of the head is begun. Accompanying spells guarantee the functioning of the eyes, mouth, ears, and nose, as the oil from the anointing soaks into them. The final anointing of the head accompanies spells to ensure that the deceased will appear triumphant in the netherworld and will not be deprived of his head. The hands are then wrapped, with spells protecting the entire mummy of the deceased and assuring that the deities Isis and Nephthys are mourning and helping him. Finally, the legs and feet are anointed, perfumed, and wrapped, while spells are recited rendering them effective and allowing the deceased to walk. Concluding spells ensure the resurrection and rejuvenation of the deceased.

[*See also* Burial Practices; Coffin Texts; Funerary Literature; Mummification; Offerings: Offering Formulae and Lists; Opening of the Mouth; *and* Pyramid Texts.]

## BIBLIOGRAPHY

Altenmüller, Hartwig. *Die Texte zum Begräbnisritual in den Pyramiden des Alten Reiches.* Ägyptologische Abhandlungen, 24. Wiesbaden, 1972. An attempt to reconstruct the rituals of the royal funeral, based on the Pyramid Texts of the Old Kingdom.

Altenmüller, Hartwig. "Bestattungsritual." In *Lexikon der Ägyptologie,* 1: 745–765. Wiesbaden, 1975.

Barta, Winfrid. *Aufbau und Bedeutung der altägyptischen Opferformel.* Münchener Ägyptologische Studien, 3. Munich, 1963. A discussion of the contents and evolution of the compartmental offering list or "menu," focusing principally on the Old Kingdom.

D'Auria, S., et al. *Mummies and Magic: The Funerary Arts of Ancient Egypt*. Boston, 1987. The introductory essays, particularly those of H. te Velde, J. Allen, and A. M. Roth, deal with funerary beliefs and rituals.

Lapp, Günther. *Die Opferformel des Alten Reiches*. Mainz, 1986. A study of the offering formula (*ḥtp di-nswt*) and its variants during the Old Kingdom period.

Leprohon, Ronald. "The Offering Formula in the First Intermediate Period." *Journal of Egyptian Archaeology* 76 (1990), 163–164.

Settgast, Jürgen. *Untersuchung zu altägyptischen Bestättungsdarstellungen*. Glückstadt, 1963. A study of the depictions of funerals in nonroyal tombs.

Wilson, John A. "Funeral Services in the Egyptian Old Kingdom." *Journal of Near Eastern Studies* 3 (1944), 201–218. A survey of several of the Old Kingdom depictions of the funeral.

ANN MACY ROTH

**FURNITURE.** By the New Kingdom, the quality of Egyptian "furniture" (*ḥtwt*) was renowned throughout the ancient world. It was often sent as tribute to the rulers of neighboring countries. Its origins can be found in the early Predynastic period. Then, poorly constructed furniture was made from roughly cut branches that were simply lashed together with rope; the timber was cut and formed with stone and flint tools. Flint knives have been found from that period with serrated teeth along their cutting edge, which enabled the woodworker to use them like a simple saw. Since the blade was quite thick, however, it was difficult to saw through thick wooden elements. Indigenous woods often provided Predynastic woodworkers with timber of inferior quality, which produced only short lengths of small cross-sectional area. The working of timber into furniture during the early Predynastic period was, therefore, an arduous process. Although the quality of the finished artifact may appear to be primitive, those few pieces discovered exhibit a great deal of functionality combined with simple elegance.

**Types of Furniture.** The small amount of furniture made during both the late Predynastic and Early Dynastic periods—mainly bed frames and some stools—appear to have been designed to be taken into the tomb after serving the individual during life. This pattern continues and even increases throughout the dynastic period, since large amounts of surviving furniture have been protected from destruction by the Egyptians' overwhelming need to furnish their tombs for the afterlife. The quality of furniture steadily increased throughout the Middle Kingdom and into the New Kingdom, when many eighteenth dynasty tombs were elaborately furnished with chairs, stools of various types, bed frames, and chests. The furniture placed in tombs was a mix of specifically designed funerary furniture, often of lesser quality than the better household items that were modified for the tomb on the death of the individual. Modifications included the painting of religious text or the carving of inscriptions on the furniture.

Some of the earliest known furniture has been found at Abydos, Saqqara, and Tarkhan, preserved in the tombs of the kings of the Early Dynastic period and those of their nobles and officials. In the early 1900s, at Tarkhan, W. M. Flinders Petrie discovered a significant collection of early bed frames, which have legs finely carved in bovine form. This indicates the strong influence that royalty had in the lives of the people, for the king was associated with the bull from as early as the first dynasty. The introduction of copper woodworking tools by the late Predynastic period allowed carpenters to carve and cut sophisticated joints in timber elements, which had been impossible to achieve before. Bovine-shaped stool legs of beautiful proportion and striking anatomical detail were also manufactured from hippopotamus ivory. In the second dynasty royal cemetery at Helwan, a number of "ceiling" stelae have been discovered that show the stool as commonly used. It had tall bovine-shaped legs, with a seat strung of plaited rush cord wrapped around the seat rails before being woven across the frame. One important stela at Helwan, of the same period, shows a member of the royal family seated on a chair with a high back, which perhaps represents an early throne.

During the third dynasty, the design and construction of furniture progressed rapidly. Painted wall carvings in the tomb of Hesyra at Saqqara show a typical collection of furniture that would have been used in the households of high-ranking officials. Some bed frames have bovine-shaped legs while others have legs made from bent timber elements. They are designed to slope toward the foot of the bed, where a vertical frame was placed to prevent the bedding from slipping to the floor. Some stools and chairs are also seen having bovine-shaped legs, while others with straight legs have curved braces below the seat. The paintings show that Hesyra also possessed a number of elegant boxes, which have their panels decorated with *djed* and *tyet* signs. The application of hieroglyphs to furniture continued throughout dynastic times; they were found, for example, on a number of boxes in the tomb of Tutankhamun.

From the Old Kingdom, the importing of timber for structural work and boat building created opportunities for carpenters and cabinetmakers. In the fourth dynasty tomb of Queen Hetepheres I at Giza, George Reisner found the remains of an important collection of gold-covered wooden furniture. It took many years to restore this furniture (which can now be seen in the Egyptian Museum, Cairo; copies are in the Museum of Fine Arts, Boston). That furniture provides us with a rare glimpse of

pattern border and the cartouches of her husband and his Horus-name, as well as other religious symbols.

Within the canopy two armchairs were placed and a bed frame, on which there was a headrest. Egyptians did not use pillows, which would have been uncomfortable during the hot sultry nights; instead they used a wooden rest to cradle the head. Examples have been discovered with padded head supports; those used by the royal family were covered in gold foil. One of Queen Hetepheres' armchairs was reconstructed, since enough gold foil had survived to establish its construction. It has lion-shaped legs, while the back and seat frame—on which would have been placed a linen cushion stuffed with goose feathers— were each fitted with plain wooden panels. Within each of the spaces created by the armrests was fastened a carved decorative spray, of three tied papyrus flowers, the heraldic plant of Lower Egypt. From the time of Queen Hetepheres until the end of the New Kingdom, royal furniture continued to display a quality of craftsmanship that was rarely surpassed in any part of the ancient world.

During the Middle Kingdom plain utilitarian furniture was introduced. At the necropolis of Beni Hasan, a number of simple stools have been discovered, with tapered legs, and some tables that have tops edged with a *cavetto* cornice and torus moulding—a design that was continued into the New Kingdom. First seen on the roof of the *heb-sed* pavilion within the step pyramid complex at Saqqara, this architectural feature was quickly incorporated into both box and table design. Stools represent the largest surviving corpus of furnishings and were popularly used in the home by both children and house guests. Animal-leg stools were featured. The bull-legged type was used during the second and third dynasties, but by the Middle Kingdom a number of gazelle-legged and lion-legged stools are known. The lion design continued to be popular, as it is found throughout dynastic times. By the Middle Kingdom, folding stools were also made for ease of storage and transportation; they had two rectangular interlocking frames pinned together with bronze rivets. Examples from the New Kingdom have the ends of their cross spindles finished with ivory-inlaid goose heads, whose bills act as the joint with the floor rail. Lattice stools were made from a framework of thin rails strengthened by angled braces; they have a double cove seat, made from either curved slats of timber or from cord, on which would have been placed a thick cushion. Three legged stools were popular with the artisan class, as can be seen in the wall paintings of many New Kingdom tombs at Thebes. Their design allowed for firm resting on an uneven workshop floor. They were designed with a dished seat, under which the three legs were jointed at an angle.

As early as the seventeenth dynasty, round-legged stools were used. They were illustrated in a number of

FURNITURE. *Depiction of second dynasty stool with bovine shaped legs, from the stela of Nefer-mer-ka at Helwan.* (After Saad, *Ceiling Stela in Second Dynasty Tombs,* Cairo, 1957, fig. 9)

the range and quality used by the royal family at the time that both the Saqqara and Giza pyramids were being built. An equally remarkable collection of furniture was shown in the wall reliefs of the Giza tomb of Queen Meresankh III. Elaborate portable canopies were used by both queens, under which their furniture was placed. (Interestingly, the wall poles of a bed canopy are shown in the earlier paintings in Hesyra's tomb.) Around these canopies, curtains and netting were supported on small hooks fixed to the underside of the roof beams, providing privacy and protection from insects and the chill of the desert night air. Each of the wooden entrance jambs of Queen Hetepheres I's bed canopy is carved with inscriptions that bear the name of her husband, Sneferu, with his titles. The entire canopy has been covered with gold sheet, burnished onto the wooden elements. Where the canopy would have been damaged by the wear of its repeated assembly and dismantling, protective copper sheaths were placed over all the vulnerable joints. The curtains and netting were stored in a long gilt box inlaid with a faience feather-

important eighteenth dynasty Theban tombs. On close examination, they may be classified into two distinct types. First, those legs which have been rounded entirely by hand; they have a spike, which protrudes from the top and was used to support the leg as its profile was cut. The spike was then used to join the leg to the underside of the seat frame. In profile, these legs are clearly not symmetrical, and the lines decorating them are uneven. The second leg type, of similar age, are regular in profile and have a pivot hole below the foot, which indicates that at some stage during their manufacture they were supported on a fixed center. That mark could also indicate that the leg was turned, although the first illustration of a turning lathe is not seen until Ptolemaic times, in the tomb of Petosiris at Tuna el-Gebel.

**Materials.** Until the Old Kingdom, Egyptian carpenters relied on native woods, such as the Nile acacia (*šndt*), sycomore fig (*nh*), and tamarisk (*isr*). Although much of that wood was of poor quality, it was still being used in New Kingdom times. Since indigenous timber was scarce, the need for conservation created associations with a number of deities. The goddess Hathor was connected with the "Lady of the Sycomore," as were the goddesses Isis and Nut. With the importation of timber, which is recorded as early as the fourth dynasty in the Palermo Stone, a notable change occurred in the size and quality of the furniture manufactured. The Palermo Stone also records that during the reign of Sneferu, shipping routes had been opened to the Syrian coast, where coniferous trees such as cedar (*r'š*) were felled and brought back to Egypt. Hardwoods were imported from the regions south of Egypt. During the New Kingdom reign of Hatshepsut, scenes were painted in her mortuary temple at Deir el-Bahri that show Egyptians venturing into the southern land of Punt, where they and Puntites are seen felling small African ebony (*hbny*) trees, which were then shipped to Egypt.

At Saqqara, within a passage in the third dynasty Step Pyramid a broken coffin was found made of a "plywood" construction; alternating layers of wood were at right angles to one another and then pegged together. The surface of this coffin was carved with a corrugated pattern before being covered with gold sheet. The fifth dynasty tomb of Ti at Saqqara has wall reliefs that show carpenters making furniture with adzes, saws, chisels, and a bowdrill. Two carpenters are shown smoothing the lid of a box with sandstone rubbers; they sand in the conventional way, along the grain, so as not to scuff or damage the wood. In the Middle Kingdom tomb of Meketra, a model of a carpenters' workshop (*whryt*) was discovered. Carpenters are seen squatting in the shade of the high workshop walls; they appear to be repeating the same practical task, as if part of a team making batch-produced furniture. There is a striking difference between the

Middle Kingdom woodworker and the multiskilled New Kingdom carpenter, who sat on a three-legged stool and worked at a bench made from a log that was altered to help hold the timber on which he worked. He used a wide range of tools, including a try square, a straight edge, a cubit rod, and a miter-cutting aid. Illustrations show that jobbing carpenters stored their tools in a basket similar in design to a modern carpenter's holdall tray.

Furniture workshops were always engaged in making primary funerary materials, such as coffins and canopic boxes. Coffins manufactured during the Predynastic period were crudely made from irregularly shaped cleaved boards, in which the body was placed in a flexed position. The introduction of copper woodworking tools made it possible to construct coffins from sawn boards, as seen at Tarkhan; however, the saws were short, so it was difficult to convert the timber, as indicated by saw lines that cut across the face of the boards at many angles. The use of foreign timbers and the introduction of the bronze pull-saw allowed Middle Kingdom carpenters to construct very large rectangular coffins made from accurately sawn boards having mitered joints. The feather-painted *rishi* anthropoid coffin case of the New Kingdom was designed either to lie prone or to stand upright for the religious ceremonies involved in interment; accurately made from a patchwork of wood, they were often beautifully embellished.

**Joinery.** Once felled, timber had to be transported to woodworking centers, where it was converted and seasoned before it could be formed into furniture. The physical properties of the various woods were thoroughly understood, and Egyptian carpenters developed a number of furniture joints which are still commonly used. The butt joint was the earliest method encountered for fastening the cleaved wooden planks of Predynastic coffins. A simple miter joint was used to connect the corner of an early burial frame. The lap or rebated butt joint was discovered on two trays in a first dynasty tomb at Saqqara (the rebated butt requires the removal of only a small piece of wood from one element of the joint). Early Dynastic period bed frames were mortised and tenoned together; the Egyptians realized that the strongest joint had a tenon one third the thickness of the rail it would penetrate. At Tarkhan, the mortises and tenons have curved or scribed shoulders molded against the opposing rail. Since the Egyptians did not use glue until the fifth dynasty, they relied on mechanical methods of joining timber. Early Dynastic bed frames were held with leather thongs that passed through holes in the top of the leg before being bound around the adjoining pole. The thongs would have been soaked in water, so that as they dried they shrank and pulled the assembly together. Through mortise-and-tenon joints, they were secured by wedges driven between the mortise and the cheek of the tenon. The stub mortise-

FURNITURE. *Eighteenth dynasty box from the tomb of Tutankhamun.* It is now in the Egyptian Museum, Cairo. (Photograph by Lorraine March-Killen)

and-tenon joint (where the mortise is stopped in the timber) could not be wedged, so pegs were inserted through the side of the joint to secure it. The fourth dynasty furniture of Queen Hetepheres I was constructed with many elaborate joints, including the first known dovetail, used to join the roof poles to the roof beams of her bed canopy. The boards used to make boxes and chests were often so narrow that they had to be edge jointed to make a panel of sufficient width to fill the frame. Several methods were used to secure such boards, including, during the earliest periods, tying the boards together with leather thongs. Later, loose tenons or edge dowels were fitted. Other joints invented by carpenters included the housing, halving, bridle, coopered, scarf, and shouldered miters.

**Finishes.** Much of the batch-produced furniture had an application of a thick plaster, made from gypsum (a hydrated form of calcium sulphate), which occurs naturally in Egypt; it was first used to disguise the quality of the timber. Maybe the coating, a white protective film, also imparted some religious significance. When paint was to be applied to a piece of furniture, gesso (*im*) was used as the foundation. Gesso was also used as the adhesive that held inlays of wood, faience, colored stone, and/or gold foil to some elaborate examples of furniture.

Tutankhamun's furniture was embellished with a number of important decorative techniques. For example, the panels of two small boxes were exquisitely applied with thousands of tiny slivers of alternating ivory and ebony, in a parquetry technique of geometrically arranged herringbone, diamond, and criss-cross patterns. Marquetry roundels, rosettes, and lily-petal shapes were used to decorate the king's furniture. Veneering was extensively used to decorate boxes; thin strips of good quality timber were applied to the plain solid carcase of boxes to give the appearance that the box was manufactured from a frame and panel construction. The seams down the edges of the legs were carefully disguised with a comb pattern of alternating pieces of wood and ivory, while the imitation panels were made from thin sheets of red-stained ivory, outlined with a stringing of ivory and ebony. One of Tutankhamun's large shrine-shaped boxes had a lid panel made from sheets of ivory, carved in low relief, and stained with scenes that show the king and his young wife; similarly carved ivory side panels are stained with scenes of scampering animals surrounded by a floral border. Tutankhamun is also seen on the sides of an elaborately painted box, leading an army against his Nubian and Syrian enemies; he stands in a chariot drawn by a pair of horses and is attended by his servants and fan-bearers. His army is arranged in three registers behind him, with charioteers in the top two rows and the foot soldiers below. The victorious pharaoh is ready to shoot

FURNITURE. *Child's chair from the antechamber of the tomb of Tutankhamun, eighteenth dynasty.* (Courtesy David P. Silverman)

another arrow, although the bodies of his enemies lie before him. The painted detail is surprisingly realistic, and Egyptian foot soldiers are examining the bodies of the fallen, brutally hacking off their heads and hands. The surface of the barrel-vaulted lid is decorated with painted scenes that show the king hunting game.

Tutankhamun's tomb also included a number of ornate chairs and a sumptuous golden throne, with legs of lion form, clad in thick gold sheet, placed on bronze drums. Blue-glass claws were carefully cut, polished, and inlaid into the lion's paws. Above the throne's front legs, attached to the corners of the seat, are a pair of gold-covered lion heads. The seat, made from a solid board, was inlaid with over one thousand square pieces of gold, calcite, and faience. Below the seat was placed a decora-

tive gilt-on-wood spray of the intertwining stems and flowers of the papyrus and Upper Egyptian lily. This feature was often used on royal furniture to symbolize the unification of the lands of Upper and Lower Egypt. Each arm panel is emblazoned with a winged *ureaus*, wearing the double crown of the Two Lands. The seat's backrest is inlaid with a scene that shows the young king lounging on a chair (in a style similar to Amarna period illustrations). He is shown being anointed by his wife, Ankhesenamun. Their bodies have been chiselled and polished from red glass and their wigs are of delicately cut blue faience. They are dressed in clothes made from silver sheet, decorated with calcite, faience, and colored glass. The king is shown resting his feet upon a footstool. Some footstools discovered in the king's tomb were elaborately

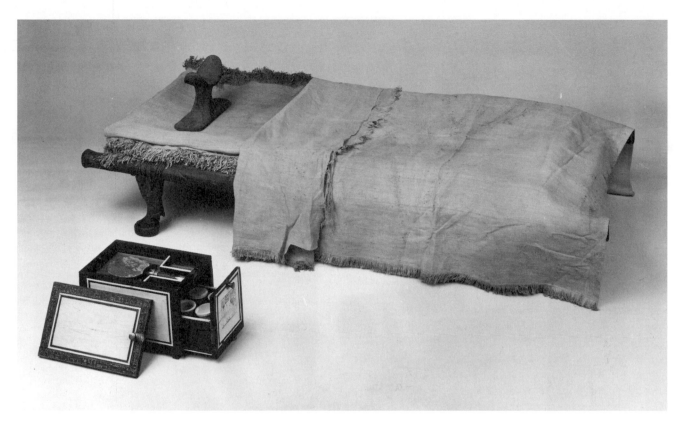

FURNITURE. *Eleventh dynasty wooden bed and twelfth dynasty cosmetic chest of cedar, ebony, and ivory.* A wooden headrest (Old or Middle Kingdom) and linen sheets (eleventh dynasty) are on the bed. The chest contains a mirror and calcite (Egyptian alabaster) cosmetic vessels. (The Metropolitan Museum of Art. 86.1.39,41 [bed & head rest]; 26.3.14,16–18 [sheets]; 26.7.1438 [chest])

decorated with scenes of bound Nubian and Syrian captives, prostrate before him.

**Economics.** Carpenters worked for a temple or the state in a regulated workshop that provided their housing and wages (made to them in grain). Money was not used until the end of the Late period; before this, transactions between individuals were based on bartering. Egyptians developed a sophisticated system in which goods were valued in comparison with a copper unit known as a *deben* (*dbn*). Records from the New Kingdom workmen's village at Deir el-Medina demonstrate how that community valued a range of goods, including furniture. The price of furniture was not rigidly set by type, which possibility suggests that size and quality also influenced cost. Chairs (*ḳniw*) ranged from 12 to 20 *deben*, bed frames (*ḥ'ti*) 12 to 25 *deben*, tables (*ṯt*) 15 *deben*, footstools (*hdmw*) 1 to 10 *deben,* and folding stools (*isbwt*) 1 to 30 *deben.*

Trade with foreign powers was illuminated by the Amarna Letters. Gifts sent to the Egyptian court were accompanied by written requests for goods, such as furniture, to be sent in exchange. The gifts received in Egypt were distributed by the pharaoh to his officials and nobles in recognition of their service to the court. What is clear from the Amarna Letters is the high regard held by rulers of neighboring countries for the quality and workmanship achieved by Egyptian carpenters. One record of furniture gifts given by Amenhotpe III to the Kassite king included four ebony bed frames overlaid with gold and ivory, a headrest of ebony, and five gilded ebony chairs. Ebony is one of the world's hardest woods, and one of the most difficult to craft into furniture.

The elaborate thrones and beds used by Ramessess III are shown in the engravings made by Ippolito Rosellini (1800–1843) of tomb paintings he found at Thebes. They are upholstered with thick cushions, which have covers decorated with star and check patterns. Some are made in the traditional lion-legged form, while one has a folding-stool frame similar to the ceremonial chair discovered in the tomb of Tutankhamun. Another throne has round legs, incised with a pattern, and gilded.

No examples of furniture have been found in the royal tombs of the twenty-first and twenty-second dynasties discovered at Tanis. That may indicate a change in religious thinking or, as records show, a lack of quality wood. Only a few pieces of furniture survive in Egypt from the Greco-Roman period, and their quality suggests that much of the furniture manufactured then was poorly executed and roughly decorated. A crudely constructed funerary couch shows that furniture painters incorporated traditional Egyptian deities within patterns that were strongly Aegean. An exceptional series of wall reliefs in the tomb of Petosiris at Tuna el-Gebel shows carpenters manufacturing furniture with distinctive Hellenistic traits. An unusual piece of furniture, a trapezium-shaped lattice framework, stands on short legs, perhaps made from the stems of palm fronds or thin timber struts; such furniture is still commonly used in the Middle East.

The art of wood turning flourished in Egypt during the Greco-Roman period, and a primitive lathe is shown in the tomb of Petosiris, as well as a stool with turned legs. Many intricately turned legs, from the Faiyum region, date to that period; they are elegantly worked into ball, spool, and vase profiles. The quality of work is very fine, showing that turners had become highly skilled, and they used a variety of shaped chisels. They produced items such as stool and couch legs, often finished with bell-shaped feet and highly polished. This type of turned leg—which is also seen painted on Greek vases and in Roman wall frescos—shows that this style and type of furniture had become desirable, accepted and widely used in Greco-Roman Egypt.

[*See also* Woodworking.]

**BIBLIOGRAPHY**

Aldred C. "Fine Woodworking." In *A History of Technology*, vol. 1, pp. 685–703. Oxford, 1954. Examines the decorative techniques applied to furniture.

Baker, H. S. *Furniture of the Ancient World, Origins and Evolution 3100–475 B.C.* London, 1966. A generalized history of furniture in the ancient world.

Davies, N. M. *Tutankhamun's Painted Box.* Oxford, 1962.

Eaton-Krauss, M. "Walter Segal's Documentation of CG 51113, the Throne of Princess Sat-Amun." *Journal of Egyptian Archaeology* 75 (1989), 77–88. Comprehensive account of one of the thrones discovered in the tomb of Yuia and Thuiu, using illustrations by the German architect Walter Segal.

Killen, G. P. *Ancient Egyptian Furniture, 4000–1300 B.C.* Warminster, 1980. Describes in detail and with working drawings the construction of bed frames, stools, chairs, thrones, tables, and vase stands; has a valuable list of furniture preserved in major world museums.

Killen, G. P. *Ancient Egyptian Furniture, Boxes, Chests and Footstools.* Warminster, 1994. Continues the theme of the 1980 volume and contains a second list of furniture preserved in minor world museums.

Killen, G. P. *Egyptian Woodworking and Furniture,* Princess Risborough, 1994. A valuable pocket-sized book for those seeking general information on furniture.

Reisner, G. A., and W. S. Smith. *A History of the Giza Necropolis,* vol. 2: *The Tomb of Hetep-heres the Mother of Cheops.* Cambridge, Mass, 1955. Excavation report, contains excellent working drawings of the queen's furniture, with photographs before and after restoration.

Wanscher, E. *Sella curulis, The Folding Stool: An Ancient Symbol of Dignity.* Copenhagen, 1980.

GEOFFREY KILLEN

# EGYPTIAN KING LIST

## Mesolithic Period (8500–5500 BCE)

## PREDYNASTIC PERIOD

### Neolithic Period (5500–3100 BCE)

| | |
|---|---|
| Badarian | 5500–4000 BCE |
| Amratian (Naqada I) | 4000–3500 BCE |
| Gerzean (Naqada II) | 3500–3150 BCE |

### Dynasty "0"

| | |
|---|---|
| ["Uj" occupant] | c.3150 BCE |
| Iry-Hor (?) | |
| Ka | c.3100–3050 |
| "Scorpion" | |

## EARLY DYNASTIC PERIOD

### First Dynasty
### (Thinite)

| | |
|---|---|
| Narmer; Aha; Djer; Wadji; | c.3050–2850 |
| Den; Enedjib; Semsem; Ka'a | |

### Second Dynasty
### (Thinite)

| | |
|---|---|
| Hotepsekhemwy | c.2850–2820 |
| Ranebi | c.2820–2790 |
| Ninuter | c.2790–2754 |
| Wadjnas | c.2754–2734 |
| Senedy | |
| Peribsen | c.2734–2714 |
| Khasekhemwy | c.2714–2687 |

## OLD KINGDOM

### Third Dynasty

| | |
|---|---|
| Djoser | c.2687–2668 |
| Nebka | c.2688–2682 |
| Sekhemkhet | ? |
| Khaba | ? |
| Neferkare | c.2679–2673 |
| Huny (?) | c.2673–2649 |

### Fourth Dynasty

| | |
|---|---|
| Sneferu | c.2649–2609 |
| Khufu | c.2609–2584 |
| Djedefre | c.2584–2576 |
| Khafre | c.2576–2551 |
| Menkaure | c.2551–2523 |
| Shepseskaf | c.2523–2519 |
| [2 unknown kings] | c.2519–2513 |

### Fifth Dynasty

| | |
|---|---|
| Userkaf | c.2513–2506 |
| Sahure | c.2506–2492 |
| Neferirkare Kakai | c.2492–2482 |
| Shepseskare | c.2482–2475 |
| Raneferef | c.2475–2474 |
| Newoserre Any | c.2474–2444 |
| Menkauhor | c.2444–2436 |
| Djedkare Izezi | c.2436–2404 |
| Unas | c.2404–2374 |

### Sixth Dynasty

| | |
|---|---|
| Teti | c.2374–2354 |
| Userkare | ? |
| Pepy I | c.2354–2310 |
| Merenre Antyemsaf | c.2310–2300 |
| Neferkare Pepy II | c.2300–2206 |
| [Antyemsaf] II | c.2206 |
| Nitokerty (Nitocris) | c.2205–2200 |
| Neferka the child | [c.2200–2199] |

| | |
|---|---|
| Nefer | c.2199–2197 |
| Aba | c.2197–2193 |
| [ . . . ] | c. 2193–2191 |
| [ . . . ] | c.2191 |

## FIRST INTERMEDIATE PERIOD

### Seventh Dynasty
Numerous ephemeral kings

### Eighth Dynasty

| | | |
|---|---|---|
| "18 kings" | | c.2190–2165 |
| Merenre Anty-emsaf II (sic) | Ny-kare | |
| | Neferkare Terer | |
| Neterkare | Neferkahor | |
| Menkare | Neferkare | |
| Neferkare | Pepysonby | |
| Neferkare Neby | Sneferka-'anu | |
| Djedkare Shemay | Kakaure | |
| Neferkare Khenedy | Neferkaure | |
| Merenhor | Neferkauhor | |
| Sneferka | Neferirkare II | |

### Ninth and Tenth Dynasties
### (Herakleopolitan)

| | | |
|---|---|---|
| "18 kings" | | c.2165–2040 |
| Akhtoy I | Shed[ . . . ] | |
| . . . | Hu-[ . . . ] | |
| Neferkare | [6 kings] | |
| Akhtoy II | Akhtoy III | |
| Seneni (?) | Merikare | |
| . . . | . . . | |
| Mer[ . . . ] | | |

### Early Eleventh Dynasty
### (Theban)

| | |
|---|---|
| Antef I | 2134–2118 |
| Antef II | 2118–2068 |
| Antef III | 2068–2061 |

## MIDDLE KINGDOM

### Late Eleventh Dynasty
### (All Egypt)

| | |
|---|---|
| Nebhepetre Montuhotep I | 2061–2011 |
| Se'ankhibtowy | |
| Montuhotep II | 2011–2000 |
| Nebtowyre Montuhotep III | 2000–1998 |
| (Civil Strife 1998–1991) | |

### Twelfth Dynasty

| | |
|---|---|
| Amenemhet I | 1991–1962 |
| Senwosret I | 1971–1928 |
| Amenemhet II | 1929–1895 |
| Senwosret II | 1897–1877 |
| Senwosret III | 1878–1843 |
| Amenemhet III | 1843–1797 |
| Amenemhet IV | 1798–1790 |
| Sobekneferu | 1790–1786 |

### Thirteenth and Fourteenth Dynasties

| | |
|---|---|
| Khutowyre Sobekhotpe I | 1786–1763 |
| Sekhemkare Amenemhet-sonbef | 1783–1780 |
| (13 kings) | c.1780–1760 |
| [ . . . ] | |
| Sekhemkare Amenemhet | |
| Sehtepibre | |
| Afni | |
| Seonkhibre Ameny-intef-Amenemhat | |
| Smenkare | |

| | |
|---|---|
| Sehtepibre Qemau si-Harendotes | |
| Sewadj-kare | |
| Nodjemibre | |
| Sobekhotep I | |
| Rensonbe | |
| Awibre Hor | |
| Sedjefakare Qay-Amenemhat | |
| Sobekhotpe II | 1750–1756 |
| Khendjer | 1756–1751 |
| (3 kings) [ . . . ] | 1751–1749 |
| Sekhemkare Sobekhotpe III | 1749–1747 |
| Khasekhemre Neferhotpe I | 1747–1736 |
| Sihathor | 1735 |
| Khaneferre Sobekhotpe IV | 1734–1725 |
| Khahetepre Sobekhotpe V | 1725–1721 |
| Wahibre Ya'ib | 1721–1712 |
| Merneferre Aya | 1712–1700 |
| Merhotepre An | 1700–1698 |
| Se'ankhenre Sewadjtu | 1698–1695 |
| Mersekhemre Neferhotpe | 1695–1692 |
| Sewadjkare Hori | 1691 |
| Merkare Sobekhotpe VI | 1690–1688 |
| (14 kings) | 1688–c.1665 |

| | |
|---|---|
| Merkheperre | Djedkherure |
| [3 or 4 kings] | Seonkhibre |
| Nehesy | Nefertumre |
| Khatire | Sekhem[ . . . ]re |
| Nebawre | Ka[ . . . ]re Kem |
| Sehebre | Neferibre |
| Merdjefare | [ . . . ] |
| Sewadjkare | Kha[ . . . ]re |
| Nebjefare | Akare |
| Webenre | Semen[ . . . ]re |
| [3 kings] | Djed[ . . . ]re |
| Awibre | [6 kings] |
| Heribre | Seneferre |
| Nebseure | Men[ . . . ]re |
| [ . . . ] | Djed[ . . . ] |
| Sekheperenre | |

## SECOND INTERMEDIATE PERIOD

### Fifteenth Dynasty (Hyksos)

| | |
|---|---|
| Maa-ibre Sheshy | c.1664–1662 |
| Mer-userre Ya'akob-har | c.1662–1653 |
| Seuserenre Khayan | c.1653–1614 |
| [ . . . ] Yansas-adoen | c.1614–1605 |
| Aa-woserre Apophis | c.1605–1565 |
| [ . . . ] Hamudi | c.1565–1555 |

### Early Sixteenth Dynasty
### (Hyksos)

| | |
|---|---|
| 22 kings+ 65+ years | c.1665–1600 |

### Late Seventeenth Dynasty
### (Theban)

| | |
|---|---|
| Sekenenre Ta'o | c.1600–1571 |
| Senakhtenre Ta'o | |
| Kamose | c.1571–1569 |

## NEW KINGDOM

### Eighteenth Dynasty

| | |
|---|---|
| Ahmose | c.1569–1545 |
| Amenhotpe I | c.1545–1525 |
| Thutmose I | c.1525–1516 |
| Thutmose II | c.1516–1504 |
| Thutmose III | 1504–1452 |
| Hatshepsut | 1502–1482 |
| Amenhotpe II | 1454–1419 |
| Thutmose IV | 1419–1410 |